'OPS'
VICTORY AT ALL COSTS

Tattered Flag Press West Sussex

'OPS'
VICTORY AT ALL COSTS

ON OPERATIONS OVER HITLER'S REICH
WITH THE CREWS OF BOMBER COMMAND
THEIR WAR – THEIR WORDS

Andrew R.B. Simpson

Published in Great Britain in 2012 by
Tattered Flag Press
PO Box 2240
Pulborough
West Sussex RH20 9AL
England

office@thetatteredflag.com
www.thetatteredflag.com

Tattered Flag Press is an imprint of Chevron Publishing Ltd.

Ops
© Andrew R.B. Simpson 2012

All rights reserved. No part of this book may be reproduced, stored in a retrieval system, transmitted in any form or by any means, electronic, or mechanical including by photocopying or scanning, or be held on the internet or elsewhere, or recorded or otherwise, without the written permission of the publisher.

Jacket Design: Tim Brown and Mark Nelson
Cartography © Tim Brown 2012

Tattered Flag Press wishes to acknowledge the kind contributions of Murray R. Barber, Tim Brown, Eddie J. Creek, Ken Merrick and ww2images during the preparation of this book

British Library Cataloguing in Publication Data
A Catalogue Record for this book is available from the British Library

ISBN 978-0-9555977-6-3

Design by Mark Nelson, Sydney, NSW

Printed and bound in the UK by the
MPG Books Group, Bodmin and King's Lynn

Copyright
Illegal copying and selling of publications deprives authors, publishers and booksellers of income, without which there would be no investment in new books. Unauthorised versions of publications are also likely to be inferior in quality and contain incorrect information. You can help by reporting copyright infringements and acts of piracy to the Publisher or the UK Copyright Service.

For more information on books published by Tattered Flag Press visit:
www.thetatteredflag.com

Also by Andrew R.B. Simpson:
Another Life: Lawrence after Arabia, 2007
ISBN 978-1-86227-464-8

'Never a day passes that you don't remember those days. You shake your head in disbelief that you managed to come through. Years afterwards I found it easy to delude myself, to think that, after all, it had been no more than an exhilarating adventure. In truth, those who survived were the tip of the iceberg of the dead. Only a few of us were real warriors, but we saw some very ordinary men do some extraordinary things.'

DON CHARLWOOD, NAVIGATOR, 103 SQUADRON
from *Journeys into Night*, 1991

'It was the wartime RAF that gave a direction and a discipline to my life, and taught me that professionalism and teamwork are the prerequisites of all human achievement. There I was shown what men and women can achieve when they are united in pursuit of a common goal clearly defined as just and good, and which they know they must attain at all costs.'

LEONARD CHESHIRE, CO, 617 SQUADRON
from *The Hidden World*, 1981

CONTENTS

Preface	viii
Foreword by John Nichol	ix
Author's Introduction	x
Exposition	xiv
Acknowledgements	xvi
Glossary	xviii
Maps: The Operational Squadrons of Bomber Command – 30 March 1944	xxiii
'Night of the Strong Winds': 24/25 March 1944	xxiv

PART ONE — FIRST STEPS

Chapter One	'… OTHERWISE I MAY END UP IN THE ARMY' First Steps	3
Chapter Two	'THAT'S THE LAST TIME YOU WILL EVER BE AT THE CONTROLS!' Training	11
Chapter Three	'IT SEEMED TO TAKE QUITE A LOT OF PUNISHMENT WITHOUT FALLING OUT OF THE SKY' The Aircraft	23
Chapter Four	'A GRAND MOB OF FELLOWS' The Crew	40
Chapter Five	'A JUGGLE WITH JESUS' OTU: Part One	58

PART TWO — ON SQUADRON

Chapter Six	'ENOUGH TO FRIGHTEN THE DEVIL OUT OF US!' First Operation	73
Chapter Seven	'THERE'S A BLOODY DUCK IN MY BED!' Squadron life	80
Chapter Eight	'A DEADLY SERIOUS AND DANGEROUS GAME' Operations	109
Chapter Nine	'OUR BOMB DROPPED RIGHT IN THE MIDDLE' First Tour	150
Chapter Ten	'WITH ENGINES – OR NO ENGINES' OTU: Part Two	171
Chapter Eleven	'YOU CAN CALL ME MEIER' The German defence	176
Chapter Twelve	'HE SHOULDN'T HAVE JOINED IF HE COULDN'T TAKE A JOKE' Morale	194

PART THREE	**THE CHOP**	
Chapter Thirteen	THE 'BIG CITY' Battle over Berlin	207
Chapter Fourteen	'OUR WORST HEADACHE' The Transportation Plan	251
Chapter Fifteen	'RATHER LIKE HAVING MISSED THE LAST BUS HOME – BUT MUCH MORE FINAL' The dangers and trauma of a 'final' operation	260

PART FOUR	**EVASION**	
Chapter Sixteen	'I SET ABOUT PADDLING FOR THE SHORE' Evasion by sea	287
Chapter Seventeen	'NOT THE MOST POPULAR PERSON IN THE REGION' Evasion by land	293

PART FIVE	**THE CAMPS**	
Chapter Eighteen	'I TOLD YOU IT WASN'T A SPITFIRE' *Dulag Luft*	315
Chapter Nineteen	'VERMIN-FREE WITH ABOUT FORTY PRISONERS TO A ROOM' *Stalag Luft* III, Sagan	340
Chapter Twenty	'THE WORST JOURNEY IN THE WORLD' The Long Marches	377
Chapter Twenty One	'IS GOD MY CO-PILOT?' The haunted many	394

Epilogue	399
Conclusions	405
The Crews	408
Chapter notes	412
Sources and Bibliography	440
Index of Personnel	443

Preface

THIS book originated following long conversations with my father about his service in Bomber Command during World War Two, life in *Stalag Luft* III and his thoughts on the war generally. My Dad was an Australian from New South Wales. He returned to Australia with his new English wife for a brief spell after the war, but then circumstances dictated a return to England. Eventually, over the years, he lost touch with most of his former aircrew apart from one. Gradually they died off, until in the 1990s only three of them remained. Then, out of the blue in 1992, we were contacted by the son of his first flight engineer, who had been killed during the war. This led much later, to a brief telephone call to his first rear gunner, Wally Maltby, in 2005. Sadly Wally died shortly after this and eventually, in 2007, my Dad also succumbed. He fell over one morning outside the local grocery shop, going straight down onto his forehead without protecting himself. He told a local person that he had been blinded by the sun. Within a few minutes he was taken into the local hospital.

We managed to contact the paramedic who sat beside him in the ambulance. He said he had seemed a very nice man, and had spent most of the time talking about the war. It was the last conversation he had. Shortly after that he passed into a coma in which he remained until passing away two and a half days later. We were all very shocked, but glad that it was over quickly. If he had survived he would have been wheelchair-bound and have lost almost all his memory.

After my Dad died I was overwhelmed by a terrible sadness. This wasn't so much for him alone, but it was for an era that I felt had ended; for a generation of men who had 'done something' very important that was fast disappearing, never to return. I have heard young men scoff at 'old fogies' reminiscing about the war. I pity them in their ignorance. But it wasn't this that was so upsetting. In the present age, when there is so little respect, people like 'the boys in blue' – the 'bomber boys' of the RAF – are not being replaced. The world will never see their like again.

In order to ease my feelings I instigated my own catharsis. I set about contacting as many veterans as I could. I had always heard this 'one story': now I wanted to hear others like it first hand. It makes a difference when you talk to people personally. They all have a similar quality: they are all people with an underlying self-respect, not a pride, but a self-respect for having contributed to something great. In these vastly different times it may be difficult for youngsters over two generations below them to relate to their experiences. I hope that this book, in some way, may alter that. Without being melodramatic, they are a generation to whom we owe our lives.

Andrew R.B. Simpson

Foreword
by
John Nichol

I HAVE written a number of books involving the Bomber Command crews of the Second World War. I have always been staggered by the stories the veterans told me of the horrors they endured and the dangers they faced. The death toll amongst the aircrews of Bomber Command was horrendous: it had one of the highest casualty rates of any combat unit during World War Two. Of the 110,000 men that joined the force, 55,573 were killed. Put simply, they had an evens chance of dying. And die for their country they did, in terrible ways – shot, burned, drowned or literally blown out of the sky in pieces. One veteran told me of a jaw-dropping fact that put the dangers they faced into horrifyingly simple terms: on one single night in March 1944, more men from Bomber Command were killed than the RAF's *total* aircrew casualties during *the whole* of the Battle of Britain.

I have read many books about aircrew in World War Two and few seem to talk about the reality of warfare. For the most part, they concentrate on the jolly japes, the heroics and the 'fun' side of life in the military. Having served in the RAF for 15 years I can testify that there is much bravery and always plenty of 'fun'. But the reality of seeing friends die, facing death yourself, and more importantly, facing the fear of death, can be a traumatic experience.

Recording the memories of the Bomber Command aircrew is crucial in understanding the sacrifice they made during the darkest hours of World War Two and books like *Ops* form an important part of military history.

Lest We Forget.

John Nichol
Military Historian
July, 2010

Author's Introduction

IF this is a book about war, then it is also a book about people. I make no apologies for this: in a war it is people who are killed and people who kill them. 47,268 men of the Royal Air Force were killed flying on operations against Germany in World War Two. The majority of them were what historian Sir Max Hastings described as 'very ordinary men'. If you passed them in the street you probably wouldn't notice them. Around 1,000 of them remain today: 'ordinary' men, the majority of whom looked 'ordinary', had 'ordinary' names, and did 'ordinary' jobs, but, when it was required of them, they did extraordinary things.

These 47,268 airmen were part of over 125,000 engaged on operations; the majority were aged between 20 and 30 – some younger. The actual gross total of the dead at the end of the war was 55,573, including 8,305 killed in accidents. This is a staggering figure considering that since the end of World War Two the gross total of British casualties in all services, in all wars, is less than 3,000.[1]

The people in Bomber Command, whether they were called up in the early part of the war or later, all volunteered; they came from all over the world, from all classes, and from all backgrounds. There were all sorts of characters and all sorts of nationalities: as well as the English, Scots, Welsh and Irish, there were Australians, New Zealanders, Canadians, South Africans, Free French, Poles, Dutch, Norwegians, Lithuanians and Americans. By 1945 this epitome of international co-operation had turned from being an under-strength, ineffective and inaccurate fledgling into a massive, sophisticated and technologically advanced machine for the systematic destruction of the German homeland.

The technology of guns used or aircraft employed did not really interest me in researching this book. It was the psychological stresses the aircrews endured, both on operations and afterwards in imprisonment, how they coped with their fears, and what the long-term effects were (and there were many), that interested me most. When 7,000 airmen go on a raid, such as the first 1,000 bomber raid, much energy is expended, much stress is felt, a huge amount of human vibrations are given off, both negative and otherwise, and fear is rampant. Hundreds of books have been written about Bomber Command. But the further one gets away from the event the more the myths increase, myths that have to be corrected. For instance:

Myth 1) The Avro Lancaster won the war. Anyone who knows anything about the air war and the machines involved will be aware that the Lancaster made an important contribution, but so did a number of other aircraft.

Myth 2) The 'lions led by donkeys' syndrome disappeared with the end of the First World War. This is also untrue. There was still much erroneous decision making by staff 'donkeys' in World War Two. One has only to read Air Vice-Marshal Bennett's autobiography, which suggests that he was the victim of inter-staff rivalry and jealousy in 1944, and that this was one of the causes of the Nuremberg disaster, to appreciate this.

Myth 3) Aircrew morale fell dramatically after the 'Battle of Berlin' of 1944. This was, according to one veteran, 'utter nonsense – morale was always very high in spite of sometime heavy losses.'[2]

My father once said that present day authors had a tendency to glamorise and make 'larger than life' events that were fairly every-day episodes in the war. He also said, referring to the morality of 'area bombing', that it was very easy to criticise the bombing with hindsight, but there were ongoing decisions that had to be made from day to day [by staff] in order to try and win a war that could very easily have been lost. At the time no-one knew what the consequences of these decisions would be. In 1943 the air war was the only European front and it was making a great contribution to raising morale at home. In the bomber war it wasn't all 'good' and 'bad': there were a large number of grey areas. There was no certainty that the decisions made were the right ones; a clinical diagnosis would show many 'uncertainties': e.g. i) The damage caused by 'area bombing' wasn't nearly as great as had been predicted, and the German public proved to be far more resilient than had been suggested; ii) The effectiveness of the bombing was restricted to a much larger degree by the German defences than had been expected; iii) Disagreements within the High Command about the variety of aims, as well as the weather conditions, retarded their fulfilment.

The attitude of the British public to Bomber Command changed dramatically after the war. Arthur W. Cole, a bomb-aimer with 158 Squadron[3] recalled: 'The civilian world had a lot of time for us in those days. It was only after that they came to regard us as war criminals.'

Alec March, a wireless operator with 103 Squadron remembered: 'During the war years, especially early on, people were glad to feel the war was being carried to Germany.' In present times however '…to say I flew with Bomber Command was to be treated like a pariah. Being asked once the question, "Did you not appreciate what you were doing?" I replied "Yes, we wanted to defeat the Nazis".'

There has been a tendency in modern times to try to rewrite history. An iconoclastic, myth-destroying approach has become fashionable in historical books and television programmes, sometimes purely for the sensation it creates. The recent meticulous research into Douglas Bader's last wartime flight, for instance, which suggested that he had deliberately misled his biographers as to what happened, is an example. Bomber Command included a number of personalities similar to Bader in its ranks, 'born leaders' whose exploits were later celebrated, but they were not always the 'supermen' they were made out to be. Two of the most renowned were Guy Gibson and Leonard Cheshire. John Leakey, who served with Gibson in 83 Squadron in 1939, described him as just another 'junior officer', but Richard James who flew as his navigator when he did a tour on Beaufighters in 1941, found him to be in a 'different league' to himself and 'completely oblivious to danger.' He was struck by Gibson's 'cool efficiency.' But Gibson's violent end in September 1944 was far from efficient.

Leonard Cheshire has also been held up as an icon: the suave, intelligent leader, who became a great humanitarian. Engineer Bill Higgs's recollection of him was slightly different. He described him as 'mad as a hatter', recalling an occasion when, while serving with Cheshire's 76 Squadron crew, they had chased some horses around a field at zero feet and forced them into a pond. The raid Cheshire led to Mailly-le-Camp in May 1944 was one of Bomber Command's biggest disasters of the war. One has to wonder where the truth ended and the myths began. Former aircrew whose stories have been featured in published books complained to me that the authors altered what the men said for dramatic purposes. Also, my father once pointed out to me that modern authors tended to use expressions that were current at their time of writing but which were not in use during the period concerned. I would hope to avoid such mechanisms in this work.

Authors can also make classic 'blunders'. Patrick Bishop's book *Bomber Boys: Fighting Back* became a bestseller, but implied that the playwright Terence Rattigan had been in Bomber Command and left his career to 'join the RAF as a wireless operator/air gunner.' Jim Mitchell, who was in 51 Squadron in 1945, served at A.H.Q.W.A.[4] Freetown in 1942 and recalled that Rattigan was actually a wireless operator there on Sunderlands.[5]

When writing a book about the exploits of 125,000 people it is extremely difficult to find a focus for a story. One has only to talk to a handful of veterans and read a small number of personal memoirs to appreciate that, although their experiences bore similarities, the exploits of each individual airman were peculiar unto himself. Because of this I realised that the only way for this book to work was for the men to tell their story themselves.

The slaughter in Bomber Command was unprecedented: over 41 per cent losses – higher even, in relative terms, than those suffered by the British officer corps on the first day of the Battle of the Somme. The total British Empire and Commonwealth fatalities from 1939 to 1945 were 452,000; since losses in Bomber Command totalled over 55,000, approximately 13 per cent of all British and Commonwealth deaths were on bomber crews. Here, these 'very ordinary men' were asked to take on an almost suicidal task, with little hope of survival, and generally volunteered for the job, a phenomenon that continued until the end of hostilities. After it was over little official recognition was given to the effort. 'Bomber' Harris became the scapegoat for policies that originated with Churchill and Portal, and retired disillusioned to South Africa. And it didn't need Remembrance Sunday to remind families of their loss. Colin Hatton's grandparents lost both their son and son-in-law in Bomber Command in World War Two, without trace. 'Neither was ever talked about,' he said, 'both were mourned forever in silence.'[6] Many veterans felt inclined to put aside the experience of the war and get on with their lives and it was only with age and a resurgence of interest in the 1970s that things began to be reconsidered.

Some of the injuries the men suffered were horrific. The chances of being burnt alive in mid-air, drowned in the cold waters of the Channel, or maimed for life as the result of high velocity explosions were common. Don Cruden, an Australian navigator, recalled:

'People were there today and then they were gone tomorrow. The poor devils, they are not buried somewhere or other. They are a puff of smoke up there, because you didn't get out of that thing too easily.'[7]

Despite the use of the parachute there were many cases of men falling thousands of feet to their deaths. Even with parachutes airmen would land in bizarre places: not only the branches of forests (which could prove as fatal as they were lifesaving), but also in waterlogged areas, on railway lines and, at least once, on a factory chimney. Sometimes a few members of an aircrew would bale out after the first warning, only to find that the remainder of the crew had returned safely to base.

Often the reception that greeted the men on the ground was hostile: there were numerous cases of aircrew, both British and American, being hanged by German civilians and aircrews regularly reported the hostility of crowds. These airmen were mainly youngsters in their late teens and early twenties, prematurely aged by operational strain – many a pilot of the big four-engined 'heavies' could fly before he could even drive; many were unmarried and only shortly out of school, ridiculously inexperienced in the ways of the world. This book uses as a central 'spine' quotations from my father's *RAAF Service Diary* written from his enlistment in 1941 until the end of the war in May 1945. He was between 23 and 27 years of age when he wrote it, and his youthful enthusiasm shows through in places. Despite this, his honesty, courage and compassion are continually evident.

The consequences of fighting an extremely hazardous war were, in terms of men's physiology and psychology, protracted, painful, and ultimately long-lasting. Some aircrew had nightmares for years after the war. But despite the suffering, privations and hardships that they endured, many veterans still said later that they would 'never have missed it'.

So, this book is written in memory of my Dad and his kind, and also as a sincere tribute to the courage of such young men who confronted so many dangers and fears: it is due to them that most of my generation has never had anything remotely similar to face. May we all learn a lesson from it.

Andrew R.B. Simpson
Devon, 2012

Exposition

WHEN I first started writing this book I really had no idea as to how things would develop. All I knew was that I wanted to write about the ordinary man's war in RAF Bomber Command and that, obviously, my father's story was going to form the backbone for this; and it was my sadness at his passing that was really the motivation for writing it – before time inevitably eroded my memories of the friendship and conversations we had before his death. I was very deeply influenced by his experience of the war, or of what he told me about it, and of his post-war service in the Royal Auxiliary Air Force.

Inevitably, through talking to other men, I was able to learn more than I already knew about Bomber Command's war in the air. Over a period of three years I received a multitude of letters, CDs and emails from people who obviously still found it a very important part of their or their relations' lives, in some cases *the* most important part. I began to be overwhelmed by a miasma of superficially unconnected tales from all over the world, but particularly from England and Australia. These were largely from men I'd never even heard of, and I realised that I would somehow have to connect these together.

Earlier, I had been fortunate to have a book published about T.E. Lawrence which was itself, coincidentally, loosely connected with the RAF. But from what I began to accumulate now I realised that I had a much more complicated subject to deal with; in fact the book was incredibly difficult to structure. I realised that the only way to do this was *chronologically* and then, subsumed to that, *thematically*. Various themes immediately suggested themselves to me from the men's similar experiences, such as the Thousand Bomber Raids, their first operation, their final operation, the Hamburg raids and evasion. Initially two subjects really caught my interest, mainly because of the obvious psychological effects they had on aircrew: these were the phenomenon of 'Lack of Moral Fibre' ('LMF') and *Luftwaffe* interrogation techniques at *Dulag Luft* and I asked, wrote to and questioned a large number of the respondees about their experiences of these.

I realised that all men had been trained, only a relatively limited number of aircraft types were used, all men had gone to OTU and then to squadron, the majority had been shot down, and a large number of them had experienced the deprivations of prison camp life. So the book evolved into a work of five parts arranged chronologically. As well as correspondence, I used archive files at the UK National Archives, the Imperial War Museum and the RAF Museum in London. I was also able to locate, from a contact at the Australian War Memorial, files that dealt with my father and his two crews that I never previously knew existed. Although the majority of his two crews had by then passed on, I received considerable help from the sons of five of these. This contact was quite moving at times as people I had only known of as names in conversation began to reveal stories of their own.

So Part One of the book you now hold covers the 'first steps' of entry into RAF service and their reasons for it; the training that they experienced in England, Canada, the USA, South Africa and Australia; the peculiarities of the different aircraft in which they flew; and the selections and roles played by the crews themselves, and of my father's first period at an Operational Training Unit.

Part Two recounts the life of men on squadron; their first operation, the joys, humour and miseries of squadron life, experiences on operations, the effects on morale; and like many authors on the subject of Bomber Command, I felt bound to try to present the German side of things – if only touching upon it. There are also chapters covering my father's first tour, based upon his own diary account, and his second period at Operational Training Units.

Part Three deals with the final operation, drawing upon fifteen separate personal accounts. An analysis of Harris's 'main offensive', the Battle of Berlin, and the complicated Transportation Plan before D-Day are also covered.

Part Four covers airmen's experiences of evasion, both on land and sea, including thirteen separate personal accounts, many continuing the stories related in Part Three.

Part Five deals with the prison camps, particularly *Dulag Luft* and *Stalag Luft* III, but there really wasn't enough space to include all the stories received. There is then a rather lengthy chapter on the 'Long March' away from *Stalag Luft* III based upon six previously unpublished accounts which, I sense, may be the most detailed presentation of this tale that there has been up to the present time. The final chapter covers the psychological effects experienced by former aircrew after the war. The conclusion incorporates an examination of the effects of the bombing and of Sir Arthur Harris's role in it.

I hope that anyone who reads this book will learn something from it and enjoy what they read. There were great moments of alternately, excitement, horror, misery, humour and happiness in the young men's experiences in Bomber Command, and I would hope that this book somehow conveys a little of this. I would sincerely like to thank anybody who was kind enough to contribute to my researches for this work, particularly to the many veterans who wrote lengthy letters to me of their recollections, and the personal memoirs they sent, a large number, of which, unfortunately, I have been unable to use.

The one thing that struck me more than anything else in researching this book was the detail that these old men, many now in their late eighties, were able to recall. I would particularly like to thank Dom Nunn for his father's personal memoir, Lewis Parsons, Sandy Rowe, and Alec March for their lengthy recollections and, in Australia, Arthur Schrock (Jr.) for reminiscences of his father, and, particularly, Ron Searle, my father's first wireless operator, for his numerous mailings.

Andrew R.B. Simpson
February 2012

Acknowledgements

I WOULD like to thank the following ex-aircrew for kindly talking of their wartime experiences with me:

Dennis Bateman, Ted Boorman, Reg Brown, Arthur Cole, Henry 'Roger' Coverley, Fred Danckwardt, Ken Edwards, George Flanagan, Ted Groom, Bill 'Shiner' Higgs, Phillip Jenkinson, Graham 'Kiwi' Korner, Deryck Lambert, Howard Pearce, Keith Pendray, Harry 'Sparky' Sparks, Les Whitton, Joe Williams.

I would also like to thank the following, or their next of kin, for kindly sending me their personal memoirs and photographs:

Derek Hodgkinson, Roy Child, Reg Cleaver, Henry Wagner, Alec March, George Cross, Cal Younger, Dick Raymond, Tom Baker, Arthur Clarke, Fred Dilnutt, Sid Duplock, Roy Finch, Bernard Frisby, Fred Hockin, John Leakey, John Nunn, Don 'Jock' Wilson, Steve Jackson, Ray Racey, Ken Brown, Eric Foinette, H.M. Farrington, Alan Fuller, John Grimer, 'Sandy' Rowe, Peter Skinner, Peter Hughes, Bill Higgs, Stan 'Paddy' Hope, Eddie Scott Jones, Bob Kirby for Jack Cheeseman, Aubrey Niner, Geoffrey Willatt, Eric Yates, R.V. Drake, Bob Kemley, Ronnie Cartwright, Frank Stone, Joseph Smith, Ron Brown, David Howell, Ron Coulson, R.B. Farren, Ron Warburton, Alan Castle, George J. Barrett, Leslie Holes, Jack West, David Fraser, Harry Jones, John Dean, Dorothy Wallis, James Mitchell, G.R. Lang, Jack Brook, Edith A. Nunn, W.E. Sutton, Beryl Pearce, Ken J. French, Reg Levy, Ella Banyard, John Geddes, Les Hill, Robert Vollum, Lewis Parsons, Frank Dennis, Phillip Bates, Ken Johnson, Russell Margerison, Ron Searle, John Rydings (Jr.), Arthur Schrock (Jr.), Susan Slade, Muriel Mould, James A. Hinwood, Ted Blackmore, W. Wetherill, Laurence Latham, R.E. Kendall, Gerald A. Lane, Graham Holloway, the East Devon Branch of the Aircrew Association and Jochen Mahncke.

Finally, I wish to thank the following for responding to my enquiries:

Bob Burns, Stan Hurrell, Mary Barsh, D. Jane Bryan, Peter Gibby, Reg White, Maurice Mayne, Douglas Robinson, Andy Wiseman, Gabrielle Wilson, W.E.M. Davies, Vitek Formanek, W.R. Chorley, Rosemary Irwin, Sheila Winlow for Denis Lloyd, H. Lloyd Lyon, Dennis McCaig, Geoff Parnell, Trevor Phillips, Norman Elford, Ken Trott, Susan Banks, Florence M. Sutton, Sylvia I. Jarvis, A.M. Norman, Jean Holes, John Funnell, Frances Farren, Betty Burns, Robert H. Gill, E.V. Richman, Jim Allen, Audrey Laverick, Margaret Everitt, Anne Smith, John Dean, John Roberts, Joy K. Goodman, Ken French, Donald Mason, S.A. Ramsey, Erik Rees, Ken Knott, John Wroughton, Robin Murray, Elsie J. Taplin, Trevor Phillips, Phil Potts, Beryl Cheeseman, Carol Holloway, Alan Bryett, Joy Goodrum, Vicki Sparks, Roland McClements, Jean L. Silver, R.W. Thomas, Reg Levy DFC, Linda A. Dolata, Peter King, Chris Maltby, Steve McLeod, Dom Nunn, Betty Howard, Robin MacDonald, Ian Fuller, Beatrice Fox, Don Mason, Betty Burns, Hazel Newsome, Norman Rolfe, Marion Clark, Tom Wilson, G.A. Laing, Florence M. Sutton, Alan W. Clarke, Nancy Woodhead, I.W. Watts, B.A. Lane, Harold Norcross, Roseanne Rockingham, Patricia Jones, Jean Adam, Leah F. Cross, Peter Donaldson, Ella Fernie, A. Griffiths, Norman Gregory, Denis Thorpe, Bernard Warren, Mary Applegate, Gertrude Taylor (nee MacDonald), Jill Skeet, David Fellows.

I would also like to express particular thanks to Craig Tibbetts of the Australian War Memorial, Canberra, Stuart Haddaway of the RAF Museum, Hendon, and to John Nichol for kindly supplying a Foreword. Also to David P. Williams, author of *Nachtjagd*, Jeremy Whitehorn of Heartland Old Books, Tiverton and Cal Younger for proofreading the text.

I would like to thank the RAF Museum, and in particular Peter Elliott, Senior Keeper at the Department of Research and Information Services, for his advice on raid navigation and the Nuremberg Raid, and for supplying me with the DFM citation for James Nairn; also the Australian War Museum for supplying the DFC and DFM citations for Hugh I. Edwards, David Holford, Graeme C. Keys, John Osborne, and L.J. Simpson.

Author's Note

Alec March is a pseudonym. The contributor wished to remain anonymous for personal reasons. Unfortunately the following contributors are known to have died since commencing the project: W.G. 'Bill' Carman (June 2007), Deryck Lambert (2007), Howard Pearce (2009), Derek W. Hodgkinson (January 2010), and Bill 'Shiner' Higgs (June 2010).

Although Wally Floody and Robert Stanford Tuck were fighter pilots in the RCAF and RAF respectively, their stories are included because of their relevance to the section on *Stalag Luft* III. W.R. Chorley suggested that the Glossary at the front was too lengthy, however the author felt that it was necessary to record as many of the RAF terms from the period as possible before they are forgotten for good.

It may be that, due to the large number of quotes and retelling of personal stories included herewith, some former aircrew or their families may be offended by some of the tales. If this should be the case, the author would like to apologise in advance, as any offence caused would be entirely unintentional. The author would be pleased to hear of any inaccuracies found in the text.

Glossary

AC 1	Aircraftman First Class.
AC 2	Aircraftman Second Class (a lower rank than AC 1.)
A.C.R.C.	Aircrew Reception Centre (or 'Arsy-tarsy'.)
AFU	Advanced Flying Unit.
Airborne Cigar (ABC)	Bomber aircraft fitted with RCM equipment that flew in a bomber stream. Jammed enemy night fighter frequencies by broadcasting aircraft's own engine noises. The equivalent in England was termed 'Ground Cigar'.
Annie	Epithet for the Avro Anson.
Appell	Roll call in a prison camp.
AOC	Air Officer Commanding.
Arsy-tarsy	Aircrew Reception Centre (or A.C.R.C.).
ASI	Air Speed Indicator-
Astro Compass	The 'hanging compass' in a bomber. Located in the fuselage, on a Lancaster near the rear exit door. It was suspended from the roof so that it moved with the aircraft, remaining upright, as opposed to the main compass which was fixed inside the cockpit.
ATA	Air Transport Auxiliary. ATA pilots were ferry pilots, often females from the wealthier classes of society.
ATS	Auxiliary Territorial Service.
Bags of flap	Application of a large degree of aircraft flap control during take-off or landing; alternatively, time of extreme squadron activity at the time of a full moon (with related night fighter activity).
BAT	Beam Approach Training: a very basic form of navigation aid, where the pupil flew down a radio beam to his home airfield. In conditions of low visibility a series of radio beacons, located on the ground below the beam, emitted vertical zones of radiation in the form of inverted cones to indicate the aircraft's proximity to the airfield. These normally consisted of an outer beacon two miles from the airfield, an inner beacon on the airfield perimeter, and a main beacon in the centre of the airfield. As the aircraft passed over the beacon, a warning signal sounded superimposed over the beam emission. A red light also glowed in the cockpit. The inner beacon was normally crossed at about 100 ft. BAT flying was extremely frustrating as you had to watch the Air Speed Indicator, Rate of Climb needle, altimeter, compass, beam needle, listen to the beam note and visualise where you were and what to do next, all at the same time.
'B' bombs	'B' bombs were a type of mine which, when dropped, would remain just below the surface, and detonate whenever a ship passed overhead.
Beacon crawling	Technique of flying from one radio beacon to another.
Berlin Twitch	An involuntary contracture of the sphincter muscle caused by times of stress or great danger. Resulted in a nervous tick or twitch, or swivelling of the head.
Bomb Trainer	Bombing simulator. A platform the bombardier lay on under which a film of the landscape passed. When the target appeared underneath the trainee pressed the bomb toggle and a light flashed on the map where the bomb hit.
Boomerang	An 'early return'. Normally if a crew had to abort an operation and return early for whatever reason, a crewman would enter 'Boomerang' in his Flying Logbook beside the target details.
Box Barrage	Where the enemy had put up a barrage of anti-aircraft fire directly in front of a formation in a particular area of the sky.
Brevet	Winged badge indicating an airman's role in the aircraft; normally sewn above the left battledress pocket.
Browny type	Army officer.
Bullseye	Mock bombing attack.

CAS	Chief of the Air Staff.
Cat's Eye	Night fighter that flew over the bomber stream at a high level before diving to attack.
CGI	Chief Ground Instructor.
C-in-C	Commander in Chief.
Circuits and bumps	Practice take-off and landings. Done in order to accustom a crew to taking off and landing; this training found to be useful when the stacking system for returning aircraft approaching an aerodrome was used.
Cocked Hat	Triangular junction of three radio beams.
Compass Point	Circular turntable; on an airfield where an aircraft's main compass was reset by rotating it manually to compensate for the effect of magnetic material in the aircraft affecting compass readings.
Cookie	4,000 lb high-explosive bomb.
Cooler	Solitary confinement cell.
Corona	RCM: transmission of fake orders by German-speaking RAF controllers to *Luftwaffe* night fighters.
Corkscrew	Manoeuvre devised for a bomber evading enemy fighters. The aircraft climbed and turned to port simultaneously; then dived and turned to starboard simultaneously. The manoeuvre was repeated until evasion was successful or otherwise.
Creep Back	Effect of bombs dropped from a bomber stream gradually landing further and further away from the target. Caused by crews dropping a bomb load before the 'aiming point', the landing point 'creeping back' progressively as more aircraft unloaded early.
DF Loop	Direction Finding Loop. A rotatable circular loop aerial normally located on the top of a fuselage. It acted as a focus for beam emissions when navigating. For radio location finding the aircraft would take two bearings from two separate transmitting stations. The aircraft's approximate location was where the beams intersected. When flying along a beam, i.e. at right angles to the DF Loop, a continuous tone was heard. If the pilot deviated to the left the signal changed to a series of dots; if he deviated to the right a series of dashes was heard. The DF Loop was also used during BAT flying.
DNCO	Normally entry in an airman's Flying Logbook during operations indicating 'Duty Not Carried Out'. The antonym of this was 'DCO' i.e. 'Duty Carried Out'.
DREM lights	Lights encircling an airfield.
Early Return	Where a bomber crew may have returned before it was due, having intentionally dropped its bombs prior to reaching the target.
EFTS	Empire Flying Training Scheme, or Empire Flying Training School.
Elsan	Toilet at rear of aircraft: small cylindrical metal can, emptied after an operation. The name derived from the manufacturer Elsan Ltd., which still produces sanitary equipment today in East Sussex.
ETA	Estimated Time of Arrival.
F700	Official RAF form, a 'certificate of airworthiness' required to be signed before an operation.
Feather	Term used to describe the method of adjusting and fixing the pitch on propeller blades to face forward and prevent 'windmilling' of the blades, which created extra drag.
FFI	Freedom from Infection parade: inspection for sexual diseases.
FIDO	Fog Intensive Dispersal Operation.
Flap	Moveable surface fixed to the wing of an aircraft, increasing lift during take-off and drag during landing; alternatively state of panic.
Flare Path	Lights parallel to and illuminating a runway.
Forecast Winds	See 'Wind-finding'.
Funnels	Parallel lines of lights leading to a runway; they appeared to be arranged like a funnel, diminishing into the distance, as one attained a sufficiently low altitude on the approach. Also to be seen in daylight. Alternatively, the command indicating the approach to these.
Gardening	Minelaying flight, often off the enemy coast: mines were referred to as 'vegetables'.
Gash Bod	An airman who was 'no good' i.e. unreliable company.
GCA	Ground Controlled Approach.

Gee	An early navigation system for fixing the general position of an aircraft based on a grid of three intersecting radio beams. Influenced by the early German X-*Gerat* and Y-*Gerat* systems, it was developed by the Telecommunications Research Establishment near Swanage. The term has been said to have derived either from 'G' for grid or Ground Earth Emissions.
Getting a Green	Point during the take-off procedure where an aircraft received a green light (for go) from the airfield controller's caravan.
G-H	Blind-bombing aid.
George	Automatic pilot: it enabled an aircraft to fly in straight and level flight, and automatically compensated for any alterations in roll, pitch, or yaw, using three gyroscopes. When straight and level flight was interrupted, the gyroscopes would return the aircraft to correct trim by a pneumatic system, controlled by compressed air, or an electrical system controlled by servo motors.
Going hand-in-hand	Flying in close formation with another aircraft.
Gone for a Burton	Killed: said to derive from an RAF station where the Morse Testing School was located in the same building and above the local branch of Burtons' the outfitters. Hence when the feared final examination arrived, airmen were said to have 'Gone for a Burton'. (For alternative definition see Nelson p.76).
Goon	A German: more particularly, a German guard in a prison camp. Said to derive from a character in the 'Popeye' cartoons.
Gremlins	Small mythical goblin-like creatures rumoured to inhabit aircraft, being held responsible for any unaccountable malfunction.
Hallybag	Epithet for the Handley Page Halifax.
Headless Crew	Crew without a pilot.
HCU	Heavy Conversion Unit.
H2S	Airborne radar capable of picking up ground contours by bouncing radar emissions off the surface of the earth. Results were displayed on a cathode ray tube. Name said to derive from 'Home Sweet Home' or, alternatively, from the chemical formula for Hydrogen Sulphide, due to an occasion when an inspecting staff officer pronounced: 'It stinks!'.
IAS	Initial Air Speed.
IFF	Identification Friend or Foe.
ITW	Intensive Training Wing.
Kriegie	Prisoner of War, derived from the German *Kriegsgefangener*, epitomised by the cartoon character 'Kriegie Joe'.
Kripo	German Criminal Police.
Lancaster Ear	Permanent damage caused to the inner eardrum by the noise of four aero engines. Particularly applied to Lancaster crews, where five of the crew were located in the nose near the engines.
Link Trainer	Early flight simulator, named after its American inventor, Ed Link. It featured a small enclosed cockpit and miniature fuselage complete with stub wings, tailplane and fin. The whole structure was mounted on four supporting bellows, contained in a turntable on a square base. Using a vacuum turbine the bellows were inflated or deflated in pairs as appropriate, employing an intricate valve system linked to the control column. The trainer could reproduce the movements of a full size aircraft. An automatic recorder, the 'crab', traced a detailed graph of the course flown on the instructor's desk, which had a duplicate instrument panel to that in the cockpit.
LMF	Lack of Moral Fibre.
Mae West	Inflatable life jacket; named after the blonde Hollywood star due to its bright yellow colour.
Mag drop	Fall in the electrical supply from the magneto, which provided the electric current to the spark plug.
Main Force	The main part of a bomber stream.
Main spar	In a cantilever monoplane, the laminated timber beam or spar that extended the length of both wings, and through the fuselage.

Mandrel	Radar.
M gear	Supercharger gear.
MI9	Military Intelligence Department 9: set up in World War Two to monitor escape and evasion.
MO	Medical Officer.
Monika	Short-lived tail warning airborne radar whose emissions were found able to be received by enemy aircraft from as far away as 1.5 miles.
Mu/g	Mid-upper gunner.
Nachtjagd	Lit. 'night hunters' – German night fighter force.
Nachtjagdgeschwader	Night fighter wing.
Nav (b)	Navigator/Bomb-Aimer: derived from the old pre-war 'Observer', the Nav (b) had to be able to double up on all other jobs in the aircraft as well as to navigate. Largely outmoded with the arrival of the four-engined heavy bombers.
Newhaven	Pathfinder aiming-point marking flares designed to ignite at ground level for visual idenitification.
NJG	*Nachtjagdgeschwader* (see above).
Nothing on the clock	Altimeter reading zero.
Oboe	Sophisticated form of radio location device. Name derived from the tone of the signal.
OC	Officer Commanding.
OO	Orderly Officer.
Op	Bombing operation.
ORB	Operations Record Book.
OTU	Operational Training Unit.
Pancake	Land an aircraft.
Parametta	Pathfinder aiming point ground working by radar.
Penguin	Ground staff at an OTU; alternatively sand dispersal man in POW camp.
PFF	Pathfinder Force.
PFI	Pathfinder Indicator flares.
Photoflash	Delayed action photographic flare dropped after the release of a 4,000 lb 'cookie', intended to illuminate the explosion.
Pilot Officer Prune	Archetypal bungling airman.
Pitot tube	Tube to measure air pressure and hence air speed, located on leading edge of a wing.
Pongo	Army officer.
Predicted	Radar predicted Flak: tended to creep across the sky towards a target aircraft.
Putting up a black	Bad misconduct, possibly leading to disgrace.
QDM	International 'Q Code' signal giving course to steer to reach transmitting station: navigational quick reckoning.
QFE	International 'Q Code' signal giving barometric pressure reading required to reset an aircraft's altimeter so that it read zero at ground level.
RCM	Radio Countermeasures.
RAAF	Royal Australian Air Force.
R Aux AF	Royal Auxiliary Air Force.
Reaper, the	The Grim Reaper, i.e. death.
R of C	Rate of climb indicator.
Rotate	Climb, i.e. 'rotate upwards'. Term used by a pilot's assistant when telling a pilot to climb after take-off – 'rotate' being more easily distinguished phonetically than 'climb'.
SAAF	South African Air Force.
SBO	Senior British Officer.
SBC	Special Bomb Containers.
St Elmo's Fire	Static electricity emissions that could appear on leading edges and aerials of an aircraft as blue flames during an electrical storm.
Schräge Musik	Literally 'Slanting Music' or 'Jazz Music': twin cannon mounted at an angle within the cockpit on Bf 110, and behind the cockpit on Ju 88, night fighters. Designed to fire upwards

	and forwards at a bomber's underside.
Screen	Vetting procedure conducted upon a crew's completion of a tour of operations.
SD	*Sicherheitsdienst* – the German Security Service.
Second Dickey	Term for a pilot or other member of crew sitting in with another crew to gain experience before his first operation.
Serrate	British airborne radar developed to pick up radar emissions from enemy aircraft. Normally used on Mosquito aircraft.
SFTS	Service Flying Training School.
SOE	Special Operations Executive.
Sortie	A single operational flight by one aircraft as opposed to a multi-squadron operation.
Stooge	Fly slowly and unplanned; alternatively POW observer in prison camp.
TAS	Theoretical Air Speed.
Tail-end Charlie	Rear gunner.
Tallboy	20,000 lb, aerodynamically-designed bomb, invented by Barnes Wallis in order to destroy earthworks, tunnels, and submarine pens. Effectiveness caused by delayed subterranean explosion creating underground pressure waves.
T.I.	PFF target indicator flare.
Tiger Moth	de Havilland Tiger Moth: the standard RAF single-engined trainer.
U/s	Unserviceable (out of action).
Village Inn	Code name for a facility designed to give greater protection to bombers. Its technical name was the Automatic Gun Laying Turret, or AGLT. The AGLT turret had a small radar transmitter installed at the base of the turret that sent out a signal, which coned an area behind the aircraft. If the radar picked up a contact there would be a 'beep' heard in the aircraft's intercom system which signalled the crew to be on the alert and the rear-gunner to check out. This he could do by screening the object through a small telescopic device. If he detected an infra-red signal, it would be another RAF aircraft: all bombers were fitted with a device, code-named 'Z', which sent out a signal from a screen in front of the bomb-aimer's position. If there was no such signal, the gunner would assume that it was a night fighter and would keep better watch.
WAAF	Women's Auxiliary Air Force.
WAG, W/ag or Wop/ag	Wireless operator/air gunner.
Wakey-Wakey Pills	Benzedrine tablet stimulants taken by aircrew before or during an operation to keep them alert.
Wanganui	Pathfinder sky-marking at release point by radar.
Whimpy or Wimpy	Nickname for the Vickers-Armstrong Wellington, said to derive from a character in the 'Popeye' cartoons.
Wind-finding	Procedure where an aircraft was sent ahead of the Main Force to determine the meteorological conditions: it then transmitted the results back to base or the rest of the bomber stream as 'Forecast winds'.
Window	Thin aluminium strips, used as a radar countermeasure, blackened on one side and tied into bundles, which were hand-fed into flare discharge chutes and dropped over targets by RAF bombers at the rate of one per minute. As the cloud of foil strips fluttered to earth, they reflected back radar pulses to confuse German defences.
WO or W/O	Warrant Officer (i.e. officer by warrant): a temporary appointment whilst an NCO awaited a commission.
WOP or W/op	Wireless operator – Wireless operator/air gunner.
W.T.	Wireless Telegraphy.
Y	Early code name for H2S.

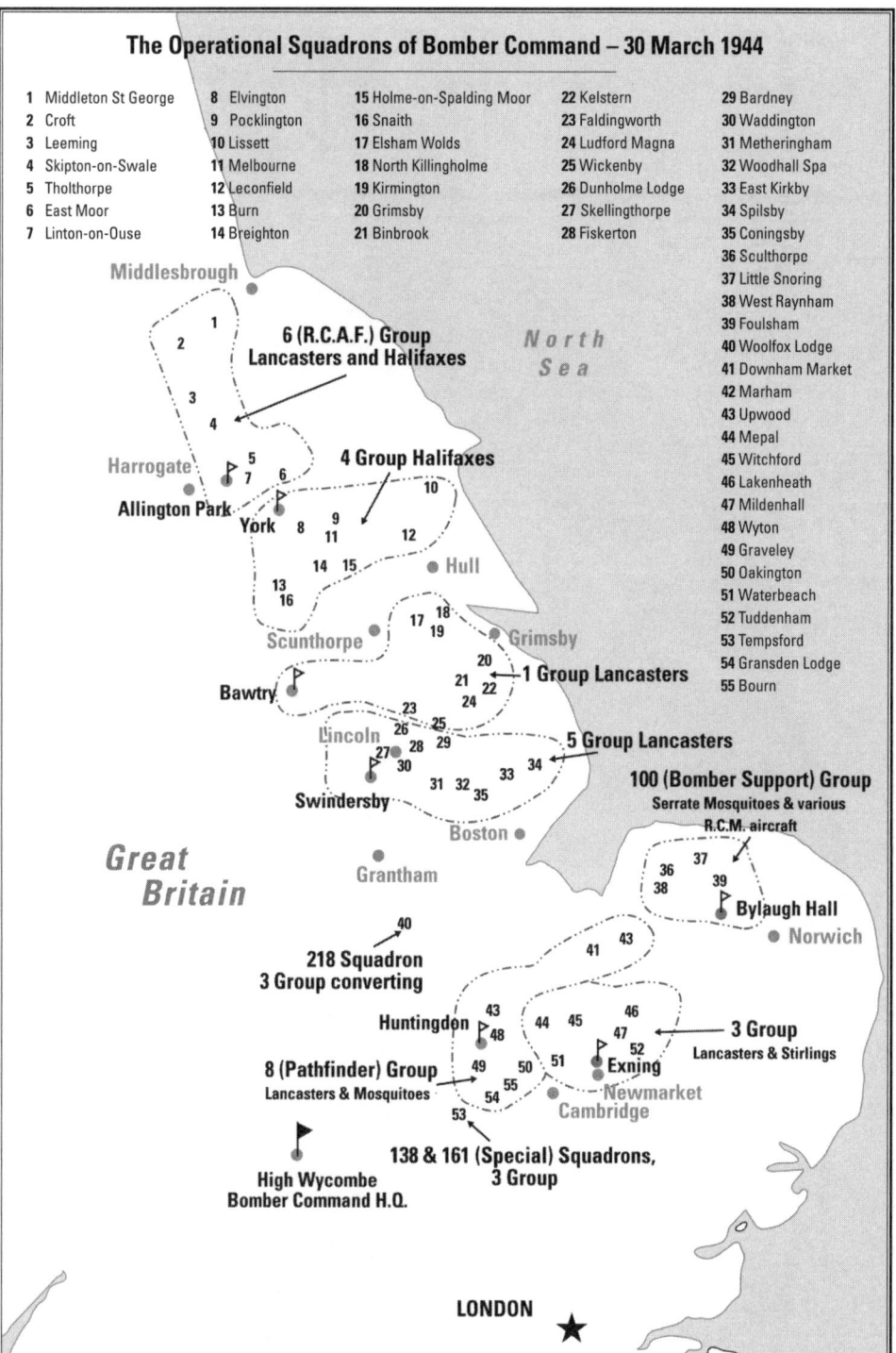

xxiv

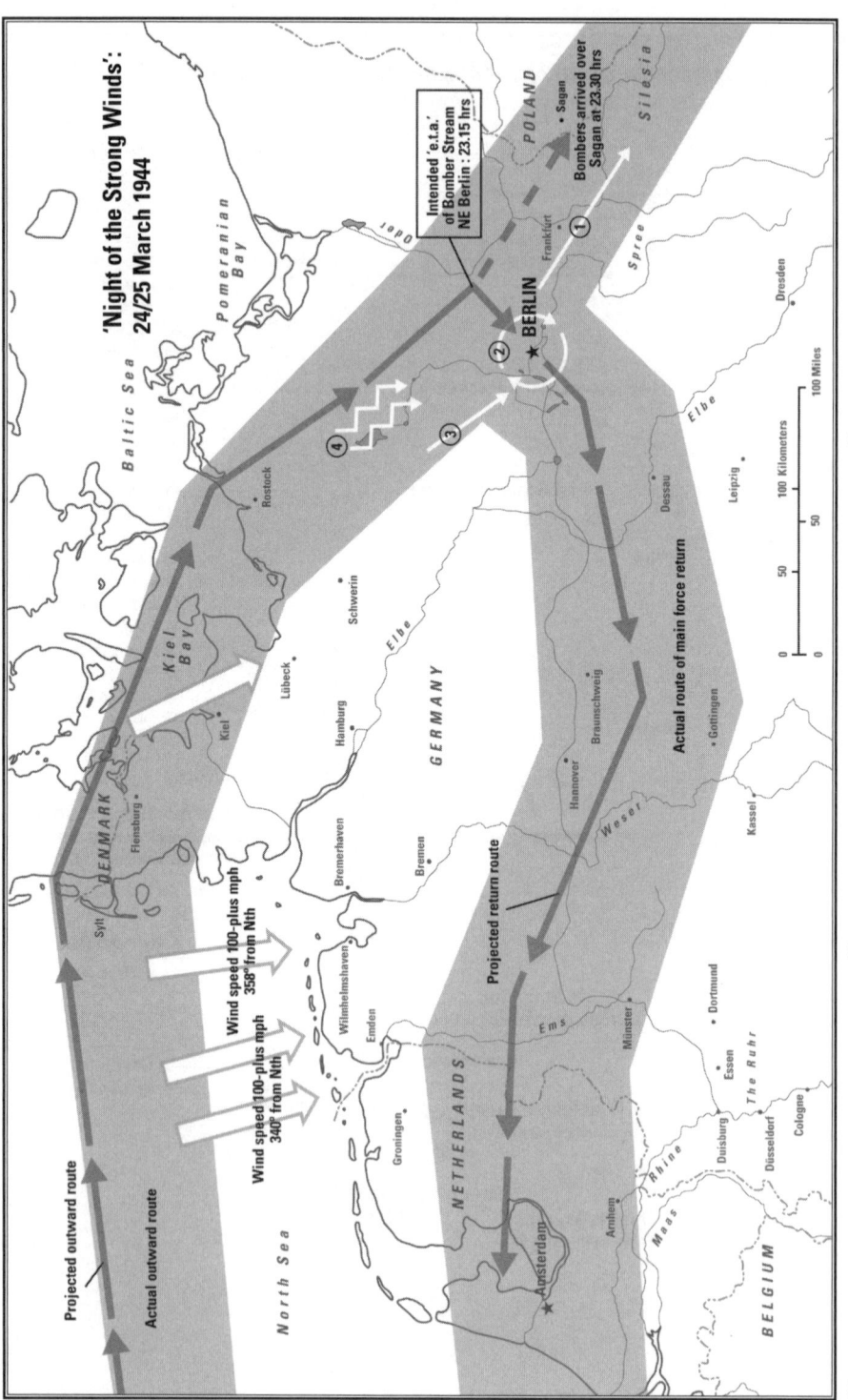

Part One

FIRST STEPS

'There were all sorts, mostly from nineteen years old to their early twenties, a few in their late twenties or sometimes even over thirty. They came from all walks of life, the serious minded, the flippant, the brash or raucous. At times they appeared undisciplined by some standards, but on duty in the air all were members of a team and as one in their application and dedication to the job which had to be done.'

GROUP CAPTAIN TOM SAWYER, 4 GROUP STATION CO,
from *Only Owls and Bloody Fools Fly at Night*, 1982

CHAPTER ONE

'... OTHERWISE I MAY END UP IN THE ARMY'

First Steps

THE 1930s have been described as 'The Devil's Decade': a time of mass unemployment and privation, the origins of which had been the General Strike of 1926 and the Wall Street Crash of 1929. The financial world fell into a trough of depression and in Germany reparations payments bankrupted the country and inflation was rife. In Britain the economy was in a dangerous state with the foreign markets hedged in by protective barriers, exports shrinking, and businesses collapsing. All of this led to more unemployment, people having to find work below their capabilities. In 1931 unemployment benefit cost the government £120 million. Hunger marches were staged as late as 1938, and five days before Christmas 200 unemployed men laid down in front of traffic lights in Oxford Street and stayed there for 24 hours.

Amidst all this misery one bright light seemed to shine through the omnipresent gloom – the rise of the aeroplane. Prospects of appreciating this new wonder were limited however. Opportunities to fly, or to learn to fly, were generally only the province of the rich and famous. Les Hill, a flight engineer, pointed out that 'before the Second World War very few people had flown in an aircraft; commercial flights were only affordable by the rich, mainly on short hops from London to Paris.'[1] Gradually however, this restriction began to be corrected. One pioneer, who inherited the mantle from the barnstormers of the 1920s, and was the origin of many a young man's fantasies, did offer affordable flights. This was Alan Cobham.[2] Ten year-old John Goodrum, who would spend his entire working life in aviation, received the free gift of a flight in Cobham's 'Youth of Britain', an Armstrong Whitworth biplane with a 500 hp Armstrong Siddeley engine. The flight was paid for by a dignitary to stimulate underprivileged children's interest. Bob Burns was brought up in Sheffield and also experienced Cobham's opportunity. In 1935 Cobham's 'Flying Circus' arrived at Coal Aston landing field, four miles from Sheffield city centre and 15 year-old Burns won a competition for a 20-minute flight in a Handley Page H.P.35. Gerald Lane was 12 when his father took him to Lympne airfield to see the 'Flying Circus' in 1928. He paid five shillings for a flight and Gerald was so impressed by it that he maintained his interest with copies of *Flight* magazine, eight years later joining the RAF on a Short Service Commission.[3]

Henry Wagner was 11 years-old in 1934. He recalled having his first flight with Cobham when scraping the finances together to fund such flights was difficult. 'Paying for the flight was just not on', he recalled. 'Sir Alan Cobham's Air Circus was due to come to Henley that year and, by way of publicity, coupons were printed in the Henley Standard. The first ten to be drawn out were to be awarded a free flight. I went round all the houses in the neighbourhood asking if I could have their coupons, and sent in a whole batch of them. One of them brought home the bacon.'

These flights with early pioneers like Cobham whetted the appetite of many young men. There had been an expansion in higher education in the 1920s: increased government expenditure meant that university places rose by more than 100 per cent by 1939,[4] and it was educated individuals such as Wagner who became the lynchpin of the new RAF. Then came war. Wagner went to Reading University in 1940 to study for a French degree and enrolled in the University Air Squadron. 'In August 1942 my call-up papers arrived and I reported to the Aircrew Reception Centre at St. John's Wood, London. After a medical with other students of the squadron… we went to a Holding Unit in Brighton.'

Already regular RAF when war broke out, John Leakey had been brought up to go into finance, but found the routines of ordinary office work difficult to hold down. 'I had two or three jobs in a rather short time and was far from happy', he recalled. 'I had always enjoyed being with a crowd and found it hard to stick to the rules and regulations of an office. As I was working in central London I found it easy to get to the air force recruitment office in Kingsway from where my life took a change.'[5]

Robert Vollum was born into a working class family near Sheffield and educated at a council school before going to Nether Edge Grammar School. He was bright and started work in a local accountants/estate agent's office in 1937, aged 16. Early in 1940 he volunteered for the RAF and passed all the medical examinations and interviews with flying colours. But although he swore an oath of allegiance to the King, disappointingly he was put on 'deferred service'. He recalled: 'I was finally called up to begin my training on my 19th birthday and posted to Blackpool.'

This holding over of recruits continued for some time. In 1942 Peter Banyard had not quite finished school. He added 12 months to his age and volunteered for flying duties with the RAF at Ipswich. But, despite passing all the tests and medical, he was deferred for 12 months – poetic justice some would say.

Russell Margerison was born in 1925 and brought up in a 'two up, two down' workers' house in the backstreets of Blackburn, Lancashire. The last surviving of seven children, he was employed as an apprentice compositor before joining the air force.

Ray Thomas's father was a Fleet Street journalist prone to alcoholism, which was an occupational hazard. Ray's mother divorced him, returning to Cardiff to live with her mother. It was in the middle of the Depression and times were hard: she was only 33 with three young boys to look after. Although passing his Eleven Plus exam, Ray was obliged to leave school at 14 to help with family finances. He received '…the princely sum of 8/4d a week minus stoppages.' His mother made many personal sacrifices: she '…had to have recompense from the Social Services of the day', Ray recalled. 'The indignity of this must have been hard for her to bear.' Social Services had supplied his school uniform and text books. After being called up Ray went to train in Canada.

Dick Raymond was brought up in North Devon. His father ran a small family bakery business founded by his grandfather. This had two delivery men: one drove a motor van, the other a horse and cart. Because they were in the Territorial Army both men were soon called up and Dick was taken out of school and put on the delivery round with the horse. 'It was not an enviable job in winter', he recalled. 'My friends were slowly joining various services, so at the age of seventeen I volunteered for the RAF and was sent to the receiving centre in Exeter. I had been hoping to get an aircrew medical grade, but was told I was unfit for service, but could return in a few weeks time.' The result was that he was assigned as medical grade 3, (unfit for flying duties), but could enrol as an aircraft hand, under training as a flight mechanic. 'I thought maybe I should accept this,' he recalled, 'otherwise I may end up in the army.'

Ron Brown was born in 1921 before his parents' marriage and brought up in the coalfields of Derbyshire. His father was a miner who worked in 'horrendous conditions' and his grandparents were Bible-thumping Christians, which made things difficult. His grandfather could not face the stigma of a bastard grandson in the home and evicted Ron's mother, saying '*Never darken my doors again*', which left Ron sceptical of religious hypocrisy. He joined the RAF in 1939.

Just before the Dunkirk disaster in 1940, Geoffrey Willatt was working for a firm of surveyors in Bloomsbury, driving back and forth daily to digs in Dover. The Germans were shelling the port: 'You could see the flash from the guns 20 miles away in France', he reminisced. Every day a flag on Dover Castle would indicate if shelling was imminent. His landlady refused to have her bath before her daughter checked the flag. 'White or yellow was safe for a bath, but red meant shelling and no bath!' he recalled. After the Dunkirk evacuation the whole country felt exposed. In his London office Willatt became swept up in a feeling of near panic: 'I went round to a Recruiting Office off Euston Road,' he said, 'and signed up for the RAF.'[6]

Lew Parsons worked in a Chelmsford factory in a reserved occupation when war was declared. His mother and stepfather had moved from Clacton-on-Sea to Coventry to find war work, but were bombed out during the German 'Moonlight Sonata' air raid on the city. Lew, consequently, felt the RAF was the logical service for him to join and was accepted in August 1941.

Arthur Cole was born in 1923 and brought up in Broadstone, a small town near Poole, Dorset. He attended the local grammar school. His mother had an unduly high opinion of him and pushed him on. Thus he was 18 months younger than the average age in his class and, when all his friends left to join up after war broke out, he was too young. At 16 he tried to get into the air force but was rejected and not accepted until a year later.

Steve Jackson was brought up in Gloucestershire and served an apprenticeship in Dursley at Maudsleys Ltd, which made dynamos and undertook secret radar work. The production of materials for war was important and hours were long. 'We had to work 12-hour shifts for six days or nights a week and no excuse would allow you time off', he recalled. Initially, the war had little effect upon him, but '…over a period, things became more difficult to obtain and eventually rationing of food and clothing came into effect. We began to know that we were at war.' He was in a reserved occupation, could not be conscripted, but equally could not volunteer. The only exceptions were for aircrew and submarine work. 'I wanted to join up,' he recalled, 'and certainly did not want to go on submarines, so I volunteered for aircrew.'

John Nunn, born in 1923, was brought up in the depths of the Suffolk countryside. He left school aged 14 in 1937 and worked for the local village builder to learn carpentry. His foreman had served with the Royal Flying Corps (RFC) in the First World War and had trained as a rigger on the wood and canvas biplanes which equipped the RFC's squadrons. Whilst working, he told John stories of the RFC aircraft on which he had worked. In the late 1930s the RAF was expanding through a scheme for apprentices inaugurated by Lord Trenchard, who had commanded the Independent Air Force in 1918; there were advertisements in the papers every day for staff. But when he looked at the standards required, John realised that his youth and poor village schooling were not good enough to qualify. He could only dream of flight.

Don Wilson was better equipped. A pre-war student at Edinburgh Veterinary College, and a member of the Senior Division Officer Training Corps, he trained for 'mounted cavalry' with the Dragoon Guards but within a year the War Department had dismounted the regiment and sold its horses. So he transferred to the 10th Hussars, Royal Armoured Corps at Aldershot for tank training. But, as he was not too happy with tanks, he joined the RAF.

Peter Gibby, a ground crewman, recalled that the circumstances of his taking up a trade were unusual, not reflecting his initial leanings: 'I hoped to follow my brother, who was three years older, and become a wireless operator/air gunner: he did a tour on Whitleys and then went on to Training Command.' Their parents thought that he was safe but, one night, awaiting take-off, another Wellington landed on them and most of the crew, including Peter's brother, was killed. His parents wanted Peter to stay on the ground, so he became an electrician.[7]

John Geddes was a Metropolitan Policeman serving in London's Dockland during the Blitz in 1940. In 1941 the Police were permitted to volunteer for aircrew duties, so John applied to be an RAF navigator.

Although brought up in Plymouth, Fred Danckwardt was of Danish/German origin. In 1941 he was evacuated with his school, Devonport Boys High School, to Penzance. His grandfather was born in Holstein,[8] then a Danish state, but left at 18 and went to England. 'My grandfather spoke German', Fred recalled. 'He didn't speak Danish, but his travel documents said Dane – so they didn't know whether he was Danish or German; but he spoke German.' During the First World War he was interned: 'The Saxe-Coburg-Gothas became Windsor; the Battenbergs became the Mountbattens, but my granddad didn't anglicise his name so they put him on the Isle of Wight.' Fred was in the Penzance Home Guard at school: 'I never saw a gun; but we had an "offensive weapon" – a metal pipe with a bayonet stuck in the end.' As soon as he was eighteen, while still at school, Fred volunteered for the RAF.

Laurie Simpson – my father – was born in 1918 and brought up in Deniliquin, New South Wales at the centre of Saltbush Country: 26,000 square miles of extremely dry plains in the south-west of the Riverina, an area bounded by the Murray, Darling and Murrumbidgee Rivers. Laurie's father, Joe, was a builder and carpenter, owning a small brickworks in the town, where Laurie worked as a youth. His upbringing was Roman Catholic. He was an altar boy and learned to throw the boomerang with Aboriginal boys when visiting the local Catholic mission. It was a beautiful but unforgiving land and, years before, with no hospital in the ramshackle town, exhausted men met their deaths on the arid plains or, if they had money, put up in a local hotel to die. If they were destitute they were thrown in the jail and died there. The killer of outlaw Ben Hall was made Police Inspector of Deniliquin in the 1890s, and Ned Kelly himself was reputed to have once visited. Laurie's teenage friend Gertrude MacDonald remembered Laurie as 'one out of a box'; 'a lovely fellow', tall, dark-haired and handsome, with a quiet, understanding nature.[9] The Simpsons were not from convict stock, but originated in the pioneer folk of Australia, whilst Laurie's mother was from the Dennis family from the 'Lorna Doone country' of Exmoor. In the autumn of 1938 Laurie joined the local militia, the 39th City of Bendigo Regiment. After a month's training he was promoted to

Sergeant, but soon became bored with the inactivity. So, in January 1939, he joined the air force at the battalion HQ.

American Robert Raymond, who joined the RAF before Pearl Harbor, was brought up in Kansas City, and served as a volunteer ambulance man during the Battle of France. He was from a strict, religious background – his grandfather had been a Methodist preacher in Eastern Kansas in the days when wagon trains crossed the prairies. Men had to work ten hours a day, six days a week, just to eat in those days. It was this background of competitiveness, and a desire to excel, that led Raymond, a boyish-looking, short, 28 year-old with a slight stammer, to succeed as a bomber pilot.

An Australian from even more obscure origins than Laurie Simpson was Queenslander, Jan Goulevitch. 'John' Goulevitch, as he preferred to be called, was born in February 1919 close to the border of Siberia and Manchuria. His family had emigrated from central Russia to take up new land. They lived in Shanghai for a number of years, but on 1 April 1925 Jan arrived in Townsville, Queensland in the ship the SS *Tango Maru* after travelling from Yokohama in Japan. The holds were full of refugees and migrants. His father and mother had arrived six months earlier: when they disembarked, they saw so many sunburnt dockworkers on the quayside that they concluded Australia to be full of Negroes. They falsely gave their identity as Polish and the whole family subsequently moved to Ayr in Queensland, where they remained for many years. Jan became a carpenter and cabinetmaker there. In 1943 he enlisted in the RAAF.

These were but a few of the 125,000 or so men who served as aircrew with Bomber Command from 1939 to 1945. They had travelled to England for one purpose: to fight.

Forging the Weapon
Largely due to his work with the Independent Air Force, the most significantly influential figure in British bombing strategy development before World War Two was General Sir Hugh Trenchard. The Independent Air Force, founded in France in June 1918 under Trenchard's command, was part of the new RAF, and equipped with Handley Page's 0/400 and enormous V/1500 'Bloody Paralyser' biplane bombers. Trenchard, actually sceptical of any use of an independent bomber force, was ordered to attack Germany's 'densely populated industrial centres', the aim being to destroy their morale;[10] however, only a limited number of tactical attacks and even fewer strategic industrial attacks were carried out before the Armistice was signed.[11]

Trenchard considered the morale impact of bombing 20 times greater than the material impact. A phrase originally coined by P.M. Stanley Baldwin and used by proponents of bombing strategy for years afterwards, largely out of context, was the popular '*the bomber will always get through.*' Baldwin was actually trying to raise public awareness of the dangers of bombing: there '…was no power on earth,' he said, that could prevent 'the man on the street' from 'being bombed', qualifying this with the even more controversial '*The only defence is offence*', i.e. one has '…to kill more women and children more quickly than the enemy' in order to win.

On 21 May 1935 the Cabinet held a special meeting which approved plans to accelerate the expansion of the air force. A broad timetable was set for any future building work and, the same day, contractors received instructions to proceed with the construction of new RAF stations in Lincolnshire and Shropshire. These were but a drop in the ocean of future airfield development, but there was a real fear that the German Air Force would carry out strategic attacks against British targets. However, the *Luftwaffe* had been developed primarily as a tactical force to support the *Wehrmacht*, and its equipment reflected this, although the Cabinet was unaware of this fact. British thinking concerning bombing developed completely independently from that in France and Germany, partly reflecting the fact that British cities had been the object of bombing by the first 'heavy' bombers – the German Zeppelins and Gothas of the First World War. Ever since the formation of the Independent Air Force, the British 'powers that be' had been committed to the principle of strategic bombing by a unit independent of other forces.

The formation of Bomber Command in 1936 was part of the general drive to expand the RAF, although this was late in the day considering how advanced Germany's militarization had become. But even though it had a defined purpose of long-range attack, the RAF did not have the tools to fulfil this mission. Much of its equipment, including bomb sights, had been inherited from the First World War. Biplanes such as the Heyford, a 'heavy' bomber in the parlance of the period, were still considered front line aircraft. Only with the introduction of modern monoplane bombers, such as the Armstrong Whitworth Whitley and the Handley Page Hampden, could the RAF be considered in any way capable of strategic attack, and such aircraft rapidly became obsolete. So there was a futuristic concept with antiquated equipage.

At the outbreak of war on 3 September 1939, there was a certain naive feeling amongst some senior British staff officers that the war would continue where it had left off in 1918, making no allowance for developments in the interim period. A succession of well-meaning civil servants in the 1930s had contrived to resist moves to rearm, ignoring Churchill's cries from the 'wilderness', and discouraged any financial expenditure on the RAF. Their somewhat misguided thinking was that a weak Britain was less likely to be attacked than a strong one.

Senior RAF staff had no idea what course the conflict would take. Throughout the 1930s there had been a series of switches in strategic thinking, from offensive to defensive conduct. A theory developed, which was later adopted by Hitler during the area bombing of Germany, that the only acceptable way to counter a bomber offensive was to have a bomber force equal to or greater than the enemy's. There was also the consideration of range. If the Germans invaded France or Belgium, they would have only 22 miles to travel across the Channel to reach British targets. British aircraft attacking Germany, however, would have much further to travel and German defences consequently would have more forewarning than the British, giving them time for preparation. As important as this, German centres of population and industry were far more widely dispersed than in Britain, especially in the east of Germany where they were beyond the range of British attacks.

When Bomber Command was formed in 1936 simultaneously with Fighter, Coastal and Training Commands, it was not proposed as a night force and preparatory training was poor. It was difficult to replicate in 1938 what would have been the impenetrable blackness of a wartime blackout. Ideally this could only be achieved over the sea, but night-flying practice at that time was generally undertaken near well-lit home airfields. The comparative ratio of daylight to night-flying hours practised in 1938 for most crews was 10:1.

There was also a sparseness of thinking in the Air Ministry on the protection of the bombers. Losses were so high amongst the Hampdens, Whitleys and Wellingtons early in the war that by April 1940 the decision was made to switch them to night raids. After the first few night ops, crews realised that the problems of distance, darkness and bad weather were very real. In aircraft like the Wellington, the second pilot was the navigator. However, when single pilot aircraft were introduced, such as the Hampden, all the thinking behind navigational techniques had to be reconsidered, and it became gradually accepted that long-range navigation at night was highly specialised work, in days when navigation equipment was extremely basic and often inaccurate.

In 1937 Chamberlain's government, despite apparently adopting a stance of appeasement, realised that Hitler represented a substantial threat, and that some form of detailed plan for aerial action would be required if a war broke out. This led to the Western Air Plans. These were drawn up by the Air Staff in 1937 in response to a government request: a list of 13 objectives, divided into four groups, was prepared for all RAF Commands. The most important of these were Group I, Plans 1 to 5, three of which applied to Bomber Command. In a condensed form these were: WA 1 for an attack on the *Luftwaffe's* striking force; WA 4 for an attack on *Wehrmacht* areas of concentration, and for breaking any communications supporting an attack into Belgium, Holland and France; and, most importantly, WA 5 for attacking industrial concentrations in the Ruhr, Rhineland and Saar. Only WA 5 was viewed by Bomber Command as 'useful and realistic'. Its aim was to neutralise the whole of the Ruhr's armament industry by attacking Germany's main sources of power, its power and coking plants, with 3,000 operations in 14 days. Predicted losses for these were 176: optimistic in the light of later developments.

However, although the Bomber Command's new C-in-C, Sir Edgar Ludlow-Hewitt,[12] was enthusiastic about WA 5, before it could be implemented a list of priority targets had to be drawn up. This was done at the beginning of 1938 by a sub-committee of the 1934 Air Intelligence Centre, which led to the problem of deciding what the key elements were for the functioning of a large-scale industrial system. From this arose two separate factions: one for attacking rail and canal networks, and the other for attacking the electric power supply.[13] However it was soon realised that a huge number of individual attacks would be necessary before any of these strategies could be effective.

The Chiefs of Staff, unimpressed with the sub-committee's conclusions, finally decided against any preparations for implementing WA 5 and, in April 1938, the British and French commanders officially decided against any intentional bombing of civilians. However the initial objection to WA 5 ceased automatically when Germany invaded France and the Low Countries in May 1940.

• • •

At the beginning of the 1930s England was still suffering from the effects of a worldwide depression. Many thousands were out of work and, as in Germany, the gearing up for war meant employment. New developments in technology meant new skills had to be learned. The majority of men who enlisted in the new Bomber Command, particularly in the ranks, generally came from very humble and deprived backgrounds. There was no conscription for aircrew and throughout the war aircrew service was entirely voluntary: for the ordinary man aircrew was a much more attractive and exclusive option than the infantry or submarines. In the army one never knew where one was going to be, but it certainly was not so in the air, and death at sea was a far more chilling prospect than death in the air. The motivation for joining could vary considerably and many were deeply influenced by events in the society around them.

The Dunkirk evacuation, the bombing of Coventry and the London Blitz affected many, particularly those who had lost friends, homes and relations, or knew people who had. Many joined simply because they were following in colleagues' footsteps. Some had already served in a uniformed service, whilst others had been RAF regulars before the war. Some came straight from university and were influenced by the pioneers such as Sir Alan Cobham. Some like John Nunn, with very little formal education, were still able to eventually obtain high rank. Others were advised to avoid aircrew duty altogether because of the dangers involved. Bush pilots, cowboys, and men from even more obscure backgrounds came to the bomber war by some unbelievably indirect and varied paths.

With the Nazi warhorse rearing its head, these young men were offered an unprecedented opportunity to fly in extremely high-tech aircraft. Developments in aviation and military strategy were eons away from the primitive thinking of 1918, despite some staff officers' outdated thinking. The new monoplane stressed-skin bombers could deliver a relatively large payload at heights and speeds unequalled by existing designs.

These were the beginnings of a relatively inflexible organisation that evolved into a colossal professional force dedicated to wholesale destruction, although no one saw it thus at that time, or realised what it would lead to. The aircraft were there; the men were there; but they had to be trained.

CHAPTER TWO

'THAT'S THE LAST TIME YOU WILL EVER BE AT THE CONTROLS!'

Training

IN September 1939 the Royal Air Force was inadequately equipped to counter the threat of a modern, battle-tried air force such as the *Luftwaffe*, already blooded in the skies over Spain. Immediately after war was declared a massive air-training programme was set up involving all the air forces of the Commonwealth. The Empire Air Training Scheme has since been described as '…the single largest aviation training programme in history'. It was responsible for training nearly half the pilots, navigators, bomb-aimers, gunners, wireless operators and flight engineers of the Commonwealth air forces in the Second World War. Under an initial agreement of December 1939 it was planned that 50,000 aircrew would be trained each year for as long as was required: 22,000 were to come from Britain, 13,000 from Canada, 11,000 from Australia, and 3,300 from New Zealand. Elementary training was to take place in the various Commonwealth countries and advanced training in Canada. Canada was the optimum location for the 'The Plan' because of its ample fuel supplies, open spaces, industrial facilities for the supply of trainers, parts and supplies, lack of threat from Axis forces, and distance from the war theatres. At its peak 'The Plan' incorporated 231 training sites, 10,000 aircraft and 100,000 administrative personnel. Of 167,000 students, 50,000 were pilots.

Ronnie Cartwright, who became a wireless operator with 49 Squadron, recalled:

'The first few weeks in the Royal Air Force were tough with foot drill, arms drill, strict discipline and general fitness exercises. I wasn't physically fit when I started, but I was when I finished. Getting up at 6 am, polishing, cleaning, having breakfast and being on parade at 8 a.m. were foreign to us all. The instructors appeared to be ruthless and almost inhuman, using a rare form of English with a combination of uncommon, unusual, obscene and lewd words. First impressions were not encouraging, but I later learned that the instructors had to instil in us a sense of rigid discipline in a short period and that harsh treatment was the only way to break us from our mother's apron strings.'

RAF staff often played pranks on inexperienced trainees. One instructor at Binbrook in Lincolnshire, when tired with an AC2[1] acting up at lectures, sent the erk off to the stores to collect some 'tappet clearances' and a bucket of 'propeller pitch', to get him out of the way. The aircraftman never found them.[2]

Alan Castle, who later became a navigation leader with 101 Squadron, also suffered from pranksters as a trainee: 'I suspect that I looked much younger than my actual age of 19, as I was only 9 stone, but 6 ft tall. One day I was called to the CO's office and given a requisition form for an 'oxometer' and told to collect this from the stores. When I presented the requisition I was told that the 'oxometer' was out on loan to the MO. I went there and was told that it had been taken by the Adjutant. The Adjutant's office told me that it had gone to another department. This went on all afternoon until eventually I returned to the CO's office and told him I had been unable to find the 'oxometer'. He just told me to take no further action. It was not until over a year later that I learned that an oxometer was a machine for measuring bulls' testes!'[3]

John Nunn ended up at the Number 9 Reception Centre at Blackpool, after Warrington and Padgate, and was subsequently declared an Aircraft Hand, General Duties, Second Class. He was then posted to the No. 3 School of Technical Training, at Squires Gate, near Blackpool, where there was also a Vickers Aircraft factory producing Wellington bombers. He left a particularly fascinating and detailed account of his early training as a Flight Mechanic (Engines), which illustrates the lengths to which, even in those days, the RAF was willing to go in order to attain the precision necessary for its technical work. Nunn had received only very limited schooling at his village school as a young man. On his course the majority of trainees had been to grammar or secondary schools and had a much higher standard of education than the four or five of the 'entries' who had left school at 14 or 15. 'This had a marked effect', he said. 'It was very noticeable that they seemed to absorb everything easily whereas we had to work very hard to achieve the same results.'

Keith Slade was also assigned to Squires Gate and had previously been to Yardley Grammar School where 'people simply didn't steal'. On the first day of his three months at No.3 S.T.T. he had his fountain pen stolen. 'Most of the chaps had a very poor education and, whilst they could express themselves volubly with some highly unusual language… I doubt if many of them could have ventured further than "the cat sat on the mat".' He passed his mechanics' course with flying colours, achieving the highest mark ever given, and was awarded his 'Props' (a winged cloth badge with the image of a propeller indicating that the wearer was a qualified air mechanic).

Nunn found it more difficult. 'I had a full week in the classrooms, taking Maths and English; they even tried to teach me some algebra but with little success.' On 17 September 1942 he started basic training:

> 'The first two weeks were designated to basic training and to assess if we were suitable. There was some classroom work, where we were told about different tools etc., files, hacksaw blades, metals and the colour codes, various types and uses of nuts and bolts. The practical work consisted of us taking a piece of mild steel plate and producing a test piece that was about three inches long, by an inch and a quarter wide and about a third of an inch thick. It had to be in two pieces and joined in the middle by a dovetail joint. The whole thing had to be produced to a tolerance of plus or minus two thousandths of an inch. To achieve this level of accuracy, we had to learn to use a micrometer and Vernier Gauge, scribers and a scribing block to mark the metal and a rubbing block to check that we had filed it level and flat.
>
> 'We all passed this phase except for one chap. His uncle was in the RAF and he had been continually telling us what would happen and what we would have to do. At the end of the first week, he was told that he was not suitable and was taken off the course. He had to pack his kit immediately and was posted. After the second week, we were tested on what we had been taught, our test piece was checked for size and we were told that we had all passed.'[4]

Keith Slade also started from scratch with basic training: 'We had two blocks of aluminium about 4 ins by 3 ins, more or less oval, with a scoop out of each. We had to scrape the surfaces, using engineer's blue [paste], to get them as flat as possible, before drilling and tapping six holes for studs and fastening them together. We then had to drill into the joint and screw in a Schrader Valve, to pressure test our work. One can imagine the leaks.'

But even Slade's work had bubbles: 'It seemed to me that almost no one had any idea about how to use a file or engineer's blue', he concluded. At grammar school he had had a proficient metalwork teacher, '... so I coped very well, not only with the basic training but also with my grasp of the detailed workings of both radial and in-line engines.' Ignition and magnetos, carburettors, superchargers and boost controls were all grist to the mill and 'the variable pitch propeller I found to be a most absorbing engineering contrivance.' After a week's leave Slade was posted to RAF Waterbeach at Cambridge.

John Nunn recalled one character he subsequently met on his course at No. 9 'Arsy-tarsy',[5] Blackpool:

'Life at Blackpool was not service life as you would imagine it. It was more like civilian life, going to the office each day from eight until five with the rest of the time your own. There were none of the fatigues, drills, parades or petty restrictions we would have had on a camp and when we finally did get posted to a camp, we certainly noticed the difference.

'There was a chap called Humphries from the West Country. He was the only one amongst us who spoke and acted as if he had been to public school, and had a terrific sense of humour. He was very fond of chocolate and was always trying to scrounge from the others. One day, someone had the bright idea of buying a bar of *Exlax* (the laxative chocolate) and feeding it to him in the hope that he would get the "trots" and be cured of his addiction. The plan backfired though, because it had absolutely no effect on him. On his return from our forty-eight hour leave, he told us a lurid tale about how he had picked up a girl on the train to London and spent the weekend with her at the Strand Palace Hotel. Whether it was true or not, he was certainly a good raconteur and had us all in stitches as he recounted his experiences, many of which would not bear repeating. I will always remember how he stood in front of a fire notice and pretended to read it: "*If you discover a fire, try to put it out. If this is impossible, pour some petrol on to keep it going while you fetch help*".'[6]

Russell Margerison recalled his experiences of the Aircrew Selection Board procedure whilst at RAF Padgate in November 1942. After two days of peculiarly unusual aptitude tests, both physical and mental, that could only have originated with the RAF at that time, he was asked to appear before the selection board. In a large interview room he was confronted by a line of ageing RAF officers 'with enough decorations on their chests to cover a snooker table', he later commented. Always, at the end of an interview, a prospective airman was asked, in order to test his initiative, what Margerison termed 'a silly question'. One candidate was confronted, typically, with: 'What would you do if you were on sentry duty on the fringe of a wood and were attacked by a submarine?' To which the young man responded: 'I would throw my cap at it sir.' He was successfully accepted for Aircrew training.

At the Officer Training Unit at Uxbridge in 1937, Derek Hodgkinson, a pilot with No. 1 Coastal Operational Training Unit flying Hudsons, met a character named 'Dismal' Devitt who was an acting pilot officer:

'The opening address of the course was given by the station commander, an elderly, irate-looking group captain, on 'The Behaviour Expected of an Officer and a Gentleman'.

He banged on for about twenty minutes whilst we all sat bolt upright in our chairs trying to look interested in this extraordinary subject, when suddenly he stopped. The ensuing silence would have been shattering, had it not been for the rhythmic sound of snoring: the snoring of a heavy sleeper. The group captain, who had turned slightly white with shock, transfixed the back row of his audience with a terrible stare: we all turned round, and there was Dismal, comfortably stretched out in his chair with his head sunk on his chest, oblivious to the world. He jumped at least a foot when he was awakened by a strangled cry from the stage: "*Adjutant, place that officer under close arrest, and have him before me at 0800 hours tomorrow!*"[7]

Devitt later became CO of the RAF's Advanced Training Squadron.

Eric Foinette, whose family were of Huguenot extraction and had holidayed in Germany before the war, became a navigator with 12 Squadron. He remembered one particular individual who was on his course at Prestwick:

'At nine weeks Bispham, who had bluffed his way past the CO to remain on the course, was caught cribbing in a test to see if he had progressed. That finished him and he was suspended. He went on leave but did not report back, and so a warrant for his arrest was ordered. Two regular "S.P.s" were sent to collect him and bring him back to Prestwick. When found, he was wearing sergeant's stripes and wings and was chargeable on quite a few counts. But, upon reaching Prestwick, he slipped his guards and disappeared. He had made himself both objectionable and unpopular – no one knows how he got as far as he did because his educational standard was low for a budding observer.'[8]

Eric Foinette (Foinette)

Years later, when Foinette was in *Stalag Luft* III a pilot named Thompson arrived. Another *Kriegie*,[9] who had been with Foinette at Prestwick, called him over to ask if he recognised Thompson. 'I immediately identified him as Bill Bispham. He at first denied it all and we reported the matter, because he was the only survivor of his crew and we feared he may have been a plant.' But eventually Thompson admitted the truth, and then said he had changed his name in Ireland and enlisted for pilot training. This time, Foinette assumed, he had made the grade. 'How he got a commission, though, was beyond our comprehension because he was quite an unpleasant character.' Although the SBO accepted the story, Bispham was taken away for court martial, allegedly for having struck a guard, and the Germans ultimately shot him. Foinette had no idea why. 'He was given a jail sentence and was not heard of again. Maybe he was really a plant but removed by the Germans when we reported him', Foinette concluded.[10]

Australia

Laurie Simpson started his flying training on 4 May 1941 at No. 3 Elementary Flying Training School, Essendon, Victoria. After nine-and-three-quarter hours' dual instruction he did a ten-minute solo on his 21st flight. He had developed a carbuncle on the back of his neck during training and found it very difficult to loop the aircraft, which was a standard DH. 82 Tiger Moth. Not only did pupils have to be familiar with the cockpit layout and controls, and be able to taxi, fly straight and level, climb, glide and stall and perform medium turns, but they also had to be able to take off into the wind, make both powered and gliding approaches and landings, spin, slide slip, fly low (with an instructor), make steep and climbing turns and force-land. 'Easy stuff' with an instructor, but the course became progressively more difficult, culminating in instrument flying, restarting the engine in flight and aerobatics, to name just a few elements.

After Laurie's final test on 24 June, having flown 25.03 hours dual and 25.5 hours as a pilot, the Chief Flying Instructor stated that he was an 'average' pupil. Points to be watched, however, were that he was '…generally inaccurate and careless of detail'. It was a mediocre beginning. By 19 August 1941, after six weeks at the Service Flying Training School at Amberley, Queensland, with 49½ hours under his belt on twin-engined Ansons, he was an 'average' pilot.

By the time Laurie had boarded a troopship for England, the SS *Themistocles*, (a requisitioned, coal-fired liner of World War One vintage), his flying was still 'average', as was his navigation. The trainee aircrew were going via the Cape of Good Hope and they envied those on a boat bound for the USA with the opportunities to see the sights over there. Earlier, on 11 November, Laurie had expressed his feelings on what awaited them:

'*Armistice Day*
A doubtful day as to the weather and my feelings. The latter were very mixed as I left Spencer's Street station for God knows what. To say au revoir to my family, my sweetheart and my friends would be unbearable except for the companionship of my fellow aircrews. This promises to be a wonderful adventure and, if we come through on top, an invaluable experience. But then it is tough on the folks left behind.'

The trainees were given £5 Sterling for the trip and eventually boarded the *Themistocles* on 17 November 1941. The following day, after awaking with a 'nasty cold', Laurie began to perk up:

'*[It] was queer for me to be gazing at an endless vista of sea, sea and more sea. Had an escort of various sea birds whose tireless gyrations caused us endless enjoyment. Wish I could handle an aircraft the way they handle themselves. Saw my first sunset at sea and it made me think of my loved ones so near, yet so far. Still, let's get on with our job and finish it, then we'll come back for our just heritage.*'

Wilson's Promontory – the southern extremity of Victoria – was eventually sighted and the ship soon steamed west into the Bass Straight. Despite being close to home, paravanes[11] were launched due to the threat of Japanese mines and the vessel was continuously pitching in a heavy swell. They ran into a storm on the 20th and Laurie was given charge of a team to supply shells to the aft naval gun. On the 24th they sighted land and berthed at Albany. When they went ashore they had a whale of a time, playing billiards, drinking spirits and meeting girls. Laurie was developing a close friendship with a fellow pilot he had met at Essendon named Graeme Keys: '*Graeme and I seem to be stuck everywhere together viz postings, commissions, berths, boat stations etc. Really a remarkable coincidence*', he wrote. It was the same 'remarkable coincidence' that was to take them to the same Advanced Flying Unit, the same Operational Training Unit and the same Heavy Conversion Unit. In fact they would both be posted to the same bomber squadron and both serve as Flight Commanders simultaneously. They would start and finish their tours at the same time, and both be awarded the DFC together. The friendship, which seemed to be based on a subtle chemistry, would end only when one went missing and the other was killed on operations.

On 27 November they were halfway out of King George's Sound at 05.00 hrs. On the 29th they arrived at Fremantle and left on 5 December: '*It is now 6.30 and*

Australia has just disappeared below the skyline', Laurie wrote. *'This time it is quite definitely gone for many, many months. Still I'm glad to be getting on with the job. I wonder what the people we leave behind think and feel at this moment.'*[12]

Little did he know that it would be over three-and-a-half years before he would see his homeland again. Many of those with him, including Graeme Keys, would never see it again.

South Africa

A number of RAF aircrews trained abroad, away from the war zone. Postings to Canada were popular, but there were also training centres in exotic places such as the Bahamas. Henry Wagner did most of his early training in South Africa:

'Tropical kit was issued to us so we knew we were headed for somewhere warm. We travelled by train to Liverpool and were marched from the station to the docks, to embark on a troopship – the 23,000-ton SS *Strathmore*. Ten days after setting out we sailed into Freetown, Sierra Leone. Three days later we put to sea again, to arrive in Durban, South Africa a fortnight later. South Africa was a new world to all of us, far removed from the wartime austerity of England. There were no blackouts, the shops were full of everything, and no ration books.'

Wagner spent three weeks at Roberts Heights, which he regarded as 'time wasted', waiting for a vacancy at the Navigational Training School. Eventually he was posted to No. 43 Air School, where he learnt the rudiments of navigation.

'For the first three weeks of training nothing much happened. We did a lot of PT, played rugby, and regularly marched the drill square with and without rifles. It was during a rifle drill one day that the station warrant officer, Warrant Officer Barnett, came out to watch us. Observing the drill manoeuvre "Put down arms", when the rifle had to be laid on the ground, he shouted, *"You lot remind me of a lot of WAAFs getting down on a jerry!*[chamber pot]" *"What a common man,"* I thought, *"how does HE know what a WAAF would actually look like getting down on a jerry?"*'

On 22 December 1941, the SS *Themistocles* steamed into Durban. *'Awoke to find us steaming slowly into the roadstead outside Durban'*, Laurie Simpson wrote. *'Around us are some 20 odd ships all waiting their turn to dock. Ships of British, Norwegian, Belgian, Argentine and French nationalities are here.'* On 18 January 1942 the ship reached Freetown, but it was found that there had been a big mistake: *'It seems that we should never have left Newcastle (Australia) with 160 fully trained aircrew aboard; should never have left Cape Town unescorted; should never have come to Freetown. Someone blundered, at our expense. Two submarines chased us three days out from here, the Navy got one. Half-a-dozen of us saw the depth charges that got it, but didn't realise it at the time. No doubt about this ship – she's dead lucky.'*

Canada

Bob Kemley became a navigator with 427 Squadron. He joined the RAF in 1941 as a Trainee Observer and did his ground training before going to Canada. Under the Empire Air Training Scheme, his instruction was at Charlottetown, Prince Edward Island:

'In those days air navigation was a continuous task of establishing wind velocity which is, in essence, the movement over ground of a vast column of air in which your aircraft is flying and with which it is being taken. Air speeds were then relatively slow and a wind velocity of 30 knots would significantly alter the aircraft's direction and/or speed over the ground, and would have to be allowed for. There were several methods of calculating wind velocity, all involving the solution of a triangle of velocities, and this would vary according to the data available.'[13]

At Prince Edward Island all these methods were practised and, flying out of sight of land over the Gulf of St. Lawrence, coastal navigation was undertaken. But taking bearings and map reading was done over land. Astro-navigation could be done anywhere after dark.[14]

The RAF had a prerogative for changing its plans if it was thought necessary. Howard Pearce originally went to Hastings in Sussex for his initial training but, since that was too close to France, he was transferred to Torquay. He was then to be posted to Africa, but there was some confusion:

'The funny part was they said, "*You're going abroad for training, so here's your khaki and sun helmet – you're going to Africa.*" Then, at the very end, they said, "*Have it all back, you're going to Liverpool, and then by boat over to Canada.*" So that's what happened – they changed their mind. It's a little complicated as I was in the second batch of RAF characters sent to Canada. I wasn't a bomb-aimer then: bomb-aimers hadn't been introduced – the navigator did the bomb-aiming. I passed my navigation course, and shone at signals, so they said, "*We want signaller/gunners at present, not navigators. If you do a course on signals you'll get an automatic commission.*" I thought "*Well that's good enough for me.*" I loved Canada, the training was terrific, and the girls beautiful: it was a great place. So I stayed there [and trained as a signaller] at Montreal. I think I was over there for a year and a bit altogether, from 1940. Then I came back, went to Cranwell, then to Newmarket on a gunnery course, and then to squadron.'[15]

Ted Boorman, who became a navigator/bomb-aimer with 102 Squadron at Pocklington, also trained in Canada.

'We were at Belle Vue first where it was freezing cold with only the uniform on. Then we trained to be observers at Ainsi-Lorette in Quebec. It was summer and was very nice there. They got me onto a navigator's course. It was a 24-week course, which meant every fortnight one course would finish, and so upon arrival, you went to the back of the queue. The first course in front got their half wings, and then every fortnight it would start again. Every fortnight you moved forward a stick. Later we did bombing training on the St. Lawrence in winter. We used to mark out circles on the ice when it was frozen. We dropped dummy bombs from an Anson, which were actually smoke bombs so they didn't make a hole in the ice.'

After the course had ended, Boorman took a fortnight's holiday in Buffalo. On return he was told he was being posted to Miami to go on Catalinas, but he first had to do a course for 'Navigator Overseas'. He sat the course and passed the exam, but things did not turn out as he expected: he was due for another week's leave and was intending to return to Buffalo, but when he went to collect his tickets,

'…the Sergeant said: "*You're not going to Buffalo: you're going back to England. You're not going on Catalinas: you're going to Bomber Command.*" I thought Miami would have been lovely, so I lost out on that. I don't know why. They wanted more people in Bomber Command, I suppose. They wanted crews.'

Whilst Ray Thomas was in Canada training to be a navigator he heard that his mother was dying. She was 43. 'My love for her was so deep,' he recalled, 'that when I knew she was very ill I spent several hours in the camp chapel at night, heartbroken and offering my life on ops if God would spare her.' But his beloved mother died. 'The effect on me,' he said, 'a very unworldly "just" 20 year-old, 4,500 miles from home, was absolutely devastating.' He had no counselling from officers or padres, and his contemporaries did not know how to cope with his despair. 'With no chance of compassionate leave,' he said, 'I was reprocessed and carried on somehow to graduation.'

Pilot training was a specialised, highly skilled discipline that normally took anything from 18 months to three years of intensive training: one had to learn to fly several different types of aircraft. The selection method was rigorous, and many people who failed found that they had to accept other skills as second best. There was a variety of different reasons for this, not always because of a lack of ability, but often due to bad luck and the intense pressure of 'The Plan' to produce the large numbers of qualified pilots required in a limited time. As the war progressed recruitment increased and the authorities began pushing them through as fast as possible.

Capable men often failed their pilot training. In some cases the cause of the problem was partly the aircraft: the Tiger Moth was a very light aircraft and trainee pilots found judging its correct height above ground when landing difficult, sometimes having to make several approaches. Some causes were medical. Other cases were attributable to a trainee being too slow and taking too long to perform set tasks. Others were occasionally due to airmen being sent to the wrong establishment. Despite this, trainees accepted the decision against them and went on to fight the war in a different capacity, sometimes outside the more elite 'PNB' scheme.[16]

Eric Foinette's instructor had been dissatisfied with his handling of the Tiger Moth; however one morning the man told Foinette to go solo. His trouble was the aircraft's lightness: it would bounce if dropped from a great height. Foinette found judging the height above ground when making a gliding approach without engine difficult. His first solo was probably his best: he made an almost perfect landing. Unfortunately, this did not continue. After 22 hours, the instructor took him up for a test: 'Although I had finished top of the theoretical subjects,' he remembered, 'he decided to ground me. If the war had gone on for a long time, probably I'd have made a pilot, but time was essential.' Foinette became a navigator with 12 Squadron.

Henry Wagner had similar problems: 'After I had flown ten-and-a-half hours solo an incident occurred which put paid to my dream of becoming a pilot.' His instructor '…got out of the aeroplane, took his control column and off I went. But as I came in over the wire to land I could see I was too high, so I increased speed and went round again.' This happened three times. On the third attempt he had to get down at all costs: 'On touching the ground and having no brakes I could do nothing to arrest [the Moth's] progress and finally stopped two yards from the boundary wire.' He turned the aircraft around manually and then scrambled aboard and taxied back to where the instructor was waiting. '"Right, Wagner", the man said, "Fly me back to Kroonstad and make a good job of it because it's the last time you will ever be at the controls!"' Wagner retrained as a navigator and went to 51 Squadron.

Tom Lees was posted to South Africa to train as a pilot after joining the RAF in late 1939. He had already completed, in six months, the first year of a Cambridge engineering degree, part of an RAF scheme. However, in South Africa, he suffered the misfortune, whilst on exercises, of being shot accidentally in the eye by a fellow trainee, which ended his prospects of ever becoming a pilot. He spent the remainder of his life partially blind.[17]

Arthur Cole trained in Florida on Stearman biplanes, which he found interesting but it only lasted three-and-a-half weeks. 'I had this bad sinusitis problem,' he recalled, 'and they treated me in the sick bay with heat packs and ice packs, and when that didn't work they sent me to a civilian specialist in Miami.' That didn't suit the air force at all so he was posted up to Trenton in Canada by train, to '… a big air force place in Ontario. There I had an operation and was there for some weeks.'

Cole terminated flying training firstly since, although he was still on a pilot's course, he had lost confidence in his 'ability to land', and secondly since he was 'frantic' to get on operations, 'largely because it was the thing to do in those days', he said. Cole wanted to get on ops. 'I volunteered for the relatively new trade of bomb-aimer and trained at a Bombing/Gunnery School at Picton, Ontario.' Cole later became a bomb-aimer with 158 Squadron.

Ted Boorman started off pilot training but, because of an inflexible eight-hour rule, he missed qualifying by half-an-hour.

'You had eight hours to go solo in the war – that's a day! I did all my basic flying, spinning, etc. in a day – you didn't get a second chance! My last instructor said: "All you need is another half-hour to polish a couple of things up; I would send you solo, but I can't because you've had your eight hours."'

Ted's explanation was '…because of the war they were pushing people through, and couldn't mess about!' He retrained as a navigator and went to 102 Squadron.

Graham Korner had been accepted for pilot training but things went wrong:

'I don't know what happened. I tried to join up but when the war broke out I was too young. I got sent home and tried again later, and got accepted for pilot training. But there was a hold-up on training in 1941 and I got put on "deferred service". I was on this for nine months and getting panicky, thinking the war would be over. Eventually my call-up papers arrived and I had to report to Cardington. I thought, "*Wow, wonderful, I'm off!*"'

He arrived at Cardington and the Medical Officer asked what he wanted to do. Korner replied: 'Spitfires. I want to fly Spitfires!' The MO said 'Not here, mate.' Korner asked 'What do you mean, "not here"? I've been called up for pilot training.' The MO responded 'Not *here*. There's no aircrew *here*.' So Korner said he would go home and take it up with the Air Ministry. The MO bristled: 'You walk out the gates, mister; you'll be done for absence without leave.'

Korner felt his best option was to do the shortest course. The medic told him air gunner was fastest, but there was no aircrew at Cardington as it was a ground station. One option was for him to re-muster and join the new RAF Regiment. Although he did not want this, Korner felt it was his only option:

'I kept putting in applications for aircrew, but nothing happened. I was afraid that the war would end. Then, one day, a wing commander came round and they had a parade. He tried to talk us into becoming air gunners, so I got up and explained that I'd been trying to transfer ever since I arrived there. The Wingco turned to his Flight Lieutenant and said "Get this man up to St. John's Wood right away", and the next morning I was gone.'

Graham Korner became a rear gunner with 640 Squadron.

New Arrivals

The trip on the SS *Themistocles* across the Indian Ocean and up into the Atlantic had been not without interest. Laurie Simpson was 23, going on 24 which, he once remarked, was quite old for aircrew. Graeme Keys was seven years older, having been born in 1911. This suggests that, upon enlistment, he must have been at the absolute upper age limit for flying duties. Whilst they were still steaming north, 13 February came and went. Despite being 'Friday the 13th', it was '... *a beautiful sunny day with flat calm seas*', Laurie wrote. A Catalina flew overhead and proceeded to sweep the convoy perimeter. The aircraft were a great comfort, he felt, and gave the men a feeling of security. He noted philosophically: '*When I stop and consider that we are almost in England and entering the War Zone, I find it very unbelievable, and if the "Cat." hadn't flown over today, I'd have thought the war was over.*'

On 16 February, at about midday, they crossed the bar into the Mersey Estuary. As the requisitioned liner steamed upstream they could see the wrecks of ships on either side of the channel. They dropped anchor at 4 pm. It was the first time Laurie had been to England, but his impression was not a clear one: '*It was through a murky fog which made it difficult to distinguish anything*,' he wrote, '*although I believe there are seven miles of docks here.*' Events nearer home also disturbed him. '*I should feel very thrilled, I suppose, but in the face of the events in the East I find it hard to muster enthusiasm. When we land tomorrow we'll see England really for the first time.*'

They berthed on the 17th at 9 a.m. and by 10 a.m. they were on a train to London. They arrived in the capital in the early afternoon and later caught a train to Bournemouth, where there was an Aircrew Reception Centre. The train pulled into Bournemouth Central shortly after 7 pm. Laurie had travelled halfway around England in a day and seen much of the countryside and liked it: '*Seems green and very fertile,*' he wrote, '*and presented a quaint picture with snow occasionally and frozen streams. Our first sight of London was impressive, though bomb damage has been cleared up.*'

The next day he and his friends accepted an invitation to tea at Lady Frances Ryder's Headquarters at the nearby White Hermitage Hotel as part of the 'Lady Frances Ryder and Miss MacDonald of the Isles Hospitality Scheme': the two ladies had had experience of looking after soldiers of the Empire in the First World War and now they tried to match the likes and dislikes of young men from the Dominions with English families.

For the first time the Aussies met English women, whom they found on the whole charming. '*They are not quite as attractive as Australian girls,*' Laurie concluded, '*nor have they figures to compare with our girls, but they all have beautiful peaches and cream complexions.*' He found an earlier scepticism was unfounded. '*Another thing is their conversation,*' he wrote, '*which is very friendly and entirely devoid of lack of confidence, which is the opposite of the impression we've always had.*'

The Australians were offered a week's stay in the countryside with some 'well-to-do people'. They decided that they would take advantage of this and Laurie had nothing but good to say about the Lady Ryder scheme: '*The Lady Frances Ryder Organisation is an amazing show which is solely to send Colonial troops, particularly Aussies, to spend their leave at any place in the country they wish to go, and usually to big manors or well-to-do people in the towns. I take my hat off to this wonderful woman.*'

On the 19th the Aussies took a tour of the local area and enjoyed the trip immensely. They inspected Christchurch Abbey, Whitecliffs Towers (where Kaiser Wilhelm visited in 1907), 'Ye Hendesborough Tap' (dating back to 1603), beautiful old manor houses, and '...old English villages with narrow winding streets and [a] quaint style of architecture'. But, whilst Beaufighters and Spitfires swept overhead, Laurie still felt concerned about the news from the East: '*I'd love to be back there fighting the Japs*', he noted.

A Safe War
Englishman Frank Dennis found himself purely by accident flying operations with a Canadian squadron, No. 419. Whilst training as a flight engineer at St. Athan, he had seen 'a number of brand new Mk 2a Halifaxes from a Coastal Command Maintenance Unit on the airfield.' They were gleaming white, with the old style fin and rudder, four-bladed Rotol props, and four-gun mid-upper turret. To him they looked magnificent. At that time in the war, March 1944, Bomber Command had been suffering very heavy losses and Coastal seemed a much safer option. Dennis later recalled:

'Being of a rather cautious nature I reasoned that my possible chances of survival might be slightly better if I could be crewed on one of those. They were listed as a choice along with a few personnel needed for Stirlings. My fellow trainees thought I was bonkers, but with a little persuasion some decided to join me.'

He was posted to a Heavy Conversion Unit at Topcliffe where a number of Merlin-engined Halifax Mk 1s and Mk 5s were stationed. There were a few Canadian aircrew in the vicinity and Frank thought they were Coastal Command, since Canada was a maritime nation. The new trainees were sent to play cricket and await developments. Presently some Canadian pilots appeared and a lanky one invited Frank onto his crew. Frank then realised that the cricket match had merely been a ruse to allow the Canadians to make their crew selections surreptitiously. He then found, much to his chagrin, that he was posted to No. 6 Canadian Group[18] – which had 14 bomber squadrons. His plan for a 'safe' war had backfired on him.[19]

A Late Starter
Although he was attested in July 1943, Joseph Smith missed the war entirely. He was called up to Lords Cricket Ground for kitting out and to receive inoculations in August 1943 and, after initial training, passed out as a sergeant signaller, but did not arrive on squadron until early 1946. One of the causes of this was a large backlog of crews available for further training in mid-1944. Since the aircraft were becoming more and more sophisticated, there was a large number of failures amongst pupil pilots who had to convert to the four-engined 'heavies'.
Smith recalled:

'I completed my training on 2 June 1944. I was a "Sergeant Signaller Aircrew".[20] From then, until December of that year, we had no further training. We understood that there were insufficient pilots to form crews. We recommenced training in December 1944 for three months at Wigmore, doing three-hour flights over west Scotland, providing bearings on radio beacons to assist the navigator plotting a position. A lot of these were at night.

'At the end of May 1945 we were posted to Abingdon for "crewing up" and training on Wellingtons. This lasted until the end of December 1945.'

In early January 1946 Joseph Smith was posted to Cottesmore H.C.U., Oakham for conversion to Lancasters. He had missed the war altogether.

Despite the RAF having the best of intentions, some men failed to end up where they wanted to go. There was a vast range of abilities in the air force and some people naturally found the training easier than others. Although many were selected for pilot training the selection process soon weeded out the weaker contenders and frequently men had to choose second best in order to get into aircrew.

Some trainees found travelling from the home country almost as dangerous as being in the war itself, while training outside the 'war zone' offered many Englishmen the chance of instruction in sunnier climates where they would never have expected to have gone. Others, however, tried to engineer their placements to where they wanted to go but, like Frank Dennis, failed to achieve their wishes; whilst others still, like Joseph Smith, never saw operations at all.

Now that they had received their initial and advanced training, the aircrews of Bomber Command had to be geared up to fly in some of the world's most highly sophisticated, purpose-designed aeroplanes, in a constantly changing force that would suffer disturbingly high, sustained casualties for the duration of the war – all of them young men who had volunteered unhesitatingly for the task.

CHAPTER THREE

'IT SEEMED TO TAKE QUITE A LOT OF PUNISHMENT WITHOUT FALLING OUT OF THE SKY'

The Aircraft

BOMBER COMMAND was in a constant state of adjustment throughout the war. As the bomber war escalated after 1940, so technology had to change to keep up with this. Due to the foresight of men like Sir Wilfred Freeman[1] and Winston Churchill, the future Prime Minister, who was at that time out of office, a move for rearmament came between 1935 and 1937. This resulted in a number of tenders for new aircraft being put out, particularly for the radically new twin-engined and four-engined 'heavy' bombers after it was realised that antiquated machines like the Heyford were hopelessly out of date. As production work proceeded on medium bombers such as the Manchester, the Whitley, the Hampden and the Wellington, so the strengths and weaknesses of the aircraft began to become apparent; and as the new aircraft went into operational service, so the Air Ministry realised that much of the equipment it had to call upon was already out of date. Certain technical equipment, particularly in-line engines like the Rolls-Royce Vulture and Goshawk, fell far short of what was required of them and this led to the use of radial engines as stopgap replacements. This was less than 40 years after the Wright Brothers, and British aircraft engineers such as Roy Chadwick and Frederick Handley Page were still learning the intricacies of aerodynamics; consequently many of the early designs fell hopelessly short of what was required. The original Halifax design was unstable which led to many fatal accidents, whilst the high angle of incidence of the wings on the Stirling and Whitley were radical solutions to the problem of a limited take-off run, and would never have been considered at later stages of the war. Aircraft like the Hampden and Manchester were hopelessly cramped inside, reflecting their designers' lack of experience of operational requirements. At that time the only real familiarity the RAF had with operations of an overseas character were the Middle Eastern insurgency wars of the 1920s which were by then long past, and which bore little relation to the problems of attacking the German mainland at night. In fact the only real precedent for night attacks by heavy bombers had been that of the German Gothas against London in 1918. But as we shall see, design mistakes on aircraft like the Manchester and early marks of the Halifax would soon become the foundation of what were, in both cases, much superior aircraft – the Lancaster and the later Halifaxes.

Whilst Bomber Command was still in a fledgling state from 1939 to 1942, three aircraft became its mainstay large bombers. These were the Vickers Wellington, the

Handley Page Hampden and the Armstrong Whitworth Whitley. Of these, by far the most successful and important was the Wellington.

The Wellington
The Vickers Wellington was designed by a then relatively unknown engineer, Mr. B.N. Wallis. Wallis had previously worked on the R100 airship, a privately funded venture which out-performed and outlasted its rival, the government-backed R101. He had also designed a monoplane day bomber for Vickers, the Wellesley, which used a revolutionary form of construction in its airframe, the main structural principle being a 'geodetic' framework of diamond-shaped lattices. This design was inherently very strong and stress resistant. Exactly the same system would be used in the Wellington, which resulted in a very hardy and battle-resistant aircraft. The Wellington was designed to an Air Ministry specification for a twin-engined medium day bomber. Its required strength factor was 6, but under testing at Farnborough this reached a factor of 11 without any indication of failure but, because the geodetic frame elongated under tension, it failed as a glider tug. Previously, the Air Ministry's specified tare weight for the aircraft had to be strictly adhered to but, by 1933, this yardstick had been removed and Vickers was able to upgrade the bomb load and engine size accordingly. With the increasingly tense European political situation, the company eventually received a production order of over 260 machines, announcing that it aimed to produce one per day: the first was assembled in less than 24 hours. Terry Kearns, a Wellington pilot with 75 Squadron, recalled:

> 'From a combat point of view they were fantastic because you could shoot up to 50% or more of the aeroplane away and it would still fly. This geodetic construction was quite fantastic, it really was. The only problem was that if you lost the fabric off your wing or the fuselage… you lost lift. I've seen aeroplanes coming back with so much stripped off that you'd hardly believe they flew. But they did – they were a very solid old bit of kit.'[2]

The Wellington, or 'Wimpy', was indeed a tough aircraft but it had its limits. The fitting of wooden, fixed pitch, three-blade propellers to the early aircraft could cause problems as these were vulnerable to shrapnel. On 8 May 1942, 101 Squadron navigator Alan Castle took part in a raid on the small Baltic port of Warnemünde. The target – a factory complex – was a diversionary target.[3] But the attack was spoilt by inadequate planning. It had been intended to bomb at 50 feet and 170 mph, but at this height and speed it was almost impossible to see the target.

> 'There was a small jetty jutting out into the sea so we were told to fly down this and, reaching the end, turn sharp starboard 90 degrees, then count up to 10 seconds, and release our bombs.[4] The first problem was that Warnemünde was not poorly defended; there were several machine guns on the jetty and they started firing at us as soon as we reached its sea end, and continued after the 90 degree turn. Also several searchlights picked us up.'

In the nose, Castle was blinded by searchlights and unable to see the ground. He recalled: 'There was a church spire dead ahead which we would have hit if the pilot had not managed to turn far enough to port to avoid it.' The whole attack was spoilt and other aircraft were distracted. Aerial photographs later showed that all the bombs had missed the aiming point. Castle's crew also suffered a near fatal mishap: 'As we flew over the target we felt our plane give a small "shudder" and shortly afterwards it started to vibrate in a high frequency/low amplitude manner. Our pilot established fairly quickly that the vibration was being caused by the port engine. He decided to feather the propeller, but the feathering mechanism did not respond and continued to fail after several attempts.' The crew concluded they would have to endure the vibration for the remainder of the flight back; the main concern was that three hours of this might lead to progressive wing damage.

Castle tried to keep up navigation entries but found that his pencil was vibrating so violently that it was impossible. After they touched down at Bourn the strength of the Wimpy's construction was again confirmed. Although deterioration appeared negligible, inspection of the port engine revealed that each prop blade had lost over 4 inches from its tip and consequently each blade was unequal in weight and, as the propeller boss was crushed completely, attempts to feather the motor failed.[5] They seemed, he thought, to have '…collided with a barrage balloon cable, which wrapped itself round the boss and crushed it.' The blade tips were whipped off and snapped with the violent twisting action. Reconnaissance photographs later confirmed that a barrage balloon that had been there before the raid had disappeared.

David Fraser was a rear gunner on Wellingtons with 115 Squadron at Marham, Norfolk. His aircraft was shot down on 10 May 1941 during an attack on the Blohm und Voss factory at Hamburg, when he suffered the same frustrations with equipment as many tail gunners did. 'As we were about to release our bombs, a heavy burst of Flak at close proximity threw us off course, and we decided to make another run.' This was successful, and with the observer's shout of '*bombs away*' his aircraft headed for home. 'The Flak was still heavy so we took evasive action, but after a few minutes we were picked up by an unusually powerful searchlight, followed by several others.' They were being 'coned'. Then there followed 'a real belting' from the defences and they felt the hits, and smelt the cordite. 'After a few minutes the firing stopped, and we then knew there must be a night fighter in the area. It was then that Sergeant Kerr in the astrodome sighted a Messerschmitt Me 110 on the port quarter.'

Fraser attempted to engage the Messerschmitt but a Flak burst had caused the perspex of his turret to become covered in oil and hydraulic fluid – the turret was immovable, and the electric gun sight u/s.[6] 'The first burst from the fighter must have struck my turret, and the leaking oil and fluid caught fire.' He shouted to his skipper, who instructed a crew member to grab an extinguisher, but by the time they reached Fraser the fire was out. 'Another burst from the fighter set the port engine alight,' he recalled, 'and the fire appeared to be spreading along the fuselage.' Despite several violent manoeuvres the fire continued spreading, and at last a 'bale out' was ordered.

With his turret jammed solid, Fraser gave up attempts to rotate it and squeezed himself through a 12-inch gap to try to find the fuselage hatch, but the fighter kept firing. A badly wounded, semi-conscious member of the crew was lying beside the diamond-shaped exit. 'I put him through the hatch,' recalled Fraser, 'after placing his hand on the D-ring and saw his parachute open immediately he left the aircraft.' Fraser followed, landing successfully but injuring his back.

The most traumatic mission Sergeant Observer Ron Coulson ever experienced was a daylight op to the shipping lanes off Stavanger on 12 April 1940. 'Six Wellingtons from 38 and 115 Squadrons based at Marham were despatched to drop "B" bombs[7] in the shipping lanes off the Christiansand Fjord', he remembered. 'We approached the Norwegian coast at low level, but were soon spotted by a German recce aircraft as we prepared to drop the bombs.'

Six Me 110s soon formed up on either side before carrying out beam attacks, so the RAF men dropped the mines and turned fast for home at low level. The Messerschmitts then started a running battle, attacking from both sides, but they were reluctant to do so from the rear, because of the defensive fire from the four-gun tail turret. Coulson manned the astrodome, which had a good all-round view. 'I reckoned the best defence was to wait until the fighters started their beam attacks, then to instruct the pilot to turn towards the attacker.' This, he hoped, would force them to steepen the attack and overshoot. 'The tactic was successful,' he said, 'although the sea was churned up by bullets close to our tail.' Other aircraft were not so lucky and three Wellingtons went down.[8]

The Whitley

Another early mainstay of Bomber Command was the Armstrong Whitworth Whitley. Armstrong Whitworth had manufactured front line aircraft since the First World War and in the 1920s it brought out the first of the RAF's post-war single-seat biplane fighters, the Siskin. The Whitley was designed to an Air Ministry specification for a bomber/troop transport. Due to its slow speed it was restricted to night-bombing, its nickname 'The Flying Barn Door' was due to its broad, rectangular, low aspect ratio wing.[9] It was the first of the trio of early 'heavy' bombers put into service, with the Hampden coming second and the Wellington third. Dennis Bateman, a navigator/air gunner with 77 Squadron, recalled: 'I did quite a lot of operations on Whitleys in the rear turret. It was slow of course, but it seemed to take quite a lot of punishment without falling out of the sky. You'd come back with a lot of odd shots here and there, but you'd come back: that's quite a strong aircraft.' The strength was due to the fuselage being a monocoque[10] construction of light alloy rolled sections, pressings and corrugated sheets, with a metal wing covering, but not of the stressed skin type.

Don Wilson, a Scot with 51 Squadron, found the Whitley 'sturdy, robust, and able to absorb a great deal of battle damage.' It was '…easy to fly and responded very well to the controls', he said, but he found it 'uncomfortable': the nose was very cramped and '…it was not very easy to climb down from the [front] gun position to use the bomb sight.' Henry Wagner, also on 51 Squadron, agreed about the restricted interior:

> 'It was not a pleasant aircraft to fly in, being very cramped, cold, lumbering and having no radar navigational equipment. Also it was very difficult to get out of in an emergency. The wing chord was very thick; the two wings were joined by a main spar across the fuselage, a narrow tunnel through which one had to crawl down to reach the escape hatch. The Whitleys we trained on were tired and worn out, and would not get above 12,000 feet.'

The peculiar 'nose down' attitude of the Whitley in flight was due to the high angle of wing incidence: because wing flaps generally had not been introduced when the aircraft was designed, the angle of the thick, high lift wing was increased to 8.5 degrees to facilitate take-off. It carried three main fuel tanks, two in the outer wing leading edges and one in the fuselage roof. Eventually the Whitley was phased out of front line duties but subsequently it performed diligent service as a troop carrier, glider tug and also with Coastal Command on anti-submarine and convoy escort duties.

The Hampden

The RAF's third important early bomber was the Hampden. It was named after John Hampden, a 17th century defender of civil liberties, and represented a compromise between either taking a large load further, or a small load faster. At first sight it was a better design than the Whitley as it did not have the thick wing and awkward drooping nose of its contemporary. But a design that focused its crew at the front made it 'extremely cramped, uncomfortable and difficult to leave in emergencies.' This, and the slender tail, resulted in its nickname 'The Flying Tadpole'; it came from the same stable as the Halifax and was the last of the twin-engined medium bombers. Entering RAF service during the pre-war expansion period, by the end of 1938 there were 38 Hampdens operating. But although it was equally as flawed in design as its larger stablemates, the Hampden did have a lot of factors in its favour: it was faster than the Wellington or Whitley and nearly as fast as the Blenheim, a light bomber. Manoeuvrability was also superior to that of the other 'mediums', Bristol Pegasus radial engines being installed after the Rolls-Royce Goshawk in-line engines, a first choice, were found to be inadequate. But to install radials, its all-up weight had to be cut. Despite this, on ops, it did not live up to pre-war expectations and its use with the Wellington in early daylight raids proved disastrous: the static turrets and antiquated Vickers 'K' guns were ludicrously inadequate for their purpose, and even doubling up the guns in the dorsal and ventral turrets was not enough. In 1940 83 Squadron lost 81 crewmen killed, with 12 taken POW. By 1942 this had risen to 108 killed, with 19 POWs: the total losses in two years amounting to 220 men. Thus Hampdens were soon relegated to night ops.

John Leakey was a wireless operator/air gunner on Hampdens with 83 Squadron at Scampton in 1939. He remembered: 'The Hampden was cramped and only three feet across the fuselage. The rear gunners were uncomfortable, particularly the lower gunner, who spent the whole journey with his knees up, practically under his chin.' Bulky flying kit made emergency egress difficult, but '…every crew member had a clear exit, navigator and lower gunner through doors in the floor.' Leakey did not think it particularly noisy, compared to the four-engined aircraft.

It was a characteristic of large bombers like the Stirling and Lancaster to swing to port (and occasionally to starboard) on take-off due to massive engine torque. Leakey: 'I didn't notice if the Hampden swung to either right or left, but pilots used to fly in the same aircraft and most knew how to overcome swerving.' The lack of power-operated turrets became the Hampden's Achilles heel: 'The guns were in many ways defective,' commented Leakey. 'For instance it was possible to shoot off the rudder from the top gunner's position.' Before modifications were made to its fuselage, any twin-engined German aircraft could fly immediately to the right or left of a Hampden without fear of being shot at. 'The lower guns were restricted in their field of fire,' Leakey recalled, 'but unless hit in the engines or controls, the Hampden coped well.' Rear gunners applauded the thin, pencil-like rear fuselage, representing less of a target for the enemy Flak.

'Rookie' second pilots often acted as navigators when first on squadron, which gave them experience of a raid before flying their 'own' aircraft. Leakey: 'Usually, the navigator occupied the [lower] nose. If the intercom failed he would communicate with the pilot by pulling his trouser leg, or climbing up behind him.'

In June 1940, just before 'Operation Sea Lion', the planned German invasion of England, Leakey's crew was off the coast of Holland. 'We spotted a couple of ships, each pulling a convoy of barges in the direction of France', he recalled. The skipper, P/O Svendsen, instructed navigator Barber to send a message indicating the barges' position. Leakey put this into code and transmitted it: 'I've often wondered if this was the first definite information on the "Sea Lion" invasion attempt. Barber gave me the position in English which I encoded from a sheet changed daily, and I sent off the message in Morse.'

The Blenheim

Bomber Command's front line light bomber in 1939 was the Bristol Blenheim. When it first appeared in 1937, it was something of a revelation as it was faster than any of its biplane contemporaries: it was a development of a civilian aircraft, the first production batch appearing on RAF squadrons in 1937. With the declaration of war, the long-nose Blenheim IV superseded the Blenheim I on home-based RAF squadrons. It had improved navigator accommodation and the rear turret possessed double the armament of the Mk. I. There was also a rearward-firing .303 chin barbette under the nose.

No. 2 Group Blenheim IVs were actively engaged in attacking enemy shipping from Norway to the Bay of Biscay during the first six months of 1941: more than 70 enemy vessels were sunk. On 27 December Blenheims of 114 Squadron, operating from northern Scotland, attacked an enemy airfield at Herdla in Norway in support of the first British Combined Operations raid against the German-held islands of Vaagso and Maaloy. Navigator Tom Baker recorded an account in his operations diary:

> '*Something big has been in the air for days, and it was with no surprise that the crews heard that they had to move. The first ship took us as far as Driffield on Dec 22nd and on Dec 23rd we flew to Lossiemouth. The stay at Driffield was due to weather conditions. On the 24th W/Cdr Jenkins practised getting data for the coming operations. Christmas Day was not celebrated by the squadron. Sqn/Ldrs Newberry and Pollard and Flt/Lt Adam practise-bombed, the CO swung his compass all in preparation[11] for the "big op". Dec 26th was a duff day but the squadron was "briefed" for the operation. It proved to be a combined service effort: the Army and Navy raiding Norway. Our task was to bomb the runways on the aerodrome at Herdla near Bergen, so grounding a/c and putting the aerodrome out of action.*
>
> '*The attack was to be made at 250 feet. Dec 27th was fairly fine and the squadron took off at 0920. 12 crews were flying. The squadron flew at 50 feet all the way across the North Sea, picked up the Norwegian coast, and turned up for the target as planned. The aerodrome turned up and the squadron climbed to 250 feet to attack in flights: a creditable piece of navigating and map reading.*
>
> '*Each flight had its own area of the target to attack; the attack was carried out to perfection and numerous hits were observed on the runways. One Me 109 crashed on take-off, running into a bomb burst and is claimed as destroyed. Five enemy aircraft were seen in the target area but no attack was made.*
>
> '*An unfortunate incident occurred after bombing: Sgt Davis and Sgt Fisher crashed and were seen locked together when they hit the water. It is thought that Sgt Davis was hit by Flak.*
>
> '*The other eleven aircraft returned safely. The whole show was a credit to the squadron and was taken as the best show in 2 Group[12] for many months.*'[13]

THE 'HEAVIES'
The Stirling

Three heavy bomber types saw service in the RAF during World War Two: the Handley Page Halifax, the Short Stirling and the Avro Lancaster. The Stirling and Halifax always assumed the role of ugly sisters to the Lancaster in the public's eye, and the short-lived Short Stirling was by far the largest of the three. Almost 20 ft longer than the Lancaster, it had a fuselage 87 ft 3 ins compared to the Avro machine's 69 ft 6 ins. Stirlings were also higher off the ground than Lancasters at 22 ft 9 ins to 20 ft.

The Stirling was designed to an Air Ministry specification of 1936. It was the first heavy bomber to enter RAF service and was designed from the outset to carry four engines, unlike the Halifax and the Lancaster. But it was soon relegated to second-line duties because of a major fault in its design which resulted in a relatively low service ceiling: when the Lancasters and Halifaxes were flying at 24,000 feet they welcomed the

Stirling crews on a raid as the Stirling's altitude capability was limited to less than half that height which could have daunting consequences if enemy ground fire was active. Originally intended to have had the same 112-ft wingspan as its seaborne stablemate, the Sunderland, Air Ministry officials, ignorant of the aerodynamic consequences, decided that for the Stirling to be accommodated in standard RAF hangars anywhere in the world (which had a maximum width of 100 feet) and also to enable maintenance out in the open, six feet had to be chopped off each wing. This gave it a ludicrously inadequate span of 99 ft 1 ins. It has been suggested that a reduced span was inevitable because of the aircraft's high all-up weight (31 tons), i.e. the wing area had to be restricted if the wing's loading was to be within reasonable limits. Another factor was that the reduced span was intended to limit the take-off distance to fit standard RAF runways. Whatever its true reasons, the decision was a short-sighted, ignorant one, turning what should have been a superior aircraft into the equivalent of a clipped-wing duck.

Originally, large trailing edge flaps were fitted to reduce Stirling take-off and landing runs. However a small experimental model revealed these runs to be excessive and test pilots realised that an operational aircraft with full bomb and petrol loadings would require an even longer run. An increase in the wing incidence from 3.0 degrees to 6.5 degrees was suggested to correct this but, since production was already advanced, the only option was to increase the aircraft's undercarriage length, to give the necessary incidence. This resulted in a characteristic 'nose-up' appearance.

Despite the Stirling's limitations many aircrews loved it. James Hinwood, a pilot with 218 Squadron, flew 10 operations on the type and piloted both the other 'heavies'. 'The best aircraft to fly', he recounted, 'was the Stirling: it handled like a light aircraft – but it had to be "flown"; the pilot had to be in sympathy with the machine.' The Stirling also gained approval because it had a much roomier cockpit than the Lancaster or Halifax. All three bombers were mid-wing cantilevered designs, the root of the wing being bolted halfway up the fuselage, with a continuous timber 'main spar' going straight through the airframe. This could cause crews great problems if they had to go to the Elsan toilet at the rear of the aircraft while in mid-flight. In the Stirling the navigator and engineer were on a lower level to the two pilots, sitting directly behind them, and the wireless operator was behind them, immediately in front of the spar.

Eric Homewood, a Stirling flight mechanic/engines, was with 90 Squadron:

'Life on squadron in those days meant looking after one engine of a four-engined bomber, the Stirling. Later it was a case of one flight mechanic and all four engines, and signing the F.700 as to their serviceability.[14] I liked the Stirling myself; they were so beautifully built, but probably not as good as the Lancaster ...

'There wasn't much difference in the servicing carried out on the Hercules radial engines on the Stirling Mk III, or on the Merlin in-line engines on the Lancaster. There was a different access problem because the mainplane of the Stirling was so much higher off the ground. I didn't like climbing up into the undercarriage nacelle of the Stirling: I always thought it might fold up on me, as it had been known to do. The main servicing points were plugs, magnetos and carburettor. The engines were run up, checked for "mag drops", and we listened for audible sounds that indicated something amiss. We removed, cleaned and checked the sparking plugs once a week in any case, but neither type of engine was a lot of trouble. One of the big differences was fuel tanks – seven in each wing on the Stirling and three in the Lanc.'[15]

Norman Elford, a wireless operator/air gunner on Stirlings with 15 Squadron at Mildenhall, was shot down in May 1943 during an attack on Dortmund. He and one other crewman survived. He remembered returning from Germany on one occasion, short of fuel, and asking the airfield at West Malling in Kent if the aircraft could make an emergency landing. As they turned onto the circuit, three German fighters followed them. The Stirling landed; one of the Germans landed, another was shot up by AA fire and the third one got away: the Germans had confused a local river with the Channel, assuming that they were in France. 467 Squadron rear gunner Fred Danckwardt commented:

'Once or twice we were on the circuit and a night fighter followed us in and shot people down while they were preparing to land. You couldn't really relax until you were in the dispersal and the engine stopped. They very often followed us over. It was most unusual for the aircraft to be lined up [on the runway], because a German fighter coming in would destroy the whole lot.'[16]

John Dean, a navigator with 77 Squadron, recalled his most frightening experience on Stirlings. During a raid on Leipzig his crew was assailed by a Ju 88: 'The attack caused a lot of damage to the aircraft which forced us to make an emergency landing away from base at Silverstone.' The local artillery fired on them as they landed because they had no navigation lights, or r/t communication with the ground. 'Fortunately, no one was hurt,' Dean recollected, 'but we were lucky to get away unscathed.' He also recalled a dramatic confrontation on a raid to Montlucon. Although other bombers in the stream could not be seen, these were often detected by slipstream buffeting. In some cases aircraft unintentionally flew directly over each other on a bomb run. On this occasion a Stirling released its load 50 feet above Dean's Halifax. 'We were attacking a factory making ball bearings for German tanks', he recalled, 'and, due to the need to flatten the place, were instructed to bomb at 8,000 feet.' Two of the Stirling's bombs hit them. One 'went straight through the fuselage and exited without exploding. The other came into the fuselage near the tail and stayed there.' Fortunately they were only small 12 lb oil bombs and the short distance they had fallen was not enough to detonate them. 'The flight engineer went to the back of the aircraft and threw them out,' he recalled, 'another 50 feet and I doubt if I'd be telling the tale.'[17]

Charlie Potten, an Air Mechanic, had a great affection for the Stirling, nicknamed 'Queen of the Skies'. 'When in flight it was considered to have great manoeuvrability, especially at lower levels, and in the event of fighter attack or being caught in searchlights, a good skipper – and a strong one – could throw it about the sky to some effect.' Harry Yates, who flew both Stirlings and Lancasters, recalled: 'There was a marked tendency to swing off line under take-off acceleration and on landing. One had to work on the throttles to keep it straight on the runway. But, oversize or not, the Stirling was transformed in the air and a delight to fly.'[18]

Air Mechanic Keith Slade had a friend whilst at RAF Waterbeach named 'Tug' Wilson who, one September evening, was on 'Kite Guard'[19] at 'Compass Point'.[20] Although night-flying was on that night, any 'circuits and bumps' would have been difficult because a thick mist had settled by 02.00 hrs. Two Stirlings were awaiting clearance for take-off at runways 1 and 2. As there was very little wind, No. 2 was ordered to be the main runway and the Controller's caravan was moved nearer to this: the flare path had already been laid on one side. Take-off permission was given and the Controller flashed a 'green'[21] at the aircraft on No. 2. However, after a few moments both Stirlings were speeding down the two runways at 80 mph respectively. At the intersection they collided. Fortunately neither aircraft carried a full fuel load. An undercarriage came adrift from one of the aircraft, which skidded to a halt, a write-off. Slade recalled '...but all the crew members suffered only a shaking. The other shot across the grass and collided with the aircraft standing on Compass Point. By good fortune "Tug" had been awoken by the noise and leapt out of the rear door, not stopping until he reached the safety of H block!'[22]

'Kite Guard', one of the most disturbing tasks for many air mechanics, was an overnight duty where a ground crewman would sit in an operational aircraft to guard against fifth column saboteurs or other illicit intruders. Edmund Dolata was a Polish fitter on 300 Squadron who had formerly served as a despatch rider during the German invasion of Poland. He had trained on the Polish railways and been called up in August 1939, aged 24. He soon became a skilled mechanic and welder. After the Poles 'ran out of everything' – tanks, aircraft and ammunition – the Polish Air Force evacuated south, through Rumania, and Dolata made his own way by motorcycle until it ran out of petrol. He then hitched and walked, sleeping in haystacks, to Batlyk on the Black Sea. There he made his way by boat to Marseilles via the Dardanelles and Malta, where he worked with *l'Armee de l'Air* for a time.

When France fell the RAF put out a request for volunteers and Dolata was one of 80 who responded. With his previous training as a mechanic/welder he was posted to 300 Squadron, then at Bramcote. 'One of the saddest things,' his daughter recalled, 'which upset him throughout his life, was being put to guard a Lancaster overnight.' It had got its injured crew home, but had landed and burnt, 'and those on board (all friends of his) had died there.' He also '... often had to fly down to Manston to replace engines on planes which had just managed to limp home.'[23]

Keith Slade described Kite Guard as 'something else'. It lasted all night and no company was allowed to relieve those on duty: 'On a moonlit night,' he recalled, 'it was more than a little eerie, sitting entirely alone in an aircraft, which a couple of nights earlier had been shot up over the Ruhr, and in which the mid-upper gunner had been killed. Around midnight one could imagine the screams until one could almost hear them, and one was very glad when the night was over.'[24] Jack Hewittson, an air mechanic with 218 Squadron at Woolfox Lodge, remembered ground crews took it in turns to guard the H2S airborne radar equipment in his squadron's Lancasters overnight, around the time of 'Operation Taxable'.[25]

Eric Yates was on Stirlings, Halifaxes and, later, Lancasters. He found the Stirling a far heavier aircraft to handle than the Lancaster, both on take-off and landing, and thought it was difficult to land and had to be 'wheeled in'[26], whereas it was relatively easy to make a three-point landing or 'a three-pointer' on the Lancaster. 'My main thoughts upon take-off on both was to build up as much air speed as possible before lift-off. But the Stirling was much slower and heavier, inhibiting [this].'

Yates only took part in a few 'distraction' or 'diversion' raids, not major operations: 'The ceiling height was a problem and you were fortunate if you could get above 14/15,000 feet.' Contradicting Homewood, Yates stated: 'Unfortunately the Stirling was notorious for its engine failures: I lost one on return from one raid and had to land on three engines.' He also stated that it was '...dangerous to land in a crosswind – when the undercarriage could be lost.'[27] Charlie Potten explained the reason for this:

> 'The considerable area of "keel" surface of its [single] tail rudder and fin and the long-legged undercarriage with its fairings gave plenty of resistance for the slipstream and wind to play

upon. The swing on take-off increased when the wind was from starboard. Manipulation of the throttles, strong arm and leg muscles lessened the difficulties, but there were many flying accidents on landing Stirling aircraft and not a few on take-off.'[28]

From another perspective, Stan Berry was a member of a Stirling squadron fire tender crew. His job was to stand by on the crash wagon outside the Watch Tower with the ambulance whilst the bombers took off:

'The officer on duty in the Watch Tower said to us and the ambulance crew, "*Right, you can relax now until it is time for them to return*". This would be in five or six hours. It would be a time of great worry because we did not know who would come back. If they ran short of fuel some aircraft would land at the nearest place they could. If this was not the case, we would take it they had crashed in Germany.'[29]

The Manchester

The Avro Manchester resulted from an Air Ministry specification of 1936 for an all-metal, mid-wing, medium bomber powered by two Rolls-Royce Vulture engines. But it was a white elephant. Engine design was critical to the success of these bombers and the Vulture engines suffered frequent mechanical failures. The main reason for this was poor engineering. One of the most successful Rolls-Royce engines of the 1930s was the Kestrel. The Vulture employed four Kestrel-type engine blocks of six cylinders each, arranged in-line but diagonally opposed to one another, in an 'X' arrangement. This was a bulky, high-drag configuration, contradicting Henry Royce's original principles for simple, efficient designs. The root of the problem was that the Vulture employed a single crankshaft with a master rod on each crank pin, three articulated rods, and a bolted joint.

Since the Vultures were unreliable, and because a twin-engined bomber was considerably less forgiving than a four-engined one, the pilot often had a crisis on his hands in mid-air. Keith Slade:

'It was a struggle to keep them flying. One of the modifications was to blank off two hydraulic pipes to the air intakes. We had no proper blanks and the Airframe Fitters merely cut the pipes and peened over the ends. This was all very well if it was done carefully, but often there was an hydraulic leak, and as a result a fine spray of oil was directed at the engine. One morning I was starting up a Manchester for a crew to do a "cross-country" when the port engine burst into flame. I grabbed an extinguisher and succeeded in controlling the flames, waving to the crew to cut the engine. Another airman gave me a fresh extinguisher when the first one was empty, so I put out the fire. The crew had meanwhile left the aircraft and gave me a vote of thanks. Not so my Chiefy, who had come over to see what was going on: "*You stupid sod*," he said, "*I've been trying to get rid of that clapped-out kite for two years, and when it looks like it's a gonner, you put the fire out!*"'[30]

When they took the cowlings off, the ground crew found the jet of hydraulic oil was spraying directly onto the exhaust manifold, igniting when it was sufficiently hot.

Another reason for the Manchester catching fire was the design of the exhaust manifold itself. These were on each side of the engine, but the gasket between the manifold and the exhaust port was a composite of copper and asbestos: this did not compress uniformly and could cause a gasket to blow eventually, back pressure from the manifold diverting hot exhaust gases past the gasket and onto the ignition harness which burnt away. If the propeller was not feathered, the engine caught fire.[31]

Avro eventually abandoned the twin-engined concept altogether, replacing the Vultures with four Merlins and extending the wings on each side by 5 ft 11½ ins, giving a total span of 102 ft with a greater aspect ratio (approximately 3:1 as opposed to the earlier 2:1). This produced an airframe of greater operational ceiling height and more powerful engines and was originally named the Manchester III.[32]

The Lancaster/Halifax controversy

The Halifax and Lancaster found their origins in the Air Ministry specification of 1936 for an all-metal medium bomber. In the Lancaster's case this led to the development of the Avro Manchester. In the Halifax's case there was an original mini-Halifax design, the twin-Vulture-engined HP56, which was abandoned after a shortage of Vultures was predicted. Whatever the failings of both these original designs, the Air Ministry's policy was visionary: a 1936 decision to invite tenders '…for a four-engined aircraft able to exploit alternatives and a very heavy bomb load… was a far-sighted decision that altered the course of the war.'[33]

The 'controversy' concerns whether the Lancaster was a better aircraft than the Halifax. Many 'Hallybag' crews swore unremittingly by the Halifax and found the Lancaster's epithet of 'the best heavy bomber in the world' was anathema to them. Ted Boorman, who was a nav (b) on Halifaxes, stated: '…Better to be in a Hally: a Hally on three engines would pass a Lanc without a following wind. The Lancaster only had such a good reputation because they did the run on the Möhne Dam – that was all! If it hadn't been for that it would just be another aircraft.' Bill Higgs, an engineer in 35 Squadron, thought there was more room in a Hally: 'It had a smaller bomb load: we carried 10- or 11,000 pounds whereas the Lanc carried 13 or 14. "Butch" Harris wanted it like that, and the reason was that the Halifax was almost a two-level aircraft – the centre of the fuselage had the engineer and pilot one behind the other, then, two steps down sitting underneath the pilot was the wireless operator; and forward of him the navigator. In the Lancaster the bomb bay continued forward – that's where they got the extra bombs in. You could run through a Halifax.' Philip Bates, who flew in both aircraft, commented: 'The Lancaster was very cramped and difficult to escape from in an emergency. The Halifax was much easier, partly because several crew positions were in the nose, close to the escape hatch.' Frank Dennis found the Halifax had '…far more space to move about with greater headroom.' Unlike the Lancaster the flight engineer had his own 'office', although the fuel controls were 'midships'.

The Halifax I had a limited ceiling of 22,800 ft, but the Halifax VI with the Hercules 100 had a ceiling of 24,000 ft and, with a top speed of 312 mph, could outperform any Lancaster. Gerald Lane, who flew both Halifaxes and Stirlings, converted to 'heavies' on the Mk. I Halifax. He recalled that it was '…a beautiful aircraft, no turrets or equipment – light as a feather.' They collected their aircraft from Radholt: 'Mine was 3rd off the production line', he remembered. The staff were keen to meet the pilots due to fly it: 'They asked what we were afraid of on operations. I had to reply, so I said "Being shot up the arse!"' As a result Lane was given a piece of armour plate 'to fit in my seat' he recounted. But there were problems, particularly with the hydraulics for the wheels and flaps. In fact Lane recalled that the consequences of hydraulic failure caused at least one crew to be lost before operations even started.[34]

Whilst at Lichfield Heavy Conversion Unit on 25 September 1942 Laurie Simpson wrote: '*We are to scrub the Halifax and change to Lancasters, the best heavy bomber in the world.*' They were '*thrilled to the core!*' Ron Searle, his wireless operator at that time, stated: 'From Lichfield we went to 460 at Breighton where they [originally] operated Wellingtons. Luckily for us they decided, before we did any ops, to change over to the Halifax, and so we were posted to Lindholme for a conversion course. We only did two training flights before we [converted onto] the Lancaster, the best heavy bomber ever produced up to that time and for the rest of the war. Anyone who says the Halifax was better obviously never flew in a Lanc or had rocks in their head.'

There were two types of Halifax: the early Rolls-Royce Merlin in-line-engined Mk I and Mk II, and the subsequent marks with Bristol Hercules radial engines. When the Merlin was installed in the Lancaster, it was a remarkably successful marriage, but on the Halifax the Merlin was a failure. The main reason for this was the way the engines were hung: on the Halifax, the Merlin Xs were mid-slung on the airframe, not sitting well because the line of the propeller thrust was above the wing aerofoil centre line. This was inefficient and produced excessive drag. But on the Lancaster the Merlin XXs were underslung, and the propellers' thrust line aligned with the aerofoil centre line, producing minimal drag. The Halifax Merlin Xs were also of greater cross-sectional area than the Lancaster's Merlin XXs, with a more rounded cowling, due to the Halifax's specification for temperate and warm climate work. Arthur Cole, a navigator with 158 Squadron, commented: 'The Halifax had the engine size increased all the time, partly because of its heavier equipment and because more speed was required. So they upgraded the engine, until they got up to the Merlin XX, toward the end of 1943, when the Halifax III came into force.'

The Bristol Hercules on the Mk III was a more compatible stablemate. Phillip Bates, an engineer with 149 Squadron, recalled: 'Several of my friends flew Halifax aircraft, most marks of which were inferior to the Lancaster. However the Mark III, with Hercules engines, was probably on a par, except for its load-carrying capacity.' Arthur Cole: 'The Mark III was a great step forward because of two main changes: firstly it was fitted with Hercules XVI radials, the other was that the tail fins were converted from a triangular shape to a rectangular shape. We never came across it ourselves, but the problem with earlier marks of Halifax was that in certain conditions the controls locked over, and the aircraft spun into the ground. This was eventually put down to the design of the tail fins, so that's why the Mark III and subsequent marks had rectangular fins.'

It was the adaptability of the Merlin that made it such a fine engine. On bomber operations particularly it developed a reputation for an ability to run for long periods at high power. This was the beauty of four-engined aircraft: even if one engine failed, the other three would absorb the load and continue running, completely outside of normal operational limitations. In combat as opposed to civilian flight, when taking evasive action, the engines had to keep running, whatever the power demanded. Provided a sick engine could give power and was not a danger to the aircraft, it was kept running. There were remarkable cases on ops: a Merlin X on one op to Nuremberg in a Wellington Mk II, using maximum revs and boost, ran for five hours without any display of hardship.

The Merlin was a V 12 engine with two banks of six cylinders opposed to each other around a shared crankshaft. On the Lancaster it was fitted with constant speed propellers. These enabled it to perform intricate manoeuvres such as the 'corkscrew' without any loss of power. The de Havilland constant speed unit (c.s.u.) was first fitted to the Hurricanes and Spitfires of the RAF during the Battle of Britain. Before this, these fighters had fixed pitch propellers; in other words the blades had to be switched manually from coarse to fine pitch. This was impractical in combat since it meant that pilots would spend valuable time performing the action. So de Havilland was asked to supply Fighter Command with a constant speed unit that could perform the actions automatically. At coarse pitch, with open throttle, the blade was at an acute angle to the slipstream, allowing it to 'grab' plenty of air. At 'fine' pitch, more or less head on to the slipstream, less air was 'grabbed', the airscrew travelling further through the air when the pitch was 'coarse'. Using the c.s.u., the optimum settings for airscrew and engine revolutions would be set automatically.[35]

As mentioned, Halifax Mk Is and Mk IIs with a V-shaped leading edge to the tailfins were inherently unstable. Many crashes ensued. My father made 14 flights in early Halifaxes. Towards the end of September 1942, at Lichfield HCU, as his crew continued doing 'circuits and bumps', he went to collect the mail. Whilst he did so, his Halifax took off with the rest of the crew, went into a spin and crashed, killing all on board: *'Another Halifax crashed today,'* he wrote, *'and in it was John Faulkner & F/O Percival, two crack pilots. I was lucky as they left me on the ground after we landed when they went up to do rudder stalls.'* He found the aircraft 'difficult especially for take-off', but eventually pulled off a 'sizzling landing'.

The total wingspan of the Halifax Mk I was 98 ft 10 ins. This was later increased to 104 ft 2 ins giving the wing a higher aspect ratio and an increased ceiling. Bill Higgs: 'The Lanc and Halifax were pretty well exactly the same size. Because the Halifax was designed and built earlier than the Lanc, there were rules on it which were amended for the Lanc. She had rounded wing tips whereas the Halifax had square wing tips – as far as I know the wing tip design had to be a certain amount for some reason.'[36]

The Lancaster was not an easy aircraft to stall, especially if it had a full fuel load. Frank Dennis: 'The amount of height lost trimming it out was a few thousands of feet.' The Halifax seemed inherently more stable: '…when put into a steep dive,' he said, '[it] tended to pull itself out.' But the Lancaster was visually the most appealing of the new bombers; it was an aerodynamically more balanced design and its longer wingspan gave it a greater service ceiling. However it did not withstand longitudinal stress so well and attempts to use it as a glider tug were abandoned. Halifaxes conversely performed more than adequately as tugs during and after the invasion of Europe.

Take-Off
The procedure for take-off and departure from an aerodrome was both stressful and hectic. After leaving the ground aircraft had to return to their home airfield and circle round getting their course bearings – an extremely involved few minutes and, with landing, one of the most dangerous periods on an operation. Certain fuel tanks had to be used for the period of greatest activity, i.e. take-off, landing and over the target. The flight engineer or navigator would assist the pilot in controlling the throttles, the rear gunner would turn his turret sideways in case of an emergency exit and the bomb-aimer would be wise not to occupy the nose.

Steve Jackson recalled: 'When fully dressed, you jumped into a lorry and were taken out to dispersal. Here your ground crew would be waiting for you. As take-off time got closer it was last fag and we would climb aboard, settle down and put our equipment in their respective places.' After the engines started they taxied out and queued for take-off. When the green light came, all four throttles were opened up.

'The runway always looked too short with a full bomb load and the end seemed to be approaching too soon,' he recalled, 'but at the last moment you could feel life and we were off.' Bombardiers had to have some knowledge of how to fly as they may have to fly the aircraft home. In some planes this was the engineer's job 'but mostly it was supposed to be the bomb-aimer', Arthur Cole recalled:

> 'I had certain jobs to do: one was to help the pilot on take-off. He pushed the four throttles as we were going down the runway. My hand would be behind his, and eventually he would let go to concentrate on the steering column. I would thrust the four columns hard forward and hold them there. There were four other levers which controlled the airscrews, and when you got safely into the air, if you looked out from the nose, you could see that this airscrew was turning perhaps that fast and that one was turning perhaps faster or slower; and by adjusting the four levers that control the pitch of the four airscrews, you could synchronize them.'

On the 'heavies', when the throttles were opened the 'butterfly' valves in the carburettors would be set to a specific position. At ground level, since the aircraft was built to perform at height, if these were opened *too far* the engine would blow up. This meant the only way to reduce speed was to alter the propeller pitch. The c.s.u. adjusted the pitch automatically from fine to coarse without interrupting the rotation speed of the blades, whilst the engine revs were fixed simultaneously. There was also an 'overriding factor': this was the 'Automatic Boost Control', an aneroid capsule installed in the throttle control, regulated by barometric pressure, which acted as a 'governor', restricting throttle movement and preventing the carburettor 'butterfly' valve from opening too wide if the air pressure was excessively high.[37] As height increased and air pressure fell, the governing action automatically reduced. In an emergency (e.g. take-off or during a 'corkscrew', when extra power was needed) a contingency arrangement allowed one to override the aneroid governor and push the throttles through the restricting 'gate' on the control column. This could only be done for five minutes or so, or for a 1,000 ft height increase – after that the engines blew up. So the pilot's assistant had to force the throttles through the gate and hold them there on take-off. Ted Boorman:

> 'The pilot held the control column with one hand and the throttles with the other. I would put my hands round his, to make sure he pushed it forward if the throttles slipped back. We used to go down the runway at night like that. I'd sit in the right seat – he looked straight ahead, hands round the bar ready. Then you wait. When you get the green signal you say "OK, we've got a green!" Movement builds up, and then you count the speed off. If you get it wrong you've had it because you'd got to do all the umpteen checks again.'

Some of these pre take-off checks for the Halifax included:

Running Up
Throttle up to +4 lbs/sq. in. boost.
Test switches. Max drop 100 revs.
Pitch back to 200 rpm.
Throttle back slightly. Watch revs drop and then build up to original figure. Test both suction pumps.
Open up to full boost +9 and full revs 3,000.
Throttle back to 1,000 rpm.

Cockpit Drill
Brake pressure.
Inst. suction 4 ins.
Switch cages up.
Altimeter 0°. Gyro caged on 0°.
Flaps 35°.
Rudder, aileron and tail trimmers.
'M' gear, weak mixture, cut out up.
Revs fully fine and locked.
[All engines running at 1,000 rpm all the time.][38]

The Merlin 24 engine used on the Lancaster late in the war needed 3,000 lb rpm and +18 boost to take off.[39] This should have been reached after 100 yards of runway. If the target was a distant one, such as Berlin, which required 1,760 gallons of fuel, or Nuremberg, which required 1,840,[40] with an 8,000 lb bomb load, almost 2,000 yards of runway was required. Reg Brown, a flight engineer with 115 Squadron, recalled: 'I did the flaps, the throttles etc. on take-off: the four-engined craft needed that. The pilot would open the throttles at various stages and then you'd take over when they were fully open for take-off, and screw them in the forward position. Then you'd be responsible for bringing the flaps in and selecting the undercarriage.' The four throttles were close together, and worked with one hand. The undercarriage was hydraulic and worked by lever. 'Part of the drill was maximum revs and wheels up. The flaps were down for take-off, and had to be gradually lifted up, so *"Flaps up!"* was called and then one settled down.'

Take-off power would be held until the aircraft was clean off the deck and well into the climb. Then the engines were throttled back to 2,850 rpm with +9 lb boost (12 lb available as a contingency). Ted Boorman:

'You were sitting on a bomb, with the speed building and the nav pressing the pilot's hands into the throttles. You'd say "80. 90. One ton. 110. 120…" and when you get to 125, "Rotate! Rotate!" That means "Take off!" like in a circle – going up. The pilot isn't looking at the dials; he's looking ahead all the time. He's got to keep it straight. Pitch dark when you look down the runway. Once you're in the air, at about 2,000 feet, he can throttle back to whatever speed he wants. Then you clamp the throttles in position so that they don't slip back – you're going full throttle all the time. He takes his hands off and then puts them on the control column.'[41]

Gordon Stooke, a Lancaster pilot with 460 Squadron at Binbrook in 1943, wrote an account of his experiences many years later:

'At 2300 hrs a green flare from the Duty Pilot and the first Lancaster rolls forward, turns left, then, accelerating, disappears over a crest in the runway [and] struggles into the air. One by one 460 become airborne. All the while we wait, our engineer watching the engine temperatures like a hawk. Too high and we will have to shut down to cool them off.

'It is our turn on the runway. First a burst of throttles, then left turn and we line up. I put down ten degrees of flaps, pitch fully fine, mixture rich, trim controls centre. Brakes on; throttles to 1000 revs. A green from the Duty Pilot's Aldis lamp and I release the brakes. When I open the throttles "D-Donald"[42] trundles forward, slowly at first, then accelerating. I lead the left two throttles in advance of the right and a slight swing to the left is corrected. Then, as the slipstream increases, push the stick forward slightly to raise the tail. 50 mph reached. Rudders establish direction control. I push the throttles fully forward, then hand them over to the engineer who ensures they are fully home, locking them by tightening a friction nut.

'Engines 3000 rpm +14 boost. Speed 110 mph. I ease back on the stick and "D-Donald" heaves itself up. 1,500 gals of fuel, 11,000 lbs of bombs and seven men into the air. 130 mph, undercarriage up; 140 mph, flaps up; 160 mph, engines down to +9 boost, 2,850 rpm. We check oil and coolant temperatures. All OK. I trim the control surface for climb. We are at 500 feet.'[43]

For the following half-hour aircraft would rendezvous with other machines as they gained height until, at 10,000 feet, oxygen masks went on. The reason for height gain over the home airfield was that Lancaster and Halifax crews were normally briefed to bomb at 20,000 feet. With a short-range target like the Ruhr it was impossible for heavy bombers with an all-up load to attain this. Jack Currie, a Lancaster pilot with 12 and 626 Squadrons,[44] recalled: 'You couldn't reach 20,000 feet by the time you got to the target even if you climbed hard all the way.'[45] Reg Brown: 'Things began to get serious and one only spoke when necessary. Even though we were still over England, with so many aircraft milling around it was crucial that we observed other bombers' positions.'

Ted Boorman:

'You've got to circle back to the aerodrome to "take off", because the navigator's getting the course to set. The nav gives him the compass bearing as soon as you reach the aerodrome, the skipper sets his compass and you're on your way. From there up to 20,000 feet you chug along at 200 feet per minute.'

At standard operational height of 20,000 feet the motors would be throttled back to 2,650 rpm, with +6 or +7 lb boost. Pilots normally aimed for the highest operating height possible – 22,000 feet. Joe Williams was a rear gunner with 625 Squadron:

'As we climbed out and turned to port, the noise and reverberation pulsating through the aircraft was acute, but later our dulled senses became accustomed to it. The spire of Louth Church passed beneath us. I would turn the turret to port and look up: the aircraft appeared to be hanging in the sky, a thin film of petrol venting from the tanks spread across the wing and flicked off the edge, and I thought of the eight tonnes of high explosive we were sitting on: life was precarious.'[46]

While the bomber gained height so the atmospheric pressure reduced relatively. Because the Merlin was a small, highly boosted, liquid-cooled engine, 'sprog'[47] pilots felt inherent difficulties would be involved, particularly regarding its vulnerability to external damage. But the Merlin could run for long periods outside operational limits, without the risk of overheating and seizure. Reg Brown:

'The navigator gave his course setting for the first leg after a time, and we turned onto it, still climbing. There was no radar in those days so it was imperative that we map read as much as possible, recognising landmarks and giving [the navigator] everything he needed to check wind speeds and direction. Presently he said "*Enemy coast ahead*" and then the serious times began.'

The need to strike deeper into enemy territory later in the war demanded that more attention be paid to the problems of 'range flying', i.e. how to determine the most economical combination of throttle control and engine revs boost at altitude to minimize fuel consumption.

. . .

Aircraft designs became progressively more complicated as the war outplayed its course since machines were required to carry heavier and heavier bomb loads, travel greater distances and endure greater punishment than could have been envisioned by any Air Ministry man pre-war. It was the farsightedness of men like Churchill and Ludlow-Hewitt that laid the foundations for what became one of the most formidable and highly trained bomber forces in the world. The specifications issued in the 1930s for bombers were far-sighted and exceptional in such appeasing times. The early twin-engined designs were soon outmoded as the war escalated and technology developed to enable aircrew to solve the problems of long-range navigation, heavier ordnance and a more potent enemy.

As the game increased in sophistication, so men like Wilfred Freeman ensured that the bomber force had the aircraft it required to survive. The High Command adjusted to the strategic demands that Churchill and Portal's[48] plans laid upon them and the Lancaster increasingly took over from the older 'heavies'. Taking off from an airfield at the beginning of a mission was, with the bomb run, and landing, one of the three most dangerous periods in an operation, and as the aircraft became more complicated, so the roles of the airmen flying in them grew to be more sophisticated and dedicated to the job in hand.

CHAPTER FOUR

'A GRAND MOB OF FELLOWS'

The Crew

THERE were a number of characteristics of the seven-man crews on the RAF's heavy bombers that were unique. To perform effectively the men had to rely upon each other to work as a team. This led to a form of comradeship that was most unusual and has been said to have no parallel in any other military unit, certainly not in the air. Peter Banyard, a bombardier with 514 Squadron, recalled:

> 'When we were flying on operations, every member of the crew had to rely on each other to play their part, and the friendships that were built were very special – this was something that I had never experienced before and it was quite unique.'[1]

My father, Laurie Simpson, always said that he never found quite the same friendships as those he experienced during the war; he placed a special value on 'the crew' to the end of his days, once describing them as 'a grand mob of fellows'.

Essentially, the leader of the team was the pilot, whom almost all crews referred to as 'skipper' during an operation. He was in command of the aircraft and all final decisions were his. Many bomber pilots could fly before they could drive and a lot of them were aged under 25. When asked if he was scared during an operation my father simply responded that there was 'too much to do to be afraid'.

Crews displayed a hierarchy, both in terms of training and responsibility. The pilot had the longest training of all at over two years, and the navigator, the man who ensured the ship got there (and back), had almost as lengthy a training as the pilot. He and the skipper were part of the 'PNB' scheme with the bomb-aimer, who had to ensure that the ordnance reached its target, although the bombardier had little to do when not over the objective and often doubled up on other functions. Men who failed their pilots' course would often take navigator or bomb-aimer as second option. But the other members of the crew also had a huge responsibility. The gunners worked in co-ordinated 'arcs of fire' designed to give an aircraft maximum protection. The mid-upper turret had a 360-degree arc of fire that was constricted only by the twin tailfins on the Lancaster and Halifax. The Lancaster's central turret was designed by Avro with a contoured fairing around it to prevent bullets hitting the aircraft. The .303 Browning machine guns used for most of the war by the RAF were totally inadequate and regarded by most gunners as 'pop guns', having only token effect. This was of great disadvantage particularly in the rear turret, which became crucial for defence during rearward attacks by night fighters. Only with the limited introduction of the 'Rose Rice' tail turret with .5 Brownings towards the end of the war did the RAF have anywhere near the firepower that the Americans carried. The front gun turret, particularly on the Lancaster, was almost redundant.

The roles the crews played became increasingly sophisticated as the war progressed. Modern navigational equipment took the navigator's skills far in advance of pre-war days, whilst the new trade of 'flight engineer' had been introduced to supervise the two extra engines. As gun turrets became increasingly sophisticated and effective, so the air gunners became more skilled. It is possible that the crews of the early twin-engined mediums of 1940 (which were the only operational bombers at that time) would have been incapable of performing their trades in the advanced aircraft of 1945; by then the war had become a 'business' rather than an adventure.

The Navigator

At the beginning of the war the specific role of 'navigator' did not exist. The early twin-engined medium bombers would normally have a complement of five. Sergeant Ron Coulson,[2] was an observer with 38 and 218 Squadrons. In 1940, his role was termed a 'nav (b)'[3] – as well as being a navigator he could double up on all the other roles in the aircraft, including pilot:

'In the early days on Wellington aircraft I had a triple role; in addition to navigating the aircraft I was expected to man the "dustbin" which was a twin machine gun under-turret on the Mk 1a which descended hydraulically under the belly of the aircraft. I also dropped the bombs from a prone position in the nose. There is no wonder that, due to these distractions, navigation was not all that it should have been and we were frequently unsure of our position. We relied heavily on QDMs obtained by our wireless operator, which gave us a course to steer for base.'[4]

Often the early Wellingtons would fly with both a pilot and a second pilot. This could prove extremely costly in terms of aircrew losses because a pilot was expensive to train. Consequently the second pilot's role was soon replaced by the navigator/bomb-aimer. The nav (b) had to serve as bomb-aimer, but also be able to master all the other tasks in the aeroplane, including pilot, wireless operator and air gunner. This was in case of an emergency. Only with the introduction of the four-engined bomber did the roles of navigator and bomb-aimer become separate functions. Later in the war, on some operations in 1944 and 1945, both nav (b)s and navigators worked together in the same aircraft.

Ted Boorman flew as a nav (b) with 102 Squadron from Pocklington:

'I did everybody's job. I was the co-navigator and radar operator, and the bomb-aimer as well. One night we were on a training flight in a Wellington and the skipper was not well. He said *"Take over and fly, I'm going to sleep; wake me up when we get back."* This sort of thing was normal in those days. So I was happily sitting there flying the aircraft when suddenly a line of barrage balloons appeared on each side. I thought, "God! What do I do?" We were running down an avenue of barrage balloons!

'I had no idea where we were. There was some cloud cover, but the balloons were above that: normally balloons would be below the cloud. I thought, "What do I do now? If there's one at the end of the alleyway, we've had it – but if I turn to the right or the left, I don't know what's there." I also thought, "If I say anything to the rest of the crew they'll probably all bale out." So I kept quiet and by luck we ran out of balloons – no one said anything about it. When we got back and were debriefed, I moaned like the clappers: "What were all those barrage balloons doing up?" I demanded. I knew the Army ought to have been told about it. The CO said later that some Army bod had phoned them up and said the balloons shouldn't have been there – they'd forgotten to take them down and were sorry. I was incensed – they had been told we were flying in the area that night!

'For air gunnery training we used a Bolingbroke with a dustbin-type gun turret in the tail. There were three of us in it, without parachutes and with one machine gun. And they took us up to a couple of thousand feet, and then a drogue was towed by and we took turns to fire at it. It came from either the beam, the aft, or the tail. The bullets we fired were all marked with a different colour for each of us: red; green and blue; or red and green. When we landed they would count the bullet holes in the drogue and from the colour they knew who had fired them.'[5]

Keith Pendray served with the 2nd Tactical Air Force in Normandy in 1944 where nav (b)s came into their own. They were the only trade suitable for light bombers such as the Mitchell and Boston, as these did not have enough space for both a navigator and a bomb-aimer. Keith recalled:

'I didn't like night ops. Had I been either a navigator or a bomb-aimer I might have gone onto the "heavies", but the daylight bombers could only operate with nav (b)s and they never carried a straight navigator and bomb-aimer like the "heavies" did.'

Pendray found the Mitchell idiosyncratic:

'On some Mitchells there was a .5 inch [gun] in a ball mounting in the nose, but quite often it wasn't there. On one aircraft someone had stuffed the tube the gun was mounted in full of rags, and about halfway out the op I was hit in the stomach by this ball of rags. We were flying close to 240 mph, which was quite a pressure; so I had to sit sideways to make sure I was out of that 240 mph draught. But I never actually used the gun for anything. We did once or twice come back at low level over parts of Northern France and it was a case of, "anything that moves – shoot it!" But we never saw anything moving.'[6]

The navigator proper, as already mentioned, did not appear until later in the war with the introduction of the 'heavies'. Navigation was still a fairly rudimentary skill before the introduction of electronic aids and much of it was done by 'dead reckoning'. By this the navigator estimated the aircraft's position with his knowledge of airspeed and course. This was a seemingly simple technique but one subject to accumulative errors: for example if the estimated speed was inaccurate, then the aircraft's estimated location would also be inaccurate, the disparity increasing with time. Bob Kemley flew as a navigator with 427 Squadron:

'In the early years Bomber Command missions had failed often to reach their target due to the lack of direction-finding equipment. We had a Mercator chart, ruler, pencils, protractor, sextant and a computer. This was called the "Dalton Computer" – a metal box, 7 inches by 4 inches, having on its obverse side a circular slide rule for all calculations, with a little window to calculate TAS from IAS, height and outside temperature. It was, as one navigator put it, like "sitting in a freezing cold under-stair cupboard with the door shut, a Hoover running, and trying to do calculus".

'I was very fortunate in that I started my operational service just as the first airborne radar was being introduced, called "Gee". It measured the aircraft's distance from two widely separated ground stations to give the aircraft position as the intersection of two arcs on the Gee chart. I was fortunate because it got us off to a good start: it enabled the navigator to fix his position extremely accurately on reaching the operational height, then to obtain another fix after 30 minutes, from which an accurate wind velocity could be calculated for that operational height. This would then be compared with the wind velocity forecast by the Met people at briefing and adjusted, if necessary, in the light of the forecast synoptic situation.'

Kemley concluded:

'Wartime Met officers were extremely good in view of the paucity of information available for the Atlantic. It was a compliment to them that navigators would check their work before using a found wind velocity which was markedly different from that forecast… As we got near the enemy coast, Gee would be heavily jammed and therefore no longer available, but at least it gave us the luxury of a good fix on entering enemy airspace. From then on one relied almost entirely on astro-navigation.'[7]

As the 'heavies' started to appear, the dual role of nav (b) began to be phased out and the navigator's job became more dedicated. Navigational equipment became more sophisticated and training more technically demanding. A strong academic background was necessary, particularly in maths. Navigation training was shorter than that for pilot but, at over a year, lengthier than a bomb-aimer's. Much of the catchment for navigation came from the educated middle classes, particularly academics such as former or future schoolmasters, but although men may have selected navigation as second best, the work was not necessarily easy. David Howell:

'The job of navigator did not come naturally or easily to me. I was a nurseryman, fresh from seven years hard work on the land in Scotland. Thus, it was no easy transition to take a compass and computer in my hand instead of the habitual spade and hoe! Navigation for me was always hard work since the days when I sweated it out at the "Pan American Navigation School" in Miami. I was never one of those who could take it easy from time to time. From the moment my good old Stirling took off from the Norfolk flatlands, I had my eyes and nose glued to the chart.'[8]

Reg Frayers was another who did not find navigation easy:

'With me it was almost a technical job. You sat at the table trying to work out what the wind was, and correcting that as far as possible. Any time the pilot had to take evasive action you made a note. You kept a log going the whole time, making notes of whatever action there was. And, if he had to change course – say perhaps we'd [encountered] some great cumulus clouds – you go round. If there was any sort of danger, he would have to change direction, and you noted that in the log and kept the "dead reckoning" going.'[9]

Frayers was so concerned with this work, that he was not worried about what may have been happening outside the aircraft, particularly the threat from Flak.

Henry Wagner realised that his navigation training in South Africa was next to useless in practical terms:

'On training flights you were either first or second navigator. The first navigator was responsible for plotting the course, working out the wind direction, calculating the ground speed and the time of arrival at the destination. The second navigator undertook the photography, and obtained navigational fixes and bearings using the loop aerial and astro compasses. It sounds straightforward, which it may well have been in broad daylight in the clear skies of South Africa, but it was not much use in Europe, where the ground was usually obscured by cloud and most sorties were at night.'

Wagner also found the taking of star fixes impractical:

'The second navigator took sights of the stars using a sextant. These astro-fixes were far from reliable: sights would be taken of two stars and the reading converted into position lines, using the Air Almanac, but it could take 20 minutes to get a fix plotted, by which time you had moved on about 40 miles!'[10]

Alec March opted to teach at Ground School after his first tour where his duties included giving lectures to all crew members on every aspect of W.T. One of Bomber Command's main concerns was poor navigation: 'What surprised me was the poor standard of education shown by many students,' March recalled, 'which made life difficult for us. It was important that a bomber stream flew as close together as possible. Accurate navigation was essential to this end. Navigators' logs in many cases showed that the wind speed and direction calculated was most inaccurate.'

John Nunn's navigator, a very proficient Yorkshireman named Ron Evans, finished his tour before the rest of his crew in December 1944 and, as a temporary replacement, Nunn's crew took on an Australian flight sergeant. On 12 and 13 December the crew flew two daylight trips to test the new recruit: all navigation and map reading had to be done alone by the 'Aussie', although he could have help with H2S. During the second flight, which lasted over three hours, Nunn recalled:

'I still have a vivid memory of this chap saying to Doug, "*OK skipper, you can lose height now, we're approaching Lincoln and are nearly back to base.*" I looked out of my window and could see a town. I remarked, "*If that's Lincoln, John Player has moved his effing tobacco factory!*" I had recognised the building from the cigarette packets and the town was, of course, Nottingham. He adjusted the course and we soon landed back at base. We were very apprehensive about our new navigator but he had a lot to live up to following the high standards set by Ron. The Group Captain saw Doug in the mess that night and asked him how his new navigator was shaping. Doug said something along the lines of "I think he'll be all right, given time."'

But the group captain must have compared notes with the station navigation leader, as the Australian was subsequently posted back to Navigation Training School.

'It was decided that in an attempt to gain greater accuracy,' recalled Alec March, 'certain squadrons should provide just one nav who would be operationally experienced, and competent to transmit the wind and ground speed to Group.' All this data would be correlated and passed to all aircraft. The method of passing such information to Group was usually done by the w/op. 'I always advised my pilot', March continued, 'when I was about to start transmitting: he would usually start to corkscrew quite gently in case my signals were being picked up by the enemy.'

Bob Kemley was appointed squadron Navigation Officer of 432 Squadron at Skipton-on-Swale, flying Lancasters, in September 1943. His responsibilities included analysis of logs and charts of the previous night's operation, discussion of problems and any remedial action for the future. Extreme efficiency in astro-navigation was vital so they had to make it a habit to take around 30 star shots a week, doing the calculations and plotting within three-and-a-half minutes.

> 'The daily routine was to listen with the CO to the morning 6 Group briefing on the scrambler telephone to hear whether we would be required for ops that night. If so, I would then take down the return route to target, prescribed operational height and forecast wind velocities for each leg; then prepare the flight plan from which the number of air miles to be flown could be calculated and then passed to the Engineering Officer so that he could work out how much petrol would be needed and hence the available bomb load weight. I would also work out take-off times from which briefing and other activity times would follow. I would then prepare my briefings both for main crews and, separately, for navigators. Meanwhile the CO and the two Flight Commanders would select the crews to take part; if the CO was flying I would be his navigator.'[11]

As well as a job of huge responsibility, navigation leader could be extremely hazardous. On some squadrons, in a time of 'maximum effort', the 'nav leader' was required to sit in as a replacement if the regular navigator was unavailable. Alan Castle:

> 'One might have to fly with an inexperienced crew and, although not completely borne out by statistics, there were strong feelings that lack of experience caused many losses. Imagine my feelings when I first had to join a crew whose navigator was too ill to fly, and the target that night was Essen.'

The Bomb-Aimer

The bombardier had to know how to fly the aircraft in an emergency: it was his job to take the control of the aircraft on the bomb run, the pilot following his instructions. Arthur Cole felt that the popular notion of the bombardier repeating 'Left... left....' and 'Right... right...' was a misrepresentation: 'As we got experienced I didn't do that. I would say "Left a bit" or "Right a bit" to indicate that I didn't want much movement. That was quite unofficial, but it worked for us.'

To drop the bombs Cole pressed a button, the 'tit', on the end of a piece of flex. After release, the bombs fell forwards, then downwards by gravity. To his right was a pointer that moved round a dial when each bomb dropped. The idea was to attempt to drop the load together. But because, aerodynamically, each bomb performed in a different way, this was impossible. Tail finned, high-explosive ballistic bombs dropped straight down, but the hexagonal 4 lb incendiary sticks, blunt at both ends, with a different gravitational pull, dropped haphazardly; they had a different rate of fall and so had to be released separately.

The innovative Mk XIV bomb sight had a cross-like, illuminated graticule on it. During the bomb run '...you'd see a group of markers ahead,' Cole recalled, 'and would estimate the middle of them, directing the aircraft to that point. When the point reached where the short arm crossed the long arm on the cross, you released the bombs.'

When not bombing or conducting the after-bombing check, the bombardier also checked for 'hang-ups'. The dial showed each successive bomb condition: if, when a switch underneath this was pulled, a red light came on, then a hang-up had occurred. He also doubled up as front gunner, but this was not practicable after the front turret on the Halifax was replaced by a perspex nose with the inadequate Vickers 'K' gun.

The Wireless Operator

Originally, in the early stages of the war, wireless operators, like nav (b)s, were required to double up as air gunners. The wireless operator/air gunner in the cramped 'mediums' would man the upper rearward-firing gun or beam guns in aircraft such as the Wellington; sometimes this was only an antiquated Vickers 'K'. However, when the 'heavies' arrived, air gunners came into their own, leaving the wireless operator to concentrate on the radio and new radar fittings. Previously the 'wop/ag' or 'w/ag' had worn an air gunner brevet but now, after qualifying, he gained an 'S' (Signals) brevet.

In fact, although having a lower status than the navigator or bombardier, the w/op's training, combined with an air gunnery course, was longer than that of any other course except the pilot's. After their basic training, including Morse operating, trainees attended a 'wireless school' which included all aspects of signals training, plus fundamentals such as valve and electronic theory. Morse had to be transmitted at a rate of 22 words per minute (wpm) and the drop-out rate was high.

Robert Vollum volunteered for the RAF in 1940, and was recommended for w/ag training. At that time, with a rush of volunteers, all the training schools were full and, like many others, he was put on deferred service. He started Morse training in the Blackpool Winter Gardens: for the initial course the speed required was 12 wpm and those who survived were sent to No. 2 Wireless School, Yatesbury, where they had to achieve 20 wpm: most raised this to 24 wpm. They were also introduced to the W.T. sets. They made practice flights in Dominie trainers, with five pupils practising

Robert Vollum (Vollum)   in-flight use of a set but, on two-seater Proctors, the W.T. practice was much more difficult. The gunnery schools were by then full up so, after 14 days' leave, Vollum was posted to 35 Squadron at Linton-on-Ouse: 'I was stationed [there] until the end of May 1941 helping ground operators to do daily inspections on the aircraft and working the station Wireless Department. I was then posted back to No. 2 Wireless School to be brought up to date on the new Marconi receiver and transmitter.' This was for six weeks, including airborne practice again in Dominies and Proctors, and then Vollum was posted to No. 25 OTU at RAF Finningley to do cross-country exercises and simulated day and night bombing raids. He was awarded a wireless operator's/air gunner's brevet and promoted to sergeant: pay was six shillings and eight pence (34p) a week.[12]

The Flight Engineer

In 1942, with the introduction of the 'heavies', the trade of flight engineer was born. This had not existed before and it was only with the increasingly complicated amount of work created by two extra engines, with more involved fuel balancing in flight, that a trained man was needed. It was the one aircrew trade where experienced non-commissioned men, particularly fitters and flight mechanics, could progress to operational flying duties. Before the introduction of the 'heavies', on aircraft such as the Wellington, a second pilot or nav (b), would monitor how the aircraft's engines were performing with fuel consumption, revs, propeller pitches, etc. John Nunn:

> 'With the advent of the new bombers, it was difficult for the pilot to cope with all the gauges, controls, etc. They had been using a second pilot to assist and this meant that every time an aircraft was lost, two fully trained pilots were lost. Volunteers were requested from the ground staff and sergeants and corporals who were mechanics or fitters were given a short course to train as pilots' assistants. It was not long before the RAF realised that by using these men (who were mostly trained in peacetime), they risked losing the nucleus of their highly trained personnel and that maintenance and servicing of the aircraft would suffer. It was clear that they were just as important as those who flew the aircraft. It was for these reasons that [in August 1942] the idea of the flight engineer was born. Men would be taken straight from civilian life, sent for basic training, given a six-month flight mechanic's training course, put on a station to gain some practical experience as a flight mechanic, and then sent on a flight engineer/pilot's assistant course.'[13]

The disadvantage with the 'Direct Entry' system was that the new engineers had no experience of operations. Former Chelmsford factory worker, Lewis Parsons, who upgraded from ground crew to flight engineer, pointed out that Direct Entry was satisfactory, but that 'the majority of crews preferred to have someone with practical ground staff experience if there was one available.'

Originally, without an engineer, Bill Higgs recalled: 'If an aircraft landed away from base nobody knew how to manage the engines, but with the introduction of engineers, if there was trouble, they could get out and tell the ground crew what to do – they knew where the fuel tanks were for filling up etc.' In flight there was a set procedure for how to use the tanks: 'We would do this, but at times you had to make changes to balance the fuel supply. All the time you were flying you kept a log sheet and worked out the fuel consumption, calculating the average for the tanks.'

It was really a question of the load on the airframe affecting the aircraft's performance. Laurie Simpson:

> 'You were transferring fuel all the time to even up the loading on each side; you'd got to do it and you'd got to do it manually. You had to open the cocks and turn on the pump, so that it pumped from one tank to the other. They were self-sealing tanks, but [whether they resealed after an attack] would depend on the size of the hole. For the light stuff [light Flak and bullets etc.] they would, but for heavy stuff [heavy Flak and shrapnel[14]], they wouldn't.'[15]

The Flight Mechanic

On operational flights, ground crew were divided into two tradesman levels, Group 1 and Group 2, and were not allowed to fly on operations. When the trade of flight engineer was introduced, however, many flight mechanics used their skills to get onto aircrew. Before that, for the Group 1 trades, aircrew was a closed door. This was because mechanics were 'screened' personnel: a skilled man was a valuable asset to his home station, and stations needed skilled men. The more useful he was, the more reluctant his superiors were to promote him, and any mechanic requesting transfer to aircrew had to be vetted or 'screened'.

Keith Slade found it very difficult to get onto a fitter's course as it meant a three month absence from his squadron at a Technical Training Centre. It was only when his Engineering Officer went on leave that he was able to persuade another officer to submit an application for him to Group HQ. On completing the course, he converted from Flight Mechanic Group 2 Tradesman to Group 1 Engine Fitter, with a consequent rise in salary. After being at HCU he was posted to RAF Waddington in September 1942 to help form a conversion flight.[16] Upon arrival, he was surprised to find that the two squadrons on his station, Nos. 9 and 44, flew every night, weather permitting. Although Waddington had grass runways, on most nights the bombers were off soon after dark. 'Having been in a comfortable H block, and working in the relaxed atmosphere of a Conversion Unit, with most Saturdays and Sundays free,' he recalled, 'it came as a bit of a shock to work on the flights in all weathers. In addition we worked shifts that totalled 101 hours per week.'

The long shifts and limited time off were not helped by a restricted tool kit. Slade found that the RAF did not supply its mechanics with all the tools they needed. The standard tool kit consisted of two hammers (one hide-faced), three spanners, a set of feeler gauges, and a set of 2-in.-long Terry's spanners (2, 4 and 6BA spanners being riveted together): these were useful for any normal size nuts and bolts but, because of Rolls-Royce's lack of standardization at that time, the many unusual thread sizes appearing on the Merlin or Vulture engines were not catered for.

Slade recalled that he and his friend, L/Ac Hatcliffe, were the only conscientious mechanics at Waddington: 'Whether it was a block change on a Merlin, or even a coolant pump that had to be replaced, we were called upon, because we were the only ones with the tools to do the job.' This lack of provision seems to have been an administrative oversight on the part of the RAF, suggesting that the air force's Supply Branch was in some areas ignorant of the new engines' servicing requirements. The lengths to which Slade and his friend went to find their tools were amazing. Through a friend employed at an engineering firm they had them made up: '11/16-in. and 13/16-in. spanners could never be found in the shops, or on the Flights, and the type "C" spanner was needed in many places.' Slade recalled later that he was only able to work because he had the right equipment.[17]

Converting to Flight Engineer

Typical cases of ground crew who converted to flight engineers included George Hockin, who had originally been posted to RAF Cranwell in May 1942 as an engine fitter, but that July went to the RAF Technical School at St. Athan, to do an engineer's course. The following month he was detached for a three-week aerial gunnery course at Pembrey in South Wales. He returned to St. Athan and passed out as an engineer. Bill Higgs was a corporal fitter with 610 Squadron during the Battle of Britain, and volunteered to become a flight engineer in March 1941. To enable him to double up as an air gunner, before any engineering training, he went on a three week aerial gunnery course at No. 6 Bombing and Gunnery School. He was then posted to 35 Squadron at Linton-on-Ouse, Yorkshire, the first unit to be equipped with the Halifax. 'Here we were instructed on the fuel system and how to use the various tanks for operational and local flying, the hydraulic system, and operation of undercarriage and flaps', he recalled.

Reg Brown initially trained on Sunderland flying boats: 'I joined when I was 18 as a flight mechanic, and became a flight mechanic (airframe) – an AC1. Later I upgraded to fitter.' He was offered the chance of flight engineer training and took it because he wanted to get into aircrew. 'This meant that I had to convert to engines, in addition to airframes. It was a technical training, with no flying element, and we trained to a particular type, in this case Sunderlands.'

Dick Raymond, who had been previously classified unfit for flying duties, was posted to RAF Locking in Weston-super-Mare to do a flight mechanic's course:

'We had periodic tests and if you failed you were put in the RAF Regiment. You can imagine this made me work so hard, I passed out amongst the top of the entry, and was posted to the number one school of technical training at RAF Halton. Approximately halfway through the course, a notice was posted stating that volunteers were wanted for flight engineers. I volunteered and was sent to London for a selection board and medical. To my delight I passed both. To this day I do not know whether my health had improved or they were desperately short of flight engineers.'

In 1942 Ted Groom was training as a fitter at St. Athan when he heard that the RAF wanted engineers. He joined a course but it was cut short because, due to the high losses, there was an urgent need for replacements on operational units:

'I did my engineers' course. It was only three months at the *very* most. They put us on an eight week course, and two weeks of that were up at Avros at Woodford, which was ideal. You learned more, because you went in with the aircraft as it was being built, and watched it right the way through the production line. They were on 24-hour rotation, so if you returned the next day they put you back on where you left off. In between times we'd be having lectures by civilians.'

Fuel Balancing

As mentioned, it was the flight engineer who was responsible for balancing the fuel tanks, maintaining a log of the flight, and assisting during take-off (unnecessary on the Lancaster). The full fuel load on a Lancaster was 2,154 gallons. There were six tanks, three in each wing: two small 114-gallon tanks on the outside; two 383-gallon intermediate tanks, and two main 580-gallon tanks adjacent to the wing root. There were two engine data panels on the Lancaster: the flight engineer's panel, to the right of the pilot's seat, and the pilot's auxiliary panel. Reg Brown:

'...I had a "jump seat" next to the pilot, and you'd fold that up. And you had an instrument panel, in addition to the one at the front, on the fuselage side.'[18]

The pilot's panel was very basic, with engine temperature gauges, propeller safety switches and cowling gill information, all in quadruple. The engineer's panel was more comprehensive. This contained four oil dilution push buttons, four oil pressure gauges, four oil temperature gauges, four fuel content gauges, four electric fuel pump switches, and two fuel tank selector cocks which enabled the engineer to transfer fuel to the port or starboard engines as required. The main fuel transfer cock on the Lancaster was centrally located on the cockpit floor, immediately in front of the main spar.

Reg Brown:

'Every 20 minutes the engineer had to make a log entry of the fuel position. On landing you would take any faults to the ground crew and explain what they were. You were normally on main tanks for starters, [then] you'd go onto number two tanks, and you seldom needed to go onto number three.'

Each tank used either an electrical 'immersion' pump or, alternatively, an hydraulic 'pulsometer' pump, to transfer fuel. John Nunn:

> 'I kept the immersion pumps on all the time we were using a tank and it was my job to keep the aircraft balanced by using each tank in turn. There were three tanks in each wing[19] and they were covered by about three inches of some type of latex material. This would seal up any leaks if the tank was hit by bullets and I believe it was very effective....'

The outer tanks were not connected to the engines: it was the engineer's job to transfer these to the main tanks as soon as space became available.

> 'Fuel could also be pumped from one wing to the other to prevent loss if a tank was holed. This fuel could then be used to feed the engines on the damaged wing. When we were over enemy territory, I would try to keep the fuel spread as evenly as possible so as to minimise the potential loss should one of the tanks be holed.'

On one occasion, Keith Slade was ordered to change the immersion pump on a Lancaster centre tank. It was just after midnight and he had been working since 06.00 hrs the previous morning: 'The centre tank on the Lancaster held 383 gallons of 100 octane aviation fuel and the immersed pump was about one-third of the way down from the top. This meant that one had to be quick and accurate to pull out the old pump, and push the new one in with as little loss of fuel as possible.' That night there was some light snow and the bad weather meant aircraft were being recalled early. Slade and his friend, L/Ac Hatcliffe, heard the aircraft circuiting the airfield. The job seemed impossible in such conditions – 383 gallons of aviation fuel weighed over a ton, but after slackening off a circular aluminium ring nut, and much thumping with a hide-faced hammer, the pump came loose. 'The petrol was forcing itself past a neoprene washer and we had to be ready to pull it out, and push the new one in, in a fraction of a second.' Somehow they whipped out the old pump and put the new one in position. They had lost about 20 gallons of fuel – but the night would have an explosive end.

The two men retired to the Flight Office to thaw out. Flight Office stoves had kidney-shaped lids which were soon lost if they fell into the fire, and a blue brindle brick was placed on the stove top as a replacement. As it was cold the stove was blazing away merrily and the bottom plate was open, so the coke had become very hot. Slade recalled that 'The RT came over with news that our flight had landed, and we all had to get the aircraft into dispersals before the snow became really heavy.'

They went to work. Suddenly there was a tremendous bang from inside the hut followed by the sound of shattering of glass as the office window blew out. They returned to a scene of devastation: the blue brick on the stove had disintegrated. Slade: 'It was only by the greatest good fortune that the place was empty, as an exploding brick would have caused some casualties, if not worse.'[20]

On Stirlings the aviation fuel was contained in 14 tanks of 2,254 gallons' capacity. Charlie Potten recalls:

> 'There were seven in each wing, numbered 1 to 7 port and starboard with seven different capacities. No. 2 and 4 tanks were the two largest tanks and these were used for all take-offs and landings and in the target area, as they had the greatest "heads" of petrol to the engines. The main job of the flight engineer was to maintain as much fuel in these four as possible and

to keep an account of all fuel remaining throughout the flight. This became a juggling act with the tanks being used on a specific flight. By using prepared graphs, the engineer computed the fuel used by the engines at any given power setting, multiplied by the length of time at that setting.

'A calculated amount of fuel allowed for take-off, for any evasive action, and for time spent over the target: the amount used varied according to the conditions and how prudent the manipulation of the throttles was.'

Charlie Potten commented: 'Getting your arse out of the line of fire and "Guesstimate" became the rule of thumb.'[21]

Gunnery and Turrets

On the 'heavies' the bomb-aimer would often double up as front gunner. But the Lancaster front turret was not efficient as the streamlining was poor and the installation was difficult to climb into and get out of, wasting time. Fred Danckwardt recalled:

'The front turret was useless. If they'd faired the turret and just had a .5 gun in it, instead of a couple of little .303s, it could have been much more effective; and then the bomb-aimer could have reached it immediately. But in order to get into the turret, the bomb-aimer had to stand up and get "into" it. And by the time he'd done that the target had disappeared. I don't recall that there's any record of any aircraft being shot down using a front turret. It was useless. But if they'd faired it like a Heinkel He 111 it would have first of all made the aircraft much more aerodynamic, and a gun turret is a very heavy and complicated piece of machinery – it didn't need it!'[22]

Peter Banyard, a bomb-aimer with 514 Squadron, who was also a front gunner, recalled that every member of his crew had to do pre-flight checks. During standard pre-flight tests he had to check routinely both the Bombing Switch Gear in the bombardier's position and the two .303 Browning guns in his front turret before a flight. 'One time when I tried to cock my guns they wouldn't work, so we had to remove all the guns and send them back to the armoury for checking. Everything had to be done by the manual. On my guns the breach blocks were fully rusted in and had to be released and completely cleaned.'[23]

The mid-upper and rear turrets became the principal forms of defence on 'heavies' and the tail gunner was the most crucial: he had over 180 degrees of visibility and fighter attacks on the tail were common before the Germans introduced their *Schräge Musik* tactic. Boulton Paul had had an early association with the airborne turret. Its Overstrand was the first RAF bomber to feature a power-operated turret in the nose, which was a great success and air-to-air gunnery in training improved five-fold because of it.[24]

Turrets for the early bombers were originally designed specifically for the aircraft but, by the middle of the war, after lengthy experiments, firms such as Frazer Nash and Boulton Paul had introduced purpose-designed, industry-standard equipment. These were hydraulically operated and equipped with quadruple Browning .303 guns, but generally they remained ineffective because of their limited range. A Boulton Paul tail turret was fitted to the early marks of Halifax. The standard fitting on the Lancaster was the Frazer Nash FN20. Joe Williams:

'I didn't like the Boulton Paul turret. The guns were up by your face and you could only just see out between them. The Frazer Nash was better – the guns were at your waist and you had a bigger window area to look out of. With size 10 or 11 flying boots your feet fitted inside the turret wall, but it was very cramped and, with all this up in front of you, you couldn't see out the side much. The Boulton Paul was more rounded. I didn't like the thing at all, but people got used to it.'[25]

The rear gunner's job was arguably the most dangerous and certainly the coldest, most lonely and isolated of any of the crew. From the beginning of a mission until the end, the gunner's only human contact was the voices of other crewmen on the intercom. Jim McGillivray, a non-commissioned rear gunner, recalled the Frazer Nash:

'It was hydraulics, with electrical [control]: when you pressed the triggers it fired. It had a "Fire on safe" on each gun, so you could put it on "safe" and press the trigger and it didn't fire. If you were getting into the turret, you always made sure that it was on "safe", because if you touched the triggers it would fire – which was noisy. But we never had ear muffs, even with four guns blazing away at once. With the hydraulics, when you squeezed the handles (like a tap) then it was "on". You twisted the handle up for the guns to go up, and down to go down. There were two triggers: one and two would fire all the guns with a [Bowden] cable.[26] You moved the handle – like a bicycle handle – to turn [the turret]: then the whole turret moved round. It was all done on hydraulics, no effort at all.'[27]

The interior of a Lancaster was bleak indeed. Inside the structure, fuselage formers and longerons were all exposed, revealing a bare metal skin. Running the length of the fuselage walls were metal pipes, rods, and all manner of plumbing and wiring for hydraulic fluid and power to flow where needed.

The rear gunner would be the first member of the crew to enter the aircraft. He would pass the Elsan toilet to his right, scramble over the tailplane spar, pause to stow his parachute, then squeeze into a cold and cramped position, shutting the turret's armoured doors behind him. From the point of take-off he was unceasingly vigilant, yet tail gunners had the shortest life expectancy of all crewmen. Before the Germans deployed *Schräge Musik*, the attack from underneath and the rear – '*von unter hintern*' – was the most favoured form of approach by the night fighters but, if he was lucky enough to survive a tour, a tail gunner may well have done so without once seeing an enemy aircraft.

Ivor Turley of 218 (Gold Coast) Squadron wrote a vivid, detailed, and unusually animated description of the tribulations of a rear gunner:

'"Okay, boys," came [skipper] *Harry's voice, "Stand by to take oxygen: oxygen on, Tom."*

'"*Okay, Harry, oxygen going on," replied Tom. He was in charge of the tap that supplied oxygen.*

'*I watched the needle on the oxygen meter between my legs swing to "on". I connected my oxygen mask to the bayonet tube on the meter, held the mask to my cheek and waited for the puff of oxygen to tell me everything was okay.*

'*I gripped the turret controls tighter. We started cutting the upper layer of cloud, leaving long furrows from our slipstream. It was getting colder, and the slipstream was whipping through the open front of my turret, making my cheeks smart and eyes water. By squeezing further back in the turret I found I could escape some of the draught. I closed my eyes: they felt tired and the glare from the white cloud was intense. The goggles steamed up, but when I raised them the slipstream hit my eyes again. I shivered, the chill running sharply up and down my spine and my flesh crawled with the intense cold. I switched on my electric* suit and felt the warmth percolating through my underwear. It wasn't really warm, but it took the bite from the cold away, and felt better.

'I turned my attention to the guns, cocking them to see if they were okay. I then realised I should have had them cocked as soon as we got airborne. I looked at my fire and safety mechanisms: they were all on "Safe". Frantically I switched them to "Fire" and cursed and cursed. I had been sitting all this time in a gun turret with four machine guns that between them could not have fired a cork, let alone a bullet. A fine ruddy Gunner I was turning out to be!

"I searched the sky in detail but couldn't see any fighters. My operating of the turret controls was now fully automatic: port to starboard, starboard to port. What monotony. Search, search and search again. The cramp was maddening. I yearned to stand up and run. In front and past the gun sight – clear vision; open space where the perspex had been cut away. No armour: this had been removed to give clearer vision downwards. I wanted to squeeze out, jump onto the cloud layer below and just walk. By leaning over my ammunition feed mechanism and with my head nearly out of the turret, I found that I could straighten my legs and get as near as I could to a bent forward standing position. I felt the numbness leaving my knees and legs. Oh what relief at last!

'I pushed my head further out of the turret and could feel the slipstream rushing by, then realised that I could look virtually straight down. With relief I sat down. Within two minutes the numbness was back, so I gave up… They weren't kidding when they said it was cold at 20,000 feet!'[28]

Fred Danckwardt also remembered how cold it could be on ops. During his time with 467 Squadron[29] his crew normally flew at about 22,000 feet, because they had a Canadian-built Lancaster with paddle-bladed propellers.[30] These were larger and more rectangular in shape than conventional props (which normally tapered to a point). The paddle blade had a larger surface area and when set at full pitch could chop through a higher volume of air than normally. This improved an aircraft's performance particularly in the climb and at higher altitude where the atmosphere was rarefied.

'On one trip my heated suit failed,' Danckwardt recalled, 'and my left leg was being burnt and my right leg was being frozen; so I had to turn the heating off. Our heated suit had a thing you had to plug in, so I had to pull that out. Then I was sitting in a freezing metal box with the temperature of minus 40. The pilot called me frequently to make sure that I was OK, but I lapsed into unconsciousness with hypothermia: I became completely comatose so he had to reduce height, which meant we were coming back over Germany on our own, below our normal operational height. I became completely "out of it" and when we landed they literally lifted me out, and took me to the hospital. I had frostbite. It took me a day or so to recover.'[31]

Joe Williams remembered the privations of high-altitude flying:

'Night temperatures at 18-20,000 feet in winter were always minus 30 degrees and often fell below minus 40 degrees. Soon after we had started operations, only rear gunners were issued with the "Taylorcraft Flotation Suit": a massive yellow garment, it was quilted and electrically heated with built-in Kapok flotation pads, so no "Mae West"-style life jacket was needed. Some assistance was required to get into it and, once in it, mobility, in the aircraft, was reduced. Only with very low temperatures did I decide to use it, being much more comfortable in the Sidcot inner and outer flying suit. With both suits, electrically heated slippers and gloves were worn and the oxygen mask and microphone were heated. With either suit it was a normal additional requirement to wear silk-lined long pants, fisherman's jumper and long socks. To protect the hands, five pairs of gloves were put on and a woollen Balaclava helmet was worn under the flying helmet.'

Climbing into the rear or mid-upper turret could be a cumbersome exercise. Having entered the aircraft, Wyn Morgan, Williams's Welsh radio operator, assisted him.

'Stepping up onto the Elsan, I clambered up onto the tailplane spar and then slid feet first down a plywood board into the turret. Wyn would come up, put his boot in the middle of my back and slide the doors closed behind me. At the end of each operation it was Wyn who let me out again. He would also come down the fuselage when we returned over the North Sea, and pass a coffee through the side window. Shortly before start-up time he often broke into "Off we go into the Wild Blue Yonder" – I can still hear his Welsh voice now, raised in song.'[32]

Graham Korner recollected the tribulations of being a rear gunner with 640 Squadron:

'Usually the rear turrets with two guns had two ".5s", which were a much better and heavier gun.[33] The standard quadruple .303s were nothing really, because the German fighter could open fire at about 1,000 yards and, with an ordinary Browning, your maximum accurate range was only 400 yards. So they had a great advantage over you: you couldn't open up until they got within that distance.

'In those days all we had was the old "ring and bead" sight, which was an illuminated sight, but was the old round ring with a cross on it. After the war, when I came back, they had this reflector sight. And they were much better, because all you had to do was get your ring and bead on the aircraft and, as you turned, the deflection was laid off automatically whereas, with the old ring and bead, you had to aim at it and allow one or two radiuses off – it was a bit of a crude business really. The only time I ever opened fire was when I went to clear my guns over Reading one day and the things went off! Once, towards the end of the war, we were attacked by an Me 163 rocket fighter coming head on. The wireless op shouted "*Fighter! Fighter!*" and then this "tail pipe" shot past, and it was gone.

'Another time I was in my turret and down below was another Halifax. If you're bombing above cloud, there's a terrific reflection up through the haze and you can see anything silhouetted against it. I saw this Focke-Wulf 190 fly up and do a wonderful bit of firing: a full 90 degree shot! The Halifax just turned over and went straight down – they must have all been killed, they could never have got out of it.'

Crewing Up

One of the most bizarre procedures practised by the RAF in the 1940s was the method of sorting newly trained aircrew into seven- or five-man operational crews. 'Crewing Up' was highly improbable in its method but, as most airmen agreed, it worked. When men first arrived in Bomber Command they were sent to an Operational Training Unit: in Laurie Simpson's case this was 27 OTU at Lichfield, Staffordshire. It appears that 'crewing up' in its final form did not really develop until 1943. Crews were generally formed whilst men were in their initial period at an OTU or at a Heavy Conversion Unit and it was normally the prerogative of the pilot to finally decide who was 'in' and who was not. If a crew became 'headless', that is to say suffered the loss of its pilot, it might be some time before a replacement could be found, during which time it could be non-operational.

Alan Bryett recalled the more formal and unhurried selection of his Wellington crew in the early part of the war.

'There were 250 of you assembled and they were all sorts of people: they were all qualified, the lowest rank was Pilot Officer, there were some chaps who were Flying Officers and some who were Flight Lieutenants. There were people from all over the Empire, all dumped together, and the pilot's job was to get himself a crew, by quietly and unofficially, unbeknown to us, going through the records and the backgrounds of the various crews who were there. They then came out and would talk and chat and there were various social events. There was no hurry; it lasted for ten days to a fortnight.'

The pilot was told not to rush but to have a crew selected by the end of the fortnight.[34] By 1943 the process had become less protracted, but more haphazard. Steve Jackson recalled: 'The way crews were picked was most peculiar: all the various trades – pilots, navigators, engineers, bomb-aimers, wireless operators and air gunners – were put into a large room and one went around looking for one's crew. It was very hit and miss, but it meant that you had a real cross section of ability and social background. When you finally found your crew, the real training commenced.'[35]

Joe Williams was crewed up after D-Day, on Tuesday 11 July 1944. He gathered in a hut with 150 airmen from all the Bomber Command trades: 'The officer addressed us: "Get yourselves crewed up".' Like so many people at a large party, aircrew moved around, politely asking, "Are you fixed up?" Pilots with half a crew in tow, and looking for the remaining member, would approach and ask, "Would you like to join my crew?" Within a few minutes, Joe was a member of a crew that included a whole cross section of nationalities.

Leslie Holes thought crewing up very 'hit and miss' indeed: 'Numbers of newly qualified aircrew were sent to an appropriately sized airfield equipped with aircraft that they would train on. Then all of them were told: "By mutual consent, sort yourselves into crews." And this seemed to work. It was a kind of courtship.'

Holes had been an instructor before this: 'My crew were probably influenced by the sort of wisdom that "pilots who had been flying instructors were the safest!" On returning to our billet, I heard that two gunners had been looking for me who had been friends at Gunnery School. I needed two gunners and that they were already friends appealed.'

'Haphazard and amusing' was how one could describe Ted Boorman's experience:

'When you'd done all your training and come back to this country, they sent you to Harrogate. You were then told to report to a station somewhere with hundreds of other aircrew, and then you flew home for the weekend. On Monday morning you were braided ['sorted' into crews] – they said: "There are 700 aircrew here; by Thursday we want 100 crews."

'You walked around and had a chat with people; and it sort of came to about Tuesday and I hadn't done much. I thought, "Bloody hell!" Wednesday I picked up with two Aussies: they were wandering around. So we got chatting. They said, "Let's get together then, shall we?" I said "OK, fair enough, that's OK." So we did. Then on the next day we said, "We want a pilot now," and I think one of them said, "I know of a pilot, he hasn't got a crew yet, but he's not very tall" – he could just see over the rim of the cockpit. So someone said "Right!" So we went and had a word with him. Then they said, "Now we want a couple of air gunners." So we wandered around. All of a sudden somebody said, "Well I know two – they're horrible blokes and I wouldn't trust either of them, but they haven't got a crew." So then we said, "Now we want a flight engineer, that's the last bloke." Someone said, "Well we know of one, but nobody wants him." So we went and saw him, and his father was a parson. "I'll tell you straight away," he said "I don't drink, I don't smoke, and I don't go with women. But if you want to go to a knocking shop, I'll wait outside and hold the money!" So we said "We'll have you!"'

But 'crewing up', although generally favourable, did have some failures. For a number of reasons not all crews gelled successfully: occasionally attitude, personality clashes, or ill health could cause a problem. Sometimes a crew could be broken up during operations due to personal squabbling, in which case men were obliged to find a place on any available aircraft. Arthur Cole found the procedure 'somewhat imperfect':

'I mean it's always written up as something that was unlikely, but very effective. I don't believe a word of it. To start with, the crew that I started out with had a South African squadron leader who was an odd character to say the least. But the navigator was an Irishman, and he and I didn't like each other, and he was offensive – continually offensive. And after one cross-country at OTU we finished up by having a flaming row in the crew room shouting at each other, and the authorities then broke up the crew. The crew that I was finally with, they didn't like their bomb-aimer, and he was ejected from their crew and they chose me to fill in the gap.'

Miles 'Mike' Tripp, a bomb-aimer with 218 Squadron, recalled that he 'felt like a girl at a dance and cringed at the thought of being a wallflower.' As a bombardier he held what he termed as '…an unacknowledged but undeniable status distinction' over air gunners in particular. But by the end of the first day he remained crew-less. That evening in the local pub he met a navigator, Jack, who was still looking for someone. They agreed to team up and the following day Jack excitedly told him that he had met an Australian pilot, who had a wireless operator. The nucleus of Tripp's crew was formed at that point. The last man to join them was the flight engineer, a 19 year-old from a Norfolk village who loved football. Tripp recalled their first meeting at HCU:

'Ray and I enjoyed a natural animosity from the start. He had close-cropped hair. Mine was long. He had no time for music and literature; I sneered at technical know-how. He would spend an evening sweeping and polishing his bed space; the ration of coal was stored under my bed space where it was reckoned safe from other crews. In general he was as intolerant of arty-craft types as I was of swede bashers. We were destined to form a love-hate relationship in which the love was derisory.'[36]

Tripp's navigator, Jack, had to fly out with more veteran airmen to gain navigational experience shortly after crewing up. The others went to a satellite airfield to practise 'circuits and bumps'. The next thing they knew Jack was dead, killed in a Wellington which had blown up on approach.

Occasionally unforeseen circumstances created problems. Airmen, although crewed, did not always last the course. Alec March's first skipper on 103 Squadron had a slovenly appearance that eventually proved to reflect his flying skills: 'He was a large fellow with extremely broad shoulders, a mop of tousled hair the colour of old hay, and his dress most untidy.' March found this image '…nearing the point of unacceptability', but was advised by the navigator not to be 'fooled by his appearance'. He was forced to accept it until the man's flying standard dropped noticeably. After he made two radical errors during a practice 'overshoot' at night, 'we the crew, decided we must consult our CO, otherwise we would all have little wooden crosses before we had dropped a single bomb.' Their CO took them on a cross-country flight with the pilot to assess them: 'I will not only assess the skipper's ability to continue flying,' he said, 'but yours as well.' Next morning they reported to him and were told their skipper had 'fallen below the standard required and his flying career had been terminated.' The performance of the rest of them was satisfactory.[37]

Russ Margerison lost three of his crew very early on after forming. The pilot performed two 'duff' landings within a week, writing off both aircraft. The navigator went down with appendicitis and also disappeared. Finally, the bombardier took fright in mid-air and jettisoned the escape hatch inadvertently: 'Panic in the air could not be tolerated', Margerison related. The man was packed off to another crew.[38]

The British 'crewing up' system appeared successful, probably because the men were allowed to select the comrades they felt most suited them, and the procedure took place after training had ended: thus, generally, none of those concerned had any operational experience. Men who thus found themselves selected then had to be 'blooded' and, perhaps, it was being 'partners in adversity' that welded them together. The unusual ergonomic nature of a bomber demanded mutual interdependence for airmen to survive: anything interrupting this could be potentially life threatening but, generally speaking, despite having a haphazard and uncertain nature, most veterans agree that 'crewing up' worked. Men saw someone they liked, or had heard about, and made straight for them. Apart from airmen who had met earlier, it was very much a 'hit or miss' affair, likened to 'love at first sight'. It was an unpredictable success. Many crews lasted for the duration of the war, but some failed abysmally: those who initially appeared compatible did not always prove to be so. The procedure was never adopted by the USAAF where men were merely assigned to an aircraft – an arrangement which one would expect to perform less well, but the survivors of my father's crew, who were all allocated to each other, rather than being 'crewed up', kept in contact right up until he passed away.

The comradeship shared by the crews of the heavy bombers of Bomber Command was almost unique. For the first time each member of a crew had to have his own specialist training, but they would be mutually dependent upon one another. Of the seven, perhaps the pilot and navigator were the weakest links in the chain, for if their equipment or they themselves failed to perform properly, it may lead to a failure of the entire effort. A crew without a 'head' may take weeks to find a replacement; a crew without proper navigation equipment, or its operators, was unable to perform efficiently. The gunners, wireless operators, bombardiers and flight engineers were less critical, but the 'flightys', as they became known, had a critical role in fuel calculations and balancing when the four-engined aircraft arrived. Despite 'crewing up' being remarkably successful, it was never adopted by the Eighth Air Force.

• • •

By the beginning of 1943 the eight Groups of Bomber Command were coalescing into one of the largest bombing forces ever assembled up to that time in the war. Some of the most highly trained jobs were undertaken by the men of Bomber Command and, although not every man was able to become a pilot, they accepted the alternate courses that were offered to them as an opportunity. It was not easy finding a crew that was compatible: for some it took a long time before they found those whom they could trust with their lives – perhaps one of the most stressful relationships imaginable. It was the quality of training they received before operations, sometimes lasting over two years, and spreading across three continents, that ensured their survival.

CHAPTER FIVE

'A JUGGLE WITH JESUS'

OTU: Part One

FOR most pilots Operational Training Units had two purposes. One was to initiate them into the stresses of operational flying before they were posted to squadron. The other was to allow those who had completed a first 'tour' of ops to return as instructors for five months before they went back for a second tour as 'old lags'. The situation became more hopeless as time went on, as the chances of completing the second tour were reducing all the time, eventually becoming minimal, and the fatality rate on OTUs, largely due as much to overworked machines as poor piloting, was disturbingly high. After the first four-engined bombers were introduced, pupils were obliged to go to a Heavy Conversion Unit following OTU, normally on Halifaxes. Then, when the Lancaster became front line in 1942, trainee aircrew went to a Lancaster Finishing School. They would then be posted to squadron.

The year 1942 was crucial for Bomber Command. It was then that it had to build up its front line strength from the inadequately trained and under-equipped force employed on the initial German raids of 1940/41, to a force strong enough to undertake Harris's planned 'main offensive', the 'siege' of Berlin, for which he was preparing all through 1942 and for the most part of 1943. There were a number of factors, however, restricting his objective, one of which was the employment of trainees emerging from the OTUs. In 1942 Bomber Command OTUs were training crews to serve all over the world and, with Montgomery's victory at El Alamein, the Mediterranean Theatre was seen by the chiefs of staff as the main active front. Consequently a large proportion of crews leaving British OTUs were siphoned off to serve in the Mediterranean. Whilst squadrons in England struggled to maintain their quotas, a large number of men in the Middle East were either misemployed or bone idle. In order to keep the same number of squadrons whilst manpower was being drained off to other theatres, the number of men on each British unit had to be reduced proportionately. Thus, up to May 1943, the majority of Harris's squadrons were running at less than 80 per cent of their front line strength: although 19 new squadrons had been created in 1942, 13 of these were sent overseas and three transferred provisionally to Coastal Command. For most of 1942, over 84 per cent of Harris's original force was assigned elsewhere. This disparity was eventually corrected with the introduction of OTUs within the Middle East itself, specifically training for the Mediterranean Theatre. Harris himself stated that 'the demands from overseas and Coastal Command'[1] was the main reason Bomber Command failed to expand in 1943.

Another factor affecting the build-up of Harris's forces was the introduction of the four-engined bomber. With this, all medium bomber crews had to be retrained – a much more involved and lengthy process than had been initially envisaged. If this had not been done, however, and the force had confined itself to bombers such as the Wellington, it would have required twice the number of pilots. Aircraft like the Lancaster carried twice the ordnance of the Wellington, but still had had only one pilot: in other words, a force of Wellingtons required twice as many men to fly half the ordnance, which would have put undue strain on OTUs. The early contracts put out for four-engined aircraft in the 1930s were indeed far-sighted.

Like Laurie Simpson, most pilots arriving at Bomber Command OTUs in 1942 had already spent over a year in elementary and initial training schools. This, with 'further education' at the operational and heavy conversion units, meant the cost of training one pilot alone in 1942 could amount to well over £10,000, an astronomical sum in those days. Not only that, but crews had to pass 'a specialist course in bomber operations'[2] to work as a mutually dependent unit; this was not a scheme aimed at nurturing individuals. The training cost of a seven-man crew could thus exceed £70,000. The OTU courses normally lasted five months with 80 flying hours per man. At one point the course could have been reduced, lowering the training standard, but this fortunately was avoided.

Simpson went to 27 OTU three times: once between 9 and 20 July 1942 with 460 'Conversion Flight' when based at Lichfield, Staffordshire, and once with 460 'Operations Flight', also at Lichfield, from 26 July to 1 September 1942 – on both occasions as a pupil. His third time at OTU was in 1943 at Church Broughton in Derbyshire, after his first tour.

No. 15 (P) AFU, Leconfield, Yorkshire, 1-30 April 1942

At the end of March 1942, shortly after arriving in England, Laurie Simpson was posted to Leconfield, Yorkshire, where he arrived on 30 March. He noted: '*Arrived here at 11 o'clock. Had supper and after mucking about getting our luggage, eventually bedded down at 2.30. What a day!*' His time here was to last until the end of June, apart from one week at a 'BAT flight'. '*Our first impression of this station is excellent*', he wrote the next day. '*The food is first rate, our quarters leave absolutely nothing to be desired and the atmosphere is generally very friendly… The officers in the mess seem to be a grand crowd and we got along very well.*'

Laurie Simpson
(Simpson)

The following day they had their first real taste of lectures which '*weren't really so bad*'. In the afternoon Laurie made his first flight since leaving Australia, in an Oxford. The Airspeed Oxford had entered service in 1937 as part of the RAF expansion programme and was built by the firm that the author Neville Shute[3] had helped to found, based at Portsmouth and Christchurch. Along with the Avro Anson, the Oxford was the standard RAF trainer and a three-seater intended for all types of aircrew. 1 April was '*… a bad day with strong, cold, gusty winds.*' Laurie concluded, however: '*I like these crates. They're comfortable, solid and feel good.*'

A Blenheim and a Spitfire were on station and a Defiant landed that day. Up over Beverley Laurie noticed a large, old cathedral which he hoped would be worth seeing:

'*As we flew along the coast towards Flamborough Head,*' he wrote, '*it seemed strange to think that just across the North Sea Jerry lives.*'

Three days after that he '*flew with Wing Commander Robinson today and learnt quite a lot. Later in the morning went up with P/O Morris again.*' My father flew seven times with Alec Morris as first pilot at Leconfield. Morris, an Australian, already had a DFM and was instructing following a first tour but was very young.

After his flight with Morris, Laurie was eventually allowed to fly solo: he wrote '*Felt very confident and did quite a fair landing.*' In the afternoon a squadron leader and the flight lieutenant in charge of lectures took the course to Hull, which they enjoyed immensely and they saw a show in the evening. Laurie was surprised by the reaction of the civilians to the Australian presence:

> '*I don't think Hull has seen many of the RAAF because we were the cynosure of many curious eyes, and the word (as they pronounce it) "Oustralyens" was whispered behind our backs often. One woman who has a son flying at Haventon, Victoria pulled us up and asked if we were real Australians.*'

The city of Kingston-upon-Hull had '*copped the Blitz*' much more than any other town he had yet seen. '*Whole blocks are ruined and innumerable places have been gutted by incendiaries*', he wrote. '*The damage is simply terrific.*'

On 5 April he did an hour's solo and a '*...flip around the countryside*'. But the haze and murk were so thick that not much could be seen: '*I made one good and one bad landing today*', he noted. The Chief Flying Instructor and Officer Commanding happened to be watching, and it was the impression he created that worried him, when his flying was still classed as 'average'. He found it '*hell trying to make a good landing*' as the winds had been fierce and gusty and on the runways mostly crosswind. '*What I wouldn't give for some good old Australian sunshine and the tang of gum leaves and some of George Hall's beer or a camp by the Billabong with the boys*', he mused. '*Nil desperandum!*'

On Easter Monday, the 6th, he got in a couple of hours more flying but, with strong gusty winds and the visibility zero above 1,000 feet, found it, '*...as the boys put it, "one continual Juggle with Jesus."*' But his landings were quite safe and he felt '*rather gratified*'. 7 April was '*another ruddy awful day*'. He '*stooged around the countryside*' between Leconfield and Market Dreighton and '*as usual*' once managed to get temporarily lost. At about 16.30 hrs another strong gusty wind caused flying to be scrubbed.

The following day the weather was still 'B.A'. Flying was confined to the morning with lectures in the afternoon: '*I flipped over to York but the thick haze at 800 ft and the number of aircraft pushing through it made me decide to scram.*' He later found a gap in the clouds and '*basked in beautiful sunshine*'. By the 10th, he had clocked 17 hours' flying time which was '*quite satisfactory*'. It was an exceptional day with bright sunshine over broken cumulus but the '*usual ruddy 40-50 mph gale*'. He was managing to keep his standard up and his time down, despite the constrictions of 'The Plan', which cannot have been easy. Men were still being scrubbed from flying despite it being an 'Advanced' unit.

On 9 April Laurie complained that the weather had come down again. '*Dammit!*' he wrote, '*Ceiling 800. Winds 40-60 mph. Conditions generally SH.*' So he did an hour's blind-flying. '*I chased air speed indicator needle, altimeter needle and R. of C. needle damn near all round the clock. Then, after I came down had an hour on the Link [Trainer] doing beam approaches and landings. Phew!!!*' He and Graeme Keys had been invited to a party in the mess the following Saturday night which promised to be '*a bit of a thrash*'. That day Laurie was quite philosophical about the course of things:

'The God of War seems to be really sharpening his tools of trade in preparation for the thaw in Russia and for something in Libya, not to mention India and the Pacific. I often wonder where and when the hell it is going to end.'

The weather improved on Friday, 10th. Sunshine with broken cumulus cloud and visibility of up to 10 miles made it '*quite an exceptional day*'. The English countryside continued to enthral him when viewed from above. That evening he developed what he described as '*a touch of the ta-tas*', probably brought on by a letter he had received from home concerning a former girlfriend. On 11 April, Laurie had his first near accident. The wind was milder, but visibility at 1,000 ft was '*practically nil*'. Commencing a cross-country in an Oxford from Askern to Rippon, he found that he could not see anything:

'*While doing a circuit later on I saw a crate on its nose on the edge of the runway and received a red light and so I had to open up everything and go round. I was at 100 feet at the time and heading straight for a tower across the aerodrome, and the damn crate wouldn't climb with full flap down. So I was losing height with houses all around underneath me and very little prospect of getting away with it.*'

Pupils were taught never to let the flaps up under 500 feet because the aircraft would consequently drop 100 to 200 feet like a stone. At 50 feet above the houses Laurie thought '*Simpson, old boy, the writing's on the wall unless this bloody thing climbs pretty quick!*' There was only one hope and that was '*...to get the flaps up and hope like hell that she didn't drop much!*' So very gently he let the flaps up – and it worked. As soon as they were up, the aircraft began to climb and his interest in life became renewed. He wrote, '*Even though it was a spot I wasn't worried – which amazes me!*'

The '*old thrash*' in the mess that night was '*a great show*'. At about 2.30 am, feeling the worse for wear, Laurie decided he had had it for the night and sought out Graeme Keys who had disappeared about an hour earlier.

'*I found him in the lavatory in his underwear with his underpants up and his trousers, coat, shoes and socks rolled into a neat ball in various unorthodox positions around the said lav. Graeme was seated on the seat fast asleep. So I woke him and told him it was bed time and he mumbled some unintelligible gibberish and allowed himself to be led to bed, undressed and put between the sheets in his birthday suit. Boy was it a funny show.*'

No. 1518 Beam Approach Training Flight, Scampton, Lincolnshire, 3-8 May 1942

After changing trains five times Laurie eventually arrived at Scampton in the afternoon of 2 May. This was an operational base. For the first time he saw crews flying out on ops and encountered the Avro Lancaster: '*We were delighted to see the huge aircraft here*', he wrote. '*Lancasters, Manchesters, Hampdens, all "heavies". This station is inhabited by 49 and 83 Squadrons, so us little blokes feel small change in comparison with the boys here. More or less feel out of it too. It is now 9.45 and the big ships are taking off in succession for their various jobs over there.*' These were 'Nickel raids' (leaflet-dropping flights): the crews may not have been fully operational but were crews in training. Eleven bombers went to France without loss.

He continued: '*The four-engined Lancaster is a particularly interesting thing. It is simply huge and like a flying block of flats. The wheels are almost as tall as a man. I'll bet they give Jerry a helluva headache.*'

Laurie did not find beam approach work easy. It was four days before he started to get the hang of it. The idea was to aid navigation. An aircraft flew along a radio beam and if it deviated to the left or right, a note sounded in the earphones. At first it was easier than the Link flight simulator, but Laurie soon became afraid that the continual shrill note of the beam would drive him 'crackers'. He found the work *sometimes good, sometimes rotten*', but generally '*exasperating*' as he tried to watch simultaneously the Air Speed Indicator, Artificial Horizon, D.G. [probably Directional Gyro], Rate of Climb, compass, beam needle and listen to the beam note, as well as trying to visualize where he was – all at once. On the 6th: '*At last! At last! I'm beginning to master the beam procedure. How I've sweated and fought that aircraft to try and do a good job and at last I'm getting somewhere.*' On the 7th he finished his Link Trainer programme and in flying excelled himself: '*Gosh, it was good to hear the instructor say, "Well you seem to have got that taped now"*', he wrote.

Operational aircraft continued to fly out from Scampton. '*The squadrons here are always flying at night*,' he wrote, '*mostly "Nickel" raids.*' [These were flown mainly by medium bombers.] '*Nothing big has been pulled off since we've been here*', he noted. He passed much of his time in the Ops Room which was '*…time well spent because it gives me the low-down on all operations, and an insight into our espionage system.*'

On 8 May, Graeme and Laurie finished the BAT course and got themselves cleared '*after much ado*'. They were ready to go on leave first thing the next morning. However, the effects of a party that night almost ensured otherwise.

9 May

'Woke up at 0600 hrs feeling terrible and dragged Graeme out. Arrived at Lincoln station to see the train pulling out, so I rushed along and demanded that the guard stop it, which strangely he did. We tried our hardest to get over the night before, but didn't succeed too well.'

No. 15 (P) Advanced Flying Unit, Leconfield, Yorks, 13 May-20 June 1942

Laurie Simpson arrived back at Leconfield station on 12 May at 10.45 hrs: '*Had some beer and sandwiches and so to bed.*' The next morning he felt '*…a glow of satisfaction with memories of a pleasant leave.*' He reconciled himself to being back to earth: '*Well anyway Leconfield is such a small station and it is good to be back with the boys.*'

The next day: '*Had some dual this morning from P/O Alec Morris and as he is a wonderful chap I found time well spent.*' Morris appears in Don Charlwood's book *No Moon Tonight*. Charlwood was discussing crews leaving Elsham Wolds for an operation in 1943: '*Soon the crews about me began leaving… In their hands they carried red packages of escape equipment … in case tonight they were shot down, but survived. It occurred to me how young they were and how foreign to their task. There was Morris who at nineteen was so soon to die.*'

Laurie wrote on the 14th: '*We were issued with bicycles today to replace the bus which isn't running any more, and I think it is a grand idea.*'

Bicycles may have been a convenient solution to the transport problem at Leconfield in 1942 but at Binbrook in 1944 they proved a liability. Illegal 'borrowing' of bikes after hours was not uncommon on 460 Squadron and a local 'bobby' was continually kept busy with reports of thefts. Thinking he could put a stop to this, the man rode to Binbrook to confront the station adjutant requesting that aircrew be ticked off and the illegal pilfering cease. Rather pleased that he had put his message across, the policeman prepared to leave only to find that his bike, too, had been stolen.

On 16 May 1942 there was heavy fog at Leconfield until midday which made everything unusable. That afternoon Laurie started a form of synthetic night-flying in an

Oxford using sodium runway lights and special goggles. But a gremlin beset him: '*I had trouble because my glasses misted over with moisture at the critical moment of each approach*', he wrote. Life on training units was still dangerous and there were many fatalities. Then something happened on the 18th that shook Laurie out of any complacency:

18 May

'Was watching a formation of twelve Spitfires go over today when suddenly two collided and both spun in from 2,000 ft. A big gush of flame and then smoke. We flew over and saw the wrecks and they were absolutely burnt out. It shook me more than I like to admit, because it isn't nice to see two boys end that way.'

On 19 May: '*Did some formation and two cross-countries today all with Graeme and enjoyed it immensely.*'[4] At lunchtime they heard that one of the 'boys', Sgt Judge Rutherford, had gone 'into the deck'.[5] Later they learned that '...while formating with Bill Paterson their wing tip and tail planes collided and Judge went in.'

Rutherford had been in training with Laurie since Queensland. '*Poor old Judge*,' he wrote, '*he was a grand little guy, a Westralian*[6] *and a perfect gentleman.*' It shook him to know that another of his friends had '*gone west*'. His one wish was, '*Dear old Judge may you go to a world where there [are] no wars to take nice kids like you away from your loved ones.*'

On 22 May they buried Rutherford in Leconfield churchyard. Leconfield was a small village with an ancient church that Simpson hoped would '*stay with him*'. Rutherford was one of the first of his friends to be killed; they were a long way from home and he felt '*very touched*' when he stood at the foot of the grave and gave a last salute. The inscription on the coffin was poignant '*Sgt. Rutherford R.A.A.F.*' – but he also perceived it as defiant: '*We'll be seeing you old boy*,' he wrote, '*where all good airmen go. Au revoir Judge old man!*'[7]

During his last week from 16-20 June, Laurie did a number of cross-country, low-flying and sodium-assisted landing exercises.[8] On the 15th and 19th he flew with Graeme Keys. His total airtime by then was 326 hours, 26 minutes, and his 'proficiency as pilot on type' was recorded as 'Above the Average'. Although for the majority of his time at Leconfield Laurie was training on Oxfords, he appears to have had some ground experience, at least, of the Vickers Wellington. In a final note at the end of the course, before moving to Lichfield, he was certified as understanding '...the petrol, oil, ignition and hydraulic systems of the Wellington aircraft.' Bad news arose, however: he and Graeme learnt that they were to be posted to different units.

23 June

'Word of our posting came through – me to Lichfield. Graeme to Wing. Disappointed at being separated. Everybody expressed their sorrow but "it is inevitable" they say. Only Asst. Adj. "Jolly" Rodger holds out hope. Rang Air Ministry on 23rd and it worked like a dream. Incredible.[9] *Our mess party Saturday night was quite good, but I didn't enjoy it much. Our farewell party with the boys was much better. Started in Beverley Arms at 7 p.m. To sergeants' mess at 10.30 and back to our own mess at midnight – we were finished at 2.30 after putting Peter Lines to bed with a bunch of flowers.'*

Once again the 'boys' found that their paths corresponded.

No. 27 OTU, (Conversion Flight) Lichfield, Staffordshire
24 June 1942-20 July 1942

OTU was the location where men 'came of age', acting as a place of initiation:

'It was at OTU that the trainees began to use the air force language – technical, comic and evasive – that helped to bind them together. So they began to talk of a *'shaky do'*, *'piece of cake'*, *'kite'*, *'bags of'*, *'gen'*, *'stooge'*, *'chop'*, *'prang'*, and *'line shoot'*... To use air force slang before OTU was pretentious; to use it later was to demonstrate graduation.'[10]

On the 24th Laurie and Graeme caught the bus on time and after going into Beverley and Burton-on-Trent arrived at Lichfield at about 19.00 hrs. They found the station *'not nearly as elaborate as Leconfield'* but the boys had *'a good small room'*. The food was fair and the mess convenient. *'So we are quite content,'* he asserted, but then added after more consideration, *'...as yet.'*

27 OTU was formed on 23 April 1941 to train aircrew on Wellingtons and form crews before going to squadron. Lichfield was originally known as RAF Fradley, and was constructed in 1939 and early 1940. Work at 27 OTU was involved with the Wellington Marks I, Ia and Ic. These would have been ex-operational aircraft and, from a handling point of view, past their best. *'They have Wellingtons (Mark Ic) here,'* Laurie Simpson wrote, *'and they certainly are much bigger and more complicated than the Oxford. But I reckon I'll be able to cope.'* By 27 June his flying was judged as *'above average'*.

29 June: *'We were initiated into the knobs and tits of the Wimpy today and I think she should be OK.'*[11]

'My crew is lined up now', he wrote. *'The observer is a small young Aussie; the bombardier is a browny type of bloke*[12] *who almost got his pilot's wings so should be handy when I get tired. The w/op I haven't met yet nor the rear gunner, but they are Aussies except the A.G.*[13] *who is of the RAF. They look a nice bunch and I hope we get along OK.'* This crew consisted of Simpson, as pilot; Sgt Alistair Kennedy RAAF, as navigator; Sgt Colin McLeod RAAF, as bombardier; Sgt Ronald Searle RAAF, as wireless operator; and Sgt Ken Sutton RAF, as rear gunner. This suggests that the crew was actually assigned to Simpson rather than being formed through the normal 'crewing up' process, since he had met only Kennedy and McLeod before the other two, and

Colin McLeod (Searle)

Ken Sutton and Ron Searle (Searle)

Alistair Kennedy (Searle)

there is no record in his diary of a 'crewing up' procedure. They did not actually fly together as a crew until 28 July.[14]

By 6 July Laurie had not received any mail from Australia for almost eleven weeks. Conversely, Graeme, who was married, had received half-a-dozen letters; but there was no correspondence from Laurie's old girlfriend at Deniliquin. He wrote, despairingly, '*According to mother's letters Joy had left me like a shag on a rock. What can I do about it over here?*'

A North American B-25 Mitchell landed that weekend, an aircraft which struck them greatly. '*They are the last word in efficient aircraft*', Laurie observed. They also witnessed a formation of six B-17 Flying Fortresses passing overhead but he was '*not impressed with them*'. On the 9th they were due to start flying the Wellington: '*I hope I can manage the Wimpy alright, shouldn't be too difficult.*'

Bruce Richards was another friend killed during training. They had been together since the early days at Amberley in Queensland. From 16-19 July the unit lost five trainers – four Wellingtons and an Anson with more than 15 aircrew killed. Richards, cryptically nicknamed 'Ace', was the first to go: it was thought that he crashed into the North Sea.[15] Then a Wimpy dived into a hill with only the bombardier surviving. On the night of the 18th, a third Wimpy 'went off on fire' and an Anson went missing. The following day an Australian who had come over on the *Themistocles*, Eric Longbottom, a particular friend of Richards and Simpson's, was killed. It was, Simpson wrote, '*very bad luck*'.

25 July: Laurie and Graeme finished their conversion course and were now qualified as 'captains of Wellington aircraft'. Laurie found the Wellington '*heavy and with a totally different landing attitude to the Oxford*', but liked it just the same. The weather was improving on the night of the 25th when his girlfriend, Dorothy Holmes, arrived from Bournemouth.

27 OTU (Operations Flight), Lichfield, Staffordshire, 26 July-1 September 1942

By 26 July, Laurie Simpson's crew had transferred to the 27 OTU's 'Operations Flight'. He made four '*long flips over England*' in three different Wellingtons with his crew on 28 and 31 July, and 4 and 5 August, and they did well. The navigator, Al Kennedy, was '*a real hot merchant*'. Bomb-Aimer Colin McLeod ('Mac') co-operated with Kennedy well and made '*a good fist*' of the job. Ron Searle, the wireless operator, was '*extra good*' and pounded away at his Morse key '*unceasingly*'. Ken Sutton, the RAF air gunner, was '*a really nice lad*' in whom Simpson had plenty of confidence. He summarised them all as '*a grand mob of fellows. Mac with his slow drawl; Al with his definite ideas; Ron the Morse key-basher; and Ken the grand little gunner.*'

On 27 August Laurie's crew made its second cross-country trip from Lichfield over the Irish Sea area, via Rhyl, Douglas, the Skerries, Rhyl and back to Lichfield. The Wellington was equipped for infrared bombing, carrying 10 bombs, but they experienced '*St. Elmo's fire amidst very sticky weather*'. He wrote:

> '*The port motor iced up four times and we once ran into an electrical storm. We were bathed in a phosphorescent light from sparkles on the trailing aerial. The front turret went up in a flash of blue flame, the props were blazing arcs of blue and every raindrop created a spark on the windshield. So we went down out of it. However everything was OK and we plugged along and completed the exercise.*'

From 5-18 September he went on leave. '*The final days at Lichfield awaiting a posting and it is to 460 Australian Squadron in Yorkshire*', he wrote. He was to convert onto the

Halifax immediately and Graeme later. That Thursday he went to visit friends in Tamworth and then took the train to Bournemouth.

Don Charlwood

Don Charlwood was an Australian navigator who wrote one of the most admired books on operational life in Bomber Command, *No Moon Tonight*. My father and some of his second crew, including mid-upper gunner Johnny Rydings, knew Charlwood's pilot Geoff Maddern, at 27 OTU, Church Broughton in Derbyshire during 1943. Charlwood was from Melbourne and had wanted to write ever since he was a teenager. Originally he tried to get work with Keith Murdoch, the newspaper baron in Victoria, but subsequently found work as a farmhand, writing occasional short stories. He volunteered for the RAAF after training as a navigator in Canada, went to 27 OTU, Lichfield in 1942, and then to a Heavy Conversion Unit. This was undoubtedly the same course that my father took, 1656 Conversion Unit, Lindholme. Charlwood was posted to 103 Squadron, Elsham Wolds where, at 27, he was quite old for aircrew. He recalled his first encounter with 27 OTU:

Don Charlwood
(via M. Rowe)

> 'The atmosphere there was different from anything we had known, for at Lichfield all instructors had completed a tour… Before lectures began, the senior Lichfield officers introduced themselves. These men with their ribbons, their moustaches and slang gripped our imagination. They had operated, they were skilled, they had about them an elusive air – something I could never define.'[16]

Of the 20 navigators Charlwood trained with, only five survived the war. Three of these did their initial training at Somers, Victoria where Laurie was in February 1941. Among the 20 was Flight Sergeant W.R.K. 'Bill' Charlton who sat in as a replacement with Laurie's crew on an aborted raid to Hamburg on 30 January 1943. Charlton was killed on the disastrous Pilzen[17] raid of 17 April 1943. Another 460 Squadron man in the '20' was Tom McNeill; he was Flight Sergeant Dave Charlick's navigator and was killed on a raid to Berlin on 29/30 March 1943. Charlick flew as a 'second dickey' with Laurie on a raid to Cologne on the 26th. The only man to get out of Charlick's aircraft was Flying Officer 'Frankie' Falkenmire, who went to *Stalag Luft* III. The third navigator Laurie knew from Charlwood's '20 men' was 'Blue' Freeman. Freeman did 30 ops with 103 Squadron and then a second tour as navigator to Squadron Leader (later Wing Commander) Bill Brill, a 460 Squadron flight commander, who later became CO of 467 Squadron. His total number of ops was 50. Ted Freeman gained a reputation for irreverence and high spirits, once holding the distinction of having his activities mentioned in the House of Commons. He set fire to a Land Army cottage on display in Trafalgar Square and on 21 April 1943, Cliff O'Riordan, 460 Squadron's resident barrister, defended him at a Courts Martial, which was presided over by the station CO, Hughie Edwards. Freeman was acquitted on every charge.

A deeply thoughtful and reflective man, Charlwood survived his first tour of ops and, realising how fortunate he was, wrote two books after the war that became classics – *No Moon Tonight* and *Journeys into Night*,[18] later described as 'among the finest autobiographical works on Bomber Command'.

460 Squadron Conversion Flight, Holme-on-Spalding-Moor, Yorkshire, 20 September-14 October 1942

Laurie Simpson was assigned to Holme on 20 September, shortly after being posted to 460 Squadron. The crew went there to convert to Halifaxes and he found '*a good lot of blokes*' there, noting, '*Had a yarn and a game of billiards with Flt/Lt Falkiner, one of the big family, and discovered that more than half the officers of 460 Squadron come from the Riverina.*' The Riverina area of New South Wales produced the finest wool in Australia and John Falkiner's family owned great tracts of land there.[19]

Henry Coverley,[20] a 76 Squadron Halifax pilot, reported Holme to be a very primitive, absolutely chaotic station, where the only accommodation was in Nissen huts. From here Laurie went on five flights, four in Halifaxes. There was little doing for several weeks and he became '*thoroughly browned off*' until 14 October when he went up in a Manchester as a second pilot. This was for half-an-hour of 'circuits and bumps' with a flight sergeant.

> '*At last on the 14th was taken up by Shorty Fahey for some dual on a Manchester. The other pilot Dan Murphy did a couple of ropey landings and the u/c* [undercarriage] *went u/s so I didn't get at the controls.*'

On 27 September a Halifax crashed at Holme and Flt/Lt Falkiner was killed in the aircraft with one other, both men being regarded as crack pilots. By 14 October two new members were added to Simpson's crew: Freddy King as flight engineer and Walter Maltby, mid-upper gunner, both roles being needed on four-engined bombers. Then news was received that the whole squadron was to convert to Lancasters. During the third week in October there was little flying. '*Hanging about looking at our beautiful Lancasters*', Laurie wrote, '*isn't as good as flying them.*'

Freddy King (King)

On the 20th a Manchester went down:

> '*Kev Murphy, Roger Wood, Lennie Forrester and a South African Flying Officer Hoorn were killed when they hit a tree in a Manchester down near Lichfield on the 20th. Graeme, Mac, Quicky and I are to go to the funeral tomorrow. Lots of rumours are in the air at present: about the date of our receiving ops, shifting south to the Humber, moving to Lindholme, going back home etc. Aw hell! Our C.O., W/Cdr Kaufman has been recalled to Aussie, lovely man. B Flight O.C. Sqn/Ldr Bailey has been posted to a new Aussie squadron at Driffield and he is a good man for the job.*'[21]

Kaufman was replaced by Wg/Cdr J. Dilworth DFC, who was subsequently replaced by Wg/Cdr C.E. 'Chad' Martin DSO, DFC.

1656 Conversion Unit, Lindholme, Yorkshire, 2 November-13 December 1942

On 2 November Laurie's crew moved to Lindholme. The night before they had a small party in the local hostelry: '*Wound up in the "Fairy" at 2.30 a.m.*' he wrote. Eventually, on the 2nd, the crew moved by road to Lindholme where they found '*....a glorious station on permanent lines*'. Such superlatives were undoubtedly a reaction to the squalor of Holme.

Lindholme airfield was located about five miles east of York, its construction having begun in the spring of 1938 and it was officially opened in June 1940. The airfield took up 250 acres and an adjacent camp and support facilities added a further 150 acres. 1656 Conversion Unit was a Heavy Conversion Unit where fledgling crews converted from the twin-engined Wellington onto the Halifax and, if they were lucky, the Lancaster. Ted Groom recalled one 'awful' incident that occurred when he was posted there:

> 'We arrived at Lindholme and there were some traffic lights where the runway crossed the aerodrome. Of course the aircraft were taking off straight across the road only a few feet up. We had to stop at these lights: they were operated by Flying Control when aircraft were taking off or landing. We sat in the bus and all of a sudden a plane went over the top and "Boom!" – it went straight in. A Halifax! One of the problems with the Halifax was that the undercarriage and flap levers were identical and side-by-side in the cockpit. You had to have seven degrees of flap to take off – the pilot would say eventually, "Undercarriage up". But while landing here he pulled the undercarriage up instead of the flaps!'[22]

Despite the base being glorious, the staff there left something to be desired as they treated the new boys as 'very raw pupils'. It was 'terrible compared to squadron life', Laurie commented. In his diary he recorded the suppressed anger this gave rise to, especially towards the non-flying staff:

> 'The staff officers, particularly the "Penguins", seem to adopt a very antagonistic attitude towards us, which is wrong to glory [in]. However they'll learn the hard way. Damn their stupid hides. They seem to think they can subdue us "Aussies" the same way they do their own Pongoes.'

This was not an unprecedented reaction. Ken Newman, a South Londoner who had trained as a pilot in South Africa and visited Germany before the war, had been flying Wellingtons before being sent to Lindholme to convert to Lancasters. He was also disgusted by the way the staff behaved: 'The whole atmosphere changed', he recalled. 'They treated us like shit. We were all apprehensive about the future but they acted as if we were all about to desert. They were very heavy-handed.'[23] Similarly Robert Raymond, an American sergeant pilot, was 'the happiest mortal on earth' when he transferred from a 'miserable' Advanced Flying Course to an OTU, but he was 'unfavourably impressed' by the attitude of the RAF officers upon arriving. They deliberately mistreated the colonial trainees, particularly air gunners and w/ops: 'Some are rather rough,' Raymond commented, 'but they should be treated more considerately.' He was equally critical in a diary entry of 16 April 1942: 'The officers cannot conceive of anyone talking in the breezy staccato manner that is their natural mode of expression, or of being equal to [them] in intelligence and efficiency.' He saw this as applying throughout English society. How, Raymond wondered, could crew relationships work on long operational flights? He saw the easy-going Canadian aircrew as 'flint and steel compared to RAF officers'.[24]

For Laurie, there were other frustrations: '*Coming to Lindholme meant forfeiting our six days leave and God knows when we'll get it again. We have no aircraft here yet, so the conversion which should only take three weeks will take ages.*' It was not until 29 November that he received his certification as 'First Pilot (Day)' on Halifaxes. It was signed 'D. Holford'.

David Holford

Whilst at Lindholme, on 21 and 23 November Laurie flew across Lincolnshire on two training flights, the purposes of which were described as 'dual check and weather test'.

This was in essence a dual flying check on the Halifax which, unlike the Lancaster, had two pilot seats. In each case he noted meticulously in his logbook that the 1st Pilot was '*S/L Holford DSO, DFC*', the Officer Commanding 'B' Flight at Lindholme. When Don Charlwood was first posted to 103 Squadron in 1942, his crew was put under the authority of an officer whom he described as a 'pale, boyish-looking squadron leader, who wore the ribbons of the DSO and DFC over his battledress pocket.' Charlwood remembered little of what he said, but could not forget the man's 'dark staring eyes'[25]: 'I felt that he had looked upon the worst,' Charlwood recalled, 'and on looking beyond it found serenity.'[26] This was David Holford. Holford was a phenomenon in the RAF. He had been awarded the DFC at 19 years of age in October 1940 and the DSO at 21. A native of Kingston upon Thames, he was commissioned in 1939 and completed two tours. According to his DSO citation on operations he was '...*an outstanding captain who performed his duties, both in the air and on the ground, with a thoroughness rarely found*.' Such was his determination to hit back at the enemy that he 'performed sorties at every opportunity'.

One day in February 1942, when a daylight op was announced at short notice, Holford so organised his air and ground crews that they were able to take off well within two hours of being briefed. On many occasions he had made three or four runs over a target to ensure the bombing was accurate, or to enable a photoflash record to be made. He had participated in most of the operations in which 103 Squadron had engaged.

In 1943 Holford was the Base Commander at Lindholme. Charlwood recalled hearing a flight sergeant say that if he returned for a third tour, half the station would follow him. Eventually 'one foggy night, as Holford came into land, he crashed and was killed.'[27] What Charlwood did not mention was that this occurred on one of the worst nights ever for Bomber Command – 16 December 1943 when 382 aircrew lost their lives in a single night, nearly half of them over England.

On 17 February 1942, four days before his 22nd birthday, Holford had been promoted to Wing Commander. By December 1943 he was the CO of 100 Squadron based at Waltham, Grimsby and the youngest 'Wingco' in the RAF. On the fateful day his wife of only a few weeks was staying at the Ship Inn in nearby Grimsby. A total of 483 Lancasters and 10 Mosquitoes set out that night to attack Berlin. They encountered night fighters over the Dutch mainland and also on the way to the target. But on the return flight, opposition was avoided by taking a more northerly route out over Denmark. Despite this, 25 Lancasters were lost. However worse was to come. The night became known later as 'Black Thursday' – a night when 29 aircraft crashed or were abandoned after a thick fog developed over the home airfields. One hundred and forty-eight airmen were killed.

Holford attempted to land in the fog at Kelstern some time after midnight. His Lancaster, JB560 'N-Nan', clipped a hillside just short of the airfield. One of the two survivors thought that he was lost and became dazzled by the fog funnel lights as he approached. The Lancaster went in nose first and exploded. G.R. Fawcett, a pilot with 101 Squadron, found his crew confronted by circuit lights upon his return, glowing through a hole in the fog: down below was Grimsby. On the run in he made out a burning wreck:

> '*The final approach was well lit by the burning remains of a Lanc that didn't quite make it... I found out later that this contained the C.O. of 100 Squadron, Dave Holford.*'[28]

Holford was blown clear by the blast and broke his ankles; his frozen corpse was found the next day in a snowdrift.[29] The rear and mid-upper gunners were also blown clear but survived. Holford was '*an outstanding leader whose skill and courage have set an inspiring example*', his citation ended.[30] Don Charlwood concluded that he was 'one of the most striking men we met in the RAF' and '…the personification of all that was best in the RAF.'[31]

Men like David Holford epitomised the spirit of the instructors in OTUs who had been willing to face, in some cases, greater dangers at the hands of inexperienced, half-trained aircrew than those that threatened them on operations. Air Marshal Harris had a lot to say for the men at the OTUs. After the war he decried the fact that the work of the instructors and the risks they ran were never officially acknowledged:

'It is not generally recognised how astonishingly good was the work of the OTUs. They produced an endless flow of crews whose ability to cope with every conceivable sort of weather was far in advance of what any pre-war crew, civil or service could have achieved. All this was done by instructors during what were called their "rest periods" between operational tours, and it was not done without casualties. It was quickly realised that only aircrew with operational experience could train the OTU crews, and until the last year there was a continual shortage of men who could serve as instructors, and particularly of pilots with operational experience, so that they all had to work overtime.'[32]

Now Laurie's crew was ready for the big test at Breighton, and the hard work of men such as David Holford was to come to fruition. They found that they had to face their initiation over what Laurie would later describe as '*the world's hottest target*'.

Part Two

ON SQUADRON

'I should point out that the bombing of a German target on one single occasion was the equivalent of going through the Battle of Jutland or any other great battle. An ordinary bomber crew in one tour of duty experienced thirty such battles.'

AIR VICE MARSHAL D.C.T. BENNETT CBE, DSO, AOC PATHFINDER FORCE
From *Pathfinder*, 1958

'There is no parallel in warfare to such courage and determination in the face of danger. It was… a clear and highly conscious courage, by which risk was taken with calm forethought… It was the courage of men with long-drawn apprehensions of daily "going over the top".'

AIR MARSHAL SIR ARTHUR HARRIS, C-IN-C BOMBER COMMAND
From *Bomber Offensive*, 1947

CHAPTER SIX

'ENOUGH TO FRIGHTEN THE DEVIL OUT OF US!'

First Operation

THE first operation was the proving ground for most aircrew. If one could endure that and the next four, one may have a chance of completing a tour. Reg Brown:

> 'The odds were stacked against you over the first five, because you were a new crew and you didn't really know much. You knew what you were doing but... hadn't really knitted together. But as it went on, it became somewhat easier from the crew point of view. Certainly statistics show that more people were lost on the first five raids than any other time during a tour.'

Often crew members, particularly pilots, for their first op would go on a flight with another crew as 'second dickeys' to gain experience. Ronald Farren, a navigator with 44 Squadron, recalled: 'The policy for the first operational trip was for the pilot and navigator to go as "dickeys" with experienced crews: this was embarrassing and at times could cause problems, particularly if either or both were shot down; then the remainder of the crew were either split up amongst other crews or awaited a replacement.' John Wroughton, who was a w/op/ air gunner, was sent to a Heavy Conversion Unit at Pocklington to convert to Halifaxes from Wellingtons. His crew became 'headless' after its pilot was killed on a 'second dickey' trip. The crew remained at Pocklington with 102 Squadron, Wroughton filling in with other crews – an experience, he remembered, that led to a number of 'dicey moments'.[1]

One of the first operations of the war
On 2 September 1939, the day before war was declared, Don Wilson of 51 Squadron was allowed to get married and stay with his wife until one minute to midnight. He was refused permission to leave his base at Linton-on-Ouse as 51 Squadron was a front line squadron. The following day he flew on the first raid of the war: 'All the aircrews assembled in the crew room listening to an old radio and heard Chamberlain announce, "...and that consequently, this country is at war with Germany."

One could have heard the proverbial pin drop. Doubtless we were all wondering if we would be fortunate enough to survive.'

Eighty aircrew were to crew sixteen Whitleys. This first attack was a propaganda flight to Frankfurt-am-Main where four million leaflets were to be dropped, in 'Jock' Wilson's words '…telling the cursed Hun to leave Poland or else!'[2]

Wilson's lengthy round trip involved simple navigation down a pre-arranged corridor from Linton-on-Ouse to the south coast of England, made easy by good weather conditions. Since the RAF component of the BEF had not yet been sent to France, a stop was necessary at an *Armée de l'Air* base at Villeneuve on the outskirts of Paris. They then flew to Rheims, aided by a string of flashing ground beacons. The Whitleys landed, refuelling commenced and they took off again at twilight. They then unpacked bundles of leaflets and prepared them for dropping. At that period Holland was a blaze of lights by night, but Germany was in complete darkness; opposition on the trip was light and it seemed like a joyride. But to the enemy, leaflets were a hollow threat: German aircrew were better trained, the *Luftwaffe* had more aircraft than the RAF and it had been blooded in the Spanish Civil War. Leaflets would not deter them.

'Having completed the task of distributing the "toilet paper",' Wilson recollected, 'we set course from Frankfurt to the Cherbourg Peninsula.' The coastline was bathed in bright moonlight with sparkling sea and silver sand. 'We had just altered course over the Channel, when the tranquillity was disturbed by a frantic voice on the intercom – "*Christ! We're out of fuel!*"'

The Whitley banked through 180 degrees, sinking slowly towards the French coast. They scraped over a sand dune, port engine spluttering, undercarriage down, and made a remarkable landing between the high and low water marks. Immediately, the aircraft was surrounded by French Marines: 'Once it was established that we were not the *Luftwaffe*, they conducted us through the dunes to an antiquated fisherman's hut.' The French then arranged for an old caterpillar tractor to retrieve the aircraft. Whilst this was being done, a farmer appeared with a barrel of cider, but it was very dry and very unpleasant: 'Our crew was fortunately able to hide its true feelings about this kind, if unappreciated, gesture', Wilson recalled.

A first operation could be the most daunting. Men often failed to survive it even after years of training. Alec March, an operationally experienced tutor at an OTU, had one pupil who came from a privileged background having attended two public schools. His father was a high-ranking Army officer and the young man had been commissioned while still training. Despite the 'string-pulling' he was incapable of understanding decimals – a necessary skill for operating Gee. March spent many late nights giving him extra tuition and had almost given up before feeling 'satisfied he was competent'. But '…finally news percolated through to us that he and his crew were lost on their first op.'

John Nunn knew a fellow at Elsham Wolds who had trained with him at St. Athan: 'I still think of him as "the piano player" as I can't recall his name', he recorded. 'He wanted to know what it was like flying on ops as he had only just arrived on the camp and had just done his cross-country. He was lost on his first trip.' Howard Pearce remembered his initial operation with 115 Squadron, a unit that had flown the first bombing raid of the war:[3]

> 'My first op was scary indeed. Although I was commissioned they said, "Look we haven't crewed you up yet; this is the Wing Commander." I flew with him first: Wing Commander Freeman. He was as mad as a hatter, had a double DFC and a DSO, and ran our squadron very well. He announced to me: "You're going in the front." So I became the front gunner.

You can't visualize it, but when you're hit by searchlights and so on, you feel that you've been exposed in the toilet with no door on. But you grinned and bore it. Freeman was quite gung ho: "While we're at it," he said, thinking of the searchlight, "I'll do a bit of a dive and see if you can knock the bugger out."'

But, in his excitement, Pearce missed:

'I opened the machine gun up but nothing happened!' he recalled. 'We were with 218 Squadron at Marham in Norfolk. 115 and 218 together, with the boss of the whole lot Group Captain McKee, the station C.O. 'Square' McKee he was called;[4] wonderful man! Big chap: everybody liked him.'[5]

Robert Vollum flew his first op as a w/op/ air gunner with 420 RCAF Squadron from Waddington on 23 April 1942: 'I flew as a gunner in a Hampden to Rostov. It was an uneventful trip, except that on the way back the starboard engine started throwing out streams of sparks and we thought it was going to pack up.' The pilot asked the navigator for a course to steer to Sweden; however the engine settled down and Vollum and his crew flew back to base where they landed after 8 hours 45 minutes.

Fred Danckwardt's first trip was not with his regular crew: 'It was 3 December 1943, to Leipzig. I arrived at Waddington on 2 December. The following morning – I hadn't even unpacked – I was going around the station: you had to go around the station to get this chitty signed in at various places in order to pay accounts and at the medical centre; you even had to go round to the cycle shed on the other side of the airfield. Suddenly there was a message on the tannoy to say that I should go to 467 Squadron immediately! They'd had a flu epidemic and were missing a rear gunner. So I flew with this chap and I couldn't recognise their faces afterwards; I was just bundled into an aircraft and that was it. But actually that crew went on to Pathfinders. Then the next time, I flew with my own crew. But normally pilots did one trip with an experienced crew. In fact I did my first trip before my pilot did.'

In February 1942 the two German battle cruisers *Scharnhorst* and *Gneisenau*, and the heavy cruiser *Prinz Eugen*, broke out of Brest harbour and made a spectacular and audacious daylight dash through the Straits of Dover back to Germany. Strikes by the Royal Navy and the RAF against the ships all proved unsuccessful and suffered cruel losses. Bill Higgs was with 35 Squadron; his first ever raid was to Brest:

'I was on the squadron from May 1941, and I couldn't get on operations. I'd turn up at the "pool" time after time, and couldn't get a crew. I got fed up with it! On 11 May they sent me to Brest where the German battleships were [still] in dock. Of all the places to choose, the Navy gave us Brest! Aircrew were usually given an easy trip for their first, such as a target on the French coast, but as I was flying with a comparatively experienced crew I went to a real hot spot. We flew down from Yorkshire and crossed the English coast at Bridport. In the sky I could see flashes and asked the pilot what they were. He said, in a clear Aussie voice, "*Fireworks!*" In my ignorance I thought what a funny Navy we have, playing about like this. About half-an-hour later I asked the same question and got the same reply. Then I thought I saw balloons and said so over the intercom. The aircraft started weaving violently and the pilot asked, "Where are they?" I said, "All around us!" The skipper replied in unmistakable Aussie: "They're Flak bursts with the moon shining on them!"'[6]

Higgs's Halifax passed through masses of searchlight beams, the bomber bobbing about in the night sky like a cork. 'I was terrified and sweating like mad', he recalled. 'Somehow we came out of this and turned towards England. I gave a sigh of relief, only to find we were turning around to go in again! The navigator couldn't see to drop his bombs: smoke had been laid all over the ships. So we made a timed run from an aiming point on the land. This time the bombs dropped and we left the area, much to my relief!' Higgs realised that even with so much Flak, '…you could get through and survive. I was never so afraid again.'

Arthur Cole:

'The first raid I was on was to Dortmund, and for some reason my bombs were plotted about five or six miles short of target. I never found out why. I was given the most horrible grilling by the crew afterwards – I was quite sure I had not deliberately dropped them early. Eventually the controversy ended when I stabbed my finger on a marker which was shown on the intelligence photograph, the target indicator, and my bombs were planted well on top of that. I think it's a bit unlikely that I was that accurate but, on the other hand, at that time target-marking by Pathfinders was subject to a lot of difficulties: for one thing the Pathfinders might not get it right; for another they were more likely to be shot down than the rest of us, and if they were there would be a blank period when there were no markers visible. If one of them had to release their bombs early because the aircraft was so damaged that it had to drop them, then the odd bomb may have been short and it could have been that which I bombed. There's no real explanation.'[7]

Laurie Simpson's wireless op, Ron Searle, remembered: 'Our first op was to Essen, and what a trip that was: only 5 hours 10 minutes flying, but enough to frighten the devil out of us! We were holed by Flak and one very close shell blew our escape hatch off, which resulted in most of our papers being sucked out into space and our main concern was then holding the papers down. We were at 20,000 feet and the air that came in was like ice.'[8]

Laurie later commented: 'It was 4 January 1943 and at pre-flight briefing we learnt our first op was to be a raid on Essen in the Ruhr. On our run-up to the target and over it, we encountered heavy Flak, and that was an experience I shall never forget. My first thoughts were "*How could we possibly survive this?*" But our experience that night taught us that you can. We reached the target and dropped our bombs and then set course to get out of the area.'[9]

Laurie's diary entry from 4 January 1943 stated:

'At 10.30 a.m. Tammy, our flight commander, told us that we were on for ops tonight. So some frantic organising took place. Briefing 2.30 [p.m.]. Took off at 5.30. Climbed to 1500 feet over the 'drome with bags of vapour trails streaming out behind. Set course at 1823 and it was on. Climbed all the way and reached 1900 odd at the enemy coast. Turned for the target – ESSEN – one of the two hottest in Germany, at the Zuider Zee, and soon saw the blaze of searchlights and Flak. Got in, and bombed the PFF[10] aiming point at 1951 and boy, was I glad to feel that 4000-pounder go – not to mention the 700 incendiaries. Then some violent weaving dodging hundreds of searchlights, heavy Flak – all lit up by the glow of the fires down below. Had our escape hatch torn off in a screaming 300 mph dive when a Flak burst came a little too close.'[11]

Laurie later reflected: 'The Flak was heavy, but to the west we could see it was quieter so we flew in that direction. It was only quiet until *we* arrived! Then they threw everything at us. We survived but it was a mistake we never made again.'[12]

'*Violent evasive action got us clear of the target area after what seemed interminable hours – actually ten minutes – and turned for home. Weaved all the way but didn't strike any trouble. Sighs of relief when the enemy coast was crossed south of Rotterdam and cries of joy when the English coast came up – dear old home – everyone relaxed – hot Bovril was handed round – chocolate was eaten. I took off my oxygen mask and wiped my face which was wet with perspiration. Had trouble with our undercarriage over base, but landed OK amid bad visibility. We bombed at 21,000 feet. Al, Ron and Freddy practically passed out going to the tail of the machine* [i.e. going to the Elsan closet] *as the portable oxygen bottle was nearly empty. All the boys behaved very well. I was much too busy to be scared. Mac acted as if we were over the bombing range instead of over a heck of a nasty target. Al and Ron didn't say much as they both had one long look out and then ducked back to their tables deciding ignorance was bliss – Wally was quiet and seemed a little overawed; Ken was as excited as a schoolboy and shouted with joy as we lost the various searchlights; Freddy was a bit shaken by the near miss by Flak as he was standing right near the escape hatch when it blew off. It was only two feet behind my head and made an awful row. All got back feeling very pleased with ourselves.*'[13]

Ron Searle: 'I think the skipper may have been thinking of a different op when he said Al, Freddy and I made a dash for the toilet.'[14] I can't remember ever using the Elsan on the aircraft, and I'm pretty sure Al didn't that night either. Perhaps he was thinking of the night Al did go to the "toot". On his way back, I noticed him struggling to get over the 4 ft high main spar that ran across the plane just behind my seat. When I went to help him, I discovered he'd forgotten to use his portable oxygen tank and, at 20,000 feet or more, that's not a good idea. So I gave him my tank. I was still connected to the main supply of oxygen, and, within a minute or two, was able to help him over the spar and he was all smiles again.'

After the Simpson crew's first operation, Ron kept a scrapbook of newspaper cuttings for each of the thirty operations of their first tour: as the tour progressed so the articles became more extensive and increasingly detailed. The first three were from the *Yorkshire Post*, the *Daily Mirror* and the *Daily Express* for that day. '*Another Raid on the Ruhr*', the *Post* stated: '*There was intense anti-aircraft fire over the area. Several pilots saw the glow of fires through the thick clouds which hung over the targets.*'[15] This was the second Essen raid in two nights, but the Censor's covert hand was working: 'The Ruhr' was mentioned as the target, but not 'Essen'. Laughably, German radio admitted only 'minor damage'.[16] The 'relatively small losses' were put down by the *Express* as due to (a) the bad weather and (b) the much smaller scale of the attacks compared to the previous summer. '*Many people have thought our small losses recently may be due to the transfer of enemy ground defences from Western Europe to Tunisia,*' the *Express* continued, '*where the Flak is said to be very heavy. This is not true. Bomber pilots back from northern France and western Germany report that Ack-ack fire there is as fierce as ever.*'[17]

Oxygen failure
Prolonged oxygen failure was a serious concern when flying at operational height, and the correct and continuous supply of it was vital. It was the w/op's duty to ascertain that it arrived correctly at all crew stations during his pre-flight checks. Gunners, due to their exposed positions, were particularly at risk because their breath froze in their masks and blocked the flow. Bill Carman, a wireless operator/air gunner with 49 Squadron, recalled a problem with oxygen failure on his first operation: 'On leaving the target area there was no response from the mid-upper gunner. The skipper sent the bomb-aimer and myself to check him out. We found him slumped unconscious; his oxygen mask had filled with

moisture – condensation, from his breath – which had frozen, cutting off his life-supporting oxygen supply.' The two men pulled their comrade out of the turret with difficulty then carried him to a rest bed by the main spar. They plugged him into the portable oxygen supply, but it was some time before he came round.[18]

Alan Castle remembered an experience in 1942 with a 'second dickey' pilot to Essen. The only bombs on board were 36 flares intended as rudimentary pathfinders.[19] As a nav (b), Castle found it a nuisance approaching the target to have to leave his chart table, go into the nose and aim the bombs. He decided, since flares did not require any aiming, to ask the 'second dickey' to do it. He was required only to go into the nose when Castle instructed, and press the flare release. All went as planned until the pilot informed Castle that the 'second dickey' had not returned to the cockpit.

'I went to investigate,' Castle recalled, 'and found him lying unconscious beside the bomb toggles. I established that this was because he had not plugged in his oxygen supply after moving into the nose.' It was an easy mistake for a novice to make. Battle-tried veterans sometimes made the same error. 'I plugged his oxygen in,' Castle continued, 'and had to wait a few minutes before he came round.' By the time Castle returned to his desk, a close burst of Flak had forced the pilot to veer off the nav's recommended avoiding action course: 'In effect, we were lost over an unfriendly Ruhr, but after a worrying ten minutes, we got back on track.'

In a village near their airfield, Alec March and his crew had been befriended by two maiden ladies in their sixties who kept a respectable public house:

> 'Quite early one evening, just after we arrived, our pilot got out of his chair and started to walk towards the door. Then, without warning, he collapsed onto the floor. We were all quite sober. We carted him off to see the MO, who, without a moment's hesitation, said, "Yes, this is the delayed effect of inadequate oxygen. He'll be fine." Fortunately it did not happen in the air.'[20]

The Elsan

Ronald Farren: 'The wireless operators had the task of procuring and looking after a one-gallon can; the Elsan in the Lanc was at the rear of the aircraft and for any front-end member of the crew this was a hazardous journey when at operating height (20-25,000 feet). With a full parachute harness, Mae West, parachute and portable oxygen bottle, it took 8 to 10 minutes for the total journey, and the life of the oxygen bottle was 10 minutes. Furthermore, because of the extremely low temperatures, normally -30 to -56 deg C, you were liable to suffer frost burns. The solution was keep the can by the wireless operator (who had all the heating) and pass it around when needed. W/ops weren't very pleased with this arrangement because, during a "corkscrew", the "G" forces would occasionally get the can airborne with sometimes disastrous results.'[21]

One problem with the Elsan toilet was that it had to be emptied, and a 'can' it was. It was rather like a bucket – but there was no lid to it. A 460 Squadron Lancaster had a cryptic sign supplied by the 'LNER'[22] mounted on the rear of its fuselage above it. This read: '*Do not pull the chain while the train is standing in the station.*' Below it some wag had written, '*Except over enemy territory!*'

Mary Corran, a WAAF MT driver stationed at 21 OTU Wellsbourne near Stratford-upon-Avon, once had the unenviable task of disposing of a load of Elsans. This was not strictly a WAAF job, but one day in autumn 1943 she arranged to meet her brother, a bomb-aimer on Lancasters, in Stratford-upon-Avon. To get the afternoon off she agreed with the MT sergeant to drive the station sanitary wagon. 'It was a load of Elsan buckets on a sideless low loader,' Mary recalled, 'I took a downhill corner too fast, and the buckets slid off, with results best left to the imagination.'[23]

• • •

The first operation, although a big hurdle, was not by any means a definitive test for a crew. There were many long, stressful hours in the darkness awaiting them that could be even more challenging. As the war progressed the relatively straightforward operations of 1940 became inevitably more complex with increased demands on airmen. The planning beforehand was more involved: a quartet of engines, and the systems relying upon them, required further attention and were more susceptible to attack; superior navigation systems necessitated specialist training, and German countermeasures and tactics grew more sophisticated.

Some airmen had to do their initiation with complete strangers. Others, despite not being the cause of errors themselves, had to suffer interrogation by their colleagues after these were made. The extreme heights (for those times) and unusual environmental conditions (rarefied air) at which the 'bomber boys' flew, could put unusual and unaccustomed stresses on them that would have delayed effects. Despite this they adjusted to the demands of life on operations, surviving to continue their unusual way of life, engendered by the consequences of war. Reacting to the stresses of living 'on the edge' they occasionally exhibited extremes of behaviour.

CHAPTER SEVEN

'THERE'S A BLOODY DUCK IN MY BED!'

Squadron Life

IN January 1942, 460 Squadron RAAF transferred from Molesworth in Huntingdonshire to Breighton, a few miles south-east of the cathedral city of York. Yorkshire, and its neighbouring county Lincolnshire, was fast becoming enveloped in airfields by that time in the war, and Breighton, unlike 460's later airfield at Binbrook, which was built during the pre-war expansion scheme, was one of 4,000 sites selected by the Air Ministry after hostilities began, for civilian contractors to develop into aerodromes.¹ The criteria that had been used pre-war for this became far less selective and, consequently, standards fell. By the end of the war the original 220 aerodromes in the UK had trebled in number, 360 acres of land being ploughed up, and 160 million square yards of concrete being laid by tens of thousands of men, all at a total cost of £600 million.² In 1942 a pinnacle in construction was reached with one airfield being completed every three days on average.³

Laurie Simpson's crew arrived at Breighton in September 1942. First thing every morning they would run around the perimeter track prior to getting the 'gen' on operations for the night. This 'gen', however, was not normally revealed to them until after 10.00 hrs, for it was not until that time that 'Bomber' Harris had conducted his 'Morning Prayers' conference at High Wycombe. Around that time all the Groups in Bomber Command would be told if there was to be a raid, and all the station commanders would then be informed by their respective Group HQs whether 'ops' were 'on' or not.

On each base, every snippet of information on base activity was monitored by the station's 'watchkeepers'. These were normally WAAFs who kept a 24-hour watch in three shifts from a tiny room in the station Flying Control Tower.⁴ They knew every detail of an operation even before the aerodrome's station commander. Dorothy Wallis was employed on various Halifax squadrons of 4 Group between 1943 and 1945 as a 'Clerk-Special Duties' or 'watchkeeper' and she recalled that every morning, when full details of that night's operations from Group HQ arrived, the watchkeepers would pass these orders for the day on to each section (e.g. bomb load to the armoury, the quantity of aviation fuel required to the fuel dump etc.). Thus no one section had a complete picture of what was happening. It was all a question of security: the clerks had the overall picture, but only transmitted orders that were relevant to the individual sections, the Air Ministry's intention being that no one individual would be able to conclude what the target details were.

Bill Higgs, a flight engineer on 35 Squadron at Graveley, Huntingdonshire in 1942, compiled a meticulous account of his daily routines:

> 'We rose between 0730 and 0800 hrs, washed, dressed, made our beds, tidied the room and made our way to the mess where we had breakfast. We then proceeded to the hangars where the crew room was situated; there we checked to find out what duties we were to perform. Should we find we were to carry out night-flying tests, it was fairly safe to assume that we would be flying on an operation that night.
>
> 'During the morning we would carry out a flight of about one hour, maybe flying out over the sea and testing our guns together with other equipment. In the afternoon we would attend a briefing and discover where our target was, take-off times, route and weather conditions. Certain targets could send a shiver down our spines as we knew they were well defended or were long flights across enemy territory. The Ruhr was known as "*Happy Valley*": it had towns such as Cologne, Essen, Duisburg and Dusseldorf closely bunched together, and in the "*Happy Valley*" there were 600 Flak guns from Dusseldorf to Duisburg, and searchlights were counted in hundreds. The long flights were of the order of Berlin and Nuremberg.'[5]

The Briefing

Before a raid could take place, all the crews involved in each Group in that night's operation, had to be 'briefed' or instructed on the relevant background details of the mission. This 'explanation of intent', and the procedures to convey it, were as a rule held in the station Briefing Room which, in many cases, was a Nissen hut. At one end of the room, mounted on a wall above the speaker's stage, would be a large-scale map of Europe, which included all the targets currently considered active. Before the briefing this would normally be obscured by short black curtains. Just before the Officer in Charge of Flying mounted the rostrum, the curtains would be drawn back to reveal the route for that night's raid, marked out with a red ribbon stretched across the map and pinned to its surface at the turning points. The shock of this was often registered audibly by the crews, but many would perhaps already have determined the target from the bomb and fuel load. After the Officer i/c Flying had introduced the target, the force that would take part, the take-off and bombing times, and the predicted bombing height, he would be replaced by the navigation leader. The 'nav leader' was responsible for all the squadrons on that station. He would explain the route, turning points, adjustments to height, indicated air speeds, and broadcasting of corrected wind information, collated by wind-finders.[6]

The nav leader would be replaced in turn by the bombing leader. He would outline the bomb and fuel loads, aiming points, PFF-marking, crosswinds, avoidance of 'creep back', rate of 'Window' delivery and other associated factors. Next, the Meteorological Officer, an RAF man, would describe any warm or cold front activity, high or low pressure areas, forecast cloud, precipitation, and wind speed, height and direction. Finally, the Intelligence Officer would explain the background to that night's operation plan, with reasons for any dog-legs, 'spoof' raids, accompanying operations, likely ground defences, and predicted night fighter activity. Rear Gunner Ivor Turley was present at a pre-op briefing for the crews of 218 Squadron on 12 December 1944:[7]

> 'And so to briefing: what was it really like? Suddenly it seemed I was confident as we made our way to the Briefing Room. The clump, clump of air gunners in their heavy, fur lined boots, the muffled chatter of other bods as in groups we converged on the Briefing Room door. Through the door into the locker room, past the S.P.[8] on the inner door, I saw the well-lit room full of

men in stages of aircrew dress. The long table with navigators' bags on: the navigators were briefed an hour before us. There was a flurry of activity, navigation maps everywhere: navigators' drawing lines, flight engineers working on charts, pilots gazing at maps. *God!* What confusion!

'We joined the rest of our crew at a long table and sat down. Harry was there, smiling as usual. The focus of attention was the stage at the end of a long hut: a large map of Germany was the backcloth. From a red-knobbed pin in England, which represented our airfield, ran red tape to other pins, over the top end, down the bottom end and back to base.

'The briefing began with a roll-call for skippers' aircraft. I was absorbed, excited, and unafraid, realising that this was the point of no turning back. The target was written: *Germany.* Oil and coking plants at the far end of the Happy Valley. Frankly, we'd never heard of it! The Met men gave us the weather conditions: clouds to avoid, icing up, how to get out of it, where to expect it. Temperature 35/40 below freezing: that's cold, I thought. Visibility 3 miles: cloud cover 4/5 tenths, thickening to 5/8 tenths in the south and over base at 4,000 feet.

'The bombing and intelligence office told us this was a virgin target: it produced oil and coke – reconnaissance had shown it as a very busy target, and it was time it went out of production. The aiming points were to be large coke ovens.

'The briefing was over. In the changing room sitting on low benches we put on our clothing, stuffing things in our pocket. Handkerchiefs in right-hand Sidcot flying suit pocket, escape pack in back pocket – no, that would be uncomfortable. That can go in Sidcot left pocket. Wakey-wakey pills? Yes. Put those in a twist of paper and put them in this little square pocket of my Sidcot left breast pocket: Mae West over the lot, the straps tight. I didn't want that floating off!'

Crew relationships

Although they flew together on operations, often crews did not mix with each other off ops. There were various reasons for this. Officers had separate accommodation to other ranks generally and a different mess. So in some cases this was difficult. Often there just was not time for crews to mix off operations. Ron Searle:

'We didn't socialise much as a crew; I can only think of one occasion where the seven of us went to the 'local' together. We didn't even get together after we had finished our tour and we virtually lost contact. One of the reasons we didn't fraternise was because the skipper was commissioned and the rest of the crew were either Flight Sergeants or Sergeants and consequently ate etc. in a different mess and slept in different quarters; officers led a different lifestyle. It was just how things were and we all accepted it.'

Harry Jones was a mid-upper gunner with 106 Squadron. His skipper at Syerston on his last and several earlier trips was Flight Lieutenant Les Brodrick[9], but like Searle's crew they did not get together much: 'We didn't say a lot to each other when on camp because there didn't seem to be time, apart from a bit of boozing if we had the money', he said. Alan Bryett, of 158 Squadron at Lissett, had fonder memories of relationships with his crew: 'We knew everything about each other's girlfriends, and backgrounds, and what they'd done and where they'd been on leave. We'd been out together and knew each other intimately. We knew each other's abilities; we knew each other's educational backgrounds. We knew more about each other than I've ever subsequently known about any group of people with which I've worked.'[10]

Any distinction between officers and other ranks varied according to the squadron. 12 Squadron, which was one of the RAF's oldest squadrons, had an established social hierarchy in which there was a distinct 'them and us' attitude between the officers and the other ranks. This was generally unusual for Bomber Command and especially amongst the Canadians and Australians the opposite applied.

Alan Castle, a navigator with 101 Squadron and the only commissioned man on his crew, recalled 'For the whole of my first tour, I was the only officer in my regular crew and I cannot recall any situation in which I felt that the others were deferring to me in any way, and I was always careful never to "pull rank". I never saw any evidence that other officers were different. Apart from the fact that officers and NCOs had their own separate messes, I can recall no class distinction at all.' And Eric Foinette, who served on 12 Squadron early in the war, recalled, 'As an officer, I must admit I lived separately in the officers' mess, but I am unaware of any ill feeling from the NCOs in our crew. I flew in a Wellington from Binbrook. Maybe the circumstances changed when 12 Squadron moved to Wickenby, but by that time I had been in *Stalag Luft* III for nearly a year.'[11]

But Robert Raymond, an American sergeant pilot with 44 Squadron, was shocked by the class distinction he found whilst training in July 1942:

> '*Unlike the US Army Air Corps, commissioned rank is not conferred on all. Ordinarily they're granted only to those with the Old School Tie and/or those who play rugger. Seriously, the situation is just that.*'

He noted in his diary: '*I sometimes feel that England does not deserve to win this war. Never have I seen such class distinctions drawn and maintained in the face of a desperate effort to maintain a democracy. With powers of regulation and control inevitably centred in the hands of a few, the abuse and preservation of the Old School Tie is stronger than ever on every side.*'

By 1943 the RAF was less than a quarter of a century old. It had always been more egalitarian then the Army or the Navy. Even the oldest squadrons in the command, like No. 12, had been formed at the beginning of the First World War and were relatively young units compared to those in the other services, which had hierarchies dating back centuries. Australian, Canadian and other Dominions' units were even younger, mostly being formed during the Second World War, and generally they had a more relaxed attitude towards rank.

John Nunn had a number of experiences of the 'them and us' attitude. On one occasion his crew took their ground crew out to the *Saracen's Head* pub in Lincoln, a city with a cathedral and 'half-timbered buildings along narrow, winding cobbled streets'[12] which Laurie Simpson described as a '*cramped, stuffy, old fashioned place*'. 'Unfortunately some senior officers were dining at the next table,' Nunn recalled, 'and a couple of days later it was on orders that the hotel was out of bounds for other ranks. Even after four years of war, the Colonel Blimp syndrome was still operating.' On

John Nunn and below, on the right. (Nunn)

another occasion, near the end of his first tour, he had been put forward for a commission. 'I went for an interview with the Wing Commander of 103 Squadron. I think his name was Nelson. When he learned that I had only attended a village school and that my education ended when I was fourteen, he didn't ask me any more questions.'[13] Nunn later found out that the man had served as an equerry to the Queen. It has to be said that Nunn, because of his social background, may have been more sensitive towards any hierarchy and the behaviour of others towards him.[14]

Many officers' experiences contradicted this. Robert Raymond saw operational squadron life as the reverse of that in Training Command:

> 'Having heard much about daily life on a squadron, I found the realities even more pleasant than I had anticipated. There was an air of casualness and restfulness on the station far different from that which we have been accustomed to under Training Command. I became convinced that the apparently inefficient, meddling ways of this organisation are one of the reasons why it can upon rare occasions put up a tremendous effort without strain.'[15]

Henry Coverley, in spite of being a commissioned public schoolboy, found little discrimination in his unit. Apart from himself, all his crew were NCOs:

> 'In Bomber Command there was no distinction between officers and sergeants: *none!* I called them all by their Christian names, and when I went drinking with them we sat at the table all together, drinking. We were in uniform, and the Army kicked up a colossal outburst about it! They made complaints to the RAF that they'd seen officers sitting and drinking with sergeants in the mess! *"This can't be allowed!" "Raise a couple of fingers to 'em."* Only on ops was there a difference: if anything had to be done they called you "Skipper", any other time it was "Roger", and all my crew members I only knew by their Christian names.'[16]

Robert Raymond: 'I shall risk being misunderstood and make a few objective remarks about RAF pilots, the only breed I know. They have an aesthetic appreciation of the ease and beauty of this form of travel, of doing a job all by themselves in which every moment you feel like a king... I have found no representative type, no particular kind of mental equipment, no manner of thinking, talking or reacting that is common to them all and have therefore concluded that, more than most in the armed forces, a pilot remains an individual.'

Englishman Ted Groom had a lot to say for the Australians:

> 'The chaps I flew with at Binbrook – the Australians – I knew them all. I don't know why it was but you knew all the pilots. I knew those that got shot down and those that were killed. It was altogether different [to the English units]... We had a good CO – Hughie Edwards, the brilliant VC. He didn't believe in bullshit or anything, or CO's Parade. We had a CO's Parade in the morning, "But," he said, "you come in your working clothes so there's no time lost in getting the aircraft serviced." The whole of the station, 2 or 3,000 men, went on the CO's Parade.
>
> 'I thought 460 was a very good squadron. I think it was the attitude, because it was Australian: in a nutshell there wasn't the "them and us" attitude between the officers and the men. There wasn't the "old school tie" type of attitude; you had discipline admittedly, but not like it was at Wickenby.'[17][18]

A touching story illustrates this. There was a strong affinity between the non-commissioned ground crew and the rest of 460 Squadron. Early in 1945 a very bad winter occurred and for a period Binbrook was cut off and food rationed. As milk was in short supply, a notice was displayed in the sergeants' mess announcing that it was only available for those on flying duties. But for three days not a single drop was drunk and every churn was returned unopened until the notice was removed.

Peter Gibby, an electrician on 460 Squadron, was an Englishman amongst Australians: 'I think most of us were young lads, dead keen, and thrilled to bits to be working on Lancasters. If any of us wanted a hand we only had to ask and an airman of any trade would come and help. There was no "not my job": it simply wouldn't have crossed our minds. Likewise the kites had to be bombed up and serviced regardless of how long it took, or if we decided we might go into Grimsby for the night. I had a nasty shock when the European war ended and I went to India with another squadron.

'There is no doubt that being on 460 was the greatest experience of our lives for many of us ground staff. My son once asked me, "How was it so good working every day on three Lancasters in our weather?" I replied, "Son, you will never know."'

Fred Danckwardt was another Englishman on an Australian squadron, No. 467:

'The Australians sent over a lot of pilots, bomb-aimers, but very few air gunners. I was a rear gunner at the time, and my pilot actually came over with his brother, who was a rear gunner but they decided not to fly together to increase the chances of one of them going home. So that's when I joined them. My pilot came from Oodnadata and our aeroplane was called *The Orphan from Oodnadata* because it was coded 'O-*Oboe*', and we had a nice naked lady – the orphan – painted on the side. The trouble is, after we left, the crew that took over from us did the raid on the *Tirpitz* and were shot down.

'We had quite a few German names among the Australians because a lot of them came from the area around Adelaide, where the Germans started vineyards. A lot of these were German, German families; we had Stromberg, Girsch, all sorts of German names there.'[19]

David Fellowes was a rear gunner with 460 Squadron in 1944-45. He joined an Australian squadron because his Aussie skipper, Arthur Whitmarsh, took his crew with him from OTU. On Fellowes' first trip, the base CO Hughie Edwards took the whole crew to Freiberg as 'second dickeys' and they had the misfortune to be hit by American anti-aircraft fire over France. Fellowes remembered Edwards as a 'smashing chap' who had joined the RAF as a regular before the war, and did not mess about with 'airs and graces'. Fellowes, who commenced his tour in November 1944, and had always been 'a bit of a loner', was a lanky six-footer. He preferred the rear turret to the mid-upper, which he found rather 'stuck out'. He trained at RAF Hixon OTU in Staffordshire on Wellingtons in 1944 and, whilst at the 1 Group Heavy Conversion Unit at Lindholme, he flew on a 'spoof' raid over enemy territory to distract the radar. His crew's most serious incident was a mid-air collision with another Lancaster on a raid to Munich in February 1945. The other crew was killed.[20]

The Canadians were also relaxed in their attitude, but never developed quite the same wild reputation as the Australians. Frank Dennis, an English engineer in 6 RCAF Group, formed a good opinion of them:

'The Canadians were very smart like us Brits, and fiercely loyal to their country and the Commonwealth. They were invariably well-mannered and easy to get along with. I think it remarkable that [the Commonwealth nations] all decided to come over and fight for the "mother country" in the hour of need. They were in it from the outset. Generally speaking I found Canadians very pleasant and easy going on the ground, but in the air most professional.'

Dennis found no differences between NCOs and commissioned officers amongst RCAF aircrew: 'As far as we were concerned once you were "crewed up" rank didn't come into it. You were known by your aircrew trade and it was assumed that you knew your job because the lives of six other crew members depended upon that.'[21]

The desire to fight for the 'mother country' by men from the Commonwealth was explained by Australian Cal Younger.[22] He was three months short of his eighteenth birthday and in bed with measles when the Australian Prime Minister announced on the radio that as Britain had declared war on Germany, Australia also was at war:

> 'I am often asked why I volunteered to come and fight for Britain. The answer is that in those days we were British first and Australian second. As soon as I heard the announcement I wrote offering my services to the Navy. They were a bit slow, so… I applied to the RAAF.'[23]

Unlike Breighton, all the rooms at 460 Squadron's pre-war base at Binbrook were centrally heated, as they were at Lindholme. Dave Fellowes confessed that he preferred the Australian units because their government determined that they be stationed at these better quality pre-war purpose-built bases. Jim Mitchell, a nav (b) with 51 Squadron, commented: 'RAF camps were mainly Nissen huts around an airfield. Bill [Mitchell's skipper] got us to RAAF Driffield [home of 466 Sqn RAAF]; Australian and Canadian crews were usually on pre-war brick camps.'[24]

Binbrook was a base station with satellite stations attached to it, drawing personnel from all of them if necessary. Crews lived together, both officers and NCOs, in the married quarters, one crew to each quarters, which were two-storey houses. John Nunn's first glimpse of a peacetime station was when his crew made a courtesy call to Binbrook to pick up an aircraft on loan.[25]

Alan Castle joined 101 Squadron on 31 December 1942, the day that his wartime base RAF Bourn was completed. Bourn was a satellite aerodrome of RAF Oakington and the accommodation was in Nissen huts, but unlike conditions at Elsham Wolds, Castle felt things were 'quite comfortable'. At Ludford Magna, also a wartime base, the flood table was close to the surface and conditions on the airfield were almost frequently muddy. When 101 moved to 'Mudford', the officers had batmen.

Fred Danckwardt's 467 Squadron base at Waddington was pre-war. He recalled:

> 'We were fortunate in that it was a permanent base. I was a sergeant then, so I didn't have batmen. It was rather odd because we had a Station Commander, and then there was a Base Commander, who had several stations. He was called Air Commodore Hesketh and the Station Commander was called Bonham-Carter. You often hear the name. I think one of his great, great granddaughters is always in the news.[26] This Base Commander used to come round to all the aircraft before we took off. Of course, by that time we were the senior crew on the station by far. He approached me the trip before the end trip and virtually said that as an Australian squadron the gongs would be going to the Australians, but "…could you put your commissioning papers in tomorrow?" So I did, and then Forbes, the Wing Commander who was with us for two days, signed them.
>
> 'The day after that, I went to see Bonham-Carter. He had a deaf aid, and in those days deaf aids were not very good – they had a huge battery and didn't last very long. He was not supposed to fly on ops but when the Base Commander was away he used to gather a crew together and fly. Every now and again he had to turn the battery off to save power, and then the engineer would dig him and tell him to switch it on again. So I went in for the

commissioning interview and he had all his logbooks and said, "Would you care to volunteer to fly with me if we have a spare night?" I wasn't very keen, but I couldn't really say no. Fortunately, though, I was soon posted, so it never happened. But he survived the war OK.'

Group Captain David Bonham-Carter was the station CO of 467/463 Squadron at Waddington from the end of March 1943 until 14 April 1945.[27] As Fred Danckwardt recalled, although he was deaf and had to wear a hearing aid, he often joined crews on operations, when the ground staff would assume that he was 'elsewhere' or off station. His favourite Lancaster was R5868 PO-S 'Sugar' which originally had been with 83 (Pathfinder) Squadron, with whom she completed 68 ops. 'Sugar' flew 70 operations with 467, making her a 'ton-up' Lancaster having 138 ops to her credit.[28]

Bomber Command Watering Holes
One of the most celebrated hostelries in Yorkshire in 1943/1944, which became a focus for the post-operational gatherings of 4 and 6 Groups, was the famous *Betty's Bar*. Henry Coverley: 'We used to meet at *Betty's Bar* after we got back [from an op]. You used to go down there and drink yourself silly on "near beer", it was practically water coloured.'[29] Alan Bryett also had fond memories: 'It was really quite wonderful because it was an "intelligence room" and when you got there you met your friends from other stations. And if you went and drank in *Betty's Bar* (and it was quite heavy drinking there) you would pick up all the "gen" that was going on: you'd know what the losses were; you'd actually get buzzes on what the future ops were going to be.'[30]

Betty's became a focus for many air force men. F.J. McGovern recalled: 'York seemed to be the hub of activity for the whole of the RAF, because of course there were numerous squadrons around Yorkshire, and most of them within about 30 miles seemed to find themselves drawn in to the centre of York, and in particular to *Betty's Bar*.'[31] Ron Searle never had the opportunity to go to *Betty's* – it was too far away.

> 'There was the *Mucky Duck* pub in Breighton but we used to prefer the other one; it was run by three ladies and known as the *Six Tits*.[32] We didn't just used to fly and drink ourselves silly. Usually we'd only have two or three ales. We mainly went to the pubs for companionship and to relax. Wally [the mid-upper gunner] and Freddy [the flight engineer] used to socialise together; they appeared to prefer the company of the opposite sex, probably with future marriage in mind.'

Whilst riding back from the nearby village of Holme-on-Spalding-Moor one night, a group of 460 Squadron aircrew decided to cycle in formation with one of them acting as an attacking German fighter. Without warning a local 'bobby' suddenly appeared in the road and commanded them to halt. His orders were that they be clear of the area in half-an-hour. The Aussies pulled on their outback charm and persuaded him to partake of a drink. They then borrowed his helmet, replaced it with a party hat and, as the bewildered 'bobby' swayed drunkenly in the centre of the road, made cycling attacks on him, dividing formation at the last second as they passed each side.

Shortly after 'Chad' Martin took over as Breighton CO, two local policemen arrived to ask if he could devise a way to prevent the unwarranted requisitioning of bicycles from outside the *Black Swan* and *Seven Sisters*. They would disappear at closing time only to be retrieved by their correct owners from near the camp gates the next morning. This 'wanton pilfering' was generally abhorred by the Breighton personnel and, after much discussion, it was agreed that the air force bicycles would be painted white all over. The two constables were shown the door, only to discover that their bicycles *too* had disappeared.[33]

Ron Searle: 'Whilst we didn't socialise much, when it came to operations it was a different matter. We worked together, each one respecting the other's capabilities and were confident about them carrying out their duties. We had plenty of luck and, when it all boils down, luck has got to be on your side at all times to survive.' Peter Banyard, a bomb-aimer with 514 Squadron, corroborated Searle's view that mutual respect and dependency were essential features of crew relationships. 'When you were flying on operations,' he added, 'you quickly learned to live for today and to hell with tomorrow, so you worked hard and played hard!'[34]

Because the four-engined bombers required more complex fuel handling and had a mid-upper turret, the flight engineer and mid-upper gunner normally joined the original five-man crew at a Heavy Conversion Unit. This probably accounts for the friendship between Wally Maltby and Freddy King. They joined Laurie Simpson's crew at the beginning of October 1942. Simpson described them at the time as '*nice lads*', but they had divergent personalities. Short, tubby, home-loving Maltby, the mid-upper gunner, was aged 21 and quiet and reserved. Despite having a secure job before the war as a Boots employee at Beeston, Nottinghamshire, he had felt it was his duty to volunteer for aircrew. He also regarded the cause as important enough to return voluntarily for a second tour. King, the engineer, was an Australian from Oatley, a suburb of Sydney, was more flamboyant and sported a moustache like Clark Gable's. Both got married in September 1943 – Maltby to a girl from his home town, King to a Yorkshire girl. Laurie noted the occasions in his diary, an indication of the closeness of a crew: '*Sept 11th-26th. Wally was married in Nottingham and I went up to Freddy's marriage at Goole.*'

Mess Antics

At Elsham Wolds there were often ribald antics in the mess: 'What we had expected of the mess on an operational station I don't quite know,' Don Charlwood wrote, 'perhaps a gathering of aloof, highly-decorated men in a chilly atmosphere. We found the opposite. Bike races occurred; men left footprints on the ceiling; the pianist was plied with beer by grateful singers; the furniture was turned upside down so that aircrewmen could fling themselves over it.' In June 1942 'a rip-snorting party' had been in progress at Leconfield when Laurie Simpson returned to 15 Advanced Flying Unit after leave in Bournemouth. The chief perpetrators were a Squadron Leader Powell and a Major Meakin: '*Chairs, waste paper baskets and cushions were being tossed around; soda siphons used as Tommy guns; glasses as skittles and lighted newspapers as flares.*' It was a '*good show*' but there was, he said, '*a stink in the morning*' when the Group Captain stuck his head in the ante-room and '*didn't like it at all*'. Christmas was an excuse for even greater excesses:

> '*Our Xmas eve was the wildest I've yet been to. Motor bikes in the ante-room. Foot holes in the ceiling. Our coats off, shirts hanging out, ties around our waists and initiations with glasses of beer thrown over head and shoulders. Wound up about 3.30 a.m. but carried on next day. The party spirit still prevails and will do so until 460 operates again.*'

Former barrister Cliff O'Riordan mentioned a '460 special' in his diary entry for Saturday, 15 May 1943, which was drunk by all those present under the threat of being shot with a Verey pistol. O'Riordan subsequently tried to ride a horse in a field and fell off. He was then given a lift back to base in an airman's car, but found there were neither clutch nor brakes. He bought another officer's car on the spot and drove himself back to Binbrook. The upshot of this was that his arm remained sore the following day and the station MO put it in a splint. An X-ray in Grimsby on the 17th proved that there was a fracture of the lower radius. On his return by bus from the hospital 'an old dear', seeing him bound up 'like a Red Cross parcel', offered him a seat and he 'felt a fraud'. But worse was yet to come.

The following week there were no ops until Sunday 23rd, which was the biggest effort yet by Bomber Command. The following day Flight Lieutenant Burnham's 'kite' UV-B 'Beer' was what O'Riordan described as 'an awful mess' with '150 holes by fighters', but no one was hurt.[35] The same day, Monday 24th, 'gongs' were given to Ted McKinnon, Geoff Heath and two others.[36]

On Thursday 27th O'Riordan had his moment. Five aircrew were told to parade outside the officers' mess at 10.00 hrs. They had no idea why they had been chosen until His Majesty King George VI and the Queen arrived an hour later. 'I tried to hide behind Lamb,' O'Riordan commented, 'but the King asked me what had happened to my arm. The AOC was there and I told the truth. He [the King] laughed like hell and said "Did you borrow the horse or scrounge it?" I told him I had scrounged it.'[37]

Squadron Leader 'Bill' Brill and his friend, Arthur Doubleday, like Laurie Simpson, had been brought up in the Riverina, New South Wales. Brill and Doubleday were pilot officers in 460 Squadron at Molesworth in the early days in 1941. According to Hank Nelson, who interviewed Doubleday and was allowed access to Brill's papers by his wife, Brill practised one particular party trick of 460: a cry of '*Clear the runway, Bill Brill will do the impossible!*' went up in the squadron mess, whereupon Brill would sprint shoeless across the mess floor along a route cleared of furniture, to where a settee had been set up across his path, an upturned armchair behind it. He grabbed the back of the settee, somersaulted, and landed on the chair, his momentum turning it upright! Others, encouraged by drink, tried to repeat his performance but 'pranged' hopelessly, ending up against the wall or surrounding objects.[38]

The Strand Palace Hotel
The Australians were well known for their wild behaviour on operational squadrons. When in London they would often meet at their favourite venues, of which the Strand Palace Hotel was one. During the war the Australians made the Strand their own; it was at the centre of an area bounded by Charing Cross, Trafalgar Square, Fleet Street, St. Paul's Cathedral, Waterloo Bridge, the Thames Embankment and Covent Garden. At 372 the Strand, the Hotel was 'an art deco showpiece'[39] and considerably more sophisticated than many of the pubs and guest houses in the area. My father spent two days in London at the end of July 1943 with his new wife:

> '*On leave for seven days. Met Dorothy at Waterloo. Stayed at Wellbeck Hotel near Lavender Square. Saw play "Heartbreak House" by G.B. Shaw – Robert Donat was grand. Visited Madame Tussaud's and Strand Palace Hotel. Had supper at Argentine café near Piccadilly [and] next day visited Dorothy's relations at Ealing.*'

Another popular calling place was the Boomerang Club in Australia House just north of the Strand. Australia House opened in early 1942 as a venue for men wanting to find accommodation, write letters and generally relax. The Boomerang Club occupied two floors of the building, and there was a reception area off Melbourne Place where aircrew could find news of old comrades. This could sometimes have unsettling consequences. Whilst at Leconfield on 12 May 1942 my father '...*caught the 10.20 train for London. Had three hours in London and spent it at Australia House and lunched at our own Boomerang Hotel.*' Here he met 'another old friend' from training days, Bob Burns: '...*he told me that Dick Horne had been scrubbed and returned to Australia.*' On 15 June Laurie '*caught the train from B'mouth West to Waterloo*', had '*ale at the Club in Australia House and then boarded another train at Kings Cross for Manchester, changed there for Hull, and then for Beverley.*' Here he '*fluked a taxi ride back to camp*'. After proposing to Dorothy in January 1942 he called into Australia House and as it was Australia Day (the 26th) he found it very crowded: '*I met Doc* [from 460], *George Burniston, Bruce Andrew, Bruce Gaston and others, all from the old "Themistocles". Also met my W/Op Ron and Denham Hardy.*' Hardy had been in the Deniliquin Militia with him.

The bomber war was fought on a peculiarly half-English, half-German battlefield. Geoff Willatt: 'Unlike life in the army in the front line, with constant danger to everyone, existence on a bomber station was unsettling – safe in England or even at home for a few hours, and then over Germany in extreme danger the next night or nights. This life, or half-life, had a severe effect on some people.' Ron Coulson was a sergeant observer with 38 and 218 Squadrons: 'The war was unusual for me as I lived out with my wife in a small village seven miles from our base at Marham, Norfolk. My pilot lived in the same farmhouse. It was strange to leave home to participate in a bombing raid over Germany and then to return, hopefully, each morning: it was just like going to the office! Occasionally, if we had been diverted to an alternative airfield because of bad weather, we didn't get back punctually.'

On 26 November 1943, bombardier Sergeant Alan C. Fuller was with 76 Squadron at Holme-on-Spalding-Moor. Take-off in their Halifax V LK946 was at 16.51 hrs just as dusk fell. Less than three hours later, when the winter night was pitch black, and while approaching the target of Stuttgart, they encountered quite heavy Flak which hit them and started a fire in one of the port engines. They found that it proved difficult flying asymmetrically with a full bomb load and became easily visible to 24-victory night fighter ace *Oberleutnant* Eckart-Wilhelm von Bonin, the *Kommandeur* of II./*Nachtjagdgeschwader* 1, who was on patrol flying a Messerschmitt Bf 110 night fighter. Bonin shot them down at 19.30 hrs. Heavy cannon fire hit the fuselage, starting fires, and they all baled out except the 18 year-old Canadian rear gunner, E.J. Berndt, who was killed by the Flak. He was one of the youngest Canadians to die in Bomber Command in 1943.[40] Fuller dived out and ended up suspended in a tree. He extricated himself, then hit the ground with a bump, leaving behind his parachute and a pistol he carried with him on operations, to avoid being shot if he was caught.[41] The sudden contrast between the cosy surroundings of Yorkshire and the uncertain environment of hostile territory was pronounced. His son recalled: 'He used to make mention of the fact that one moment he was sitting down for tea at home, then just a few hours later he was wandering through the Black Forest having just jumped out of a burning aircraft.'[42]

Inevitably, humorous situations arose on squadrons. Ronald Wakeman, a pilot, recalled his life during the first days on squadron in Yorkshire:

> 'I thought "We'll go and have a look at the local hostelries; we'll do some cross-countries before we get onto ops, we should be alright – we'll go and have a few jugs at the local tavern."

So we got the "liberty truck" down to Beverley, where we found *The Valiant Soldier*. We went in for a game of darts, had a few beers, [and] came back at about midnight.'

He confessed he didn't have a clue about the aerodrome: he had no knowledge of where the aircraft were, and knew little else about the base. But at 03.00 hours a tannoy speaker blared right outside his room that his crew were at the top of roll call for a briefing at 04.00 hrs. His w/op banged on the door and announced they were on ops that night! "It can't be tonight," Wakeman replied, "it's tomorrow morning! Get the crew out... get down to briefing." I hadn't got a clue.'

They went to the Briefing Room and a Flight Commander with a 'very English' accent accosted them: 'Hello, old boy,' he said, 'Sorry about this but the operation is to attack some gun positions over in France.' Wakeman thought: 'No problem, we don't have to do a cross-country for that.' But then he realised he had no idea where his aircraft was: 'Yes, well, where are the aeroplanes?' he asked. The man replied, 'Oh don't worry about that, old boy, the WAAF drivers know them all!'[43]

Bert Wolstenholme's skipper suffered from that 'old demon alcohol' when he was on aircrew in 1943. They were about to go on an op, but it was repeatedly cancelled. Wolstenholme recalled:

'At 2 o'clock it was scrubbed. They said: "Come back at 4." So I came back at 4 and the weatherman said, "Scrubbed again." So, off we go down to town as usual: we used to "pub crawl". Then at 6 o'clock they put the trip back on again! The skipper's still up there [at the airfield] – he didn't come with us. We were down in town, so he had to get a taxi – and he had half a pint in each pub until he found us! By the time we got back to camp, he'd had half a pint in each one – and we had to fly out at 7 o'clock!

'I don't remember a lot until I heard the navigator, Johnny. We heard him say we were crossing the coast of France: and it was then that I started to realise exactly where I was! But up to that point I didn't know; and I don't know how the skipper ever got the aircraft off the floor, the state he was in!

'The funny thing was that after the war, I went to a reunion and one of the chaps, my old Flight Commander, told me that he was in the aircraft behind us and watched us taking off. He said the take-off was just like an elephant taking off!'[44]

While at Woolfox Lodge in Norfolk with 218 Squadron, Len Gillies, an Australian, found a nice pub in the village of Essendine, a few miles north-east of Stamford. The landlord, Reg Straker, and he became good friends, having common interests in cars, shooting and fishing. One evening Len was out wandering quietly along the edge of a lake with his 12-bore shotgun in hand when, with a loud '*honk honk*', a large, grey goose flew past. There were 4 or 5 'erks' nearby and they leapt up and shouted excitedly, '*Shoot it, sir!*' Encouraged by this, Len raised his gun and opened fire. Being a first-class wildfowler he could hardly miss and the bird fell in a heap in a marsh.

After a while he took the goose back to his hut where a few aircrew were billeted. They had a chat and put the goose in Airman Gregory's bed, who was up at the bar. The goose, tucked up with its head on the pillow, awaited his return. In due course Gregory arrived quite well 'oiled'. All was quiet for a few seconds, and then he cried, '*There's a bloody duck in my bed!*' Soon the whole hut was roaring with laughter.

The next question was what to do with it. It was decided to hang it up by the neck in the hallway, at face height beside the door. At that time the RAF employed WAAFs as batwomen whose duties included making early morning tea at the officers' mess between 06.00 and 07.00 hrs and delivering it, then making beds, cleaning rooms, pressing uniforms, and taking laundry. At about 06.00 hrs a WAAF batwoman named Helen entered the airmen's quarters and ran straight into the bird. Her horror-stricken shriek was the best reveille the squadron ever had.[45] Arthur Cole:

'The thing is you're lumped together. When you're not flying you get drunk together. Occasionally the pilot got hold of a small Morris 8 and sometimes we'd all pile into that and go to a pub where we were served black market food: the civilian world had a lot of time for us *in those days*. It was only after [the war] that they came to regard us as war criminals – but we were all heroes then and they put up with some awful behaviour; we used to sing vulgar songs in pubs and make a lot of noise, and get drunk and so on… You had to get on with your crew because you relied upon each other, and to a certain extent you became friends. But friendship didn't last after the war, to tell the truth. We were all too different for that. We were all different types: I was a grammar school boy; the pilot went to a very superior public school – I believe his father was a senior army officer – there was a lot of difference in those days. I was the youngest in the crew. The rear gunner was only about a month older than I was. He was probably the most popular member. He was an East Ender.'[46]

Steve Jackson, a wireless operator with 35 Squadron, had fonder memories:

'My rear gunner, "Punch" Weatherill, was the son of Weatherills the tailors, an exclusive West End establishment. His uncle later became Speaker of the House of Commons and he was never broke. He owned an Austin 7 car and would quite often go out drinking on his own, and would come down to Flights next morning having no idea where he had left it. I would have to pretend that something was wrong with my radio so that we could get airborne and look for it. So imagine a huge Lancaster bomber with a crew of seven scanning the countryside looking for a small Austin 7. It was usually left on the roadside, but on one occasion it was in the middle of a field and the pilot decided we ought to have a practice bomb on it. We went through the procedure with bomb doors open and "Punch" begging the bomb-aimer not to release. We never bombed, but at the time it was quite funny.'[47]

In 1943 four young airmen from 460 Squadron went one up on 'Punch' Weatherill. Ron Whitney, Bob Appleton, 'Digger' Hammett and 'Mick' McGrory were returning by bicycle from a night on the tiles at nearby Goole, when they came across a steamroller parked on the roadside. Abandoning their bicycles, and observed by a small crowd, the semi-inebriated men drove the beast back to within a mile of Breighton camp when, after careering over a ditch and through a hedge, it came to an abrupt and final halt. The young airmen dismounted and completed their journey by foot. According to McGrory the crew took off on exercise the following morning and, uncertain where it was, '…flew around for a bit to see if we could spot it.' But the steamroller had disappeared.

Nothing more was heard of the incident for five days until Wing Commander Kaufmann, the station CO, ordered all aircrew to the briefing room and asked if anyone had 'thieved, borrowed or left a steamroller somewhere between Goole and Breighton.' No one was willing to own up, but then one of the culprits volunteered that there was one parked in a hedge about a mile from the camp. After the local Council had retrieved it, the vehicle was returned to its home, but when not in use 'the controls were always carefully padlocked!'[48]

Leonard Cheshire

Bill Higgs recalled an incident with Leonard Cheshire while they were on 35 Squadron in June 1941:

> 'I was flying on "Chesh" Cheshire's crew, only locally – I never went on ops with him – but I flew locally with him. He was mad as a hatter! We picked up a new Halifax – we used to go and pick them up ourselves then – and we were coming back and he did some hedge-hopping. He saw some horses in a field; there was a big pond there, and he said, "*I bet I could make those horses jump in that pond!*" And everybody was laughing over the intercom. So, next thing we know we're chasing horses round the field: and he got one to go into the pond! As we were flying along we came to a road, higher virtually than we were flying, and a car approached. Old Cheshire said: "*We'll frighten the life out of this chap!*" And, as the car got nearer we began to close in on it and I got panicky. There were trees on the bank the car was on. I looked out and thought "*Trees... oh Christ!*"'[49]

Cheshire saw them and pulled the Halifax up, and as it was climbing it hit one of the trees and lost a wing tip! Later this was replaced. 'Chan' Chandler,[50] a tail gunner on 617 Squadron, recorded his first encounter with Cheshire:

> 'My first meeting with Cheshire was at Petwood. I shared a room and was just unpacking when there was a shot outside the window. I looked out and saw this chap with a revolver in his hand; I called him a bloody lunatic and asked him what the hell he thought he was doing. He replied that he thought the place needed waking up! It turned out to be our new CO, and my first words to him were to call him a "bloody lunatic!"'[51]

Cheshire was Henry Coverley's CO in 76 Squadron in 1942:[52]

> 'Cheshire got to know everybody's Christian name in the mess. How he did it I don't know. I was a very junior officer then and he was a Squadron Commander. But on one occasion after the war, I was flying a Handley Page HP 81 Hermes in September 1963 from Gatwick to the Middle East, taking a load of Catholic pilgrims. Leonard Cheshire turned to Catholicism after the awful business in the Far East,[53] and the hostess said: "Do you know who we've got on board?" And I said, "Who?" She replied: "Group Captain Cheshire". I just said, "Oh". Well, always on these trips – about halfway through, you'd invite somebody up to the front, and I said to the hostess, "When we get into cruising, I'll signal and ask him to come up". And he came up front. Of course we didn't have helmets on or anything, just headgear. And between the two of us there, he looked at me and he said, "Ah! Roger!" Now how did he remember that? But he did. But, in the mess he'd remember everybody by their Christian names, as well as the new ones. I found that extraordinary.'[54]

Jimmy Marks

Another inspirational leader, but one less well known to the public, was James Hardy Marks. He became, at 23, the youngest wing commander in the RAF, being appointed the leader of 35 Squadron, Pathfinder Force, after Donald Bennett specifically asked for him. Marks hugely impressed Cheshire when he first met him at RAF Topcliffe in May 1942. Cheshire described him as 'the greatest pilot in the room, if not in the whole of Bomber Command', adding 'his greatness lay in the phenomenal strength of his willpower and in his complete calm.'

Bill Higgs was Jimmy Marks's flight engineer four times:

'Hamish Mahaddie wrote: "...if ever there was anyone who was going to become 'Air' rank it was Jimmy Marks." He was the youngest Wing Commander in the RAF; he was involved a lot with Bennett and the other staff and Squadron Commanders; he would have been the youngest Group Captain, and would obviously have gone on. He was tall, good-looking, with these huge hands and wide shoulders and he had a brain...

'I was sitting in the crew room one day and I thought I was in trouble, and I was sitting up on this tabletop with a cigarette in my mouth, and my field service cap stuck on the back of my head, swinging my legs. At that time I was flying with my Flight Commander, and the door opened and in walked Jimmy Marks. I jumped up off the table and stood to attention, and he said, "How'd you like to be my Flight Engineer?" I said, "Well, I can't because I'm already on Squadron Leader Peveler's crew". He brushed this aside: "Don't worry about that; would you like to be my Flighty now?" I simply said, "Yes please!" So that's when I joined him...'

Higgs was 'Flighty' on his final op. Marks was killed during an attack on Saarbrücken on 19 September 1942.[55] He had to put in one more operational flight to complete his tour:

'I was on his last mission when he died... If Jimmy Marks hadn't decided to try and push in one final operation he would have still been alive today. He would have gone on. Instead of that he pushed this other trip in, and got killed.'[56]

James Hardy Marks was born in 1918 and educated at Newport Free Grammar School from 1931-36. He excelled at sports and was known to have a 'quietly authoritative presence'. Commissioned in the RAF in May 1937, he was Mentioned in Despatches in May 1940 and awarded the DFC for attacking a bridge during the Battle of France. Flying through heavy Flak he made three passes over the target before bombing. On another occasion, during a raid on Emden in a Whitley, he was attacked twice on the bomb run by a night fighter, losing the starboard engine and the rear turret hydraulics. On the fighter's third pass, it clipped one of the Whitley's rudders with a wing and dived away steeply. Flying flaccidly over hostile France, Marks released all the bombs from the Whitley, now at 700 feet, but one, a 500-pounder, became hung up. The observer eventually jettisoned this, and Marks landed at Bircham Newton.

In 1942 Marks led his squadron against the German battleship, *Tirpitz*, twice. Despite extremely heavy defences he dropped down to 200 feet to press home his attack, releasing the bombs on – or almost on – the enemy vessel. In April 1941, Marks was promoted to squadron leader, and in July of that year he was awarded the Distinguished Service Order (DSO). Marks's DFC recommendation stated:

'In addition to his own magnificent example of courage, his superb leadership, sense of duty, enthusiasm, cheerfulness and determination which he exhibited at all times were responsible for the gallant way in which the other crews of his squadron went into the attack.'

L'amour and the 'Special Clinic'

In terms of relationships between the sexes in Bomber Command, different sources have conflicting reports. For security purposes, the three watchkeepers on Dorothy Wallis's Halifax squadron in 4 Group were instructed to say that they worked in the Cookhouse, and had separate sleeping quarters to the rest of the station in a small building out in the woods. Otherwise they lived in the aircrew mess. 'We knew most of the men, of course,' Dorothy recalled, 'but there was surprisingly little promiscuity – sex was not mandatory as it is today, and we all had other loyalties. We acquired a kind of screen though – we were able to accustom ourselves to empty places on the dining tables and losing familiar faces almost every night.'

Occasionally on a base, aircrew would break the rules and agree to take WAAFs or girlfriends up for a joyride. Les Hill was a flight engineer at Wickenby with 626 Squadron.[57] He recalled one occasion, during operations, when his crew were the 'Duty Crew'. The job they had that day was to air-test a new engine: ground-testing was not sufficiently rigorous for a new engine about to go on operations. The bomb-aimer, Benny, had a girlfriend, Molly, and the pilot was a Canadian called Scotty.[58] Molly was anxious to experience a flight and was soon fitted with a parachute and flying helmet. The crew bribed a transport driver with cigarettes to pick her up from the NAAFI. It was a beautiful sunny day with a few small clouds and the remaining Lancasters on squadron were being tanked up and armed for the night's operation:

> 'Everything went smoothly. No one was looking as Benny bunked Molly through the rear door and deposited her on the rest bed and fitted her helmet. We all made our pre-flight checks and got into our positions to set off. We went round the perimeter track as we had done many times before to the take-off runway.'

As there were no bombs, incendiaries and little fuel on board, Les knew there was nothing to worry about.

> 'As usual I assisted the captain on take-off, pushing the throttle levers up to full power, the aircraft increasing speed down the runway. We were halfway along, going quite fast, when the recently fitted engine gave a loud cough and burst into flames. The mood swiftly changed to that of panic.'

It was the worst thing that could have happened. They could either continue the taxi run ending with a sudden pull-up (a hedge at the end of the runway presented a good reason for not doing this), or continue to get airborne. Campbell had to make a quick decision. He plumped for a take-off, which had its own hazards. The burning engine would have to continue turning: losing power on one side could be dangerous. Les Hill recalled: 'I shouted, "*What do we do?*" "*Take off!*" yelled Scotty. So I pushed the throttles to full power and waited for what seemed like a long time for us to rise to a safe altitude.'

They then feathered the propeller blades and shut the engine down.[59] After leaving a trail of white smoke, the fire went out. Les Hill: 'We circled round to land, the engine to be tested having failed on the first hurdle. Unfortunately for us the whole incident had been witnessed by the Station Commander, going round checking preparations for the night. Scotty made a wonderfully smooth landing on three engines.' The Lancaster taxied to a dispersal point. As they were shutting off, the Station Commander arrived in his chauffeur-driven car. It was a court martial offence to carry civilians in operational aircraft and Benny's girlfriend was still on board. Hill: 'Benny put her under the navigator's table and told her to stay put until the all clear.'

The CO watched them get out and line up by the rear door: 'I say, you had a bit of a flamer there', he said in typical RAF fashion. 'Still you followed the drill alright. Good show.' The man, ignorant of the girl's presence on the aeroplane, continued chatting to the deaf ears of the crew, who watched helplessly as a tractor drew up and towed the aircraft away. 'Follow that plane, we have left something inside it', the crew told a transport driver who had just arrived. Before the tractor reached the hangar the crew headed him off and 'brought out a bewildered Molly' to the amazement of the drivers. They then dropped her off at the NAAFI and returned to camp.[60]

Roy Finch, a pilot with 101 Squadron, had the promise of an amorous experience cut short by war:

'Late in the afternoon of 30 November 1941 I was sitting in the sergeants' mess feeling bored out of my mind. I had checked the Battle Order and yet once again my name was not on it. To date, I had only done two operational trips as second pilot and was desperately anxious to complete the five or six required to be given my own crew. On two previous occasions my name had been withdrawn at the last minute. Neither of the two Wellingtons returned to base. Suddenly the telephone rang and, on answering it, I found myself talking to a young lady who wanted to speak to a chap who I recognised as being listed to fly that night. Having informed her that he was not available, I started up a conversation and quickly realised that I was talking to a very attractive barmaid who worked in one of the Cambridge pubs and whom I had had my eye on for some time. Much to my great astonishment and delight she agreed to let me act as a substitute for the other fellow. A few minutes later, just as I was thinking I had better get myself smartened up ready for the date, I was informed that my name *was* on the Battle Order. Thinking that I was being teased, but being somewhat curious, I decided to have another look. Sure enough there was my name replacing somebody else's. I looked at my watch and realised I had only a few minutes to get ready to board one of the trucks used to transport crews from Oakington to Bourn. There was no time to get a message to the young lady.'[61]

Finch was shot down in Wellington R1778 that night on a raid to Hamburg and later taken prisoner. He still wonders what sort of evening he would have had.

One lived for the moment in wartime and a girl, unlike in normal circumstances, may have been willing to go 'a bit further' than she would ordinarily.[62] For the first time many English girls, who in peacetime may have led a relatively sheltered existence, had the opportunity to meet a profusion of young men who appreciated their company more than normally. A conversation radio telephony operator Pip Beck had with a parachute packer in her billet, upon first arriving in Bomber Command, was: 'Ops tonight', the girl nonchalantly said. 'This is a bomber station, you know. You'll have a good time here. You can have a different boyfriend every night if you want to. Its wizzo!'[63]

Alec March: 'On our first morning after leave I overheard the w/op of another crew relating to his Canadian bomb-aimer the wonderful time he had been given by a "young lady" he had met in a local public house. The Canadian, in beautifully descriptive language, which would not have been employed in the drawing rooms of 1942, said he would surely find himself in the "special clinic" (the usual place to go in such circumstances).' March continued:

'Postings to squadrons were slow to come through and for several weeks, crews were kicking their heels; meanwhile we were still "headless"[64] and also waiting aimlessly. At breakfast one morning we noticed the w/op who had an amorous leave was missing. It seemed that his Canadian friend had quite correctly forecast the biological result from his enjoyment on leave. This crew was also without a mid-upper gunner due to an eyesight problem. The CO did not have to look far to find replacements for both men and my Canadian mid-upper gunner and I were moved across to fill the gaps.'[65]

For some time trainee aircrew had been undergoing regular Freedom from Infection (FFI) parades. John Nunn recalled his experience of this during his initial training at No. 9 Aircrew Reception Centre in Blackpool, the town that was a night life centre for the north-west. 'Every so often we had to go for an FFI parade. A medical officer checked us for VD and also to see whether we had developed a hernia.' Dick Raymond, when a naïve young trainee engineer at St. Athans, recalled seeing on the toilet wall a notice warning '*Beware of Crabs*', and wondered what 'crabs' were doing in the airmen's toilets. John Nunn lost his virginity to an ATS girl at Elsham Wolds in a haystack in September 1942: he recalled that, as the result of a second liaison, 'I returned to camp covered in nettle stings and itched for a couple of days having discovered that a ground sheet was not much help in a bed of nettles.'

> 'If we had seen ATS girls back to their camp it meant missing the last train back to base. The first time this happened we asked a policeman where we could get a cheap night's lodging. This would have been about eleven thirty and he directed us to a place that we had already heard of called "*Irish Maggie's*". We had assumed that this was a "house of ill-repute" but it was just a boarding house of sorts. Maggie was a kind lady who, with her husband, put up stranded servicemen for five shillings a night.'

Alec March: 'I think it was early in 1944 when venereal disease became a real problem for the Command. So much so that it was having an effect on crew availability. This resulted in an order which stated that any aircrew member found to have this disease would return to duties when cured, but all previous trips would be written off. This, no matter if one or twenty-one trips had been carried out.'[66]

In 1944 Muriel Mould was an airwoman in the WAAF, stationed at RAF Newton, near Nottingham. One of her recollections illustrates the extent of the spread of the disease. Along with two other airwomen she volunteered to donate her blood for transfusion. For some reason this could only be done at RAF Cosford which, for them, was a long and tedious journey:

> 'On arrival we were told to wait in a huge hut until receiving further instruction. The hut was bursting at the seams with dozens of airmen who greeted us with wolf whistles and much laughter. Eventually the men were called outside by a time-expired Sergeant using very fruity language, until he spotted us ladies cowering in a corner, when he went bright red and almost swallowed his tonsils! The upshot was that the airmen were receiving treatment for VD! Three very bewildered airwomen finally got to the right hut, gave a lot of blood, and returned to Newton about 11 p.m.'[67]

The Germans too, had problems with the consequences of sexual promiscuity. Derek Hodgkinson was shot down during the third Thousand-Bomber raid of 1942, and afterwards was transported with a *Luftwaffe* captain to Leeuwarden, a night fighter airfield in northern Holland:[68]

> 'I was taken in and told to sit on a bench in a very draughty corridor outside what appeared to be the Station Commander's office. The *Hauptmann* knocked and went in. Opposite me was

a notice board containing a sheet of white cardboard to which were affixed the photographs of some thirty to forty women. Across the top in bold lettering was the word "*Verboten*". My mind was working so slowly that I just could not imagine what it was all about; then the penny dropped and I realised I was staring at a picture gallery of the local whores who were forbidden to the troops. Why it should be displayed outside the CO's office defeated me.'[69]

When WAAF Mary Corran was stationed at 21 OTU, Stratford-on-Avon, she worked as the CO's driver. On one occasion there was a jitterbug dance in the town to an RCAF band. 'It was a super night,' she recalled, 'until I found myself and one of the Canucks jiving centre floor with everyone clapping in tune, including the WAAF Sergeant, WAAF officer and station CO.'

Whilst chauffeuring the CO's car the next day, the CO, in order to maintain protocol, tried to suggest that he hadn't noticed her and said, after a strained and embarrassed silence, 'You missed a good dance last night.'

Mary recalled that the camp was a 'happy and willing one in which to work', and although it was customary to routinely check for aircrew canoodling with WAAFs in the air raid shelters, there was no impropriety found. This was because, she said, '…the CO usually mentioned any impending camp inspection to his WAAF driver.'[70]

My father Laurie Simpson confirmed that 'hanky panky' did occur on the bomber stations. I recall we were driving past Binbrook airfield some time in the late 1960s when he pointed out an old hangar, stating '…the erks used to take the WAAFs behind there.' 'That's life', was his attitude.[71]

Laurie got married during the war. One evening in 1942 whilst on leave at the Aircrew Reception Centre, Bournemouth, he had been introduced to a girl named Dorothy Holmes in the White Hermitage Hotel. For 5-18 September 1942 he wrote in his diary: '*The final days at Lichfield awaiting a posting and it is to 460 Australian Squadron in Yorkshire. I am to convert onto the Halifax immediately and Graeme [Keys] later. On Thursday Eileen Bastian invited me to her aunt's place at Tamworth so I spent a night there and then off to Bournemouth. Dorothy met the train and Mrs. Holmes gave me a great welcome when we arrived at Wood House. I'm afraid Dorothy is getting rather serious about me. I think the world of her too but somehow don't think it fair to marry the kid as "Ops" are coming on and even then would I be able to afford to take her back to Australia and keep her? And after Joyce*[72] *dropping me like a hot coal I'm not so sure that love is as everlasting as the poem book says it is.*'

Laurie took a week's leave from 17-26 January 1943 to visit Dorothy at Wood House, her home in Ferndown, Dorset. He wrote:

'*After dinner when everyone had gone to bed I did what I'd waited two months to do. I asked Dorothy to marry me, she said "Yes" and so it was sealed. Gosh, I love her and she loves me. Bought the ring next day and as we were sitting in a restaurant I slipped the ring on just as the singer began to sing the words "I'll walk beside you through the passing years". Gee, I hope those words are prophetic.*'

Before he left, his new fiancée gave him a gold signet ring that he '…*liked wearing very much.*' Their intention was to get married as soon as his tour had finished, not wanting to wait any longer than necessary.

'*So concluded the happiest week I've spent since I left home,*' he wrote, '*and I find myself engaged to the sweetest most loveable girl in the world.*'

There was much sunshine from 10-12 March 1943 and Laurie went to see Dorothy again: '*We talked things over and decided to be married on my next leave (20 April). Much preparation followed.*' They decided to honeymoon in Devon.

John Nunn recalled his days courting a WAAF at St. Athan whilst on his flight engineer's course. There was still a traditional attitude to love and marriage then, despite some 'home truths':

'We decided, one evening, that we were enough in love to think about marriage at the end of the war, always provided we both survived. I remember Edith saying that she had expected and was expecting to do a lot more than kissing when we had decided. I told her that my father had said to my mother that if things went too far, he wouldn't have married her. My mother had told me this, but since my eldest sister was a "seven month" baby, I wondered about the truth of it.'[73]

Couples who got married during the war still had problems. Beryl Pearce was a Bomber Command nursing orderly and her future husband a navigator:

'I remember counting the planes going out and counting them returning and wondering if he had made it. We married during the war. We had to change the date three or four times as we couldn't arrange our leaves together. I was on a different station. My brother, a pilot in Transport Command, was to be our best man.

'On the morning of [the wedding, in June 1944] we were all up and busy. My mother had made the cake from small gifts of a bit of sugar, fruit, etc. from many friends [despite the rationing]. My dress had been sent from America.

'By 9 a.m. we were getting worried as we'd had no word from my brother. We switched on the radio to hear "*This is D-Day*" and realised why Don had been unable to contact us. Soon after, our vicar arrived. On being told there was no best man, he said, "Leave it to me…" jumped on his bike and cycled round, asking if any of the youth club were on leave. He found one and told him to put on his uniform and be at the church by 2 p.m. It was a relief to arrive there and see an old friend. Later we learned that my brother had been sworn to secrecy on that day.'[74]

Laurie Simpson returned to Breighton on 13 March 1943 to find that '*duff*' weather had prevented the squadron from flying a single op since he had left. 'Chad' Martin, the squadron CO,[75] informed Laurie that although his flying officer appointment was still to come through, he had been recommended for Flight Lieutenant. On 26 March the squadron went to Duisburg. This was '*disappointing*': the 10/10 cloud cover '…*didn't stop Jerry's gunners from being very accurate.*' Berlin was the target on the 27th. From Laurie's diary: '*We had a good trip but it was long and tiring. It was 10/10 cloud all the way to within 5 minutes of the target and then it cleared up miraculously. There was moderate heavy Flak and then intense, combined with many searchlights which we evaded successfully.*'

Laurie's crew had just begun to relax when, immediately off the coast of Denmark on the way back, a Flak ship – and Flak ships bristled with guns – opened fire and nearly hit them.

'Chad' Martin (via Johnson)

The Lancaster returned safely, however, and Laurie was due for happier times. On the 29th his promotion to Flight Lieutenant finally came through. His diary entry for 21-29 April 1943 reads:

> 'The happiest week of my life: Dorothy and I were married in the Holy Cross Church at Stapehill near Wimborne by Sqn Ldr Pearce, RAAF Padre. Al was my best man and Anne [Holmes] was the bridesmaid. Had lunch at Wood House – entrained at Broadstone – arrived in time for dinner at the "Rosemullion Hotel" in Budleigh Salterton – lovely little room overlooking the red cliffs and the town – very nice meals – drinks in the bar before lunch and before dinner.'

Dorothy made him very happy. He commented: '*She is really a sweet lovely young thing and we are very much in love.*' The journey back to camp he described as 'rotten'. He met Colin McLeod and a few others at the *Mucky Duck* in Breighton and had a repetition of his bachelor party. He once told me that a married man would have less of a tendency to be single-minded than a bachelor: whilst flying, the attachment could distract one's mind and lead to accidents. I believe he said that some fatal incidents were caused by this. The couple's happiness, however, would soon be disturbed by the war.

Graeme Keys

In August 1942 Laurie wrote a frank diary entry about his friend Graeme Keys whom he had first met at an EFTS at Amberley in Queensland in 1941. For some reason, probably because they were both quite seriously minded men, they gelled. Keys was concerned because his rear gunner was due to go into hospital for three days and his navigator, Arthur Quick, was also unwell and looked like being grounded for a week. As they were due to pass out in five days it was very worrying. Also – '*...Graeme is very friendly with a lass on a farm near here and seems to think that she is the moon and the stars. I am surprised that a fellow of his age and experience can't see through her. He thinks she is the sweetest, most innocent girl ever, but I think I know better. Anytime Graeme is flying she asked me to come over and sample the goods. Yet Graeme can't see it... I don't think this lass is good for him.*'

Graeme was my father's closest friend during the war. On 1 May 1942 Laurie arrived back at No. 15 AFU at Leconfield, Yorkshire before lunch and set about getting their clearances for posting to a BAT flight signed:

> 'We learnt that we were posted for our course to Scampton, so a farewell party was decided upon and the whole course gathered at the Beverley Arms. The place waxed hot and strong and some of the boys allowed themselves to be sidetracked by women.
>
> 'At 2.30 Graeme and I finished the remaining bottle and [went] off to bed. At least I did. When the batman woke me in the morning Graeme's bed hadn't been slept in. Eventually found him in the bath idly making ripples on the water with his fingers. He had only been there asleep... for 3½ hours. It is just a wonder he hadn't got pneumonia or something. Why he went there at 2.45 in the morning I guess we'll never know. But hell I thought it was damned funny.'

Keys was actually married before the war. On 17 June Laurie wrote: '*Feeling very "cheesed off" today and am longing for a posting. Graeme and I do a cross-country together tonight – should be swell. Graeme received two letters from his wife today. I wish some would come through to me... The flowers down in Dorset have just penetrated my memory: Rhododendrons, Lilac, May, Lupin, Chestnut, etc. all growing freely – were a real delight. The summer seems to have passed, the few days of it we had [were] equivalent to mild Spring in Aussie – aw hell!!*'

Laurie frequently also heard of old friends 'going west': on 13 June in Bournemouth he '...*read of the death of Flight Lieutenant Hunter, our OC of ATS at Amberley on a casualty list.*' He concluded it was '...*the long arm of coincidence*'. In June, '*Neil Yarman had gone for a Burton while teaching two pupils at a BAT course.*' He '...*liked poor old Neil and felt sorry he had gone*'. One of the pupils was also killed. '*That makes at least four of the boys who won't see "Ops".*' In addition a friend on operations was killed: '*Weir an A.G died when an incendiary was dropped on their plane over Cologne...*'

In the last week of June, at the end of their time at Leconfield, Graeme and Laurie's confidence in their abilities received the boost it had much needed since leaving the old country. My father's diary entry for 23 June:

> '*Next day we were told that we were the outstanding pupils in the whole two years the A.F.W.*[76] *had been going. Blow me! Also both Graeme and I were assessed "above the average" for flying. Good show! Then the Wingco was very complimentary to us also.*'

This is very uncharacteristic of my father who, nearly all his life, had a tendency to understate himself. It seemed to reflect a continuation of the 'dual careers' both he and Keys had experienced. Laurie's final comment: '*Said cheerio to Terry tonight* [his batman] *and I guess I'll miss the cup of tea at 10.30 am.*'

Following their departure from Leconfield, after being posted to Lichfield, the boys would partake of the 'amber nectar' at *The Bull's Head* – '*quite a pleasant place*' –only a mile or so down the road from the airfield. On the 27th they drank '*six or seven*' pints after managing '*to get sweet with the barmaid*', who '*organised drinks 40 minutes after closing time.*' The following day there was a party in the WAAF officers' mess to celebrate the third anniversary of the formation of the Women's Auxiliary Air Force. They '*had some fun*' and Laurie met an '*Aussie padre*' who was on the station – '...*a wizard bloke*'.

At the end of June Graeme, 'Quickie' and Laurie went '*for a few jugs*' at *The Bull*: '*There was a rip-snorting party in progress in the mess when we arrived back so we joined in.*' He went to bed before Graeme, who was trying to write a letter to his wife, Alice: '*He finished two pages and they were ludicrously funny*', Laurie wrote. '*Nothing made sense and* [he] *just seemed to ramble on in disjointed phrases.*'

Ron Searle recalled Keys' character: 'The skipper was great mates with Graeme Keys known as "The Baron", mainly because he looked like a German with his cropped hair cut flat, and the moustache, very straight backed, like most of the German officers that you see in films.' In Laurie's diary on 18 March 1942 there is a reference to Keys' imaginative nickname. It was a Wednesday and there had been an announcement in the papers that General Douglas MacArthur had just taken over command of all Allied troops in Australia. It was '*real news*'. Laurie felt he was the right man for the job. He had proved himself in the Philippines as possessing '...*initiative, resourcefulness, and doggedness*'. MacArthur had an '*offensive spirit*' which meant they could escape the British '*stodginess*'. To celebrate, Graeme and Laurie went to the Circle Club in Bournemouth to '*nudge their excellent beer*'.[77] It was the funniest night they had experienced:

> '*We talked, laughed and sang and not once did we sink to a low level. The Doc's frantic cry of "I want something to eat!" and our reply of "OK, Doc, just another one for the road!" carried on throughout the evening. Graeme's exhibition of the new RAF entrance exam balancing movement took the house by storm, and was the Baron's face red!*'[78]

Ron Searle: 'Graeme's crew and ours started ops together and finished on the same night – the first crews to do a full tour for some time on 460. I didn't get to know Graeme, he was also in the officers' mess, but I always thought of him as a very serious character who wouldn't stand any nonsense. He was awarded the DFC and was killed flying a Mosquito, I think with a Pathfinder squadron. I heard he had crashed on landing.'[79]

Cliff O'Riordan noted in his diary: '*Thursday, 24th: Fighter affiliation in morning. Baron Keys came over*[80] *in the afternoon and seemed quite happy at Lichfield.*' Nearly a year before, in August 1942 at Leconfield, Keys and Laurie had applied to join the Pathfinder Force, but their application had been quashed because the CO thought it would be 'too tough' for them. Laurie noted:

> '*Graeme and I volunteered for the Pathfinder Force, who are the boys that go in first and light up the target for the rest of the mob. A special "gen" box is installed which navigates the aircraft very accurately to the target. It seems that you do 60 sorties instead of the usual 30, and 6 months screened at an OTU and then 20 more sorties, so if we get it we'll do the lot at once.*'[81]

After his time at Lichfield Keys was seconded to 139 Squadron based at Upwood in Huntingdonshire. It was just as he and Laurie had planned the year before: 139 was part of No. 8 (Pathfinder) Group and was a founding unit of the Light Night Striking Force, which Don Bennett initiated in 1943 to make small-scale raids deep into the Reich. The LNSF was often utilised for 'spoof' raids to distract enemy fighters away from the primary target, with large amounts of Window being employed to give the illusion of a far larger force. The size of these operations gradually increased from a handful of aircraft to over a full squadron by late 1944. Some crews found 'spoof' raids more stressful than going to the actual target.

Sometime between the end of his 460 Squadron tour and being transferred, which would have been around the middle of July 1943, Graeme Connor Keys was awarded the DFC, the citation for which stated that he was employed '*for some time... Captain of an aircrew... which had completed a number of successful raids on enemy objectives.*' These included '*...no less than six attacks on Essen, two on Berlin and many others on the most heavily defended targets in enemy territory.*' One operation showed remarkable similarities to one of my father's own experiences: '*During one of his missions to Berlin, one engine ceased to function while still 30 miles from the target. Despite this handicap, Flt/Lt Keys continued and completed the sortie effectively.*'[82]

When one reads DFC and DFM citations it is difficult not to be sceptical of the content due to the eulogistic nature of them. Of course, there is a distortion with time: an empathetic understanding of the forces these young men faced, or the climate of the times, is difficult to make over 60 years later. '*This officer has invariably set a fine example of courage and devotion to duty...*',[83] Keys' citation concluded.

Graeme was killed in 1944 in a Mosquito IV in the early morning of 5 May, the day after the big RAF attack on Mailly-le-Camp. 139 Squadron was performing target-marking duties[84] during a minor raid by 28 Mosquitoes on Ludwigshafen. Keys' aircraft took off from RAF Upwood at 22.00 hrs and no further radio contact was heard.[85] According to Graeme's logbook[86] he was involved in an air battle.[87] However, RAF Air Historical Branch records reveal that Keys was on the approach to the 2,000-yard runway at RAF Ramsey on return when his aircraft stalled. He had called for and received permission to land, and acknowledged it, but at the same time reporting that his ASI was unserviceable. '*He said he would take particular care on the approach*', the report stated. The '*aircraft made a normal circuit and turned into the fog funnel at approximately 800 feet. Whilst just completing the turn, or whilst straightening out after it, preparatory to the final approach, the port wing dropped and it dived into the ground at 01.32 hours.*'[88] Both Keys and his navigator, Flying Officer Hamlin, were killed.[89] It was thought that the ASI had frozen up whilst the aircraft was flying in cloud and failed to unfreeze. Graeme was buried four days later in Newmarket Road Cemetery, Cambridge. He was 33 years of age.

By late 1943 460 Squadron had accumulated a varied collection of characters: Joe Munsch, a Warrant Officer, was the only English pilot on the squadron. Ted Groom recalled: 'He was one of these pilots that flew by the book: go out at 152 knots and come back at 145 knots. Joe would stick to that; it was a question of saving fuel and everything.'

Jan or 'John' Goulevitch joined the RAAF in 1941 and had flown five ops with 100 Squadron before transferring to 460.[90] By 16 September 1944 he had 16 operational trips under his belt. When a flight sergeant, Goulevitch had 'procured' a top hat one day from a pub in Doncaster. The story goes that it was thought to have been left by an absent-minded undertaker. On one occasion, just before 100 Squadron was due to go on an operation, the hat disappeared. 'Gouley' stood up at the end of the briefing, refusing to fly until the 'pommy bastard' who had purloined his pride and joy, gave it back. It was duly returned.[91] Ted Groom flew as Goulevitch's flight engineer on the Peenemünde raid of 17/18 August 1943:

'Goulevitch used to wear the top hat on top of his helmet. When we went to Peenemünde we flew in over the Baltic, that's where we were routed. Searby was the Master Bomber and the PFF were dropping their bombs. Searby said "Do not bomb the greens,[92] they're in the water." So we went round again – hell of a danger because you've got everyone coming up behind. Anyway we got away with it, and were coming out and "Gouley" said, "OK, let's go home!" Then we got shot up by this Jerry night fighter, but "Gouley" was more concerned about his top hat than he was about himself.'[93]

Goulevitch escaped by taking evasive action. Bert Gorell, who was his w/op on the trip, wrote to him years later: '*[That] fighter attack at Peenemünde: we should have bought it there – if you hadn't dipped.*'[94] Gorell recalled other trips they had been on: 'Coming back from Cologne without part of a wing and engine, how we crossed a fighter box without getting caught. How did Ron Scarr get a rope to help pull on the stick with Archie? With a "Darkie" call[95] at Hawkinge telling you to wait for a landing – you saying "No way!" and using his airfield to bounce into Kent fields.'[96] 'But we were all mates', recalled Ted Groom. 'We'd come back over base and Joe Munsch would always be first off and last back because of his greater experience. And as we're circling Jerry Bateman, or Sharpy or Goulevitch would call him up on the r/t and say, "If you don't make it, Joe, can I have your bacon and eggs?"'

RAF airmen were believed to have a more considered approach to things than their wilder Australian contemporaries. John Nunn was 20 and a man of sensitive disposition. His wife Edith recalled that he had fears of what he had to face as soon as he finished his flight engineer training. 'On finishing his FE course at St. Athan he came on leave with me to my parents' home near Rye. We walked up on to the cliff top and sat talking. Suddenly he said, "I can't go through with it". The enormity of what he had to face caused a tearful spell and I hugged him and said, "John, you must go through now and be ready for flying on tours". I felt it was something he had to face. He calmed down and then said, "I suppose I have to carry on."'

As soon as Nunn became operational, however, things changed. 'He was sent up to Lincoln and joined his station, but he started drinking, getting really sloshed before flying. It was "Dutch courage" and difficult to stop once started.' The addiction nearly wrecked the relationship. Nunn was finding the strain of operational flying immense: 'Every time we came back from a bombing mission the pressure mounted, because others did not.' He was unable to find the strength to fly without alcohol and for a year-and-a-half the couple did not see each other. Edith, who was not happy at all, warned him that '…he could choose drink or me.' John responded: 'I said that if and when I finished my tour safely, I would consider her idea, but in the meantime I would carry on as I had been.' His wife was adamant: 'I said if he survived the drink and flying we'd see what happened later on.'[97] John 'went a little mad' then, going in to Brigg or Scunthorpe at every opportunity, often indulging in a 'skinful'.

Some other aircrew also resorted to drink but did not survive. In March 1944 the staff at the *Luftwaffe* Interrogation Centre at Frankfurt-am-Main recovered letters from the body of the dead flight engineer of a Halifax to his fiancée. He wrote:

'20.3.44. My hand is trembling so much that I can hardly write. My nerves are pretty bad at present. It must be the flying. It is very nice and I like it, but where we fly to, that's what does it. I have already done ten flights, but have another 20 in front of me.

'The night before last we did another operational flight. They get more and more and I shall be through in no time. I am looking forward to this with mixed feelings, as I have promised you to give up drinking when I have finished my tour, and that will be a hard blow for me if I do it. But [as] I get you I really will give up drinking.'[98]

Jack Brook, a flight engineer with 617 Squadron, was another airman profoundly affected by his experiences. His daughter recalled that he was '…terrified before and during every mission… He did not talk about his feelings very much at all. He had obviously seen a lot that a person shouldn't have to see in this life, and his priorities were affected by that.'[99]

These were ordinary men whose lives were transformed by the war. Laurie Simpson, also a quiet man by nature, thought his experiences 'made him'. He struggled with shyness all his life. Despite this, 'it didn't stop them making me a squadron leader', he recalled. He would look back in later life on his survival of three weeks' solitary confinement in an SS prison as a source of inner strength: but there were 'no heroics'[100]; it was a job that had to be done and men did it the best way they could. Steve Jackson, a Pathfinder w/ag, recalled the fears that came to aircrew after a briefing: 'The atmosphere was different, with most of us dressing in silence whilst some still had to joke about the Reaper waiting above the clouds with his scythe ready to chop you in half. No matter what attitude you took you knew that this could be the last time you would be doing this.'[101] Alan Bryett recounted, 'We were all frightened, and this was quite natural and had to be faced. I never was quite sure whether the fact that I sweated profusely after dressing for a flight was due to fright, or the excessive amount of clothing needed for the cold at great heights – probably both.'[102] The term 'hero' was not a title many airmen welcomed. Henry Wagner, reflecting upon his experiences, said: 'Several articles about my incident have had the word "hero" included. I wish they would not do this, as there is nothing heroic in taking vigorous steps to save your own life.'[103]

Superstition and Luck

Aircrews' lives were run by superstition, such was their fear for themselves and their colleagues. This led some men to perform personal rituals that were essential for many of them if they were to be able to continue: urinating on the tail wheel; walking once round the aeroplane before each operation; the lucky rabbit's foot; the miniature 'gremlin' in the cockpit. Any non-performance of these rituals or non-appearance of such mascots could result in a certainty of doom even before a mission had started. Wynford Vaughan-Thomas recalled witnessing this on the raid to Berlin that he covered for the BBC: 'Most of the crew had their ritualistic superstitions. Jimmy carried a little white doll. Ken always put his right hand first into the sleeve of his jacket. Con did a complicated wave with his left hand. So we propitiated the Gods.'[104]

The mechanics of such rituals were occasionally so obtuse that they were almost impossible to perform. The crew of Lancaster bomb-aimer Vernon Wilkes, had a rear gunner named Danny Driscoll who made a habit of spitting on the aircraft's rudder before take-off. His comrades were adamant that the task had to be performed before each raid. 'On one occasion,' Wilkes recalled, 'we were about to take off and the skipper asked Danny if he had spat on the rudder? Danny replied that he had forgotten.' The pilot 'slammed on the brakes and told him to get out and do it.' But in the course of the exercise the engines' slipstream blew the spittle off target. As the uncooperative sputum flew past the rear rudder, Driscoll cupped both hands to direct it. Wilkes: 'Flying Control couldn't understand why our Lancaster was holding up the whole squadron take-off and was frantically flashing green lights at us.'

The skipper was forced to commence his taxi run as Driscoll ran alongside trying to get back in. Having jumped four feet up in the air, the mid-upper gunner heaved him into the rear fuselage. After this incident, all their take-offs went smoothly. Wilkes recalled, 'Danny always claimed that his ritual of spitting on the rudder was the reason we survived 36 operations.'[105]

Such irrationalities extended to even more disturbing areas: the WAAF with a jinx; the aircraft that misperformed every operation; the code letters that brought bad luck. My father crashed twice during his service, both times in an aircraft coded 'K'. The final entry contained in his *RAAF Service Diary* was dated 25-27 January 1944, the night he failed to return:

> 'Briefed for Frankfurt, but op cancelled at last moment. Next night Berlin... At last moment was switched from "J2" to "K". A bad omen as "K" was the "Wimpy" I crashed at Church Broughton.'

Engineer Bill Higgs recalled a case of a 'jinx':

> 'One of the things we didn't like was anybody in a crew getting married. If ever a stranger came in on your crew... it was a jinx. And there was I, going to step in for Paddy O'Caine [a friend] on a daylight raid![106] I got in, and we did our air test and landed. In the afternoon we got the engines started and were taxying out... and suddenly it stopped: the op was cancelled! I breathed a sigh of relief!'[107]

UV-P 'Peter', the 'Simpson Kite' (later renamed '*The Fooship*'[108]), had its own mascot. This was 'Goody the Gremlin', a small Leprechaun-like leather and cloth doll that one of the crew had probably picked up in York. Goody featured in photographs, perched on the framework of the Lancaster cockpit's Plexiglas 'greenhouse', above the engineer's window.[109] The term 'Gremlin' slipped into RAF parlance at the beginning of the Second World War but had appeared in print as early as 1929. Possible origins of the name came from a beer, popular in RAF messes, brewed by the Fremlin Company, that combined with the term goblin, produced 'Gremlin'. An alternative suggested origin was the author Flight Lieutenant Roald Dahl, an injured fighter pilot who wrote a children's book entitled *Gremlins* in 1942. The *Daily Mail* reported that year that they were '... *"little devils"* who made things go wrong. These were the sprites who plague young fliers by dipping wing tips, clogging oil lines, jamming undercarriages, eating petrol or vanishing landing grounds.'[110] But they brought order and relief to the chaotic world of air combat, shifting responsibility for any serious problems away from the bomber men to a rather ludicrous, tongue-in-cheek creature.

Stories of obsessive behaviour generated by mascots were often near ridiculous. Some of them were tested to destruction to prove their worth. Sergeant E. Harmer, a WAAF Watchkeeper, made a small leather dog for one airman friend and then had to make one for every other member of the crew. Before the dogs were accepted they had to be tested for 'luckiness': the mascot was put down on the runway behind the bomber's wheels. If, when the brakes were released, the aircraft ran forward, it was declared 'lucky'. However, if the reverse happened, it was 'unlucky' and worthless. Airman William Davies's crew had a near life-sized duck weighing 2 lbs made for them from wool. On one occasion, when on their way out to their aircraft, weighed down by flying clothing and equipment, someone shouted, 'We forgot the duck!' One unfortunate airman then had to run back to retrieve it.[111]

Sometimes men had a premonition of their death even before getting onto an operational squadron. Lew Parsons flew ops with 75 (New Zealand) Squadron. During his initial training at Bridlington he met a recruit named Larry Hayward. The airmen met again two years later whilst on engineering courses at St. Athan:

> 'Larry was ahead of me on an earlier Flt/Engineers' course and when he passed out and was awarded his Sergeant's Stripes and Engineer's Brevet, I congratulated him but remarked he didn't look well. He was white, and physically shaking. He told me he should never have come on this course and he was sure he was not going to survive on operations. I tried to reassure him but he was obviously upset. It was my first experience of someone with a real premonition of impending doom.'

Hayward went to 467 Australian Squadron. In 1944, when Parsons was a POW in *Stalag* IVB he met Charlie Bicknell, a navigator from 467, who was in the same crew as his friend. But there was bad news: on 15 August 1943 Bicknell, Hayward and crew had attacked the secret rocket development and testing establishment at Peenemünde and 40 bombers were lost. Among these was Lancaster PO-N with the unusual moniker '*Nuts to the Nazis*'; it had been downed by a night fighter and crash-landed inland. 'Charlie told me that they had been shot down', Lew recalled. 'They had baled out over the coast and Larry was blown out to sea and drowned.' Hayward's premonition came sadly true. He was 22.[112]

Conversely, on his final mission, Parsons flew in a Stirling with a w/op who was unusually lucky. On the night of 31 August 1943, the boy's 21st birthday, they were attacked by two Ju 88s after a bomb run over Berlin. As the turret gunners returned fire the Stirling dived away to starboard. The attack crippled the port inner engine, the tail plane and elevators were badly damaged, and cannon shells had entered the fuselage.

'The rear gunner had been wounded and his intercom was u/s, but he could signal us with his emergency lamp. Dougie Box, the mid-upper gunner, was concussed in his turret and Bobbie Quelch, the wireless operator, who had been standing at the flare chute to ensure the flare had gone when Ian released the bombs, found that his jacket was torn under the armpit where a cannon shell had passed as he had his arm raised to hold himself steady in the dive.'

Quelch experienced more good luck that night. They baled out at almost zero feet after nearly colliding with a range of tree-covered hills. Parsons got caught in a tree on the way down:

'I undid my harness and dropped to the ground: I had lost my right boot when I baled out but I was able to walk away in what I hoped was a westerly direction. It was a starlit night and I walked on a gravel track that crunched under foot. As I went, I could see the flames of the aircraft burning on the hill above me. Suddenly I heard the burst of machine gun fire off to the right. My immediate thought was, "My God, they're shooting my mates."'

Parsons was picked up by the *Luftwaffe* and taken to the next village, where he met the surviving members of his crew:

'I learned from Bob that the machine gun fire I had heard was when he had been found lying on the ground: the German who found him pointed the gun at him and cocked it ready to fire, then fired it into the air to attract attention, much to Bob's relief. His second bit of luck that night.'[113]

'Lady Luck' was the Queen of the game plan alright. Dick Raymond put his survival down to 'sheer luck – nothing else'. But it was a factor that John Geddes, a navigator with 428 Squadron, did not take into account, until one op: 'In the course of training we were told survival was 50 per cent ability and 50 per cent luck, but I couldn't see that until one night over Berlin they insisted that I take a look outside. There was complete cloud cover below, so the searchlights were stationary pointing vertically, completely illuminating the clouds. Looking below was a whole collection of bombers silhouetted against these: easy pickings for a fighter above. Yes, this was where luck came in.'[114]

One member of Geddes' crew was regarded as a talisman by his comrades:

'George, our rear gunner, was a Yorkshireman, a bit of a loner and psychic. He had been ground crew and had returned from Dunkirk before re-mustering to aircrew. After all the time training for air gunner he felt it wrong to stop at 30 trips; he would carry on. We pointed out that, with losses of 5 to 10 per cent, the chances of completing 30 trips were small, but he was happy that he would survive.'

When asked about the survival of the rest of the crew, the rear gunner was non-committal. Geddes:

'Inevitably one night George was sick and we had to take a spare rear gunner. After our return, at debriefing, the mid-upper commented that he was glad the trip was over. Someone asked, "Because George wasn't with us?" Several of us had been thinking the same thing. With that on our minds our concentration was not so efficient – however we survived.'[115]

Supernatural forewarnings could affect even the lives of the high and mighty. Don Bennett, who was by then PFF leader, found that in the course of his duties he got to know his senior pilots quite well. The knock-on effect was that when any of them went missing he inevitably suffered from resultant personal grief. Bennett recalled, 'This naturally had an effect on one's nerves and spirits... and occasionally driving home from interrogation in the early hours of the morning, it was hard to avoid breaking down and shedding a few tears – which was probably a good safety valve.'[116]

On one bizarre occasion, one of Bennett's staff officers, a Squadron Leader Price, went missing in a Mosquito. Things took their course and the next of kin were informed. The following morning Bennett walked into his outer office and there, to his amazement, was Price. What struck Bennett as odd, however, was that the man was wearing the wrong badges of rank. It emerged that this was not Price at all, but his twin brother, Flying Officer Price, who had been on Coastal Command duties in Iceland. 'By telepathy,' Bennett recounted, 'he knew that his brother was missing' and had received permission from his CO to visit Britain for compassionate reasons. But upon visiting the parents he was able to inform them that their other son was alive. Price then went to PFF HQ and told the same news to the C-in-C. The forewarning proved to be right: Squadron Leader Price had survived the crash and was a prisoner.[117]

• • •

On some RAF squadrons there was still a strong class distinction – a 'them and us' attitude – between the commissioned officers and other ranks, and sometimes between the regulars and those who only joined up for the duration, which tended not to be a feature of the Australian and Canadian units. For the Australians there was more of an 'all hands together' attitude. Despite this, crews often did not mix at all with each other outside operations, and the friendships that were forged between men varied according to the individual in longevity. Airmen fought a peculiarly idiosyncratic war – one moment they could be sitting down to tea in a Yorkshire village, hours later they could be lost in the midst of the 'Brutal Reich'.

Men were still dying in the air. In the Operational Training Units untried, inexperienced pilots could cause or reap the consequences of avoidable accidents and, in these circumstances, it is hardly surprising that crews questioned or dismissed their own survivability. Any introspection or dwelling upon private fears was occasionally offset by blowing off steam at the local hostelry in the way young men always have. But still a flyer's morale could break down.

CHAPTER EIGHT

'A DEADLY SERIOUS AND DANGEROUS GAME'

Operations

BOMBER operations over Europe were perhaps the most stressful combat experience in World War Two. Colonel Mark K. Wells, an eminent American historian, once concluded: 'No other group of Western Allied combatants, except for their American daylight bombing counterparts, suffered the same huge casualties, nor faced the mathematical certainty of their own deaths so routinely and so unflinchingly.'[1] Most of these men were aged between 18 and 30 and often had no experience of the world at all: Ron Warburton was only 19 when he joined 218 Squadron:

'In 1944 I was 19 – a very young 19 – as I had lived a very sheltered existence in elementary and grammar schools in Wales, with no experiences in life to give me a semblance of growing up. After nine months of very concentrated training I was posted to a Heavy Conversion Unit, where I joined a crew of six others. We did 19 daylight and night operations before we ran out of war.'

Initially, the extent of a tour of operations in Bomber Command was indefinite. By 1943, however, this had been set to 30 missions, whereas in the US Eighth Air Force a tour was only 25 ops. As it was, the average life expectancy in Bomber Command was little more than eight missions – after that, one's chances of survival were slim. Although confidence may have increased with time, as the last few trips approached, the odds of 'getting the chop' were at their highest. Arthur Cole: 'It was a hell of a strain. It increased as time went on. I will never know whether I could have completed my tour, personally. What I do remember is that the strain of flying was enormous: you knew that somebody wasn't going to come back every time you went up.'[2]

For the uninitiated, their arrival at an operational unit, where men were dying daily, could be shocking. Ted Groom, a flight engineer with 460 Squadron, recalled: 'In June 1943, when we arrived at Binbrook, the first thing we saw was a Lanc that had been out the night before with the rear turret shot away and all the blood all running out... I think they'd only just arrived back about six or seven o'clock in the morning; they'd brought it in from Dispersal. I mean you often saw that... not just the rear gunner, other people – sometimes it would be the wireless operator that would catch it.'[3]

In the spring of 1943 WAAF Sylvia Pickering was posted to RAF Coningsby. She was to be clerk to the Senior Base Station Medical Officer there and would be the only clerk in the Station Sick Quarters (SSQ). One of her enduring memories was of the mortuary, which was located quite close to the SSQ. 'On one occasion badly burned bodies from a crash were [brought] in there', she recalled. A '...strange, sickly-sweet stench crept across from these tragic victims to the SSQ.' She remembered hearing of a girl in her hut who had arranged to marry her fiancé as soon as he finished his tour. The girl would discuss her wedding plans in the darkness of the hut with her friends.

> 'I remember... the tension which gradually increased as he got closer and closer to the magic figure of 30. Although I never spoke to her myself, nevertheless I used to listen anxiously each night to find out how many more ops he still had to do. All was going well. Six... five... four... three... two. From then on there was no more talking in the darkness each night, only weeping in the bed at the far end of the hut.'[4]

Ken Edwards, who joined the RAF Regiment as a Medical Orderly in 1940, had a gruesome encounter in a Station Sick Quarters. Although he disapproved of the war on account of his Christian beliefs, he neverthless felt bound to help in some way and so went into the Medical Branch. He recalled:

> 'Right from the beginning I was confronted with death. After six weeks' basic training, three of us were posted to Thorney Island, and we reported to the Sick Quarters. The Sergeant there informed us, "I've got a job for you; we'll toss up to see whose it is." So he tossed up and it landed on me. And the job was to lay out a pilot who'd crashed in the Channel. The body was crawling with crabs and things – he'd been in the sea for some time. I didn't feel sick: you just grit your teeth and do it, but I had to undress him – he was hard with rigor mortis, but I could recognize his face. They hadn't eaten away at his face, but there were all sorts of creatures crawling all over him. And that was my introduction to the Medical Service.'[5]

After a time squadron veterans were easily able to single out the crews that looked as if they would not survive. By the late summer of 1943, Bomber Command had been suffering 'horrifying losses', tail gunner Chan Chandler remembered. 'Replacement aircraft did not seem to be a problem,' he recalled, 'but replacement crews were...' – and they found that some of these stand-in airmen were under-trained. His unit was receiving surrogate gunners who had never done night-flying before:

> 'It was strange how you could pick out crews that were never going to make it; we used to say that they had the mark on them – the ones who were not going to come back after their first trip. It was something like "learning to look under the light" in the old Hampden days. If you complained about being dazzled by searchlights, the old hands would say, "You'll have to learn to look under the light."'[6]

Hughie Edwards

During the Second World War only three airmen were awarded the triumvirate of the DSO, DFC and VC. Two of these were Guy Gibson and 'Chesh' Cheshire. The third was the Station Commander of 460 Squadron in early 1944 – Hughie Edwards. Hugh Idwal Edwards was the most highly

Hughie Edwards (via Johnson)

decorated Australian airman of the Second World War. He was born in Fremantle, Western Australia, the son of a Welsh immigrant family, in 1914, leaving Fremantle Boys High School in 1928. In 1934 he joined the Fremantle Garrison Artillery and in July of the following year he enrolled in an RAAF pilot officer cadets' course at Point Cook, but transferred to the RAF in 1936. At 24 he was over six feet tall, of athletic physique and a celebrated sportsman. The first time my father met him, in January 1944, six years later, was when my father commenced his ill-fated second tour, and had to report to the station CO, Edwards. Laurie remarked upon how strikingly good-looking Edwards was. By that time Edwards had married the wife of a fighter pilot friend and was living in the Station Commander's residence with his son and daughter. He flew 11 ops from Binbrook.

Despite his later success in the RAF, Edwards suffered a number of misfortunes early in his career. Two serious flying accidents delayed his operational flying for over two years. One was particularly hair-raising. In 1938 he baled out after a Blenheim iced up, but his body struck the tail wheel, and his 'chute became snagged on the tail plane. Just a few hundred feet above the ground he managed to break free. The incident caused paralysis in his right leg from the knee down: it was so serious that he was told he would never fly again. Eventually, however, he was awarded a limited flying category, later converted to full. Then, in September 1940, on a training flight in the middle of an air raid, he ran out of fuel. Directing the aircraft over open countryside, the escape hatch jammed and he had to crash-land. Edwards hit a tree but escaped with minor concussion. As a result of this he was not operational until 1941.

In January 1941 Edwards was commanding 105 Squadron, a Blenheim unit based at Swanton Morley. This squadron was virtually wiped out while it was undertaking operations from Malta. 460 Squadron was Edwards' third tour, the second being on Mosquitoes with 105 Squadron. Every unit had its adventurous types.

My father recalled that a few derring-do flyers achieved notoriety (for example Gibson and Bader), but they necessarily became hardened characters in order to accomplish this, and thus were less likeable. Unknowns often achieved equally remarkable deeds, but either did not survive the war, or were sent to prison camps. Many airmen went onto bombers because they did not have the fast reactions required of a fighter pilot. A man of slower metabolism, my father typically understated himself, saying he thought he did not have enough 'zip' to be selected for fighters after initial training.

The raid for which Edwards was awarded his VC occurred on 4 July 1941 when he led two squadrons, 105 and 107, towards Bremen. It was his 36th operation. The 12 Blenheim IVs were reported by enemy shipping near Cuxhaven and the formation flew into Bremen at ultra low level – 50 feet with light Flak and machine gun fire coming at them from Bremerhaven, amid balloon cables and high-tension wires. At rooftop-level they flew in as the local populace dived for cover. Buildings, sheds, rail lines and gantries exploded in an orgy of steam, smoke and metal, and all the Blenheims were hit, with four aircraft lost. One aircraft was hit by Flak and crashed into a factory. Another was 'last seen heading away from Bremen burning fiercely.'[7] Two 107 Squadron pilots, Wg/Cdr L.V. Petley and Flt/Lt F. Welburn, the former responsible for abandoning a previous attack, were shot down, and crashed in the target area. Welburn, in Blenheim V6193, was the sole survivor of 13 airmen in four Blenheims. The bombing continued as crews flew around searching for targets: a timber yard went up and a goods train and airfield also succumbed as the eight remaining Blenheims flew out from the shattered city.

Two weeks later Edwards was awarded the VC. His DFC citation for an attack on enemy shipping on 4 June had stated that he had '...*completed numerous operational missions* over enemy and enemy-occupied country and against their shipping... at all times displayed great leadership, skill and gallantry.' Now he had the VC and the DFC. The new citation stated, 'Wing Commander Edwards, although handicapped by a physical disability resulting from a flying accident has repeatedly displayed gallantry of the highest order in pressing home bombing attacks from very low heights against strongly defended objectives.'[8] He had '...made a successful attack, and then with the greatest skill and coolness withdrew.' His navigator received the DFC and his w/ag the DFM. Joseph Goebbels, the Nazi Minister of Propaganda, quickly downplayed the attack, saying that only 'slight military damage' had been caused, which 'could be quickly repaired'. Despite the high losses and limited overall damage, it was a foretaste of things to come. The raid was hailed as the first of a series of round-the-clock attacks and a sign of Britain's determination to fight back. It also took place at a time when the general accuracy of RAF navigation and precision bombing attacks were inadequate for the job required and before the infamous 'Butt Report' which exposed the inaccuracy of normal British bombing. It was also one of a series of low-level daylight raids, such as the raid by Blenheims of 114 Squadron and other units on the Cologne power stations at Knapsack and Quadrath in August 1941, and the Nettleton raid on Augsburg in April 1942, where much daring was required.[9] On 6 December 1942, Edwards led a daylight low-level attack on the Philips factory at Eindhoven for which he was awarded the DSO. The operation that the citation mentioned stated that it '... was executed faultlessly. It demanded a high degree of skill and accurate timing.'[10]

Hughie Edwards was appointed Station Commander at Binbrook after 460 Squadron moved there in May 1943. One end of the airfield had steeply sloping ground running up to the flight path. This often made approaches to that area, where the airfield appeared to be on a plateau, difficult. Gordon Stooke, a 460 Squadron pilot in 1943, described how this unusual feature could affect a Lancaster on take-off: 'One rolled forward, turned left then, accelerating, disappeared over a crest in Binbrook's peculiar runway, to appear again, thankfully, as one struggled heavily-laden into the air.'[11] One squadron leader 'buzzed' the airfield and was severely reprimanded for it, probably by Edwards, who was more responsible than any other man for the efficient unit that 460 Squadron was to become by late 1944. Although Edwards was a fine, brave man, who would often circle a target with a new crew to give them experience, he never perfected his landing procedure, and flight engineer George Toombs recalled that his technique was so bad that the whole squadron would turn out to watch him land. There were comments that Edwards was 'flying on kangaroo juice!'

Toombs and his crew received a severe dressing-down on one occasion for the consequences of low flying. He recalled that his skipper, Pilot Officer Lester, and a best friend, often indulged in hedge-hopping in formation. One day Lester's Lancaster was so low that he had to heave back on the stick to clear a haystack, and in the back 'Fingers' Dowse, the tail gunner, cried in glee as the stack disintegrated and hay blew everywhere. But back at Binbrook Lester was ticked off by the CO as the haystack had contained a number of sleeping tramps, one of whom was blown over 20 yards along the ground and received a broken leg.

A low flyer who did achieve notoriety was Squadron Leader 'Mickey' Martin of 617 Squadron. Harold Brownlow Martin had left Sydney for England on his way to Edinburgh University and a medical degree[12] when his interest and his money were diverted. Martin was as unorthodox in the way he came to Bomber Command as he was when he got there. After joining the RAF in England, he trained as a fighter pilot, but was posted to the north and missed the fighting during the Battle of Britain.

Determined to get into the war, he applied for a transfer to bombers. Early in 1942 he put together one of the first all-Australian crews to bomb Germany but, after their first few missions, Martin decided it was inevitable that he would be killed.[13] John Elliot, who was an NCO on ground crew with 617 Squadron at the time of the Dams Raid, saw Martin fly between the Scampton control tower and a hangar as they looked down on him from the control room. 'He couldn't have been more than 20 feet from the ground', Elliot remembered. One time Martin was doing a practice run over a dam when the rear gunner called out '*Climb!*' The man was soaking – the tail wheel had hit the surface!'[14] 'Mickey' Martin survived the war.

By the end of 1941 the Air Ministry found it difficult to determine exactly the accuracy of British bombing. With no efficient target-marking force it was impossible to ensure that the relatively unsophisticated raids that had been conducted up until that time were as successful as hoped. An investigation carried out into RAF bombing led by a member of the War Cabinet Secretariat, Mr. D.M. Butt, and which became known as 'The Butt Report', was published with depressing conclusions in August 1941. One of this pamphlet's most shocking deductions was that, up until that time, '...only a third of the aircraft claiming to reach the target actually reached it.' In general the proportion of aircraft bombing within five miles of the target was as little as 25 per cent.

Until Air Chief Marshal Harris took over centre stage as C-in-C on 22 February 1942, Bomber Command was in a very nascent state. It had less than 600 serviceable aircraft, navigational aids were still very primitive, daylight raids impossible and the only night raids practicable were by aircraft flying individually: the concept of a 'bomber stream' had yet to be invented. In fact, things were in such a poor state following 'The Butt Report' that by September 1941, Churchill was forced to dispute what he had earlier stated on the efficacy of British bombing: '...its effects', he reluctantly concluded, 'are greatly exaggerated.'

Harris's predecessor, Sir Richard Peirse, had succeeded Portal as C-in-C in October 1940, but did little to improve things. He made one final effort to redeem the situation on the night of 7/8 November 1941 when he ordered 392 aircraft to attack Mannheim, Cologne and Berlin. The raid ended in disaster. That night thick clouds, strong winds and icing were predicted in the bombers' path, but Peirse was adamant. Originally it had been intended to attack the capital with over 200 bombers, but the restrictions imposed by the Hampdens meant all these 5 Group aircraft had to be reassigned to Cologne. As a result only 169 Stirlings, Whitleys and Wellingtons went to Berlin and less than 50 per cent of these even approached the target; 21 'failed to return'. In total, 118 aircrew were lost that night. Cloud obscured aiming points and Intelligence Officers later found it almost impossible to conclude how much damage had been done. Yet only one of the Hampdens bound for Cologne was destroyed – in a crash-landing, after being hit by Flak, and without any loss of life. For Mannheim 55 aircraft went out, of which seven Wimpys were shot down including three from Polish squadrons. This raid proved to be a turning point for Bomber Command and, as a result of decisions made by the War Cabinet, ops were all but shut down for the winter. The Secretary of State for Air, Sir Archibald Sinclair, drew Churchill's attention to the findings of the Air Staff and, despite Peirse's attempt to find other scapegoats, including the weather, he was relieved of his command on 8 January 1942. His 14-month reign could in no way justify the losses he had incurred.

At that time Sir Henry Tizard and Lord Cherwell (formerly Professor Frederick A. Lindemann),[15] both former physics professors, were employed as scientific advisors by the Air Ministry. They knew each other well, having been students together in Berlin before the war. If anyone ever wanted to lay charge to who was responsible for the area bombing policy, that person would have to be Professor Lindemann. According to the physicist and novelist, C.P. Snow, who was not very approving of him, Cherwell resembled '…a central European businessman – pallid, heavy featured, correctly dressed' – and, being of German descent and having been born in Alsace, had a 'faint Teutonic undertone to his English'. Historian Norman Longmate was equally disparaging: Cherwell was a life-long bachelor, teetotaller, and vegetarian, and lived a semi-monastic existence at Christ Church, Oxford, when not at his country home near Oxford, where he was protected by his wealth and 'a devoted manservant' 'from the normal trials and satisfactions which humanize and mature the personality.'[16] He was also a 'monstrous snob' and had a peculiar, malicious sense of humour, often pursuing relentless vendettas: 'Kindness and compassion, at least to those outside his own narrow social or scientific circle, were not in Cherwell's nature, only a streak of Germanic cruelty and obstinacy.'[17]

This was in sharp contrast to Tizard, who was much more balanced and rational and, in actuality, a more extroverted, good-natured Englishman. These two very different men represented the opposing sides of the bombing debate. Tizard supported the concept of steady, continuous bombing, but with priority given to destroying the U-boat fleet. Cherwell was more in favour of area bombing influenced by the success of the German raids on Britain.

On 30 March 1942 Cherwell wrote a letter to the Prime Minister advising him that statistics compiled from the *Luftwaffe's* raids on Britain suggested that de-housing the German population, i.e. striking at its morale, would be the key to winning the bomber war, rather than targeting industry specifically and precisely. His report was based upon some extremely questionable statistics that Tizard and others later came to question. Notably he calculated that the civilian population of 60 German cities could be de-housed if each of the 10,000 bombers that he thought would be available by the end of 1942, could make at least 13 operational sorties with a three-ton bomb load. These were wildly exaggerated and optimistic figures, but Portal and Sinclair were convinced by them and sent a memo to Churchill to that effect. Tizard and other scientific advisors saw the figures as erroneous and extremely optimistic. The official figure for the number of heavy bombers due to be available by July 1943 was 8,000, experience suggesting that only 7,000 of these would become operational. The Navy's chief scientist thought the statistics were too high by 600 per cent, one of the main concerns being that bombers would be taken away from naval targets. The Army similarly feared that its losses in the Middle East, such as that of Tobruk, would only be exacerbated unless it received more bombers.

In the event, Cherwell's erroneously supported arguments held sway at Downing Street. Many could never understand how Churchill could be influenced by such 'a repellent, unclubbable, un-English figure'.[18] The answer seemed to be that 'Winnie' found in the man's sanguine and calculating detachment something he did not possess himself. Churchill and Portal may have later been the orchestrators of the area bombing policy, but Cherwell certainly sowed the seeds of it.

Early Raids in 1942

In 1942 Air Chief Marshal Harris needed an operation for Bomber Command that would act as a propaganda and morale-boosting tool in the midst of a welter of operations that were of too poor a standard to have any positive effect on the public's perception of his squadrons' activities. Three raids, however, were carried out early in the year which made a strong contribution to Harris's thinking. These were envisioned as morale-boosting exercises, and two in particular set standards for many future ops. These attacks were on Lübeck, Rostock and Augsburg. At Lübeck 191 aircraft of a force of 234 found the target on 28/29 March and bombed in three successive waves from as low as 2,000 feet. Sixty per cent of the timber buildings at the heart of the old city were burned down by the combined effect of high explosive and incendiaries. The Rostock raid of 23/24 April was less successful.

Augsburg was the most daring RAF raid up to that time in the war. Twelve new Lancasters from two squadrons flew at low level (sometimes as low as 25 feet) on 17 April to attack the MAN U-boat engine works in the city. Seven of the 12 bombers were lost – four even before reaching the target. A diversionary raid of Bostons on northern France had caused a squadron of Bf 109 fighters to cross paths with the incoming 97 and 44 Squadrons. Three further Lancasters were shot down over the target. Although a sobering price to pay, it did have a considerable morale effect on the British public. This was the first time the Lancaster had been used on a deep penetration raid.

These raids impressed High Court judge Mr Justice Singleton. On 16 April 1942, Singleton opened an official enquiry into British bombing policy.

The Air Ministry realised that there was a need to resolve the continuing conflict of philosophies between Tizard and Cherwell. Singleton was instructed by the government to report on the existing position of RAF bombing and whether it would be possible to accomplish attacks in strength over the next 18 months. He examined the existing RAF records and technical advances and, on 20 May, produced a report that was strongly influenced by three attacks earlier in the year. His main conclusions were that German morale was *not* a worthwhile target; Bomber Command should concentrate on industrial centres, and an acceleration in the improvement of bombing accuracy was a fundamental requirement.

One unexpected result of these early raids was that the 'Kammhuber Line'[19] was extended to cover the whole of Denmark with many new stations, due to the RAF flying around its northern extremities in the north German coast raids. With hindsight the Singleton report can be viewed as prescient; but when it was published it became all things to all men, being used to sustain an assortment of conflicting strategies. Consequently it had little long-term effect. Harris realised, however, that if the Baltic coast attacks such as that on Lübeck had impressed Singleton so greatly, how much more inspiring would be a large-scale attack on an important German city.

The Thousand-Bomber Raids

Harris's initial proposal was to assemble 1,000 bombers to attack Hamburg. The codename eventually assigned to this operation had been earmarked originally for the Army for the Second Front. This was to be *Millennium*. Strangely enough, after the RAF had wrestled it from them, the Army resorted to an alternative soubriquet, *Fortitude*.[20] The Royal Navy was able to supply a number of usable aircraft, having an interest in attacking Germany's submarine factories. In the event however, the Navy pulled out, feeling that its aircraft were of more use protecting the shipping lanes. Harris was left to scrounge what he could from Heavy Conversion Units and Operational Training Units. Lead aircraft were equipped with Gee navigation equipment which had a limited range. This dictated the choice of target. It has been suggested that Hamburg was named as a security ruse, but this seems to be unfounded. Cologne had been the secondary target: 52 airfields were assigned as bases from which the attack would be mounted and normal operations were virtually suspended. For three nights from 27 to 29 May the weather was too poor for operations. 30 May, a Saturday night, was the last night of the full moon, moonlight being essential to avoid collisions.[21] Because training schedules had been suspended on OTUs it was the 30th or never. On 30 May 1942 Cologne was switched to the primary.

Just after 09.00 hrs that day, Harris examined the synoptic charts for the day. They suggested conditions over the continent were tending towards unsuitable. A second forecast arrived at 09.10 hrs: *Much thundery cloud with some breaks over the north-west, decreasing southwards and dispersing in the middle Rhine to relatively small amounts during the night.* Harris reviewed the charts, eventually giving the go-ahead. At 12.25 hrs the order went out: *'Thousand Plan Cologne'*. Throughout the afternoon, forecasts suggested a deterioration in conditions; only at 17.00 hrs did things appear brighter. 'Broken cloud with some large breaks' was predicted over Cologne. Forecast conditions at take-off were 'very good' with possible thunderstorm interference, and 'cloud and occasional thunderstorms' were predicted going out, with an improvement on the return. One major consideration was the conditions over the home bases: the majority of crews were unfamiliar with the airfields from which they were operating.

Howard Pearce was a navigator (b) in 115 Squadron based at Marham, flying Wellington Is and IIIs:

'I was in the first raid on Cologne – that was quite something! We hardly saw another aircraft the whole flight. It was incredible, because we were flying at different levels. That was before the days of the "bomber stream".'

Bill Higgs:

'I returned to the squadron on 21 May in time for the first Thousand-Bomber raid, with Squadron Leader Peveler as pilot. This was the most perfect operation that I had flown on. We were climbing out of Linton and I had the astrodome above me. It was still daylight, and I looked back and couldn't believe it! I said to the skipper, "There are planes coming up everywhere!" Peveler said "Well, keep an eye on them as long as you can, because when it starts to get dark we won't see them and they won't see us…" – no navigation lights or anything.

'When we crossed the Dutch coast we could see fires burning in the distance. I thought, "God! Who's going to live under *that*?" It was three-quarters of an hour before the raid was scheduled to start. Aircraft were behind us for another three-quarters of an hour.

'We had been told to bomb east of the river Rhine. But if there was trouble and there were no fires burning, we had to bomb to the west. When we got to Cologne we were wheeling over the target and I could see my log sheet from the flames down below. I cheered when I saw Cologne burn: I was at Tangmere when it was bombed out, and a land mine went off a couple of houses away from my girlfriend's home in London, and the blast blew the whole place down!

'Then another two bombers came up in formation on each side of us. There were five of us flying round: I couldn't tell what type they were, but suddenly we all started the run-up to the target – bomb doors open, and we all bombed together. Each aircraft carried two 4,000-pounders, and when they dropped off the aeroplane you could see them go! We also had forty 6-lb sticks of incendiaries in cans on the wings. So, that night, whoever was down below got a nice load! We lost 44 aircraft that night.'

For Alan Castle the *Millennium* operation was uneventful: 'On the Cologne raid the weather was ideal with a moon and no cloud cover over the target. We arrived at 1.01 am, the attack having started at 0.55 am, and already there were some big fires going. I aimed our bomb load of 810 x 4 lb incendiaries at the centre of a group of small fires from a height of 18,000 feet.'

Robert Raymond, an American pilot in the RAF, recalled that most of his squadron flew far below this. They 'bombed from 10,000-12,000 feet and used oxygen on half the trip.' Visibility was good and the target easily identified: 'Crews next morning were jubilant over a successful trip and not too much opposition. One of our gunners shot down a Messerschmitt 110. Several were caught in searchlight cones and caught some Flak.' Some aircrew reported later that they could see the fires of Cologne from 80 miles away on the return journey.

LAC Keith Slade was on Flare Path Duty at Waterbeach that night. The duty crew had to stay up all night. 'It really was a night to remember', he recalled.

Alan Castle (Castle)

'In those days there was no question of the flick of a switch and the lights came on, or transferral to a different runway; it was all hard graft. The flare path lights at that time were "goose necks": contraptions like old fashioned oil cans, with a wick in the spout. Even in a moderate breeze it was difficult to light them, and we expended many boxes of matches every night – usually our own.'

To carry all the flares a Commer 'Karrier' low-loader was used, which made it easy to lift the flares on and off the vehicle. They had to be placed on each side of the runway but, at a Heavy Conversion Unit such as Waterbeach, many of the crews were inexperienced at landing four-engined aircraft like the Stirling: in a crosswind, the aircraft would approach the runway crabwise, not landing in the centre. This meant they went down one side and blew out all the 'goose necks' and at the intersection a great many more. 'We relit them all, then heard from Flying Control that the runways were changing. All the "goose necks" had to be reloaded on the truck, and we had to start on another runway. Down comes the rain, but there was no shelter for us.'

Harris's front line squadrons were so deficient in operational aircraft that 369 ageing ex-operational aircraft – Hampdens, Wellingtons and Whitleys – had to be scraped from Heavy Conversion Units and OTUs, particularly after Harris had been refused naval aircraft. On 14 April 1942 Australian Arthur Schrock, then a 26 year-old flight sergeant, was posted to 23 OTU at Pershore, near Worcester. He had arrived in England the previous July after training as a wireless operator/air gunner in Canada, being attached to the RCAF for seven months. He spent over three months from January to April 1942 on a Group Signaller's course at Lichfield with 27 OTU. Schrock's unusually raucous character will be described in detail in Chapter Ten; suffice to say that people either loved or hated him. The RAAF assessed his character as 'very good' and his proficiency as a w/ag 'superb'.

Arthur Schrock (Schrock)

At the end of May, Schrock's crew was selected to go on the Cologne raid in one of the unit's Wellington ICs. At around 23.00 hrs they were one of the later aircraft to take off. On board was a peculiar mixture of nationalities: the pilot, Lieutenant Ernie Weyle, was an American from California serving in the RAF; the front gunner was Sergeant Val P. Kennedy from Casino, New South Wales; the navigator was Pilot Officer Nick Carter from New Zealand; the rear gunner Flight Sergeant John H. Taylor, who had been awarded a DFM; and the wireless op/ag was Schrock. Schrock, Carter and Taylor were all trainees at the OTU. Taylor and Schrock had been friends before the war and were both from Townsville, Queensland. This combination of three different nationalities worked surprisingly well. They were nicknamed the 'United Pacific Crew'.[22]

Of 1,047 that flew out from four Groups and two Operational Training Groups, only 898 aircraft claimed to reach Cologne on 30 May, but the raid had significant propaganda value. Of the 369 Wellingtons, Whitleys and Hampdens from training units that went, 17 were lost. Surprisingly there were fewer losses of pupil pilots than of instructors. A total of 1,455 tons of bombs and incendiaries were dropped and 469 civilians were killed, with over 5,000 injured.

Schrock did not arrive on 12 Squadron until nearly a fortnight later – 11 June.[23] It seems the Weyle crew met at 27 OTU, Pershore and stuck together when it went to squadron. They bombed Cologne as planned. That night, for the first time, the concept of a 'bomber stream' was practised, but on return the stream thinned out considerably. Then the crew was attacked. Schrock's mate, tail gunner Taylor, was the first to see the fighter:

'We were ten minutes from the Dutch coast when I saw an aircraft to the starboard and reported it. We went into cloud and when we came out it was sitting there waiting for us. It opened up at 60 yards range and hit us straight on the nose, a little to port. The first burst took most of the port motor away, then it raked us all the way down.'

Schrock had escaped injury by sheer providence. He was standing in the astrodome, above the wireless op's position, with Carter in the second pilot's seat. Carter's charts and table were shot to pieces and three bullets went through the w/op's position. Taylor:

'The Ju 88 did a stall turn and came back behind. I shall never forget the great, ugly looking thing coming at us with guns blazing.'

The Junkers' bullets hit the rear turret and damaged the tail plane. The hydraulics had been shot away when the port motor was hit and all the turrets were out. Taylor had to rotate his turret manually. He opened fire when the German was about 150 yards away, firing two or three hundred rounds. By sheer luck the Ju 88 did not pursue the attack. 'He broke away after I got in my first burst and disappeared leaving a trail of sparks.'

Weyle did a remarkable job that night. He made a 'beautiful landing' at Martlesham Heath, a fighter aerodrome, and he flew between the hangars to get a long run in. Taylor recalled:

'Our port engine was u/s, our wireless was u/s, the navigator had no maps left, the hydraulics were gone and petrol was pouring from holes in our tanks when we got in. We pumped the emergency gear down, but we had no brakes, and he put her down perfectly. We all climbed out and shook hands three times!'[24]

One posthumous VC was awarded to a Manchester pilot from 50 Squadron that night. P/O Leslie T. Manser had been caught by a searchlight over the target but, despite this, he held the aircraft on course at 7,000 feet whilst bombing. The aircraft started to come under heavy fire and Manser took violent evasive action, turning and then descending to under 1,000 feet, but could not avoid the defences which followed them out of Cologne. The aircraft was repeatedly hit and the tail gunner wounded. The cockpit became filled with smoke and the port engine badly overheated.

Manser was one of those forgotten VCs of the Second World War who disappeared into obscurity after the conflict. The citation stated that *'when in extreme peril, thinking only of his comrades...'* he *'...displayed determination of the highest order.'* In what today would be seen as rather archaic and eulogistic language the quote continued:

> *'Pilot Officer Manser, disregarding the obvious hazards, persisted in his attempt to save the aircraft and crew from falling into enemy hands. He took the aircraft up to 2,000 feet, then the port engine burst into flames. It was ten minutes before the fire was mastered, but then the engine went out of action for good, part of one wing was burnt and the airspeed became dangerously low.*
>
> *'Despite all the efforts of pilot and crew, the aircraft began to lose height. At this moment Pilot Officer Manser once more disdained the alternative of parachuting to safety with his crew. Instead he set a new course for the nearest base, accepting for himself the prospect of almost certain death, in a firm resolve to carry on to the end.*
>
> *'Soon the aircraft became extremely difficult to handle and, when a crash was inevitable, Pilot Officer Manser ordered the crew to bale out. A sergeant handed him a parachute but he waved it away, telling the NCO to jump at once as he could only hold the aircraft steady for a few seconds more. While the crew were descending to safety they saw the aircraft, still carrying their gallant captain, plunge to earth and burst into flames.'*[25]

Twenty-three VCs were awarded to Bomber Command aircrew during World War Two. The more celebrated awards such as those to Gibson, Cheshire, Edwards, Reid, Jackson, Middleton, Nettleton, Hannah, Garland and Gray, largely due to popular writing, have not been forgotten. Many remain unheard of by the general public, however. Who remembers James Allen Ward, Hugh Gordon Malcolm, Cyril Joe Barton, George Thompson, Robert Anthony Maurice Palmer, Edwin Swales, Ian Willoughby Bazalgette, Arthur Stewart King Scarff, Andrew Charles Mynarski, or Leslie Thomas Manser? For that matter, who will ever know of Freddie Nuttall's unrecognised action?[26]

After Cologne the Germans strengthened the anti-aircraft defences of their cities considerably. Balloons were deployed and more night fighter units stationed on airfields in Denmark and Holland.

On 1 June another 956 aircraft were sent to Essen. Ernie Weyle's 'United Pacific Crew' was among them. Bill Higgs: 'Two nights later we attacked Essen with another force of 1,000 plus and lost 35, but the smoke haze from the industrial units below made it more difficult to see the target. However Krupp [the armaments manufacturer] was hit.' Alan Castle:

> 'The raid on Essen was not a success due to cloud cover over the target as well as the ground haze, which was usual over this target. We were carrying no bombs but 36 flares which were intended to light up the target area for other aircraft. I saw the flares ignite but the ground haze and clouds made it impossible to see the target.'

The night of the Essen attack, Laurie Simpson and Graeme Keys flew down to Group HQ at Scampton:

'Flew to Scampton about 5.30 to stay the night and get the gen on operations. We were lucky because another 1,000 bomber force was sent against Essen and although we missed the briefing we saw the boys go off around midnight, followed them in the operations room and watched them come home – all but two. This was a grand experience and we stayed up all night and flew back to Leconfield after brekker.'

Ron Drake was a mid-upper gunner on the Essen raid with 15 Squadron from Wyton in Stirling LS-R, W7513. His logbook entry for 1 June states: *'Bombed target – badly shot-up on the way back over Antwerp – rear gunner wounded – crash-landed at base.'* The aircraft took off at 23.10 hrs with a crew of eight. It was their 20th operation. After crossing the North Sea they managed to avoid being coned by the searchlights, which were distracted by other aircraft. Eventually LS-R released its bombs 'into the inferno enveloping Essen'. Drake:

'On the return over Antwerp, "R-Robert" was suddenly caught in searchlights and incendiary shells. They tore into the fuselage and wings and in less than a minute the plane was riddled with holes – the gunner in the rear turret was badly wounded – his turret shattered.'

Crash-landing at Wyton, the Stirling finished up on its nose at the side of the runway, badly damaged. One of the six-foot tyres had been blown to pieces. However, Essen was hardly affected by the bombing; only 15 Germans were killed on the ground and 11 houses damaged. The smoke and cloud had rendered it almost invisible to crews and the casualty rate of 3.2 per cent, or 31 aircraft, was relatively low.[27] At this stage, before the formation of the Pathfinder Force, 'raid leaders' flew ahead of the stream and dropped the marker flares – in fact, paradoxically, this time many more than those dropped on Cologne.

On 25 June a third Thousand-Bomber raid took place when 960 aircraft attacked Bremen. Ten different types of aircraft were used, the most diverse force ever sent out by Bomber Command during the war. As Bremen was a major port, Coastal Command contributed 102 aircraft. Derek Hodgkinson, a pilot with No. 1 Coastal Operational Training Unit flying Hudsons, wrote an extremely lucid account of this, his last operation. His colleagues were either Coastal Command crews with little experience of night operations and not prepared for a high-altitude mission, instructors resting after a tour, or advanced OTU students without combat experience. The sixty-odd pilots were assembled in the ops room at Thornaby and all they knew was that they had been brought in to assist in a raid against Germany. The briefing was short and to the point. The station CO explained that it had been decided to incorporate temporarily the land-based element of Coastal Command in the raid. The aiming point would be the U-boat pens in the heart of Bremen. Hodgkinson:

'The route to and from the port was displayed on a wall map stretching the width of the stage in front of us. We were to join the main bomber stream 60 miles due east of Yarmouth.'

Their ETA at Yarmouth would have to be adhered to precisely if they were to achieve maximum concentration of force. The route thereafter was direct. The island of Texel, which lay just to the north of their track, was thought to be heavily defended, but its guns only accurate up to 12,000 feet, which posed little threat to the main stream at

25,000 feet. The briefing team then told them the 'good news': the Hudson, with its maximum bomb load of four 250-lb bombs, would be lucky to stay above 10,000 feet.

> 'Our unease at our limited performance at altitude increased when the forecaster took the floor: the weather was expected to be clear en route and over the target. There would be a full moon, and after 23.00 hrs the northern sky would be illuminated by the Aurora Borealis. In other words, we would stand out like sore thumbs in what was clearly going to be one of those "night fighter benefit" raids.'[28]

That night 15 obsolescent bombers were despatched on the raid from 15 AFU Leconfield, where Laurie Simpson was a pupil: '*The night of the 25th was the 1,000-Bomber raid on Bremen*', he wrote. '*We sent 15 from here and lost one crew, mostly Aussies. Graeme and I were on marshalling duties so were up all night until 7 a.m.*' Alan Castle:

> 'The raid on Bremen on 25 June was also ruined, this time by 10/10 cloud over the target. There was a considerable amount of Flak, so I dropped our load of 810 x 4 lb incendiaries in the centre of the Flak area. I believe that recce photos later showed some substantial damage.'

Laurie Simpson: '*Saw the boys go out and come back. Bad weather spoilt the trip and most of them didn't see the target but could see the glare through the clouds.*' Cloud cover had again prevented accurate navigation, and the casualty rate of 5 per cent, or 49 aircraft, was nearing the prohibitive. Derek Hodgkinson was shot down on this operation and spent the remainder of the war in captivity.

The 25 June was the last of the great 1,000 raids of 1942. By 1945 it would become quite common for raid quotas to easily exceed 1,000. Eighty-five civilians were killed on the Bremen raid and 497 injured. The journey to Bremen exceeded the Cologne and Essen distances by 200 miles, which may account for the loss of 23 ex-operational OTU bombers from 91 Group.

On 26 July Arthur Schrock's 'United Pacific Crew', recovered from the Cologne raid, went to Hamburg in a Wellington with 12 Squadron. They were employed to 'saturate the defences': this meant that they were in the first wave which it was hoped would force the enemy to expend as much ammunition as possible before the Main Force arrived. Weaving and jinking madly, they tried to avoid the highly accurate anti-aircraft fire. Suddenly, just after passing the Kiel Canal, there was a double explosion: the left wing was hit and the whole aircraft blown on its side. Inside there was considerable damage: the intercom system was down and the wireless antenna gone. Carter was practically scalped by shrapnel, Taylor was hit in a 'vulnerable spot' and unable to sit down for the rest of the trip, and Weyle's wristwatch had been blown off without even a bruise to the skin.

They dropped 8,000 feet down to 6,000 feet over the target, having lost the port engine. Gradually shedding height they approached the English coast and a flashing beacon came on in response to their SOS. A green light winked at them to land. Weyle:

> 'Petrol was leaking out of the main tank on the port side. The gun turret's hydraulic system had been shot up and the intercom, wireless and hydraulic systems were unserviceable. As if this weren't trouble enough, I discovered the landing wheels wouldn't come down. I tried the emergency pump but it wouldn't work. Neither would the emergency unit. Now I knew we were in for it. I fired the Verey cartridge for the emergency squad to bring out the ambulance

and fire apparatus at the field. Then I ordered the crew to crash-landing positions. The navigator gave me the thumbs-up sign and strapped me to my seat.'[29]

At 200 feet they were making a long, low approach. Weyle opened the bomb bay doors for maximum drag and dropped the air speed as low as possible: 'There had been no practice for a landing like this. It was something I had to be good at first time.'[30] He cut the switches, pressed the fire extinguisher buttons and braced himself. There was a *crump* and a *thud* as a rock hurtled through the bomb panel, hitting him on the knee and smashing against the dashboard. Clouds of smoke rolled up as the Wellington skidded to a stop with a quick jerk.

All were alive, but Schrock had narrowly escaped death. They again found three bullet holes in the w/op's seat next day. He had been sitting in the second pilot's position for most of the trip and missed the Reaper's scythe by sheer good luck. Nevertheless, the 'United Pacific Crew' was awarded the best photoflash photograph for the Group on that trip. Schrock had not used his skills as an air gunner, but on the last op to Berlin of his first tour he was given a 'probable' when two 'Bf 109s' attacked and shot up the aircraft. Weyle was in England for 14 months before returning to the United States where he transferred to the US Navy. He flew over 29 operations with the RAF, the most exciting of which, they all agreed, was the Cologne trip. The 'United Pacific Crew' survived its tour of 30 ops together.

Pathfinders

The Pathfinder Force (PFF) was created in August 1942. The man appointed to lead it was a slight and unimposing New Zealander named Donald Bennett. But appearances can be deceptive and in Bennett's case they certainly were, for Don Bennett was an experienced navigator and an exceptionally intelligent and gifted leader. Bennett's aim in 1942 was to use all the means possible to improve the accuracy and efficiency of RAF bombing, which had been so flagrantly besmirched by 'The Butt Report' of the previous August. It was the Air Ministry's Deputy Director of Bombing Operations, Group Captain Sidney O. Bufton, who first suggested a specialist 'Target Finding Force'. Sid Bufton was an experienced officer who had previously commanded two operational bomber squadrons. Although now a staff officer, he was still in contact with his former colleagues on ops, and realised that the new navigational equipment was not enough to solve Bomber Command's problems. Because of the high casualty rate, an elite unit would have to be formed and its crews be given specialist training before they could become operational.

Harris wanted nothing to do with the idea of a Pathfinder Force at first: he did not see any point in taking the best aircrew away from normal front line squadrons and dumping them in isolated 'elite' units. He reasoned that their former good influence would be subdued and their departure may lead to a loss of morale. But, after resisting Bufton's proposals for some time, despite the lobbying of his Group Commanders, Harris was eventually forced to give way when Bufton wrote to him. Under orders from 'the powers that be', he agreed to support Bennett – an officer he knew and whose ability he respected – all the way. He even introduced a special badge to be issued when Pathfinder crews were suitably experienced.

Sid Bufton recommended selecting six existing units and then honing their target-finding skills, and Portal stressed the need for 'an effective degree of illumination... in the right place and only in the right place.'[31]

There was something of a personality clash between Harris and Bufton. Bufton was rather disingenuous about 'area bombing': it was not a concept that he wholeheartedly supported, but he envisioned that Harris's 'area bombing' policy would inevitably lead to more precise attacks – which was what Bufton was pushing for. He realised that, in order to do this, a Pathfinder Force was necessary.

Bufton met Harris outside the Air Ministry, writing a carefully worded letter to him shortly afterwards, setting out his precise arguments for the allocation of six squadrons to the force plus one *good* crew from each of the other forty squadrons. All these were to be based close together. Simultaneously he wrote to a number of his colleagues setting out his ideas and asking them to complete a questionnaire. Thus he had gone surreptitiously behind Harris's back.

Harris replied to Bufton on 17 April stating that he was open minded about a PFF but 'not yet convinced'. Bufton responded by letter on 8 May arguing that recent RAF raids showed how difficult target finding was, and contesting Harris's worries about an elitist force, pointing out the need for more of a team approach. He also argued for additional operationally experienced COs rather than flightless 'staff-wallahs'.[32]

Harris coined the term 'Pathfinders' himself, the eventual arrangement being for the transfer of two squadrons from each of the existing Groups to the new PFF.

Don Bennett immediately began investigating all the existing and up-and-coming navigational equipment, and soon realised that devices such as the nascent H2S and Oboe would stand the force in good stead, but there were teething problems. Philip Hedgeland was a boffin involved in the early development of H2S,[33] a ground-scanning radar developed originally from the AI interception sets used for detecting airborne targets. By accident it was discovered that AI received quite distinctive responses when pointed at the ground – particularly buildings and water. According to Hedgeland:

'It was a bit of a struggle at first… I think the biggest difficulty really was understanding the nature of the responses from a given target. There was a tendency for people at first to think "Oh well, you will get a reflection from a town which will resemble what you got on the map". In fact that doesn't work out – particularly if the town's in a valley or has some undulation running through it: the nature of the buildings give different responses. And the understanding of what goes to make up a radar response on the tube from an H2S system was still being investigated after the war.'[34]

Pathfinder training was intense – crews were expected to do a first tour of 60 operations. Often, particularly during the early stages, this was undertaken after an initial tour of 30 ops with a conventional squadron. By the time he finished his tour, a Pathfinder could expect to have clocked up 90 trips – if he survived. Initially, five squadrons were transferred to the PFF: 7, 35, 83, 156 and 109.

As mentioned, Bill Higgs had served on 610 Squadron in Fighter Command as a flight mechanic during the Battle of Britain. This was an elite squadron of well-heeled University pilots. However, Higgs retrained as a flight engineer when the call went out for engineers for the four-engined bombers and he was posted in 1942 to 35 Squadron, a similarly elite unit which became one of the most famous of the Pathfinder formations:

'Normally on crews the discipline's good, but on the Pathfinders it was a different kettle of fish. Squadron Leader Peveler, who I was flying with, was a real disciplinarian, and before we got to know it there were no Christian names. As soon as the PFF started, particularly before it got H2S, navigation was a problem unless you could pick up some landmarks because, if you're navigating, with these winds, you've got to fly with them unless somebody can check your readings. You've got a three hour flight. You've worked out a 10 mile deviation – whichever way it is – every hour, so after three hours you're going to be 30 miles away from where you want to be.

'We went to Nuremberg and we didn't have our normal navigator on board. This one's name was Watt. *Watt!* And we were snoozin' along and I asked, "When the bloody hell are we going to get to Nuremberg, boy?" And he said, "I think we've passed it." Bob Norman [the pilot] told him, "We'll turn round again and go back: and this time you'd better find it. We'll hit it." So we went back, and Bob said, "When are we going to hit Nuremberg?" Watt said, "Is that the one we're going for? I think we've passed it again."

'So Bob said to me, "How are we doing for fuel?" I said, "If we go in the direction we're going, we should get out, but [if we] turn back and go round again, I don't think we'll do it." So Bob said, "OK, we'll go home!"'[35]

Higgs was unnerved by the inefficiency of the British anti-aircraft fire (AA) or 'Ack-Ack'. One night over Leeds while flying in a Halifax during an AA exercise with local searchlight batteries, Higgs and his crew saw some searchlights. It appears to have been pre-arranged that the aircraft make visual contact with the ground defences:

'We said, "Oh, they're the ones, possibly." So we'd turn and fly over to them, and just as we got near, they'd move. And there'd be three of them, never more than three.[36] Rather than 'corkscrewing' all over the sky, the crew were flying straight and level. [We're] chasing the blinkin' searchlights around, trying to get into them for them, and occasionally they'd get us. But as soon as they got us we did a bank and turn, and they lost us again.

'One night coming back – and this is a typical incidence of the wind being wrong coming back – we were heading for Flamborough Head, and instead of Flamborough Head as we were going along I looked out and said to the navigator, "Buddy, there's land ahead, but I can't see it in the book." So we went along. He said, "I think it's Spurn Head!" That hooked me. Spurn Head was a beautiful thing to pick up – you couldn't mistake it. The nav said, "OK, OK, we'll turn and go up the coast, so you'd better inform Bert the pilot." So [I] said, "Turn round, Bert – we'll go up the coast!" Bert said, "OK, we'll hit Flamborough Head and turn inland."

'By then we were getting a bit closer, and we started to turn. We had what they called "Colours of the Day", fired from a Verey Pistol, and we'd been told there'd be convoys going up and down the coast, and where they would be. We had to fire the "Colours" at them. Anyway as we came back, all of a sudden a searchlight came groping at us, and all round Ack-Ack started up, and guns were shooting at us. I said to Bert, "I'm gonna fire the "Colours of the Day".

'"*Bing!*" Up it goes. "*Bing!*" – flares all over the sky. Crikey, those gunners… "*Rap! Rap! Rap!*" But little Bert, he banked her hard down; we went down and they lost us! And we went up the coast. Their shooting missed! Appalling! It was abysmal! It was terrible! I don't think [they] ever shot *anything* down.'[37]

Flight Engineer Dick Raymond was posted to 83 Squadron, 8 Pathfinder Group at Wyton in Huntingdonshire in October 1943, straight from a Heavy Conversion Unit. Before joining he was required to sit a navigation course at RAF Upwood. When they first arrived he and the rest of the crew were interviewed by a 25 year-old group captain named Donald Searby[38] who, at 25, already had a DSO and a DFC. Sizing Raymond up Searby asked, 'How old are you, my man?' Dick replied, '19, sir.' 'Good God!' exclaimed Searby. Dick flew 13 missions with the PFF before being shot down.[39]

Deryck Lambert[40] was at Graveley over a year after Bill Higgs. Lambert recalled that PFF training was '…quite a lengthy process: latterly it was more intense [than normal bomber training] and you tended to be judged more, particularly so that you wouldn't get away with anything.' He was shot down on 11 September 1944 on the first operation of his first tour. ND782 'G-George' left Graveley at 16.40 hrs. 'It was extremely frustrating,' he recalled, 'infuriating in fact. It was the first thing you thought of when you landed on the ground: "Why did it happen to be me on my first op?" We were on a daylight raid to Gelsenkirchen, in the Ruhr Valley.' That day, a mixed force of 379 Lancasters, Halifaxes and Mosquitoes attacked the German synthetic oil plants at Castrop-Rauxel, Kamen and Gelsenkirchen. Both Castrop and Kamen were bombed accurately in good visibility, but at Gelsenkirchen there was a protective smokescreen. Bombing was hindered and accurate observation of results was prevented.

'It was a beautiful evening,' Lambert continued, 'and we had a good flight. The first thing that happened was we ran into some pretty accurate anti-aircraft fire. We were leading the formation, and of course we got most of the stick – and it was pretty hectic! I think it was around 18.30 hrs', he said. 'We got hit by Flak several times over – more or less to the extent that you thought to yourself, "Something's gonna happen here. I will have to get out…"' Only Lambert and the mid-upper gunner,[41] Flt/Sgt Rhodes, survived:

'It was very strange because I was talking to the pilot [F/O G. Bradburn], standing up in the aircraft… when suddenly there was a terrific bang and a flash – and smoke all over the place. He just said "We'll have to get out" or words to that effect. He didn't get out, I don't quite know why. But I suspect that he was hit, or his 'chute went – something of that sort. I have no idea. I didn't have my 'chute on at the time; I had to scramble back to find it.

'I was three quarters the way along the aircraft. I had to cross the spar, and no sooner had I got hold of it than the whole aircraft sort of bucked and fell, and I thought, "*This is it* – no way out of this lot!" I didn't mean to do something dramatic like jumping without a parachute. Anyway, luckily I found the 'chute, and got as far away from where I was as possible. I thought "What do I do now?" The aircraft was all over the place – landscape upside down and everything. It was a mess, a complete mess. It was on fire. It was all over the shop – the pilot was obviously still controlling it to some extent.

'I reckon the first few movements had been a sudden dive, I suppose due to [which] the obstructive fires were placated. The aircraft righted itself and I just dropped. And I thought "Now is obviously the time to do something". So I made my way towards the rear exit, which I knew was the only one available. When I got there, there were crew members standing, looking out down at the ground, which seemed to me to be a bit of a stupid thing to be doing at that time – looking out of the door, of the open door – so they'd opened the door. It didn't look like anybody was going to jump, so I just took one running dive and went straight through it. Height was about 16,000.

'I'm not sure what happened to the kite. I did see an aircraft in a shallow dive, smoking and burning heavily, going down. I knew it crash-landed at a place called Gladbach [in the Ruhr Valley]. The parachute opened straight away because I had my hand round it. And, because I had my hand on it, I put it on upside down. So I put my hand on the wrong side of it. I eventually found the release handle, and when I jumped, I just jumped straight out of the aircraft.

'I landed in a tree and the parachute hooked in the top of it. I was in the middle of this pine forest and I thought "How the hell do I get out of here?" And from the stars I could see which way was north: I could pick up my way from the navigator's point of view: it helped being a navigator. But on the ground, of course, it's a bit different to being in the air.'[42]

Two PFF Lancasters were lost on the Gelsenkirchen raid.

The Flying Brooms
One of the most famous of the twin-engined PFF teams was the renowned 'Flying Brooms' –Sqn/Ldr Ivor Broom (pilot) and Flt/Lt Tommy Broom[43] (navigator), who both ended the war with the DFC and two bars. The pair flew Mosquito XIVs with 571, 128 and 163 Squadrons, with crossed broomsticks painted on the nose. 'The Flying Brooms' story remained hidden from the public for years and only came to attention after a former schoolmaster, Tom Evans, who had occasionally chatted with Tommy at his local pub, published an account 'of a Portishead lad who brought honour to his village.'[44] Earlier in the war, Tommy Broom had been a navigator on Blenheims and, at one point on a raid to Cologne, crash-landed after one engine collided with a Belgian pylon. With the help of the 'Comet Line' he made his way back via the Pyrenees and two months later was in England.

Tommy teamed up with Ivor Broom in May 1944, joining 571 Squadron at RAF Oakington in 8 Group, part of Don Bennett's Light Night Striking Force. As their teamwork developed, they become noted for their high degree of accuracy at both high and low level. One of the team's notable attacks was against the Dortmund-Ems Canal in Germany, regarded as 'always the bane of Bomber Command efforts'.[45]

The canal played a crucial part in the Nazi economy, linking the heart of the industrial Ruhr at Essen and Dortmund to the river Ems which ran north to its estuary at Emden. The canal was 168 miles long, 16 feet deep and 125 feet wide and millions of tons of industrial goods travelled along it every year. One of its other, more important, aspects was that after the RAF attacks on the north German U-boat centres, such as those at Bremen and Wilhelmshaven, the Germans outsourced their work, prefabricating huge components at centres located miles inland, away from the ports, one such important facility being at Dortmund. The components were then shipped down the canal and assembled in bomb-proof underground sheds on the coast. By attacking the canal and its linking Mitteland Canal, the RAF hoped U-boat production would be delayed for many months. 617 Squadron had attempted to breach the canal with 'Tallboy' bombs in September 1943 but largely failed.

The Brooms' attack took place early on 10 August 1944 when the RAF was still attacking the French Atlantic coast pens. It was Ivor's 71st op and Tommy's 51st. They were to drop a mine rather than a conventional bomb. There was an almost dead straight stretch of the waterway near Rheine, enabling them to make a timed run from a PFF-marked point five miles away. A crucial difficulty, however, was that to make a precise bomb run, they would have to fly as low as 200 feet (many crews flew lower) and a cloudless, moonlit night was thus required. That night, however, cloud was at medium height, becoming patchy closer to the earth. The Brooms were undeterred. Just before they released the mine the Mosquito flew over a barge whose skipper gaped in terror at the sight of the British lunatics skimming above him. The Brooms made a low, flat, straight and level final 90-second flight, along 3 miles of the canal, before depositing their mine with 'inch-perfect accuracy'.[46] For this Ivor was awarded a second DFC and Tommy his first.

The other remarkable mission flown by the Brooms occurred on New Year's Day 1945, and if ever an operation promised to be the antonym of its title then this was it. 'Operation Boring' came in the wake of the great German counter-offensive on the Western Front (later somewhat flippantly referred to by the Allies as 'The Battle of the

Bulge'), which had pushed through the forests of the Ardennes from 16 December 1944. The Allies needed to sever the enemy fuel supply lines from southern Germany. One of the weak points in the German supply chain was the rail tunnels in regions such as the Eifel Mountains and the hills of the Ardennes. If the tunnels could be blocked, the supply chain would be broken. So, that night, 17 PFF Mosquitoes set out to bomb the tunnels in the Eifel, all carrying 4,000-lb 'cookies' with 10-second delayed fuses.

As anyone who has studied bomber operations knows, precise navigation is crucial to the success of an 'op' and, apparently, Thomas John Broom was an extremely accurate navigator. The tunnels were near Kaiserslautern, the link between Saarbrücken and Mannheim, and Broom ensured they arrived there with time to spare. The only certain way to put a 4,000-lb cookie in a railway tunnel is to skip-bomb it – attacking from zero feet and literally throwing the bomb into the entrance, release having to be effected split seconds before pulling away.

Approaching from the German side, with signals and telegraph poles flying past, they approached the tunnel at 50 feet, just as a freight train was about to enter it. Ivor pushed the 'tit' and the bomb bounced into the entrance, as steam and smoke poured back out. The Mosquito zoomed up two hundred feet and banked away as the cookie blew the earth below to smithereens. Thirteen other tunnels were attacked like this in 'Operation Boring'; one Mosquito crashed on take-off. Both the Brooms were awarded bars to their DFCs. How far these attacks affected the German advance can be gauged by the bitter comments of German *General der Panzertruppe* Hasso von Manteuffel, Commander of Fifth Panzer Army, made after the war on the failure of the campaign:

> 'It was not until the 26th [December] that the rest of the reserves were given to me – and they could not be moved. They were at a standstill for lack of petrol – stranded over a stretch of a hundred miles – just when they were needed.'[47]

Operations such as these illustrate how effective the Mosquito could be. It could carry the same bomb load as a B-17, it required only a quarter of the crew (and consequently casualties) of a Lancaster, and it could fly further than any four-engined bomber and faster than any German fighter except the Me 262 jet. One thus has to question whether it would have been better for Harris to replace all his heavy bombers with the type.

Some pilots seemed to have charmed lives. Pathfinder Force aviators often clocked up over 150 trips before retiring, Guy Gibson flying 176 operations before he was killed. A number of the better squadrons, such as those led by Gibson, owed much of their worth to sound leadership and solid training, rather than ability.

Mark Wells concluded:

> 'Bomber Command was never reluctant to comment on the quality of the men appointed to send [its crews] into battle. In general terms their thoughts regarding leadership, both at the time and now, indicate that they best followed men who showed courage, competence and compassion. The optimum may have been to have unit commanders with equally dynamic portions of all three characteristics, but as long as no single quality was totally lacking, for the most part, men were prepared to get on with their missions.'[48]

Cheshire trained his crews relentlessly. He demonstrated all three of Wells's leadership criteria in abundance. The success of his policy of leading from the front by force of character is evident in the reputations of the three squadrons with which he was mainly involved: 35, 76 and 617.

Crack Squadrons

A number of squadrons were harder hit by the bombing campaign and endured greater losses than others. Among these were 35, 76, 78, 101, 102, 115, 158, 460 and 467 Squadrons. There appears to be a difference of opinion as to which unit suffered most. Some say it was 158, but Alan Castle felt it was his own unit – 101 Squadron. This was mainly because 101, as the only 'Airborne Cigar' squadron, had to fly on every raid and was spread evenly throughout the bomber stream. The German night fighters, Castle supposed, could home in on their transmissions.[49] It would not be without justification to assume that a squadron with high losses would either have been the best, because of its willingness to continue flying despite dangers, or the worst, because loss of aircraft indicated poor piloting. In reality it seems the hardest hit units were those in the thick of things.

No. 460 (Australian) Squadron had been based at Breighton since January 1942 when it transferred to 1 Group, beginning operations on 13 March. Over 55,000 aircrew were killed in Bomber Command in the Second World War. Four thousand of these were Australians,[50] 1,018 coming from 460 Squadron. 460's record during three-and-a-half years of operations was astonishing. With a total of 24,856 tons, the squadron dropped more bombs per tonnage than any other RAF squadron. In 368 different attacks it flew 6,264 individual sorties at a cost of 30,856 operational hours. The formation 'suffered higher casualties than any other unit of the Australian Army, Navy or Air Force in World War Two.'[51]

As Laurie Simpson recorded in his 1942 diary, '*September 19th: Breighton after a long trip. So this is 460, the squadron that is off ops for three weeks to rebuild its strength, the squadron that has been almost wiped out, and the squadron which is one of the cracks in Bomber Command. In compensation, the whole squadron is converting to Halifaxes.*'

460 Squadron had indeed been 'almost wiped out'. By mid-1942 its maximum operational strength was 18 Wellingtons, sending off from 8 to 10 aircraft on each operation. When the 'Wimpys' were finally withdrawn in September 1942, 460 had the highest percentage losses of all the Wellington squadrons in Bomber Command: 22 aircraft were shot down in five months alone. 460 Squadron was formed at Molesworth, Huntingdonshire from 458 Squadron on 15 November 1941 as a bomber squadron equipped with Wellingtons. It was the third Australian bomber squadron but, of the other two, in February 1942 458 had relocated to the Middle East and, in April, the third Australian unit, 455, had transferred to Coastal Command. Originally part of 8 Group it moved and transferred to Breighton, Yorkshire, and No. 1 Group early in January 1942 and began operations on 12/13 March. In September 1942 the squadron 'stood down' to re-equip with Halifaxes. It was the only Australian squadron in 1 Group in 1942.

76 was also 'one of the cracks in Bomber Command'. It was formed during the First World War as a Home Defence unit, but disbanded in 1919. In 1937, on re-forming, it was based at RAF Finningley and equipped with Vickers Wellesleys. With the outbreak of war it re-formed as a Group training unit with Hampdens and Avro Ansons, but soon became a bombing unit, and was the second RAF squadron to be equipped with the Halifax bomber, moving from West Raynham to Linton-on-Ouse after a temporary disbandment. Henry Coverley, a Halifax pilot, recalled: 'Linton was a beautiful place – one of the pre-war bases. You had a room to yourself with a berth, and a WAAF would come and knock on the door and say: "Can I get you a cup of tea, sir?"[52] And they'd say,

"Everything's OK for today because there's no ops tonight, so I've left your best blue out, and I've run a bath for you", that sort of thing.' F.J. McGovern remembered Linton as 'a sleepy little village' where the local people probably only saw two or three strangers a month prior to the war. Then they were 'suddenly swamped by an army in RAF blue', but the locals did not treat the bomber boys with disdain: 'we were simply a matter-of-fact, everyday part of village life',[53] he recalled. It should be stressed that this was happening all over Yorkshire and the other counties on the English east coast at that time, with the villages of England's largest county most certainly becoming swamped with air force blue.

The Canadians were also based at Linton and wanted to take over the station when 6 Group was formed in January 1943. Coverley: 'Well, the Canadians wanted Linton for themselves, so 76 and 78 were moved right out to make room for them. I'd only done 27 ops I think, on my first tour, and we went along to instructing at Holme-on-Spalding-Moor, but it was absolute chaos – complete chaos. When we went down to Holme it was huts: very primitive – from luxury to absolute horror!'

Laurie Simpson was assigned to Holme on 20 September 1942, just hours after being posted to 460 Squadron. The crew went to convert to Halifaxes and he found there '*a good lot of blokes*'.

'Personally, I don't believe there could ever be another station like Linton-on-Ouse,' Henry Coverley commented, 'with squadrons like 76 and 78,[54] and Air Commodore Whitley as CO. When I was down there I remember Whitley turning up with white overalls on. He'd pull his moustache, and he'd go up to some sergeant, never a senior officer, and say, "I wonder… do you think I might come with you tonight?" And he did. No other squadron would have allowed it: quite inappropriate! In the end he got shot down, and walked back home into Spain and got back! In fact his wife didn't even know he'd gone down that night – she thought he was working late. But he was an extraordinary man, the example he set,[55] and with Cheshire and Tait there, flying with each other, you'd go anywhere. They went for all the nastiest trips themselves; didn't pick out the easy ones.' Coverley added: 'Looking back, it was an extraordinary bunch of characters; we were in our early 20s or late teens. The Americans would burst into tears when one of their mates got shot down, but we just used to say, "Sailor's got the chop has he? That's hard luck; he shouldn't have joined if he couldn't take a joke. Let's have a pint." And had we not adopted that attitude we'd never have been able to get through it.'

Bill Higgs on 35 Squadron recalled typical pre-operational activity: 'Depending upon the time of take-off we would have a flying supper, then make our way to the crew rooms, put on whatever gear we required and be taken to our aircraft, either by lorries or coach. Much joking took place on this short ride, especially amongst the newer crews.'

Ivor Turley recalled his pre-op fears: 'As I sat in the crew bus I realised it was daylight. Take-off was at 10.30 hrs. It was now 09.15 hrs. How long ago it seemed that I had woken up: so much had happened. My mind was numb – I was afraid again. The briefing, the excitement, the handing in of all identity in case we were shot down. I thought: what if I do get the chop? I looked at others in the bus. Had they the same thoughts? The crew bus moved and then stopped. "C-Charlie" was the call: that was us. Mac, Tom, Joe and I gathered our kit and jumped out. The crew bus moved on, leaving us standing on the grass.'

Bill Higgs commented that all the time on ops one's chances of survival were diminishing: 'I remember, so often, as we crossed the English coastline, thinking, "I wonder if I will see you again." This was not a question of nerves. It was a known fact, when I was operating in 1941-42, that we had to complete 30 operations and were losing about 5 per cent on each one.'

Collision course

Flight engineer 'Sandy' Rowe recalled one hair-raising incident that occurred after take-off from Elsham Wolds: 'We started to climb, circling over North Lincolnshire. Douglas, the pilot, was trying to maintain maximum rate of climb, to gain as much altitude as possible. I had been logging engine and fuel readings and then had a look out. Dead ahead was a pair of red and green wing tip navigation lights – red on the starboard, green on the port! Another aircraft was coming towards us! Douglas put the nose down and the bomber scraped over the top of us, its fuselage only feet away.'

Arthur Cole had a similar close call over Germany. Normally crews were briefed to do a dog-leg up to the target, then away on a different course. On this occasion the brief was to fly in and then return on only a 5 degree course alteration:

> 'We went into the target and did a steep turn after bombing to get back on this very narrow change of course, and met a Lancaster coming in. I looked up after my after-bombing check and saw this aircraft nose-to-nose, wing tip-to-wing tip. I could see the starlight faintly glinting on its canopy. I felt my hair turn white with shock, but realised after a while that the inevitable hadn't happened. There was a long silence and I said, "*Christ*, that was a near thing! How the hell did you miss him?" Skipper said, "Well I pulled the nose up." I said, "Nothing much happened then?" whereupon he pulled the stick back again and the aircraft leapt in the air.
>
> 'I realised afterwards what had happened and added, "It's a good job the other chap hadn't done the same thing, then?" We had bombed and were flying light!'

The 'Corkscrew'

'Corkscrewing', a standard evasive tactic on operations, was extremely violent, the 'G' forces created being immense. Men and equipment could be thrown around like corks in a barrel. Despite this, some experienced *Luftwaffe* pilots were able to follow the aircraft through the manoeuvre. Squadron Leader Les Holes had occasion to use the manoeuvre after being diverted to a secondary target over the Ruhr:

> 'There was a loud "*bang*" from under the port wing. Over the intercom came Cisco's[56] calm, matter-of-fact voice: "We're predicted, skip."[57]
>
> 'I immediately took evasive action known as "corkscrewing". This starts with diving and turning the aircraft, then reversing the effect by climbing and turning in the opposite direction: the object being to offer a target which is changing altitude, direction and air speed. In our case, this worked and there were no more nasty bangs.'

Graham Korner:

> 'When you do fighter affiliation you have to do what they call a "corkscrew", which is quite a complicated thing. You dive so much one way and then so much the other and then you come up another way. But they reckoned it used to work. The trouble is you can't move with the centrifugal force: you're held in. If you're sitting in the rear turret and trying to keep the guns on target, with the mask pulling off your face, then you're pulled down by the centrifugal force. Trying to fire whilst you're doing that is very hard work – hopeless in fact. So, if the aircraft hurtles down into a dive, then goes around, you're stuck in that position. You'll be very lucky to get out.'

'A DEADLY SERIOUS AND DANGEROUS GAME' 131

The 'Corkscrew' evasive manoeuvre as employed by RAF bombers to shake off an attacking night fighter

On detecting an enemy fighter, the bomber entered a steep diving turn to port or starboard into the direction of the attack (to port in this example), at an angle of bank 45 degrees, **(1)** This enabled the bomber to build up speed quickly, and make visual sighting from the fighter difficult since it placed the bomber beneath its level. After a descent through about 1,000 feet, the bomber reached a speed of around 300 mph. Then maintaining its turn to port, it pulled up and climbed **(2)** for 4 seconds. It then rolled to starboard, and turned in that direction and continued climbing **(3)** for 4 seconds, gaining 200 feet in altitude, during which its speed fell to about 255 mph. The bomber then rolled into a climbing turn to starboard and speed continued to fall to about 250 mph. If the enemy fighter was still behind, there was a good chance it might overshoot the bomber. At the top of the climb the nose was pushed down again **(4)**, and after a descent of 1,000 feet the turn was reversed **(5)**. The bomber continued its descent through a further 1,000 feet **(6)**. It then repeated the procedure from **(2)** if the fighter remained a threat. As a tactical evasive manoeuvre, the corkscrew had three outstanding features: first it gave a good chance of throwing off a night fighter; secondly, even if it did not throw off the night fighter, the latter was left with a difficult target with almost continual and changing height and deflection with fully alert rear gunners; and thirdly, since the manoeuvre could be flown along a mean heading and height, it combined the maximum possible evasion with minimum deviation from the bomber's intended track and altitude.

Ronald Farren: 'As the navigator, I sat facing the engines, and the bomb-aimer, wireless operator and myself had no safety harness. One became so used to grabbing hold of a strut for support during "corkscrews" that even when the aircraft banked you automatically braced yourself. If we were destined to crash-land we three and the mid-upper gunner scrambled back down to the rear and braced ourselves against the bomb bay bulkhead.'

Alec March recalled that when new pilots joined his squadron, they could provoke merciless rib-pulling. 'How do I get rid of a searchlight when picked up?' was a common query. March's pilot once answered with a straight face: 'That's simple: fly in a tight anti-clockwise circle, then the beam will follow you and unscrew itself. Beam extinguished – end of problem!'

Wounded in the air

One 207 Squadron wireless operator flying on ops was wounded during a near collision with a night fighter but survived to tell the tale. Harry 'Sparky' Sparks was a w/ag based at Langar, Nottinghamshire on 20 October 1943, when his squadron went to attack Leipzig. He recalled:

> 'I had a feeling that something was going to happen. You do get these feelings. I was sat right on top of the "cookie": if it went up I'd go for a Burton – all you'd get is a lot of coloured lights going up in a smoking great circle. It was exactly ten past nine at night and very dark. The pilot, the navigator and the mid-upper gunner were all on their second tour – Ken was a first class pilot; he'd already got the DFC. As we came in I was right below the astrodome: I could stand up on my seat and see all that was on the port, and all that was on the starboard, right down to the mid-upper turret.
>
> 'I knew it was ten past nine because that's when the r/t call came through. All the bases in 5 Group sent a message through at that time, on a particular wavelength, so you knew when it was due. It was altered every day. I stood up on my seat, waiting for the message to arrive.
>
> 'We were starting our run in. It was very dark, but I could see searchlights, and thin Flak curling up from cloud below. All of a sudden this tracer came from an aircraft way back, and something came straight over the top of us, just like a great shadow. This happened in points of a second. He must have dropped his load and an incendiary had come right through our aircraft. At the same time a night fighter came down and attacked us.'

This was probably what was termed a 'cat's eye' night fighter – one that was shadowing the Lancaster, observing its condensation trails[58] from above. It would dive straight down to attack from about 30,000 feet:

> 'So he swooped down, fired at the aircraft above us, hit it, burned it, swung round, and in that second suddenly found he was on top of us. He must have been fairly experienced because he flew straight down and seemed to draw another attack position without even thinking.
>
> 'His nose came round and, as he opened up, there were great lances of fire at our side, he was that close. Then he veered off because he was too near – we could almost have shook hands with him. It was all very fast, but he swung away to avoid being blown up with us!
>
> 'I was hit. It came through the fuselage and hit me low, down through the top of my legs, and lifted me up and smashed me right across the soft edge of the structure. I fell down onto the floor, ending up underneath the navigator's table which was only a short distance away. Afterwards I pulled myself up, because everything below my waist was in a hell of a pain.

Because it was dark I didn't know how it had happened, or really where I was. I'd got field dressings stuffed in the hollows between the ribs at the side of the aircraft. So I grabbed one of them, ripped it open, and smacked it underneath my leg. Then I screwed it up tight right into my groin, like a tourniquet, to stop it bleeding if it was the femoral artery.

'Lying on the rest bed I flicked on the intercom. "Ho Jimmy" (that's the mid-upper gunner); "Ho Dev" (that's the rear gunner). No replies from either of them, not a sound. But I could hear the navigator just in front of the pilot: they couldn't hear me because the intercom had gone u/s. The pilot needed to talk because the bomb-aimer was ready to let go of the bombs. It was a hell of a position to be in. I slid down under the navigator's table, pulled myself across, and in the dark ran my fingers all the way along where any wires would be, to see if there were any breaks. I could hear the pilot yelling out, "*Can you hear me? Can you hear me?*" He had no communication. So I grabbed down and felt where the wiring was breaking up, and, in the dark, got hold of it, and turned it all round. I was lying on the navigator's feet – he was a very big man.

'All of a sudden I heard the skipper's voice coming over, "OK": I'd made contact! So I said, "Hallo there," and he replied, "How are you?" and I said, "I've been hit." I dragged myself onto the seat and saw that Jimmy, the mid-upper gunner had also been hit. Then I realised we'd been hit by cannon fire. With his great yellow suit on, Jimmy was hanging out of the turret in the open with his head and helmet dangling down. All the perspex had gone and he was just hanging there in the fuselage. The cannon shell had come through the perspex. Because his head nearly touched the metal of the turret, the shell had come right across the top of it, in the centre, and punched a groove along his skull. It split his helmet wide open, perfectly, as though with a knife. Then he passed out.

'We didn't contact Les, the rear gunner, until later. His oxygen tube had been severed, so, at 19,000 feet, he just passed out, and never "came to" until we got back over the Channel – he should have been dead. He woke up, by all accounts, all "googoowoowoo"[59] with nobody to talk to.

'I yelled out to Bill, the bomb-aimer, "Have you jettisoned, yet?" He said "No!" So I said, "For Christ sake do so, we're on fire." I could see down the fuselage: all the plates, right down to the very end, were aflame, and the entire floor over the bomb load was crinkling red hot. Before you could say "Jack Robinson" he'd called out "Bombs gone".

'As the heat started to dissipate, I wrapped a big 6-foot knitted scarf around my leg to keep it warm. Jock the engineer came back. He really was a big man, an Australian, about 6 ft 2 ins, but he never took his 'chute. He was such a big boy there was only that much room between him and the side of the fuselage. When he came along he trod on my legs in the pitch dark and I shouted some very, very rude words at him. Then he went back and then returned, saying "His incendiaries must have hit our incendiaries when he dropped his load, and went off."

'There was no sound from Jimmy; his legs were just dangling there. Jock couldn't get him out of the turret because the legs were above him as he went by. So he went down to see the rear gunner, and opened the turret door, but he was completely out of it. I'd lost quite a bit of blood by then and was beginning to go white; I was all over the place mentally and physically, but still held on.

'We landed but didn't have any ailerons! That means you don't get the same degree of control, so it's very dodgy coming in, not knowing how badly your undercart, wheels or anything else have been hit. They were all waiting for us when we arrived because we were late coming back. It was around 2 a.m. They dragged me out and put me in the blood wagon with old Jimmy – he didn't know what was going on, and the rear gunner – he'd no idea, he'd been unconscious the whole time.

'I got hit at ten past nine at night and got into hospital about half past five the following morning. I must have travelled across every railway crossing in Lincolnshire that night, with the blood wagon bouncing over all of them! A fellow came with us, but I was too far gone to notice much. He handed me a packet of 20 cigarettes, and I'd smoked the whole lot before we even got to the hospital!'

After recovering from his injury suffered during the attack, Sparks had returned to Langar. Despite wishing to go back on ops to finish his tour he was declared 'Unfit Air' and 'Unfit Ground'. By that time, casualties were getting 'very, very high'. He recalled:

'They put me on "Burials". And amongst those that had got washed up on the shore on The Wash they found members of the squadron. These were brought back and buried in Cambridge. I asked if they ever came back, could I ever go along [to see any picked up] as there weren't a lot of us.'

Being wounded in the air could indeed be an ordeal. If one has experienced how debilitating an ordinary motorcycle accident can be – one moment one is relatively fit, seconds later the body has been rendered semi-useless, damaged forever – this can be only a pale reflection of the effect of molten anti-aircraft shrapnel or 20 mm cannon shells at 20,000 feet in 250 mph winds. Alan Castle, the 101 Squadron navigator, remembered forever the words of his bomb-aimer during a raid on Stuttgart in September 1944. Castle's aircraft was to pass a few miles north of Strasbourg and this the crew assumed to be weakly defended since it was a French city. They were a few miles south of the intended track – nearer the town than intended:

'I had just given the pilot a revised course to fly when our Lancaster went into a dive and, over the intercom, I heard "*I'm bleeding to death*". At first I thought it was the pilot saying this, so I tried to pick up my parachute off the floor, but it might as well have been a ton weight because I could not lift it, due to the effect of the ["G" forces].'

In fact, the pilot was unharmed, but in the nose area the bomb-aimer, Gordon Smart, an Irishman from Dublin, was seriously wounded. The engineer subsequently found a large hole in the nose. He tended to Smart, who had been hit by a shell splinter, as best he could, but Castle thought they should turn for home in order to get help as soon as possible. A consensus was formed and they agreed to abandon the target and divert to Karlsruhe, only 20 miles away. However, as the ground was obscured over Karlsruhe, they bombed blind. A few hours later they arrived back at Ludford Magna after an uneventful flight. Castle recalled:

'On landing it was established that our bomb-aimer was dead and that his injury was far worse than we had at first thought. We realised that he had probably died within ten minutes of our being hit. The hole in the nose had been caused by a single burst of predicted Flak, probably from the northern outskirts of Strasbourg.'

Forever after that, whenever Alan Castle heard Strasbourg mentioned on the media, he recalled the incident and the last words of Gordon Smart. 'Since he was an Irishman [i.e. a 'neutral'], he needn't have been with us,' Castle reflected, 'and he might have been alive today.'

The Beguiling Press

Newspaper coverage of Bomber Command operations was often misleading and sometimes completely untrue. Alec March recalled three incidences of spurious press reports that could have been extremely misleading.

First: It was often written that the station CO would attend operational briefings. 'My period on squadron lasted eight months,' March remembered, 'not once did the CO put in an appearance; furthermore, I never saw him around the station.'

Second: March's crew bombed Schweinfurt ball bearings works twice. On the second trip they were in the first phase of the stream. They found the works '…as black as the night in which we were flying', he said. 'It only came to life when our bombs hit the deck.' The next day they were surprised to hear on the radio and read in the papers '…that *fires were still burning*" when the RAF arrived; these from a raid by the Americans earlier in the day. This was quite untrue!'

Third: When, after one dangerous raid, March's pilot was awarded an immediate DFC, the event was reported in the local newspaper: 'It was reported that he had kicked open the bomb bay doors which had jammed', March recalled. 'Of course, to do so was a physical impossibility and the doors were still working… The story was purely fictional as no one from "the rag" had interviewed him.' The event evoked some humour: 'He got teased by us wanting to measure the length of his legs', recalled Alec.

Broadcast from Berlin

In May 1943 the BBC formed its War Reporting Unit (WRU). A 'Warcasts Room' was established in Broadcasting House and, for the first time, war reporting was taken to a new level. From then on correspondents were treated with respect and even awe. One member of the WRU who was to report on the work of Bomber Command was a veteran 30 year-old correspondent from Richmond-on-Thames, named Richard Dimbleby. He pipped his rival, Wynford Vaughan-Thomas, to the post for being the first to report on a bombing raid to Germany by nearly eight months.[60] Dimbleby later commented: 'It was suddenly recognised that the most important person in the operation was the man at the front line.'[61]

On 17 January 1943, 187 aircraft – 170 Lancasters and 17 Halifaxes – took off to bomb the German capital and it was this mission that Dimbleby was assigned to cover for the BBC. Up until that time, the RAF had been quite contemptuous of journalism. For his part, Dimbleby was afraid of flying: he was frequently sick, and bomber operations were '…statistically the most dangerous form of battle that the Second World War could offer.'[62] In fact as the war developed, correspondents had the opportunity of a soft option. They could, if they preferred, sit on the home field and simply wait for aircrew to return from an 'op' and then interview them. Dimbleby, however, discounted this: he insisted on completing 21 operations by the end of the war.

Laurie Simpson was on leave in Dorset at the time but his navigator, Alistair Kennedy, went as a replacement that night with another crew and was nearly killed. Laurie wrote: '*My navigator, Al, went to Berlin the second night and on return just made the coast and baled out. The W/Op, Dudley Corfe, was killed when his 'chute didn't open.*'

Kennedy had gone in UV-K 'King' as a replacement navigator with an all-NCO crew piloted by Sgt Wendon. They had taken off at 17.00 hrs from Breighton, ran out of fuel on the way back, and had to bale out over Flamborough Head at 5,000 feet. Corfe was an academic with a Bachelor of Arts and Laws. His radio leads became entangled in his parachute lines and he 'Roman Candled'.[63] All the rest of the crew survived.

That night, 24 aircraft were lost, including the Lancaster from 460 Squadron, four from 9 Squadron, 4 from 12 Squadron, 2 from 76, and 3 from 1654 Heavy Conversion Unit. Dimbleby's report of the raid was gripping and he received a telegram later from the Air Ministry, applauding his work. Before that, he had a sense of guilt at not being able to take an active part in the war, and felt he had to 'share the danger', once remarking:

> 'I only wish that there were some way of telling people in Britain what all these men are doing for them. You hear people discussing the losses and being so complacent about them.... they've no idea what it means for men to take the strain of these operations day after day and night after night, always wondering what's going to happen to them.'[64]

But, for Dimbleby, the raid nearly ended in tragedy. The aircraft in which he was flying took off at 16.35 hrs. Its pilot was none other than Guy Gibson, who was on his 25th op with 106 Squadron. The reporter, who had the concessionary rank of major, saw 40 Lancasters climbing around them and remarked that they looked 'suspended in air'. He saw German Flak for the first time as they crossed the enemy coast, but the noise from the engines drowned out almost all sound. Gibson sat up front in the cockpit, flying the Lancaster 'as if it were a toy', Dimbleby recorded. The reporter was obliged to switch on his oxygen supply as they gained height. He soon felt tired and fell asleep. The next thing he knew he was sprawled on the fuselage floor and McGregor, the flight engineer, was bending over him, adjusting his oxygen mask. He had accidentally constricted his oxygen pipe and lost consciousness. Gibson quipped: 'Want to watch that. Keep it under your arm and away from the parachute harness.'

As the target approached, in the ensuing silence, someone hissed: '*Berlin!*' Since the RAF was following the same route as the previous night's raid, the *Luftwaffe* was able to locate the incursion easily. This was only the second attack on Berlin in 14 months and although the weather had improved from the previous night, the PFF was unable to mark the city centre. For a second time in two nights, bombing fell on the city's southern areas.[65] The Lancaster of the CO of 460 Squadron, 'Chad' Martin, was attacked six times that night by Bf 110, Ju 88 and Fw 190 fighters in the vicinity of Berlin. Sgt Johnny Osborne, who was later to fly as Laurie Simpson's rear gunner, was the 'tail end Charlie'.[66]

The operation lasted for 30 minutes but, by the time it was over, Dimbleby was exhausted. Guy Gibson, he said, was 'as cold as ice' over a target – he had to be. For the first run the Flak closed right in around them: 'It seemed impossible we could miss it', Dimbleby recorded. 'One burst lifted us in the air as though a giant hand had pushed up the belly of the machine.' There was a large explosion behind them: 'All over the German capital these great incandescent flower beds [of incendiaries] spread themselves.' It was so cold that the film in the unit cine-camera jammed. Once more they began to swing round in the darkness for another run. 'I am going to bomb', Gibson said.

These were the most dangerous moments of the raid. A shell burst a few feet away and the reporter slipped and banged his head against the instrument panel. The bombardier began his destructive incantation: 'Right... right... steady... left a little... left a little... steady... *steady*. Hold it – bomb gone!' At that point Dimbleby remarked that he wondered if the 'Hitler gang' were cowering in the shelters below: 'This shimmering mass of flares and bombs and gun flashes was their stronghold... great exultation!' Despite this, hardly any important damage was done that night and not a single building was destroyed or even seriously harmed. There were only eight civilian fatalities.

As the Lancaster pulled twisting and turning into the blackness, Dimbleby's fear jolted through him like an electric shock: he vomited over the fuselage floor, missing the bombardier by inches. When they arrived back at Syerston they had to wait for 80 minutes in a 'stacking system' to land. At 01.50 hrs, when they touched down, Dimbleby said, 'I wouldn't have missed it for the world.' It was the first time a war correspondent had been on a raid over Germany and he returned straight to London to broadcast the story.[67]

Flying with the Canadians
Englishman Frank Dennis was posted to 419 (Moose) Squadron, No. 6 (RCAF) Group[68] in August 1944:

> 'I was like most Bomber Command aircrew, young and full of enthusiasm and in spite of knowing of the heavy losses still being suffered, it was difficult to imagine, at that age, your own life coming to a sudden end. However it didn't take long to realise that the war in the air over Germany was not to be taken lightly and was a deadly serious and dangerous game.'[69]

His first tour with 419 Squadron went along without much trouble until 1 November 1944 when his aircraft suffered a prolonged attack by an Fw 190. This did considerable damage to the airframe, and injured all the crew except the pilot and himself. 'We carried on flying with a scratch crew until Ron [the skipper] became ill with blocked sinuses and was sent back to Canada for a rest period.' His next crew, with pilot F/O McNeill, arrived on squadron without a 'flighty' but after a few training flights, they were ready for ops. At this point, March 1945, there was a period of inclement weather and the whole Command was stood down for the weekend until Sunday evening. 'It was an unusual occurrence, so I caught the train home on Friday evening', Dennis recalled. The rest of the crew decided to stay on station, and would either see a film or visit the local. When he returned to Middleton on Sunday evening someone in the mess shouted, 'Shame about your crew, Frank.' Dennis was bewildered: 'What have they been up to, then?' 'They went missing on ops Saturday night!'

It was true, and the circumstances were unusual. On Saturday, 7 March a 'special op' had been arranged. The Russians, advancing towards the Polish/German border, had become bogged down in fighting at Dessau and could not get around, or through, the German lines. It had been agreed at the Yalta Conference in February 1945 that if they needed assistance on the ground, the Russians could request it. At Dessau the Soviets had wanted the Allied air forces to blast a way through, and RAF squadrons, despite appalling weather, were ordered to get as many crews into the air that night as possible. Lancaster KB797 was lost, five of the crew being killed and two becoming POWs. Dennis recalled:

> 'I was crewless again, but not unduly surprised for, after all, they were a new crew on their first op with a spare F/E. They were also about four hours over enemy territory, in awful weather: their chances of returning safely were minimal.'

Robert Vollum was a w/ag with 420 (Snowy Owl) Squadron, RCAF, on the earlier marks of Wellington, based at Skipton-on-Swale in the late summer of 1942. He had a regular crew, three of which – the pilot, navigator and bomb-aimer – were Canadians, whilst the rear gunner was Australian. Vollum was the only Englishman. They made one 'dodgy' trip to Cologne when the port engine packed up as they were crossing the French coast. The aircraft turned back, making it back in time for a forced-landing at Bradwell Bay, Essex, just as the fuel ran out on the other motor. Soon after that, in October 1942, the squadron relocated to Middleton St. George near Darlington. Vollum then flew two ops to Turin that November.

On 1 January 1943 No. 1 (RCAF) Group was formed, an all-Canadian Group. After a demanding trip to Lorient the same month, Vollum's crew was broken up and he joined a 'scratch' crew, completing one trip with them in February on the new Wellington Mark X – '*much roomier than the old Hampden*', he wrote. He transferred to 427 (Lion) Squadron, RCAF, at Leeming, Yorkshire in May 1943 to finish his tour. He had flown with ten different pilots on this first tour, and subsequently would fly with another 11 in 158 Squadron on his second.[70]

In his early days with the Canadians, Frank 'Shorty' Dennis had shared a Nissen hut with a crew whose mid-upper gunner had been badly wounded by Flak. Because the boy, who was only 18, had lost much blood, his skipper decided to land at Manston aerodrome. Manston was right on the edge of the east coast in Kent, virtually on the cliff top, and was one of the hardest hit aerodromes of the Battle of Britain. As such it was frequently used as a touch-down point for emergency landings. Immediate medical attention was available and blood transfusions saved the young gunner's life. He recovered rapidly, although his back was badly scarred. 'He was sent back to his squadron,' Dennis recalled, 'to return to ops and was absolutely terrified at the thought of that. We did our best to try and cheer him up, saying such things as, "You've had your packet of trouble, it can't happen to you again. You'll be fine", to the point where he accepted what we said; sadly though, he "got the chop" a few weeks later.'[71]

John Geddes flew as a navigator with 428 (Ghost) Squadron RCAF at Middleton St. George. He met his pilot, a Frenchman named Francois Guillevan from Montreal, at HCU.[72] Geddes felt that one of the two things that contributed to the survival of his crew was Guillevan's pre-war experience in light aircraft. He had flown an aerial taxi service in Montreal before the war with wheels, floats and skis, depending upon the destination. Similar to Ted Boorman's South African skipper, Ron Heiden, Guillevan was a short man and needed blocks on the rudder bars before his feet would reach them. Despite this, the RCAF 'appreciated his experience'. The other contribution to Geddes' crew's endurance, he felt, was his own high standard of navigation training, learnt at the RAF Intensive Training Wing at Torquay.

After the loss of his second crew, Frank Dennis was posted to 427 (Lion) Squadron, RCAF, Leeming[73] where a crew starting its second tour had arrived without an engineer. After settling in, he was checked out by his flight commander:

'Sqn/Ldr Deegan told me I would be flying with a Flt/Lt Schmitt, who I'd be meeting in the mess that night. Schmitt turned out to be quite an interesting character who flew before the war as a bush pilot in North British Columbia and had flown his first tour mainly on Wellingtons of 427 Squadron, then at Croft. Apparently his father was a German immigrant to Canada and his mother a pure bred Indian squaw, which I suppose accounted for his pale brown pallor. He also had two noticeable gold teeth and was known to one and all as "Indian".'

The following day 'Indian' proved himself to be a versatile pilot. The crew flew a cross-country with H2S and undertook visual bombing practice and also – something that caught Dennis unawares – practice stalls.

'I became weightless and ended up on the cabin roof with loose Verey cartridges and a few other bits and pieces. I protested a little and asked him to warn the crew if he intended to do it again. Slyly Indian said, "OK, we'll have another go."'

When they reached 6,000 feet, Schmitt demonstrated how ineffective controls were at stall point: 'Look Shorty, no joy!' Quickly adjusting the ailerons and elevators the aircraft dropped like a stone, but the crew was prepared this time.

Schmitt was very self-confident. Some days later he announced he wanted to practise 'circuits and bumps'. To Dennis this was unexpected: Indian's landings 'greased in' beautifully, but his taxying technique was unusual:

'Whereas most pilots would use the brakes to some extent, Indian only used them to stop, rolling around the perimeter track at about 25 knots with an occasional blip on the throttles to negotiate bends. We had to stop briefly to allow a bowser to move out of the way, at which point the rest of the crew got out.'

This puzzled Dennis but he was soon to find out why. Schmitt announced that at Croft he used to take off in a Wimpy and turn inside the perimeter track at the runway's end. He wanted to do the same in a Lancaster. Dennis dismissed this as impossible, but Schmitt was adamant: '10 degrees of flap will do,' he said, 'and get those wheels up the moment we've lifted off!'

Indian did not manage to turn inside the perimeter track, but did inside the adjacent 'A1' highway. Dennis thought they were 'going in', and the WAAFs in the control tower advised them to '…save aerobatics until you get some altitude', but Indian had another trick up his sleeve: he would fly to Wombleton across the North Yorkshire Moors and 'have a bit of fun'. Wombleton was an HCU and the time-worn Halifax crews there were surprised to find a lunatic in a Lancaster chasing them across the aerodrome like a Spitfire! Indian then performed vertical banks around the control tower until 'a rather elderly officer appeared on the outside veranda shaking his fists at us.' It was time to go: seeing the controller, Indian suddenly cried out 'Christ, I don't know him!'

But Dennis was not to be let off lightly. The next day he received a severe dressing-down from the CO: 'I blame you, Dennis, for this mess', he said. 'Well I wasn't actually flying the aircraft', 'Shorty' replied. 'No,' said the CO, 'but if you had left the aircraft before it took off, as the rest of the crew did, Indian couldn't have flown it either, could he?' Dennis retorted: 'At that point I didn't know what he was going to get up to, sir.'[74]

In May 1943, 427 Squadron was adopted by MGM studios in Hollywood, whose symbol was a lion. All its aircraft were named after MGM stars and crews were awarded a free pass to any cinema showing MGM films. The company also adopted a live lion. Dennis recalled, 'I can remember one or two on the squadron visiting him at Whipsnade Zoo and were well received – no charge for admission etc. Also some of the films shown at the station cinema were sent prior to general release over here.'[75]

Australian Squadrons

As well as 460 Squadron, two other Australian squadrons made their mark in Bomber Command. 467 Squadron was formed on 7 November 1942 as part of No. 5 Group at Scampton, Lincolnshire, originally with RAF personnel, but soon Australians predominated. The squadron moved to Bottesford, Leicestershire that same month and then, a year later, transferred to Waddington in Lincolnshire. It took part in all Bomber Command's major campaigns against Germany.

463 Squadron was formed from 'C' flight of 467 Squadron on arrival at Waddington on 25 November 1943 where, as mentioned earlier, Group Captain David Bonham-Carter was the Station Commander of 467/463 Squadrons from the end of March 1943 until 14 April 1945. Its first CO was Rollo Kingsford-Smith, son of the pioneer Australian aviator, who had already flown five operations as 'C' flight commander. Kingsford-Smith completed another 23 ops as CO of 463 Squadron.

On 24 June 1944, nearly three weeks after D-Day, some miles east of Brest in occupied France, Gestapo officers aboard a train crossing the French countryside were about to arrest six Resistance fighters who were planning to make a hasty exit from the coaches. The Gestapo men closed in, but their attention was drawn by a large, black, brown and green four-engined aircraft flying parallel to them, 70 feet above the ground. The aircraft was '*Whoa Bessie*' a Lancaster from 467 Squadron returning from a raid on an ammunitions dump at Limoges. It was piloted by Bruce Buckham, an Australian flight lieutenant on his 25th op:

> 'I swung "*Whoa Bessie*" 180 degrees, descending down to about 70 feet and coming up behind and slightly to starboard of the train, which was travelling on a stretch on top of the embankment. We were quite close to it. I said to the gunners, "Fire when I tell you – and hit the engine only, not the carriages!" As we came level with the engine I gave the order to "*Fire*".'

The Gestapo men watched in alarm as red and yellow tracer from the aircraft's gun turrets crept across the terrain towards the engine. The train suddenly lurched to a halt as steam and smoke shot out of its boiler and streamed skywards. As the distracted Gestapo men gazed helplessly, the Resistance fighters made their escape. Buckham's crew flew on and attacked an uncharted airfield whilst searchlights and Flak groped towards them in the darkness.

> 'Johnny Muddle, mid-upper, and Eric Giersch, rear gunner, put the searchlights out and shot up the gun emplacements as we flew around then dived down right onto sea level and kept going. Naturally we landed well after the rest of the crews. I swore my crew to absolute secrecy and was very adamant about it as we bombers were not supposed to get up to pranks like this.'

A few days later Air Commodore Hesketh, the Waddington Station Base Commander, button-holed Buckham and asked him to explain '*Whoa Bessie's*' late return. His excuse proved inadequate. 'That's strange', said Hesketh. 'There's a report of a heavy bomber shooting up the train and "they" are trying to ascertain who was responsible. Did you see anything unusual, Buck?' 'No', a straight-faced 'Buck' replied. About a week later, Hesketh met Buckham in the mess bar and explained about the Resistance men's escape. The Gestapo were just about to arrest the six escapees but on the appearance of the Lancaster the Frenchmen disappeared into the scrub. The Underground then took them in and hid them. A British submarine picked them up later. 'They are safely back in this country', Hesketh commented. 'Isn't that great, sir?' replied Buckham innocently.[76]

On 23 October 1944, 112 Lancasters from 5 Group were briefed to attack a dyke surrounding the island of Walcheren in western Holland. Bombing time was 11.00 hrs. 463 Squadron was due to lead the attack, but that day visibility over the island was extremely poor whilst at the home airfields it was cold and wet. Take-off was delayed, and did not take place until after 14.00 hrs. Shortly before leaving, 463 was informed that it would be bombing a battery of four large guns near Flushing on Walcheren. This caused some concern as only two days previously a Lancaster from 75 Squadron had been shot down attacking a coastal battery near the town and all its crew had died, despite five baling out. Flying Officer John I. Dack, an Australian, led the 463 Squadron attack, and his flight engineer, bombardier and mid-upper gunner were fellow countrymen. At 14.22 hrs their aircraft, Lancaster JO-P, '*Piratical Pete*', took off at the head of the queue, but there was very low cloud and the squadron did not reach Flushing until 16.00 hrs. Flying at 4,000 feet '*Piratical Pete*' soon became the target for German light Flak, almost immediately bursting into flames. '*Prepare to abandon aircraft!*' Dack yelled, but the aircraft soon became filled with thick, choking, yellow-brown smoke, whilst amidst the flames the bomb-aimer, wireless op and both air gunners lay dead. The navigator, Australian Warrant Officer J.F. Maple, clipped a parachute on Dack and pushed him out but, by doing this, Maple forfeited his own life.

Barely conscious, Dack landed in the cold waters of the Scheldt, smashing his chin on his rough parachute harness whilst, a few seconds later, '*Piratical Pete*' nose-dived into the river 200 yards away in a cloud of spray. Hans Bannick, a German gunner manning a quadruple 20 mm Flak cannon on Walcheren Island and watching the Western Scheldt, caught sight of something bobbing in the water and pointed it out to one of his fellow gunners: it looked like a man's head! Beside the cannon was a rubber dinghy, and ignoring the warning of their NCO, the two men pushed this out into the grey waters of the Scheldt, abandoning their helmets and weapons in the hope that any British soldiers watching would realise they were attempting a rescue. A 463 Squadron report stated:

'Hans and his comrade rowed out against the wind and tide to see if it was indeed a person and, even if it was an Allied airman, to pull him out of the water.'

Dack was unconscious and had been badly injured in the crash. The two Germans lifted him out of the water, into the dinghy and rowed him back to shore. He was then taken, still unconscious, to an hotel: Bannick never saw him again. Flying Officer Dack, his flight engineer and the bomb-aimer all became POWs.[77]

New Zealanders in Bomber Command
There were two New Zealand squadrons in Bomber Command. 75 (New Zealand) Squadron, part of the RAF, was re-formed in 1940 from an original First World War unit, and was the first Commonwealth squadron in the command. In 1942 it was based at Feltwell, Norfolk later relocating to Mildenhall, and then Newmarket, both in Suffolk. Subsequently it moved to Mepal, Cambridgeshire, all the time remaining part of 3 Group. 487 Squadron was formed in August 1942 at Feltwell as part of the Royal New Zealand Air Force (RNZAF), a light day-bomber squadron which re-equipped from its original Venturas to Mosquitoes in August 1943. With these, it took part in the famous raids on the Amiens Prison and also the Gestapo HQ at Aarhus in Denmark in 1944 and the Gestapo HQ in Copenhagen in 1945. Its most famous alumnus was Squadron Leader Leonard Trent VC.

A total of 1,850 New Zealanders died while serving in Bomber Command in the Second World War, operating in many other squadrons apart from the two mentioned above. One can only relate a few representative stories here. An attack on Wuppertal on the night of 29/30 May 1943 was described as the 'outstanding success of the Battle of the Ruhr.'[78] Ironically, the RNZAF suffered one of its worst nights of the entire war on that raid: 21 aircrew were killed in 11 bombers. A Stirling navigator from Christchurch, New Zealand, Alan Boulton, recalled what the 218 Squadron Briefing Officer had told them:

> 'Tonight we're going to Wuppertal... a lot of the people who work in the Krupp steel plants live there. We're going to get them. They're in the war just as much as you and I. They're making shells and we're going to get them.'[79]

Despite the cold-bloodedness of the officer's speech, which shocked many of the listeners, Boulton was not perturbed. That night 75 (New Zealand) Squadron lost four out of 20 Stirlings and 12 New Zealanders were killed. Only seven baled out successfully. Ray Bennett's Stirling, BK776 JN-B, was shot down near Odenspiel, 14 miles north-west of Siegen. It had an eight-man crew, one of whom may have been a second pilot or special operator. There were five New Zealanders on the crew as well as two RAF men and one Canadian. Only three of them baled out successfully. Sgt J.B. Harrison, the RAF flight engineer, survived as did Flight Sergeant Alan Davidson, the bombardier, and Sgt Pat Middleton, the tail gunner, both RNZAF. Bennett, Davidson and Middleton had five more ops to do before the end of the tour. Middleton and Davidson had teamed up at OTU and roped in another Kiwi, Stan Kavanagh, after an earlier friend had ducked out of ops, saying he could no longer cope with it.

After a successful flight out and an early arrival, Stirling BK776 was hit by Flak at 10,000 feet. Harrison shouted, '*I can see petrol pissing out of the tanks!*' The aircraft had started to burn and Bennett advised that he was going to try and dive to extinguish the flames. As the aircraft zoomed down, Middleton shouted '*I'm off!*' and rolled out of the rear turret. Hearing this, Davidson cried '*Hooray!*', gave Bennett his parachute, and went out through the front escape hatch, surprised to see two of his fellow crewmen standing by the exit hole contemplating the prospects. Davidson, abandoning the recommended 10 second count, ticked off 'one' and pulled the ripcord in mid-air. After his 'chute opened, 'B-Bob' blew up in mid-air above him. His fellow crew members, Harrison, Davidson and Middleton, became POWs whilst Bennett and the four others were killed. Of the remaining three 75 Squadron aircraft lost that night, four airmen (including three New Zealanders) survived on Flight Sergeant Carey's Stirling which crashed near Aachen, while all those in the other two aircraft died.

Leonard Trent: 'A Very Bleak Day'

One of the heaviest single squadron losses of the entire war occurred on 3 May 1943. The operation was codenamed 'Ramrod 16', a daylight op by 487 Squadron from 2 Group, which specialised in daylight work, and consequently lay in the shadow of its sister Groups conducting attacks by night. The target was a power station on the northern outskirts of Amsterdam, the intention being to encourage the Dutch workers to resist the German occupying forces.

The Ventura was a development of a pre-war transport aircraft, the Lodestar. A light bomber with an official crew of five, with two Pratt & Whitney Double Wasp engines, it was more high powered than its maritime reconnaissance stablemate, the Hudson, and its dorsal turret was set further forward to give a better arc of fire between the twin tail fins. It also had a ventral gun position under the fuselage with twin .303 machine guns. Although 394 Venturas were delivered to Bomber Command starting in the summer of

1942, the aircraft did not commence operations until November and was active for less than a year. It served with 487 Squadron from September 1942 until September 1943, when it was withdrawn from service. In fact, compared with the Beaufighter and the Mosquito, the Ventura was obsolete.

Although 487 was officially part of the RNZAF, it had many Commonwealth aircrews in it and, at the pre-op briefing, the twelve crews had it strongly impressed upon them that this was an important target. Squadron Leader Trent, a New Zealander and pre-war regular RAF, who had been brought up in Nelson, South Island, and was later described as a 'gallant officer' displaying 'outstanding leadership', had already won the DFC. He told a colleague there and then that, irrespective of the Flak and fighters, he was determined to bomb the factory.

It was a bright afternoon when 12 Lockheed Venturas took off from RAF Methwold just before 17.00 hrs. Under a clear blue sky, with perfect visibility, the formation headed out towards Holland; three squadrons of Spitfires escorted them. They flew at low level over the North Sea, when a series of factors cruelly coalesced to seal their fate. A few hours earlier a Spitfire sweep over Holland had alerted the German defence. Also, by sheer bad luck, that day a number of very experienced German fighter pilots were in attendance at a *Luftwaffe* fighter conference at Schipol airfield, 10 miles from Amsterdam. In addition, one of the Venturas had its escape hatch blown off over the North Sea, and was forced to return. That left fifty-five relatively callow airmen of mixed Commonwealth extraction, flying eleven virtually obsolete light bombers against an experienced German defence on full alert.

As the Venturas crossed the Dutch coast, sixty-nine German fighters were in the air waiting for them. Because the high-level Spitfire escorts had arrived early, they were already low on fuel and began turning back; only the close escorts remained, much faster than the sluggish Venturas, but all had already been picked up by the Germans' *Würzburg* and *Freya* radar.

What followed was butchery. As the attack force crossed the coast, its 2,000 hp Double Wasp engines clawing at the thin air, the maximum speed the crawling aircraft could hope to attain was 300 mph. The majority of the high-level escorts had already peeled off for home when large numbers of Bf 109s and Fw 190s from II./JG 1, based at Woensdrecht, scythed into the dawdling formation. The close-support Spitfires were outnumbered by almost three to one by Bf 109s of JG 1 and 2./JG 27,[80] and the vulnerable, sluggish Venturas, closing up for mutual protection, began to plummet to earth. The first crash-landed north-east of Vijfhuizen at 17.45 hrs., its navigator, New Zealand Pilot Officer M.B. Shapiro, having been wounded severely by cannon shells. By then the Spitfires had all been recalled and, as the formation struggled to continue towards the works target, six of the doomed Venturas fell, one after another, to the guns of some 15-20 Bf 109s. Flight Lieutenant A.V. Duffill's aircraft, although mercilessly raked by German cannon shells, with mind-dogged determination managed to return, sieve-like, to Methwold.

Trent determinedly continued the approach in AJ209 EG-V with three remaining bombers in tow. Heavy Flak now began to envelope them and two more Venturas went down. Two remained. As he made the run-in, Trent fired at point-blank range with his nose guns at a Bf 109 and destroyed it.[81] Then the aircraft flying immediately behind him shook from a direct hit by the burgeoning black Flak and fell away, streaming clouds of oily smoke.[82] Trent continued the bomb run alone, dropped his ordnance, turned away but then, after going into an uncontrollable spin, broke up in mid-air and crashed into a polder at 18.00 hrs.

Trent and his navigator survived, but the wireless operator and air gunner were killed in the crash. Eleven of the twelve bombers had been destroyed and, of the 44 aircrew shot down in these aircraft, 27 died, 12 became POWs and five survived. Of those shot down 13 were RNZAF, and six of these young men, from all over New Zealand, were killed. Not one was over 30.

An entry in the 487 Squadron war diary for 3 May stated: '*It's a very bleak day... everyone is dazed by the news.*'

At the end of May, 487 Squadron left Bomber Command to join the Second Tactical Air Force for operations in Normandy and in August converted to the Mosquito. Some time later Leonard H. Trent was awarded the VC for his performance in this action. The citation concluded: '*His cool, unflinching courage and devotion to duty rank with the finest examples of these virtues in the face of overwhelming odds.*' In fact the award was not announced until almost a year after he had been returned to England from Germany in May 1945. Squadron Leader Trent had been a POW for two years, but this was not without excitement: for Len Trent was number 79 on the escape list from *Stalag Luft* III and, on 24 March 1944 when the mass breakout occurred, he was the penultimate man out of the tunnel and lying face down in the snow when discovered by a gibbering sentry. But that was before he got his VC.[83]

Wind-Finders

Initial techniques used by the RAF to bomb Germany at the beginning of the war were not a success. The 'bomber stream' system was developed to enable RAF aircraft to overcome the problems which scattered aircraft were encountering from an increasingly more efficient German defensive system. By pushing a 'stream' of bombers through the line at one point, the RAF hoped to overwhelm *Luftwaffe* defences. However this required an increased amount of co-ordination between aircraft. To facilitate this, 'wind-finders' were employed – experienced navigators who could assess the upper air winds encountered and radio their findings back to the stream. They took up a position ahead of the others. Reports received enabled the remaining aircraft to allow and compensate for a wind speed or direction that could tend to push aircraft off track. Once a navigator had calculated his compensated course using these 'broadcast wind' reports, he had to calculate the ground speed (speed over the ground). He would use this to compute the air speed (speed through the air) – the ground speed less the wind speed, allowing for the effects of height and air temperature. This was done with the 'Dalton hand-held computer'. Freddy Fish, a navigator with 153 Squadron, commented:

'In practice the actual wind would be different from the forecast wind and this would throw all your calculations out. We were then supplied with "broadcast winds" calculated from flight reports and averaged out at base. We then had Gee, from which we had to obtain fixes every six minutes until we were out of Gee range or the Germans jammed it.'[84]

He cited the Nuremberg raid of 30 March 1944 as an example of things going disastrously wrong. Bert Carter, a flight engineer with 44 Squadron, was in an aircraft on a wind-finding mission when it was involved in a serious attack of 'friendly fire':

'The 18th March 1944 started as just a normal day: we saw by the battle order we were flying again that night. With luck we thought this should be our last operation before our leave, which we were looking forward to after a couple of hectic months of operations.

'At the briefing, when Frankfurt was named [as the target], we all felt apprehensive, I know I did. I shrugged off the feeling: we were clobbered there once on the way to Berlin. We were "wind-finding" this night ahead of the Main Force and should be well on the way before we met any enemy aircraft able to climb to our altitude. On the other hand we would be a single blip on the German radar for predicted Flak, which would follow you across the sky, until the Main Force presented a big and better target.'

The journey started off as normal. It was fairly low on cloud and visibility good. At the enemy coast they encountered light Flak, but no fighters. They 'banked and searched' just to make sure.

'After about a couple of hours we picked up a faint bleep on the audible Monica [radar], the signal was so faint that it didn't register on our visual Monica screen. We carried out further bank and search routines but still no aircraft were spotted. We continued towards the target but the audible Monica signal was becoming more pronounced.'

The other aircraft had been with them for around 15 minutes. Rex Bennett, the w/op, reported a blip faintly visible on his screen, and the loud warning note that came over the intercom system indicated it was close. Bennett got a fix on the blip: it was directly below them! Carter:

'I looked out of the cockpit side blister, which enabled me to see down under our starboard wing. I hadn't expected to see anything, but the noise in my ears told me otherwise. Suddenly a four-engined aircraft appeared out of the thinning clouds down under our starboard wing and, at the same moment, it opened fire on us from its mid-upper turret. The fire hit our starboard engines and petrol tanks which burst into flames. The aircraft must have had 0.5-inch guns as we were too far away for normal .303 guns to inflict so much damage with one long burst.'

Gunfire ripped into the vulnerable wing spar and the ensuing blazing heat damaged and weakened the wing. It was impossible to see their protagonist through the ensuing flames, but Carter concluded it must have carried a very trigger-happy mid-upper gunner. His aircraft's gunners found that their limited viewing angles made it impossible to return the fire. But they themselves were far too experienced to open fire without checking the other aircraft's letter codes. Carter concluded, 'A lot of ex-aircrew would not be alive today if our gunner had been as trigger-happy as the chap on this Halifax. We had no chance of putting out the fire: if we dived down in the hope that the slipstream would put it out, the starboard wing would have folded up and we would have been unable to bale out.'

The pilot, Frank Phillips, gave the order to jump. Carter had to get out fast as he was blocking the exit for the rest. His oxygen mask was still on as he rolled out into the darkness. The mask's straps stretched, the hose broke, but the straps pulled his mask back on his face, with such a force that the microphone broke his nose. He then pulled his ripcord:

'I could see aircraft above me before the 'chute opened. At the same time the other Halifax's gunner opened up again. This burst must have raked the bomb load, and on to the tail. When our Halifax blew up, it blew the pilot, navigator, and w/op out of the aircraft. I had baled out at about 20,000 feet and just hung there.'

He concluded later that it was probably an aircraft also on a wind-finding mission for another group. Their Lancaster had a higher service ceiling than the Halifax, but later 'Hallies' had 0.5-inch guns in the upper turret. Since they were flying on an original flight plan, any German four-engined aircraft (and there were not very many of those) would have been unable to attain their height and overtake them.[85]

'Sandy' Rowe, a flight engineer on a 103 Squadron Lancaster flying on a mission to Italy in 1943, also experienced 'friendly fire' in the air:

'We reached the Alps which were covered in snow, visibility downward being excellent against the white background. I had my head in the side window blister looking down and spoke to our bomb-aimer Jock: "There is a Lancaster beneath us, slightly in front and drifting from starboard to port. Keep your eye on it." "Right," said Jock, "I can see it…" Then: "*Hell*! It's firing at us!" I could see tracer shooting up and around our aircraft.

'Our pilot, Douglas, having noted our chat, immediately swung to starboard out of harm's way. An inspection of our aircraft later in the day revealed that we had not received a single hit. At debriefing the incident was mentioned. Group Captain Dicken, the Station Commander, was listening and said: "You've got front guns, haven't you? You should have let him have it. You don't want to stand for that kind of nonsense!" I could hardly believe my ears! The CO actually suggesting that we should have a duel with another Lanc over the Alps.'[86]

Inclement Weather

A raid on Hamburg, the last of a series of five to the city, long before the 'firestorm' raids of August 1943, was the worst operation w/op Harry Sparks ever undertook, and it was caused by ice not fire. Sparks's crew was not due to fly that night. Ken, his usual pilot, was unavailable. But a friend of Ken's, who was a first-class flyer and had trained with Ken before the war, had a brand new crew and asked Harry if he would act as a replacement on it. 'You make your own mind up, old son,' Ken advised him, 'you do or you don't.' 'Sparky' decided to go for it.

'I often stood up because my seat was directly underneath the astrodome. And, as we were going along I saw way over these little [white] snakes. I thought, "Hang on a minute, this is night time". It wasn't the sort of white light you see up in a cloud. It was an eerie light I could see, above and below. I could see these things coming and I thought, "Wait a minute, they're Jerries!" Instead of these aircraft turning round, they went straight on past. In a short space of time I saw the reason why: stretching down to the deck, right the way above us, way above us, was this great black sheet. It was a storm – a monster! It was a huge great front. We went into it, and the next minute everything went haywire; the aircraft was all over the place. Gradually we began to drop, and drop, and drop. We were freezing up, and the instruments were going all over the place.

'The aircraft was being struck by lightning continuously. [As a w/op] I'd got a long trailing aerial with about 13 or 14 beads along it – lightning loves it; and that was smoking – you daren't reach down and touch it. I did once – never did it again! We carried on like that, and gradually dropped and dropped and dropped and dropped. The instruments were playing silly buggers. Near me, down [the fuselage] by the main door, there was the hanging compass – the astro compass – and that was going all over the place.'

Sparks went to the back of the aircraft and got his parachute ready. They were down low and it was still misty and he could see the tops of the trees through the mist. It was difficult to make out what shapes were: 'Am I going to be able to do it?' he asked himself, because it was not safe to bale out at less than 2,000 feet. Then the pilot jettisoned the bombs. They had been icing up, and the build-up was so heavy it took the aircraft right down low. As 12,000 lbs of bombs jettisoned, the aircraft immediately began to lift in the air. But it was not pressure waves from the bombs exploding down below that then caused the aeroplane to soar upwards: '*Boomph!* There was this terrific bang,' Harry recalled, 'and it was the bang of the ice coming off the aircraft in great lumps, and we rose up just like an elevator!'

Eventually they turned round and came back on a home bearing, but could not estimate how far off course they were. It may have been over 100 miles. Later they found out there had been a clear patch of sky over Hamburg: one or two of the force found this and bombed through it, but many did not. 'We didn't,' Harry said, 'so it was rather a futile raid, but not completely futile.'[87]

The Witten Raid

Eric Clayton, who was a pilot in 218 Squadron in 1944/45, believes that Ivor Turley's account of a rear gunner's experiences of a raid, quoted in this book, describes his first operation, which was a daylight attack on Witten in the Ruhr on 12 December 1944 by 150 Lancasters from 3 Group, including aircraft from 15, 149 and 195 Squadrons. Turley's crew was a 'sprog' crew which, Clayton thought, made the exceptionally detailed account 'even more remarkable'.

218 led the bomber stream with, at its head, AH-E 'Easy', the whole squadron flying in formation in vics of three. This was not normal practice, but some weeks earlier the unit had received a new CO straight from Training Command who insisted that they fly into and out of the target in close formation. He was immediately nicknamed 'the Vicar' by the entire squadron, his popularity not helped by the fact that he had only to go on one op a month.

It was a 'G-H'[88] raid to the Ruhrstahl steelworks at Witten, a railway town on the river Ruhr, and it was the first air raid the town had experienced. As such there should have been very little opposition. Miles Tripp, who was the bomb-aimer in AH-P, was guiding the aircraft in as its Gee set had gone u/s. Immediately to port was Flight Lieutenant Harry Warwick, (whose tail gunner was Sgt Ivor Turley), flying in tight formation with two other Lancasters. Tripp's skipper, Australian Flying Officer George Klenner, nicknamed 'Dig', suddenly asked what Tripp made of some specks ahead. '*I climbed into the front turret*', said Tripp. '*In the blue distance it seemed that a cluster of midges was darting erratically up and down; then one fell, leaving a thin spiral of smoke in its wake.*' It was a dogfight. The formation's fighter cover was attempting to cope with an attacking force of 160 German fighters, divided into groups of 40 each. What no one could understand was how the Germans had known about the raid – Witten was a 'virgin target'.

As they began the run in, huge fractious black puffs of very accurate Flak began to explode all around them and Warwick's aircraft started to stream clouds of oily smoke from its port inner engine. The *Luftwaffe* then piled in, ignoring its own Flak and Clayton recalled that the rear of his group was attacked by a swarm of seven hornet-like Bf 109s: 218 Squadron lost seven Lancasters in less than 30 seconds. 'They just made the one attack and then disappeared,' Clayton recalled, 'possibly due to fuel shortage, leaving about seven of our aircraft peeling off with smoke trailing and in trouble.'[89] Rowland Mason, a tail gunner with 218 Squadron, later recalled that the fighters '…got stuck into the middle of our stream.'⁹⁰ Tripp was about to press 'P-Peter's' bomb release when he saw a Messerschmitt closing in on a Lancaster, which turned slowly to port. The tail gunner fired wide and the Bf 109 returned fire:

> 'Suddenly the rear gunner rotated his turret and fell out backwards; for two or three seconds he rolled over and over in the sky, then he pulled his ripcord and a white parachute blossomed. A burst of flame came from one of the Lancaster's engines, its nose went down, and it spiralled away out of control.'⁹¹

'P-Peter' veered away from the target after bombing, seven other Lancasters weaving with it in precarious formation. Both Klenner's wingmen had gone down. Twelve 218 Squadron aircraft went out but only ten returned. Warwick's 'C-Charlie' was escorted part of the way back, but ditched in the sea, and 'Q-Queenie' blew up in mid-air. To top that, the squadron's flying control officer electrocuted himself at base and an 'erk' on a bicycle was run over by a petrol bowser. Seven other aircraft were lost on the Witten raid: one from 15 Squadron, two from 149, and four from 195.

George Toombs recalled that 460 Squadron made a similar daylight raid in 1944 where it was at the head of the bomber stream. The trio of Hughie Edwards, Air Commodore A.M. 'Hoppy' Wray, and the Squadron CO, their tails painted with bright yellow bands,⁹² led the attack in an immaculate formation. As the Flak started, bombers began peeling off like fighters to avoid it. The three leaders were unshaken and maintained formation as the rest of the squadron gradually re-formed behind them.

• • •

The elements that made up life on operations were a huge accumulation of opposing factors: danger, stress, personal failings, degree of confidence, individual emotions, superstitions, fate, unit pride, quality of leadership, daily routines, media attention, national character, staff rivalry, a resilient enemy, and the weather. All these contributed to the success or failure of operations.

The year 1942 witnessed the first of the large-scale RAF raids against the German homeland. The initial three 'Thousand-Bomber raids' were a hallmark of what was to come. Four-engined heavy bombers lumbered their way into service and, consequently, twin-engined crews had to be phased onto them at Heavy Conversion Units such as Lindholme. Despite the presence of inspiring leaders, such as David Holford, the attitude of many of the staff at these units left much to be desired and ill-feeling was common amongst the trainees. Airmen made stupid mistakes leading to accidents and unwanted fatalities even before operational squadrons were reached. Although crews from mixed nationalities were now working together as effective teams, some missions, such as the third Thousand-Bomber raid, appeared to be suicidal. Fear of what to expect on operations led some to seek 'Dutch Courage' whilst others tried to quell their fears with the comforts of superstitious aids. The Australians developed a reputation for wild behaviour, competition arose to be billeted at plush pre-war bases, whilst the press began to reveal to the public the truth about night-flying, but still harboured deception, and bomber crews faced the consequences of German retribution.

The year 1943 saw the beginnings of the RAF's planned wholesale assault on Germany. The Battle of the Ruhr was mounted against targets such as Dusseldorf, Cologne, Duisburg and Essen and, in addition to Hamburg and the attack on Peenemünde, the year also saw the early stages of the Battle of Berlin. Whilst all this was happening, the Germans were developing a much more efficacious defence system which led the RAF to evolve an improved and effectual method of approach to the target. Bomber Command began to introduce increasingly complicated systems of navigation to enable the 'bomber stream' to be better co-ordinated but, although bombing methods were becoming relatively sophisticated, still crews misidentified their compatriots, leading to fatal errors over the Reich.

CHAPTER NINE

'OUR BOMB DROPPED RIGHT IN THE MIDDLE'

First Tour

DURING the opening months of 1943 Commonwealth crews began to appear on operational stations in ever increasing numbers. The first few months of the year were fairly quiet for Bomber Command, allowing crews to correct a number of flaws in the new equipment and to adjust to the increasing number of Lancasters and Mosquitoes being phased in.[1] Up until the beginning of 1943 organised target-marking did not exist and navigation was fairly elementary, often crews having to rely on 'dead reckoning'. As the Pathfinder Force became established, however, more sophisticated systems of navigation such as Oboe and H2S became more prevalent, and in the first few months Bomber Command's strategic targets were being altered continually, resulting in a fractured campaign. In January a series of Oboe-supported raids against the Krupp munitions works at Essen appeared to be developing into a major battle: 460 Squadron conducted four operations against the Krupp works during the first two weeks of the month. Although the Casablanca Conference, which commenced on 21 January, specified Harris's 'primary object' to be 'the progressive destruction, and dislocation of the German military, industrial and economic system', at the top of its priority targets were the German submarine construction yards. Consequently, after six or so such attacks on Essen, following a resurgence of U-boat activity in the North Atlantic, another priority replaced this. The Air Ministry ordered High Wycombe to change the thrust of its attacks to the French Atlantic coast U-boat pens, and the battle that appeared to be developing was now redirected. A decree was issued to Harris on 14 January by the War Cabinet to this effect. When these raids failed to produce the desired results, the Command switched to attacking U-boat yards in northern Germany.

But this too failed to be the hoped-for knock-out blow, as the Germans simply withdrew their factories inland to manufacture the boats. At around the same time, there was increased activity on the North African front, obliging Churchill to make a show of attacking the Italian homeland. This followed on from a number of operations against northern Italy in the autumn of 1942. These were intended mainly to draw Axis fighter support away from the Mediterranean area, in preparation for Operation Torch, the invasion of North Africa on 8 November 1942.

Flight Lieutenant Simpson recorded the following diary entries during the course of his crew's first tour of operations:

6-10 January 1943

'For 11 days four crews were standing by for a daylight attack, but weather was unfavourable all the time. On the 8th we were briefed for a minelaying stooge up into the Baltic near Königsberg, probably the longest trip to be undertaken by Bomber Command yet. 1,800 miles, 2,154 galls of petrol and 3 vegetables (mines). A ten hour job. Weather clamped down and it was scrubbed.² Last night we were briefed again for Essen! Were the boys laughing!! Anyway after a frantic scramble we got out to "Y-Yorker" on time but had engine trouble. Then had an overload of fuel, IFF went u/s so they scrubbed it for us. The other boys went but Pete Jackson had to turn back. Graeme got there and told me again that it was very hot. I was very disappointed at not getting off, but I realise now that being scrubbed from a trip on Essen is nothing to be disappointed about. Three more days and I go on leave. Whizzo!!'

Commentary

On 8/9 January three Lancasters were lost on 'gardening' (minelaying) sorties, one from 9 Squadron at Wickenby and two from 44 Squadron at Waddington, both stations around 50 miles south of Breighton, which may have had better weather at the time. The raids against the Krupp works at Essen over an eleven night period at the beginning of January 1943 marked the start of a long anticipated intensive assault on the German heartland. Five crews were lost in two attacks from the 3rd to the 5th, including the one manning H.G. Brooks's 460 Squadron Lancaster to a night fighter on the 5th. All Brooks's crew was killed, including six Australians. These were followed by four more raids on Essen from 9/10 to 13/14 January, ten bombers being lost. Despite this, only two of the Krupp foundries were damaged, and these were soon repaired. Fifty Lancasters attacking were subjected to heavy fire from a ring of Krupp-manufactured 88 mm and other anti-aircraft guns around the Ruhr, operated by 100,000 Flak troops. Three Lancasters were lost with one survivor; 28 German civilians were killed and 127 buildings destroyed.³

11 January 1943

'Ops tonight! Briefed again for Essen. Bomber Command must have a one-track mind. Took off 4.30, arrived back about 9.45, but as Gordon Grant had pranged on the runway, we were diverted to Holme. Back at Breighton and to bed by about 2.30 a.m. Good, fairly quiet trip. Hot enough near target. 9/10 cloud but searchlights illuminated through them. Flak heavy and accurate. Attacked by fighter, probably a Ju 88,⁴ on way to target, but took evasive action and lost him both times we saw him. PFF aiming point flare failed to ignite. Fred and Wal were both sick on way back tonight. All stood up to it well.'

12-13 January

'Dragged out again at 10 o'clock for stand-by. Briefed at 4 p.m. for – Essen. This is past a joke. Owing to bad weather we took off at 3 and bombed at 6.20 on the morning of the 13th. Arrived back at 8.10 a.m. Shot at by Flak and S/L [searchlights] at Antwerp and Gladbach on way in. Flak heavy and very accurate. No fighters seen or heard. Had to stay at 20,000 feet right to English coast. Felt the 'Flu coming on all day yesterday and by the time I arrived back from Essen, I was very groggy. Went to the Doc after breakfast and was ordered to bed for two days. My leave has been put back a week – once again. And not because I'm sick either. Carried the usual Essen load 1 x 400 and 10 SBCs.⁵ 13,080 gals. fuel. About 860 miles to Ruhr and back. Very disappointed about my leave and I guess Dorothy will be filled with despair. Still everything usually happens for the best.'

Commentary

That night the PFF Mosquitoes arrived late and crews bombed on dead reckoning. This was a small force and there was a wide spread of bombing, although 20 houses were hit in Essen itself and nine civilians killed. The succession of raids against Essen between 7-13 January did not have any great effect and were fairly insignificant compared to the later raids in the spring of 1943.

14-15 January 1943

'Spent in bed; cold improving. Caught up with my letter writing. MO[6] says I will be grounded until my leave so maybe I can get a couple of extra days leave. I'm entitled to them anyway, even if people view it with suspicion. Oh gosh, I hope I can get it. Maybe things are happening for the best anyway. Who knows? Passed my 500 hours flying this week, which includes nearly 50 hours in Lancs (28½ in "Y-Yorker").

Johnny Kearns dropped in to say that the boys have gone to BERLIN tonight! Gosh that's a tough trip and I hope they all make it OK. Five crews including the Wingco and the Sqn/Ldr B Flight. Due back about midnight. This should shake the Heinies to their very foundations, damn them! We are concentrating very much on the tough targets lately. Four times on ESSEN and now BERLIN! Whew!! It only wants HAMBURG now and we'll have covered all the hot spots. It's a lousy night outside. Bad visibility, low 10/10 clouds and dark. Not bad for the trip, though – I hope.'

Commentary

Laurie Simpson's diary entry appears to have been written on the 16th. The next raid on Berlin around this period was on 16/17 January.[7] It was the first attack on the 'Big City' for 14 months. The attack that night has been regarded by some as a failure. Berlin was covered by haze, the more advanced RAF navigation systems were yet to be introduced, half the Berlin Flak personnel were away on a course and the city's air raid sirens performed inadequately. As a result 198 people were killed, including 53 POWs. This raid was the one covered by Richard Dimbleby for the BBC (see Chapter Eight). Only one aircraft, a Lancaster from 61 Squadron, was lost that night.

17-26 January 1943

'Got out of bed and was told to go on leave as soon as possible. Oh boy!! All our chaps returned from Berlin OK. Got three extra days leave as sick leave and proceeded to Bournemouth in quick time. Met Bobby Neilson in Bournemouth. He is now commissioned and in the Pathfinders.'

Commentary

At the beginning of 1943 there was an increasing threat from U-boat attacks in the North Atlantic as German submarines returned to attack the northern convoy routes. The U-boats' second 'happy time' of the war ensued as they reaped a rich harvest. On 21 January 1943 Churchill, Roosevelt and advisors met at Casablanca. A blueprint was drawn up for the strategic decisions that would affect the rest of the war. One of these was to defeat the U-boats in the Atlantic and the securing of lines of communication across it.[8] This led to the 'Casablanca Directive'. As a consequence of this, Harris was ordered to mount a series of raids against the five sites of U-boat pens on the French Atlantic coast. This order was fraught with difficulties, both tactical and political. But, despite the Air Ministry telling the Admiralty that as the ports were few in number, the raids were a waste of resources, the Navy insisted. To his frustration Harris had to obey the War Cabinet's order for an area bombing policy. The protection over the U-boat installations was formed of five metres of solid concrete. The RAF had no means of penetrating such a thickness at that time, so the obvious solution was to bomb the facilities around them. All services, communications and maintenance facilities for the submarines were to be obliterated. Top of the priority list was Lorient and after that St. Nazaire, Brest and La Pallice.

Laurie returned to Breighton on 27 January, following a visit to Dorothy at Bournemouth and meeting old friends at Australia House, London, for Australia Day. Back on the squadron there was news of surprising casualties: '*We were dismayed to learn that Sqn/Ldr Osborn had bought it over Düsseldorf whilst I was on leave. His 46th operational trip.*' Osborn was a tried veteran with a DSO and a DFC. It had been an early evening raid on 23 January and his Lancaster, UV-C 'Charlie', was attacked on its return by a Bf 110. It crash-landed on open land in Friesland. The rear gunner and w/op were killed, but Osborn was repatriated in September 1944.

27-28 January 1943
'*Bruce Oliver on his first trip failed to come back from LORIENT last night. Poor old Bruce. Hard luck.*[9] *Johnny Kearnes the adjutant was stricken with spinal meningitis and died within 24 hours. Gosh, I feel sorry because he was a grand guy.*

'*We were briefed for DUSSELDORF last night and as my rear gunner, Ken, hadn't come back home from leave we took an Aussie called Robinson. Also Al is u/s with a cold, so I had Ron Friend as a navigator. He once taught at Deni I.H.S.*[10] *However a chapter of accidents happened as soon as we got off the deck and we had to abandon the trip. Dumped our 40,000-pounder in the North Sea and landed after dodging around Hull's balloon barrage. The other boys all got back except Bob Brittingham who was on his 15th trip. Tough luck old boy.*[11] *Poor old 460 Squadron, the "bone" seems to be pointing at us once more.*'

Commentary
On the 27th 157 aircraft went out to the U-boat base on the French coast and 153 returned. Three Wellingtons[12] and one Lancaster were lost. For the first time Oboe-equipped Mosquitoes were used with ground-marking target indicators, and the bombing was unusually accurate. Laurie's '*chapter of accidents*' included trouble with the oxygen supply, the intercom system, one of the turrets, and the front escape hatch. The crew also took a Sgt Kine along to replace Freddie King as flight engineer. Flight Sergeant R.A. Brittingham's Lancaster was one of seven aircraft lost. All of his seven-man crew, which included six Australians, was killed. 420 Squadron w/ag Robert Vollum was involved in a hair-raising run on Lorient in January 1943:

'A short time before we reached the target, flying at 19,000 feet, the pilot blacked out. As we spun down about 5,000 feet, I was the only one who reached the cockpit, under a terrific "G" force, by which time the pilot was breathing stentoriously, but was starting to come round. We managed to pull the aircraft out of its dive and got safely back to base.'

The skipper was sent before a London medical board, grounded, and posted home to Canada. Vollum's crew was broken up.

29-30 January 1943
'*High-level formation in co-operation with PFF Mosquito today. Very tiring and not too satisfactory. Rang Dorothy after supper, but she is ill in bed with signs of mumps. Good kid just warded them off over my leave. Must have been sheer will power. We don't seem to have any luck without our own navigator Al. Gosh I feel fed up. Wrote to my mother last night telling all about Dorothy and I, and to Jack*[13] *today.*'

Commentary

The 'flight formation' was at 20,000 feet with a Mosquito and was probably with one of the early Oboe-equipped aircraft. This followed 'beam practice' flying which Laurie had undertaken the previous day to Lindholme and back in an Oxford, which may probably have been linked to the Oboe work.

31 January-5 February 1943

'Briefed for Hamburg, Cologne, Hamburg [again] and Turin.'

Commentary

Breighton aerodrome was a low-lying, bleak, flat and unforgiving site. On the author's visit to the area in 2001, he was struck by just how flat and exposed the site was, having little to defend itself from rain-soaked winds off the North Sea. From 29-31 January 1943 the airfield seems to have suffered a severe rainfall. On the 30th Laurie Simpson recorded: '*Briefed for Hamburg tonight, Bill Charlton as navigator but got bogged before take-off!*' At least two photographs were taken of the crew that afternoon with the equally short Charlton standing in for Kennedy. '*Very disappointed and exceedingly fed up*', Laurie wrote. '*3 others also didn't get off and Shorty Grenfell turned back.*' This was Flight Lieutenant K.H. Grenfell, an Australian, who piloted a mixed RAAF/RAF crew on the night of 29 March but was shot down over Holland by *Unteroffizier* Christian Koltringer of III./NJG 1. Only two of the crew survived. '*Promised to be a hot target,*' Laurie went on, '*– perhaps the hottest of all – and we were to have done a special reconnaissance.*' For two nights running the 'Simpson Kite' was prevented from operating because of poor ground conditions. The initial Hamburg raid was a major operation and the 'special reconnaissance' referred to the first occasion in the war in which H2S, originally intended for use as airborne early warning, was used. This was not successful. A total of 148 aircraft went out, including 135 Lancasters – 91 per cent of the force. In such an environment, H2S was not as effective as hoped. Its usefulness had been discovered after a navigator accidentally pointed the scanner at the ground and began picking up images of buildings and water. It consisted of a tiny transmitter mounted under the fuselage, normally in a streamlined radome. This produced echoes on a cathode ray tube that were sharp enough to distinguish land from water and buildings from open countryside. The magnetron valve that powered it could provide very short radio waves, measured in centimetres – hence the 'centimetric radar'. But it had teething problems: according to historian Norman Longmate: 'Of fifteen major operations using H2S, in the next few months only three were even moderately successful, and only half the sets worked properly.'[14] Unfortunately the image of a town on the H2S screen bore little resemblance to that on a map, and consequently only a skilful operator would be able to use it successfully.

On 30 January eight Lancasters were lost,[15] three of which crashed on landing.

'*Got to Cologne and bombed OK.*' The Cologne operation was another experimental trip using various Pathfinder techniques: both Oboe and H2S were used in conjunction, but the results were 'disappointing'. Aviation historians, Martin Middlebrook and Chris Everitt state: 'The target markers failed to achieve a clear concentration; the bombing was well scattered.'[16] Laurie noted: '*Moderate heavy Flak, plenty of S/L in banks of 20 or 30. Sighted five enemy fighters but lost them. First home to base.*'

The second Hamburg raid was on 3 February. A force of 263 bombers went out. Laurie wrote: '*Took off for Hamburg the second time but port inner motor cut, so tried again and this time made it.*' The engine failed before the aircraft even left the ground – a portent of what was to come. That night there were very icy conditions over the North Sea and many aircraft made early returns.[17] Laurie: '*Over base at 11,000 feet, starboard outer engine lost all power, so we dumped our bomb in the North Sea and I did my first three-engine landing. Had trouble with navigation equipment and rear turret also.*' That night's bombing showed little improvement on that of the 30th. Perhaps Laurie's crew was fortunate because 16 aircraft were shot down by the *Nachtjagd*.

On the 4/5th there was the 'ice cream' trip over the Alps to Turin: '*Last night briefed, to our joy, for Turin but on getting out to our a/c found that the bomb doors wouldn't be fitted in time. So it was cancelled.*' Out of a force of 188 aircraft, only 156 bombed the Italian city, although 'serious and widespread damage' was caused. '*Damn it!*' Laurie continued. '*Felt very fed up and disgusted so went down to the New Inn and got plastered. Had words with the Wingco[18] afterwards but he was very reasonable and we smoothed it out.*' He also got a welcome contact from his teenage friend from hometown Deniliquin, Gertrude MacDonald: '*Received parcel from home and three from Gert, very nice and so welcome.*' Gert later confessed, after Laurie died, that she 'would have married him', but for the competition.

6 February 1943
'*Stand-down from ops: anyway we have no serviceable kites. Lazy day – did one-and-a-half hours Link on new beam method of locating base – rang Dorothy tonight. She sounded very happy over the phone and that makes me happy too. I really feel quite content and not a little happy. So bed early. 8.30.*'

7-8 February 1943
'*Went to Lorient on night of 7th. Our easiest trip to date. At last moment we had to switch to "Z-Zebra" as "Y-Yorker" had a negative earth. Saw the docks beautifully and our bomb dropped right in the middle. Had no trouble and on way out, as far as the coast of Brittany, fires could be seen. Briefed for Wilhelmshaven tonight but weather closed in so it was scrubbed. Rang Dorothy after dinner.*'

Commentary
The 7th was a Sunday and the RAF bombed Lorient in two waves: the heaviest raid on the port up to that time – the 65th. There were two concrete U-boat pens in a completed state, each capable of holding 20 U-boats, and a third under construction of half that size. Because it was a much shorter trip than the Ruhr, the RAF bombers could carry their maximum ordnance. The 'Simpson Kite' bombed at 14,000 feet; the Flak was 'moderate' and two enemy aircraft were sighted. One Lancaster bomb-aimer described the target as 'a mass of flames'. 'There was a column of smoke rising up to 7,000 feet', he said. 'We made our bombing run through it and my cabin filled with the smell of burning. It was very thick black smoke, probably from oil.' From miles away a great column of smoke was silhouetted against the blaze. The same crew's mid-upper gunner remarked that he remembered occasionally seeing 'a sudden bright burst of light' as one of the 4,000 lb cookies exploded amidst the flames.[19] Bomber Command lost seven aircraft on the raid, all the crew being killed in every case.

9-12 February 1943
'*Briefed for, and got to, Wilhelmshaven despite lousy weather. Trip out quite uneventful and arrived just 2 mins after PFF flares. Bombed early in the show but on the way out glare could be seen for 100 miles. Searchlights useless because of 9/10 low cloud. Got back and landed OK. Canadian AFV instructor was sent with us for the experience and seemed to enjoy it altho' he was a little ill.*'

'Today (12th) stand-down. RAF Gang Show very good tonight. Gale still raging and "Y-Yorker" has controls broken as a result. Damn! Received letters from Dad, Joyce and Flora today.'

Commentary

The Wilhelmshaven raid on Thursday, 11 February is classed by Middlebrook and Everitt as 'interesting and important'. The raid began at 20.00 hrs. Reports came back that the weather was difficult on the way out, with severe icing periods amidst the clouds over the North Sea. Laurie recalled, *'Ran into heavy rain on way out, but old "Y-Yorker" plugged on relentlessly.'* For the first time H2S was used effectively as a blind-bombing aid, when the '9/10 cloud' was countered by the PFF dropping – in this case – highly accurate sky-marker flares. A newspaper reported that much of the Flak, which was moderate, was directed at these flares.

However, newspaper reports about the raid seem only to confuse things. Laurie Simpson's record was: *'Flak was moderate heavy but very accurately predicted.'* This also conflicts slightly with a newspaper that quoted a Lancaster pilot saying, *'Sometimes light Flak would come up in the wake of our tail, but just as the gunners seemed to be getting near us, they would go off after someone else.'*[20]

This was the 70th attack on the German submarine-building yard and four aircraft were lost,[21] one of which crashed on landing. At 20.06 hrs crews witnessed '…the biggest explosion they had ever seen.' 'It lit up the sky with a brilliant red glow,' one Halifax pilot recalled, 'and seemed to spread for miles before it died away. For a few seconds the light was so brilliant that other bombers were silhouetted beneath us.' Another report stated *'For a vast area the clouds were coloured a deep burning red.'*[22] The pilot surmised that they had hit an arsenal. In fact the bombs had fallen on a *Kriegsmarine* ammunition depot to the south of the port at Mariensiel, devastating nearly 120 acres.

13 February 1943

'Went to Lorient tonight and [as] there were 450 aircraft on, it was well pranged. Took Doug Boyer (Canadian AFV instructor) with us and he enjoyed it. First home that night. Got into no trouble at all.'

Commentary

With clear visibility over Lorient at 14,000 feet there was moderate heavy Flak, searchlights, and intense light Flak. This was the heaviest raid on Lorient during the war, and 1,000 tons of bombs were dropped. The 'Simpson Kite' UV-H 'Harry' carried five 1,000-pounders, 9 SBCs, and 1,380 gallons of aviation fuel. Two days later, the *Daily Sketch* reported that the raid was 'a double attack'. When the second wave arrived, the crews could see the glow of the fires 160 miles away: the whole dock area was 'a mass of flame'. By that time, a Stirling pilot reported that only six heavy guns were firing and five searchlights operating. This was the eighth attack on the U-boat base that year and the 56th since 1940.[23]

These attacks on the submarine pens on the Atlantic coast reflect how serious U-boat shipping attacks in the Atlantic were becoming. The 'Casablanca Directive' reached Bomber Command HQ at High Wycombe on 4 February 1943. At this time, Bomber Command was becoming increasingly effective. But many of its commanders, such as Harris and Bennett, realised that the resources they had were being squandered. The attacks on the pens were futile. The most efficient place to destroy the U-boats was where they were built. This was reflected in a famous remark Harris made: 'We said the place to find the submarine and to defeat it was where it was born, not where it went to after it grew up.' But the Admiralty was adamant, with the result that a large amount of the force Bomber Command had, which could have been employed more effectively against the German heartland, was directed against the U-boat pens. 'The idea', Don Bennett reflected, 'was that we should remove, brick by brick, the entire town of St. Nazaire in one case, and Lorient the other.' What concerned Bennett more than this, as Pathfinder leader, was that the U-boat crews actually lived in rest houses *outside* the towns along the coast. This 'simple fact', he commented, 'apparently did not penetrate as far as the Anti-Submarine Committee.'[24]

It would be the end of 1943 before Coastal Command was finally able to combat the U-boat menace. In the autumn of that year, Hitler approved the *Kriegsmarine's* decision to withdraw its U-boats from the Atlantic. Before that the campaign was, in Bennett's view, misplaced. It was a repeat of what had happened when the German surface ships *Gneisenau, Scharnhorst* and *Prince Eugen* 'holed up' in Brest harbour in 1941, when the 'Battle of the Atlantic' took precedence over the 'Battle of Germany'. Harris believed that the whole campaign against the surface ships then was a waste of lives and effort: of 1,161 operations against the Brest ships over two months in 1941, 1,655 tons of bombs were dropped, but only four hits occurred. Not only this, but the RAF effort was distracted away from what would have been a more opportune target: the U-boat pens then being constructed in the five French Atlantic ports. If the RAF had attacked these, then the 'safe houses' of the *Kriegsmarine*, where it could repair and refuel, would have been severely damaged if not destroyed. It was not until the late spring of 1942 that destruction of the pens became a priority. But, despite a number of near-suicidal RAF attacks at that time, the U-boat programme was unaffected. The official history of the British air offensive stated that, for 1942, '…the efforts of the large numbers of attacks on the ports concerned were negligible.'[25]

13-15 February 1943

'Our big day was the 14th when we were sent on our first Italian stooge. Milan was the target and we bombed it. The dagos' searchlights and Flak, while there in quantity, were pathetically ineffective. The Alps were an amazing sight in the brilliant moonlight as they were snow-covered. We passed over Mont Blanc and I was enraptured at the scene. Got back first again and was in bed by 6 o'clock.'

Commentary

Milan was attacked by 142 Lancasters from three Groups. Italian targets were regarded as soft or 'ice cream' targets. Milan, with a population of 1,000,000 inhabitants was bathed in brilliant moonlight. By 22.45 hrs 'fires ran in parallel lines across the city and bombs were continually exploding among them.' One Lancaster pilot commented upon a new type of Flak: 'A kind of rocket with long fingers [coming] out horizontally after bursts. Whole buildings were disintegrating by the time I left.'[26] The Milan attack followed an earlier raid on Cologne that had commenced at 20.00 hrs. Contemporary Italian newspapers reported no fighters seen, but a Lancaster of 101 Squadron later recorded shooting down a Fiat CR42 'Falco' fighter.

Many aircrew were struck by how beautiful the Alps appeared on ops. Being covered with snow, visibility downward was excellent against the white background.

16-25 February 1943

'A lousy time, although the six ops we were briefed for were all abandoned except one on Bremen. This was a hot trip. Shot at all the way from target to coast. A full 50 minutes. Our parent station, Holme,

forgot to tell us the change of route out from the target, hence we were the only eight aircraft to arrive through the Flak belt. I bet the Jerry gunners were having some fun. We got hit on the tail plane and almost severed the rudder control. Lucky!! On the 25th, bogged the aircraft just before taking off for Nürnburg. We were all bitterly disappointed.

'A crew from 460 has to go to the Pathfinders and it looks like me. I don't want to go as I wish to finish my tour here and then marry Dorothy. Have said "No" to Groupy and Wingco, so hope I'm not detailed. I'm more in love with Dorothy every day and the only thing that will cure me will be to make her my wife.

Graeme has been made deputy Flight Commander and will probably be Fl/Lieut soon. Good show!'

Commentary

Simpson's 'Flying Logbook' records that his crew attacked Lorient again on 16 February and Wilhelmshaven a second time on 18 February. Lorient was the largest raid of the series on the submarine pens. A total of 363 aircraft dropped mainly incendiary bombs from 12,000 feet. The visibility, with no cloud and bright moonlight, was so good that bomb-aimers were able to keep track of the bombs halfway to the ground. The Air Ministry had no intention of shattering the concrete emplacements. Their strategy was more to '…isolate them by creating a state of such complete dislocation in the port as to prevent its restoration for many weeks.'[27] The port had experienced great devastation and the civilian population had already been evacuated. Simpson's 'UV-V' dropped four 1,000-pounders and 10 SBCs. Four aircraft were lost, two of which crashed on landing. Al Kennedy was still sick and P/O Rust replaced him.

On Wilhelmshaven P/O McCullough sat in for Kennedy. ED354, 'UV-W' carried one 4,000-lb cookie and 12 SBCs. The Flak and searchlights Laurie recorded as '*moderate*'. Despite the PFF claiming accurate target-marking, photographic interpreters after the raid reported that most of the bombs had fallen west of the port in open country. There were two attacks in two days on Wilhelmshaven and, in all, 17 aircraft were lost. The Bremen raid was on 21 February.[28] 'UV-W' bombed from 16,000 feet with one 4,000-pounder and 12 SBCs. It was the RAF's 102nd attack on the port. Middlebrook and Everitt state that of 143 aircraft that set out, only 129 bombed, and this through cloud. Bremen was Germany's second largest port and an important shipbuilding centre with extensive U-boat yards. There were also a nearby Focke-Wulf aircraft factory, another aircraft works, oil refineries, and jute-spinning and grain-milling works. The attack began at 20.45 hrs but newspaper reports claimed that the German anti-aircraft batteries only returned fire after the first bomb exploded, and the defences were strong but ineffective, which rather contradicted Laurie's logbook report that the Flak was '*accurate all way out*'. The papers also stated that more than 100 two-ton cookies had hit the port without a single aircraft lost. By 21.15 hrs the town was ablaze.[29]

26 February-7 March 1943

'Have been very busy over this period. Bombed St. Nazaire, Cologne, Hamburg, Berlin and Essen. St. Nazaire was easy although a complete intercom failure made it very awkward. Cologne was a good trip. Hamburg was a pretty tough one. Berlin of course was the big "do" and although we saw blokes getting pasted, and there were hundreds of searchlights, we got through quite easily. A very tired crew landed eventually at Holme. Three more days will see me on leave. Gosh, it will be grand to see "Muddy Eyes"[30] again.'

Commentary

The Cologne raid took place on 26 February. A total of 427 aircraft took part and 13 aircraft went missing.[31] Flak was in 'barrage' form, but 'moderate' with searchlights. By the end of the raid, Bomber Command had been bombing Germany continuously for 48 hours. The RAF was out in force all day: formations of aircraft could be seen '…flying very high and leaving trails, going out over the Straights of Dover towards Calais… other planes also flying at great height, were heard coming back.' 'At one time,' a newspaper reported, 'the rumble of very heavy explosions, lasting for nearly ten minutes without a pause, was heard from the other side of the channel.' The Air Ministry's official communiqué for that Friday night's operations stated: '*Last night aircraft of Bomber Command made a very heavy attack on Cologne. Weather over the target was clear, apart from ground haze, and good results were seen. From these operations 10 of our bombers are missing.*'

On the 28th it was the turn of St. Nazaire. Al Kennedy had returned to the crew and the 'Simpson Kite' was back to full complement. The earlier attacks on Lorient had destroyed that port and now St. Nazaire was the priority. In the initial raid, 60 per cent of the town was flattened and 29 civilians killed. The raid commenced a few minutes before 21.00 hrs. Within 15 minutes, the place was likened to 'a burning torch, lighting up the sky for 30 miles around.' Fires in an oil depot and others in railway marshalling yards belched out flame and smoke and a massive explosion rocked a bomber 15,000 feet in the air above the blaze. In a little over 30 minutes, 1,000 tons of bombs had been dropped. The aim was to erase all the installations feeding the pens, rather than the pens themselves which were almost impregnable. The Simpson crew had taken a second pilot, Sgt Fulton, with them on this occasion. They found Flak and searchlights were moderate but, as Laurie relates, 'Z-Zebra' suffered a complete intercom failure. The PFF realised that these Atlantic coast raids created a difficulty. Since all their Oboe transmitting stations were designed for raids into Germany, in order to attack the French pens new transmitting equipment had to be set up near Sennen in Cornwall and Worth, near Sandwich in Kent, to give them the cover they needed.

By the beginning of April 1943 Lorient and St. Nazaire had both been completely destroyed. Don Bennett reflected:

> 'I should have thought… that the then "powers that be" would have been sufficiently intelligent to realise that the enormous weight of bombs that we put down on St. Nazaire and Lorient over those few months… were completely and totally ineffective from the point of view of the submarine campaign, and did a great deal of harm to our position with the French people. It was total and wanton destructiveness of the cities of an ally, and did no good whatever.'[32]

Only after the British intercepted a signal from the C-in-C *Kriegsmarine* to the Naval Commander, St. Nazaire congratulating him on the 'effectiveness of his bases as air raid precautions for Berlin',[33] were the RAF allowed to return to Germany.

Simpson's crew would make three more attacks against Berlin within 29 days that March, the first being on the first of the month. '*Berlin's Worst Raid Night*', the headlines screamed. '*Fires visible for hundreds of miles*'. '*Berlin Blazes after War's Biggest Raid*', reported the *Daily Sketch*, '*Goebbels Protests – Terror Tactics*'.[34] The raid inflicted more damage to Berlin than any earlier efforts, mainly due to the greater numbers of aircraft employed and the heavier ordnance. A pilot, who spent 15 minutes inside the city's ring of defences, said the Flak 'was not up to Berlin's usual standard'. German radio announced that a 'terror raid' had left 89 killed and 215 injured. The German capital possessed large power stations and electrical engineering works, armament works, aircraft factories and oil storage tanks. The Siemens works was one of the largest electrical factories in the world. Although 'Z-Zebra' 'got through quite easily' and Flak was 'moderate', Laurie's logbook reported that his aircraft 'Z-Zebra' was *'holed by Flak'* amid *'intense'* searchlights. The raid lasted for half-an-hour; 20 aircraft were lost, at least nine to night fighters. Crews due to arrive towards the end of the raid said that they could see the city burning for 20 minutes before reaching it. The bomb pattern spread over 100 square miles, mainly in the south-west. It was the 58th attack on the capital and the Fatherland was celebrating *'Luftwaffe* Day'. Reichsmarschall Göring,[35] the corpulent commander of the *Luftwaffe,* due to broadcast that day on German radio, was kept off the air by the first attack, and Goebbels was equally distanced by the second.

5 March–24 July 1943 – Battle of the Ruhr

The 'Battle of the Ruhr' was a series of 43 major raids ranging from Stuttgart to Aachen, but focused mainly upon the Ruhr. How effective this campaign was against the German cities was witnessed by 617 Squadron bomb-aimer, Jack Brook, after being shot down during a raid on a V2 site at Wizernes near St. Omer on 24 June 1944. Whilst on his way by rail to the *Luftwaffe* interrogation centre at Frankfurt, he glanced out of the train window: 'Despite the heavy losses suffered by Bomber Command during the sustained Battle of the Ruhr,' he recalled, 'widespread damage had been inflicted upon almost every town and city in the Ruhr Valley… I do not think any of us were prepared for what we saw. The devastation was incredible. There were piles of rubble as far as the eye could see and gaunt empty shells which had once been buildings. It was total destruction, and I can only liken it to the pictures of Hiroshima after the dropping of the atomic bomb.'[36]

From the time the battle opened, the crew of the 'Simpson Kite' was briefed for 13 ops. On 5 March, 442 aircraft attacked Essen, at the heart of which was the strongly defended *Waffenschmeide*,[37] the centre of Krupp munitions manufacture. Each year this produced over 20 million tons of shells, Flak guns, howitzers, tank bodies, and heavy and very heavy guns.[38] Due to use of PFF target-marking, directed by Oboe, the city was harder hit than ever before and only 14 aircraft were lost.

5-7 March 1943

'Essen was a hot trip but we had a good time. This was a most successful job so I think Krupp received a good belting. Have been scrubbed on Essen and Hamburg these last two nights. Our G/C and Wingco took a party to the Owl Club near Selby last night and it was quite good.'

Commentary

During the following months almost all the major centres of the Ruhr were attacked: Duisburg, Dortmund, Düsseldorf, Bochum and Aachen were all bombed by the RAF and Oboe target-marking ensured increased accuracy. In the first month of the year the raids against Krupp were fairly insignificant. It was only in March that things started in earnest and Essen was severely hit four times, most of the damage being done by incendiaries, and also by high explosive bombs, of which the 8,000-pounders were the most effective. The Krupp works were vital to the Reich's war economy and distributed over various centres within the Ruhr.

After the first Krupp attack RAF losses rose rapidly. Dr. Goebbels, the Reich's diminutive propaganda minister, stated after a raid on 13 March: 'The Krupp plant has been hard hit… twenty-five major fires were raging on the ground of the Krupp plant alone... Things simply cannot go on like this... It is expected that Göring will now do something decisive.' But he did not – could not, for the bombing campaign was overwhelming him.

8-26 March 1943
'Bombed Nuremberg (8th) and had to turn back from Munich (9th) owing to engine failure.
'Got away for my leave and caught the train from York to London.'

27-28 March 1943
'Duisburg was disappointing as there was 10/10 cloud, which incidentally didn't stop Jerry's gunners from being very accurate.
'My promotion to Flight Lieutenant came through today and I am very pleased.
Briefed for, and bombed, Berlin on 27th. We had a good trip, but it was long and tiring. It was 10/10 cloud all the way to within 5 mins. of the target and then it cleared up miraculously. There was moderate heavy Flak and then intense combined with many searchlights which we evaded successfully. A fresher crew[39] (Sgt Weber), but all came back from Berlin.
'Had letters from home including snap of the kid sisters and old Deni.[40] Gosh they've grown beyond description. Also letters from Bill, Gert and Wiggy.'

29-30 March 1943
'Mar 29th was disastrous for 460 Sqdn. Shorty Grenfell and Dave Chadwick were two who didn't come back. Eight of us took off for Berlin, two turned back, two failed to return and I was one of the few to get there after a terrific struggle with heavy icing cloud. Many times I was on the point of turning back but somehow we plugged on and made it successfully. Northern Lights were spectacular.
'Interviewed today by reporters from the "Herald" and "Age" newspapers and shot a line. Stand down today so I'm early to bed. Rang Dorothy and she is as excited as a kid at an orphan's picnic.'

31 March-5 April
'On the 3rd I made my fifth trip to the world's hottest target – Essen. Found it very clear and there were hundreds of searchlights and thousands of Flak guns. We twisted and turned in and out of the target and went flat out for home. Next day was delighted to learn that my photograph was only 2 ¾ miles from the centre of Krupp.
'Next night we set out for the naval base at Kiel and were disappointed by 10/10 cloud. The Flak was hot over the target but we didn't get into any trouble. Kay Moore and Bruce Rust[41] didn't get back last night.
'Mac and Quicky gave me a cheque for five guineas as a wedding present to Dorothy. I was dumbfounded and couldn't thank them, as I would've liked. Great fellows.
'Bert Newton who once taught at D.HI.S.[42] has arrived here as engineering officer and we've had some yarns over old times. Arrangements for our wedding are pretty well in hand now. The ceremony will take place at the Holy Cross Church, 3 miles form Wimborne, just near Dorothy's home.
'460 has had a bad week. Wilson missing on Duisburg, Shorty and Dave's on Berlin and Moore's on Kiel. Lets hope it improves pretty soon now.
'Kiel was my 22nd operation and I hope I can have 26 up to the time I go on leave. Saw old Morris for the first time since I left Leconfield, in York a few days ago. Also Ron Read and Monty both Flt/Lts now.'

Commentary
The RAF could hardly miss – the Krupp works at Essen covered six million square yards,

seven times greater in area than that of the city centre itself and even Churchill admitted that residential (to the south-west of Essen) as well as industrial areas were targeted. During his six raids against the city, Laurie Simpson must little have realised what he had unleashed his total load of 24,000 lbs of high explosive against. The Krupp family had been trading in munitions for over 350 years and the Krupp dynasty was one of the richest in Europe and, indeed, the world. The Krupp empire had supplied the Prussian army after the fall of Napoleon; Krupp guns had equipped Prussia during the Austro-Prussian War in 1866; they had bombarded Paris during the Franco-Prussian War in 1871; in 1914 'Big Bertha' guns had been used to crush Belgium. Krupp guns had also dominated the battles of Verdun (on both sides) and Jutland in 1916, and in 1918 they had shelled Paris. By the end of May 1945 1.8 million square yards of the firm's main factory space had been obliterated.

But the Air Ministry was blind to the fact that Krupp munitions were manufactured in centres other than the *Waffenschmeide*. The RAF ignored the works at Magdeburg and also, one of the most important, the foundry at Borbeck, a munitions plant directly in the path of the bomber streams which included 75,000 tons of machinery, 1,000 square miles of invaluable blueprints, and 60,000 workers manufacturing the new Tiger tank from Scandinavian ores.[43] Superseding this in significance were the forges at Rheinhausen, the 'most highly integrated steel plant in the Krupp combine'.[44]

6-17 April 1943

'Have been twice more to Duisburg,[45] to Stuttgart and to Pilzen in Czechoslovakia. Had a cable from home, letter from Bill and Xmas card from Danny Maker. My F/O has come through with £55.00 back pay – just in time for my wedding. Have only four more ops to do to complete my tour and offer a little prayer that they go OK.

'I'm troubled at the thought of our wedding next Thursday (22nd) and I know Dorothy is too.'

Commentary
The Pilzen Raid

The trip to the Skoda armaments factory in Czechoslovakia on 16 April was one of the longest operations my father's crew ever undertook: he recalled the night being '*a really beautiful one – full brilliant moon*'. The Skoda works was an important target, ranking with Krupp and Schneider-Creusot in France as one of the largest arms-producing plants in the world, and second in importance to the German war machine after Essen. The factory had been taken over by the Nazis after the invasion of Czechoslovakia in 1939[46] and was converted to armaments production for the Third Reich. As a result of the damage done by Allied bombing to the Krupp factories, the Skoda production facilities took on an increasing importance.

The mission, he recalled the following August, was flown at '*zero feet*'. It took them almost 10 hours – a 1,400-mile round trip, all of it over occupied territory. The outbound flight was made via Augsburg and Munich with operational heights generally being between 16,000 and 20,000 feet, but they would have also flown considerably lower than this. Laurie gives only a minimal record of it in his service diary, with no mention that it was at very low level. The full diary entry for the period 6-17 April 1943 was:

'Have been twice more to Duisburg, to Stuttgart and to Pilzen in Czechoslovakia. The last trip was my most trying to date. We wandered off track on the way and struck trouble over Augsburg and Munich. Couldn't reach Pilzen in time so we bombed Nurnberg. There we were covered by searchlights at 4,000

feet and Flak was all around us. We got out and then chose the long trip home. Over the English coast our port inner engine went for a burton so we landed on three.' [47]

Laurie's crew used up 2,060 gallons of fuel, carrying three 1,000-lb bombs and one 4,000-lb cookie.

On the outward trip the aircraft flew in bright moonlight. Wing Commander G.B. Warner, a Halifax pilot on his second tour after the award of a DFC, who subsequently wrote a special report on the raid, stated that the flight out was *'quiet and uneventful'*. *'Every now and then,'* he recorded, *'we saw Flak coming up from various towns on the route. There was a haze over the ground in places, but [we] were able to pick up ground details.'*[48]

Ron Searle recalled: 'We went to Pilzen in Czechoslovakia to hit the Skoda works. We never did get to Pilzen, mainly because the Met. Report we received at briefing must have been for somewhere else; it was nowhere like the weather we encountered and, consequently, we ended up south of the target, as did quite a few others. As we didn't have enough fuel to get to Pilzen and then back to base, it was decided to drop our bombs on Nuremberg, a decision that almost cost us dearly as we were covered by searchlights over the target and once that happens it's usually "goodnight". I can only put it down to the skill of the pilot and a bit of luck because we had plenty of holes in "P-Peter", which we discovered when we got back. Fortunately nothing serious had been hit by Flak. This was the longest operation we ever did, 9 hours 50 minutes, mainly over enemy territory. I used to watch what was going on through the astrodome, which was almost above my head and, on this trip, saw five of our aircraft shot down in flames.'[49]

On their return some crews complained of stiffness, but many showed little sign of the strain that they must have been under for ten hours. Two days later the late northern edition of a national newspaper quoted the captain of a Halifax,[50] '... *the whole factory seemed to be a mass of smoke with flashes from high explosives coming up through it and leaving a red glow. There were other bombers all over the place. The weather on the whole was so clear you could see for miles.'*[51]

The *Sunday Express* wildly embellished its report of the raid: *'How Skoda works was Krupped'* it stated. The exaggeration was forgivable in view of the circumstances: *'Bombers so thickly concentrated they had to dodge their own bombs; most superb RAF raid of the war: the arsenal that Hitler thought was safe...'*[52]

Wg/Co Warner, who thought he had reached the Skoda works, reported, 'When we were running into the Pilzen area, flares were being dropped and we had a clear view of the town. It was smaller than we had expected and one of the first things I saw was the large square and the Church of St. Bartholomew standing out like a model. There was no mistaking the factory – a layer of cloud at about 10,000 feet reflected the flares.'[53]

Sunday Express journalist Edward J. Hart, who claimed to be 'the only air reporter visiting any bomber station' during that morning's raid, was more guarded in his praise: 'I am assured to the best of the crews' belief that very many of their heavy bombs scored direct hits on the factory.' [54]

It was all baloney. Of the 327 aircraft that went out, there were only six confirmations of a bomb pattern within three miles of the Skoda factory. Pilzen was one of the classic PFF 'cock-ups' of the war: it was the fifth attack on the city by the RAF, and 39 aircraft were lost. Bomber Command suffered the highest casualties in a single night since the third Thousand-Bomber raid of a year before. On 13/14 May Pilzen endured another attack which again failed to achieve the desired results.

Hart qualified his earlier statement with a convenient opt-out clause: '...the target itself was hidden by a thin layer of cloud, and until daily photographic evidence is available the raid is regarded officially as "inconclusive".'

Essentially, what occurred was a navigation error. Pilzen was part of a two-pronged attack: one on Pilzen and one on Mannheim. Two hundred and seventy-one second-rate bombers[55] went for Mannheim, over 400 miles from Yorkshire, whilst 327 Lancasters and Halifaxes went to Pilzen. The take-off times varied between 20.30 hrs and 22.17 hrs according to the unit and the location; the Mannheim-bound aircraft took off after those attacking Pilzen. Although the order of the day was 'low flying', the heights chosen varied considerably: some aircraft flew lower than 1,000 feet, others flew over 17,000 feet.[56] Mannheim was an inland port on the Rhine, around 500 miles from Yorkshire. This attack was successful: Pathfinder-marking was accurate and 205 aircraft dropped a concentrated bomb pattern curtailing production of 41 industrial plants. Of 271 aircraft that set out, only 20 were lost.

Pilzen was a different kettle of fish. It lay at the apex of a 1,400-mile round trip and was 200 miles beyond Mannheim. The Main Force passed over the town around an hour *after* the first bombing. A *Sunday Express* reporter eulogised: '*To achieve the raid, the RAF had to go through four-fifths of Germany's night fighter strength.*'[57] In fact there had been over eleven attacks on the stream around Mannheim by the *Nachtjagd* before it even crossed the Czech border. At around 01.40 hrs on the 17th, five hours from England, the first of the Main Force arrived in the Pilzen area. The majority of these never even *saw* the Skoda works. The confusion was due to a number of factors:

(a) A slight drizzle had occurred and a thin veil of cloud lay over the target that night.
(b) The main attack went in from the south-west along the course of a railway line running parallel to the Radbusa River, which meandered to the east for a few miles, two-and-a-half miles south of the Skoda works, before continuing northwards. Seven miles south of Pilzen lay Dobrany,[58] which like Pilzen straddled the Radbusa. South of this, a bend in the river uncannily mimicked the meander near Pilzen and, from 17,000 feet, both bends looked exactly the same.
(c) On the outskirts of Dobrany was a large mental hospital with buildings arranged in regular blocks; a tall chimney, a boiler house and a water tower made this appear from the air to be identical to an industrial complex. To the south was also an old Austro-Hungarian barracks requisitioned as a hospital for survivors of the battle of Stalingrad, which made what appeared to be Pilzen from bomber height, 'smaller than we had expected'.

'A real cock-up ensued', one RAF man recalled. 'The Main Force was ordered to confirm the position of the Skoda works visually,' Middlebrook and Everitt state, 'the Pathfinder markers were only intended as a general guide.'[59] When the PFF came in, three white magnesium flares that were dropped to try to identify the Skoda works, actually went down on Dobrany. A minute later, a green PFF flare mistakenly confirmed that this was the factory. After several other green T.I.s, the Main Force assumed this was the target and bombed it. From 17,000 feet, because of the hazy conditions, it was almost impossible to distinguish anything. Two hundred and forty-nine aircraft bombed the hospital, and in the ensuing chaos, 300 mental patients were killed. 'The whole factory area seemed to be a mass of smoke with flashes from high explosives coming up through it and leaving a red glow',[60] Wg/Cdr Warner reported.

So the majority of Main Force attacks were made more than seven miles south of Pilzen, the actual Skoda plant being bombed, fortuitously, by only a few aircraft.

'We knew', a Lancaster pilot told Hart, 'that the perils would be unusual.'[61]

A number of other aircraft, in addition to Simpson's, dropped their bombs on secondary targets. Among these were two 460 crews. Laurie Simpson:

'460's bad luck continues as we lost three crews on the Pilzen one: Dave White, new DFM, Nem Williams and Miller; nearly 60 fellows in less than three weeks. According to the news today, 55 crews were lost last night so I had a phone call from Dorothy. Poor kid she must have been worried.'[62]

Chorley commented that this was 'the worst night in Bomber Command's history so far'.[63] 59 aircraft were lost: 39 on Pilzen, 20 on Mannheim. Five on the Pilzen run were from 51 Squadron, four from 76 Squadron and two from 78. All the 460 Squadron deaths took place on the Pilzen attack. Quite often crews took second pilots along to help out if things looked tough. On the Pilzen trip Sergeant Robert S. 'Bob' Christie accompanied Laurie's crew. He was later killed when his aircraft was shot down by a night fighter on a raid to Dusseldorf on 11 June. Laurie took second pilots along on some other occasions. Dave M. Charlick went to Cologne on 26 February, and 'Nem' Williams went twice to Berlin on 27 and 29 March.

18-20 April
'Went to the Italian naval base at La Spezia and it was a wizard trip across France and over the Alps. Bombed through 10/10 cloud. The Flak was very intense and very accurate. Thought we'd been hit. Still the hottest target imaginable. [Laurie's 'Flying Logbook' contradicts this, stating that the Flak and searchlights were 'ineffective', despite the fact that they were 'holed by Flak'.] *Briefed for Duisburg but scrubbed at last moment. The G/C and camp have allowed me to go on leave a day early – so I'm off.'*

Commentary
The crew of the 'Simpson Kite' never saw the 'Battle of the Ruhr' through to its completion. They did three more trips before completing their tour: one to Essen, one to Dortmund and the final one to Duisburg. On Friday, 30 April, they bombed Essen for the sixth time. They were timed to bomb at 02.30 hrs for 40 minutes.

When the Krupp AA fire burst in the sky around the RAF bombers, liqueur glasses on tables 20,000 feet below trembled. There was so much steel in the sky that aircrews christened the area 'Flak Alley'. One of the final entries in Laurie Simpson's 'Flying Logbook' for his first tour stated:

'Operations Essen: Ht. 20,000 ft. Bombs 1 x 4,000-lb. 12 SBCs (Special Bomb Containers). Fuel 1,500 gals. 10/10 cloud. Predicted heavy Flak and barrage intense accurate.'

Headlines in the national dailies screamed at the British public: '*Krupp is Hit Again*'; '*10,000 Tons of Bombs on Essen: World's worst hit town.*' It was, the report stated, '*...the heaviest weight unloaded so far in any single town in the world.*' In the last ten raids on Germany, one article claimed, the RAF had dropped a greater tonnage of bombs than the *Luftwaffe* dropped during the whole of the Blitz on London. Two enormous explosions in the area were seen by crews 20 miles away. There was a profusion of icy clouds to a height of 20,000 feet, with an air temperature of 20 degrees below zero – so cold, in fact, that one crew had to wipe the hoar frost away from its cockpit windows: 'Our trailer aerial was so badly coated over,' one pilot reported, 'that it broke off. The aircraft became heavier and heavier as we went on, and at one point it began to lose height while we were trying to climb.' Other crews had their aerials broken before they reached base.

Although production in the *Waffenschmeide* was curtailed after every heavy attack, the Krupp works showed a surprising ability to recuperate: even direct hits did not necessarily obliterate a factory. Modern construction techniques began to outfox the Air Ministry planners: an official Krupp report stated, 'Many of the older, brick wall structures were completely demolished, but the modern steel frame buildings sustained little more than roof damage.'[64]

Although old Gustav Krupp had been resistant to Hitler's warmongering, his young successor, his eldest son Alfried, heir to the empire, was wholly in favour of the *Führer*. The machinations of the world the chain-smoking Alfried had inherited became increasingly corrupt as he was swept up in an environment of power and double-dealing. Alfried appropriated raw materials illegally from mining works in Belgium, and employed slave labour from Auschwitz and from the Orianenburg concentration camp after native German labour began to disappear after D-Day. He knew what to expect in an air raid: 'As the engineer behind the first 88 mm guns used in Spain, Alfried could gauge exactly when a raid was approaching its crescendo. Once the drone of motors became audible, he could estimate from experience the number of attacking planes, their type and altitude.'[65]

An illustration of how far removed the Krupp family could be from the reality around them occurred one December day in 1944. A flight of Lancasters had arrived during the morning as the Krupps were about to take cocktails. Alfried paid little attention to the bombers, but later became irritated when his butler served a glass of Moselle with his meat. Aghast, Krupp asked what had become of his red wine. The man explained that there had been a fire in the servants' quarters. But how, Alfried wondered, could that affect the red? A pipe had been fractured by a bomb, the servant explained, and the chateau was waterless. *Then how had the fire been controlled?* Alfried queried. The poor man awkwardly explained that he had been forced to douse the flames with a bottle of *Chateauneuf-du-Pape*.[66]

Bomber Command lost fourteen aircraft on the 30 April Essen attack, three of them from 77 Squadron.

End of the Tour: the Dortmund and Duisburg Raids

On 13 May 1943, Laurie and Graeme's tours both finished with a final op, the 30th, to Duisburg, but they made a penultimate trip to Dortmund on Tuesday, 4 May. Dortmund was a steel, oil and transportation centre for the Ruhr. The *Daily Express* reported, '*So many RAF planes battered Dortmund, bombers almost bumped.*' It was '*...the largest fleet of four-engined bombers ever used in one operation*', another paper reported. 'It gave us quite a bumpy flight', a Canadian navigator stated. 'I broke the point of my pencil four times trying to write up details in the log.' There were '*bags of searchlights and night fighters*', and losses were '*quite heavy*', Laurie wrote, '*but we got through OK.*' A Stirling skipper, Pilot Officer L.C. Martin, reported '...at least 200 searchlights. There were so many cones working it was difficult to see the Flak.'[67]

This attack on Dortmund had been expected by the Germans. There were five attacks on the 'Happy Valley' in April, and Essen, to use an expression of the time, 'nearly went out of business'. Dortmund was the second largest town in the Ruhr and the raid had been mounted to try to strangle the great transportation system there and to devastate the factories, which were working at double time. Within ten minutes of the first attack there was a vast explosion, after a white glow from the incendiaries that turned bright red. The cockpit of the aircraft of Wing Commander Steve Gemm DFC, a second-tour man, was 'suddenly filled with light'. There was a second huge explosion fifteen minutes later, at about 01.30 hrs. 'It mushroomed up in a vast glow,' Gemm reported, 'and was followed by a column of smoke that rose to 10,000 feet.'[68] That night Bomber Command lost 42 aircraft, including six from 101 Squadron (one crashed on take-off, two on landing), three each from 78, 102 and 405 Squadrons, and one from 460 Squadron. This was flown by 19 year-old Flight Sergeant Dave Jaekel, one of the youngest Bomber Command pilots to die on ops in 1943. Graeme Keys described the raid to an Australian reporter as 'an extremely good show'.[69] Thirteen bombers were claimed by night fighters,[70] including three by *Oberleutnant* Lothar Linke of IV./NJG 1.[71]

A Stirling pilot, Sgt A.J. Sedunary of South Australia, was attacked from behind by a night fighter. After the rear gunner fired a long burst, pieces flew off the aircraft, which turned away and glided down to earth. Seconds later the crew saw the red glow of an explosion on the ground. The Lancaster of Sergeant Ernie McCrea[72] of County Donegal was hit by three bursts from a fighter which cut the elevator trim cable, holed the port aileron and damaged the aircraft's hydraulics. The captain went down on his knees under the control column to bring the bomber out of a stall and she eventually made it back to base.[73]

Graeme, Laurie and the 460 Squadron crews had to wait for over a week before operation number 30 came up. During this period the Skoda works at Pilzen were again attacked, but the raid proved another failure. The target was difficult to find, and nine aircraft were lost.

'*Eight days we waited,*' my father wrote, '*– six times we were briefed.*' This was an added misfortune as the final op was what crews most feared. It was not uncommon for men to go missing on them. '*The strain was beginning to tell a bit*', Laurie commented.

> '*At last on the 12th, the target Duisburg came. Off we got, climbed through cloud and collected some ice but eventually got to 18000 ft. Just past the Zuider Zee, Wally called out and said we were leaving vapour trails. I looked out and vapour trails nothing – our port outer engine was on fire and it was smoke he could see. So we had to stop the motor and feather it. Luckily the fire went out but our rear turret was unserviceable – and the gun.*'

Duisburg, a town of 300,000 people, and around five miles square, was centred on huge dock installations. This was a major raid, employing more than half the available strength of Bomber Command, the fourth attack that year in the Battle of the Ruhr. Ron Searle: 'Our port-outer motor "gave up the ghost" 60 miles from the target, and had to be feathered. Skipper asked each of us what we thought about going on with only three engines and each of us agreed to carry on: after all we'd waited about seven nights to do this last op, and so we went in and bombed the target.[74] Later I realised that our decision could have been disastrous: with only three engines and a full bomb load we couldn't maintain height and, by the time we got to the target, we must have been three or four thousand feet below the Main Force and, as a result, could have been hit by falling bombs and incendiaries. Luck again!'

Geoffrey Willatt, a bomb-aimer in 106 Squadron, was also on the Duisburg trip. It was uneventful for him, but more successful than some of his earlier missions where navigation had been a problem. In England he had practised 'bombing' the target in a 'Bomb Trainer'[75] but in the event the city was 'covered with fires, flashes, columns of smoke and searchlights' and was quite unrecognisable.

The raid began at 02.00 hrs. The PFF-marking was near perfect and Main Force bombing concentrated and accurate. 'A great explosion was seen 40 miles away,' a pilot reported, 'it began as an orange spark on the ground, growing bigger and bigger until it lit up all Duisburg and the country around. The glow seemed to go to the top of the sky... When it was over there were more fires than ever before.'[76] The centre of the city, with the largest inland port in Germany, was suffering severe damage. German civilians working as 'Flak helpers' stated on the radio: 'Duisburg was a cauldron; hell was let loose... Everything was ablaze.'

'All hell was let loose,' Geoffrey Willatt similarly recorded, 'but this time there was some cloud. I saw the target quite suddenly, with only a few minutes to go before bombing.'[77] Laurie Simpson:

> '*We plugged on 80 miles to the target, losing height with our speed back to 130. Eventually we got there but searchlights coned us owing to our loss of manoeuvrability and we were in a spot of bother. We managed to dump our loads close to the aiming points and by the grace of God got out after losing eight thousand feet. And so we struggled home, too slowly for my liking.*'

A reported 1,596 buildings were destroyed with 273 fatalities. An unidentified pilot recalled: 'As we turned away the place was filling up with fires. We could still see them blazing when we were 150 miles away.' Ron Searle: 'On the way home we couldn't keep up with the Main Force and could have been a "sitting duck" for a night fighter, but you don't think of those things at the time.' Laurie: '*At base the cloud was right on the deck – visibility practically zero, and it was raining. Made a scratchy landing and it was over. We'd made it!*' There were no further attacks on Duisburg during the Battle of the Ruhr due to the success of this raid.

460 Squadron was about to move station from Breighton to Binbrook in Lincolnshire. One of the men involved in organising this was the previously mentioned Cliff O'Riordan who, only a few days before, had been flown down to Binbrook with some 'erks', 'getting things in order'. On Tuesday, 11 May 1943 he had been run off his feet: '*Have signed for three hangars and four living blocks*', he wrote in his diary. '*Every detail needs a signature.*' At the end of the 12th he wrote:

> '*My birthday but no chance to celebrate. The boys went to Duisburg tonight and it was Laurie Simpson's last trip. Got through on three engines. Had a beer in the village before turning in.*'[78]

O'Riordan was a lawyer before the war and the unofficial squadron historian. After his death, another officer recorded in his diary: '*Cliff had been in the squadron since August 1942 doing his first tour and had been regarded as one of the squadron fixtures. He had acted as a defending officer to most of the Courts Martial in the Group and had the record of getting the majority of his clients off. He was a KC from Sydney and had defended many cases there. He gave his age as 34, but most people placed him as being some few years older and were probably right.*' O'Riordan was killed on the night of 29 July 1943 at 01.40 hrs on a raid to Hamburg. Twenty-four other 460 Squadron aircraft took part: two were lost. His skipper, Flying Officer Johnson, had the unhappy distinction of being the 44th victim of night fighter ace *Hauptmann* Egmont Prince *zur* Lippe-Weissenfeld, commander of III./NJG 1.[79]

The Fate of Laurie Simpson's First Tour Crew
Ron Searle returned to Australia on compassionate grounds halfway through 1943 after

his wife was injured in a car crash. He went back to teaching at an Australian OTU but found that there were so many fatalities in training accidents that it was safer to go back to ops. He was posted in 1945 to an operational unit flying North American B-25 Mitchells in Borneo which was nothing like as stressful as ops over Germany. Wally Maltby and Freddy King would soon be posted to different crews at 12 Squadron, Arthur Schrock's old unit,[80] while Ken Sutton retrained as a pilot. Before that they spent brief periods at training units.

In June 1943 Laurie had two '*very quiet*' days at Lichfield. There he met up with Freddy King, who was at Lindholme, and Wally Maltby and Ken Sutton who were at Lichfield. Maltby, characteristically, volunteered to return for a second tour and was shot down on 15 February 1944, 17 days after Laurie. It was one of the final raids of the Battle of Berlin. A force of 891 bombers went out, including 561 Lancasters, the largest force ever sent to Berlin. Maltby's 12 Squadron Lancaster 'R-Robert', flown by Flight Sergeant J.P. Jones, took off from Wickenby at 17.08 hrs. That night the German controllers ordered the *Nachtjagd* not to attack over the city, but many still did, despite it being covered by cloud. Wally's Lancaster was hit by Flak at 22,000 feet over the target and, although they all baled out, engineer Sgt E. Auty's parachute snared on the tail plane after he jumped from the nose hatch and he was dragged to his death. All the rest survived. By the time Laurie Simpson arrived at *Stalag Luft* III, Maltby was already there.

Freddy King was killed on 24/25 March 1944 during the last raid of the Battle of Berlin. After a time instructing at various Conversion Units, he was posted to 12 Squadron at Wickenby. He made four operational flights there as an engineer with three different crews. On 22 October 1943 he went with P/O Hutchinson's crew to Kassel. It was a five hour, 40 minute op at 20,000 feet. 'Hajo' Herrmann,[81] a highly decorated bomber pilot and leading tactician of the *Luftwaffe*, controlled a force of night fighters which were active that night, while the German Flak and searchlights were only moderate. On 23 November King flew with the squadron CO, Wing Commander Craven on a four hour trip to Berlin. A note in the 'Remarks' column of his logbook stated simply '*Operations Berlin. D.N.C.O. p/c failed to climb.*'[82] In the New Year on 22 March an engineer went sick on Flt/Lt Bracewell's crew on Lancaster JB359 and Freddy stood in for him. Bracewell had been awarded a DFC and was probably a 'second tour' man. It was a 5 1/2 hour op to Frankfurt. That night 816 bombers flew out, passing north of the IJsselmeer, convincing the German controllers that they were heading for Hannover. The stream then dog-legged due south to Frankfurt-am-Main. A German report later stated that the combined effect of this and a subsequent American raid perpetrated '…the worst and most fateful blow of the war' to the city, emphasising dramatically that it was 'a blow which simply ended the existence of Frankfurt.' Thirty-five aircraft failed to return.[83] One unpleasant consequence of the raid was the threatening of downed aircrew in transit to the *Luftwaffe* Interrogation Centre near Frankfurt by local civilians.[84]

Freddy went out again with John Bracewell's aircraft on the night of 24/25 March. This raid later became known as 'the night of the strong winds'. It was the last major raid of the 'Battle of Berlin' and a cataclysmic one: 74 aircraft were lost,[85] i.e. 9.1 per cent of a total force of 811. There were very powerful northerly winds that night which blew many of the raiders miles south of their plotted course. In fact, they were so forceful that the various methods used to detect their full strength failed, and the stream scattered far and wide. Many aircraft were blown so far south that they passed near Sagan, Silesia, where Laurie Simpson and Wally Maltby were, by then, incarcerated in *Stalag Luft* III. They would have been surprised if they had learnt that King was the engineer in one of the aircraft they heard thousands of feet above them. As they flew home many of the scattered bombers were brought down by radar predicted Flak. JB359 was shot up by a night fighter and crashed near Harzgerode.[86] It was Bracewell's 24th operation and all were killed, including King. They now lie buried together in the British War Cemetery at Charlottenburg.[87] German *Nachtjagd* records claimed 83 four-engined aircraft were shot down between 21.00 hrs and 00.15 hrs that night,[88] but these records appear to be wildly exaggerated when compared to RAF Operational Record Book reports, possibly due to different fighters claiming the same victim.

Ken Sutton, the 'Simpson Kite's' wiry tail gunner was, according to Ron Searle, posted to Canada for pilot training, after teaching at Lichfield OTU following the first tour. He appears to have returned to an operational squadron and flown as skipper on a number of operations before losing his life. There is little information about his background. Searle, who was his best friend on the Simpson crew, stated: 'Those days were very different to what they are now; all you worried about on leave was having a good time and you didn't care much where your mates came from; after all, the future was a bit uncertain.' Nobody really seemed to know what happened to Ken. RAF Historical Branch records reveal that, in March 1945, Sutton, by then a Flying Officer, was serving with No. 10 OTU, so he was possibly instructing after a second tour of 20 ops. On the 4th he fell from a ferry at Bablockhithe, Oxfordshire and drowned.[89] Ron commented:

> 'One expression of Ken's I'll always remember was when he used to describe how he felt when things got a bit scary. He'd say, "His ring went Half-a-Crown – Threepenny Bit", and would illustrate this by extending and contracting his fingers.'

He concluded: 'Ken never spoke of his family or where he came from, but he was a "live wire" and had a good sense of humour. I can't recall him ever saying an unkind word about anyone.'[90]

The remaining members of Laurie's first crew, Alistair Kennedy and Colin McLeod, returned with him to 460 Squadron in January 1944.

• • •

When Laurie Simpson's tour ended, his crew had undertaken only nine of the 25 trips they were briefed for during the Battle of the Ruhr. This must have created some anxiety amongst them; the relief of being 'stood down' or having to abort a mission was what led to the spate of 'early returns' with which Bomber Command was plagued during the spring of 1944. Fortunately Simpson's crew never resorted to 'funking out', even at a time when losses were proportionately higher than those of the subsequent year. During the whole of the Battle of the Ruhr, 872 aircraft were lost, averaging 4.7 per cent of the entire force despatched, mostly four-engined aircraft. 'Revolutionary advances in the technique of bombing', the Official History stated, had made Bomber Command 'into an effective bludgeon but that… had not enabled it to develop the potential of a rapier.'[91]

CHAPTER TEN

'WITH ENGINES – OR NO ENGINES'

OTU: Part Two

THE work and achievement of the Bomber Command Operational Training Units in 1942 was remarkable. This was the year when the Command had to build up strength in order to continue with the campaign. By May 1943 some squadrons in Bomber Command were beginning to get back to full strength. 'Bomber' Harris praised the hazard-fraught work of his 'old lags' who served as instructors after their first operational tour:

> 'In the most dangerous flying conditions the instructors and instructional crews ran almost as much risk as the fighting crews, and they ran these risks over a much longer period than that of an operational tour. It was and is a matter of great distress to me that recognition of their work and the risks they ran was refused.'

Laurie Simpson's third spell at 27 OTU was after his first tour, when he served as an instructor from 28 June 1943 to 7 January 1944 at Church Broughton in Derbyshire. Church Broughton was a satellite airfield of Lichfield – about 13 miles further north, just 'across the county boundary'[1] with Staffordshire. First, however, he and his colleagues had to be taught the problems of instructing inexperienced aircrew.

27 OTU, Lichfield, Staffordshire, 20-23 May 1943

At 27 OTU Lichfield many of the instructors had already completed their first tour and some became commissioned there, but this did nothing to alleviate their boredom in flying up and down the Irish Sea. However the training of crews was not without its risks. Some instructors did not survive this 'rest' period and most of them eagerly awaited a return to a squadron. On 20 May 1943, after six days' leave, Laurie Simpson's crew was posted to Lichfield to fly Oxfords. He remarked that he *'could never quite describe'* the happiness of the short time that he had spent on leave with Dorothy, his *'darling wife'*. He had passed through London and Crewe and ended up at Lichfield with *'½d in my pocket'*. After a few days of idleness, they *'visited Ma Irwin at the Anchor Inn and had a real bash.'* But he felt *'grim'* the next day.

On 26 May he attended a Flying Instructors' Course at Castle Combe, after managing *'to scrounge three days'* with his *'darling wife'*. Diary entry 26 May:

'Flying Oxfords – grand instructor F/O Tew – Tony Mattock RAF and Fred Canthell are my flying companions – good blokes – Tony a bit erratic and too fond of low flying – Fred more solid. So it goes on – "Patter" – instructors' jargon – a bit of a bind – Oxfords OK.'

That Friday Dorothy came up for the weekend and he had two days off, meeting her in Salisbury and staying the night at Chippenham. Laurie found the surroundings at Castle Combe *'very lovely'*. It was dairy country:

'Castle Combe – old town, very quaint, with shallow stream full of trout. Should be enjoyable stay here – getting the hours in nicely too. Five NZs, three Canadians, two Scotsmen, three Poles, three Aussies and a dozen RAF here. All ex-operational, mostly Middle East. Some fighter boys, Coastal, PRU, and Air Sea Rescue. Interesting to hear of other chaps' work.'[2]

No. 3 Flight Instruction School, Castle Combe, Wiltshire, 25 May-20 June 1943

By 7 June Laurie was at Castle Combe learning different methods of landings: '*…with engines – one engine or no engines.*' The weather was cloudy again with rain. That day he saw his first de Havilland Mosquito up close and confessed that he had a 'secret desire' to fly them. It was two years and one month almost to the day since he had first felt the controls of an aircraft. The bad weather ensured that, for Bomber Command, this was an 'inactive' period. During this three week course he was instructed in techniques of flapless landings, glide landings, forced-landings, and crosswind take-off and landings. He also learnt instructors' 'patter', techniques of coping with stalls, climbing and gliding, engine failure on take-off, restricted take-offs, steep turns, and low flying. He finished the course on the 17th and 'passed out with good report' – he had completed it a week early. On the 18th F/O A/F/L Simpson[3] was categorised as a flying instructor. He was back at Lichfield on Thursday, 24 June.

27 OTU, Lichfield, Staffordshire, 24-26 June 1943

After his first tour Laurie's handwriting had become much more intense and self-confident, lacking the slack, lazy curves of the year before. The losses in Bomber Command mounted. He noted in his diary: '*Bomber Command very active and losing many kites. 460 lost 11 in 8 nights inc. Lloyd Hadley on his 28th and Bob Christie (about 12th).*' On the 25th he went as second pilot with Graeme Keys on a cine-camera gun exercise in a Miles Martinet.[4] He summed up this time at Lichfield briefly: '*Two days at Lich – very quiet. Thence to Church Broughton.*'

27 OTU (93 Group Instructors' Course), Church Broughton, Derbyshire, 28 June-1 July 1943

'*Al has just received his commission and I think Ron and Col may get theirs soon. Started my week's Group Instructors' course on 28th. Don't like the Wimpy III very much. Am O.C. Night Flying tonight* [the 30th]. *Going on leave on the 9th.*'

27 OTU 'D' Flight, Church Broughton, Derbyshire, 3 July 1943-9 January 1944

In the summer of 1943 Laurie was at 27 OTU at Church Broughton in Derbyshire, where he and Ron Searle were instructing on Wellingtons. He described it as '*… a lovely spot and very handy for Derby and Uttoxeter.*' Searle was training w/ags, and Laurie pilots. They sometimes flew together in the old, ex-operational Wellington ICs which had, to a great extent, had their day. Occasionally, Al Kennedy and Colin McLeod joined them.

When not training pupils, Laurie and his crew found time for less stressful pursuits: 29 June: '*Last night Al and I played squash on Lady Vernon's court at Sudbury Hall*', he wrote.

Laurie was '*happy in the knowledge*' that he had '*a sweet, lovely wife and that she loves me*', but he was becoming despondent about the way things were going:

'*I'm sick of OTU life and the war in general. If I go back to ops, when I've finished my second tour I'll only come back to OTU. Flying for pleasure is grand fun – but the way we are now is not fun – it is drudgery – I wish the bloody war would end and I could stop and think further than the end of my nose.*'

At Church Broughton he met three airmen who would later be part of his second crew: mu/g Jack Rydings, who had just arrived from Australia; rear gunner Johnny Osborne, a warrant officer with a DFM who had done a previous tour with 460 Squadron, and a w/ag who was later to figure more prominently in his life – the 26 year-old survivor of the 12 Squadron 'United Pacific Crew', Arthur Schrock.

Schrock's first tour on Wellingtons with a mixed Australian/American/New Zealand crew at Wickenby has been described in Chapter Eight. He undertook 33 operations with 12 Squadron, not including the 'Thousand Plan' raid. He had a raucous character and was an extrovert. He variously described himself as a 'commercial artist', 'house furnisher' and 'shop assistant'. He was born in Townsville, Queensland, educated at the local state school and technical college, and served two years in the Townsville cadet battalion and three years in the local militia. He also had some flying time with the Queensland Aero Club. His final progress report at Church Broughton stated he had '…*made good progress as a lecturer and practical demonstrator*', and shown '*ability and keenness in his work as a w/ag instructor.*' Unfortunately, of Laurie's two crews, Schrock was the one person Laurie found it difficult to like: 'Schrocky: [I] didn't like him,' he once told me, 'always talking about women… I don't know how many conquests he made…' Ron Searle's impression of him was mixed: 'He was one of a type, a "loudmouth", but [there was] no harm in him.' One thing that everyone remembered was Schrock's obsession with the opposite sex: he never stopped talking about the ladies. Ron Searle: 'I certainly knew of his reputation for being "well endowed" and his reply of, "Well, can I help it if my mother only had one arm and that's all she could lift me up by?"'[5] But he was a gifted draughtsman and cartoonist and was much help to his comrades on the 'Long March' away from *Stalag Luft* III.

Despite its relatively safe environment, instructing at an OTU was not easy and quite different to operations. Alec March, a wireless operator, had been unhappy with the training he had received at Ground School. Whilst teaching at OTU, he wanted to ensure that his instruction was more thorough. He felt the job was useful, but found he was not only '…required to instruct w/ops, but also to give lectures to all other crew members on every aspect of w/t.' Tuition was difficult because many pupils had a 'poor standard of education'. He had to employ strict discipline which resulted in him being disliked by many: because of his dark complexion, his 'lazy and disinterested' Canadian pupils nicknamed him 'the black bastard'. When certain students were below standard, March would give them extra tuition. This was unpopular as they mainly preferred to be down at the 'local'. But w/ops had a certain responsibility: 'I was always at pains to stress that their duty as a w/op could be absolutely vital to their own safety, but more especially to that of their crew.'

The Wellington crash

In July 1943 Laurie Simpson experienced the first big blow to his self-confidence. In the first week of the month he was giving dual instruction on Wellingtons, and on the afternoon of the 6th he sent his first pupil off solo: Sgt Baxter, an Australian. Many of the ex-operational Wellingtons were mechanically worn out and subject to technical failures, which could be particularly dangerous with an inexperienced pilot low on flying hours. That night, the 6/7 July, a crash occurred that resulted in the loss of a life.

7-31 July 1943

'Had my first crash the other night: I was the senior pilot on a night x-country. The pupil, Noel Russell, was losing the take-off – no sooner off the ground and I knew something was wrong. Took over – immediately straightened the kite up. Starboard engine failed – visions of trees all round – hedges – an odd house – fields – what could I do? Thought we were getting away with it for a couple of secs – but actually I knew there was no hope. I called to the crew to hang on. I felt a bump as we knocked the top of a chimney off a house; closed the throttles; the back-rest broke and I no longer had control. We crash-landed in a cornfield, went through a hedge, some small trees, a dam – up over the bank. There was a terrific tearing noise, bags of dust and dirt, and the aircraft was spinning on the ground, I didn't think it would ever stop. We hung on like grim death thinking, "So this is it!" But the aircraft stopped – I was unhurt – fear of fire around me – we all got out in a few seconds. We found rear gunner's turret had been torn off, and the gunner beside it badly hurt. Three of us dragged him through a hedge just as the aircraft burst into flames.

'Ammunition started going off, Verey cartridges exploded, and the petrol tanks were going up. We carried the gunner behind a hedge, and rendered what aid we could. As we awaited an ambulance, people came from out of the night. We put the gunner on a stretcher amidst the morbidly curious crowds. I felt like bashing them all. Taken back to Sick Quarters, I was bruised but otherwise unhurt, and the rest of crew were OK except for Geoff Heath – he had a torn muscle in calf of his leg. The whole episode took a few minutes but seemed like hours – we were very lucky.

'We learned the next day that the gunner had died during the night, poor boy. I wrote to his mother expressing sympathy, and was taken up to test my nerve or something. Did not feel as confident as formerly, but I am quite OK.'[6]

Yanks

By July 1943 the Americans had arrived in England in force. Their aircraft could be seen stacked two-storeys-high on low-loaders on the major roads; their tanks and military vehicles were visible in every major town. The US presence was also felt in other ways. Laurie: 'While we were in London, Dorothy's mother had a phone call from a friend saying that she'd read in the paper that I had been awarded a DFC – proved to be correct – Graeme and Alec Masenthan also got one and Al [Kennedy] the DFM. Al has a commission now and we share a room. One of our boys, Geoff Heath, was knifed in the back by some Yanks at Scampton and feelings ran high: he is OK but has vicious wounds – we [Aussies] went down in a body next night, but no Yanks were to be seen.'

Dick Raymond: 'The mid-upper gunner in my first crew was an American who was in the RAF – Roy Webb. I shared accommodation with him at RAF Wyton. I remember going with Roy down to Huntingdon one evening, the only form of transport was a bicycle. We had a few beers and, on returning in the dark, "no light". A figure on a bike overtook us, stopped and shone a torch at us. It turned out to be a police sergeant who said, "Sorry chaps, I thought it was a couple of Yanks". You can imagine Roy's reaction. After we were blown up at Wyton, Roy was killed flying with another crew.'

Tom Sawyer, a Station Commander on various Bomber Command stations, also recalled the Yanks: 'With the Americans over here in large numbers their influence was being felt. Wireless sets had mysteriously been turned into 'radios'. The word aerodrome was old hat; the complex was now termed a 'base' and the landing area being an 'airstrip' or 'airfield'. The watch tower or control tower had now become 'flying control tower' or simply 'flying control', and instead of asking for permission to land, you merely asked, "May I pancake?" (for some completely inexplicable reason). We also had to change to the USAAF style of alphabet for r/t chat which took a little getting used to, for instead of "A – Apple, B – Beer", etc. it became "A – Able, B – Baker", to name but two.'[7]

Laurie experienced further problems with US servicemen's behaviour in early October 1943 and found their excesses disturbing:

'Just finished a very happy week's leave. Cycled to "Barn Club" in Christchurch one night – had chops and mushrooms and a few beers – was cold cycling home – Dorothy kept complaining of the way the kerb kept bending! Another night cycled to Wimborne for dance in "King's Head" – very stuffy show – too many Americans, which I find are a positive menace where women are concerned. Two Yanks grabbed a WAAF up here the other night and tried to rape her. Luckily the MO came along and they ran off across the fields – My opinion of the Yanks is at rock bottom.'

The last few weeks at Church Broughton were gloomy. On 1 December Laurie returned from leave and '*felt miserable*'. Gradually, however, he got over it and on the 9th wrote '*feel pretty good now*'. Many of the Australians on 460 Squadron were being sent back home but, with his new wife, he did not feel that was an option. However Dorothy and he were still '*dissatisfied with the set up*'. He wanted to get down to see her for Christmas but, as travelling by train was 'restricted', he did not know how he could manage it. They wanted to live together and have a baby. Events, however, were to dictate otherwise.

The weather over Nottinghamshire in December 1943 was not good for flying, with banks of fog, mist and low cloud. One particular cross-country flight on the 12th, on the other hand, was a revelation. It had been very cold with dense fog for days: 'Took off at about 6 o'clock amid murky fog, and 10/10 low cloud. So we climbed through the low strato-cu.[8] And as soon as we broke through, the change was amazing: a clear, smooth sky with the sun just set in the west and the moon rising in the east, with two filmy bars of cloud across its face. We all cried out with astonishment. From then on it was beautiful until we came between the cloud to land and back into the murk.'

Simpson finished his stint at OTU at the end of December 1943. Col McLeod and Al Kennedy wanted to volunteer to return to ops whilst the three of them were still together and, in order to facilitate this, Laurie went back to 460 Squadron slightly early: he was on leave in Bournemouth over the New Year when he got the recall. He had gone out to a Canadian officers' dance at the Royal Bath Hotel, and received a telegram. 'I'd only had about two days leave,' he recollected later, 'and I had to go back within three days.' He noted in his diary: '*Recalled from leave to return to 460 as a Squadron Leader, taking Al, Col, Arthur Schrock, Jack Rydings and Johnny Osborne with me. Seventh member is a Scot, Jock Nairn.*' Schrock, Rydings, Osborne, and Nairn had all been in the squadron 'pool' at Binbrook awaiting a crew placement.

CHAPTER ELEVEN

'YOU CAN CALL ME MEIER'[1]

The German defence

THE Germans are a well organised and meticulous people. Their perfectionism is reflected in their music, philosophy, architecture and engineering. Generations after the Second World War, the legacy of the Nazi period can still be seen in the cemeteries of small towns all over Germany. In southern Bavaria one can see memorials to the fallen. In a village near Nordlingen nine slabs have been erected to local boys who went off to fight on the Eastern Front. They never returned: '*Gemmischen im Russland*' they are inscribed – one has only the soldier's name and a year, '*1943*', inscribed on it, so uncertain were the authorities of his fate.

The German soldier, unlike Hitler, believed that God was on his side in 1943: '*Gott mit Uns*' was emblazoned at the centre of his being, cast into the alloy of his belt buckle. But the average Briton would have countered that it was the Allies who were fighting a 'righteous war' and that God was on *their* side. There was a clash of ideologies engendered by different cultures. The militant character of the Germans, Hitler's '*Mitteleuropa*' and '*Lebensraum*' policies, and perverted Nazi anti-Semitism, had collided head first with a culture nurtured by an outdated imperialism, a free country that itself contained a host of contradictions. The Allies faced a 'perverted science' nurtured by the corrupt and evil thinking 'Hitler Gang' – as the Nazi leadership was labelled. Despite this, German ingenuity produced some of the most radical and best engineered military equipment of the war. Few would deny that the Tiger tank, the Me 262 jet fighter and the V2 rocket were the forerunners of a new generation of weaponry.

In 1943 the Germans came up with an ingenious idea that nearly cost the RAF the air war. On the moonlit night of 17 August 1943, 600 aircraft took off to attack the V2 rocket base at Peenemünde. By the following morning 43 bombers had been lost from 26 squadrons, at least ten shot down by night fighters.[2] In August 1941, the German night fighter pilot, *Oberleutnant* Rudolf Schoenert of I./NJG 1, revised a weapons system that had been proposed originally during the First World War. This involved a machine gun bracketed on the upper wing of an aircraft to fire upwards and forwards.[3] Its adaption in 1943 was straightforward: a pair of twin Oerlikon 20 mm MG FF cannon was mounted in the upper fuselage of a fighter, behind the cockpit, arranged to fire upwards and forwards at an angle of between 10 and 20 degrees from the vertical. To sight them the pilot used an extra reflector sight, mounted above his head. This tactic immediately rendered the RAF 'corkscrew' manoeuvre, and even the most effective lookouts, obsolete:

> 'For the RAF aircrew one of the worst aspects of bomber operations in 1943 was that crews often did not know exactly what had destroyed the aircraft flown by their colleagues. Bombers would simply explode for no apparent reason. It was not until mid-1943 that aircraft returned home with evidence that the German flyers had upward-firing cannon in their night fighters. Little could be done to counter this weapon as [aircraft] fitted with H2S aft of the bomb bay had no room for what was needed – a manned gun turret.'[4]

With the abandonment of ventral turrets, a bomber's underside was virtually blind to attack from below. Previously the only option for a *Luftwaffe* attack from underneath was to fire with a slightly nose-up attitude, the fighter aiming its forward guns at the centre of the target bomber, after arriving 50 yards astern of it. This was the *'von unter hintern'* ('from behind and below') method of attack. With *Schräge Musik* (literally 'Jazz Music' or 'Slanting Music'), the game became even more deadly and scores of bombers were brought down. 'The hunter closed on his victim, endeavouring to get into a firing position without being seen', as aviation historian, Dr. Alfred Price, put it. 'Like that of the infantry sniper, the task of the night fighter crew amounted to little short of cold-blooded murder.'[5]

It was, indeed, merciless. A simple, almost faultless surprise attack ensued as, directly under the belly of the bomber, the fighter could fire straight into the bomber's wing tanks. As the German cannon used invisible, explosive non-tracer rounds, British crews never knew what had hit them: aircraft simply blew up in mid-air. In late 1943 a theory developed that German Flak units were using hoax shells nicknamed 'scarecrows' designed to simulate a bomber exploding. After a period, however, as more reports came back, RAF Intelligence Officers realised the truth of what was happening.

The most vulnerable points on the Lancaster were its oil tanks. These supplied hydraulic pumps that pumped oil to, and operated, the gun turrets, bomb doors, undercarriage, flaps, air intake shutters and fuel jettisoning system. A very large capacity tank was required to do this. On the Lancaster these tanks were located in the two inboard engines. In fact, there were two oil pumps on each inboard engine. The first one operated the turrets, the second all the additional systems. It became obvious to German pilots that aiming at the bomb bay was foolhardy and, as soon as it was realised where the Lancaster's hydraulic systems were centred, the *Luftwaffe* changed tactics.

On 12 September 1944 w/op Bob Kendall was shot down. It was his crew's 20th op, a mission to Frankfurt, and their 15 Squadron radial-engined Lancaster II was the victim of a *Schräge Musik* attack. 'On the way to the target,' he said, 'as we neared Mannheim we were coned by searchlights and immediately attacked by night fighters. The rear gunner ordered evasive action and we went into a violent "corkscrew".' As the aircraft weaved and rolled, the 'G' force pressed them against the equipment. 'The Browning guns were chattering away from the rear turret,' Kendall recalled, 'then suddenly a terrific bang and an explosion occurred under the wireless equipment and the navigator's table. We were consumed by a Dante's Inferno. My brain was numbed by the explosion, cordite fumes seared my throat, and flames were enveloping my body.' By then the whole cabin became engulfed by flames and thick, choking smoke: 'Flames spurted through the floor and fuse panel,' he remembered, 'as we had been hit smack bang in the bomb bay, which was loaded with canisters of incendiaries and a 4,000-lb cookie.'

Kendall's parachute lay on the floor under the wireless equipment table: 'I snatched up my 'chute from amidst the flames and clipped it onto my harness', he recalled. The bomb load had been jettisoned but the whole aircraft was ablaze and the pilot gave the order to abandon. 'I made for the nose. The bomb-aimer and engineer were trying to open the forward escape hatch, and I stood alongside the pilot, still skilfully handling the controls.' The engineer went out, followed by the navigator, the bombardier and then Bob Kendall.

'As I parachuted down,' Kendall recalled, 'I was illuminated by a searchlight which followed my descent until nearing the ground.' Bob Kendall was picked up and interrogated, and then sent to *Stalag Luft* VII Bankau.[6]

Warrant Officer Ken Knott suffered a *Schräge Musik* attack on 28 September 1943 with an RAF Film Unit on board:

> 'We were a senior crew on 166 Squadron. I was sent for on the morning of the trip and asked to volunteer to take two photographers whose task it was to take photos over the target. We would be in the first wave. The guns had been taken out of the front turret, we had no automatic pilot and the Lancaster I would only reach 19,000 feet.'

It was the crew's second trip to Hannover and they were attacked over the target by a Ju 88 with twin upward-firing cannon. 'Our gunners had spotted two Ju 88s behind us which appeared to be acting as decoys to distract our attention', he recollected. 'They warned me and I waited for their instructions to take evasive action.' *Schräge Musik* was then a new development and such attacks were unexpected. 'Our attackers fired their cannon after we had dropped our bombs and were on the photograph run.'

It was a good time for an attack as the Lancaster was running straight and level. Of the crew of nine, three – the mid-upper gunner, the bombardier and the flight engineer – were all killed. 'I managed to keep the aircraft under control [until] finally it disintegrated', he said. 'The rear cameraman and rear gunner baled out from the back door. The front cameraman and bomb-aimer baled out from the front hatch. Those of us still in the aircraft were blasted out.'

During the time that Knott and his crew were on operations they were unaware of the *Schräge Musik* tactic. 'This was a new development by the *Luftwaffe* which proved to be very successful', he recalled.[7] Knott was captured and sent to *Stalag* 357.

The Kammhuber Line

New German ordnance in the air, however, was only partly a solution to Harris's determination to burn, in his own words, the Nazis' '...black heart out'. In July 1940, a former bomber commander, *Oberst* Josef Kammhuber was appointed head of the *Luftwaffe* night fighter force – the *Nachtjagd*. The German night fighter defence at the beginning of the war was, like the British bomber force, very rudimentary and cobbled together from existing equipment. It was only with Kammhuber's appointment that the situation began to be reversed. He was teetotal, and in some ways bore similarities to British Pathfinder leader, Don Bennett, in as much as he was not physically imposing, but had an austere dedication to his job.

Initially the Germans had a simple searchlight and night fighter system stretching all the way from Denmark to France. However, by the last week in May 1942, RAF reconnaissance flights had proved that all the searchlights had been moved back to Germany. There was a political reason for this. That month there had been three major raids against Mannheim, Warnemünde and Stuttgart, and Göring's boast that 'no enemy plane would fly over Reich territory' had been proved empty. In the light of this, and in order to reassure the Germans that their protection took priority, Hitler ordered the searchlights back to Germany.[8]

A chain of small radar stations which controlled individual night fighters replaced the searchlights. Each station oversaw an area of the night sky known as a *raum* or 'box'. Thus a system of 'boxes' was developed called the *Himmelbett* (literally 'bed in the sky') line, stretching from Jutland to Brest, and the tactics were called *Raumnachtjagd* ('box night fighting'). In any box below 18,000 feet the Flak was free-ranging, or free of any incursion of the space by night fighters; above that was the night fighters' kill zone.

For the British, much of the intelligence-gathering ground work on the so-called Kammhuber Line was undertaken by Belgian agents who would send their reports back via France and Lisbon. One such agent worked as the fireman on an express train and concealed his documents under lumps of coal in his cab, ready to be shovelled into the fire box if necessary. Up to 15 cwt of these reports was collected in Lisbon at one stage. The Belgians had a long history of occupation and readily adapted to espionage. Professor R.V. Jones, who was Scientific Officer to the staff of the British Air Ministry in 1939, and in 1940 was involved in the breaking of the German *X* and *Y-Geräte* radio direction beams,[9] spun a yarn about this. He found some documents in the workplace of his Belgian Liaison Officer:

> 'He waved towards his top shelf, and told me that there might be a map "up there"... After a few minutes I found the map: it was a breath-catching moment for, as I unfolded it, I saw that it must show the deployment of a whole searchlight regiment covering the entire northern half of Belgium. I like to think that one of our Belgian friends, daunted by the prospect of cycling round the countryside laboriously plotting the sites of individual searchlights, thought that it would be simpler to break into the headquarters of the Regimental Commander and remove his map, for this is what it was.'[10]

From this document Jones and a colleague worked out that the Kammhuber defence was based on three types of radar; these worked in close co-operation according to their capabilities. At 32 kilometre (20-mile) intervals along the coast was a line of long-range grid aerials called *Freya*. These could scan through 360 degrees and had a range of up to 160 kilometres (100 miles). The *Freya* was the first to pick a bomber up and would transfer its data to two *Würzburg* detectors – narrow beam, high definition, circular dish radars, with a range of 48 kilometres (30 miles): one would fix on the intruder whilst the other fixed on a night fighter. The *Würzburg* tracking the bomber had a three-light squad (or *Zug*) of radar-controlled searchlights around it. Some miles behind this was a unit, or *Abteilung*, of 27 more searchlights which responded to the first *Zug's* reports.

Scientists were also able to use Ultra[11] to crack the secrets of the line. When the Bletchley Park decoders broke a cipher which covered reports from named Kammhuber Line sectors sent back to the German control, British scientists led by R.V. Jones compared these details with Air Ministry records of bomber operation routes to determine the sector locations. On 9 September 1942 they found the location of one *Raum* [sector], no. 7, in southern Belgium. Sector 7 gave away the numbering of the whole system. It was brilliantly simple: the Belgian agent's map suggested that each sector was roughly rectangular and had a fixed 90-kilometre frontage. Since the night fighter zone followed the line of the coast from Jutland to France, one had simply to project that the first 90 kilometre (56 mile) sector was in Schleswig Holstein and work down, fitting the sectors together like pieces in a jigsaw. Thus Sector 7 *was* located in southern Belgium.

The third radar in the system was an airborne device named *Lichtenstein* carried by the night fighters themselves. After the bomber had been located by ground radar and its location passed to the attacking aircraft, the *Lichtenstein* set on the fighter was used to home in on a bomber at close range.

Arthur Cole was caught by radar-controlled searchlights on an operation to Berlin in August 1943:

> 'It's a particularly nasty experience. They worked in groups, maybe six or eight in a group, and one of them would be radar-controlled, the beam of which was blueish. That fastened on us, and then about half-a-dozen others immediately joined it. So we were caught in this absolutely blinding light. In my opinion, the purpose of that was not so much to direct Flak but to illuminate the aircraft for a fighter, which would have been directed underneath.'

Bill Higgs recalled his own experience over Germany: 'Suddenly a line of searchlights came flying up – about 30 or 40 of them – although we didn't rate their searchlights very highly. But they were using a marker searchlight operated by radar – that's usually a big blue one – and it was straight on us. The aeroplane had to get out of the way quickly, because they put a cone of about 60 lights on us, all gathered around so there were no gaps [between them].'

Himmelbett was superior to the earlier German system; however it was not foolproof. The problem was that only one fighter could operate in a 'box' at a time. British scientists realised this and, in the winter of 1941/42, bombers began to be sent through a box closely bunched up, and as fast as possible; this was to push as many through whilst the fighter was engaged with another target. It was reasonably successful: during the course of an interception 40 or so bombers could pass through a 'box'. It was estimated that a closely-bunched bomber stream would take four 'boxes' to pass through the defence line. This left the remainder of the line and its fighters inactive.

On the return, the likelihood of fighter attack increased. This was because the differences of speed and navigation between each bomber resulted in the stream being strung out. One has only to look at various RAF squadron 'Operations Record Books' to realise that large numbers of aircraft were being shot down on the homeward journey. Ernie Weyle's Wellington Ic was attacked by a Ju 88 whilst returning from the first Thousand-Bomber raid on Cologne; Steve Jackson's Lancaster was shot down by a night fighter when returning from a raid on Coubronne; and Frank Mannion's Halifax was downed by a night fighter on the return from a raid on Neuss.

But the *Himmelbett* system was too rigid, soon becoming outmoded, and the *Lichtenstein* set's range was too limited – it only worked at extremely close range. Kammhuber responded to the British concentration tactics by expanding the Line to a defence in depth, incorporating many more fighter stations. By the end of 1943 these had increased to 200. His creation stood like a Maginot Line of the skies. To counter it, the Allies came up with a solution so straightforward it was almost naïve – Window.

'Window'

Like most good ideas, Window was simple but ingenious. It was first used during Operation 'Gomorrah', the four night attack on the Hamburg submarine and aviation works in July 1943: but it was a long road to its denouement. For years the

Telecommunications Research Establishment (TRE), at Worth Matravers, near Swanage in Dorset had tried to find an effective way to jam the German radar defences. As far back as 1933 it had been realised that radar could be blocked by dropping metallic strips, 'tuned dipoles', which would resemble an aircraft on a cathode ray tube – but there was considerable resistance to its introduction. One of the main arguments which obsessed Bomber Command in 1941 and 1942 was that German Flak was more of a threat to attacking bombers than night fighters.[12] In 1937 R.V. Jones had suggested the use of 'spurious reflectors' to the Radio CounterMeasures (RCM) Board, which had been formed to discuss the possibility of introducing RCM, but he found the Board had a strong reluctance to do this. This resistance continued up until the end of 1942, and found its root in R.A. Watson-Watt, who had been Superintendent at the Air Ministry Research Establishment at Bawdsey Manor when the idea was first suggested in 1937: he prevented trials taking place. The whole project disturbed Watson-Watt (who had invented radar), because it meant devising a means to jam his own creation (despite the radar being in German hands). This was at a time when radar was yet to be generally recognised as an effective defence weapon. Whatever success the British may have had in jamming this detection method, in using countermeasures like 'Window' there was a risk of a loss of faith in radar on the part of the Air Ministry. Watson-Watt was succeeded as the Superintendent at Bawdsey by A.P. Rowe, but Rowe had heard no mention of an 'RCM War' in 1941: he told R.V. Jones after the war that it was simply 'not done' to question the workability of Watson-Watt's creation. There was also, of course, the fear of 'reciprocation': an Air Ministry report of January 1942 on the German detection methods stated: *'The true reason against undertaking countermeasures is that, ultimately, the enemy will learn to overcome them, and that it is only during the period of his education that we shall reap the advantage.'*

In 1942 two reports were published on enemy developments, collated in 1941 from research carried out that year. The first, on German radar, became available on 10 January, and the second, on German night fighter control, became available on 29 December. The first report suggested that producing a large number of pulses simulating the echoes of an aircraft formation would be preferable to a total 'obliteration' of enemy radar transmissions (by 'jamming'). But there was a danger that the enemy would learn from any such countermeasures and imitate them. Thus there was, initially, much reluctance amongst the British authorities to use such means.

Following the acquisition of this new knowledge, after years of work and speculation, at the end of 1941 and the beginning of 1942 trials *were* undertaken at the TRE at Worth Matravers in Dorset of a new type of radio countermeasure. This was by Joan Curran, a researcher who was under the direction of a Dr. Robert Cockburn, the head of the RCM technical design section. There was a form of 'lateral thinking' involved in this research: since the Germans had difficulty in identifying their own fighters, and having no form of IFF, would they not have greater difficulty in identifying an Allied bomber? Curran focused upon the theory of 'spoof', i.e. since the enemy deduced an aircraft's position from 'evidence', would it not be possible, by deliberately adding to or distorting this evidence, to deceive him as to the aircraft's true location? The question was how to do this. Simply put, radar works by bouncing radio waves off an object. The intensity of the returned wave and the delay in receiving it tell one, respectively, how large the object is and how far away it is. In order to create a 'spoof' or false reading one can either create echoes from spurious objects, simulate echoes, or alternatively obliterate echoes altogether. Obliteration may be produced by using a form of 'smokescreen' which, although not a 'spoof' in itself, can be manipulated to create a 'spoof'. Unfortunately the more one repeats the use of a 'spoof' reading the more one erodes the element of surprise. Thus use of obliteration a number of times before separate attacks serves to forewarn the enemy when another 'spoof' will occur. Curran experimented with an assortment of reflectors, varying from wires to leaflets, roughly A4 exercise book size. Finally she found the answer to the interminable problem with a strip of aluminium foil 25 centimetres long and 1 to 2 centimetres wide.

On 30 May 1942, Window packets were actually loaded on some bombers for Operation 'Millennium', but then there was a last minute prohibition of their use. One of the reasons for this was the resistance of the Chief Radar Officer of Fighter Command, Dr Derek Jackson, a pre-war research scientist who had been a night fighter radar operator. He had similar emotional qualms to Window's use as Watson-Watt. Jackson conducted experiments using Window with an RAF night fighter squadron. His conclusion was that the British radar was vulnerable to being jammed, and he predicted that only one bomber in a thousand would owe its survival to Window; Harris predicted that using Window would cut losses by a third. Jackson by then had converted Churchill's scientific advisor, Lord Cherwell (formerly Professor F.A Lindemann who, as we have seen, deeply influenced the Prime Minister's opinions),[13] from being a supporter of Window to an opponent. The Germans by that time had already developed *Düppel,* their own form of Window.

The device that eventually went into service was a 27 cm-long strip of black paper, 2 cm wide, with a rectangle of aluminium foil glued to the back of it. It was codenamed 'Window' by A.P. Rowe, the Superintendent of the TRE, and was intended to be released in thousands from host aircraft to swamp the enemy radar. Ted Groom:

> ' [The Germans] had got a fantastic radar system that ran from Norway the right way down through France along the coast, and they could pick us up, eventually, where we took off, it was so good. All their fighters were in boxes. Well, Window put a stop to that because they couldn't get their instructions from the radar people, since the radar couldn't tell the difference between the Window dropping and the aircraft. But very shortly afterwards they devised a system whereby they could pick us up just the same. Of course all we did was alter the length of the strips – the wavelengths. All sorts of things went on like that.'

Despite all R.V. Jones's efforts, men like Jackson, Watson-Watt and Cherwell continued to resist Window's introduction. This delay bears similarity to the initial use of the Tank on the Somme in 1916. The authorities were very hesitant to use it at first, despite its advantages, and it was not exploited to the full initially.

On 4 November 1942, Jones helped to organise a meeting between Portal, Sholto Douglas of Fighter Command, Bob Saundby (Harris's deputy), and Cherwell. Portal recognised the lateness of the hour from Jones's indignant responses, and agreed to test the effect of the new jamming device on both British and German radar. At the end of that year Bomber Command losses began to fall as a result of successful jamming of the German *Würzburg* transmitters and the r/t communication between German ground control and their night fighters, but introduction of Window was still refused.

It was only with the German defeat at Stalingrad, in early 1943, and the accumulated losses suffered by Bomber Command in the air, that the Air Ministry began to press its case. But Herbert Morrison, the Minister for Home Security, afraid of another German Blitz, and the Royal Navy, fearful of having its ship-borne radar jammed, resisted. There were three more top-level meetings before Window was finally introduced. Firstly, on 2 April 1943, a meeting chaired by Portal persuaded Harris to support the measure and it was agreed for its introduction on 1 May. But the Navy resisted still: before its introduction, Operation 'Husky', the invasion of Sicily, would have to be undertaken, and there were also production problems. Secondly, on 22 June 1943, a high-level Staff Conference with Churchill present was convened. Watson-Watt presented his case against that of R.V. Jones. Leigh-Mallory, the head of Fighter Command, agreed to risk Window's use even if there was a risk that the enemy might capture examples of it and introduce its own version to use against Britain's own night defences.[14] Churchill closed the conference with an approval, reputedly saying: 'Let us open the window'. Thirdly, on 15 July 1943, after further delays, at a meeting chaired by Churchill personally, Morrison, the final opponent, was overcome. Two days later Harris issued a command for a major raid, Operation 'Gomorrah', on the night of 22/23 July. The target had been selected long before: according to one historian, 'Bomber Command Operation Order no. 173 was already on file with every Group HQ'.[15]

When Window was finally used operationally, it proved its efficacy straight away: it completely swamped the German radar system and rendered it temporarily useless. Arthur Cole was on the 22/23 July 1943 raid: 'We flew on the first raid in which Window was used, which was a raid against Hamburg. On that occasion it was the wireless operator who was chosen to push the bundles down the flare chute.' Individual crews appeared to differ upon who dispensed the 'chaff'. Ted Groom: 'We went to Hamburg and it was the night of the inferno. In those days Window was dropped through the flare chute at the back: it'd be all stacked up, and it was the engineer's job to do it. We put it through in bundles, one a minute.' Phillip Jenkinson flew on three of the four 'fire raids' on Hamburg, including the firestorm attack:

> 'I threw the Window out on the Hamburg raid – that was my job as a mid-upper gunner. Different squadrons had different crews and sometimes the wireless operator did it, but mostly mid-uppers did it. You pushed it out through the flare chute [which was] just down below, by the mid-upper turret, set on the starboard side. You pushed the Window and millions of [propaganda] leaflets out – I've still got some of them.'

The practical difficulties of unloading it were soon realised: 'From 35 miles off the coast we'd be there, right the way through and back again, dropping this stuff', Ted Groom recalled. 'It would last the whole trip: you got rid of practically all of it over Germany. I mean, you were supposed to drop it every minute but, as you can imagine with 800 aircraft, they wouldn't all be there checking their watches.'

Even before the first Hamburg raid, however, Hajo Herrmann, the innovative *Luftwaffe* commander, had devised a means of outflanking Window: single-engined day fighters, adapted for night work, working with early warning ground radar and radio beacons – Bf 109s and Fw 190s that ranged untamed like '*Wilde Sau*' ('Wild Boar')[16] above the Flak levels. This led to the equally effective '*Zahme Sau*' ('Tame Boar') tactic using twin-engined fighters. Using these techniques the aircraft, no longer controlled in 'boxes', could attack along much of the route of a bomber stream. So, although Window was extremely successful to begin with, over time the Germans found a solution to it.

The effectiveness of Window was finally confirmed during the 'Gomorrah' attacks. But it had been a long journey. History records that many aircraft were lost as the result of the failure of Harris to introduce the glittering countermeasure in 1942. It was another of his controversial red herrings: he stated in *Bomber Offensive* that he had continually championed its introduction in 1942 but that the authorities' resistance had prevented it. However the official history suggests he was undecided about its effectiveness, never really pressing hard for its introduction.

The Battle of Hamburg

> 'The streets were littered with hundreds of corpses. Mothers with their children, youths and elderly people; sometimes their bodies were charred and burned, sometimes untouched; sometimes they were clothed; sometimes they were unclothed, sometimes naked, with a waxen pallor like tailors' dummies. They lay in every attitude, now quiet and composed, now hideously contorted, with the final struggle of death crying out in every line of their faces.'
>
> SS-*Obergruppenführer* Kerl, Hamburg, August 1943[17]

For some months in early 1943 Harris had been planning to use Window to break the German defence system but was delayed by the weather. However, over four nights, from 25 July to 2 August 1943, the RAF rained four attacks on the old Hanseatic port of Hamburg: on the first night it dropped high-explosive bombs first to destroy buildings and then incendiaries to feed the resulting fires. The air temperatures in central Europe had been rising steadily that summer, with hot air convection up-draughts having already developed over Hamburg city before bombing began. On the second night of the assault, the up-draughts created by fires were strong enough to turn whole aircraft upside down. Due to the use of Window to blind the defences and a 'spoof' raid by Mosquitoes to another target on the second night, the bombers suffered minimal casualties.

The free-ranging *Wilde Sau* night fighter system that Hajo Herrmann had been working on had yet to be put into practice; it would act in collusion with Flak forces on the ground and operate above a certain altitude, relying on flares and sky markers for illumination. Despite elaborate deception plans to camouflage the city's major lakes by breaking up their outline from the air using barges and pontoons etc., the use of low frequency 2 cm H2S sets enabled Bomber Command Pathfinders to bomb fairly accurately.

Accounts of the Hamburg raids differ considerably. Reg Brown found the target almost impossible to miss, whilst on one raid bomb-aimer Arthur Cole recalled that his crew could not see it at all. Reg Brown:

> 'We did three [trips] to Hamburg during the "Firestorm" raids. It was incredible because the fires didn't go out; you didn't need the Pathfinders really, because there were still fires burning from when the Americans bombed it during the daytime; and it lit into the night, it was all aglow. You didn't need any markers to mark the target.'

24/25 July 1943

For Ted Groom, Hamburg promised to be a 'walk in the park':

> 'Our pilot, who was a Warrant Officer, had gone "second dickey" on the first trip to Hamburg two nights earlier, the first night that Window was dropped. We were in bed when he came back in... in the morning. We asked, "How'd it go?" And he said, "No need to worry about anything – we only lost 12 last night."'[18]

This was the first raid of the battle and a winner. Window had passed its initial test with flying colours. Seven hundred and twenty-eight of a force of 791 bombed; 2,284 tons of bombs were dropped in 50 minutes. But it was later found that bombing accuracy had been poor, less than half of the aircraft having bombed within three miles of the city centre, and a 'creep back' of six miles had occurred to the north-west causing severe damage on the west side of the city. 12 crews were lost, including two from 103 Squadron and one from 460.

27/28 July 1943

On the second raid 787 aircraft were sent out. This was the night of the firestorm. Philip Jenkinson, mid-upper gunner with 10 Squadron, did three of the four Hamburg fire raids, including this one:

> 'There was a great fire, but we didn't know what we'd done until a few days afterwards. We were flying through solid black smoke. You could see the fire 180 to 200 miles away, out over the North Sea. I registered the explosions but never actually saw the flames – because when you get up to 18-19,000 feet the ground's three or four miles away. You look out and with a fire [that far] away all you see is a red glow.'

By this time the German controllers were beginning to recover from the initial bewilderment that Window had propagated. All the PFF-marking was by H2S, which was concentrated, but fell two miles to the east of the aiming point. However there was minimal 'creep back'. Seventeen aircraft – 2.2 per cent of the force – were lost. Ted Groom:

> 'Our first one was in July from Binbrook: 27/28 July… the night of the inferno. That was our first trip! Keen as mustard, and we'd only lost 12 [the night before]! Previous to that we'd been losing 20 to 30 odd [a night], which was a lot, but not from the same squadron. You'd turn up about 24 aircraft from each squadron, and some nights you didn't lose any. Some other devils lost four probably. Eight times we went during the Battle of Hamburg, from November right up to January, but we did other trips in between.
>
> 'We were in the last wave from 1 Group, because we were the new boys – it was no good putting the novices in first. If there were 24 aircraft, we'd be the last to take off, depending upon how many new ones there were. The others would be off as much as 20 minutes in advance of you. This happened on every aerodrome. But at night you can't see who's where, and the only thing you can do is to keep your eyes open. If you hit the slipstream of somebody, you knew it, because not everyone was flying dead straight. We were the last ones in and everything was going like the clappers.'

Halfway through the raid a chain reaction set in. The air temperature was 30 degrees Centigrade at 18.00 hours and the relative humidity had fallen from the normal 40-50% to only 30% because there had been a long rainless period and everything in the area was dry. The damage to the western side of the city two nights before ensured that many streets were still blocked by fallen debris. All the city's fire-fighting vehicles were in the western districts damping the still-smoking remains, which meant that the majority of fire appliances were unable to reach the areas of Borgfelde, Hamm and Hammerbrook to the south-east, where the bombing had caused many conflagrations. On that night 96,429 4-lb Thermite stick incendiaries fell onto every square kilometre of Hamburg, as well as 2,733 of the larger 30 lb incendiaries. Halfway through the raid the fires in the southernmost area, Hammerbrook, began to coalesce, and the ensuing blazes set up such a vast suction force (as oxygen was drawn in from the surrounding areas) that air rushing into the eye of the fire at ground level dragged men, women, children, even buses and small buildings, into a raging hellhole.

The German design for air raid precautions also had alarming consequences. Adjacent cellars that had been joined into one, now facilitated the flow of the high pressure convection currents through them. Hermetically sealed shelters that had seemed an intelligent precaution now began acting as incinerators, so that bodies became vaporized and were turned into appalling layers of flaking grey ash, and precious kitchen utensils became transformed into useless silver and black pools of molten metal. In the already sweltering city the frantic, roaring up-draughts caused an uncontrollable firestorm, in-rushing air replacing the rising thermals at ground level all over the fire-stricken city. The resultant winds reached 150 mph at ground level, caused by rising convection currents, and the smaller less threatening fires were fanned by uncontrollable winds, these fires growing and coalescing into larger ones to increase the devastation. A column of roasting hot, flame-filled air rose over three storeys high, billowing into the blackening sky above.

The RAF later used other deception techniques such as 'Corona' – trained operators, Jews, exiled dissidents, German-speaking Englishmen in England, all imitated the voices of the German controllers, giving the night fighters false orders. Aerodromes 'fog bound' was a favourite. Gradually the Germans realised what was happening with the storms of Window and started to filter it out. The RAF simply changed the length of the foil.

Ted Groom:

'We dropped the bombs and the skipper said "OK now, course for home?" Then suddenly the Lancaster was flipped over on its back: the nav never even had time to give him a course! I ended up floating in the back of the aircraft with all the Window burst open: we were losing height and upside down! We thought an aircraft had blown up in front of us and turned us over. It happened so quickly, only seconds, and we were going straight down. So we went in at 19,000 feet and ended up at 10! And my parachute was down the back amongst all the Window.

'I'd lost all communication – the plugs had come out, and I'd got no oxygen – that had come out too! But at 10,000 feet you don't lose consciousness. Because I knew where everything was in the aircraft – every socket and every nut and bolt – I plugged my intercom in and [heard] the skipper shouting out for me to get up to the front. So I clambered up and sorted things out. He was strapped in and hanging in his straps. He'd opened the throttles up, and then he said to the nav, "Are you all right, Noel?" "Yes," Noel said. "What is it, 270 then?" "Yes, take that," Noel said, "I've lost all my charts – I've got nothing to tell us."

'Everybody was wondering what had gone wrong. I tapped Midge on the shoulder and pointed to the altimeter; it said 10,000 feet. He shook his head, and I nodded. Then he nodded "Don't tell anybody!" We said, "We think an aircraft blew up", and we did, until I read about it much later, and realised that we'd been caught in the up-draught from the inferno.'

There was a colossal temperature variation that night over the city. Groom thought that the heat just over the ground level was about 32 degrees above freezing whilst up above it must have been 20 degrees. This compared with some nights the squadron went out, when it was minus 47! On the ground below people were lifted off by the up-draught and sucked up into the vortex. Women carrying children, and even double-decker buses, were pulled in by the powerful, uncontrollable winds to where the firestorm was raging. Ted Groom:

> 'The heat was so intense that when they came out of the air raid shelters and tried to cross the road, they would be stuck in [molten] bitumen. And they'd die like that. It was terrible. We didn't know. We didn't find out until after the war. If there was anybody else who got caught in the inferno like we did, they must have never got away with it; otherwise we'd have heard.
>
> 'We got back over the North Sea, and were flying along and I was a bit worried because the instruments had all gone haywire. The Master Compass at the back had been toppled; that wasn't working, and one or two other gauges weren't working. I was worried about the petrol side of it... that it was OK. We landed at Binbrook, taxied in, and the ground crew came round, and as we got out they said, "Where have you been then? What's happened to you?" There were panels loose, mainly on the undercarriage nacelles: the rivets had popped. And the fuel jettison trunks had come out under the wings, underneath the centre tanks. The petrol hadn't gone because we hadn't jettisoned it. But the aircraft was in a bad state, and that was only the first raid.'

As is now well known, the agonising deaths caused by asphyxiation, poisoning from the toxic gases and incineration killed around 45,000 people with many more injured and 16,000 multi-storey buildings destroyed.[19] In some cases identification became impossible where the corpses had been carbonised, the bodies hideously shrivelled by the carbonisation process. Goebbels ordered civilians to evacuate the area as far as possible after the first raid. By the time of the second attack, however, Göring had instructed Hajo Herrmann to begin the *Wilde Sau* tactics he had been practising earlier and RAF casualties rose correspondingly.

29/30 July 1943

This time 777 aircraft went out and the PFF used H2S-marking, but the strategy was to bomb the areas of the city that had so far been untouched by bombs, in the north and north-east. However the PFF came in too far to the east and marked an area south of the Borgfelde, Hamm and Hammerbrook areas, devastated two nights before. A four mile 'creep back' developed, laying further bombs on the devastated areas. There was also very heavy bombing to the areas in the north and north-east of the firestorm area. Widespread conflagrations ensued, but no inferno. Twenty-eight bombers – 3.6% of the force – were lost. Ted Groom:

> 'Then we went to Hamburg two nights later[20] and they told us, "No need to worry about fighters: with the heavy cloud and icy conditions they wouldn't be able to get off." But we couldn't find the PFF markers. As soon as they'd dropped them they'd gone through the clouds; or if they were on the clouds, the clouds were up to about 16 or 17,000 feet. We were plodding along and Noel said, "Well, we should be there by now; we should be able to see something." Couldn't see a glow... couldn't see anything. And I said to Midge, "We have four propellers, just like Catherine wheels: Ice!" I'd no sooner said that than there were lumps flying off them. The leading edges were treated with a paste to stop ice forming, but our ailerons and flaps were not there. And our elevators at the back were the same. We were stuck: we just couldn't move. And we were gradually going down and down and, this happened so quickly you didn't have time to think a lot about it. You've got to make some decisions quickly, or you could be in trouble very quickly. So I desynchronised all the engines, and we got vibrations to shake the ice off. But it was a dangerous thing to do. We were going down lower, and we were through

this cloud, and it was getting warmer as well. Cu Nim!²¹ And we got away with it; we got back. That was the third raid on Hamburg.'

St. Elmo's fire had been experienced by Laurie Simpson in 1942 during a training flight over the Irish Sea:

'The effect is that the props look like a couple of Catherine Wheels and sparks run up and down the gun barrels [and the trailing aerial]. The first time we encountered it we didn't know what it was because we'd never come across it before, and were a bit perturbed. We thought "How dangerous is this?" But apparently it's not – there's no chance of getting electrocuted. It was quite bright because we were in cloud; I suppose it was cumulo-nimbus or something. So we were flying along in a glow, through these clouds.'²²

2/3 August 1943

On this raid 740 aircraft were sent out but the operation was a failure. A large thunderstorm had developed over Germany and Hamburg was covered by cloud. A number of the attacking aircraft either aborted or bombed alternative targets. PFF-marking was impossible, and the small amount of bombing was widely dispersed. Thirty aircraft were lost. Arthur Cole:

'We didn't go on the firestorm raid, but we did three raids on Hamburg and one of them was quite useless. One way they had to report the weather over the target was to send out Mosquitoes. On the fourth raid they reported that there were thunderstorms about 200 miles east of the target. In fact, when the storms got there, they were more like 50 miles *west* of target! So we flew into these enormous great thunderheads that went up to 25,000 feet: the aircraft was tossed all over the place – it was a really heavy electrical storm. And it was the only time that I flew when the blue flames of "*St Elmo's Fire*" danced around the edges of the plane; an extraordinary sensation.²³

'The navigator was doing a theoretical course check and we did a retirement distance run²⁴ to what was supposed to be the target. Well, when we got back, not a single bomb-aimer on the squadron claimed that he'd bombed the target, except one, and he was on his first trip. I think that was a bit suspect. But the rest of us simply said that no way could we know where we dropped our bombs!

'The following day the BBC announced, "Last night our bombers attacked targets in north-western Europe." Mind you, I haven't found a single book that records the true fact of the matter: they all describe the storm to some extent, but they all say that we bombed Hamburg. Well we didn't bomb Hamburg – we don't know where we bombed! It was impossible to see anything above, below, or on either side! The Pathfinders were due to mark, but if they achieved anything that evening it was not visible.'²⁵

Mid-upper gunner Robert Gill was also on the raid of 2/3 August:

'I did three of the Hamburg firestorm raids out of four that week. They were quite spectacular as you can imagine. One of them was in a severe electrical storm, all of our navigational gear and r/t were out of action, and when we emerged from the target area, we just headed west until we reached the UK.'²⁶

German Reaction to the Air War

If we are to believe Albert Speer's widely available memoirs, *Inside the Third Reich*, Hitler had a surprisingly naive understanding of the strategy behind the European air war. In 1943 he blamed not only His Majesty's government, but also the Jews, for the RAF raids. His answer to the bombing was to build a large retaliatory fleet of German bombers, the threatened use of which, he believed, would persuade the Allies to stop building aircraft.

Hitler expected the impossible from Albert Speer. But the shrewd Armaments Minister questioned the wisdom of his orders: any increase in German bomber production, Speer pointed out, would have a knock-on effect on fighter production, which would dwindle. This is what happened in 1944/45. The original reason for this was Hitler's blindness to the seriousness of the bombing, caused by Germany's unusual ability to recover from the air attacks. He was far more shaken by the loss of his valuable architecture than by that of human life and refused the entreaties of Goebbels and Speer to visit the bombed cities, unlike Churchill who toured British cities.

By 1944 the Allies were dropping over 3,000 tons of explosives a day on German targets. But Hitler's narrow-minded response was to concentrate on developing the V2 'revenge weapon' to attack British cities, envisaging a production rate of 900 a month. This drained resources away from development of a far more useful weapon, the '*Wasserfall*' ground-to-air missile available for production from 1942, which could transport 300 kg (660 lbs) of high explosive along a radio beam to 15250 metres (50,000 feet). It was unaffected by weather and could be produced in larger numbers and at less cost than the V2. But Hitler had a natural distrust of innovations, possessing only the outdated technical experience of the 'Great War' generation. Just as he contributed to the misdirection of the Me 262 jet fighter programme, his enthusiasm for the use of the V2 as a 'revenge weapon' caused the eclipse of the '*Wasserfall*', which never appeared in any quantity.

Speer, who had apparently considered assassinating Hitler, was interviewed after the war by staff of the United States Strategic Bombing Survey. This was set up after Roosevelt realised sometime in 1944 that '…there was a large amount of exaggeration and guesswork in what the [US] Air Force was accomplishing.'[27] An independent civilian commission, the Survey wanted to know how Germany's economy had performed during the war, and the analysis that Speer provided enabled it to conclude that the effects of the bombing had been very limited. The economist, John Kenneth Galbraith, was on the American team: 'The bombing of Germany both by the British and ourselves', he said, 'had far less effect than was thought of at the time.' Despite the heaviest air attacks, '…the German arms industry continued to expand its output until the autumn of 1944.'[28] Speer had increased armaments production successfully very early in the war. This gave him the confidence to explore the economic performance and realise that, until 1942, there had been a great deal of slack in the German economy; essentially, the Third Reich had more resources than it was employing. Taking up this slack, Speer utilised these resources to expand armaments production in 1944 to unprecedented heights. J.K. Galbraith attributed the failure of the Allied bombing to three factors. First, although factory machine tools may be enveloped by wreckage after a raid, the debris could be removed and the equipment dug out in a few days. Second, the Germans realised that production could be decentralised – the reorganisation taking much less time than the Allies realised – and not be confined to one site. With typical efficiency they also utilised substitutes: after the ball bearing raids, such as the first Schweinfurt attack on 17 August 1943, their engineers redesigned their machinery to use fewer bearings. Third, the previously inadequate factory management was reorganised to perform more efficiently.[29]

The British Bombing Survey Unit, founded in 1946 with Solly Zuckerman as its scientific director and Air Marshal Sir Claude Pelly at its head, only officially assessed the destruction after two years of analysis. It became apparent that the results of the bombing were far from what was thought at the time. Arthur Tedder, then Chief of the Air Staff, restricted the circulation of these reports, probably because they endorsed what the US Survey had found: the consequences of area bombing were indecisive. Peter Johnson, who had commanded a Lancaster squadron in 1944, worked for the BBSU in 1946 and its findings came as a revelation to him. The German loss of production, which was intended to be a direct effect of the evacuation created by area bombing, appreared to be a myth. The thinking had been that if houses were destroyed, the German people could not, or would not, work. But the BBSU found that there was no evidence to suggest any loss of production due to evacuation during the entire war.[30] Although large targets such as Essen and Hamburg suffered huge death tolls, there was no indication that casualties among the workforce had any pronounced effect upon production.[31]

Corroborating this, Speer said that he found Harris's policy of area bombing 'incomprehensible'. He told the Americans that it had had very limited effect upon German industrial production. Precision bombing was more effective, he said, but the wrong targets had been chosen. Raw materials, rather than armaments, would have made more crippling targets, Just as the British did not exploit the Dams Raid, Speer told them, hesitation after important bombing operations by the RAF allowed the Germans time to recover.

Failings in German fighter production
In July 1942 Hajo Herrmann had been appointed as a junior staff officer at the *Luftwaffe* Headquarters Staff on the Havel where he had taken over the 'bomber' desk in his department. Whilst there, after a short time he discovered, to his surprise, that there was what appeared to be a fault in the administrative machinery. As he became more involved in the work, what he termed 'his front line officer's nose', not yet dulled by perfunctory administrative work, '...sensed that there was something going on that was not quite right.'

What he actually found out was shocking. There was a totally naive understanding amongst *Luftwaffe* headquarters staff as to what a threat Allied aircraft production figures presented: not only that, but projections for subsequent years, suggested that the situation would become worse. There had been a general call in the summer and autumn of 1942 for more fighters, but there was a 'pecking order' amongst the *Luftwaffe* departments and as a bomber man he wondered what possibilities there were of filling the shortages he had found on the Mediterranean front. Immediately adjacent to his hut was Department 1c, which dealt with British bomber and fighter production. What Herrmann learned, he recounted, 'worried me a great deal'. The figures suggested that by July 1943 Allied twin- and four-engined bomber production would outstrip Germany's fighter production by a ratio of 3:1. This was 10,000 German fighters (projected) to over 29,000 Allied bombers produced in a year. Even translated to front line strengths the ratio remained the same: the 29,000 figure could be divided roughly evenly between the American day and British night bombers. If the Allied air forces attacked Germany en masse, theoretically, with the support of 19,000 fighters, their total attacking strength would be over 48,000 aircraft. This represented an even more overwhelming ratio of nearly 5:1 against the projected German fighter figures. The *Luftwaffe* staff had a blinkered view of the situation: 'In 1942

I discovered that this worst-case situation in the planning of aircraft production had not been properly thought out', Herrmann recalled. 'If I considered the air war by night alone, the British had an annual production potential totalling 15,500 twin- and four-engined bombers, while our night fighter capacity totalled only 1,700 a year.' A ratio of 9:1 was suggested: impossible odds. If the Allied fleets combined into one night force, 29,200 bombers would face 1,700 night fighters, giving odds of 17:1.

German senior commanders appeared to Herrmann to be 'blindly' skirting around the threat these figures presented. He proposed solutions to curtail bomber production, and cut existing bomber capacity 'ruthlessly', enabling increased fighter production. But, as he was a junior staff officer, and particularly a restrained one, Herrmann did not cut a strong figure, and the year 1942, with the victories in the East and North Africa, and the Dieppe debacle, was an optimistic time for Germany. His suggestions never materialised: the night fighter staff advised him to 'stick to your job' whilst the day fighter staff dismissed his concerns as naive fantasy; and neither the bomber staff nor the Quartermaster General took the threat of enemy competition seriously. Their argument, 'The *Führer* will know what to do!' gave Herrmann no reassurance: it was obvious that Hitler, in this case, would not.

But although the Germans knew what they faced, it was not Harris whom Herrmann wanted to understand: 'D.C. Bennett I saw as the main imaginative genius', he wrote much later, 'and about whom I tried to gather information. I considered the Air Vice Marshal to be my personal enemy.' This led to him interviewing some of Bennett's downed airmen at Oberursel.[32] He had flown over Berlin in a German bomber fitted with an H2S set found near Rotterdam and was shattered by the advances he discovered in Allied technology. The Germans realised that the RAF, equipped with new ground-scanning radar, could attack over cloud. To combat this they planned to shine their searchlights vertically into the haze where the light would scatter. They also intended to burn magnesium flares on the ground. The upper surface of the cloud would then resemble a great milky lake and silhouette the 'Tommies' above. They had even used spoof markers fired from the ground to combat the Pathfinders' antics. But these did not prove effective initially and an alternative was to drop improved hoax markers from Ju 88s.

In the autumn of 1943, Herrmann met Albert Speer in the Flak tower in Berlin's Tiergarten Zoo. He later felt bitter about the conversation they had. Whilst the Battle of Berlin was raging outside, Speer exhorted him to hold out for further increases in production, but Herrmann sensed that any action he asked for would not be undertaken until a bomb had actually fallen on the High Command's bunker.

The *Luftwaffe* could neither catch up with, nor overtake, the Allies: Speer's huge increases in fighter production by late 1944 were too late. That summer, shortly after Stauffenberg's failed assassination attempt, Hitler interviewed Herrmann: 'I was not overawed by him', Hermann recalled. 'I had no impression of greatness or of magic, but neither did I have the impression of evil: the only impressions I had were of simplicity and clarity.' Herrmann spoke of the adverse weather conditions over Germany, '…which didn't impede enemy operations.' The poor weather situation was making the dilemma of outnumbering of their fighters even worse: it was not taking off but landing in poor visibility that was the problem. Herrmann told Hitler of his intention to fly in even the worst conditions and by 1945 this visionary staff officer's calculations were being proved correct: Allied fighters and bombers were coming across in thousands by then rather than hundreds.

Under the Bombing

In 1941 Hitler decided to conscript German high school students born between 1926 and 1927 into the *Luftwaffe* as 'air force auxiliaries' or *Luftwaffenhelfer,* young men recruited straight from the schools to man the German anti-aircraft units of the Reich. The initial intake of 41,000 was later boosted in 1943 and 1944, it being finally estimated that between 70-80,000 students served overall. The son of a *Luftwaffe* General, Jochen Mahncke was called up with the first intake of recruits. He later recalled that they were both proud to become soldiers and elated to be free of the restrictions of school. They were soon on the receiving end of an 'unfair share of incendiary sticks, bombs and phosphorus canisters and also mines.' His unit's initial equipment of six 88 mm guns, a sound locator – which 'took hours to adjust' – and a searchlight that was 'more of a hindrance than a help', was later expanded to incorporate a giant *Mammut-Batterie* of three gun batteries, each with six 88 mm, 20 mm and 37 mm guns and a *Würzburg* radar. Mahncke recalled:

> 'I remember being afraid, with a sick feeling of anticipating the inevitable. But this was only before the raids, when the female voice on our special radio frequency gave the position report of approaching bomber streams, and we waited for data to come in for the gun controls. After that, training took over, and among the din of the guns and the exploding bombs, I forgot my fear and even experienced a kind of devil-may-care-high. We graduated to battle-hardened gunners, constantly tired and on edge, and we could only relax if the weather was bad. Our alarm periods lasted from four to six hours, depending on the weather and the moon. Quite often, a lone Mosquito, aptly called a *Schlafzerstörer* or "sleep destroyer", arrived after the raids had ended and would catapult us out of bed once again to run to the guns.'

When the American daylight raids began on Berlin in 1943, all *Luftwaffenhelfer* leave was cancelled but, with only 88 mm guns, their batteries were unable to reach the heights that the USAAF B-17 Flying Fortresses achieved and they were forced to stand by and observe:

> 'They kept to altitudes which we were unable to reach. We could only watch helplessly as they bombed the city to ruins, with fire and smoke spreading across the horizon and high up into the sky, while the thunder made the ground shake under our feet. At night it was a similar picture but in full colour, with the Christmas trees descending in slow-motion from the sky…'[33]

One German civilian who did experience the effects of the bombing first hand was a 26 year-old Berliner and convinced National Socialist, Melita Maschmann. She worked at the head of the press and propaganda division of the *Bund Deutscher Mädel* (BDM – or 'League of German Girls'). On 9 August 1944 she had travelled to Darmstadt, 32 kilometres south of Frankfurt to help her parents to move house. At 20 minutes to midnight on 11 August the sirens sounded. Everyone went down to the cellar and sat shivering on wooden benches as the first wave passed over. 'The hum of the approaching engines became a roaring hurricane', she remembered. 'The crashes of the first explosions could already be heard. The light went out. Folding our arms over our heads in an instinctive gesture of self-defence, we cowered in the darkness and listened…' The bombers came over in waves. Their infernal roar drew near them, moved away, approached again and withdrew. But they returned yet again. 'For a few seconds a frantic hammering of the heart shut out all other sensations. Then came a somewhat longer pause: the explosions had receded to the edge of the town and the humming of the engines [became] distant.'[34]

The cellar turned into a prison for them: as Melita's mother cried to God for help, a fresh wave of bombers passed overhead. Escape was impossible as the building was surrounded by an inferno so, climbing out of a small window and running through a sea of fire, the girl dipped her shoes in the nearest water tank and ran back. But the window could only be opened from inside: 'The human in me collapsed', she said, 'and the animal took over.'

> 'I ran to save my life, desperately summoning every scrap of energy. There was not a house anywhere in the street which had not turned into a blazing firebrand. Above the sea of flames, a glowing cyclone raged over the town; and whenever it caught the bodies of people in flight, it shrivelled them in a second to the size of a child, and the next day they lay all over the streets, hardly burnt, but like mummified children.'[35]

That night 15,000 people died and nearly 80 per cent of Darmstadt was destroyed. Of those in the cellar the only one to escape was Melita Maschmann, the convinced Nazi.

Albert Speer also experienced life under the bombing. Some time after Speer's meeting with Hajo Herrmann in the Tiergarten Flak tower, Göring ordered the staff there not to allow the Minister out onto the platform during a raid. But Speer found the views of the bombing of Berlin an 'unforgettable sight': it was an apocalyptic vision that completely entranced him. Unlike Hitler, he would visit the bombed-out districts after an attack: 'We drove over streets strewn with rubble,' he wrote, 'lined by burning houses; bombed-out families sat or stood in front of the ruins; a few pieces of rescued furniture and other possessions lay about the pavements.' The Gothic awfulness of it besieged his senses: 'There was a sinister atmosphere full of biting smoke, soot, and flames', he commented, and he was surprised by the way the inhabitants behaved: 'Sometimes the people displayed that curious hysterical merriment that is often observed in the midst of disasters. Above the city hung a cloud of smoke that probably reached twenty thousand feet in height. Even by day it made the macabre scene as dark as night.' Despite his attempts to describe the desolation to Hitler, the *Führer* showed little concern.[36]

* * *

The *Luftwaffe* was able to remodel its defence system as the RAF attacks became more concerted. In 1942, as bomber streaming and RAF Pathfinder techniques developed, the Kammhuber Line represented a system of defence in depth that, with advances in German ground and airborne radar, was continuously adapting to the Allied countermeasures. The *Luftwaffe* eventually had come up with a system of defence that almost cost Bomber Command the air war. The Air Ministry subsequently devised a simple but ingenious countermeasure that proved extremely adaptable,[37] and so the system of measure and countermeasure continued until a 'secret war' in the night skies over Germany evolved. The success achieved by the Third Reich in the Battle of Berlin was due as much to the unpredictability of the weather (which proved more potent than *Schräge Musik*) than to any foreknowledge the *Luftwaffe* High Command had. But, despite this, and the organisational genius of Speer, Hitler's blindness to the necessity for more fighters spelled the end for the German defence.

CHAPTER TWELVE

'HE SHOULDN'T HAVE JOINED IF HE COULDN'T TAKE A JOKE'

Morale

'There will be a residuum of cases where there is no physical disability, no justification for the granting of a rest for operational employment, and in fact nothing wrong except a lack of moral fibre.'

Charles Evans, Air Ministry official

LMF (Lack of Moral Fibre) was not so much a medical condition as a badge of dishonour. It could, in the present day, be loosely described as combat fatigue; but in the Second World War, when the *'Theirs not to reason why, Theirs but to do and die'* mentality was only just beginning to fade, and when an understanding of the psychological stresses men underwent in combat conditions was still nascent, the bitter acronym 'LMF' was a stigma that carried a promise to scar men for the rest of their lives. However, LMF was a broad term: it could cover a number of states, and be caused by a number of different circumstances, but it was the one tag most feared by aircrew. Today, in an age of more advanced understanding, after the horrors of Vietnam and Northern Ireland, and recent conflicts such as Iraq and Afghanistan, it could be termed 'Post Traumatic Stress Syndrome', but in the 1940s, when there was still little sympathy for any signs of apparent cowardice, those aircrew showing evidence of its symptoms were stripped of their rank and taken off station immediately.

Reg Brown, a flight engineer, who became a wing commander after the war, recalled: 'A chap who had flown 20 ops would say, "I don't want to go any more" and that would be it. This was very unusual. He'd lose all rank, and if he was an officer, forfeit his commission, and go. There was no counselling in those days; no psychiatrists were around the corner or anything like that. It was a horrible thing.' Thousands of bomber airmen had breakdowns which ended their tours prematurely. It has been estimated that 5% of the total complement of Bomber Command was affected, air gunners being in the majority. Bernard Frisby, a w/ag with 75 (New Zealand) Squadron, recalled that, as early as 1941, the front gunner on his Wellington declined to fly again after an attack on Dunkirk docks: 'We encountered severe Flak, especially as we made a second run over the target to take a photograph. On return to base he refused to continue operations and was therefore charged with LMF and reduced to the ranks.'[1]

Various airmen had their own views of the condition. John Dean, a navigator with 77 Squadron, recalled: 'The only time I ever came across a case was at a briefing prior to a trip to Berlin when a navigator, whom I knew slightly, suddenly threw his navigation bag on the ground and said in a loud voice, "I've had it, I'm not doing any more!" He was immediately bundled out of the Briefing Room by RAF police and we never saw him again.'[2]

The old remedy from the First World War of shooting a man for 'cowardice in the face of the enemy' had been used *'pour encourager les autres'*: it had been employed to keep a large body of men focused on their jobs and to prevent the spread of panic. In the Second World War, however, such barbarity was unacceptable. With this new war, aircrew who could not stand the strain and refused to fly were still treated very harshly, and stripped of their rank and flying badges; this was despite any track record of previous operations successfully completed – but it was not a capital offence. Such treatment struck navigator Alan Castle as unjust: 'On one occasion I had to fly with a crew that had only just arrived on squadron because the navigator was too scared to fly. This could, and did, occur at any stage of operational training, and sometimes to men who had completed numerous trips. Everyone had volunteered to fly, and to be treated, in effect, as a coward after doing say 10 trips to places like Essen was, in my view, unreasonable.'[3]

Russell Margerison, a gunner with 166 Squadron, recalled the case of a nineteen year-old mid-upper gunner who witnessed his own aircraft's tail and rear turret being sliced in pieces by the props of another Lancaster, taxying on the perimeter track.[4] The gunner, whom Margerison knew well, sat there 'speechless' and 'petrified' as the monster 'which had just gobbled up his best pal', bore down on him. He eventually climbed out and, ignoring all those present, threw his helmet to the ground, proclaiming, 'I shall never climb into an aircraft again.' He was immediately posted off squadron.[5]

By 1942, in the face of mounting losses, the staff of General Ira Eaker of the US Eighth Air Force was forced to review the acceptable number of trips that a daylight operations crew could perform in one tour. They calculated, as realistic for survival, a minimum of 25 ops and a maximum of 30. RAF bomber crews by the spring of 1944 were flying 30 on their first tour, and 20 on their second. For RAF crews it was considered that there was a 17% chance of completing a first tour, and a 2.5% chance of a second.[6] Pathfinder crews, who were generally regarded as more skilful, had to fly 60 ops on their first PFF tour, and this was often a man's second actual tour if he had transferred from normal duties.

The knowledge of having to return for a second tour affected many men, particularly Americans.[7] Before August 1944, after completing their first tour, US Eighth Air Force crews were sent back to the United States for 30 days leave. However they then had to return to the European Theatre of Operations (ETO) for a second period of duty. This could, and did, have a marked effect upon their psychology. The Eighth had suffered many cases of acute combat fatigue: the British attitude of '…he shouldn't have joined if he couldn't take a joke' was not as common among the American crews. In August 1944 a new rotation policy was introduced: after completing their first tour, Eighth Air Force personnel were returned to the US for reassignment elsewhere. From that point 'cases of chronic and acute combat fatigue' dropped by more than 50%, and the less severe anxiety reactions dropped by 90%.'[8]

Frank Dennis felt that '…the continual stress and strain would take its toll. There were a few aircrew who found that they could go on no longer and just gave up.' Although they knew they would be branded LMF, stripped of their rank, their brevet[9] and moved off squadron, Dennis suggested that 'maybe… the humiliation and degradation was tolerable if it helped [them] to retain their sanity!'[10]

Reg Brown noticed a 'serious flaw' in British flight engineer training. At the early stages of the war many of the new engineers had never been up in an aeroplane before they arrived on squadron. He recalled that '…two of the chaps I went through training with got onto a conversion unit, and decided "this is not for me" and went. They lost their flying badges; lost their stripes.' Bill Higgs of 35 Squadron recalled, 'I knew of one case – an accidental case. It was on a daylight raid and the chap, who was an air gunner, said, "I don't fancy this at all", and was taken off the crew, and another gunner put in. So the first was taken up on LMF and stripped of his rank; but he had to keep the brevet up. He was then made what they call ACH – Aircraft Hand – who cleaned the latrines and all those sorts of jobs. Of course, anybody who saw somebody cleaning the latrines with a brevet up, understood immediately that he'd been stripped. But he came back on ops: I saw him – it must have been eight or nine months later – in our [aircrew] pool. He was killed later.'

Henry Coverley's second crew was a 'headless crew' when he met them: 'I was given [them] suddenly because their skipper had gone LMF, and I felt very sorry for them. But we were more frightened of LMF than Flak or Jerry fighters. It was the most frightening thing in Bomber Command. To think that you'd be branded with LMF and those letters would stay with you until you died, was more frightening than anything.'

Arthur Smith, a bomb-aimer on Halifaxes, was himself branded. He recalled: 'It was a very gradual thing. I was getting very, very frightened: if the aeroplane started doing anything odd, such as unusual movements in flying, my heart would go into my mouth. It just seemed to be a general fear of flying. We went up on to this particular trip, probably about the 21st mission, and as we climbed to height, I did literally freeze with fear. The jobs I had to do, like taking navigational fixes etc. – I just couldn't do them. The navigator realised there was something wrong, and so they turned back after going out for an hour or so, and landed with a "sick air bomber" on board: that's what was radioed back.'[11]

The total number of LMF cases in the Second World War is difficult to quantify precisely because many of the official case records have disappeared. The label was peculiar to aircrew and cases increased as the war went on. Estimates range from 4,000 to around 6,250 cases, but sympathetic treatment by medical officers and relegation to instructor duties by COs meant the actual figure may have been far higher. Many men reported as having LMF were dealt with harshly. This was recognised at a high level but felt to be unavoidable. 'Bomber' Harris, aware of the dilemma, feared a risk of contagion and many senior officers had a blinkered view of the problem: any 'LMF' cases had to be crushed. Arthur Smith was taken to his station CO and severely dressed down. He was informed that '…in the First World War it would have been termed "turning my back to the enemy" and I would have been shot. I was divorced from all contact with my crew, in fact anybody on the aerodrome… then I was taken to a centre where they took cases of LMF.' He was interviewed by an RAF psychiatrist: 'What he said made me realise that my family would know about it; my girlfriend would know about it; all my friends would know. Wherever you were sent, and whatever jobs you did, there would be whispers behind your back: it would have been a terrible atmosphere.' Smith concluded that it would be better to return to ops than to suffer such a stigma.[12]

No one was devoid of fear on operations, but it was seldom expressed openly, and remained in the mind of the individual. As men approached the halfway mark on a tour, when the odds of survival were nil,[13] the look of strain on their faces was difficult to ignore. Group Captain Tom Sawyer: 'I don't mind admitting now that I certainly had the odd moment of doubt during my second tour when, in the small hours, I would very occasionally be unable to sleep and lay wishing I could break a leg or catch pneumonia and get away from it all with a cast iron excuse. It would not have been human to have felt otherwise.'[14]

Arthur Cole:

> 'You didn't really know whether people had gone LMF because they would be taken off the squadron and you wouldn't know about it. I've got this theory: it's not derived from me, its something I've read in the past – that everybody is endowed with a certain reserve of courage but it was not the same for everyone. We had a Scottish mid-upper gunner, he was at least 35 years-old, which was old for aircrew, and he started to drink; I didn't know that he drank, he was quite a friend of mine and he was an officer.
>
> 'The officers' mess at that time was built around a quadrangle, and there was a rough square of grass in the middle. I was walking along a corridor, and I heard my name being called in a drunken way and looked out of the window at this square of grass, and there he was, crawling on his hands and knees, hopelessly drunk.
>
> 'We ordered stuff from orderlies, and we didn't go to the bar; but the bar was down a corridor, in a cubbyhole. He had persuaded the staff to let him in, and as I understand it, he would order a beer with a double whisky, and then cider with a double rum: his nerve had gone. I suppose you would call that LMF, but perhaps not typical LMF. But I know we relied upon each other, and I had to report him immediately and he was off the squadron the same day. And that is roughly what happened with people who were LMF. I suppose he got drunk simply because he couldn't stand the strain of operational flying any longer.'[15]

Engineer 'Sandy' Rowe recalled how LMF affected – or rather did not affect – him during his time on 103 Squadron:

> 'One afternoon at Elsham Wolds, I walked into the lounge of the sergeants' mess with the intention of getting a drink. I noticed that there were very few – maybe less than half-a-dozen chaps – present. A small group were chatting in a corner, and one fellow was sitting alone at a table. I decided to join him. I did not know him or whose crew he flew with.
>
> 'I sat down and greeted him: "Hiya, how you doing?" "I'm in trouble", was his reply. I queried his problem, and he told me that he had resolved not to continue flying. I was startled: I had heard of such people but had never encountered one before.
>
> 'He then told me about his last flight which was horrific, with dead and injured aboard and the aircraft in a very poor state. It soon became clear to me that he was quite unfit to continue to be crew and that his decision to discontinue flying was correct. Unfortunately for him the decision should have been made by the medical officer and not by himself.
>
> 'I decided that he had done his bit, and felt sorry that his experience had affected him so much and sincerely hoped that the authorities would not humiliate him but treat him with kindness. Eventually, I gave him my best wishes and left.
>
> 'Within a couple of days I went on leave and there was no sign of him on my return nor did I hear any mention of him. [Rowe thus suggests that he had been sent off squadron, charged with LMF]. I am of the opinion that, apart from myself, the remaining members of his crew, and the official who had to deal with him, no one else on the airfield knew about him. This type of thing was not publicised: the old idea of stripping a chap of his chevrons on a public parade had, I believe, long been forgotten.[16] I knew nothing about any damaged aircraft the "LMF" had referred to, and in fact never saw any damaged aircraft at all during the 6-7 months that I was at Elsham Wolds, except my own.

'Strangely his story had no effect upon me at all, however. It's something that I do not understand: I consider that I'm a sensitive person, but back at that time I seemed to be immune to these happenings. One night after returning from an op, an aircraft from Binbrook crashed a couple of fields away.[17] Returning to my hut, and thinking that I might be able to help, I went to the scene: I was the first and only one there. With all the petrol about, it was blazing from end to end and I could do nothing. Eventually the crash crew arrived and I stayed awhile, watching them dragging the shrunken bodies from the wreckage with long iron bars. Then I left, went to my hut and was sleeping within minutes.'[18]

During a period of being 'stood down' on 218 Squadron, Miles Tripp befriended a young fellow bomb-aimer, Warrant Officer P.M. Nicholls, nicknamed 'Nicky', who had been deeply affected by operational stress. The man was something of a loner and one who was not easy to get to know: 'One obtained his acceptance rather like winning the confidence of a wild animal,' Tripp recalled, 'by frequent contacts and allowing him to sense there was no danger of any sort of aggression.' He was a most unusual character, whom Tripp saw as 'completely brutalised', his nerves were in tatters, and yet he was a compulsive risk-taker who saw 'violent death in action' as 'a fitting end to a human life'.

'Nicky' had the isolated air of a 'contemptuous misanthropist' that made Tripp want to get to know the young man better. His behaviour reassured Tripp, as the bombardier appeared more scared than himself, and he wore a frozen, emotionless expression beneath his fair hair and deep-set blue eyes. There was a duality about him. He would give ruthless illustrations of the worst in human nature, but then be amused by another human being's distress; he seemed to be as horrified by the prospect of his own death, as he was excited by it.

'In 1943 he had been nearly killed over Essen and the memory of that raid haunted him. Through a quirk in his temperament he was utterly opposed to dying in a raid against Essen. To die in a raid over Cologne, or Frankfurt, or Nuremberg would be an acceptable end, but to die over Essen was somehow disgraceful.'[19]

Tripp later discovered that his companion was estranged from his parents, and was the father of a three year-old boy. Eventually 'Nicky' disgraced himself in front of the whole squadron: Tripp, who had not heard from him for some time, approached one of his crew, who told him that the young bomb-aimer was off the crew. During an open night at the mess, and in the presence of ladies, Nicholls had unzipped his flies and urinated contemptuously on the floor. The next day he was packed off to the Aircrew Refresher Centre at Sheffield for a three week disciplinary course. Tripp was bemused: if 'Nicky' had been attempting to alienate himself from others with a deliberate 'show of contempt for ordinary behaviour', he had succeeded.[20]

Warrant Officer Nicholls returned to ops but was killed on 24 April 1945, on 218 Squadron's last operation of the war. The Lancaster he was in, NF955, took off from Chedburgh at 7 o'clock in the morning to attack Bad Odesloe, but the starboard engines lost power and the aircraft crashed into a hedgerow near the WAAF quarters. As the crew tumbled onto a wing, a bomb blew up and killed all. The explosions continued for over half-an-hour.[21]

Fred Danckwardt of 467 Squadron recalled a disturbing case of LMF on his own crew. His mid-upper gunner had been killed on an op in circumstances that Danckwardt found particularly upsetting: 'It's *very* difficult to get into a mid-upper turret; but when a person is completely unconscious, it's *extremely* difficult to get them out. We had to first unstrap him, and he was quite a heavy chap and it was difficult. He became unconscious with his hand on the control and the turret was still spinning round, which didn't help. The crew eventually did get him out but they ran out of oxygen bottles. So we came down low. After we'd left the enemy coast, the pilot told me to go back to see what I could do. I was holding him in my arms and I thought I saw his eyes flickering, but then he died.

'Another chap came to us for the next trip, and he had a complete mental breakdown in the air, just as we were about to attack Berlin. He started shouting, screaming, and firing his guns willy-nilly, that sort of thing. It took a long time for the pilot – and our pilot was a pretty strong character – to calm him down. We got through all right, and then when we landed he disappeared and I never saw him again. I don't know what happened to him; I'm not sure where he came from, but he just disappeared. He went completely berserk: it was his first operation and I think he just couldn't take it.'

David Howell, a navigator, was one of very few airmen who confessed to having a whole belief system that helped him control his fears: 'I was as much subject to fear as anyone – especially when our aircraft was being hit, or on fire – as twice happened. My main preoccupation at such times was, naturally, to keep track of our movements, and to continue to "press on regardless" with work on my chart. What creates "morale" in a bomber crew? I had friends who had taught me to base my life on four moral standards: honesty, purity, unselfishness and love – all absolute. "Live by those standards", they told me, "and you will create a new moral climate around you."'

Howell recalled that he had a 'Super-Radar' aid on operations that enabled him to overcome fear: 'There was no box, no mechanism. It was the strict discipline of silence and acceptance of God's will, and the obedience to the thoughts which entered the mind during that silence, no matter what the conditions were like.' He found that it was easy to pray to God in moments of extreme urgency. 'It was also my habit to jot down the thoughts that came in the silence, and then to obey them implicitly and with faith.' Fear went when perspective came in. 'We were fighting a war of faiths on a world scale,' he recalled, 'a war of which 1939-45 was but an episode. The moment I made a conscious effort, enlarging my mind and heart with the perspective of a world transformed, then all fears were knocked to bits.'[22]

Unsurprisingly, given the relentless pressure, there were some men who chose to remove themselves from the affray by means of self-inflicted wounds – a frequent escape from the stresses of the First World War, known as 'Blighty Ones'. Geoffrey Willatt recalled, 'Merle [a friend] said he'd been posted back home to Africa. After an evening on the town, we all went to see him off at the railway station. As the train started, he pulled me close and whispered in my ear, "That's what lighter fuel in your eyes does for you".' Willatt had heard of one airman staying up all night staring at a light bulb: 'I found it hard to blame people like this, and quite understood why – they were no good for the job in hand anyway.'

Henry Coverley's recollection of his second tour, in the spring of 1944, around the time of the Nuremberg raid was '…there were some colossal casualties; very, very high; outrageously high.' Around this time medical officers at air bases across England began to notice an increasing number of 'early returns': crews aborting missions and returning to base with purported technical problems. As this phenomenon increased, questions began to be asked, putting more pressure on pilots. Alec March:

'Morale of aircrews on squadrons was at an extremely low ebb in early 1944. This can, perhaps, be understood as not a single crew [on March's unit] had been "screened" in six months since we arrived on squadron.[23] The usual question asked by new crews upon arrival was, "How long does it take to complete your tour here?" The reply from older members, prefaced by a cynical laugh, was, "What do you mean 'complete your tour'? No one ever does." Command must have been aware of low squadron morale as six senior crews, of whom we were the most senior, were "screened" suddenly before completing a full tour of ops. Only two were needed for us to reach the magic number of thirty. I have often wondered if we would have returned safely had we been made to fly them.'[24]

Russell Margerison, whose crew was on the ill-fated Nuremberg operation, was adamant that the notion that aircrew morale fell dramatically after the 'Battle of Berlin' was '…utter nonsense – morale was always very high in spite of sometime heavy losses.'[25]

Miles Tripp's crew found they had great trouble in completing their tour in early 1945. On their 24th operation – a raid on an oil installation in the Ruhr at Wanne-Eickel – they were forced to turn back after the main supercharger gear failed. Although only having six operations to go, after three months on ops their tempers were beginning to fray. Then, following what would have been their 25th mission, the skipper, George Klenner, was informed of an order that had been issued: any crew that had not completed 25 ops that morning would have to continue for another 5 before being 'tour-expired'. This meant that, because of the 'early return' on Wanne-Eickel, the crew had a further 10 trips to do. The cause of this order was bad weather, which was reducing the number of new crews passing out at OTUs. This meant that any veteran crew approaching the end of its tour would have to continue on ops until the gap in personnel was filled. After Klenner's next trip the restrictive order was amended: a tour was to include forty ops 'over enemy or enemy-occupied territory'.

Alec March had a replacement mid-upper gunner assigned at one time to his crew: a thin, pasty-faced Londoner, who had failed to complete his first tour because of illness. 'He gave us all a fright on his first night when he shouted, "*I don't want to go to Berlin!*" several times. The poor lad was having a terrible nightmare.'[26]

On 3 March 1945, Ray Thomas, a navigator with 10 Squadron based at RAF Melbourne, went with his squadron on a raid to Kamen in the Ruhr. The RAF had planned two raids that night: one on the synthetic oil processing plant at Kamen; the other to the Dortmund-Ems Canal near Ladbergen. A total of 234 aircraft went to Kamen and 222 to Ladbergen. Before crossing the Dutch coast Thomas's aircraft lost an engine and the crew decided to return home, jettisoning their bombs in a designated area of the English Channel.

It was fortuitous that on the 13th op of their tour they had made an 'early return'. It was the night of *Unternehmen Gisela*, an operation of unexpected deceit in which 200 German night fighters crossed the North Sea to shoot down RAF bombers returning over the home circuit. The intruders entered British airspace between the Thames Estuary and the North Yorkshire Moors and, in the ensuing chaos, 20 operational aircraft were shot down with five from Heavy Conversion Units. German losses were around 24 – all Ju 88s.

The problem with 'early returns' was that in some cases they were genuine. Navigator John Geddes recalled his second trip with 428 Squadron. His aircraft was crossing the

Channel into France when his engineer started to complain about a pain in his arms: 'In no time he was screaming with pain and we decided to return. Next day we were all up before the Wing Commander and went for an interview with the MO.' Apparently the aircraft had flown through an extreme temperature change, producing in the engineer an affliction similar to divers' 'bends', when nitrogen bubbles build up in the tissues. The MO was reluctant to accept this but, because the crew was adamant it had not happened on a previous trip, '…our engineer was saved; otherwise he would have been taken off flying duties – LMF.'[27]

In Sandy Rowe's case his crew's 'early return' in 1943 was nearly disastrous. They were heading out over the North Sea when oil pressure on one engine dropped: 'I told Douglas [D.W. Finlay – the skipper] that the engine would have to be stopped before the needle reached zero… we would get no thanks if we ruined the engine.' As Rowe was the oldest crewman at 27, Finlay asked him his opinion. Rowe felt that there would be enough trouble ahead without taking more with them. 'I reminded him that the final decision would be his,' Rowe recalled, 'but mine would be to return.' Finlay decided to turn back. They dropped the cookie in the sea.

When they arrived over Elsham Wolds there was no need to jettison any fuel or bombs because the aircraft was the correct landing weight. Rowe: 'The airfield lights were lit and we received permission to land. We were coming in nicely and were nearly down to the runway. Suddenly all the lights went out, and we were in darkness. The language was strong! I opened the throttles and started raising the wheels and Finlay managed to lift the machine over the high ground ahead. As we reached its peak we were surprised to see another fully lit airfield in front of us.' This was Elsham: they had tried to land at Kirmington.

Unbeknown to them they had suffered a narrow escape at Kirmington, since there had been another aircraft on the runway. 'The controller, seeing our lights approaching his runway,' Rowe recalled, 'realised it was too late to fire a red flare in front of us, and pulled the master switch.'

In 1941 a 'Secret Order', A.M.O.S.1141/S.7.C (1) was issued; this dealt with '…the disposal of members of aircrew whose conduct may cause them to forfeit the confidence of the Commanding Officer in their determination and reliability in the face of danger in the air.' A Special Cases Committee was established to judge whether a man was lacking moral fibre, inefficient, insubordinate, or just medically unfit, but the RAF's final classification of 4,000 LMF cases did not include the last three conditions.[28] Evidence suggests that many men who were reported as having LMF, were harshly dealt with. Although this was recognised at a high level it was felt to be unavoidable, the thinking being that it was 'better to misjudge the unfortunate few than allow the slow decay, and subsequent collapse, of the entire force.'[29]

Ted Groom experienced three cases of LMF in his first crew on 460 Squadron. His rear gunner had served on Blenheims in the Middle East but found operations over Germany far more traumatic. It was a sure case of 'contagion': he infected the other gunner with his conversation. They were the first to be reported and subsequently disappeared off the squadron. The wireless operator, whom Groom described as 'a nice chap', went sick on a trip to Italy. They were coming back from an operation to Milan and got 'iced up' near London. The ailerons, elevators and other control surfaces were coated with ice and became unresponsive. The one trick they could use, which was not recommended because of the way it affected the airframe, was for the engineer to desynchronise the engines so the ice would be shaken off by vibrations. In doing so they fell 10,000 feet but still could not get rid of the ice. So the crew went into 'jump' positions. Eventually, at 3,000 feet, they broke cloud base and the controls became more responsive. Everyone went back to their positions except the wireless operator, who stood traumatised by the rear escape hatch. The navigator, Noel Knight, went back to help him onto the rest bed, and they subsequently landed without permission at Lakenheath and forced him, against his will, to return to Binbrook. The unfortunate w/op was then taken off squadron.[30]

But the bomber war could affect men in even more disturbing ways than this, some even ending their own lives. Reg Frayers recalled at least one pupil at Arcadia, a training establishment in Canada, doing so after elimination from pilot training; and Fred Danckwardt remembered an NCO on his squadron shooting himself in the head: 'An Australian wireless operator in the room next to mine in the sergeants' mess actually shot himself: there were bits of his brains all over the ceiling. He just couldn't stand it any more.'

Flight Lieutenant 'Roy' Maurice Skeet was an extreme case. He had taken part in the first two Thousand-Bomber raids with 158 Squadron in early 1942 but, later that year, conscience-stricken by the policy of 'area bombing', he took his own life. After the war Skeet's son made a lengthy examination of the circumstances of his father's death. He found that the subsequent RAF enquiry had tried to cover up what had happened, stating that Skeet had killed himself due to financial difficulties. A corporal fitter who knew him in Iraq and respected him, suggested that his action was actually typical: Skeet abhorred injustice, was unafraid of his superiors, and was perceived to have a sensitive nature.

As a flight commander, a responsible position normally given to officers of special qualities or outstanding experience, Skeet would have been able to inspect any reconnaissance reports of the damage caused by area bombing. In a letter to his mother, he said how troubled he was by the consequences of the bombing policy and was worried that his opinions might affect men under his command. An air gunner who happened to speak to him the day before he ended his life, said his decision to do so was '…related to the indiscriminate nature of the area bombing offensive.' He believed Skeet was probably unable to reconcile his conscience with his duties.[31]

In some cases of extreme stress a peculiar twitch became recognisable on ops. Alec March concluded that although crews were cleared as medically fit for operations, by the time a tour was over few were free from symptoms of the strain caused by it. 'Many problems were due to the nervous system,' he said, 'and perhaps the best known of these was the "Berlin Twitch", usually facial, but not necessarily so.'[32] John Nunn:

> 'Near the end of a tour, especially if a crew had had several narrow escapes, men could, and often did, develop a nervous tick or twitch of the head. They would continuously swivel their head as if searching for fighters. Two or three tour men had this twitch for years. I think it was prompted by an involuntary contracture of the sphincter muscle in times of great danger.'

One pilot in Nunn's squadron, a squadron leader, became very jumpy as no one had finished a tour for some time. 'The first thing pilots did after an op,' Nunn recalled, 'was to check to see if this squadron leader was on the operations board. I don't think he actually finished his tour: he was lost on his 29th or 30th trip.' Arthur Cole recalled another character who was unable to control his nerves:

'We did four operations in seven days to blood us in: God it was tough! The fourth was to Essen. We had a flight engineer who'd got the DFM, and he was on his second tour: he'd definitely got the twitch to some extent. As we approached Essen, the whole sky was illuminated because there were masses of searchlights, and there was always a haze over the Ruhr. You could see ahead, and as you came in they had a "box barrage" up – an area of sky that was so full of shells you didn't feel you could fly through it!

'The flight engineer came over on the intercom as we were on the bombing run and, probably because of the stress, I started the bombing run too early. He came over the r/t – which he wasn't supposed to do, yelling, "*Christ, look at the shit going up!*" After no comment from anybody else, he said, "Haven't you dropped those bloody bombs yet, bomb-aimer?" At that point the pilot told him to shut up.'

Men often found a release from physical and psychological stresses of ops in the language they used. Post-war the wartime RAF may have been represented with ridiculous 'handlebar moustache' expressions like 'wizard prang', but the reality of RAF terminology on operations was far removed from that popularised in the comic books. Russell Margerison commented that if he had used the actual expletives his crew employed in the dialogue for his book *Boys at War* it would have been classed as an obscene publication.

The psychological injuries suffered by aircrew could also have longer term effects. Fred Danckwardt recalled: 'Immediately after the war, our bomb-aimer had a sort of nervous breakdown; he was an architect and he never worked again, and my pilot died shortly after the war of a heart attack.'

• • •

Being declared LMF could have dire consequences, and men could be removed from a unit immediately. Even operationally experienced crews, particularly air gunners, could resort to opting out, but in some staff circles this was not tolerated. Contagion was a very real concern, not only due to men who simply did not want to fly, but also caused by irresponsible conduct in the air, such as Fred Danckwardt's over-reactive mid-upper gunner or Arthur Cole's flight engineer. There was, initially, little understanding of the need for what would now be called 'rest and relaxation' when uncontrollable physical reactions became apparent. However a more considerate approach later developed and calculated limits were placed on tour lengths. Despite this, cases of LMF continued throughout the war. These were not always due to a simple 'fear of flying' but, as in the case of one officer, whose troubles took him further than simply 'opting out', a man's awareness of the consequences of area bombing could break him. The spring of 1944 witnessed entire crews taking any acceptable option they could – for example, mechanical malfunctions – to avoid difficult operations, although some men were more able to bear the stresses of operations than others.

After the war those declared LMF would have that stigma attached to them for the rest of their lives, a major factor determining Arthur Smith's decision to return to ops. The dangers of flying on operations were daunting, but they could lead to experiences that men would reminisce about for the remainder of their days. Harris's attack on Berlin was to exacerbate many psychological disturbances.

Part Three

THE CHOP

'A tour consisted of 30 trips. Average losses were about four per cent, therefore after 25 trips a man was statistically dead and therefore again, the average man could expect to last 12 or 13 trips. Some, of course, went on their first trip, and some on their thirtieth, and, obviously, you needed a lot of luck on your side. It was not so much a matter of skill, as of luck...'

HENRY WAGNER, Navigator, 51 Squadron

CHAPTER THIRTEEN

THE 'BIG CITY'

Battle over Berlin

IT had been Air Marshal Sir Arthur Harris's contention, ever since being appointed C-in-C of Bomber Command in 1942, that if he could ruin Berlin and break the morale of its people, he would have won the war: there would thus be no requirement for an invasion of Europe. But there were certain restrictions upon how Harris could do this, and the primary ones were the concurrent tactical plans that acted as building blocks for the overall strategy of D-Day. The means by which two important strategic directives issued by the Combined Chiefs of Staff in 1943 were reinterpreted by Harris illustrate how far he was willing to go to realise his intentions.

The Casablanca Directive
The Casablanca Conference[1] of early 1943 had put the reins on Harris's attempts to go all out for German industry. By the directive it issued – the Casablanca Directive – submarines, aircraft, transportation and oil were to take precedence over industrial targets. The instructions to the heads of the Allied bombing forces, Portal and Harris, and Spaatz and Eaker, were contained in this well-known communiqué:

> 'Your primary object will be the progressive destruction and dislocation of the German military, industrial and economic system and the undermining of the morale of the German people to the point where their capacity for armed resistance is fatally weakened.'[2]

This Directive changed the operational control of things and, by its ruling, authority now came to Harris from the British and American Joint Chiefs of Staff rather than the Air Ministry or Churchill's War Cabinet. The policy originated in the United Kingdom and Portal was responsible for directing it, but not for its practical implementation.

Harris was controlled by the tactics and pragmatics of it, and he did not like it. It spelled doom for his plan to attack German industry. It must be remembered that the bomber commanders had been receiving directives from the government air staffs since the beginning of the war. They arrived once a month, on average, and their aim was to ensure that the strategies implemented were within the general structure of Allied concerns. The historian Robin Neillands suggested that after contemplating this new Directive for weeks, Harris actually altered the wording of it to more closely correspond to his ambitions. He 'came back with comments which modified his instructions and the part he proposed Bomber Command might play.'[3] Harris's own wording of the Directive, some three weeks after it was issued, was:

'The primary objective of Bomber Command will be the progressive destruction and dislocation of the German military, industrial and economic system aimed at undermining the morale of the German people to the point where their capacity for armed resistance is fatally weakened.'[4]

This reinterpretation implied that the undermining of the German peoples' morale would be a consequence of attacks on German industry, rather than attacks on German industry and attacks on German morale being two separate issues. It was a subtle, deliberate misreading and allowed him the freedom to assault the German industrial centres.[5] At that time Churchill still thought the Americans were capable of night attacks. Consequently daylight attacks received a lack of emphasis in the Directive, being mentioned only in Paragraph 5 of a seven-paragraph ruling. This oversight allowed Harris, in his own mind, to mount operations independently of the USAAF, which would concentrate on precision targets.[6]

Harris's post-war justification of his actions in his 1947 autobiography built on this misreading. He stated, 'the subject of morale had been dropped', and by giving priority to attack certain aspects of German industry such as oil, submarines and aircraft production, the Directive had allowed him to attack 'pretty well any industrial city with 10,000 inhabitants or above'. Neillands and Charles Messenger point out that this interpretation was wholly incorrect. One of the priorities of the Casablanca Directive was the destruction of the German U-boat force because of the threat it imposed upon the build-up of US resources in Britain prior to 'Overlord'. Harris concurred with any attacks on the North German construction yards but (as stated elsewhere) realised that attempts to destroy the bases on the French Atlantic coast were pointless as they were so strongly fortified. However, the three main attacks on Hamburg that July/August had completely destroyed the homes of the U-boat construction workers. These successes, coupled with the industrial bombing of the Battle of the Ruhr, and the Peenemünde raid, meant that Harris had much increased his clout in the corridors of power at Whitehall. Now he wanted to go all out for the Reich capital. In the previous few months nineteen German cities had been either severely damaged or destroyed: this was the 'half completed' programme about which he wrote to Churchill in November 1943. 'We have not far to go' he remarked. But he mistakenly thought the Americans would be ready to attack Berlin much sooner than they were. After pointing out the foolishness of disasters like the Ploesti attack,[7] he famously stated: 'We can wreck Berlin from end to end if the Americans will come in on it.' He might have been implying by this that the Americans should start bombing by night. Middlebrook suggests that a direct communication by the C-in-C of Bomber Command to the Prime Minister like this was completely outside normal procedure and 'totally improper': the correct recipient of the missive should have been Portal at the Air Ministry.

Churchill had, in fact, been lobbying the Air Ministry for attacks on Berlin ever since *Operation Barbarossa* in 1942 when the Soviet Union joined the Grand Alliance. In early 1943 he requested attacks on the 'Big City' to take the pressure off Russia. He repeated this on 19 August, expressing approval of the Hamburg bombing and also of the American attacks on Regensburg. Portal forwarded this to Sir Douglas Evill, the Vice-Chief of the

Air Staff, but was then informed that Harris would commence attacks on the German capital anyway at the beginning of the next moonless period.

It soon became clear that the USAAF would not be able to attack Berlin: the high casualties associated with unescorted daylight operations made flying to long-distance targets like Berlin almost impossible, before the introduction of the P-51 Mustang escort fighter. The alternative for success, Harris informed Portal in December 1943, was to give the Lancaster full production priority. He stated, '...the Lancaster force should be sufficient, but only just sufficient, to produce in Germany by 1 April 1944, a state of devastation in which surrender is inevitable.' Although after the first two raids of August and September, when Stirlings and Halifaxes were withdrawn temporarily from the front line and, later, Stirlings completely, his statement proved to be more than optimistic: it appears that he completely overestimated the effect of area bombing upon the Germans – if anything, their resistance *increased* because of it.

The Pointblank Directive
In June 1943 a new directive was issued. This came in response to the increased expansion of the German fighter force. In order for the prospective invasion of Europe to take place within the following year, the Allies had to have total air supremacy. To achieve this, the absolute destruction of the German fighter force would have to be carried out. The most logical way of doing this was to attack the manufacturing centres, i.e. the aircraft and ball bearing factories like Schweinfurt and Regensburg. The new order, which subsequently was dubbed the 'Pointblank Directive', stated that although destruction of German industry and morale was still a priority, the *Luftwaffe,* and particularly its fighter squadrons, would have to be smashed first. But Pointblank involved two air forces, not one: the US Eighth Army Air Force would also have to be involved before the Directive could become effectual.

The Pointblank Directive found its origins in a plan formulated in April 1943 by the American General Ira Eaker which called for all-out attacks against selective targets involving, where tactically possible, round-the-clock precision raids. This became known as the 'Eaker Plan' or 'Combined Bomber Offensive'. In addition to this, night area bombing would also have to be carried out against associated cities. In May 1943, however, the plan went to a conference of the Combined Chiefs of Staff in Washington. Here Eaker's plan suffered some significant changes: it was stated that 'precision targets bombed by the Eighth Air Force' by day, should be completed by the RAF bombing 'the surrounding industrial area by night'. The conference acknowledged that the chief problem in perpetrating the core of this plan – the US daylight attacks – was the growing German fighter force. Eaker's was a tactical plan, but it was also part of the overall strategy for D-Day. The raids on the Atlantic coast U-boat bases in May 1943 were also part of this overall strategy, as were those on the fighter bases and fighter production. Because of the strong German fighter force, the instructions of the Casablanca Directive regarding the reduction of the Third Reich's industrial might were not possible. Consequently, it was imperative for two reasons that the German fighters be destroyed. ('Pointblank' was actually the codename of the combined bombing offensive. Different factions put different interpretations on the 'primary object' of the Casablanca Directive. Although the RAF and USAAF saw the 'fatal weakening' of Germany's 'capacity for armed resistance' as crucial for overall victory in Europe, Churchill, Roosevelt and various other Chiefs of Staff thought that the 'fatal weakening' was the lynchpin for the invasion, rather than the final victory.)

At the Air Ministry Air Vice-Marshal Bottomley was responsible for redrafting the Pointblank Directive before it was passed to Harris and his American equivalent, Eaker. The primary objective was still the progressive destruction of the German military/industrial/economic system, but now the German fighter force had to be eradicated as a priority, and this had to be done before 1 April 1944.[8] Neillands contended that Harris employed the administrative confusion created by Bottomley's redrafting, and its apparent conflicts with the Casablanca Directive, to interpret the two commands whichever way he wanted: he used selective instructions from both decrees 'to fight the bomber war as he wished'.[9]

Harris had two arguments against Pointblank. First, he regarded the bombing of selected industrial targets[10] as a waste of time, his thinking being that only the destruction of the large industrial centres, like Essen, would bring the Germans to their knees. Second, the targets that Pointblank suggested were beyond Oboe range, and outside the RAF's capability. Harris won his way. Pointblank was revised to allow German industry, and (by Harris's reading) consequently morale, to remain the RAF's main aim. The USAAF would attack the aircraft plants and ball bearing factories. This led to the catastrophic American attack on Schweinfurt and Regensburg in August 1943, when 19% losses were suffered.[11]

Harris had been able to circumvent the Pointblank decree. Its final draft appeared in June 1943 and illustrates how far he had fulfilled his wishes. Neillands points out that, although the destruction of *Luftwaffe* fighters was still a priority, the Americans had the precise charge of reducing German fighter power and fulfilling the six objectives of the Casablanca decree, whilst Bomber Command was to 'be employed in the general disorganisation of German industry.'

The 'Big City'
Berlin, the 'Big City',[12] was the seat of government, the heart of Hitler's Reich, where he and his scurrilous henchmen – Göring, Goebbels, Himmler and Speer – held sway. It was an administrative and political centre, rather than an industrial city, and was capital of the old kingdom of Prussia. It was therefore a morale and propaganda target, as well as a strategic one and, at 22 kilometres across, was the third largest conurbation in the world with many parks and open spaces. Its southern half was engaged in full war production, with Tiger tanks included in the manufacturing output, whilst in the north, at Siemensstadt, radio and radar aides were produced for all three services. Berlin was also the centre of 12 strategic railway complexes, had the second largest port in Europe from its connection to the German canal system, and contained the manufacturing firms Siemens and Daimler-Benz, Heinkel, Dornier, Focke-Wulf and AEG. But Berlin was beyond Oboe range, had very poor H2S characteristics, a much dispersed industry and, being a city of apartment blocks, was difficult to burn.

The anti-aircraft defences of the city were phenomenal: a ring 64 kilometres across, with a searchlight belt around it that was itself 100 km deep. There were an inner and an outer ring of Flak guns, the core of these being twenty-four enormous 128 mm guns mounted in pairs on three massive, almost impregnable, concrete Flak towers in the Tiergarten Zoo, and in the Friedrichshain and Humboldthain areas. The lower levels of these towers housed vast public air raid shelters, and their construction was so strong that they remained standing in the British and French Zones until long after the war, when they were demolished or converted into apartment blocks.

Route Planning

Route planning[13] for any Bomber Command operation into enemy territory was complicated and normally finalised on the day of the attack. Looking back with hindsight over 60 years makes it difficult to understand the thinking that applied in the winter of 1943. There were day-to-day decisions that had to be made in order to help win the war. The distance to Berlin from Lincolnshire was just less than 600 miles, meaning a round trip of over 1,000 miles. When Harris said 'Bomber Command fought 1,000 battles' he was not understating things: Pathfinder leader Don Bennett pointed out that each Bomber Command attack 'was the equivalent of going through the Battle of Jutland or any other great battle'[14] in a single night. From the end of November 1943 to late January 1944, seven major attacks took place against the city of Berlin. The planning for these was conducted at Bomber Command Headquarters, High Wycombe, a location selected by the Ministry of Defence because of its proximity to London and its topographical obscurity. Each morning shortly before 09.00 hrs, Harris would arrive at his underground HQ for 'Morning Prayers', the derisory title he gave to his morning conference. He would welcome the butterfly-collecting Air Marshal Robert 'Sandy' Saundby and his other minions with the greeting 'Good morning, gentlemen', then take a seat at his desk and, as his entourage gathered attentively behind him, light a cigarette, as a USAAF liaison officer sat down beside him.

Harris then had to consider the results of the previous night's operations, the consequences of which would affect his decision that morning. After that, the principal meteorologist, a civilian named Magnus Spence, would give him a summary of the predicted weather conditions for that night. Priorities for an operation's success were good take-off weather; no large convective cloud en route (with icy conditions); a cloudless, visible target for PFF-marking; a high cloud base and no fog on landing. On a number of raids during the Berlin campaign the forecasting did not prevent a disaster, particularly on 'Black Thursday' in December, and the Nuremberg Raid of March 1944.

Usually, after 40 minutes, the 'target for tonight' was selected and Harris returned to his office at ground level. It was then up to Saundby and around ten other staff officers, who had remained underground, to plan that night's operation. Each morning an effective bombing route was determined. The ideal criteria for this were: minimum flying time, minimum fuel use, maximum bomb load, and minimum exposure to the German defences. The RAF had two main schools of thought on this:

1) Direct flight in/direct flight out: flying a path, ideally with no deviation, straight to the target and straight back. The advantages of this were: easier navigation (no turning points), shorter flight time (less fuel consumption: greater bomb load), lower crew fatigue, less time over enemy territory (and exposure to defences). The major disadvantage of a direct route, however, was that it gave the enemy an optimum chance to intercept the stream.

2) The multi-leg indirect route: this would appear superficially to be the safer choice. The change of direction at the beginning of each leg was designed to hoax the enemy into misidentifying the target. However all the advantages of philosophy 1) above were negated by this: navigation was more difficult (finding way points), flight time was longer (more fuel and thus fewer bombs), and greater crew fatigue and time over enemy territory (longer exposure to German defences) would all occur.

Bob Saundby and his colleagues had a daunting choice to make and one upon which hundreds of men's lives depended. They had over 250,000 square miles of airspace to play with, from the north of Denmark to south of Frankfurt-am-Main. In an area stretching from Hamburg in the north to Stuttgart in the south, they were confronted by 25 fighter stations with over 2,000 night fighters. In some cases an outward route was used on a later operation as a return route, and vice versa. In fact, due to the target nearly always being Berlin, there was a limited choice of routes. Examination of the nineteen major operational raids of the Berlin campaign gives some idea of how the planners' thinking developed: the most direct routes took place on 22/23 and 23/24 November 1943, 2/3 and 29/30 December 1943, 2/3 January and 28/29 January 1944. The one advantage Berlin had over targets in southern Germany was that the stream could spend an optimum time over the sea by flying north, around or over Denmark, then parallel to or over the Swedish coast, and across the Baltic towards the capital. This reduced the amount of time the stream was exposed to the German defences. Similarly with the return route.

Although some of the routes taken to Berlin were similar, they were never exactly the same. John Nunn: 'We never took the same route twice, sometimes going overland and on other occasions spending more time over the North Sea and crossing the coast as late as possible.'

The Building Up of the Bomber Stream
Before the bomber stream could take shape for an operation each individual base (the 'base' being a particular unit of RAF organisation) had to send its aircraft to a specific 'assembly point'. The overall route for an operation was normally peculiar to each Group and the 'way points' for each of these units were specified at a Navigators' Briefing before a raid. There were two main 'assembly points' (actually more points of convergence) by 1944:

1) Over a specific point in the middle of the North Sea. This was for targets in northern Germany, such as Bremen and Hamburg.
2) Over Reading. This was for targets in mid and southern Germany, France and Italy.

In the case of the Nuremberg raid of 30/31 March 1944, the first way point for No. 1 Group and all the other Groups, 5150N, 0230E, was also the assembly point of the stream, a specific point over the North Sea about 50 miles due West of the Hook of Holland. From here No. 1 Group had to alter course twice in order to reach the target, at points 5030N, 0435E and 5032N, 1058E, and then head SSE, adjusting speed according to what 'time over target' was given beforehand. There was no attempt for formation flying in the dark: each aircraft would take off and try to attain the correct height over base, but if this was impossible, set course and climb to reach the height specified over the enemy coast. Leaving the target after the attack all five Groups had to make four further alterations in course for the long flight back westwards, crossing the English coast over Selsey Bill and dispersing to their seperate bases over Reading.

Up until 1942, for targets in mid-Germany the bases in Lincolnshire and Yorkshire would send their aircraft down over East Anglia to get to northern Germany. After the Americans arrived in England in 1942 the Eighth Air Force bases grew to around 60, and by 1943 they were sending 3,000 aircraft by daylight on a single raid. Since these would be returning in late afternoon/early evening, any Bomber Command aircraft flying out for a night raid, could meet them coming back, with the possible result of a collision. Consequently, to avoid this, the British raids going to southern targets had to fly west of

East Anglia and south on individual routes, converging on Reading. They would then turn south-east towards Beachy Head. Any of the well-known photographs showing huge formations of bombers flying over England would have been taken on the route from Reading to Beachy Head where the bomber stream was taking shape (it did not 'assemble' as such – i.e. there were no aircraft milling around over Reading). If the stream had flown due south of Reading it would have crossed the coast over Portsmouth, with the attendant chance of being shot at by the local AA guns.

On the Nuremberg Raid the converging Main Force Groups, heading for southern Germany, all flew across East Anglia to reach the assembly point over the North Sea. The first RAF bomber did not take off until 21.16 hrs, and so there was no danger of a clash with any returning USAAF aircraft.

The Initial Phase
During the period 18 November 1943 to 30 March 1944, sixteen important raids took place on Berlin. The first generally recognised phase of the Battle lasted from 19 November to 31 December 1943. The second was from 1/2 January 1944 ending with the raid against Nuremberg on 30/31 March 1944. However there were some initial raids on the city before November 1943 which bomber historian Martin Middlebrook believes marked the opening attacks of the campaign. From 23 August to 4 September three operations occurred: on 23/24 August, 31 August/1 September and 3/4 September. There was also an aborted raid for 8 September planned whilst there was no moon. However this was cancelled, as was one the following day, presumably due to poor weather. At that point the new moon began to wax and so all Berlin operations were put on hold.

Middlebrook suggests that these five planned and three performed raids indicate that 23/24 August was the real start of the Berlin campaign. Bob Saundby, in his book *Air Bombardment,* supported this. Portal, reflecting a whim of Churchill, sent a telegram to Harris from Washington on 19 August to ask when the bomber assault might begin:

> 'In the present war situation attacks on Berlin on anything like the Hamburg scale must have an enormous effect on Germany as a whole.'

Although results from these first raids did not compare to those of Hamburg, 1,669 sorties were flown and suffered a rate of attrition of 7.5% (i.e. 125 aircrews). The raid on 23/24 August saw Bomber Command's highest loss rate in one night up to that point in the war. Arthur Clarke, a Stirling navigator with 149 Squadron based at Lakenheath, went on the first two raids that August and fortunately returned home. Pathfinder flight engineer, Sgt W.E. Sutton, and bomb-aimer P/O Alan E. Bryett did not.

First Raid: 23/24 August 1943
Just before 21.00 hours on 23 August, Stirling III BF438 'B-Beer' took off from RAF Lakenheath in the burgeoning twilight for an eight hour trip to the 'Big City'. 149 Squadron had been equipped with Stirlings since November 1941 and took part in the Battle of the Ruhr, Hamburg and the Peenemünde raids. Civilians sitting outside their inns around Lakenheath would have heard the roar of Bristol Hercules engines as the Stirlings taxied out and took off into the eastern dusk. Crew briefings had been held late in the afternoon. The long anticipated 'Battle of Berlin' was about to begin and great feelings of apprehension were aroused: the next three raids would be a foretaste of what

was to come. Three of the Station Commanders in 8 Group were on the battle order, but only one would return. At that time there were said to be 2,000 night fighters in north-west Germany, 1,000 of them protecting Berlin.

At Elsham Wolds the loss figure for 103 Squadron since April 1943 was approaching 200. The unit prepared for the evening's operation. Lancaster PM-H 'Harry' was at its dispersal bay, the engine test and equipment check having been completed. On the grass outside, chatting and listening to the other Merlins being tested, were navigator John McFarlane and his crew, including engineer Sandy Rowe. Presently the airfield controller's caravan gave them the green light to start engines and move out for Berlin. The crew had had a run of good luck with ops up until then and hoped it would remain that way. At the adjacent dispersal pad a ground crew was giving Lancaster PM-C 'Charlie' last-minute repairs. The bomb doors were hanging down. 'All of a sudden,' recalled McFarlane, 'there was an enormous "*clang!*" from the next dispersal: the engines of the Lanc next door had been started with the bomb doors open.' This was strictly against regulations. 'By some mischance,' Sandy Rowe remembered, 'all the bombs fell out of the bomb bay to the ground with the incendiaries and burst into flames.' In the midst of the escalating conflagration were a 4,000 lb cookie and several 1,000-pounders. 'H-Harry' was only 150 yards away.

McFarlane's crew flung themselves to the ground. Then, almost immediately, Wing Commander Slater, the squadron CO drove up, yelling, '*Get your aircraft away!*' They scrambled aboard, but it was impossible to start the two inner Merlins. In the cockpit, pilot Doug Finlay and engineer Rowe, with the help of the ground crew, managed to get the two outers going. McFarlane noticed the cookie was still visible amidst the smoke and flames as they began to taxi towards a safer spot. 'As we rolled out,' McFarlane recollected, 'we had to turn back towards the burning bombs to follow the peri-track.' 'When we were at our closest,' said Rowe, 'the whole lot exploded, both the bombs and the aeroplane, complete with its 2,000-plus gallons of petrol. A huge flame developed outward and upward and I thought we would be engulfed.'

On the other side of the airfield John Nunn's crew was about to board its Packard Merlin-engined Canadian Lancaster III, LM335 PM-V, when they heard the explosion:

> 'We had got out to our aircraft and were chatting to the ground crew when we saw a plume of smoke on the other side of the aerodrome. There were several muffled thumps and two or three aircraft were taxying away from the smoke. It later transpired that the ground/flight switch that isolated the aircraft batteries while the plane was on the ground, had been switched on. The armourers hadn't finished arming the plane with bombs and they all dropped from the bomb bay to the ground. The incendiaries dropped out of their canisters and ignited. The resulting heat caused the plane's fuel tanks to explode and the four thousand pound bomb split open and burned. I'm not sure whether the one thousand pound bombs exploded, but I do know that one or two other planes were damaged and were unable to take off. Groupie and Wingco came round and said no one was hurt. We were told that take-off would be at the normal time and that we should try not to look at the wreckage as we took off almost over the burning plane.'[15]

The explosion had interfered with and stopped the starboard outer engine on 'H-Harry': the aircraft swung through 90 degrees towards the inferno. With the Lancaster fully bombed up, and thinking there was a chance of more detonations, McFarlane recalled that the crew jumped out of the front hatch and did not stop running until they were several hundred yards away. Sandy Rowe subsequently stated that shrapnel had penetrated and badly damaged 'Harry' and thus it became the first fatality of the Battle of Berlin: 'Large lumps of exploding bombs came hurtling past and through our aircraft', recalled McFarlane. Sgt Harry Wheeler, the wireless op, was struck on the head by a large chunk of metal and killed instantly. 'I seem to recall', John Nunn stated, 'a w/op in the astrodome of another aircraft, looking out as they moved away, being hit by some debris.'

'Our luck had changed', concluded Rowe.[16] He later recollected: 'They said the sound was heard in Grimsby about 20 miles away, but I didn't hear a thing because I was in the centre of it.'[17]

Meanwhile, en route for the 'Big City', of the 727 aircraft that took off, 635 were flying almost due east out over Holland, with accurately forecast tailwinds driving them on. John Nunn:

'We took off and set course for Berlin, leaving three or four aircraft, unserviceable because of the explosion, behind. Our usual point for leaving our coast was Mablethorpe and when crossing the North Sea it was not unusual to see flashes and explosions in the water. We all assumed that these were caused by aircraft dropping some of their bombs in order to make themselves lighter: no one could prove anything unless they dropped their four thousand pound bomb, when the photo flash would automatically go off. If this was indeed what was happening, it seemed such a waste to me. We all went five or six hundred miles over enemy territory, running all the risks entailed and there seemed no point in not dropping the maximum bomb load when we got there. Berlin was, to us, just another target.'[18]

Despite the near perfect flying weather some of the 124 Stirlings on the operation were icing up and, due to poor Pathfinder marking caused by inefficient H2S readings, the centre of Berlin was overshot and the target markers dropped on the southern environs of the city. Many crews in the Main Force, due to make their attack from the south-east, actually undercut the approach and flew in from the south-west, causing further inaccuracies. Nunn:

'Bombing short was an understandable human trait because a lot of crews were only too eager to drop their bombs as soon as possible and get away from the target area. Max [the bomb-aimer] was always very conscientious and made sure that he reached the target. This was borne out by the photographs and was in spite of the crew telling him to "Drop those bloody bombs!" Doug [pilot] usually cut in and told us to keep quiet and let Max do the job we had come to do. Berlin was bigger and more heavily defended than most others. Over the target, it was like daylight and, although I wasn't supposed to take a look, I usually did. Ron [wireless op] would come forward to look, but his night vision was not so important.'[19]

Wilf Sutton's 77 Squadron crew had completed seven operations from Elvington before deciding to volunteer for Pathfinders and, on 23 March, was posted to 35 Squadron at Graveley. Although their CO approved, he decided that they needed a new bombardier and Flt/Lt John Annetts was assigned. Berlin was their '22nd and a ½' operation, the '½' denoting a so-called 'milk run' – a relatively less dangerous mission – and, since this was 1943, it had probably been a minelaying sortie. It was a beautiful night and the moon and stars could clearly be seen; but they were an ill omen. The Monika tail warning radar had been blipping all the way across Europe[20] and the crew agreed to switch it off. But as the aircraft broke through a cloud bank 125 miles short of the target, at around 23.15 hrs,[21] a Ju 88 attacked the Halifax II TL-A 'Apple'. Sutton recollected:

'I was sitting on the rear spar, putting Window through the flare chute, when a fighter came in from the port and strafed our aircraft all along the starboard side. It was amazing that no one was hit.'

Cannon shells had missed the flight engineer by inches, but knocked out two engines and set fire to the wing on the starboard side. John Annetts recalled: 'The starboard inner was in flames and there was a big hole in the side of the aircraft. In spite of feathering, fire extinguisher and diving, the fire spread and the captain gave orders to abandon aircraft.' Sutton:

'Len, the mid-upper gunner, asked me if I could do something about the flames, so I crawled up the fuselage and tried to put them out with a small extinguisher. But putting foam through a cannon shell hole and with a slipstream of 250 miles per hour – what a hope!'

Sgt Len Such then climbed down from his turret and tapped Sutton on the back: the Australian skipper, P/O Les Hahey,[22] had ordered 'Abandon plane'. Annetts went back, patted Hahey on the shoulder, gave the thumbs up sign, and jumped out. Such and Sutton '…both went to the escape hatch,' the engineer recalled, 'right next to where I was lobbing the Window out.' Although the pilot had been engaging in violent evasive manoeuvres, Sutton's parachute was still where he had sat on it. 'I put it on', he recalled, 'and Len and I baled out from 18,000 feet.' Sutton landed in a potato field which, he concluded, '…was a soft place to finish, and no harm done.'[23] The *Luftwaffe* recorded 32 aircraft shot down over Berlin that night.[24] All Sutton's crew survived and became POWs.

Alan Bryett's 158 Squadron Halifax HR079 NP-L 'Leonard' was based at Lisset, Yorkshire. His aircraft was shot down on this raid with five others from the same squadron; they crash-landed nearly 17 miles NNW of the target. Although Window was jamming the radar, it was being partially filtered out by the German controllers and at least 150 *Wilde Sau* night fighters arrived over the city. Bryett's crew was attacked at 23,000 feet[25] by multiple fighters flying 2,000 feet above them. Of the seven-man crew, two Australians – pilot Flt/Lt Kevin Hornibrook and the tail gunner Flt/Sgt G.A.G. MacLeod – were both killed, as well as the RAF mu/g, Sgt L.G. Chesson. In fact they had been 'coned' by searchlights. A bomb-aimer from another squadron, F.J. McGovern, commented upon such an experience:

'You suddenly find yourselves "coned": first one searchlight, and then another, and then another. And in no time at all you have five or six searchlights concentrating on you alone. Once that happens you can't see a damn thing. You're bathed in light, you can see nothing outside the aircraft, and you're a sitting target for enemy night fighter action. Our evasive action was so intense on one occasion that I was airsick.'[26]

Engineer Reg Brown remembered some violent evasive action after being 'coned' on his first operation: 'The pilot and myself hadn't strapped ourselves in. We got over the target at Wuppertal one time and were coned by a radar searchlight – they were the blue ones; they picked you up and then the ordinary searchlights would cone in on the blue one. And the skipper immediately pushed the nose down so far that he and I both ended up in the canopy. So we went from 20,000 down to about 13,000 before he was able to get hold of the trimming wheel, which gave you the fine adjustment, and got us back level again. We'd gone to a much lower level and got the hell out of there.'

But, for Bryett's crew, evasive action was not enough:

'The German fighters, 25,000 feet above us, dived down on *all* the coned planes. We were worried because we were in the middle of it all. But there were other planes that were coned as well. They dived down on these and killed the rear gunners. Our rear gunner was already dead, but they came round firing and then there was another burst of shenanigans. I was at the front with Kevin Hornibrook. The navigator, flight engineer and wireless op were all underneath his feet. This burst of fire went round and Kevin said, "Go back, Alan. See what the trouble is – how's Mac?" And I went back: Mac [the mu/g] was dead in his turret [slumped in his harness] – just as Mac shouted "*Corkscrew*", he had been killed. The rear gunner was terribly injured. He came out of his turret and had been hit by machine gun bullets – they'd cut through the whole of his face and head – it was terrible. He collapsed on the floor; he couldn't speak and was just lying there. His head was… it was absolutely terrible… Anyway he just lay on the floor and died – just like that'[27]

Although both the air gunners were dead, the navigator, wireless op and engineer all jumped clear.

'That left Kevin and myself in a plane on fire with two gunners dead and going down out of control… racing to the ground. Kevin could no longer control it! The ruling with parachutes was that when you got within quarter of an hour of the target you clipped your 'chute on. So we got our parachute packs on, all ready to go out. But we couldn't do it because the aircraft was twisting and turning so we couldn't get to the escape hatch, which was in the floor near the perspex nose. One minute I was upside down on top of Kevin, and then he was [upside down]. It was twisting and turning, going on for a minute or a minute-and-a-half. But all the time I thought "*This is death! We're going to be trapped in this plane – we can't get out – we're going to crash with it!*" Eventually Kevin got down to the escape hatch by the bomb-aimer's position and got hold of the trap door – which was like the trap door in a house – and pulled the thing open. Then he literally got hold of me, pulled my feet down, and pulled me to the trap. He pushed me out saying, "I'm following!" So I went out with my 'chute on, with him waiting, ready to follow me. We both knew we were low, but we didn't know how low!

'I got clear of the plane, pulled my parachute cord and the canopy opened. I was on the 'chute for two or three *seconds*! The plane crashed about 200 yards away, and burst into flames with all the bullets going off and there was a great fire. The thing that I didn't know at the time [was] Kevin couldn't get out! He was in the plane when it crashed [and was killed].'[28]

Alan Bryett was sent to *Stalag Luft* II.

Arthur Clarke's 149 Squadron Stirling OJ-B, BF438, was also hit over the target but suffered little damage. However his was one of the Stirlings that had iced up. He recalled, 'Our troubles were caused by "coring": icing and oil freezing affecting the engine performance. As a lame duck we needed cloud protection but also new winds at these lower heights, with no "met" forecasts being available as a guide. We were able to take bearings on a lake to the east and on Berlin itself, establish a position and the wind and fly 353 degrees to the Baltic then, with engine trouble, head for Denmark.'

The aircraft was becoming dangerously short of fuel. By the time it crossed the Danish coast the crew could see Flak coming up from the German naval base at Flensburg. From this they were able to get an astro compass bearing and, coupled with a dead reckoning fix, Clarke calculated a surprisingly accurate 'most probable position'. He recalled:

'The new position, wind direction and speed showed we had sufficient fuel to get to the English coast with five minutes to spare, or turn the aircraft out to sea and bale out if we ran out of fuel. A later wind change gave us even more time. Crossing the coast we were rather low to bale out and, as our fuel would now run out over base, we called "Mayday... Mayday..." – the distress signal. We arrived back home with empty tanks, but made a good landing.'[29]

Second Raid: 31 August/1 September 1943
Clarke's crew was not so lucky on the second raid of this series. On 31 August, 622 aircraft took off, including 106 Short Stirlings. Total losses for the night were 50, of which 17 were Stirlings (34%). The 'Summary of Operations' of Bomber Command for the fortnight ending 12.00 hrs, Sunday 12 September stated: '*Weather was unfavourable for the first of these raids. Markers were not well concentrated and a scattered attack to the S.W. of the aiming point developed.*'

Clarke's crew, like many on his squadron, flew four ops that week (23 August to Berlin, 27 August to Nuremberg, 30 August to Mönchengladbach/Rheydt and 31 August to Berlin) and was attacked by night fighters on three of these. As they approached Berlin on the 31st, high-flying Ju 88s dropped 'fighter flares' – long strings of parachute flares that acted as an airborne flare path, illuminating the bombers' route to and from the city. These blinding lights turned night into day and heavy Flak was centred on them.

The German defences were ferocious. Eighty-six aircraft made 'early returns' and a number of losses occurred over Hannover, a heavily defended area: the city appeared to be less densely guarded by searchlights, but this was a deliberate illusion, acting as a snare, and the ground erupted, the resulting heavy AA devouring any unfortunate aircraft above them. Over Berlin, difficulties with H2S equipment and the aggressive defence resulted in the PFF flares being well to the south of the city centre, and the Main Force bombing was far away from the original aiming point. Spread over a wide area, 'creep back' appears to have occurred.

As Clarke's crew bombed the *Hauptbahnhof* (central railway station) area, they were attacked by a Ju 88 and an Fw 190 working together. Clarke remembered:

'With the fuselage on fire and flames around his feet, our mid-upper gunner stayed at his post, shot down the Ju 88 and beat off the Fw 190. The rear gunner was unconscious and the front gunner acting as a co-pilot. Then a burst of Flak took out the starboard outer engine.'

A gaping hole was left in the fuselage to Clarke's right, a cannon shell smashing that end of his bench seat. He found himself under the bench with his head spinning and feeling very sick, but had the presence of mind to locate his oxygen mask. Although the intercom was still operating, two of the pilot's compasses had been knocked out and, in the back of the aircraft, the flight engineer was fighting the fire. Clarke went back with an extra extinguisher but, although the blaze was extinguished, the Distance Reading Master Unit had been hit by a cannon shell and was u/s. Clarke was now without any compass or distance analysis ability and had to use astro-navigation[30] and dead reckoning to determine a course for home, first giving the pilot a south-west heading and then a long southerly to west route.

When they arrived back at Lakenheath, the rear gunner was found to have a head wound, the flight engineer was suffering from smoke inhalation and Clarke, sent to the

RAF Hospital at Ely, had a large bruise in his back, due to Flak hitting his bench seat. That night's raid had been a failure: there had been cloud over the target, difficulties with H2S, and poor PFF-marking which caused the Main Force to bomb well off the centre with much 'creep back'. As a result of his injuries on this raid, Arthur Clarke was still being treated for a prolapsed disc six months after the war ended.[31]

Pilot Officer A.W. Cole was a bomb-aimer in Halifax II HR937 HP-P of 158 Squadron which attacked Berlin that night. It took off from Lisset at 20.29 hrs. The squadron's gunnery leader, mid-upper gunner Flt/Lt W.A. Gorton, was on board. 158 Squadron was one of the hardest hit RAF squadrons in World War Two. No fewer than 336 of its airmen were shot down and became POWs, second only to 337 on 35 Squadron. These figures were a reflection of both squadrons' overall losses. 158 Squadron was formed in September 1918, but disbanded two months later when the First World War ended. It was re-formed in February 1942, taking part in many of the major raids on naval and industrial targets, first with Wellingtons, then Halifaxes.

Cole could not remember much about the flight across Germany. 'It was a disastrous raid because there were strong winds which were not as forecast,' he recalled, 'so to start with the Pathfinders marked the wrong part of Berlin, which was a very big, straggly target anyway.' The raid plotters had drawn a course which took them to the target, and then back. 'This was ridiculous,' Cole recalled, 'because a lot of people made the mistake of turning where they first saw the Pathfinder Force markers, instead of flying on and back.' At this point HR937 was coned by radar-controlled searchlights.

'We flew on and bombed. And immediately after we bombed, when I was still doing my after-bombing check, pulling on the switches to see if there were any hang-ups, we got a first burst of cannon fire. The pilot checked if we were alright, and I dived into the nose and saw this Ju 88 about 100 feet below. I believe [it was a] *Schräge Musik* attack. I dare say he shot at the fuel pipes but didn't hit them. He put one engine out of action. This was feathered and another one on the opposite side of the aeroplane was running extremely rough. It had clearly lost part or the whole of a blade or two of the propeller.[32]

'The wireless op came on the intercom and said, "There's blood dropping on me" and the pilot said, "Yes, I know, its mine. I've been hit in the leg – I don't know how badly." It was then that this piece of shrapnel flew past my eye and I carried a pink mark for about 20 years before it disappeared. I was otherwise unhurt. The pilot must have left his intercom on because I heard him say, shakily, "*I can't hold the thing*": to lose one-and-a-half engines would make life difficult. What other damage there was there's no way of telling. We then received a second burst of cannon fire. The fighter had been waiting for us to drop our bombs before he attacked. When we had that second burst, the intercom went dead, and lights came on in the nose section, which shouldn't have. There was no means of communication, other than movement of the blackout curtains which shut off where the wireless operator and navigator were working. These parted and they told me that we'd been ordered to bale out. I was then in a panic. I tried to go through the curtains and found that I was held back by the intercom flex – the plug was still plugged into the socket. I tore my helmet off, went back through the curtains and found the navigator and the wireless operator standing by the forward escape hatch. They seemed to be hesitating. I thought, "What the bloody hell are they doing waiting?" Then I said, "This is no time to argue: I'm an officer, I'd better lead the way." So I dived out head first.

'That's all I remember because we were at about 15,000 feet – we had turned our oxygen on at 9,000 feet if we needed to do anything energetic. Then I blacked out.

'The two gunners were killed, but the rest of the crew got out. The pilot regained a measure of control and flew on hoping to get home, but he didn't get very far. They had another burst of fire – I'm sure it was the same fighter. And the pilot couldn't find his 'chute: he told me that it had rolled down into the forward compartment, at a lower level, but he didn't know this then. He'd more or less given up when he suddenly found the 'chute, a chest pack, and put it on. He reckoned he baled out at 2,000 feet, which was low. I jumped at maybe 15,000 feet: we'd been flying at 16,000 feet and hadn't gone into a dive, so we were pretty high up. I never found out where I came down: an investigation by German researchers [after the war] suggested that the aircraft actually crashed at Dahlen, but the squadron record book says it was Görzke.

'I blacked out and when I came to, I felt for my parachute handle which should have been on my chest pack, but it wasn't there. My immediate reaction was to close my eyes and assume that this was the end, and just wait to hit the earth. But after a while I realised I wasn't going down very fast and I opened my eyes and saw that my parachute was there and was open. I must have jumped with my hand on the handle and pulled it. It was very dark and the next thing I remember there was something odd about my feet. I looked down and my flying boots had gone – they'd been ripped off in the slipstream, although I had tied them on with string. I'd got three pairs of socks, but two of them had been removed – I remember one was hanging off. I looked down and I thought I could see the dark shape of the ground a long way below. I thought, "I've got 5,000 feet to go." So I shut my eyes with the intention of drifting off to sleep again. But next second I hit the earth.'

Cole's Halifax crashed at Dahlen and both Gorton and the rear gunner, Sgt F.H. Thacker, were killed. Cole went to *Stalag Luft* III.

Third Raid: 3/4 September 1943
The third of the initial raids against Berlin, on 3/4 September, was a Lancaster-only operation. Because of the high level of losses on Halifaxes and Stirlings in the previous two raids on the capital, Harris decided to pull them out of front line operations for a while. That morning the Allies invaded southern Italy: it was the fourth anniversary of Chamberlain's declaration of war. The outward route would prove similar to the later Nuremberg raid of 30 March 1944. The complicated dog-legging of recent routes was now abandoned and crews now flew one straight, long leg of 350 miles after crossing the North Sea over Holland and north Germany. Since the *Luftwaffe* no longer seemed to be concentrating its *Nachtjäger* over the target, there was less chance of raiders being attacked on the inbound flight.

Although there was a forecast tailwind it had changed direction slightly and caused a delay before aircraft reached the target area. Thick cloud covered northern Europe up to 18,000 feet which hindered the night fighters, as did the possibility that the long straight leg (at first sight, a foolish tactic) was simply a ruse. Shortly before the 'Big City' the sky cleared and the PFF was able to use Newhaven ground target indicators rather than Wanganui sky markers.[33] The original T.I.s were plumb on the aiming point, but most late indicators fell between two and five miles to the west, which would have caused a major 'creep back' with a larger force. As it was, most bombs fell within the city area, if not on it.

On 3 September wireless op Harry 'Sparky' Sparks of a 207 Squadron crew from Langar (see Chapter Eight) was assigned to a 'special duty'. Wynford Vaughan-Thomas, the broadcaster, was to make an airborne recording of the raid for the BBC. Sparks recalled:

'It was a terrific experience – the first time a raid was broadcast across the radio. Remember there was only radio then. So you had all the little radio sets up and down the country, which everyone tuned into, to hear any comments about anything, all switched on. You all listened in and got the news of what was going on. Somebody told the BBC what it was like on ops – because nobody knew! Nobody knew anything about anything. Don't forget there was a blackout on all news, not like now with Afghanistan. There was nothing like that at all – you couldn't give any information like that to anyone.'[34]

On the night of 3/4 September Sparks's skipper, Ken Letford, and his crew were ordered to fly Vaughan-Thomas, a member of the BBC War Reporting Unit, and a BBC sound engineer named Reg Pidsley, in Lancaster 'F-Freddie' from Langar to Berlin. A force of 316 Lancasters took off and 22 were lost. Vaughan-Thomas later wrote a graphic account of the experience. A 'Warcasts Room' had been established in Broadcasting House four months earlier which took war reporting to a new level – for the first time correspondents were treated with respect and even awe. Richard Dimbleby commented: 'It was suddenly recognised that the most important person in the operation was the man at the front line.'[35]

They took off for Berlin at around 21.00 hours. 'All we ask you to do,' the AOC of 5 Group told Vaughan-Thomas at Grantham, 'is describe exactly what you see. No window dressing.' Letford's crew not only took the BBC men to Berlin and back, they also shot down a night fighter to boot. Vaughan-Thomas was nicknamed 'Taffy the Talk'. Reg Pidsley, his engineer, Sparks recalled, was 'a very, very brave man; very brave and very quiet.' They crossed the Dutch coast and were soon witnessing tragedy after tragedy. Target-marking, and bombing for the force, approaching from the north-east, had fallen short. As they approached the 'Big City', Vaughan-Thomas noted:

'…again that awful moment when a beam rested on us and lighted up the whole cockpit: Ken at the controls, Bill Bray now lying forwards in the bomb-aiming position in the nose, Jock and myself all frozen at our posts – and then it passed on to grip the Lancaster behind us. Again the fierce uprush of Flak: the [other] Lancaster shuddered and suddenly seemed to disintegrate in seconds. The wings seemed to split apart, but now I had to look away for we had entered the bullring. The sky above us was full of lights, burning chandeliers falling down on us, bursting rosettes of Flak everywhere. I pressed as close to the perspex as I could and looked down. Below was the awe-inspiring and beautiful, yet macabre spectacle of Berlin burning in its death agony. The ground below looked as if someone had been throwing jewellery down on black velvet. The bombs burst like glowing rubies. There were emeralds flashing fire and sapphires of dangerous delight; horrible but beautiful.'[36]

Vaughan-Thomas and Pidsley survived the attack. The recording they cut was later broadcast by the BBC as '*Broadcast from Berlin*' and issued as a gramophone record.

One of the unique characteristics of this raid was the return. The surviving force was ordered to fly directly north, over the Baltic Sea, then deliberately to violate neutral airspace by flying across the south-east tip of Sweden and up the Swedish Kattegat coast to Gothenburg. It would then turn west. Although this was against international law, it was apparently taken with a pinch of salt by Air Ministry planners. At least one other Bomber Command raid violated Swedish airspace around that time – to Stettin, on 5 January 1944. Ted Groom recalled his squadron's illegal flights across Sweden:

'Sometimes the stream would be more than three miles wide, depending on where it was. We crossed the English coast at Mablethorpe, and normally you crossed the enemy coast wherever you were plotted – it could be anywhere. It could be dog-legged. Sometimes we went up to the north of Denmark, crossed over to Sweden, then came down the west coast of Sweden to Berlin. Sweden was neutral territory and the Swedes used to fire at us: they'd be all lit up down below, but their ack-ack only came up to about 10 or 15,000 feet, so we were alright. I don't think they had night fighters: I think the ack-ack was just to let you know where you were. We came down the coast, crossed over the Baltic down towards Berlin on some of the Berlin raids. Other times we'd go over the south of France… come up that way. There were several routes.'[37]

On 4 September the returning stream crossed the southern tip of Sweden, flew due north just inside the Swedish coast for 120 miles, then turned off after Gothenburg, across the top of Denmark, west to the North Sea. Three 460 Squadron aircraft went down that night. One crashed near Utrecht with two survivors, one was shot up by a night fighter and crashed near Ringkobing in Denmark. The third, Flying Officer F.H. Randall's Lancaster, lost two engines over Berlin due to Flak and fighters. One man had already baled out when they were over the island of Zeeland and Randall ordered the rest of the crew to jump. One airman, Flt/Sgt N.J. Conway RAAF, drowned; two, the bomb-aimer and wireless op, were arrested by the Germans; and one, the flight engineer, Sgt A.H. Jones, escaped to Sweden with the help of the Danish Resistance. Randall and the mid-upper gunner landed in the sea, were picked up by a Swedish vessel and interned. Their aircraft crashed in Sweden and Randall was awarded the DFC, but later was killed on 'Black Thursday' in December 1943.[38] A 57 Squadron pilot recalled the Swedes that night had laid their searchlights out horizontally across the Skaggerak as a guide to bombers as they turned west. The RAF lost 24 Lancasters, with 18 sorties aborted and 130 airmen killed.

THE BATTLE PROPER
The First Phase: 18 November–31 December 1943

After 3/4 September there was a lull in the campaign and, for the next two monthly 'no moon' periods, Bomber Command was stood down from the German capital, but continued to attack other targets in Europe, such as a raid to Munich on 6/7 September. Author Henry Probert suggests that two of the reasons for this were the high casualty rates of the three initial raids – 7.9% of the total force – and an attempt to try to improve critical target-marking inadequacies. The result was a 1.8% drop in the overall casualty rate. The total number of operationally serviceable Lancasters committed increased in number by 142, but the total number of operationally serviceable Halifaxes committed remained the same. Although the Halifax and the inadequate Stirling were reprieved on 3/4 September after their heavy losses in the first two raids of the 'Initial Phase' of the battle, they were still classed as front line machines, and had to face the 'Big City' again.

During this pause in operations a number of technical advances occurred. The new H2S Mk III ground-scanning radar was introduced, but finding crews with navigators to train for it was a problem. Only PFF crews were suitable and had to face an extension to their normal 45-op tour; and, as such, efforts to locate such crews were soon abandoned due to lack of interest. In October, 101 Squadron became a radio countermeasures unit, commencing operations with ABC (Airborne Cigar – radio jamming equipment). A German-speaking operator was normally included in the crew. Also, a new home-based RCM facility was introduced at Kingsdown, Kent: 'Corona' transmitted hoax instructions by German-speaking RAF operators to the German night fighter controllers. 100 Group, the Bomber Support Group, was also formed, representing a revised thinking on the part of the Air Ministry as to the importance of combating the *Luftwaffe* night defence with RCM.[39]

In the Reich the *Luftwaffe* overcame RAF jamming with even more potent transmitters and also retaliated with music, using certain tunes to represent particular instructions. A new German night fighter division, 30. *Jagddivision*, was set up by Hajo Herrmann in September 1943. This was due to the *Wilde Sau* tactics, which had been introduced after the success of Window at Hamburg, proving ineffective for twin-engined aircraft.

6/7 September and 2/3 October: Munich

Although these two raids were not part of the 'Battle of Berlin', they are included because they figure in the overall chronology of the series of raids carried out during the lull in the Berlin campaign and because of one crew's peculiar experience. There were 31 POW survivors from the two raids: the first, from 6/7 September, resulted in 29 POWs;[40] the second, the 2/3 October, saw eight POWs being taken.[41] Mid-upper gunner Philip Jenkinson, whose 10 Squadron Halifax II[42] went down on the first raid, suffered the ignominy of being returned to the city he had bombed and was threatened with execution:

Philip Jenkinson (Jenkinson)

'The Germans were so incensed by what we did to Munich, by the orders of Hitler the majority of the survivors were taken from prison camps to be paraded around Munich and shot. That was by the end of October 1943. We were right up in East Prussia [at *Stalag Luft* VI], and it was a two day trip down to Munich by train.

'We were shot down by night fighters – two of them. We got the Me 109, the single-engined one, but the other one, a Ju 88, came up from underneath and killed the rear gunner and the pilot never got out: missed me by inches; took the whole of the starboard side out and set all the fuel tanks on fire. The leads to the bomb bay were cut where we carried magnesium and phosphorus incendiaries. In seconds there was a hell of a fire but it didn't last very long.'

Jenkinson was on the run for nine days. It was the first time he had used a parachute: 'When they were issued,' he recalled, 'you were told that if you didn't get it right you wouldn't be back for another one.' Howard Pearce, the 115 Squadron navigator, recalled the fatal experience of one of his skippers, an officer named Sword:

'Sword DFC, AFC – a silly man: he could have survived, but he was shot down. But it was in the summer and he had his parachute webbing on too loose, and it killed him! It twisted around him, and got him in the balls and everywhere. Because of the terrific pull, if you're not strapped tight, that will happen, and it did with him.'

Jenkinson: 'It took 15-20 minutes to descend by parachute, and when I came to there was another 'chute a short distance away from me.' Two of the crew, the pilot and rear gunner, were killed, but Jenkinson's friend, navigator Kevin Murphy, came down in Leeder and was captured immediately and the 'flighty' and wireless op were arrested two days later on a German airfield.

Jenkinson buried his parachute in a wood and set out to look for the other RAF man, his bombardier. Calling out in the pitch darkness, the bomb-aimer heard him and replied. Jenkinson attempted to reach Switzerland with him, but found that he had been saddled with a 'gash bod'. Their normal bomb-aimer had been taken ill and Sgt N.W.J. Simmonds had been put in as a replacement. But, '…he'd been chucked out of a crew', stated Jenkinson.

> 'The opportunity was golden to get away, no Germans about and right out in the wilds, but he had no escape kit whatsoever. They reckoned that you could live comfortably with what you carried on you for a week, as long as you could get water; but we had no water… and I carried him for nine days.'

After walking 130 miles, they reached the town of Immenstadt near the Swiss border. Attempting to walk through its streets after nightfall, they were accosted by two soldiers who took them at gunpoint to the nearest police station. Jenkinson eventually ended up in *Stalag Luft* VI at Heydekrug in East Prussia. Then, when he was in the prison camp:

> 'One day, about four o'clock in the morning, two German guards came in with a big Alsatian, and my name was called out. Usual thing – rifle and bayonet – you had to do what you were told. At the main entrance were two or three others, including our bomb-aimer. We then realised that we were all survivors from the Munich raid. Then another officer came in and told us that we were going to be taken back to Munich, paraded around and shot by Hitler's orders. Now that is not a very nice feeling.
>
> 'They looked after us very well. We went to an airfield. They said they were going to shoot us but they didn't. They paraded us all round the city and showed us all the churches and everything except the military targets. Then they took us to the Opera House and Göring was supposed to come and address us. But he never turned up. We were there for well over an hour when a senior German officer said, "Take them back to the camps". It was as near as that. This was totally against the Geneva Convention. It was an atrocity that would have been committed if Göring had turned up.'

After the war there was no official record of the incident anywhere. 'The Germans were very methodical in their records', Jenkinson remembered. 'All through the prison camps, going out for medical purposes, dental purposes, help with the Red Cross parcels, help with the mail, etc., all was recorded, but not the prisoners that went on the parade to Munich.' [43]

In the next 'no moon' period, during the second half of November, there were four raids on Berlin – 18th/19th, 22nd/23rd, 23rd/24th, and 26th/27th, with thick cloud over the target for the first three.

18/19 November 1943

This operation was the jump-off point or Harris's 'main offensive' against Berlin. The force was unfortunately split: although a uniquely Lancaster force of 440, with a few Mosquitoes, was sent to Berlin, an almost equal mixed force of 395 aircraft was despatched to Mannheim. The latter contained 248 Halifaxes and 114 Stirlings. Total losses were 5.8% of the force: 12 Halifaxes and 10 Stirlings failed to return. Although Lancaster crews were at one time ordered to remain at the same altitude as the less powerful Halifaxes and Stirlings, when the fighters came in and crews had to make a decision, the Lancasters went for height. Combined, the two attacks represented the largest raid since the Thousand-Bomber raids of 1942, but the Berlin attack was a failure. According to the *Weekly Résumé* to the War Cabinet, in this attack, '…the markers, although punctually dropped, were widely scattered, and no concentration of bombing was achieved. A number of fires was started, the glow of which was reflected on the clouds.'[44]

Bert Carter was a flight engineer in 44 Squadron at Dunholme Lodge, Lincolnshire at that time. At the controls of his Lancaster DV263, KM-L 'Leonard', was Flying Officer Frank Phillips. Also on the crew were Flt/Sgt W.R. 'Bill' Taylor, bomb-aimer; Flt/Lt J.L. 'Jim' Gourlay, RCAF, navigator; Warrant Officer T.E. 'Terry' Dowling, RAAF, rear gunner; Pilot Officer R.K. 'Rex' Bennett,[45] wireless op; and Flt/Sgt D. Curtiss, mid-upper gunner. Both Dowling and Curtis were later killed in action. Carter's crew made nine attacks on Berlin between 18 November 1943 and 15 February 1944 plus two aborted sorties: a remarkable 11 attempted attacks. In November they flew four sorties to Berlin in eight days: on the 18th, 22nd, 23rd and 26th. On the operation of 18 November, 411 Lancasters reached the target, but the attack was not a success: Berlin was covered by thick clouds, tops between 10 and 12,000 feet. The PFF target indicators soon became lost in the murk and the Wanganui sky markers replacing them were too few to guide the force successfully. Not only did changes in the wind cause bad timing, but the H2S sets on the PFF Blind Marker aircraft malfunctioned, the thick cloud cover not helping the situation, and many navigators were unable to find Brandenburg, the start point of the bombing run. Carter's crew took off at 16.50 hrs. Their raid lasted eight hours ten minutes:

'I well remember the first Berlin raid in November. When we arrived at our target we must have been ahead of our ETA, because everything was in darkness. We thought that our navigator, Jim Gourlay, had dropped a clanger and put us in the wrong place. Jim was quite sure that Berlin was below the clouds, so we started to circle the target area and then, after a while, the markers and T.I.s started to fall, so we lined up onto our bombing run and dropped them without meeting much Flak. That was the only time we pranged Berlin with ease: I think Jerry must have been asleep that night. For all the remaining raids he was on his toes: in the end he was sending up a trelliswork type of Flak.'

After bombing, the Main Force deviated sharply south. To the north, a small force of Mosquitoes dropped hoax fighter flares, which successfully drew off the *Nachtjäger*. After flying south the Main Force turned due SW for 200 miles, then WSW for 100 miles, then flew 230 miles due west before crossing the Channel. An unexpected southerly wind scattered many of the returning bombers back north over Kassel and the Ruhr, as John Nunn's navigator predicted:

'On 18 November we went to Berlin again. This trip took seven hours, fifty minutes. The wind details given by the Met Officer at briefing were all haywire. We bombed on time and by this stage, we were reaching heights of 28-28,500 feet, trying to get as far as possible from the ack-ack. On the way back, Ron reported to Doug that the forecast winds were way out and that a lot of crews would be in trouble if their navigators were not on the ball. Ron had his H2S but backed this up by taking star shots when the skies were clear enough. The extra time taken on this trip could have been because we took a longer route than that taken four nights later.'

That night the RAF lost ten Lancasters out of a total of 440. Forty-three airmen were killed.

22/23 November 1943
Over five days that November, Dick Raymond, flight engineer with 83 Squadron, was scheduled to go on three trips to Berlin, the first of which was the third op of his first tour. On the 22nd, the target was enveloped by cloud: although the markers were accurately placed and well maintained throughout, results were difficult to assess and Intelligence Officers could only estimate what the effect of the attack had been. Although Raymond had 'nothing to report', this operation is on record as being the most effective attack on Berlin during the war: the greatest force sent by the Command to the 'Big City' up until that time. A total of 764 aircraft went out and 26 were lost. A significant feature of this was that it was the last time the Stirling flew against Berlin. Fifty went out as opposed to 465 Lancasters – nearly ten times as many – and five Stirlings went missing while 11 Lancasters were lost. The Stirling had been Short Brothers' ultimate folly. During the first three-and-a-half months of the Battle of Berlin, 109 were shot down. This was largely due to the poor performance relative to the other 'heavies': low altitude and a slower speed meant that they were plum targets for the *Wilde Sau* pilots. One sad side effect of their withdrawal was a marked increase in the number of Halifax losses: nearly 10% casualties from December to 15/16 February. The Germans were using dummy night fighter airfields, complete with dummy cows and artificial lakes,[46] to confuse RAF intruders. RAF Intelligence knew about these. John Nunn:

> 'On one of these trips, over Germany, I reported seeing the lights of an airfield on our port side. Ron came out, checked the position and logged it. We reported it to the Intelligence Officer at debriefing and after we confirmed that we were sure of what we had seen, he said that they had no record of an airfield at that position and it was probably a dummy. It seemed typical to us: if they didn't know about it, then it wasn't there!'[47]

23/24 November 1943
83 Squadron went out from Wyton again on the 23rd with the Main Force, all flying the same route as before, some equipped with the new H2S III sets. This was classified as a 'major raid' although almost half the number of aeroplanes, 383, of the previous night took off. Early arrivals over the target reported fires still burning from the night before, and a Mosquito, which flew over Berlin two hours after the attack, reported nine large fires forming a circle with two additional fires to the south-west. Hoax instructions from German-speaking controllers in England caused much annoyance to those co-ordinating the *Nachtjagd* operations. A game of plot and counter-plot developed: the *Luftwaffe* began to use a female commentator, but was soon upstaged by a female voice from the UK. Although flight engineer Sergeant Dick Raymond did not attach much importance to this raid, 20 Lancasters were lost.

26/27 November 1943
'*Berlin again and then things started to happen*', Dick Raymond wrote for the 26th. A force of 443 Lancasters took off and 28 were lost, with 14 others crash-landing 'somewhere in England'. The three raids of 22, 23 and 26 November caused much confusion in the German capital. That afternoon Raymond's Lancaster did not even leave the dispersal pad. 'We were taken out to the aircraft as usual and I had a number of checks to do both

inside and outside the aircraft', he wrote. 'I remember seeing an armourer working on the photoflash which was shaped like a torpedo.' The photoflash was designed to be dropped at the same time as the main bomb load, and explode and light up the whole area whilst a photograph was taken. Raymond recalled:

'On leaving the aircraft, as was customary, I went into the ground crew's Nissen hut for a cup of tea. The next minute I found myself under a pile of rubbish. The aircraft, which had been fully bombed up, had exploded. I had only superficial injuries, but it had killed a number of people, including three of my crew. The navigator's body was never found; amongst the others killed was a WAAF transport driver.'[48]

But the raid went on. It seems that the *Luftwaffe* followed the stream as it penetrated European airspace. The size of the force would have been calculated by high-powered listening devices in Germany picking up the short wave signals emitted as RAF wireless operators tuned in their r/t equipment. Ju 88 reconnaissance aircraft were sent up to fly parallel to the Main Force and to radio back its size and position. Other German aircraft were subsequently ordered to fly over the stream and drop parallel lines of magnesium parachute flares to form a blinding white avenue of illumination along its track. One of the unusual features of this operation was a diversion to Stuttgart by 157 Halifaxes and 21 Lancasters. This was the reason for the stream taking such a southerly direct route across Belgium, then just north of Frankfurt. These were clever tactics that successfully fooled the German controllers into thinking that Frankfurt was a major raid. All the night fighters were therefore deployed there, whilst the Main Force dog-legged to the north-east towards Berlin, and then turned right again, ENE, for the final run to the target. Only five aircraft went missing to Stuttgart, but 28 Lancasters were lost on Berlin, and a further 30 crashed on or approaching fog-ridden English airfields, 15 of thesepermanently wrecked. Total aircrew fatalities that night were 196. Bert Carter remembered:

'This particular flight plan had been laid on for a raid on Berlin which should have taken place 24 hours earlier, but which was cancelled at the last moment. The same plan was put in operation the next night: same times, same route, same turning point.[49] On this particular raid, our route was lined with fighter flares on both sides – we were sitting ducks. That night on the way to the target we had to pass Frankfurt, and that was when we were clobbered by cannon fire: our gunners couldn't see the fighters due to the flares. Anyway, the rear turret was put out of action – we discovered next day that a cannon shell had exploded under the gunner's seat, knocking out the electrics and hydraulic system – and shell splinters had sprayed out from the impact of hitting the hydraulic pump under the centre seat and had perforated all round the edge of it.

'We called up Terry Dowling, the rear gunner, and he said that he was OK, but his turret was out of action. He would not come forward but said that he would stay in his useless turret to look out for fighters. His electrics were knocked out – only his intercom was working. Although his heated flying suit was useless he sat there whilst we continued. Our cockpit cover was damaged and a piece of the canopy had dropped down my neck, and at first I thought that I had been hit.

'We carried on to the target and dropped our load on Berlin, which was well alight and we started back home. One of our petrol tanks had been hit, so we had to juggle our petrol feed using the cross balance cock. We at last crossed the coast and made for the nearest aerodrome. A couple of our aircraft had already touched down.

'When we had permission to land we made our approach, and checked the undercarriage to make sure that everything was working OK. We touched down and then put the runway out of action. One of the tyres had been shot up and our aircraft, which had now lost flying speed, tried to settle on the damaged undercarriage wheels but slewed across the runway and eventually came to a rest.

'The next morning, having tried to no avail to get a couple of hours' sleep on chairs in the mess, we went out to see the aircraft. When we climbed into the fuselage it looked like a colander: there were holes everywhere! Cannon shells had gone through the main spar and wings and the port petrol tank. The jettison pipe was hanging down out of the wing just like an elephant's trunk. We couldn't fly the aircraft back to Dunholme Lodge as it was a "write-off".'[50]

Sgt D.J. Edwards was a bombardier on Lancaster DV247 with 166 Squadron that night. It was an all-NCO crew apart from the pilot, J.E. Thomas, who was a warrant officer with a DFC. They took off from Kirmington at 16.45 hrs. Edwards recalled that, because the PFF had been taking heavy losses around that time, it was decided that the Main Force would lead the attack using high-explosive bombs alone. This would prevent incendiary fires breaking out and they would draw off some of the defence:

'We arrived over Berlin – I reckon we must have been one of the first – because I suspect some of the others held back a little. It was a very, very tough trip over Berlin that night; and it was quite a relief when you got through and came out the other side. We used to put the aircraft into a shallow dive so that we could increase the speed coming out, so that we could get away from the target quickly. Then you used to get back up to your correct height for the rest of the trip.'

But things did not turn out quite as expected: coming away from the target, silence reigned until they reached the German-Dutch frontier. At this point a searchlight snapped on and caught them, like a moth, in its beam:

'The next thing we knew we had a fighter attacking us with 20 mm cannon tracer shell. I can remember seeing two streams of it going past the aircraft, And then – I think it must have been another attack – we were hit underneath, and I was hit. I was kneeling in the front throwing out Window. I was forward, I had my hand down and my knees behind me, and I was hit by something.'[51]

At this point a part of Edwards' left hand was shot off and he received a large thigh wound, probably the result of a *Schräge Musik* attack. Sgt W. O'Malley became trapped in the tail turret, and the mid-upper gunner A.V. Collins, a second tour NCO, went to his aid. But the aircraft went down, probably over Dutch territory. Edwards, the pilot, and the rest of the crew all baled out and survived, but the two air gunners remained trapped in the aircraft. Collins broke his ankle, presumably upon landing, and W.G. Bell, the navigator, with Edwards and the w/op E.M.L. Davies, was sent to *Stalag Luft* IV at Gross Tychow, from where he made numerous escape attempts. Bell finally returned to England on 7 May 1945.

Subsequent to the 26 November raid Carter and Phillips's crew appear to have gone on leave. They then had to find a replacement for their Lancaster DV263 'L-Leonard'. This was encapsulated in veteran aircraft LM306 which had flown 11 earlier operations with 49 Squadron from Fiskerton, Lincolnshire as EA-F 'Freddy': it had taken part in the first two Hamburg raids of July 1943, the Peenemünde raid and also the Berlin raids of 2 and 18 November. 44 Squadron received LM306, also coded 'L', on 10 December 1943. The crew flew to the German capital in it seven times: on 29 December, 1, 2, 20, 27 and 30 January and on 15 February 1944. The attacks of 23 November and 1 January were both 'boomerang' raids, or aborted sorties. Carter recalled one of these Berlin ops, during which circumstances became farcical:

> 'On another raid on the "Big City" we were making our way back home to base. I think we must have been ahead of the first wave and minding our own business, with thoughts of the bacon and eggs waiting for us back at base. In front of us all seemed quiet, no sign of Flak or searchlights when, all of sudden, all hell broke loose. Flak and searchlights picked us out, and we were blinded for a few seconds. Fortunately, before other searchlights could cone us, a couple of shells exploded nearby, and our aircraft dropped like a stone and out of the searchlight beams.
>
> 'Our wireless operator declined to use the Elsan closet at the rear of the aircraft during trips over Germany. Instead, to ease the call of nature, he had obtained a large open tin can, which he used frequently during our trips and usually it was nearly full during return trips. Unluckily, at this particular time, it was almost full and, as the aircraft dropped, we felt as if we were floating in mid-air, our feet left the floor of the cabin and, at the same time, the can that usually reposed on the wireless op Rex Bennett's table, slowly left the worktop and rose upwards towards the fuselage roof. During this time Bennett was unable to move, but just had to sit in mid-air and watch as his tin can slowly reached the roof and gradually tilted over, spilling its contents all over him!'[52]

Rather than examining all the subsequent raids that went to Berlin before 30 March 1944, when the campaign ended, we shall study nine in particular.

16/17 December 1943 – 'Black Thursday'
The raid of 16/17 December deserves some examination because it had the highest casualty rate up to that time in the campaign, but only 43% of these casualties were caused by enemy action. The great protagonist on the final part of this raid, the return, was provided by the one factor which, more than anything else, affected the success of an operation: the weather. On every op Magnus Spence at Bomber Command HQ faced a daunting task and, even though his staff's calculations generally proved accurate, occasionally an operation would end up a failure. On 22/23 November, for example, the meteorological conditions were predicted as 'near perfect' – all UK bases would be clear; Germany would be covered by low cloud and fog, and Berlin only broken cloud at medium level. In fact, the weather deteriorated markedly and there was cloud at all levels. Over the target the winds were lighter than forecast; there was thick cloud up to 16,000 feet and PFF sky markers had to be dropped, which soon became swallowed up by the murk.

There was a full moon for 12 nights after 4 December, but on 16/17 December it was decided to mount another raid. By this period in the campaign the Stirlings had been phased out for operations over the Reich. Many Bomber Command staff that night thought ops would be scrubbed as so many airfields were enveloped in mist. On the 15th Laurie Simpson took off at 18.00 hrs amidst '*murky fog*' and '*10/10 low cloud*', and on return landed '*back into the murk*'. On the 16th, 483 Lancasters and 15 Mosquitoes took off around 16.00 hrs, flew out, assembled over the North Sea, and took a direct 600-mile route due east to Berlin after crossing the Hook of Holland. John Nunn's 103 Squadron crew, with a replacement navigator, was amongst them:

'On 16 December, we were briefed for an op to Berlin. We took the navigation leader as navigator. Our plane was JB730, "P-Peter". It was stressed that, because of the very low cloud, we were to take off and climb straight ahead until we reached the clear skies above. The airfield was shrouded in low cloud with a base of about 150 feet. It was drizzling, but was safe to take off because the runway lights were clearly visible. We were told (correctly) that we would break through the cloud into brilliant sunshine at about one thousand feet and (incorrectly) that the cloud would be gone by the time we returned. We were scheduled to take off at the end of the queue and had not yet got into our aircraft when the first aircraft started lifting off. We were just climbing into our plane when the skies lit up and there was a loud bang. We realised that two planes had collided and that the crews had little chance of surviving. It didn't do our nerves or those of the other crews any good at all. Eventually we took off and climbed into clear skies at about 1,000 feet.'[53]

The two Lancasters that collided in mid-air, three minutes after take-off at Elsham Wolds, were from Nunn's 103 Squadron and from 576 Squadron, which had been formed less than three weeks before from 'C' Flight of 103. All 14 crewmen were killed. The 576 Squadron Lancaster UL-B2 'Bob Squared' included two Australians; their engineer was the youngest Bomber Command man to die on operations that year, 18 year-old Sgt Cull.

Despite the apparent foolishness of the route, the operation was carefully planned. Later in the night, a three-quarter moon was due to rise – any bombers caught in a clear sky on a direct flight by its light would be slaughtered. This was what had happened on 30 March. But Saundby and his staff were very clever. They planned an early take-off so that the stream would arrive over the target before the moon rose. By this point in the campaign, time over the target had been reduced to a minimum: 14 minutes. Bombing started at 17.58 hrs. Having bombed, the force would then turn due NNE and head out towards the Baltic before the moon rose, flying across mainland Denmark and out over the North Sea. The Met men suggested that the German night fighter bases would be fogged in. However there was also a possibility that fog may cover the home bases during the course of the night: a prediction that proved to be true.

The direct route proved doubly effective. There had been a raid on Leipzig on 3/4 December when the Main Force had flown a route due east, directly towards Berlin. Rather than bombing the 'Big City', however, 80 miles before it they veered off south and attacked Leipzig. Now, seeing the RAF stream heading directly to Berlin, the German controllers assumed that this was again a feint and did not direct their fighters towards the capital: so far so good. The stream then turned north after successfully bombing Berlin. As the moon began to appear the *Nachtjäger* were unable to follow and the bombers headed out over Denmark: only 25 Lancasters had been lost.

That night one of the most highly decorated crews of the time went down: Lancaster JB216 GT-W from 156 Squadron at Warboys, one of the four founder squadrons of the PFF, had an eight-man crew which included five Australians and one Canadian. All of these were second tour men, with DFCs or DFMs, and there was additionally an RAF squadron leader, R. Hadley DFC, flying as a special duties navigator. The regular navigator, Flt/Lt Samuel DFC was a graduate from Melbourne University, and the Australian w/op, P/O Smith DFC, was an agriculturalist. This highly experienced crew disappeared that night 'without trace', all lives lost.

Back over the home country things were taking a turn for the worse. This night became infamous amongst RAF circles as 'Black Thursday'. It was eight days before a

Christmas that Laurie Simpson would call '*a very busy period*'. A WAAF Met assistant at RAF Bourn wrote, '*A real pea soup fog descended on eastern England while the squadrons were out, so that they came back to find every airfield shrouded in gloom.*'[54] Thirty-seven of the returning bombers crashed on English soil or in the North Sea.[55] Due to the appalling conditions over Binbrook three 460 Squadron crews were amongst these. The worst case was Flying Officer Randall's JB657 which took off for Berlin at 16.32 hrs, clipped a tree at 23.12 hrs over England, fired off Verey cartridges 36 minutes later, but then crashed into a wood at Market Stainton, Lincolnshire: all on board – six Australians and one Englishman – were killed. At 23.12 hrs Warrant Officer Stafford's Lancaster DV173 crashed into a field near Caistor in Lincolnshire: the rear gunner, P/O Garment, died and the engineer, Sgt Dixon, was injured. At 23.57 hrs Lancaster JB704 undershot the runway at Binbrook and crashed into an adjacent field without casualties. John Nunn recalled his own crew's experience:

'On our return we expected to see clear skies but could only just make out our searchlights breaking through the cloud. We called up the base, got our stacking position, runway number, etc. and were told that cloud base was at 250 feet. Another voice chipped in and told us not to believe a bloody word of it. "I'm down to 200 feet, I'm still in effing cloud and they won't give me a diversion!"[56] He was told to be quiet, stick to r/t procedure and remember that there were WAAFs manning the r/t. He then made some remark about the WAAFs knowing all the words and knowing their meaning through experience! Our turn came to land and we made a dummy run on the heading of the runway to find out for ourselves how low the cloud base was. We broke through at about 175 feet and Doug said he would stay down and attempt to land at the next approach. We continued down the length of the runway until we got to the outer circle of the airfield or DREM lights. We followed these around as best we could, cross wind, down wind, cross wind and funnels. As we passed over each light (these were on poles and pointing skywards) we would be in darkness for a few seconds before we picked up the next one. Fortunately, there are not many hills around Elsham and we eventually landed safely but it was still a very frightening experience. The round trip had taken seven-and-a-half hours.'[57]

Total Bomber Command fatalities for that night were 382, nearly half of them killed when the raid was almost over. Twenty-nine Lancasters crashed or were abandoned. 1 Group lost 13 aircraft, and in 8 Group, 97 Squadron lost 7 – total fatalities were 148.[58]

The Second (Final) Phase: 1/2 January to 30/31 March 1944
1/2 January 1944
The first raid of the New Year was on 1/2 January. On this raid 421 Lancasters went out and 29 aborted. Although the RAF ordered a spoof force of Mosquitoes to branch off north to Hamburg, away from the Main Force, this was ignored by the German controllers. One interesting aspect of the raid was an alteration in the outward route. Originally this had been planned to go out over the neck of Denmark and across the Baltic, but a delay was caused by concerns about the weather. The return route was a long southerly one south of the Ruhr, across Belgium, the northern tip of France and the Channel. The delay meant the force did not take off until after midnight. Since the hours of available darkness were fewer than originally planned, the raid was forced to take a near direct route to the target across northern Holland and the Zuider Zee. Although there was a strong tail wind, 28 Lancasters were lost and 168 men killed. This was nearly double

the casualties of two nights before, which had a larger force: on 29/30 December a mixed force went out (457 Lancasters and 282 Halifaxes) and 81 airmen were killed. The Lancaster had a higher fatality rate than the Halifax[59]: during the whole of the Berlin campaign a total of 2,461 Lancaster men were killed compared with 703 on Halifaxes and 183 on Stirlings.[60]

2/3 January 1944

The next raid saw 362 Lancasters and nine Halifaxes despatched with, curiously enough, almost exactly the same losses as the previous night: 26 Lancasters and 168 aircrew. This was an unpopular raid: the order to go out again at midnight, so soon after the New Year's Eve celebrations and an eight-hour trip to the 'Big City', led to near mutiny on some stations. The original route was again changed to a near straight in-straight out route, with a slight dog-leg north after passing south of Bremen. The unpopularity of the raid undoubtedly contributed to an abnormally high abort rate of 60, but included in this were 15 Lancasters which misread a return signal sent to a Wellington force over the Bay of Biscay.

21/22 January 1944: Magdeburg

The day after a Main Force operation to Berlin, in which 769 aircraft took part and 35 were lost, Harris ordered a raid on Magdeburg, a city 100 km from Berlin, which had not been attacked before. News that the target would not be Berlin came as a welcome relief to the crews of many squadrons who had been on the recent string of operations to the capital. On the same night 22 Lancasters and 12 Mosquitoes flew a decoy operation to the 'Big City'. However the Germans did not fall for the 'spoof' raid: some *Nachtjäger* actually diverted away from Berlin to engage the main attack. Bill Carman, an engineer with 49 Squadron, flew on the hoax flight to the capital. It was his seventh mission:

'The last of our five trips to Berlin was, to our dismay, a "spoof" attack, comprised of 30 aircraft, to draw the night fighters away from the main stream attack on Magdeburg. Fortunately for us the "ruse" didn't work and we had an uneventful journey. That didn't stop us sweating it out, though, at the time – all the way there and all the way back. These long trips acting as a "decoy", with some eight hours in the air, most of the time over enemy territory, were an even greater strain on each and every one of the crew [than normal ops].'[61] [62]

The results of the Magdeburg raid were horrendous: 55 aircraft went down, including over 15% of the Halifaxes.

The previous night, after five days of bad weather, there had been another attack on Berlin and, for the first time, *Zahme Sau* tactics had been used. These resulted from the Germans' introduction of SN-2, an airborne radar device which enabled the operator to filter out any Window interference, giving a truer picture. Twin-engined night fighters, Bf 110s and Ju 88s with specialist operators, could thus roam free of ground control. If the ground operators were able to track the inbound and outbound path of the stream, the night fighters could then locate and attack it independently. On most raids it was the Main Force, not the diversion, which carried H2S, and using an airborne device named *Naxos* (and its ground-based equivalent, *Korfu*) which detected H2S transmissions, the Germans identified the Main Force, and thus the diversion.

27/28 January 1944

This was an all-Lancaster raid and 515 aircraft went out (accompanied by 15 Mosquitoes) on what was described as 'the cleverest tactical plan yet employed on the Berlin raids.'[63] Saundby and his staff decided to confound the enemy further by sending out a 'spoof' force of 80 Stirlings and Wellingtons into the German Bight, accompanied by 21 H2S-equipped Halifaxes which mined Heligoland. This convinced the *Luftwaffe* to despatch part of its *Nachtjagd* into the North Sea. At first the Main Force followed this 'spoof' raid, but then dog-legged south-east, flying across northern Holland, suggesting to the enemy that targets for the raid, following this route, were perhaps Magdeburg and Leipzig. Meanwhile six Mosquitoes dropped dummy route markers and fighter flares to the north-east of the stream, indicating Hannover or Brunswick as targets. Thus any one of four major cities were 'spoofed' as possible subjects for attack. After over 300 miles the Main Force then dog-legged north-east towards an area north of Berlin, whilst three Mosquitoes, continuing on the south-east route, dropped Window and dummy fighter flares as another diversion. The rapidity of these moves put great pressure on German night fighter controllers. At a point approximately 60 miles from Berlin, the bombers veered due east for the final approach. But the target was cloud covered and, although the PFF's Wanganui sky markers were accurate, the strong following wind blew them east along the line of the bomb run and the bombing became widely dispersed. Thirty-three Lancasters were lost, three of them from 460 Squadron. A total of 1,704 tons of bombs was dropped, 38 aircraft aborted, 172 airmen were killed and 55 became POWs. Sixty-seven civilians were also killed.[64]

This attack on Berlin, on 27/28 January, tested the strength and abilities of crews to the absolute limit, and was to prove to be one of the last concerted attempts by Harris to bring the capital to its knees. In his history of 460 Squadron, *Strike and Return*, pilot Peter Firkins wrote:

'In the period 18 November 1943 to 30 March 1944, Bomber Command attacked Berlin on 16 occasions as well as 14 other major targets… It was Bomber Command's most devastating period in six years of war when 1,117 aircraft were lost, including 36 from the squadron; among them were the crews of three flight commanders: Squadron Leaders E.G.M. Corser DFC, L.J. Simpson DFC and E.A.G. Utz DFC.'

During December 1943, 460 Squadron had lost 11 crews. In January and February 1944 another 14 were shot down. In those miserable three months, 25 crews were lost on 21 operations. By the end of the war 460 Squadron had sent more aircraft on operations both generally and to Berlin (385 sorties) and lost more Lancasters than any other squadron in 1 Group – and in the whole of Bomber Command. Its total losses by the end of the war were 169 aircraft. On the night of 27/28 January, of the force sent out, 6.4% failed to return even though half the night fighter force was lured north and the opposition was less intense than normal.

This was Laurie Simpson's final operation. His aircraft took off from Binbrook at 17.40 hrs, with what was almost a 'scratch' crew, which had not flown on previous ops and had made only a couple of daylight cross-countries together. For mid-upper gunner, Johnny Rydings, who had arrived from Australia at the end of the summer, it was his first trip, as he had only previously been to 27 OTU before going into the 460 Squadron crew 'pool'. All the rest were fairly experienced with three DFMs and one DFC between them. Laurie Simpson, Col McLeod and Al Kennedy had decided to go back on ops early in order to stick together, and rear gunner Johnny Osborne,[65] wireless op/air gunner Arthur Schrock and James 'Jock' Nairn the engineer, a Scot, and the only non-Australian on the crew, had all done earlier tours: Osborne with 460, Schrock with 12 Squadron and Nairn with

101 Squadron. Schrock volunteered for a second tour because he wanted to avoid the 'sprog crews' he had been teaching at Church Broughton if he was to have any chance of survival. Although the odds of completing another 20 ops were minimal, they were less so with inexperienced crews at a training unit. Kennedy, Osborne and Nairn had all received DFMs at the end of their first tour. Soon after Laurie arrived at Binbrook, a new station for him, he had to report to the Station CO, Group Captain Hughie Edwards.

Only one photograph survives of the crew of the 'Simpson Kite' from this period:[66] taken by Alistair Kennedy it reveals a bedraggled group of six men who look considerably more war weary than the pristine, over-confident first tour crew of January 1943. Apart from Rydings, who appears less 'broken-in' than the others, they were all veterans of an earlier tour. Thirty operations and six months at OTU had changed my father and his way of looking at things. He was by then married and had been away from Australia for over two years. He had witnessed numerous friends being killed, and had himself experienced a number of 'close shaves'. He must have realised, even before they did the series of cross-country flights leading up to the first operation, that their chances of survival were negligible.

Lancaster JB296, AR-K 'King', was actually a reassignment after their original Lancaster, 'Jig 2', had become unavailable. That night, after bombing Berlin and having escaped the attention of the German night fighters, 'K-King' was holed in a fuel tank by Flak and they were losing fuel.

Laurie gave his own account of the mission:

'We'd just finished our stint at OTU. We didn't finish the whole term because Alistair and Col, the two members who were still with me, wanted to go back on ops again while we were still together, before we got split up. So we applied and that's what we did. I was on leave with my wife at the end of 1943 and I got a recall, and I had to go back. I'd only had about two days leave and we'd been to a Canadian Officers' dance at the Royal Bath Hotel in Bournemouth, and I had to go back within three days. And so we went back. We picked up a new rear gunner, Johnny Osborne, a new flight engineer, 'Jock' Nairn. They were in the pool at the home squadron, waiting to make up crews. Arthur Schrock from Queensland was the wireless op and the mid-upper gunner was Johnny Rydings from West Australia. We did a couple of night "cross-countries", and then we went on ops. And from the first op we, unfortunately, didn't get back. The reason – and we thought about this quite a lot – was that as we flew over complete cloud cover all the time, right to the end, we weren't able to check our navigation or our wind to see whether it corresponded with the forecast.'

Laurie made four operations to Berlin in his two tours. He later described how serious the night fighter activity could be: 'There were fighters everywhere on the night runs to Berlin and their tracer bullets criss-crossed the sky. What was sickening from our point of view was that we could see our colleagues being shot out of the skies and with every aircraft went seven men. In truth we would probably only lose six or seven aircraft, but it always seemed much more at the time.'[67] He recalled the 27 January raid:

'We reckoned the winds were probably 40 mph stronger than predicted but we couldn't prove that.[68] And they were coming in a northerly or north-westerly direction, probably northerly,[69] because when we sighted the glare through the clouds where Berlin was, we had to turn towards the north to get up to where we should be for our bombing run,[70] and then we came away.

'At that stage we were hit by Flak over the target. There was so much bursting around us that, in a way, we didn't realise we had been hit. I didn't see any tracer coming up; in fact I didn't see any at all. So it wasn't light Flak, it was the heavy stuff.[71] We must have been hit in one or two of the fuel tanks, because later on we suddenly found the gauges had jammed on full. They were self-sealing tanks, but it would depend on the size of the hole [whether they resealed]. For an ordinary bullet hole, for the light stuff, they would, but for the heavy stuff, they wouldn't – and it was a big hole. But we didn't realise this: we just thought ourselves lucky to be getting away in one piece.'

One of the reasons for the failure of the flight was poor navigation: the H2S and some other navigational equipment failed, and there were very strong northerlies that night:

'We set on a slightly west of south course: we should have gone down to the Ruhr and then turned west of north-west, then around the Ruhr and back up to base. But we weren't able to check how our navigation was doing, at any stage, by sighting the ground. It was only when we'd gone onto a westerly course after we thought we'd gone round the Ruhr, that Alistair took a couple of astro-shots; and the position he worked out put us so far south of where we should have been that he didn't believe them: he thought he'd made a mistake. In retrospect they were somewhere near right, a bit too right, and if we'd known that was the true position at that time, the remedying action we would have taken would probably have got us back alright. But we didn't, and we were still over 10/10 cloud: we couldn't see a thing. At the time our ETA – the time we were due to cross the English coast on the return journey – was up. We thought: "We've got to find out where we are somehow!"'

The difficulty of taking astro-shots on operations was explained by Don Charlwood:

'About an hour from our target, an astro-fix showed us 40 miles south of track. On training flights my star shots had brought good results, but I regarded this fix with extreme doubt. Astro on operations was a different proposition. With surprise attacks by fighters always a probability, none of us regarded straight and level flight with much enthusiasm, with the result [that we] tended to work hurriedly and less accurately. To alter course on this one check appeared to be inviting trouble. To get another fix was soon complicated by the development of high cloud. Our Gee and our radio were both out of order and, in any event, we were beyond the range of British transmitters. I continued with dead reckoning for almost two hours. For all that time a strong wind blew us further and further south of track. Supposedly at Caen... we must in fact have been in the northern reaches of the Bay of Biscay.'[72]

Laurie Simpson:

'Quite a way before then [Brittany] the H2S had packed up, so we weren't getting any ground pictures. We weren't able to get the homing beam because, it seemed to us, it was being bent by the Germans – it should have passed through the DF Loop, which picked up directional beams from the transmitting stations, [but wasn't].[73] So, at the time we were due to cross the coast we thought we were going to have to break cloud anyway, and the cloud base was down to about 2 or 3,000 feet; lower perhaps. We did see some coastline but it was so dark, there was no moon and the cloud base was so low, that we couldn't see far enough in any direction to give us an idea of the general run of the coast; we could only see what was immediately below us, and it didn't seem to correspond with where we should have been. But we couldn't decide where it might be.

'So we thought we'd better send out distress signals and then we could get a course to fly from the receiving station. So we did this and then we went on... I think we turned onto a north-westerly course. We thought, "we must be going in the right direction", but there was so much traffic on the air that we couldn't get through. And then we were left with the decision about what to do as we hadn't got very much fuel left.'

Although wireless op Schrock's 'Maydays' were picked up in England – they were heard '...on the w/t saying they were experiencing severe problems with the fuel supply' – efforts to establish the position of JB296 failed.[74] One of the reasons for this was the large amount of radio traffic on the air that night, which prevented any accurate fixes being made. The crew decided to bale out over Brittany.

'We eventually came to the conclusion that we were quite a lot south of where we should have been, quite a lot south, and that what we were looking at [below] was the Cherbourg Peninsula. Instead of coming down in a south-westerly direction, the wind had taken us in a southerly direction after we left Berlin. So instead of flying westerly, then north-westerly, we had gone south of the Ruhr and were flying towards the south-west, then west, rather than north-west. The wind had been taking us further away from where we wanted to be.

We wondered if we'd overshot England and [whether] the coast that we saw (which was a westward facing coast), was of the Bristol Channel, in which case we would have gone right across England. That's what we thought we might have done; but, not being able to get a ground sighting, or to get a pinpoint or a course to steer from, we were blundering on a bit. Then we decided it was the Cherbourg Peninsula.'

The crew discounted any option of ditching in the Channel: the winter of 1943/44 was one of the coldest winters on record that century:

'We weren't going to be able to get across the Channel: there were very heavy storms that particular period of the year, early January, and ditching would have been impossible. Consequently there was no way we could have glided home: it was stormy and the seas were very rough because of the gale-like conditions. It was also pitch black: it was late January, and at that time of year the nights were very dark, and if you had gale conditions coming from either the south-west or the north-west, even from the east, the English Channel could be very rough indeed. We talked about this, and everybody agreed that we'd never make a ditching: the waves were 20 foot high. We were going to have to abandon the aircraft. So I turned it on a southerly direction. The gauges had jammed: when "Jock" Nairn the engineer tried to transfer fuel for two of the tanks it was just pumping air – there was nothing pumping through! So that was our reserve that would have got us home – but we didn't have it!

We all went out through the nose hatch because they couldn't get the rear door open. Two of them tried to unjam it but found it too difficult. So they all went past me and I was the last one out. I set it on "George" – auto – we were flying in a circle by this time and I thought we must be over land. I could see the coast: the maximum height I could get, and still see the coast, was two-and-a-half thousand feet.

Everybody got out safely, and landed safely: nobody was injured. Johnny Rydings found himself suspended in a tree. Arthur Schrock landed in a lake; and I think Colin and Alistair landed on a town. It might have been Dinard, because I'd turned the aircraft south once we thought we were over Cherbourg. We had no idea at all what our chances of getting back to England were.'[75]

All seven of the crew survived, five going to *Stalag Luft* III, and two to *Stalag Luft* VI at Heydekrug.

28/29 January 1944
Jack Whitehouse was a wireless op with 35 Squadron, part of 8 (Pathfinder) Group based at Graveley in Huntingdonshire under Wing Commander S.P. Daniels. His crew's first op in its Halifax II was as a 'supporter' on an attack on a 'special target' in north-west France. 'Supporters' were inexperienced PFF crews who accompanied the Main Force dropping Window or bombs to confuse the enemy. The next mission on 21 January was also as a 'supporter', throwing out T.I.s and bombs. On 27 January they raided Heligoland. Then Whitehouse experienced his first attack on Berlin:

'28/29 January was the big one for us – Berlin. We took off at five minutes past midnight, arriving at the target at 03.47 hours at 19,000 feet. With T.I.s and bombs we bombed on green target indicators. The red glow in the clouds could be seen from the enemy coast on return. The duration of the flight was just over eight hours. This flight was without incident for us, but the German ack-ack was very heavy indeed and much too accurate for my liking. The noise on the Halifax's fuselage made it feel as if we were flying through a wall of steel.'

This was a 'maximum effort' raid against the 'Big City' with extensive diversions, following on from the success of the previous night's hoax attacks. Three Mosquitoes took off at around 20.00 hours on a 'spoof' raid to Berlin, the intention being to convince the enemy that no major attack on the capital would be made that night. Four Oboe Mosquito attacks were made on the important German night fighter airfields in the Netherlands, including Leeuwarden, and Stirling minelaying attacks were made on Kiel Bay. A hoax raid by Mosquitoes on Hannover was also made around the time that the Main Force assembled.

There was a further raid against Berlin on 30/31 January (540 aircraft despatched, 33 lost). As was customary there was then a lapse in operations, because the first part of the new month was a lunar period. But the ensuing prolonged stand-down for thirteen nights was unusual. It was a period for what would now be termed 'R and R',[76] allowing Harris time to increase his stock of Lancasters. This period of refrain from ops was prolonged by snow and bad weather which resulted in the 13th and 14th being days of cancelled missions. Harris's next raid was on 15/16 February when 561 Lancasters, 43 Halifaxes and 16 Mosquitoes went out. Forty-three went missing – nearly 5% of the force – and 75 aborted.

19-20 February 1944: Leipzig
The city was a priority target and came under the Pointblank Directive with its aircraft factory being second in precedence to Schweinfurt. The raid has been described as 'probably the most important of the Battle of Berlin', not because it was a success, but because it was a failure. Rear gunner Roy Child's 7 Squadron Lancaster MG-U, JB468 took off from Oakington at 23.59 hrs, one of 823 aircraft that went out, including 561 Lancasters.

'Autumn had now become winter and the war in the air over Germany had continued unabated, as did our casualties. Each nightly bombing raid meant the loss on average of two of our squadron aircraft. Into February the losses began to mount and the feeling abounded that there was little chance of getting through a tour. There was also a feeling that the Germans were starting to win the battles against our bombers. The RAF lost more and more planes and could not supply the new crews that were needed. "Old Lags" would look at new airmen and bet on how long they would last. As it turned out, after the raid on Leipzig there was only one more major raid during the winter and spring of 1944. In the raid against Leipzig we lost 79 planes over Germany and another 30 crashed in England or into the sea. On that night, we set out from Oakington with the Met officer forecasting "good weather, with some winds": *some winds!* They turned out to be very strong, blowing from the west and, within an hour, we were well ahead of our time.'

The problem with the winds affected the whole stream and resulted in many aircraft arriving over the target early. A 'steady head wind' had been forecast, but there was, as Martin Middlebrook records, a 'light wind from the north'. This caused the stream to break up. Some of the 'old lag' navigators persuaded their pilots to dog-leg more than once in order to ensure they arrived over Leipzig after the PFF. But less experienced navs did not correct the broadcast wind reports, and the stream became unusually extended and was soon attacked. Roy Child:

'From the start bandits were among us: the *Luftwaffe* fighters attacked us as soon as we crossed the coast. The crew of "U-Uncle" had another big worry because over the sea we had checked our guns, and "George" the automatic pilot was not working and we should have returned home. Instead we voted to carry on: this was a big mistake!'

That night there was a diversionary minelaying raid in Kiel Bay by four H2S-equipped PFF Halifaxes and 45 Stirlings, and another by 15 Mosquitoes to Berlin, but the Germans only partially took the bait. A large part of the *Nachtjagd* was available to assault the Main Force when it crossed the Dutch coast, and soon Bf 110s were harassing the stream, reinforced by other fighters returning from the north. Child's navigator, Flying Officer R.F.B. Powell, realised how inaccurate the Met Officer's forecasts were, and that they were considerably ahead of schedule.

'In order to try and delay the time we were due to bomb, and to allow the Pathfinder flares to illuminate the target, the skipper, against my advice, started to zigzag across the bomber stream. At one stage another bomber flew over the top of us, about 30 yards from my turret. I reported this to the skipper who turned into the bomber stream. We had by this time seen a number of aircraft being shot down. One was close to us when it blew up: we knew the crew had no chance to survive. The stream was heading straight for Berlin to try and persuade the German controllers to think that was our target. But within 70 miles of the city the bombers turned [south] and headed down to Leipzig. Ahead we could see the target, already alight.'

The unexpectedly strong winds were causing some aircraft to arrive prematurely. To make matters worse, cloud obscured the objective. Untimely arrivals had to circle Leipzig and an anarchic situation developed in which four aircraft collided. Child:

'Bombers had arrived early and were bombing the city; but there were few PFF flares going down. I had been alert during the entire trip and looking down saw a twin-engine German plane below us. I yelled to the skipper to dive to port but it was too late. Tracer, bullets and cannon fire were coming towards us and the plane was hit. The wireless op was killed and "U-Uncle" was on fire.'

JB468 was attacked over Wittenberg and abandoned by five of the crew, leaving the pilot, Sqn/Ldr K.G. Davis, and the wireless op, F/O K. Marriott DFM, who had done his first tour with 115 Squadron. The attack occurred at 18,000 feet. In fact quite a large number of attacks that night were high – up to 22,000 feet; Chorley lists 15 reported attacks, mostly by Bf 110s and Ju 88s between 19,000 and 22,000 feet.[77]

'The skipper said he could not control the plane and we should bale out. I fought my way through fire and smoke and, at the same time, saw the other gunner coming along towards me. I opened the rear door, put on my 'chute, and jumped out. When my 'chute opened I saw our plane coming down and I could hear the German fighter flying around. It was only then that I remembered "George" was not working and the skipper could not get out: he would have to force-land. This has lived with me over the years. He did, in fact, try and land the plane but was killed. I landed in thick snow and was soon taken prisoner by German troops. They were to give me a rough time. I felt hopeless: I was now a prisoner of war in the hands of the Germans.'[78]

It is believed that Davis force-landed the aircraft because Marriott was wounded and neither man could bale out: they both died in the crash. The 'other gunner' was Flight Sergeant Alan Grange, also with a DFM. Although officially recorded as a 'POW', Child stated that he believed Grange had subsequently been killed by the Germans: his body was never found. The four survivors became POWs.

Also on the Leipzig raid was Pilot Officer Stanley W. Payne, a mid-upper gunner with 106 Squadron based at Metheringham. Payne was an RAAF man from Perth, Western Australia. His Lancaster ME630 ZN-P was attacked over the target area by what was identified as an 'Me 210' at 21,000 feet, in a *Schräge Musik* attack. The pilot, Flying Officer E.R.F. 'Dickie' Leggett, like so many others that night, had dog-legged to the target after the initial forecast winds proved to be inaccurate. Leggett put the Lancaster into a starboard dive, and as he did so the enemy fighter shot out the main port fuel tank which ignited, before raking the entire length of the bomber's fuselage. Leggett immediately shouted at the crew to bale out, and the bomb-aimer, navigator and wireless op went out through the front hatch. Stan Payne, Leggett and tail gunner, Sgt John Harrison, were still in the aircraft. Payne struggled to get the rear door open, but it had been buckled by the German attack. Leggett then told them to get to the nose hatch, saying he would hold the aircraft as long as he could. Payne dived through the front hatch. Harrison hesitated, and looked back at Leggett, who gave him a 'thumbs up' sign, then also dived out. They were at 10,000 feet.

Six of the crew survived the attack. Harrison went to *Stalag Luft* VI. Dickie Leggett rode the aircraft down and crashed into a lake. His feet became jammed under the rudder pedals; he was unable to get out and was killed. The survivors later submitted for a posthumous award for him, but it was never ratified.[79] Payne went to Block 109 at *Stalag Luft* III. On ANZAC Day 1944, Payne, Johnny Rydings, Keith Murdoch, Paul Royle (a survivor of the Great Escape),[80] and all other West Australian POWs in the camp, were photographed by the German official photographer.

Of the total force that went to Leipzig, 82 aircraft went missing, with 20 lost to Flak. The raid was important because it caused three important revisions to the machinery of Bomber Command:

a) To prevent aircraft from arriving over the target early due to incorrect wind forecasts, 'Zero Hour' would henceforth be advanced or retarded at will on the r/t by the Bomber Command controllers.
b) The Halifax Mks II and V, with in-line engines, nineteen of which had been lost on Leipzig, were to be withdrawn from front line service immediately, resulting in four squadrons being stood down until their aircraft were replaced.
c) Harris decided to curtail the Battle of Berlin forthwith. Since so many aircraft had been lost on a secondary target (9.5% of the force), how many more would be lost over Berlin? This, together with the German *Nachtjagdwaffe* appearing more effective than ever, and there being little evidence of the capital's resilience or morale crumbling, led Harris to concede defeat. One could suggest that the Germans had stalemated him.

Harris had frequently modified or rejected the directives sent to him in order to pursue his primary aim – the destruction of Berlin. This was now impossible and he must have realised that the preparations for D-Day would take the situation out of his hands. On 1 April he was subordinated to Eisenhower: the moment was past.

24/25 March 1944: 'The Night of the Strong Winds'
The 24/25 March raid later entered Bomber Command parlance as 'the night of the strong winds'. It was the last major raid of the 'Battle of Berlin' and equally cataclysmic: 74 aircraft were lost,[81] i.e. 9.1% of a total force of 811.

A powerful wind from the north carried the bombers south at every stage of the flight.[82] The RAF navigators had various methods to detect the wind force and direction. Both H2S and Gee could be used, but Gee was jammed by the enemy as soon as the force came within range, about halfway across the North Sea. Two Master Bombers were to be used and one of these, the Deputy Master Bomber, was in a high-flying Met Flight Mosquito. The stream was to fly out over the neck of Denmark ESE, make landfall on the German coast and veer SE towards the north of Berlin. Then, 30 miles from the capital, the bombers would dog-leg SW for the final run in. The forecast winds over the North Sea were predicted to vary from 21 mph increasing to 44 mph, but in the event navigators began picking up even stronger winds on their Gee equipment. As soon as these became jammed, however, there was around a half-hour gap before the stream could make revised calculations when H2S picked up the coast of Denmark. During that period they relied upon the estimated and forecast winds they had received, via England, from 'wind-finder' aircraft. Although the wind direction remained steady during this period, the strength had increased. Expecting to arrive north of the Danish island of Sylt, they were 30 miles south of where they should have been. Winds of 130 mph were recorded by some navigators. This led to much confusion in the air and the stream became widely dispersed. Many bombers tried to fly north to regain their original track or to try and pick it up later, wasting much time and causing further confusion. This was not helped by highly inaccurate wind readings that were broadcast back to the stream – much lower than originally calculated due to a general downgrading caused by disbelief, on the part of the Met officers and staff concerned, over the high velocities recorded. This resulted in accumulated error.

The bombers had been expected to arrive over the north-eastern outskirts of the 'Big City' at 23.35 hrs. However 700 aircraft were now approaching the capital spread out over a front 70 miles across – known in RAF parlance as a 'gaggle'. Tail-gunner Jim McGillivray explained:

'"Gaggle" – that was the official word for it. Each bomber followed its own course; it didn't follow the leader over – you're going the same way, of course. All flew at different heights... some would be at 18,000, some would be at 17,000 feet. And when we reached the turning points you tried to be on time. If you were too early you used to do a dog-leg, where you'd zigzag to lose a bit of time. If you were late you could cut a corner to get up. The main thing was to get over the target when they wanted you there, because that saturates the defences.'[83]

That was the ideal situation. Freddy King, Laurie Simpson's former flight engineer, now on the 12 Squadron Lancaster crew of Flt/Lt John Brabewell, an experienced second tour man with a DFC, like everybody else ended up over the capital much later than predicted. Flt/Lt King, who was commissioned after his first tour, was the only Australian on the crew and all the way to the target he would have been balancing the fuel tanks using the fuel cocks by his seat. The bomb run was one of the most dangerous periods of the mission. Some of the initial crews to arrive were blown right across the city and had to attack any target they found. Others, approaching later, bombed the aiming point of a PFF marker and skated across the city at a welcome high escape velocity. Others made the hazardous decision to turn around and make a second run: this was a 20-minute trip over the most heavily defended city in the world, against a head wind of over 100 knots.

An interesting situation developed where the Canadian Master Bomber was swearing four-letter expletives of encouragement at the bomber force; the Deputy Master Bomber, lying flat on his stomach in the Mosquito, was occasionally commenting in educated English; some bombers were struggling backwards against winds exceeding 100 mph; whilst down below, the clouds that obscured certain areas of the city took on a translucent quality as Hajo Herrmann instructed great bonfires of phosphorus to be lit, housewives to open their blackout curtains and searchlights to shine directly at the underbelly of the clouds: all this to help the night fighters.

Aircraft flew out from the target to the south-east, following a return course with three dog-legs. It was during this period that the majority of raiders fell: over 66 aircraft, including Freddy King's. Three of these were from 115 Squadron, a radial-engined Lancaster II unit from No. 3 Group. They had taken off from Witchford, 20 miles north of Cambridge, between 18.37 and 18.49 hrs, climbing out towards the coast of Holland.

115 Squadron was one of the best in 3 Group from 1941 through most of 1942. It carried out more operations than any other squadron at that time and was one of Harris's prime units, flying 5,392 sorties during the war and dropping nearly 23,000 tons of bombs.[84] When the Pathfinder Force was formed, Harris wanted to train the squadron up for that role, but it transferred to Mildenhall from Marham in Norfolk in September 1942 and, in the words of one veteran, 'stopped being so good'.[85] Harris decided on another unit for the PFF.

Reg Brown was a flight engineer in 115 Squadron in 1943 and 1944 and commented upon the Hercules-engined Lancaster IIs:

'They were very powerful low down, but couldn't get the altitude of the Merlins. Our particular squadron, one of five Lanc II radial engine squadrons, had one of the best records of all squadrons in the war: so they were very effective. But we had a bit of a struggle to get to the 20,000 foot mark.'[86]

Brown was on the squadron at the end of 1943 waiting for his last op, having bombed Berlin a number of times:

'Berlin was a nasty one because it was so long – tremendous defences around Berlin, but there were also defences around the Ruhr. The weather was particularly grotty, so we were sweating on our last trip. We did nine raids on Berlin. It was quite an experience really, but an incredible amount of luck for people who survived. You'd see an aeroplane, say a Lancaster, quite near you, and it was hit and [it would] go up in a ball of flames. The entire time one was over the target you could hear the tinkling of the shell cases on the fuselage. Fortunately we didn't see any exploding ones, apart from the time we were damaged over the Zuider Zee, so we were very, very lucky.'[87]

Of the three 115 Squadron Lancaster IIs that took off for Berlin on 24 March, one was DS664 coded A4-K. The other two were LL694, coded KO-N, which departed first, and DS678, coded KO-J. The skipper of 'K-King' was Flt/Sgt John Newman. On board were Sgt Geoffrey Burwell, wireless op, Sgt J. P. Cleary, navigator, and Sgt Nicholas Alkamede,[88] tail gunner. All three of the 115 Squadron Lancasters were miles off their planned return route when they were shot down, each one by a night fighter. As it came away from Berlin, the stream was spread across a front 50 miles wide which soon stretched back over 150 miles,[89] the 100 mph-plus winds blowing the whole 'gaggle' well to the south of the intended route, so that many aircraft began to stray over the Ruhr. Around an hour after DS664 left the target area, a Ju 88 approached from the rear and raked it at 19,000 feet with cannon fire from its *Schräge Musik* installation. The whole aircraft was soon engulfed with flames. In the rear turret Alkamede fired his four .303s and hit one of the Junker's engines which started to burn, but he soon found he had problems.[90]

DS678, flown by Canadian P/O L.M. McCann, was blown so far south that it ended up over Leipzig at 20,000 feet. Roaming the night skies around Berlin that night were some of the *Luftwaffe's* leading night fighter aces: *Oberleutnant* Martin Becker, *Staffelkapitän* of 2./NJG 6; *Oberstleutnant* Helmut Lent, the *Kommodore* of NJG 3; and *Oberleutnant* Heinrich Schnaufer, *Gruppenkommandeur* of IV./NJG 1. But the man who attacked McCann's Lancaster was probably *Hauptmann* Iro Ilk, the *Gruppenkommandeur* of III./JG 300, who claimed a four-engined 'Tommy' over Leipzig at 22.53 hrs. Only the bombardier and the Canadian navigator survived. LL694 was shot down by *Hauptmann* Martin Drewes of III./NJG 1 in a Bf 110. This was claimed in the squadron Operational Record Book as crashing 4 km SSE of Deventer at 00.20 hrs, and corresponds to Drewes' claim for an attack on a Lancaster 50 km west of Rheine, Germany (thus in Holland) at 00.10 hrs.[91]

In DS664, Sgt Alkamede was faced with an horrific situation. He later recounted his experience to *Scangriff*, the Prisoner of War newspaper of *Stalag Luft* III:

'We got through the Flak and searchlights belts safely, and an hour or so later found ourselves in the radio-controlled fighter belt. Though keeping a good lookout and carrying out banking searches, we received a surprise attack from a Ju 88 night fighter. Our aircraft sustained serious damage from cannon and heavy machine gun fire, the starboard wing and fuselage catching fire and blazing furiously. My rear turret also received a direct hit from a cannon shell, blowing out all the perspex and setting part of the hydraulic gear on fire. I managed to get my guns depressed to give a long burst to the enemy aircraft, at the same time reporting my impressions to the captain of the aircraft. I saw my gunfire take effect by the bursting into flames of the port engine. He then dived away as if out of control. Meanwhile the skipper had found the aircraft unsafe and unmanageable and gave the order to "bale out". This I proceeded to do. I centralised my turret by hand and opened the doors to get my 'chute, stored in the fuselage. It was at the centre of an inferno. Absolutely useless! I pulled myself together and shut the doors again. What was I to do? I had the choice of staying with the aircraft or jumping out. If I stayed I would be burned to death – my clothes were already well alight and my face and hands were burnt, though at the time I scarcely noticed the pain due to my high state of excitement… I decided to jump and end it all as quick and clean as I could. I rotated the turret to starboard and, not even bothering to take off my helmet and intercom, did a back flip out into the night. It was very quiet, the only sound being the drumming of the aircraft engines in the distance, and no sensation of falling at all. I felt suspended in space. Regrets at not getting home were my chief thoughts, and I did think once that it didn't seem very strange to be going to die in a few seconds – none of the parade of my past or anything else like that.

'I "blacked out" about then; it may have been lack of oxygen or the concussion from the aircraft exploding – I don't know. The next thing I knew I was coming to my senses lying on my back in deep snow, gazing at the stars through the tops of some young fir trees. I was alive! I guess I was the one airman who didn't mind being a POW.

'I next checked my limbs and found I was uninjured apart from burns, bruises, a small scalp wound, a flesh wound, also small, in my thigh, and a twisted knee. The knee and bruises were the only damage sustained in my fall. I afterwards estimated that fall to be one of 18,000 feet!'[92]

Meanwhile, Burwell and Cleary, were still in the aircraft. The r/t was down and communication impeded. Then the Lancaster exploded and both men were blown out. Cleary's parachute opened automatically, despite being damaged, and he lost a boot. Burwell, like Ted Boorman and others, found his 'chute trailing behind him but managed to pull the D-ring. Both men landed in pine trees. When Alkamede was picked up by the Germans they refused to believe his story. At *Dulag Luft*, 'Even chaps who listened to Goebbels wouldn't believe me', he said. 'On instructions from me they investigated my 'chute harness that I was wearing and found it sealed; also the absence of any canopy at the spot where I was picked up helped to convince them.'[93] Alkamede was given the title of 'the luckiest man in Germany' and sent to a transit camp. The remainder of the crew all perished.

Many aircraft on the raid were blown so far south that they actually flew near Sagan, Silesia, 100 miles south-east of the capital, where *Stalag Luft* III was located. This was the night of the 'Great Escape' from the camp. Because the stream passed close by, the Germans switched off the camp's electricity supply and all the searchlights went out. This prevented the POWs from increasing the volume of traffic escaping through the tunnel. (Partly as a result of this, only 76 prisoners got out rather than the 200 hoped for).

German *Nachtjagd* records claim 83 four-engined aircraft were shot down between 21.00 hrs and 00.15 hrs that night,[94] but these records appear to be wildly exaggerated when compared to RAF ORB reports, possibly due to different fighters claiming the same victim. This was the final attack on the German capital during the Battle of Berlin: 72 aircraft were shot down, 392 airmen were killed, and 131 became POWs.

30/31 March 1944: the Nuremberg Raid

This raid could be seen as Harris's 'final fling' before switching to operations relating to D-Day. He wanted to employ the attack on Nuremberg as a final opportunity in the Battle of Berlin to prove the efficiency of his policies.

Historically, Nuremberg was a significant city to the Nazis, as well as being an important transportation centre. But in the British official history of the bomber offensive[95] Sir Charles Webster and Dr. Noble Frankland state that the raid 'abandoned most of the tactical precepts which for a long time had governed Bomber Command operations… The normal ruses gave way to a straightforward declaration of intention and the German fighter force was presented with a unique opportunity.' In other words, the RAF made no serious attempt to disguise the route by changing direction halfway, which would usually have been the case. Harris had been a friend and old colleague of Don Bennett, the Pathfinder Force leader. Normally Pathfinders would have flown a dog-leg or jinking route to the target; but the plan that Bennett put forward to High Wycombe, which practised this, was overruled by the Group Commanders for the Main Force representing 1, 3, 5 and 6 Groups. These non-operational staff plumped for a straight leg of 350 miles.

A low pressure area over Norway and a slow moving cold front coming from Ireland could have provided the cover the bombers needed on the outward flight, and it was these weather conditions, cloud moving southwards, that led Harris to consider a target in the south of Germany, despite this contravening a directive received earlier in the month.[96] The reason Harris gave for ignoring some of the directives he received was to save his crews, the 'old lags', from harm: if Bomber Command could not bomb large targets like Berlin, Frankfurt and Stuttgart successfully, how could they hope to hit smaller industrial targets, which required greater time and accuracy, without losing more lives?

He insisted on continuing with the Nuremberg plan despite it being a half moon period. After receiving a final report from a weather Mosquito indicating that the target would be obscured by cloud and the hoped-for cloud cover on the long outward leg would not be there, Harris for some reason unbeknown to his staff – Saundby included – continued to go ahead with the operation. This was despite a general feeling that it was the wrong move. Saundby later told Martin Middlebrook that he assumed Harris's decision had been affected by 'some top secret political decision', but later reneged on this. But the raid proved to be a disaster. In the event, *any* cloud conditions forecast as advantageous to the raid proved to be inaccurate. Furthermore, 100 mph tail winds at 20,000 feet blew directly onto the stream as it turned for its long leg and this, with a bright, unshielded moon, ensured a complete debacle.

The 'long leg' over Germany was where the majority of Bomber Command's losses were experienced that night. It was 350 miles long, passing alarmingly close to two night fighter beacons. The early forecast of protective cloud issued before the weather Mosquito returned at 15.25 hrs proved incorrect: there was no cloud shield at all and consequently the Main Force flew out into bright moonlight, exposed to any attacks the enemy chose to make. A half moon lit 3,180 condensation trails like fluorescent tracks of cotton wool. It was also forecast that the target would be clear of cloud interference, but in fact the opposite occurred, and Nuremberg was covered in cloud. These circumstances set up a classic example of what Derek Hodgkinson described as a 'night fighter benefit' raid. Ninety-seven out of 795 aircraft of the attacking force were lost. Pathfinder leader Donald Bennett, when writing of the catastrophe, was adamant that the failure was primarily the result of misguided planning: '…it was *caused* and not simply accidental', he wrote.

Poor forecasting also played a part in the slaughter on the return. Unpredicted Westerlies blowing at speeds of up to 125 knots towards the returning stream caused much higher fuel consumption, forcing many of the beleaguered 'kites' to ditch in the North Sea. It was the 'lions led by donkeys' scenario once again. This analogy of the First World War where, so some sources have held, the General Staff led lives and had conceptions completely divorced from the realities of the front line, deserves explanation. Bennett felt that none of the senior RAF officers at the time of the raid had any 'firsthand operational experience in the current war', and were 'at a grave disadvantage in any tactical planning'. He could not understand how these blinkered men could be so critical and impatient of methods – the 'normal ruses' – that previously had saved many lives. At its most basic level he attributed the disaster to staff jealousy: 'it seemed merely human weakness that they should revolt against the loss of their power to a youngster in another group',[97] (i.e. himself).

John Geddes, a British navigator in a 428 (Ghost) Squadron Canadian Halifax from Middleton St. George, felt that the Nuremberg raid was his most impressive trip: 'We flew across the North Sea,' he recalled, 'then turned just south-south-east on a long leg over Germany to the target.' The Halifax got to max height, but there was a tail wind of 100 mph:

> 'I was expected to record any incident a crew member wished to report, and was getting numerous reports of shot-down aircraft, until I had to say that that was enough. It was clearly getting hectic outside, but all these interruptions were interfering with my calculations.'

At debriefing they reported all the aircraft they had seen shot down, but other crews maintained that these were 'spoof' shells or 'scarecrows'. 'Scarecrow' was a nickname the 'bomber boys' gave to a Flak detonation they assumed was deliberately designed to resemble a bomber exploding; such was the beauty of its pyrotechnics. This was later discredited, but there still seems to be some uncertainty about this.

For Russell Margerison, Nuremberg was his first raid with 625 Squadron. For two-and-a-half hours he and his crew watched helplessly as bomber after bomber went down. By the time they had turned off the 'long leg' they had witnessed 15 bombers destroyed. Like John Geddes, Margerison's navigator also attempted to record the losses, but after half-a-dozen or so, the demoralising nature of the process rendered it pointless:

> '"Halifax going down port side", I said.
> '"Got it, Russ", replied the navigator.
> '"Lanc falling to the rear", came Gib from the tail.
> 'No sooner had he got the words out than I watched mesmerised as a Lanc's wing folded at right-angles to the aircraft like a drop-leaf table and it just toppled over, quickly disappearing from view. An excrescent flash of orange flame from another Lanc soon enveloped the whole plane and it skidded out of sight below us.
> '"Another Lanc..."
> '"Let's just forget it Gib", I interrupted.'[98]

It was 'like shooting fish in a barrel', Fred Watts, a pilot also in the attacking force, concluded. 'With full strato-form cloud and the moon behind them, the Main Force was silhouetted perfectly against the cloud, which covered the whole of Western Europe.'

It was the air gunners' duty to announce any aircraft exploding or other incident in the sky so that the navigator could log the position:

'After the gunners had reported something like 20 going down, I told them not to report any more because I didn't think it was doing very much for the morale of the crew, especially those poor boys, the navigator and the wireless operator, who were just sitting there and couldn't see out... I also noticed that on the track we were keeping... most of them were going down over on our port side. So I altered course just a few degrees away, and then paralleled my course with the navigator's assistance. I like to think we just kept out of the main stream where everybody was going down. And then when we got nearer to Nuremberg or what we thought was Nuremberg – because it was all under cloud – we eased over and went through and bombed what we hoped was [the target].'[99]

Henry Coverley was humming the popular song '*Paper Doll*' to himself as he flew down the 'long leg'. His 76 Squadron Halifax II was suddenly hit by Flak:

'I went down on the ninth trip of my second tour. It was a clear night – [the weather report] was wrong because the Met [officer had] told us it would be overcast and the fighters wouldn't be able to get up. But there was no cloud – wasn't a bloody cloud in the sky! However there was nothing much you could do. I did notice a hell of a lot of aircraft going down all around us, and at the time thought it was special shells... "*Scarecrows*!" We thought the Germans were putting those up to make it look like it was an aircraft going down. They were going down quite fast – I was [about] the thirtieth [casualty] on the way out.'

All Coverley's crew, apart from the navigator, Sergeant Motts, baled out and Coverley subsequently went to *Stalag Luft* I, Barth:

'I'd never carried a parachute – in those days we had ones you slipped on. And I put this thing on, but I put it on wrong. I can't remember getting out of the aircraft, and I couldn't find the handle to pull [the ripcord]. But we were at 24,000 feet, so I had plenty of time to think about it.

'The rest of the crew went out first. One caught fire as he jumped out. The parachute caught fire – I think it was the engineer, and it was just a mass of flames. I couldn't leave: two engines had gone on one side; I was fighting the controls, and the thing was on fire. The only way I could get out was to leave the controls, take a couple of footsteps to the other side of the aircraft, go down a couple of steps to the escape hatch in the front. By that time the aircraft was upside down, doing God knows what. There was no question of just opening a door and jumping out.

'The other thing was the standard harness I had was not my size and we'd ban anyone who took his own.[100] I didn't think it would be any use anyway; and the strap that should have been across was in front of my nose. I was awfully sick on the way down; I landed in some trees. I couldn't see anything – something had hit me in the face before I'd jumped out and I couldn't see very well. I was suspended from these trees and I didn't know how far I was from the ground – I couldn't see. Eventually after swaying around in this tree for a while, I thought I'd better get myself out and my feet were about six inches from the ground! So then I started walking. I was lucky. The rear gunner, who got out all right, was shot by one of our own Spitfires at the end of the war, on the [long] march back west.'

Another typical victim of the raid was Flt/Sgt Don Gray. His 50 Squadron Lancaster took off from Skellingthorpe at 22.13 hrs. Just three of the crew of seven NCOs survived.

Jean Silver, Gray's cousin, who lived next door to his family in Ilford, remembered that all those who knew Gray 'adored him' and were 'very proud of him'. 'He was so handsome', she wrote. 'I can remember he took me out to see a film and tea many times when he was on leave.'[101]

Gray's mission was jinxed from the start. There was a WAAF at Skellingthorpe who appeared to carry bad luck, what was termed a 'chop girl', i.e. every airman who dated her failed to return. She was a cheerful NCO and approached Gray in the sergeants' mess before the op, saying a few words to him. His immediate thoughts were: 'That does it! We're in for it!' She later appeared at the end of the runway when they took off and waved them away. It proved to be a bad omen. On the outward leg the Lancaster was hit by Flak or cannon fire and Gray and two others were blown out when their 4,000 lb blockbuster exploded over Waldbreitbach. Gray subsequently found that he was descending head first, as his parachute harness had become entangled around his ankles, which were locked tightly together. He repeated a 'limited repertoire of prayers', narrowly missing crashing head first onto an autobahn. Unable to find any survivors he was later picked up and sent to *Stalag Luft* VII.[102]

Flight engineer Dick Raymond recalled the Nuremberg trip with 83 Pathfinder Squadron:

'The only trouble we had was on landing. The weather was terrible, snow everywhere. On our first approach Ken decided to overshoot and as I pushed the throttle forward and Ken pulled on the control column, his seat collapsed and he found himself level under the blind-flying panel. How he got out of that no one knows. Ken swears we were below stalling speed.'[103]

Ever since the war ended there have been intimations that there was something more sinister behind the operation. Dr. Alfred Price, who wrote the definitive book on radio countermeasures in World War Two,[104] *Instruments of Darkness* (1977), stated '…suggestions [were] that the Germans had some foreknowledge that the night's target was to be Nuremberg and had arranged their defences accordingly.' Harris himself admitted that the raid was Bomber Command's '…one real disaster and we were lucky not to have had a dozen.'[105]

The idea that the Germans had prior knowledge of the raid was supported by Anthony Cave Brown in his book *Bodyguard of Lies* (1975). This contained a number of somewhat sensational and intriguing theories: for example that Coventry was allowed by Churchill to be bombed in 1940 to protect Ultra and that Reinhard Heydrich's assassination had been carried out to save the neck of the head of the *Abwehr*, Admiral Wilhelm Canaris. Cave Brown stated that in the 1970s he had talked to Sir Francis de Guingand, Field Marshal Montgomery's Chief of Staff in 1944. De Guingand informed Cave Brown he had, '…been told that the identity of a target in Germany "for major air attack" had been revealed to the Germans in order to ensure the continuing credibility of [an] agent.'

In 1944 De Guingand was concerned with the Operation Fortitude deception plans developed to ensure the success of the D-Day invasion.[106] By the time of the Nuremberg attack on 30 March 1944, two months before D-Day, all German agents in England had either been incarcerated or turned into double-agents by J.C. Masterman's 'XX Committee'. Cave Brown suggested that, at that time, anything the Allies could do to sustain Germany's trust in reports from these double-agents would be justifiable, enabling them to feed false information back to Germany to support the Fortitude deception.

The old General remembered the target was probably Stuttgart, but he made no mention if it was the target of either an RAF or a USAAF attack.

Martin Middlebrook, whose book *The Nuremberg Raid* was published less than two years earlier, did not accept Cave Brown's theory. There had been four raids against Stuttgart in February and March 1944, one mounted by the USAAF, and three by the RAF, the last being on 16 March. Middlebrook contacted the authorities in Stuttgart after *Bodyguard of Lies* was published, and queried Cave Brown's suggestions. He was informed that the late former head of the city's *Flugwachtkommando*, a *Major* Engelhorn, related before he died that they had been warned by Berlin on 16 March that Stuttgart was to be the target of the RAF that night: this was long before any bombs fell. Consequently 'the city's sirens sounded 36 minutes before the first bombs dropped', he said.

Cave Brown dismissed de Guingand's suggestion of Stuttgart as the target. He adopted a classic, generally erroneous technique of making 'links by association', i.e. concluding that Nuremberg was the target – sacrificed to maintain a double-agent's credibility, thus supporting a theory he had heard that the Nuremberg disaster was caused by an 'intelligence leak'.[107]

Another Cave Brown suggestion was that, following the raid, aircrew prisoners at *Dulag Luft*, the *Luftwaffe* prisoner interrogation centre, were told by their captors that the *Luftwaffe* had been forewarned of an attack. Middlebrook contacted *Oberst* Killinger, the former German CO at *Dulag Luft* at the time of the raid, and Killinger denied this.[108] Cave Brown appears to have formed sensational conclusions seemingly based upon insubstantial facts.

• • •

The Battle of Berlin was a magnificent failure. No fewer than 3,347 men were killed, over 77% of the force: 2,461 on Lancasters, 379 on Halifaxes and 183 on Stirlings. The highest numbers of sorties[109] were flown by squadrons with three flights. Top of the list came 460 Squadron with 385 trips, followed by 101, Alan Castle's Airborne Cigar squadron, (both in 1 Group), with 363 trips, followed by three Pathfinder squadrons from 8 Group, 156 Squadron with 362 trips, 7 Squadron with 353 trips and 97 Squadron with 342 trips. 460 Squadron lost 28 aircraft and 135 men, 101 Squadron 25 aircraft and 133 men, and 7 Squadron 156 aircraft and 97 men. The Pathfinder Force squadrons all lost 26 aircraft with 146, 168 and 120 men dead respectively.

After the war Harris explained his philosophy of the area bombing campaign:

'We weren't aiming particularly at the civilian population. We were aiming at the production of everything that made it possible for the German armies to continue the war. That was the whole idea of the bombing of factories; including, as I said, the facilities for the construction of submarines, and the armament industry throughout Germany, and the people who worked in them – they were all active soldiers to my mind. People who worked in the production of munitions must expect to be treated as active soldiers. Otherwise where do you draw the line?'[110]

Leonard Cheshire described his own feelings:

'…We're not going into the question of the rights and wrongs of area bombing: nobody really enjoyed area bombing. You'd far rather have a precise military target, which you knew you could hit without taking civilian casualties…

'If you start to give too much of your sympathy to the people you've got to attack, you wouldn't do it. So you've either not got to do it, or you've got to do it… In the conventional bombing of Germany, the odds were against us. We were suffering far more casualties, proportionately, than the Germans who were on the ground. The average… we were losing, 4.5 to 5% a night. So 20 trips was about all you could hope for, 20 to 25. And, I know this doesn't stand in logic, but it felt "fair"…'[111]

More than anything else the one thing that stands out upon studying the campaign is how often the weather worked against Harris. This happened time and time again, whether through inaccurate forecasting, inadequate recording or, in the case of Nuremberg, simply through ignoring the obvious. During the 19 major attacks of the Battle of Berlin, a total of 625 aircraft was lost.

Two major factors led Harris to abandon the Berlin campaign. The first was the proximity to D-Day: Harris had promised the Combined Chiefs of Staff that he would be able to defeat Berlin by 1 April 1944. From then on he would come under the command of Eisenhower, and the destruction of the German rail infrastructure in France would become a priority, in the build-up to the invasion. There would be no more major raids on Germany before the invasion was well established. The second factor was that Harris realised that the casualties he was incurring, particularly in the last two raids, totalling 937 dead, were insupportable. There was no way his force could sustain these losses for an indefinite period. Of the 19 major raids only one, on 22/23 November, could be counted as exceptionally effective. The majority of them, particularly those on 26/27 November, 16/17 December, 24/25 March and 30/31 March, were inglorious failures. Indeed the latter three raids when 1,319 men were killed, are regarded as disasters. Neillands put the Nuremberg raid's failure down to 'bad weather, bad luck and the shrewd use of the night fighter force by the German controllers' and this précis could be applied to the whole campaign. As Berlin was so remote from the bomber bases – nearly 600 miles with a direct route and well over this on indirect flights – Harris was obliged to attack in winter with its longer hours of darkness. The lunar period meant he had only slightly over two weeks in a month to launch his attacks. Consequently, over seven months, operations could only be feasible for slightly more than half of this period. Poor weather forecasting, particularly on 'Black Thursday', 'The Night of the Strong Winds', and the Nuremberg raid, led to tragedy.

Only later in the campaign, after the inadequate Stirlings and early Halifaxes had been phased out, and more sophisticated RCM and navigation equipment phased in, did Bomber Command become truly effective, and even then it was matched, and often outpaced, by the guile of the Germans. One could say that Harris was blind to the hopelessness of his task. His one aim of the war, the key to victory, he thought, was a 'maximum effort' against Berlin – what would be termed a 'Big Push' in an earlier war. But Harris did not take into account the innumerable variables that he would have to contend with: a high proportion of aborted raids, ordnance abandoned over the North Sea, the effectiveness of the German defences, and the difficulty of persuading his superiors of the campaign's importance. More than anything else, the weather – erratic and treacherous – had defeated him.

Harris was obdurate in his memoirs that the campaign had not been a failure, but it is difficult not to refute this. Don Bennett believed his chief had achieved a 'great victory', but this does not stand up to clinical examination: Berlin still stood; the German people had proved unusually resilient; the German war engine was unpredictable in its ability to recover; and the USAAF had not come into the Battle. Thus Harris's theory of wrecking

Berlin from end to end was flawed from the outset. Some said it was a disappointing end to what many saw as Bomber Command's major campaign of the war: there had been no real precedent for it, and there would be nothing quite like it in subsequent years. In Harris's case the tail in his chain of command had wagged the dog too many times.

CHAPTER FOURTEEN

'OUR WORST HEADACHE'

The Transportation Plan
The interdiction of the German communication
lines in France, April–June 1944

> *'Our worst headache has been a panacea plan devised by a civilian professor whose peacetime forte is the sexual aberrations of the higher apes. Starting from this sound military basis he devised a scheme to employ... the entire US and British forces for three months...in the destruction of targets... in France or Belgium.'*[1]
>
> AIR CHIEF MARSHAL ARTHUR T. HARRIS, C-IN-C RAF BOMBER COMMAND
> TO ROBERT LOVETT, US ASSISTANT SECRETARY FOR AIR, 3 APRIL 1944

THE debacle of Nuremberg had finally sealed the fate of Harris's 'main offensive' against Berlin, and on 14 April 1944 Bomber Command came under the ultimate control of General Eisenhower, Supreme Allied Commander. At this point, Harris had to devote his squadrons to supporting the land invasion due early in June and the Plan that was developed in the months before that to demobilise the German transportation system in France.

Harris was eventually allocated 37 targets to destroy as part of this Plan, an assignment that caused him months of anxiety. Increased German night fighter activity, witnessed at Nuremberg, obligated Harris to attack multiple targets, rather than concentrating his force on one a night. Not only had Harris to contend with this, but there was also the problem of the German 'revenge weapon': V1 launch sites had been sighted in northern France as early as November 1943, and a plan was formulated to deal with this, to be known as Operation 'Crossbow'. The first Crossbow attacks were carried out that December. Precision bombing was raising its head as a priority. In this respect No. 5 Group was split from the Main Force and received three Pathfinder squadrons – 83, 97 heavy bomber and 627 (Mosquito). A very specialised precision bombing unit, 54 Base, was also formed from 106 Squadron and 617 Squadron, a unit retained following its deployment in the Dams Raid.

F.J. McGovern, who was on aircrew around that time, recalled that many airmen gained confidence from the fact that fighter cover had become available for British daylight attacks and that the H2S radome had been removed from their aircraft and a .5 mid-under gun placed centrally in its place:

'[There] seemed to be a split between the necessity for the preparations for D-Day... and the necessity to control the despatch of these "buzz-bombs", the V1s and V2s – V1s particularly. So we would often be called at short notice, when our "powers that be" were informed of the location of one of these sites. We would be bombed up and off within a couple of hours to attack that particular target, sometimes during that day, sometimes at night.'[2]

With attacks on France now counted as 'half' an operation, the crews looked on this as a 'relatively easy period', feeling that 'life was becoming much more tenable'.

The man mainly responsible for the design of the so-called 'Transportation Plan' which, up until the day of the invasion, had priority over all other targets, was a South African born, former anthropology Professor lecturing at Oxford, named Solly Zuckerman.

Solly Zuckerman

Solly Zuckerman later described his research as being 'focused mainly on problems that entailed experiments with monkeys'.[3] Zuckerman had conducted an earlier study on bomb effects in England in 1941/42, and later did work on army co-operation with the Desert Air Force in North Africa. In Cairo in 1943 he had attended a series of meetings with Sir Arthur Tedder – later described by Harris as 'one of the most brilliant minds in any of the services' who had recently become Deputy Supreme Commander under Eisenhower – and Lieutenant General Carl 'Tooey' Spaatz, then C-in-C, Western Mediterranean Air Forces. Before the invasion of Sicily, Zuckerman was employed as a group captain, although still being paid by Oxford University, to devise a bombing attack on the island of Pantelleria, a small island halfway between Tunis and Sicily, less than nine miles long and six miles across.

On 10 July, after the report by Zuckerman on this bombing plan was completed, Sicily was assaulted by the Allies. Before the invasion, however, Zuckerman was invited by Tedder to prepare a coherent plan for the bombing of the island itself, and of southern Italy, as there was, at that point, no clearly co-ordinated proposal for such an operation. Zuckerman commented:

'As I saw it, the enemy depended on the rail system for major military traffic, and I had learnt that lines and small bridges could not be dealt with by the "precision bombing" that was possible at the time, whereas rail centres were not only big enough targets, but that every bomb dropped on them counted, with the consequence that the marshalling of rolling stock, the signalling systems, and the repair of locomotives would inevitably be disrupted.'[4]

On 22 July Patton's Seventh Army took Palermo. Zuckerman was allowed by Tedder to set up an HQ in the town to make a survey of the effects of three years of bombing on the island, particularly relating to the rail yards. The conclusion of his findings, he informed his chief, was that the more the attacks concentrated on the rail centres 'where the movements of trains were marshalled and regulated', the greater the return would be 'in terms of the dislocation of military traffic.'[5] As a consequence of this he was offered, but passed up, an invitation to join Mountbatten's staff in South East Asia, and was also asked by Leigh-Mallory to be scientific advisor to the Allied Expeditionary Air Force.

Zuckerman returned to Palermo in mid-October 1943, heading a staff instructed to make a detailed survey of the effects of bombing on the town, local shipping, airfields, and enemy movements generally. Accurate field surveys, statistical analysis of reams of data, and 'the study of bomb craters to make sure we knew what bombs had caused what damage' were made. Zuckerman found that although only six rail centres were attacked, this had almost paralysed the entire Italian rail system. Arthur Harris later stressed the importance of statistical analysis:

> '*In war it is of enormous value to substitute a statistical probe for an experimental operation, and the work of the large research section[6] at my command saved thousands of lives and hundreds of aircraft.*'[7]

In late November 1943 the Tehran Summit was convened in Iran, attended by the 'Big Three' – Stalin, Roosevelt and Churchill, with Portal, Eisenhower and General Sir Alan Brooke (Chief of the Imperial General Staff) in attendance. This conference, and the Cairo Conference of only weeks before, had been convened to hammer out the fate of 'Overlord', which was viewed as the supreme and decisive operation of the war. Roosevelt and Stalin were *for* the invasion of occupied France as soon as practicable, but Churchill, seemingly irritable, unwell and prejudiced towards an encroachment into the Eastern Mediterranean,[8] was reluctant to see the English Channel choked with the bodies of '*three hundred thousand dead British soldiers*.'[9] Stalin, who had not met the two other statesmen before and was on his first excursion outside the USSR since the Revolution, was, Churchill sensed, in 'cahoots' with the American President. Roosevelt and Stalin were adamant: there had to be an invasion before June 1944: Stalin warned Churchill that if Overlord was delayed, the exhausted Red Army would be unable to hold on, leaving an unpleasant suggestion that he would have to make peace with Hitler.

On his way back from Tehran in mid-December, the Chief of the Air Staff, Portal, met Zuckerman in Tunis. At dinner that night it was suggested, for the first time, that Zuckerman should put the lessons he had learned in Sicily to good effect: they would be used in the preparatory phases for the invasion of France. Portal informed Zuckerman that Eisenhower was now Supreme Commander in preference to the expected appointment of General George C. Marshall, Chief of Staff of the US Army, with Tedder as his deputy. Zuckerman was told he would have to leave for England before January.

New Year's Day 1944 thus witnessed the genesis of the Transportation Plan: Zuckerman, having completed his reports on the attacks on Palermo and the Italian railway system, met Portal and Leigh-Mallory in England. The following night he was introduced to Harris at the Bomber Command Chief's residence, Springfield, at Great Kingshill, five miles from High Wycombe. This was in order to explain what had been learnt. But Harris, Zuckerman recalled, 'did not want to know.'

The initial Transportation Plan prepared for the Army and Air Chief Marshal Sir Trafford Leigh-Mallory's Allied Expeditionary Air Force (AEAF) was never adopted. It was shown to Zuckerman on his first day back in London. It suggested that any rail attacks should be undertaken at the same time as the landings, cutting the railway system at 20 points in a semi-circle 50 to 60 miles behind the invasion beaches. Zuckerman's first thoughts were that this would not work: the idea depended on good weather and accurate bombing. Also, *crucially*, and presumably from his experiences in Sicily, he was first to suggest that any straightforward 'cut' to a line could be repaired quickly, i.e. within a few days. The answer to this, as Harris had realised and pointed out, was to hit the repair centres, but no one in the AEAF understood this up until that time.

12 February 1944

Eisenhower decided that, following suggestions from the British, Leigh-Mallory should be made C-in-C of the Allied air forces, and that his command would include tactical bombers. At 53, Leigh-Mallory had been a Cambridge graduate and was the son of a clergyman. British historian David Irving has described him as 'round-faced, with a neat toothbrush moustache, and the soulful eyes of a spaniel.' Due to his rather difficult personality he was not well liked, particularly by Spaatz, who had by this time been appointed to command the US Strategic Air Forces in Europe. Both he and Harris felt that since Leigh-Mallory's only previous command had been Fighter Command, and because of his slightly unorthodox views on bombing, he was not suitable for the job. Consequently it was not originally intended that he should command the strategic bomber force, but this was what Leigh-Mallory began pushing for. Initially both the US Eighth Air Force and Bomber Command were of too high a status to be allotted to the AEAF, but Eisenhower insisted that he should be able to use them when he needed them: their participation was essential to the success of the invasion. Both Spaatz and Harris were against taking orders from Leigh-Mallory and their opposition was strong enough to persuade Churchill, the 'old man', to place them under the more affable, but brilliant, pipe-smoking Tedder: Spaatz would take his orders from Eisenhower and the stubborn, carrot-topped Harris from Tedder himself.

15 February 1944 – Stanmore meeting

The discussions that took place during the second half of 1943 and early 1944 about ways to destroy the *Luftwaffe* fighter force and gain control of the air before the invasion, were long and protracted. Leigh-Mallory, for whom Zuckerman now worked, planned to shift the bombing emphasis away from the defeat of the *Luftwaffe* and over to the Overlord campaign early in March. He suggested that the combined Allied air forces 'pulverise the French and Belgian railroad system for ninety days before the invasion.'[10] This would be from the coast all the way back to Germany and would, he said, incite the German fighters to retaliate. But his opinions on how the fighters should be overcome were contentious. Spaatz wanted to destroy the fighters before the invasion by making strategic attacks on German oil centres, to ensure that the *Luftwaffe* came up to meet the bombers. To Spaatz's despair however, Leigh-Mallory refused to take on the Germans before the landings started. As Montgomery had stated emphatically in 1943 that the air battle had to be won before an attack on land or sea could take place, Leigh-Mallory's view bluntly stood in the face of this.

Spaatz was incensed: he was uncertain whether or not the *Luftwaffe would* retaliate, and if they did not, he said he would have to attract them into the air by attacking other targets, namely the synthetic oil plants. Leigh-Mallory opined that Spaatz's Strategic Air Force should come under his command on 1 March, which increased Spaatz's fury and made him completely unwilling to limit his targets. Leigh-Mallory's plan for the rail attacks obviously would not work. Harris entered the affray with guns blazing: Leigh-Mallory was deceived – there was no way all the rail transport in the suggested area could be disrupted sufficiently to prevent military traffic. Harris believed that he knew the limitations of his own force, and that what was asked was beyond its capability.[11] With Spaatz, he contemptuously dismissed Leigh-Mallory's plan as impractical.

Leigh-Mallory then turned to Zuckerman, his scientific expert. Zuckerman suggested that the most economical way to dislocate the rail system was by the 'destruction of its nodal points'.[12] According to David Irving's account of the Allied High Command at this time:

'Zuckerman turned to the theory of attacks on railroad systems. He concluded that they were like any other nervous system, and that damage to any part would affect the whole. It all sounded a bit too pat to the other bomber barons.'[13]

The central aim now discussed was to bomb the key French and Belgian rail centres right back into German territory. This would ensure that economic as well as military traffic was disrupted. Zuckerman recalled that, initially, although this revised plan found favour, '…all manner of objection was raised.' This was early February 1944 with, by Stalin and Roosevelt's reckoning, only four months to the invasion.

Harris was reluctant to commit his forces to lesser tactical attacks, ostensibly because 'there was little reason to think that the whole force could be switched to the destruction of small targets.' There were other considerations: Bomber Command's aircraft were poorly armed and in the face of 'any serious opposition', could not operate in daylight. Harris's men could not hit precision targets by night unless the opposition was negligible, and the weather and light unusually good. Harris vehemently concluded that it would be extraordinary for such conditions to concur for a prolonged time; it would also be 'almost impossible' to perform any sustained nocturnal operations against 'a number of small targets'.[14] In fact Harris's true motive for his disinclination towards the Transportation Plan was a fear of interrupting his fight against the cities: any lull in these operations might allow the Germans to rebuild their industry and defences.[15]

The March attacks on French rail centres

In order to test Harris's views, on 4 March Portal ordered him to carry out attacks on six[16] French marshalling yards which continued for a three week period from 5 to 26 March. Among the targets were Le Mans, Amiens and Laon, on 13/14, 15/16 and 23/24 March respectively. Total losses on these three operations were 11 aircraft.[17] Other towns were Trappes, Aulnoye, Lougeau and Courtrai.

Eisenhower was becoming exasperated by the British reluctance to hand over the British strategic bomber force to his control. On 23 March, one week before the Nuremberg debacle, it was finally agreed that he would be allowed to direct all the air forces he needed. Eisenhower had appointed Tedder as his deputy because air supremacy was imperative and Tedder had experience of air command in Italy, where 'Ike' had witnessed his genius.

On 24 March, Spaatz presented his case against the Transportation Plan: he suggested that US bombers could flatten the entire German synthetic fuel, ball bearing and fighter production centres, and then rubber and bomber centres, within a fortnight. Then they could undertake tactical operations. He felt that an attack on the transportation system would be misdirected: intelligence reports indicated that the Germans needed fewer than 80 trains in the invasion area daily – a small proportion of their total available capacity. Consequently any attack on the enemy rail system would prove ineffectual. Spaatz believed that only oil targets were crucial to the enemy and would draw the fighters up. Statistically, he suggested, the transportation targets did not hold water: 80 per cent of Germany's fuel and oil was produced by 14 synthetic oil plants, whereas 14 rail yards, of approximately similar scale, were but a fragment of Germany's rail traffic potential.[18] Although Tedder agreed with this it was apparent to him that such synthetic oil targets would be difficult to locate, difficult to bomb and difficult to obliterate, in the eight or nine weeks left before the invasion.

25 March 1944 Meeting

Following the success of the March raids against the French marshalling yards, Portal chaired a meeting on 25 March to try to beat out the structure of the Allied air campaign prior to D-Day. Present were Eisenhower, Tedder, Leigh-Mallory, Spaatz, and Harris. The air commanders all disagreed about how the campaign should be carried out. The logistics of how to destroy the German transportation network were extremely complicated. It all rested on which target scheme would be most likely to lure the German fighters into the air: oil or transport? The question of stockpiled supplies was also crucial to the validity of either scheme. Portal pointed out that even if only a small number of trains infiltrated the bombing, their goods, plus any stockpiled supplies, would make Leigh-Mallory's plan ineffective: fractured rail lines could be repaired within days. Indeed, as Harris later recalled:

> 'Railways are extraordinarily difficult and unrewarding targets for air attack. Main lines can be repaired in a few hours, and "through lines" in wrecked marshalling yards in a few days, provided there is an efficient organisation to do the work.'[19]

Initially Eisenhower had agreed with Spaatz that control of the air had to be accomplished before the invasion could start but, on 25 March, he reneged on this: Ike had become convinced that a transportation attack was the only solution. A Ministry of Economic warfare expert then left Spaatz gazumped by suggesting that, if the Germans had large stockpiles of oil in the west, which they undoubtedly did, these would leave their invasion defence unaffected, even with the *complete destruction* of the oil plants. Out on a limb, Harris still felt that Bomber Command's proper role in Overlord was to continue the attack on German cities; but eventually he was persuaded to toe the line.

The plan devised by Tedder, Zuckerman and Leigh-Mallory to attack 79[20] key French and Belgian rail centres was at last submitted to the War Cabinet following the 25 March meeting; 37 of these were to be attacked by Bomber Command and the remaining 42 by the Americans and tactical forces.

As previously stated, the crucial solution to the problem of attacking railways was not to cut the lines themselves, but to destroy their repair centres. Harris wrote '...it was not the principal aim of this campaign to damage the marshalling yards or destroy rolling stock.' Seventy-nine rail centres were selected, in each of which there was an important repair shop:

> 'Nearly all the shops and depots [were] situated in or beside railway marshalling yards, and the plan was to select one or more aiming points in the marshalling yards in such a way that a heavy and effective concentration of bombing round these aiming points would destroy or severely damage the repair centres.'[21]

Harris and Leigh-Mallory came head to head during the 25 March meeting over the controversial factor of French civilians in the target area – there was a danger that hundreds, if not thousands, of them would be killed. (Churchill feared this may turn the French against them, when they most needed their help). Leigh-Mallory was reluctant, he said, to 'go down in posterity' as being responsible for the deaths of thousands of Frenchmen. Reportedly Harris sneered: 'What makes you think you are going down in posterity at all?'[22] Portal solved the problem by instructing the RAF to drop leaflets within a mile of the target, warning civilians to clear the area.

Graduation Day march past at the Elementary Flying Training School at Amberley, Queensland, Australia, 15 September 1941, following the award of wings by the Governor General of Australia, Lord Gowrie. L.J. Simpson is at the extreme left of the front rank, nearest the camera. The EFTS course lasted two months, in this case from May to June 1941, on the DH 82 Tiger Moth and the Link Trainer. At the completion of the course, the pupil flew solo, and if he passed, he was awarded his wings. (Author)

A De Havilland Tiger Moth of the Empire Flying Training Scheme flying over cumulus cloud in Canada, 1942. Note the enclosed hood due to the low temperatures. The DH 82 was the standard basic trainer used by the EFTS and introduced thousands of men to flying. As an elementary trainer it was used for training both fighter and bomber pilots. It was reputedly not easy for an inexperienced pilot to land it. The Avro Anson was used subsequently for further training for Bomber Command pilots. (Goodrum)

'These are the buses we are flying at present... twin-engined reconnaissance job,' wrote Laurie Simpson on the back of this photograph of an Avro Anson trainer while at the EFTS at Amberley in Queensland in 1941. 'Powered with two Armstrong-Siddeley Cheetah IX engines each having 7 cylinders. Cruise at 130 mph and have a top speed of about 160 in level flight. Carry a normal crew of four. We call them "Annies" now, but called them other things at first. Quite easy to fly with no apparent vicious qualities. The turret sticking out of the top of the fuselage is for the gunner, while the compartment in the nose is where the bomb-aimer lies and sights for bombing.' (Author)

Graeme Keys (top left) and Laurie Simpson (top right) while with No. 12 Course, 3 EFTS, Essendon, Victoria, Australia, autumn 1941. Of the 30 members of this elementary flying training course, six were killed in action (including Keys), five were scrubbed from training, one became a POW, and four 'came through OK'. Of the remaining 14, there was no news. (Author)

Of the three bomber types that bore the brunt of RAF Bomber Command's offensive during the first three years of the war, the Armstrong Whitworth Whitley had the lowest performance. Its broad, low aspect ratio wing caused it to be nicknamed 'The Flying Barn Door', its engines being set at such an angle that it had to be flown in a characteristically nose-down attitude. This example, a Mark V, belonged to No. 102 Squadron based at Finningley in Yorkshire before the war. At the outbreak of war, the Whitley was largely relegated to the role of night raider, and it flew many of the early leaflet-dropping missions over Germany. The Mark V – the main production version – cruised at 210 mph at 15,000 ft and for defence was equipped with four Browning .303-inch machine guns in the rear turret and one in the nose turret.

Handley Page Hampden Mk Is of No. 144 Squadron climb in formation over their base at Hemswell in Lincolnshire. The Hampden was nicknamed 'The Flying Tadpole' for obvious reasons. This twin-engined bomber had a maximum speed of 265 mph and the armament, three .303-inch Vickers guns, was hopelessly outdated, the rearward firing Vickers being in two fixed turrets. The Hampden flew its last operational sortie with Bomber Command in September 1942.

The Short Stirling was the first of the modern four-engined bomber types to enter service with Bomber Command following the outbreak of war, commencing ops in February 1941. The Mark I, seen here, cruised at 215 mph at 15,000 ft and was fitted with four Browning .303-inch machine guns in the rear turret, two in the nose turret and two in the dorsal turret. This photograph shows the classic high angle of incidence of the Stirling's fuselage and its unusually long undercarriage, required to shorten the take-off run following the removal of six feet from each wing tip. Unlike the Lancaster or Halifax, the Stirling also had two retractable tail wheels.

Don Wilson's 51 Squadron Whitley which crashed in a canal near Wunsdorf, following a bale-out after Flak caused a loss of control while returning from a raid to Hannover in May 1940. (Wilson)

Ground crew prepare to load a Short Stirling of No. 149 Squadron with its 500 lb bombs during the summer of 1942. The Stirling, unlike the Lancaster, had its bomb bay divided into short sections that restricted the size of bombs it could carry. This, together with its low operational ceiling, resulted in it being phased out from operational duties.

The crew of a Vickers Wellington prepare for a flight. The dress of these airmen suggests that they were a non-operational crew early in the war.

Eric Foinette's 12 Squadron Wellington II, Z8410 waiting to take off at Binbrook for an operation to Kiel on 25 February 1942. It was photographed by a member of the ground crew that evening. Following engine failure, the aircraft force-landed near Odense in Denmark around 03.00 hrs the following morning. (Foinette)

Lancasters at dispersal. These are believed to be aircraft of 428 (Ghost) Squadron, RCAF, at Middleton St. George seen during preparation for an 'op', probably in the summer of 1944. The aircraft on right, (NA-W) has completed seven operational sorties. All of 428 Squadron's Lancasters were Lancaster Xs, some with paddle-bladed props.

103 Squadron Lancaster ED724 PM-M on the flare path at Elsham Wolds in 1943. One Lancaster on 103 Squadron, ED888 PM-M2 ('Mike Squared'), completed 140 operational sorties (974 hours) – more operations than any other aircraft in Bomber Command. (H.R. Rowe)

Right: On 9/10 April 1943 a press photographer appeared at RAF Breighton in Yorkshire to photograph 460 (Australian) Squadron personnel before and after a raid to Duisburg. This photograph shows the crew of UV-P 'Peter', ED315, being interviewed by an RAF Public Relations Officer, Flight Lieutenant I.N. Smyth, following their debriefing. Left to right: Sergeant W. Maltby RAF, Flight Sergeant A. Kennedy RAAF, Sergeant K. Sutton RAF, Flight Lieutenant L.J. Simpson RAAF, Sgt F.J. King RAAF, Flight Sergeant R. Searle RAAF, and Flight Sergeant C.W. McLeod RAAF. Sutton and King were both killed during the war. (AWM)

In February 1942, Air Marshal Sir Arthur Harris (left) assumed leadership of RAF Bomber Command. Under this vigorous new commander, the force rapidly built up its strength and effectiveness. This posed photograph, probably taken at the height of a raid, shows Harris at Bomber Command headquarters at High Wycombe, pointing out the area of the Ruhr Valley to his deputy, Air Vice-Marshal Robert Saundby. Saundby had been Harris's Flight Commander on 45 Squadron in Iraq before the war.

Below: A Halifax of 77 Squadron having its port inner engine checked forms a background to the autumn harvest of 1943. Produced in the last week of March 1943, this aircraft was lost in the attack on Kassel on 3/4 October 1943, brought down at Wernswig, 5 km south-west of Homberg, with only two men, Sergeants R. Searle and D. Griffiths, surviving from Sgt H. Cracknell's crew.

Looking back and upward at the wireless operator of a Halifax bomber in his position directly beneath the pilot illustrates the depth of the aircraft's fuselage. In the Halifax, the wireless operator was separated from the navigator's position by a bulkhead on which radio equipment was mounted. The horizontal bar is the control linkage rod to which the second pilot's controls could be fitted when needed. The bulkhead behind the pilot was fitted with armoured glass panels and the flight engineer is standing on the steps leading down to the front fuselage compartment. The flight engineer had a folding seat, part of which is visible on the left. When in use it was swung up and locked into the frame of the pilot's floor section.

The bomb-aimer's prone position in the Halifax was just forward of the navigator's table (on left). To his right are the bomb fusing and release panels, while the ammunition bins for the C Mk I nose turret flank his head and shoulders. The standard bombsight in these early Halifaxes was the CSB (Course Setting Bomb Sight). The gunner's folding seat is hanging in its down position. In the lower left corner of the photograph is the vertical mounting frame for the target camera, which had a circular window set in the belly of the nose section.

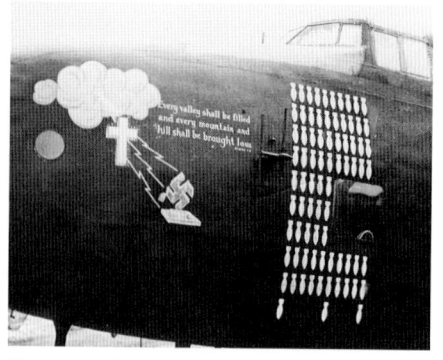

Some crews of Bomber Command emulated the Americans and adorned their aircraft with nose art. However, it was not always humorous or risqué. There were those who put their trust in faith which, as in the case of this Halifax of 432 Squadron, seems to have proved providential, the B Mk VII having already completed 65 operations with another squadron before passing to 432 where the artwork was applied. It depicts a light blue cloud and the Cross, with three yellow lightning bolts striking at a Swastika and factory. A further 13 operations were recorded before the Halifax was flown to 45 MU and struck off charge in August 1947. The text, from the Gospel of St Luke 3:5 reads: 'Every valley shall be filled and every mountain and hill shall be brought low' and was to prove true by May 1945 when most German cities lay in ruins, 78 contributions having been made by this Halifax and its various crews. (W.E. Miller via M. Wright and K.A. Merrick)

Left: 'The Baron', Flt/Lt Graeme Keys, at the controls of his 460 Squadron Lancaster I on a muddy dispersal at Breighton in the early evening of 9 April 1943. This was taken at sunset as the ground crew prepared the aircraft for a big raid on Duisburg that night when 31 aircraft were lost. Take-off was at 20.40 hrs. The figure in the background and the booted figure to the right appear to be members of the crew. Note the accumulator trolley by the starboard undercarriage. Keys was nicknamed 'The Baron' because of his Germanic appearance. (Author)

Below: Airmen of No. 460 Squadron, RAAF, sit on 500 lb bombs in front of Lancaster AR-Q, 'Q-Queenie'. 460 Squadron was part of No.1 Group and replaced its Halifaxes with Lancaster B.Is in October 1942. It eventually used a mix of B.I or IIIs. It moved to Binbrook in May 1943 and then to East Kirkby in July 1945. The last flight carried out by the squadron was in October that year when RF191 photographed the Australian War Memorial in France. The figures in dark blue battledress are RAAF personnel, the remainder being RAF and other Dominions aircrew. The whistles hanging from some of the men's collars were to aid identification if they crashed at sea. The airmen in the foreground appear to be trying on Mae Wests and other paraphernalia under supervision. (ww2images)

A posed photograph of RAF armourers fitting American 'square tails' to bombs, which were not ideally suited for fitting into the bomb bays of RAF bombers. On several occasions, the United States supplied bombs to RAF Bomber Command when its supplies ran short. The Lancaster in the background has an H2S radome under its rear fuselage, in place of the proposed ventral turret. This, plus the profusion of other aerials, suggests that the photograph was taken late in 1944. The tail fin of the aircraft on the right reveals that this was 'R- Robert', confirmed by the letter on the wheel chock between the two 'erks' to the left. (ww2images)

Marshal of the RAF Lord Portal of Hungerford inspecting a unit of the Royal Auxiliary Air Force after the war. The second officer behind him, in the forage cap, is L.J. Simpson. Portal, with Churchill, had been responsible for introducing the area bombing policy during the war. (Author)

View into the cockpit of a Lancaster. When in flight the Flight Engineer had the option of a fold-down seat although many rarely used it. The thin cables in the canopy roof were for sun shades which could be pulled forward to alleviate glare. The flat plate with the yellow disk painted on it, behind the pilot's head, was the only piece of armour plate in the whole aircraft. (ww2images)

The navigator in a Lancaster sat sideways behind the pilot. Seen here is Flying Officer Ingleby of No. 619 Squadron. This view illustrates the sparseness of the Lancaster's interior. (ww2images)

Behind the navigator, facing forward, was the Wireless Operator. Sitting next to the cabin heating outlet, the w/ops could always be spotted on crew photographs as they always wore the least amount of flying clothing. The w/op sat directly below an astrodome on the fuselage roof, and could stand on his seat to make observations. From here the navigator could take 'star shots'. (ww2images)

A bomb-aimer sitting at a Mark XIV bomb sight which was standard equipment for most of the aircraft of Bomber Command. It was introduced into RAF service in 1942 and was designed for area bombing. It was also known as the 'Blackett bomb sight' after Patrick Blackett, the physicist who invented it. (ww2images)

The rear turret on the Lancaster was the most isolated position in the whole aircraft and, at 20,000 feet, could get extremely cold. Entry and egress was by the two tiny doors that slid back to allow access to and from the fuselage. In some cases gunners would slide down a wooden plank resting on the tail spar to get into the position. Men of a larger build often opted for the mid-upper turret since it was more comfortable for them. (via Garbett and Goulding)

Left: A Lancaster rear gunner glances out from his FN20 rear turret with its four .303-inch Browning machine guns. The arrowhead aerial for the 'Monica' tail warning radar is clearly visible beneath the turret. Note the gunner has removed some of the turret's perspex to give him clearer vision. Since the turret anyway was always extremely cold at height, the difference to inside temperature was minimal. (ww2images)

A press photograph of the crew of Lancaster Mk I ED315 UV-P 'Peter' after their return from the big raid on Duisburg the night of 9/10 April 1943. Foreground left to right: Ken Sutton (RG), Colin McLeod (B/A), Laurie Simpson (Pilot), Al Kennedy (w/op), Ron Searle (Nav). Background, on the ladder: Freddy King (F/E) and, behind, Wally Maltby (mu/g). (Author)

Right: Outward bound. A photograph taken in 1943 by Ron Searle from the astrodome above the w/op's position of UV-P, ED315, during an operation in the Battle of the Ruhr and looking back along the fuselage of 'Peter' at Wally Maltby in the mid-upper turret. Maltby was a former Boots employee from Beeston, Nottinghamshire, who felt it was his duty to join the RAF. He returned after OTU for a second tour, this time with 12 Squadron, and was subsequently shot down. (Searle)

Lancaster I OJ-E of 149 Squadron based at Methwold, Norfolk, on a cross-country flight over eastern England in late 1944, taken from pilot John Goodrum's OJ-M. Note the semi-glazed H2S radome under the rear fuselage. The squadron flew its first Lancaster op on 17 September 1944, and dropped nearly 16,000 tons of bombs on Axis targets during the war. (Goodrum)

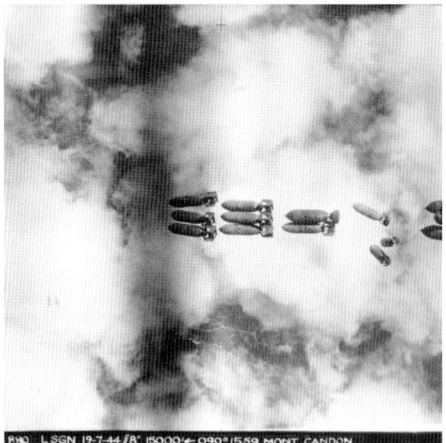

In the third week of July 1944, 950 Bomber Command crews attacked five German strongpoints east of Caen in support of General Montgomery's troops. On 19 July 1944 at 15.59 hours, a 582 Squadron Lancaster from 8 (PFF) Group based at Little Stoughton, piloted by Sqn/Ldr Sooby, drops a cluster of eleven 1000-lb and three 500-lb bombs on Mont Candon, France from 15,000 feet. Note both the round and US square tailed bombs. (ww2images)

Caught by the camera in F/O Nixon's Halifax HX268 A of 433 Squadron: a 346 Free French Squadron's Halifax passes over the Fôret de Nieppe at 15,000 ft on 3 August 1944. Nixon's Halifax was carrying sixteen 500-lb bombs, the type of load favoured for attacks on V-1 storage sites.

A dramatic time exposure photograph taken from the upper story of a residential building showing a typical scene across Germany between 1942-45 as anti-aircraft tracer fire, or 'Flak', arcs through the night sky, targeting RAF bombers. Crews found light Flak far less lethal than the 'heavy stuff'. (Barber)

Below: A Messerschmitt Bf 110 night fighter of NJG 1 runs up its engines prior to another flight from its base in Holland in 1942. The aircraft is finished in overall black night camouflage and carries the distinctive 'Englandblitz' emblem on its nose. Prior to the installation of airborne radar, the German defence system relied on ground controllers directing night fighters to within visual range of their targets, hence the lack of any antennae on this Bf 110.

'The Simpson Kite'. Lancaster UV-P, ED315, 'Peter' on its dispersal pad at Breighton, Yorkshire, during the Battle of the Ruhr, 1943. The sparse background illustrates the bleakness of the Yorkshire landscape.

Above: A stellar line-up of German Nachtjagd aces at St. Trond in 1944: (from l-r) Hauptmann Heinz Schnaufer of IV./NJG 1, the most successful of the German night fighters; Hauptmann Martin Drewes of III./NJG 1; Major Hans-Joachim Jabs, the Kommodore of NJG 1; Hauptmann Paul Förster of I./NJG 1; and Hauptmann Eckart-Wilhelm von Bonin II./NJG 1. Together, these men would account for more than 200 'kills' scored at night by war's end. Schnaufer shot down George Flanagan's 77 Squadron Halifax on 18 August 1943. Von Bonin shot down Alan Fuller's 76 Squadron Halifax on 26 November 1943.

Right: Flight Lieutenant L.J. Simpson and Miss Dorothy Holmes after their marriage at Stapehill near Wimborne, Dorset in April 1943. (Author)

A Junkers Ju 88 G-6 night fighter believed to have been photographed at Grove in Denmark in 1944. It was probably flown by the Kommandeur of II./NJG 3, or perhaps the Kapitän of one of the Staffeln which comprised that Gruppe. The machine was equipped with SN-2 radar.

The port side of the nose of Lancaster UV-P, ED315, 'Peter' under the pilot's position. Each of the 24 kangaroos represented a completed operation, the red and white 'roos indicating Italian trips. The 'gong' to the right symbolised L.J. Simpson's DFC. The boomerang symbol below indicated an aborted trip or 'boomerang'. The 'Fooship' logo was applied by another crew after Simpson's crew completed its first tour. This aircraft, re-coded AR-P, was written off after a 'wheels-up' landing at Binbrook on 28 June 1944, in which all four engines were destroyed. Three other 460 Squadron Lancasters dubbed 'Fooship' followed this – 'The Fooship II', 'The Fooship III' etc. (Author)

'Goody the Gremlin' perched on the cockpit glasshouse framing of Lancaster ED315, 'the Simpson Kite', above Freddy King, the Flight Engineer's, position at Breighton sometime during the Battle of the Ruhr in the spring of 1943. Goody was a small leather doll one of the crew picked up in the York area and he was adopted as the crew's mascot. Gremlins were peculiar little imps that the bomber crews blamed for any malfunctions on an aircraft during an operation. (Author)

Six of the 'keep 'em flying lads'. ED315's ground crew during the Battle of the Ruhr with the removed rear door after it had been covered in tongue-in-cheek graffiti. Kneeling on the left in the doorway is navigator, Al Kennedy. The lettering reads: 'For terms: see Ken (rear gunner?). For hire 6 days only, only gen crews need apply. Chow house included. See sunny Italy by moonlight. Distance no object. Rations and guide supplied. Extra special coffee from Sergeants' Mess.' (Searle)

Photograph taken by Ron Searle from the astrodome above the w/op's position on ED315 as 460 Squadron Lancasters fly out to Germany during an operation in the Battle of the Ruhr, April 1943. (Searle)

New South Wales POWs on ANZAC Day 1944 at Stalag Luft III, Sagan, Germany, taken after the mass breakout of 24 March. Of those numbered: '1' is Flt/Lt Frank Falkenmire of 460 Squadron; '2' is Sqn/Ldr L.J. Simpson; '4' is Flt/Lt Alistair Kennedy; '11' is F/O Colin McLeod; '16' is Flt/Lt Paul Brickhill. (Author)

West Australian POWs on ANZAC Day 1944 at Stalag Luft III, Sagan, Germany. This appears to have been taken at the same location and on the same day as the previous photograph. Both were taken by the German camp photographer, suggesting a group was photographed representing each Australian state. Fifth from the right is F/O Johnny Rydings, from whose POW logbook the photo came. Fifth from the left is Paul Royle, who escaped on 24 March 1944 with Howard Pearce's friend, Edgar Humphries. On Royle's left is P/O Stan W. Payne from Block 109, the 106 Squadron mu/g shot down on 20 February 1944. Second from the right in the bush hat is Keith Murdoch from Block 105. (Rydings)

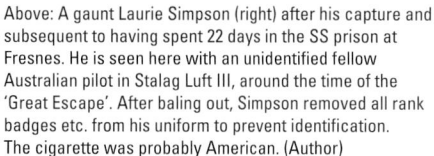

Fighter ace Robert Stanford Tuck (left) and Roger Bushell in Stalag Luft III before the mass escape. Bushell had been Tuck's CO in 92 Squadron. This picture was taken after Bushell's torture by the Gestapo following the assassination of SS-Obergruppenführer Reinhard Heydrich, and his gaunt appearance contrasts strongly with pre-war photographs. Bushell, then head of the escape organisation, had a slight disfigurement to the right eye, the result of a pre-war skiing accident, which gave him a rather sinister appearance. His cold penetrating eyes, coupled with a dominating personality, could quell a man with a look. (via Burgess)

Above: A gaunt Laurie Simpson (right) after his capture and subsequent to having spent 22 days in the SS prison at Fresnes. He is seen here with an unidentified fellow Australian pilot in Stalag Luft III, around the time of the 'Great Escape'. After baling out, Simpson removed all rank badges etc. from his uniform to prevent identification. The cigarette was probably American. (Author)

Below: Photograph taken by Howard Pearce with a German camera of Edgar Humphries (left) and other members of his hut in Stalag Luft III before the 'Great Escape'. Humphries and some of those shown were described by Pearce as 'very boring characters' who habitually read very advanced mathematics, 'always messing about with paper, writing it down, that sort of stuff'. Humphries was executed by the Gestapo after the breakout. [Pearce]

Air Chief Marshal Sir Douglas Evill (centre) at the closing down of 3617 Royal Auxiliary Air Force Fighter Control Unit, commanded by Wg/Cdr L.J. Simpson (left), at Bournemouth in January 1961. Evill was Vice-Chief of the Air Staff in 1943. On the right is Sir Hugh McGregor, C-in-C Fighter Command. (Author)

Graeme Keys' headstone in Cambridge City Cemetery, 2008. Keys and his navigator were killed on 5 May 1944 when his PFF Mosquito crashed on landing at RAF Ramsey. His age suggests that he must have been at the upper limit for aircrew when enlisting. (Author)

Harris's men came under the official command of Eisenhower at 12 noon on 14 April 1944. There is some suggestion that his post-war account of the bombing war, *Bomber Offensive*, was slightly watered down for political reasons: one imagines that he was reluctant, after all the controversy surrounding the campaign post-war, to tread on any official toes, as General Patton had done on innumerable occasions in 1943/44. Referring to Solly Zuckerman he stated:

> 'To the working out of the plan of campaign for the destruction of the French railways, Tedder brought a genuinely scientific mind, with all the detachment of the scientist.'[23]

However Harris's cynical, biting wit had come to the fore earlier concerning this in the missive he wrote to Robert Lovett, the US Assistant Secretary for Air, on 3 April 1944 when he mocked Professor Zuckerman's pre-war anthropology studies at Oxford as having little relevance to the devising of a plan for the entire Allied forces to destroy French and Belgian rail targets.[24]

THE ATTACKS

On 3 May a four-pronged attack was launched by Harris in an attempt to disperse the Germans' night fighter umbrella. Mailly-le-Camp was one of four targets with Montdidier, Châteaudun and Ludwigshafen, together with 'gardening' sorties. In fact, the Mailly-le-Camp attack became almost as notorious as the Nuremberg operation.

At Mailly-le-Camp Leonard Cheshire, then CO of 617 Squadron, acted as Master Bomber. Five weeks before D-Day, he led four 617 Squadron Mosquitoes on the raid, against an SS training and troop facility assembled on the site of an old French Army camp in Normandy. The threat posed to the invasion was obvious. Although the subsequent attack was completely successful, a number of things went wrong. 617 Squadron's target-marking went well but, for reasons unknown, Cheshire's radio was mistuned[25] and an American forces' radio broadcast interfered with communications. Perturbed, Cheshire called for an abort but, circling 15 miles north of Mailly, none of the 300 Main Force Lancasters of 1 and 5 Groups heard him. The ensuing delay meant the target had to be re-marked,[26] causing further delay, which allowed a large number of German night fighters to impregnate the raid. Eventually the Deputy Master Bomber took over and the force began to move southwards.

The anticipated 'milk run' turned into a nightmare. R/T discipline broke down almost completely as fear-filled crews lost control. Men began to swear and talk at odds with each other on the intercom. Simultaneously, a brilliant moon in its third quarter meant that German night fighter crews picked out the bomber stream easily, and aircraft were exploding in mid-air all around the tracer-filled sky. Alan Castle, navigation leader for 101 Squadron that night, recalled that Sgt J.E. Worsford, a 19 year-old rear gunner on one Lancaster which was operating from Ludford Magna on Airborne Cigar electronic countermeasure duties, escaped miraculously. During one attack:

> '...his rear turret had been completely shot away at 9,000 feet, and he fell to earth still sitting in the turret and, although injured, survived and became a POW. All of the other crew members were killed.'[27]

It was Bomber Command's worst disaster since the Nuremberg raid: 42 aircraft were lost, all Lancasters,[28] with 44 out of 360 airmen killed. The scapegoat for all this was Cheshire – crews assuming his meticulousness had caused the delay. He was even shouted at over the r/t. The following day his name was castigated on airfields all over Lincolnshire.[29]

By D-Day, Harris's crews had made 60 attacks on key Belgian and French rail centres in seven weeks as part of 'Operation Clarion', two-thirds of the targets being put out of action. A total of 13,349 sorties[30] was flown, and 52,347 tons of bombs dropped. Harris's men welcomed the break from the stresses of attacking German targets. Casualties over four months were, on average, as low as 2.6%, although these trips were regarded generally as 'milk runs' – compared to those on Germany – and, when added to the tally for a tour, they represented only half an operation. Far fewer than the 10,000 civilian deaths, feared by Portal, occurred. The transportation attacks required extraordinary precision: Zuckerman concluded that Harris's forces had 'contributed more to the dislocation of enemy communications than any of the rest', and Harris was genuinely surprised by the accuracy of his men. He wrote:

> 'Our attacks on the marshalling yards proved to be astonishingly accurate, never before had there been such concentrated bombing... Bomber Command's night bombing, from this point onwards, proved to be rather more accurate, much heavier in weight, and more concentrated, than the American daylight attacks, a fact which was afterwards clearly recognised by SHAEF when the time came for the bombing of German troop concentrations within a mile or so of our troops.'[31]

Initially, the Americans had blindly ignored British warnings about the dangers of daylight raids. This was to their cost. Very few of their navigators had been trained to navigate in the dark and, aside from a tentative experiment in the late summer of 1943 when the 422nd Bomb Squadron flew night missions in conjunction with Bomber Command, it was not continued. Joe Williams, a rear gunner on 625 Squadron in 1944/45, had some scathing criticisms to make of the alleged American 'precision bombing'. Their suggestion had often been that they could 'drop a bomb in a pickle barrel'. On one occasion two American Flying Fortresses, coming back over eastern England, got lost and landed at Kelstern, Lincolnshire, home of Joe's squadron, after their formation was jumped on by enemy fighters and broke up. Williams recalled:

> '...their navigator was talking to our navigator in the officers' mess and said "Would you like to come over and visit our ship?" So we went out and climbed into the B-17 and there was a Gee Box.[32] Bill Patrachenko, our navigator, said to the American, "Oh, I see you've got Gee then?" "Oh sure we've got Gee", the Yank replied. Bill asked, "Where are your *maps*?" "Oh, we don't have any *maps*", the Yank replied. How completely useless! So Bill said, "Well how do you use it?" "Oh, we get *approximations*", the Yank said. Approximations! – I suppose if he was a lead navigator he could bloody work it – they had all the gear, but they weren't trained!
>
> 'They had navigators, but they just followed the lead ship. When it came to a briefing on the American bases, as we had before we went, their lead ship crews and their lead ship navigators would have a briefing before the general briefing. Of course when they got to the target, the lead navigator would take over, and as they approached it they all switched on VHF. And the lead bomb-aimer would say, "Open bomb doors..." And when he pressed the tit, they all pressed the tit! If that's not blanket bombing I don't know what is!
>
> 'Then, when they bombed on radar, they bombed using H2X[33], which was blind of course. But they hid behind an attitude of, "When we bomb on radar we still hope to hit a pickle barrel." It was a load of bullshit!'[34]

Graham Korner, tail gunner on 640 Squadron, was involved in one of the attacks on V-1 flying bomb sites made after D-Day where captured Soviet troops had been pressed into *Wehrmacht* service:

'On 4 August we attacked the flying bomb site at Le Chatellier.[35] Intelligence told us that it was "…nothing really, they've got Russian gunners there." We got absolutely plastered! I came back with ulcers! Russian gunners? They were bloody good Russian gunners!'

In that operation two Bomber Command aircraft were lost: one was another 640 Squadron Halifax III, LK757, flown by Flight Sergeant D. Barr, which crashed on landing. Korner was also involved in one of the raids on German troop concentrations near the front line in August 1944, two months after the invasion. He recalled:

'On 7 August 1944 we were briefed to bomb troop concentrations at a place called May-sur-Orne.[36] This was intended to back up the invasion and what happened that night? We killed 1,000 Canadians!

'They were supposed to fire star shells to mark the target, something that had never been done before. In the meantime the troops moved up, for some reason, and we were actually on our bombing run, had the bomb doors open, and on the run-up. Then the Master Bomber came over the intercom, I forget what his codename was, but the codename for "Abandon Mission" was "Canary". And he announced; "Master Bomber to Main Force: '*Canary! Canary! Canary!*'" I thought "Oh, no!" But they were still bombing and he said, "Master Bomber: for Christ's sake, *stop bombing!*" I remember it clearly.

'Anyway, we closed our bomb doors and turned back. But we were too heavy to land, so we had to fly the Halifax out over the North Sea and drop a couple of the bombs. We did that, and Jock the bomb-aimer, said "I'm safe!" I was looking out of the rear turret and they went off and hit the water, and there was a convoy underneath! I don't think they hit anybody. And we understood that all these Canadians, about a thousand, had been killed that night.'[37]

The Transportation Plan attacks of early 1944 had been meticulously planned and required months of organisation and discussion – largely contrary to Harris's wishes. But, despite his worries, all 37 targets were eventually destroyed successfully. The achievement of the D-Day invasion in lodging a bridgehead on the Normandy coast, within 24 hours, is a testimony to its success. Despite this, due to poor tactical planning, and sometimes an unfortunate combination of circumstances, many lives, both in the air and on the ground, were unnecessarily lost in 'bodged' operations. But, regardless of being sidetracked from his true intent, and placed under Eisenhower for a few months, Harris soon was back in the driving seat, continuing his attacks on the German heartland. The campaign was now steering towards its iniquitous climax: the 'Thunderclap' operations of 1945.

CHAPTER FIFTEEN

'RATHER LIKE HAVING MISSED THE LAST BUS HOME – BUT MUCH MORE FINAL'

The dangers and trauma of a 'final' operation

THE standard formula for a crew's final operation, as oft quoted, was that it '…took off, flew out, bombed, and returned.' Sometime during the intervening period any number of incidents could occur, and most of the cases, although similar, differed in detail. For instance: in American George Harsh's case, a string of circumstances resulted in his failure to return from an op; sheer providence on three different occasions resulted in Bill Wetherill's survival; and, for years after he was shot down, Steve Jackson thanked God for saving his life as the result of the sacrifice of two of his friends.

This chapter contains fifteen separate accounts of final operations either sent to the author by Bomber Command veterans, discussed with him by survivors, or discovered during the course of research. They are presented in chronological order, and have been selected principally for their descriptive detail. In all cases, although other factors played a hand, most men owed their survival purely to luck.

Donald J.R. Wilson
51 Squadron, Whitley, raid to Hannover, 18/19 May 1940

Donald 'Jock' Wilson was shot down on 19 May 1940 flying in Whitley N1408 on an operation to Hannover where his crew had been ordered to bomb an oil refinery. The pilot was Squadron Leader W.H.N. Turner DFC and the bomb-aimer, Flying Officer A.C. Peach. The wireless op was Sgt D.S. Edmondson and the rear gunner AC2 G.B. Smith. N1408 took off from Dishforth in North Yorkshire at 20.20 hrs. 51 Squadron was a disbanded First World War Home Defence squadron which had re-formed as a night-bomber squadron in 1937. It had been based at Dishforth since December 1939, having previously been at Linton-on-Ouse. It was equipped with Whitleys early in 1938 and had undertaken Bomber Command's first attack on a land target on 19/20 March 1940 against Hornum on the island of Sylt. On 11/12 May the squadron had made the first big attack on the German mainland against rail targets in Mönchengladbach.

Wilson, who qualified as a doctor after the war, recalled:

'We headed for Flamborough Head where we altered course for the target area. Hannover was approximately five hundred miles from base, so we required additional fuel to complete the return journey. We therefore replaced two 500-lb bombs with an extra fuel tank and were to attack the oil refineries with two 500-lb and six 250-lb bombs. Fortunately for me, as the air observer, I had most to do during the flight, and therefore had little time to contemplate the coming battle and its possible consequences. Before darkness fell, I checked our position by dropping an aluminium sea marker[1] – a box of aluminium powder which spread over the waves when it hit the sea. I then checked the aircraft's drift by using the tail drift sight, in order to calculate the wind speed and direction. Accuracy is of an absolute necessity for successful air navigation. We had a further two checks to ensure we were flying on the correct track. After dark we dropped a flame float[2] and again calculated the drift. However the flashing beacon on Terschelling Island in Holland was a more efficient method of calculating our position, and it was comforting to see it to the south on the starboard side.

'After crossing the north German coast, everyone felt the tension when searchlights swept across the dark evening skies, trying to pinpoint us for the local Flak batteries. We reached the Hannover area a little after ETA, and the town was clearly recognisable, but finding the target was much more difficult. I confess we spent at least ten minutes circling the town trying to locate the oil refineries with its roadway, railway lines and canal.

'Much to our astonishment and intense relief, we had so far encountered only minimal opposition, and we were able to line up for the bombing run. Having completed aiming procedures and released the cargo, I did not feel the usual buffeting which happens when the heavy bombs leave the aircraft. I personally did not see any bombs dropping, nor did the tail gunner see any explosions. I was assured by the Captain and other members of the crew that the task was completed, and we set course for Dishforth.

'I was still worried about the possibility of landing with bombs aboard and asked the Captain to test the bomb bays to ensure that all had gone. The result of the test was devastating, as all the bombs were still in place. It was then that we discovered a fault in the bomb release mechanism, which we successfully repaired. The captain decided that we had enough time and fuel to return for a second attack and still be able to make our way home. We completed the task, dropped our bombs, and set course for base. As we left the target the Flak defences opened up a terrific barrage and we received the first hit at the moment the second pilot and I were in the well of the aircraft. The shell ruptured the oil pipe line from the port Merlin operating the front gun turret, showering us with oil. This was warm and of the consistency of blood and, as the blast had propelled us with considerable force against the fuselage, it was only too easy to believe that we had sustained some injury. Having cleaned our faces with the silk inner lining of our flying boots, we were very relieved to find oil, not blood.

'We hastily returned to our respective crew positions and almost immediately we sustained a much more serious hit, which slammed us violently across the cabin. We were somewhat dazed but, on recovering, I saw the pale, grinning face of Sgt Edmondson, the w/op, looking past a pile of shredded metal which had been our transmitting and receiving sets. Shrapnel had also destroyed part of my navigation table, satchel of maps, and of course part of the floor. My Irvin trousers had slits torn above and below the knee of the left leg and I sustained a small cut on the left side of my neck. This was the closest I came to meeting the man with the scythe. The Merlin engines appeared to have escaped serious damage, but because of severed control cables, the machine was impossible to fly. The Captain warned us that he couldn't carry on much longer and ordered us to don our parachutes. Soon after, he told us to abandon the aircraft.

'I reached the trapdoor first, stood aside and let the second pilot get out. However, he said I should "jump", but, a few seconds later, the skipper smartly disappeared through the escape hatch and I followed him. As soon as I was clear, I pulled the ripcord and the parachute opened instantly. My descent now seemed painfully slow especially as the Flak continued to fire up towards us. The shells came up in groups of five, indicating that they were 30 or 40 mm calibre.

I was completely unprepared for a landing and, on hitting the ground, my knees buckled and hit my chest so violently that I temporarily lost consciousness. I awoke, gasping for breath, not realising what had happened. My parachute and harness were pulling my body along the ground so I quickly pressed the release mechanism and gathered together the folds of the parachute. I remembered emergency instructions to hide the equipment if possible, and get as far away from the crash site, as the Germans would be searching for survivors. Having deposited my equipment in a ditch at the edge of a field, I ran away until I collapsed, exhausted, behind a hedge.'

Bill Wetherill
207 Squadron, Manchester, raid to Berlin, 12/13 August 1941

Bill Wetherill was a w/ag with 144 Squadron and completed his first tour in December 1940. He was eventually shot down with 207 Squadron on a trip to Berlin in a Manchester on 13 August 1941. Of his six-man crew, he was the sole survivor. 207 Squadron, originally an RNAS squadron, was redesignated when the RAF was formed on 1 April 1918, and was the first unit to operate the Handley Page 0/400 – Trenchard's 'Bloody Paralyser'. In August 1941 it was based at Waddington, Lincolnshire, with Manchester Mk Is.

Wetherill's story came to light following recent research by two German historians who found a photograph of a crashed aircraft in an old German magazine from 1941. This was identified as L7377, EM-G, a Manchester I, shot down near the village of Grossbeeren, during an attack on Berlin. In April 2001, the story was published in the British magazine *Aeroplane* under the title *One Way Ticket to Berlin*. It was quite an involved story, suggesting that Wetherill survived purely by chance. The aircraft had a crew of two pilots, an observer, a tail gunner and two wireless operator/air gunners, Bill Wetherill and Flight Sergeant G.R. Birt. Wetherill was operating the r/t set on the outward flight, and Birt was in the mid-upper turret. They agreed to swap places on the return.

As they flew out over the North Sea, one Manchester turned back due to 'tail flutter' and another, EM-R, L7381, was shot down as it approached the target. Wetherill's skipper, Squadron Leader Taylor DFC, had difficulty dropping the bombs after his aircraft was 'coned' by searchlights, and gradually the Flak got closer until an explosion directly in front of the aircraft inflicted some minor damage. Just before 02.00 hrs they received the *coup de grâce*: a shell hit the back of the Manchester, setting fire to the rear fuselage, the mid-upper turret (where Bill Wetherill was due to be on the return), and blowing the rear armour-plated door up the fuselage to the w/op's position. Birt's turret was by then engulfed in flames. Bill clipped on his parachute but found three men trying to force open the forward escape hatch, which was jammed solid. There was an exit window on the starboard side of the cockpit glasshouse. As he tried to open this, Bill's hand was severely burnt, but he stuck his helmeted head out only to be confronted by a maelstrom of rotating prop blades. At that point, as the flames burned his legs, he became stuck and passed out. Coming round, he found that he was falling earthwards without a parachute. He pulled the D-ring, and within seconds hit the top-most branches of a tree, hanging suspended there until a German search party cut him down.

At that point Bill faced a further trial: a German officer threatened to shoot him until a young boy interposed and redeemed him. Pure chance had saved Bill Wetherill's life three times that night: a replacement in the mid-upper turret, his Manchester blowing up in mid-air and the help of a youngster. He was sent to *Stalag* VIIIB, and later repatriated.'[3]

Eric Foinette
12 Squadron, Wellington IC, raid to Kiel, 25/26 February 1942

Eric Foinette was a 12 Squadron navigator shot down in a Wellington IC on 26 February 1942 during an attack by his squadron on Kiel. One of the oldest RAF squadrons, 12 Squadron was formed in February 1915 at Netheravon, Wiltshire, going to France that September equipped with the B.E.2c light bomber. It was disbanded in July 1922, but re-formed in April 1923 with DH 9 bombers. In 1935 it moved to Aden for a year to reinforce Middle East Command during the Abyssinian crisis. The squadron re-equipped in 1938 with Fairey Battles and relocated to Bicester from Andover in 1939. It became part of the Advanced Air Striking Force in France that year. The skipper on the Kiel raid was Sqn/Ldr R.B. 'Abie' Abraham, and his second pilot an Australian, W/O D.R. Wardhill.

Foinette: 'We set out for Kiel on the night of 25/26 February and met heavy, rainy conditions on the way out. We crossed the Danish coast in the area of Sylt, some 50 miles north of track, and as we ran in, a salvo of anti-aircraft shells was fired and there was a heavy explosion underneath the plane, which lifted us several feet in the air. The Flak must have penetrated the cooling system as the starboard engine started to heat up. With the prop feathered we began to lose height, so we jettisoned and turned back.'

The official report stated that 'they were last heard on the w/t at 0300 advising severe engine problems and that course had been set for Sweden.'[4] Foinette: 'Conditions over the North Sea made the crossing extremely hazardous, and we retraced our track in an endeavour to reach Sweden. George [wop/ag Sgt G.R. Duckham], was able to report back to Binbrook accordingly. Had we not turned back initially, in all probability we would have reached Sweden before getting too low. We lost height continuously, and tried to lose weight by throwing sextants and other items overboard. The camera wouldn't come undone and the gunners were reluctant to dispose of ammunition. By now we were flying at around 90 mph into wind, so the ground speed was pretty low and we started to fly over water, but had dropped to about 2,000 feet. "Abie" decided that the descent could not be checked and to bale out over the sea in very cold weather was not on. So we again turned westwards and as soon as land was reached again, the order to jump was given. Frank Payne [Sgt C.F. Payne] had been alarmed at being stuck in the front turret and called for us to let him out: there was a bulkhead door between the turret and the main fuselage, which could only be operated from inside the aircraft. Frank went out first, then David Wardhill, followed by George Duckham, then me and subsequently Abie, who got out at about 1,500 feet. Ev Littlefield [wop/ag WO2 E.E. Littlefield RCAF], of course, had gone out of the rear turret as soon as the order was given.

'George claims he had managed to perform some somersaults when he jumped so he must have left opening his parachute fairly late. I must admit that I had my hand on the release handle when I went out through the nose. Fortunately we fell below the aircraft so that even early release was pretty safe. Later we discovered that George had not wound in or jettisoned the trailing aerial, which could have caused a nasty wound if we had hit it. I had kept my leather helmet on and, unfortunately it slipped down over my eyes as I fell, so I had little chance to survey the landscape, nor to enjoy fully the sensation of the jump. The other recollection I have was of the silence after leaving the noise of the aircraft engines. I landed in deep snow in a field, gathered up and buried my parachute in the snow, together with my helmet and flying suit. I well remember the feeling of bewilderment immediately on landing – rather like having missed the last train or bus home, but much more final. The uncertainty of one's exact whereabouts didn't help either.'

Foinette's aircraft was forced down 5 km SE of Odense, Denmark and all survived. His evasion was short-lived. As a result of gyrations in the air and headwinds, he had lost his 'air plot' and could only guess where he had landed. He began walking through deep snow and eventually spotted the lights of a farm and wondered, as there was a blackout in Britain, whether he may have landed in Sweden. He approached a man and woman outside a cattle shed but they did not respond to his broken German, or tell him where he was. They took him into the farmhouse where the farmer and his wife gave him coffee and sandwiches, but the man had presumably telephoned the Danish police as, shortly afterwards, a uniformed policeman arrived. He searched Foinette for weapons and then apologised, saying that he had to be held in custody since the Germans were on the lookout for the crew of an aircraft that had crashed locally. Subsequently a lorry arrived and Foinette recalled: 'I was collected, meeting up with the rest of the crew, and we were taken to an army barracks in Odense.' He later thought that if they had landed in Jutland or Zealand rather than Funen where there was no Resistance movement, they might have been more fortunate. They were later transported to *Dulag Luft* and Foinette then went to *Stalag* 6B and later *Stalag* 21B and *Stalag Luft* III.[5]

Edward G. Ratcliffe
57 Squadron, Wellington III, raid to Hanau, 1 April 1942

Nav (b), Ted Ratcliffe, a navigator, was 22 years-old when he was shot down. His Wellington carried a six-man crew: a second pilot, a Canadian Flt/Sgt Lundy, had been included, who proved to be a liability. Unfortunately Ratcliffe lost his 'Flying Logbook' when he was shot down: 'It was usual each morning', he recalled, 'for the ground crew to empty any cabinets in the crew room and destroy or redirect any papers and effects of the missing from the previous night.'

Although his logbook was destroyed, Ratcliffe believed he undertook at least six months of ops, because he was awarded the European Star at the end of the war, the qualification for which was six months minimum on operational service. Earlier, Ratcliffe had the distinction of being on a crew that contributed to the end of the German capital ship, *Gneisenau*. The *Gneisenau* was bombed in Kiel harbour a fortnight after 'Operation Cerberus', the famous 'Channel Dash' of 12 February when the German capital ships, *Scharnhorst*, *Gneisenau* and *Prinz Eugen* broke out of Brest harbour and successfully ran the gauntlet of British air and sea attacks, through the English Channel to reach North Germany. The *Gneisenau* never saw active service again.

Ratcliffe was in a Wellington Mk IC from Feltwell:

'We were [ordered] to bomb the city of Kiel, being routed beyond the target, turning back from the Baltic Sea and heading west. When it came to turning to port, a chorus of three other crew members called on the skipper for us to go home then.'[6]

Ted's pilot altered course, turning through 260 degrees to fly over Kiel harbour. 'We found ourselves just behind another Wellington and followed it', Ted recalled.

'The plane ahead was constantly bracketed by Flak, whereas no one shot at us – we enjoyed watching them suffer at the time. They weren't hit, which of course was good to know.' Below them Ted noticed a large ship. 'I jettisoned our bomb load,' he said, 'aiming at an area of water a little inland. Automatically our plane took photographs of our bomb bursts.'[7] Six aircraft were lost on the Kiel raid that night. This identifies Ratcliffe's attack as being part of the Bomber Command raid on Kiel of 25/26 February, 1942 when five Wellingtons and a Stirling were lost.[8]

After his landing, Ratcliffe gave '...an honest account' of the operation to his Intelligence Officer.

'The next morning,' Ratcliffe recalled, 'the CO called for the skipper and me to report to him. He told us that our complete load of bombs, each 250 or 500 lbs, had hit a large ship. It was the battlecruiser, *Gneisenau*, the remains of which were moved up the Baltic, where it was written-off due to excessive damage.'[9] Both men were recommended for a commission. But this was not to be.

Less than a month later, on 1 April 1942, Ratcliffe's New Zealand first pilot, Flight Sgt R.E. Knoblock, took off from RAF Feltwell in Norfolk bound for Hanau, 10 miles east of Frankfurt-am-Main, in Wellington X3748 at 21.25 hrs. He then handed the controls over to the Canadian, but Lundy, who had had inadequate training, flew the aircraft very badly. Ted later considered the whole trip was intended to be a training exercise for Lundy, under Knoblock's supervision. The Wellington originally was a good aircraft, Ted recalled, but by the time he was shot down, it was too slow for the job. 'Our flying from west to east attracted close Flak continuously', he recalled. The aircraft had been coned by searchlights and was hit by Flak from all quarters. At 8,000 feet the Wimpy was on fire, and the two pilots were unable to control it as it spiralled down. 'We heard a crump just behind and below the rear gunner', he said. 'He screamed and the skipper told me to get him out of the turret. Hearing this on the intercom, the gunner leapt out, and bowled me over when coming forward.'

Knoblock was late in ordering a 'bale out', hoping that he would be able to get the aircraft away. They were down to 500 feet and almost all the fabric on the aircraft had burnt off. Sgt R.O. Thomas, the tail gunner, had yet to put on his parachute when Knoblock called for the crew to leave. Ratcliffe:

> 'We were tardy in accepting that attacks by a twin-engined fighter on our beam had set alight our port engine. I put the parachute on the chest of the rear gunner and pushed him out of the front. Knowing that the two others had baled out, and having ensured that both pilots had parachutes, I followed the gunner and landed on a hillside close by him. Both of us were close to each other and landed between the huts of some *Luftwaffe* personnel. Whilst dropping, I heard the plane crash, killing both pilots.'

The two airmen had landed on the roof of a *Luftwaffe* sound detector unit and were soon captured. 'We learned later that we had flown over *Dulag Luft* in flames', he recalled. The aircraft appears to have veered west after passing over *Dulag Luft*: it crashed at Sprendlingen in the Rhine Valley, over 30 miles south-west of Hanau. Ted was never awarded his commission: he was subsequently put behind barbed wire at *Stalag* VIIIB in Silesia for three years.[10]

Cal Younger
460 Squadron, Wellington IV, raid to Gennevilliers, 29/30 May 1942

Australian Sergeant Cal Younger was shot down on a raid on Gennevilliers, near Paris, on 29 May 1942. It was his 13th operation of his first tour with 460 Squadron, and the night before Harris's first Thousand-Bomber raid. Six aircraft were shot down that night, including two from 460 Squadron. Z1388 'J-Johnny', flown by Australian Flying Officer T. Bourke, took off at 23.43 hrs and was lost over the target area: only the tail gunner, Sgt Holborrow, survived. Sgt Younger's Wellington Z1391 'R-Robert' took off one minute earlier, and was hit by Flak and crashed near Dreux. Only Younger, who was navigator, and Sgt Graham Loder, the rear gunner, lived to tell the tale. The pilot, Flying Officer R.A.O. Jones, an Australian, and the two RAF wireless operator/air gunners were killed. Not all the aircrew on RAAF squadrons were Australians. Younger recalled: 'It had to be 70%, or 75%', he said. 'I actually had three Australian and two Englishmen in my crew.'

Cal Younger (Younger)

'I was shot down on my 13th op, on Wellingtons. We were shot down by Flak. It was a terrific sight as we approached the target. The Germans knew we were coming. We hadn't expected to face a lot of opposition, but I later met a POW who had been in hospital near the target, who said that the Germans told him we were coming over and were going to get a hiding. They put guns on the roof of the hospital!

'The target was just a sea of colour, with all the tracer coming up and we flew straight into it! We were hit somewhere amidships first: that knocked out the intercom, and I suspect the wireless operator was killed then – he was back in the astrodome. I was down at the bomb sight when that happened. So I went back to the pilot and we agreed we'd bomb on the red and green lights. But then we got another dose that seemed to go through the nose: actually it went right along the starboard wing, and set it on fire! And, in the end, only the rear gunner and I got out: just two of us. There were only three survivors from all six aircraft lost. The rear gunner from the other aircraft from our squadron also got out. So the three that got out were all 460, two rear gunners and me. All the rest were killed.'

Younger was on the loose in France for eight days. He later recalled:

'I got well away from Paris. I stayed in barns mostly. After I baled out – I don't know what height it was when I jumped, but it was treetop height when my parachute opened. A tree broke my fall and knocked me out for about half an hour! It was twenty to three when I was shot down, so I probably walked for a couple of hours until it was about half past five.'[11]

He arrived at a village called Sarong where a festival was taking place in the local church. A young woman came out to throw some dead flowers over the hedge he was hiding behind and saw him:

'It was thought I was a drunken German and a lively old lady came fearlessly to send me packing. Unable to follow her diatribe, I smiled and said: "*Je suis un aviateur Anglais.*" She fetched her daughter, who spoke some English, and I was taken to a clinic, fed and put to bed."[12]

The women later woke him up and said that the Germans had found his parachute and were searching the area so they had to get him away. He was given a mackintosh, a beret and a haversack with some food, brandy and tobacco. They then sent him on his way. He was later picked up after curfew by the French Police. When Younger returned to the area after the war he met the chief of the local Resistance who told him that the *Gendarmerie* had known very well that Younger should have been handed over to him, and then he would have been hidden and flown back to England. But he was not. Over 200 airmen shot down in that area during the war made it back to England, but only one was taken prisoner: Cal Younger was that one.

George Harsh
102 Squadron, Halifax II, raid to Dusseldorf, 5/6 October 1942
George R. Harsh, an American in the RCAF, was squadron gunnery officer with 102 Squadron at Pocklington on 5 October 1942. For a fortnight the unit had been suffering a high casualty rate resulting in a number of untried crews arriving from OTUs. As one such crew's Halifax prepared to take off, the pilot suddenly waved distress signals to Harsh and his friends. The gun sight in the rear turret was defective and the gunner, a solid Yorkshire farm lad, did not have a clue what to do. Harsh wasn't actually scheduled to fly at all that night, but climbed in to take the gunner's place; if anyone could hit a fighter without a gun sight, he could. As they flew out over Flamborough Head he began to have second thoughts. The parachute harness was much too large for him and there was a lot of slack around the crotch, which would not be very comfortable in a bale-out.

Harsh believed the target to be Dusseldorf and the Intelligence reported only light Flak to be expected; in fact the squadron ORB[13] records that the target was Aachen, 50 miles south-east of Dusseldorf.

After about an hour from base Harsh noticed that there were no other aircraft visible, yet they should have been in the centre of a stream. 'Slowly I swung the turret round on its full arc', he recalled, '– nothing out there but an occasional fleecy patch of white cloud, shimmering in the bright moonlight. And then I looked down at the ground eight thousand feet below us... The Kolner Dam! The majestic spires of Cologne Cathedral were pointing into the sky at me... There we were, right on top of Cologne... alone!'

At that point the pilot, a novice New Zealand warrant officer named F.A. Schaw, asked the navigator [Flt/Sgt G. McGowan] where they were: 'Hallo navigator!... Where are we?' There was dead silence, then, in a well-bred, English public school accent, the nav replied, 'I'm f.....d if I know, old boy.'[14]

'The groan of despair did not even have time to escape my lips,' Harsh wrote later, 'before everything seemed to begin happening at once.' A purple master searchlight latched on to them, and soon the entire Cologne air defence system was zeroed in on the Halifax: they were 'coned'. 'Having seen this happen to other bombers,' Harsh recalled, 'I knew there was no escaping it.' They were a sitting duck.

There was a standard evasion tactic to adopt when coned: essentially, it boiled down to a case of 'nose down, throttles wide open, go like hell', the idea being the faster you went, the harder you were to hit. Lumps of shrapnel flew past the aircraft as the bucking, jumping machine, surrounded by oily brown explosions, began to receive direct hits, and eventually it burst into flames.

Fire streaked from the wings and Harsh realised that they would have to abandon the aircraft. By that time the intercom was out and the rear turret hydraulic system was u/s too. Harsh, who had spent 12 years on a Georgia chain gang, was undeterred by this and hand-cranked the turret rotation system around so that he could fall out backwards. Then a burst of light, and fine shrapnel sprinkled his back: 'It felt as if a dozen white hot pokers had suddenly jabbed into me', he recalled. 'My one prayer at that moment was that the Flak had not cut the parachute harness draped over my back.' As he descended, Harsh pulled the slack in the harness up into his stomach, simultaneously jerking the ripcord. He free-fell and amid dead silence; a single searchlight followed him down. Then the parachute opened and he lost consciousness.[15]

George Harsh survived the fall and was sent to *Stalag Luft* III. That night 18 bombers were lost on the Aachen raid and, of the rest of Harsh's crew, all lived except Schaw. An inexperienced crew, a damaged gun sight, faulty navigation and, finally, Flak, removed George Harsh from the war.[16]

George Flanagan
77 Squadron, Halifax II, raid to Mönchengladbach, 30/31 August 1943

Bomb-aimer George Flanagan was with 77 Squadron at Elvington, Yorkshire in August 1943. He was shot down when attacked apparently by more than one enemy fighter, on an operation to Mönchengladbach on the 31st of that month in a Merlin-engined Halifax II serial JD460, coded KN-D. Four of the crew survived including Flanagan, but when they crashed in the target area, mid-upper gunner Sgt Les Letts, w/op Sgt Jack Naylor and Sgt Robin 'Jock' Hunter, the rear gunner, were all killed. They had taken off from Elvington at 00.22 hrs.

Flanagan discovered after the war that one of his attackers was probably the *Luftwaffe* night fighter ace, Oberleutnant Heinz-Wolfgang Schnaufer of NJG 1. Between June 1942 and March 1945 Schnaufer shot down 114 British bombers during 164 night missions. He became known as the 'Night Ghost of St. Trond' by British aircrews. Flanagan: 'The attack came from the stern and below. The gunners engaged the stern attacker but the one underneath with upward-firing guns, he got us. It was a *Schräge Musik* attack – and you *know* it! There were two of them: one was the decoy and the other was the "action man" and that was Schnaufer! They were both Me 110s and we were well alight on the port side.[17]

'The command from Johnny our skipper was loud and clear: "*Prepare to abandon aircraft!*" I clipped on my 'chute and then Johnny's last command to us: "*Abandon aircraft! I can't hold her...*" During the first part of the attack, I heard Letts talking on the intercom, but I think that he was hit and killed later, because I saw him afterwards – he had all his head blown away. Robin "Jock" Hunter, our rear gunner, couldn't rotate his turret as the port inner engine was well alight, and this controlled the hydraulics. John Goulding, the captain, and the navigator tried unsuccessfully to extinguish the blaze. Bob Whyte, our flight engineer, left his table and began to move back to the rear turret to help Jock. Hunter couldn't swing round on the beam and push himself out, which rear gunners normally do. They just rotate it round and fall out backwards. But he couldn't do that – he just crashed with the aircraft.

'Sid the navigator calmly folded his seat. Jack, our wireless operator, stood up. We dropped everything and clipped on – because you had front clip-ons – and that's how I got near to the escape hatch. I moved back near the escape position. Johnny all the time

George Flanagan (Flanagan)

wrestled with the now useless controls. Suddenly the aircraft lurched over and there was a flash, and I was thrown against the inside of the aircraft and remember no more.'

(In the ensuing explosion Flanagan, Whyte and Sid Ellingstad, the American navigator, were all blown out of the aircraft. The remaining four crewmen were killed. Neither of the other two survivors could recall exactly what happened). 'They don't remember *how* they got out of the aircraft, just that they know they got out of it. When it exploded it must have blown *them* up and *me* down! They had a longer fall, so they were able to pull their 'chutes sooner. I "came to" flying through the air, cold air on my face, and the 'chute clipped to my chest. I pulled the D-ring and the pack opened. It broke my fall, although I hit the ground very hard, falling through some trees and my flying boots had come off, but I never found out where.

'I lay there winded but alive, and thought, "Am I the only one?" I could hear the bomber stream above returning to their bases. The impossible had happened: most aircrew adopted the attitude it might happen to anybody else, but not to us. But it *had* happened to us! After a while I tried to pull the 'chute down from the tree, but it was caught on a branch, so I gave up.'

Then Flanagan discovered that his smoking habit had probably saved his life: 'I reached for my cigarette case in my top left battledress pocket to find it was bent completely in half: so it had struck something hard!

'I landed, or fell down, and tried to get over a barbed wire fence. I fell off the fence, crashed onto the ground and flopped. It wasn't dark, but getting light by then, because it had been quite a late take-off. Then a German Home Guard man approached me; he had a great big rifle and a huge, snarling Alsatian dog, and indicated to me to empty my pockets. So I started doing this when suddenly a soldier came up: "*Nein! Nein!*" He pointed – "*Put it back!*" Then he said: "*Kom! Kom!*" So I said, "I can't walk." Then he bent down, put my arm around his neck, lifted me up and we walked to the edge of the wood, where there was a small Volkswagen field car. He put me in that and then drove me to the area where the remains of our aircraft were. That's when I saw the lads that were dead.[18] Amongst the wreckage as I got close, I could make out three bodies: Jack the wireless operator had his 'chute, still packed, clipped to his chest – killed by the impact; Les, the mid-upper had been hit in the head by a bullet; and Jock the rear gunner was lying halfway out of the remains of his turret. No sign of Johnny the skipper, Sid the navigator or Bob, the flight engineer.'[19]

Flanagan was subsequently taken to the village of Rheydt and put in the local jail. He was still under the impression that he was the only one who had survived. Suddenly there was a lot of noise outside, opening and shutting of doors, and then Bob Whyte, the flight engineer, was thrown into the cell. Flanagan informed him that three of the crew had been killed. 'I think we were both still too dazed to take it all in', he said. Later that day another airman was put in the cell, whom they concluded was a 'stool pigeon': 'He said he was a navigator on Lancs,' Flanagan recalled, 'but he asked too many questions, so we kept quiet and he was then taken out of the cell.' Although he was unable to walk, George considered himself lucky: he later met an airman on Frankfurt station who had two broken arms and 'such a swollen face that he couldn't see'. Flanagan and Whyte were subsequently both sent to *Dulag Luft* and after they had been there a day Sid Ellingstad, their American navigator in the RCAF, was brought in, but he could not recall how he had got out of the aircraft. New Zealander John Goulding, the pilot, was killed in the crash and his body never found.[20]

Norman E. Gregory
101 Squadron, Lancaster III, raid to Dortmund, 22-23 May 1944

Sergeant Norman Gregory was a bombardier in a 101 Squadron Lancaster on Airborne Cigar duties which flew out from Ludford Magna to accompany an attack on the Ruhr. His first op had been the disastrous raid to Mailly-le-Camp on 3/4 May. This was his fifth or sixth operation. The crew had bombed Duisburg the night before, then, on the raid to Dortmund, became the victim of Flak and fighters.[21] The specialist radio operator, the eighth man on the crew, was a Canadian, Sergeant C.M. Beauregard, who probably spoke German. *Luftwaffe* records state that within the space of 11 minutes, seven four-engined aircraft were attacked and shot down by night fighters between 00.44 and 00.55 hrs that night over the city. Two of these were identified as Lancasters.

Only three of Gregory's crew survived the ensuing *Schräge Musik* attack; Gregory himself, P/O L.N. Davidson, the New Zealand pilot, and the navigator, Flight Sergeant I.D. Jacobs. Gregory recalled: 'In the target area we were attacked from below and set on fire. We were on fire from the main spar to the tail. Five of the crew were killed.' At 23,000 feet Gregory jumped from the front escape hatch but seconds later the Lancaster 'Q-Queenie's' controls burnt through, her nose dropped like a stone and she tumbled out of control. Negative 'G' forces threw the navigator Jacobs and the skipper, Davidson, out through the canopy roof. Jacobs floated down but the aircraft fell into a lake. Gregory:

> 'The fuel tanks burnt and the lake was on fire. The skipper fell into this lot and was badly burnt but survived. My chest pack parachute deployed violently, caught me under the chin and knocked me out. Then, when I "came to", my boots had fallen off and I was in the beam of a searchlight. My landing was rough and I could only crawl. The local policeman put me on the crossbar of his bicycle and pushed me along. A day later I was in the cell at Dortmund airport where I joined the skipper and navigator. We were transferred by lorry to *Dulag Luft* where conditions were far from pleasant.'

Davidson ended up in *Stalag Luft* III, and Gregory and Jacobs went to *Stalag Luft* VII Bankau. Overall RAF losses that night were recorded in RAF ORBs as 19 bombers. The *Luftwaffe* claimed 38 RAF four-engined aircraft, including a Halifax north of Dortmund.[22] An RAF flight engineer was killed with 166 Squadron who was 45 years-old, probably one of the oldest fatalities on operations.

Steve Jackson
35 Squadron, Lancaster III, raid to Coubronne, 23/24 June 1944

Steve Jackson was a wireless operator/air gunner who had flown many hours before the trip to Coubronne in Lancaster ND734, TL-H. This was an operation to mark a flying bomb site in France in view of the threat of attacks on England. Four of his 35 Squadron crew had already finished one tour and were decorated and experienced men: pilot, Squadron Leader Geoff Ingram DFC; flight engineer, Flight Sergeant Doug Gerrard DFM; mid-upper gunner, Robert H.J. Gill DFM; and rear gunner, Pilot Officer D.A. 'Punch' Weatherill DFC. Jackson owed his life to the sacrifice of Weatherill and Ingram in the last moments of the trip when, after being shot up by a night fighter near Dunkirk, they were both killed. The rest of the crew, Canadian V.J. Murphy, G.W. Rushbrook, M.J. Spencer, Gill and Jackson survived.

Jackson: 'On the night of 23/24 June we made a raid on Coubronne, on the Belgian border, to bomb V2 rocket sites, and this was to be my last raid. That night we were

Master Bomber in the Pathfinder's group, which meant that we were first in at 6,000 feet, [we had to] drop our flares and bombs and tell Main Force where to bomb. Looking back, being Master Bomber meant you had to fly around giving instructions; it was a mug's game because at the end you were flying on your own, always a dangerous thing to do. The raid seemed to be a great success, however, and we had turned for home when we were attacked by a night fighter.

'The first thing we knew was, the centre of the aircraft was on fire and it wasn't long before the order to "abandon aircraft" was given: this meant clamping on your parachute and jumping out. I then witnessed the bravest thing I have ever known and probably anyone could witness. For the rear gunner to get out he had to rotate his turret round 180 degrees and fall out backwards. The hydraulic system was out of action, but the turret had what was known as a "Dead Man's Handle" whereby you could rotate it by hand and still get out. As I moved up to take my turn to bale out, I plugged in my intercom and heard Punch say, "It's no good Harry I can't rotate the turret" and Ingram replied, "Keep trying, Punch, I can hold her up a little longer." With that I jumped. The plane went on flying in flames and 15 seconds after I jumped out, it blew up in a large explosion; so two very brave boys lost their lives.

'I must place on record that these two knew they were probably going to their death, but there was no sign of panic as they spoke to each other. Even now I feel very humble when I think of it, proud to have known such wonderful and brave people. As for me, I have to thank God for giving me those 15 seconds that allowed me to live a long, happy and loving life, knowing the joy of having a wonderful wife and family.

'I drifted down to earth, but because it was so dark I did not see the ground and, although we had been trained how to fall, I fell heavily and hurt the bottom of my back. I was winded and in pain, but I gathered up my parachute and walked on to a road to be picked up almost immediately by a German with a horse and cart.'[23]

Robert Gill recalled:

'I was the mid-upper gunner on the raid on Coubronne. Steve Jackson was the wireless operator. The eighth member of the crew was Spencer, along for the training. He was injured when we were attacked and spent some time in hospital. I could not open the door in the fuselage to bale out and had to go up to the escape hatch in the nose. I was the last one out, just behind Jackson, who told me later that the rear gunner could not open the turret doors, which did not surprise me – I did over 40 trips in the rear turret and could never open the doors when we were in the air.'[24]

Jim Philpot
300 (Polish) Squadron, Lancaster III, raid to Stuttgart, 24/25 July 1944

Jim Philpot was a mid-upper gunner on Lancaster, MD-P ND984 on an all-English crew in 300 (Pomeranian) (Polish) Squadron based at Faldingworth, Lincolnshire. 300 Squadron was originally an all-Polish unit, a training formation, which transferred to No. 1 Group in August 1941. In 1940, when the squadron was formed, British advisors, technical specialists and an adjutant were also employed. By July 1944 there were all-English crews on the squadron.

'It all began on the night of the 24/25 July 1944. We were briefed to bomb Stuttgart for the second time in a week. The first time we found the target very heavily defended – plenty of Flak and night fighters. The powers that be decided to use the same route again, hoping it would fool the Germans. But of course it didn't. As we approached the target the welcome was very hostile to put it mildly.'

Often veterans' recollections are not that accurate. According to Middlebrook and Everitt the 24/25 July attack 'was the *first* of 3 heavy raids on Stuttgart in 5 nights'. The second of these raids was on 25/26 July when 15 aircraft were lost, and the third on 28/29 July when 40 went missing. Philpot's attack on Stuttgart appears to have actually been on 25/26 July. The only major attack on Germany that month before 24/25 July, was a raid on Homburg in southern Germany, on 20/21 July when 23 bombers failed to return.[25] So the *first* Stuttgart attack, conducted soon after the Homburg operation, using a similar route specifically to fool the enemy, was on 24/25 July: unwise as it turned out as 23 aircraft were lost.

Philpot and his crew took off at 21.15 hrs. As they approached the target they saw a Lancaster picked out by a blue master searchlight, which led to the inevitable 'coning', and it became the focus of all the Flak in the area. Soon a 'flamer' developed, and the unfortunate bomber went down vertically.

'It's enough to frighten the living daylights out of you', thought Philpot, whose aircraft carried on towards the target where '... bombs were going off all over the place!' Although 'P-Peter' bombed and did a smart diving turn out of the target area, almost immediately a blue searchlight had them. 'It was like being in a raging furnace', Jim recalled. 'The light was so intense it almost blinded you.' After some violent evasive action by Dave Harkin, the flying officer in charge of ND984, to the crew's great relief, they escaped, but had dropped from 20,000 to 9,000 feet in a few minutes and were on their own, way below the Main Force.

Shortly after 02.10 hrs a twin-engined fighter, probably that piloted by *Unteroffizier* Buhlmann of 11./NJG 5, (who claimed a victory at 02.25 hrs 80 kilometres north-west of Stuttgart for his first ever 'kill'), fired at them from below in a *Schräge Musik* attack. 'It just wasn't our night', Jim remembered. 'We were suddenly hit by cannon shells which ripped through the port wing, knocking out both engines on that side. The flames were streaming out alongside my mid-upper turret: the tail gunner [Sgt Ben Couchman] and I both saw the fighter make a turn in towards us, so we let fly only to see our tracers falling short.[26] Another belt of cannon shells came close but luckily did not score a hit.' Skipper Harkin tried to keep control on the two remaining good starboard engines but 'he could not hold it', recalled Jim. The order to bale out was given.

'I scrambled out as fast as I could', he said. 'Picking my 'chute up on the way, I clipped it on and headed for the rear door.' Philpot then saw that Sgt Couchman had rotated the rear Frazer Nash turret so that he could fall out backwards and was on his way to safety. The tail structure loomed out of the darkness behind him as Jim prepared to exit. 'I opened the door and looked out, and the thought flashed through my mind, "How on earth can I jump without being swept back against the tail?"' The next thing he knew Sgt Dave Berry, the w/op, was pushing him out of the rear side door 'in no uncertain manner', at the same time yelling 'For Christ's sake get out!'

'Well I was out now and didn't have time to see how close I had come to the tail. I immediately pulled the ripcord and the 'chute unfolded above my head, and I was pulled up with a sudden jolt.'

'It felt very weird floating down in the dark,' Jim recalled, 'so peaceful after the noise from four engines throbbing away, hour after hour.' He later reflected that he would 'probably have enjoyed the thrill of it under different circumstances' but, as it was, he was glad to be alive. In the distance 'P-Peter' was 'blazing furiously' in mid-air.

He saw its final moments as the 'plane crashed straight into the ground' in the area of Ochsenbach at 02.15 hrs.²⁷ ²⁸

Philpot came down in a forest, ripping his clothing and scratching his face, which was soon covered in blood. He came to an abrupt halt about twenty feet above the ground. The time was around 3.30 a.m. He released his 'chute, dropped down and started walking, soon coming to the edge of the trees, and found he was on top of a hill, about a mile away from a small village. He decided to hide up for the day in a ditch behind a hedge at the edge of a field of turnips. His escape pack did not have much food in it. 'I'd rather have my bacon and egg', he thought. Around 8 a.m. he heard voices. 'I found to my horror that a crowd of men and women were hoeing weeds between the rows of turnips', he recalled. They were moving very close to where he was hidden. 'When they reached the top of the field most of the men sat down and pulled out their pipes and cigarettes, while the women carried on down the field.' As they were only a few yards away, Philpot made himself as small as possible, but one of the men turned towards him to relieve himself. 'Thank the Lord he hadn't taken a few more steps as I should have copped the lot', he stated. As dusk fell the workers disappeared. A nearby road threaded its way down the valley, lying between two forests. He ran down the hill and up the other side into the opposite tree line, deciding to head south for Switzerland. At that point the going became exhausting and he seemed to make little progress:

> 'I was ploughing through dense undergrowth. My feet were killing me. I can assure you that walking in flying boots is no joke: the perspiration was pouring off and my clothes were sticking to me.'

Around 2 a.m. he heard the sound of Merlin engines in the sky above; the 'bomber boys' were back. He reached the edge of the forest as the dawn came up and presently found a stream: 'Joy of joys,' he recalled, 'the water didn't look too good but I cupped my hands and scooped up a mouthful. It didn't taste too bad.' He washed his face and blistered feet, then slipped back into the forest to sleep, having decided to travel only by night. That evening he awoke, sampled some more water, and then realised he had to find some food. He would take to the road when it was dark. Presently he came to a village. Advised procedure was to skirt around villages, which he did, pursued by barking dogs and encountering barbed wire and unexpected ditches. Returning to the road, after 15 or so miles he came to a second village. Then he made a mistake. It was the early hours and very quiet and, abandoning advised procedure, he decided to 'chance it and go straight through.' About halfway along an air raid sounded and, as there was no one about, he started to run.

> 'I was suddenly confronted by a large man in some sort of uniform who had a rifle in his hands. He called out something and pointed his gun at me. So I had no alternative but to stop. Before the blinking of an eye there were dozens of men surrounding me.'

Jim was taken to the local police station, searched and his possessions removed. Subsequently he received the stock phrase in broken English: 'For you the war is over.'²⁹

Frank Mannion
10 Squadron, Halifax III, raid to Neuss, 23-24 September 1944

Flight Sergeant F.P. Mannion's Halifax, flown by Flying Officer G.R.G. Kite, a Canadian, took off from the 4 Group station at Melbourne, Yorkshire at 17.25 hrs. It was bound for Neuss, west of Dusseldorf on the banks of the Erft. This was the crew's 33rd operation. It had been particularly badly hit on its 30th op on 13 September during an attack on the oil production works at Gelsenkirchen, also in the Ruhr. This had been a daylight raid with intense Flak and four aircraft were lost, one from 158 Squadron and three from 640 Squadron – two of which crashed on take-off at Leconfield, one with engine failure the other with its ASI unserviceable. Both were controlled crashes. Only the 158 Squadron Halifax was hit by Flak. Seventeen 10 Squadron crews went out on the Gelsenkirchen raid, twelve suffering Flak damage – over 70% of the force.

Mannion's crew had been the last to take off and the last to bomb. They turned for home after some normal small talk from the bombardier. That night, *Hauptmann* Ernst-Wilhelm Modrow of 1./NJG 1 was on the prowl in a *Schräge Musik*-equipped night fighter. He located and attacked the Halifax from below at 23.11 hrs, 73 kilometres west-north-west of Dusseldorf.[30] For rear gunner Mannion this was not his first encounter with night fighters. He recalled a major post-D-Day op in which 11 Bomber Command aircraft were lost, two from 10 Squadron: 'On 30 June 1944 we were attacked on two separate occasions by fighter aircraft whilst bombing the marshalling yards at Blainville – that was hectic! The first aircraft was seen to be badly hit whilst gaining position to the rear of us and dived away steeply with flames in its wing. The second aircraft, I think, was being flown by an inexperienced pilot; he flew straight into our cone of fire and just seemed to blow up.'[31]

'After the debriefing,' Mannion continued, 'I was told that I was to be recommended for an award; somehow this did not take place.' For the Blainville operation the normal mid-upper gunner had been replaced by a Scotsman, Hanz Beck. Beck 'received the immediate award of the DFM after the mission', explained Mannion,[32] 'I believe it was for the action he was involved in with the two [enemy fighters] that attacked us on that trip.' Mannion felt that his part had been misrepresented: 'I was directly responsible for what happened to those two German fighter aircraft', he said. He found that Beck's citation in the official records stated that the Scot was the rear gunner, which was incorrect. For every one of the operations in which Mannion took part he was listed officially as the mu/g, whilst he was actually the tail gunner.[33] The ORB crew listings falsely recorded Beck as being the tail gunner on the Blainville op. The DFM award was officially given to F/O Kite's tail gunner, as listed in the crew records, which should have been Mannion. Although Mannion contacted RAF records about this, the error was never corrected.[34]

The operation against Neuss on 23 September was the final op of Mannion's crew:

'I was straining my eyeballs in the tail turret as usual: it was very dark and cloudy. Then it happened. An almighty bang around what I took to be the port inner [engine] followed immediately by a thud just behind me. At once the order to abandon aircraft was given. It wasn't your polite, "This is the pilot: prepare to abandon aircraft." Oh, no. This was a bawled, "Eh, fellas, *get out!*" from the skipper. The next voice I heard was our navigator checking, in his quiet Canadian drawl, "Did you say bale out, skipper?" The answer to that was very affirmative and then the other members of the crew acknowledged the instruction.'[35]

Mannion attempted to leave his turret but the doors were jammed solid and would not move. Although his headgear was still on and he was plugged into all the aircraft's services, he found all around him was 'strange and unreal'. The doors still refused to budge. 'It is a funny thing, but people never know how they will react when faced with a desperate situation', he wrote. 'In my case I felt very calm and resigned. I didn't think I was going to get out of that aircraft.' He recalled biting at a piece of chocolate he had placed on a tray near his left hand, and at the same time unwittingly bumped against the turret control stick. The machinery began to move.

> 'Turning round I again tackled the doors. This time they opened. I felt that I had tempted fate long enough: on went my 'chute, the turret on the beam, and I was just about to roll out backwards when I decided to make a last check. It was as well that I did so: I had only secured the 'chute on one side. This was soon rectified and out I went.'

He had been impressed by the behaviour of the aircraft as there had been no violent movement. Although he knew the front of the Halifax was damaged, he thought he was the last one on board, and heard nothing more from Kite after the 'bale out' order. But Kite and the w/op, Flt/Sgt Saunders, were still on board. Kite flew the aircraft towards the Allied front line in Holland and crashed it when attempting to land near the town of Zwier Wimburg, which was occupied by the US First Army. Both men were killed.[36] None of the rest of the crew could understand what had happened: they assumed both men were in good order when they exited. 'One can only assume,' Mannion wrote, 'that some disaster, perhaps an injury or parachute problem had befallen the w/op, and the skipper set aside his own safety in an attempt to save Saunders.' Mannion made a bad landing after baling out but survived. A few days later he was picked up by the German Home Guard and put into a local village gaol. He was sent to *Dulag Luft* and then *Stalag Luft* VII.

Keith Pendray[37]
226 Squadron, B-25 Mitchell, raid to Deventer, Holland, 15 October 1944

Flight Sergeant Keith Pendray was a nav (b) on a North American B-25 Mitchell, 'W', FW106, of 226 Squadron, piloted by W/O F.F. Turner, attached to the 2nd TAF based in Normandy. On 15 October 1944 12 Mitchells of 226 Squadron went to bomb the rail bridge over the Yssel River, at Deventer, near Nijmegen. The aircraft was hit by Flak near Arnhem after an inexperienced flight leader made a tactical error. All three crew got out safely following a crash-landing, and were taken prisoner:

> 'We were always flying daylights in boxes of six. We were going to a railway bridge over the Yssel River after the Market Garden operation at Arnhem. We were leaving the target, going south to a little place on a level with Arnhem and then south-east to Eindhoven; then into our new French base in Normandy. That was the flight plan. Unfortunately the chap who was leading the box was Number 2 and he was "pitched in" rather. On the way the Box Leader said his bomb sight was u/s, and so number 2 changed over to number 1. And we went in and bombed, not very well, but did spread our load over a railway track: but we didn't get the bridge. Instead of going down south and then south-east, we went almost direct to Eindhoven, and that meant very close to Arnhem. By that time the Arnhem battle had ended, so all the "88s"[38] were pointing upwards instead of south. Our Cockney gunner asked, "Can we take our Flak suits off, please?" I replied, "No, we're too near Arnhem", and just at that moment there appeared – deadly accurate – four little black puffs. And this chap leading the box, who obviously wasn't very experienced – took us very, very gently slightly down and slightly away from the Flak; which is roughly what the gunners expected him to do! And the next lot got us.

'It wasn't a direct hit. A direct hit, even on a Mitch, which is a very solidly built aircraft, blows it to bits! But it was nearby. We lost our starboard engine, insofar as it couldn't be shut down. I should think what happened – unless Freddy, my pilot, had a bit of finger trouble – was the engine lost its control over the pitch of the airscrew, and it was going "fully fine". If you've ever seen a Pratt and Whitney with 4,300 rpm on it, when the normal maximum was 2,900, then you've seen something! In front of the crank case and behind the spinner there is about 100 mm visible of prop shaft, and it was sparking! But we had the biggest field in Holland to land in. We landed without using wheels and were just behind the German lines. We flew right across the Salient, which was a bulge in Montgomery's front line, and just outside the west of it! The Germans were *around* the Salient; Monty's men were *in* the Salient. The Salient was south of Arnhem and aligned south-west/north-east. By the time I had got the second gunner over the bomb bay and out through my hatch, the ground was going past like a rocket! I then realised my parachute was on the other side of the hatch. So I wasn't going out like that.

'It looked like we wouldn't land *anywhere*, because we were going down in a steady turn and the machine was more or less uncontrollable. You blow out one engine and get 4,000 rpm on the thing – you haven't got a flying machine, you've got a streamlined brick! Because the two gunners baled out first, they came down nearer to the front line than us. [After we flattened out and landed] a bunch of *Luftwaffe* men being used as ground troops came galloping up, and we were POWs within about 90 seconds! The gunners were taken prisoner as well: they were just behind the German line and we were a little bit further back. We were the only aircraft shot down.'

Graham Korner
640 Squadron, Halifax III, raid to Bochum, 4/5 November 1944

Rear gunner Graham Korner's 640 Squadron Halifax MZ930 C8-K was shot down during a raid on Bochum in the Ruhr. 640 Squadron had been formed as a heavy bomber unit at Leconfield, Yorkshire on 7 January 1944, from 'C' Flight of 158 Squadron. Its first two missions were flown from Lissett – 158 Squadron's base. Subsequently it was transferred to Leconfield. Korner's crew had been together for a number of ops. Dutch Flying Officer, Kais Goemans, the heir to a family bulb-growing business, was killed almost instantaneously by a Flak burst near the cockpit when they were hit. W/op Freddie Nuttall, a former butcher's boy, went down with the aircraft after he took over control when it burst into flames. Mid-upper gunner 'Paddy' Finnigan jumped out with Flight Sergeant H.D. Patterson, but failed to strap himself on to Patterson and fell to his death as the parachute opened. The other four became POWs. The navigator, Flight Sergeant Ron Purcell, was badly burnt before he baled out, and Korner had difficulty extricating himself from his turret:

'It was 4 November 1944. It was our last op and we were bombing an oil refinery in Bochum. We took off about seven o'clock[39] in the evening and we had to bomb from 16 or 18,000 feet. Once we bombed the target we went straight down to 12,000 [feet], and then came home at 12,000. I saw a fighter and there was quite a bit of Flak over the target when we got there. The fighter was attacking another aircraft, but as soon as we saw that happen – we were all eyes: we figured he might come up and have a go at us – but we didn't see him any more after that.

'We got our bombing run in and did our bombing; got it all on target, and everything was OK. Once we'd bombed, the pilot stuck the nose down and we turned. The navigator gave him a course and he went straight down and dived off – all you want to do is get away from the target! With hindsight it was stupid: we should've kept weaving really, but we didn't. It had been quiet, we were just drifting along, on the way home, while the navigator was getting a fix and setting his course. Then we were hit: I could see these four shells coming towards us. I shouted to the pilot *"Dive!"* and he no sooner did than, *Boom... Boom... Boom... Bang!* and that was it – the last one got us. No doubt this was predicted fire it was so accurate. And the aircraft gave a lurch, and the fourth shell went right through the nose and burst... I heard it too! It came in from the starboard side, through us, and out. It set all the nav instruments and other equipment on fire.

'The shell had burst outside, beside the pilot and he got hit in the head. Despite being strapped in, he was blown clean out of his seat and right down into the well of the aircraft, jammed across the front escape hatch. His parachute came undone. He was killed – he got half his head blown off...

'The wireless op, Freddie Nuttall, was standing beside him when we were hit. The w/op normally does nothing over the target, just sits tight, because over the Ruhr he had to keep an eye out for fighters. Also if they got into a dive the skipper might need a bit of help. Freddie Nuttall – he was a character. He was a butcher's boy before the war, and you could never make out how he'd got into aircrew. He said he hated going upstairs on buses! He was a funny bloke: but if it hadn't been for him none of us would have got out. When the pilot was hit and the aircraft caught fire, he got into the pilot's seat, grabbed the controls, and held the aircraft steady. And when the navigator and bomb-aimer finally got out, he was sitting there screaming, with all his hair on fire – the flames were blowing back on him: but he held it long enough for all of us to get out.

'Ron Heath was about to go out, and the flight engineer came running up to him and said, "My 'chute's burnt!" We had lost the previous engineer on the 11th op. He was replaced by this lad, Paddy Finnigan, only 19. He came up, and said "My 'chute's burnt, I'll have to go out with you!"

'With hindsight I suppose you'd say. "Yes, we'll do that: we'll put the parachute on, one clip on me and one clip on you." If they'd done that, sitting side by side, they'd both have come down: you'll come down a bit faster because there are two of you, but you will come down. Or they could have lain on the floor; and you had what they called "dinghy clips" on, and he could have clipped onto those. But Finnigan went out hanging onto Heath. And, of course, as the mid-upper gunner's parachute opened, the engineer fell off: just went off without his 'chute. His body was found later that night. I suppose in the panic of the moment they didn't think about clipping on: I mean at any moment the thing could have exploded! It had a bad effect on Ron Heath.

'When we were hit, I could see these shells – *Whoof... whoof... whoof...* coming towards us. Then the aircraft caught fire – all I heard the pilot say was "Ouch!" and nothing more. I thought "Bloody hell, what's happening?" I felt the aircraft side-slip. I thought: "Time for me to put the parachute on!" All of a sudden the aircraft seemed to straighten up for a minute – that must have been when Freddie held the controls.

'The nose of the Halifax was formed of a big glass canopy. When we were first hit, the navigator and bomb-aimer apparently both passed out in the nose for a minute. Jock Patterson fell right into it, probably so he'd be away from the flames. The navigator got burnt on his hands and face when the fire started. I heard him say to the bomb-aimer: "Give us the extinguisher, Jock." He got the extinguisher alright, but it was red hot and burnt his hands. The next thing I heard him say was. "Jock, get the front escape hatch open!" I thought, "That's it, they're on their way out!" The navigator's 'chute was also on fire, but they put it out. The engineer had been burnt – his 'chute was on fire, but they put that out.

'The bomb-aimer tried to open the escape hatch but, Kais, the pilot, was jammed across it with his parachute, so they had to come back, past Freddie, who was sitting at the controls in the cockpit. They came up a couple of steps beside him and, as they were going past they shook him and said "Coming?" But he shook his head. So they said "Fair enough", and went back, climbed over the main spar, got down and went out the rear door, one after the other. As our navigator went down he remembered watching his parachute burn above him. But finally, he and the bomb-aimer ended up in somebody's backyard in Düsseldorf with a hell of a crash, not far from each other.

'I turned my turret round on the beam, and looked down inside, and all I could see were green flames coming down the fuselage. I suppose it was the electrics burning – all the cables that were coated with stuff. The flames were quite green. I thought the others were going out the front, so I leaned out, got one turret door open – that was a job – got the second one open, sat back on the turret ring, leaned out a bit, and thought, "I've got to go". I'd got my flying boots on, but because you've got a belt feed mechanism, bringing all the ammunition up through the bottom of the turret, there wasn't a lot of room. Your feet can feel each other and you sit there and ease further back. I gave a push and away I went!

'I didn't know how high we were: it was about 12,000 feet. I thought, "You're supposed to count". So I counted five, or six, or seven and went to pull the ripcord but it wasn't there! *Oh God!* Then I thought, "Other side": I'd put it on the wrong way round. The ripcord came away so easily, I thought I'd broken it. The ring came out, and it went *Pheeeyoo* – with a flash of white. Then I slowed up and there I was happily floating down.

'The next thing I knew I could hear *Whoo… whoo… whoo….* I looked round and there was another aircraft coming towards me – it was a Halifax with radial engines. It was so near I could see the glow in each engine. I thought *"Blooming heck!"* It seemed to be coming straight towards me – too near for my liking anyway. So, pulling onto the shroud lines, I tried to slip away. Afterwards I thought, "I wonder how many blokes that has happened to?" Anyway it went past, so I was alright.

'It was a fairly moonlit night and I thought I was over water. I couldn't understand it because we hadn't been that long off the target. If we'd been over Holland, I could understand it. But it was the moon shining on these fir trees. I saw a patch of dry land, pulled the shroud lines up and hit the deck: God! I'd landed in a cobbled farmyard – backwards! I went over with a terrible crash and cracked my bum, and hit my head. I sat up and thought *Whew!* – and as I did so our aircraft flew overhead. It had obviously circled right round, and it was on fire from head to tail. It went right over and the machine guns were going off – the rounds must have got heated up. It was fairly high, but it was coming down, and it disappeared behind some trees. All of a sudden there was a *Whoo* and it was gone. The reason it went so quickly, apparently, was because it landed in the Rhine, actually in the river, at a place called Rhein. The pilot was never found. I should imagine the nose was smashed to pieces when it went in and the aircraft broke up. But they found the wireless operator's body washed up on the shore, and he's buried in the Reichswald Cemetery.

'When I got picked up a day or so later, I was taken down into Düsseldorf to a big hutted camp, and they brought Jock and Purc out. Poor old Purc, he looked awful; his hair and eyebrows were all singed, his face and hands were done up in paper bandages, and his trousers were burnt and pinned together with safety pins. He was in a hell of a state! I don't know why he was burnt more than the others – I suppose he was nearer the fire, probably where all the instruments were and tried to put them out. But it was hopeless.'

Ted Boorman
Halifax III, 102 Squadron, raid to Hannover, 5/6 January 1945
Ted Boorman was a nav (b) on a Halifax with 102 Squadron based at Pocklington,

Yorkshire when his crew raided Hannover in January 1945. He had the unnerving experience of free-falling for 18,000 feet before he could get his parachute open.

His Halifax took off at 16.52 hrs with a crew of eight, the eighth man being Sgt A.I. Johns, a bomb-aimer who was doubling up as a third air gunner on the crew. The navigator was Flight Sergeant W.A. 'Bill' Quill. At 19.22 hrs, near Hannover, the 42-victory German night fighter ace and holder of the Knight's Cross, *Hauptmann* Hermann Greiner, *Gruppenkommandeur* of IV./NJG 1, claimed a Halifax shot down for his fourth victory in ten minutes.[40] The bomber was recorded as crashing at 19.25 hrs. Ted Boorman lends credence to Greiner's claim: 'I reckon it was a night fighter', he said.

With the exception of Boorman, all the rest of the crew, including the diminutive South African pilot, Captain Ron Heiden, were killed in the crash, probably caused by baling out too late as their parachutes were still wrapped around the aircraft when it went in. Ted was soon picked up and became a POW in *Stalag Luft* I.

'We were on the bombing run, and I was down in the nose getting all the bombs ready. The Germans used to have upward-firing guns mounted in the top of some of their aircraft's fuselage – *Schräge Musik* – and that night they got our port inner engine. At the same time the skipper was killed – because the only thing we heard him say was "*Bale out!*" and that was it, never another word…

'Then Bill and I tried to get out. He was Australian, and for navigators in Australia he was at the top of the age limit for aircrew – 33. He made it by one day. As we prepared to get out, Bill and I picked up the navigator's table and strapped it back. Our parachutes were still hanging up. We put them on and unlocked the escape hatch. In the Halifax you sit on the escape hatch and it's very handy to get out.

'Then there was a "*bang*" and I was outside the aircraft, one leg caught inside and the door shut. I had no idea whether I might get out or not. So I pulled the foot out of my flying boot: it was generally cold up there and I'd got frostbitten more than once. The only thing that worried me was that if I did manage to get my foot out, would the tail wheel hit me before I fell away?

'Then I went to pull the ripcord but it wasn't there! I thought: "Hell, where's it gone?" There was a flapping noise: I looked up and there was the 'chute. It had caught on the edge of the escape hatch and the straps had been broken and were now hanging loose. It was attached to me by cords from the harness, and the harness was up above my head. So I had to get it down.

'If you catch hold of the cords and try to pull them down, you go up. But if you pull up on the harness, you drop down. I kept doing that and thought: "What am I going to do? How am I going to get the 'chute down?" I kept on trying, and it was floating around above me in the slipstream. By then I was doing 120 miles per hour, [the terminal velocity for a body in free fall], going straight down feet first – I didn't somersault! I was getting worried: falling through cloud you can't see anything and it was difficult to work out how long I'd been falling for. I was more interested in getting the parachute open. I supposed that if I broke cloud level at 2,000 feet, at 120 miles per hour, I'd have a few seconds left before I hit the deck.

'I finally managed to open the 'chute just as I broke cloud level: I'd fallen from 20,000 feet to 2,000 feet, and after it opened, I fell another 2,000 feet to the ground. It took about 10 seconds, roughly, and I landed in a ploughed field. I don't remember any more because I passed out and didn't come round for two hours.

'[When I came to] I could see our aircraft down in the road with German soldiers walking round it. I don't know how I ended up in the same location. The aircraft was on fire with bullets going off in the guns, the engine had exploded and there was petrol everywhere.

Fortunately the bombs hadn't been fused so they were safe – but the bullets kept going off. There were parachutes all around, so everybody else had been killed. Bill didn't get out: they were all dead.'

Joe Williams
Lancaster I, 625 Squadron, raid to Chemnitz, 5/6 March 1945

At 16.39 hrs on 5 March 1945, Warrant Officer Joseph V. Williams, a rear gunner in Lancaster, NG240, CF-F2 'Fox Two', took off from Kelstern in Lincolnshire for Chemnitz in eastern Germany.[41] 625 Squadron was formed at Kelstern on 1 October 1943 as part of 1 Group, the main nucleus coming from 'C' Flight, 100 Squadron which was based at Waltham, near Grimsby. Kelstern was 420 feet up on the Lincolnshire Wolds, a range of long chalk hills. 'It was agricultural land up there', Williams stated. 'There was a lot of water, and the rest of it, but it was flat on top. Obviously there were straight and level bits which were long enough and flat enough to have a lengthy runway.'

Joe Williams (Williams)

Williams was to suffer the alarming experience of suddenly finding he had no parachute when his Flak-damaged aircraft caught fire.

'We had been to Chemnitz before and on that occasion had been airborne exactly nine hours. Shortly after passing Beachy Head,[42] the starboard outer engine began streaming smoke; quickly it was shut down and the propeller feathered. Cliff Lear, our flight engineer, diagnosed the problem: the Merlin 24 had blown one of its cylinder head gaskets and was burning glycol coolant, so our Canadian skipper, Jim Alexander, consulted the crew. The dead motor drove an oil pump which operated the mid-upper turret which was therefore useless. It also drove a generator which provided power for the navigational aid Gee. "Can you still search, Joe?" asked Jim. "I can manage alright," I replied. Bob Pyett's mid-upper turret was immobile, but he could still see in some directions. The navigator, Bill Petrachenko, said he could manage without Gee. Cliff did his calculations for three-engine consumption: "We shall get back to England", he said, "but we won't get back to base."

'Over Poix we turned due east. Soon it was time to gain altitude, so the starboard outer engine was restarted and the throttles adjusted to give climbing power. Very quickly it became obvious that the faulty engine was in serious trouble and again it was shut down. This time, though, it was necessary to operate the Graviner fire control system, which injected foam into it.'

The three remaining engines were adjusted to maximum climbing power, and the aircraft headed for the Cologne Gap, between Bonn and Koblenz where the Flak was less intense than in the industrial centres to the north and south. However, the Germans, aware of the RAF use of the 'Cologne Gap', had set up a line of night fighter control beacons, *Ida* and *Elster*, with *Otto*, near Frankfurt, to cover the area. Williams:

'With the engines still at maximum climbing power, "Fox 2" was gaining altitude only slowly and the cylinder head and coolant temperatures were rising dangerously. It was becoming obvious that we would be unable to reach our bombing height and, worse still, because we were falling behind our timed position, if we ended up alone at the end of the bomber stream we would lose the protection of Window. We reached our turning point directly over the Rhine and turned on a new heading.'

Close to Bad Hersfeld they turned 18 degrees to port on a north-easterly heading, pointing directly at Berlin, 200 miles away. As the engine temperatures were dangerously high, they decided to reduce power and therefore could not reach the bombing height of 18,000 feet. Fortunately for them, the night fighter activity was taking place at the front of the bomber stream. This meant that the Germans had plotted the stream's route and height, and all the bomber force would pass through their interception area; therefore 'Fox 2's' lower altitude was a protection at this time. North-west of Halle, the stream made two major course changes: 270 aircraft attacking Böhlen separated from the main stream, turning 60 degrees starboard; 700 aircraft attacking Chemnitz turned south 50 degrees to starboard. 'Fox 2' had 43 miles to target. The attack was due to start at 21.37 hrs. The timing for the attack was in three phases to prevent all the bombers from arriving simultaneously: the first phase from 21.37 to 21.39 hrs; the Main Force at 21.42 hrs to 22.11 hrs; and the last phase from 21.41 to 22.03 hrs. The Main Force was an all Halifax force from two different Groups, and the last phase was exclusively Lancasters, probably due to their higher operational ceiling. As 'Fox 2' approached Chemnitz there was little Flak. Williams:

'We were late and there seemed to be no one around: they had all gone home. Scanning the night sky behind us I saw a fighter approaching: "Ju 188, starboard quarter down, converging on us…" I reported. "What shall we do?" Jim asked. "Do a gentle turn to port to see if he's seen us", I advised. We turned to port: so did the fighter. "Do some flat turns", I ordered, and opened fire. The fighter, undoubtedly equipped with *Schräge Musik*, was intent on rushing in beneath us and closed rapidly. Firing my guns fully depressed, he passed below us out of my line of sight. I ordered "Corkscrew starboard" and down we went in a steep dive to starboard. This should have brought him into view again. Not so. Obviously this fellow had done battle with "corkscrewing" bombers before and knew the precise routine – he went through the "corkscrew" with us: down starboard, rolling, down port, changing, up port, rolling, up starboard. With the reduced power from our three engines, the "corkscrew" was probably not as vigorous as it would be on full power. Half standing and craning downwards, I continued to fire the guns fully depressed, knowing he was beneath us somewhere. In the nose, bombardier Floyd Chapman could see the fighter tucked in beneath us. Now the cannon shells were coming in. Bob Pyett later remembered the incident: "I can hear those shells now, banging in all along the fuselage." In my rear turret I heard nothing more on the intercom. Then the hydraulic power went, my guns stopped firing, and the turret was useless. In seconds it was burning and the hydraulic hoses were like torches. It was time to get out!'

The aircraft began to break up: escaping fuel had set both wings ablaze and the tailplane was coming apart piece by piece. Jim Alexander ordered 'Bale Out', punching a button that flashed a warning light in each crew position. There was no response from Joe Williams. Bob Pyett, the mu/g, climbed out of his turret, grabbed and clipped on his 'chute pack, and made his way back to the rear exit. The ammunition supply to the rear turret ran along feed tracks on each side of the fuselage and this was exploding with loud pops and bangs as it burned. Pyett opened the rear door and flung himself out, pulling his 'chute's D-ring release simultaneously. But the slipstream blew him back and the parachute spilled out in a heap at his feet in the fuselage. Desperately, he gathered the silk in his arms, sat on the opening, and rolled out backwards. As he passed under the tailplane he released the silk bundle.

'In the next few moments Joe Williams faced a nightmarish situation. The doors on his turret had jammed. He worked the port one slightly open, only to find the turret rotated to one side and great sheets of orange flame streaking past. Using the hand rotation lever, he wound the turret to line up with the fuselage, but the other door was still jammed. He recalled:

> 'I thought at that moment I was going to die. I sat back in my seat and shouted, "*For God's sake get me out of here!*" Maybe He did hear, for when I attacked it again it opened.'

Williams tore off his oxygen mask and climbed over the rear spar, only to witness blue-green flames spiralling down the fuselage.[43] His next sight was horrific: he saw his parachute pack burning in its stowage rack. In a split second he recalled a minor incident from the previous day. Williams, Petrachenko, Alexander and Pyett had gone to the Waterloo pub in Laceby, near Kelstern. During the evening Alexander mentioned a 'spare parachute' and Joe immediately asked where it was stowed. 'Behind Jim's seat', someone had said.

> 'I put my hand over my face and made a dash up the fuselage. The plane made an awful lurch and I thought I wasn't going to make it. Then I went over the bomb bay, over the rear spar, over the high main spar and into the cockpit. Jim was just going down under the instrument panel to the forward escape hatch in the nose compartment. I grabbed him. He shouted, "*What do you want?*" "*Spare parachute!*", I shouted back. "*Behind the seat...*" he shouted and then, getting into his seat, took the controls again.'

But the Lancaster had lost almost all its elevator control and required the pilot's entire strength to stop it stalling. Desperately Williams followed his simple instruction, but the pack was not behind the seat: 'I groped a little further back, behind the blackout curtain and under the navigator's table. There it was – in a stowage rack against the fuselage!' He quickly snapped the 'chute to his chest and, looking out at the port wing, saw blue flame shimmering on the top of it. Smoke was pouring into the cockpit: 'I shouted "OK!" and slid down to the nose escape hatch bending my knees. I went out head first.' Turning over and over in the slipstream he pulled the D-ring release and, with a tremendous jerk, the canopy opened. Suddenly Joe was floating down in complete silence – alive![44]

Reports after the war of the loss of a German twin-engined aircraft in the area on the same day, suggested to Joe Williams the possibility that he had, after all, shot down the night fighter. He had mistakenly identified it as a Ju 188 due to its pointed wing tips. It was, in fact, a Ju 88. After the Lancaster caught fire it fell out of control into occupied Czechoslovakia. As it descended, the rear turret and the back of the fuselage wrenched off. The front landed around 2 km away, crashing vertically into solid rock. The force of its dive was such that the four Merlins drove deep pits into the rock face and disintegrated.

In 1986 the wreckage of Williams's turret was found by Czech researchers and the main crash site shortly afterwards. They told him that the wreck had included at least one crew member – the pilot.[45] Williams has since visited the site. From the scene he recovered part of the aluminium framework of the FN20 rear turret with a 7.62 mm bullet hole in it, two spent 20 mm linked cartridge cases, and a segment of the rear turret traverse mounting ring. At the main wreck location he found at the bottom of the engine 'pits', a constant speed unit, a cylinder block holding-down bolt, an engine inlet valve, a supercharger torsion drive shaft, an oil pump drive gear, and a supercharger lower gear change fork.

• • •

In summary: this chapter presents a very small sample of aircrew who suffered at the hands of fate: Don Wilson's Whitley suffered a bomb 'hanging up', causing his crew to make a second 'bomb run' as a result of which they were shot down. The fact that Bill Wetherill did not move into the mid-upper turret before his aircraft was attacked, and that it blew up in mid-air, probably saved his life. Poor weather and indecision prevented Eric Foinette's crew reaching Sweden. Since the enemy knew the raid in which Cal Younger flew was coming, it was devastated, preventing Younger from flying on the first Thousand-Bomber raid. Replacing a less able gunner and poor navigation on the part of a 'rookie' pilot, led American George Harsh, once a long-term convict, to play a major part in the 'Great Escape' from *Stalag Luft* III. Ted Ratcliffe, who contributed to the demise of the *Gneisenau*, suffered confinement in prison camp due to a poorly trained pilot and an obsolete aircraft.

The tales of these men, although having a root in similarity, all exude contrast: George Flanagan was blown downwards out of his Halifax and so suffered greater injuries than his fellow survivors; although Norman Gregory survived the attack on his Lancaster, his pilot was badly burnt in the fire it created, and Gregory was transported to prison by bicycle; Steve Jackson owed the rest of his long life to the sacrifice of two of his young comrades; and a foolish attempt to deceive the enemy by attacking the same heavily defended target in a week, resulted in Jim Philpot's crew 'failing to return'.

And so the list goes on: although Frank Mannion's role in his aircraft was misrepresented a number of times in his squadron ORB, resulting in him being overlooked for a DFM, he was a brave man. On his last operation his turret failed to turn during an attack, but then responded and he was able to bale out, escaping the violent death that befell his two comrades; Keith Pendray's Mitchell went down partly due to an inexperienced flight leader; Graham Korner's Halifax was flying too low and too slowly, and its evasive action was too late; Ted Boorman succumbed to a *Schräge Musik* attack on the run-in and finally Joe Williams's Lancaster was late over the target, and also suffered a *Schräge Musik* attack. Williams survived by sheer good fortune.

Fifteen airmen, their lives intrinsically separated by the mysterious phenomena of time and distance, all bore a similarity of experience on their last operation, yet each case was entirely different. And all had to face the same bleak prospect of survival alone within enemy territory.

Part Four

EVASION

Awake! For morning in the Bowl of Night
Has flung the stone that puts the Stars to flight:
And lo! The Hunter of the East has caught
The Sultan's Turret in a noose of light.

OMAR KHAYYÁM

'It seems to me that a man can never be so lonely as when he is alone and hunted like an animal in a strange and hostile land, cold and hungry, where he can be sure every man's hand will be turned against him.'

HENRY WAGNER, NAVIGATOR, 57 SQUADRON

CHAPTER SIXTEEN

'I SET ABOUT PADDLING FOR THE SHORE'

Evasion by sea

IN November 1938, a few weeks after the Munich Agreement, two War Office staff officers began to work towards the setting up of a revamped version of MI 1a, a First World War organisation created after it was realised that Prisoners of War were a valuable source of intelligence. One of these officers was J.C.F. Holland, a specialist in irregular warfare and the creator of the Commandos. He realised that a 'very thorough organisation' would be needed in the impending conflict to help POWs during their possible evasion, imprisonment, escape or release. His paper on the subject was referred to the 1935 Joint Intelligence Committee, an Intelligence umbrella organisation which represented all three services. The man Holland recommended to lead his prospective organisation was a 45 year-old stockbroker and former infantry officer named Norman Crockatt.

Evasion for shot-down RAF aircrew was still a fairly hit or miss affair in 1940. 'Jimmy' James, a navigator with 9 Squadron, recalled: 'At that time there was very little training given in evasion and escape; it was too early for the establishment of resistance movements and escape lines in occupied countries, populations were demoralised and the evader was on his own in a shadowy and unreal world with every man's hand against him.'[1] To help overcome these restrictions, Military Intelligence Section 9 (MI9) was set up in December 1940 as part of the War Office, charged with assisting Allied troops behind enemy lines and resistance organisations in occupied territories. It was based in the Metropole Hotel, London and initially took some time to develop.

As the Allied bombing campaign intensified, and downed flyers grew in number, particularly from the beginning of 1943, the demands of 'escape and evasion' became increasingly complicated. Escape routes were required in order to repatriate aircrew to their home countries. In order to monitor these routes and their subjects, MI9 had to become increasingly sophisticated in its organisation.

Throughout the war there were basically three geographical areas in Europe where an RAF airman could come down: firstly, in occupied territory, i.e. Germany, France, Belgium, Holland, Denmark and Norway; secondly, in unoccupied territory such as Vichy France; or, thirdly, in the sea. Occasionally some men came down further afield such as in Italy or Poland, or others were interned in the neutralities. The following accounts elaborate on this.

The ocean offered little real hope of salvation. Although the chances of arrest were minimal, in areas such as the Channel and the North Sea ditching near the English coast did not necessarily mean that aircrew would survive. There were a number of cases of British aircrews landing within a few miles of the English coastline and not being picked up, particularly in the early part of the war when no organised Air Sea Rescue Service existed. Coming down in a wind-blown, cold, choppy sea with a high swell, in mid-winter, was not a welcome prospect. There was also no certainty that an aircraft would remain afloat, or that its dinghy would inflate, assuming that it survived a crash.

Peter Hughes, pilot, 489 Squadron, 7 August 1944, Norway
Peter Hughes was shot down in a Bristol Beaufighter on 7 August 1944 during an anti-shipping strike on a convoy off the Egero Lighthouse, Norway. His 489 (RNZAF) Squadron was based at Langham.[2] He landed in a sea that was flat and warm, jettisoned his parachute, undid the K-type dinghy from his harness and activated its air bottle. After it inflated he climbed in, then saw a disturbance in the water to the west and assumed it was where his aircraft had ditched. His main concern was for his navigator, of whom there was no sign. Years later he found out that his nav had jettisoned his hood[3] and been sucked out into the slipstream, but he had failed to attach his parachute. That he had not exited before his crewmate was the only consolation Hughes had:

> 'I was some ten miles off the coast. I could see the tops of the mountains and a lot of smoke where the convoy was. There were some fishing boats away to the North so I fired a distress flare but there was no response. I set about paddling for the shore. A [German] search and rescue Heinkel He 115 flew almost over me, but I kept quiet as I hoped to get ashore and evade.'

He continued paddling towards the coast. 'Around midnight, after a long time in the water, I landed on a flat rock and looked around, but there seemed to be more sea inland before the mainland. I thought it best to wait for daylight before making another move.' He hid his escaping money, which was in Kroner, under the insole of a flying boot and rested. At dawn a rowing boat appeared and its Norwegian occupant indicated that he should walk to a German Flak battery at the cliff top and give himself up: 'I communicated that if he could be of no more help than that he should leave – which he did. But soon a posse of German soldiers arrived with the standard phrase, "For you the war is over." Apart from that we were unable to communicate.'

Ivor Turley, rear gunner, 218 Squadron, 12 December 1944, Witten, Germany
Ivor Turley, a tail gunner with 218 Squadron, had a vivid recollection of events on 12 December 1944 when, after the Witten raid, his aircraft crashed into the North Sea, 50 miles from Felixstowe. The Lancaster had been hit in the main and secondary port wing tanks. Soon, with three engines out, they were losing height:

> '"Can't see a bloody thing yet", came Harry's voice, "we're still in cloud." Once more the engine cut and the nose dipped. I waited for it to roar into life again: it didn't. The wind started to howl. "Two thousand feet", shouted Harry. "One thousand feet." "God, we're going in fast", I thought. Sweat broke on my skin: Mac looked at me as though to say, "What happened to two thousand feet?" I looked at him, gently held him closer and shook my head, listening hard. I felt Mac start to tense his body: he too probably realised we were going to hit fast and hard.

'Suddenly, with a cough and a roar, the engine started again: the airplane swung, the nose pulled up and the tail went down a little. "I see it", shouted Harry. "Four hundred feet. Stand by for impact." I squeezed Mac's shoulder and we braced each other. I squeezed harder several times, quickly turning my head to Mac. I tried with my right hand to grab the side of the fuselage and then "*Wham!*"'[4]

The inside of the aircraft blurred with the vibration. Turley was not conscious of any stopping or slewing round – there was just a great surge of water from somewhere. Then suddenly he could stand up. A wave poured through the open escape hatch in the roof and Mac [the navigator] moved to the emergency dinghy release cord housing along the top right-hand side of the fuselage. It was stowed in a long tube with convenient gaps in it so it could be pulled like the communication cord on a train. He tugged at the cord but it came away easily, so he had to pull it hand-over-hand until he found the broken end. He waved to Turley, saying that it was broken by the impact.

'I was now conscious of the up and down movement of the floor. We were still floating – but for how long? I glanced back, and to my horror saw that the aircraft had broken in two just aft of the bomb bay. The tailplane and my turret were beginning to float away. Must get out quickly now, I thought: this lot will go down any minute. Sea water sprayed and slopped around our feet. Mac was signalling quickly to use the escape hatch. I pushed him up through it as he swung himself up: I pulled myself up. Mac was kneeling on top of the fuselage: he grabbed my arm and shoulder and pulled them as I squeezed and struggled through the hatch. My bulky flying clothing didn't make it easy.'[5]

At last Turley was on top of the fuselage. Another man was pulling himself through the escape hatch. For a moment Turley sat on the edge on top of the canopy facing backwards. As he pulled his legs clear he looked around and grinned. 'Well boys, we made it!' he shouted. A look of triumph was on his face. For a brief moment Turley felt that it all was over and then, just as quickly, he realised that now they had to survive. All the crew were later picked up by Air Sea Rescue.

Ronnie Cartwright, wireless operator/air gunner, 49 Squadron, 5 September 1940, Stettin, Germany

Ronnie Cartwright was a w/ag with 49 Squadron based at Marham, Norfolk, who was shot down in a Hampden I in the English Channel on 5 September 1940. All his crew got out safely to board their dinghy after ditching and paddled away from the aircraft before it sank. However, the boat was punctured and they had to partly abandon it, holding on to it, using whatever buoyancy remained to keep close together for rescue. Their Mae-Wests kept their heads above the water until a boat appeared in the distance. Cartwright recalled:

'At that time I was still under the opinion that our own troops had shot us down. Thoughts then began to enter my head – had I switched on the IFF equipment when approaching our coastline? It sent out a message to anti-aircraft gunners that we were friendly. It wasn't until the boat came near that I realised that they weren't British.'

The navigator had assumed that the coastline was that of England, but through a navigational error they had flown across the coast of France and he had not recognised the crossing point. The truth began to dawn on the crew: they were off occupied France. Cartwright remembered: 'I was exhausted and lost consciousness before they got me out of the water. It was only when I came to and heard a strange voice say *"For you ze vor is over…"* that the truth dawned on me.' All were rescued safely apart from the homing pigeon.[6]

Derek Hodgkinson, pilot, 1 C.O.T.U., 25 June 1942, Bremen, Germany

On 25 June 1942 the third Thousand-Bomber raid took place when 1,006 bombers were ordered to strike at Bremen. As it was a major port, Coastal Command contributed 102 aircraft. Derek Hodgkinson was a pilot with No. 1 Coastal Operational Training Unit flying Hudson Mark IIIs and was shot down on the return leg:[7]

Derek Hodgkinson (Hodgkinson)

'All was quiet. The moon was right overhead and visibility unlimited, but for an unbroken layer of cloud below us, looking like snow in the moonlight. I relaxed and plugged in "George", ordering coffee to be brought up. Then, half a mile to our port bow, an aircraft at the same height was flying opposite and parallel to us. I alerted the crew and, as the aircraft came abeam, turned to port to keep it in sight. I also put the nose down to be nearer the cloud cover. It was a Bf 110, and it started a climbing turn to get on our tail. I opened throttles to the maximum and pushed the stick hard forward. Just as we entered cloud we were hit from stem to stern by cannon and machine gun fire. I felt the aircraft shudder and buck as shells slammed home: the noise was as if we had exploded. We burst into flames and the cockpit filled with dense smoke.

'I dreaded being burnt alive; in my imagination I had pictured it, and it formed the subject of my worst nightmares. To my surprise I found that my mind had become crystal clear and I was able to plan what I had to do with a cold, detached deliberation.

'The reflection of the fire on the cloud made all around like a furnace at full blast. By leaning well forward, I could just see the instruments which enabled me to keep the aircraft the right way up. The controls and engines were OK, but the intercom was dead, and there was no sign of the crew. In case they could hear, I shouted *"Abandon Aircraft!"* as loud as I could. I closed the throttles and levelled off. My two big fears were that the fuel tanks would explode, or that our attacker would put in a second burst. I had no idea what had happened to the crew and could not possibly jump out until I was certain that they had jumped before me. The only way of jumping from a Hudson was through the back door or the hatch in the nose, and both were now in the midst of an inferno.

'We broke cloud, and I saw a bright light on the sea some miles distant on our port quarter. I turned towards it and it looked exactly like a lighthouse. Beneath it, stretching to either side, I thought I saw the dark shape of a coastline. My mind was made up. The greatest danger was that the tanks would blow. Why they had not done so was because they were self-sealing tanks – the Hudsons I had flown previously would have blown up immediately! I would have to accept the risk of a second attack and try to ditch as near that light as possible.

'I started a shallow dive towards the sea, heading directly for the light. Then things started to happen fast. I saw through the smoke two crew members struggling with the starboard cockpit window, obviously trying to jump. The noise suddenly increased and a gale-like draught swept through the cockpit, sucking up the flames from the nose so that my feet on the rudder pedals, and my legs, began to be scorched. At the same time the smoke increased so that I could no longer see the instruments. I took my feet off the rudders and attempted to open my side window. The catch at the front lower corner of the window was smashed and I could not get it to move. I finally put my hand through the hole in the glass and yanked it aft, badly cutting the palm of my hand. The cockpit cleared a little and I could see that the starboard window was open – but no sign of the crew. If they had jumped, they must have realised that their chances of making it alive were virtually nil as they were certain to hit the tail plane.

'The draught was intense, causing flames to roar through the rudder pedals. There was nothing for it but to climb onto my seat – difficult as my parachute was strapped to my backside – and thrust my head and shoulders through the open canopy into the slipstream. My helmet was immediately torn off, but I could at least see, and kept hold of the control column with my right hand. We were the right way up and the light was ahead. It looked to be at our level and I judged we were not far off the surface. In a few moments I saw the extraordinary sight of the wave tops illuminated by fire from our aircraft. I eased back on the stick and my last memory before I yanked it fully back was of large, green, white-topped waves coming towards me.'[8]

Hodgkinson 'came to' underwater in pitch blackness. He was free of the aircraft but his lungs were under great pressure:

'I struggled upwards and, after what seemed ages, broke surface, spluttering and coughing. About twenty yards away was the aircraft, its back broken so that the twin tails hung over the nose – but, miraculously, it was still afloat, though only for a few more moments. As I started to swim towards it, it gave a lurch and disappeared beneath the waves. All that was left on the surface was one of the main wheels, bobbing up and down in what seemed a pretty rough sea.'

His parachute was still attached to him and beginning to pull him down. He tried to activate the CO2 bottle to inflate his Mae West, but it failed. So, as the parachute began to drag him under, he swam across to the still buoyant wheel:

'Clinging to it, I found Vic Cave. I asked him if he was alright but, even in the moonlight, I could see that he was in poor shape. He said that he had been hit in the legs and was not feeling good. I asked him if he knew what had happened to the others. He said he thought they must have jumped as, when he went aft to look for his parachute, there was no sign of them.'

Hodgkinson was still having trouble with his parachute, and had to make a determined attempt to get it off. He dived under the water several times to release the catch – but to no avail. Eventually he was so exhausted he could only cling to the wheel as the parachute became heavier and heavier: 'The effort to keep my head above water became more and more exhausting. I felt I had swallowed half the North Sea.' In a semi-stupor he began to contemplate letting go altogether. Then a miracle happened:

'With a "*whoosh*" and a "*plop*" a large, dark object surfaced a few yards away. We could not believe our luck; it was the Hudson's dinghy, which must have inflated itself and worked its way loose from the wreckage. We struggled over to it; Vic had no trouble climbing in but, despite his help, I could not make it. I was completely unable to drag the dead weight of the now sodden parachute over the side. I knew I would drown unless I did something desperate about it. I let go of the dinghy and sank, whilst I struggled with both hands to release the catch. Suddenly, thank God, I was free.'

On board the dinghy Vic was lying in a pool of blood and water. His face was as white as a sheet and there was an awful rigidity about his stare. Hodgkinson spoke to him but there was no response. He could see that he was breathing but was obviously near to unconsciousness. All the stores, flares, and other equipment essential for survival, were missing from the dinghy. An aircraft flew overhead but the engine noise suggested it was German and it passed by at about 500 feet. The dawn was just breaking, which suggested it was about 04.30 in the morning.

The dinghy was slowly sinking lower into the water. Hodgkinson, kneeling down to look over the side, saw a stream of bubbles on the outer wall. There was no bailer and the wooden plugs designed for such an emergency were missing. The sea was becoming increasingly rough, and very soon they were being tossed about in the heavy surf, with the wave tops sweeping over them. Then the dinghy capsized as an extra large wave broke behind them.

> 'I swum from under the dinghy and clung to the ropes on its side – but there was no sign of Vic. I dived under again, found him and was kicking down to drag him out – when I hit the bottom with such a force that I thought for a moment I had broken my leg! I stood up with Vic in my arms and, to my amazement, found that we were only in about three feet of water. If the situation had not been so desperate it would have been hilariously funny.'

Twenty or so yards away was a sandy shore. Hodgkinson stumbled across to the beach, keeping his companion's head above the water, and dragged him above the waterline. 'He looked dead. His face was green and I could see that his legs were in a very bad state with flesh and blood showing through his torn trousers. I knelt by him and discovered that he was still breathing.'

They were on a beach some 400 yards long, flanked by sand dunes, 30 yards inland. Hodgkinson knew that he had to find out what lay beyond the dunes. The beach might be mined, but Vic needed help. He took one step towards the dunes when a shot rang out: 'A bullet whistled uncomfortably close to my head and I stopped in my tracks. I saw a file of German infantry running towards me from the left.'

Standing by his friend, Hodgkinson raised his hands. A German *Unteroffizier* called out '*Kommen sie mit uns!*' and marched him across the beach, leaving a soldier to guard the exhausted Vic.

• • •

These four accounts are but an extremely brief illustration of the type of experiences airmen suffered when they crashed into the ocean. Often they didn't survive at all, some were lost without trace. Others, like Les Whitton and Dick Sewell's 432 Squadron Wellington crew, returning from a raid on Hannover, crashed almost within sight of the English coast, but remained in the water for days until picked up by a German E-boat. They were then, like a multitude of others, sent to *Stalag Luft* III. In that sense, although landing in hostile territory presented serious threats in some ways, it could offer more chances for survival than the cold and hostile waters of 'the Drink'.

CHAPTER SEVENTEEN

'NOT THE MOST POPULAR PERSON IN THE REGION'

Evasion by land

EVASION on terra firma by the men of Bomber Command almost always occurred in mainland Europe. In the following nine examples the airmen's individual evasion experiences are presented chronologically from 1940 to 1945. Two of these evasion reports continue from final operation accounts in Chapter Fifteen.

Donald 'Jock' Wilson, navigator, 51 Squadron, 19 May 1940, Hannover, Germany

Don Wilson was shot down in a Whitley V of 51 Squadron on 19 May after taking off from Dishforth on 18 May at 20.20 hrs to bomb an oil refinery at Hannover. Wilson, who had baled out and parachuted down amidst a hail of AA fire, had landed violently, briefly losing consciousness, and was dragged along the ground by his parachute and harness. He managed to free himself and hide his equipment in a ditch. He recalled what happened next:

'It was then that I checked my direction of flight, only to discover that I was running eastwards into Germany, instead of west. It was indeed fortunate that I retraced my steps to my landing site, because on the ground was a bright red notebook containing codes for the day and other secret information. I really felt physically sick knowing that, had the Germans recovered it, they would be able to intercept and decipher all radio communications for the following twelve hours. I sat down and tore every page into pieces smaller than postage stamps and threw them into the wind. I then started the impossible task of trying to reach friendly forces which, unfortunately, were several hundred miles to the west. I felt alarmed but somewhat proud of myself in successfully evading a squad of soldiers in "skirmishing order" accompanied by dogs, obviously looking for me. This was, however, only a temporary success, because I was discovered and captured by troops of a local Flak battery.

'It was understandable that I was not to be the most popular person in the region as we were always accused of bombing churches, hospitals and civilians. The suspected beating up by my captors was luckily avoided by the swift intervention of a *Luftwaffe* Lieutenant who was driving past in a Volkswagen. He searched me for weapons and ordered me into his car. He explained that according to the news, the raid in which I had taken part had allegedly killed a hundred civilian workpeople in the adjoining village, hence the hostile reception!

'This Lieutenant drove me to his Headquarters and took me to the kitchen where he spread black bread with margarine and sausage. He also handed me the remainder of the loaf, saying that it might be a long time before I got anything to eat – his assumption was correct!'

Jack Cheeseman, observer, 207 Squadron, 12 October 1941, Hüls, Belgium

Flight Sergeant Jack A. Cheeseman was a bombardier flying in an Avro Manchester L7312 EM-L on an operation to attack a synthetic rubber factory at Hüls in the Ruhr Valley. Eleven Manchesters and 27 Hampdens set out and, apart from Cheeseman's aircraft, only one, a Hampden of 144 Squadron was shot down, this by *Oberleutnant* Helmut Lent of 4./NJG1. For one of the senior pilots on 207 Squadron, Cheeseman's skipper, P/O Derek B. Bowes-Cavanagh, was a protégé. Apart from Cavanagh all the remainder of the crew were non-commissioned. Over northern Holland a Bf 110 flown by *Oberfeldwebel* Paul Gildner[1] of the same unit as Lent, raked the Manchester from close range near NJG 1's base at Leeuwarden. Sgt Ian H.D Passy, the rear gunner, failed to see the Messerschmitt. The Manchester caught fire and Bowes-Cavanagh told Cheeseman to go to the nose and bomb. But the fire was out of control and Bowes-Cavanagh ordered the crew to jump. Cheeseman, aged only 20, dived out through the front escape hatch, ignored the 10-second free fall count, and pulled his ripcord. The harness straps were loose and the lack of deceleration when the canopy opened caused him a sharp pain in the crotch and severe friction burns on the inside and top of his legs. The Manchester went down 27 km NNE of the port of Antwerp. Cheeseman then noticed that the aircraft had crashed and exploded almost immediately below him and that he was drifting towards the burning wreckage, but the rising hot air filled his canopy and lifted him clear. However, his ordeal was only just beginning: because he was reluctant to discuss what happened next, his friend Dr. Robert Kirby had to piece together the remains of the story from Belgian sources and ex-POWs.

Cheeseman was the only survivor from his crew and twisted his ankle badly as he landed in a field of cows which showed a natural curiosity in him. Uncertain of their intentions, he panicked and painfully hobbled off, later receiving a rudimentary dressing from a local doctor who had been awakened by the crash. Cheeseman was then arrested by some German troops, but little of what followed could be said to be within the boundaries of the Geneva Convention. The Germans drove him around the local town in the sidecar of a motorcycle combination. Robert Kirby explains what followed:

'The entire township had been violently shaken from their beds by the crash and explosion and many were out and about. Jack's captors proceeded to drive him round and round the streets herding the townsfolk into groups: laughing, exhibiting and humiliating Jack with the intention of reinforcing their supremacy and the hopelessness of any Belgian resistance. Next, as dawn broke, the Germans, with their 20 year-old "exhibit", drove to the crash site. A horrific scene greeted them. A crater marked the impact point, with widely scattered small airframe debris littering the field. Soldiers wandered amongst the wreckage. Local residents had either been goaded or driven by their oppressors to the crash scene, or drawn by their innate curiosity. The dismembered remains of the other crew members were also lying around. Local people, and doubtless Cheeseman himself, were sickened and disgusted in equal part to see a German guard dog trotting around with a quite unmistakable airman's leg fragment in its mouth.'[2]

Cheeseman was subsequently transported via Antwerp and Brussels to *Dulag Luft* where he was interrogated and was then in five different prison camps, including *Stalag Luft* I, IV, and III, for three-and-a-half years.

Bill Higgs, flight engineer, 35 Squadron, 19 September 1942, Saarbrücken, Germany

W.E.G. 'Bill' or 'Shiner' Higgs was shot down in Halifax II W67657 TL-L on 19 September 1942 during a raid on Saarbrücken. His pilot was Wing Commander Jimmy Marks DSO, DFC, who was one of the youngest and most promising wing commanders in the RAF, CO of 35 Squadron, and on his second tour. He had been awarded his Pathfinder badge that day; Higgs was awarded his badge two days later. Marks had been responsible for modifying the nose of the Halifax: the front turret on the Mk I was little used, and the Boulton Paul dorsal turret on the original Mk II had been found to be too cumbersome. These were both abandoned, along with the flame-damping exhaust muffs, to improve performance. Marks redesigned the nose as a solid cone, which increased the aerodynamic qualities, and flew it down to Boscombe Down for approval. This became the Halifax II Series I Special and later led to the fully Plexiglas nose of the Mk II Series Ia.³

Bill Higgs (Higgs)

Higgs:

> 'On the Halifax Mk I we didn't have a top turret: we had a couple of windows inside which we'd take out, and push two VGO [Vickers Gas Operated] guns out: they had a drum on the top that fired .303 bullets, which weren't much good against a modern fighter – it was like spitting peas.'

'Chesh' Cheshire, CO of 76 Squadron, also had modifications made to his Halifax. He stripped everything removable from the aircraft, including the flight engineer's armour plated door.

On 19 September 1942 Jimmy Marks's crew took off from Graveley, Huntingdonshire at 20.01 hrs. Graveley was 35 Squadron's base for the entire duration of the war from 20 August 1942. Marks and his crew were unable to locate the target because of low mist, even after a square search of an hour at 2,000 feet, so Higgs, who had previously served for a short time on 76 Squadron, advised his skipper that if they could not bomb and had to take a full fuel load back home, they had better turn immediately. Marks responded by asking the navigator for a course to base. Shortly afterwards, on the return, at 00.30 hrs, they were shot down by a Messerschmitt Bf 110 near the town of Vitry le François in France. The port fuel tanks caught fire and the Halifax crashed at Blesme on the Marne. The two other survivors on the six-man crew were the w/op, Flt/Lt N.H. Wright, an Australian, and the mid-upper gunner, P/O R.J.L. Saunders. The navigator/bomb-aimer, Flt/Lt A.J. Child, was a second-tour man with a DFC and was killed with the rear gunner, who had the distinction of bearing a triple-barrelled surname, P/O R.L. Leith-Hay-Clark. Marks was also killed. Higgs remembered:

> 'I was the last to leave the plane and, when I passed the captain on my way to bale out, he was having to fight to keep the aircraft in any sort of trim. As there was plenty of height when I left, I felt that as soon as he abandoned the controls, the aircraft would have gone haywire and made baling out for him impossible. When I left the aircraft, I momentarily got my harness hooked on the inside frame of the hatch and, hanging half in and half out of the fuselage, my

flying boots were pulled off so I went down in my socks. I was suspended freely in my 'chute and suddenly heard an "*Awrrrrr*". I looked round and saw this 110 coming towards me: I could see it quite clearly. It was banking around, and I got hold of the straps on my harness and pulled up, and then I pulled my knees up. I put my hands across my face, and waited. I waited for the cannon shells to come thudding into me, because we'd heard they were killing blokes in the air. I was hanging on, just waiting there, and next I heard "*Yarroomm*" and he'd flown past me – he'd gone back after the aeroplane again. But, not long after that, the plane hit the ground: there was a tremendous flash and fire – *Boom, boom, boom!*'

Higgs had not made a parachute jump before. As he descended he remembered somebody telling him that, on landing, '…you had to put your hand on the 'chute, pull down on a strap, put your knees together, and as you come to ground, pull your knees up, pull your arms up, and cushion the landing.' But this man had forgotten to tell him that he had landed in daylight, whereas Higgs was landing at night. 'Coming down,' Bill recalled, 'I saw some trees, and swung the 'chute to miss them.' He thought the trees seemed to be waiting for him. But, as he swung the parachute, he came in backwards: 'I was looking over my shoulder at the ground,' he recalled, 'and grabbed the straps to pull myself up. Then I hit the ground with an almighty thud and broke a leg. I didn't know for years afterwards that I'd cracked and crushed the fourth vertebra in my back. I must have shouted out, but nobody heard!'

Bill had landed in a tiny field near the small town of Vitry le François, south of Rheims. The parachute collapsed, and he crawled onto it, waiting for the Germans to appear; but nobody came. In the evasion talks his squadron had been given at home, they were told to get away from the drop area as quickly as possible, so he unclipped the 'chute and dragged himself up to a hedge at one end of the field. But he could not get through – it was full of barbs – so he crawled back down again and lit a cigarette. He attempted to burn the parachute, but it just smouldered and would not ignite.

'I crawled on again and came to a railway line. I'd broken a leg on landing and, although it wasn't hurting, I knew I'd injured it. Then I saw this railway bridge and crawled onto it. I got on the edge, and looked down, and thought, "What am I going to do?" There was a drop of six feet down to the lines below. I started crawling across the tracks in the dark. Then I suddenly heard, "*Woooh!*" I thought, "God! There's a train coming! Where is it? Is it behind, or in front of me?" I looked down the line and thought: "Just keep crawling; if you crawl into it, it's too bad." So I kept dragging myself across the tracks.'

Higgs came across a railway signal and, grabbing hold of the base of it, pulled himself up and began calmly to think out his situation. He hid behind the signal post as a blacked-out train went by and then, making out one of the rail tracks, dragged himself over it, continuing until he came to some spiked railings. Pulling his body over these, he snagged his battledress trousers on a spike. But, heaving himself across the top, he managed to unhook the snag and swung his legs gradually down the other side. Then he let go and fell to the ground.

'I started crawling up a path and began to feel pain in my leg. When I got some distance up the path I saw a light under a door. So I crawled across towards it and thought: "I'd better get some help." There were a couple of steps and I pulled myself up these. I banged on the door, it opened and somebody looked out. I was on the floor. The chap looking out shouted but didn't see me. So I banged again to get his attention. Then he came out, got hold of me and dragged me up the steps – it was the *Gendarmerie*! So that was the end of me! He helped me inside and sat me on a table. I explained I was trying to escape, but couldn't get any help.'

Eventually, at about 01.30 hrs, the *Gendarme* telephoned the Germans. After some time a big German guard appeared, with a huge rifle. He poked Higgs in the chest with it and demanded: "*Wo haben sie bomben?*" ('Where have you bombed?')

> 'There was something strange about him: his ears were big and his lips swollen; I concluded this was probably from frostbite on the Russian Front. Since I didn't speak German, I just sat there trying to figure out what he meant: "*Wo haben sie bomben?*"'

That night Bomber Command had flown a 'split raid', the first one ever, and the whole stream was headed for Munich. But a small force turned off before the target and bombed Saarbrücken at midnight, so the Germans would be caught 'with their pants down': they wouldn't have time to put any Flak up.

> 'My brain was racing. I thought: "If I tell him the wrong target I'll probably still be with him tomorrow and away after that." But, "if I tell him the right target – what will happen?" Then I thought: "if I say Munich – that's a big city, but Saarbrücken is only a little place." (Saarbrücken had an ordnance factory.) So I thought: "I'll say Saarbrücken if I'm going to say anything."'

The guard was drunk, and hit Bill in the chest again: he nearly fell off the table. "*Wo haben sie bomben?*" he repeated. But Higgs was obdurate: "*Nein!* Name; number; rank."

Then the German came at him again, thumping him: '*Nein!*'

The guard loaded his gun, and picked it up. 'I was watching his fingers like mad', Bill recalled. 'He was about to hit me again, so I said, "*Nein!* Name; number; rank!"' Then the German took the safety catch off: 'I saw his finger come round inside the trigger guard,' Bill said, 'and thought: "If he hits me with that now, it'll go off."'

> "Wait!"
> The man laughed at him, again demanding, '*Wo?*'
> "Saarbrücken!"
> "Good!" the guard said in German. "I live in München!"'

It was a lucky choice.

They dragged the 35 Squadron engineer off and slung him in a lorry. He was later put into a cell and left on the floor. Next morning they dragged him out again and put him on another truck, which took him to the *Luftwaffe* station at St. Dizier. The nearest place to where he was shot down was a village named Blense, with only one or two streets. Higgs revisited the site after the war and the French had built a memorial to his crew there, inviting him to the presentation ceremony.

At St. Dizier an English-speaking German inspected his leg, pronounced that the femur was broken and that it would take six weeks to mend. Bill recalled:

'Then I was taken to the guardroom by mistake, and dumped on the floor overnight, on a mattress. A night fighter pilot came in to see me: "I shot you down", he said.
"Good shooting!" I said.
"I saw you fly across the moon", he replied.
'We'd been told in the past, that one could never get through a tour: we were given lectures by [the Intelligence] people who had told us that the German night fighters didn't have radar and that they were directed on to us by controllers who had to pick us up as best they could.'

As Higgs was carried off the lorry towards the guardroom, he had noticed a Bf 110 standing outside, with some nose aerials and big crosses on it. He later commented:

'It had radar![4] That was a morale-booster really, as I knew then why they were hitting us and why we never saw them. [Intelligence had] told us lies – what a waste of time!'[5]

Bill Higgs spent the remainder of the war as a POW in four camps including *Stalag Luft* I and VI. He received the nickname 'Shiner', which he was very proud of, during a boxing match in *Stalag Luft* I Barth, when he was given a black eye. Someone shouted, 'Come on, Shiner' to encourage him, and the name stuck.

L.J. Simpson, pilot, 460 Squadron, 27/28 January 1944, Berlin, Germany

On 28 January 1944 Laurie Simpson's crew was lost returning from a raid on Berlin, one of the final ops of the 'Battle of Berlin'. As mentioned in Chapter Thirteen, the whole crew baled out over the Brittany Peninsula near St. Malo after running out of fuel, as a result of high southerly winds, a holed fuel tank and non-functioning navigational equipment. It was Laurie's first parachute jump, although he had made practice jumps before from a tower. The only crew member with any experience of an operational jump was Alistair Kennedy, who had baled out over Flamborough Head on 17 January 1943.[6] Laurie later recalled: 'We all went out the front hatch, and everybody got out safely.' Laurie had been instructed how to control the parachute by twisting the shroud lines over each other to turn. Once out, he attempted to do this, to try and gain control, but soon realised he was in trouble:

'I did it very vigorously and found myself spinning one way, and then back the other. Of course we weren't very high and, because it was very dark, I couldn't see where the ground was, which came up very quickly: the top of the trees and the ground was almost instantaneous. I found that my 'chute was tangled up in what looked like brambles and, although it was of white silk, it was so dark that I couldn't be sure what they were. I tried to get the 'chute out, but was getting nowhere. I didn't bury it because I couldn't get it free, and it was a big thing, and all the rigging was tangled up in this stuff. So I thought the best thing to do was to leave it. My immediate idea was to get as far away from the spot as possible.

'I was wearing a battledress jacket. I didn't wear leather flying jackets because they were cumbersome and Lancasters weren't really that cold. I didn't feel the need for them. As it was we had Long John underwear. The boys further back might have been colder, but at the front it wasn't too bad. There was enough heat in the aircraft to stop the windscreen icing up inside, anyway.'

'We'd already had talks about evasion and button compasses. I had a map sown into the lining of my flying boots, and a pipe with a compass built into it. We had been warned that the French river water was not "potable" and were issued with a chemical you could put into it, to make it safe. The only rations we had consisted of a bit of chocolate, and some English tea. Unfortunately I could speak very little French, *"Bonjour"* and *"Au revoir"* – that was about it.'

The whole crew jumped out safely to land unharmed in French territory: it must have been around 02.00 hrs. No one was injured, although all seven men were scattered some distance away from each other. Laurie recalled:

'Johnny Rydings found himself suspended in a tree. Arthur Schrock landed in a lake; and I think Colin and Alistair landed on a town. It might have been Dinard, because I'd turned the aircraft south once we thought we were over the Cherbourg Peninsula. We had no idea at all what our chances of getting back to England were.'

My father, as far as I know, never saw either Johnny Osborne or 'Jock' Nairn again after they baled out.[7] In fact, after *Dulag Luft*, they were both sent to *Stalag* 357 at Heydekrug on the Baltic Coast in East Prussia.[8]

We now examine the 'evasion reports' of members of Laurie's crew, prepared after the war for MI9.

Colin McLeod was the 26 year-old navigator (b). He had been in the air force since June 1941. His son described him as 'a man's man… of high ideals and morals', who 'could be tough at times but with a soft heart… who loved his family dearly… He was mostly quiet until something needed saying and he would certainly make himself heard.' Col sprained his ankle when he hit the ground. He buried his 'chute and destroyed his maps and decided to wait until daylight before making off. The next morning he approached some farmers and told them that he had been shot down that night. They gave him a meal, but could not help him further:

'I set off in a southerly direction and reached Plancoet. I hid until dark and then went to another farmhouse and got another meal, but no further help – except an atlas map covering the district of Rennes. At 21.00 hrs I reached the district of Plancquet.'[9]

McLeod walked all that night, making for the railway line to Rennes. At first light he saw a farmhouse. Approaching the farmer he explained that he wanted to go south to Rennes, and then to Paris. The farmer advised him to go by train and volunteered to buy a ticket for him. 'At nine o'clock we left for the railway station,' he recalled, 'and on reaching the village I was promptly stopped by the local policeman.'[10] He was handed over to the *Luftwaffe* at Dinan on 29 January.[11]

Arthur Schrock, the flamboyant character from Townsville, Queensland, wrote a sober account of his own evasion experience:

'[We] baled out in the St. Malo district near Wassea. I landed in a lake and sank both my parachute and harness, and when I reached the bank decided to walk south-west. I walked all that night and at dawn crawled on top of a haystack and slept all the next day. In the morning of 29 January I was in the stack when I was woken by a dog barking over me; then a little boy came across and questioned me. I told him who I was, that I wanted to keep quiet, and he covered me up and went away to fetch his parents.'

The boy's parents took Schrock into their house and gave him a bath, dried his clothes and served him a meal. Five farmers in that area had recently been shot for harbouring airmen, so they did not want him loitering. They then informed him that another of their sons was walking south to [take the train to] Paris, and suggested that he could take Schrock with him. 'We started walking to the station,' he wrote, 'when the *Gendarmerie* stopped us and arrested me.' He was then handed over to the Germans, who took them to Plancoet army barracks, nearby. On 30 January Schrock was escorted by train via Paris to *Dulag Luft*.[12]

Laurie Simpson evaded for longer than either McLeod or Schrock. He was picked up on the morning of 2 February 1944, having been on the run for five days. Years later he would tell his wife that he had never been as scared as when he had to stay at the Lancaster's controls over Brittany whilst the others baled out:

'After landing I stepped over a low hedge and, not being able to see anything, fell down a six-foot drop into a cutting. I thought I'd damaged myself, but hadn't and, probably because it was so unexpected, I fell limply. It wasn't a drainage ditch: I think it was a farm track. So I struck off across country and soon found that the fields were very boggy. I ended up, around about dawn, in the loft of a farm, and slept for an hour or two…'

He spent the night in the loft, having arrived there at about 04.00 hours, and awoke on 29 January at 10.00 hrs.

The following report is a day-by-day account of Laurie's evasion. Entries in italics are based on his MI9 Evasion report of 1945: *Secret Statement by S/Ldr Lorraine Joseph Simpson, D.F.C.*[13] The text in quotation marks is from an interview conducted in 1995.

1st Day: 28 Jan
Laurie spoke to some farmers who gave him something to eat; got a rough idea of his position and made westwards. He walked till about 20.00 hours that night.

1st Night: 29 Jan
He decided to walk along the roads by night. He walked for an hour-and-a-half then came across a road block. He was challenged and dodged into a ditch.

'The next night I was walking along a road and I came to a wire chain-fenced barrier, it looked as if there was some sort of military establishment behind it, because there was a ditch on either side and I heard some people talking in German – I presumed it was German – coming towards a big gate in this enclosure. So I crouched down in a ditch at the side of the road till they'd gone.'

A French civilian followed him and they passed through the barrier together. Laurie tried to pass the barrier again alone, but ran into barbed wire barricades.

'Then I crossed the road and went on to see if I could find a way round this enclosure. But I couldn't. It went on for a long, long way: it might have been an airfield.'

He retraced his steps for a mile, passing Plelan (S.W. of Dinan) and slept in a hayloft.

'I just found the hayloft. I wandered [around] and had to find somewhere to use for cover, if only for a short time. I had to get a bit of warmth. It was the end of January and very cold. January and February are the coldest months in the year [in Western Europe].

2nd Day: 29 Jan

'When I woke up in the morning, I looked out of the loft and could see military vehicles going by [including a soldier in an open-topped Volkswagen] and they were German. I thought at first they were RAF, and thought "Ah, good!" but soon realised that they weren't: [they] just looked too different. Then I knew I was in France. A woman came up the steps: she might have come up to get some straw, but when she saw me, she nearly fell off the ladder.

'The next day I was given an overcoat and a beret [by some French peasants, but they did not seem to want to know anything about him].

'I wanted the loft for the daytime, but soon felt that the people at the farm wanted me to move on. So I did, and went into a very small village called Plelan-le-Petit, into a bar, and ordered a beer – for I had a little bit of French money – and waited to see what would happen. It was like a café. By this time I'd taken off my badges of rank. My flying boots were made so that you could take the top off[14]; so I took these off and they looked like shoes, but it must have been pretty obvious to those people who I was. They seemed to be very suspicious.'

He walked until night fell.

2nd Night: 30 Jan

'The next night I was at the edge of another village and went around behind a house, and found, again, a barn full of hay. So I bunked down there for the night and could hear German soldiers walking home from having a night out on the booze, singing songs and generally making a lot of noise. It was probably around midnight.'

3rd Day: 30 Jan

Laurie went to a house near the hayloft where an old lady gave him some food and drink and an old French Air Force cap which he made into a beret.

'The next day I thought I'd better move away from there before nightfall. So I struck across country, and came to a house on the edge of a village. Then an old lady came out and invited me in. She told me that she had a son in the French Navy, and she made me understand that she didn't speak any more English than I did French. And she gave me an overcoat and a beret, and black coffee [laced] with Calvados: and that warmed me up. Then she gave me something to eat, and [after an hour or so] I cracked off again.'

3rd Night: 31 Jan

That night Simpson found another barn to sleep in and passed an uneventful night.

4th Day: 31 Jan

Next morning he followed a track through some nearby woods for most of the day and at night slept in a haystack.

'I hid up most of the day in a wood. I ended up going in the direction of Rennes, but had difficulty pinpointing exactly where I was.'

At first light he followed a road and soon arrived in the village of Caulnes. He clearly wasn't trying to avoid settlements owing to his need for food.

'About dawn I came to a village. I went into the local Catholic Church and the Priest in the confessional box told me to clear off: he didn't want anything to do with me! So the best thing I could do was to push off.'

4th Night: 1 Feb
That night it was biting cold. He arrived at a house, and went round to the back entrance. An old villager opened the door, invited him, and let him dry himself out in front of a fire. Simpson slept that night again in a hayloft. He ate the food in his escape box, buying some more at a café.

5th Day: 1 Feb
The day broke still and misty. He walked cautiously out of the village in the general direction of Rennes, soon arriving at a large house, which he approached from the rear.

'I went to the edge of the village and I went into this house... through a wall with a gate in it. It was raining by now, and cold, and I wasn't feeling very happy. I didn't have very much money, just what the RAF gave me. All I had were French francs, no German money.'

A man, who was a gardener or a servant, took Simpson into the building and they discussed his position with the owner of the house, who offered to hide him and gave him his overcoat. He suggested that he should go to Paris and that they should ride down on bicycles to a nearby village next morning. They offered him dinner and a bed, so he sat down in front of a big fire, dried his clothes and went to sleep.

'I went into this place that looked like a farm. A chap came out of a farm labourer's quarters, twigged who I was, took me up to the house and they took me in. A man and a woman, middle-aged, gave me breakfast, which was bacon and eggs – and it was good. Then they took me into their sitting room and sat me in front of an open fire to dry out.

'I told these people who I was, and they'd arranged that I should cycle with them to the nearby station. Not the main station, but another, a small station close by. And they gave me the name of a contact in Rennes, the Abbé St. Vincente, a Catholic priest. That was where I *should* have ended up, except the Germans spoilt it by picking me up and taking me away.

'Having been up all night, with not much sleep the preceding nights, and now being warm and comfortable, I fell asleep. I woke up at about 2 a.m. I'd heard the stamping of feet across the floor in the main room, then a party of German soldiers burst in and picked me up.'

The Germans said they knew he was an English pilot, and searched him.

'I don't know whether the couple gave me away: the Germans sort of said they did. The only reason I could think was that we were in a Forbidden Zone, and at that time – it was not very long before D-Day – the Germans were very suspicious about a landing. I think it was 15 or 20 miles from the coast – and you could be shot on sight.

'The *Wehrmacht* took me to a *Luftwaffe* base, where I was put into an empty cell. I wasn't there very long. One or two German officers came to see me; they were quite jovial, but they didn't invite me up to their mess for a drink or anything, and the next day they drove me to Rennes. They took me to the prison there run by the *Wehrmacht*, or whoever did that sort of thing for the German Army. I was then interrogated and they tried to establish who I was.'

In October 1942, largely in response to Allied Commando raids on the Atlantic Coast, such as those at Bruneval and Dieppe, Hitler instituted his 'Commando Decree'. In contravention of the Geneva Convention, this measure declared that any commando units, whether 'soldiers in uniform or demolition parties with, or without weapons, were to be exterminated to the last man in battle… Even should these individuals… make as if to surrender, all quarter was to be denied on principle…' This made things extremely difficult for POWs later in the war, particularly those who landed near the French coast before D-Day, such as Laurie, who were faced with the possibility of being shot as spies. Laurie continued:

> 'A small, brown-shirted guard found a crucifix on me and was ranting and raving – he wasn't at all pleased with the cross, but I didn't know if he was SS or *Wehrmacht*, because the uniform was basically the same in the 'other ranks'. He was a nasty little man. Then I was charged and put on a train to Paris – I don't know whether they knew I was Australian or not, because I didn't have the "Australia" tag on any more.'[15]

Fresnes

Fresnes was an old prison used by the Germans to house captured British SOE agents and members of the French Resistance. It was purpose-built of concrete and steel and four storeys high with its outside walls centred on a hollow rectangle. Conditions were extremely unpleasant and a number of prisoners were tortured and executed there throughout the war. A British navigator, Stan 'Paddy' Hope, was in Fresnes for a number of weeks in 1943 after being picked up by the Germans at a farm near the French Pyrenees with Dedee de Jongh, the main organiser of the 'Comet' evasion line. On 15 January they were almost on the point of crossing the mountains into Spain when they were betrayed by a local farmhand.[16] Initially Hope was imprisoned in Bayonne in the south-west of France. But the officer there was a gentleman, he recalled, despite using 'all sorts of tricks' to get information from prisoners: 'I remember him asking me one time which side of the street I had stayed on and I just sort of said, "I don't know", and waved one hand and he said, "On the right side". Immediately he spotted which hand I had moved. He was very cunning indeed. He could get answers out of you which you didn't even know you had given away.'[17]

Hope made contact with a Frenchman named Jo Reman who was in the cell below him in Fresnes and they spoke through the ventilation shaft. Reman had been imprisoned for sabotage in the German-supervised factory he had worked in. Hope recalled as 'very comforting' news shouted between the cells every evening by fellow prisoners. He met a young Welsh RAF pilot who, whilst evading, by speaking Welsh had pretended to be a foreign worker.

Hope was later sent to the Avenue Foche, the Gestapo HQ in Paris. His experiences there, he stated, were almost 'too painful to recall'. He was transported to a special 'torture place' outside the prison by the Gestapo and threatened with torture. They drove him, handcuffed and blindfolded, between two Frenchmen, whom he described as 'horrible types'. The Gestapo man, he said, was '…a particular brute'.

> 'They told me that they would keep me there overnight and take me down to the cellar below the house and that I would eventually talk.'

Faced with such a prospect, being at a very low ebb, and 'having lied so many times before, and told so many stories', he was unable to take any more and told them where he had received help in Brussels (i.e. where the Comet Line started).

He was then returned to Fresnes and met a German sergeant in charge of the cells who had been on the Russian Front. 'When he found out I was RAF',[18] Paddy recalled, 'he sent me up extra food.' The German sympathised with Paddy because he was a serviceman. The sergeant was also a soldier and had been wounded in Russia and gave Hope extra soup and English books. Paddy occasionally talked to the other prisoners. The German warden 'wasn't too bad', he recalled, but it was the Gestapo who were tough.

Laurie Simpson was in Fresnes for over three weeks. From Rennes, on 5 February 1944, he was taken by train to Paris, via Le Mans. On arrival in the French capital he was taken by car to the outskirts of the city. It was a three-quarter-of-an-hour drive past the *Arc de Triomphe* and through built-up areas. On arrival at Fresnes, as they proceeded through the big main gate, it was half dark. He was forced to take his clothes off, which were put through a big cylindrical steam chamber, and then herded through some hot, steamy showers for delousing. He was allocated a cell in one multi-storey block, measuring eight feet by seven feet, with a lavatory in one corner and a hard bed in the other. The door had a circular spyhole in it, with a small trap, which was movable on the outside. There was space at the end of the bed to stand up, and the flagstones on the floor were very cold, especially in winter as there was no heating.

At the time of his arrival, Simpson's squadron still had no knowledge of his fate. The first that was heard back home was when Dorothy received a telegram. She telephoned 460 Squadron, but the adjutant couldn't believe it, as nothing had yet been heard through official channels. Dorothy remembers vaguely that the message came from a prisoner who had met Laurie in one of the prisons and brought news of his survival with him, possibly after being repatriated.

Laurie remained in solitary confinement for 23 days with no knowledge of what was to happen to him. He always said that his spell in Fresnes was one of the defining moments of his life: he would later point to this experience as an example of overcoming hardship by determination and willpower. Occasionally, when in Fresnes, he was taken for a shave with the French barber, and, like 'Paddy' Hope, made contact with a Frenchman, a man named Henri David who cleaned the lavatories and lived in Nouilly. This human contact was one of the few things that kept my father sane during the early period of his solitary confinement. David brought him a packet of playing cards, a toothbrush and a newspaper. My father wrote to Henri David after the war and received a reply. In the cell next door was a man who identified himself as an American flyer. On one occasion, David brought a message in from him and the two prisoners conversed in Morse Code, tapping on the wall. When the American eventually came into his cell Laurie was washing his feet in a basin and stood up. 'Don't let it get you down', was the Yank's advice on solitary. He was a little man who said he had been shot down over Guernsey. It occurred to Laurie that he may have been a German plant.

Simpson was interrogated on four or five occasions, the first being chiefly to determine who he was. His interrogator was an English-speaking man who had lived in London before the war and said that they knew all about him, reciting the name of his CO and various squadron details.[19] Because he had been picked up in an area within 30 miles of the French coast, the Gestapo was uncertain whether or not Laurie was a flyer or a 'terrorist': although he was a squadron leader, it was not normal for RAF prisoners, even officers, to be sent to an SS prison. The Gestapo wanted to know about RAF tactics in the air, bombing strategy, the defensive capability of the Lancaster etc. One of the interrogators had been on the German ambassador's staff in South Africa and was in Hamburg at the time of the firestorm raids, whilst another was what Laurie later described as a 'buxom blonde'. The variety of his interrogations suggests that the Germans were anxious to get as much information as they could out of him.[20] But on 28 February he was taken by car to the Gare du Nord in Paris and put on an overnight train to Frankfurt.[21]

Jack Whitehouse, wireless operator, 35 (Pathfinder) Squadron, 20 February 1944, Stuttgart, Germany

Sgt Jack Whitehouse was shot down in Halifax II, JP121 TL-U, of 35 (Pathfinder) Squadron during a raid on Stuttgart, having taken off from Graveley in Huntingdonshire at 00.31 hrs. It was the last Merlin-engined Halifax II lost on a major operation over Germany during the war, and the last from 35 Squadron. Six of the crew abandoned the aircraft, baling out. But the Canadian tail gunner, Sgt F.N. Paisley, RCAF, remained on board, surviving the subsequent crash. All lived and became POWs. Whitehouse recalled:

> 'I had dropped into a small valley and I noticed a little higher up, on one side, ran a railway line; a goods train was travelling along it: it stood out quite clearly against the snow. According to the small compass from my escape kit, the line was running south, which meant towards the Swiss border.
>
> 'It was about 04.00 hours; the snow was very cold and very deep. I decided to climb up onto the line with the idea of getting onto a goods truck to make an escape. It took me 20 to 30 minutes to climb up to the line in the thick snow, only to come face to face with a member of the "*Volkssturm*" (Home Guard), who not only had a rifle slung over his shoulder, but a vicious German Shepherd dog straining at the leash. That was sufficient deterrent for me: I had no intention of having myself torn to pieces by an animal.
>
> '"For you, the war is over", he said in broken English. He took me to a small farmhouse down the valley and phoned for transport. The farmer and his wife were kindness itself: I was given a piece of dark brown bread and a cup of milk. The children just glared at me. Then I was taken to Freiburg civic jail, and given some black coffee and black bread. The next day, under armed guard, I was taken by train to Oberursel.'

John Grimer, flight engineer, 77 Squadron, 22 April 1944, Laon, France

P/O John Grimer was shot down in Halifax, LK710 KN-S 'Sugar' on 22 April 1944. His aircraft took off from Elvington at 21.00 hrs on a raid to bomb the railway marshalling yards at Laon. The raid was mounted six weeks before D-Day and was part of Solly Zuckerman's 'Transportation Plan'. One hundred and eighty-one aircraft went out and attacked in two waves, causing a large amount of damage. Nine bombers were lost. LK710 'Sugar' was flying at 7,000 feet when, without warning, she was attacked from below by a night fighter. The pilot, Sqn/Ldr K.F.P. Bond, was killed, and navigator P/O Hobgen quickly captured. The rest evaded. Grimer:

> 'I came to earth and my 'chute caught up in some trees. Looking down, I saw the reflections of stars in water. Imagining I was over a canal, I turned and pressed my quick release, to fall some fifteen feet into a large two-inch deep puddle, almost breaking my back! Only when I attempted to stand did I find my right leg to be shattered below the knee. Such I suppose is the analgesic effect of shock.

'After I had taken my Benzedrine tablets, I applied a tourniquet to my right leg and started to crawl through a small wood, and across several fields, until eventually I reached a local village. I can remember calling out: "*Je suis aviateur Anglais – je suis blessé – aidez moi!*" ("I am an English airman – I am wounded – help me!") But the only responses were a few curses and shouts of "*Taisez vous!*" ("Shut up!") from angrily opened windows.

'Surprised and discouraged, I crawled through the village to the door of a small farmhouse on which I banged repeatedly. It was eventually opened by an old couple who, seeing my plight, helped me in and treated me with utmost kindness. They gave me brandy, hot soup and a bowl of raw eggs. They sat me on a chair with my wounded leg on a stool. I had loosened my tourniquet every half-hour during my crawl – and now did so again. As the blood dripped onto the stone floor one of the farm dogs started to lap it and, I must confess, I retched!

'These good people sent for the local doctor, who bandaged and put a splint on my leg. The doctor said that I might be able to be moved – even walk with crutches – in about six weeks and the elderly couple offered to hide me in their barn until I could be moved to a safer place.

'After two days or so in the barn, in spite of receiving much kindness as well as food, which I could not eat, I was running a very high temperature and was semi-delirious. Accordingly, I asked my hosts to send for the Germans and to tell them that they had just found me in one of their fields. This they did, and a few hours later, two German soldiers with a motorcycle and sidecar arrived to collect me. My hopes of getting to hospital were, however, dashed when, after a painful journey in the jolting sidecar, I was eventually carried into what was obviously a prison, where I was locked in a small cell containing nothing but a wooden board and a bucket with a "peephole" in the door which was opened periodically. To this day I do not know how long I was there – perhaps only hours – perhaps two days. In my lucid moments I can recall hearing French patriotic songs and at one time gunshot volleys as if from a firing squad. You can imagine my despair.

'I have the vague recollection of being taken out in a stretcher later and put into an ambulance. Eventually I was taken to an operating theatre where the German "*Hauptmann Doktor*" saved not only my leg, but possibly my life. I saw this good doctor on several occasions during the next four to five months of my stay in the prison ward of the former First World War American Military Hospital in Rheims.'

Graham Korner, rear gunner, 640 Squadron, 4 November 1944, Bochum, Germany

New Zealander Graham 'Kiwi' Korner baled out during a raid on Bochum in the Ruhr on 4 November 1944 after his Halifax was hit by predicted Flak. The pilot, flight engineer and wireless operator had already been killed:

'I landed in a cobbled farmyard in moonlight. The 'chute came down draping itself across the yard and the main road. I could see a barbed wire fence on the other side of the road, and pulled the 'chute to avoid it and rolled it up. Then I tried to climb up into an open Dutch barn, but couldn't get in. So I took the 'chute and jammed it into a ditch, and put grass over it. I then took my Mae West off and I threw that up into the barn; then shot across the farmyard, went through a hole in the fence and into some fir woods. We had been issued with an Escape Kit, and I got this out to get the compass. All of a sudden I heard footsteps coming along the road, crunching on the gravel. It was dark and I had black silk gloves and an RAF uniform on, but my pullover was navy blue. I stood behind a tree, my hands over my face. A woman came along and walked right past me, then walked into the farmyard where some people were singing – they had a piano accordion going and never knew I was out in the back yard.'

Korner made his way through the forest. Although he wore his 'escape' type flying boots, where the top could be cut off for evaders, he found it hard going. After a time he encountered a canal and, seeing that a tree had fallen across part of it, took a flying leap, landed on the tree and walked across to the other side. He then came to some cabbage fields, traversed these and arrived at a railway embankment. He began to climb it, when a train approached, so he retreated rapidly down the embankment again. The train went past and he crossed back across the railway tracks, ending up in some marshes. By this point he began to grow exasperated with his predicament. Emerging from the marshes, he was walking through some grass, when he heard a shot and, looking up, saw a figure running on the hill above him. He considered afterwards that it must have been the mid-upper gunner, Ron Heath, under pursuit.

'I kept going. I was getting so fed up walking through these fields, when suddenly I came to a road. But I thought it better to walk in the ditch. It was a straight road, surrounded by fir trees all the way to the horizon. You could see hardly anything at all.

'Walking quietly down a verge, I suddenly came upon these huts with signs on them. I looked at them, and was wondering if anyone was in them, when a voice suddenly shouted something like, "*Hoo, hooa, hey, hoo, hoch!*" I turned round and there was this little German with a huge rifle! He was one of the old *Volkssturm*, the Home Guard. I think if I'd upped and run, he wouldn't have known what to do. But he had this bloody great rifle, and was a typical Giles cartoon character with his hat pulled down and he was wearing an enormous greatcoat. He again said, "*Ho, hoo, ho, hoo, hoo!*" So I just said "RAF!" But he kept on… "*Ho, hoo, ho, hoo, ho!*"

'Then he took me into this place which was like a Home Guard hut. There was a picture of Hitler on the wall and the guards were all in there. I was so thirsty I said, "Can I have a drink?"

'They said, "*Trinken?*"

'"No, drink," I said – misunderstanding them, "I want a drink." They gave me some *Ersatz* coffee but it tasted foul. One of them shot off into an end room, and a chap came out looking just like "Wee Willy Winkie"! He had a long white nightshirt on and a red cap with a bobble! He was obviously the senior man, either an officer, or a sergeant, or something, but looking at him I just couldn't believe it! "*Vor you zee var is over, ja?*" he said.

'I said, "So you say."'

The Germans gave Korner a drink and he sat down. They then phoned up a local *Luftwaffe* unit and two Flak officers subsequently arrived to pick him up. They were evidently experienced in dealing with downed flyers, because the first thing they did was turn the top of Korner's boots down, where there was concealed a small knife. They removed this and all his other flying gear. "*Kommen*" they said, escorting him out. One had a bicycle, and the other was on foot, and they walked back very nearly to where Korner had landed, finally arriving at a village police station. Korner was taken inside, and confronted by the old station sergeant, who looked just like von Hindenburg.

'He was miserable! He had a square head with a walrus moustache, and looked fierce. He took everything off me… then read something out – I suppose it was charges for being an enemy alien. Then he said to an old bloke who ran the cells: "Take him down to the cells!"

'The guard, who was a little German policeman, took my pipe off me, which was empty, and I got clumped in this cell. It was just a plain cell with a wooden bench and a hatch in the door. I didn't know how many had got out of our plane. I didn't know what had happened.

I had heard once that a bloke had jumped out of his aircraft and the rest of the crew had gone back home without him.

'The following morning, an air raid siren went off and they took me out and down to a shelter. They parked me in a corner and the local populous came in and looked at me; they hated me, shouting "*Terror Flieger!*" This beautiful girl was down there on the radio. They had a very good air raid warning system in Germany, with radios, and whenever a raid started they would radio ahead which way the attack was going. This passed all the way down the line, and she was obviously in charge of it.'

A day-and-a-half later, a truck rolled up and an SS officer with a black leather coat signed for Korner. 'His teeth were filed to a point and he was a horrible looking bastard', Korner observed. He was put into a lorry with three Germans and driven off. Korner concluded that they were back near the Rhine. Two of the men got out and left him with the third. The two then went across a field and into some trees. They came back carrying a body between them, tied to a spar for support. Korner noticed one was holding what appeared to be a head rolled up in paper. Then they dragged the body up into the van and dumped it there.

'I wanted to look, but didn't like to. Then they drove round to a cemetery, brought a wheelbarrow out, pushed the body into it, dumped the head in, and went off. That was it! It could well have been one of the crew: it might have been old Freddy Nuttall [the wireless op]; I didn't want to look. Then they drove off and when an air raid started, they all jumped out the back and ran off down the road to a shelter. They left me standing in this truck. But then they stopped and looked back. I thought: "What am *I* supposed to do?" and wondered if they were waiting for me to make a bunk for it, so I could be shot trying to escape. I just sat in the back of the truck. I felt sorry for the people who were under the bombing: you could feel the ground shaking…'

Graham Korner was later transported to *Stalag Luft*VII at Bankau on the Polish border.

Henry Wagner, navigator, 51 Squadron, 17 December 1944, Duisburg, Germany

Henry Wagner was shot down on 17 December 1943 by a *Schräge Musik* attack during a raid on Duisburg. It was a night take-off at 02.49 hrs from RAF Snaith, in Halifax III, MH-A 'Apple' NR248. A total of 523 aircraft from three Groups went out including 418 Halifaxes, eight of which were lost. The aircraft had been flying at 14,000 feet. After keeping a fighter at bay, Wagner recalled he heard '…a rapid series of thumps on the starboard wing and almost immediately we were on fire.' As he exited through the Halifax's nose the cord holding the parachute pack straps to his harness broke and the pack ended up above his head, the release ring facing backwards. He hauled the pack down to pull the release ring – doing all this behind his head. Suddenly the 'chute opened with a tremendous jerk. 'After a few seconds there was an enormous flash as the Halifax blew up', he said. 'I couldn't tell if anyone else had escaped.' The remainder of the crew were all killed. Wagner:

Henry Wagner (Wagner)

'One of the advantages of being the navigator was that I had a pretty good idea of where we were. I knew we were over the British side of the lines, but knew also that there was a strong westerly wind which would probably carry me back inside Germany. If you take an average wind speed on the way down of 80 mph, I was going to drift some 20 miles. It was about 6.30 a.m. and still dark – perhaps just a hint of daylight – *"dawn's left hand was in the sky"* [Omar Khayyám] – so I could not see where I was going to land and, in fact, plunged down through the branches of a tree and hit the ground. The advice was that, when you landed, you were supposed to roll your parachute up and hide it. I realised that this was not on as it was draped over the tree; furthermore it was an apple tree in the back garden of a house, and the curtains in one of the bedroom windows parted and a face peered out. So I took off my life jacket, dumped it, and went down the side path and out of the front gate. Turning left, I heard the sound of marching feet approaching, so I turned right, and in a few minutes was out of the village and in open country.

'It was now getting light and the thing to do was to find concealment wherein to lie up for the day. Soon I found a wood of fir trees and took refuge. First, judging from the sound of gunfire from the west, I knew I was in Germany. Then I examined the contents of my evasion pack. This was a flattish plastic box, slightly curved to fit inside the thigh pocket of a flying suit. It contained a map on silk, razor, rubber water bottle with a packet of Halazone water purifying tablets, energy tablets, Horlicks tablets, barley sugar, and chewing gum, also a small compass of about 1-inch diameter. Also there was a small slab of nut toffee.'

The man responsible for designing much of the RAF evasion equipment was Charles Fraser-Smith. One of Fraser-Smith's particular inventions, a hollowed-out lead pencil, had the lead partially removed and replaced by a slim metal ferrule in to which a minute compass was slipped. Also contained in the pencil was a tiny rolled-up cloth evasion map. Fraser-Smith's inventions were largely manufactured by a factory in Keswick, in the English Lake District. The gadgets were so high on the 'secret list' that, of the thousands of workers employed, only six of the management staff knew of the actual contents of the device, and they were responsible for inserting these after the rest of the factory had retired at the end of the day. Wagner:

'My clothes were by this time wet through and it was cold as well, so I did not have a comfortable day. I set off walking south as soon as it was dark, keeping clear of the roads and going across country...

'It was a bad time of year for evasion, there being nothing in the fields in the way of berries, fruit or vegetables. I drank from streams or troughs, using the water bottle and purifying tablets. I set off at dusk and walked until about 4 a.m. I came across a barn and stepped inside.

'At daybreak I saw what appeared to be a dilapidated farmhouse, and I approached with the intention of sleeping there. A middle-aged woman came out and must have recognised me for what I was. I followed her inside and she indicated I was to sit at the table. She gave me a few small apples, two slices of bread, and two cups of coffee. It was now broad daylight so, after leaving, there was not time to look for a good place of concealment; the best I could do was a copse with wet brambles in it. So I hid up there for the day, although only half a mile from the farmhouse.

'I decided it was no use going south, the distance to the lines being too great, so I turned back north towards Holland. The reasoning was this: there was no way of getting through the lines by going due west – the river Rhine was in the way, and that would be well guarded. However the British advance northwards into Holland had been very rapid, and looked like continuing. So I thought I would head north-west, around the corner in the lines, and either hide up or fall in with the Dutch Resistance until the fighting moved further north.

'That night, 21 December, it rained hard again. Towards dawn I wandered about looking for somewhere to sleep. I stayed for a while in a shed beside the road, then it stopped raining, so I carried on for another three miles. I found a stack of loose straw, so I dug some out and made a cubbyhole, climbed in and went to sleep. I got out at dark, put on my flying suit and set out again. That night it froze, and my flying suit, being wet, froze stiff and the zips would not work, so I could not get out my ration pack, and suffered pains from cramp again. I then walked all night, breaking ice on puddles to drink from.'

By this time, for various reasons, Wagner was becoming light in the head and not thinking clearly. He came to a railway embankment and, climbing up, thought that the easiest thing to do would be to simply walk along the line until he came to a station. At that point, he could 'get a train home'. He walked along the track for 20 minutes, but seeing the lights of a station ahead and hearing voices brought him to his senses, so he got down off the track and pushed on. At daylight he bedded down in a partly cut wood of fir trees as American bombers passed overhead, and pressed on again that night. Then he met his undoing:

'Without thinking what I was doing, I went through a village instead of skirting around it as usual. At the far end there was the click of a rifle bolt and a voice called out, "*Halt! Wer da?*" So I knew that was the end of my run. "*Englische Flieger*", I said, and the reply came: "*Hande hoch!*" I had run into a sentry post. The soldier approached and indicated with his rifle that I should go into the post, which was a dugout about ten feet square, entered by going down some steps. In it there was a table, a chair, and a bench. It was heated by a wood burning stove and lit by a pressure lamp.'

The sentry, an older man, possibly a reservist, appeared well meaning and not one to make life difficult; he did not seem to want any trouble and Wagner was in no state to give him any. He patted the chest of his flying suit: '*Ich habe hier eine kanone.*' ('I have here a gun.')

The man indicated that he should put the gun on the table, meanwhile watching Wagner closely and gesturing that anything else in his pockets should be brought out: 'After that the atmosphere became less strained, and he provided me with a bowl of soup.'

The next morning, Christmas Eve, the guard's relief arrived and, being apprised of the situation, he went to fetch help. Wagner was then escorted for 8 km by two guards to a fighter aerodrome at Alpen. In the officers' mess he was asked all sorts of questions by the *Luftwaffe* staff, but not of an operational nature. None of them spoke English but, having been educated in France, Wagner conversed with one in French. The German was an experienced aviator and translated for his comrades: he asked how many times Wagner had been over Germany. 'Eight', he replied. That was nothing, the German scoffed: *he* had been over *London* 66 times. Wagner's flying gear and the contents of his evasion pack also interested them. 'They gave me some of their dinner,' Wagner recalled, 'which was a sort of spaghetti bolognaise, but I was shunted aside into an alcove to eat it on my own.'

He was then handed over to the Military Police and made to sit on a stool in the middle of a room, watched over by a hostile policeman with a rifle. 'After several hours of this, my back ached, so I moved the stool against the wall, but an outburst of rifle-waving indicated I should stay where I was put.' Wagner was then taken down to a cellar and locked in. It was warm and he slept until the following morning, Christmas Day.

He left Alpen the next day with a guard and was walked 5 kilometres, before picking up a lift to the nearest railway station. From there they made their way gradually to Oberursel. Occasionally, Wagner was accosted by noisy crowds, shouting '*Terror Flieger!*' He would spend the remainder of the war in *Stalag Luft* VII.

Sid Duplock, mid-upper gunner, 227 Squadron, 22 February 1945, Gravenhorst, Germany

Sidney A.F. Duplock,[22] who flew 28 ops as a mid-upper gunner with 50 and 227 Squadrons, had a remarkable experience towards the end of the war. He was shot down on 22 February 1945 during a raid on the Mitteland Canal in Lancaster PB690, SJ-V, after taking off from Balderton, Nottinghamshire at 17.29 hrs. His aircraft had been attacked by a *Schräge Musik*-equipped Bf 110. All the crew baled out: five became POWs and the pilot, Flt/Lt J.B. Osborne, and navigator, Flt/Sgt T.O. Kidd, evaded.

Duplock later thought that his capture was the best thing that could have happened to him:

'I jumped out at 1000 feet into a reforestation centre and my 'chute got caught up in a tree. I ran with one foot in an irrigation channel full of water, and jumped over a stream, after filling my water bottle, then climbed over a barbed wire fence, laid on wet ground and went to sleep. I was awakened by the noise of aircraft overhead, looked out of the bush [I was in] and saw a number of Ju 88s: I had climbed onto a German airfield.'

Two *Wehrmacht* soldiers with a large dog arrived and took Duplock to a farmhouse where a Lancaster had pancaked on the roof. They gave him a shovel and told him to search for dead bodies; he found two. He was then taken to the local town hall and interrogated by a young lady who asked him why the RAF was bombing Germany.

'So I asked "Why did you bomb Britain?" She seemed surprised, and also asked why I showed no emotion when I dug up the dead bodies. I told her I had dug up dead bodies and identified them when the Germans had bombed Britain. I said I was 15 years-old at the time. I was taken to cells in a basement and given a meal of red cabbage, potato and meat sauce. I complained about the food and was told that they had given up a meal to feed me.'

He was removed to a lunatic asylum and locked in a cell with the American pilot of a Douglas Boston bomber; then, after two days, the door opened and a wing commander walked in covered with medals, including a DSO and Bar. The man was not happy as he had led his wing to aid some USAAF Mustangs in a combat engagement and one of them had shot him down in an act of 'friendly fire'. The asylum was located close to a German airfield and they could see the outside through a small clerestory window. On one occasion they saw a *Luftwaffe* aircraft shot down as it came in to land, a sight not appreciated by the guards. On the way to Frankfurt they were strafed by American P-47 Thunderbolts and the whole party had to take cover. After interrogation at *Dulag Luft*, Duplock was taken with his rear gunner, R.W. Sheen, and bomb-aimer, R.A. Scutt, to a *Stalag Luft* outside Nuremberg,[23] but with the approach of the advancing Allies, they were marched out a few weeks later, and almost immediately they were, again, strafed by Thunderbolts. The small party marched on, travelling by train in cattle trucks:

'We were walking towards Munich one night and sleeping in a hayloft when I experienced terrible stomach pains. I managed to get out of the barn and was sick and had diarrhoea. After two or three days I could hardly walk, but knew that I dare not stop. Suddenly, a German staff car pulled up and a major got out: he said he was a doctor and would examine me. He concluded that I had appendicitis and would arrange for a good night's rest for me, and would pick me up next day and get some help.

'The major took me to a convent where the nuns put me to bed: I must have looked and smelled terrible. The next morning the major returned and took me to a POW camp where they had an operating theatre staffed by POWs. I was operated on by a British surgeon who, in exchange for penicillin, had been allowed to parachute into the camp, to operate on wounded POWs.'

After the operation the surgeon asked Duplock if he did a lot of swimming as he had a very large lung capacity. Duplock confirmed this and was told that the appendicitis had developed into peritonitis, and at the point the surgeon had started to operate, Duplock had only about 30 minutes left to live. He was injected by a Polish nurse with penicillin every three hours: the nurse apologised every time because the needle was blunt.

Later the camp was liberated by Patton's US Third Army and Duplock was taken for a few days to a US Army field hospital. The British surgeon and staff there shook hands with him before he left for his next hospital, another American establishment, where he noticed that a French doctor smoked every time he cleaned his wound. When asked why, the physician replied 'Because of the smell!'

Duplock was flown by a DC 3 air ambulance to a US airbase in the UK, arriving on 7 April 1945,[24] just before VE Day.

• • •

The evasion experiences suffered by the aircrew described in this chapter are remarkable for their variety. The fact that men could survive in such extreme conditions, often having had no previous experience of being 'on the run' in hostile territory, or of having to fend for themselves alone, when 'all men's hands were turned against them', is equally extraordinary and a testimony to the grit and determination they exhibited, despite their situation appearing to be, superficially, hopeless. However the privations of these experiences and the airmen's eventual arrests were frequently to prove but a foretaste of what was to come.

Part Five

THE CAMPS

'We found that it was up to the individual to develop tolerance, restraint, and to keep unruffled in the most trying circumstances. To a great extent this was accomplished despite the fact that the course of events did not always run smoothly.'

L.J. SIMPSON, RAAF, POW

'Living in a room with other men day in, day out was absolute hell. We argued, we had spasms of hating each other almost, and being placed in the Cooler was almost like a holiday.'

A.W. COLE, RAF, POW

CHAPTER EIGHTEEN

'I TOLD YOU IT WASN'T A SPITFIRE'

Dulag Luft

'On arrival at Frankfurt, the guards told us that there had been an air raid the previous night and as we walked across the station forecourt, we were harassed by some of the crowd. There was a rope with a noose at one end, slung over the station clock. The guards drew their pistols, surrounded us and led us to safety in a basement room. On our way to Oberursel station we saw seven US aircrew hanging from a tree by their necks.'[1]

THIS was the kind of brutal treatment that many shot-down Allied airmen, upon their arrival in Germany, narrowly avoided. The *Luftwaffe* was determined to obtain as much information as it could from its prisoners in order to know the strategy and tactics that Bomber Command was using, and would use, to attack German cities and industry. This would enable it to plan more thoroughly any countermeasures and predict how future operations would develop.

As the bomber war escalated and techniques became more sophisticated, so the need for new information increased. Consequently the *Luftwaffe* set up its own interrogation centre and transit camp at Oberursel, just outside Frankfurt-am-Main at the foot of the Taunus Mountains, and called it '*Dulag Luft*',[2] a name that became synonymous amongst Allied airmen with extreme techniques of cross-examination. *Dulag Luft* was where all shot-down aircrew went for questioning. Every time a new airman was picked up he had to be interrogated and his details recorded before he was sent to a prison camp. Following the commencement of Operation *Barbarossa*, the German invasion of Soviet Russia, a second interrogation camp was established in the East but, until that time, *Dulag Luft* Oberursel was the sole *Luftwaffe* interrogation centre. My father wrote a report for MI9 after the war that commented upon Oberursel:

'*It was divided into two sections, 1) The Interrogation Camp just outside Frankfurt at Oberursel and 2) the Transit Camp in Frankfurt itself.*'[3]

The German authorities had to find space for their new internees. They also had to transport them from various parts of Europe to the interrogation centre, during which time their safety was frequently threatened. The CO of *Dulag Luft* in 1940 was Harry ('Wings' or 'Pricky') Day, who had served as a Royal Marine in the First World War before transferring to flying duties with the RAF. He led the 1931 Hendon Air Display Team with Douglas Bader, was chief flying instructor at Netheravon, and had been shot down on a reconnaissance mission in a Blenheim of 57 Squadron during the 'Phoney War'.[4] Soon after his arrival, Day became responsible for all incoming Allied prisoners. John Leakey, the Hampden wireless operator who passed through the centre in August 1940, recalled: 'I don't think at this stage of the war the Germans were so aggressive as they were later towards RAF prisoners. To them, the war would soon be over and in their favour.'[5]

The behaviour of the British permanent staff at Oberursel, which was responsible for the administration and general care of the British prisoners, convinced many incoming POWs that they were soft-soaping the Germans and collaborating with them. This caused much trouble for Day and his staff until two British officers, who were vetting the establishment covertly, informed MI9 that this was incorrect. Day actually had more considered intentions.

Harry Day's opposite number at *Dulag Luft* was Theodore Rumpel, who had flown fighters in the First World War in the 'Richthofen Circus' with Göring. After the war he became a *Major* in the *Luftwaffe* Intelligence Service, accepting the job at *Dulag Luft* after previously making many British business friends whilst working in the Far East.[6] Day cultivated an especially amicable relationship with Rumpel in order to enable the British to devise a way of escaping from the camp. On Day's permanent staff was Flying Officer Mike Casey,[7] who had been in Spangenberg Castle[8] with him in 1939, and who was shot after the 'Great Escape'. Another was Major John Dodge, DSO, DFC, nicknamed (inevitably) 'The Artful Dodger'. A relation by marriage of Winston Churchill, he had served at Gallipoli in 1915 and in the Battle of France in 1940, but was captured by the *Wehrmacht*. He escaped and was then recaptured by the *Luftwaffe*.

One of the first POWs to make a successful escape from Oberursel was Roger Bushell, a squadron leader and former CO of 92 Squadron, who was shot down on 23 May 1940 at the time of the Dunkirk evacuation. Bushell was a natural leader, a first-class German speaker and a qualified barrister, and he turned all these abilities to his advantage as soon as he arrived at the camp.[9] Bushell was part of Day's staff from the early days in 1940, when the Germans had as much to learn about finding tunnels as the British had about digging them. His first escape was ignominious; an incongruous exit that occurred the night before a major tunnel was due to break out. He had been made 'head of escape, security and supply' in the camp, and was enthusiastic about tunnelling, with a natural talent for detecting useful information from the Germans. A week before the main tunnel was due to break, Bushell told Day he had a simpler plan. Adjacent to the camp was a field where POWs exercised, in which a goat lived in an old brick shed, and Bushell hoped to conceal himself in the shed the afternoon before the breakout, then go over the wire that night. He exited the shed shortly after evening roll call on the day appointed and, the next night, whilst a diversion was being organised, the tunnellers broke out of the tunnel and escaped: all of these men were recaptured, only two making it further than 20 miles from the camp.

Bushell, who went out earlier, got as far as the Swiss border. When passing through a small village within yards of the frontier he was accosted by a guard, and tried to bluff his way across by impersonating a drunken skiing instructor.[10] The guard almost believed him, but Bushell bolted when asked to go to the local police station, became trapped in a cul-de-sac and was arrested. With Day, however, he would go on to greater things.

One consequence of the air war increasing in intensity, and one which affected the *Luftwaffe* adversely, was that the number of downed aircrew grew exponentially with each aircraft shot down. Every USAAF B-17 added 10 POWs to the bag and every Lancaster, seven. By December 1943 1,000 prisoners per month were passing through Oberursel, a number that doubled by December 1944, and the Germans had to find space for them. In mid-1943 there were 128 cells in the isolation block and by the end of the year, three whole new wings had been added, one with 24 cells. In the new basement, a POW reception room, a strip-search room, and additional interrogation cells, in the area known as 'The Snake Pit', were added.[11]

Many airmen reported being greeted by extremely hostile crowds when they arrived in Germany. After his arrest, Dick Raymond, the 83 Squadron flight engineer, was taken by train down the Rhine Valley to Oberursel. But for the circumstances, it would have been an enjoyable journey:

'On arriving at Frankfurt, we discovered that the city had been bombed the previous night. We received, quite understandably, a rough reception, bearing in mind that we were still wearing flying clothing. They were trying to hit us with anything they could lay their hands on. The German guards kept them off, and we boarded another train to take us to the interrogation centre at Westlaw. Once again luck was on our side: as there were so many British and Americans arriving, the Germans were swamped, so it was only the odd unlucky ones that got the full treatment, and we were not amongst them.'

Laurie Simpson arrived at Frankfurt on the last day of February 1944. When he dismounted from his train, two guards accompanied him. However, a crowd on the platform gathered, screaming '*Terror Flieger!*'; one old man got more and more worked up, and waved his fists and spat. 'There seemed to be hundreds, but there was probably only a dozen', he recalled. Engineer Reg Cleaver also remembered being threatened by German civilians: 'When we arrived in Germany we had to change trains. While we were standing on the platform waiting, I became aware of some people pointing at me and a crowd starting to gather, shouting '*Luftgangster!*' and '*Terror Flieger!*'. At this, the German guards closed tightly around me with their pistols drawn. I was very glad of their company, or I would have been dangling by the neck from the nearest lamp post.'

It was only the protection of the guards that prevented anything more serious happening to Graham Korner:

'They took us down to Dusseldorf railway station, and led us downstairs telling us to stick together. "Keep together," a chap said, "because last week they got hold of 52 aircrew here and hung them up on lamp posts!"

'Underneath the railway station were huge, extremely deep, air raid shelters; and they led us down and into a room – it must have been about 10-foot square: we were packed in with only enough room to stand side-by-side, but there was a gap above the steel door. They slammed this shut and that was it! We're standing packed in there and we could hear a woman outside – obviously remonstrating with a guard. One of the Yanks, a first generation American named Schultz, could speak fluent German: "God damn!" he said, "She's trying to get his rifle off him! She's trying to shoot through the door!" So we all pushed away from the entrance. That went on for quite a time, and then finally the door opened and we found the guards had rounded up all the servicemen they could find: *Luftwaffe, Wehrmacht, Kriegsmarine,* everybody. They'd made a corridor for us to get through, and were holding the crowds back – who were trying to have a go at us with umbrellas and briefcases! Cripes! Did we shoot through there!'[12]

Henry Wagner arrived at Oberursel after a 'bitterly cold' train trip. 'Civilians sitting opposite were much interested in the nature and quality of my flying gear,' he recalled, 'especially my boots.' On the platform at Düsseldorf, however, he had noticed 'a rat-faced little man going from person to person, talking to them and indicating at me with a nod of his head. A few people started drifting in my direction, and I didn't like the look of things at all.' Wagner's guard, observing this, unshouldered his rifle and they soon lost interest.

George Cross, a Mosquito intruder pilot with 23 Squadron, had been shot down on his 41st operation during which he had attacked a Flak train and came out second best. In the afternoon prior to their take-off Cross and his navigator, 'Jock' Irvine, flew a quick test flight and realised that something was wrong with their parachutes. Irvine's 'quick release was sticking, but he decided to carry on with it as it was', recalled Cross. 'My 'chute had been impounded [by the station parachute department], but as our sergeant fitter cycled over a mile to my quarters that morning and got me out of my bed to tell me, I borrowed one, and was OK.' During the attack, after the port wing caught fire and the elevator was left flapping, Cross baled out at 500 feet. But Irvine, whom he later described as 'the best friend I ever had', having a faulty parachute, did not get out and was killed.

Cross was on the run for two days. After being picked up he was escorted to Oberursel:

'We arrived in Frankfurt about 10 o'clock. In the full moon I could see fairly well, and the RAF had really been on the mark. Brunswick and Hannover had not been nearly so damaged as this town had. The amount of damage was astounding and I felt sorry for the civilians for all they must have gone through in, and after the raids – but then I remembered Coventry, Bath and a few other British cities and I realised that the Germans had brought this on themselves. I was told later that 30,000 people had been killed in one recent heavy raid on Frankfurt. When we got off the train, the guard took me to a railway enquiry bureau staffed by German Red Cross nurses. From here we went back to the platforms. Then we left for Oberursel.'[13]

Deryck Lambert, a navigator with 35 Squadron, had a very pragmatic recollection of his captivity: 'When we were transferred by train to *Dulag Luft*, I got kicked up the arse by an officer for refusing to carry his suitcase for him. I thought, "It's no good protesting here, they've got the upper hand": I had to do what I was told.'[14]

Arthur Cole:

'There must have been a lot of aircrew who had been shot down at that time, because I was taken to a solitary barrack hut surrounded by barbed wire, and was soon in a room with a number of other people. I don't think we talked to each other much because we were all suspicious of the place being wired for microphones and so on. I don't remember if we were given any food. I was there for about ten days. If we needed a toilet we hammered on the door and the guard escorted us down to a room with a bucket in it in a different part of the block. I remember that there were Americans there because one of them was constantly laughing in a loud voice.'[15]

The initial impression that a non-commissioned American airman, R. Livingstone, had of *Dulag Luft* when he arrived at the end of April 1943, was comical, despite the misery of the circumstances: the first sight that greeted him was a sign over the main gate stating: '*I told you it wasn't a Spitfire!*' Bob Kendall was picked up on 12 September

1944 – the same day that he had baled out over Mannheim. He entered *Dulag Luft* shortly afterwards:

> 'I arrived there in the evening and was put in a cell which already contained nine American airmen. We each had a wooden chair to sit on and there was just about room for the ten of us. The heating was turned up and we sat there all night sweating profusely. The next morning we were taken out singly to interrogation.'

Henry Wagner had all his flying gear, except his boots, confiscated when he arrived. He was 'shoved into a cell' measuring some eight foot by four foot. Along one wall was a bench with a blanket, also a small, high, barred window and, in the ceiling, a light which never went out. The radiator below the window came on during the day but was turned off at night. Wagner found it hard to sleep because of the cold and 'to make matters worse', his footwear was taken away.

In his report for MI9, Laurie Simpson described the design of the prison huts: '*At the Interrogation Camp*', he wrote, '*there were a number of wooden huts divided into small cells, size 8 ft x 5 ft. The lavatories were inside the hut and on a sewer system.*' Henry Wagner gave a detailed description of the processes for going to the toilet:

> 'There was a spyhole in the door, and beside the door, a handle, which caused a signal arm to clang down in the corridor outside; this brought a guard, who escorted one back and forth. Outside each cell was a box containing toilet paper. The first time I took two sheets, but it was made very plain to me that the standard ration was just one: hard luck on anyone who happened to be suffering from a common prisoner of war complaint known as the "squitters" or "screamers".'[16]

Derek Hodgkinson, the Coastal Command pilot based at Silloth shot down on the second Thousand-Bomber raid, recalled one annoying feature of his cell at *Dulag Luft* in 1942:

> '...the window was at a reasonable level, and I could look out at the barbed wire about twenty yards away and the slopes of the ridge beyond. There were some buildings on the opposite side of a road that ran between the base of the ridge and the Camp, and one of them had a clock tower. The clock struck four as I looked at it. I was to discover, as the day went on, that it had the charming, and to me novel, ability to strike the exact time every quarter of an hour; at a quarter past four it gave four strokes, followed after a pause by one; at half past, four followed by two, and at a quarter to five, four followed by three. As I lay awake that night it nearly drove me round the bend.'[17]

Laurie Simpson gave an account of the rations prisoners received: '*We were fed twice a day; morning and afternoon. The early meal consisted of two slices of black bread, one spread with either Ersatz margarine or jam. The late meal was a bowl of hot, indescribable soup and a slice of bread. In the morning we had a jar, kept permanently in the cell, filled with not very warm, weak coffee.*'

The German interrogation team developed a very refined procedure for destroying, in the shortest possible time, the mental resistance of a prisoner. '*The average stay in these cells*', Laurie Simpson wrote, '*was usually three to five days.*' Henry Wagner: '...the object of this solitary confinement, without seeing anyone else and with absolutely nothing to do, was a sort of weakening-up process, to make one more willing to talk when the time came for interrogation. It didn't bother me a lot though, as I have always been somewhat solitary by nature.'

From lectures and films shown by their squadron Intelligence Officers many men knew almost exactly what to expect from the interrogators. Consequently several RAF aircrew acted during their interrogation like the actors they had seen in films back in England. It was obvious that the Gestapo could extract the information they wanted no matter how hard men tried to resist, but *Dulag Luft* was run by the *Luftwaffe* and '…between Göring's *Luftwaffe* and Himmler's Gestapo there existed a professional jealousy that bordered on ill-feeling'.[18] The *Luftwaffe* was thus not averse to treating prisoners according to the Geneva Convention within reasonable limits, but the interrogators overlooked nothing. A record of each interview was minutely examined by staff afterwards and the prisoner's 'likes, dislikes, habits and powers of resistance' were determined by a meticulous psychological study.[19] If an airman could not be persuaded to collaborate, he was treated with care and respect, but still had to suffer long periods of isolation. Bomber Command personnel received the attentions of a pre-war Professor of Medieval Literature at Heidelberg University, Burt Nagel; *Hauptmann* Waldschmitt, a Professor of Indiology at the University of Göttingen; or *Leutnant* Ulrich Haussmann, another English-speaking interrogator. But one of the most successful of all these interrogators was a man who was non-commissioned: *Obergefreiter* (Corporal) Hanns Scharff.

Hanns Scharff

Many men who were questioned by Scharff later stated that they could not believe that he was only a corporal. His father had been wounded in the First World War and Scharff gradually worked his way up until he became the most respected interrogator in the camp. Although of only lowly rank, he succeeded, by his subtle interviewing techniques, in deceiving many POWs into thinking that he was an officer. He would wear a grey suit rather than a uniform, thus further deluding his subjects into treating him with respect. Indeed, these subtle techniques made him one of the most successful of all the German interrogators. He concentrated mainly on American fighter pilots, and later confessed that he used a fairly simple technique to extract information. He would spend hours telling his subjects things about themselves and their unit, all factual. In many cases this could be quite off-putting for an airman. His aim was to convince the prisoner that the Germans' information was so complete, that nothing they could tell him would be news. It was thus essential that the subject should be put at ease to prevent any possibility of him 'clamming up'.[20] One simple technique Scharff employed was to place a photograph of a well-known pilot in the interview room. Pointing this out, he might remark, 'Isn't that a swell photo of Hubert Zemke?' Whereupon the subject may reply, 'No, that's Frances Zabreski.' Thus, when these well-known pilots were eventually captured, Scharff would immediately recognise them.

In retaliation, Allied aircrew in England were briefed in advance by their Intelligence staff on the Germans' interrogation techniques.[21] Repatriated or escaped POWs would give advice to MI9 and identify specific individuals on the *Dulag Luft* staff. The standard prisoner's response was to divulge nothing other than name, rank and number.[22] Scharff, however, would ask his subjects to question the worth of this, particularly if the POW had been aided by an escape line and was arrested in civilian clothes. The 'holy trinity' would not prove he was a combatant; he may be shot as a spy or German deserter.[23]

Bert Carter, a flight engineer with 44 Squadron, recalled that his squadron's Intelligence Officer had warned them of *Dulag Luft* and its staff's methods of obtaining information.

'When we arrived at the camp, we were locked in a large cell together, in the hope that we may mention our squadron details or anything else that would have been of use to the Germans, who would be listening to us from hidden microphones in the cell. But they were unlucky as we had been warned about this trick, and also about the bogus Red Cross forms they used. The guards monitoring our talk finally got fed up with our guarded conversation and took us off to be searched again. This time the camp staff carried out a thorough search. We had to strip naked and stand on a stool, so that every part of our body could be inspected for hidden escape aids.'

Carter was cross-examined by two interrogators:

'When I was first questioned there were two interrogation officers: one ranted and raved, calling me a spy, as I had no badges or stripes on my battledress… I would be shot etc. The other played the good guy; they took it in turns to question me. "Of course we know all about you and your crew" they said, which rather surprised me. I thought he was bluffing, until he said, "You are from 44 (Rhodesia) Squadron." I could only guess the Germans had obtained our squadron number from the letters on the side of our crashed aircraft…

'Then the ranting and shouting officer left the room and the guards were still standing by the door. The remaining officer told me to sit down; there was a chair in front of his desk. He offered me an English cigarette and then went to a large bookcase, which nearly filled one wall of the room. He took down a thick, heavy volume, and I saw the 44 (Rhodesia) Squadron crest on the outside of the front cover. He read things out about our squadron that I was not aware of and also the names of different aircrew in it. His knowledge of our squadron and its past happenings was far greater than mine. He was still trying to gain information, so I blew my nose and it started to bleed again. I suppose he didn't fancy my blood dripping onto the floor of his office, so he told the guards to take me back to my cell.'[24]

The Bogus Red Cross Form

At *Dulag Luft* POWs were subjected to a variety of interrogation techniques, many of which they had been informed about previously by RAF Intelligence. But still some fell foul of them. Two such examples were a counterfeit Red Cross form, and a priest who turned out to be a German. Bert Carter:

'I think I was questioned about six times; sometimes in my cell and sometimes elsewhere. The bogus Red Cross form duly arrived but I only filled in my name, rank and number and left the remaining questions unanswered.'

Jack Whitehouse, a wireless op with 35 Squadron, also had to strip semi-naked and sign the form. He remembered arriving under armed guard:

'I was put in a single cell, stripped of my clothing, with the exception of my underpants, vest and socks. I was then interrogated by an English-speaking *Luftwaffe* officer, who gave me the Red Cross form. I refused to write down anything, and gave only my name, rank and number. I was amazed when the man then proceeded to give me information about my squadron, type of aircraft, squadron commander etc. My uniform clothes were returned to me and the small compass I had hidden in my blouse top buttonhole was still there – thanks to German thoroughness!'[25]

Derek Hodgkinson also encountered both the fake Red Cross form and its presenter:

'…an hour after the morning meal a civilian was let into the cell and announced that he was from the Red Cross. He spoke, behaved and dressed as if he was an Englishman, and I believed that he was. He said that he was based in Geneva and that his job was to look after the interests of prisoners and to see that they were correctly treated. First, it was necessary to let my relatives and my Commanding Officer know that I was safe; "would I please fill in this form?" He gave me a pencil and, all without suspicion, I began to fill in the answers to various questions. Name, Rank, Number – I filled them in. Name and address of next of kin – without thinking I filled in my wife's name and address. Then I saw the questions that followed: unit, station, command, aircraft flown and more of that ilk – and realised that all was not as it should be. I asked him why he wanted to know the answers to questions such as these which could only be of interest to the Germans. His answer was sickeningly plausible. It was all, he said purely routine and, of course, entirely confidential to the Red Cross. How, he asked, were they to let my CO know I was safe if they did not know where to write to? I said, nevertheless I was not prepared to answer any more questions on the form.

'This obviously riled him. He snatched the form away from me and made as if to leave. I asked him not to be in such a hurry; since he represented the Red Cross, there were some questions I wanted to ask him. I told him about Vic Cave and what I thought had happened to the rest of my crew and asked if he could find out anything about them. He said he would see what he could do and then left the room. It was all pretty unsatisfactory, and I kicked myself for being such an ass as to go further than Name, Rank and Number when I gave my wife's particulars.'[26]

Arthur Cole was similarly bemused by the interrogators' subterfuge::

'I was given a Red Cross form before I was interrogated. One look at it was enough to persuade me that it was something I shouldn't go very far with, because it started with my name, rank and number, and I think the next question was the number of my squadron. Well, that was a step too far… bomb load and so on followed, but I only scanned it. So I filled in my name, rank and number and then made a mistake: I was asked to sign the form, and at the same time a form purporting to be signed by a group captain was shoved under my nose, so I signed the form, which of course left the Germans the opportunity to fill in the whole thing. But then I suppose they must have had plenty of forms to do this so I don't really feel very guilty about it.

'I was then sat in front of a desk. Behind it was a chap wearing an Intelligence Officer's uniform. He spoke good English. I don't think I'd heard about this kind of interrogation before. I accepted a cigarette. I proceeded to ask the meaning of all his badges and his epaulettes and his rank, and all sorts… anything I could think of. When I eventually ran out of steam, he started to ask me questions and I said, "I can only give my name, rank and number…" – which I duly did; I then said, "I can't answer any further questions." Whereupon he got a bit irate, and so I said, "Well, you put yourself in my position: would you be able to answer any more questions?" And it was at that point that he said, "Well, you're wearing a civilian shirt," – which I was. He said, "As you won't answer any more of my questions you will be handed over to the Gestapo, and because you're wearing a civilian shirt, you'll be treated as a spy and shot." I didn't believe this chap, and simply said to him "You must do what you have to do." I was then put into solitary confinement, but only for about three or four hours, and then moved into a transit camp.'[27]

Commonwealth POWs in *Dulag Luft*

To Cal Younger the cells at Oberursel 'engendered a sense of utter blankness, a feeling of being emptied. There were none of the traditional bugs to tame or even nails in the door to count.'[28] He was ordered to strip, his clothes removed, and he was searched, and then given a rough Polish uniform and clogs he could hardly walk in.

George Harsh, an American in the RCAF, who ended up in Oberursel at the end of October 1942, described his cell as 'small, wooden' and 'bare of any furniture other than a cot'. After a hot shower and having his dressings changed, he was left there naked for three days. Even the guard refused to talk to him, and he soon realised the man was under orders not to do so. This led Harsh to devise a childish form of personal entertainment. Every time the sentry unlocked the door to deliver the twice-daily slop bucket and cabbage soup, he would, to bait the man, expound elaborately prepared speeches in schoolboy German, such as – 'It is rumoured in certain parts of Austria that Hitler's mother used to run out from under the front porch and bite the postman in the leg.' The guard's neck would turn a fiery red: Harsh recalled that it was the only means he had of retaining the 'tattered shreds' of his sanity.[29]

Laurie Simpson noted in his MI9 report: '*We were taken out at periods to the other side of the camp into well-appointed huts for interrogation. The interrogating officer started off by being very generous and charming with cigarettes etc. but quite often became coldly stern or raving mad later on. Usually these interviews were done on four or five separate occasions during the period spent in the cells.*'

Henry Wagner's interrogation occurred at the end of his second day in the cooler:

'After two days, I was taken out in the evening and up to a comfortably furnished, softly-lit room, smelling richly of cigar smoke, where an officer started off with general small talk, then came to air force matters.'

Wagner offered the obligatory 'holy trinity', but was then asked how long it had been since he was shot down: 'I saw no harm in answering that correctly, but when the interrogator said "That would be the night of an attack on Duisburg", I thought I had said quite enough.' The German then asked about his squadron number and aircraft type, but Wagner refused to divulge any more. The interrogator persisted for a while, and then gave up, and Wagner was taken back to his cell for a few more days. Later he was returned for a second interrogation: if a prisoner was unable to identify himself as RAF aircrew he could be faced with execution as a spy. 'This time the approach was somewhat different', Wagner recalled. 'He began by remarking on the fact that I wore no identification discs. There were two of these: one round red one, and one green oblong one, with the corners chipped off. They were made of some sort of fibre and the red one was fireproof. They were normally worn around the neck, but the string on mine had broken the day before the last flight, and I was intending to renew it when I got back.' His interrogation went something like this:

Interrogator (referring to Wagner): "We have an airman who has been wandering about in Germany for six days, claiming he has been shot down, but we have no others of the crew and, to crown it all, no wreckage of the aircraft he came from. How do you explain this?"

Wagner: "I jumped out over Holland and drifted back into Germany on the way down. Presumably the aircraft disintegrated over British-held territory."

Interrogator: "Well, as it happens, Sergeant Wagner, I know more about you than you think. You come from 51 Squadron, Snaith, flying Halifaxes. The commanding officer is Wing Commander Holford, and…" (He went on to name the Navigation Leader, Bombing Leader and Signals Officer.) "You see, I have had other crews from 51 Squadron, and they have said more than you are saying. Now, what I would like to know is: what operation you have been on, what was your route and height to Duisburg, and what was your bomb load?"

Wagner: "The bomb load was no concern of mine – I don't know what it was. The height varied continually, and I can't remember the exact routing. Even if I could, the Geneva Convention only permits me to give number, rank and name."

Interrogator: "There are two things that worry me, Sergeant Wagner. Here we have one single man in RAF uniform who cannot, or will not, identify himself, and who claims a German name. How do I know you are who you say you are? Some details of your last flight might help to clear things up."

It was a veiled threat of fifth column involvement but, having explained the problem of the 'dog tags', Wagner refused to say more and was returned to his cell. The following morning he was roused at 02.00 hrs, given a piece of bread and some coffee, and departed *Dulag Luft* two hours later with 50 other airmen, mostly Americans.

Graham Korner, a New Zealander, remembered that his time in solitary – before his interrogation – was for 'a couple of days':

'Then they came and picked me up and took me down to an office where a *Luftwaffe* officer was sitting. He gave me loads of bullshit about this, that and the other, which I'd already heard about in England. I said, "Just number, rank and name." But they knew what squadron I was on. They'd obviously put two and two together when they found our aircraft, because our whole squadron had black and yellow squares on the tail. Well if they found that they probably already knew that it was from 640 Squadron.'

Korner made a mistake regarding the markings. He assumed that the Germans had spies watching his squadron's home airfield at Leconfield; however it is more than likely that the Germans gained their information from crashed aircraft or crews who had been shot down earlier.

The interrogator offered Korner a foolscap folder saying, 'Have a look yourself'. Korner thought, 'All he's waiting for me to do is to turn up where my squadron is'. Going through the folder, he found what he saw difficult to believe: the Germans had the entire American and British Bomber Groups' data on file, everything – navigation leaders, gunnery leaders, bombing leaders, COs – and more. He worked through it gradually, spending time on each page. Then he came to his own squadron, and found they had it all correct except for one thing: the navigation leader had been posted up to Group Headquarters the previous week, but they still had him down as 'nav leader'. Korner hastily closed the page, trying not to show his shock, and carried on reading.[30]

The Administration Block

By 1943, the Germans had accumulated a huge amount of intelligence data. This came not only from interrogating airmen, but also from scanning foreign newspapers and magazines, meticulous examination and recording of equipment and objects found at an aircraft's crash site, as well as monitoring enemy intercom traffic. The latter was conducted not only in the air over European territory, but broadcasts from the enemy air bases were intercepted.[31] All this data was stored in the *Dulag Luft* Administration Block which had ten rooms, each with an individual specialisation:

1) Document Evaluation Room: produced 80 per cent of the centre's data, collected from Allied publications, captured aircrew, and salvaging crash sites.
2) Yellow File Room: collected biographical information on Allied personnel from foreign and German publications, awards lists, radio broadcasts, and even censored POW mail.
3) Squadron History Room: information was collected here on every Allied squadron.[32]
4) Map Room.
5) Attack Room: where British and American air operations of the previous 24 hours were displayed.
6) RAF Situation Room: showed the progress of recent raids.
7) USAAF Situation Room: (ditto for USAAF raids).
8) Press Evaluation Room: here staff scoured Allied newspapers for data.
9) Technical Room: contained a museum of flying instruments and a library on Allied equipment.
10) Crash File Room: plotted all the Allied air force crashes in German or occupied territory. Each crash was numbered and location, crew, aircraft type and marking details were filed. The room supplied information of the missing, dead and imprisoned to the International Red Cross.[33]

Allied airmen were instructed to carry personal identification photographs, known as 'Pimpernel' photos, with them on ops. These were individual passport type photos, of different poses, taken by a service photographer at the beginning of a tour, in order that aircrew could use them in forged passports if they were shot down. One American bomber group had these in an unusual brown colour. This easily identified the group to the Germans. Sometimes the same photographer would be used by a number of squadrons in a group, and often every subject wore the same suit. Thus the type of clothing a man wore could identify his unit. Even minor items like railway tickets or food and clothing chits, issued by particular RAF stations, could reveal things. Despite their instructions not to carry personal papers and other such documents on operations, many aircrew continued to do so. If a station clerk made a particular pen mark on a chit, the Germans could identify the unit from it if they added all the clues together.[34]

Many POWs were amazed by the amount of information the Germans knew. Henry Coverley's interrogation shook him at one point: the man told him his father was in the Foreign Office in Portugal:

> 'I came from Portugal and my father was a Consul in the Consulate at Oporto. During the war Portugal was neutral – so the Germans could find out what they wanted about the British community there – who'd joined up and what they'd done, etc., just as we could about them.'[35]

'They were very clever, the *Dulag Luft* crowd', Coverley commented. He realised later that they were using shock tactics, it being their hope that prisoners would 'drop the name, rank and number thing' once they thought, 'Well, they know it all'.

Jim Philpot, was a mid-upper gunner with 300 Squadron:

'My crew was split up and each member taken into a room where they were interrogated. After we refused to give more than name, rank and number, we were dragged off to solitary confinement. This was a small cell with nothing more than a bare board for a seat or bed, plus a bucket. The light in the high ceiling was blazing away night and day. Food consisted of their idea of bread, which was dark brown, hard as nails, and tasted like sawdust, and some water. I was kept there for three days, and then interrogated again. They again requested details of where I was based, what aircraft I was flying, what special equipment was on board, etc. They then said, "OK, we know all these facts: you were born in London, joined the RAF in 1942, you were based at Faldingworth etc." So it made me wonder why they went to such lengths, when they already knew so much.'[36]

Peter Hughes was also impressed by the amount of correct information his interrogator introduced. 'He offered me cigarettes and sympathised with my damaged face,[37] which, he opined, "was not 'cultured'" although he stopped short of apologising. I added nothing to his description of the situation as he saw it and was dismissed, two days later.'

To update its interrogation methods the *Luftwaffe* invited Franz von Werra, a fighter ace who was the first German POW to make a home run from America to Germany,[38] to visit Oberursel. But von Werra's assessment of *Dulag Luft*'s set-up and intelligence-gathering process was generally negative. His interrogation by the British at Trent Park, Cockfosters in 1940 had been much more thorough. He recalled that his RAF interrogator tried to drain his morale and 'assassinate' his character by referring to thoroughly researched files on von Werra's background. Nothing like this had been tried at *Dulag Luft* up to that time, where methods were comparatively amateurish. The staff at *Dulag Luft* learned a great deal from von Werra's visit.[39]

Hajo Herrmann, the night fighter leader, was another German flyer who called in at Oberursel. He found Bennett's Pathfinder tactics a 'jigsaw puzzle', and wanted to interview Allied POWs to understand these devices better. He was allowed to conduct a number of interrogations himself:

'The majority of them curtly gave me their service number and name, nothing more. They would not confirm their squadron even when I named it and the commanding officer. One man did weaken under the torture of having to go without cigarettes for a number of days. He inhaled greedily the secondary smoke from my cigarette and began to talk hesitantly. I borrowed this man from the camp *Kommandant* for two days and flew him in my *Storch*[40] to *Schloss* Allner, where he was able to smoke to his heart's content.'[41]

This airman was deliberately feted with good food and drink and eventually told Herrmann that he only knew Germany from the air, but still believed it to be 'a den of thieves'. Herrmann understood Bennett's tactics better after he made a return visit to the centre.

Heat Treatment

The Germans began to increase the prisoners' ordeal by manipulating the temperature of the cells to extremes of hot and cold for long, antisocial periods. Henry Coverley: 'I was in solitary confinement, and they turned the heat on when you said it was too warm, and they turned the cold on when you said it was too cold. It was miserable: a room, a quarter the size of a small living room – and food? I didn't get any food, only soup.'

Howard Pearce also experienced the heat treatment:

'It was a lovely June day and they had me in the cooler. They decided that, because I was the only one of the crew who'd survived, I might be fruitful. They put me in a cell and locked the windows, put three radiators on and made me squirm. I mean I was sweating like a pig and they didn't give me anything to drink for 24 hours. Anyway a chap came in and he was dressed in a sort of German uniform with a clerical collar. He said how sorry he was to see me there and asked where I came from. I gave him my address at home. He reassured me they would make quite sure through the Protecting Power that England would learn very quickly that I was in the land of the living. He asked "What school did you go to?" and I replied, "Just an ordinary grammar school". And he said "Ah yes, play games?", to which I said, "Cricket and football" and we chatted about cricket. Then he drifted around to my squadron, and I didn't say anything at all. He left some cigarettes with me and said, "Look, this is bad! I'll make sure that the windows are open and they're cutting out the radiator. I'll come back some time." He came back dressed as an officer in the *Luftwaffe*! The same man; and he was very different. But he didn't get anything out of me. I hadn't got much to tell him anyway.'[42]

Jack Brook, a bombardier with 617 Squadron, who was exposed to severely brutal treatment, remembered the excessive heat in his cell:

'A pipe on the same wall as the [window] grille, presumably a heating pipe, was hot to the touch. I tried to settle down, making a pillow out of my battledress blouse, but without much success, as no matter how I twisted and turned, the uneven boards continued to dig into my back. Furthermore I could not escape from the glare of the light which was shining directly into my eyes. I changed positions continually, but it made no difference at all. It was like being in an oven and most uncomfortable.'[43]

Peter Hughes recalled:

'The *Dulag Luft* staff knew all the tricks: my uniform was taken away and returned with the magnetised buttons, intended for use as compasses, cut off and the whistle removed. The cells were steam-heated to an unbearably hot temperature, but there was some entertainment: RAF Lancasters, clearly identifiable by their sound, attacked the nearby Opel works at Russelheim and made a lot of noise which caused the staff to rush around in near panic.'

The 'sweat box' techniques were probably introduced at the instigation of the Frankfurt Gestapo who were occasionally permitted to interrogate prisoners. One particular German, *Oberst* Braeder, has been described as 'a thoroughly nasty piece of work'.[44] At one end of each isolation cell, under a barred window obscured by paint, was a 1.5 kilowatt heater. The cells were about 10½ feet long by 5½ feet wide, varying slightly depending upon their location in the building. Books may have allowed the prisoner some distraction, but generally he was left alone with his thoughts and to contemplate threats of being handed over to the Gestapo. The single light in the high ceiling could be switched on and off only from outside. The walls were of thick cement, and acted like a sauna, retaining the heat:

> 'Frequently the temperature in the room became almost unbearable, rising high enough at times to singe a towel laid on the radiator and making the bed and all the metal hot enough to scorch bare flesh.'[45]

The 'advantage' of this was that it made the POW look forward to any escape from the cell – the only one being a visit to an interrogator.

A Strange Coincidence

Alan F. James was a policeman in civilian life, a 'reserved occupation' until 1941, when he was released and joined Bomber Command. His crew was shot down west of Cologne in a 102 Squadron Halifax, JB964, on 13 May 1943. They were on their way to Bochum when they were attacked by a night fighter. James, the navigator, was one of two survivors, and landed in a bombed-out building, damaging his backside. He was taken to a hospital and put in a small, guarded room with a picture of Hitler on one wall and Göring on the other. Eventually, a boy was found who could speak English. On the way to Frankfurt, James concluded that as the civilians were showing little animosity towards him, they must be travelling through an area which had suffered little bombing. He was put in a convalescent hospital upon arrival and soon received the obligatory Red Cross form, most of which he refused to complete. However he did give his home address and former occupation. Although he had been a serving police officer, he did not consider it wise to mention this. 'To refuse could arouse suspicion,' he recounted, 'so I said I was a farmer living at Edwalton, a small village about three miles from Nottingham.'[46]

Alan James (James)

James was from a farming family and thought this would suffice, but an uncanny coincidence almost caused the ruse to backfire on him. He recalled that his first interrogator was '...an obnoxious, aggressive individual' who asked him about his 'base, squadron, crew, and bombing targets'. James declined to co-operate and was returned to his cell. The next interrogator was different '...an older man in civilian clothes', he recalled, who was 'more cultured in appearance and manner, with a softer approach'. Eventually, after repeating the same questions as those of the first German, the interrogator said, 'I see you come from Edwalton?' James replied that he did, and the German said, 'I have visited Edwalton. Do you know Colonel Brewell?' James:

> 'I knew that Colonel Brewell had retired from the Army and been engaged in business in Nottingham, and had died some years previously. I was able to say that I did not know him personally, but knew of him, and that he had lived in a large house in the outskirts of the village of Edwalton. He then told me that Colonel Brewell had been a prisoner in the previous war and that he, himself, had been an officer in the old German Army and had become friends with him as one of his captors, and that he had been a guest of Colonel Brewell after the war ended.'[47]

James met his interrogator a number of times and 'even had discussions on German policy, treatment of the Jews, etc.', but he still refused to co-operate. After three weeks in solitary he was told he would not be allowed to leave unless he could prove he was aircrew. The interrogator said that he had seen a slip of paper with the name of Sergeant Brown, the bomb-aimer on James's crew, on it. But his suggestion that Brown was in Oberursel was contradicted by the story that Coughlin, the mid-upper gunner,[48] had told James that all the rest of the crew had been killed, and that their bodies had fallen near the crashed Halifax. Later, after refusing to participate in a radio broadcast in English, Alan James was transferred to the POW section at *Dulag Luft* and subsequently to *Stalag Luft* III.

To put prisoners at their ease Hanns Scharff and the Oberursel team would take subjects for long walks in the countryside or to the cinema. Meals in the German officers' mess were intended to convince prisoners that they would not be intimidated by the tactic of 'wine, women and song' that RAF Intelligence Officers had spoken of.[49] Laurie Simpson recalled: 'I was taken over twice to the officers' mess and given a meal: the *Ersatz* coffee didn't taste a lot like coffee; it was just a bitter taste.'

Hans Scharff recalled how, on one occasion, while on a walk with a prisoner, he encountered a red ants' nest which led to an interesting political discussion. Close examination of the nest led the American to comment that the ants were like soldiers... the Queen resembled a President... American ants had freedom of speech, but red ants must be Communist etc. Scharff commented:

> 'This little incident was the origin of a long series of political interrogations at Oberursel. Just because I had noticed how easy it was to get Americans involved in arguments reflecting upon political and economic outlooks, differences and conditions, I led many another POW along this path...'[50]

Officers particularly, being generally better educated, felt obliged to defend their views, which could cause them to disclose information without realising it. Scharff used the ants' nest technique repeatedly. Laurie Simpson:

> 'The interrogations were normally just within the rules of the Geneva Convention: "name, rank and number" – no problem there. There was a certain amount of discussion, but they started off by telling you who you were, and your rank, what squadron you came from, and the name of the CO of the station. They knew the squadron because they collated this information from people coming in all the time: some people must give some information away. Once they'd established that, they tried to put you off your guard. They knew so much about you, so there was nothing much you could tell them – that is what they wanted you to think. They asked how you bombed, whether in formation etc.'[51]

A Collaborator

'*Some people must give some information away*': Laurie was never aware how accurate his statement was. Files now residing in the British National Archives in London confirm limply that many RAF prisoners did supply the Germans with the information they wanted: these files contain dozens of reports made after the war by MI9 officers on interrogations conducted at *Dulag Luft*. Amongst these was the following entry:

'*Crash No. KE86A 'Lancaster' (RAF) 28.1.44, 01.30 hrs*
Place: in the vicinity of St. Malo
No. 460 (B) Squadron; Binbrook (GB) No. 1 Group.'[52]

Upon encountering this file record I realised immediately that this was my father's Lancaster. Only three Lancasters from 460 Squadron were lost on the night of 27/28 January 1944. One, JA860 AR-C2, piloted by Australian Flight Sergeant W.R.McLachlan, took off five minutes before my father's, and a second, JB637 AR-B, piloted by Warrant Officer R.J.Power, took off 10 minutes before McLachlan's. Power's aircraft crashed in Berlin and all on board were killed, while four of McLachlan's crew were killed and buried in Poland, which indicates that the aircraft crashed well to the east of Berlin. Only one 460 Squadron aircraft crashed near St. Malo on the night of 27/28 January 1944 – Laurie Simpson's. This implies that at least one member of my father's crew had 'talked', under interrogation, to the Germans at *Dulag Luft*.

One particular report in an adjacent file in the National Archives was of a 101 Squadron Lancaster from Ludford Magna shot down on 15 February 1944. This contained much important information about the work of specialist operators in this RCM squadron. However the 460 Squadron report was not as disturbing. The interrogation concentrated mainly on 'Development of Methods of Attack' and 'General Information about Losses'.

This *Dulag Luft* report, which was typical of those found by the British occupying forces and recorded by them, stated that the airman concerned had told the interrogator that he '…had carried out his first operations in 1942' and he spoke of the difficulties of integrating 'the first Lancasters into the bomber stream,'[53] (which mostly consisted then of Wellingtons). He also told them that '…it was not altogether easy to calculate the flying times so that the Lancasters arrived either separately or as the last wave over the target.' He explained to them '…the beginnings of the Pathfinder technique,' but 'believed… that even after two years the procedure then adopted was not followed…[54] No fundamental alterations in the Pathfinder technique were being taught in the OTU and he had noticed none when he returned to operations.'[55]

The man also told the Germans about the new Halifax Mk III, the aircraft that, it was hoped, would equal the performance of the Lancaster: 'It had long been expected that Halifax III aircraft would operate with Lancaster aircraft in one wave, as it was generally known that the Halifax III was not inferior to the Lancaster.'[56] So far as the prisoner knew, the combination of Halifax Mk IIIs and Lancasters was attempted for the first time on the raid to Berlin on 27/28 January 1944.

The airman also gave them some general information on crew awards and tour completions: 'Of the crews which entered No. 460 (B) Squadron in September 1942, about 50% of the first line crews had survived 30 flights up to April 1943.'[57] But not all crews automatically received awards after completing a tour: 40% of these crews, the report recorded, 'had been awarded the DFC or DFM'. He even described to the Germans the psychological effects of a first tour: '…the last 5 operations were the most difficult, because one asked oneself nervously whether one would reach the 30th flight.' On an operational squadron, he told them, 'silent losses', (losses where the fate of the crew was unreported), in 'operational and war flights[58] were generally not more than 2% per flight.' With added losses occurring on 'practice flights, the total is not more than 10'. He then revealed, 'In the last 14 days, No. 460 Squadron had actually lost three aircraft on practice flights, but this number was far above the average.'[59]

The prisoner's answers suggest that the Germans convinced him that they knew a great deal about the workings of his squadron and Bomber Command, and much of the information he divulged may have been thrown in as chance remarks or replies to apparently innocuous questions in general conversation. The interrogators, in fact, may not have known half of what they suggested. We will never know.

Isolation

Lew Parsons went to *Dulag Luft* at the beginning of September 1943, with the three other survivors from his crew. They were put into solitary cells to await their interrogators. 'We knew that we only had to give our name, rank and number,' he said 'but of course they wanted a lot more than that.' A 'stool pigeon' was then introduced:

'Each of us was visited by an airman who claimed he had been shot down over Berlin and had a blood-stained bandage on his hand. He asked too many questions to be trusted and we each said later that we had told him nothing of significance. His name was Sgt R.D. Hughes of 467 Squadron, POW No. 821.[60] At the end of the war he was charged and found guilty of treason. He was sentenced to five years in prison.'[61]

Graham Korner heard after his own interrogation that the *Luftwaffe* used to put English-speaking Germans in RAF uniform in *Dulag Luft* – men who would listen to the prisoners' conversations, 'earwigging, picking up bits of information'.[62]

Peter Skinner, a gunner with 158 Squadron, was in the cooler for six nights, before being 'educated':

'I spent six nights in solitary confinement during which time I had many an interview, mainly by a *Luftwaffe* major and a lieutenant. For four nights and days all they got was my name, rank and number. I was also visited by the alleged "Red Cross" representative, (from OTU training we had been warned of this ploy), who was such an obvious fake that I felt bold enough to tell him to "bog off".

'Another civilian visitor was a younger man who questioned me about the mine recovered from the wreckage [of our aircraft]. On his second visit I think I convinced him enough that air gunners were not privy to bomb loads, targets or anything mechanical, only ammunition. I had also maintained that when being interviewed by the officers. I honestly think they believed my "innocence"; that I was just another air gunner who was not privy to pre-knowledge of target and purpose of mission.

'At one such interview I was shown some charred maps; on one of them, the plotted dropping zone in the Kattegat was clearly marked. To hide whatever I was feeling, I know I put on a pretence of great interest and asked the interrogator how was I to know it wasn't a fake because air gunners of my rank were never shown such things as maps. Anyway, on the fifth day after midday soup the major came into my cell and banged a black leather bound dossier on the table. Looking at me squarely he said, 'Well, Sergeant, you don't seem able to help us, let me help you to know something about your squadron.' After he had left I was amazed, and educated, on the squadron's dates of re-forming, training schedules, type of Wellington aircraft used on its initial raids, its Halifax aircrew conversion programme, and subsequent raids up to three weeks before Christmas. They knew of absolutely every movement, raids and losses and, more to the point, names of the commanding officer(s) and flight leaders. I got to know more about my squadron in the next few hours than probably anyone still serving back at base.'[63]

Lew Parsons tried to use the same technique of pulling the wool over his interrogator's eyes. He was questioned about the sea mines dropped by Stirlings by an officer who appeared to be a member of the *Kriegsmarine* in a dark blue uniform. Parsons gave the stock response, saying he was the flight engineer and knew nothing about what load they carried. The German became exasperated by his negative replies, but then appeared initially pleased when the Englishman requested if he could ask a question: 'Why did you scuttle the *Graf Spee*?' Parsons asked furtively. The officer became very agitated, uttering a number of native expletives, and then replied in broad English: 'The *Graf Spee* was scuttled on the orders of the *Führer*.'[64] It would appear that here the German was deliberately misleading Parsons in order to avoid further embarrassment.[65]

Long Confinement

Occasionally prisoners were in the *Dulag Luft* cooler for considerably longer than three to five days. Bob Kendall put only name, rank and number on his Red Cross form. The German officer interviewing him immediately became insulting and threatening, and informed him that he would most certainly be shot. 'I was removed to a cell and spent the next eight days in solitary confinement', Kendall related. He was then taken for interrogation with a different officer whose manner was more emollient: 'He told me I could not give him any useful information as he had all the information he wanted.' Two days later Kendall was transferred.

Eric Hookings, a 619 Squadron Lancaster pilot shot down on a raid to Gravenhorst on 6 November 1944, was incarcerated for ten days in the solitary block, but has no idea of the reason for it: 'I only know that they felt there was far more that they could glean from me about "Village Inn"[66] at the latter end of 1944', he said. 'I was physically abused and threatened, dragged from my cell at any time of day or night, and roughly handled by those questioning me, who were intent upon finding out about H2S or "Village Inn".'

From 1 July 1944, Jack Brook, the bombardier with 617 Squadron, was in solitary for thirteen days, suffering much brutal treatment and many interrogations. At the end of this he was totally broken in spirit. He had been involved in Operation Taxable, a deception plan using Window and his squadron's Lancasters to represent a large formation of ships crossing the Pas de Calais the day before D-Day. He was also involved with the early use of the Tallboy bomb. Upon release from Oberursel he reflected upon his captors' change of heart:

> 'I have often wondered why I came in for their special attention. After all, I was only a small cog in a large wheel and there was little I could have told them. The conclusion I finally came to was that [the interrogator] obviously knew I was a member of 617 Squadron, and we happened to be the first crew from 617 to be shot down since D-Day.'[67]

Brook was subjected to an unusual amount of psychological torture, as well as physical. He found it almost impossible to sleep in his cell due to the high temperatures and the electric light being on all night. His mud-covered boots were taken away but returned the following morning. The first afternoon he had his first interrogation with a middle-aged German who spoke fluent English. Brook had been given a bogus Red Cross form earlier. The man explained:

'Did I not realise that the form was designed to separate the genuine cases from the terrorist flyers? In [his] experience, the only airmen who refused to complete the form were those with something to hide.'

The *Luftwaffe* was under considerable pressure from the State to hand British flyers over to the civilian courts, where they could be sentenced to death or sent to a labour camp if found guilty. Although Brook was shaken by the German's declaration, he was still convinced that the man was bluffing. He was returned to his cell. There was a list of former inmates' names scrawled on one wall of it. He scratched his name with a pin and added two lines for each day he had been there.

Deryck Lambert recalled finding a message in *his* cell: 'There were various writings scrawled on the wall,' he remembered, 'and one of them was something like, "Don't speak. Don't say anything. Three days solitary." Lambert thought he would give that a go to see what happened, and didn't say a thing for three days. It worked. He was duly removed and sent to the slightly more tolerable confines of a prison camp.[68]

Jack Brook was subjected to further stress in the night, aside from being unable to sleep:

'I decided to try and sleep on the floor and at some point I dozed off only to be awakened by the guard bursting into the cell, shouting at me to give my number, rank and name. He hauled me roughly to my feet, banging my head as he did so.'

Brook was also told he was not allowed to sleep on the floor and from then on would be closely scrutinised. The guard said that since he was so fond of only divulging his name, rank and number, he would be forced to repeat them day and night until he was fed up with doing so.

On 5 July, although initially appearing affable, after asking if he was ready to co-operate, the interrogator told him, '[He, Brook,] belonged to a squadron which had been involved in specific terror raids against the German people, and that the civilian government was pressing him hard to hand [Brook] over to them.' Brook then told him that under the Geneva Convention he was only required to give his name, rank and number. Since his crew had attacked solely legitimate targets, he felt exempt from civil prosecution, and under the protection of the *Luftwaffe*. Furthermore, the German had no right to threaten him with reprisals: '[The interrogator's] face changed hue', Brook recalled, 'and I thought he was going to burst a blood vessel. He stood up from his chair, his face distorted with anger. He leant across the desk, calling me arrogant and stupid, and knocked the cigarette out of my mouth. Still continuing his verbal assault on me he ordered me to my feet. He made me retrieve the cigarette and stub it out on his ashtray. For my indiscretion I was made to stand to attention for the remainder of the interview.'[69]

After that the interrogator informed him that '…he would see to it personally that I was locked up in solitary for the duration of the war'. The alternative was to be handed over to the Gestapo: 'I could expect a very different type of interrogation then', he was told. Brook was escorted back to his cell and 'collapsed on the bed shaking like a leaf', torn between national loyalty and self-preservation. He lay tormented by hunger, lack of sleep and mental despair:

'How I managed to survive the next five days I shall never know. I was now in a very poor state, mentally and physically. Never a night went by without them bursting into the cell at all hours, demanding my number, rank and name.'

On 10 July he was sent for again and subjected alternately to threats and promises of leniency. Soon he was almost at the end of his tether. Another interrogation followed on 13 July. The German told him, 'I had reached the end of the line and that he could not help me further.' An 'ominous' civilian sat in on the interrogation, not speaking. Brook was sent back to his cell: 'I sat with my head in my hands feeling utterly dejected and terrified. This was one of the worst moments of my captivity.'

He began to sink into the trap they had created: he resolved to complete the Red Cross form and tell them anything they wanted – it was irrelevant as they appeared to know everything anyway. He would concoct what he did not know. 'I had resisted the pressures for as long as I could and could not take any more of it', he recalled. He returned to his tormentor. Brook had to communicate his decision: 'My mouth was dry and I could hardly get a word out, although I had rehearsed them enough, but in that vital instant something told me to bluff it out a little longer.'[70]

After reiterating that he was an airman and not a gangster, there was an agonising pause. Eventually the Nazi informed him that he had decided to terminate the interrogations. Such unhappiness led Jack Brook later to ruminate at length over this experience. It was after the 'Great Escape' of March 1944 and German POW security was becoming increasingly tight. It is possible his interrogator had been truthful when threatening him with the Gestapo. He realised that although the enemy had been interested in 617 Squadron operations, particularly the use of Tallboy, he had been '…lucky that the Germans had gained sufficient information from other sources', he recalled. His daughter later commented:

'One of the things that distressed him the most, was how close he came to being broken physically, mentally and emotionally during his interrogation, and how he may have given up information had it continued much longer. He felt unbelievable guilt and shame for this for many years. He felt let down that his training had not prepared him for this.'[71]

After the war Brook was able to converse with many ex-POWs who had suffered similar experiences. He realised '…that my behaviour was in no way unique. I had been reduced to that state by men specially trained in the art of psychological warfare and interrogation.'[72] 'Only reading the memoirs of other forces personnel', his daughter wrote, 'convinced him that his behaviour was not only normal but totally understandable; that he was not an exceptionally weak character, and that he had nothing to feel guilty or ashamed about.'[73] This evokes reflection when one considers, as previously stated, that dozens of *Dulag Luft* interrogation reports in the British National Archives suggest that many airmen gave away information to the Germans under considerably less ruthless circumstances.

George Cross, the Mosquito intruder pilot shot down on 30 September 1944, was kept in the cooler at *Dulag Luft* for over a month, but still refused to talk. The techniques of his interrogation were typical of those employed on other prisoners. He wrote a day-to-day account of this:

'At this place every possible trick was used to glean information from unsuspecting prisoners. I was taken into an office where I was given what was supposed to be a Red Cross form to fill in. I had been warned of this trick however and half of the queries I just scored through with my pencil. I was then sent into the next room where I waited for about 10 minutes before a German came in and got me to strip down for him to search me. This he did very thoroughly indeed. After this I was taken to a small room where I got into bed.

Tuesday October 3rd 1944
I was awakened at about eight in the morning by a guard who was giving me breakfast. This consisted of a sandwich made up of two fairly thick slices of black bread, one of which had had some jam put on, then scraped off again, also a cup of German coffee. I managed to eat my breakfast easier than previously, for by this time I was getting a little hungry and thirsty. After breakfast I finished off getting myself dressed. My shoes, which I had been told to leave outside the door the night before, had been placed inside for me. I made my bed up very quickly; all I had to do was fold one blanket up. The bed itself was of fairly solid wooden construction with several loose boards on the bottom on which was a mattress half filled with wood wool. I dare not shake it up as I would lose more of the filling which leaked out and dropped through the boards badly enough as it was. The room itself was 10 feet long, six feet wide and 10 feet high. The walls were made of some fibrous material and practically soundproof in between rooms. It had a fairly big window with frosted glass panes and bars. For heating purposes a radiator was fitted with a four-way switch outside the door, as was the light switch. The room was very clean and to call the guard a handle was turned which let drop a red arrow just by the door outside.

At about 9.30 a.m. a guard took me over to the building where the interrogation was carried out. Here an Oberfeldwebel, who said he had been shot down over London, been a POW in Canada, and repatriated, presented me with a form which he said I had to complete to prove that I was what I claimed before I was accepted by them as a POW and my name sent to the International Red Cross. I took the form, filled in number, name and rank and gave it back to him saying, "I am afraid I am unable to complete it any further." Whereupon he told me that until I completed the form he would not be able to accept me as a POW and would remain there until I was willing to co-operate. He then tried to draw me into conversation, telling me amongst other things that "Jock" [the navigator] had been buried at a place called "Grasseln" near Brunswick. Shortly, I was dismissed to my room where I found under the pillow a book which I started reading. At about 12.30 my door was opened and I was given a dish of very good, thick soup which I enjoyed. In the afternoon I was taken over to be interrogated by a captain. After refusing to answer his questions or enter into conversation I was taken back to my room. At 5 o'clock I was given a cup of coffee and two thick slices of black bread, one with margarine on, for my tea. I was not seen again except for meals until Friday, October 6th.

I was again interrogated and presented with the same uncompleted form. On refusing to be drawn I was sent back to my room where on the door was a white sheet of paper. This meant loss of privileges, i.e. no book, no water during the night and windows constantly closed.

Friday, October 13th
Getting extremely fed up with my own company and daily routine of getting up at 8 for breakfast, making my bed, sweeping out room, light off, blackout opened; 12.30 soup up; 2.00 numbers of rooms called out for chaps being taken over for interrogation, never mine though; 5.00 tea; 5.30 light on, blackout closed; 6.00 guard looks in to check, I put my shoes outside door and get into bed quickly before the door is locked and light put out to close another day.

Tuesday, October 17th
At 4.00 was interrogated by two airmen who told me my officer was ill. They gave me a drink of coffee with milk in it and a roll with jam. I tried bags of soft soap with no effect. Got chit to wash, shave and

draw library book. Drew second book out in case one got taken away from me, also got a chit to get my window opened.

Thursday, October 19th
Awoken in the middle of the night and asked for number, name and rank by a Jerry who wrote it down and went away.

Saturday, October 21st
Interrogated again by two airmen who once again gave me some coffee and some slices of bread with jam. They are on the old soft soap again, telling me what a great life I would have in a POW camp. Finally they said, "If you just give us the number of your squadron that will be sufficient for us to check your identity by, and then tomorrow you will be sent to a POW camp." I want to get away from here but with some effort, I stuck it out. I was given a chit for shave and one to get them on the phone if I changed my mind.

Tuesday, October 24th
AM: Interrogation Officer back from illness: his questioning was much harder to evade than that of the two airmen. He is on the soft soap now, giving me a pear to eat. He went outside for a few minutes, so I took advantage of this by looking at a much enlarged photo of a board showing all the squadrons in the Mediterranean with their bases and COs. (I judge it to have been taken last December.)[74]

Wednesday, October 25th
PM. Over to Interrogation Officer. He finds I still won't come clean and the mailed fist is on with a vengeance. Threatening me with being turned over to the Gestapo, says I am a spy and will get shot. Loss of privileges again.

Thursday, November 2nd
First thing in morning over to IO, who still says I stay here until I give my squadron etc. After five weeks of solitary confinement I am beginning to wonder how long I will be kept here if I keep my mouth shut. Decide to give him a cock and bull story made up from gen I had seen on Louden and Tennant's sheet.[75] He had shown me this interrogation sheet several times amongst others. Over to him again in afternoon, to my relief, he did not see through my story and seemed pleased as punch at his apparent triumph. Gave me chit to shave and wash and promised to send me a plate of soup over for tea. Back over to room and cleaned. Got a plate of soup which I never expected to see, then was taken over to outer compound with several bods. Boy! It's wizard to be able to talk to someone at last.'[76]

Fifth Columnists

Some prisoners' accounts suggest the Germans almost certainly had agents on the RAF bomber stations. Bill Higgs related the story of an airman he met from his unit, 35 Squadron, at *Stalag Luft* I, who told him of his interrogation at *Dulag Luft*. Higgs's friend gave the Germans his name, rank, and number:

'The interrogator said, "You're from 35 Squadron. In your crew room there are names." In the crew room at Graveley there was a board listing the crews for the night. My mate thought, "This is from Graveley, where they're flying Halifax bombers. The letters are 'TL'." Some of our aircraft had crashed, and had broken up and had 'TL-C', 'TL-M' etc. on the sides. Anyway my pal said "I don't know anything about this." So then they brought in a photograph of the crew list for the night he was shot down, and said: "That's you. That's your crew isn't it?"

"Yes."

"We've got you," they said. "We've got five other of your crews that were shot down that night."

My mate looked at the photo: it was a copy of the operations schedule for that night, a crew list for a 35 Squadron raid. "I couldn't believe it!" he said. "I'd only been there for three or four days, plus ten days in solitary, and they'd got these photographs of the board up on the wall at Graveley." Then he remembered: there was a little warrant officer in the mess, and everyone was suspicious of him because, whenever we went on ops, the bloke would go down into the crew room and have a chat with the lads, saying "best of luck" and all that. I reckon he had a camera, and he photographed that board. The Jerries had pigeons and he sent them with the photos back across the Channel. There was no other way to get them back. So the Germans had a photograph of the list of crews that were flying that night!'[77]

Derek Hodgkinson recalled realising that there was a fifth columnist on his squadron. He had originally been cross-examined by a German disguised as a member of the British Red Cross:

'I was surprised and angered when the English Red Cross gent turned up in the full rig of a *Luftwaffe* lieutenant. When I remonstrated, he brushed the whole thing off by saying that in war, little deceptions such as that were quite permissible. In fact, in my case, he went on, it was really unnecessary as they already knew all there was to know about me. He then proceeded to read out my service record from a folder he was carrying.

The details that Hodgkinson's interrogator then went into suggested the *Luftwaffe* had sources far beyond Germany:

'If I was taken aback by the detail of his knowledge so far, I was astounded by what followed: "How are Dismal Devitt and Hank Niven?" and he mentioned others of my friends. "Have you been to the Skinburness Hotel lately? If you have, you will have noticed that the clock over the main bar has been stopped at ten past one for the last few weeks." He went on in this vein for some time, making it clear that he had an intimate knowledge of Silloth and all that went on there.

'I was convinced then that the Germans must have had an agent at Silloth who not only had access to confidential documents, but who also was fully in touch with the day-to-day life of the station.

'One man fits the bill only too well. I had known him for some time and counted him as a friend. He was a typical product of Eton: charming, accomplished and highly intelligent. However, he was a homosexual and could have been blackmailed. He had also, I am aware, spent some time in Germany before the war and knew people in the *Luftwaffe*. He made no secret of his determination never to see action and indeed, on one occasion shortly before I was shot down, said to me, "You're a bloody fool, Derek. You will go back to your squadron and get yourself killed…"'[78]

Because he had no proof of this, Hodgkinson never confronted the man with his suspicions (ironically the miscreant later became very successful in the City of London), but felt 'in his bones that it was him'. Hodgkinson later said that most prisoners regarded the interrogation centre as 'a place of ill repute'. He did not like the atmosphere of the camp 'particularly the attitude of the SBO (Senior British Officer) (i.e. 'Wings' Day) and his staff' when he was there.

Sid Duplock, who was shot down on 22 February 1945, was told specifically that there were spies on the Bomber Command bases:

'They locked about 12 prisoners in a room 8 ft by 10 ft, but I was put on my own in a room which had about 12 stools in it. The room temperature varied from freezing to very hot. I put all the stools together and went to sleep. Next morning I was taken before an officer who asked me if I'd had a good night. I said, "Yes". He seemed surprised and then asked some questions: "What group? What squadron?" I said that all I could tell him was my name, rank and number. He then said that he used to live in Notting Hill Gate and had supported Chelsea. I replied that I supported Arsenal, and that we all hated Chelsea and that was the end of that.

'He then produced a 227 Squadron battle order for the raid, together with a pilot's route map, which should have been destroyed. He must have seen my surprise because he then said that the Germans had an agent on every RAF station.'[79]

Corruption on the Bomber Command stations may be questioned by the average reader, but there is much evidence to suggest that this did exist and it was not confined to fifth column work. Alec March became aware that theft of personal property went on in his squadron. He found on one occasion, when returning late from an operation, after having first landed at another base, that there was a silver cigarette case in his tunic pocket that was not his. It emerged subsequently that an NCO in the squadron Intelligence Section had been stealing aircrews' possessions if he heard that they had not come back from a raid. In March's case his crew returned late and the man had to replace the objects quickly, but he had put them back in the wrong tunics. The NCO, he later discovered, was also wanted by the civilian police.

• • •

We can conclude that *Dulag Luft* was a place of extremes of experience where some men were in solitary confinement for many weeks. Despite the increasing accuracy of RAF Intelligence lectures, airmen still fell foul of their inquisitors and became trapped into giving more than 'name, rank and number'. Deprivation of heat, food and sleep created deliberate hardship, but there were few cases of serious physical brutality. Some men were toughened cases and so able to endure more easily the cross-examining than others, but most airmen were amazed by the amount of information the Germans knew. However, the technique of persuading the POWs that they knew more than they actually did, at which Hanns Scharff was a past master, did not always fool the victim.

Jack Brook was really an atypical case. He, in some ways, felt 'badly let down by the RAF'. He thought he had received little preparation for his interrogation which, in the event, was unusually lengthy. 'I was shocked with myself for even thinking of collaborating with the Germans,' he recalled, 'in order to save myself from being handed over to the civilian courts.' Despite this he concluded that the enemy had 'all the aces in the pack… Once you had been softened up sufficiently, so that you could no longer think logically, they had almost won.' He felt that the RAF simply did not have time to prepare aircrew for what may have been only a few days isolation. Any rehearsal, he conjectured, could have the opposite effect to that desired, i.e. simply alarming aircrew. There were also political considerations: the RAF's decision not to discuss, or even understate, *Dulag Luft's* methods could be due to its reluctance to admit that similar treatment occurred in British interrogation centres such as the 'London Cage'.

But some men were quietly affected by the 'education' they received at *Dulag Luft*. As a *Luftwaffe* camp, unlike a Gestapo and SS establishment, the staff generally had a mutual respect for their fellow aviators, and consequently many prisoners got off fairly lightly. However, in the future, in the main camps, the new prisoners would have to countenance far more prolonged and exigent hardships than they were prepared for.

CHAPTER NINETEEN

'VERMIN-FREE WITH ABOUT FORTY PRISONERS TO A ROOM'

Stalag Luft III, Sagan

THERE were 260 Prisoner of War camps in the German-occupied territories of Europe from 1939 to 1945. Ten of these were *Stalag Luft*[1] camps run by the *Luftwaffe* and 63 were *Oflag* (officers' camps) run by the *Wehrmacht*, as were the 231 *Stalag* (other ranks' camps), of which 88 were the larger *Stalag*. The main *Luftwaffe* camps were *Stalag Luft* I (Barth), III (Sagan), IV (Gross Tychow), VI (Heydekrug), and VII (Bankau). The four main *Oflag* were: *Oflag* IVC (Colditz), VIIB (Eichstatt), IX (Ziegenhain), and 79 (Brunswick [Braunschweig]). The 12 main *Wehrmacht* other ranks *Stalag* were: IIIA (Luckenwalde), IVB (Mühlberg), VIIB (Moosberg), VIIIB (Teschen), VIIIA (Görlitz), XIA (Altengrabow), XIB / 357 (Fallingbostel), XIIIC (Hemmelberg), XIIID (Nuremberg [Nürnberg]), XXA (Thorn), XXB (Marienburg), and 344 (Lamsdorf).

Barth was located on the edge of the Baltic in Pomerania, where the water table was so high it was almost impossible to dig underground. *Stalag Luft* VI at Heydekrug was one of the most isolated of the *Luftwaffe* camps, located in East Prussia, near the old border with Lithuania, 25 miles north-west of Tilsit. It had three compounds. *Stalag Luft* VII Bankau was on the Polish/German border, east of Breslau. *Stalag* IVB Mühlberg-am-Elbe was a Transit Holding Camp bordering Saxony. It held a wide range of prisoners from many nations, at a time when the *Luft-Lager* (camps for aircrew prisoners) were becoming overfilled. *Stalag* VIIIB Teschen was located in the south-east corner of Germany, one of the furthermost points of the Reich, on the frontier with Czechoslovakia and Poland. By the end of April 1944 one of the most notorious of all the camps had become the large *Luftwaffe* camp in Silesia: *Stalag Luft* III.

24 March 1944, Sagan, Silesia
It was an unusual night. In one hut in the compound, despite it being late, with snow on the ground, steam rose from all the windows. Entering through the door at one end of the block, the smoke would have proved almost overwhelming – enough to choke you in an air thick with it. Cigarette smoke: the cigarettes of tired men smoking earnestly to calm their jaded nerves. Two hundred extraordinary men: extraordinary because they were not dressed in the clothes normally worn by *Kriegies*[2] – the rough workmen's trousers, old worn out battledresses, American infantry greatcoats, Polish overcoats. No, these clothes were designed to fit precisely; they were tailor made.

There were 15 huts in this particular *Stammlager*, and in each hut were 13 rooms: seven on one side, six on the other, with a central corridor, just over a metre wide, like a school dormitory. On one side there was also a small kitchen, a washroom, and a night lavatory. Into this tiny timber and brick construction that night, were jammed over 200 men who had been selected to participate in one of the greatest POW breakouts in history. The date was 24 March 1944: this was the *Luftwaffe's* third *Stammlager*, and the third compound to be built on the site – the notorious *Stalag Luft* III North Compound.

In the other huts in the camp, men were aware something 'big' was going on, but they didn't want to know too much about it, unless they were directly involved, for there was a fear of giving something away. The huts in the compound faced roughly north-north-west. At the northern edge of the site was the *Vorlager*, the front of the camp, in which stood a coal shed, a small brick parcel store with an adjacent solitary confinement block (the 'cooler'), and a sick quarters or 'hospital'. These had direct access to the main gate and guardroom.

What many people today do not realise, largely due to the fantasies of what has been described as a 'silly' film made over 16 years later, is that there were over 10,000 Allied prisoners of war in *Stalag Luft* III. The Hollywood recreation was a scaled down and much simplified version of the original camp. In fact there were five compounds at Sagan. Not only was it a very large camp, but the North Compound was also designed from the outset to be a relatively lavish one. Eric Foinette remembered: 'The North Compound was considered to be a luxury camp, constructed at Göring's instigation on the theory that, if the prisoners were comfortable, there would be less enthusiasm for escape.'[3]

How wrong he was.

There were four other compounds in the camp. The earliest was the East Compound which had hosted an ingenious escape utilising only three prisoners and a physical training vaulting horse. Laurie Simpson wrote a 'Top Secret' report on *Stalag Luft* III for MI9 after being repatriated in 1945:

> '*Stalag Luft III consisted of five compounds, East, Centre, North, South and West, and a compound a few miles away at Bellaria. Bellaria and East were all RAF and Dominion aircrews, North was mixed Allied personnel, and South, West and Centre were American. The Compound described in this report was the North. Here there were about 1,200 British aircrew, 500-600 Americans, and a few hundred mixed Allies, namely Polish, Norwegian, Dutch, Free French and Belgian.*'[4]

The East Compound
Derek Hodgkinson's arrival at the East Compound at *Stalag Luft* III was uninspiring:

> '[We were] marched across the *Vorlager* to the main gate of the camp proper. The wire on either side was lined by *Kriegies* and the gate itself guarded by a couple of sentries under a junior NCO, all heavily armed. A strong wind was blowing under a grey, leaden sky and the whole scene looked cheerless and menacing. Then as we drew near, they gave us a ragged cheer. The gate was opened and the inevitable cry went up: "*Abandon hope all ye who enter here.*"'[5]

Eric Foinette arrived at 'the new RAF camp' in May 1942:

> 'The East Compound consisted of eight residential huts with rooms to take eight persons [each].[6] There was also a cookhouse/canteen plus three external washhouses and earth latrines or 'aborts'. The arrival of the first US senior officer, Lt Col Albert Clark, who was a hygiene

expert, led to modifications to the latrines. Because urine and faeces went into the same pit, the place was infested with flies and worms, causing epidemics of the "squitters" or "runs" (gastroenteritis).'[7]

Bert Clark persuaded the Germans that urine should be drained off separately and other improvements, in accordance with the US Army manual, were introduced with beneficial results. This work involved digging slit trenches to a new sump, near the trip wires. While this was proceeding, three officers, Goldfinch, Lamont and Best, utilised the trenches to excavate a shallow tunnel to the wire by 'moling' (burrowing very close to the surface). They got out after 36 hours, but were caught five days later.

'The East Compound held on average 1,400 officers of various Allied nationalities', Derek Hodgkinson commented, 'British, South African, Canadian, Polish, Norwegian, American and Czechoslovakian, to name a few. The accommodation consisted of eight wooden barrack blocks. They were designed to house 100 in 10 rooms, each measuring 24 ft by 16 ft, but most of the time we were well above this.'[8]

Hodgkinson gave a very honest account of his feelings towards camp life in his memoirs:

'For the first two or three months one was so glad to be alive, and the situation one found oneself in so novel, that life seemed interesting and exciting. Then, gradually, the monotony, frustration and uncertainty for the future began to creep in, until eventually it dominated one's whole being and became intolerable. After I had been in the camp for a year, I reached the stage when I would wake up in the morning, survey the prospect of yet another ghastly day, and be physically sick. I would try to keep myself busy for every moment of the sixteen hours of wakefulness, but no matter how hard I tried, the stark blankness of existence would obtrude and a feeling of nausea overcome me.'[9]

One of the first people he talked to was the SBO, Group Captain Herbert Massey, who had a room to himself in Block 62, known as 'the Flagship'. Massey informed him, 'For you the war is definitely NOT over.' Hodgkinson was told that this was the start of another tour and his duty was to escape. He drew an affectionate portrait of Massey, often depicted at a distance in most accounts of *Stalag Luft* III:

'Poor Massey; he was given command of a bomber station and, although well over age for operational flying, he decided he must have a go, and formed a crew out of the station leaders (Navigation, Signals, Gunnery, etc.) and was promptly shot down on his first raid. His leg was broken and had not healed properly, so he always walked with a stick and was often in pain. He was of the old school and, I used to think, rather pompous and fuddy-duddy. He was eventually repatriated[10] and... on arrival in London was summoned to give evidence [on the 'Great Escape'] at a secret meeting of the House of Commons, and was able to give a first-hand account of what had happened.'[11]

Eric Foinette recalled the antics of a number of characters in the East Compound. Squadron Leader Roger Maw[12] '...celebrated Christmas [by] getting well drunk on our camp "hooch"', Foinette remembered. 'He proceeded to roll a wooden bath tub through Barrack Block 63 but, as it was wider at the top, this proved a difficult operation'. Maw shared a small end room with the heir to Viscount Allenby's peerage, a prisoner named Wentworth. Maw created a number of Heath Robinson-type gadgets for their room.

'It was alleged that he bashed a ferret's[13] finger with a mallet when the goon[14] shoved it through a hole in the floor,' Foinette remembered, but thought that this was probably one of a number of 'line shoots' told by the imaginative POWs.

Another character was D.A. ffrench-Mullen.[15] That same Christmas, Foinette recalled, ffrench-Mullen '…got well pickled and climbed into one of the brick incinerators with another POW and proceeded to shout rude things at the guards in the "goon boxes".[16] The sentries soon replied with bursts of machine gun fire as ffrench-Mullen popped his head up.' He was rescued by German officers but, taking umbrage, they confiscated all the rum and raisins in the camp's Red Cross parcels as a punishment.

Derek Hodgkinson remembered another amusing incident that occurred in the East Compound:

'We had a new *Lager* officer, a magnificent creature, clad in an immaculate uniform, from the shoulders of which flowed a gorgeous long cape lined in scarlet. His highly polished riding boots were spurred and his left hand rested on the hilt of one of those peculiar, ornate dress daggers so beloved by the Germans. It had been raining heavily the night before and as he distastefully minced his way towards me over a sea of thick mud, he was greeted by roars of laughter and wolf whistles from the chaps.

'It was definitely not his day. The counting did not go well for the Germans, as it so happened that an hour before the *Appel*, one of our chaps had gone through the main gate in the bottom of a refuse cart and we wanted to give him time to get clear. The prisoners consequently were breaking ranks and messing around, so that in the end, the senior NCO had to report the figures hopelessly astray.'

After a recount with similar results, the *Lager* officer was chattering with rage. He ordered Hodgkinson to call the parade to attention and, in halting English, shouted:

'"*You British must be made to realise we are not playing a game of cricket! I will call the guard!*" With that, he drew himself up to his full, gorgeous height, saluted, threw his cloak around him and about-turned smartly.'

The effect, unfortunately, was ruined: his spurs became crossed and he fell full length into the mud at Hodgkinson's feet: 'The parade fell about with laughter,' Hodgkinson recalled, 'the sight of him stomping off, covered from head to foot with mud, was too much to bear!' Armed guards duly arrived to complete the count, and the escaper had a two hour start. The *Lager* Officer was never seen again.[17]

Alan James was in the East Compound from June 1943. He remembered that there was plenty of activity in the camp, most of it being – weather permitting – to walk around the perimeter track, which was a quarter of a mile long; also there were deck tennis and football to play, and 'a reasonable library with a fair selection of books', one of which was a paperback copy of D.H. Lawrence's *Lady Chatterley's Lover*. The only trouble was, James recalled, the book had been read so many times that it had become split up into several sections, such that '…when you came to the end of your section you had to find the person with the next part'.[18]

Many of the POWs had their wristwatches confiscated when they entered the camp, and then it was discovered that Rolex in Switzerland had agreed to send their own watches to British POWs on the condition that they would pay for them after the war.[19]

'Such confidence in 1942 in a British victory was pretty amazing', Eric Foinette recalled. But many POWs applied for and received the goods until HMG stopped the trading.[20]

The Wooden Horse Escape

Stalag Luft III was a difficult camp from which to escape – but it was not impossible. By 1943 a maze of aborted tunnels honeycombed the subterranean surface of the camp. The main reasons for the failure of these tunnels were German seismographs located all around the perimeter at a short distance below the surface. Although many prisoners felt that tunnels were a useless effort, others considered they offered escapees their only hope. Cal Younger isolated the problem:

> 'The solution seemed to lie in either shortening the length of the tunnel, which involved finding a way of beginning in open ground, or in digging very deep so that the vibrations of the digging were lost in the earth.'[21]

The escape that encapsulated the first method became known as the 'Wooden Horse' escape, made from the centre of the parade ground. The other method, using tunnels set deep in the earth, was personified by the 'Great Escape' of March 1944.

The 'Wooden Horse' venture took place in the summer of 1943, the brainchild of three men. They were Eric Williams, who was later awarded an MC for his venture, Oliver Philpott and Michael Codner.[22] Eric Foinette was in the same room as Philpott: 'We went into Block 62 and Room 12 was formed with Oliver Philpott as room "*Führer*".'[23] On their way to Sagan, Foinette recalled, the *Kriegies* tried to saw through the wooden floor of their cattle truck: 'Oliver Philpott, Roy Hester and I tried to loosen the barbed wire over the ventilator in the side of the van, but neither effort came to fruition and we arrived at Sagan to be surrounded by armed goons for the half-mile march to the new camp.'[24] After the war, Williams wrote a book about his escape, *The Wooden Horse*. In fact this was his third book. The first, *Goon in the Block*, was written in 1943 after Williams had returned to England. The second, *The Tunnel*, was written after the war. *Goon in the Block* included some of the material that *The Wooden Horse* contained but, because hostilities were still in full swing, certain details of the escape had to be excluded.

In *The Wooden Horse* Williams described the germination of the idea: whilst walking around the circuit in the East Compound, Codner suggested a new method of escape to Williams. Codner's idea came from a wooden horse the Ancient Greeks had used to enter the city of Troy during the Trojan Wars. The Greek wooden horse was a deception: an assault machine, disguised as a gift, which carried alien warriors into the city. Codner's idea was to build a trap in the centre of the parade ground and disguise it with a wooden vaulting horse containing a digger, for a few hours each day, during daily PT practice. The horse was what Williams described as '…a square thing with a padded top and sides that went right down to the ground.' Digging had to be done from inside the horse whilst PT-practising *Kriegies* jumped over it. 77 Squadron navigator Dennis Bateman was one of those participating:

> 'We had to jump over the damn thing doing gymnastics. They said, "Come on lads, join in the fun", that sort of thing – so the guards could see what we were doing. It was high enough to jump over if you were careful, but it was knocked over once or twice by careless people, although hastily put back again. They said there was an escape going on, and we knew there

were people down below, but they said, "Do nothing – don't ask any questions." So we kept absolutely quiet about it, apart from those immediately concerned.

'When the time came to finish exercising, we'd ease off and the *Kriegie* standing by it would call "time" for the chap to come up, and then they'd wheel it back to the hut. It took a while to dig the sand out – it must have been some weeks.' [25]

Codner envisioned the horse as being foolproof: it would be carried out every day and vaulted over, with a trap that was a foot below the surface. But Williams was sceptical, envisaging sand dispersal as a big problem. 'We'll have to take it back with us', Codner suggested; 'use a kitbag or something…'[26]

The horse was eventually built by *Kriegie* carpenters in the East Compound, having been designed by one of Eric Foinette's former COs at Binbrook, the ubiquitous Roger Maw. Derek Hodgkinson was Security Officer on the Escape Committee for the East Compound and Williams, Codner and Philpott had to clear their scheme with the Committee before it was allowed. Hodgkinson recalled:

'The carpenters made an excellent job of the horse. It was built out of wood with three-ply packing cases with a pad along the top made of sacking stuffed with wood shavings. Inside the frame there were sufficient cross pieces for two, or even three, in an emergency to wedge themselves in. The bar to hang the sausage-shaped sandbags ran its length under the top padding, and there were holes on each side of the horse through which long poles could be pushed so that four men could lift and carry it.' [27]

The tunnel was begun on 8 July 1943. By that time Philpott had left Foinette's room and was bunking with Williams and Codner. All three of them escaped on 29 October and successfully made 'home runs'.

Oliver Philpott recalled the night of the escape:

'When we reckoned it was dark, Williams said: "We're breaking now… follow me!" I crawled along the tunnel and suddenly he said, "Keep quiet now! We're breaking!" And I could hear Michael Codner; he was obviously cutting the way through the roof at the end of the tunnel on the freedom side. And it was falling in: *Thud, thud, thud!* I was following Williams's kit bag and suddenly it wasn't there! I realised that these two had actually got out! They'd got out and were presumably in the woods, among the pine trees, across the little road. You can't wait in a thing like that, so I go up to the front of the tunnel, and there I could see the night sky above. And I looked up and I saw the German looking in – he's looking *in* to the camp, fortunately. Well there was no time to study him or anything, so I hoiked my bundles up one after another, and followed them up, hauled myself out, and then streaked across the little road and into those heavenly pine trees which gave cover. There was no shot, no shouting, no nothing. We had all said we'd crawl across this road like commandos – highly disciplined people – but we'd gone across that road, each of us in turn, at a hundred yards sprint speed, without any doubt! We wanted to get away from that lit-up area.'[28]

Alan James was in the East Compound after the tunnel broke:

'It was discovered about 11 p.m., and the guards checked the rooms to determine who was missing. The escapees' beds had been filled by other prisoners, their own beds being left empty. The following morning there was a photo check, but we were instructed that, contrary to usual practice, we were not to co-operate, to give the escapees more time before an accurate description could be circulated.'

Another check was called for and a squad of armed soldiers filed into the compound. 'Most of us thought that discretion was the better part of valour,' James recalled, 'and made tracks for the parade ground.' However a few brave souls were slow to respond until some shots were fired. Then a wing commander shouted out, "Don't worry boys, they're only blanks!" It was revealed later, however, that there were a number of bullet holes in one building.'[29]

Of the three escapees, Oliver Philpott didn't return to England for over five months as all three of them were detained temporarily in Sweden. In *Stalag Luft* III, Derek Hodgkinson recalled: 'The first we knew about it was when a member of their room received a watch he had not requested from Rolex in Switzerland, and engraved on the back was a Trojan Horse!'[30] In April 1944 Peter Hughes was in the bar of the officers' mess at RAF Leuchars when a stranger walked in. A greeting rang out and someone exclaimed, 'Hello Ollie, I never knew a Beaufort could stay up this long!'

> 'It transpired that this was Oliver Philpott of "Wooden Horse" fame, who had left Leuchars in a 42 Squadron Beaufort some two years earlier and failed to return. But here he was, and he told us he had just landed from Sweden travelling in the bomb bay of a BOAC Mosquito. He gave us a preview of the now famous "Wooden Horse" escape from *Stalag Luft* III by which he and two companions had made a "home run". Little was I to know that five months later I would be in the very compound from which he had made his escape.'[31]

The Centre Compound

From March 1942 Ronnie Cartwright was in the Centre Compound for non-commissioned men. '*Luft* III was vermin-free with about 40 prisoners to a room', he recalled. 'Lights out at 10 p.m. so one prisoner would remain up with a spring-operated gramophone and play countless Vera Lynn records. Ablutions and toilets were primitive,' he said, 'and still no hot water.

'There were two incidents which remain firmly with me', Cartwright remembered. 'An Irish friend, who obviously couldn't take the strain, tried to commit suicide by cutting his throat. He [climbed up into] the ceiling in the ablutions and was discovered when someone noticed blood coming from the ceiling. When revealed, he was resting quite comfortably with his hands behind his head – just waiting for death.

'On another sad occasion, a prisoner, whose nerves must have cracked, suddenly charged the perimeter fencing quite near an armed sentry box. The guard in the sentry box opened fire and killed him instantly. The prisoner fell, but got entangled in the barbed wire and hung there until the Germans came and removed his body. It was sheer murder.'[32]

Peter Buttigieg[33] was another prisoner in the Centre Compound. When he entered it early in the autumn of 1942:

> '...there was a confusion of bearded faces with home-made hats all eagerly welcoming the new prisoners and asking questions about the state of the war. When did we think it was going to end? Had we seen any preparations made to open the second front etc. etc? Of course we only had very vague answers to all of these. We didn't know any more than they did.'[34]

Very soon after his arrival, Buttigieg had to report to Sgt James A.G. 'Dixie' Deans, the NCO who was the camp's 'Man of Confidence'.[35] Deans had been in 77 Squadron when it was based at Linton-on-Ouse in Yorkshire in 1940. He was the pilot of a Whitley V that was lost during a raid on Bremen on 10 September 1940. The aircraft crashed in Overijssell, north-east Holland. All the crew members survived. Despite being non-commissioned, Deans had developed a reputation during the war of being a reliable camp leader that equalled or possibly, in some sense, even surpassed that of Roger Bushell.[36] This was regarded as being the case by the German *Luftwaffe*, the British Air Ministry and also the Swiss Protecting Power. Buttigieg, who was Maltese by birth, recalled his first meeting with Deans:

'When it was my turn to face "Dixie", I felt he inspired respect and dignity. He looked at me with soul-searching effect and I got the impression he knew my innermost thoughts; yet I felt he was sympathetic and understood my every worry and anxiety which he inexplicably seemed to put to rest.'[37]

Another arrival in the Centre Compound at that time was navigator, Sergeant Cal Younger, who had been shot down on 29 May 1942 – the night before the first Thousand-Bomber raid. He met and befriended Buttigieg at *Dulag Luft*. But Younger's first impression of the camp at Sagan was not positive:

'*Dulag Luft* was small, and in a way intimate. *Stalag Luft* III, which we could see as we struggled down the road from the station, had a forbidding bleakness. Long wooden huts huddled together in tidy rows. The wind whipped the sand around the spindly legs on which the barracks perched, scuffled it through the wire, beneath the ugly, squat sentry boxes, across the sandy, stump-punctuated wasteland surrounding the camp, into the frigid pine trees that loomed beyond.'[38]

Upon arrival he too was interviewed by Deans. Younger was surprised by the respect a German guard showed the NCO when asked by the new arrivals if their parents would know they were safe. The *Feldwebel* held up one hand and told them that any queries they had would be answered by Sergeant Deans: a measure of how high an opinion the Germans held of 'Dixie'. Younger's record of meeting him was similar to Buttigieg's – one of awe:

'When I stood at his table he regarded me steadily, and I felt that in those few moments he isolated my every virtue, laid bare my every weakness, and gently pushed aside my every pretence; revealing nothing of himself, save his strength.'[39]

'Deans was an elected leader,' Younger later wrote, 'and he kept order by the sheer weight of his personality. There were men his senior in rank, but they, like everyone else, were loyal beyond belief… In three years I never heard a murmur against his benevolent despotism.'[40]

A further newcomer at that time, who later formed a 'combine' of three[41] with Younger and Buttigieg and shared Hut 140, was Canadian Thomas Breech Miller, a Flight Sergeant from 78 Squadron. Miller was a navigator shot down three days after Younger, whose Halifax had been blasted by Flak on the way to Essen; the rudders stalled and the aircraft went into a flat spin off the Dutch coast. Miller, who liked to be known as 'T.B.', and the rear gunner, P/O P.J. Jones, were thrown clear when the aircraft hit the sea and the fuselage broke in two. But both were badly injured. The dinghy ejected on impact and Jones climbed in; 'T.B.' was left floating and paralysed on his back until Jones pulled him aboard. They then spent four days afloat until picked up by an E-Boat. Younger remembered Miller, appearing as 'an extraordinary figure' in the camp: dressed only in a winter singlet tied round the waist, he '…walked barefoot, head prognathically forward, shoulders hunched, hair flopping over his eyes.'[42] 'T.B.' always carried a tin into which he would put any cigarette butts he found in the sand: these were later smoked in Younger's pipe.[43]

Up to the time of Buttigieg's arrival no one had escaped from *Stalag Luft* III and the *Stammlager* gained the reputation of being impregnable. But Buttigieg soon came up with what he described as 'a modest plan': he intended to go out as a Spanish worker. With the approval of the Escape Committee, he climbed under the chassis of a lorry delivering swedes and potatoes to the camp. The truck drove out through the first, inner gate and then the second, main one. Once outside the camp, however, the vehicle turned around and re-entered to collect some rotten potatoes from the German officers' kitchens. By this time Buttigieg was feeling extremely uncomfortable, with bolts sticking into his back. His body sagged. He was soon discovered and hauled out amidst a burst of shooting. This led to the appearance of Bader, 'Wings' Day, the SBO, Massey, and several others.

Buttigieg was then thrown in the cooler. The Germans were under the misconception that he was an officer, until numerous confused headcounts at evening roll call suggested that he should not have been in that section of the camp at all. Whilst in solitary he became involved with an idea for a tunnel. He had already assisted on one failed project in the Centre Compound which had earned him the nickname 'The Human Mole', such was his digging speed. This time, however, he hoped for more success. There was a rectangular lavatory block, 60 feet from the perimeter wire with a cesspit underneath. *Kriegies* would sit and 'do the business' on a plank, 14 inches above ground level with circular holes cut in. The idea was to dig a two foot diameter circular tunnel from one of the side walls of the cesspit to come out under the nearest guard tower, a distance of around 96 feet. This had to be done in four days, before the cesspit was emptied again. To assist Buttigieg in his endeavours, he teamed up with a fellow POW nicknamed 'the Monk' – Sergeant Salvage, who supplied him with a chisel.

As the tunnel developed they had to employ two other men to kick the sand back away from the tunnel face, into the cesspit. In three days they had cleared 80 feet. But this was inadequate with a four day schedule, and so the complement was increased to six to speed up work. By that time the Germans were hot on their trail: 13 'ferrets' appeared in the vicinity of the latrine in the course of one hour. The POWs intended to go out after evening *Appel* but, by the time they went on parade, Buttigieg was disturbed to notice that there were a huge number of 'ferrets' walking around the compound. The count was delayed and delayed. Eventually he got away and sauntered discreetly towards the latrines. To his shock he saw '…about two dozen "ferrets" digging in the sand with prodders.' They were looking for the tunnel.

The young escapees' hearts were raised, however, as the Germans put the 'prodders' away. But it was a forlorn hope. A tractor later appeared, entered the 60-foot wide area between the warning wire and the perimeter fence, and the tunnel collapsed! It was Buttigieg's last escape attempt from Sagan. Their hopes dashed, his disheartened comrades consoled themselves with the thought that it was too cold to spend the night out of doors in any case. The following June, Buttigieg was transferred to Heydekrug where escape was more difficult.

The North Compound
Laurie Simpson's MI9 report stated:

> 'The size of the compound was approximately 150 yds x 250 yds. In this area there were fifteen huts, size roughly 36 ft x 130 ft. Each hut had 14 rooms: twelve to the ten large rooms, and four to the smaller ones; the average hut accommodation being 120 to 150 men. To each large room there were two 25 or 40 watt light bulbs, one stove, one or two tables, four to eight chairs or stools, six double tier bunks, and four to six lockers. In every hut were a small lavatory and a washroom. The water supply here was fairly good except in mid-summer when there was a shortage during the main part of the day. Fuel ration in summer was practically nil, but a little better for the winter. We supplemented our fuel supply by digging up the tree stumps with which the compound was pitted. There was a washroom in the compound and we had hot showers once or twice a week.
>
> 'The food rations issued by the Germans were fairly good at first, but by a series of cuts gradually became less and less. Except for some commodities the basic ration such as bread, potatoes and barley were fairly regular.
>
> 'Red Cross supplies were very good, until the end of August 1944, when the camp went on to a half parcel per week issue. Full parcels were resumed at Christmas.
>
> 'As Stalag Luft III was the central camp for air force POWs we received fairly regular deliveries of mail and personal parcels. After 'D-Day', except for the month of October, this service became very spasmodic. For recreation we had sufficient area for a rugby and a soccer ground. At various places around the camp there were spaces on which volley ball courts were located.'[44]

Laurie was quite disorientated when he first arrived at Sagan, for reasons he later explained:

> 'When you first go to a prison camp, after you've jumped out of an aeroplane, and wandered around France for a bit, and been in prison at Fresnes and in Frankfurt, and eventually arrive, your thoughts are getting a bit muddled. You've been living day by day and that still goes on for a while when you first arrive at the camp, and your memory of the first few days there is pretty hazy.'[45]

Laurie Simpson arrived at *Stalag Luft* III on 12 March 1944. The rest of his crew were already there, apart from 'Jock' Nairn and Johnny Osborne who went to the NCO camp *Stalag Luft* VI at Heydekrug, East Prussia. Laurie was taken to the *Vorlager* and shoved into a cell in the cooler with a man whose aircraft had blown up over Berlin and who woke up lying across a railway line. After a few days Laurie was marched to the camp gate and saw Wally Maltby, the mid-upper gunner from his first tour, walking around inside. Maltby had evaded capture for a few days after being shot down in his 12 Squadron Lancaster on 15 February. He was eventually captured by a local policeman, handed over to the Gestapo and interrogated. Laurie was taken to a hut, given a pack of Red Cross food and a food cereal form, and then a substantial quantity of cigarettes, including some Canadian ones. He later received a shirt, a pullover, a red coat and an American infantryman's greatcoat. He had arrived twelve days before the mass breakout and he discovered that everybody wanted to go. He was assigned to Hut 123, and Room 6.[46] In the bunk immediately below him was a Flight Lieutenant Wylton Todd, a former navigator on Mosquitoes, who had been a very successful architect in America before the war. He later designed the memorial to the 50 escapees shot after the 'Great Escape'.

The manner in which aircrew were assigned their billets in the camp appeared to be haphazard to Laurie: 'I don't know how we got allocated to our rooms', he later recalled. 'I think that they know when you're coming in; the Senior British Officer's office asks for the allocation to be made with former crew members.' So Laurie was placed in Block 123 on the south-west side of the camp with four others from his crew: Alistair Kennedy, Colin McLeod, Arthur Schrock and Johnny Rydings.

Alan Bryett, a bomb-aimer with 158 Squadron, arrived in *Stalag Luft* III at the end of August 1943 and was assigned to Hut 122, east of 123:

> 'When you first got there, the first thing was to be 'kitted out'. That was a bit of a joke really because the stores were very sparse. You went to one particular room, and it was a room in Hut 123, which was the next hut to mine, which was the stores room. One of the RAF prisoners was in charge of the stores, and he would go there and say to you, "Well, what have you got?" I had my flying boots with me, so I had a decent pair of shoes. But my trousers, jacket, shirt, pants, and vest were either filthy or covered in blood. You hadn't changed since you were shot down; so you got rid of all your old clothing and were given a "hotchpotch". I had a pair of army trousers and two vests, I think, and two pairs of pants, an RAF shirt, and an RAF blouse. That was all.'[47]

When he moved into his hut, Bryett noticed it was 'very bare', with ten bunk beds in a room in stacks of three. He found he always ended up in the top bunk because he was 'a little fellow' while at the bottom were 'the hefty fellows'. There was a table in the centre with six to eight chairs – '…a wooden chair, a German chair and maybe one or two made out of Red Cross boxes.' Every occupant had a limited amount of personal space and personal possessions were put in an empty Red Cross box. Each hut had a washroom about 12 ft by 12 ft, with three washbasins each side and water running into a sump in the middle of the floor. A single toilet at the end of each block consisted of a wooden seat, with no flushing mechanism: all excrement went into a pit which was emptied by Russian POWs every 10 days, with a suction machine mounted on a four-wheeled horse-drawn cart, nicknamed the 'honey wagon'. The CO in each hut, normally a squadron leader or wing commander, had a small room for two people, of slightly better standard. Finally there was a primitive kitchen with gas stove and simple cooking facilities, with three or four pots and pans.[48]

There were only 15 huts in the compound at Sagan. Conditions were better than those in the 'other ranks'' compounds, but paled into a level of insipid hedonism compared to Auschwitz.

Also bunking in Block 123 was a fresh-faced young English navigator from 432 Squadron, named Dick Sewell. He was nicknamed 'Wimpy', probably due to the fact that he and his Wellington crew had ditched in the North Sea in September 1943, returning from an op on Hannover. All five members of the crew survived but were confined in the aircraft's dinghy, in appallingly hostile conditions, for four-and-a-half days. The bomb-aimer, Les Whitton, was a Scot on his 15th operation:

> 'I was shot down on 23 September 1943, and I didn't get into *Stalag Luft* III for about two weeks. I came down in the "Drink", in the North Sea. We were coming back from Hannover and we got attacked from below: the guy that shot at us had hit the tanks. We just kept going,

and knew roughly where we were, and we made for the nearest point towards the English coast. The navigator [Sewell], because he had nothing to go by, reckoned that we were heading towards Yarmouth, which he thought was the nearest point. Later the skipper noticed there was only a small amount of fuel in the tanks, about the quantity of that in a cigarette lighter, so he said: "*We're going to have to ditch.*" Then the engines cut. Anyway we carried on with no engines towards what we thought was Yarmouth. We could have been just off the English coast. Skipper did a wonderful job in ditching and we all got out of it, into this bloody dinghy! It was a bloody marvellous landing. It wasn't funny – four-and-a-half days in "the Drink"!'[49]

Whitton was allocated to Block 122, where the aborted tunnel 'Dick' commenced. Because he was a friend of Sewell's, Whitton often dropped into Block 123 and got to know some of the fellow prisoners there. Laurie Simpson was senior officer in the block: 'Each hut must have had 10 rooms, eight to a room, say 80 to a block,' he recalled, 'there must have been in excess of 1,500 in the camp.' A sketch plan made of Room 6, Block 123 at the time shows that eight men lived there: Michael Raye ('Mickie'); D.W. Finlay ('Bish'); N.F.Lewis ('Deacon'); L.J. Simpson ('Laurie'); Arthur R. Schrock ('Doc'); F.R. Kennure ('Fosannack'); L.R. Sewell ('Wimpy'); W.C. Hawke ('Admiral'); and J.A. Rydings ('Johnny'). Rydings was a tough, moustachioed, mid-upper gunner from Western Australia who did not mix easily and whom Les Whitton found to be '...an aloof sort of person'. 'He didn't make friends easily', Les commented. Arthur Schrock, nicknamed 'Doc' in the hut, Simpson's wireless operator, was the complete opposite, a noisy, gregarious man whom many found irritating because he had a tendency to steer any conversation his own way. Whitton:

'Well he had one subject of conversation, and you could be talking about anything, any subject under the sun, and he'd direct it onto women. Quite incredible! He'd a big heart – at heart he was nice, a good fellow: he'd have given you his last loaf of bread.'

Two other POWs in Hut 123 were Alistair 'Shorty' Kennedy, and Colin McLeod. Kennedy was the navigator on Simpson's last crew. He was the best man at Laurie's wedding, and was from the Arncliffe area of Sydney, but had been brought up in Stirlingshire, Scotland. He and Laurie had shared officers' quarters at Binbrook. Before joining the RAAF, and training as a navigator in Canada, Kennedy had worked as a local government audit department surveyor in New South Wales. Colin McLeod, the bombardier, was the second tallest man on the 'Simpson Kite'. Formerly a wool classer and sheep shearer from New South Wales, he was described by Laurie as a 'rough, tough roustabout'.

Another 460 man in the North Compound at that time was Flying Officer 'Frankie' Falkenmire, shot down on 29 March 1943 on a raid to Berlin. News of his fate did not reach 460 Squadron until the beginning of May 1943. Laurie noted: *'Word of Shorty Grenfell's crew (all killed except Dunn and Webb) and Dave Charlick's crew, of which Frankie Falkenmire was the only one to get out. He is a P.O.W.'*[50] On ANZAC Day 1944 a German photographer at Sagan photographed all the Australian POWs in the camp region by region. Falkenmire was snapped together with all the other New South Wales POWs in a group.

The fighter ace Robert Stanford Tuck was in the North Compound at that time, although he was shortly to be moved away to Belaria, on the other side of Sagan town, with 'Wings' Day and a few others just before the breakout. Two of those in the Belaria contingent were an RCAF Spitfire pilot, Wally Floody, and George Harsh. Floody's experience of working in dangerous conditions, constricted, dark spaces, choking dust, and trolley trucks in the Canadian mines before the war, put him in a good position for advising on the construction of the tunnels in the North Compound.[51]

George Harsh must have been the only POW in *Stalag Luft* III who had been a long-term prisoner before, in civilian life. In fact, the story of Harsh's life before the war was like an odyssey in itself. His original imprisonment occurred at the height of the Depression, the seeds of it beginning during the Prohibition era in America when, with a gang of four teenagers, all from well-to-do families, he planned a perfect crime.

For weeks the gang raided various establishments for the excitement of it. Then, one night in October 1928, Harsh was elected to hold up a grocery store and a gun battle ensued, in which George accidentally shot one of the two assistants, who let off a stray shot which killed the other assistant, then died. Harsh was caught, tried and sentenced to the electric chair. However this was commuted to life imprisonment due to the money in his family and a sympathetic judge. He then spent eight years on a Georgia chain gang and, eventually, although having no medical qualifications, performed a life-saving emergency medical operation and was granted a state pardon. He travelled to Canada and enlisted in the RCAF and was commissioned. Then, in due course, he became a rear gunner and squadron gunnery officer with 102 Squadron at Pocklington. He was shot down in October 1942 and sent to Sagan.

Wally Floody was the only person in the North Compound who knew of Harsh's past. They had met in 1942 when George was put in the same room as Floody in the East Compound. Floody volunteered to send details of Harsh's survival to his wife in Toronto, and she communicated the news to Harsh's family. This led to a friendship that would last beyond the war. George eventually told Floody of his background, something that Floody revealed to no one. When Roger Bushell, who was the appointed leader of the 'X Escape Organisation', was looking for a Security Chief, Floody realised that Harsh would make a perfect choice and suggested this to Bushell, who was ignorant of the American's background. Initially Harsh wanted nothing to do with the 'X Organisation', although since he felt that he owed Floody a favour, he agreed to contribute his services. George turned out to be the ideal man for the job: there had always been a system of 'stooges' in the camp, but Harsh's knowledge of how prisons worked enabled him to make it more effective.[52]

A 'stooge' was a lookout man employed by the 'X' organisation during the preparations for the breakout at various points in the camp to monitor the movements of the German guards. Laurie Simpson, Eric Hookings and Arthur Cole all acted as such for the North Compound escape: they would stand for hours at specific points with good visibility monitoring the Germans. The POW watching the main gate was called the 'Duty Pilot'. Laurie:

> 'I knew a little about the escape as I was on the surveillance side of it, where you watched who came through the gate and reported it back to the central escape committee – that so-and-so was on the compound. Then they'd nominate someone to follow him to see just what he got up to.
>
> 'We knew something was going on. But we weren't quite sure. We didn't want to know quite what, because a whisper or a peep out of hut number so-and-so could ruin the whole thing.'[53]

Cole:

'"Stooges" were people who watched everyone that came into the compound. There was a room at one of the blocks where there were a couple of blokes on duty, and they logged everyone who came into, and went out of, the compound, and the times.

'When I became active in the escape organisation, the job that they gave me was dependent on the fact that it was in winter at the time when the tunnel "Dick" was being used to disperse the sand from "Harry". I was given a lantern for the hours of darkness before the huts were closed down. There was only one ferret on duty at that time. He was followed, and would often go into a room for a coffee or an English lesson. This was not allowed, but these chaps were cultivated by POWs who spoke German. They were allowed to contact them and the ferrets were buttered up until they came in for coffee and so on. There would be a stooge in the corridor near the room where the ferret was expected. When the ferret went into the room, the stooge outside the room would signal to another stooge at the end of the hut. He would signal to me standing in the path, not far away. And I would shine a green light down the path. My position was carefully chosen so I couldn't be seen from a watchtower, and sand dispersal would commence.

'When the ferret came out the procedure was reversed and I shone a red light down the path to indicate that dispersal should stop. One night it did not, and I was wandering casually down the track with the lantern concealed beneath my greatcoat, and I pretty well bounced, in the darkness, into a chap carrying a kitbag full of sand. I said, "*Get out of sight, you fool, there's a goon ten yards behind me!*" I've often thought to myself, if I hadn't bumped into him and he'd been discovered, that maybe that would have stopped the tunnel, and saved the lives of 50 people. This chap presumably had not seen the red light. You couldn't hang about; you just flashed the light and left. I think the lamp had a slide on it which you could move so that it shone green, yellow or red. We didn't use the yellow, just green or red. Of course it was forbidden stuff and had to be brought inside quickly.'[54]

Bob Stanford Tuck[55] was one who caused Roger Bushell a great deal of concern. A great individualist, Stanford Tuck would often stalk the North Compound circuit alone. Geoffrey Willatt related that Tuck used to wander around on a hot day, sunbathing, hoping that he would soon be as brown as a berry – the aim being that all the girls would love him when he got back to England. He also recalled that Tuck's non-commissioned brother was in the camp, whom Tuck refused to talk to. Arthur Cole was in Block 105, adjacent to Tuck's block:

'Tuck was in Block 106. I didn't know him personally, but I do know that Roger Bushell, head of the escape organisation, "Big X" as we called him, was the CO of Tuck's squadron. He was Stanford Tuck's hero. But Bushell was shot down without any decorations; and Stanford Tuck took over from him, and Tuck was, of course, covered in decorations.'[56]

Tuck's solitary behaviour became a great worry for Bushell, who was a personal friend. The solution was to put Tuck in charge of a 21 year-old bomber pilot named Danny Pearson, whose mind was going. Pearson was due to be considered for repatriation after attempting suicide a number of times and Tuck was made responsible for him until then, becoming his confidant. Pearson was put in a hut full of Canadians who kept an eye on him, ensuring he did not repeat the attempt. But, whilst in the same room as the other *Kriegie*s, Pearson slashed his own tendons and nearly died. The Germans forced the

Swiss Protecting Power to refuse to repatriate him – the main reason for this being that they knew some POWs had earlier feigned madness to be returned home. The Swiss could re-present Pearson's case in six to nine months, so he was returned to the camp hospital.

Eventually the 21 year-old stole out onto the hospital roof one night and made his way across the warning wire to the outer perimeter fence. The watch tower guards waited until the last moment as he was climbing the outer fence before a warning shot was fired across his head. Pearson ignored this and also shouts from the guards, and then he was shot dead.[57] Tuck blamed himself for his death, but Bushell, Massey and others assured him that nothing could have been done. The Germans could not be blamed for refusing to accept Pearson's case as genuine.

Laurie Simpson recalled that he had heard of other people being killed:

'One chap was shot when we were there. I think he was doing a deal with one of the Germans for eggs, or coffee; we had Nescafe come with the Red Cross parcels, and they would give their lives for that. This chap had arranged to go to the wire and exchange this coffee for eggs, or whatever, through the wire – there might have been a different guard on one of the lookout posts. He'd crossed the trip wire, which was about 20 yards from the main wire, and the warning was that if you crossed that you'd be shot. The guard heard the noise, saw the bloke, and he was shot. This was in the evening, because we all heard the shot, but we didn't know what happened until the next day, and by this time we were all locked up in our huts.'

On another occasion Simpson remembered lining up at the main gate to collect Red Cross parcels from the German guards, when a guard pulled out an MP 40 machine-pistol and someone shouted a warning:

'We used to do dealing with the Germans, mostly at the main gate. We would take what we had and the guards would offer us eggs or something like that. Quite often it got to the stage where there were eight or nine blokes standing in a queue, waiting to speak to the guard on the other side. I was five or six back in the queue, and something was said up front which I didn't understand, and everybody in front of me dropped flat. I thought, "Gosh! I'd better join them!" Either someone was having them on, or somebody had said something that suggested someone was going to open fire. It might have been a misunderstanding, but they weren't taking any chances, and obviously their German was as limited as mine.'[58]

Occasionally prisoners were taken outside the camp on work parties and there were a number of times when these sorties were used for escape attempts. Often prisoners would go out under escort to unload parcels at Sagan station. Laurie recalled that on the way they would be met by a group of German children and that the POWs made it a practice to give them small amounts of chocolate as well as teaching them a nursery rhyme. As the party approached, the children would line up by the roadside and recite, 'Good morning Mr RAF officers: up Hitler's chuff for a bag of nuts. God save the King!'[59]

Howard Pearce, the 115 Squadron navigator, remembered that there were escape attempts taking place all the time in the North Compound, with many tunnels being dug. The German in charge of security was *Hauptmann* Pieber. Pieber knew most of what was going on because his 'ferrets' told him everything: 'He also prided himself in speaking colloquial English', Pearce recalled. 'And what he did daily was to count us. He got us out in the morning lined up, more or less on parade. Having counted us successfully and believing that there was no one missing, he said: "Shentlemans, before you go, you think I know bugger nothing! But, you are wrong – *I know bugger all!*" That did it; we just fell about on the ground with laughter – a funny man.'[60]

Eric Hookings, the 619 Squadron Lancaster pilot shot down on 6 November 1944, who had done ten days solitary at *Dulag Luft*, recalled one event at Sagan that still stands out in his memory:

> 'We were told that the camp was to be visited by the famous German boxer, Max Schmeling. We were called on parade and lined up by our CO with "special instructions" and when, to the delight and pride of our German captors, Max Schmeling arrived and drove slowly through the camp gates, all the POWs turned away and completely ignored him.'[61]

Steve Jackson, the 35 Squadron w/ag, met Schmeling at Stalag IIIA Luckenwalde in January 1945: 'He had no doubt that Germany had lost the war,' Jackson recalled, 'but I got an autographed photograph of him for two cigarettes.'[62]

The POW Logbooks
A personal comfort many found, and a relief from the boredom, was the *Wartime Log for British Prisoners* issued by the YMCA and other similar organisations. These were sent to most air force prisoners for their personal use, but their distribution appears to have been patchy – many veterans of POW camps couldn't recall using them.

Arthur Cole:

> 'In the North Compound of *Stalag Luft* III none of us were issued with any such document, and we were chronically short of writing material. We were, I think, issued by the Germans, possibly via the Red Cross, with a letter form, and we were allowed to write one letter only each month. These were written in pencil because we were allowed no pens, although the Escape Organisation had some, smuggled in via concealment, bribery or blackmail.'[63]

Despite these assertions a number of these books still exist in private collections. Arthur Schrock received his from 'The War Prisoners' Aid from the YMCA', based in Geneva. This was implemented following the success of logbooks already issued to American and Canadian POWs, their purpose being, '...*to bring you greetings from friends*' and to facilitate the recording of your experiences '*during these eventful years*'.

POWs were advised that: '*Your own ingenuity may suggest to you many other ways of using this book, which comes to you with our greetings and good wishes.*'[64]

One of Cal Younger's friends at Fallingbostel was collecting in his logbook the thoughts of acquaintances whom he thought may be able to add interesting comments. The *Kriegie* asked Younger to contribute, having seen a poem Cal had written earlier for another prisoner: 'Having logbooks brought to me was no new experience,' Younger wrote, 'but usually I was asked to "draw something funny" – and this at a time[65] when I no longer believed in humour.'[66]

In Room 6, Block 123, 'Doc' Schrock went to town with his. In Les Whitton's words he was 'an above average artist' and the drawings in his logbook demonstrate this. It would appear that at least the occupants of Block 123 doubled up on their work, copying from one book to the other. Both Johnny Rydings and my father's logbooks have copies of 'Doc' Schrock's drawings, as well as those of other artists. These were mostly humorous, but some were serious, and included copies of the warning issued to POWs after the shooting

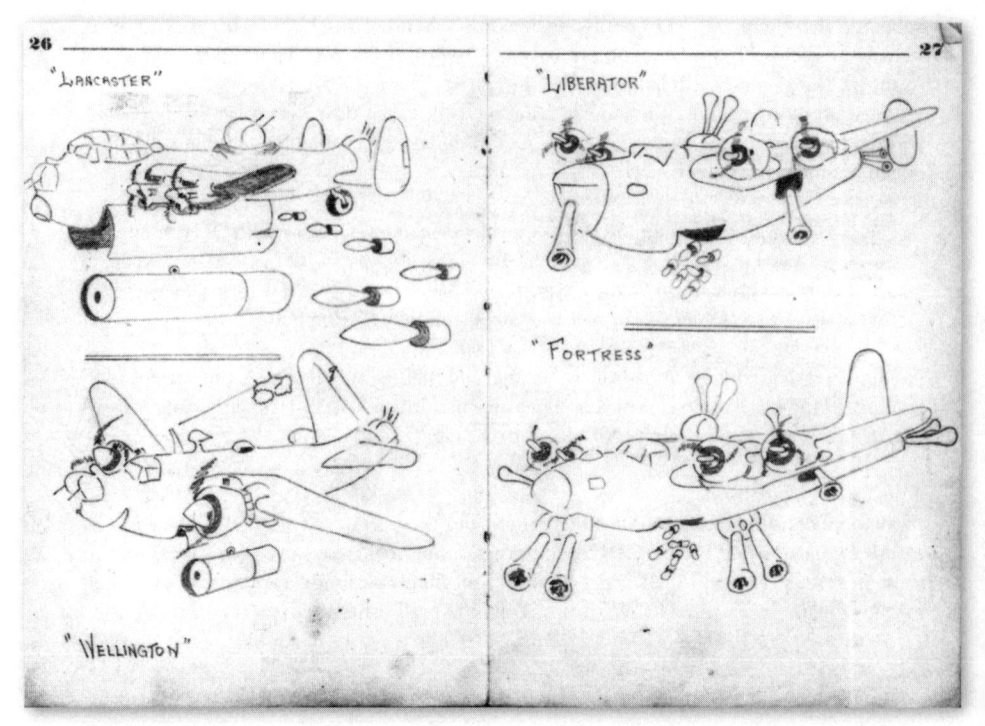

In Room 6, Block 123, at Stalag Luft III, Arthur Schrock, 'an above average artist', produced numerous sketches in his POW logbook, many of them cartoons. One of these consisted of amusing caricatures of the various Allied heavy bombers that the POWs had flown in, including the Lancaster, Wellington, Halifax, Flying Fortress and Liberator. This cartoon, plus 'Where is this now?', also appeared in Johnny Rydings and Laurie Simpson's logbooks. (Schrock)

of 50 of the escapees in the March 1944 'Great Escape': '*To all Prisoners of War! The escape from prison camps is no longer a sport!*' In my father's book there is a sketch map of his evasion route. One set of drawings that occurred more than once in books from Block 123 were cartoon caricatures of the Halifaxes and Wellingtons they had flown in.

In 1988 one of these books, that of Polish fighter pilot, Sqn/Ldr B. Arct, was published entitled *Prisoner of War: My Secret Journal*,[67] with all 152 pages reproduced in full colour. One page is titled '*The Life and Death of the Word Goon*'. Arct wrote: 'The "Goon" was ideally suited to the needs of the POW as a word for their captors.' He then described how the term had become outlawed: the SBOs and Senior American Officers in the Main and North Compounds at his camp, *Stalag Luft* I, Barth, received this instruction on 2 July 1944 from the *Kommandant*:

'The use of the word "goon" was granted to the POW by the Kommandant under the condition that this word would not have any dubious meaning. It has however, been reported to me that the POW have been using the word "focking goon up", the meaning of which is beyond any doubt. Consequently the use of the word "goon up" or "goon" is prohibited, severest punishment being in future for any disobedience against this order. gez. Schroder. *Major u. Gruppenleiter.*'

In 'Doc' Schrock's logbook one page is headed *'Extracts from Letters to POWs'*. These are, for the most part, quotes from wives' and girlfriends' love letters. In fact in the camps these missives were referred to as 'Mespots', a term originating from RAF policing duties in Mesopotamia in the 1920s when men were jilted in such numbers that a 'Mesopotamian letter' came to have a special connotation.[68] Many of these letters contained unintentional wit – to the amusement of the men, and this correspondence was often pinned up with the 'Foodaco'[69] notices in the camp to amuse the *Kriegies*, for example:

'So, I have to spend two weeks in hospital and I can't blame you this time.'
'Do you attend lectures for your BSc at a German university?'
'I hope you don't return passion dead.'
'Try and get to Dresden and have a look at the picture gallery. The blue 'Madonna' is worth seeing.'
'I've married your brother, so I'll still be in the family.'
'I'm having a baby, don't worry I'm being paid 10/6 a week and the American Corporal is sending you some cigarettes.'
'I'm so glad you were shot down before flying became dangerous.'[70]

The men, who were a long way from home, gained great strength from any correspondence they received from loved ones.

Life in the camp

Derek Hodgkinson wrote a very honest account about how he felt about being away from his wife and the service whilst in the prison camp:

'The things that mattered to me most, I suppose, were my wife, flying, fighting and my career in the RAF. Suddenly, I was cut off from all of them and I was singularly ill-equipped to adapt myself to life without them. I loved my wife, dearly, and being without her was a sort of death in itself. Sex, or the lack of it, was difficult to start with, but nature really is a wonderful healer, and after a time the urge had gone – I used to worry about it ever coming back! The prospect of years without being able to fly appalled me, and to hear and see an aircraft, albeit German, fly overhead, was almost too much to bear. The war, and fighting, terrified me to death, but it had so completely absorbed me and become a way of life that to suddenly find oneself impotent to do anything about it, except to try and escape, was unimaginable.'[71]

In his 1945 MI9 report Laurie Simpson commented:

'Life of a Prisoner of War must be considered from many angles [in order] to obtain a full and accurate view of the feelings experienced by those fortunate – or unfortunate, as the case may be – enough to have spent months or years behind barbed wire. A psychologist could probably tell us a lot about the general temperament and reasoning behind the reactions of the Kriegies.

'Food seemed to be of No. 1 importance to all. When he is continually hungry there is a certain amount of nerve strain; he might normally be of a very even temperament and have unbiased views, but hunger can make him very irritable and develop a quite intolerant and narrow-minded attitude.

'We found that it was up to the individual to develop tolerance, restraint, and to keep unruffled in the most trying circumstances. To a great extent this was accomplished despite the fact that the course of events did not always run smoothly. The small courtesies of everyday life, so easily forgotten, were practised and it

was the little things such as these which helped us to remain fairly normal and on good terms with each other through the long waiting days.'[72]

Despite this experience of 'unruffled tolerance', Arthur Cole found the reality of men living together in cramped, less than savoury conditions, extremely difficult: 'Living in a room with other men day in, day out, was absolute hell. We argued, we had spasms of hating each other almost, and being placed in the cooler was almost like a holiday.'[73] Howard Pearce was equally realistic: '...there were days when you didn't want to speak to anybody: you went into a sort of shell. It's just the way people are made I suppose. You just went into yourself and got on your bunk and read and slept to get away from people, but you couldn't get away.'[74] Eric Hookings: 'Of course there were dissents and minor skirmishes between hundreds of men confined in a prisoner of war camp, but I was never involved as such.'

Ronny Cartwright, a flight sergeant in *Stalag Luft* I, however, found a lot of good in his POW experience:

'Harmony within the compound was a necessary ingredient and that element was there in abundance. It was amazing to see how many people from different nationalities and different persuasions could co-operate, show goodwill and share in the common good. Of course there were differences, but understanding and caring led the way. It taught me to accept and live with my neighbour. It was for the common good of all.'

But life could be unendurably dull, and escaping provided a source of 'entertainment' if nothing else. Al Kennedy wrote home:

'Sunday in a *Kriegie* camp – what a life! We don't get treated harshly here, but one gets bored having to stay in one place. Transport facilities have been suspended for the duration, so I guess I shall just have to suffer it. At present I have almost finished my apprenticeship in dishwashing and making tea and coffee. We do all our own cooking here, and we manage to have some weird and wonderful dishes concocted out of Red Cross parcels.'[75]

Phil Bates, flight engineer with 149 Squadron,[76] recollected camp life as '...almost two years of utter boredom beyond belief. I scrounged as much food as I could, kept myself reasonably clean and free of lice, etc. and played a great deal of rugby football. That was it.' Howard Pearce also found POW life '...boring as hell! All you could do all day was to read and walk and play the odd game if it was a decent day; and to wait for the next film to be shown, or play to be put on.'[77]

Roy Fernie was one of the many who found ways to escape the lack of stimulation. He had been a navigator in 158 Squadron in a Halifax named '*The Menace*' which was shot down on 15 October 1942. He did not arrive at prison camp until over a year later. His aircraft had come under heavy fire from a night fighter and Roy was hit by cannon shell splinters many times in his leg. He managed to parachute out and, on landing in Holland, crawled to a nearby cottage, but was the only survivor. The family there gave him first aid and he was taken to a hospital in Arnhem where he remained for a year. At Sagan he earned the nickname 'Alvar Liddell' as he would read the news each day to his fellow *Kriegies* (from the camp's secret radio). His wife recalled: 'He maintained his sanity by playing bridge at all hours.'

The 'Great Escape'

In 1943 an RAAF flight lieutenant was shot down in a Spitfire over Tunisia and parachuted into a minefield. Eventually the Germans picked him up and sent him to *Stalag Luft* III. He was an ex-journalist from New South Wales named Paul Brickhill. Paul was billeted in Block 103 with fellow journalist Conrad Norton, and was a member of the 'X Organisation' responsible for co-ordinating all prisoner escape attempts. Brickhill and Norton realised their situation offered them a unique opportunity:

> 'During the war in Europe, some 100,000 men fell with their aircraft over hostile soil. Of them, about 10,000 lived. And in 10,000 ten-to-one chances for a man's life in air battle, there were going to be some fabulously slim chances that came off.'[78]

They set about recording as many of these stories as they could. My father recalled meeting Brickhill when he first arrived at Sagan:

> 'I wasn't interrogated when I was in the camp. The only interrogation I got was from Paul Brickhill. He wanted to know my story. Everybody who came in, he got their story, and the more spectacular ones, of course, appeared in his book. He was quite a nice bloke: I liked Paul. He was a journalist before the war, and he knew what he was about.'[79]

Les Whitton recalled Brickhill:

> 'I met him, but I wasn't on Christian name terms with him. I knew who he was; I doubt if he knew who I was. He was quite a personality.'

Of the 76 prisoners who escaped from 'Harry', the tunnel that was finally used for the 'Great Escape' of 24 March 1944, 73 were caught, 50 of these being murdered by the Gestapo on Hitler's orders. At the end of the war this incident '…remained among the great untold adventure stories of the war' because those who knew about it had 'been exiled for weary years behind barbed wire in the midst of the enemy.'[80]

The first account appeared in a limited edition book produced at the end of 1945, *Spotlight on Stalag Luft III*, produced by the editorial staff of *Scangriff*,[81] the camp newspaper, which included Brickhill, Norton, and the camp artist Ley Kenyon. This contained a story by Brickhill, described as 'an ex-journalist Spitfire pilot', which was a transcript of a broadcast by the BBC Overseas Service to Australia. 'Yes, I was in that camp,' Brickhill recounted, 'but now I find it hard to believe all the fantastic things that happened.' The light-hearted eight-page story was very basic, and included three drawings by Kenyon. For this first description, the breakout was named 'the great break'. Brickhill concluded, 'And now I hope we are through with tunnels for good. I would much rather take a bus.'

In 1946 the story went public with the publication of Brickhill and Norton's *Escape to Danger*. As well as describing the breakout's mechanics, it also related several of the dramatic survival stories told to the boys by other prisoners. The road from prison camp to publication was a long and dangerous path. The budding authors were forced to hide their manuscript for a year from the Germans: '…sometimes in a secret wall panel, sometimes down another tunnel called "Dick" and sometimes by the simple expedient of putting it in the barrack block that the Germans had searched last, knowing that it would wait its turn before being searched again.'[82]

They had to memorise a great deal of the story of the escape, it being too dangerous to write down any descriptions of the mechanics of it. Not only this but, during the march west from *Stalag Luft* III in 1945, Brickhill had to carry his manuscripts on his back, in blizzard and ice, in a huge sack, chained like Prometheus to his own endeavours. But the stories survived. Laurie Simpson:

> 'When we were moved from camp, at the beginning of the [long] walk, everybody was taking the essential foods and things, but he took all his notes; and there were quite a lot of them too. He had a great big pack, and it paid him off after the war.'[83]

Of the tales, of course, many never made publication. It was only the more remarkable ones that were marketable, and as a consequence, a great deal disappeared from history.

The planned exit from the North Compound was one of the most ambitious escapes of the war. It was intended that more than 250 POWs with full documentation and disguised clothing would escape along a 350-foot long, 30-foot deep tunnel to eventual freedom. Nothing was left to chance and, as has more than adequately been described before, a complex network of security, deception and digging teams was employed to carry out the preparatory work.

As is now well known, three tunnels were dug for the 'Great Escape': 'Tom', 'Dick' and 'Harry'. In fact there had been a suggestion that they be named 'The Father', 'The Son' and 'The Holy Ghost', but Bushell vetoed that 'for fear of offending the Almighty'.[84] 'Dick' was dug from Block 122, 'Tom' from Block 123, both going out west, and 'Harry' from Block 104, going north.

One of the key members of the 'X Organisation' was the previously mentioned Flight Lieutenant Ley Kenyon who was shot down on 16 September 1943 in a 419 Squadron Halifax during his second tour, and was captured near Dax in south-west France eleven days later, probably trying to escape across the Pyrenees into Spain.[85] Kenyon was asked by Massey, the SBO, to record the progress of the digging of 'Harry' but, as number 120 on the escape list, he failed to escape on the night of the breakout. 'Working in extremely difficult conditions he made – and hid – a complete portfolio of drawings which were retrieved after the Russians overran Sagan at the end of the war.'[86] Howard Pearce remembered being sketched by Kenyon:

> 'I do remember meeting Ley Kenyon who was excellent at painting and drawing. He did me, and in the kerfuffle of leaving the camp and marching God knows where, it went: I lost it. He did a very good one, I thought; very well worth a couple of cigarettes – which is what I gave him.'[87]

Kenyon's drawings were used to illustrate *Escape to Danger*.

On 4 March 1944, less than three weeks before the mass breakout, SS-*Gruppenführer und Generalleutnant der Polizei* Heinrich Müller, the head of the Gestapo, issued the notorious *Kugel Erlass* or 'Bullet Decree'. This was an instruction to the Security Police and SD which provided that certain categories of prisoners of war were 'to be discharged of prisoner of war status' and handed over to the Secret State Police. The subjects were sent to Mauthausen concentration camp where they were shot. This covered all POWs of all nations, except Britain and America. British and US POWs had a special order applied to them by the *Oberkommando der Wehrmacht* (OKW – German military High

Command). In fact, the 50 RAF POWs shot after the Sagan breakout were also 'discharged from prisoner of war status' by Hitler's order.

A decree issued by Goebbels in 1943 had instructed the German police not to interfere with any crowds lynching downed Allied bomber crews. At the end of February 1944, less than a month before the breakout, under instructions from Himmler, *Generalfeldmarschall* Wilhelm Keitel, head of the OKW, issued the order *Stufe Roemisch III.* Escaped officer *Kriegies*, other than US and British, were to be handed to the Gestapo on recapture. Recaptured British and US POWs would be kept in police or military custody until the OKW decided their fate. All this would be clandestine – the POWs being classed as 'Escaped and Not Recaptured.'

The Nazis' aim was the creation of an atmosphere of terror and secrecy that would prove anathema to any resistance. Thus the *Nacht und Nebel* (Night and Fog) decree provided that all suspected resisters who could not be shot out of hand, were to be sent in utmost secrecy to Germany, where their fate would be concealed, even after death.[88] Recaptured officers, other than those who were British and American, would be transported to Mauthausen concentration camp where they would be shot. This was the atmosphere in Germany before the 'Great Escape'.

At the time of the *Kugel Erlass* decree, Himmler had sent word to all prison camp commandants that sterner measures were to be taken against escapers, and hinted that from then on, the Gestapo would reclaim recaptured officers as their prisoners, and they would be dealt with as saboteurs and spies.[89] *Stalag Luft* III's 64 year-old *Kommandant*, Oberst Friedrich Wilhelm von Lindeiner-Wildau, was informed by the Gestapo of this. The Gestapo even suggested that von Lindeiner should shoot offending POWs within his compound. He ignored this, but summoned all the British senior officers, chaplains and doctors to a conference, giving them a sincere warning of the Gestapo's intentions towards mass escapes.

Shortly before the March breakout, 19 POWs were transferred to Belaria, the external compound around 10 km away from the main camp. Belaria was a cluster of huts surrounded by clear, flat ground. The group included Stanford Tuck, George Harsh, Wally Floody (whom Bushell had put in charge of tunnelling), and Peter 'Hornblower' Fanshawe. All those transferred cursed their luck at the time, not realising how fortunate they were. It was assumed that they had been 'purged' because they were 'troublemakers'. But Bushell was not among them. His supposed involvement in the camp theatre production of *Pygmalion* had successfully deceived the Germans into thinking he was portraying Professor Higgins rather than organising an escape.

Frank Stone moved into the North Compound from the East just before the 'Wooden Horse' break. He remembered the discovery of tunnel 'Tom':

> 'The Germans had evacuated Hut 123 and had taken a week of concentrated searching. They were about to give it up as a bad job when one of the ferrets accidentally found the trapdoor. They certainly celebrated their discovery: a number of high-ranking officers were invited to see their success before the tunnel was blown up with disastrous results to the roof of Hut 123.'[90]

Stone was also involved with helping to supply the electric lighting to 'Harry':

> 'I was very much aware of the tunnel being dug and was involved with obtaining the two reels of electric cable that was used down the tunnel. A fellow orderly and myself were collecting a large box of boiled potatoes from the Cookhouse when "Red" Noble, who had just been

This painting by Geoffrey Willatt was done around the time of the 'Great Escape', 24 March 1944, when it was 'very cold, with snow on the ground and a severe frost at night.' This was probably painted in Willatt's own hut, showing the view from Room 19, Block 106 looking south-east. Immediately in front and to the left is Block 105, which was adjacent to Block 104, where the escape tunnel 'Harry' was dug. On the right is Block 108, which was immediately adjacent to Block 122 where Laurie Simpson's crew was billeted and from which the unfinished tunnel 'Dick' was commenced. Each hut had its floor set a foot or so above ground level to enable the German security guards to guard against any tunnelling activity. The tree stumps are evidence that the whole camp had been built on a cleared forest, although occasional individual trees were allowed to remain. (Willatt)

released from a spell in the cooler and was carrying his blanket and overcoat, saw the two reels which two workmen were intending to use to replace the tannoy system. He seized the reels and dumped them in our box, draped his coat and blanket on top and escorted us to Block 104.'[91]

One of Stone's jobs,[92] as an orderly, was to remove the diggers' sand in Block 104: 'To sweep up the sand we made soft brushes from Red Cross string,' he said, 'which ensured that every grain was swept up. Generally it was only small quantities, which were disposed of amongst the general rubbish. In addition we scrubbed the corridor every second week.'[93]

George Harsh had been made Head of Security in *Stalag Luft* III a few months after he arrived in the camp. At the beginning of 1943, well over a year before the final breakout, Floody invited Harsh for a walk around the perimeter track. He told him that there was to be a military-style escape attempt. The idea was Bushell's from the start; such was his hatred of the Germans. This hatred appears to have originated from Bushell's torture by the Gestapo, following his arrest in Prague in the wake of the assassination attempt on the senior SS leader and Deputy Reich Protector of Bohemia-Moravia, the feared *Obergruppenführer* Reinhard Heydrich, on 29 May 1942 and his eventual death from the ensuing wounds the following month. Bushell, with his companion, Jack Zafouk, a Czech RAF officer, had escaped from a train travelling from Lübeck to Barth and they were being sheltered by civilians in a flat in Prague. But the caretaker of the building had 'grassed' on them and the Gestapo broke in to the apartment and arrested them, part of the mass reprisals occurring in Czechoslovakia subsequent to Heydrich's death. The Gestapo was out for blood. Over 1,200 civilians were executed and the entire village of Lidice bulldozed to the ground: one hundred and seventy-two members of the male population were shot. The family sheltering Bushell and Zafouk were also butchered. It was coincidental that Bushell was in Prague when the assassination occurred, but to be an escaped POW held little water for the Gestapo. Both RAF men were viciously interrogated. Zafouk was bundled off to Colditz, a high security prison, whilst Bushell was the recipient of more savage treatment. In an environment of violence, he was mercilessly and brutally interrogated in rooms besmirched with human blood. Amidst the agonized screams of the tortured and the death rattles of the innocent, Bushell's attitude changed. A hardened, unrepentant loathing for anything Nazi – the corrupt Gestapo, the brutal SS – consumed him. He was transported to Berlin where, in the dank, dripping cellars of the Gestapo's headquarters on Prinz Albrecht Strasse, described as a 'pit of organised torture and injustice',[94] and encrusted with the putrid remains of human suffering, he was further 'educated'. Here victims' bodies and spirits were broken by robotic inquisitors 'who knew how to be affable and bland when occasion demanded', and 'how to beat a man until he whimpered for mercy.'[95]

However the *Luftwaffe* was aware that Bushell was missing. The chief censorship officer at *Stalag Luft* III, von Masse, who liked him, and had a high-ranking brother in the *Wehrmacht,* arranged for him to be transferred to the North Compound. Here Roger Bushell was told that if he escaped again there would be no saving him.

It was intended to empty *Stalag Luft* III's North Compound of all its inmates for the breakout of 1944 – 600 men. However, 600 did not in the event prove to be a practicable proposition.

Arthur Cole was in Block 104 on the night of the escape:

'I remember I was asked to take a message down to the room opposite where the tunnel entrance was, and when the door opened in Block 104 the room was full of cigarette smoke; I'd never seen it so thick anywhere – you could cut it with a knife. And in there, there were German businessmen, one or two Germans in uniform – all bogus of course! And many of those people would have been amongst those that were shot.'[96]

Laurie Simpson:

'We knew there was going to be an escape that night. We didn't quite know which hut it was going from, but we were told which huts to keep away from. I didn't know which hut the tunnel was in. I knew where one of the tunnels was, but I didn't really want to know anything that I didn't have to know. Most of us only wanted to know what we had to know, to enable us to do our small part in the escape.'[97]

Howard Pearce was also in Block 104 on that night. He had planned to go out with one of his close friends and room-mates, Edgar Humphreys: 'He and I chatted about it and decided that we'd had enough, but the others in the room weren't interested.' Edgar Humphreys was a flight lieutenant, a pilot who had worked his way up through the RAF and been shot down in a Wellington. Pearce: 'He was married; I know he had a child. He was there when I arrived and they wanted a spare bod in the room, and I was the spare bod.' He remembered him as '...an absolute wizard – I've never known a man like him. No wonder they kept him in the air force. He and a friend of his used to pick up books on very advanced mathematics and read them instead of a novel at night. I found them very friendly, but somewhat boring characters. I just couldn't understand it, and nor could the other "normal" characters. It was really advanced stuff; and they used to chat to one another about it. They were always messing about with paper, writing it down, that sort of thing.'[98]

'Jimmy' James, 39 on the escape list, found a similar small group of intellectuals, 'pseudo-philosophers', as he called them, 'who did not fit into any category'. These were men '... who found it hard to integrate...', 'individualists with extreme views, nurtured on Engels, Junge and Freud, on all activity from politics to bird-watching... Some rooms were found for them where they could drive each other round the bend.'[99]

Four of Ken Rees's room-mates were on the escape list, together with Johnny Bull, who had closed the end of the tunnel ten days before, at the top. Rees and 'Red' Noble were due to go out after the first 80 as 'hardarsers' – those who would be travelling overland in disguised uniforms they had made for themselves, chosen from those who did not speak German or any foreign language, thus preventing them from masquerading as foreign workers. They had a slim chance of success with the ground covered in snow and conditions below freezing, having to travel across country, keep low, avoid police and guards, and move by night and live off 'scrounged' food. They had several hundred kilometres to go before reaching friendly territory and their chances were minimal.

Johnny Bull[100] had been working with 'Crump' Kerr-Ramsay, who had taken over from Wally Floody as head of tunnelling operations. As they dug the exit shaft they '...came to some pine roots, which made them think they must now be about two feet from the surface.'[101] They then put a temporary timber plank roof across the top of the shaft, still some feet below ground level, and packed it solidly with sand to prevent any patrolling Germans from falling into it. The roots they discovered probably persuaded them that they had come out in the forest surrounding the camp. This was to have serious consequences.

Charles Hall, a 26 year-old photo-reconnaissance pilot, who acted as the camp meteorologist, confirmed to Bushell that the nights of 23 to 25 March would be moonless. That decided it and all the forged passports and passes were stamped for the 25th. Although the diggers had ceased work, all the forgers, tailors and compass-makers were still working the week before the escape. Arthur Cole:

> 'One of the people I knew particularly well was Charles Hall, the camp photographer. The other was Brian Evans. They were on the first 200 list and because they were in Block 105 I knew them to some extent. They shook hands with me [before escaping] and said, "See you in a fortnight, Coley."
>
> 'I knew a lot of the others by sight, but one that I do remember was Henri Picard, a Belgian. I remember him because I wanted to learn some French and a Frenchman who was in the Free French Forces introduced me to him.'

Flight Lieutenant Brian Evans, a 24 year-old Welsh Hampden pilot, had trained as a surveyor pre-war, which made him very useful to the 'X Organisation'. Evans had been shot down in December 1940, and Hall in December 1941. Hall, Evans and Picard were all shot after the escape.

On the night of the breakout, as 'Shag' Rees and 'Red' Noble entered Block 104 together just before 8 p.m., 'Shag' got the shock of his life when he encountered 'Wings' Day's Polish escape partner, Tobolski, kitted out as a German *Unteroffizier*: 'Tobolski's German uniform, even up close, was a masterpiece, every badge and belt in the right place.'[102] 'Jimmy' James recalled that David Torrens, the block commander for the night, and a tall, powerfully-built *Kriegie*, had the fear of God put upon him on seeing Tobolski and '...set off up the passage at fast stride, preparing to tower over the little Corporal.'[103] He had not been forewarned, but realised his mistake in the nick of time. Rees: 'There were about 200 of us spread evenly in the rooms throughout the hut... An odd collection of *Kriegie*s were crowded in the corridor.'[104] There were slick-suited "businessmen" with suitcases, and "hardarsers" carrying blanket rolls, and dressed in any conceivable garb. They all suffered from fear: a nervous, constant checking of papers, personal details, and escape rations, without which their life was forfeit.

Roger Bushell was going out as a French engineer and had a small attaché case to make him look the part. He wore an RAF greatcoat disguised as an overcoat, dyed with black boot polish. Each escaper's kit had already been 'censored' by a team of *Kriegie*s to ensure they looked the part, but scores of mistakes were made. Dutchman, Bob Van der Stock, a former medical student who worked in the camp hospital, was picked up by Security for the mistake of wearing a sweater labelled 'Gieves Ltd., Old Bond St., London', with his Dutch name marked on his socks. He had served in the Dutch Air Force before the war and was going out as a Dutch guest worker. His experience of living in occupied Holland proved invaluable to the 'X Organisation'. He was one of only three to make a 'home run'.[105] Even Bushell made a mistake. Although travelling as a French aircraft engineer employed by Focke-Wulf, he had initially included a hairbrush stamped 'Kent of London' in his kit.[106] These early errors were soon ironed out.

Also waiting in 104 that night was bombardier Arthur Cole who, as a helper to the 'X Organisation', had his name put down on the escape list. But he was not in the first 200:

> 'One thing about The "Great Escape", which is not common knowledge, is that although our superiors planned to get out 200 people, Wing Commander Day,[107] who was on the Escape Committee, said, "Look, supposing everything goes perfectly and we get out 200, what are we going to do then? We've got nothing prepared." So they created a reserve list, and tickets were drawn for this for people from the escape organisation: I got one, I think it was 227. This suggests that the reserve list had 50 people on it. We had papers which were cruder than those who had been on the list of 200, but we were in the escape block like the rest of them.'[108]

'Jimmy' James[109] had a farewell meal in his room on the night of the escape: 'We ate in silence', he said. 'It was as though impending doom had thrown a dark shadow to chill the intense excitement in the air.'[110] He was due to go out with Sortiras Skanziklas, a Greek fighter pilot, who would escort him down the Danube to Greece. They met in 104, Skanziklas looking like a Greek worker in a cut-down overcoat. 'The block was fast filling up with odd-looking characters in an assortment of clothing,' commented James, 'ranging from smart business suits and trilby hats to plus fours, workers' trousers, old coats, berets and cloth caps, carrying suitcases, bundles and packs.' Massey, the SBO, dropped into the hut to wish them luck: as a consequence of von Lindeiner's earlier warning he advised them to '...avoid provocation if caught'.

Around 10 p.m. as a guard closed the doors on Block 104, the silence was enough to hear a pin drop: when the German left 200 men breathed a sigh of relief. Les Brodrick: 'All the windows were open, but all the lights were put out immediately inside the hut and we sat there all quiet and waited and nothing seemed to be happening. It got so hot in there with all the bods that you could see steam coming out of the windows.'[111]

'Wings' Day moved amongst the waiting crowd, cheerfully easing tension by suggesting that they tear off the destination labels on any wagons they found in any goods yards. Feeling more peaceful than he had ever been before an escape, he suggested some slogans in German – such as '*Deutschland Kaput!*' – which the escapers could write as graffiti on walls when the opportunity presented itself.

Day was going out as 'Colonel Brown', an Irish officer made a POW in 1940 who was converted to National Socialism, the story being that von Lindeiner had allowed him parole to go to Berlin to see the devastation. Tobolski was to be his '*Luftwaffe* escort'.

'Shag' Rees and 'Red' Noble, as tunnellers, had a place in the first 200, but quite far back. They went down the entrance together. The third man, after Bull and John Marshall, was Sydney Dowse, who was due to haul through the first 20 POWs. Following were Bushell and his partner, Bernard Scheidhauer, a lieutenant from the French *Armée de l'Air*, also masquerading as a businessman. He had been a POW since November 1942. Their aim was to reach Paris.

The escape proper began just after 22.00 hrs when Bull and Marshall, taking it in turns, gradually pulled through the wooden shoring and turf at the tunnel's exit, but the timber had swollen, making its removal difficult. Prior to Bull breaking open the trap, the tunnel had to fill up with escapers, which took 40 minutes. It was 22.15 hrs before Bull and Marshall were able to break through the tree roots, only to discover that they were short of the surrounding woods by 15 feet.[112] Not only that, but they had come up in open ground only 45 feet from a sentry box and the well-lit perimeter wire. Bushell, number 4 on the list, had to make a quick decision: he knew that there was no chance of a delay – all the forged passes were stamped for Saturday 25th so it was then or never.[113] He and Scheidhauer, in the chamber at the base of the shaft, were surrounded by would-be escapees, all 'lying more or less on top of each other'.[114] It was 22.30 hrs before they decided what to do.

The system used to engineer the exit of each escapee was simple. Only a few feet inside the wood and close to the exit hole was a 'ferret fence' (for Glemnitz, the chief security guard and his troops, to observe the compound). If a length of rope was strung from the base of the exit shaft to the fence, a waiting controller could give two tugs on the rope every time a patrolling sentry reached the end of his beat, thus informing waiting escapees when to emerge. But this inevitably slowed down the pace. An hour had passed before all the mechanics of the system had been explained to those in the tunnel, and, for the first two hours after 23.00 the rate of exit was only one POW every 12 minutes.

However, other things began to go wrong. A *Kriegie* carrying the bulk of a suitcase caused a tunnel collapse and 'Cookie' Long, one of the tunnellers, took a long time to fix it. In Hut 104 Les Brodrick became tired of all the delays because no one would tell them what was happening. Since they could not make any noise, the men in the hut could only sit and wonder. Brodrick thought 'it was a hell of a long time to be sitting silently... just thinking.'[115]

'Wings' Day was number 20 on the list. Just as his number came up, an hour after the escaping started, seconds after midnight, an air raid siren wailed, the electrics were cut, and Block 104 and 'Harry' were plunged into darkness. Howard Pearce: 'There were a few hold-ups and then the lights went out when the air raid was on.'[116] This was the 'Night of the Strong Winds' and there was a raid on Berlin. Laurie Simpson would have been saddened to hear that the flight engineer from his first tour, Freddy King, was killed that night.

As the siren wailed, Block 104 shook with the distant pounding of bombs. With Berlin slightly less than 160 km away, the camp was only occasionally affected by diversionary flights coming down from the capital. On this night, however, the unforecast high altitude winds scattered the bomber stream to the east of the target[117] and the Main Force, attacking from the south, passed right over Sagan.[118] Bushell hoped that this would enable them to speed up the exit rate, but the power cut meant that the tunnel's fat-burning lamps[119] had to be lit as replacement lighting, and it was 35 minutes before this was achieved, inevitably slowing things down.

Day went down the 28-foot escape shaft clutching a cardboard suitcase to his chest. At the base of the shaft were three chambers, one for maintenance, one for storage, and one for an air pump. Day passed a Frenchman laboriously pumping the bellows in and out, and careered down the tunnel on a trolley. At the base of the exit shaft he met Sydney Dowse, his puller. Dowse climbed the shaft as Day took over, pulling Tobolski up from the 'Leicester Square' halfway house to the exit. 'Tob' climbed the 20-foot ladder to the open air and, in the confusion and delay caused by the raid, Day eventually exited at 35.

Humphreys and Pearce were going out together, but Humphreys was higher up the escape list than Pearce, in the first 76. 'Both of us went to 104,' Pearce recalled, 'with all the others in a huddle. It was absolutely thick with tobacco smoke and he and I were dressed as Belgian workers. I could speak a fair bit of French, but very little German.'

'Jimmy' James, number 39, was going out with 12 other POWs, posing as local sawmill workers, 'hardarsing' it to a small town south-east of the camp, and then splitting into groups and continuing by train and foot to the Czech border. The group, led by a Pole, included Bull, Johnny Dodge and a 57 year-old *Kriegie* named 'Pop' Green.

Les Brodrick, number 52, was due to be travelling with Denys Street, son of the British Permanent Under-Secretary of State for the Air. When they reached the shaft Brodrick found the base of the ladder was a foot above the tunnel bottom and had great difficulty in getting up it. The shaft was so narrow he could not get his feet on the ladder without becoming wedged in. Hauling himself by his hands, Brodrick was exhausted when he reached the top, but had sufficient adrenalin to make the short dash to the woods. There he met Henry Birkland. He gazed back at the camp and was surprised to see steam coming out of the tunnel mouth.

James, Dodge, Bull and nine others went out at 01.30 hrs. By the time 'Shag' and 'Red' went down the entrance shaft there were only two hours of darkness left. Humphreys, Australian Jimmy Catanach[120] and some 80 others had already successfully gone through when Noble took up his position as hauler at 'Piccadilly Circus', the first halfway house, while Rees went on to 'Leicester Square'. They had to haul up 20 men before they could be relieved. Rees replaced Tony Bethell who was 65 on the list. After Rees had hauled through 15, it was 04.45 hrs and 'Crump' Kerr-Ramsay and David Torrens decided, in view of the encroaching light, that it was time to call it a day. Kerr-Ramsay sent down a team of three *Kriegie*s to close up the shaft after the final man had got out. Rees pulled up his room-mate, 'Sax' Saxby, to 'Leicester Square', who told him that that was it and he had to follow him out. Heart beating with excitement, Rees pulled Noble up from 'Piccadilly' and set off towards the exit shaft. But as they neared the end he heard a shot.

Up on the ground strange things were happening. At around 04.00 hrs Roy Langlois,[121] number 60, had just reached the 'ferret fence' when he saw a group of

There were eight sentry or 'postern' boxes set immediately outside the barbed wire perimeter of Stalag Luft III at intervals of about 150 metres around the circumference of the 300 metre square compound. Each one was manned by at least one sentry equipped with an MG 42 machine gun on a bipod and a manually-operated searchlight, with a wide field of view across the adjacent part of the compound. If a POW stepped over the infamous 'warning wire', a single strand of wire set one foot above the ground and 10 metres from the inner fence (which here appears to be a solid board), he could be shot. Each 'Goon Tower' was a square, timber frame structure, with a pyramidal roof, set on stilts about 10 metres above the ground level. It was accessed by an external timber staircase. The double perimeter fences were strung with twenty strands of barbed wire, the gap between them packed with great coils of additional barbed wire, so dense one could hardly distinguish anything through them. This rendition was painted by Geoffrey Willatt around the time of the 'Great Escape'. (Willatt)

Germans march along the perimeter road only seven yards from the exit hole: the guard was changing.

Different reports emerged about exactly what happened next. The critical thing, which Brickhill pointed out, and the screen version overlooked, was that two guards came separately to relieve themselves within a few feet of the tunnel, within half-an-hour. At 04.30 the guard in the nearest sentry box began shouting. He was facing out towards the woods and for a moment Langlois thought he had been spotted. But the man was only calling to his replacement, who climbed the guard box steps to replace him. Then, to Langlois' horror, the guard descended noisily, walked straight towards the tunnel, and squatted down to relieve himself four feet from the hole.

That one guard failed to notice the tunnel, a black hole in the surface of the snow, with steam rising out of it, was a miracle. That a second guard also almost missed it, was beyond belief. Brickhill concluded that the first German was probably blinded by the camp searchlights. The second guard sat there for five minutes before hitching up his trousers, still oblivious to the escapers' slushy trail in the snow.

Numbers 76 to 80 were at the exit shaft. 76 was Lawrence Reavell-Carter,[122] 77 and 78 were, respectively, Flt/Lts Keith Ogilvie and Mick Shand.[123] 79 was Len Trent, the New Zealander who had led the attack on the Amsterdam power station the year before.

Around 04.50 Reavell-Carter crawled out of the hole towards the tree line. He was 'a big, burly air gunner'[124] and his efforts were making a deep furrow in the slush. Ogilvie and Shand followed him out. Reavell-Carter made the 'ferret fence' and ran into the woods. At that point 12 *Kriegies*, including Langlois, were near the tunnel exit: one at the 'ferret fence', one in the woods, one at the exit, one on the ladder, and eight at the bottom of the shaft.

Ogilvie crawled into the woods past Langlois. Shand was lying in the slushy trail in the snow, halfway between the tunnel and the forest, when a guard, returning from the eastern end of his beat, approached on the forest side of the perimeter road. This was unusual, as earlier guards had walked along the camp side of the road. Trent was beside the hole, lying prone in the snow, as the guard came within a foot of the exit, staring straight ahead, oblivious to the New Zealander. Ogilvie had reached the 'ferret fence' but Shand was only halfway there, face-down in the snow. The guard, whom Brickhill later described as 'a simple peasant type', according to Trent 'almost peed down the exit', still oblivious to the tunnel. Langlois and Ogilvie dropped down behind the fence. But the German realised something was wrong and, muttering incoherently to himself, unslung his rifle.

At this point, Brickhill suggests, the guard saw Shand, and Reavell-Carter, seeing the threat, walked forward shouting in German '*Don't shoot!*'[125] The German let off a wild shot in surprise and Ogilvie and Shand bolted into the trees. Alex Cassie, a *Kriegie* who worked for the forgers 'Dean and Dawson', recalled that the shot quivered 'throughout the whole camp'.[126] Reavell-Carter then emerged from the wood and he and Langlois raised their hands in surrender. Then Trent stood up right beside the sentry, who 'jumped about a foot in the air'[127] and Trent surrendered.

Coming out of his comatose state, but still gibbering, the guard shone his torch down the shaft and picked out *Kriegie* Bob McBride. The German blew his whistle, McBride crawled out and then the Goon covered all four POWs with his rifle. It was 04.55 and Langlois heard the sentry in the guard box telephoning the guard house, from which Germans could soon be heard running.

It was all over.

Back in Block 104 the last man, number 87, was just entering the shaft when the shot echoed out. Up in 104 Pearce was at the end of a queue of POWs still waiting to go: 'The exit was discovered about ten men before me and then the whole thing collapsed', he stated. 'The Germans came in, the dogs came in and all hell broke loose! Whistles were blown and a gun was fired.' Frank Stone remembered: 'Only one shot was fired by the guard who discovered the tunnel exit, but there was quite a lot of shouting and blowing of whistles.'

After the alarm had been raised, Brickhill records, '…a few leapt out of the windows – strictly against orders – into the lightening compound and dashed back to their huts. The guard in the goon-box by the cooler sent a couple of bullets after one of them and the practice stopped.' Arthur Cole was more specific:

'When the balloon went up in the morning and some shots [sic] were fired, I said to a chap called Jock who was in the same room as myself in Block 105, "Look, I'm not waiting here to be caught in the wrong block by the Germans when they come round, let's get out of here." So we agreed, and burnt our papers. I jumped out of a window, and dashed across the open space. There were still a few tree roots in the camp, which had not been dug up. I tripped over a root, went down on my hands, bounced up again and leapt through a window in Block 105. When the Germans came round I was in my own block and my own bed. When Jock appeared two or three weeks later I said, "Why didn't you follow me?" He said, "*You fool!* There was a guard outside the wire drawing a bead on you with his rifle. If you hadn't tripped over that tree root, you wouldn't have been *here* today."'[128]

Ken Rees and 'Red' Noble were still in the tunnel. All escaping had ceased. Rees made his way back to the second halfway house and when he got there two *Kriegies* shot past him, making for the entrance shaft. They were lucky. One of the last POWs out, a *Kriegie* named Newman, refused to listen when 'Crump' Kerr-Ramsay tried to pull him back and broke the trolley rope. After a while Newman paddled his way back angrily, unaware of the drama outside. Then the last remaining *Kriegies* started pouring out of the exit shaft, all remarking that they were being pursued by ferrets. 'Shag' and 'Red' were coming back. Rees was worried about being 'stuck in a cave-in with a bullet up my backside' and tried unsuccessfully to pull the shoring boards loose behind him. He eventually made it back to the entrance to his intense relief: 'I was the last man up,' he said: 'then they shut the trap behind me.'[129] It was 04.55 hrs and the game was up.

Edgar Humphreys had intended to wait in the woods for Howard Pearce. 'He told me,' Pearce recalled, 'that the tunnel was short of the woods. The message came back, but still the word was to 'go'. Humphreys and Pearce became separated, and Pearce was still in Hut 104: 'My friend Edgar saw what was happening,' he recalled, 'and ran off. He met somebody else, and the two then decided to go together.' Frank Stone: 'Once the tunnel was discovered, all those left behind were instructed to burn their forged passes and permits as they were no longer any use. All permanent residents of Hut 104, who were not included in the 200 selected to escape, moved out to occupy the bunks of those who were.'

'On the morning after the breakout,' Stone related, 'the Germans did a room-by-room check and all residents of Block 104 were paraded outside the hut. About midday a full roll call was held on the Appel Ground with an individual photo check.'[130] Wally Maltby thought the whole camp was going to be shot when the Germans lined them up in the snow for a headcount that morning. Laurie Simpson:

'They called the SS in because so many people had escaped, and for a day or so they were pretty hard on us. I don't think there had been any other big escapes [before]; normally it was just in twos or threes. That's why they brought the SS in; because the Camp Commandant was in trouble.'[131]

In the East Compound there were no guards the morning after the escape. Alan James recalled, however, that the sentry boxes were still manned:

'We guessed something important had occurred and soon heard that the tunnel in the North Camp had broken and a number of POWs had escaped. We knew that some had been captured by the camp staff and returned to the North Camp, where they had been put in the cooler.

About two weeks later the SBO came on parade and read out the list of names supplied. He was told verbally that they had been shot whilst trying to escape.'[132]

The fates of Edgar Humphreys and Jimmy Catanach were typical of what happened to most of those shot. Humphreys, 55 on the list, teamed up with P/O Paul Royle,[133] who was 54. They left the camp at 2.30 a.m. on the morning of 25 March, and headed southeast towards the nearest *Autobahn*. By dawn they still had not found it and hid up all day. That night they finally found the road, but there was deep snow on either side of it which prevented them from skirting around it. Then, later, they were accosted by three German Home Guard soldiers who did not believe their story and arrested them. The two were taken to jail in nearby Tiefenfurt. Subsequently they were taken to Sagan jail and then, to their dismay, to the jail in Görlitz. On 31 March Humphreys, with Brian Evans and three others was taken away by the Gestapo. They were never seen alive again.

On 15 April the details of all five men were pinned to a bulletin board in *Stalag Luft* III. Along with 42 others they had been shot 'attempting to escape'. In fact, they were taken back on the Sagan road in a lorry and let out to relieve themselves and warm up in the freezing cold. They were then shot with machine pistols by five Gestapo men. Their bodies were scattered all over the roadside.[134] Paul Royle survived.

After the war it emerged that Catanach[135] and three fellow escapees, Arnold Christensen, Halldor Espelid and Nils Fuglesang – all Norwegians – had been picked up by the police on the Danish border near Flensburg. Following a short time in prison Catanach was taken away by Johannes Post, the deputy chief of the Kiel Gestapo. Under orders from Berlin, Catanach was taken to the small hamlet of Roter Hahn. After talking to him amiably, Post told him that when the car stopped he was going to shoot him. Catanach thought this was a 'tasteless joke'.[136] With a Police inspector named Hans Kahler, Post and Catanach got out. After walking a short distance, Kahler drew his pistol and fired a shot, but it misfired. To avoid further mistakes Post shot Catanach through the heart from the back. He was 23.[137]

The three Norwegian POWs arrived and, seeing Catanach dead on the ground, tried to run off, but Post and Kahler shot two of them dead, then Post finished the third off with a rifle.[138]

Laurie Simpson had known Catanach and two or three others. Frank Stone recalled: 'The reaction to the news of the shootings was at first disbelief, followed by anger and eventually sorrow at the loss of our comrades.'

Laurie:

'I was shocked when I heard that 50 had been shot. The senior officer from each hut was called to the Camp Theatre, where I think Group Captain Massey told us what had happened, and we had to tell each room. After the 'Great Escape', escaping was forbidden, because of the threat that Allied airmen attempting to escape would be shot on capture. That was lifted after a period.'[139]

Laurie later concurred that he would probably have tried to escape if given the chance: 'There were many things to consider, of course,' he said. 'By the time the 'Great Escape' was over it wasn't long after that, that D-Day occurred, and then the attitude to escaping changed a bit, because we felt that after we [the Allies] had landed in France, after a few weeks it seemed to be going well. We thought it was only a matter of time and we'd be rescued. POWs were becoming much less cavalier in their attitude: "If we get out now, there'd be so much chaos in Germany, particularly as you get towards the frontiers of other countries, that you might be shot… just through bad luck, rather than because of people getting touchy" – that kind of thing.'[140]

On 12 December 1944, nine months after the mass breakout, and after ten months in *Stalag Luft* III, Laurie wrote to his mother in New South Wales:

> '*Everything is OK with me. Am fit and full of hope. The days are dreary and monotonous, but we manage to fill in time somehow. Every day we have our one meal at 5 o'clock to look forward to and that is something.*'

OTHER CAMPS
Stalag Luft I, Barth
Ted Boorman: 'When I left there were 10,000 of us there in five compounds. I think it was escape-proof. There were 24 in a room. It was about 18-foot square, and we used to sleep six in a row, three high! There was only an eight-foot ceiling and the bunks were about six inches off the ground, and then the next one, and the next one up to the ceiling. You slept six in a row down one side in pairs, and the other six were in the other corner. You couldn't all get up together, [or] all go to bed together. Well how could you? Twenty-four men living in a room like that size?

'It was so bloody cold you slept in all your clothes. You had a little fireplace for which you were allowed so many coal blocks a day. The only other way you could get any blocks was if you went and nicked them.'

Henry Coverley arrived in Barth in spring 1944: 'It was very difficult to get away; it was bloody cold too, because the temperature used to go down to minus 40 in the winter. I mean we had no clothes, no heating, nothing.'

Ablutions
Lew Parsons remembered Mühlberg: 'The latrines were emptied using Russian prisoners who came along with a large "Frog-Mouth" hand-pump and a long cylinder mounted on an oxen-pulled wagon. They pumped the contents of the pit under the latrines into the cylinder and took it out into the fields surrounding the camp, pulled out the bung in the back of the cylinder and the oxen moved along, spreading the excreta over the land. The smell pervading the whole area including the camp resulted from this basic form of muck spreading.'

Graham Korner remembered Bankau: 'The ablutions – well, you just sat in a row. There was a great big bench with holes in it. It was like a concrete trough all the way down – everybody crapped in there and it was just all washed down. So you sat in rows: "How you getting on, Fred?" "Oh, alright," sort of thing; and there was another bloke right opposite you doing the same thing. You'd sit there chin-wagging. There was no modesty at all. Anything like that just went by the board!'

Ronnie Cartwright recalled the Centre Compound at *Stalag Luft* III: 'There was an aspect of prison camp life which I could never accept and always suffered extreme embarrassment [about]: the lack of privacy in the toilets, which was an open structure inside a large block containing about fifty bodies sitting side-by-side with just enough room for oneself. During a call of nature you were able to have a conversation with your neighbours – [which was] most embarrassing! Camp life was made for it: rugby, soccer, hockey, theatre, lectures, debates, reading, study, and playing cards [were all discussed].'

Bill Higgs recollected Heydekrug: '*Luft* I had six in a room and we had toilets and showers; when I got up to *Stalag Luft* VI in Lithuania, near Mamon – it was 70 to a room! Washing facilities were across the wire and cold. The place was just like the Arctic. And, of course, there was snow up there most of the time – it was terrible.'

Guards

Graham Korner was at Bankau: 'The guards we mostly had dealings with, who we called "Goons", were the English-speaking guards. We had one – he was quite comical – a Cockney, a real Cockney lad: "*Wotch yer, mite*" and all that business. He was a German, but he'd lived most of his life in "*Saff-End*", where he had a "*Caf*". When the war broke out, he had to go back to the "*Muvverland*", because he was a German. He spoke English, but he was a rank Cockney! When they had what they called '*Appel*', the Germans would line all the POWs up and count them. But we used to muck them about, and move about. This guard went spare one day: "I'm not trying to teach discipline to me enemy," he said, "but we'll bloody stand here until we get it right!"

'We told him, "Up yer chuff!" He replied "When the war's all over, *I'll* go back to *Saff-End* and open the caff up." And the boys said "See *you* in South End, mister – you've had your lot!"

John Leakey was at Heydekrug: 'It was in 1943 and the Gestapo came, unannounced, to *Stalag Luft* VI and every POW was made to go outside to be searched while the huts were ransacked. I assume the officers' compound was being treated likewise. We were made to stand in batches around the fire pool.[141] Every prisoner was then made to strip to his underpants while every bit of clothing and their contents were searched, then given back to him. When my turn came, I put on my trousers etc. piece by piece, until it came to the last – my jacket. When the Gestapo chap held it out for me to take, I turned my back on him and put my arms behind me so that he could help me to dress. Of course he blew a gasket. Those who witnessed this laughed until the Gestapo man lost interest.'[142]

Alan Fuller was at Mühlberg. Around the time Germany surrendered, and it became obvious it had lost the war, the guards at *Stalag* IVB threw down their weapons and tried to leave the camp. Fuller, a bomb-aimer from 76 Squadron, took some drastic action. His son related: 'A particularly brutal guard had made [my father's] life a misery, so, when this guard gave up his gun, he walked over, picked it up and shot the guard, killing him instantly. He always maintained that had it been twenty-four hours later, he would have been regarded as a murderer but, at this juncture, the war had yet to end officially.'[143]

Escapes

Graham Korner: 'When we were at Bankau, there were two lads: one was a nice little chap from Manchester. He and another bloke tried to escape one night. Their idea was that when the air raid siren went, all the camp lights used to go out – including the floodlights around us. But what they didn't realise was that when they did this, the Germans put on extra guards with dogs! The boys got through the first lot of wire and out into the fields, where there were vegetables and everything, and they went along the trenches, and got through the outside wire. They got through underneath somehow, but they got caught up in it, and the dogs caught them. And one of the guards just came up and bloody shot them! Shot them both dead! That caused a furore, that did! It was so unnecessary – they needn't have shot them; they could have brought them both back in again. But the bloke came up and "Pop"!'

Henry Coverley – Barth: 'There was one very good attempt to get out from Barth. Outside the huts there was a great big mesh wire box thing we had to throw all our rubbish into. One chap collected all the rubbish he could, and pinned it, or sowed it, or stuck it onto his uniform. And when there was nobody around, he climbed into this box and they chucked as much in the way of tins and cans after him. He was lumbered out to be dumped outside with all the other waste. I didn't actually see this, but this is what I heard. And he was dumped outside the camp, where he lay with all this rubbish. Unfortunately some Germans used to go round the dumps seeing what they could find, and somebody pulled at one of the cans and found that there was a man attached to it. Which was rather unfortunate: so he got captured.'

Alan James – East Compound, *Stalag Luft* III: 'After the "Wooden Horse" escape there was a daring plan to build a tunnel from the parade ground whilst the twice daily parades for counting were taking place. We paraded in block order, five deep, with 100 plus POWs in each block. It was estimated that when greatcoats were worn, any activity could be screened from the guards, both those in the sentry boxes and those on the ground.[144]

The normal duration of a parade was about half-an-hour: during this period, an initially shallow hole had to be excavated and the sand from it lifted out and then concealed. As in the North Compound, the subterranean sand was much lighter and cleaner than that on the surface, and the hole had to be covered with boards and discoloured top sand. James commented: 'We were all quietly warned to be careful when walking in that part of the camp. The digging took place each time we paraded and eventually it was considered that the hole was big enough for the diggers to remain in it until the next parade and continue working.

'At one point, however, the digger had to be pulled out during the middle of the day after he sent a distress signal to the surface. A rugby scrum was arranged over the hole and he was pulled out semi-conscious. Then the hole was re-covered and the unfortunate digger carried back to his hut whilst the guards laughed at the foolish POWs injuring themselves playing rugby football. Eventually digging could proceed from parade to parade as the tunnel became larger. However by the time the camp was evacuated in January 1945 the tunnel was abandoned; incomplete and undiscovered.'

Shootings
Graham Korner – Bankau: 'We weren't all that far from Kreutzberg, which was a local town. The town had an air raid siren, but we also had one in the camp. One day the Kreutzberg siren went off about "grub time" when blokes used to go over to the cookhouse. An "All Clear" siren went off, and a Canadian shot out with his canteen, thinking it was the camp "All Clear" and he was going to be first in line. But it wasn't the camp "All Clear", but rather the siren in Kreutzberg. A guard just went "pop", picked him off, and shot him dead. We heard afterwards that because of that, the German High Command sent this guard, a ginger-haired bloke, straight to the Russian front.'

Camp Radio
Cal Younger – Heydekrug: 'In the second week of June 1944 the camp theatre was deliberately set on fire by the prisoners to protect a clandestine camp radio.' By the next morning the building had been gutted by flames. Younger recorded that '…gone was … [the theatre] the cause of ameliorating unhappiness and boredom.'

The despondent *Kriegies* searched throughout the ashes but all that remained intact was a gramophone record of Vera Lynn singing "*I don't want to set the world on fire*"!'[145]

Hunger

Cal Younger – Thorn: 'Hunger amongst the POWs was such that at Christmas 1944 in Thorn one man had bartered cigarettes for some dehydrated vegetable and, with sublime ignorance, ate it dry, then drank several cups of tea. Probably he thought he had the same bellyache as everyone else, but it was *not* the same. He literally burst, and died.'[146]

Jews

Graham Korner – Bankau: 'We got stuck in these trucks: we were going across then to Bankau. That took four days, and one day – I never realised then, but I realise now what it was – we were in some sidings, and these trucks pulled up beside us, and up in the right-hand corner there was an opening with barbed wire across it, and there were *people* in them. You could *see* them. I'm quite convinced they were Jews. I'm sure now, but we didn't know anything about them then. They must have been Jews under transport. You could only see their hands and faces…'

Bill Higgs – Barth: 'At *Stalag Luft* I Barth they used to bring women in and girls for showers, and some were gazing our way. They used to have a big 'P' on their clothes, for Polish, or a big yellow star – the Star of David. When we saw them coming in, we used to scrounge around to get chocolate and soap – things like that. We used to hurl it over the barbed wire to where they were going. They tried to pick it up, but the German sentries stopped them. Then in a little while, half of the young, fair-haired German guards, they'd go in with the girls.'

Cal Younger – Fallingbostel: 'Polish prisoners heard that the concentration camp to which the women captured during the Warsaw insurrection had been taken, had been liberated, and they went off anxiously to find relatives. They came back, dazed, horror struck. British troops had overrun Belsen.

'We remembered now the strange stench which had sometimes drifted to the camp, a stench which we knew was the reek of death, and which we believed had come from shallow graves in the camp cemetery. A few prisoners went to see Belsen; we did not.'[147]

Dennis Thorpe – Barth: A Lancaster pilot with 626 Squadron, Thorpe recalled the camp's liberation, 'We were released by the Russians. There was an aerodrome next door with several concentration camp huts which some of us visited. I still have a vivid memory of offering a skeleton-like Pole a cigarette – which he promptly ate!'[148]

Henry Coverley remembered: '*Stalag Luft* III was where they sent all the suspect POWs. Anybody suspected of having information or who had tried to escape was sent to III.'[149] The camp's five compounds encompassed an unimaginably varied assortment of bored humanity. How this humanity was able to live together in the confined, barren conditions, and yet attempt to maintain an atmosphere of 'unruffled tolerance' beggars belief. Some did, but not all.

. . .

There were entertainments with lectures, theatre shows, radio broadcasts, the inevitable Vera Lynn and, of course, tunnelling. The first few attempts to escape failed hopelessly, but gradually men became more ingenious, and with the appointment of Roger Bushell, the military style 'X Organisation' developed. Characters such as Maw and ffrench-Mullen in the East Compound, Deans, Buttigieg, and Miller in the Centre, and Harsh, Floody and Tuck in the North all made a contribution to the restrained insurrection, while leaders like Bert Clark, 'Dixie' Deans and Bushell, managed to maintain some form of order, despite the increasing overcrowding as the air war 'hotted up'.

In the other camps there were sometimes even worse privations than at Sagan. Horrors and atrocities still occurred; however amidst the humour and the misfortune, men were still able to summon up the will to survive, and even try their hand at escaping, but many of these attempts ended in tragedy. Notwithstanding the privations, deprivations and utter boredom of camp life, two major escape attempts were 'successful' at *Stalag Luft* III, using very different approaches, one going close to the wire, the other deep. The former had 100% success, all three escapees returning home. The latter had only 3.9% home runs, suffered 65% fatal casualties, and the total number of escapees was 38% of that intended. But it 'put the wind up' the Germans for months afterwards. Unfortunately there was never to be another attempt at a breakout on the scale of Bushell's 'Great Escape'. Things became more difficult then and, after D-Day, men were usually more reluctant to risk their lives. Unbeknown to them they still had to face one further trial, the suffering and privations of which were to be worse, in some ways, than those in the camps itself.

CHAPTER TWENTY

'THE WORST JOURNEY IN THE WORLD'

The Long Marches

AT the end of the Second World War, the Prisoners of War situation in Europe created a complex political problem. Nine months earlier, in August 1944, there had been 160,000 British and Commonwealth and 22,000 American POWs in Germany. This figure had increased significantly by April/May 1945. One hundred thousand of the British and Commonwealth POWs were in a zone which Germany and the Western Allies anticipated would be liberated by the Soviets. In addition there were 165,000 Russian troops in England who had been captured after D-Day while in the service of the German forces. There was a fear that any Allied POWs overrun by the Red Army would be used as bartering chips to get back the Soviet POWs in Britain who had served in the *Wehrmacht*. The problem with the Soviets was that Stalin did not recognise Russian POWs as 'legitimate', for any Red Army soldiers who surrendered were disowned by the dictator. Hence any Soviet POWs returned to the USSR, forcibly or otherwise, were liable to be shot which provoked reluctance on the part of the Western Allies to do this, the consequence of which would be increasing difficulty in having their own POWs returned from Soviet-held zones.

On 19 July 1944, Hitler issued an order from the '*Wolfsschanze*', his eastern headquarters near Rastenburg in East Prussia, concerning preparations for the defence of the Reich, part of which covered a projected rearward movement of the Allied prisoners. The POWs advanced various theories for Hitler's intentions: one was a revenge killing for the bombing of Dresden and other cities; another was a forced march to the death, from exhaustion; a third was that Hitler might use them as a 'human shield'. At the post-war Nuremberg trials, SS-*Obergruppenführer und General der Waffen-SS* Gottlob Berger, general commander of the POW camps by 1945 – the so-called '*Chef des Kriegsgefangenenwesens*' – stated that Hitler had considered executing 35,000 prisoners unless the Allied High Command agreed to peace negotiations. Himmler, he said, had made similar plans for imprisoning POWs in a castle on the Bay of Lübeck.

The so-called 'Long Marches' west from the German prisoner of war camps in the east to escape the advancing Red Army at the beginning of 1945, were routed over large expanses of Germany. All reports of these marches state that the roads were thick with snow and ice, and that conditions were extremely harsh. Graham Korner marched from *Stalag Luft* VII: 'Did we ever go on a long march! I've never forgotten that: from Bankau on the Polish border to *Stalag Luft* IIIa at Luckenwalde, 27 kilometres south of Berlin. There was thick snow and ice – we had three weeks of that on the road. I think one of the first nights we slept in a brick works. There were 1,500 in the camp at Bankau – British, Canadians, New Zealanders, and Australians. You were all RAF – there weren't any Yanks in there. But we had some odd blokes.'

Eric Yates marched from Heydekrug:

'They had about 20,000 people in the camp. There was snow and ice and we didn't know where the food was coming from – the guards didn't even know. The third day we did 42 kilometres. The seventh day, the 25th, was a so-called rest day. I'd been in the RAF Regiment before I flew, and when I got shot down I was pretty fit – but some of those poor bastards, they'd been in camp for four years! They weren't very well fed at all. We had some disappear on the way.'

The march from *Stalag Luft* III in Silesia began on 27 January 1945 and lasted over nine days. The march was in two stages. The first was by foot, when over 10,000 prisoners from all five compounds were force-marched west along icy roads for around 100 km from the prison camp in Poland to Spremberg railway station, in eastern Germany. This leg took six-and-a-half days approximately (times varied according to where in the column each group was) with the destination reached in the afternoon of 2 February. It would seem that, because Sagan station was not connected to the main German rail network, the prisoners had to trek west in order to access a railhead linked to the Reich system which could transport them north-east.

The second stage was effected by rail in French cattle trucks. These contained more than 40 men each and they rolled out of Spremberg at around 23.00 hrs on the 2nd, finishing their journey at around 16.30 hrs on 3 February, after between 41 and 48 hours travelling (estimates varied, some groups arriving later than others). The trip had taken place in appallingly unsanitary conditions, the only hygiene facility being a bucket in the centre of each wagon. The total distance covered was around 620 km. This was to Tarmstadt, the station for a German *Marlag* naval camp, 96 km north of Hannover.

After the war, the march was described by some as 'one of the greatest movements of population' and, because of the extremely low temperatures, frequently 20 degrees below at night, was also rather excessively dubbed 'one of the severest tests of endurance in history'.

FIRST STAGE
First Day: Saturday, 27 January 1945
Sagan

The trek was undertaken amidst great hardship, freezing temperatures and with snow on the ground. The *Kriegies* were underfed, under-clothed and carried most of their possessions[1] on home-made sledges cobbled together in the camp huts from any wood available. Geoff Willatt's room-mates hacked up an armchair made from two old Red Cross boxes. Many of these sledges fell to pieces after a time and had to be abandoned. Fifteen per cent of those taking part (300 out of 2,000) dropped out or died of exhaustion due to the extremely harsh conditions. Forty German guards also abandoned the trek or expired, some having to be carried by the POWs. There were many cases of frostbite and one guard had to have both legs amputated. Little or no food was supplied by the Germans to the POWs. At the very start of the march, all the remaining Red Cross parcels that the *Kommandant* of *Stalag Luft* III had stored illegally in the camp were turned out into the *Vorlager* to allow the

Kriegies to take as much food with them as they could – but there was little time for this. In addition, before they left, most men had binged on the food they had that was not possible to carry with them. The first official issue of food by the Germans did not occur until the column arrived at Spremberg in the early afternoon of 2 February.

On Saturday, 27 January 1945 the prisoners were ordered to be ready at *Stalag Luft* III to move out at one hour's notice: the Russians were reported to be breaking through at Stenian only 38 km away. There had been a rumour of this as early as the 24th and the *Kriegies* started packing. However many complained that the Germans would never attempt to march them 'in this weather!' when the SBO, Group Captain Weare, stated that there was no plan to move the prisoners.

At 21.30 hrs on the 27th a POW rushed into Geoff Willatt's room (number 19, Block 106), shouting, '*Prepare to march in an hour!*' Ted Robinson, a Halifax navigator who had been with 78 Squadron at Breighton, remembered:

> 'Bob Coulter and I were playing double patience across the table. The room was quiet for once. Then the voice of a fellow *Kriegie* came down the corridor, "The Germans have given orders that everybody must be ready to move off inside the hour" –and the flap was on. For a fortnight previously the Russian advance had caused nearly everybody to make preparations for a move, more especially when German sanction had been given for the making of rucksacks. Now, at five past nine, we had an hour to do everything we had not done before.'

In the North Compound there were feverish attempts to dispose of the remaining food stores, men eating and destroying all that they couldn't take with them. Much of this was stored in the new tunnel 'George' that was never to be used. On the night of 27 January, a year to the day after Laurie Simpson's crew was shot down, the 'flap' subsided somewhat: the camp 'Gen men'[2] were of the opinion that there was too great a number of *Kriegies* to be moved and the roads west were already crowded with refugees. At 21.00 hrs the Germans gave the order that they were to march in an hour. Arthur Schrock noted: 'Wild panic was the order and people ran here and there packing as much as they could carry in a pack and destroying all else. As the ground was frozen and the temperature sub-zero, many sleds were made and packed to overflowing.'

'After bags of panic,' wrote Johnny Rydings, 'and bets regarding removal over the last few days, "Deacon" rushed in at 9 p.m. looking pale and breathless with news to be ready to march in an hour. More panic and flap, feverish packing and frequent trips to the abort; made a hot brew of coffee, ate as much as we could and destroyed the rest. Rumours came in regarding big advances on the Western Front and capitulation on the East. Denied later.'

Geoff Willatt threw all his things out of his locker and stuffed them into a kitbag, but this was so heavy he had to remove half of them: 'We have to carry a Red Cross parcel of food each (12lbs)', he wrote, 'as well as our belongings.'

Second Day: Sunday, 28 January 1945
Sagan to Springruh

On the morning of the 28th there was snow on the ground and the roads were frozen. Willatt recorded:

> 'The ground is covered with snow and it's bitterly cold. We hack up our armchair and make a sledge – no mean feat in an hour – in addition to packing, cutting sandwiches and rushing

futilely around. I get stomach trouble and rush ceaselessly to the end of the passage. The start is postponed each hour until 1.30 a.m. and we make another sledge and sit around with hot faces in a pile of litter and wreckage.'

Ted Robinson recalled the sledge building: 'Time was at first spent feverishly packing, then in making sledges. Beds and chairs were ripped to pieces. The sledges were colossal creations, with eight men pulling, and tiny one-man affairs made from chairs. There was a foot of snow over the countryside, and every hope was that the roads would be in good condition.' In the East Compound, Derek Hodgkinson mistrusted the sledges he saw being built: 'They looked as if they would fall apart after a few miles; and what about deep snow, or the opposite – a thaw?' Hodgkinson was adjutant of the East Compound column, needed freedom of movement, and decided that the best way to survive was to be completely independent and carry everything he needed on his person:

'I took a lot of time, and great care, in converting my kitbag into a really strong and well fitting rucksack. I decided it was to be for carrying food and I filled it over half full with a combination of porridge oats, chocolate, biscuits and dried prunes, all mixed together to make a really sustaining mash. I topped it up with a few of my most treasured possessions including my Repton cufflinks, photos of my wife and the latest volume, still only half complete, of my diary. I gave away my sleeping bag to one of the fellows in my room as I thought it would be too heavy to carry, and in its place made a roll of a couple of blankets tied together at the ends so that I could sling it over my shoulder. To my subsequent cost, I completely forgot to provide myself with a pair of gloves!'

It was a moonlit night, but very cold. The snow was nearly 10 inches deep. Ted Robinson remembered his departure was put off for hours, and it was past 2 a.m. before they finally moved southward in a long column. Geoff Willatt recalled that the whole Compound, which numbered 2,000 men, eventually set off in blocks, moving in a stream of sledges to the main gate and through the *Vorlager*. He was ecstatic at being out of the camp, but found it 'difficult to get any thrill' because of the mad rush of loading the sledges. Although Arthur Schrock, Johnny Rydings and Laurie Simpson shared Room 6 with five others, according to their separate accounts they left the prison camp at different times. Johnny Rydings got away with his pack from Sagan at 04.00 hrs. Schrock said he finally marched out at 04.30 hrs after each man in the North Compound received a Red Cross parcel in the *Vorlager*, but Laurie did not leave until 08.30 hrs. Rydings was surprised to find that no one knew either their destination, or how far they had to march. 'We could not find out and I doubt if the German guards knew either', wrote 'Doc' Schrock. Derek Hodgkinson remembered coming across an extraordinary spectacle in the *Vorlager* of the East Compound:

'The contents of the parcel store had been dumped on the ground outside in huge piles. The Germans told us to help ourselves on the way out. We threw ourselves on them, ransacking them for the items that we thought would sustain us best. I filled my pockets with more chocolate and dried prunes, and topped up my rucksack with tins of meat and stew. Then we passed the Guardroom and out onto the main road.'

That day they had three main stops: the villages of Halbau, Freiwaldau and Springruh. They turned south in the direction of Görlitz, and passed forests, swamps and much snow.

Hodgkinson recalled that it was 'a very fine, cold day' with a temperature of 8°C and the 'snow was sparkling on the heavily burdened branches of the fir trees that lined the road'. As he was coming up behind the earlier compounds, at least a foot of snow had been trampled into solid ice and the going was good. Geoff Willatt was further ahead in the column than most of the Block 123 group: 'We passed through Helbau shortly after dawn', he wrote. The civilians were quite friendly. Ken Rees noticed that 'the ground became littered with discarded items – all things the over-ambitious had tried to carry but found they couldn't'. Willatt saw some German women moving in the other direction behaving in an outwardly friendly manner as they picked up food and cigarettes that the *Kriegies* had discarded: 'From now on there was a trail of broken sledges and jettisoned boxes, clothes, food, books, cigarettes', he wrote.

Derek Hodgkinson's East Compound group was some miles behind the others:

'We marched through miles of pine forests, and then the trees gradually gave way to more open country. In the morning sun, under a covering of snow, it was unimaginably beautiful. It did not take long for the column to lose all order and become a long, straggling mass. Sledges piled high with parcels and every form of personal belonging –some just could not bear to leave anything behind – were dragged along by four or even six men. Others marched singly or in groups. At the head was the *Lager* Officer who was the German in charge of the compound at *Stalag Luft* III and the SBO, and the flanks and rear were guarded by Germans with Tommy guns and hand grenades. Nobody except the *Lager* Officer knew where we were going; and even he only knew our ultimate destination.'

All along the front millions of civilians and hundreds of thousands of POWs began to take the great trek west to avoid the Russian hordes. Before reaching Freiwaldau a stream of buses travelling east passed by the North Compound contingent, carrying German mountain troops in white winter camouflage smocks, suggesting that they continued to be well-equipped, even at this stage in the war. Freiwaldau was reached at 14.00 hrs, but Laurie Simpson arrived there half-an-hour later having walked 33 km suffering from a stomach ache – he noted, probably caused by dysentery. They would stop every half-hour for a 10 minute break and every time it was recorded as being 'very cold'. Laurie:

'*Freiwaldau is the first good sized town which we reach in the afternoon. No real food yet; only hasty snacks from tins when we pause for the ten minute rest and, worst of all, nothing to drink. We sit in the gutter while it snows for three hours, and try to get a decent cold meal, scrounging hot water from houses.*'

'Doc' Schrock had a more positive impression:

'...this stop was amazing as the inhabitants were most friendly and the *Kriegies* just about took the place over. POWs were in houses and hotels talking to, and laughing with, the civvies; at one time it was thought we would stay overnight, so all the lads got busy getting billets for themselves. They met with good luck and all was set, until our guards and commander ordered us to move on and so the march was resumed.'

It was decided that it would be better to march to Lieppa, six kilometres further on. Johnny Rydings' feet were blistered and starting to play up. He went into a house and filled a billycan with water: '*Added half a tin of coffee and sugar,*' he wrote, '*and Charlie,*

Wimpy and self had a hot drink.' Geoff Willatt noticed a *Kriegie* '*striding across the marketplace with a leg of mutton under his arm*'. The man disappeared into a house but was pulled out by a guard. '*You can buy almost anything with a tin of coffee or cigarettes*', Willatt wrote. Rydings' group resumed the march at 15.00 hrs.

A long way behind them, Derek Hodgkinson was progressing at a snail's pace, almost coming to a halt as the weather deteriorated and it was bitterly cold and snowing once again. 'The going, especially for sledges,' he wrote, 'became difficult, and for the first time one began to notice the odd pile of clothes and other belongings dumped by the roadside.' Sledge crews were tired and the guards began to shout at, and threaten, the stragglers. After 17 kilometres they approached Helbau. The roads were crammed with refugees and the column had to struggle to make its way to the main square, which was packed with civilians.

> 'These were a sorry sight. Whole families, including the aged and children, tramped alongside carts drawn by horses and oxen laden to the brim with household possessions of every description. They had obviously been on the road for many days and were hopelessly bedraggled, the men unshaven, and all frozen stiff, as they shuffled along with a blank look of misery and hopelessness on their faces. We pitied them.'

Up ahead, the snow beat against Willatt's group in the open country and the walking periods became shorter and shorter, eventually reducing to 50 yards at a time. A penetrating cold went right through their clothes and, as there was no shelter, at each stop they sat huddled together at the sides of sledges for protection. Then, when the light went, the temperature fell. Willatt observed: '*It starts to get dark and we're still out in an exposed place in 22 degrees of frost – now almost at a standstill, but something must be happening at the front of the column to cause the hold-up.*' Johnny Rydings' feet and body were numb with cold. 'Our boots became frozen on our feet.' 'Doc' Schrock wrote, 'some of our men were collapsing from fatigue and cold, [but] we kept on until we reached Springruh.'

In fact, it grew so cold that even the guards, who were mainly comprised of ageing *Volkssturm*, were more concerned with keeping warm than carrying out their sentry duties. '*Escape would be easy but what's the use?*' wrote Geoff Willatt, *you'd perish in the snow in a very short time.*' At Springruh, which was reached around 19.30 hrs, they waited almost three hours in the middle of an open plain, shuffling forward a few steps at a time. Ken Rees had been on the road for sixteen hours, having covered 36 kilometres. They waited in the dark for four hours, the temperature was minus 20, which he described as 'horrible': 'You've gone numb long since,' he recalled, 'and lack the energy even to worry about freezing to death.' Laurie Simpson complained that '…*after 35 kms everyone was exhausted and frozen in the bitter cold. We had been on the road for 15 hours with packs up.*' 'Doc' Schrock was 'forced to stand out on a causeway until the Germans, goaded on by our SBO, found us billets in barns, where we lay in the straw utterly exhausted and then lapsed into a sleep interrupted by fits of shivering.' He and 'the Bishop' (D.W. Finlay), Laurie Simpson, Mike Raye and Johnny Rydings were in a barn with 50 others. There was 'no organisation at all', Schrock remembered and he shivered all night. Geoff Willatt was in another barn:

> 'We were herded into a farmyard and made a rush for a large barn. On entering the door it was completely dark and we stumbled forward, falling over a carpet of people who had already bedded down in the straw. I climbed up a ladder to the loft.'

Ken Rees's friend, 'Red' Noble, found a pitchfork and threatened to stick it in anyone he found smoking. The hay was warm, inviting and sweetly scented. Willatt noticed that Noble was doing good work fitting bodies in where any minute spaces were left. 'He deserved a medal for that', Willatt commented. But then Noble fell off the ladder onto occupants of the barn below, who were too tired to swear at him. Many had frostbite and were vomiting. Rees found his socks frozen to his boot soles, and his feet were so cold that he shoved them 'under some bloke's bottom'. Amidst the coughs and snores of 400 men, he drifted off to sleep, reminded of scenes from Antarctic explorer Apsley Cherry-Garrard's book *The Worst Journey in the World*. Back in Halbau town square the East Compound group was having difficulty finding shelter. The mayor of the town had nothing to offer – he had thousands of displaced Germans to cope with and Hodgkinson's *Lager* Officer was at his wits end trying to sort it out. For two hours the men of East Compound stood in rows, freezing, and then an empty school was found on the outskirts of the town. Hodgkinson had a miserable night:

> 'By the time we got in, we were not only frozen but exhausted. I and my 12 room-mates found ourselves in a room 18 ft by 10 ft crammed to bursting point with 17 others. We had something to eat out of our pockets and then lay down head to tail, like sardines in a tin, and tried to sleep. My hands (no gloves) were frostbitten, and as they thawed out I went through agonies. I also wanted to urinate badly, but knew that if I got up and tried to get to the door I would lose my place on the floor.'

Third Day: Monday, 29 January 1945
Springruh to Muskau

On Monday, 29 January the North Compound group arose at 07.00 hrs after ten hours' rest. The Germans' headcount lasted half-an-hour and was 'ineffectual' according to Rees. Only when the prisoners organised themselves into groups, with one person in charge of each group, was anything achieved. They moved off between 08.00 and 09.00 hrs, still heading south. The final destination that day was to be the village of Muskau. It appears that the men from Room 6 in Block 123 at Sagan became gradually dispersed along the column, as their records of arrival and departure times differed considerably. Schrock: 'At 09.00 hours on the 29th we started our second day's drudge – same weather, same snow and bitter cold.'

The surface of the road was packed hard. Laurie noted that '*the use of sleds made things much easier*', and Johnny Rydings saw that 'Doc' Schrock and Laurie had 'knocked up a sled to carry the packs', whilst his feet were playing 'merry hell'.

Hodgkinson's East Compound was still at Helbau. It was a 'sparkling sunny day', he recalled, and they were warm again. The *Lager* Officer, realising how near to disaster they had come the previous night, decided to go ahead in a car to see if he could arrange accommodation for the next night. The rest of the group remained in the town all day.

Johnny Rydings' group, after walking between 2 and 3 km, left the Görlitz road at noon and turned north-west towards Priebus, where the column stopped for a 'lunch of frozen bully beef'. Arthur Schrock:

> '…hot water was given us by the German women, who brought it to us where we stood on the roadside. After a short spell we carried on until we reached Muskau at about 8.30 p.m.'

They passed a Russian POW camp. By now people were beginning to drop out in scores. Geoff Willatt noticed men '...sitting in the road at the wayside with a glazed look in their eyes and going to sleep where they sat'. The German guards were too exhausted to help, but Willatt observed that local farmers assisted, picking up 'some of the unfortunates in carts and carrying them on to the next village. As we got more and more exhausted, the villagers appeared increasingly friendly, and we once got hot water or coffee for nothing, although the stops were very infrequent.' He noticed that the guards' attitude changed according to whether they were fresh or tired: 'Most of the time they trudged along near the rear, too exhausted to bother whether we escaped or not.' He had a vivid impression of one undersized German '...limping along painfully with a cork stuck in the end of his rifle, a "last gasp" look on his face.' Many of the guards dropped out, one lying asleep in the snow as the column passed by. Some of them had not even the strength to carry their own packs, and abandoned them, and 'Doc' Schrock noticed a *Kriegie* helping a guard, who was sat in a ditch, put his pack back on: 'He staggered for a bit, threw away his tin helmet and finally threw away his whole pack!'

Derek Hodgkinson's overriding priority was to find some form of protection for his hands.

'I had a "housewife"[3] in my rucksack, so in no time at all, I was able to cut a double thickness mitten for each of my hands out of one of the blankets and sew them together. I attached a length of string to the cuffs so, when not in use, they hung round my neck. They proved to be ideal; although it took some time for the effects of frostbite to wear off, my hands were never cold again.'

The group opened a few tins of meat, made some milk from 'Klim' tins[4] and gradually their spirits rose. 'Despite the circumstances,' Hodgkinson recalled, 'it was really terrific to be out of that damnable camp and fending for ourselves.'

The North Compound reached Muskau at 19.00 hrs 'in very weary condition'. It was still snowing and bitterly cold. Laurie noted that they had marched 71 kilometres, and entered the town after dark, having walked the last 33 kilometres in 10 hours. Schrock: 'At Muskau, being a fair-sized town, we were billeted in factories and a cinema. The civilians were friendly and in some cases went out of their way to help us; bags of black market trading went on and onions, bread and many other things were bought for cigarettes.'

Geoff Willatt's group had to stagger the last three kilometres uphill to a glass foundry on the 29th,[5] and was then billeted in its air raid shelter. He found it 'cramped, stuffy, dirty, but gloriously warm.' They boiled water in tins by the furnace doors and slept on straw over the ovens –'too hot below, but cold and draughty above', he wrote. For the next two days Laurie Simpson's group of 300 men were billeted in the cinema 'with barely room to stretch out', which Johnny Rydings found 'extremely crowded, but dry and warm.' They were at last able to get a hot drink, but not a hot meal. They had walked 30 kilometres and Rydings' feet were 'played out'. Conditions were so cold that he developed 'frostbite in both big toes' with blisters under the toenails.

Fourth Day: Tuesday, 30 January 1945
Muskau
Tuesday 30th was a quiet day and the North Compound group remained in the cinema.

The East Compound contingent marched out of Halbau at 06.30 hrs. 'The conditions were much the same as on the first day,' Hodgkinson recalled, 'good to start with but deteriorating as the day wore on.' The North Compound men took advantage of the black market that was operating in Muskau and traded cigarettes, soap and coffee for bread, onions and beer.

Johnny Rydings recorded: '*Americans leave us tomorrow presumably en route for Nuremberg; it's rumoured we are to go to a place near Bremen.*' The POWs were treated well by the local populace and plenty of black market trading took place amongst the Polish prisoners and German-speaking POWs, and the foreign workers and their German 'management'.

The East Compound passed through Freiwaldau and finally reached the village of Lieppa. A barn was commandeered by the *Lager* Officer, but Hodgkinson found it full by the time he arrived:

> 'I espied a small platform built on the rafters of the roof, with a stepladder leading up to it. It was precarious to say the least, but by laying our kitbags and rucksacks around its edges, we were able to ensure that it would be reasonably safe to sleep on. Hot air rises and, being reasonably close to the roof, it was remarkably warm. We passed out as if hit by sledgehammers as soon as we lay down.'

Fifth Day: Wednesday, 31 January 1945
Muskau

On Wednesday 31 January the North Compound contingent was still at Muskau. Geoff Willatt recalled that the Americans had left with only half-an-hour's notice: they were marching to Nuremberg. '*Americans leave at noon today giving us more room in the cinema*', Rydings noted. On the march they had passed large groups of refugees who made their way through Muskau in one long stream. '*Departure still held up,*' Rydings wrote, '*they don't seem to know what to do with us.*' There were no hot meals; just brewed up tea or, alternatively, *Ersatz* coffee, the Germans supplying them with one-sixth of a loaf of bread per man.

Meanwhile, the East Compound left Lieppa at 06.00 hrs. They marched towards Muskau, passing by Buchenwald,[6] and after 28 kilometres arrived at Muskau in very poor shape. It had been 10 degrees below all day and, although Hodgkinson felt alright, some of those towing the sledges were 'at the end of their tethers'. But at Muskau they found the locals as friendly as the earlier groups, and drank their first hot drink since Sagan:

> 'The women in the houses on either side of the road came out with pots of tea and coffee in their hands. We all had mugs with wire handles ...we held them out and the women filled them. One or two of the guards tried to stop them, but the women paid no notice.'

Geoff Willatt's group was still lying up in the large glass foundry when the East Compound party arrived. The foundry was a miracle in the circumstances, as its furnaces were going full blast – hot water was readily available, and they could dry their clothes. The furnaces were red hot so the *Kriegies* cooked stew on the edge of them. It was 'pure heaven' Hodgkinson said. The Germans served them their first hot meal since leaving Sagan - vegetable soup with rice – and told them that they could rest there for 24 hours. Then, oddly, the snow began to thaw – a month before its usual time: 'The winter had been hard for so long,' Hodgkinson wrote, 'that when, later in the evening, the snow began to melt on the roofs, few believed it was more than a temporary change.'

Sixth Day: Thursday, 1 February 1945
Muskau to Graustein

By morning a great deal of the snow had disappeared, and it had started to drizzle. Muskau had metamorphosed into an improvised transit camp, the continuously arriving prisoners bedding down wherever they found cover. Some, using sledges, clung to the hope that the snow-covered roads would be compact enough for use, whilst the more enterprising *Kriegies* bartered cigarettes and food for wheeled vehicles. The march went on and on. They had been travelling for five days. At this point the East Compound group was told that it would be divided up into two groups: one contingent would join the North Compound and continue the march to the railhead at Spremberg, where it would entrain on the 2nd for Bremen. The other would join 2,000 POWs from Belaria and march for Nuremberg on the 3rd. There was some discussion as to which group was more fortunate, i.e. which one had most chance of being liberated. Hodgkinson recalled:

> 'It really was quite traumatic. Quite a number of the chaps applied to change places, and a few were allowed to do so. In the few hours remaining, people said their goodbyes. Men who had lived together for three years or more were suddenly parted without knowing when, if ever, they would meet again. Many who had been devoted friends missed each other that night, never to meet again.'

Geoff Willatt's group began early: '*At 22.30 hrs we left Muskau at an hour's notice. Why is it that we always move and always get billeted in the dark? All my clothes and food are in my kitbag strung from my shoulders – a total load of approximately 50 lbs, which doesn't seem too much at first, but it is back-breaking after a few hours.*' Johnny Rydings: '*Thawing and rain outside, this will mean the sledges will be useless.*'

They were told to be ready to leave at 11.00 hrs in the morning but did not depart finally until late that night in the dark and rain. 'Doc' Schrock: 'At 23.00 hours we started an all-night march to Graustein.' Derek Hodgkinson's group left at 22.45 hrs in the pitch dark, its destination Spremberg:

> 'We met up with the North Compound column on the outskirts of Muskau and moved together into the open countryside. The conditions were appalling. The snow had been replaced by thick slush and mud. It quickly became apparent that sledging was near impossible. A few hardy individuals struggled on, but sledge after sledge had to be abandoned with their contents. After an hour or so the clouds cleared and the moon came out – to reveal the full horror of the situation. It looked like the retreat from Moscow. Sledges were upended with their contents spread all over the roadside verges; prisoners frantically trying to stuff as much as they could into kit bags, which they then had to carry over their shoulders or under their arms. Perhaps the most pathetic sight I saw was a chap sitting, crying, on his sledge, the sole contents of which were the heaped pages of the book he had spent the last three years writing; he knew he could not carry them, and yet he could not bring himself to abandon them.'

The snow continued to thaw, making the large, heavy sledges next to useless. After 44 kilometres many of these had to be abandoned because of the slush. Abandoning the sledges meant they had to carry all the food from them on their backs. 'Doc' Schrock: 'The thaw had set in and so sleds were discarded and packs put on.' Rydings 'trudged through the whole night' finding it very heavy going due to the extra weight; 'No one knew definitely where we were going,' he recalled.

Derek Hodgkinson:

'As the night wore on the situation became more and more chaotic and the prisoners more and more exhausted. The two columns became inextricably mixed together, and guards abandoned their duties and mingled with the column. Many of them were aged reservists and finding the going too much. Prisoners took compassion on them and one saw the odd sight of *Kriegies* carrying rifles and machine guns whilst the guards hobbled beside them. Some prisoners formed themselves into groups so that they could march in a disciplined fashion with regular halts for rest. However, even this broke down as almost to a man they fell asleep as soon as they halted. It was like waking the dead to get them on the move again. Others just fell asleep as they marched and ended up in the ditch beside the road; their friends, noticing their absence, then had to retrace their steps to rescue them.'

Hodgkinson himself had the extraordinary experience of falling asleep as he marched, having dreams in vivid colour, but always coming around before collapsing.

Seventh Day: Friday, 2 February 1945
Graustein to Spremberg

At dawn the North Compound group reached the small hamlet of Graustein where it staggered into barns. The East Compound contingent reached Graustein just after dawn. It collapsed in barns filled with hay and Hodgkinson recalled: 'I just lay down in the biggest bundle I could find and went out like a light.' 'Doc' Schrock: 'After another seven to eight hour trudge we reached the village and were once again herded into barns for a three hour rest.' Laurie Simpson noted that they arrived at Graustein at 07.00 hrs after marching 89 kilometres. Geoff Willatt: '*Although very tired we are cheered by the news that there are only eight kilometres more, hot soup and then a train.*' At 11.00 hrs they were on the move again. 'We rested for five hours,' Laurie recalled, 'and set off again for Spremberg.'

The column reached Spremberg at 14.00 hrs – '*tired out*', noted Rydings, '*total distance since leaving Muskau: 33 kms.*' Schrock's group arrived later: 'Spremberg was reached at 14.30 hrs and we were taken to an Army Barracks and marched into garages. Here we received our first meal supplied by the Germans.' Hodgkinson recalled that, in the early afternoon the East Compound had reached a barracks of a German armoured division. 'It was a huge place,' he said, 'and I can remember wondering at the grand scale in which it was built with palatial barrack blocks and large hangars for tanks, all extremely well equipped.' Johnny Rydings' group was billeted in the same tank garages 'of a German military barracks' where the Germans supplied them with their first hot meal since the prison camp, 'a small portion of soup', he said.[7] Rydings' group left at 16.30 hrs, walked another 2-3 kilometres, and then reached Spremberg junction at 17.30 hrs. 'Doc' Schrock's group arrived thirty minutes earlier: 'We were marched another 4 kilometres to a railway siding, and loaded into cattle trucks', he recalled. Rydings and his companions were '…packed into cattle trucks at 18.30 hrs: 40 men per truck. There was hardly enough room to lie down.' Geoff Willatt: 'We had three glorious hours of rest and then moved off across a common to the station, arriving there at dark, to be herded into old French cattle trucks: "*40 hommes ou huit chevaux*!" We tried to bed down, but it was impossible,' he recalled. These were the infamous French rail trucks designed for 40 men or eight horses. In some cases as many as 60 to 80 people were confined in these trucks, which were particularly unsanitary, stank of urine and faeces, and had only one metal container to serve as a communal toilet.

An hour after entering the tank garages, Hodgkinson's group set out on the last kilometre to the Spremberg sidings:

> 'On the way we passed through a steep-sided defile and, as we did so, a new batch of heavily armed guards appeared on the skyline on either side. A terrifying thought entered my mind – they were not going to entrain us, they were going to mow us down in the defile and then fill it when they had finished. Others voiced the same thought and, for a moment, we considered making a run for it. But nothing happened.'

This reflected the fears that many POWs had throughout the war – what was the Third Reich going to do with all its Allied prisoners? Ronnie Cartwright recalled a camp rumour that, after the first Thousand-Bomber raid on Cologne, 'Hitler was so enraged that he ordered the assassination of all RAF prisoners of war, a thought we had to live with for many months.' By 1945 the fear was that the *Führer* would use the POWs as his last card, and threaten to murder all of them unless the Allies came to terms, although in many camps the prisoners were prepared to make a break or fight for it.

The Run up the Road
No one had any doubt about the atrocities that the Nazis were capable of. In one infamous incident on 19 July 1944, 900 men travelling from *Stalag Luft* IV Heydekrug to *Stalag Luft* VI at Gross Tychow in Pomerania, were crammed into the stinking hold of a captured Russian coaling ship, the *Insterburg*, at Memel, for a trip of 60 hours to Swinemünde on the estuary of the Oder. After disembarking, they were forced to remove their boots and were handcuffed together in pairs. For a few hours they travelled by train to a tiny siding where they dismounted. Then followed one of the most notorious POW atrocities of the war: this became subsequently known by ex-*Kriegies* as 'The Run Up the Road'. Six hundred men were divided into three equal groups and, led by a huge German officer acting as pacemaker at the helm, were forced to run the gauntlet of a great number of fanatical teenage *Kriegsmarine* cadets who kicked, slashed and stabbed at them with knives and bayonets, the normal guards standing back or, with ravenous dogs, participating. Cal Younger described the scene:

> 'Officers, riding bicycles, fired off their pistols: "That's for Hamburg, that's for Essen, that's for Berlin", they chanted with each shot... The athletic young guards were tireless, lunging with their bayonets in rhythm with each step, sometimes striking with rifle butts. Still the worse was to come, for now the guard dogs were set loose, and flung themselves into the prisoner stampede.'

On each side of the forest track, the column was covered by heavy machine guns, their gunners threatening to shoot any of those who tried to escape. All this was filmed by a German cine unit and overseen by a pistol-waving *Major* shouting orders from a Mercedes. Percy Carruthers, a 25 year-old pilot shot down in a Martin Baltimore over North Africa, took part in the run. He recalled:

> 'Dogs were being riled and tormented, then given a long lead to lunge into the flanks and take the first available victim. A *Feldwebel* was fast losing what little patience he had remaining.

He drew his revolver, pushed it into the ear of an imperturbable airman and, with a beetroot type complexion and protruding eyeballs, squeaked, "*Run, English swine, run!*" [He] had become so worked up that his attempt at bellowing hatched out the weakest of tortured squeaks...

'The *Feldwebel* was now quite overcome with fury, as the dispassionate English swine just ambled along as before. The German withdrew his pistol from the boy's ear and, with a very determined expression, firmly flicked the safety catch off... Judy [Garland – a fellow prisoner] felt sure that the sound was loud enough to travel the length of the column, irrespective of the rifle shots, barking dogs, bellowing guards and cursing *Kriegies*...'

The run continued. Those at the front and back of the column were oblivious to what was happening in the centre where, to the relief of the *Kriegies* involved, the pace of the column gathered momentum. The SBO tried to reason with the German *Major*, but was dismissed out of hand. He went to the front to try and regulate the pace:

'The guards now intensified their activity. Stabbing by bayonets increased to an alarming level, becoming even more dangerous as they elevated the blades in an attempt to slash the pack shoulder straps, intent in cutting them free. Rifle butts were rained down on shoulders... The dogs were goaded and encouraged, making them devastatingly aggressive, jumping, snarling and ravaging legs, thighs and hands.'

At one point Carruthers fell into a roadside ditch and was so exhausted that he was unable to continue until two Germans came up and threatened to shoot him. 'I leapt up in a flash,' he said, 'shot past both of them, knocking one off balance and, before they realised what had happened, was back in the column.'

After some miles the *Kriegies* came to the end of the run, only to be greeted by a further gauntlet of guards who beat and clubbed them. Six hundred exhausted POWs then entered the new camp and were immediately herded into kennels 16 feet by eight feet and four feet high – ten at a time. Hundreds had suffered serious wounding – the official recorded number of 106 probably being far less than the actual total. A German camp doctor refused to treat the injured – one American had 64 bayonet wounds, and at least one POW died from his injuries.

Consequently in 1945 there was little feeling of innocence amongst the Allied POWs as to what the Germans were capable of. At Spremberg, Hodgkinson's group was confronted by the news that between 40 and 50 people had failed to make it to the railhead. Whilst one Bill Jennings was responsible for the North Compound group, Hodgkinson and Peter 'Hornblower' Fanshawe[8] entrained the East Compound. At 22.30 hrs Hodgkinson's group was locked in, 43 men to a coach, so that they could barely lie down. 'Somehow', he recorded, 'we all managed to find a bit of space on the floor, and covered ourselves with blankets.' Laurie Simpson noted: '*The train pulled out at 23.00 hrs and set off for north-west Germany.*'

SECOND STAGE
Eighth Day: Saturday, 3 February 1945
Spremberg to Halle

News coming from the Eastern Front was 'very good', Derek Hodgkinson reported: Frankfurt-an-der-Oder had fallen, the Russians were 80 kilometres from Berlin, and 50 from Stettin, and it looked as if the war was almost over. '*It is all very exciting,*' he wrote, '*one wonders if we will reach our destination before it is over.*' At Hohenbacha Johnny Rydings awoke from a doze at 08.00 hrs. Then followed Ruhland, Plessa, where the country was flat and featureless, and Falkenberg. They crossed the Elbe at 15.20 hrs at Torgau and went on to Eilenberg, Delitzech, reaching Halle at 20.30 hrs. The East Compound train arrived at Hohenbacha, halted, was unlocked and stayed there for an hour. Hodgkinson was relieved to get out of the overcrowded, stinking carriage and onto the tracks. But he was so tired that night that he was oblivious to the conditions. At that point, he recalled, he '....had a very fine crap by the side of the tracks!' As the train moved off his friend 'Butch' Brodie fainted and fell out onto the line. 'Luckily he was not hurt,' Hodgkinson commented, 'and we hauled him in just as the train was getting under way.'

The members of the group had been issued with a food parcel each and the previous night had shared a loaf of bread. As the train travelled west, they spent the time sitting, sleeping, chatting and smoking. Hodgkinson estimated they were travelling at about 40 mph, which was 'not bad going for a goods train' and were routed via Torgau, at Eilenberg branching right for Magdeburg. At Halle the train stopped for an hour, leaving at 21.30 hrs.

Ninth Day: Sunday, 4 February 1945
Hildesheim to Tarmstadt

Johnny Rydings awoke at Hildesheim at 07.30 hrs. '*Fine morning with a big chance of air attacks*', he noted. At that stage of the war the Allies had almost complete mastery of the skies over the German Reich and enemy transportation was a priority target. 'Apart from the conditions,' Hodgkinson remembered, 'the thing that worried us most during the two-day journey was the possibility of being bombed by our own aircraft. We passed through many marshalling yards and railway junctions and the thought of being caught in a raid on one of them, locked in cattle trucks, was not pleasant.' Geoff Willatt: 'We were all frightened of Allied aircraft strafing our train, particularly as we passed the outskirts of Hannover, where there was a lot of bomb damage. The bad weather saved us.'

Henry Coverley, shot down on the Nuremberg raid of 20 March 1944, recalled that his own rear gunner died in a strafing attack on the march back west: 'The Spits saw these chaps and presumed they were Germans advancing. They opened fire and he was killed.'

'*Looks like we're definitely en route for Bremen*,' Rydings noted, '*Hannover at 0800 hrs – some bomb damage. Nienberg (river Weser) 1045 – Verden, 1130 – Zeven 1300 to 1500 hrs: the first and only water during whole trip.*' But they had suffered '*atrocious treatment generally*' and it was snowing again. '*At last we arrived at Tarmstadt station – 40 miles from Bremen and 60 from Hannover.*' Willatt's account of the arrival at *Marlag Nord*, a special camp for naval prisoners near Tarmstadt, illustrates the frustrations they had:

> '*We quickly tumble out of the train and then move off slowly up the road, with frequent stops, to arrive at a Navy camp in the dark. Instead of going straight in – and I don't think I shall ever be so glad to see a POW camp – we stand in the slush and cold for three hours. This wait is absolutely the end – exhausted, dirty, hungry, and thirsty – and so near rest and warmth!*'

Rydings, with 'Doc' Schrock and Laurie, was delayed for even longer – over six hours:

> '*Tarmstadt at 1630 hrs – left train and marched 3 kms to a Marlag – reached it at 1800 hrs but kept waiting in heavy fog and mist on a waterlogged road until after midnight while 2,000 POWs were*

individually searched. This was the last straw. Quite a few collapsed waiting to enter the camp. Finally we got to sleep on the brick floor of a hut with a bit of wood straw at 0230 hrs.'

Effectively, Arthur Schrock and Laurie gave the same account of this incident and their time outside the camp was the same as Rydings, suggesting they were all together at that point. Schrock: 'After entraining we marched another four kilometres to a naval Camp where we stood for six hours in rain on a muddy and bitterly cold road whilst the Germans searched us before we were let into a compound and thence to huts.' Laurie: 'We walked for an hour to the camp, but had to wait six hours in the misty rain on a slushy road while being searched in groups of twenty and thirty men. Eventually [we] had some warm coffee and went to bed on damp straw at 02.30 hrs. Not once on the trip did the authorities give us any food or water. We carried our food on our backs and scrounged water the best way we could. Gastric flu and heavy colds were the main physical complaints after the trip. Absolutely nothing was awaiting us on arrival at Tarmstadt.'

'Many of the prisoners had dysentery and had to relieve themselves repeatedly where they lay', Derek Hodgkinson commented. 'Others were suffering from frostbite, with hands and feet going gangrenous. We had food but were desperate for water. The wait of six-and-a-half hours outside the wire at Tarmstadt was the last straw. It rained heavily and many of the ill and exhausted collapsed and had to be carried in...'

Tenth Day: Monday, 5 February 1945
Tarmstadt

In a report written for MI9 after repatriation in 1945, Arthur Schrock stated that he had arrived at *Marlag Nord* on 5 February where the conditions were 'filthy'. John Hartnell-Beavis, a former 10 Squadron Halifax pilot from Melbourne, Yorkshire, who had been shot down returning from an op to Essen on 25 July 1943, described it as 'the most derelict collection of huts I ever set eyes on.'[9]

The men lived in crowded conditions, 14 to a room, with wooden, three-tier bunks, poor lighting and a lack of heating. The sanitary and washing facilities were worse than those at Sagan. Schrock deemed all this to be the fault of the Camp *Kommandant*. The only clothing he had for 15 months was Red Cross issue, including one pair of pants, a second-hand tunic and a pair of boots. *Luftwaffe* and Naval behaviour he found 'quite OK' but Police and Gestapo conduct was 'very bad'.

He wrote in his diary: '*The total march was 264 kms, 165 miles (88 klms 1st day, 85 klms 2nd day, 90 klms 3rd day). With the exception of the meal at Spremberg and a little bread, we received no food or drink from the German Air Force, who treated us like dogs and tried to degrade and belittle us as much as possible. The German women were the only ones to help us and then it was only in the way of hot water; they would have given us more, but I believe their short rations and general lack of food prevented them from doing so. Wherever we were billeted we were so overcrowded it was impossible to rest, and whatever little organising there was, was carried out by our own senior officer and his staff. The march throughout was a terrible nightmare and was nothing short of an atrocity. (Believed 25% failed to complete the march.)*'

After they eventually entered the *Marlag*, Johnny Rydings noted: the '*...boys sorted ourselves out and made up a room of 13 Kriegies comprising Laurie, 'Bish', 'Polly', 'Doc', Mike, 'Wimpy', 'Fagan' and Charlie from the old room '6' at Sagan and Col, Al and Ted from the old Room 10 and a Canadian Johnny Taylor. So at last the old crew are all together in the one room.*'

Marlag Nord was controlled by the *Kriegsmarine* and situated about 25 kilometres north-east of Bremen. It was 'small, dirty and wet', according to Rydings. There were no beds, palliasses, fuel or cooking gear, and the lighting was 'very poor': in fact there was a general shortage of everything. 'Ninety per cent of the *Kriegies*', he noted, 'were ill with gastric flu and "the squits" due to exposure and exhaustion.'

From Bremen, Schrock later told MI9, they were marched to the north-east of Hamburg and *'exposed to strafing and bombing'*, with *'insufficient German rations'*. Finally, in April 1945, they received *'rough treatment'* at the hands of civilians at 'Buduslo'. All these he listed as *'atrocities'*, as he had the shooting of the 50 officers at Sagan.

May 1945
Laurie Simpson: final Service Diary notes

My father joyfully recalled the day of his and his friends' liberation. On 2 May 1945 he heard the sound of shooting growing steadily closer to where his party was camped: 'Gradually it passed by on either side,' he recollected, 'and then at 12.04 hours, amid wild cheering, a jeep drove up and we were prisoners no longer. Mad exultation and terrific excitement filled everyone.' The Cheshire Regiment, attached to the 11th Armoured Division, British Second Army, had released them. 'After we had cooled down a little,' he recalled, 'we all wrote to next of kin and waited to go home.'

The next day it rained again and there were 'POWs all over the countryside as far as Lübeck, Bad Oldesloe and down to Ratzbeck.[10] Most commandeered cars and all were busy collecting souvenirs.' On 4 May he set out with Johnny Rydings to see the local district. Things were grim: it was at this time that they witnessed a group of Hitler Youth throwing a stick grenade into a lake, killing all the fish; on another occasion, Laurie turned a street corner and saw a British armoured car run over a dog. They were picked up by a signals lieutenant and driven round in a captured Opel. *'Saw thousands of Goons waiting to give themselves up,'* he wrote, *'but they received no gentle treatment from the Tommies. Everything was looted but there was no brutality. Refugees and foreign workers were streaming on the roads.'* The *'arrogant Wehrmacht'* was humbled before the *'overwhelming might of the Second Army'*, he commented. They arrived back in camp at Trenthorst and went by truck across a long pontoon bridge over the Elbe to Lüneburg.[11]

On 6 May they set out in trucks for Solingen,[12] crossed the Weser and went to *'a much battered and blitzed aerodrome at Diepholz'*, he wrote. There they slept in a big mess building named after Oswald Boelcke, the First World War German fighter ace. The following day the POWs were flown to Brussels in Dakota transports. There was *'terrific activity with thousands of POWs coming in on thousands of aircraft.'* All nationalities, all colours, and all ranks were present; all in various states of health. They waited for eight hours, but there were no aircraft available that day.

On 8 May they went out to the airport and 'eventually got a lift for Blighty in a Lanc'. It was Laurie's first flight in an aeroplane for over a year. They crossed the English coast at 17.30 hrs and landed at 18.00 hrs. 'There was a warm welcome for all,' he recalled, 'with delousing again for a third time and tea.'

They were back home.

Reunited

The 'Long Marches' were an extreme test of endurance for all those involved and repatriation after so many months must have come as a very welcome relief. Afterwards Laurie returned to his young wife at Ferndown in Dorset. Their marriage was to last for 64 years. His diary entry for 10 May contains the following comment:

'*Decided to visit Dorothy as soon as I got some clean clothes. Arrived at Wood House around 7.30. Dorothy rushed out and the world stood still. Nothing can describe the joy of that moment.*'

The war was over but, for the majority of those involved, a huge portion of their lives had simply gone missing. For many it may have seemed a waste of time; for others it had been an unmissable experience; for thousands it was time to start again. But there was much rebuilding and reconstruction to be done before the peace could be exploited confidently.

• • •

On 19 June 1945, a Garden Party was held at Buckingham Palace by King George VI for the thousands of ex-POWs who had returned to England. Laurie attended and reflected that the members of the Royal Family were 'charming people'. He thought the Queen 'very sweet and Elizabeth very charming.' '*Margaret Rose*', he wrote, '*would be a very, very coquettish little girl because her large blue eyes fairly dance with mischief.*' He had a couple of words with the King, who was an extremely thin man, not very well and did not have a great presence. After asking Laurie if he'd received his DFC, the King remarked that:

'…as there were still 40,000 gongs to be given out, he'd "be an old b….. by the time he did them all."'[13]

CHAPTER TWENTY ONE

'IS GOD MY CO-PILOT?'

The haunted many

IN July 1944 a replacement RAF padre, the Reverend John Collins, arrived to work at Bomber Command headquarters at High Wycombe. Later in the year he was invited by the Minister of Aircraft Production, Sir Stafford Cripps, to give a talk to Bomber Command Headquarters on the supremacy of the individual conscience in the bomber war, titled 'Is God My Co-pilot?' Collins had found his posting 'soul destroying and depressing' when he first arrived but, despite reports to the contrary, he actually liked Harris, and the two men developed a mutual respect for each other. Collins's speech, however, upset the C-in-C. The Reverend suggested that men should agree to fly on a bombing operation only if they believed it was militarily and 'morally justified'. He was harangued by his audience over the practicalities of this, in view of its effect on discipline and the war effort. Harris responded to it by asking Harry Welldon, his personal staff officer and a philosophy don from Magdalene College, to give a lecture on 'The Ethics of Bombing' which would require compulsory attendance. At the end Collins promptly got up and mockingly suggested the talk should surely have been called 'The Bombing of Ethics'. This battle between these two strong-minded protagonists, Harris and Collins, continued until the end of the war.

Another cleric whose views drew much public attention was Dr. George Bell, the Bishop of Chichester. Bell made an oft-quoted speech to the House of Commons on 9 February 1944, following the publication of an article he had written the previous September in his local diocesan gazette, protesting against the morality of area bombing. Before speaking in the House, he had prepared his speech by 'drawing heavily on material in the neutral press he had seen during a visit to Sweden'. It is worth bearing in mind that the 'visit to Sweden' had actually been a diplomatic one concerning the safety of the European Jews in the light of events in Germany. It must have strongly affected Bell, who was a conscience-driven man with his concerned finger in many pies. To him, a 'convinced and consistent' anti-Nazi since 1933, Hitler was 'a barbarian'; but he deplored any 'lowering of moral tone' or allowance of British actions to be dictated by 'a spirit of revenge'. Whole towns, he explained convincingly, were being indiscriminately obliterated.

Bell's speech received extensive coverage in the press, but the Church viewed his performance glibly and he was passed over when the Bishop of Canterbury's see became vacant that October.

A popular Noel Coward song of 1940 *Don't Let's be Beastly to the Germans*, featured in a *Daily Mail* cartoon of 21 February, eventually lost its savour: Group Captain Peter Johnson, a Lancaster squadron commander, reflected upon visiting Belsen concentration camp in 1945, that the spirit of Coward's ditty had lost its attraction.

It is very difficult for modern society to understand the stresses of those times. There were 'no counsellors for stress, no flowers by the roadside, no little vigils'.[1] Ted Groom commented: 'People have no idea today what it was like. We lost 55,000 airmen; a hell of a lot considering nothing else was being lost at that time in the war.' And John Wynne, a vastly experienced pilot and OTU instructor, reflected:

> 'It was totally different then. The world events were so monumental that you had no time to think about the people who had fallen by the wayside. If we had had today's attitudes, we would never have won the war.'[2]

John Nunn, who died in September 2006, completed his tour on Lancasters. Like many of his contemporaries, although escaping bodily injury, his nerves were shattered by incidents during the war and recollection of them became a nightmare for him. It was 47 years before he was able to record his experiences, but the writing of his memoirs became a kind of palliative for him. Records he had of his operational career were few: only his flying logbook and a signed photograph of his crew survived. Despite this, and not being an especially eloquent man, he was able to produce a remarkably detailed and intelligent account of what had happened to him. He wrote:

> '*On the twentieth of January 1992, I sat down with pen and paper, to write down what I could remember about my service in the Royal Air Force. This was exactly fifty years from the day that I went to London for my Aircrew Selection Board.*'

He was very honest in his admittance of how the process was a healing one:

> '*The task of writing has laid a few ghosts for me and I no longer have so many spells, in the long reaches of the night, recalling those times.*'

Jack Cheeseman, the 27 Squadron bomb-aimer, was not so fortunate. The horrific experiences he had suffered dogged him for the rest of his highly troubled life. After the war, when he returned to England, his health was still fragile and, despite improving physically, he suffered a complete mental breakdown. Marriage, a family and a job helped, but his wartime demons still clung to him. He would refuse to discuss his experiences subsequent to his baling out, and falsely claimed amnesia.

Arthur Schrock also suffered from suppressed memories. In fact, despite leading a fairly carefree existence as a young man, his life became beset by troubles after 1945. He returned to his pre-war wife, but they lost their first child after a rushed forceps delivery. When he returned to his family in Queensland they had little empathy for what he had suffered. The area bombing offensive weighed heavily upon his conscience for years and his enduring nightmares had violent side effects. His son has a clear recollection of his mother, Mabel Schrock, telling him that on a number of occasions she found herself on the bedroom floor after receiving an almighty kick in the back. 'Dad was thrashing around in bed yelling '*Get out! Get out!*' He would wake in a cold sweat and be very apologetic and tell her about trying to clear the escape hatch.'

Ron Heath, Graham Korner's mid-upper gunner, who jumped from their Halifax after an attack on Bochum, also suffered long-term flashbacks. For years after the war he would recall how the engineer, 'Paddy' Finnigan, had clung onto him as they baled out together. Finnigan fell off as soon as Heath's parachute opened. Korner remarked; 'It affected Ron badly. For years afterwards he would bale out of bed in the middle of the night: his wife said he ended up with his legs up in the wardrobe!'

Ray Thomas, whose mother died whilst he was training in Canada, did not arrive on squadron until 1944: 'We all coped in different ways on ops', he said. 'Being young helped, I suppose.' He was fortunate in not suffering from post-war nightmares: 'I had no real after-effects, but then I wasn't operating in 1943 when losses were much greater. I have every admiration for those who did a full tour of 30 ops or more.' Although not suffering long-term he was taken aback and made to think when an old lady asked him years later 'if I ever thought of the death and destruction I may have caused. Saying "They started it" didn't really cover it.'

There are countless cases of traumas pursuing airmen and they were not always the result of experiences in the air. Wally Maltby, Laurie Simpson's diminutive mid-upper gunner on his first tour, suffered from nightmares long afterwards. He would wake up pouring with sweat some nights recalling the ill-treatment he had received as a prisoner of war. Bill Higgs wished to forget his tunnelling work in *Stalag Luft* I: 'A fall of sand trapped me. I was a face digger and last out of a tunnel. It was about 80 feet long and the other lads had loosened the sand as they went out. Peter Buttigieg came back into the tunnel to free me, but the incident had made me claustrophobic and I never went into a tunnel again. I think I had worked on about eight or ten by then.'

Bomb-aimer Jack Brook's daughter was struck by one after-effect of her father's POW experience:

> 'He was generous to a fault, money was just money: "There are no pockets in shrouds" was his attitude. However I believe that his POW experiences resulted in a need to horde things and he could not tolerate waste, self-pity, laziness and ingratitude.'

She noticed that a number of people corroborated that they, or their relation, displayed similar behaviour, which appeared to be directly due to the deprivation they had suffered.

The comradeship that heavy bomber crews shared during the war had been unique: each member relied upon the others to survive. Philip Bates, flight engineer with 149 Squadron, commented: 'When I returned to England, where I was not greeted as a hero, my one desire was to regain life as a member of a bomber crew and go east and bomb Japan. How naive can you get? There were still thousands of active, but redundant, aircrew ahead of me in the queue.' Navigator Frank Dennis retrained as an Equipment Officer and finished his post-war career at the RAF Hospital in Ely. Whilst there he shared a room with a psychoanalyst on the medical staff named Bickerstaff. Bickerstaff asked him one day what life was like on an operational bomber squadron; some of his patients were ex-aircrew who needed help and advice. 'Apparently the most common factor that ran through their troubles,' he said, 'was the fact that after operational flying, the camaraderie that existed on squadrons, and particularly between crew members, was no longer there. This seemed to be the main factor that exacerbated their problems.'

Of his time as a POW at Heydekrug, Eric Yates recalled: 'I have always felt that these experiences gave me an insight into my fellow men in good times or bad.' Laurie

Simpson once said that the whole experience of the war 'made him' what he was, and Ted Boorman recalled of his RAF and POW experience that 'it stayed with you for the rest of your life'.

How men dealt with the awfulness of what they had perpetrated varied according to the person. My father once told me that there simply was no time on operations to consider the consequences of what one was doing. He said he had thought about it after the war however. 'I think we were all affected by our experiences and had to deal with them in our own particular way,' Frank Dennis recalled, 'which often took some time. There are some who will not, or cannot, talk of those now "far off" days.'

Reg Brown, the 115 Squadron flight engineer, worked in the RAF with NATO after the war:

> 'Even now, I'm convinced that it had to be done. We never had any real briefings other than about the town or the place we were attacking. You would never admit that you would be going to a housing area, but it was obvious that there would be fallout during blanket bombing and so forth. There was always a defined target which you did your damnedest to hit but, inevitably, you sometimes missed. We were all too young to sit back and think about it.'[3]

On the concentration camps he commented that aircrews' knowledge was very limited: 'That unfolded bit by bit, but nothing was really known until after the war, not to the extent that it is today. We just thought that Hitler had to be beaten; we had to survive, and that was the way to do it.'

Dr. Deryck Lambert was able to look back at what he had done in the war and realise what an important part it had played in his life post-war. 'Being a member of an aircrew played a crucial part in what I've done since', he reflected. This was not just in terms of saving people's lives, but also 'concentrating on certain aspects of life: teamwork, working with other people; our whole lives depend on teamwork.'[4]

Leonard Cheshire concurred with this: 'It was the wartime RAF that gave a direction and a discipline to my life, and taught me that professionalism and teamwork are the prerequisites of all human achievement. There I was shown what men and women can achieve when they are united in pursuit of a common goal clearly defined as just and good, and which they know they must attain at all costs.'[5]

• • •

At a squadron reunion at Middleton St. George, the Battle of Britain Memorial Flight Lancaster gave a flying display. Afterwards veterans were invited to look around inside the aircraft but one ex-airman bluntly refused to go: 'He was in tears and apologised, saying that it was an acute reminder of all the friends and colleagues he had lost on operations.'[6]

EPILOGUE

AFTER the war Laurie Simpson and Dorothy sailed back to Australia on the 'Stork Ship'.[1] Laurie appears to have lost his accent during the war. When he arrived back in the home country he quickly telephoned his friend from his Deniliquin days, Gertrude Lawrence. 'Gert' was by that time married as Mrs Lewis. Her husband answered the phone and briefly announced, 'There's some "Pom" on the phone for you.'

Laurie was glad to be back home, seeing old friends and family. Despite the war 'Gert' thought he had changed little. Laurie and Dorothy rented a flat in Melbourne and he went to work for Massey-Harris Co., the agricultural equipment manufacturer, in Queensland, travelling back and forth once a week. But Dorothy was homesick and very lonely looking after their first child, who was born in 1946, and eventually they returned to England. When the war ended, like most men, Laurie wanted to get on with his life, but he always appreciated and never forgot his experiences in Bomber Command and as a Prisoner of War.

'Doc' Schrock disembarked at Sydney docks on 8 September 1945, where some of his personal papers were pilfered. He had spent four years and ten months outside the continent with the RAAF. This included eight months training in 1940 and 1941 in Canada at Calgary and Halifax. He had arrived at 12 Squadron on 11 June 1942, made 34 operational trips with Ernie Wyle's 'United Pacific crew', and was on 460 Squadron by 16 January 1944. 'Doc' made a statement for the Australian military forces at the RAF Receiving Centre in Brighton in 1945, after his repatriation, in which he mentioned that he had been '…captured by Germans in a French farmhouse after walking 36 kilometres.' He had been in *Stalag Luft* III for 352 days, from 9 February 1944. The 'Long March' from Sagan in mid-winter, the worst winter the Germans had experienced for over 40 years, was 150 miles. During the cattle truck rail journey from Spremberg to Bremen, he and his fellow prisoners had 'no water for over 48 hours'. Schrock pronounced the '*Haupt Deutsch*'[2] responsible.

Schrock's case is typical of men who served in Bomber Command, ended up in prison camp and partook in the 'Long Marches'. His summary of the treatment he received is, however, an indication of what men suffered at the end of the war as well as the Germans' attitude towards them.

Cal Younger also went back to Australia, but the economic climate was such that he decided to return to England where he would be better able to pursue his interests in writing and cartooning. In 1949 he revisited the scene of his evasion and gradually began to unravel the actual circumstances of his arrest. His first book, *No Flight from the Cage*, was published in 1956: the original draft was twice as long as published: 'They had to cut it', he recalled. 'I probably took a couple of years over it. I started it in 1952.' The book was an account of his experiences as a POW, written mainly to expiate himself of his memories of the war, and was not intended to be an 'escape' book. Afterwards Younger was thanked by a number of the wives of ex-POWs for enabling them to understand what their husbands had been through.

Younger did not really know James 'Dixie' Deans during the war, despite being in the same camp as him. Deans had gone to work for the London School of Economics, a job he was grateful to have because of his multiple sclerosis. It was only after Younger crossed paths with him in London one day, when Deans reprimanded him for not greeting him, that they began a firm friendship, a relationship that continued until Dixie died in 1989, after battling his illness for 50 years. Their inaugural encounter, when Deans invited him to join him and a couple of the 'boys' for drinks, led eventually to the forming of the RAF ex-Prisoner of War Association, an organisation which subsequently grew to have thousands of members worldwide. In 1961, when the BBC was filming 'This is Your Life' with 'Wings' Day as the subject, Deans, Younger, Massey, and Paul Brickhill all contributed, and Younger recalled having a long conversation with Brickhill after the show. Brickhill had worked as a journalist in England, Europe and Australia after the war and was the most successful of the ex-POW journalists. Three of his books, *Reach for the Sky*, *The Dam Busters*, and *The Great Escape* were all filmed, the latter by Hollywood. As well as *No Flight*, Younger also wrote a novel about growing up in Depression-era Australia, *Less than Angel,* and three books on Irish history (despite his having Scottish origins). He married a widow, became a stepfather to her two children and later worked as an administrator for various charitable organisations, a job which he said he found very rewarding.

Don Charlwood, the 103 Squadron navigator who survived his first tour, wrote one of the most celebrated accounts of life in Bomber Command, *No Moon Tonight*. He returned to his home country and took up journalism, later also producing *Journeys into Night*, the story of six of the men he trained with as a navigator. He married, had four children, and went on to write a number of other books about Australian life and growing up in the 1920s. In 1992 he was made a Member of the Order of Australia (AM) for services to Australian Literature.

Of a few others whose stories are included in the text:

Dennis Bateman remained in the RAF on ground duties. To his surprise, whilst working at the Demob Centre in Brighton in 1945, he met his bomb-aimer, Morris Crabtree, and had to sign him out. Crabtree had evaded and got back to England via Switzerland and was later posted to India.

Ted Boorman worked as an engineering draughtsman and illustrator for various firms.

Reg Brown became an administrative officer for the RAF with NATO in Europe, eventually being promoted to Wing Commander. He was awarded the MBE for his services. About the morality of area bombing he reflected:

'You got to realise that the harrowing tales told by these people were true – what happened to their families and so on at the hands of British bombing – Hamburg and so on. One particular girl, had lived through the hell of Hamburg when she was about 10 or 11 years old. But then we had people who'd been in London and suffered at the hands of the Germans. In NATO it was accepted that these things happened. The Germans in NATO weren't bitter – they were glad to be accepted, to shake off the Hitler cloud...'

Henry Coverley became an RAF pilot flying troop carriers to the Suez Canal Zone in the 1950s, and later to the Far East. He recalled transporting Group Captain Sydney Smith, T.E. Lawrence's former CO at RAF Mount Batten in the 1920s, from Luca to Fayed in the Nile Delta, and having many fascinating talks with him at Fayed airport about 'Aircraftsman Shaw' (Lawrence's incognito in the ranks) into the 'early hours of the morning, over large tumblers of gin.'

In 1945 John Grimer joined the RAF's Missing Research and Enquiry Service and worked in all four zones of occupied Germany. George Harsh found employment with a publishing company in New York as a sales representative, and then took up market gardening in New Jersey. He died in Toronto in January 1980. Graham Korner, the 640 Squadron tail gunner, went back to New Zealand after repatriation, but returned to the UK and signed on for a regular RAF engagement for three years flying on Wellingtons. He subsequently joined the police force. Ron Heath, Korner's mid-upper gunner, became the director of a large London typewriter firm based in King's Cross. He went to a local Guild meeting one night, suffered a heart attack and was, according to Korner, 'dead before he hit the floor'. Peter Hughes did the Empire Central Flying School course in 1945 and stayed on as a tutor for two years. Steve Jackson thanked God for saving his life after the sacrifice of his two friends 'Punch' Weatherill and Harry Ingram, over France in 1943. He married Rose, brought up three children and remained in good health for the rest of his days. He felt that, despite the loss of life, the area bombing campaign was justified for the sake of the security of England and the rest of the world.

Deryck Lambert, who returned to general practice and worked for some time as a consultant in a paediatric hospital near Liverpool, was awarded an MBE for his work. Howard Pearce became a quantity surveyor and company technical director after the war and then was made assistant Town Clerk at Ringwood Town Council. Jim Philpot was dissatisfied with working as a fitter's mate after demob and did a course in clock and watch repair, which he found 'right up his street'. He subsequently worked for 16 years for a jeweller in Gloucester.

Arthur Smith, the Halifax bomb-aimer charged with Lack of Moral Fibre, declined to take the soft option, returned to operations and survived the war. Henry Wagner continued the academic career he had begun pre-1939 and taught French. Geoffrey Willatt trained as a chartered surveyor. Philip Jenkinson and Joe Williams both returned to the agricultural world, in which Joe remained until retirement. Philip continues in farming to this day.

Of George Flanagan's crew, American Sid Ellingstad returned to the USA after the war and Bob Whyte went back to Glasgow. Both have since died. Following liberation by the Russians from *Stalag* IVB Mühlberg-am-Elbe, George escaped from a Russian-controlled German army barracks with four others and made his way to the American front line. He was subsequently flown back to Brussels and repatriated. He lives today in Highcliffe, Bournemouth.[3]

Leonard Cheshire converted to Roman Catholicism after witnessing the dropping of the second atomic bomb on Nagasaki. After leaving the RAF he was at a loss to know what to do and took in an old man who was terminally ill, and nursed him. He later accommodated and nursed a number of other sick old men, which led eventually to the formation of the Cheshire Homes organisation, now a worldwide charity. Guy Gibson was killed on 19 September 1944 flying a 627 Squadron Mosquito XX when acting as Master Bomber for an attack on Rheydt. Like Cheshire and Hughie Edwards he had been awarded the VC, DFC and Bar, and DFM and Bar. He crashed on the return flight, possibly after being engaged by a night fighter. Ken Brown, his fellow 617 Squadron dam buster, later concluded that Gibson's lack of experience on Mosquitoes probably contributed to this.

Of Laurie Simpson's two crews, Ken Sutton and Freddy King were both killed during the war. Freddy's only son, Peter, was born in 1945 and Freddy's wife remarried in 1953. Alistair Kennedy survived *Stalag Luft* III and the 'Long March' and returned to Australia, but died in the 'fifties from a heart attack. Wally Maltby went back to working for Boots in Nottingham. He wanted to put the war behind him and, like many men, forget about it. He was fairly unambitious, and wished only to do a nine-to-five job and have no other responsibilities. He had one son. The family kept themselves to themselves and my father never heard from him again until 2006 when, out of the blue, Freddy King's son, Peter, located him and put them in contact. There followed a brief telephone conversation, but they never met again: two weeks later Wally died aged 83.

Arthur Schrock opened a drapery business which failed in the early 1950s. He then worked for the family building business until he began running a pub in the 1970s. He was in his element: *The Centenary Hotel*, owned by the Schrock family company, was built with him as the driving force behind it. Arthur died aged 60 in July 1977 from cancer of the throat. His son had a lot to say about him. When he was told his cancer was terminal Schrocky 'was very calm and accepting of it,' his son recalled, 'telling a relation "Christ only knows how many people I've killed, why should I expect to be any different?"' But he wasn't ashamed of his wartime service and was proud to have been a member of Bomber Command.

Jack Rydings[4] went back to Perth and had two sons. He rejoined his old firm, a South Australian wine company, as a travelling sales representative, visiting hotels and liquor outlets in Perth and most Western Australia country towns. In the early 1950s he was appointed State Manager, a position he held until his retirement. Jack wrote to my father in 1985 from Como, Western Australia, by which time he had arthritis in both hands:

> '*I saw Colin McLeod some time in the '60s. He was still in the wool business and called in during a business trip in this state, but have not heard from him since. Geoff Maddern,* [Don Charlwood's skipper], *who you would remember from Church Broughton, lives two streets away in Como and we often meet in the shops. Allen Ellis (Block 110), Keith Murdoch (Block 105) and Stan Payne (Block 109) have all died before reaching 65. Harold Roberts, the next room in 123, is with the Swan River Conservation Administration and, although I haven't seen him for some time, I believe he's still going strong.*'

Jack Rydings died in 1987.

Colin McLeod returned to Australia and, in Sydney in December 1948, married Eve, a widow he had met near Breighton during the war. She had with her two daughters. Col went back to the wool trade and found a good job with a Sydney firm which involved some overseas travel. They had two boys. Eve died in 1967, aged 50, when Col was managing a wool processing plant at Bathurst. He was heartbroken. Col remarried in 1969 and had two further sons. Col died in January 1999 after a long illness.

Ron Searle remained in Australia after his service in Borneo and worked in sales for a commercial broadcasting station in New South Wales. He married Mavis, the girl he had known before the war, and had three sons. He later moved into selling with an international insurance company but then became, with his wife, an agent for the Totalizator Agency Board, although they had no personal interest in horseracing or betting. In the new millennium he returned to England, met Freddy King's son, and was taken for a joyride over Breighton aerodrome by a local flying club which he greatly appreciated. He had intended to meet my father whilst in London, but Laurie was under-the-weather and the rendezvous never occurred. Sadly Ron passed away after going into palliative care on 2 September 2011. Boys changed into men overnight when they were on aircrew: his youngest son remembered him as 'ten foot tall and bullet proof'. 'Goody the Gremlin' is, in 2012, the only survivor of my father's two crews.

. . .

A campaign medal for Bomber Command was never struck. Attlee's post-war Labour government gave Harris's men little recognition for the six-year offensive, and many of the air and ground crews of the Command had little with which to console themselves apart from the Defence Medal. Such was the disgust of Harris at the lack of official acknowledgement of his men's efforts that, when he was awarded the CGB in 1946, it caused him great distress and embarrassment. When the Conservatives returned to power Churchill offered him a peerage, but Harris refused it. He felt particularly strongly for his ground crews, who had to work at all hours in often abominable conditions.

Before the official history of the bombing campaign, *The Strategic Air Offensive against Germany*, was published in 1961, the authors were prevented from including the Portal-Harris correspondence, largely due to the efforts of Portal; and, to his bemusement, Harris was never consulted by them whilst the writing took place. Following publication the press deemed the bombing campaign a 'costly failure', although this was not the judgement of the book's authors.

Harris eventually returned to South Africa and became an executive with a South African shipping firm. He never lost touch with his 'old lags', and when the Bomber Command Association was formed in 1983, he became the first president and regularly attended its functions.

Marshal of the Royal Air Force Sir Arthur Harris passed away, aged 91, on 5 April 1984. On 31 May 1992 a statue of him was unveiled by the Queen Mother outside St. Clement Danes Church on the Strand in London to a mixed reception. At the present time the official Bomber Command Memorial is still in the process of being built near Green Park, London, and a further smaller memorial is due to be erected on Beachy Head, largely due to the efforts of Joe Williams and friends.

In 1947 Harris wrote:

> '*There are no words with which I can do justice to the aircrew under my command. There is no parallel in warfare to such courage and determination in the face of danger over such a prolonged period... It was moreover, a clear and highly conscious courage, by which the risk was taken with calm forethought... the courage of the small hours of men virtually alone, for at his battle station the airman is virtually alone... Such devotion must never be forgotten.*'[5]

"Lest We Forget"

An elegiac cartoon, showing a deep reverence for friends who had passed away on operations. Arthur R.B. Schrock flew on operations from the first Thousand-Bomber raid with his 'United Pacific Crew' of 23 OTU, Pershore, on a Wellington Mk Ic, up until the 'Simpson Kite's' final operation with 460 Squadron on 27/28 January 1944 to Berlin on a Lancaster I from Binbrook. The cartoon depicts a Wellington, a Lancaster and a Blenheim heading out of the sunset towards the silhouette of a wooden crucifix, with a pilot's helmet slung from it, thrusting organically from the grave of the European mainland. (Schrock)

....

'Born of the sun, they traveled a short while towards the sun
And left the vivid air soaked with their honour.'

STEPHEN SPENDER

CONCLUSIONS

GENERAL William Tecumseh Sherman was the first person to voice the oft misquoted remark 'War is hell'. Few would deny that statement, even in the present day, and hardly anyone would disagree that it is a more than adequate description of the bombing campaign. If there can be any broad conclusion about this book it must be that the work is hopelessly flawed. It is almost impossible to describe the Bomber Command experience effectively unless you have been there, and I have long since concluded about any on-the-edge experience such as this, that the best books on these subjects are always written by the people who *were* there. From Bert Harris and Don Bennett, to the works of men such as Don Charlwood, Miles Tripp, and Paul Brickhill, to name a few: these accounts get much closer to the reality of the experience than any second or third-hand writer could possibly hope to do. However I do feel that I was at least able to present a work from a slightly different perspective – from that of one who wasn't there, or alive at the time, but was brought up on the stories of the campaign. The two salient things that impressed me more than anything else in researching this book were firstly, how awful it must have been and secondly, how did men endure it? And if this work succeeds in depicting the first point and answering the second then at least it has achieved something – but only the reader can judge that.

Sir Arthur Harris's area bombing policy was misrepresented after the war: it came nowhere near having the effect that the Air Ministry and the British Government had hoped for, and the Allies severely underestimated the German economy's ability to recover from its effects. The bombing campaign was badly mismanaged from the first: poor weather forecasting contributed to disasters like the Nuremberg raid; poor Pathfinder marking made a large contribution to notable 'bog-ups' like the Pilsen raid and the fourth raid in the Battle of Hamburg. The inconsistencies of bombing accuracy were also obvious: the number of cases of 'creep back' that occurred, such as on the second Berlin raid of August 1943, before the Battle of Berlin itself, which caused bomb patterns to be hopelessly overspread, are an example of this. Despite the horrific consequences of attacks such as of the Hamburg 'firestorm' raid, the demoralizing aims of the bombing, for example the attempt to break the will of the German people, was hardly achieved at all; in fact exactly the opposite resulted if anything.

Although 'Bert' Harris was a brilliant, natural and diligent leader, he was also an imperfect one, as witnessed by the inconsistencies of his command.[1] Consider policies of his that could be deemed questionable:

1) His reluctance to bomb the U-boat pens.
2) His reluctance to bomb northern Italy, where there were 'soft' targets that would draw the enemy away from the Mediterranean Front.
3) His reluctance to start up a separate Pathfinder Force.
4) His delay of the employment of Window for over a year until the Hamburg raids of July 1943.
5) His encouragement of 'propaganda' raids after he became C-in-C, such as the bombing of Lübeck, Rostock, Augsburg and Cologne. These were all deliberate 'morale-boosting' operations that succeeded – but at a cost.
6) Harris more than any other person was responsible for implementing the area

bombing policy, and pursued it wholeheartedly, even when it became obvious that it was not bringing Germany to its knees, and that he had not 'wrecked Berlin from end to end'.

7) If Harris had had his way and continued with his campaign against Berlin in 1944, and had never allowed his squadrons to became involved in the plan to destroy the French transportation network before D-Day, a possible consequence of this may have been the driving of the invasion force back into the sea.

The organisation on the squadrons in Bomber Command was, in some cases, appalling, but understandable in the circumstances. Flight engineer Sandy Rowe recalled the instance of his 103 Squadron Lancaster landing at the wrong airfield due to confusion with the controller's instructions, and almost colliding with another aircraft. Numerous cases occurred of bombers crashing into each other over the home airfield on take-off. There were also the huge number of fatalities on Operational Training Units that were as much due to poor instruction and timeworn aircraft as to inexperienced pupils. Even on operations things inevitably went wrong. Operational aircraft were in far from pristine condition. Although Ron Searle extolled the virtues of the Lancaster, the fact is that, after its first operation, and before 'The Battle of the Ruhr', his crew was briefed for twenty-five operations and sixteen of these had to be 'scrubbed' for various reasons. Many of the misfortunes that plagued the aircraft during the winter of 1943 were unpredictable and expensive. The 'Simpson Kite's' operational record reads like a succession of unwanted disasters – aircraft bogging down, engine, bomb door and hydraulic failures, negative earths, broken controls and so on. By the end of January 1943, of the aircraft's eight operations, three had to be scrubbed due to inclement weather and two were mud-mired. From 31 January to 5 February of that year Simpson and his crew were briefed for four trips and only got to the target once – a raid on Cologne. The subsequent week they seem to have experienced unbelievably bad luck when two operations had to be aborted. On Hamburg, the first op, the port inner engine cut out after take-off. This was corrected, but over the airfield the situation deteriorated and the trip had to be abandoned. For the Turin operation on the 5th, the bomb doors could not be fitted. In the first two weeks of February 1943 the 'Simpson Kite' had nine projected operations and actually carried out only four – less than 50 per cent.

So, in typically English style, Bomber Command got through the war with a succession of 'bog-ups', 'cock-ups' and 'muddle throughs'. Navigational equipment, such as H2S, and the later GH blind-bombing aid, often failed, causing unpredictable problems. Miles Tripp recalled the story of a complete operation in 1945 being aborted after all his squadron's aircraft's GH bombing aids malfunctioned over the target. In the light of all this one could tentatively ask, '*How on earth did we win?*' or even '*Did we win?*' In many senses Bomber Command did not win the bomber war. Although it destroyed cities, it did not destroy the German people; neither did it destroy the German economy.

The RAF's bombing campaign in World War Two had, by the end of 1944, become a thankless, expensive and unfulfilled task. Thankless in that after the war, aircrews and air staff received little public recognition; expensive, in terms of the loss of many highly trained men and relatively sophisticated equipment; unfulfilled in that the results fell far short of what Harris and Portal had envisioned. The myths that developed after hostilities ceased tended to disguise the reality of what had really happened.

One has also to take the report of Albert Speer's post-war views of the consequences of the Allied bombing with a pinch of salt. His talks with the US Strategic Bombing

Survey were conducted over a period of ten days in May 1946; that is before the Nuremberg trials, when he was anxious to appease the Americans and impress them with his lack of complicity in the overall Nazi war plan, particularly the Holocaust.

A much more thought-provoking exposition of Speer's views was given by 'Marshal of the RAF' Harris at a Bomber Command Reunion in London in April 1977.[2] Harris delivered an after-dinner speech in which he related a number of the comments Speer had made to him. The German, Harris recounted, had told him that in all the histories of the war he had read, the effect of the strategic bombing of Germany was 'always under-estimated': the bombing campaign, Speer felt, was the Germans' 'greatest lost battle' of the war. Hitler had declined to authorise work on the building of an atomic bomb because it would utilise 'Jewish science.' For Speer this was fortunate, because it was necessary to use the people who would otherwise have been involved in building it, 'to repair the bomb damage to the German armament industry'.

Speer also concluded, Harris stated, that, by the end of 1943, bomb damage to German industry had deprived the *Wehrmacht* on the Russian Front of '10,000 of their bigger calibre guns and 6,000 of their heaviest and medium heavy tanks.' One reason for the strategic bombing offensive being Germany's 'greatest lost battle' was that 20,000 dual-purpose 88 mm anti-aircraft/anti-tank guns had had to be relocated haphazardly throughout Germany due to the unpredictability of the Allied bombing targets. This reduced German anti-tank ability on all fronts by half. Hundreds of thousands of troops were seconded from active fronts to provide anti-aircraft defence. Harris concluded that the bombing offensive 'deprived the German armies of well over a million men and half their anti-tank ability.' This gave a completely different complexion to things, rather contradicting Speer's earlier statements to the US Strategic Bombing Survey.

British High Command policy was to destroy cities. It was a policy Harris was directed to carry out by his superiors – and he pursued it with vigour. The deaths in Krupp's Essen factory were recorded as between five and seven thousand, with between 11 and 15,000 being injured. Hamburg suffered around 50,000 deaths. However, one has to bear in mind that, although the casualties from the bombing were, by normal standards, high, they pale in comparison to those caused by the Nazis in the extermination camps: 6,000 Jews were being gassed and cremated daily at Auschwitz in late 1944. Despite the different motivations, both systems represented highly organised forms of industrialised destruction such as the world had never witnessed before.

One must additionally consider that if there had not been a bomber front, which at one point was the only active front in Western Europe, and the German economy had continued performing as it had done despite the bombing, how much more effective would the Nazi war machine have been? All these questions are hypothetical however. The fact is that the bombing did contribute to the ultimate victory and it did retard German wartime production, even though it did not cripple it, despite the targets chosen not always being the best ones, or the fact that operations were not always carried out in the most suitable way. But then nothing is perfect: in war everyone loses.

CREWS

Alan Castle's 101 Squadron crew at Ludford Magna, 12 April 1942. Despite appearances, there was no social distinction between navigator Castle, the only officer on the crew, and the rest of the men, who were all NCOs. The photograph was taken by an airman from another 101 Squadron Wellington just before a raid on Essen; there was no time to arrange a pose. (Castle)

Bill Higgs's 35 (PFF) Squadron crew with their Halifax I at Graveley, Huntingdonshire. Left to right: Norman Long, front gunner (KIA); W.E.G. Higgs, flight engineer (POW); Harry 'Ollie' Olsen, Canadian tail-gunner (POW); Leslie Izzard, w/op (later Sqn/Ldr); 'Wattie' Watt, navigator (POW in 1943); Bob Norman, Australian pilot, later W/Cdr (POW); Sid Palmer, bomb-aimer (KIA while attacking the Tirpitz in Norway, April 1942). (Higgs)

Left: L.J. Simpson's first 460 Squadron crew at Breighton, January 1943. Left to right: Sutton, Maltby, Simpson, Kennedy, King and Searle – all fresh-faced and full of confidence. Searle was transferred to Australia after the tour on compassionate grounds. Simpson, Kennedy and King wear the darker blue RAAF uniforms. (Author)

Right: L.J. Simpson's first 460 Squadron crew at Breighton. Taken on 30 January 1943 when Bill Charlton, third from left, temporarily replaced navigator Al Kennedy, who was sick. They were due to attack Essen but, due to muddy conditions, caused by severe rainfall the previous day, ED315 bogged down on take-off and the trip was abandoned. (Author)

Left: Ron Drake's 15 Squadron crew in front of their Stirling W7513 LS-R 'Robert' in the summer of 1942 at Wyton, Huntingdonshire. Flt/Sgt R.V. Drake, the mu/g, is third from the left under the 'L'. The eighth man on the team was the 2nd pilot, P/O King, probably standing in front of the open entrance door. This aircraft and its crew took part in the first two Thousand-Bomber raids against Cologne and Essen on 30/31 May and 1/2 June 1942. Drake was later awarded the DFC. He carried a small, hand-sown rabbit on all his operations for good luck. (Drake)

R.H.J. 'Sandy' Rowe's 103 Squadron crew with Lancaster III JB952 PM-H 'Harry' and three groundcrew (sitting) at Elsham Wolds in 1943. The pilot was F/O Douglas W. Finlay DFC, centre standing. Sgt Rowe DFM, engineer, is third from right. The remainder of the crew included navigator J. H. McFarlane; bomb-aimer W/O I.A. Fletcher DFM; w/op Flt/Sgt W. H. MacDonald; mu/g Flt/Sgt R.J.F. Vivers RAAF and rear gunner F/O W.C.C. Gillespie RCAF. MacDonald and Vivers were both killed when JB952 was shot down approaching Mannheim on 24 September 1943. (R.H.J. Rowe)

Left: L.J. Simpson's second 460 Squadron crew in 1944. This photograph was taken at Binbrook during a period of low flying exercises before the first and final operation to Berlin on 27/28 January. Left to right: Schrock, McLeod, Simpson, Rydings, Osborn, Nairn. Osborn, Nairn and Kennedy (who took the photograph) had all been awarded DFMs and Simpson the DFC. These medals were not necessarily granted at the end of a tour. The crew's battle-worn, dishevelled appearance contrasts noticeably with that of the fresh crew of the year before. (Schrock)

Right: Bert Carter's 44 Squadron crew at Dunholm Lodge in 1944. H. Carter, engineer, extreme right; Frank Phillips, pilot, centre; Bill Taylor, bomb-aimer, second from left; R.K. 'Rex' Bennett, w/op third from left, with Lancaster - R 'Robert, possibly during the Battle of Berlin. (Carter)

Ted Boorman's crew with their 102 Squadron Halifax taken at Pocklington in early January 1945. From left to right: Sgt R.O. Jones, mu/g; Flt/Sgt J.F. Valery (RAAF), w/op; Flt/Sgt W.K. Quill (RAAF), nav; Capt R.W.F. Heiden (SAAF), pilot; P/O E.M. Boorman, obs./b-aimer; Sgt A.I. Johns, r/g; Sgt P. Morgan, flt/eng. All the crew were killed on 5 January on a raid to Hannover except Ted Boorman, who freefell 18,000 feet before his parachute opened. (Boorman)

Below: Graham Korner's 640 Squadron crew at Leconfield in 1944. Left to right: F/S 'Freddie' Nuttall, w/op; Sgt Ron Purcell, navigator; Dutchman F/O Kais Goemans, pilot; Sgt H.D. 'Jock' Patterson, bomb-aimer; New Zealander Sgt G.V. Korner, rear gunner. The engineer, Sgt Paddy Finnigan, and the mu/g, Sgt Ron Heath, are missing from this group. Nuttall was recommended for a posthumous VC after their final operation. (Korner)

Above: Frank Dennis's 419 (Moose) Squadron, RCAF, crew at Middleton St. George in 1944. All were commissioned and were members of the RCAF apart from Dennis. P/O Dennis, RAF, is in rear row, third from left, while in front row kneeling second from left is Flt/Lt W.H. 'Bill' Schmitt, a half German/half Indian former bush pilot nicknamed 'Indian'. [Dennis]

Above: John Nunn's 103 Squadron all-NCO crew at Elsham Wolds in 1944. This consisted of left to right: Ron Evans, navigator; Max Greenwell, bomb-aimer; John Nunn, flight engineer; Doug Warren, pilot; Frank Palmer-Smith, w/ag; Norman 'Joe' Bolt, mu/g; and Bill Russell RCAF, rear gunner. (Nunn)

CHAPTER NOTES

Author's Introduction

1. Figure up until 2000.
2. Russell Margerison, letter to author May 2009.
3. A squadron was Bomber Command's basic operational unit, and was led by a Wing Commander. The average bomber station contained either a three flight squadron of 30 bombers, or a two flight squadron of 40 bombers.
4. Air Headquarters West Africa.
5. James Mitchell, letter to author, March 2010.
6. C.M. Hatton, letter to author, 2009.
7. *Australian Week Ender*, 6/7 December, 2003. Of 9,000 Australians in Bomber Command in England in WW2, 4,050 died.

Chapter One

1. Les Hill, letter to author, May 2009.
2. Cobham became one of the pioneers of in-flight refuelling.
3. G.A. Lane, letter to author, February 2010.
4. G. Horseman, *Growing up in the Thirties*.
5. J. Leakey, letter to author, 2008.
6. G. Willatt, *Bombs and Barbed Wire*.
7. P. Gibby, letter to author, 2008.
8. Later part of Schleswig-Holstein.
9. G. Taylor, conversation with author, 2010.
10. This command by the British Air Staff must surely have been the origin of Bomber Command's 'area bombing' policy of the subsequent war.
11. Overy, *Reaping the Whirlwind: Bomber Command 1939 – 1945*, Harper Collins, 1997.
12. Appointed in September 1937, Ludlow-Hewitt was unusually pragmatic in regard to Bomber Command's extremely limited capability at that time. He forewarned the Air Ministry that the Command was, in strategic terms, virtually powerless against Germany, predicting a 'major disaster' if the force was called to attack. This was a total contradiction of the 'Trenchard Doctrine'.
13. Even at this early stage, consideration was given to attacking the Ruhr dams.

Chapter Two

1. AC2. An Aircraftman 2nd Class or 'erk' was the lowest rank and thus regarded as the lowest form of life in the RAF.
2. E. Groom, conversation with author, September 2008.
3. In his letter to the author Mr Castle actually wrote 't.......s'. Alan Castle, letter to author, April 2009.
4. J. Nunn, *My War*, 1990s.
5. Aircrew Reception Centre. See Glossary.
6. J. Nunn, *My War*, 1990s.
7. D. Hodgkinson, personal memoir, 1987. Air Chief Marshal Sir Derek Hodgkinson, KCB, CBE, DFC, AFC, was a wartime Coastal Command pilot and the Air Secretary, 1973-76. Born on 27 December 1917, he died on 29 January 2010, aged 92.
8. Eric Foinette, personal memoir, 1990s.
9. Colloquial term used by POWs for a prisoner: an abbreviation of the German *Kriegsgefangener*, literally 'war prisoner'.
10. Eric Foinette, personal memoir.
11. The paravane was a form of towed underwater 'glider'. Developed initially to destroy naval mines, the paravane would be strung out and streamed alongside a towing ship, normally from the bow. It would make contact with enemy mines and detonate them harmlessly.
12. L.J. Simpson, *Service Diary*.
13. R. Kemley, letter to author, 2008.

14. Astro-navigation was dangerous to employ on operations, because of the requirement to fly straight and level for a prolonged period over hostile territory. Consequently, it was later abandoned by the Americans in their training schools.
15. Howard Pearce, interview with author, July 2008.
16. Pilot, navigator, bomb-aimer.
17. Sir Thomas Lees (an inherited title) later became well known in Evangelical Christian circles in the 1970s as the owner of Post Green Community, Lychett Minster, Dorset. He was a J.P., agriculturalist, and Chairman of the Secondary Education Committee, Dorset County Hall.
18. 6 Group had 13 squadrons all belonging to the RCAF, commanded by a Canadian officer, with most of its finance met by Canada, but fully integrated into Bomber Command.
19. F. Dennis DFM, correspondence with author, May 2009.
20. 'Sergeant Signaller' was the new name for the wireless operator/air gunner trade, which had become more specialised.

Chapter Three

1. Freeman was then the Air Ministry's Air Member for Development and Production. He became Vice-Chief of the Air Staff in November 1940, where he remained for two years. He has been described as 'one of the most important officers in the history of the RAF', and was largely responsible for setting up the new heavy bomber force. His knowledge of the Allied aviation industry, senior RAF officers, and his perception of the fundamental essence of the air war made him of boundless value to Portal.
2. IWM Sound Archive.
3. 15 aircraft were involved in this, whilst the Main Force of 200 attacked Rostock, a few miles south.
4. Delayed action: 2 x 1000-lb and 2 x 500-lb.
5. A damaged, undriven propeller may 'windmill' with consequent increase in airflow drag. 'Feathering' fixes the blades in one position, with their angle to the slipstream set at a minimum, to reduce this.
6. Unserviceable.
7. 'B' Bombs were a type of mine designed to lie below the surface and detonate whenever a ship passed over.
8. This encounter was reported in the Jan-March 2009 edition of *Air Mail* by one of the German pilots. *Oberleutnant* Helmut Waltersdorf claimed to have shot down five Wellingtons, including that of 38 Squadron's Squadron Leader Nolan. Don Coulson: 'I actually witnessed Nolan's aircraft being shot down. It was on our port side heading for home when suddenly its undercarriage dropped down and it dived into the sea and disappeared.'
9. The aspect ratio was the ratio of the chord, or width, of the wing to its length at the leading edge. Thus a wing with a span of 25 ft and a width of 5 ft would have an aspect ratio of 5:1. As the chord increased so the ratio fell; conversely if the span increased the ratio rose.
10. Single shell, or hull, as in boat construction.
11. This would have been on a 'compass point'.
12. Between Bomber Command HQ and the operational squadrons were three intervening command levels; group, base and station. By March 1944 the Command contained seven operational groups, three training groups, and a signals group. The base was a small extra link recently included in the chain of command. It was directed by an Air Commodore and housed on an operational airfield. The station was a permanent organisation on a bomber airfield led by a group captain, with facilities for squadrons operating from it.
13. T. Baker, *Operations Diary*, 1942.
14. The F.700 was a form the pilot had to have signed before take-off, being the equivalent of a 'Certificate of Airworthiness'.
15. From *7 x X x 90*, Charles Potten, K. Gandy & C. Potten, Ely and Hove, 1986.
16. Nav (b) James Mitchell of 466 Australian Squadron, Driffield, recalled one time when his crew went to York racecourse to collect a new Halifax. After a week's leave they returned to the squadron and were told to be careful when landing. The aircraft they had collected and one other had been shot down on the home circuit by a *Luftwaffe* aircraft. Letter to author, 2009.
17. John Dean, letter to author, April 2009.
18. Harry Yates, *Luck and a Lancaster*.
19. An overnight duty where aircraftmen sat in an aircraft to prevent vandalism etc.
20. This was an anti-magnetic circle on an airfield where individual aircraft compasses could be reset using a master compass.
21. 'Getting a green.' See Glossary.

22. Keith Slade, unpublished personal memoir, 1990s.
23. Linda Dolata, correspondence with author, 2009.
24. Keith Slade, *RAFly Speaking*, personal memoir.
25. The operation on D-Day by 617 and other squadrons to create a spoof invasion force attacking across the Pas de Calais using false radar echoes produced by Lancasters ejecting 'Window'.
26. Make a two-point landing on the main undercarriage without the tail wheels touching the runway surface until the end.
27. Eric Yates, letter to author, May 2009.
28. Charles Potten, 7 x X x 90, privately published account, 1986.
29. S. G. Berry, letter to author, April 2009.
30. Keith Slade, unpublished personal memoir, 1990s.
31. Ibid.
32. This was later changed to Lancaster.
33. Charles Potten, 7 x X x 90, privately published account, 1986.
34. G.A. Lane, letter to author, February 2010.
35. J.V. Williams, interview, 26 June 2010.
36. This would be associated with hangar access.
37. All Merlins had superchargers or 'blowers' fitted, i.e. a device that increased or 'boosted' the mass of air drawn into the engine by raising the intake pressure. The superchargers had a gearing mechanism within them, the 'M' gear. With increased height, e.g. above 10,000 ft, one had to raise the gearing on the 'blower' to another level to compensate for the reduced air pressure.
38. L.J. Simpson, *Service Diary*.
39. Boost was measured in lb/sq. in. The engineer would call out: '3,000 and plus 18!'
40. Pilzen required 2,060 gals from Breighton. For all of Laurie's long-distance trips the standard bomb loading was 1 x 4,000-lb 'cookie' with 12 Special Bomb Containers (SBCs).
41. E.M. Boorman, interview with author, 2008.
42. Lancaster AR-D, W4320.
43. G. Stooke, *Flak and Barbed Wire*, Australian Military History Publications, 2008.
44. 626 Squadron was formed from 'C' Flight of 12 Squadron on 7 November 1943 at Wickenby.
45. Jack Currie, quoted in *Lancaster at War Vol. 1*, M. Garbett and B. Goulding, 1971.
46. J.V. Williams, *A Timely Reminder – No Turning Back*, personal memoir, 1990s.
47. i.e. an inexperienced crew, untried on operations.
48. Charles Frederick Algernon Portal, later Lord Portal of Hungerford and Marshal of the RAF, was Chief of the Air Staff. 'Peter' (as Harris and many friends referred to him), was born in 1893, and was from an affluent upper class background. Educated at Winchester College, Oxford, in 1914 he started as a dispatch rider with the Royal Engineers. Being a natural leader, in December 1914 he took command of all the dispatch riders in 1st Corps HQ, Signal Company. A year later he transferred to the RFC, was promoted to major and made CO of 16 Squadron, where he served with Major H.C.T. Dowding (later C-in-C Fighter Command). Eventually, Portal became a highly decorated lieutenant-colonel with an MC and a DFC, aged only 25. By the time he was 44 in 1937, Portal was an air vice-marshal and Director of Organisation at the Air Ministry, having previously commanded the British forces in Aden. At the Air Ministry he was responsible for finding sites for new airfields despite much landowners' opposition. Thanks to Portal's work, 30 new RAF stations, mainly for Bomber Command, were under way by 1939 and a further 56 satellite stations had land set aside for them. In February 1939 Portal was made Air Member for Personnel on the Air Council, despite many of his fellow contenders being senior to him. He was then promoted to C-in-C of Bomber Command, serving from April to October 1940, subsequently becoming Chief of the Air Staff. He numbered amongst Churchill's most trusted confidants.

Chapter Four

1. Peter Banyard, unpublished memoir, 2008.
2. Later Group Captain R.L.S. Coulson, C.B.E. Coulson retrained as a pilot after 34 missions and was employed towing gliders from Dakotas with 233 Squadron. He also served in Burma.
3. Navigator/bomb-aimer.
4. R. Coulson, letter to author, 2008.
5. E.M. Boorman, interview with author, 2008.
6. K. Pendray, interview with author, 2008.
7. R. Kemley, letter to author, 2008.
8. David Howell, letter to author, March 2009.

9. R.J. Frayers, IWM Sound Archive.
10. Henry Wagner, *Pilot to Navigator, 'Where are We?*, unpublished manuscript.
11. R. Kemley, letter to author, 2008.
12. Robert Vollum, unpublished memoir, 2009.
13. John Nunn, unpublished memoir, 1990s.
14. Shrapnel consisted of small fragments of metal contained within a shell case, deliberately designed to have jagged and sharp edges in order to create as much damage as possible.
15. L.J. Simpson, interview with author, 1993.
16. This would be for conversion from medium to heavy bombers.
17. Keith Slade, unpublished memoir, 1990s.
18. R. Brown, conversation with author, 2008.
19. On the Lancaster.
20. Keith Slade, *RAFly Speaking*, unpublished memoir, 1990s.
21. Charles Potten, *7 x X x 90*, K. Gandy and C. Potten, 1986.
22. F. Danckwardt, conversation with author, 2009.
23. Ella Banyard, letter to author, April 2009.
24. Thetford, Owen, *Aircraft of the Royal Air Force 1918-1966*, Putnam, 1966.
25. J.V. Williams, interview with author, 28 June 2010.
26. The Bowden cable operated similarly to the brake cable on a bicycle.
27. Edited from J. McGillivray, IWM Sound Archive.
28. From *218 (Gold Coast) Squadron Newsletter* no. 24. For further comment upon this operation of Turley's see 'The Witten Raid' in Chapter Eight.
29. 467 Squadron was formed at Scampton, Lincolnshire on 7 November 1942 as a heavy bomber squadron in No. 5 Group. Later that month it relocated to Bottesford, Leicestershire, and a year later moved to Waddington back in Lincolnshire.
30. The Canadian-built Lancaster, the Mark X, was produced by the nationalised Victory Aircraft Ltd in Ontario. By 1945, 430 had been built, the majority being allocated to No. 6 (Canadian) Group.
31. F. Danckwardt, conversation with author, 2009.
32. J.V. Williams, unpublished memoir, 1990s.
33. Korner refers to the 'Rose-Rice Turret' conversion that was carried out on some Lancasters.
34. Alan E. Bryett, IWM Sound Archive.
35. S. Jackson, *Steve Jackson's War 1939-1946*, unpublished memoir, 2008.
36. Miles Tripp, *The Eighth Passenger*, 1993.
37. Alec March, *Lady of the Night*, unpublished personal memoir.
38. R. Margerison, *Boys at War*, Northway Publications, 2005.

Chapter Five

1. Sir A.T. Harris, *Bomber Offensive*, 1947.
2. Ibid.
3. See *Slide Rule*, N. Shute.
4. This was in N6428 firstly, a formation flight. In the second, in R6277, Keys was the Safety Pilot. This was a cross-country flight. The different cross-country routes were given numbers. This was No. 7.
5. Wartime expression for 'crashed'.
6. West Australian.
7. Rutherford's gravestone can be found in Leconfield churchyard today. The inscription, which reads 406540 Sergeant B.P.R. Rutherford Royal Australian Air Force. 19th May 1942. Age 22', appears to be by his mother: at the base is inscribed: 'To the world an airman, to me the world. His brother Alan is buried at Duns, Scotland'.
8. Sandy Rowe and a former Halifax veteran friend had never heard of 'sodium-assisted' flying. Their conclusion was that Laurie was practising night take-off and landings. These would be done with the assistance of sodium vapour lights located at each side of the runway – an electrical discharge in sodium vapour produced a yellow light.
9. It appears that Assistant Adjutant Rodger telephoned the Air Ministry subsequently and Graeme Keys was reassigned to 27 OTU, Lichfield.
10. Hank Nelson, *Chased by the Sun*, 2002.
11. Vickers Wellington; nicknamed after the character 'J. Wellington Wimpy' in the 'Popeye' cartoons.
12. Probably a reference to a tough, outdoor type of character.
13. Air Gunner.
14. The flight engineer and mid-upper gunner joined them when they went to a Halifax Conversion Flight at Holme-on-Spalding Moor that September.

15. Sgt Bruce William Richards RAAF died on 16 July 1942.
16. *No Moon Tonight*, Charlwood.
17. The anglicised, phonetic, spelling of this name is commonly 'Pilsen'. 'Pilzen' used here throughout is closer to the original Czech.
18. *Journeys into Night* is the story of the '20 men'.
19. C. Younger, *No Flight from the Cage*. A Spitfire flying relation of Falkiner ended up in Heydekrug POW camp with Cal Younger in 1942.
20. Inevitably Henry Coverley was nicknamed 'Roger' by his crew and all who knew him. This arose from the character 'Sir Roger de Coverley', whose name and emblem were painted on the nose of Coverley's Halifax in 76 Squadron.
21. 466 Squadron, equipped with the Wellington until September 1943, when it converted to Halifaxes.
22. E. Groom, interview with author, 2007.
23. K. J. Newman, unpublished memoir, IWM archive file 06/12/1.
24. R.S. Raymond, *A Yank in Bomber Command*, 1977.
25. Reminiscent of the '1,000 yard stare', a physiological symptom many combat veterans suffered from, i.e. staring, unfocused into the far distance.
26. Don Charlwood, *No Moon Tonight*, 1954.
27. Ibid.
28. G.R. Fawcett, quoted in *The Berlin Raids* (Middlebrook).
29. Richard Knott, *Black Night for Bomber Command*.
30. RAF Museum, *Air Ministry Bulletin No. 7757* and *Notes on Careers*.
31. Charlwood, *No Moon Tonight*.
32. Sir A.T. Harris, *Bomber Offensive*, 1947.

Chapter Six

1. Wroughton, by then commissioned, was shot up by a night fighter in 1943 on his 19th trip. His crew had bombed on three engines after a difficult start and, in what was a typical *Schräge Musik* attack, lost their second port engine. The crew 'got out pronto', but the navigator died in the fall: they never discovered what happened. After *Dulag Luft*, the six survivors were fortunate to go by passenger train to *Stalag Luft* I.
2. D. Wilson, letter to author, 2009.
3. Against Stavanger in April 1940.
4. Later Air Marshal Sir Andrew McKee, CBE, DSO, DFC, AFC.
5. H. Pearce, interview with author, 2008.
6. W.E.G. Higgs, interview with author, 2008.
7. A.W. Cole, interview with author, 2008.
8. R. Searle, letter to author, 2008.
9. L.J. Simpson, interview with G.R. Holloway. Quoted in *Touchdown East Devon*.
10. Pathfinder Force.
11. L.J. Simpson, *Service Diary*.
12. L.J. Simpson, interview with G.R. Holloway. Quoted in *Touchdown East Devon*.
13. L.J. Simpson *Service Diary*.
14. R. Searle, letter to author, 2008.
15. *Yorkshire Post*, 4 January 1943.
16. *Daily Mirror*, 4 January 1943.
17. *Daily Express*, 4 January 1943.
18. W.G. Carman, *Three Times Lucky*, personal memoir.
19. This was before the PFF was set up.
20. A. March, letter to author, 20 April 2009.
21. They were only allowed three shillings and three pence for cleaning their uniforms. R. Farren, letter to author, 2009.
22. London and North East Railway.
23. M. Corran, *Just One WAAF*, BBC *Peoples' War* website (www.bbc.co.uk/ww2peopleswar).

Chapter Seven

1. Only 10% of these were actually built.
2. £15 billion in modern currency.
3. Graham Smith, *Devon and Cornwall Airfields in the Second World War*, Countryside Books, 2000.

4. This was an American term, introduced by the Eighth Air Force in 1942. They were originally called 'watch towers'.
5. W.E.G. Higgs, *My Bomber Command Story*, 2008.
6. Wind-finders were selected aircraft that went ahead of the Main Force to determine the upper air winds on the target route. All the readings collated were then averaged. It appears that, in the case of a pre-op briefing, the wind-finder information was radioed back to High Wycombe before a raid. Normally wind-finder readings were recorded during the course of an operation and radioed to the Main Force. These could often differ markedly from the readings or predictions of the Air Ministry's meteorological section. (See sub-section 'Wind-Finders' in Chapter Eight).
7. See section on The Witten Raid in Chapter Eight.
8. Service Policeman.
9. Brodrick was one of the 76 RAF men who broke out of *Stalag Luft* III in March 1944.
10. Alan E. Bryett, IWM Sound Archive.
11. E. Foinette, letter to author, 20 July 2010.
12. R.S Raymond, *A Yank in Bomber Command*, 1977.
13. J. Nunn, *My War*, 1992.
14. Despite his humble background John Nunn became a group captain after the war.
15. R.S Raymond, *A Yank in Bomber Command*, 1977.
16. H.D. Coverley, interview with author, 2008.
17. The 12 Squadron base.
18. E. Groom, interview with author, 2007.
19. F. Danckwardt, interview with author, 2008.
20. D. Fellowes, conversation with author, 2010.
21. F. Dennis, letter to author, September 2009.
22. Younger became one of the founders of the RAF Ex-Prisoner of War Society and was a close friend of POW leader, 'Dixie' Deans. His strongest desire after the war was to write and, as well as producing a novel and some other works, he wrote *No Flight from the Cage*, a classic account of his experiences in the war.
23. Cal Younger, script for '*The Bomber Command Roadshow*', 1990s.
24. James Mitchell, letter to author, March 2010.
25. It was quite common for aircraft to be loaned if a station had high losses or not enough new aircraft were available.
26. Helena Bonham-Carter, the actress.
27. 463 Squadron was formed from 'C' Flight of 467 Squadron on 25 November 1943 at Waddington, Lincolnshire.
28. R5868 'S-Sugar' is now on display in the RAF Bomber Command Museum, Hendon. It was one of 'Sugar's' former 467 Squadron ground crew who found her after the war, refurbished her, and presented her to the museum.
29. The celebrated hostelry in the centre of York: the main bar was below ground level and still exists today.
30. A.E. Bryett, IWM Sound Archive.
31. F.J. McGovern, IWM Sound Archive.
32. The 'Mucky Duck' or 'Dirty Duck' was actually *The Black Swan*. The 'Six Tits' was *The Seven Sisters,* or 'Fourteen Titties'. The *Swan* was a popular haunt for over half a dozen 1 Group stations in the area.
33. Story from *Strike and Return*, P. Firkins.
34. Peter Banyard, unpublished memoir, 2008.
35. There is no entry for Flt/Lt Burnham in W.R. Chorley's *Bomber Command Losses*, suggesting that he survived the war.
36. Probably end of tour DFCs.
37. Unofficial diary of Flying Officer C.T. O'Riordan K.C. AWM 3DRL/4164.
38. To 'prang' was RAF jargon for a crash or faulty landing with unfortunate consequences.
39. Hank Nelson, *Chased by the Sun: The Australians in Bomber Command*.
40. Chorley Vol. 4.
41. Some aircrew carried handguns with them on ops to avoid being burnt alive in mid-air.
42. I. Fuller, correspondence with author, March 2009.
43. R. Wakeman, IWM Sound Archive.
44. A. Wolstenholme, IWM Sound Archive.
45. From *218 Squadron Newsletter No. 25.*
46. A.W. Cole, interview with author, 2008.
47. S. Jackson, *Steve Jackson's War 1939-1946*, unpublished memoir, 2008.

48. P. Firkins, *Strike and Return*.
49. W.E.G. Higgs, conversation with author, April 2008.
50. Chandler was nicknamed 'Chan' by Ken Rogers, the 617 Squadron gunnery officer, who disliked his real name, Basil. Rogers likened Chandler's grin to that of 'Charlie Chan'.
51. Chan Chandler, *Tail Gunner: 99 Raids in World War Two*.
52. 76 Squadron was formed at Ripon, Yorkshire as a Home Defence unit in 1916. The squadron disbanded in 1919, but re-formed in 1937 at Finningley. At the beginning of the war it became a No. 5 Group training unit with Ansons and Whitleys. By 1940 it was absorbed into No. 16 OTU, but it rose from the ashes with No. 4 Group in May 1941 as the second heavy bomber squadron to be equipped with the Halifax bomber at Linton, where it remained until June 1941, before moving to Middleton St. George.
53. Cheshire witnessed the dropping of the second atomic bomb at Nagasaki.
54. H.D. Coverley, interview with author, July 2008.
55. See Bill Higgs's entry, Part 4 under 'Germany 1942'.
56. W.E.G. Higgs, interview with author, April 2008.
57. 626 Squadron was formed from 'C' Flight of No. 12 Squadron on 7 November 1943. It was often the case that new squadrons were formed from single flights when units became larger as the war progressed.
58. His actual surname was Campbell.
59. When a propeller was feathered the magnetos were turned off and the propeller blades turned edge-on so that they did not 'windmill' in the slipstream. In this case fire extinguishers were then set off. This was an extremely difficult operation and had to be undertaken carefully. Engineers had been known to stop the wrong engine or press the wrong extinguishers.
60. Les Hill, *Molly's Air Trip*, 2008.
61. R. Finch, communication with author, 2008.
62. Richard Todd: interview for *Bomber Command: Reaping the Whirlwind*, Cinecam Productions, 1997.
63. Pip Beck, *Keeping Watch*.
64. A 'headless' crew was one without a pilot.
65. Alec March, *Lady of the Night*, unpublished personal memoir.
66. Statistics record that the total cases of VD dealt with at civilian treatment centres in Great Britain, which included service cases, rose from 121,754 in 1940 to 142,377 by 1943. This dropped slightly the following year and then rose to a wartime high of 145,387 by the end of 1945.
67. Alec March, letter to author, 2009.
68. Leeuwarden is still in use today by the Royal Netherlands Air Force.
69. D. Hodgkinson, personal memoir, 1997.
70. M. Corran, *Just One WAAF*, BBC Peoples' History website.
71. My father was always a fairly moral person, probably because of his Catholic upbringing, and as far as I am aware, there was no infidelity in his marriage. His attitude to life was that it was something that had to be faced.
72. A former girlfriend.
73. J. Nunn, *My War*, 1992.
74. Beryl Pearce, letter to author, April 2009.
75. Wing Cdr C.E. Martin received a DFC in February 1942 after his first tour. One of the raids included a solo attack on Berlin in 1941 when his crew failed to receive a general recall for the op. He penetrated the centre of the 'Big City' alone and bombed. His crew successfully reached the home airfield, landing in thick fog. He was later awarded the DSO for supervising the extinguishing of a burning Lancaster at Binbrook in July 1943 after another had exploded accidentally.
76. Advanced Flying Wing.
77. The Circle Club was located in either the White Hermitage Hotel or the Norfolk Hotel, Richmond Hill, Bournemouth. The beer it served, Laurie thought, was 'the best over here'. Women were allowed to enter the premises unaccompanied during the war. The Royal Bath Hotel however, (another Bournemouth hotel frequented by service personnel), would not allow young women to enter alone for fear of admitting prostitutes.
78. Probably balancing a pint of beer on one's head.
79. Flight Lieutenant Keys was second in command of 'A Flight' 460 Squadron in March 1943 while Laurie Simpson was second i.c. 'B Flight'. Later they both took over full command.
80. To the new 460 Squadron base at Binbrook.
81. L.J. Simpson, *Service Diary*.
82. On the last trip of Laurie's first tour, one engine gave out before entering German airspace, but it was decided to complete the mission.
83. AWM file AWM65(3007).

84. A suggestion: target-marking was the main duty of 139 Squadron at that time.
85. Chorley Vol. 5.
86. Now in AWM archives.
87. The AWM advised that 'air battle' was a very general term often used in official reports for a number of different incidents.
88. Air Historical Branch (RAF), Ministry of Defence, letter to author, July 2010.
89. Laurie noted in his *Service Diary* in mid-May 1945, after repatriation, 'Have heard very disturbing news of the boys who have gone since I went down. Graeme (4-5-44), Merv. Powell, Ted McKinnon and many others…'
90. Hank Nelson, *Chased by the Sun: The Australians in Bomber Command*.
91. Nelson. Surprisingly, Goulevitch, despite being awarded a DFC, was never promoted beyond Pilot Officer.
92. Green target indicator flares.
93. E.G. Groom, conversation with author, 2008.
94. B. Gorell, Shipley, West Yorks, to J. Goulevitch, 14 December 1994. 'Archie' was Flt/Sgt Archie Elwing, the bomb-aimer, who died in 1988. 'Reggie' was Sgt Reg A. Moynagh, rear gunner, killed on a Berlin raid with another crew on 16 December 1943. The only other regular member of Goulevitch's crew to survive the war was Ted Anderson, the mid-upper gunner, who died in October 2007. 'Gouley' passed away on 24 December 1995.
95. The 'Darkie' system was a method of enabling an aircraft to return to base when all the main r/t systems had gone down. The pilot would switch to the D 'Darkie' channel on his four channel VHF radio and broadcast a 'Darkie' call until picked up by the nearest RAF station. As the VHF only had a range of 10 miles it was very limited. All RAF stations had a 'Darkie Watch' in the control tower. If they picked up the signal they would instruct the pilot to flick his identification lights on and arrange to have any nearby searchlight batteries and the Royal Observer Corps guide him home.
96. B. Gorell, Shipley, West Yorks, to J. Goulevitch, 14 December 1994.
97. John Nunn survived the war but his addiction to alcohol had side effects and he developed pancreatitis. He was forced to remain sugar and alcohol free for six months. The couple met again after the war and married on 19 May 1945.
98. UK National Archives, AIR 40: *Dulag Luft* files.
99. C. Holloway, letters to author, May 2009 / July 2010.
100. L.J. Simpson, conversation with author, 1990s.
101. S. Jackson, *Steve Jackson's War 1939-1946*, unpublished memoir, 2008.
102. A.E. Bryett, IWM Sound Archive.
103. H. Wagner, letter to author, July 2010.
104. W. Vaughan-Thomas, *Trust to Talk*.
105. Vernon T. Wilkes to Dr. Vanessa Gale, 2006, quoted in a PhD thesis of Dr. Gale on the impact of reliance on the supernatural during the first half of the 20th century, *Fighting Chance: War, Popular Belief and British Society 1900-1951*, University of Liverpool Press, 2011.
106. O'Caine occasionally flew as Cheshire's flight engineer.
107. W.E.G. Higgs, interview with author, 2008.
108. '*The Fooship*', ED315, eventually met its end after Laurie's tour, with a different crew on 8 June 1944, when it undershot on approach to Binbrook and crash-landed. There were three other 460 Squadron Lancasters similarly named; respectively, '*Fooship II*', '*Fooship III*' and '*Fooship IV*'.
109. It survives to this day, although in a slightly more threadbare form.
110. *Daily Mail*, 28 October 1942. Article quoted in Dr. V. Gale's PhD thesis.
111. Dr. V. Gale, PhD thesis.
112. Forty-three bombers were lost that night. Peenemünde was a low-level attack, carried out at between 4,000 and 5,000 feet, considerably reducing chances of survival. The crew's two fatalities, Sgt L.C. Hayward and Sgt P. Lowe, both drowned after being blown out over the Baltic. They were buried in the Berlin War cemetery. Lew Parsons, unpublished personal memoir.
113. Lew Parsons, unpublished personal memoir.
114. J. Geddes, letter to author, 2008.
115. Ibid.
116. Bennett, Air Vice-Marshal D.C.T., *Pathfinder*, Goodall Publications, 1983.
117. Ibid.

Chapter Eight

1. Mark K. Wells, *Courage and Air Warfare: The Allied Aircrew Experience in the Second World War*.
2. A.W. Cole, interview with author, 2008.
3. 460 Squadron lost 20 aircraft in three months from December 1943 to February 1944. By the time it disbanded in 1945 169 aircraft and 1,083 crewmen had been killed or became POWs; i.e. nearly 2.3% of all the fatalities, and over a quarter of all the Australian losses in Bomber Command were on 460 Squadron.
4. S. Pickering, *Tales of a Bomber Command WAAF*.
5. K. Edwards, interview with author, October 2011.
6. Chan Chandler, *Tail Gunner: 99 Raids in World War Two*.
7. Chorley Vol. 2.
8. VC citation for Air Commodore Sir Hughie Idwal Edwards, 22 July 1941, AWM.
9. The Cologne attacks were diversionary, hoping to draw German fighters away from the Russian Front.
10. Hughie Idwal Edwards was promoted to full Air Commodore on 1 July 1959 and was knighted in August 1974. He died on 5 August 1982, aged 68.
11. G. Stooke, *Flak and Barbed Wire*. Stooke was shot down during a raid on Wuppertal, 24 June 1943.
12. This was when degree courses were considerably more difficult to get on to than today.
13. Hank Nelson, *Chased by the Sun: The Australians in Bomber Command in World War Two*.
14. Max Arthur, *Dambusters*, Virgin, 2009.
15. F.A. Lindemann had been Professor of Experimental Philosophy at Oxford University and Head of the Clarendon Laboratory in 1919.
16. Norman Longmate, *The Bombers: the RAF Offensive Against Germany, 1939-1945*, Hutchinson, 1983.
17. Ibid.
18. Ibid.
19. See Chapter Eleven.
20. Which became the codename for the D-Day deception plans.
21. The predicted collision rate over the target was 'two'. At Swinderby, when crews heard the announcement, one comic remarked, 'Have the boffins worked out which two?'
22. It was not unusual for a Bomber Command crew in those days to include two, three, or even more nationalities.
23. AWM archives.
24. *United Pacific Crew*, RAAF Overseas HQ, Press Bulletin No. 99, London, 21 April 1943. Ernie Weyle was later killed in the Pacific theatre.
25. Moyes, P.J.R. From a VC citation in *The London Gazette*, 23 October, 1942.
26. Nuttall was a 640 Squadron flight engineer who burned to death whilst maintaining control of a burning Halifax in 1944. His recommendation for a posthumous VC was not instigated. See entry in Chapter Fifteen.
27. R.V. Drake survived the war, completing two tours; one of 33 ops in five months, the other 20 ops in four-and-a-half months. He was awarded the DFC on 21 September 1945 and promoted to Flight Lieutenant just over a fortnight later.
28. D. Hodgkinson, personal memoir, 1987.
29. Lieutenant E. Weyle, '*Midnight Raid*', *Flying*, December 1943.
30. Ibid.
31. Portal to Harris, 12 June 1942.
32. Sourced largely from Probert.
33. There are various explanations for the origin of H2S's peculiar acronym. One was that it was originally HSH for 'Home Sweet Home'. A second, more plausible and better known possibility, is that a senior staff officer was once inspecting an aircraft with it installed. Upon examining the equipment he remarked caustically 'It stinks! Call it H2S.'
34. Philip M.S. Hedgeland, IWM Sound Archive.
35. W.E.G. Higgs, interview with author, 28 April 2008.
36. German searchlights often worked in groups of up to 60.
37. W.E.G. Higgs, interview with author, 28 April 2008.
38. This may, or may not, have been the famous Pathfinder leader, Air Commodore John Searby, misnamed Donald.
39. A detailed account of Dick Raymond's PFF operations is contained in Chapter Thirteen on The Battle of Berlin.
40. D.M. Lambert later became a GP and was awarded the MBE for his work.
41. Chorley said rear gunner.

42. D.M.Lambert, interview with author, May 2008.
43. No relation.
44. *Squadron Leader Tommy Broom DFC*, Tom Parry Evans, Pen and Sword, 2007.
45. *The Times*, 4 June 2010.
46. Evans, Tom Parry, *Squadron Leader Tommy Broom DFC*.
47. Quoted in Liddell Hart, *History of the Second World War*, Pan, 1970.
48. Wells, op cit.
49. 101 Squadron was formed at South Farnborough, Hampshire on 12 July 1917. It was a night-bomber squadron and from August 1917 operated over the Western Front. By 1939 the squadron was based at West Raynham on Blenheims, flying daylight raids. It switched to night ops, but took part in the Channel Dash operation. By June 1941 it had converted to Wellingtons, and in June 1943 it moved from Holme-on-Spalding-Moor to Ludford Magna ('Mudford Magna'), where it remained for the rest of the war. It got a new lease of life in October 1943 when it re-equipped with Airborne Cigar (ABC) R.C.M. fitted Lancasters, the only RAF squadron to do so.
50. Figure from Nelson, *Chased by the Sun: Australians in Bomber Command*.
51. *History of 460 Squadron*, Peter Firkins. Firkins was a former pilot on ops with 460 who wrote the unit history *Strike and Return*.
52. About one-third of Bomber Command's 54 airfields were built before the war. These had 'extensive facilities and comfortable accommodation' (Middlebrook) and were known as 'gin palaces'.
53. F.J. McGovern, IWM Sound Archive.
54. 78 Squadron was originally formed as a Home Defence unit in Kent in 1916. It disbanded in 1919 but re-formed in 1936. When the war broke out it was based at Dishforth, Yorkshire, but then moved to Linton in December 1939, moving back to Dishforth in July 1940. By September 1942 it had returned to Linton and was commanded by Wing Commander J.B. 'Willy' Tait who led the squadron until October that year.
55. John Whitley's evasion story is told in Paul Brickhill's book *Escape or Die*.
56. William 'Cisco' Kidd, Holes's tail gunner.
57. 'Predicted Flak': Flak predicted by German ground radar that could creep unremittingly towards an aircraft.
58. Aircraft always gave off unavoidable condensation or vapour trails (contrails) at operational heights due to the very low temperatures.
59. i.e. semi-conscious.
60. For an account of Wynford Vaughan-Thomas's work with the WRU see Chapter Thirteen on The Battle of Berlin.
61. Dimbleby, Jonathan, *Richard Dimbleby*.
62. Ibid.
63. Chorley Vol. 4.
64. Dimbleby, Jonathan, *Richard Dimbleby*.
65. Middlebrook, Martin and Everitt, Chris, *The Bomber Command War Diaries*.
66. AWM records.
67. Sourced from Dimbleby, Middlebrook, Chorley Vol. 4, and Cooper.
68. 419 Squadron was formed at Mildenhall Suffolk on 15 December 1941 as the third RCAF bomber squadron overseas. Originally part of No. 3 Group, it transferred to No. 6 (RCAF) Group when that was formed on 1 January 1943. From Mildenhall it moved to Leeming, Topcliffe and Croft, before establishing itself at Middleton St. George, where it remained until the end of the war. The squadron first operated Wellingtons, later converting to Halifaxes and then Lancaster Xs. 'Moose' was in memory of the squadron's first CO, Wing Commander John 'Moose' Fulton, lost on a Hamburg raid on 29 July 1942.
69. F. Dennis, correspondence with author, September 2009.
70. Robert Vollum, unpublished personal memoir, 2009.
71. F. Dennis, correspondence with author, September 2009.
72. The French-Canadians had their own squadron in No. 6 Group – 425 (Allouette) Squadron – but Guillevan had been instructing and came through training without a crew, so he was assigned to Geddes' crew. 'Ghost' Squadron was so named because of its high loss rate.
73. 427 Squadron was formed at Croft, County Durham and was briefly with No. 4 Group, before transferring to No. 6 (RCAF) Group. It flew the Wellington III and X, and later Halifax V, Halifax III and Lancaster I and III. The squadron transferred to Leeming, Yorkshire in May 1943 where it remained until after the end of the war.
74. F. Dennis, *Flying with the Canadians*, unpublished memoir.
75. F. Dennis, correspondence with author, October 2009.

76. B.A. Buckham, *Shoot the Train*, personal memoir.
77. 53 years later Bannick was reunited with Dack after another German read about the incident in a newspaper. Bannick later went over to meet Dack in Melbourne. According to Chorley they had risked their lives since Dack had landed in a minefield.
78. Middlebrook, *Diaries*.
79. A. Boulton, quoted in *Night After Night*, M. Lambert.
80. Eric Mombeek, *Defenders of the Reich – Jagdgeschwader 1 Volume Two: 1943*, pgs.126-127 and Jochen Prien & Peter Rodeike, *Einsatz in der Reichsverteidigung von 1939-1945 – Jagdgeschwader 1 und 11 teil I 1939-1943*, pgs.299-301.
81. Two pilots are known to have been reported by JG 1 as lost in this action (see Mombeek and Prien & Rodeike).
82. Different sources give different accounts of this, but it seems to be generally accepted that Trent was the only pilot to reach and bomb the target.
83. Sourced from Max Lambert's *Night After Night*; Ralph Barker's *Strike Hard Strike Sure*; Chorley Vol IV and P.R. Moyes *Bomber Squadrons of the RAF*.
84. F. Fish, quoted in *The Bomber War*, R. Neillands, 2000.
85. M. Carter, communication with author, 2007. H. Carter, unpublished memoir.
86. H.R. Rowe, letter to author, 2007.
87. H. Sparks, interview, May 2009.
88. A type of radar, similar, but more advanced than Gee.
89. E. Clayton, letters to author 2009 and 2010. He mistakenly recalled their aircraft as Stirlings.
90. Miles Tripp, *The Eighth Passenger*.
91. Ibid.
92. The yellow bands indicate that this was also a G-H raid.

Chapter Nine

1. *History of the Second World War*, B. Liddell Hart, Cassell and Co., 1970.
2. According to Middlebrook and Everitt's *Bomber Command War Diaries* 73 aircraft undertook minelaying operations in the Baltic that night off the Danish and German coasts.
3. Middlebrook and Everitt, *Bomber Command War Diaries*.
4. Junkers Ju 88 night fighter: in its C and G variants, it was one of the best night fighters of the war.
5. Special Bomb Containers.
6. Medical Officer.
7. Middlebrook & Everitt.
8. D. Stafford, *Roosevelt and Churchill: Men of Secrets*. Other decisions included the invasion of Sicily, the build-up for D-Day, and an increased US Eighth Air Force participation in the bombing war.
9. Sgt H.B. Oliver. His aircraft W4837 UV-M and all its crew was lost without trace.
10. Deniliquin High School, New South Wales. This is abbreviated elsewhere as 'D.HI.S.'
11. F/S RA Brittingham RAAF, W4817 UV-K.
12. Chorley. Middlebrook and Everitt stated two.
13. Laurie's brother, Jack Simpson.
14. Norman Longmate, *The Bombers: the RAF Offensive against Germany 1939-1945*.
15. Chorley. Middlebrook stated five.
16. Middlebrook & Everitt.
17. Ibid.
18. Wg/Cdr C.E. 'Chad' Martin.
19. *Daily Express*, 7 February 1943.
20. Searle Archive.
21. Middlebrook & Everitt state three. The German propaganda ministry claimed two, then increased this to seven.
22. *Daily Express*, 11 February 1943. The various reports in the Press for that day were slightly different, but obviously all came from the same origin.
23. *Daily Sketch*, Monday, 15 February 1943.
24. Air Vice-Marshal D.C.T. Bennett, *Pathfinder*.
25. C. Webster and N. Frankland, *The Strategic Air Offensive against Germany 1939-1945*.
26. *Daily Express*, 14 February 1943.
27. *The Times*, 16 February 1943.
28. Chorley Vol. 4 has no entry for this raid.
29. *Daily Express*, 20 February 1943.
30. Dorothy.
31. Chorley Vol. 4. Middlebrook stated ten.

32. Bennett.
33. Ibid.
34. *Daily Sketch*, 1 March 1943.
35. Hermann Göring was a minor aristocrat, born in 1893, who became leader of *Jagdgeschwader* I, the famous *Richthofen Geschwader*, when the renowned 'Red Baron', Manfred von Richthofen, was killed in April 1918. Disaffected by the consequences of the Armistice, he became attracted to Hitler's cause and was severely wounded during the Nazi Beer Hall *Putsch* of 1923. As a result of his recovery from this, he became addicted to morphine for the remainder of his life which resulted in him being slightly emotionally unstable. Göring was the founder of the Gestapo, was made President of the *Reichstag* in 1932 and also head of the Nazi rearmament campaign in 1934. Hitler chose him for this, in preference to Hjalmar Schacht, the economics genius, after he had helped to orchestrate the murder of Ernst Röhm in the infamous 'Night of the Long Knives' that June. From 1933 he was responsible for building up the new *Luftwaffe* over six years and, in 1936, was made Plenipotentiary of the Four Year Plan. With this appointment he came into complete control of a 'well-conceived' plan of the German High Command's Armaments Office for converting the Reich economy to war. Albert Speer stated this plan was never carried out. In 1939 Göring was selected to be the *Führer's* successor, being appointed *Reichsmarschall* in July 1940.
36. J.H. Brook, *No Bacon and Eggs Tonight*, Creativelines, 2002.
37. An abbreviation of *Waffenschmiede des Reichs*, or 'Arsenal of the Empire'.
38. Manchester, William, *The Arms of Krupp 1587-1968*.
39. First operation.
40. Deniliquin.
41. Flying Officer K. Moore DFC's crew, in Lancaster W4310, UV-C, were all killed after being hit by *Kriegsmarine* Flak over the target. Pilot Officer B.K. Rust was the navigator.
42. Deniliquin High School.
43. Manchester, William, *The Arms of Krupp 1587-1968*.
44. United States Strategic Bombing Survey (USSBS).
45. 22 Bomber Command aircraft lost on first trip 9 April 1943; 460 Squadron lost one (Sgt. J.H. Ball RAAF). Nine aircraft lost on 2nd trip 10 April 1943; 460 lost one, (W/O D.I. MacDonald RAAF).
46. Pilzen was located 50 miles ESE of Prague in Bohemia-Morevia, over 600 miles from Lincolnshire. The city and the Skoda factories were overrun on 15 March 1939 when Bohemia-Morevia was occupied by Germany after the Munich Crisis.
47. The attack was actually carried out on 16/17 April.
48. *Sunday Chronicle and Sunday Referee*, 18 April 1943.
49. R. Searle, communication to author, 2008.
50. Wg/Cdr G.B. Warner.
51. *Sunday Chronicle and Sunday Referee*, 18 April 1943. This report featured in a number of daily newspapers and was obviously prepared by the Ministry of Information.
52. *Sunday Express*, 18 April 1943.
53. *Sunday Chronicle and Sunday Referee*, 18 April 1943.
54. *Sunday Express*, 18 April 1943.
55. Stirlings and Wellingtons.
56. UKNA AIR 40/310.
57. *Sunday Express*, 18 April 1943.
58. Its German name was Weisengrund.
59. Middlebrook, Martin and Everitt, Chris, *The Bomber Command War Diaries*.
60. *Sunday Chronicle and Sunday Referee*, 18 April 1943.
61. *Sunday Express*, 18 April 1943.
62. L.J. Simpson Service Diary, entry date 16-17 April 1943.
63. Chorley vol. 4.
64. Report of the USSB, *Gusstahkfabrik* (Krupp cast steel works), 1947.
65. Manchester, William, *The Arms of Krupp 1587-1968*.
66. Ibid.
67. *Daily Express*, 4 May 1943.
68. Ibid.
69. *The Non-Stop Blitz on Germany*, Australian newsletter, 22 June 1943.
70. Chorley Vol. 4. Foreman, Matthews and Parry record 24.
71. Foreman Matthews and Parry state four.
72. The author has been unable to find any of the names mentioned in the newspaper articles in either Chorley or Clutton-Brock suggesting that the names may have been fabricated for security purposes.
73. *Daily Express*, 4 May 1943.

74. Around that time in the war MOs at air bases across England noticed an increasing number of 'early returns': crews aborting missions and returning to base with purported technical problems. As this increased, questions began to be asked, putting more pressure on pilots. This may have affected the crew's decision.
75. A platform the bombardier lay upon under which a film of the landscape passed. When the target appeared underneath the man pressed the bomb toggle and a light flashed on the map where the bomb hit.
76. Searle archive.
77. G. Willatt, *Bombs and Barbed Wire*.
78. Extract from Cliff O'Riordan's diary, Australian War Memorial, 3DRL/4164.
79. This was Lippe-Weissenfeld's 44th victory according to Foreman, Matthews and Parry. It occurred at 01.40 hrs over Hagbluer Holz.
80. 12 Squadron apparently undertook special operations in 1942, including supply flights to Yugoslav partisans. After the war Schrock recognised one of the Yugoslavs whilst he was working on a ship in Queensland. The man was a seaman on an English merchant ship and became a regular visitor to Schrock's home in Townsville afterwards.
81. 'Hajo' was a diminutive of Hans-Joachim.
82. F.J. King, *RAAF Flying Logbook*, 1944. Peter King collection. Engineer Sandy Rowe suggested to the author that 'p/c failed to climb', meant that aircraft 'P' of 'C flight' had failed to climb. This was probably due to an engine failure on the outward flight. Consequently the flight entry was marked 'D.N.C.O.' i.e. 'Duty Not Carried Out', indicating that the aircraft did not bomb. The normal logbook entry would have been 'D.C.O.' i.e. 'Duty Carried Out'.
83. German archives claim 41 bombers were shot down on the 23rd: Foreman, Matthews and Parry.
84. Middlebrook and Everitt, *The Bomber Command War Diaries*.
85. Chorley Vol. 5.
86. Ibid.
87. Middlebrook, *The Berlin Raids*.
88. Foreman, Matthews and Parry.
89. Air Historical Branch (RAF). Ministry of Defence, letter to author, 8 July 2010.
90. R. Searle, communication with author, 2010.
91. From Webster and Frankland, *The Strategic Air Offensive Against Germany, 1939-1945*, Vol. II, and L.J. Simpson *Service Diary*.

Chapter Ten

1. Nelson, Hank, *Chased by the Sun: Australians in Bomber Comnmand*, Allen and Unwin, 2002.
2. L.J. Simpson *Service Diary*.
3. Flying Officer / Acting Flight Lieutenant.
4. The Miles Martinet was a high-speed target tug introduced into RAF Training Command after the final Miles Master advanced trainer was built in 1942, which it superseded. It included many elements from the Master.
5. Communication with author, May 2008.
6. 27 OTU lost 19 non-operational Wellington IIIs in 1943. 201 were lost throughout Training Command that year, the highest total for any training aircraft in 1943.
7. *Only Owls and Bloody Fools Fly at Night*, Group Capt Tom Sawyer.
8. Strato-cumulus cloud.

Chapter Eleven

1. From a well-known quote by Hermann Göring of August 1939 boasting of the Reich's air defences: 'If an enemy bomber reaches the Ruhr, my name is not Hermann Göring: you can call me Meier!' Meier was a well-known music hall performer and is the second most common surname in Germany. Also 'I want to be called Meier if ...' is a German idiom to express that something is viewed as impossible.
2. Chorley vol. 4. The figure was almost certainly considerably more than this.
3. This was probably intended to fire outside the propeller arc.
4. Ken Knott, correspondence with author, May, 2009.
5. Alfred Price, *Duel over Germany*, Purnell vol. 4.
6. R.E. Kendall, correspondence with author, 2009.
7. Ken Knott, correspondence with author, April/May 2009.
8. R.V. Jones, *Most Secret War*, 1978.

9. Jones, whose celebrated book *Most Secret War* (1978) was a best-seller, was also involved in the Air Ministry's investigation of Germany's airborne and ground-based radar systems, the Bruneval Raid, the development of Window, the attacks on Hamburg and Peenemünde, and the campaign against the German 'V'-weapons, to name only a few.
10. R.V. Jones, *Most Secret War*, 1978.
11. The Top Secret intelligence reports decoded by 'Station X' at Bletchley Park from German Enigma machine high-level communications cyphers. See *The Ultra Secret*, F.W. Winterbotham, and *Station X: the Codebreakers of Bletchley Park*, M. Smith.
12. R.V. Jones believed that 70 per cent of RAF losses were due to Flak, and 30 per cent to night fighters. Bomber Command calculated 50:50.
13. R.V. Jones was a former physics student of Lindemann's, who came into conflict with him over the design of infrared detectors, and initially left the Clarendon Laboratory because of it, until invited back. Lindemann, as Churchill's scientific advisor, wrote the 'final rationalisation' of the Bomber Command offensive; he opposed the introduction of Window for fear of reprisals; he persuaded the Prime Minister to accept the Morgenthau Plan for de-industrialising Germany post-war, which was ultimately rejected; and he was involved in the decision to use the atomic bomb.
14. In spite of such a threat, on 15 July 1943 Churchill sanctioned personally the introduction of Window. The Germans had earlier produced their own similar countermeasure, codenamed '*Düppel*', but trials of it in 1942 proved a disaster.
15. Norman Longmate, *The Bombers*.
16. *Wilde Sau* (Wild Boar): the name the *Luftwaffe* adopted for this tactic.
17. Quoted in *Apocalypse 1945, Destruction of Dresden*, David Irving.
18. This was 12 aircraft from the entire force of 791 aircraft, i.e. 1.5% – an indication of how effective the first use of Window was.
19. McKinstry and Probert.
20. Groom's descriptions suggest that this may actually have been the final raid of four on 2/3 August.
21. Cumulo nimbus thunderstorm clouds.
22. L.J. Simpson, conversation with author, 1992.
23. A.W. Cole, interview with author, July 2008.
24. To calculate the return distance from the theoretical position of the target to home base.
25. A.W. Cole, interview with author, July 2008.
26. R.H. Gill, letter to author, December 2010.
27. J.K. Galbraith, quoted in *The Good War* by Studs Terkel, 1985.
28. Ibid.
29. Ibid.
30. P. Johnson, *The Withered Garland*.
31. Ibid. One has also to remember that Hitler was affected enough by the bombing to transfer his resources away from conventional projects onto 'revenge weapons'.
32. See Chapter Eighteen on *Dulag Luft*.
33. J.O.E.O. Mahncke, *The German Air Force Anti-Aircraft Auxiliaries (Luftwaffenhelfer) 1943-1945*, unpublished memoir, 2008.
34. M. Maschmann, *Account Rendered*, 1954.
35. Ibid.
36. Speer, *Inside the Third Reich*.
37. The 'Operation Taxable' D-Day deception was an example of the varied use of Window.

Chapter Twelve

1. Bernard Frisby, letter to author, January 2009.
2. John Dean, letter to author, April 2009.
3. Alan Castle, letter to author, April 2009.
4. i.e. the 'perimeter track' that circumnavigated the airfield.
5. R. Margerison, *Boys at War*.
6. W. Holden, *Shellshock: the Psychological Impact of War*. The figures for chances of survival vary considerably: in this case they probably refer to the chances at the beginning of a tour.
7. The difference between starting a first and a second tour was quite noticeable. The photographs of Laurie Simpson's crew at the start of their first tour in January 1944 show a markedly more fresh and self-confident looking group than the dishevelled and tired looking men who began the second tour a year later.
8. Marshall de Bruhl, *Firestorm: Allied Air Power and the Destruction of Dresden*.
9. Winged badge.

10. F. Dennis, communication to author, September 2009.
11. A. Smith, *Whispers in the Air*, Channel 4 documentary, 1990s.
12. Ibid. Arthur returned to operations with the same crew. On his 30th op his aircraft crash-landed; two of the crew were killed, and he was badly burned.
13. i.e. the further one got into a tour, the more the odds diminished.
14. Group Captain G.W. Sawyer DFC, *Only Owls and Bloody Fools Fly at Night*, Goodall Publications, 1985.
15. A.W. Cole, interview with author.
16. There were some documented cases of this type of disciplinary procedure occurring in the RAF in World War Two.
17. Rowe was told the aircraft had an Australian crew, in which case it was almost certainly from 460 Squadron.
18. M.R. Rowe, letter to author, September 2010.
19. Miles Tripp, *The Eighth Passenger* (revised edition), 1993.
20. Ibid.
21. Chorley vol. 6.
22. David Howell, letter to author, March 2009.
23. 'Screened' was normally procedure for vetting a crew at the completion of 30 operations. March's crew's case was an exception.
24. March's crew lost both their mid-upper and rear gunners in one operation.
25. Russell Margerison, letter to author, May 2009.
26. Alec March, unpublished personal account, 1990s.
27. John Geddes DFC, unpublished personal account.
28. J. Douglas Harvey RCAF, *Cowards*, unsourced article, 2008.
29. Mark K. Wells, *Courage and Air Warfare*.
30. E. Groom, conversation with author, October 2008.
31. Michael Skeet, *An Airman's Son*, BBC *Peoples' War* website.
32. Alec March, letter to author, April 2009.

Chapter Thirteen

1. The German secret service never attempted to interfere with the Casablanca Conference. They misinterpreted the title as a code for an assembly at the White House.
2. Extract from the Combined Chiefs of Staff report on American-British Strategy in 1943, 31 December 1942 (see Neillands and Messenger).
3. Robin Neillands, *The Bomber War: Arthur Harris and the Allied Bomber Offensive 1939-1945*.
4. This is actually a quote from a letter from Harris to the Air Ministry (i.e. Portal) on 6 March 1943.
5. Charles Messenger (1984) appears to have been one of the first people to publish details of this interpretation. Air Marshal Harris in fact, to protect his crews, habitually either ignored or disobeyed the directives he received.
6. Sir Charles Webster and Dr. Noble Frankland, *The Strategic Air Offensive against Germany 1939-1945*.
7. Ploesti was located in southern Rumania, around 30 miles due north of Bucharest. The refineries there served the only major oilfield the Germans controlled and, as such, it was an 'oil bottleneck'. Oil, like ball bearings, was regarded by Harris as a 'panacea' target, i.e. a remedy for all ills, and semi-frivolous. In the minds of Allied target-planners, if the Ploesti refineries could be destroyed, the Germans would have to rely upon either their own synthetic oil sources or capture oilfields in the Caucasus and Middle East. The heavily defended oil plants were given attack priority mistakenly over other 'panacea' targets such as the ball bearing factory at Schweinfurt and the Messerschmitt aircraft plants at Regensburg and Weiner Neustadt in Austria. On 1 August 1943, 177 B-24s of the US Ninth Air Force took off from bases in North Africa to attack ten refineries at Ploesti, a round-trip of 2,700 miles. In a confused attack, at very low level – sometimes 30 ft, the target was seriously damaged, but not critically. A 1945 figure estimated 73 B-24s were lost, over 40% of the force.
8. Charles Messenger, *'Bomber' Harris and the Strategic Bomber Offensive, 1939-1945*.
9. Robin Neillands, *The Bomber War: Arthur Harris and the Allied Bomber Offensive 1939-1945*.
10. This would entail 'precision bombing', rather than 'area bombing'.
11. Robin Neillands, *The Bomber War: Arthur Harris and the Allied Bomber Offensive 1939-1945*. For a personal account of this see Elmer Bendiner's *A Fall of Fortresses*.
12. Berlin was dubbed the 'Big City' by RAF crews because of its wide expanse and, more particularly, because of the length of time it took to fly across it.
13. Much of this was sourced from Martin Middlebrook's *The Nuremberg Raid*.

14. Bennett, Air Vice-Marshal D.C.T., *Pathfinder,* Goodall Publications, 1983.
15. J. Nunn, *My War*, personal unpublished memoir.
16. R.H. Rowe, letter to author 2008, and J. McFarlane, quoted in M. Middlebrook's *The Berlin Raids*.
17. R.H. Rowe, quoted in *Bomber Boys*, K. Wilson, 2005.
18. J. Nunn, *My War*, personal unpublished memoir.
19. By this, Nunn means looking at a burning target for a long period could temporarily blind an airman and was not recommended particularly for pilots and navigators.
20. The noise emitted could be a terrible irritation since the radar picked other bombers in the stream as well as night fighters.
21. Their ETA for Berlin should have been around 23.45 hours.
22. Quoted from Sutton's memoir, and named P/O L.E.N. Hahey RAAF in Chorley Vol. 4. Middlebrook identified the pilot as Australian Pilot Officer Laurie Lahey.
23. W.E. Sutton, personal memoir, 2009, and J.W. Annetts, quoted in Middlebrook's *The Berlin Raids*.
24. Foreman, Matthews and Parry.
25. The maximum operational height of the Halifax II was 22,800 feet.
26. F.J. McGovern, IWM Sound Archive.
27. A.E. Bryett. IWM Sound Archive.
28. Ibid.
29. A. Clarke, letter to author, 20 October 2010.
30. Astro-navigation was removed from RAF training courses in the USA in World War Two after it was deemed to be too dangerous for operational use because of its complexity and the need for an aircraft to be flown straight and level whilst star shots were taken.
31. A. Clarke, personal unpublished memoir and letter to author, October 2010.
32. It was about a 600-mile flight out and therefore, averaging around 250 mph, they should have reached the target area around 23.15 hrs. Bomber Command lost 50 aircraft that night, 20 of them Halifaxes. Foreman, Matthews and Parry record 13 Halifaxes shot down that night after 23.20 hrs, including one by von Bonin of NJG 1 at 23.30 hrs (no location), one by *Leutnant* Johannes Haager of NJG 1 at 00.53 hrs (SW Berlin), and one by Helmut Lent of NJG 3 at 00.54 hrs (SW Berlin). The bombs were dropped after turning back, which may have added ten minutes to the flight time, i.e. they arrived over the target around 23.30 hrs. From these figures, since there is no location for von Bonin's 'kill' and the attack must have come on the west side of the city, their most likely protagonist was either Haager or Lent.
33. See Glossary. These were names selected by Harris's personal staff.
34. Harry Sparks, interview with author, May 2009.
35. J. Dimbleby, *Richard Dimbleby*.
36. From BBC radio programme *Broadcast from Berlin*, 1943.
37. E.A. Groom, interview with author, September 2008.
38. See section on David Holford in Chapter Five
39. For a fuller account of the work of 100 Group see Martin Streetley's *Confound and Destroy: 100 Group and the Bomber Support Campaign*, MacDonald and Janes.
40. 19 aircraft from 13 squadrons were lost on the Munich raid of 6-7 September 1943. The total attacking force consisted of 257 Lancasters and 147 Halifaxes. Official POW numbers were 29 from eight crews. Six men were injured on a 9 Squadron crew that returned to England. One Lancaster from 156 Squadron landed but was 'beyond economical repair'.
41. Total losses on 2/3 October 1943 were nine aircraft, i.e. 63 men, out of an attacking force of 294 Lancasters and 2 B-17s. There were also eight men who returned to England, one picked up by Air Sea Rescue.
42. Jenkinson's 10 Squadron lost two aircraft. (Chorley Vol. 4).
43. Philip Jenkinson, interview with author, May 2009. Also interview for *Quest for Freedom*, DVD film, 2009.
44. UKNA: Official War Cabinet Weekly Résumé No. 221, of the '*Naval, Military and Air situation from 0700 18th November, to 0700 25th November, 1943.*
45. Rex Bennett survived the war. In his eighties he became a drummer in a jazz band.
46. These are detailed in Len Deighton's novel, *Bomber*.
47. J. Nunn, *My War*, unpublished personal memoir, 1992.
48. R.A. Raymond, unpublished personal memoir.
49. In fact this plan was almost a reverse of the flight plan of 18/19 November.
50. A. Carter, personal unpublished memoir, 2005.
51. D.J. Edwards, IWM Sound Archive.
52. A. Carter, personal unpublished memoir, 2005.
53. J. Nunn, *My War*, unpublished personal memoir.

54. Joan Beech, *One WAAF's War*.
55. Chorley vol. 4.
56. This was another 103 Squadron pilot named 'Boozy' Bassitt.
57. J. Nunn, *My War*, unpublished personal memoir.
58. Six men were also presumed lost at sea.
59. The Lancaster was much more difficult to bale out from than the Halifax, with a smaller escape hatch; it also had a larger bomb load than the Halifax.
60. Figures from Middlebrook, *The Berlin Raids*.
61. W.G. Carman, *Three Times Lucky*.
62. Shortly after that, Carman's crew was transferred to the PFF and 83 Squadron.
63. Middlebrook, *The Berlin Raids*.
64. Ibid.
65. Flying Officer Alfred George Osborne, born Raymond Terrace, New South Wales, 9 June 1922.
66. This had remained 'undiscovered' in the Schrock family's personal archive until after my father's death.
67. L.J. Simpson, interview by G.R. Holloway, 2000. Quoted in *Touchdown East Devon*, East Devon Aircrew Association.
68. These were figures recorded by the crew themselves. When these were transmitted to a Group they may also have been disbelieved and reduced. The same process could occur when the data arrived at squadrons. Consequently many 'broadcast winds' might actually have been far stronger than suggested.
69. The fact that there were high winds that night is confirmed by other sources: although the PFF skymarkers were dropped on the target accurately, 'strong winds blew them rapidly along the line of the bombers' route (to the south-east)'. A German night fighter also reported 'strong winds against us' as he flew north. (Middlebrook).
70. The stream had originally been on a south-east course in order to confuse German controllers as to its destination. In fact, the whole raid was planned to veer to the north-east, south of Brunswick, in order to get to the position for the bomb run. Simpson may have misunderstood what was happening at this point.
71. This contradicts a report in Middlebrook's *Berlin Raids* that the 'Flak barrage was noted as… particularly feeble'. One 57 Squadron Lancaster reported being shot down by 'rockets' over the target (Chorley). Total RAF losses that night were recorded as 34, but Foreman, Matthews and Parry indicate that 26 of these fell to night fighters. From this, and allowing for crash-landings, one could assume that very few bombers were actually downed by Flak over the target.
72. Don Charlwood, *No Moon Tonight*, 1956.
73. The homing beam which passed through the DF Loop on top of the fuselage.
74. Chorley Vol. 5.
75. L.J. Simpson, interview with author 1993.
76. Rest and recuperation.
77. W.R. Chorley, *Bomber Command Losses Vol. 5*, 1997.
78. R. Child, personal memoir.
79. Additional material from *Men of Air*, Kevin Wilson.
80. Paul Royle was still alive in October 2010, and wrote to the author. See section on 'The Great Escape' in Chapter Nineteen.
81. Chorley Vol. 5.
82. Middlebrook, *Diaries*.
83. J. McGillivray, IWM Sound Archive.
84. Moyes.
85. Howard Pearce, interview with author, 2007.
86. Reg Brown, interview with author, 2008.
87. Ibid.
88. *Scangriff* magazine spelling.
89. Wilson.
90. This is based on Alkamede's 1945 report and disagrees with a later account by Burwell which stated that they were attacked as they were coming out of the city.
91. Foreman, Matthews and Parry.
92. Warrant Officer N.S. Alkamede. Originally published as *The Luckiest Man Alive?* in *Spotlight on Stalag Luft III*, by *Scangriff*, 1945. Apart from orally recited accounts in the camp, this must be the earliest and probably one of the more accurate accounts of Alkamede's fall. It was the furthest freefall by an airman up to that time in the war. Chorley Vol. 5 records that Alkamede's Lancaster was flying at 19,000 ft and that the gunner submitted a report that another airman had fallen from

22,000 ft without a parachute but Alkamede, the first, 'did come off slightly better'. Nicholas S. Alkamede died in 1987.
93. Ibid.
94. Foreman, Matthews and Parry.
95. C. Webster and N. Frankland, *The Strategic Air Offensive Against Germany 1939-1945*.
96. This was a diversification from the Pointblank Directive which listed, as its priority, six centres of aircraft or ball bearing production: Schweinfurt, Leipzig, Brunswick (Braunschweig), Regensburg, and Augsburg in order of priority. Nuremberg was not even on the list.
97. Bennett, Air Vice-Marshal D.C.T., *Pathfinder*, Goodall Publications, 1983.
98. R. Margerison, *Boys at War*, 2005.
99. Frederick H.A. Watts, IWM Sound Archive.
100. i.e. a personally fitted harness.
101. J. Silver, letter to author, July 2009.
102. Middlebrook, and Chorley Vol. 5. Donald G. Gray died in 2007.
103. R.F. Raymond, *My Service Life*, personal memoir, 1990s.
104. Instruments of Darkness.
105. A.T. Harris to H. Probert, 9/11/79.
106. One of these was the famous use of General Patton to support the hoax of the existence of a 'First United States Army Group' poised for the invasion in East Anglia.
107. Many of these stories, based purely on 'hearsay', arose after the war.
108. For an expansion of this see Middlebrook Ch. 17. 1980 revised edition.
109. Individual aircraft flights.
110. Air Marshal Sir A.T. Harris, IWM Sound Archive.
111. L. Cheshire, IWM Sound Archive. Qualifying this, Cheshire stated that the bombing of Hiroshima and Nagasaki, which he had witnessed, was correspondingly 'unfair'.

Chapter Fourteen

1. Harris Archives, Folder F28, RAF Museum.
2. F.J. McGovern, IWM Sound Archive.
3. *S.Z. and the RAF*, Lord Zuckerman, chapter in *High Flyers*, Greenhill Books, 1993. Zuckerman was invited to become advisor to the Research and Development department of the Ministry of Home Security in 1943, subsequently becoming Scientific Advisor to the Combined Operations HQ, Allied Expeditionary Force and then Supreme HQ, AEF.
4. Ibid.
5. Ibid.
6. Bomber Command Operational Research Section.
7. Harris. Arranged experiments concerning the effectiveness of bombing operations were far less accurate than statistical analysis of raid reports.
8. Specifically an alliance with Turkey.
9. Quote from the diary of General 'Hap' Arnold.
10. David Irving, *The War between the Generals*.
11. In this he was later proved wrong.
12. *S.Z. and the RAF*, Lord Zuckerman, article in *High Flyers*, Greenhill Books, 1993.
13. David Irving, *The War between the Generals*.
14. Harris.
15. In fact Speer, using slave labour, was able to rebuild the bombed factories far faster than Harris realised.
16. Probert. Other sources indicate seven target yards.
17. Chorley vol 5. Chorley indicates no casualties on any other French targets during this period.
18. David Irving, *The War between the Generals*.
19. Harris.
20. Harris. Probert stated 74.
21. Harris.
22. Probert.
23. Harris.
24. See quote at beginning of chapter.
25. Alan Castle, letter to author, April 2009. Richard Morris, Cheshire's biographer, thought that 83 Squadron's Master Bomber was off tune, meaning it was impossible for him to give bombing orders.
26. Morris, Richard, *Cheshire: the Biography of Leonard Cheshire VC, OM*, Viking, 2000.
27. Alan Castle, letter to author, April 2009.

28. It has been confirmed that during this time six Lancasters were claimed by one Luftwaffe pilot.
29. Morris.
30. A sortie was an operation flown by a single aircraft.
31. Harris.
32. 'Gee' was the system whereby three transmitting stations on the English coast, a master station 'A' and two slaves 'B' and 'C', sent out radio signals simultaneously. An aircraft flying along a line from its airfield to the target could calculate its position on the line from the difference between the master and the slave transmission received. A similar transmission from the master to a second slave established the aircraft's position on a second line which crossed the first. The point of intersection of the lines gave the aircraft's location. In the Gee Box a cathode ray tube display showed the two lines. When blips of the separate transmissions appeared, it was possible to relate these to a map.
33. American version of H2S.
34. J.V. Williams, interview with author, June 2010.
35. Le Chatellier, a small village around five miles north-east of Fougeres, Brittany. According to Chorley (Vol 5) the only losses that night were against flying bomb storage sites at Bois de Cassan about 10 miles north of Paris, and Trossy; three Halifaxes were lost on the first raid and two Lancasters on the second, all to Flak. There were 21 fatalities.
36. May-sur-Orne was some six miles south of Caen. Chorley records that three aircraft were lost on an attack on Caen that night: two Halifaxes and a Lancaster. Both Halifaxes returned with their ordnance intact, (after being instructed by the Master Bomber not to bomb), and crashed on landing, probably because of this.
37. G.V. Korner, interview with author, 2008.

Chapter Fifteen

1. Daytime navigation aid.
2. Night-time navigation aid.
3. Sources: A. Wetherill, letters to author 2010; Chorley Vol. 2; A. Metzmacher, *One Way Ticket to Berlin; Aeroplane* magazine April 2010.
4. Chorley Vol. 3.
5. Eric Foinette, personal memoir, 1990s.
6. E.G. Ratcliffe, letter to author, 1 November 2008.
7. E.G. Ratcliffe, letter to author, 3 November 2008.
8. Chorley Vol. 3.
9. Guy Gibson's 106 Squadron bombed the *Gneisenau* in the port of Gydynia in Poland, on 27 August 1942 to little effect.
10. E.G. Ratcliffe, letter to author, 1 November 2008.
11. C. Younger, interview with author, 2011.
12. C. Younger, *No Flight from the Cage*, 1956.
13. Operations Record Book.
14. G.R. Harsh, *Lonesome Road*, 1971. What may have happened was that whilst the Main Force went to Aachen, Harsh's navigator had taken them halfway between Aachen and Dusseldorf, 25 miles north-east of where they should have been, and over Cologne. This may mean that they had actually flown to the wrong target.
15. This normally happened due to lack of oxygen.
16. G.R. Harsh, *Lonesome Road*, 1972, and Chorley Vol. 3.
17. Foreman, Matthews and Parry record Schnaufer as shooting down two Wellingtons on 30/31 August, and one Halifax on 31 August/1 September, but at 22.41 hrs, south-east of Kuinre.
18. G. Flanagan, interview with author, 2008.
19. G. Flanagan, personal unpublished memoir, 1990s.
20. Based upon G. Flanagan's personal unpublished memoir, 1990s and interview with author, 2008.
21. Chorley Vol. 5.
22. Foreman, J., Matthews, J. and Parry, S., *Luftwaffe Night Fighter Combat Claims, 1939-1945*. Either the pilot misidentified the Halifax, or *Luftwaffe* records were incorrect. The only Halifax losses Chorley records for that night were three from 6 Canadian Group on a raid to Le Mans, and a 77 Squadron one on Orleans.
23. S. Jackson, *Steve Jackson's War 1939-1946*, unpublished memoir, 2008.
24. R.H. Gill, letter to author, December 2010. Gill recollected that on the Nuremberg raid of 30 March 1944, only three rear gunners survived on 97 aircraft lost. Weatherill had been an apprentice jockey before joining the RAF and was quite successful, riding several winners. He was 'quite a short, squat chap', bearing some resemblance to the 'Punch' of Punch and Judy shows: hence his nickname.

25. Chorley Vol. 5.
26. This is a good illustration of the inefficiency of the .303 Brownings.
27. Inevitably there is some discrepancy between the RAF report of the time of the aircraft's demise and that of the *Luftwaffe*. Buhlmann's report comes from the records of the *Oberkommando der Luftwaffe* and the *Abschüsse Kommission*, responsible for victory listings. These did not come to light until the last ten years.
28. Chorley Vol. 5.
29. Based upon *Jim's Story*, J. Philpot's unpublished memoir, 1990s.
30. Foreman, J., Matthews, J. and Parry, S., *Luftwaffe Night Fighter Combat Claims, 1939-1945*.
31. F. Mannion, letter to author, 2008.
32. Ibid.
33. In Chorley Vol 5, based on ORB reports, F.P. Mannion is listed as the mu/g.
34. 'Whilst not disbelieving my observations about all of this,' Mannion wrote, 'RAF Records will not even correct their files as to my correct position.' Letter to author, 13 March 2008.
35. F. Mannion, letter to author, 2008.
36. Chorley erroneously records that Mannion, rather than Saunders, was killed. Chorley Vol. 5.
37. Author's note: Although Pendray was serving with the Second Tactical Air Force (2nd TAF), this account is included here because of its interest.
38. Reference to the German 88 mm Flak gun.
39. Chorley Vol. 5 states 17.35 hrs.
40. Foreman, J., Matthews, J. and Parry, S., *Luftwaffe Night Fighter Combat Claims, 1939-1945*.
41. Chemnitz, with Leipzig, Dresden and Berlin made up the four target cities of 'Operation Thunderclap' which aimed to disrupt German communications and Axis troop movements behind the Eastern Front, coincident with the flow of refugees. The Allied Chiefs of Staff hoped that, whilst the Allies were temporarily stopped in the west, the attacks would aid the Red Army's advance – a final 'knock-out' blow was still impossible. Chemnitz, Dresden and Leipzig were in Saxony, a traditionally socialist state. This was the night after *Unternehmen Gisela*, the *Luftwaffe* raid against Bomber Command as it returned to its home airfields. It was also one of the last raids of 'Operation Thunderclap' and thirty-nine crews were lost, seven shortly after take-off due to bad weather. This raid's losses were nearly five times as many as on the Dresden operation less than three weeks previously.
42. After the Eighth Air Force 'took over' East Anglia, Bomber Command was forced to re-route its outward trips to fly over Reading, to avoid the approximately 3,000 American aircraft that could be over the North Sea; its aircraft then dog-legged due east, departing the English coast over Beachy Head.
43. These were obviously from electrical lines burning, similar to those witnessed by Graham Korner.
44. J.V. Williams, *A Timely Reminder: No Turning Back*, unpublished personal memoir, 1995.
45. Chorley's book (Vol. 6) records, apparently erroneously, that the entire crew of NG240 survived.

Chapter Sixteen

1. B.A. James, *Moonless Night*, Pen and Sword, 2008.
2. Although Hughes was not serving in Bomber Command, his account is included here because of its relevance to this chapter.
3. The navigator had a separate cockpit behind the pilot in the Beaufighter.
4. From *218 (Gold Coast) Squadron Newsletter* No. 24. Turley was the rear gunner; 'Mac' was Flying Officer A. Scott, the navigator; Harry was Flt/Lt Harry Warwick, the pilot. (Chorley, Vol 5.)
5. Ibid.
6. Homing pigeons were standard equipment on RAF bombers early in the war when targets were closer to home. They could be resorted to if r/t communication failed.
7. Although Hodgkinson was not in Bomber Command, the account is included because the raid was part of an important bombing operation.
8. D. Hodgkinson, unpublished memoir, 1987.

Chapter Seventeen

1. Chorley Vol. 2. There is no record of Gildner shooting down a Manchester in Foreman, Matthews and Parry.
2. Dr. R. Kirby, *Jack Alfred Cheeseman - Airman*, 2005.
3. Account in Newport Free Grammar School article *Old Ons*.
4. This was probably a *Wilde Sau* aircraft.

5. W.E.G. Higgs, interview with author, 2008.
6. See Chapter Eight.
7. This was not unusual. There were so many people in Bomber Command at that time, that it was difficult to keep track of one's fellow countrymen, particularly after landing in occupied territory. Word of mouth – 'the Bush Telegraph' – was the normal facility.
8. Clutton-Brock.
9. Plancoet and Plancquet were two different villages in Brittany.
10. From AWM archives, MI9/S/PG/LIB/146. File 19/SECRET. Interview: 19 June 1945.
11. Bombardier Colin McLeod survived the war after spells in *Dulag Luft*, *Stalag Luft* III and the 'Long March'.
12. From AWM archives, MI9/S/PG/LIB/327. File 19/SECRET. Interview: 5 July 1945.
13. AWM archives, MI9/S/PG/LIB/300. File 19/SECRET.
14. Designed by Charles Fraser-Smith, these boots were not as efficient as had been originally hoped and tended to let water and cold into the top. They were later abandoned by MI9.
15. L.J. Simpson, interview with author, 1995.
16. See Foot, M.R.D. and Langley, J.M., *MI9*, Bodley Head, 1979, p. 142, Ottis, S. G., *Silent Heroes: Downed Airmen and the French Underground*, University Press of Kentucky, 2001, p. 135 and *Saturday at MI9*, Airey Neave, Hodder and Stoughton, 1969.
17. This account is based on transcript from a taped interview with S. Hope, Tape 335, September 1999.
18. The majority of inmates were political prisoners, Communists, and saboteurs.
19. This information would have been available from the Intelligence files at *Dulag Luft*.
20. Around that time the SOE agents Odette and Peter Churchill were in Fresnes.
21. L.J. Simpson, interview with author, October/November 1984.
22. Duplock's surname is erroneously given as 'Diplock' in Chorley Vol. 6 and Clutton-Brock.
23. This may have been Nuremberg-Langwasser, a *Wehrmacht/Luftwaffe* camp a few miles ENE of Nuremberg.
24. Chorley, Vol. 6.

Chapter Eighteen

1. Sidney A.F. Duplock, unpublished personal memoir, 2008.
2. The name was an abbreviation of *Durchgangslager der Luftwaffe* (Air Force Transit Camp).
3. From a report on *Dulag Luft* written for MI9 by L.J. Simpson after he was repatriated in July 1945. This refers to the situation in February 1944. By mid-July the US Military Intelligence Service, War Dept. 15, stated that *Dulag Luft* had three sections: the interrogation centre at Oberursel, a transit camp at Wetzlar (supplanting the original Transit Camp in Frankfurt-am-Main), and a hospital in Hohemark.
4. On 13 October 1939.
5. J. Leakey, letter to author, 2009.
6. Sydney Smith, *Wings Day*, Collins, 1968.
7. F/O M.J. Casey was a Blenheim pilot with 57 Squadron shot down on a daylight reconnaissance flight from Etain, France to Wesel-Bocholt whilst based at Roseieres-en-Santerre, west of St. Quentin on 16 October 1939. 'Wings' Day was his squadron mate, shot down three days earlier flying from Metz to reconnoitre the Hamm-Hanover area. All the rest of Day's crew were killed.
8. Spangenberg Castle was a high security prison that had housed French prisoners during the Franco-Prussian War and Allied POWs during the First World War. A classic German edifice, it was oval-shaped with a central courtyard, turreted and set upon a rock 400 feet above the local village. Intended to be escape-proof, it was surrounded by a dried-up moat.
9. Bushell's sister, Elizabeth, commented after the 1962 film *The Great Escape* was released that: 'Roger had tremendous charisma – he wasn't a bit like the dour and short Richard Attenborough.' Douglas Bader, who had known Bushell at Sagan, agreed that 'to anyone who knew Roger... the part must seem badly written.'
10. Bushell had been on the British Olympic skiing team before the war.
11. *Dulag Luft. After the Battle* No. 106, 1999.
12. G.V. Korner, interview with author, 2007.
13. G. Cross, unpublished personal memoir.
14. D. Lambert, interview with author, May 2008. Lambert qualified as a doctor after the war and was later awarded the MBE for his work.
15. A.W. Cole, interview with author, July 2008.
16. H. Wagner, unpublished personal memoir.

17. Hodgkinson, Derek W., *Per Adua ad Astra* [edited extracts], 1988.
18. G.R. Harsh, *Lonesome Road*.
19. K.W. Simmons, *Kriegie*, 1960.
20. Raymond Toliver, *The Interrogator*, 1978.
21. For some reason, at least in 1942, according to Derek Hodgkinson, Coastal Command crews were left in ignorance of the existence of *Dulag Luft*.
22. In fact, by the laws of the Geneva Convention, only two elements of this 'holy trinity' had to be divulged.
23. *After the Battle* No. 106.
24. A. Carter, *Bert Carter's Wartime Memories*, 2008.
25. J. Whitehouse, letter to author, 2008.
26. Hodgkinson.
27. A.W. Cole, interview with author, 2008.
28. C. Younger, *No Flight from the Cage*.
29. G. Harsh, *Lonesome Road*.
30. G.V. Korner, interview with author, June 2008.
31. To counter w/t interception of any form, it was forbidden for wireless operators to test their equipment when a squadron was preparing for a raid.
32. From leading personalities to postal addresses to current equipment.
33. *Dulag Luft*, ATB 106, 1999.
34. Durand.
35. H.W. Coverley, interview with author, July 2008.
36. J. Philpot, personal memoir, 2006.
37. Hughes had been beaten up before arriving at Oberursel.
38. See *The One that Got Away*, Kendall Burt and James Leasor, 1956.
39. *After the Battle* No. 106.
40. Fieseler Fi 156 *Storch* (Stork), a light, single-engined liaison aircraft used by the *Luftwaffe*.
41. Hajo Herrmann, *Eagle's Wings*, 1991.
42. H. Pearce, interview with author, 2008.
43. J. Brook, *No Bacon and Eggs Tonight*, Creativelines, Southport, 2002.
44. *After the Battle* magazine, No. 106, 1999.
45. Durand.
46. F.A. James, personal memoir, 1995.
47. Ibid.
48. W.R. Chorley recorded mistakenly that Sgt J.A. Coughlin RCAF was killed in the attack, but Clutton-Brock confirms that he survived.
49. There was a mistaken belief on the part of the US Military Intelligence Service in mid-1944 that interrogation techniques at *Dulag Luft* varied from 'the deluxe, with wine women and song' (which was untrue), to the exceedingly harsh, with solitary confinement, little food and threats of physical violence (which was more accurate).
50. Raymond F. Toliver, *The Interrogator: The Story of Hans Scharff, The Luftwaffe's Master Interrogator*, Aero Publishers Inc., 1978.
51. L.J. Simpson, interview with author, 1995.
52. UK National Archives AIR 40/2317.
53. The Lancaster was introduced to Bomber Command operations in April 1942.
54. The Pathfinder Force was created in August 1942.
55. If this were so, he must have been ignorant of the fact that 28 experienced crews from Laurie Simpson's 1 Group were sent out as 'Supporters' that night for the first time over Berlin. These were crews from non-Pathfinder squadrons learning Pathfinder techniques. They went at the front of the stream with the 'primary marker' aircraft to thicken up the Window and help jam radar-predicted Flak.
56. The Halifax I and II were far inferior to the Lancaster in performance.
57. This knowledge implies that the airman started his own tour in September 1942 and ended it in April 1943.
58. In this case an 'operational flight' may be a training flight, i.e. an 'air test' whilst on an operational squadron, whilst a 'war flight' would be an operation against the enemy – a 'flight' in this case being a mission, rather than an administrative unit of aircraft.
59. UK National Archives file AIR 40/2317.
60. Hughes was shot down on the Peenemünde raid of 17 August 1943 in a 467 Squadron Lancaster and went to *Stalag Luft* VII. In fact, by strange coincidence, his aircraft was ED764 PO-N 'Nuts to the Nazis', the same aircraft that navigator Charlie Bicknell and Parson's friend, the ill-fated Larry

Hayward, had been brought down on. For further information on R.D. Hughes, see Clutton-Brock p. 187-190.
61. Lew Parsons, unpublished personal memoir.
62. G.V. Korner, interview with author, 2008.
63. P. Skinner, letter to author, 2008.
64. Parsons, personal unpublished memoir.
65. This concerns the incident that occurred in December 1939 when the three British cruisers, *Ajax*, *Achilles* and *Cumberland* were blockading Montevideo Harbour in Uruguay waiting for the German pocket battleship, *Admiral Graf Spee*, to come out of the River Plate estuary and confront them. This was after the 'The Battle of the River Plate' of 13 December. The British managed to convince the *Kriegsmarine* that strong Royal Navy reinforcements were approaching, and the German Naval Command advised the *Graf Spee's* commander, *Kapitän zur See* Hans Langsdorff, to fight his way to Buenos Aires in Argentina or destroy the ship. In the event Langsdorff, when advised that internment in Uruguay was impossible, and with insufficient ammunition to fight his way across the Plate, scuttled the ship on the 18th rather than sacrifice her. Hitler had no part in this. It was Langsdorff's own decision and he took his life on the 20th.
66. Automatic Gun Laying Turret, or AGLT. An electronic sensor that detected enemy aircraft.
67. J.H. Brook, *No Bacon and Eggs Tonight*, Creativelines, 2002.
68. D. Lambert, interview with author, 2008.
69. J.H. Brook, *No Bacon and Eggs Tonight*, Creativelines, 2002.
70. Ibid.
71. C. Holloway, letter to author, May 2009.
72. J.H. Brook, *No Bacon and Eggs Tonight*, Creativelines, 2002.
73. C. Holloway, letter to author, May 2009.
74. This board showed Cross's own 23 Squadron based at Alghero, Sardinia, CO W.C. Burton-Giles. 23 Squadron had moved from Luqa, Malta to Alghero on 23 December. If he told them his squadron was 23, the Germans would realise that it was operating from England and not the Mediterranean.
75. Louden and Tennant were a crew from another Mosquito Intruder Squadron, also stationed at Little Snoring, who had been shot down a week before Cross and Irvine.
76. Flt/Lt George Cross, *A Wartime Log for British Prisoners*, 1944.
77. W.E.G. Higgs, interview with author, 2007.
78. Hodgkinson,.
79. Sidney A.F. Duplock, unpublished personal memoir, 2008.

Chapter Nineteen

1. An abbreviation of *Stammlager der Luftwaffe*. *Stammlager* is a compound word derived from *Lager* or camp, and *Stamm*, i.e. 'basic' or 'lower'. In other words a *Stalag* was a lower ranks camp. An officers' camp was an *Offizierslager* or '*Oflag*'. Because RAF aircrew flew in mixed groups of officers and NCOs, officers, as well as other ranks, were sent to *Stalag Luft III*.
2. Colloquial term for a prisoner of war; from the German *Kriegsgefangener*.
3. Eric Foinette, personal memoir, 1990s.
4. From Australian War Memorial archive files.
5. D. Hodgkinson, personal memoir, 1987.
6. There were generally around 22 bunk rooms to a hut.
7. Eric Foinette, personal memoir, 1990s.
8. D. Hodgkinson, personal memoir, 1987.
9. Ibid.
10. Group Captain H.M. Massey DSO, MC, was lost on a raid to Essen on 1 June 1942 in a 7 Squadron Stirling flown by Flt/Lt N.E. Winch an experienced Stirling pilot. According to Chorley, Massey was flying as a flight engineer. He had been awarded an MC in 1917 with the RFC and, due to an injury to his leg suffered when baling out of an aeroplane, was repatriated on 11 April 1944. He died in 1976.
11. Hodgkinson, Derek W., *Per Adua ad Astra* [edited extracts], 1988.
12. Wing Commander R. Maw was CO of 12 Squadron, Binbrook on Wellingtons in early 1942, and was shot down over the Western Desert in August 1942 whilst CO of 108 Squadron. He had studied carpentry at school.
13. 'Ferret' was the POW expression for a German security guard, the name coming from their ferret-like activity around the camp huts.
14. The name 'goon' was a derogatory term for any German within a prison camp and derived from a peculiar muttering anthropoid in a loincloth that featured in the *Popeye* cartoons.
15. Flight Lieutenant D.A. ffrench-Mullen was the pilot of a 10 Squadron Whitley V shot down on 9

July 1940 off Heligoland, whilst on a raid to Kiel. He was on an attachment from 78 Squadron. He survived the war and contributed a number of sketches and lyrics to the *Stalag Luft* III review 'Back Home' held at the Haymarket Theatre, London SW1 in 1945. He later became a priest.
16. A 'goon box' was a sentry box, i.e. a guard station, set up to observe any illegal activity around the perimeter wire. These boxes were timber hut-like constructions on stilts built about 30 feet above the ground. There were 10 'goon boxes' at *Stalag Luft* III North Compound. Three of these were slightly smaller than the others as they overlooked the *Vorlager*.
17. Hodgkinson, Derek W., *Per Adua ad Astra* [edited extracts], 1988.
18. A.F. James, personal memoir, 1995.
19. George Harsh recalled that he and Wally Floody gave up their Rolexes in February 1945 during the Long March west from Belaria in exchange for some Schnapps and black bread.
20. Eric Foinette, personal memoir, 1990s.
21. C. Younger, *No Flight from the Cage*, W.H. Allen and Co. Ltd., 1981.
22. P/O E.E. Williams was shot down by Flak and fighters and crashed in northern Holland whilst a bomb-aimer in 75 Sqn Stirling, BK620, during a raid on Fallersleben on 16 December 1942. Oliver Philpott was the pilot of a Bristol Beaufort of 42 Squadron, Coastal Command, shot down in 1942. The author has been unable to locate details about Michael Codner.
23. Eric Foinette, personal memoir, 1990s.
24. Ibid.
25. Dennis Bateman, interview, 29 June 2008.
26. Eric Williams, *The Wooden Horse*, Collins, 1949.
27. Hodgkinson.
28. O. Philpott, IWM Sound Archive.
29. Alan F. James, personal memoir, 1995.
30. Ibid.
31. Peter A. Hughes, personal memoir.
32. R. Cartwright, personal memoir.
33. Sgt P.A. Buttigieg was a tail gunner shot down in a 50 Squadron Manchester on 3 June 1942 during a raid on Bremen. Four of his crew were killed and Buttigieg was, at one point, threatened with execution by an SS firing squad whilst in Apeldoorn Prison in The Netherlands. He was later posted to *Stalag Luft* VI.
34. P. Buttigieg, *We Weep No More*, Aquila Services Ltd., Gibraltar, 1997.
35. The 'main man' in the camp; i.e. one who could be trusted by all. Derived from the French term '*homme de confiance*' used in the 1929 Geneva Convention. *Vertrauensman* was the German equivalent.
36. Deans was only 28 in 1942 but all who met him deemed him as 'the wisest head on young shoulders', Cal Younger recalled.
37. P. Buttigieg, *We Weep No More*.
38. Younger.
39. Ibid.
40. Ibid.
41. A 'combine' was an important social unit in NCO camps, where three or more prisoners would pool their resources and generally look after one another.
42. Younger.
43. Like Buttigieg and Younger, 'T.B.' survived the war.
44. From Australian War Memorial archive files.
45. L.J. Simpson, interview with author, 1992.
46. Block 123 was located adjacent to the perimeter wire on the west side of the camp. It was from here that the tunnel 'Tom' – originally the main escape tunnel of the March 1944 breakout until it was discovered by the Germans and blown up – was commenced.
47. Alan E. Bryett, IWM Sound Archive. Bryett knew 'only a handful of those' in Block 123.
48. Ibid.
49. L.M. Whitton, interview with author, London, February 2009. Alan Bryett knew Les Whitton well in Block 122. They remained in contact after the war. A. Bryett, letter to author, April 2008.
50. Both Grenfell's and Charlick's aircraft were downed by night fighters from III./NJG1. Webb was the tail gunner on Grenfell's crew. It was reported that, with the mid-upper gunner, he returned fire and shot down the attacking fighter. Charlick had previously flown as a second pilot with Laurie on 26 February 1943.
51. Floody has been described in some books on the 'Great Escape' as a 'mining engineer'. This is something of a misnomer. In fact he only worked in the Canadian mines from June 1936 to September 1938, and then his work was restricted by his height – he was six foot two when he was 15.
52. Hehner, Barbara, *The Tunnel King*, Harper Trophy Canada, 2004.

53. L.J. Simpson, interview with author, 1995.
54. A.W. Cole, interview with author Nettlecombe, Dorset, 12 July 2008.
55. Wg/Cdr Robert Roland Stanford Tuck DFC. Although Tuck was a fighter pilot his story is felt to be relevant in this case and in context.
56. A.W. Cole, interview with author Nettlecombe, Dorset, 12 July 2008.
57. This was possibly the inspiration for the end of Angus Lennie ('Ives the Mole') in the Hollywood interpretation who became 'wire happy' or 'stir crazy' i.e. so tired of prison camp life that he was willing to do anything to escape.
58. L.J. Simpson, interview with author, 1993.
59. L.J. Simpson, *Flying with 460 Squadron RAAF*, 1984, unpublished memoir, author's collection.
60. H. Pearce, interview, 22 July 2008.
61. E. Hookings, letter to author, 2008. In fact Schmeling, heavyweight champion of the world in 1931, was not the beast the Sagan POWs took him to be. He saved the lives of two Jewish boys during the *Kristalnacht* pogroms of 1938, had an American Jewish manager and fraternized with German Jews. He refused to join the Nazi Party and, as a consequence, Hitler had him drafted into the paratroops. Schmeling fought and was wounded at the Battle of Crete in 1941, being subsequently dismissed. He appears to have made a tour of the German camps: he appeared at Auschwitz in 1943 and also visited American POW camps as well as *Stalag Luft* III, later trying to improve POW conditions. Schmeling lost the world title to Joe Louis in 1938, but later paid for Louis's funeral. He died in 2005.
62. S. Jackson, *Steve Jackson's War 1939-1946*, unpublished memoir, 2008.
63. A.W. Cole, letter to author, 23.12.09.
64. A.R.B. Schrock, *POW Log Book*.
65. April 1945.
66. C. Younger, *No Flight from the Cage*.
67. ISBN 0-86350-229-6. Webb and Bower have since ceased publishing.
68. C. Younger, *No Flight from the Cage*.
69. 'Foodaco' was a bartering system in *Stalag Luft* III standing for 'food account', with its own trading counter and storage area, the idea originating in another camp in Silesia. The system operated initially purely from the contents of Red Cross parcels, based on some commodities being preferred to others. A deposit of 50 cigarettes was required from each prospective dealer to form the sound basis of dealing. After a time, a sliding scale of prices was introduced that varied according to supply and demand. Foodaco worked on a credit system: a dealer deposited an article and received so much credit according to its current value. To buy, one withdrew an article from the store and its current value was subtracted from one's credit. After September 1944, an auctioning system was introduced. All profits were returned in the form of prizes for sports, competitions and theatre shows. Prices remained stable until the camp went on half-parcel issue, when they soared for about a fortnight then, gradually, they returned to normal, until Christmas when they rose again for food ingredients. Foodaco was staffed by camp inmates. Some profits were sent to the camp kitchen and messes, but a priority was given to keeping goods in reserve for bribing the German guards. [Source: File 19. SECRET. MI9/S/P.G./LIB/300. '*Description of Stalag Luft III, Marlag and Marlag Nord, and Dulag Luft*', S/Ldr L.J. Simpson, 31 July, 1945. Australian War Memorial].
70. Quoted from *Prisoner of War Log Book*, A.R.B. Schrock, courtesy of A. Schrock Jnr, 2008.
71. Hodgkinson.
72. L.J. Simpson, *Stalag Luft 3*, MI9 report, May 1945, Australian War Memorial.
73. A.W. Cole, interview with author Nettlecombe, Dorset, 12 July 2008.
74. H. Pearce, interview, 22 July 2008.
75. F /O A. Kennedy DFM. *Stalag Luft* III to his mother at 45 Wollongong Rd., Arncliffe, New South Wales. From an unidentified New South Wales newspaper, 1943. Author's personal collection.
76. Sgt P. Bates was shot down in a 149 Squadron Stirling from Lakenheath by night fighters and Flak at 13,000 ft. during a raid on Mannheim on 5 September 1943.
77. H. Pearce, interview, 22 July 2008.
78. *Escape to Danger*, Faber and Faber, 1946.
79. L.J. Simpson, interview with author, 1993.
80. P. Brickhill and C. Norton, *Escape to Danger*, Faber and Faber, 1946.
81. Derived from 'Scandal' Press and '*Angriff*', a German newspaper title.
82. Brickhill and Norton.
83. L.J. Simpson, interview with author, 1993.
84. G. Harsh, *Lonesome Road*.
85. Kenyon, who received the DFC, died in 1990.
86. *The Sunday Times Magazine*, 1989.
87. H. Pearce, interview with author, 2008.

88. The Decree issued to the Security Police by Himmler, conceived by Hitler, was targeted specifically at those 'guilty of offences against the Reich or against the occupation forces in occupied areas'. It was intended to create a situation that would 'leave the family and the population uncertain as to the fate of the offender:' a deterrent deemed by Hitler to be as equally effective as execution.
89. L. Forrester, *Fly for Your Life*, 1958.
90. Frank Stone, letter to author, 2008. The discovery of 'Tom' occurred on 8 September 1943, six months before Laurie Simpson arrived in the camp, but surprisingly he never noticed any damage to the roof of hut 123.
91. Ibid.
92. Stone recalled being an orderly for the 'X Organisation' security chief, George Harsh, and also to Wally Floody, who supervised the digging.
93. Frank Stone, letter to author, 2008.
94. Edward Crankshaw, *Gestapo*, New English Library, 1956.
95. Ibid.
96. A.W. Cole, interview with author, 2008.
97. L.J. Simpson, interview with author, 1995.
98. Howard Pearce, interview with author, 2008.
99. B.A. James, *Moonless Night*, 1983.
100. Bull was a Flight Lieutenant with a DFC who had been shot down in a Wellington in 1941. He had originally been in the East Compound where he had unsuccessfully participated in some of the 100 plus tunnels dug. Despite having a wife and young child, he was one of the 50 shot.
101. Ken Rees, *Lie in the Dark and Listen*, 2004.
102. Rees. Tobolski spoke fluent German. His uniform was the Forgery Department's *pièce de résistance*. Despite this he was later captured and shot.
103. B.A. James, *Moonless Night*, 1983.
104. Ken Rees, *Lie in the Dark and Listen*, 2004.
105. Anton Gill, *The Great Escape*, Review, 2002.
106. Sydney Smith, *Wings Day*, William Collins Sons and Co. Ltd., 1968.
107. 'Wings' Day with Group Captain Massey was one of the senior British officers in the North Compound in 1944 and a prominent member of the 'X Organisation'.
108. A.W. Cole, interview with author Nettlecombe, Dorset, 12 July 2008.
109. Described by Day's biographer as 'a slight, deceptively modest young man who had tried every "Over, Under and Through" escape in all the *Luftwaffe* prison camps to which he had been consigned'.
110. B.A. James, *Moonless Night*, 1983.
111. Gill.
112. Ken Rees, *Lie in the Dark and Listen*, 2004. 'Jimmy' James recalled it as 10 feet.
113. The crucial factor about the date stamping was that all the forged passes would become out of date when the month changed.
114. Ibid.
115. Gill.
116. H. Pearce, interview with author, 2007.
117. *After the Battle*, No. 87.
118. Ken Rees, *Lie in the Dark and Listen*, 2004.
119. These fat-burning lamps consisted of small tins filled with boiled down *Ersatz* margarine and a pyjama-cord or bootlace wick. They burned for around an hour before requiring a refill, but were sooty, smelly and above all dangerous. It was intended to use them only for emergencies, which in the event, they were. The tins were probably cut down American 'KLIM' or powdered milk tins, supplied by the Red Cross. These were also used for the air supply ducting.
120. Sqn Ldr James Catanach was a 23-year old Australian pilot and fluent German-speaker who had formerly flown Hampdens. He was shot down on 6 September 1942 and crash-landed in Norway. He was the one escaper from the tunnel that Laurie Simpson knew personally.
121. Flt/Lt R.B. Langlois DFC was shot down on 5 August 1941 whilst piloting a 12 Squadron Wellington from Binbrook on a raid to Aachen. He evaded for almost two months, and was arrested on 2 October 1941 and sent to *Stalag Luft* I.
122. P/O L. Reavell-Carter, later described by Brickhill as 'a 'big burly air gunner' was from a 49 Squadron Hampden, on a minelaying trip from Scampton on 26 June 1940, which was hit by Flak and crash-landed in the Kaiser Wilhelm Canal.
123. Shand was a New Zealand Spitfire pilot.
124. Brickhill.
125. Accounts differ. Brickhill thought Reavell-Carter shouted '*Nicht shiessen, postern! Nicht schiessen!*'

According to Ken Rees, however, it was Len Trent who got up and shouted, with Reavell-Carter right beside him. Reavell-Carter, Rees said, thought Trent mispronounced it and shouted '*Nicht scheissen! Nicht scheissen!*' In other words '*Don't shit! 'Don't shit!*' only adding to the German's confusion.

126. Gill.
127. Brickhill. Gill thought Trent was 'halfway out' of the exit, rather than lying on the ground.
128. A.W. Cole, interview with author, Dorset, July 2008.
129. Ken Rees, *Lie in the Dark and Listen*, 2004.
130. F. Stone, letter to author, 2008.
131. L.J. Simpson, interview with author, 1995.
132. A.F. James, personal memoir, 1995.
133. P.G. Royle was a former Whitley pilot from Western Australia who was shot down on his first operation. He survived the war.
134. Gill and Alan Burgess, *The Longest Tunnel*, 1990.
135. Catanach was a fluent German speaker who had formerly flown Hampdens. He was shot down on 6 September 1942 and crash-landed in Norway.
136. This was detailed in Gill's version of the Great Escape, and appears to have been based on a post-war German eye-witness report.
137. Post was captured in 1947 and gave an account of what happened in March 1944 to the British. He was an unregenerate Nazi and showed no remorse. He was tried in February 1948, found guilty of murder, and hanged with Kahler and seven others.
138. Gill.
139. L.J. Simpson, interview with author, 1993.
140. Ibid.
141. Every German POW camp had a small fire pool in case of emergencies should a fire occur.
142. J. Leakey, letter to author, 2008.
143. R. Fuller, letter to author, 2008.
144. A.F. James, personal memoir, 1995.
145. Ibid.
146. Ibid.
147. C. Younger, *No Flight from the Cage*.
148. D. Thorpe, letter to author, 2008.
149. H. Coverley, interview with author, 2007.

Chapter Twenty

1. The amount of possessions a POW had varied according to the person. In *Stalag Luft* III many important papers were stuffed down the new tunnel 'George' to be reclaimed after the war. Johnny Rydings '…ate as much as he could and destroyed the rest'. Geoff Willatt had to leave behind half the essential things he had put aside earlier, including all his notebooks 'representing 18 months' work for exams.' Paul Brickhill, as stated, carried all the notes he had made about the escape from 'Harry' and of the interviews that he had conducted with newly arrived POWs, in a huge sack on his person. Food was an essential and given priority. Consequently many personal accoutrements had to be left behind by heartbroken *Kriegies*, either in the camp or along the wayside during the great trek.
2. Prisoners who knew the latest 'gen', or information, on what was happening.
3. A 'housewife', in this case, would probably have been a roll of material or a small bag containing a needle and thread, a pair of scissors or a small knife, some string or thread, and possibly surgical bandages.
4. 'Klim' was an American milk substitute supplied by the Red Cross in sealed tins. These proved extremely useful when constructing the air ducting for the tunnels in *Stalag Luft* III.
5. Willatt's book erroneously states 19 January.
6. This was not the Buchenwald with the concentration camp, which was further to the south-west.
7. Rydings suggests that the Germans had not given the North Compound groups a hot meal for seven days, whereas Hodgkinson's East Compound contingent, from his own account, received their first hot meal on 31 January – two days earlier. These accounts were compiled entirely separately and make no account of lapses in memory.
8. Peter Fanshawe was a former lieutenant commander in the Fleet Air Arm who had led the escape committee in *Stalag Luft* I and was responsible for sand dispersal during the 'Great Escape' from *Stalag Luft* III. His character is recognisable as one of the leading personalities, Ashley-Pitt, in the Hollywood representation of the escape which was based upon him. He received his nickname because he was 'very Dartmouth', i.e. an officer with an aristocratic bearing.

9. Quoted in Nichol and Rennell's *The Last Escape*. Sqn/Ldr F.J. Hartnell-Beavis, a former 76 Squadron pilot who had the DFC, was on his second tour when he was downed by *Major* Werner Streib of I./NJG1. All of his crew, apart from the w/op, Sgt R.A. Smith, were killed. Hartnell-Beavis was arrested after nearly two weeks of evasion, at Eindhoven.
10. These towns are all well to the east of Hamburg, which itself was over 20 miles east of Tarmstadt, suggesting that Laurie and his comrades had left *Marlag Nord* some time before their liberation and were in another camp at Trenthorst. It was not uncommon for German guards to leave their prisoners to their fate before the Allies arrived.
11. i.e. they crossed over the Elbe from the east back to the west.
12. Now Sulingen.
13. L.J. Simpson, *Service Diary*.

Chapter Twenty One

1. Quoted in *Tail End Charlies*, J. Nichol and T. Rennell, 2008.
2. Ibid.
3. R. Brown MBE, interview with author, 2008.
4. D.M. Lambert MBE, interview with author, 2007.
5. L. Cheshire, *The Hidden World*, Collins, 1981.
6. P. Bates, letter to author, 2008.

Epilogue

1. The 'Stork Ship' was so named because many of the homebound wives of ex-servicemen who were on board, were expectant mothers. There was a post-war baby boom in 1946.
2. 'Top Germans' – in other words, the German High Command.
3. Based upon G. Flanagan's personal memoir, 1990s and interview with author, 2008.
4. Johnny Rydings preferred to be called 'Jack' in later life.
5. Harris.

Conclusions

1. There are some sources that claim Harris never visited his operational squadrons. This is untrue. It should be stated that photographic evidence in the Australian War Museum archives shows that Harris visited at least 460 Squadron, meeting Hughie Edwards and the No. 1 Group commander, AV-M Rice, at Binbrook on 16 September 1943.
2. This was one of a number of speeches Harris made after the war where he made similar remarks.

SOURCES AND BIBLIOGRAPHY

Archive Sources
UK National Archives, Kew, London.
Imperial War Museum, London, (Sound Archive).
RAF Museum, Hendon, London.
Australian War Memorial, Canberra.
National Archives of Australia.

Unpublished Personal Memoirs
Baker, Tom, *RAF Notebook for Workshop and Laboratory Records*, 1941–42.
Banyard, Peter, unpublished memoir, 2007.
Buckham, Bruce A., *Sink the Tirpitz*, and *Shoot the Train*, unpublished memoirs.
Carman, W.G., *Three Times Lucky*, privately published memoir, 2001.
Carter, Bert, *Bert Carter's Wartime Memories*, unpublished memoir, 2008.
Cartwright, Ronald, *The Royal Air Force*, 2008.
Child, Roy, unpublished memoir, 2008.
Clarke, Arthur, *The Battle of Berlin*, unpublished memoir, 2009.
Cleaver, Reginald, *Life as a Kriegie*, 2008.
Cross, Roy, *POW Log Book*, 2008.
Dennis, Frank, *Flying with the Canadians*, 2008.
Duplock, Sidney A.F., unpublished memoir, 2008.
Farren, Ronald B., unpublished memoir.
Finch, Roy, *World War 2 Memories*, 2008.
Flanagan, George, unpublished memoir, 1990s.
Foinette, Eric, unpublished memoir, 1990s.
Frisby, A.B., *POW Diary*, 2005.
Geddes, John, unpublished memoir, 2008.
Grimer, J.A., *Recollections and Anecdotes*, 2008.
Higgs, Bill *The Last Flight of Halifax Mk. 2 W7657*, 2007.
  My Bomber Command Story, 2008.
  My Experiences as a Prisoner of War from 19 Sept. 1942-1 May 1945, 2008.
Hill, Les, *Molly's Air Trip*, 2008.
Hodgkinson, Derek W., *Per Adua ad Astra* [edited extracts], 1988.
Hope, S. 'Paddy', *Transcript of Tape 335*, 2008.
Hughes, Peter A., *My War 3*, private memoir, ca 1990.
Hughes, Peter A., *My POW Experience*, private memoir, ca 1990.
Jackson, S., *Steve Jackson's War 1939-1946*, 2008.
James, Alan F., *Letter to Squadron Leader Jack Curry* (inc. memoir), 1995.
Knott, Ken, *RAF Bomber Command: One Pilot's Story*, 2008.
Latham, Sgt. R.A. DFM, *Brief Accounts of World War II Experiences (Selected from The Turret, the Journal of the Air Gunners' Association)*.
Mahncke, J.O.E.O. (Jochen), *The German Air Force Anti-Aircraft Auxiliaries 1943-1945 (Luftwaffenhelfer)*, unpublished personal memoir, 2008.
March, Alec (pseudonym), *Lady of the Night*, unpublished memoir and other recollections, 2008.
Nunn, John, *My War*, unpublished memoir, 1992.
Parsons, Lew, *The Wartime History of Warrant Officer Lewis Patrick Parsons, RAF Volunteer Reserve*.
Philpot J., *Jim's Story*, unpublished memoir, 1990s.
Raymond, R.F. 'Dick', *My Service Life*, unpublished memoir, 2008.
Rowe, H.R. 'Sandy', unpublished memoir, 2007 and other recollections.
Rydings, J.A., *POW Log Book*, 1944–1945.
Schrock, A.R.B., *POW Log Book*, 1944–1945.
Searle, Ron, personal newspaper archive collection, 1943.
Simpson, L.J., *RAAF Service Diary*, 1941-1945. *Flying with 460 Squadron RAAF*, unpublished memoir, 1984.
Skeet, Jill, *Enemies No More*, unpublished 467 Squadron memoir, 2003.
Slade, Keith, *RAFly Speaking*, unpublished memoir, *1990s*.
Wagner, Henry, *'Pilot to Navigator, Where are We?' The Personal Account of a Wartime Navigator*.
Williams, J.V., *A Timely reminder – No Turning Back* and *W.O. J.V. Williams Service History 29/11/43 to 14/1/45*.
Younger, Calton, extract from *Bomber Command Roadshow* script, 1990s.

SOURCES AND BIBLIOGRAPHY

Periodicals
After the Battle magazine Nos. 87 & 106.

Published books
Andrews, C.F. *The Vickers Wellington I and II*, Profile Publications Ltd, 1966.
Arct, Squadron Leader B., *Prisoner of War: My Secret Journal*, Webb and Bower, 1988.
Arthur, Max, *Forgotten Voices of the Second World War*, Ebury Press, 2008. *Dambusters*, Virgin, 2008.
Barker, Ralph, *Strike Hard, Strike Sure*, Pan, 1963.
Beck, Pip, *Keeping Watch*, Goodall Publications, 2004.
Bennett, Air Vice-Marshal D.C.T., *Pathfinder*, Goodall Publications, 1983.
Bingham, Victor, *Major Piston Engines of World War II*, Airlife Publishing Ltd, 1998.
Bishop, Patrick, *Bomber Boys: Fighting Back 1939-1945*, Harper Press, 2007.
Bowman, Martin, W. & Boiten, Theo, *Raiders of the Reich*, Airlife Publishing Ltd, 2003.
Bowyer, Chaz, *Guns in the Sky: the Air Gunners of World War Two*, J.M. Dent and Sons Ltd, 1979.
  Tales from the Bombers, William Kimber and Co. Ltd, 1985.
Brickhill, P., *The Great Escape*, 1951.
  The Dam Busters, Pan, 1955.
  Reach for the Sky, Fontana, 1968.
  Escape or Die, Cassell, 2003.
Brickhill, Paul & Norton, Conrad, *Escape to Danger*, Faber and Faber Ltd, 1946.
Brook, John Heath ('Jack'), *No Bacon and Eggs Tonight*, Creativelines, Southport, Lancashire, 2002. (ISBN 0-9542841-0-0)
Bushby, John E.P., *Saltbush Country: History of the Deniliquin District*, privately published, 1980.
Buttigieg, P., *We Weep No More*, Aquila Services Ltd, 1992.
Carruthers, Percy W., *Of Ploughs, Planes and Palliasses*, Woodfield Publishing, 1992.
Chandler, Chan, *Tail Gunner: 99 Raids in World War Two*, Airlife Publishing Ltd, 1999.
Charlwood, Don, *No Moon Tonight*, Goodall Publications, 1984.
Chorley, W.R., *Bomber Command Losses 1939-1945, (Vols. 1-9)*, Midland Publishing, 1994–2000.
Churchill, Winston S., *The Second World War*, Reprint Society, 1946.
Clutton-Brock, H., *Footprints in the Sands of Time*, Grub Street, 2003.
Cockburn, Claude, *The Devil's Decade*, Sedgwick and Jackson, 1973.
Cooper, Alan, *Born Leader: the Life of Guy Gibson*, Independent Books, 1993.
Crankshaw, Edward, *Gestapo*, NEL, 1973.
Currie, Jack, *Lancaster Target*, Goodall Publications, 1981.
Darlow, Steve, *Five of the Many*, Grub Street, 2007.
De Bruhl, Marshall, *Firestorm: Allied Airpower and the Destruction of Dresden*, Random House, 2006.
Deighton, Len, *Blood, Tears and Folly*, Pimlico, 1993.
Dimbleby, Jonathan, *Richard Dimbleby*, Hodder and Stoughton, 1975.
Durand, Arthur A., *Stalag Luft III: The Secret Story*, Patrick Stephens Ltd, 1988.
Dymond, F.E., *A Very Special Lancaster*, RAF Museum, 1976.
Evans, Tom Parry, *Squadron Leader Tommy Broom DFC*, Pen and Sword, 2007.
Foot, M.R.D. and Langley, J.M., *MI9*, Bodley Head, 1979.
Foreman, J., Matthews, J. and Parry, S., *Luftwaffe Night Fighter Combat Claims, 1939–1945*, 2004, Red Kite.
Forrester, L., *Fly for Your Life*, Panther, 1958.
Gale, Dr. Vanessa, *Fighting Chance: War, Popular Belief and British Society 1900–1951*, University of Liverpool Press, 2011.
Garbett, Mike and Goulding, Brian, *The Lancaster at War*, Ian Allan Ltd, 1971.
Gilbert, Adrian, *POW: Prisoners of War in Europe, 1939–1945*, John Murray, 2006.
Gibson Guy, *Enemy Coast Ahead*, Michael Joseph Ltd, 1946.
Grayling, A.C., *Among the Dead Cities*, Bloomsbury, 2007.
Haddaway, Stuart, *Missing Believed Killed*, Arms and Armour Press, 2008.
Harris, Marshal of the RAF Sir Arthur, *Bomber Offensive*, Pen and Sword, 2005.
Harsh, George, *Lonesome Road*, Sphere, 1976.
Harvey-Bailey, A.H., *The Merlin in Perspective: The Combat Years*, Rolls-Royce Heritage Trust, 1987.
Hastings, Max, *Bomber Command*, Pan, 1982.
Hehner, Barbara, *The Tunnel King*, Harper Trophy Canada, 2004.
Herrmann, Hajo, *Eagle's Wings: the Autobiography of a Luftwaffe Pilot*, Guild Publishing, 1991.
Holloway, Graham R. (ed.), *East Devon Aircrew and Airfields*, East Devon Aircrew Association, 2000.

Touchdown: East Devon, East Devon Aircrew Association, 2003.
Final Touchdown, East Devon Aircrew Association, 2005.
Irving, David, *Apocalypse 1945: The Destruction of Dresden,* Focal Point Publications, 1995. *Hitler's War,* Focal Point Publications, 2001.
The Mare's Nest, Panther Books, 1985.
The War between the Generals, Penguin, 1982.
James B.A. 'Jimmy', *Moonless Night,* Pen and Sword, 2008.
Johnson, *RAAF over Europe,* Eyre and Spottiswoode, 1945.
Johnson, Peter, *The Withered Garland,* 1995.
Knott, Richard, *Black Night for Bomber Command,* Arms and Armour Press, 2007.
Lambert, Max, *Night after Night: New Zealanders in Bomber Command,* Harper Collins, 2005.
Lewis, Bruce, *Air Crew,* Orion, 1995.
Macksey, Kenneth, *Military Errors of World War Two,* Cassell, 2002.
Manchester, William, *The Arms of Krupp, 1857–1968,* Michael Joseph, 1969.
McKinstry, Leo, *Lancaster: the Second World War's Greatest Bomber,* John Murray, 2010.
Messenger, Charles, *'Bomber' Harris and the Strategic Bombing Offensive, 1939–1945,* Arms and Armour Press, 1984.
Middlebrook, Martin, *The Nuremberg Raid,* Allen Lane, 1980. *The Berlin Raids,* Pan, 1990. *The Battle of Hamburg,* Cassell and Co., 2000.
Middlebrook, Martin and Everitt, Chris, *The Bomber Command War Diaries,* Viking 1985.
Morris, Richard, *Cheshire: the Biography of Leonard Cheshire VC, OM,* Viking, 2000.
Moyes, P.J.R., *Bomber Squadrons of the R.A.F. and their Aircraft,* Macdonald and Janes, 1976. *The Handley Page Halifax, B. III, VI, VII,* Profile Publication Ltd, 1965.
Neillands, Robin, *The Bomber War,* John Murray, 2000.
Nelson, Hank, *Chased by the Sun: Australians in Bomber Comnmand,* Allen and Unwin, 2002.
Neufeld, M.J. and Berenbaum, M., *The Bombing of Auschwitz,* University Press of Kansas, 2003.
Nichol, John & Tony Rennell, *The Last Escape,* Viking, 2002. *Tail End Charlies,* Penguin/Viking, 2004.
Niner, Flt. Lt. Aubrey, *Low Level Casualty,* from *A20 Boston at War,* by W. Hess, Ian Allan Ltd.
Norris, Geoffrey, *The Short Stirling,* Profile Publications Ltd, 1966.
Ottis, S. G., *Silent Heroes: Downed Airmen and the French Underground,* University Press of Kentucky, 2001.
Ovary, Richard, *Interrogations,* Allen Lane/The Penguin Press, 2001. *Reaping the Whirlwind: Bomber Command 1939–1945,* Harper Collins, 1997.
Pickering, Sylvia, *Tales of a Bomber Command WAAF,* Woodfield, 2002.
Pitchfork, Graham, *Shot Down and on the Run,* National Archives, 2003.
Pitt, Barry (ed.), *History of the Second World War Vols. 1–8,* Purnell, 1967-68.
Potten Charles, *7 x X x 90: the Story of a Stirling Bomber and its Crew,* K. Gandy and C. Potten 1986.
Price, Alfred, *The Junkers Ju 88 Night Fighters,* Profile Publications Ltd, 1967.
Probert, Henry, *Bomber Harris His Life and Times,* Greenhill Books, 2003.
Raymond Robert S., *A Yank in Bomber Command,* David and Charles, 1977.
Rees Ken, *Lie in the Dark and Listen,* Grub Street, 2004.
Rees, Lawrence, *The Nazis: a Warning from History,* BBC Books, 1997.
Rolfe, Mel, *To Hell and Back,* Grub Street, 1999. *Hell on Earth,* Grub Street, 1999.
Rowe, Mark, *The Day the Dump Went Up/ One in a Thousand / The Flying Kangaroos,* privately published, 2004.
Sawyer, Group Captain G.W. 'Tom', DFC, *Only Owls and Bloody Fools Fly at Night,* Goodall Publications, 1985.
Scangriff (*Stalag Luft* III newspaper), *Spotlight on Stalag Luft III,* 1945.
Scotland, Lt. Col. A.P., *The London Cage,* Evans Brothers Ltd, 1957.
Smith, Graham, *Devon and Cornwall Airfields in the Second World War,* Countryside Books, 2000.
Smith, Sydney, *Wings Day,* Collins, 1968.
Speer, Albert, *Inside the Third Reich,* BCA, 1971.
Sweetman, John, *Bomber Crew: Taking on the Reich,* Abacus, 2005. *Tirpitz: Hunting the Beast,* Sutton Publishing Ltd, 2000.
Taylor, James and Davidson, Martin, *Bomber Crew,* Hodder and Stoughton, 2005.
Thetford, Owen, *Aircraft of the Royal Air Force 1918-1966,* Putnam, 1966.
Toliver, Raymond, *The Interrogator: The Story of Hans Scharff, The Luftwaffe's Master Interrogator* Aero Publishers, 1978.
Tripp, Miles, *The Eighth Passenger* (Revised Edition), Wordsworth Editions, 1985.

Vourkoutiotis, V., *Prisoners of War and the German High Command*, 2003.
Watt, Clive (ed.), *Upside Down and Nothing on the Clock: Memories of the Woking Branch Aircrew Association*, 1990s.
Wells, Mark K. *Courage and Air Warfare: The Allied Aircrew Experience in the Second World War*, Frank Cass and Co. Ltd, 1995/2000.
Willatt, Geoffrey, *Bombs and Barbed Wire*, Upfront Publishing, 1995.
Wilson, Kevin, *Bomber Boys: The Ruhr, the Dams and Bloody Berlin*, Weidenfeld and Nicholson, 2005.
  Men of Air: the Doomed Youth of Bomber Command, 1944, Weidenfeld and Nicholson, 2007.
Yates, Harry, *Luck and a Lancaster: Chance and Survival in World War Two*, Airlife, 2005.
Younger, Cal, *No Flight from the Cage*, Frederick Muller, 1956.
Zuckerman, Lord Solly, *S.Z. and the RAF*, Chapter 30 in *High Flyers*, Greenhill Books, 1993.

INDEX OF PERSONNEL

Abraham, Sqn Ldr R.B. 'Abie', 263
Adam, Flt Lt, 28
Alexander, Jim, 280-282
Alkamede, Sgt Nicholas, 242, 243
Andrew, Bruce, 90
Annetts, Flt Lt John, 215, 216
Appleton, Bob, 92
Arct, Sqn Ldr B., 356
Attlee, Clement, 403
Auty, Sgt E., 169
Bader, Douglas, 111, 316, 348
Bailey, Sqn Ldr, 67
Baker, Tom, 28
Baldwin, Stanley, 7
Bannick, Hans, 141
Banyard, Peter, 4, 40, 51, 88
Barnett, Warrant Officer, 16
Barr, Flight Sergeant D., 259
Barton, Cyril Joe, 119
Bastian, Eileen, 98
Bateman, Dennis, 26, 344, 400
Bateman, Jerry, 103
Bates, Phillip, 33, 34, 358, 396
Baxter, Sgt, 174
Bazalgette, Ian Willoughby, 119
Beauregard, Sergeant C.M., 270
Beck, Hanz, 274
Beck, Pip, 96
Becker, Oberleutnant Martin, 242
Bell, Dr. George, 394
Bell, W.G., 228
Bennett, AVM Donald, 93, 94, 102, 108, 122, 123, 126, 142, 156, 157, 159, 178, 191, 211, 244, 245, 249, 326, 405
Bennett, Ray, 142
Bennett, Pilot Officer R.K. 'Rex', 145, 225, 229
Berger, SS-Obergruppenführer und General der Waffen-SS Gottlob, 377

Berndt, E.J., 90
Berry, Sgt Dave, 272
Berry, Stan, 32
Bethell, Tony, 367
Bicknell, Charlie, 106
Birkland, Henry, 367
Birt, G.R., 262
Bispham, Bill, aka 'Thompson', 14
Boelcke, Oswald, 392
Bond, Sqn Ldr K.F.P., 305
Bonham-Carter, Group Captain David, 86, 87, 140
Bonin, Oberleutnant Eckart-Wilhelm von, 90
Boorman, E.M., 'Ted', 17, 19, 33, 36-38, 41, 55, 138, 243, 278, 279, 283, 372, 397, 400
Bottomley, Air Vice-Marshal, 210
Boulton, Alan, 142
Bourke, Flying Officer T., 266
Bowes-Cavanagh, Derek, 294
Box, Dougie, 107
Boyer, Doug, 156
Bracewell, Flt Lt John, 169, 170, 241
Bradburn, F/O G., 125
Braeder, Oberst, 327
Bray, Bill, 221
Brewell, Colonel, 328
Brickhill, Paul, 359, 360, 368, 369, 400, 405
Brill, Wg/Cdr Bill, 66, 89
Brittingham, Flight Sergeant R.A., 153
Brodie, 'Butch', 390
Brodrick, Flt Lt Les, 82, 366, 367
Brook, Jack, 104, 160, 327, 332-334, 338, 396
Brooke, General Sir Alan, 253
Brooks, H.G., 151
Broom, Sqn Ldr Ivor, 126

Broom, Flt Lt Thomas John 'Tommy', 126, 127
Brown, Ken, 402
Brown, Reg, 37, 38, 48, 49, 73, 184, 194, 196, 216, 241, 397, 400
Brown, Ronald, 5
Brown, Sgt, 329
Bryett, P/O Alan E., 54, 82, 87, 104, 213, 216, 217, 350, 351
Buckham, Bruce, 140
Bufton, Group Captain Sidney O., 122, 123
Buhlmann, Unteroffizier, 272
Bull, Johnny, 364, 366, 367
Burnham, Flight Lieutenant, 89
Burniston, George, 90
Burns, Robert 'Bob', 3, 90
Burwell, Sgt Geoffrey, 242, 243
Bushell, Roger, 316, 347, 352-354, 360-367, 375, 376
Butt, Mr. D.M., 113
Buttigieg, Peter 346-349, 375, 396
Campbell, 'Scotty', 95
Canaris, Admiral Wilhelm, 247
Canthell, Fred, 172
Carey, Flight Sergeant, 142
Carman, Bill, 77, 232
Carruthers, Percy, 388, 389
Carter, Bert, 144, 145, 225, 227, 228, 321
Carter, Nick, 118, 121
Cartwright, Ronald, 11, 289, 290, 346, 358, 372, 388
Casey, Flying Officer Mike, 316
Cassie, Alex, 369
Castle, Alan, 12, 24, 25, 45, 78, 83, 86, 117, 119, 121, 128, 134, 195, 248, 257
Catanach, James, 'Jimmy', 367, 371
Cave, Vic, 291, 292, 322
Cave Brown, Anthony, 247, 248

Chadwick, Dave, 161
Chadwick, Roy, 23
Chamberlain, Neville, 9, 73, 220
Chandler, 'Chan, 93, 110
Chapman, Floyd, 281
Charlick, Flight Sergeant Dave, 66, 351
Charlton, Flight Sergeant W.R.K. 'Bill', 66, 154
Charlwood, Don, 62, 66, 69, 70, 88, 235, 400, 402, 405
Cheeseman, Flight Sergeant Jack A., 294, 395
Cherwell, 1st Viscount (Frederick Alexander Lindemann), 113-115, 182
Cheshire, Leonard, 93, 110, 119, 127, 129, 248, 257, 295, 397, 401
Chesson, mu/g, Sgt L.G., 216
Child, Flt Lt A.J., 295
Child, Roy, 237-239
Christensen, Arnold, 371
Christie, Sergeant Robert S. 'Bob', 165, 172
Churchill, Winston, 8, 23, 39, 113, 114, 150, 152, 162, 182, 183, 189, 207-209, 213, 247, 253, 254, 256, 316, 403
Clark, Lt Col Albert, 'Bert', 341, 342, 375
Clarke, Arthur, 213, 217-219
Clayton, Eric, 147
Cleary, Sgt J. P., 242, 243
Cleaver, Reg, 317
Cobham, Sir Alan, 3, 4, 10
Cockburn, Dr. Robert, 181
Codner, Michael, 344, 345
Cole, Arthur W., 5, 19, 34, 36, 56, 76, 92, 109, 130, 180, 183, 184, 188, 197, 202, 203, 219, 220, 318, 322, 352, 353, 355, 358, 363, 365, 369
Collins, A.V., 228
Collins, Reverend John, 394
Conway, Flt Sgt N.J., 222
Corfe, Dudley, 135
Corran, Mary, 78, 98
Corser, E.G.M., 233
Couchman, Sgt Ben, 272
Coulson, Ronald, 25, 26, 41, 90
Coulter, Bob, 379
Coverley, Henry D. 'Roger', 67, 84, 87, 93, 128, 129, 196, 199, 246, 325-327, 372, 373, 375, 390, 401
Crabtree, Morris, 400
Craven, Wg/Cdr, 169
Cripps, Sir Stafford, 394

Crockatt, Norman, 287
Cross, George, 318, 334
Cull, Sgt, 230
Curran, Joan, 181-182
Currie, Jack, 38
Curtiss, Flt Sgt D., 225
Dack, Flying Officer John I., 141
Dahl, Flight Lieutenant Roald, 106
Danckwardt, Fred, 6, 30, 51, 53, 75, 85-87, 198, 202, 203
Daniels, Wg/Cdr S.P., 237
David, Henri, 304
Davidson, Flight Sergeant Alan, 142
Davidson, P/O L.N., 270
Davies, E.M.L., 228
Davies, Airman William, 106
Davis, Sqn Ldr K.G., 239
Davis, Sgt, 28
Day, Wg/Cdr Harry ('Wings' or 'Pricky'), 315, 316, 337, 348, 351, 365-367, 400
Dean, John, 30, 194
Deans, James 'Dixie', 347, 375, 400
Deegan, Sqn Ldr, 138
Denham, Hardy, 90
Dennis, Frank, 21, 22, 33, 35, 85-86, 137-139, 195, 396, 397
Devitt, 'Dismal', 13, 14, 337
Dicken, Group Captain, 146
Dilworth, Wg Cdr J., 67
Dimbleby, Richard, 135-137, 152
Dixon, Sgt, 231
Dodge, Major John, 316, 367
Dolata, Edmund, 31
Doubleday, Arthur, 89
Dowling, Warrant Officer T.E. 'Terry', 225, 227
Dowse, Sydney 'Fingers', 112, 366, 367
Drake, R.V., 'Ron', 120
Drewes, Hauptmann Martin, 242
Driscoll, Danny, 105
Duckham, Sgt George R., 263
Duffill, Flight Lieutenant A.V., 143
Duplock, Sid, 311, 312, 338
Eaker, General Ira C., 195, 209, 210
Edmondson, Sgt D.S., 260, 261
Edwards, Grp. Capt. Hughie, 66, 84, 85, 110-112, 119, 148, 228, 234, 402

Edwards, Ken, 110
Edwards, Sgt D.J., 228
Eisenhower, General Dwight D., 240, 249, 251-257, 259
Elford, Norman, 30
Ellingstad, Sid, 269, 401
Elliot, John, 113
Ellis, Allen, 402
Engelhorn, Major, 248
Evans, F/L Brian, 364, 371
Evans, Charles, 194
Evans, Ron, 44
Evans, Tom, 126
Evill, Sir Douglas, 208
Fahey, 'Shorty', 67
Falkenmire, Flying Officer 'Frankie', 66, 351
Falkiner, Flt Lt John, 67
Fanshawe, Peter 'Hornblower', 361, 389
Farren, Ronald, 73, 78, 132
Faulkner, John, 35
Fawcett, G.R., 69
Fellowes, David M., 85, 86, 165
Fernie, Roy, 358
ffrench-Mullen, Flt. Lt. D.A., 343, 375
Finch, Roy, 96
Finlay, D.W. ('Bish'), 201, 214, 351, 382
Finnegan, Paddy, 276, 277, 396
Firkins, Peter, 233
Fish, Freddy, 144
Fisher, Sgt, 28
Flanagan, George, 268, 269, 283, 401
Floody, Wally, 352, 361, 362, 364, 375
Foinette, Eric, 14, 18, 83, 263, 264, 283, 341-345
Forrester, Lennie, 67
Fraser, David, 25
Fraser-Smith, Charles, 309
Frayers, Reg, 43, 202
Freeman, Ted 'Blue', 66
Freeman, Sir Wilfred, 23, 39
Freeman, Wg/Cdr, 74, 75
Friend, Ron, 153
Frisby, Bernard, 194
Fuglesang, Nils, 371
Fuller, Alan, 90, 373
Fulton, Sgt, 159
Galbraith, J.K., 189
Garment, P/O, 231
Gaston, Bruce, 90
Geddes, John, 6, 107, 138, 200, 245
Gemm, Wg/Cdr Steve, 167
Gerrard, Doug, 270

INDEX OF PERSONNEL

Gibby, Peter, 6, 85
Gibson, Guy Penrose, 110, 111, 119, 127, 136, 402
Giersch, Eric, 140
Gildner, Oberfeldwebel Paul, 294
Gill, Robert H.J., 188, 270, 271
Gillies, Len, 91
Goebbels, Dr. Joseph, 112, 159, 160, 187, 189, 210, 243, 361
Goemans, Kais, 276, 277
Goodrum, John, 3
Gorell, Bert, 103
Göring, Reichsmarschall Hermann, 160, 161, 179, 187, 210, 224, 316, 320, 328, 341
Gorton, W.A., 219, 220
Goulding, Flying Officer John, 268, 269
Goulevitch, Jan/John, 7, 103
Gourlay, Flt Lt J.L. 'Jim', 225
Grange, Flight Sergeant Alan, 239
Grant, Gordon, 151
Gray, Flt Sgt Don, 119, 246, 247
Green, 'Pop', 367
Gregory, Norman E., 270, 283
Gregory, Airman, 91
Gregson, Gordon, 90
Greiner, Hauptmann Hermann, 279
Grenfell, Flight Lieutenant K.H., 154, 161, 351
Grimer, P/O John, 305, 401
Groom, Ted, 49, 68, 84, 103, 109, 182-187, 201, 221, 395
Guillevan, Francis, 138
Guingand, Major-General Sir Francis de, 247, 248
Hadley, R., 230
Hahey, P/O Les, 216
Hall, Charles, 364
Halldor, Espelid, 371
Hamlin, F/O, 103
Hammett, 'Digger', 92
Hampden, John, 26
Handley Page, Frederick, 23
Harkin, Dave, 272
Harmer, Sergeant E., 106
Harris, Air Chief Marshal Sir Arthur T 'Bomber', 33, 58, 59, 70, 80, 113-117, 122, 123, 127, 150, 152, 156, 157, 171, 178, 182-4, 190, 191, 196, 207-211, 213, 220, 224, 232, 233, 237, 240, 241, 244, 247-249, 251-259, 266, 394, 403, 405-407

Harrison, Sgt J.B., 142, 239
Harsh, George, 260, 267, 268, 283, 323, 352, 361-362, 375, 401
Hart, Edward J., 163-165
Hartnell-Beavis, John, 391
Hatcliffe, L/Ac, 48, 50
Haussmann, Lt. Ulrich, 320
Hawke, W.C. ('Admiral'), 351
Hayward, Larry, 106
Heath, Geoff, 89, 174
Heath, Ron, 277, 307, 396, 401
Hedgeland, Philip, 123
Heiden, R.W.F., 'Ron', 138, 279
Hermann, Oberst Hans Joachim, 'Hajo', 169, 183, 184, 187, 190, 191, 193, 223, 241, 326
Hesketh, Air Cdre., 86, 140
Hester, Roy, 344
Hewittson, Jack, 31
Heydrich, SS-Obergruppenführer Reinhard, 247, 362
Higgs, W.E.G., 33, 35, 47, 48, 75, 76, 81, 93, 94, 105, 116, 119, 123-125, 129, 180, 196, 295-298, 336, 372, 375, 396
Hill, Les, 3, 95
Himmler, Reichsführer-SS Heinrich, 320, 361, 377
Hinwood, James Alan F., 29
Hitler, Adolf 8, 9, 157, 163, 166, 176, 179, 189, 191-193, 210, 223, 224, 253, 303, 307, 323, 328, 354, 359, 361, 377, 388, 394, 397, 407
Hobgen, P /O, 305
Hockin, Federick George, 48
Hodgkinson, Derek, 13, 97, 120, 121, 244, 290, 290-292, 319, 322, 337, 341-343, 345, 346, 357, 380, 391
Holborrow, Sgt, 266
Holes, Leslie, 55, 130
Holford, Wg/Cdr David, 68-70, 148, 324
Holland, J.C.F., 287
Holmes, Anne, 100
Holmes, Dorothy, 65, 80, 89, 90, 98-100, 151, 153, 155, 158, 161, 162, 165, 171, 172, 174, 175, 304, 393, 399
Homewood, Eric, 29, 31
Hookings, Eric, 332, 352, 355, 358
Hoorn, Flying Officer, 67
Hope, Stanley, 'Paddy', 303, 304
Horne, Dick, 90

Hornibrook, Flt Lt Kevin, 216, 217
Howell, David, 43, 199
Hughes, Peter, 288, 326, 327, 346, 401
Hughes, Sgt R.D., 331
Humphreys, Edgar, 'Hunk', 13, 363, 367, 370, 371
Hunter, Robin, 'Jock', 268
Hunter, Flt Lt, 101
Hutchinson, P/O, 169
Ilk, Hauptmann Iro, 242
Ingram, Geoff, 270
Ingram, Harry, 401
Irvine, 'Jock', 318
Jackson, Dr Derek, 182
Jackson, Pete, 151
Jackson, Steve, 5, 35, 55, 92, 104, 119, 180, 260, 270, 271, 283, 355, 401
Jacobs, Flight Sergeant I.D., 270
Jaekel, Flight Sergeant Dave, 167
James, Alan F., 233, 328, 329, 343, 345-347, 365, 370, 374
James, B.A., 'Jimmy', 287, 364, 365, 367
Jenkins, Wg Cdr, 28
Jenkinson, Philip, 183, 185, 223, 224, 401
Jennings, Bill, 389
Johns, Sgt A.I., 279
Johnson, Group Captain Peter, 190, 395
Johnson, Flying Officer, 168
Jones, Sgt A.H., 222
Jones, Harry, 82
Jones, Flight Sergeant J.P., 169
Jones, P.J., 348
Jones, Flying Officer R.A.O., 266
Jones, Professor R.V., 179, 181-183
Jongh, Andree de, 'Dedee', 303
Kahler, Hans, 371
Kammhuber, General Josef, 178
Kaufman, Wg Cdr, 67, 92
Kavanagh, Stan, 142
Kearnes, Johnny, 152, 153
Kearns, Terry, 24
Keitel, Generalfeldmarschall Wilhelm, 361
Kemley, Robert, 'Bob', 16, 42, 45
Kendall, R.E., 'Bob', 177, 178, 318, 332
Kennedy, Alistair, 'Shorty', 64, 65, 77, 100, 135, 153, 154, 158, 159, 170, 174, 175, 203,

233-236, 298, 299, 350, 351, 358, 402
Kennedy, Val P., 118
Kennure, F.R. 'Fosannack', 351
Kenyon, Ley, 359, 360
Kerl, SS-Obergruppenführer, 184
Kerr, Sergeant, 25
Kerr-Ramsay, 'Crump', 364, 367, 370
Keys, Flt Lt Graeme Connor 'The Baron', 15, 16, 20, 60, 61-67, 98, 100-103, 120, 151, 158, 166, 167, 172, 174
Keys, Alice, 101
Kidd, Flt Sgt T.O., 311
Killinger, Ernst, 248
Kine, Sgt, 153
King, Flt Lt Freddie, 67, 77, 88, 153, 169, 170, 241, 367, 402, 403
Kingsford-Smith, Rollo, 140
Kirby, Dr. Robert, 'Bob', 294
Kite, F/O G.R.G., 273-275
Klenner, Flying Officer George, 147, 148, 200
Knight, Noel, 202
Knoblock, Flt Sgt R.E., 265
Knott, Ken, 178
Koltringer, Unteroffizier Christian, 154
Korner, Graham V., 19, 20, 54, 130, 259, 276, 283, 306-308, 317, 324, 331, 372-375, 377, 396, 401
Krupp, Alfried, 166
Krupp, Gustav, 166
Lambert, Dr. Deryck, 125, 318, 333, 397, 401
Lane, Gerald, 3, 33
Langlois, Roy, 367-369
Lawrence, Gertrude, 399
Lawrence, T.E., 401
Leakey, John, 4, 27, 316, 373
Lear, Cliff, 280
Lees, Tom, 18
Leggett, Flying Officer E.R.F. 'Dickie', 239
Leigh-Mallory, Air Chief Marshal Sir Trafford, 183, 252-254, 256
Leith-Hay-Clark, P/O R.L., 295
Lent, Oberstleutnant Helmut, 242, 294
Lester, P/O, 112
Letford, Ken, 221
Letts, Sgt Les, 268
Lewis, N.F. 'Deacon', 351

Liddell, Roy 'Alvar', 358
Lindeiner-Wildau, Oberst Friedrich Wilhelm von, 361
Lines, Peter, 63
Linke, Oberleutnant Lothar, 167
Lippe-Weissenfeld, Hauptmann Egmont Prince zur, 168
Littlefield, WO2 E.E., 263
Livingstone, R., 318
Lloyd, Hadley, 172
Loder, Sgt Graham, 266
Long, 'Cookie', 366
Longbottom, Eric, 65
Lovett, Robert, 251, 257
Ludlow-Hewitt, Sir Edgar, 9, 39
Lundy, Flt Sgt, 264, 265
MacArthur, General Douglas, 101
MacDonald, Gertrude, 6, 155
MacLeod, Flt Sgt G.A.G., 216
Maddern, Geoff, 66, 402
Mahaddie, Hamish, 94
Mahncke, Jochen, 192
Malcolm, Hugh Gordon, 119
Maltby, Walter 'Wally', 67, 88, 169, 349, 370, 396, 402
Mannion, Frank P., 180, 273-275, 283
Manser, P/O Leslie Thomas, 119
Manteuffel, General der Panzertruppe Hasso von, 127
Maple, Warrant Officer J.F., 141
March, Alec, 44, 48, 56, 74, 78, 96, 97, 132, 135, 173, 199, 200, 202, 338
Margerison, Russell, 4, 13, 57, 195, 200, 203, 245
Marks, Wg/Cdr James Hardy 'Jimmy', 93, 94, 295
Marriott, F/O K., 239
Marshall, General George C., 253
Marshall, John, 366
Martin, Wg/Cdr C.E. Harold 'Chad', 67, 87, 99, 112, 113, 136
Martin, Pilot Officer L.C., 166
Maschmann, Melita, 192, 193
Masenthan, Alec, 174
Mason, Rowland, 147
Massey, Grp Cpt Herbert, 342, 348, 354, 360, 365, 371, 400
Masterman, J.C., 247
Mattock, Tony, 172
Maw, Roger, 342, 345, 375
McBride, Bob, 369

McCann, P/O L.M., 242
McCrea, Sergeant Ernie, 167
McCullough, P/O, 158
McFarlane, John, 214
McGillivray, Jim, 52, 241
McGovern, F.J., 87, 129, 216, 251
McGowan, Flt Sgt G., 267
McGrory, 'Mick', 92
McKee, Group Captain 'Square', 75
McKinnon, Ted, 89
McLachlan, W.R., 330
McLeod, Sgt Colin, 'Mac', 64, 65, 100, 170, 172, 175, 233, 234, 236, 299, 300, 350, 351, 402
McNeill, F/O Tom, 66, 137
Meakin, Major, 88
Meikle, Sgt, 243
Middleton, Sgt Pat, 142
Miller, T.B., 347, 348, 375
Mitchell, Jim, 86
Modrow, Hauptmann Ernst-Wilhelm, 274
Montgomery, Field Marshal, 58, 247, 254, 276
Moore, Kay, 161
Morgan, Wyn, 54
Morris, P/O Alec, 60, 62, 161
Morrison, Herbert, 182, 183
Motts, Sergeant, 246
Mould, Muriel, 97
Mountbatten, Lord Louis, 252
Muddle, Johnny, 140
Müller, SS-Gruppenführer Heinrich, 360
Munsch, Joe, 103
Murdoch, Keith, 66, 239, 402
Murphy, Dan, 67
Murphy, Kevin, 67, 223
Murphy, V.J., 270
Mynarski, Charles Andrew, 119
Nagel, Burt, 320
Nairn, James, 'Jock', 175, 233, 234, 236, 299, 349
Naylor, Sgt Jack, 268
Neilson, Bobby, 152
Nelson, Hank, 89
Newberry, Sqn Ldr, 28
Newman, Ken, 68
Newman, Flt Sgt John, 242
Newton, Bert, 161
Nicholls, W/O P.M., 'Nicky', 198
Niven, Hank, 337
Noble, Joe 'Red', 361, 364-367, 370, 383
Norman, Bob, 124

INDEX OF PERSONNEL

Norton, Conrad, 359
Nunn, John, 5, 10, 12, 13, 44, 47, 50, 74, 83, 84, 86, 97, 99, 103, 104, 202, 212, 214, 215, 225, 226, 229-231, 395
Nunn, Edith, 99, 103, 104
Nuttall, Freddie, 119, 276, 277, 308
O'Caine, 'Paddy', 105
O'Malley, Sgt W., 228
O'Riordan, Cliff, 66, 88, 89, 102, 168
Ogilvie, Flt Lt Keith, 369
Oliver, Bruce, 153
Osborn, 'Johnny'/'Jack', 136, 153, 173, 175, 233, 234, 299, 349
Osborne, Flt Lt J.B., 311
Paisley, Sgt F.N., 305
Palmer, Robert, 119
Parsons, Lewis, 'Lew', 5, 47, 106, 107, 331, 332, 372
Passy, Sgt Ian H.D., 294
Paterson, Bill, 63
Patrachenko, Bill, 258, 282
Patterson, H.D., 'Jock', 276-278
Patton, General George S., 252, 257
Payne, Sgt C.F., 263
Payne, Pilot Officer Stanley W., 239, 402
Peach, Flying Officer A.C., 260
Pearce, Beryl, 99
Pearce, Howard, 17, 74, 75, 100, . 116, 223, 327, 354, 358, 360, 363, 366, 367, 369, 370, 401
Pearson, Danny, 353, 354
Peirse, Sir Richard, 113
Pelly, Air Marshal Sir Claude, 190
Pendray, Keith, 42, 275, 283
Percival, F/O, 35
Petley, Wg/Cdr L.V., 111
Petrachenko, Bill, 280
Peveler, Sq Ldr Donald, 'Don', 94, 116, 123
Phillips, Flying Officer Frank, 145, 225
Philpot, Jim, 271-273, 283, 326, 401
Philpott, Oliver, 344-346
Picard, Henri, 364
Pickering, Sylvia, 109
Pidsley, Reg, 221
Pieber, Hauptmann, 354
Pollard, Sqn Ldr, 28
Portal, Marshal of the RAF Charles, 39, 113, 114, 122, 183, 207-209, 213, 253, 255,

256, 258, 403, 406
Post, Johannes, 371
Potten, Charlie, 30, 31, 50, 51
Powell, Flying Officer R.F.B., 238
Powell, Squadron Leader, 88
Power, R.J., 330
Price, Squadron Leader, 108
Purcell, 'Ron', 276, 278
Pyett, Bill, 280-282
Quelch, Bobbie, 107
Quick, Arthur, 100, 101
Quill, Flight Sergeant W.A. 'Bill', 279, 280
Randall, Flying Officer F.H., 222, 231
Ratcliffe, Edward G., 264, 265, 283
Raye, Michael 'Mickie', 351, 382
Raymond, Sgt Dick, 4, 49, 68, 97, 107, 124, 174, 226, 247, 317
Raymond, Robert, 7, 68, 83, 84, 117
Reavell-Carter, Lawrence, 369
Rees, Ken 'Shag', 364-367, 370, 381-383
Reman, Jo, 303
Rhodes, Flt Sgt, 125
Richards, Bruce, 65
Roberts, Harold, 402
Robinson, Ted, 379, 380
Rodger, Asst Adj 'Jolly', 63
Roosevelt, Franklin D., 152, 209, 253, 255
Rowe, 'Sandy', 130, 146, 181, 182, 197, 201, 214, 406
Royce, Henry, 32
Royle, Paul G., 239, 371
Rumpel, Theodore, 316
Rushbrook, G.W., 270
Russel, Noel, 174
Rust, P/O Bruce, 158, 161
Rutherford, Sgt Judge, 63
Ryder, Lady, 20
Rydings, 'Jack'/'Johnny', 66, 173, 175, 233, 234, 236, 239, 299, 350, 351, 355, 379-392, 402
Samuel, Flt Lt, 230
Saundby, Air Marshal Robert 'Sandy', 211, 213, 230, 233, 244
Saunders, P/O R.J.L., 295
Saunders, Flt Sgt, 275
Sawyer, Group Captain Tom, 175, 196
Saxby, 'Sax', 367

Scarff, Arthur, 119
Scarr, Ron, 103
Scharff, Corporal Hanns, 320, 329, 338
Schaw, F.A., 267, 268
Scheidhauer, Bernard, 366
Schmelling, Max, 355
Schmitt, 'Indian', 138, 139
Schnaufer, Oberleutnant Heinz-Wolfgang, 242, 268
Schoenert, Oberleutnant Rudolf, 176
Schrock, Arthur R.B. 'Doc', 90, 117, 118, 121, 122, 169, 173, 175, 233, 234, 236, 299, 300, 350, 351, 355, 357, 379-384, 386, 387, 390-392, 395, 399, 402
Schrock, Mabel, 395
Scutt, R.A., 311
Searby, Donald, 103, 124
Searle, Sgt Ronald 'Ron', 34, 64, 65, 76, 77, 82, 87, 88, 101, 102, 163, 167, 168, 170, 172, 173, 203, 403, 406
Sedunary, Sgt A.J., 167
Sewell, Richard, 292, 350, 351
Shand, Mick, 369
Shapiro, Pilot Officer M.B., 143
Shaw, Aircraftsman (see also Lawrence, T.E.), 401
Sheen, R.W., 311
Sherman, General William Tecumseh, 405
Shute, Neville, 59
Simmonds, Sgt N.W.J., 224
Simpson, Jack, 153
Simpson, Joe, 6
Simpson, Laurie J., 6, 14-16, 20, 21, 34, 35, 40, 47, 54, 57, 59-68, 70, 76, 77, 80, 83, 88-90, 98-102, 104, 105, 111, 120, 121, 128, 129, 135, 136, 150, 152-156, 158-162, 163, 165-175, 188, 203, 229, 231, 233-235, 241, 298-300, 304, 305, 315, 317, 319, 323, 329, 330, 341, 349, 350-352, 354, 355, 357, 359, 360, 363, 367, 370-372, 379-384, 387, 389-393, 396, 397, 399, 402, 403, 406
Sinclair, Sir Archibald, 113, 114
Singleton, Mr Justice, 115
Skanziklas, Sortiras, 365
Skeet, Flight Lieutenant 'Roy' Maurice, 202
Skinner, Peter, 331

Slade, Keith, 12, 13, 30-32, 48, 50, 117
Slater, Wg/Cdr, 214
Smart, Gordon, 134
Smith, Arthur, 196, 203, 401
Smith, AC2 G.B., 260
Smith, Joseph, 21, 22
Smith, Group Captain Sydney, 401
Smith, P/O, 230
Snow, C.P., 114
Spaatz, Lieutenant General Carl 'Tooey', 252, 254-256
Sparks, Harry 'Sparky', 132, 134, 146, 220, 221
Speer, Albert, 189-191, 193, 406, 407
Spence, Magnus, 211, 229
Spencer, M.J., 270, 271
Stafford, Warrant Officer, 231
Stalin, Josef, 253, 255, 377
Stanford Tuck, Robert 'Bob', 351, 353, 354, 361, 375
Stauffenberg, Graf Claus von, 191
Stone, Frank, 361, 362, 369-371
Stooke, Gordon, 37, 112
Straker, Reg, 91
Street, Denys, 367
Such, Sgt Len, 216
Sutton, Sgt Ken, 64, 65, 169, 170, 216, 402
Sutton, Sgt Wilf E., 213, 215
Svendsen, P/O, 27
Swales, Edwin, 119
Tait, Sq Ldr J.B., 129
Taylor, G.R., 262
Taylor, John H., 118, 121
Taylor, Johnny, 391
Taylor, Flt Sgt W.R. 'Bill', 225
Tedder, Marshal of the RAF Sir Arthur, 190, 252-257
Tew, F/O, 172
Thacker, Sgt F.H., 220
Thomas, J.E., 228
Thomas, Ray, 4, 18, 200, 221, 396
Thomas, Sgt R.O., 265
Thompson, George, 119
Tizard, Sir Henry, 113-115
Todd, Flt Lt Wylton 'Wilbur', 349
Toombs, George, 112, 148
Torrens, David, 365, 367
Trenchard, Sir Hugh, 6, 7, 262
Trent, Sqn Ldr Leonard H., 141-144, 369
Tripp, Miles 'Mike', 56, 147-148, 198, 200, 405, 406

Turley, Sgt Ivor, 52, 81, 129, 147, 288, 289
Turner, W/O F.F., 275
Turner, Sqn Ldr W.H.N., 260
Utz, E.A.G., 233
Van der Stock, Bob, 365
Vaughan-Thomas, Wynford, 105, 135, 220, 221
Vollum, Robert, 4, 46, 75, 137, 138, 153
Wagner, Henry, 3, 4, 16, 18, 26, 44, 104, 308-311, 318, 319, 323, 324, 401
Wakeman, Ronald, 90, 91
Waldschmitt, Hauptmann, 320
Wallis, Sir Barnes, 24
Wallis, Dorothy, 80, 94
Warburton, Ronald, 109
Ward, James Allen, 119
Wardhill, W/O David R., 263
Warner, Wg/Cdr G.B., 163, 164
Warwick, Flight Lieutenant Harry, 147, 148
Watson-Watt, R.A., 181-183
Watts, Fred, 245
Weare, Group Captain, 379
Weatherill, D.A. 'Punch', 92, 270-271, 401
Webb, Roy, 174
Weber, Sgt, 161
Welburn, Flt Lt F., 111
Welldon, Harry, 394
Wells, Colonel Mark K., 109, 127
Wendon, Sgt, 135
Werra, Franz von, 326
Wetherill, W., 'Bill', 260, 262, 263, 283
Weyle, Ernie Lieutenant, 118, 119, 121, 122, 180
Wheeler, Sgt Harry, 215
White, Dave, 165
Whitehouse, Sgt Jack, 237, 305, 321
Whitley, A.W., 260
Whitley, Air Cdr John, 129
Whitmarsh, Arthur, 85
Whitney, Ron, 92
Whitton, Les, 292, 350, 351, 355, 359
Whyte, Bob, 268, 269, 401
Wilkes, Vernon, 105
Willatt, Geoffrey, 5, 90, 167, 168, 199, 353, 378-387, 390, 401
Wilson, Donald 'Don', 6, 26, 30, 73, 74, 161, 260, 283, 293
Williams, Eric, 344, 345
Williams, Joe, 51, 38, 53-55,

258, 280-283, 344, 345, 401, 403
Williams, 'Nem', 165
Wolstenholme, Bert, 91
Wood, Roger, 67
Worsford, Sgt J.E., 257
Wray, Air Commodore A.M. 'Hoppy', 148
Wright, Flt Lt N.H., 295
Wroughton, John, 73
Wyle, Ernie, 399
Wynne, John, 395
Yarman, Neil, 101
Yates, Eric, 31, 378, 396
Yates, Harry, 30
Younger, Sgt Calton 'Cal', 86, 266, 267, 283, 323, 344, 347, 348, 355, 374, 375, 388, 400
Zabreski, Frances, 320
Zafouk, Jack, 362, 363
Zemke, Hubert, 320
Zuckerman, Solly, 190, 252-258, 305

Statistical Theory and Methodology
In Science and Engineering

A WILEY PUBLICATION IN APPLIED STATISTICS

Statistical Theory and Methodology
In Science and Engineering

Second Edition

K. A. BROWNLEE
*Associate Professor of Statistics
The University of Chicago*

John Wiley & Sons, Inc., New York · London · Sydney

COPYRIGHT © 1960, 1965

BY

JOHN WILEY & SONS, INC.

All Rights Reserved

This book or any part thereof must not be reproduced in any form without the written permission of the publisher.

16 15 14 13 12 11 10 9 8

ISBN 0 471 11355 7

LIBRARY OF CONGRESS CATALOG CARD NUMBER: 65-12717

PRINTED IN THE UNITED STATES OF AMERICA

Preface

The original intent of this book—to serve for a three-quarter sequence in statistical methods—remains unchanged. The main objective is to develop competence and self-confidence in the use of statistical methods, which require some understanding of the theoretical background and some practice in the application of statistical methods to actual data.

This edition assumes that the reader has had a one-year course in elementary calculus. This change has permitted a substantial expansion in the number and scope of the exercises.

Topics discussed at greater length than in the first edition include transformations of density functions (Sections 1.13 and 1.14), two × two tables (Section 5.4), Bartlett's test (Section 9.5), the confidence interval for the entire line in linear regression (Section 11.11), the effects of errors of measurement on observations from a bivariate normal population (Section 12.8), and the partial correlation coefficient (Section 13.4).

Material added to this edition includes Bayes' theorem (Section 1.7), curtailed binomial sampling (Section 1.11), sampling inspection (Sections 3.15–3.17), queuing theory (Chapter 4), estimation of the parameter of an exponential distribution from truncated observations (Section 5.5), the distribution of numbers of runs of elements of two types (Section 6.3), the Friedman χ_r^2 and Cochran Q tests (Sections 7.9 and 7.10), the regression fallacy (Section 12.5), correlation coefficients between indices (Section 13.5), and the likelihood ratio test for goodness of fit in multiple regression (Section 13.8).

Room for the foregoing material has been made by omitting from this edition the discussion of weighted regression and the chapter on the multiple regression approach to the analysis of variance.

This text is in a form that permits wide choice in the sequence in which the material is read. The sketch below shows which chapters are prerequisite to the succeeding chapters:

```
              ┌─4
           ┌─3┼─5
           │  ├─6
           │  └─7
     1─2─┤
           │        ┌─11─12─13
           └─8─9─10─┤
                    └─14─15─16─17
```

More compression is possible; Chapter 12 can be taken up after Section 11.4 and Chapter 13 can be taken up after Section 12.4.

Chicago, Illinois   K. A. BROWNLEE
September 1964

Acknowledgments

The body of statistical theory and techniques expounded in this book is largely due to Professors R. A. Fisher and J. Neyman and their associates. I am deeply conscious of how feeble and anemic present-day statistical theory and practice would be without their work.

My thanks are due R. R. Blough, W. H. Kruskal, H. V. Roberts, and several anonymous reviewers who commented on parts of an earlier draft of this textbook. I am particularly indebted to D. L. Wallace and G. W. Haggstrom, who made very many valuable comments and suggestions. The foregoing obviously have no responsibility for any inadequacies of the present form.

My thanks for permission to reproduce data are due the editors of the *American Journal of Public Health*, *Analytical Chemistry*, the *Astrophysical Journal*, the *Australian Journal of Applied Science*, *Chemical Engineering Progress*, *Food Research*, *Industrial and Engineering Chemistry*, the *Journal of the American Chemical Society*, the *Journal of the Chemical Society*, the *Journal of Hygiene*, the *Journal of the Institute of Actuaries*, the *New York State Journal of Medicine*, the *Philosophical Transactions of the Royal Society*, the *Proceedings of the American Society for Testing and Materials*, the *Proceedings of the Berkeley Symposium on Mathematical Statistics and Probability*, and *Science*. My thanks are also due Chapman and Hall for permission to reproduce data from *Principles of Biological Assay*, by C. W. Emmens, and the *New York World-Telegram and Sun* for data from the *World Almanac and Book of Facts*.

I am indebted to Professor Sir Ronald A. Fisher, Cambridge; to Dr. Frank Yates, Rothamsted; and to Messrs. Oliver and Boyd, Edinburgh, for permission to reprint parts of Tables III and V from their book *Statistical Tables for Biological, Agricultural and Medical Research*. I am also indebted to Professor E. S. Pearson and the Biometrika Trustees for permission to quote extensively from some of the tables in *Biometrika Tables for Statisticians*, volume 1, edited by E. S. Pearson and H. O. Hartley, and to Dr. A. Hald and John Wiley and Sons for permission to quote extensively from some of the tables in *Statistical Tables and Formulas*.

K. A. B.

Contents

CHAPTER | PAGE

1 MATHEMATICAL IDEAS — 1

1.1 Introduction, 1
1.2 Concept of Sample Space, 2
1.3 Probability, 6
1.4 Conditional Probability, 9
1.5 Independence, 11
   Exercises 1A, 16
1.6 Bayes' Theorem, 18
1.7 Permutations and Combinations, 20
   Exercises 1B, 23
1.8 Random Variables, Probability Functions, and Cumulative Distribution Functions, 24
1.9 The Binomial Distribution, 30
1.10 Curtailed Binomial Sampling, 32
   Exercises 1C, 35
1.11 Continuous Frequency Functions, 36
1.12 Examples of Continuous Distributions, 42
1.13 Transformations of Probability Functions and Density Functions, 45
1.14 Another Example of the Transformation of a Density Function, 48
1.15 The Concept of Expectation, 51
1.16 The Expectation of a Function of a Random Variable, 55
1.17 The Concept of Variance, 57
   Exercises 1D, 61

1.18 The Properties of the Standardized Normal Distribution, 63
1.19 Discrete Bivariate Distributions, 67
1.20 Continuous Bivariate Distributions, 70
1.21 Conditional Continuous Density Functions, 72
1.22 Independent Continuous Random Variables, 74
1.23 Expectation in the Multivariate Case, 75
Exercises 1E, 76
1.24 Covariance and the Correlation Coefficient, 77
1.25 The Variance of a Mean, 80
1.26 The Addition Theorem for the Normal Distribution, 81
1.27 The χ^2 Distribution, 82
Exercises 1F, 84

2 STATISTICAL IDEAS   87

2.1 Statistical Inference, 87
2.2 Some Principles of Point Estimation, 88
2.3 Maximum Likelihood Estimation, 91
2.4 A Weighted Mean Unbiased and of Minimum Variance, 95
2.5 Some Principles of Hypothesis Testing, 97
2.6 A Criterion for Choosing between Alternative Tests, 101
2.7 A One-Sided Test of an Observation from a Normal Population with Known Variance, 105
2.8 A One-Sided Test of an Observation from a Binomial Distribution, 110
2.9 The Testing of Composite Hypotheses, 111
2.10 A Two-Sided Test of an Observation from a Normal Distribution with Known Variance, 113
2.11 A Two-Sided Test of an Observation from a Normal Distribution with Unknown Variance, 118
2.12 The Comparison of Two Means, 119
2.13 The Concept of P Value, 120
2.14 Confidence Limits: The General Method, 121
2.15 Confidence Limits for the Mean of a Normal Distribution with Known Variance, 124
2.16 Confidence Limits: The Pivotal Method, 127
2.17 Confidence Limits for the Parameter θ of a Binomial Distribution, 129
2.18 The Relationship between Confidence Limits and Tests of Hypotheses, 130
Exercises, 133

3 THE BINOMIAL, HYPERGEOMETRIC, AND POISSON DISTRIBUTIONS 136

3.1 The Normal Approximation to the Binomial Distribution, 136
3.2 Testing Hypotheses about the Binomial Distribution with a Normal Approximation, 140
3.3 The Angular Transformation and Other Variance Stabilizing Transformations, 144
3.4 Testing Hypotheses about the Binomial Distribution with the Angular Transformation, 146
3.5 Confidence Limits for the Parameter of a Binomial Distribution, 148
3.6 Comparison of Two Observed Frequencies with the Normal Approximation, 150
3.7 The Correlated Two × Two Table, 154
   Exercises 3A, 157
3.8 The Hypergeometric Distribution, 158
3.9 An Application of the Hypergeometric Distribution to Wild Life Population Estimation, 162
3.10 Fisher's Exact Test for Two × Two Tables, 163
3.11 The Poisson Distribution, 166
3.12 An Alternative Derivation of the Poisson Distribution, 169
3.13 Tests of Hypotheses about the Poisson Distribution, 172
3.14 Confidence Limits for a Poisson Parameter, 173
3.15 Simple Sampling Inspection, 174
3.16 Relationship between Sampling Inspection and Hypothesis Testing, 177
3.17 Rectifying Inspection, 177
3.18 Double Sampling, 180
3.19 The Addition Theorem for the Poisson Distribution, 181
3.20 The Comparison of Two Poisson-Distributed Observations, 181
3.21 The Comparison of Two Poisson-Distributed Observations with the Parameters in a Certain Hypothetical Ratio, 183
3.22 An Application to Vaccine Testing, 185
   Exercises 3B, 185

4 AN INTRODUCTION TO QUEUING THEORY 190

4.1 Introduction, 190
4.2 Single-Channel, Infinite, Poisson Arrival, Exponential Service Queues, 191

- 4.3 Queues with Arbitrary Service Time Distribution, 195
- 4.4 Single-Channel, Finite, Poisson Arrival, Exponential Service Queues, 198
- 4.5 Multichannel, Infinite, Poisson Arrival, Exponential Service Queues, 200
- 4.6 Inventory Control, 203
  Exercises, 204

5 THE MULTINOMIAL DISTRIBUTION AND CONTINGENCY TABLES   206

- 5.1 The Multinomial Distribution, 206
- 5.2 The χ^2 Approximation for the Multinomial Distribution, 207
- 5.3 Contingency Tables, 211
- 5.4 The Two × Two Table, 215
- 5.5 Life Testing, 217
  Exercises, 219

6 SOME TESTS OF THE HYPOTHESIS OF RANDOMNESS: CONTROL CHARTS   221

- 6.1 Introduction, 221
- 6.2 The Mean Square Successive Difference Test, 221
- 6.3 Runs of Elements of Two Types, 224
- 6.4 An Approximation to the Distribution of the Number of Runs of Elements of Two Types, 226
- 6.5 Runs above and below the Median, 231
- 6.6 Control Charts for the Mean and Range, 232
- 6.7 Control Charts for Poisson-Distributed Observations, 235
  Exercises, 236

7 SOME NONPARAMETRIC TESTS   241

- 7.1 The Assumption of Normality, 241
- 7.2 The Sign Test, 242
- 7.3 The Median Test, 246
- 7.4 The Mean and Variance of a Sample from a Finite Population, 248
- 7.5 The Wilcoxon Two-Sample Rank Test, 251
- 7.6 The Adjustment for Ties in the Wilcoxon Two-Sample Rank Test, 253
- 7.7 The H Test, 256
- 7.8 The Wilcoxon One-Sample Test, 258

7.9 The Friedman Rank Test, 260
7.10 The Cochran Q Test, 262
Exercises, 265

8 THE PARTITIONING OF SUMS OF SQUARES — 271

8.1 The Distribution of Sample Estimates of Variance, 271
8.2 The Partitioning of Sums of Squares into Independent Components, 276
Exercise, 280

9 TESTS OF EQUALITY OF VARIANCES AND MEANS — 282

9.1 Introduction, 282
9.2 Uses of the Sample Estimate of Variance, 282
9.3 The Variance Ratio, 285
9.4 The Interrelations of Various Distributions, 288
9.5 A Test for the Equality of Several Variances, 290
9.6 The One-Sample t Test, 295
9.7 The Two-Sample t Test, 297
9.8 The Two-Sample Test with Unequal Variances, 299
9.9 A Comparison of Simple Tests for Means and Medians, 304
Exercises, 305

10 ONE-WAY ANALYSIS OF VARIANCE — 309

10.1 Introduction: Models I and II, 309
10.2 One-Way Analysis of Variance: Model I, 310
10.3 The Problem of Multiple Comparisons, 316
10.4 One-Way Analysis of Variance: Model II, 318
10.5 Interpretation of a Model II One-Way Analysis of Variance, 321
10.6 An Example of a Model II One-Way Analysis of Variance with Equal Group Sizes, 325
10.7 An Example of Model II One-Way Analysis of Variance with Unequal Group Sizes, 327
10.8 Simple Sampling Theory, 329
10.9 The Power Function of Model II One-Way Analysis of Variance, 330
Exercises, 330

11 SIMPLE LINEAR REGRESSION 334

- 11.1 Introduction, 334
- 11.2 The Model, 335
- 11.3 An Analysis of Variance Representation, 338
- 11.4 An Example of Linear Regression, 342
- 11.5 The Use of the Regression Line in Reverse, 346
- 11.6 The Comparison of Two Regression Lines, 349
- 11.7 Parallel Line Biological Assay, 352
- 11.8 An Example of Parallel Line Biological Assay, 354
- 11.9 Regression through the Origin, 358
- 11.10 The Use of the Regression Line through the Origin in Reverse, 361
- 11.11 A Joint Confidence Region for α, β, 362
- 11.12 Linear Regression with Several Observations on y at Each x, 366
- 11.13 An Example of Linear Regression with Several Observations on y at Each x, 371
- 11.14 The Comparison of Several Regression Lines: Simple Analysis of Covariance, 376
- 11.15 Simple Analysis of Covariance, 388
- 11.16 Exponential Regression, 391
- 11.17 Regression with Error in the Independent Variable Exercises, 391
  Exercises, 393

12 THE BIVARIATE NORMAL DISTRIBUTION AND THE CORRELATION COEFFICIENT 397

- 12.1 Introduction, 397
- 12.2 Transformations of Bivariate Distributions, 397
- 12.3 The Bivariate Normal Distribution, 401
- 12.4 Some Properties of the Bivariate Normal Distribution, 404
- 12.5 The Regression "Fallacy," 409
- 12.6 Estimation of the Parameters of the Bivariate Normal Distribution, 410
- 12.7 Tests of Significance for the Correlation Coefficient, 413
- 12.8 The Effects of Errors of Measurement, 414
  Exercises, 417

13 REGRESSION ON SEVERAL INDEPENDENT VARIABLES 419

- 13.1 Introduction, 419
- 13.2 Linear Transformation of the Variables in a Bivariate Normal Distribution to Give Independent Variables, 419
- 13.3 Regression on Two Independent Variables, 422
- 13.4 The Partial Correlation Coefficient, 429
- 13.5 Correlation Coefficients between Indices, 431
- 13.6 Regression on Several Independent Variables, 433
- 13.7 A Matrix Representation, 439
- 13.8 A Test of Whether Regression on r Variables Gives a Significantly Better Fit than Regression on q Variables, 441
- 13.9 Polynomial Regression, 447
- 13.10 Further Uses for the c Matrix, 447
- 13.11 Biases in Multiple Regression, 452
- 13.12 An Example of Multiple Regression, 454
  Exercises, 462

14 TWO-WAY AND NESTED ANALYSIS OF VARIANCE 467

- 14.1 Introduction: The Model for Model I Analysis, 467
- 14.2 The Analysis of Variance, 471
- 14.3 Computing Forms for Two-Way Analysis of Variance, 475
- 14.4 Two-Way Analysis of Variance: Model II, 478
- 14.5 The Interpretation of a Model II Analysis, 481
- 14.6 Two-Way Analysis of Variance with Only One Observation per Cell, 482
- 14.7 Nested or Hierarchical Analysis of Variance, 482
- 14.8 The Two-Way Crossed Finite Population Model, 489
- 14.9 Discussion of the Two-Way Crossed Finite Population Model, 498
- 14.10 Nested Classifications in the Finite Model, 499
  Exercises, 501

15 THREE-WAY AND FOUR-WAY ANALYSIS OF VARIANCE 504

- 15.1 The Model, 504
- 15.2 Models I and II, 508
- 15.3 Mixed Models, 511
- 15.4 Confidence Limits in Three-Way Analysis, 512
- 15.5 An Example of Three-Way Analysis of Variance, 514

CONTENTS

- 15.6 Orthogonal Contrasts, 517
- 15.7 The Partitioning of Interactions into Orthogonal Contrasts, 520
- 15.8 Four-Way Analysis of Variance, 524
  Exercises, 526

16 PARTIALLY HIERARCHICAL SITUATIONS — 530

- 16.1 A Partially Hierarchical Situation and Its Model, 530
- 16.2 Calculation of Sums of Squares, Etc., 532
- 16.3 The Expectations of Mean Squares in Partially Hierarchical Models, 538
- 16.4 Confidence Limits in Partially Hierarchical Models, 540
  Exercises, 543

17 SOME SIMPLE EXPERIMENTAL DESIGNS — 547

- 17.1 Completely Randomized Designs, 547
- 17.2 Randomized Block Designs, 548
- 17.3 The Split-Plot Situation, 550
- 17.4 Relationship of Split-Plot to Partially Hierarchical Situations, 553
  Exercises, 554

APPENDIX

- Table I   The Cumulative Standardized Normal Distribution Function, 558
- Table II Fractional Points of the t Distribution, 560
- Table III Fractional Points of the χ^2 Distribution, 562
- Table IV Percentage Points of the F Distribution, 564
- Table V $y = 2 \arcsin \sqrt{x}$, 570
- Table VI Values of d_n and Fractional Points of the Distribution of the Range, 572
- Table VII u_P, 572
- Table VIII Logarithms of $n!$, 573
- Table IX Fractional Points of the Studentized Range, 574
- Table X   Fractional Points of the Largest of k Variance Ratios with One Degree of Freedom in the Numerator, 576
- Table XI Random Sampling Numbers, 577

PARTIAL ANSWERS TO SELECTED EXERCISES — 579

INDEX — 585

Statistical Theory
and Methodology
In Science and Engineering

CHAPTER 1

Mathematical Ideas

1.1. Introduction

This is primarily a textbook on *statistics*, not on *probability*, and we will deal with the latter only as much as is necessary. The two disciplines are, however, closely related, and are often confused. In *probability*, a branch of mathematics, we specify the structure of a problem, construct a mathematical model to correspond, specify the values of the *parameters* (the numerical constants of the system), and then deduce the behavior of the system, e.g., the distribution of the relative number of times each possible outcome will occur. In *statistics*, we assume the structure of the system and the corresponding model, but not numerical values for the parameters, and from a set of observations on the system we attempt to infer, e.g., the values of the parameters.

These characterizations will be clearer from a simple example. A random sample of size n is taken from a lot of N electric light bulbs containing a proportion θ of defectives. What is the distribution of the number of defectives, X, in repeated random samples? Specifically, suppose $n = 100$, $N = 10,000$, and $\theta = 0.1$. We will not get exactly $100 \times 0.1 = 10$ defectives in every sample. Often we will get 10, in fact more often than any other outcome, but we will also often get 9, and 11, and 8, etc. What proportions of the time in repeated random samples will X equal $\ldots, 6, 7, 8, \ldots$ etc.? This is a question in *probability*. Conversely, suppose that we take a random sample of size n and actually observe X defectives. What can we say about θ? For example, what is the most likely value of θ, and what is the range of values of θ that is reasonably plausible, i.e., consistent in some sense with our observations? These are questions in *statistics*.

Modern statistics is the product of many diverse influences, and some potentially important contributions were lost in the mists of indifference of their time. A conscientious historian would have to disinter these and give due credit even though he may be almost the first man to read them since their publication. Nevertheless, some of the main landmarks are generally agreed upon. Studies of gambling problems by the French mathematicians Pascal and Fermat in the year 1654 were the first significant investigations in probability. Over the next two centuries astronomers were interested in the theory of observational errors; in the early nineteenth century Laplace and Gauss made important contributions. For a general account up to the middle of the nineteenth century, see Todhunter [1]. By the beginning of the twentieth century a school under the leadership of Karl Pearson [2] in London was active in statistics, initially from the point of view of its application to biological measurements. An associate of this group, W. S. Gosset, published in 1908 under the pseudonym "Student" a solution to the important problem of the comparison of the mean of a small sample of normally distributed observations with a hypothetical value [3].

Modern statistics may be said to have begun with the appointment in 1919 of R. A. Fisher to the staff of the Rothamsted Experiment Station in England. Fisher's contributions [4–6] are threefold: first, a broad attack on the fundamental principles of estimation and inference, second, the solution of a large number of mathematical problems in distribution theory that were roadblocks to further progress, and third, the creation of the science of the design of experiments, involving three main principles, namely, the essentiality of replication and randomization, and the possibility of reduction of error by appropriate organization of the experiment.

In the 'thirties J. Neyman, at that time in London, developed with E. S. Pearson [7] the theory of hypothesis testing and confidence intervals. In the 'forties, A. Wald and his associates of the Statistical Research Group at Columbia University created the ideas and techniques of sequential analysis [8] and statistical decision theory [9]. In recent years the volume of publication has become relatively enormous, much of it inspired, sometimes rather remotely, by the wide variety of practical problems to which statistics is now being applied. It is now difficult to be expert in more than one or two subdivisions of the field.

1.2. Concept of Sample Space

The concept of *sample space* is a convenient method of representing the outcome of an experiment. By *experiment* we mean some procedure upon which we embark and at whose completion we observe certain results. For example, we may feed a vitamin supplement to a group of hogs and observe their weights after a certain number of weeks, or we may

CONCEPT OF SAMPLE SPACE

toss a coin a certain number of times and observe how many times it falls with the head uppermost.

The set of all possible outcomes of an experiment is represented by the sample space S. Each possible outcome is represented by a sample point. For example, if our experiment is to drop two light bulbs in sequence, with possible outcomes U = undamaged, F = filament broken, and G = glass envelope broken, then the possible outcomes are as represented in Table 1.1, where the ordering of the symbols within the parentheses ( ) corresponds to the time sequence. Here the sample space contains 9 sample points.

Table 1.1

(U, U)	(F, U)	(G, U)
(U, F)	(F, F)	(G, F)
(U, G)	(F, G)	(G, G)

An *event* is the sum of sample points with some specified property. Thus for Table 1.1 the event "both undamaged" consists of the outcome (U, U). In this case the event consists of only one sample point: Such an event may be called a *simple event*. The event "one or more glass envelopes broken" is made up of the sample points (U, G), (F, G), (G, U), (G, F), and (G, G); such an event, which can be decomposed further into a set of simple events, may be called a *compound event*.

Suppose now that we consider a particular experiment. This will give rise to a fixed sample space. Consider an event E defined as a particular set of the sample points. Then all the sample points not in this set form the complementary event "not E," denoted by E^c.

Consider the foregoing experiment of dropping two light bulbs. Define the event E_1 as "one or more undamaged." Then E_1 and E_1^c are as in Figure 1.1.

Also, events E_1, E_2 may be defined such that a particular outcome may belong in more than one of them. The event $E_1 \cap E_2$, called "E_1 intersection E_2", is made up of those sample points belonging to both E_1 and E_2. For example, if the event E_1 as before is "one or more undamaged"

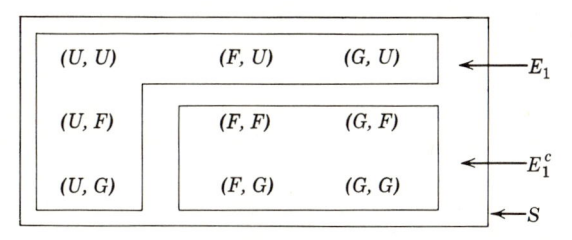

Figure 1.1

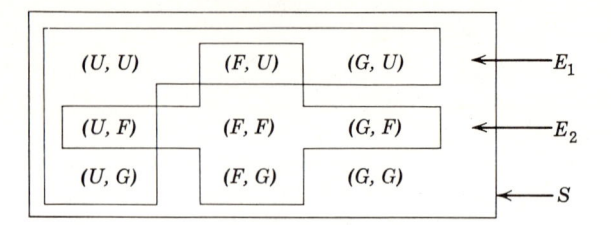

Figure 1.2

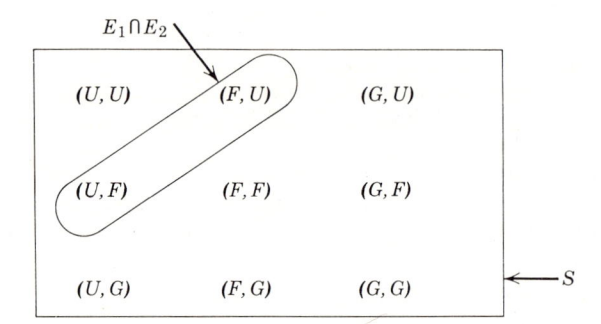

(Diagram showing a 3×3 grid of sample points (U,U), (F,U), (G,U), (U,F), (F,F), (G,F), (U,G), (F,G), (G,G), with E_1, E_2, and S indicated.)

Figure 1.3

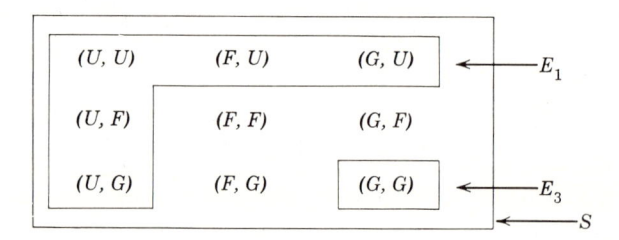

(Diagram showing the same grid with $E_1 \cap E_2$ indicated, enclosing (U,F) and (F,U), and S indicated.)

Figure 1.4

(Diagram showing the same grid with E_1, E_3 (enclosing (G,G)), and S indicated.)

and the event E_2 is "one or more filaments broken," then E_1 and E_2 are as in Figure 1.2, and $E_1 \cap E_2$ is made up of the points (U, F) and (F, U), as in Figure 1.3.

It is possible for two events E_i and E_j to be so defined that $E_i \cap E_j$ is empty of sample points; in other words, the event $E_i \cap E_j$ is impossible. We then say that E_i, E_j are *mutually exclusive* events. For example, if we define E_1 as before as "one or more undamaged" and E_3 as "both glass envelopes broken," then $E_1 \cap E_3$ is empty of sample points (Figure 1.4).

SECT. 1.2   CONCEPT OF SAMPLE SPACE   5

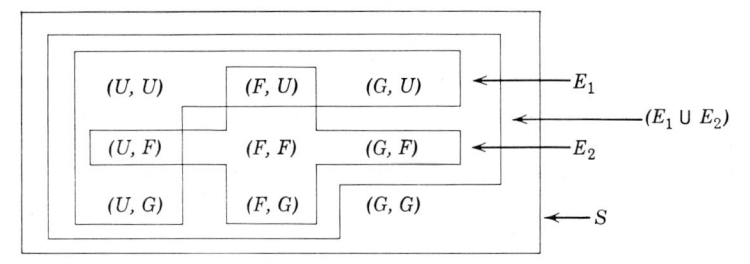

Figure 1.5

A further piece of symbolism is useful. By $E_1 \cup E_2$, read "E_1 *union* E_2," we mean the event "at least one of the two events, i.e., either E_1 but not E_2, or E_2 but not E_1, or E_1 and E_2 together." For the previous definitions of E_1 and E_2, $E_1 \cup E_2$ is shown in Figure 1.5.

More generally, for events E_1 and E_2 defined on an arbitrary sample space S by Figures 1.6a and b, Figures 1.6c and d illustrate $(E_1 \cup E_2)^c$ and $(E_1 \cap E_2)^c$ and the relationships

$$(E_1 \cup E_2)^c = E_1^c \cap E_2^c, \tag{2.1}$$
$$(E_1 \cap E_2)^c = E_1^c \cup E_2^c, \tag{2.2}$$

which can be proved from the axioms of elementary set theory.

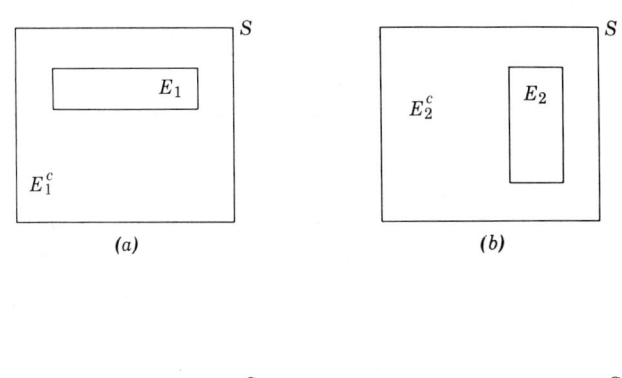

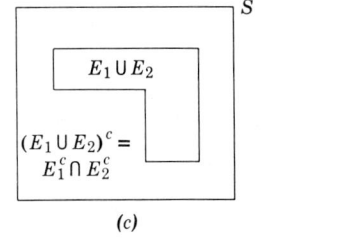

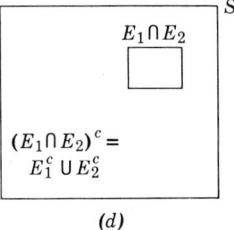

Figure 1.6

1.3. Probability

As an axiom we associate with every point A_k in the sample space a number, called the probability of A_k, denoted by $\Pr\{A_k\}$. These probabilities must be nonnegative and comply with the condition that

$$\Pr\{A_1\} + \Pr\{A_2\} + \cdots = 1, \tag{3.1}$$

where the summation is over the entire sample space. We further suppose that the probability of an event E, $\Pr\{E\}$, is the sum of all the probabilities of the sample points A_k in E.

These axioms lead to some useful rules. In (3.1), if a certain set of the points A_k corresponds to an event E, the complementary set will correspond to the complementary event E^c, so E and E^c will have associated with them the entire set of points, and therefore

$$\Pr\{E\} + \Pr\{E^c\} = 1. \tag{3.2}$$

When the events E_i and E_j are mutually exclusive, there are no sample points belonging simultaneously to both E_i and E_j; i.e.,

$$\Pr\{E_i \cap E_j\} = 0. \tag{3.3}$$

In this situation, $\Pr\{E_i \cup E_j\}$ is the sum of the probabilities of the sample points lying in E_i and those lying in E_j, there being no points lying in E_i and E_j simultaneously, and

$$\Pr\{E_i \cup E_j\} = \Pr\{E_i\} + \Pr\{E_j\}. \tag{3.4}$$

This equation holds only when E_i and E_j are mutually exclusive.

If events $E_1, \ldots, E_k$ are all mutually exclusive, then there are no sample points belonging simultaneously to E_i and E_j for any combination of i and j, and (3.3) holds for any pair of events E_i and E_j. Also,

$$\Pr\{E_1 \cup E_2 \cup \cdots \cup E_k\} = \Pr\{E_1\} + \Pr\{E_2\} + \cdots + \Pr\{E_k\}. \tag{3.5}$$

If the events $E_1, \ldots, E_k$, in addition to being mutually exclusive, are also *exhaustive*, so that

$$E_1 \cup E_2 \cup \cdots \cup E_k = S, \tag{3.6}$$

then

$$\Pr\{E_1 \cup E_2 \cup \cdots \cup E_k\} = 1. \tag{3.7}$$

Consider now the case where E_i, E_j are not mutually exclusive, so that the event $E_i \cap E_j$ is not empty of sample points. In Figure 1.7 we see that the region E_i can be split into two parts, $E_i \cap E_j^c$ and $E_i \cap E_j$, and the region E_j can likewise be split into parts, $E_i \cap E_j$ and $E_i^c \cap E_j$, the part $E_i \cap E_j$ being common to both E_i and E_j. It follows that the event

$E_i \cup E_j$ can be regarded as made up of three mutually exclusive events, so

$$\Pr\{E_i \cup E_j\} = \Pr\{E_i^c \cap E_j\} + \Pr\{E_i \cap E_j\} + \Pr\{E_i \cap E_j^c\}. \quad (3.8)$$

We can simultaneously add and subtract $\Pr\{E_i \cap E_j\}$ to the right-hand side leaving the equation unchanged:

$$\Pr\{E_i \cup E_j\} = \Pr\{E_i^c \cap E_j\} + \Pr\{E_i \cap E_j\} + \Pr\{E_i \cap E_j^c\}$$
$$+ \Pr\{E_i \cap E_j\} - \Pr\{E_i \cap E_j\}. \quad (3.9)$$

Now $E_i^c \cap E_j$ and $E_i \cap E_j$ are mutually exclusive events, so by (3.4)

$$\Pr\{E_i^c \cap E_j\} + \Pr\{E_i \cap E_j\} = \Pr\{(E_i^c \cap E_j) \cup (E_i \cap E_j)\}$$
$$= \Pr\{E_j\}. \quad (3.10)$$

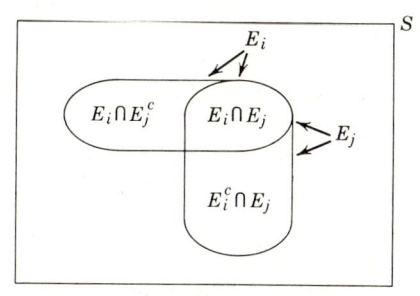

Figure 1.7

Likewise

$$\Pr\{E_i \cap E_j^c\} + \Pr\{E_i \cap E_j\} = \Pr\{(E_i \cap E_j^c) \cup (E_i \cap E_j)\}$$
$$= \Pr\{E_i\}. \quad (3.11)$$

Thus, substituting (3.10) and (3.11) in (3.9),

$$\Pr\{E_i \cup E_j\} = \Pr\{E_i\} + \Pr\{E_j\} - \Pr\{E_i \cap E_j\}. \quad (3.12)$$

As an illustration, consider the experiment of drawing a single card from a well-shuffled deck. The sample space will consist of 52 sample points corresponding to the 52 possible cards that might be drawn. Intuitively, if the deck is well shuffled this implies that the probability of any one card being drawn is the same as that for any other card, i.e.,

$$\Pr\{A_1\} = \Pr\{A_2\} = \cdots = \Pr\{A_{52}\}. \quad (3.13)$$

But these 52 outcomes are the entire sample space, so by (3.1) $\Pr\{A_i\} = 1/52$ for $i = 1, 2, \ldots, 52$. Now define the event E_1 as the occurrence of a heart. E_1 will contain 13 sample points, all of probability 1/52, so

$$\Pr\{E_1\} = \Pr\{\text{heart}\} = 13 \times \frac{1}{52} = \frac{1}{4}. \quad (3.14)$$

Also define the event E_2 as the occurrence of an honor card (ace, king, queen, jack, or ten). There are $4 \times 5 = 20$ honor cards in the deck, so

$$\Pr\{E_2\} = \Pr\{\text{honor}\} = 20 \times \frac{1}{52} = \frac{5}{13}. \tag{3.15}$$

Further, there are 5 heart honors, so

$$\Pr\{E_1 \cap E_2\} = \Pr\{\text{heart honor}\} = \frac{5}{52}. \tag{3.16}$$

We can now use (3.12) to give us

$\Pr\{\text{a heart or an honor or a heart honor}\} = \Pr\{E_1 \cup E_2\}$

$$= \Pr\{E_1\} + \Pr\{E_2\} - \Pr\{E_1 \cap E_2\} = \frac{13}{52} + \frac{20}{52} - \frac{5}{52} = \frac{28}{52}. \tag{3.17}$$

This we can readily check as there are 13 hearts, including the 5 heart honors, plus 3×5 other honors, making a total of 28 cards which are either hearts or honors or heart honors.

We will now develop a formula for the probability of the union of three events, analogous to (3.12). We first note that

$$E_1 \cap (E_2 \cup E_3) = (E_1 \cap E_2) \cup (E_1 \cap E_3). \tag{3.18}$$

We omit a formal proof of this, but in effect it would be a translation into mathematical language of the following argument. The left-hand side defines elements x which belong to E_1 and which also belong to either E_2 or E_3 (or both): the right-hand side defines elements y which belong either to E_1 and E_2 simultaneously or to E_1 and E_3 simultaneously (or to both E_1 and E_2 and E_1 and E_3 simultaneously); i.e., to E_1 and to either E_2 or E_3 (or both). Thus any x is a y and any y is an x. We will assume without proof the generalization of (3.18):

$E_1 \cap (E_2 \cup E_3 \cup \cdots \cup E_k)$
$$= (E_1 \cap E_2) \cup (E_1 \cap E_3) \cup \cdots \cup (E_1 \cap E_k). \tag{3.19}$$

We now consider $\Pr\{E_1 \cup E_2 \cup E_3\}$. The event considered here can be regarded as the union of E_1 with $E_2 \cup E_3$, so from (3.12)

$$\Pr\{E_1 \cup E_2 \cup E_3\} = \Pr\{E_1\} + \Pr\{E_2 \cup E_3\} - \Pr\{E_1 \cap (E_2 \cup E_3)\}. \tag{3.20}$$

For the last term on the right-hand side we use first (3.18) and then (3.12):

$\Pr\{E_1 \cap (E_2 \cup E_3)\} = \Pr\{(E_1 \cap E_2) \cup (E_1 \cap E_3)\}$
$$= \Pr\{E_1 \cap E_2\} + \Pr\{E_1 \cap E_3\} - \Pr\{(E_1 \cap E_2) \cap (E_1 \cap E_3)\}. \tag{3.21}$$

The last term here can be written as

$$\Pr\{(E_1 \cap E_2) \cap (E_1 \cap E_3)\} = \Pr\{E_1 \cap E_2 \cap E_3\}. \qquad (3.22)$$

Substituting this in (3.21), substituting (3.21) in (3.20), and using (3.12) for the term $\Pr\{E_2 \cup E_3\}$ in (3.20), we get

$$\Pr\{E_1 \cup E_2 \cup E_3\} = \Pr\{E_1\} + \Pr\{E_2\} + \Pr\{E_3\} - \Pr\{E_1 \cap E_2\}$$
$$- \Pr\{E_1 \cap E_3\} - \Pr\{E_2 \cap E_3\} + \Pr\{E_1 \cap E_2 \cap E_3\}. \qquad (3.23)$$

1.4. Conditional Probability

Suppose that the events E_1, E_2 are among the possible outcomes of an experiment and that we are interested in $\Pr\{E_1\}$. Suppose that we are informed that E_2 has occurred. What can we now say about the probability of E_1 which we now write as $\Pr\{E_1|E_2\}$ (read as "the probability of E_1 given E_2")?

We now are operating, not on the original entire sample space, but on the restricted sample space made up of the points belonging to E_2. This implies that the probabilities of the now restricted set of points A_i, say $\Pr\{A_i|E_2\}$, must be adjusted so that they sum to 1 in the new sample space. This can be achieved by multiplying all the original $\Pr\{A_i\}$ which lie in E_2 by $1/\Pr\{E_2\}$; i.e., we write

$$\Pr\{A_i|E_2\} = \frac{1}{\Pr\{E_2\}} \times \Pr\{A_i\}, \qquad (4.1)$$

since if we sum the $\Pr\{A_i|E_2\}$ over the entire E_2 space we get

$$\sum_i^{E_2} \Pr\{A_i|E_2\} = \frac{1}{\Pr\{E_2\}} \sum_i^{E_2} \Pr\{A_i\} = \frac{1}{\Pr\{E_2\}} \times \Pr\{E_2\} = 1. \qquad (4.2)$$

To obtain $\Pr\{E_1|E_2\}$ we sum the $\Pr\{A_i|E_2\}$ over those points which lie in E_1; note, however, that we are already confined to E_2, so this summation is over points in $E_1 \cap E_2$. Thus

$$\Pr\{E_1|E_2\} = \sum_i^{E_1 \cap E_2} \Pr\{A_i|E_2\} = \frac{1}{\Pr\{E_2\}} \sum_i^{E_1 \cap E_2} \Pr\{A_i\}$$
$$= \frac{\Pr\{E_1 \cap E_2\}}{\Pr\{E_2\}}. \qquad (4.3)$$

This implies

$$\Pr\{E_1 \cap E_2\} = \Pr\{E_2\} \Pr\{E_1|E_2\}. \qquad (4.4)$$

Clearly an analogous argument will give

$$\Pr\{E_2|E_1\} = \frac{\Pr\{E_2 \cap E_1\}}{\Pr\{E_1\}} \tag{4.5}$$

and

$$\Pr\{E_2 \cap E_1\} = \Pr\{E_1\} \Pr\{E_2|E_1\}. \tag{4.6}$$

For example, suppose that we have a deck of cards from which the 5 diamond honors have been removed. Let the experiment be to draw one card at random from the $52 - 5 = 47$ cards in the abbreviated deck. Let the event E_1 be that the chosen card is an honor and the event E_2 be that the chosen card is a heart. Then the event E_1 consists of 15 sample points each with probability 1/47, so

$$\Pr\{\text{honor}\} = \Pr\{E_1\} = \frac{15}{47} = 0.319. \tag{4.7}$$

The event $E_1 \cap E_2$ is the appearance of an honor heart. The number of sample points in $E_1 \cap E_2$ is 5, each with probability 1/47. The number of sample points in E_2 is 13, each with probability 1/47. Thus if we catch a glimpse of the card and know that it is a heart, we can then say that the probability that it is an honor is, by (4.3),

$$\Pr\{\text{honor}|\text{heart}\} = \Pr\{E_1|E_2\} = \frac{\Pr\{E_1 \cap E_2\}}{\Pr\{E_2\}} = \frac{5/47}{13/47} = \frac{5}{13} = 0.385,$$

which is substantially greater than the unconditional figure of 0.319. This is a mild illustration of the bridge proverb, "one peep is worth two finesses."

Considering this situation from another viewpoint, we can calculate the probability of getting a heart honor in two ways, using either (4.4) or (4.6):

$$\Pr\{\text{honor heart}\} = \Pr\{\text{honor}\} \Pr\{\text{heart}|\text{honor}\}$$
$$= \Pr\{E_1\} \Pr\{E_2|E_1\} = \frac{15}{47} \times \frac{5}{15} = \frac{5}{47}, \tag{4.8}$$

or

$$\Pr\{\text{heart honor}\} = \Pr\{\text{heart}\} \Pr\{\text{honor}|\text{heart}\}$$
$$= \Pr\{E_2\} \Pr\{E_1|E_2\} = \frac{13}{47} \times \frac{5}{13} = \frac{5}{47}. \tag{4.9}$$

Equation (4.4) extends to three events: write $E_2 \cap E_3$ for E_2 to get

$$\Pr\{E_1 \cap E_2 \cap E_3\} = \Pr\{E_1|E_2 \cap E_3\} \Pr\{E_2 \cap E_3\}$$
$$= \Pr\{E_1|E_2 \cap E_3\} \Pr\{E_2|E_3\} \Pr\{E_3\}. \tag{4.10}$$

1.5. Independence

Suppose that the probability of the event E_1 is the same whether or not the event E_2 occurs, i.e.,

$$\Pr\{E_1|E_2\} = \Pr\{E_1|E_2^c\}. \tag{5.1}$$

We then say that E_1 is *independent* of E_2. Equation (5.1) constitutes a satisfactorily intuitive definition of independence, but we will now show that it implies

$$\Pr\{E_1 \cap E_2\} = \Pr\{E_1\}\Pr\{E_2\}, \tag{5.2}$$

as this latter form is usually more convenient and is often given as the definition. From (4.3) we have

$$\Pr\{E_1|E_2\} = \frac{\Pr\{E_1 \cap E_2\}}{\Pr\{E_2\}}. \tag{5.3}$$

We can substitute E_2^c for E_2 to get

$$\Pr\{E_1|E_2^c\} = \frac{\Pr\{E_1 \cap E_2^c\}}{\Pr\{E_2^c\}}. \tag{5.4}$$

Now if our definition of independence, (5.1), is satisfied, then the left-hand sides of (5.3) and (5.4) are equal, and hence

$$\frac{\Pr\{E_1 \cap E_2\}}{\Pr\{E_2\}} = \frac{\Pr\{E_1 \cap E_2^c\}}{\Pr\{E_2^c\}}, \tag{5.5}$$

whence

$$\Pr\{E_1 \cap E_2\}\Pr\{E_2^c\} = \Pr\{E_1 \cap E_2^c\}\Pr\{E_2\}. \tag{5.6}$$

But by (3.2), $\Pr\{E_2^c\} = 1 - \Pr\{E_2\}$, so

$$\Pr\{E_1 \cap E_2\}(1 - \Pr\{E_2\}) = \Pr\{E_1 \cap E_2^c\}\Pr\{E_2\} \tag{5.7}$$

and hence

$$\begin{aligned}\Pr\{E_1 \cap E_2\} &= \Pr\{E_1 \cap E_2\}\Pr\{E_2\} + \Pr\{E_1 \cap E_2^c\}\Pr\{E_2\} \\ &= (\Pr\{E_1 \cap E_2\} + \Pr\{E_1 \cap E_2^c\})\Pr\{E_2\} \\ &= \Pr\{E_1 \cap E_2 \cup E_1 \cap E_2^c\}\Pr\{E_2\} \\ &= \Pr\{E_1\}\Pr\{E_2\}. \end{aligned} \tag{5.8}$$

We note also, substituting this in (5.3), that in the case of independence

$$\Pr\{E_1|E_2\} = \Pr\{E_1\}. \tag{5.9}$$

Thus we have shown that our definition of independence, (5.1), implies the usual definition (5.2). The arguments can be used in reverse to show that (5.2) implies (5.1); these two definitions are therefore equivalent.

Presumably because the word *independent* and the phrase *mutually exclusive* have related connotations in ordinary English usage, their probabilistic definitions and implications are sometimes confused. Assume that $\Pr\{E_1\} > 0$ and $\Pr\{E_2\} > 0$. If the events are mutually exclusive, then the event $E_1 \cap E_2$ is impossible, and therefore $\Pr\{E_1 \cap E_2\} = 0$. But if $\Pr\{E_1 \cap E_2\} = 0$, then (5.2) cannot be satisfied, and therefore the events E_1 and E_2 cannot be independent. Conversely, if the events E_1 and E_2 are independent, (5.2) is satisfied, and therefore $\Pr\{E_1 \cap E_2\} > 0$ and so the events E_1 and E_2 cannot be mutually exclusive.

It should be noted, however, that it is possible for two events E_1 and E_2 to be not mutually exclusive and not independent. For example, let E_1 be the event picking a heart and E_2 be the event picking a heart honor or diamond honor. Then $\Pr\{E_1\} = 1/4$ and $\Pr\{E_2\} = 10/52$. Since $\Pr\{E_1 \cap E_2\} = 5/52 \neq 0$, the events are not mutually exclusive, and since $5/52 \neq (1/4) \times (10/52)$ equation (5.2) is not satisfied and therefore the events are not independent.

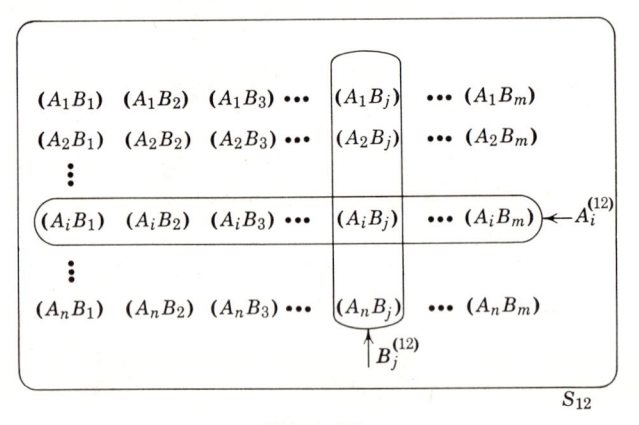

Figure 1.8

We now need to consider compound experiments made up of two separate independent experiments: consider, for example, the compound experiment formed by first throwing a 6-sided die and secondly drawing a card from a 52-card deck. The outcomes of the first experiment can be represented by points A_i, $i = 1, \ldots, n = 6$, in the sample space S_1 with probabilities $\Pr_1\{A_i\}$, and the outcomes of the second experiment can be represented by points B_j, $j = 1, \ldots, m = 52$, in the sample space S_2 with probabilities $\Pr_2\{B_j\}$. The outcomes of the joint experiment can be represented by the ordered pairs $(A_i B_j)$ in the joint sample space S_{12} with probabilities $\Pr_{12}\{(A_i B_j)\}$; see Figure 1.8. In this sample space we

SECT. 1.5 INDEPENDENCE

can define the event $A_i^{(12)}$ as the union over all j of the points $(A_i B_j)$:

$$A_i^{(12)} = (A_i B_1) \cup (A_i B_2) \cup \cdots \cup (A_i B_m). \tag{5.10}$$

Likewise,

$$B_j^{(12)} = (A_1 B_j) \cup (A_2 B_j) \cup \cdots \cup (A_n B_j). \tag{5.11}$$

The intersection of $A_i^{(12)}$ with $B_j^{(12)}$ is $(A_i B_j)$.

We now assume that the separate experiments are independent, so that in S_{12} we have

$$\Pr_{12}\{(A_i B_j)\} = \Pr_{12}\{A_i^{(12)}\} \Pr_{12}\{B_j^{(12)}\}. \tag{5.12}$$

We further assume that the probability of A_i is the same whether we consider A_i as occurring in S_1 or S_{12}:

$$\Pr_1\{A_i\} = \Pr_{12}\{A_i^{(12)}\}. \tag{5.13}$$

Likewise,

$$\Pr_2\{B_j\} = \Pr_{12}\{B_j^{(12)}\}. \tag{5.14}$$

These assumptions give, on substituting (5.13) and (5.14) in (5.12),

$$\Pr_{12}\{(A_i B_j)\} = \Pr_1\{A_i\} \Pr_2\{B_j\}. \tag{5.15}$$

Now suppose that E is an event defined on S_1 as the union of all points A_i conforming to the definition E; i.e., $\bigcup\limits_{i \in E} A_i$, and likewise F is defined on S_2 as $\bigcup\limits_{j \in F} B_j$. Represent E in the joint sample space S_{12} by E_{12}, i.e.,

$$E_{12} = \bigcup_{j}^{m} \bigcup_{i}^{i \in E} (A_i B_j).$$

Likewise

$$F_{12} = \bigcup_{i}^{n} \bigcup_{j}^{j \in F} (A_i B_j).$$

The occurrence of E in the first experiment and F in the second experiment, i.e., the ordered pair (EF) in the joint experiment, is equivalent in S_{12} to the intersection of E_{12} and F_{12}, i.e., to

$$\left\{ \bigcup_{i}^{i \in E} \bigcup_{j}^{m} (A_i B_j) \right\} \cap \left\{ \bigcup_{j}^{j \in F} \bigcup_{i}^{n} (A_i B_j) \right\} = \bigcup_{i}^{i \in E} \bigcup_{j}^{j \in F} (A_i B_j). \tag{5.16}$$

Then

$$\Pr_{12}\{(EF)\} = \Pr_{12}\left(\bigcup_{i}^{i \in E} \bigcup_{j}^{j \in F} (A_i B_j) \right) = \sum_{i}^{i \in E} \sum_{j}^{j \in F} \Pr_{12}\{(A_i B_j)\}$$

$$= \sum_{i}^{i \in E} \sum_{j}^{j \in F} \Pr_1\{A_i\} \Pr_2\{B_j\} = \left(\sum_{i}^{i \in E} \Pr_1\{A_i\} \right) \left(\sum_{j}^{j \in F} \Pr_2\{B_j\} \right)$$

$$= \Pr_1\{E\} \Pr_2\{F\}. \tag{5.17}$$

Thus the probability of observing in the joint experiment E followed by F is the product of the probability of E in the first experiment with the probability of F in the second experiment, it being assumed that the separate experiments are independent.

Equation (3.12), or the lack of it, is the basis of a common probabilistic fallacy. Suppose that two missiles are fired at a target independently and that each has a probability of 0.2 of destroying the target. The popular misconception is that the probability of the destruction of the target is $0.2 + 0.2 = 0.4$. The fallaciousness of this argument is evident if the probability of either missile destroying the target was 0.6; this argument would give $0.6 + 0.6 = 1.2$ as the probability of the destruction of the target, an obviously impossible result. The correct answer is obtained as follows. Let E_1 be the event "target destroyed by first missile" and E_2 the event "target destroyed by second missile." By (3.12)

Pr{target destroyed}

= Pr{target destroyed by first missile, or second missile, or both}

$$= \Pr\{E_1 \cup E_2\} = \Pr\{E_1\} + \Pr\{E_2\} - \Pr\{E_1 \cap E_2\}. \quad (5.18)$$

Here $\Pr\{E_1 \cap E_2\}$ is the probability of the destruction of the target by both missiles. By (5.17) when the events are independent, $\Pr\{E_1 \cap E_2\} = \Pr\{E_1\} \Pr\{E_2\}$, so

$$\Pr\{\text{target destroyed}\} = 0.2 + 0.2 - 0.2 \times 0.2 = 0.36. \quad (5.19)$$

As a similar example, consider an experiment consisting of drawing one card from a deck, replacing it, and drawing another. Let E_1 be the event of getting a spade on the first draw and E_2 be the event of getting a spade on the second draw. Then $\Pr\{E_1\} = 13/52 = 1/4$ and $\Pr\{E_2\} = 13/52 = 1/4$. Then

$$\Pr\{\text{both cards are spades}\} = \Pr\{E_1 \cap E_2\} = \Pr\{E_1\} \Pr\{E_2\}$$

$$= \frac{1}{4} \times \frac{1}{4} = \frac{1}{16}, \quad (5.20)$$

since the two draws are independent. We might note in passing that

$$\Pr\{\text{at least one card is a spade}\} = \Pr\{E_1 \cup E_2\}$$

$$= \Pr\{E_1\} + \Pr\{E_2\} - \Pr\{E_1 \cap E_2\}$$

$$= \frac{1}{4} + \frac{1}{4} - \frac{1}{16} = \frac{7}{16}, \quad (5.21)$$

SECT. 1.5 INDEPENDENCE

or alternatively,

Pr{at least one card is a spade} = $1 - $ Pr{neither card is a spade}
$$= 1 - \Pr\{E_1^c \cap E_2^c\} = 1 - \Pr\{E_1^c\}\Pr\{E_2^c\}$$
$$= 1 - \frac{3}{4} \times \frac{3}{4} = \frac{7}{16}. \qquad (5.22)$$

We might also note that

Pr{exactly one card is a spade} $= \Pr\{E_1 \cap E_2^c \cup E_1^c \cap E_2\}$
$$= \Pr\{E_1 \cap E_2^c\} + \Pr\{E_1^c \cap E_2\}$$
$$= \Pr\{E_1\}\Pr\{E_2^c\} + \Pr\{E_1^c\}\Pr\{E_2\}$$
$$= \frac{1}{4} \times \frac{3}{4} + \frac{3}{4} \times \frac{1}{4} = \frac{6}{16}. \qquad (5.23)$$

To illustrate the difference dependence may make, consider the related experiment in which first one card and then another are withdrawn from the deck, this time without replacement of the first card. Here

$$\Pr\{\text{both cards are spades}\} = \Pr\{E_1 \cap E_3\} = \Pr\{E_1\}\Pr\{E_3|E_1\}$$
$$= \frac{13}{52} \times \frac{12}{51} = \frac{1}{17}, \qquad (5.24)$$

since on the second draw, if a spade has already been withdrawn from the deck on the first draw then there are only 12 spades in the remaining 51 cards. The result of the second drawing is dependent on the result of the first drawing.

Given three events E_1, E_2, and E_3, we say that they are *pairwise independent* if the following equations are satisfied.

$$\Pr\{E_1 \cap E_2\} = \Pr\{E_1\}\Pr\{E_2\}, \qquad (5.25)$$
$$\Pr\{E_1 \cap E_3\} = \Pr\{E_1\}\Pr\{E_3\}, \qquad (5.26)$$
$$\Pr\{E_2 \cap E_3\} = \Pr\{E_2\}\Pr\{E_3\}. \qquad (5.27)$$

We say that the events are *(completely) independent* if in addition to (5.25)–(5.27) the following equation is also satisfied:

$$\Pr\{E_1 \cap E_2 \cap E_3\} = \Pr\{E_1\}\Pr\{E_2\}\Pr\{E_3\}. \qquad (5.28)$$

It can be shown that the above definition implies a commonsense equivalent, i.e.,

$$\Pr\{E_1|E_2 \cap E_3\} = \Pr\{E_1|E_2^c \cap E_3\} = \Pr\{E_1|E_2 \cap E_3^c\}$$
$$= \Pr\{E_1|E_2^c \cap E_3^c\}. \qquad (5.29)$$

and two similar equations obtained by cyclically permuting the suffices.

We will prove only the first part of (5.29). Starting with (5.28) and using (5.26), we have

$$\Pr\{E_1 \cap E_2 \cap E_3\} = \Pr\{E_1 \cap E_3\} \Pr\{E_2\}$$
$$= \Pr\{(E_1 \cap E_2 \cap E_3) \cup (E_1 \cap E_2^c \cap E_3)\} \Pr\{E_2\}$$
$$= [\Pr\{E_1 \cap E_2 \cap E_3\} + \Pr\{E_1 \cap E_2^c \cap E_3\}] \Pr\{E_2\}$$
$$= \Pr\{E_1 \cap E_2 \cap E_3\} \Pr\{E_2\}$$
$$+ \Pr\{E_1 \cap E_2^c \cap E_3\} \Pr\{E_2\}. \quad (5.30)$$

Therefore

$$\Pr\{E_1 \cap E_2 \cap E_3\}(1 - \Pr\{E_2\}) = \Pr\{E_1 \cap E_2^c \cap E_3\} \Pr\{E_2\}. \quad (5.31)$$

Substituting $\Pr\{E_2^c\}$ for $(1 - \Pr\{E_2\})$ and dividing both sides by $\Pr\{E_2\} \Pr\{E_2^c\} \Pr\{E_3\}$ gives

$$\frac{\Pr\{E_1 \cap E_2 \cap E_3\}}{\Pr\{E_2\} \Pr\{E_3\}} = \frac{\Pr\{E_1 \cap E_2^c \cap E_3\}}{\Pr\{E_2^c\} \Pr\{E_3\}}, \quad (5.32)$$

or

$$\frac{\Pr\{E_1 \cap (E_2 \cap E_3)\}}{\Pr\{E_2 \cap E_3\}} = \frac{\Pr\{E_1 \cap (E_2^c \cap E_3)\}}{\Pr\{E_2^c \cap E_3\}}, \quad (5.33)$$

so

$$\Pr\{E_1 | E_2 \cap E_3\} = \Pr\{E_1 | E_2^c \cap E_3\}, \quad (5.34)$$

which was to be proved. The other parts of (5.29) can be proved similarly.

EXERCISES 1A

1A.1. One card is drawn at random from a standard 52-card deck. Consider the events defined as the card being E_1, a spade; E_2, an honor (A, K, Q, J, 10); E_3, the ace of spades; E_4, the ace of hearts. Answer the following questions, giving reasons for your answers: (a) Are E_1 and E_2 independent? (b) Are E_1 and E_2 mutually exclusive? (c) Are E_3 and E_4 independent? (d) Are E_3 and E_4 mutually exclusive? (e) Are E_2 and E_3 independent? (f) Are E_2 and E_3 mutually exclusive?

1A.2. E_1 and E_2 are two events, not identical, defined on the same sample space, and $0 < \Pr\{E_1\} < 1$, $0 < \Pr\{E_2\} < 1$. Rank in increasing order of magnitude, using less-than signs and equality signs where appropriate, the following quantities:

$$0, \quad \Pr\{E_1 \cap E_2\}, \quad \Pr\{E_1\} + \Pr\{E_2\}, \quad \Pr\{E_1\},$$
$$\Pr\{E_1 | E_2\}, \quad \Pr\{E_1 \cup E_2\},$$

(a) under the assumption that E_1 and E_2 are mutually exclusive, (b) under the assumption that E_1 and E_2 are independent.

1A.3. The event E_1 is a sub-event of E_2; i.e., if E_1 occurs then E_2 certainly occurs, but if E_2 occurs E_1 may or may not occur. You are also given that $0 < \Pr\{E_1\} < 1$, $0 < \Pr\{E_2\} < 1$. Rank in increasing order of magnitude, using less-than signs and equality signs where appropriate, the following quantities:

$$0, \quad 1, \quad \Pr\{E_1\}, \quad \Pr\{E_2\}, \quad \Pr\{E_1 \cup E_2\}, \quad \Pr\{E_2|E_1\},$$
$$\Pr\{E_1 \cap E_2\}.$$

1A.4. Prove that if E_1 and E_2 are independent, then

$$\Pr\{E_1 \cup E_2\} = 1 - \Pr\{E_1^c\}\Pr\{E_2^c\}.$$

1A.5. If E_1 and E_2 are two events, not independent, defined on the same sample space, prove that $\Pr\{E_1\}$ lies between $\Pr\{E_1|E_2\}$ and $\Pr\{E_1|E_2^c\}$.

1A.6. You roll two fair dice, one red and one pink, without observing the outcome. What is the probability that the sum is greater than or equal to 10, conditional on the following two situations: (*a*) an observer says "the red die is a five," (*b*) the observer is color blind and says "well, one of them is a five" (not intending by this remark to exclude the possibility that both are five)?

1A.7. A deck of cards consists of just 4 cards, namely the ace of spades, the ace of hearts, the 2 of spades and the 2 of hearts. Two cards are dealt sequentially at random face down to Smith. Consider the following four circumstances: (*a*) He looks at both his cards and says, "I do have at least one ace." (*b*) He looks at both his cards and says, "I do have at least the ace of spades." (*c*) He looks at the first card which was dealt to him and says, "I do have an ace." (*d*) He looks at the first card which was dealt to him and says, "I do have the ace of spades." For each circumstance, calculate the probability, conditional on his remark, that he has both aces.

1A.8. *The New Republic*, (October 13, 1958) discussing the perils of certain foreign policies, remarked that when "... you are playing Russian Roulette, there is a five to one chance that the hammer will strike on an empty chamber. But there is equally a near certainty that you will be dead after pulling the trigger six times." Under the implied assumption of a one-to-five chance, i.e., a probability of 1/6, of hitting the loaded chamber, calculate the probability the author has in mind.

1A.9. Jones and Smith commute jointly to work by automobile and each drives alternate days. When Jones drives the probability of being on time is θ_1 and when Smith drives the probability of being on time is θ_2, where $\theta_1 > \theta_2$. At the end of one week their boss warns them that they will be fired unless they are on time for four or more days in a row in the next five days. Jones says that since his probability of being on time is greater than the probability of Smith being on time, he (Jones) should drive Monday, Wednesday, and Friday and Smith should drive Tuesday and Thursday. Check his claim.

1A.10. An automobile dealer has eight automobiles on his showroom floor. Of the optional equipment power brakes, power steering, and automatic transmission, one automobile is without any, one has power brakes only, two have automatic transmission only, two have power steering only, one has power steering and automatic transmission, and one is "loaded" (i.e., has all three options). Let an automobile be selected at random and let E_1, E_2, E_3 be the events has power steering, has power brakes, and has automatic transmission respectively. (*a*) Are the events E_1, E_2, E_3 pairwise independent? (*b*) Are the events E_1, E_2, E_3 completely independent?

1.6. Bayes' Theorem

A formula due to the Reverend Thomas Bayes [10] can be used in a particular situation, the nature of which will be clearer after some definitions. Let $E_1, \ldots, E_n$ be n mutually exclusive and *exhaustive* events. By *exhaustive* we mean that one of the events E_i must occur: since they are mutually exclusive only one can occur. We assume that each of the events E_i has positive probability: if its probability is zero, then it is simply omitted from consideration. We assume, therefore, that

$$\Pr\{E_i\} > 0 \quad \text{for all } i, \tag{6.1}$$

$$\Pr\{E_i \cap E_j\} = 0 \quad \text{for } i \neq j, \tag{6.2}$$

$$\sum_{i=1}^{n} \Pr\{E_i\} = 1. \tag{6.3}$$

Let F be another event on this sample space. We want to develop a formula for the probability of E_j given that F has occurred. By (4.3)

$$\Pr\{E_j | F\} = \frac{\Pr\{E_j \cap F\}}{\Pr\{F\}}. \tag{6.4}$$

For the numerator we can use (4.4),

$$\Pr\{E_j \cap F\} = \Pr\{F \cap E_j\} = \Pr\{F | E_j\} \Pr\{E_j\}. \tag{6.5}$$

We obtain an expression for the denominator as follows. Equation (3.19) is valid for any set of E's, so it will be valid if we substitute F for E_1 and $E_1, \ldots, E_n$ for $E_2, \ldots, E_k$:

$$F \cap (E_1 \cup E_2 \cup \cdots \cup E_n) = (F \cap E_1) \cup (F \cap E_2) \cup \cdots \cup (F \cap E_n). \tag{6.6}$$

But in the present case the E_i, $i = 1, \ldots, n$, are exhaustive, so by (3.6) the left-hand side of (6.6) is just $F \cap S = F$, so we have

$$\Pr\{F\} = \Pr\{(F \cap E_1) \cup (F \cap E_2) \cup \cdots \cup (F \cap E_n)\}. \tag{6.7}$$

Here the events $F \cap E_i$ and $F \cap E_j$ are mutually exclusive for $i \neq j$. Therefore we can use (3.5) to write (6.7) as

$$\Pr\{F\} = \Pr\{F \cap E_1\} + \Pr\{F \cap E_2\} + \cdots + \Pr\{F \cap E_n\}. \tag{6.8}$$

We again use (4.4) for each term on the right-hand side to get

$$\Pr\{F\} = \Pr\{F|E_1\}\Pr\{E_1\} + \cdots + \Pr\{F|E_n\}\Pr\{E_n\}$$
$$= \sum_{i=1}^{n} \Pr\{F|E_i\}\Pr\{E_i\}. \qquad (6.9)$$

Substituting (6.5) and (6.9) in (6.4) gives Bayes' formula:

$$\Pr\{E_j|F\} = \frac{\Pr\{F|E_j\}}{\sum_{i=1}^{n} \Pr\{F|E_i\}\Pr\{E_i\}}\Pr\{E_j\}. \qquad (6.10)$$

As an example of the use of Bayes' formula, suppose that we have three urns with contents as follows:

Urn 1: 4 white balls, 3 black balls,
Urn 2: 4 white balls, 5 black balls,
Urn 3: 3 white balls, 7 black balls.

Suppose that an urn is chosen at random, and that the probability of any particular urn being selected is 1/3. A ball is drawn at random from the urn selected. Suppose that the ball selected is black. We ask, what is the probability that the urn was urn 1?

There are 26 balls which might be chosen so the sample space has 26 points, 7 having the property E_1 (i.e., coming from urn 1), 9 the property E_2 and 10 the property E_3. Fifteen of the points in the sample space have the property F, namely being black. Clearly $\Pr\{F|E_1\} = 3/7$, $\Pr\{E_1\} = 1/3$, etc., so (6.10) gives

$$\Pr\{E_1|F\} = \frac{\frac{3}{7} \times \frac{1}{3}}{\frac{3}{7} \times \frac{1}{3} + \frac{5}{9} \times \frac{1}{3} + \frac{7}{10} \times \frac{1}{3}} = 0.254,$$

which differs from the a priori probability of 0.333. It is obvious that since the urns differ in content knowledge of the result of drawing a ball at random from the urn selected must affect our opinion as to which the urn was.

As another example [11] of the application of Bayes' theorem, suppose that a diagnostic test for cancer has a probability of 0.95 of being positive when the subject does have cancer and a probability of 0.05 of being positive when the subject does not have cancer. In other words, if E_1 is the event "has cancer," E_2 is the event "does not have cancer," and F is the event "reacts positively," we suppose $\Pr\{F|E_1\} = 0.95$, $\Pr\{F|E_2\} = 0.05$. This hypothetical test has a proportion of 5 per cent "false positives," i.e., of a population without cancer only 5 per cent are reported as positive, since $\Pr\{F|E_2\} = 0.05$. This test has a proportion of 5 per cent "false negatives"; i.e., of a population with cancer only 5 per cent are reported as negative, since $\Pr\{F^c|E_1\} = 0.05$. Now suppose that this test is applied to a population in which the probability of any individual having cancer is 1/200, i.e., $\Pr\{E_1\} = 0.005$, $\Pr\{E_2\} = 0.995$. We can now ask: What is the probability that an individual from this population, reacting positively to this test, actually has cancer:

$$\Pr\{E_1|F\} = \frac{\Pr\{F|E_1\}\Pr\{E_1\}}{\Pr\{F|E_1\}\Pr\{E_1\} + \Pr\{F|E_2\}\Pr\{E_2\}}$$

$$= \frac{0.95 \times 0.005}{0.95 \times 0.005 + 0.05 \times 0.995} = 0.0872.$$

Thus of those tested and showing positive, only 8.72 per cent (1 in 11.5) actually has cancer.

1.7. Permutations and Combinations

Assume that we have n distinguishable objects and a row of cells numbered $1, 2, \ldots, r$, where $r \leq n$. We wish to know the number of different ways in which a selection of r of the n distinguishable objects can be placed in the r distinguishable cells, one object to a cell. The standard symbol for this number is P_r^n.

For filling the first cell we have a choice of n objects. For filling the second cell we have a choice of only $n - 1$ objects, since one object has already been allocated. The total number of ways in which we can fill the first two cells is therefore $n(n - 1)$. Continuing down the row of cells, when we come to fill the rth cell $r - 1$ objects have been used up in filling the previous $r - 1$ cells, leaving only $n - (r - 1)$ objects available from which to make our final choice. Thus

$$P_r^n = n(n - 1)(n - 2) \cdots (n - r + 1). \tag{7.1}$$

The factorial symbol ! is such that $n! = n(n - 1) \cdots 3 \times 2 \times 1$. We can thus write

$$P_r^n = n(n - 1) \cdots (n - r + 1) \frac{(n - r)(n - r - 1) \cdots 2 \times 1}{(n - r)(n - r - 1) \cdots 2 \times 1}$$

$$= \frac{n!}{(n - r)!}. \tag{7.2}$$

We note that $1! = 1$. Also, in general, $n! = n(n - 1)!$, so $(n - 1)! = n!/n$. To have this equation hold when $n = 1$ we define $0! = 1$.

SECT. 1.7　PERMUTATIONS AND COMBINATIONS

In the special case where we are placing n objects in n cells, i.e., we are using all the objects, the number of possible arrangements, or permutations, is given by putting $r = n$ in (7.1), so

$$P_n^n = n(n-1) \cdots 2 \times 1 = n! \tag{7.3}$$

Equation (7.2), with the convention $0! = 1$, gives the same result:

$$P_n^n = \frac{n!}{(n-n)!} = \frac{n!}{0!} = n! \tag{7.4}$$

Now consider that our n objects are not completely distinguishable, as supposed so far, but instead fall into k different groups; the different groups are distinguishable one from another, but within a group the objects cannot be distinguished from other objects of the same group. Let there be n_1 objects of the first kind, n_2 objects of the second kind, etc., and let $\sum_i^k n_i = n$. For example, we might have n_1 red balls, n_2 yellow balls, etc. If all the n objects were distinguishable, and we were to arrange all of them in a row, the total number of permutations would be $P_n^n = n!$. Now temporarily label the n_1 indistinguishable objects of the first kind $a_1, a_2, \ldots, a_{n_1}$; i.e., temporarily make them distinguishable. A certain subset of the whole set of $n!$ permutations will have these a's in certain cells. For example, one such permutation will be

| a_1 | | a_2 | a_3 | | a_4 | | | |

But if the a's are actually indistinguishable, this permutation will be indistinguishable from

| a_7 | | a_4 | a_1 | | a_6 | | | |

in which the same cells are occupied by a's, but the a's are permuted around amongst these particular cells. In both these cases the cells left blank are assumed to be occupied by exactly the same objects other than a's. The number of ways in which we can permute the a's around is $P_{n_1}^{n_1} = n_1!$. Similar results hold for the other groups of objects. Thus we have the identity:

Total number of permutations assuming the objects are completely distinguishable

= (number of distinguishable permutations of n objects made up of k groups of objects indistinguishable within each group)

× (number of permutations of objects within the first group assuming that they are distinguishable)

× (same for second group) × $\cdots$ × (same for kth group). (7.5)

The left-hand side of this identity is $n!$. The second, third, etc., terms on the right-hand side are $n_1! \, n_2! \cdots n_k!$, since the permutation of the objects of the first group amongst themselves can be made independently of the permutation of the objects of the second group amongst themselves, etc. Thus we have

Number of distinguishable permutations of n_1 objects of type a, n_2 objects of type b, etc.

$$= \frac{n!}{n_1! \, n_2! \cdots n_k!}. \tag{7.6}$$

In the special case where there are only two types of objects, say n_1 of one kind and $n - n_1$ of the other, then (7.6) becomes

$$\frac{n!}{n_1! \, (n - n_1)!}. \tag{7.7}$$

We now turn to the problem of determining the number of ways of choosing x out of a set of n distinguishable objects. This is known as the number of *combinations* and is represented by the symbol $\binom{n}{x}$. Other symbols sometimes encountered for this number are C_x^n, $_nC_x$, etc. Imagine that the n objects are lined up in a row beside n cells. Suppose that we have x disks labeled "choose" and $n - x$ disks labeled "do not choose." The number of different ways in which we can permute these x disks of one kind and $n - x$ disks of the other kind is, by (7.7), $n!/[x! \, (n - x)!]$. But each different arrangement of the disks determines a different choice of the objects lined up beside the cells into which the disks are placed. Thus the number of different choices of the n objects x at a time is equal to the number of permutations of the disks, i.e.,

$$\binom{n}{x} = \frac{n!}{x! \, (n - x)!}. \tag{7.8}$$

For example, suppose that we have four different letters a, b, c and d. The possible permutations of these taken two at a time are

$$ab \quad ba \quad ac \quad ca \quad ad \quad da \quad bc \quad cb \quad bd \quad db \quad cd \quad dc. \tag{7.9}$$

The number of such permutations, by (7.2), is $P_2^4 = 4!/(4 - 2)! = 12$. The possible combinations of these four letters taken two at a time are

$$ab \quad ac \quad ad \quad bc \quad bd \quad cd. \tag{7.10}$$

The number of such combinations, by (7.8), is $4!/[2!(4 - 2)!] = 6$. The permutations and combinations differ; in the former the order of the letters is relevant, so that *ab* is a different permutation from *ba*, whereas regarded as combinations *ab* represents exactly the same choice as *ba*.

Now suppose that we have two *a*'s, two *b*'s and one *c*; *a, a, b, b, c*. The possible permutations of all five letters are

$$
\begin{array}{ccccccc}
aabbc & aabcb & aacbb & ababc & abacb & abbac & abbca \\
abcab & abcba & acabb & acbab & acbba & baabc & baacb \\
babac & babca & bacab & bacba & bbaac & bbaca & bbcaa \\
bcaab & bcaba & bcbaa & caabb & cabab & cabba & cbaab \\
cbaba & cbbaa. & & & & &
\end{array}
\quad (7.11)
$$

The number of such permutations, by (7.6), is $5!/(2!\,2!\,1!) = 30$.

Equation (7.6) will give immediately the number of different ways a deck of 52 cards can be dealt 13 cards to each of four players N, S, E, and W. Consider the 52 cards laid out in a row, and 13 disks labeled N, 13 disks labeled S, 13 disks labeled E and 13 disks labeled W being laid out in a row alongside the cards. Each permutation determines an allocation of the cards to the four players, and by (7.6) the number of permutations is

$$\frac{52!}{13!\,13!\,13!\,13!} = 5.36 \times 10^{28}, \qquad (7.12)$$

using Table VIII of logarithms of $n!$ in the Appendix to assist in the calculation. On the other hand, we could reason from (7.8) that there are $\binom{52}{13}$ ways of picking 13 cards for N; then 13 cards for S could be picked from the 39 remaining cards in $\binom{39}{13}$ ways, etc., so the total number of different deals is

$$
\binom{52}{13}\binom{39}{13}\binom{26}{13}\binom{13}{13} = \frac{52!}{13!\,39!} \frac{39!}{13!\,26!} \frac{26!}{13!\,13!} \frac{13!}{13!\,0!}
$$

$$
= \frac{52!}{13!\,13!\,13!\,13!}, \qquad (7.13)
$$

as before.

More generally, an alternative form for (7.6) is

$$\frac{n!}{n_1!\,n_2!\,n_3!\cdots n_k!} = \binom{n}{n_1}\binom{n - n_1}{n_2}\binom{n - n_1 - n_2}{n_3}\cdots\binom{n_k}{n_k}. \quad (7.14)$$

EXERCISES 1B

1B.1. Suppose that a day's production schedule calls for 9000 items. Three machines, each with a daily production capacity of 4000, are available, and the probability that an item is defective is 1, 2 and 4 per cent for machines *A*, *B* and *C* respectively. On a given day 4000 items are produced on machine *A*, 4000 on machine *B*, and 1000 on machine *C*. One item is selected at random from the bulked day's production and found to be defective. What is the probability that it was made on machine C?

1B.2. A manufacturing process is turning out items and 20 per cent of these on the average are defective. The items are screened for shipment by an inspection operation which is not perfect: if an item is good, then the probability that the inspector reports it as good is 0.90; and if an item is defective then the probability that the inspector reports it as defective is 0.75. A purchaser picks an item at random from a batch shipped to him: What is the probability that it is defective?

1B.3. From a panel of ten people we are to select a committee of three. In how many ways can this be done? (a) If we are merely to select three people, (b) if we are to name a chairman, a vice-chairman, and a secretary.

1B.4. A panel of ten candidates, seven from party A and three from party B, are to sit on a rostrum facing an audience. Assuming that candidates from the same party are indistinguishable, in now many ways can the rostrum be arranged?

1B.5. We ask the same question as in 1B.4, but there are five from party A, three from party B and two from party C.

1B.6. An investment adviser draws up a list of twelve stocks. (a) In how many ways can a client form a portfolio of five stocks from this list? (b) If the list is made up of four steels, five oils and three office equipments, in how many ways can a client pick a portfolio consisting of two steels, two oils and one office equipment?

1B.7. There are ten starters in a horse race. Assuming that there are no ties, and that all horses finish the race, in how many ways can (a) the horses cross the finishing line, (b) the first three places be filled, paying no attention to the ordering 1, 2, 3, (c) the first three places be filled, paying attention to the ordering 1, 2, 3?

1B.8. Twelve mice labeled 1 through 12 are to be placed in four cages labeled A, B, C and D, each cage to contain three mice. In how many ways can the mice be allocated to the cages?

1B.9. On a camping trip you are badly rained on and the labels on your store of canned food are washed off. There were three cans of meat, two cans of vegetables and two cans of fruit (all cans are of the same size). You open three cans at random. What is the probability that you can get a standard meal, i.e., a meat dish, a vegetable and a fruit for desert?

1B.10. An experimenter is going to run a clinical trial comparing six treatments. He wishes to test every possible choice of three treatments together on a patient, each choice of three treatments to be on a different patient. How many patients will he need (a) if the order of testing a triplet of treatments on a patient does not matter (e.g., ABC is not to be distinguished from BAC, etc.), (b) if the order of testing a triplet on a patient is relevant (e.g., ABC is a different choice from BAC, etc.)? Reduce your answers to simple numbers.

1.8. Random Variables, Probability Functions, and Cumulative Distribution Functions

A *random variable* is a function that takes a defined value for every point in the sample space. For example, consider the sample space for the

SECT. 1.8 RANDOM VARIABLES, PROBABILITY FUNCTIONS

experiment consisting of the independent tossing of two fair coins. We can define a random variable X as the total number of heads observed. The values that X can take are represented by x. The sample space consists of the four points $(0, 0)$, $(0, 1)$, $(1, 0)$ and $(1,1)$, and at these points x takes the values 0, 1, 1 and 2. Let A_1 be the occurrence of a head with the first coin and A_2 the occurrence of a head with the second coin. The coins are assumed to be fair, and hence $\Pr\{A_i\} = 1/2$. The two throws are assumed to be independent, so

$$\Pr\{A_1 \cap A_2\} = \Pr\{A_1\} \Pr\{A_2\} = \frac{1}{2} \times \frac{1}{2} = \frac{1}{4}.$$

Likewise,

$$\Pr\{A_1^c \cap A_2\} = \Pr\{A_1^c\} \Pr\{A_2\} = \left(1 - \frac{1}{2}\right) \times \frac{1}{2} = \frac{1}{4},$$

etc. Thus the probability attached to each point in the sample space is 1/4. The probabilities of the events X taking the values 0, 1 and 2 are therefore 1/4, 1/4 + 1/4 = 1/2 and 1/4, respectively. This can be expressed in tabular form (Table 1.2). The probability that the random variable X takes the value x, $\Pr\{X = x\}$, is known as the *probability function* of x and is represented by $p_X\{x\}$. The sum over all possible values of x of the terms $p_X\{x\}$ must equal 1.

Table 1.2

x	0	1	2
$p_X\{x\}$	1/4	1/2	1/4

As another example, consider the sample space corresponding to the experiment of rolling onto a table a pair of fair 4-sided dice (i.e., regular tetrahedra with sides made up of equilateral triangles). Let the four faces of each die be numbered 1, 2, 3 and 4. If the dice are fair, the probability of a given face of one of the dice being in contact with the table is 1/4, and if the throws are independent the probability of obtaining the result $(1, 1)$ is $1/4 \times 1/4 = 1/16$, and likewise for all the other possible outcomes. Thus each of the 16 points in the sample space has a probability 1/16. We can define a random variable Y as the sum of the numbers in contact with the surface of the table. The points in the sample space and the corresponding values of y are as in Table 1.3. From this we can

Table 1.3

$(1, 1) = 2$	$(2, 1) = 3$	$(3, 1) = 4$	$(4, 1) = 5$
$(1, 2) = 3$	$(2, 2) = 4$	$(3, 2) = 5$	$(4, 2) = 6$
$(1, 3) = 4$	$(2, 3) = 5$	$(3, 3) = 6$	$(4, 3) = 7$
$(1, 4) = 5$	$(2, 4) = 6$	$(3, 4) = 7$	$(4, 4) = 8$

construct the probability function of the random variable Y, Table 1.4. Note that we could define another random variable Z on the same

Table 1.4

y	2	3	4	5	6	7	8
$p_Y\{y\}$	1/16	2/16	3/16	4/16	3/16	2/16	1/16

sample space; e.g., the ratio of the larger to the smaller number. The sample space, the same as before, and the corresponding values of z are as in Table 1.5.

Table 1.5

(1, 1) = 1	(2, 1) = 2	(3, 1) = 3	(4, 1) = 4
(1, 2) = 2	(2, 2) = 1	(3, 2) = 3/2	(4, 2) = 2
(1, 3) = 3	(2, 3) = 3/2	(3, 3) = 1	(4, 3) = 4/3
(1, 4) = 4	(2, 4) = 2	(3, 4) = 4/3	(4, 4) = 1

From this we can construct the probability function of the random variable Z, Table 1.6.

Table 1.6

z	1	4/3	3/2	2	3	4
$p_Z\{z\}$	4/16	2/16	2/16	4/16	2/16	2/16

The two sample spaces which we have just discussed contain only a finite number of points, actually 4 and 16 respectively. Such sample spaces are known as *discrete*. In addition, if the points in a sample space are infinite in number but can be arranged in a simple countable sequence, then that sample space is also regarded as discrete. We will encounter an example of this latter type in Section 3.11, the Poisson distribution. A random variable that is defined on a discrete sample space is known as a discrete random variable, and its probability function is known as a discrete probability function.

It is often convenient to represent discrete probability functions graphically, by raising a line on the x axis with height equal to the corresponding probability at each value of x. Tables 1.2, 1.4, and 1.6 thus give rise to Figures 1.9, 1.10, and 1.11.

Suppose that the values of x, ordered by increasing magnitude, are x_i, $i = 0, 1, \ldots, N$ (it is possible, in some cases, e.g., the Poisson distribution, for N to go to infinity). Then define the *cumulative distribution*

Figure 1.9

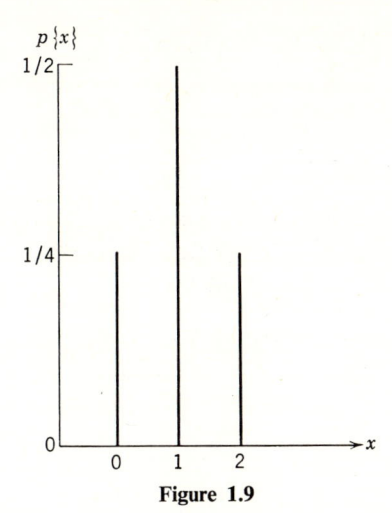

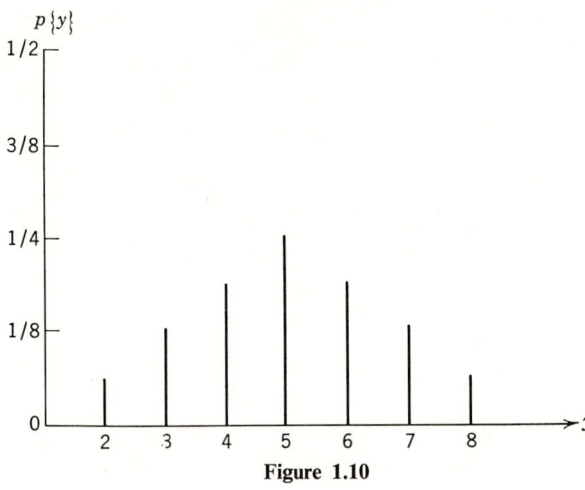

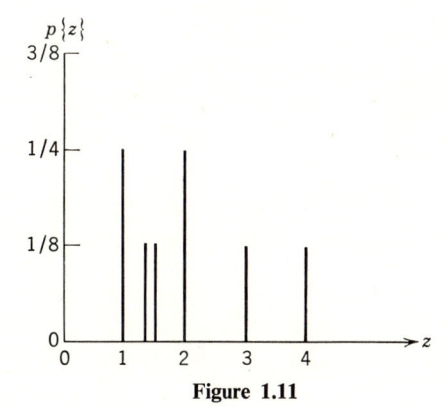

Figure 1.10

Figure 1.11

function, sometimes abbreviated as cdf, as

$$P\{x_n\} = \Pr\{X \leq x_n\} = \sum_{i=0}^{n} p\{x_i\} = p\{x_0\} + p\{x_1\} + \cdots + p\{x_n\}.$$
(8.1)

$P\{x_n\}$ is the probability that X is less than or equal to x_n. Tables 1.2, 1.4, 1.6 of probability functions give rise to corresponding cumulative distribution functions, Tables 1.7, 1.8, and 1.9.

Table 1.7

x	0	1	2
$P_X\{x\}$	1/4	3/4	1

Table 1.8

y	2	3	4	5	6	7	8
$P_Y\{y\}$	1/16	3/16	6/16	10/16	13/16	15/16	16/16

Table 1.9

z	1	4/3	3/2	2	3	4
$P_Z\{z\}$	4/16	6/16	8/16	12/16	14/16	16/16

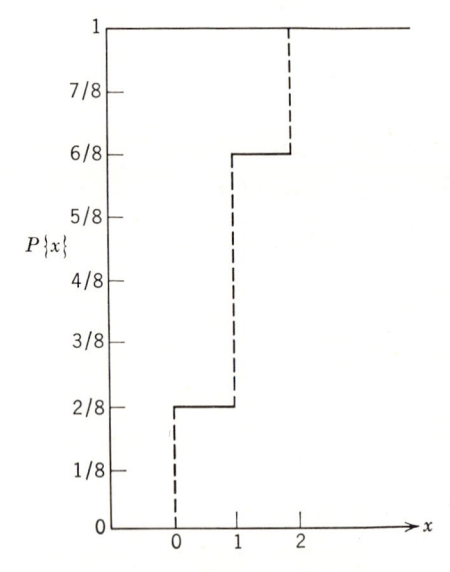

Figure 1.12

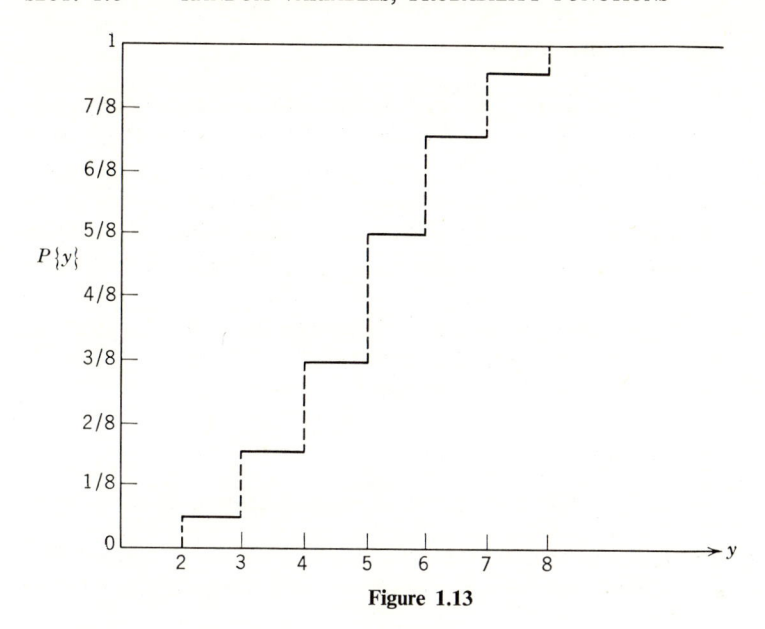

SECT. 1.8   RANDOM VARIABLES, PROBABILITY FUNCTIONS   29

Figure 1.13

These cumulative distribution functions can be represented graphically, as in Figures 1.12, 1.13, and 1.14.

It follows from (8.1) that $P\{x_N\} = 1$, and that

$$p\{x_n\} = P\{x_n\} - P\{x_{n-1}\}. \tag{8.2}$$

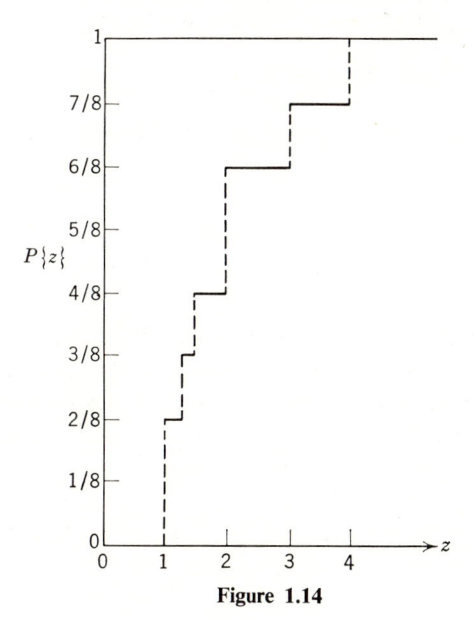

Figure 1.14

1.9. The Binomial Distribution

Suppose that we make a series of independent trials, and that the outcome of each trial is either A, a "success," with probability $\Pr\{A\} = \theta$, or A^c, a "failure," with probability $\Pr\{A^c\} = 1 - \theta$. We suppose that θ is constant for all trials and that successive trials are independent. We wish to calculate the probability of exactly x successes in n trials, $p_n\{x\}$.

First, consider the case where only two trials are made. The possible outcomes are AA, AA^c, A^cA and A^cA^c, and since successive trials are independent these outcomes have probabilities θ^2, $\theta(1 - \theta)$, $(1 - \theta)\theta$ and $(1 - \theta)^2$ respectively. It follows that $p_2\{0\} = (1 - \theta)^2$, $p_2\{1\} = 2\theta(1 - \theta)$ and $p_2\{2\} = \theta^2$. As a check we note that

$$\sum_{x=0}^{2} p_2\{x\} = p_2\{0\} + p_2\{1\} + p_2\{2\}$$
$$= (1 - \theta)^2 + 2(1 - \theta)\theta + \theta^2 = [(1 - \theta) + \theta]^2 = 1. \quad (9.1)$$

Second, consider the case where three trials are made. The possible outcomes and their probabilities are as in Table 1.10. It follows that

Table 1.10

Outcomes	Probabilities
AAA	θ^3
AAA^c, AA^cA, A^cAA	$\theta^2(1 - \theta)$
AA^cA^c, A^cAA^c, A^cA^cA	$\theta(1 - \theta)^2$
$A^cA^cA^c$	$(1 - \theta)^3$

$p_3\{0\} = (1 - \theta)^3$, $p_3\{1\} = 3\theta(1 - \theta)^2$, $p_3\{2\} = 3\theta^2(1 - \theta)$ and $p_3\{3\} = \theta^3$. Again as a check

$$\sum_{x=0}^{3} p_3\{x\} = (1 - \theta)^3 + 3(1 - \theta)^2\theta + 3(1 - \theta)\theta^2 + \theta^3$$
$$= [(1 - \theta) + \theta]^3 = 1. \quad (9.2)$$

We will now generalize to the case where n trials are made. The outcome $A \cdots AA^c \cdots A^c$, where A occurs x times and A^c occurs $n - x$ times, and any other permutation of x A's and $n - x$ A^c's gives rise to x successes. Altogether, by (7.7), there will be $n!/x!\,(n - x)!$ such permutations and each will have probability $\theta^x(1 - \theta)^{n-x}$. Thus

$$p_n\{x\} = \binom{n}{x}\theta^x(1 - \theta)^{n-x}. \quad (9.3)$$

SECT. 1.9 THE BINOMIAL DISTRIBUTION

The binomial theorem asserts that for any two real numbers R and S and positive integer n

$$(R + S)^n = \sum_{x=0}^{n} \binom{n}{x} R^x S^{n-x}. \tag{9.4}$$

Inserting θ for R and $1 - \theta$ for S gives

$$[\theta + (1 - \theta)]^n = \sum_{x=0}^{n} \binom{n}{x} \theta^x (1 - \theta)^{n-x}. \tag{9.5}$$

Thus $p_n\{x\}$ is the $(x + 1)$th term in this binomial expansion, which is why (9.3) is known as the binomial probability function. The left-hand

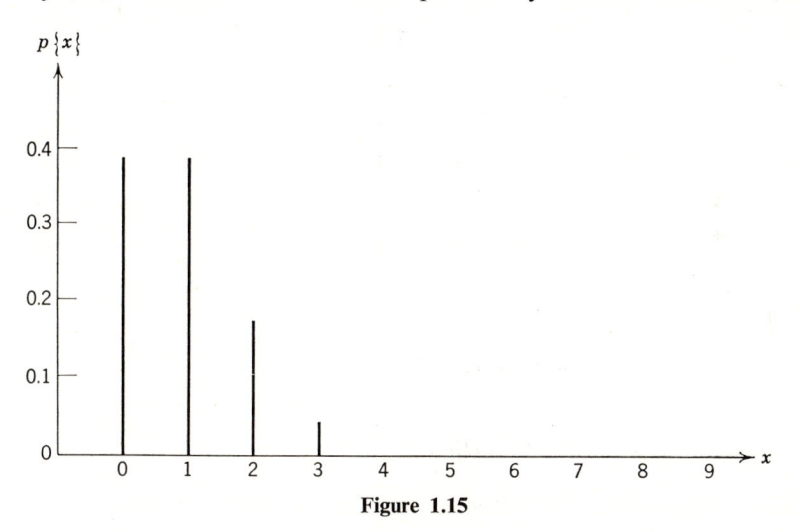

Figure 1.15

side of (9.5) is automatically equal to 1, since $\theta + (1 - \theta) = 1$, so $\sum_{x=0}^{n} p_n\{x\} = 1$, as it must. In (9.3) each choice of n and θ gives a different distribution; the constants n, θ are known as the *parameters* of the distribution.

The calculation of $p_n\{x\}$ when θ is a simple fraction and n and x are moderately small is comparatively easy. For example, if $n = 9$, $\theta = 1/10$,

$$p_9\{0\} = \binom{9}{0} \left(\frac{1}{10}\right)^0 \left(1 - \frac{1}{10}\right)^9 = \frac{9!}{0!(9-0)!} \frac{1^0 \times 9^9}{10^9} = 0.387, \tag{9.6}$$

$$p_9\{1\} = \binom{9}{1} \left(\frac{1}{10}\right)^1 \left(1 - \frac{1}{10}\right)^{9-1} = \frac{9!}{1!(9-1)!} \frac{1^1 \times 9^8}{10^9} = 0.387, \tag{9.7}$$

etc. This binomial probability function is shown in Figure 1.15: for

$x > 3$, $p\{x\}$ is too small numerically to be visible on the scale used. Figure 1.16 shows the binomial probability function with $n = 9$, $\theta = 1/2$: for $x = 0$ and for $x = 9$, $p\{x\} = (1/2)^9 = 1/512 = 0.00195$, which is too small to be visible on the scale used. For more awkward instances logarithms can be used:

$$\log_{10} p_n\{x\} = \log_{10} \binom{n}{x} + x \log_{10} \theta + (n - x) \log_{10}(1 - \theta). \quad (9.8)$$

Figure 1.16

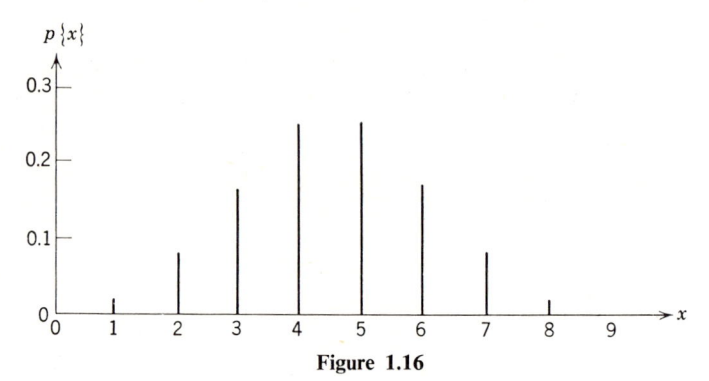

Table VIII of $\log_{10} n!$ can be used to evaluate

$$\log_{10} \binom{n}{x} = \log_{10} n! - \log_{10} x! - \log_{10}(n - x)!. \quad (9.9)$$

1.10. Curtailed Binomial Sampling

Consider a contest in which n games are played by two players P and Q. It is agreed that if P wins at least k games, then he has won the contest. Ordinarily, of course, n is odd, and determined by the equation $n = 2k - 1$. For example, it may be that to win the contest P has to win 4 games out of 7. This special relation between n and k is not essential to the problem, however. It could be that P is given an advantageous handicap so that he is declared the winner of the contest if he wins 3 games out of 8. In another example, if the fender on our automobile stays on so long as k out of n bolts do not vibrate loose, n and k are determined purely by the technology of the situation. Suppose that the probability of P winning any game is θ, and that successive games are independent. Then the probability of P winning x games is given by (9.3), and the probability of his winning the contest, say $A_k^n(\theta)$ is the sum of these terms for $x = k$, $k + 1, \ldots, n$; i.e.,

$$A_k^n(\theta) = \sum_{x=k}^{n} \binom{n}{x} \theta^x (1 - \theta)^{n-x}. \quad (10.1)$$

SECT. 1.10 CURTAILED BINOMIAL SAMPLING 33

Let us consider a particular case, say with $n = 5$, $k = 3$. Looking at the problem from first principles, each of the 5 games has 2 possible outcomes, so the total number of points in the sample space, which we will represent by symbols of the form $(WWWWW)$, $(WWWWL)$, etc., is $2^5 = 32$. The following classes of points correspond to the definition of P winning the contest:

(a) $(WWWWW)$ with probability θ^5.
(b) $(WWWWL)$, $(WWWLW)$, etc., making a total of $\binom{5}{1}$ such arrangements each with probability $\theta^4(1-\theta)^1$.
(c) $(WWWLL)$, $(WWLWL)$, etc., making a total of $\binom{5}{2}$ such arrangements each with probability $\theta^3(1-\theta)^2$.

The sum of the probabilities of these points can be found directly or from (10.1) as

$$A_3^5(\theta) = \sum_{x=3}^{5} \binom{5}{x} \theta^x (1-\theta)^{5-x} \qquad (10.2)$$

$$= \theta^3(10 - 15\theta + 6\theta^2). \qquad (10.3)$$

It is obvious that once P has won k games there is no point in playing any more: in reality, the contest will be terminated as soon as P has won k games, or as soon as Q has won $n - k + 1$ games. The previous analysis is thus unrealistic, although intuitively it is clear that nevertheless it must give the correct answer.

A more realistic analysis involves a restricted sample space, since a point $(WWWWW)$ will not exist in reality; if player P won the first three games he would be declared the winner of the contest and the last two games would never be played. The realistic sample space consists of the following classes of points:

(a) (WWW) with probability θ^3.
(b) $(LWWW)$, $(WLWW)$, $(WWLW)$, each with probability $\theta^3(1-\theta)$.
(c) $(LLWWW)$ plus other arrangements in which the first four games result in 2 W's and 2 L's, the last game always being a W. There are a total of $\binom{4}{2}$ such arrangements, all with probability $\theta^3(1-\theta)^2$.
(d) $(LLWWL)$ plus other arrangements in which the first four games result in 2 W's and 2 L's, the last game always being an L. There are a total of $\binom{4}{2}$ such arrangements, all with probability $\theta^2(1-\theta)^3$.
(e) $(WLLL)$ plus other arrangements in which the first three games

result in 1 W and 2 L's, the last game always being an L. There are a total of $\binom{3}{1}$ such arrangements, all with probability $\theta(1-\theta)^3$.

(f) (LLL) with probability $(1-\theta)^3$.

The entire realistic sample space therefore consists of $1 + 3 + 6 + 6 + 3 + 1 = 20$ points, and the sum of the probabilities of these 20 points is of course 1. Those points in classes (a), (b), and (c) conform with the definition of P winning the contest. The probability of P winning the contest, say $B_k^n(\theta)$, in this instance is

$$B_3^5(\theta) = \theta^3 + \binom{3}{1}\theta^3(1-\theta) + \binom{4}{2}\theta^3(1-\theta)^2 \qquad (10.4)$$

$$= \theta^3(10 - 15\theta + 6\theta^2), \qquad (10.5)$$

which is equal to $A_3^5(\theta)$ in (10.3).

The general form for $B_k^n(\theta)$ can be obtained by the following arguments:

$$B_k^n(\theta) = \Pr\Big\{ \underbrace{W \cdots W}_{k} + \underbrace{L\overbrace{W \cdots W}^{k-1}W}_{\binom{k}{1}\text{ permutations}} + \underbrace{LL\overbrace{W \cdots W}^{k-2}W}_{\binom{k+1}{2}\text{ permutations}} + \cdots$$

$$+ \underbrace{\overbrace{L \cdots L}^{n-k}\overbrace{W \cdots W}^{k}W}_{\binom{n-1}{n-k}\text{ permutations}} \Big\}. \qquad (10.6)$$

The xth term, for example, consists of $k + x$ games altogether, ending in a W for player P. The preceding sequence of $k - 1 + x$ games must include $k - 1$ W's, and therefore $(k - 1 + x) - (k - 1) = x$ L's. There will be $\binom{k-1+x}{x}$ such possible preceding sequences. Thus

$$\Pr\{\text{winning contest in } k + x \text{ games}\} = (1-\theta)^x \theta^k \binom{k-1+x}{x}, \qquad (10.7)$$

and the probability of winning the contest is

$$B_k^n(\theta) = \theta^k \sum_{x=0}^{n-k}(1-\theta)^x \binom{k-1+x}{x}. \qquad (10.8)$$

Since $A_k^n(\theta)$ and $B_k^n(\theta)$ give answers to two problems which must have the same answer, we must have

$$\sum_{y=k}^{n}\binom{n}{y}\theta^y(1-\theta)^{n-y} = \theta^k \sum_{x=0}^{n-k}(1-\theta)^x \binom{k-1+x}{x}, \qquad (10.9)$$

a rather remarkable identity which can be proved algebraically.

In a contest such as the World Series, in which $n = 7$, $k = 4$, the number of games required to terminate the contest, say x, is of interest. Since either team can win, we have

$$\Pr\{X = 4\} = \theta^4 + (1 - \theta)^4,$$

$$\Pr\{X = 5\} = \binom{4}{1}[\theta^4(1 - \theta) + \theta(1 - \theta)^4],$$

$$\Pr\{X = 6\} = \binom{5}{2}[\theta^4(1 - \theta)^2 + \theta^2(1 - \theta)^4],$$

$$\Pr\{X = 7\} = \binom{6}{3}[\theta^4(1 - \theta)^3 + \theta^3(1 - \theta)^4].$$

For $\theta = 1/2$, the probabilities are 2/16, 4/16, 5/16, and 5/16, and for $\theta = 3/4$, the probabilities are $328/4^5$, $336/4^5$, $225/4^5$, and $135/4^5$.

For an intensive examination of the World Series, see Mosteller [12].

EXERCISES 1C

1C.1. A professor of psychology writes the following:
"Let us now consider whether estimates of the probability of success in a given task obey rules similar to those of mathematical probability or are subject to different, psychological rules. One rule of mathematical probability convenient for such a test is the additive theorem: namely, that small, independent probabilities of a particular event add up to a larger probability. Thus if you are drawing for a lucky ticket in a pool, your chances of success will increase in proportion to the number of tickets you take. In one of our experiments we confronted our subjects with a choice between taking a single large probability or a set of smaller probabilities; e.g., they were allowed to draw either one ticket from a box of 10 or 10 tickets from 100, in the latter case putting back the ticket drawn each time before making the next draw. Mathematically, of course, the chance of drawing the prize ticket was exactly the same in both cases. But most of the subjects proved to be guided mainly by psychological rather than mathematical considerations.

"If the 10 draws had to be made from 100 tickets in one box, about four-fifths of the subjects preferred to make a single draw from a box of 10."
Comment.

1C.2. An aircraft has 4 engines, 2 on the left wing and 2 on the right wing. Suppose that the probability of any one engine failing on a certain transocean flight is 0.1, and that the probability of any one engine failing is independent of the behavior of the others. What is the probability of the crew getting wet (*a*) if the plane will fly on any 2 engines? (*b*) If the plane requires at least one (i.e., one or more) engine operating on both sides in order to fly?

1C.3. The Chevalier de Méré (1654) wanted to know the following probabilities: (*a*) probability of seeing one or more sixes in 4 throws of a 6 sided die; (*b*) probability of seeing one or more double sixes in 24 throws with a pair of dice.
The Chevalier thought that these two probabilities should be the same, but he

threw dice so assiduously he convinced himself they were different. Evaluate these two probabilities.

1C.4. Suppose that the probability that a light in a classroom will be burnt out is 1/4. The classroom has six lights, and is unusable if the number of lights burning is less than four. What is the probability that the classroom is unusable on a random occasion?

1C.5. "The United States SAC (Strategic Air Command) is supposed to be based upon about fifty home bases. If the Soviets happened to acquire, unknown to us, about 300 missiles, then they could assign about six missiles to the destruction of each base. If the Soviet missiles had, let us say, one chance in two of completing their countdown and otherwise performing reliably, then there would be ... (about) an even chance that all the bases would be destroyed, about one chance in three that one base would survive, and a small chance that two or more bases would survive." (From Herman Kahn, "The Arms Race and Some of Its Hazards," *Daedalus*, Volume 89, No. 4 of the Proceedings of the American Academy of Arts and Sciences, p. 744–80, 1960.)

Calculate the numerical value of the "small chance that two or more bases would survive."

1C.6. Large tomatoes are packaged at random three to a container. Let θ be the probability that a tomato has some flavor. Let E_1 be the event that not more than one tomato in a container has some flavor, and let E_2 be the event that at least one tomato has some flavor. (*a*) For what values of θ, excluding 0 and 1, are E_1 and E_2 independent? (*b*) As in (*a*), but suppose that a container contains four tomatoes.

1C.7. Consider making a sequence of independent trials with probability of success at each trial equal to θ. Let X be the number of trials necessary to observe a success. (*a*) Show that the probability function is

$$p_X\{x\} = (1 - \theta)^{x-1}\theta, \quad x \geq 1.$$

This is known as the *geometric* distribution. (*b*) Show that the corresponding cumulative distribution function is

$$P_X\{x\} = 1 - (1 - \theta)^x.$$

(*c*) What is the relationship between $\Pr\{x \leq 2a | x > a\}$ and $\Pr\{x \leq a\}$?

1C.8. Consider making a sequence of independent trials with probability of success at each trial equal to θ. Let Y be the number of trials necessary to achieve a successes. Show that the probability function is

$$p_Y\{y\} = \binom{y-1}{a-1}\theta^a(1-\theta)^{y-a}, \quad y \geq a.$$

This is known as the *Pascal* distribution.

1.11. Continuous Frequency Functions

So far we have only considered discrete probability functions, in which the probability is zero except for a discrete set of points on the line. We

SECT. 1.11   CONTINUOUS FREQUENCY FUNCTIONS   37

will now consider the case where X can vary continuously along the line. We will approach this question empirically.

Consider a very large population of some item, say cucumbers, from which we take a sample of 100 and measure the lengths to the nearest 4 cm, in such a way that anything between 22 and 26 is recorded as 24, etc. We can regard this as a discrete distribution, in which the cucumbers have lengths confined to nominal values 24, 28, 32, etc., and represent it by a line graph, Figure 1.17, in which the height of the line at each nominal

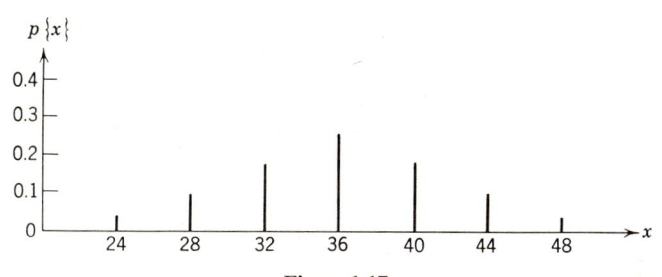

Figure 1.17

length of cucumbers is equal to the fraction of the sample with that nominal length. For the hypothetical data in Table 1.11, since the sample size is 100, the observed numbers must be divided by 100 to give the estimated values of $p\{x\}$, the fourth line in the table. Alternatively, we can replace the line graph by a *histogram*, a figure in which rectangles replace the lines, with the area of each rectangle equal to the fraction of the sample with each nominal size. The vertical scale must be adjusted so that the total area is 1. Since the base of each rectangle is 4 cm, the heights of the rectangles have to be one quarter of the corresponding lines (fifth line in Table 1.11). This is given in Figure 1.18.

Now suppose that we take a sample of twice the initial size, and measure the cucumbers to the nearest 2 cm, so that anything between 22 and 24 is recorded as 23 cm, etc. The observed numbers might be as in the eighth row of Table 1.11. We again construct a histogram in which the area of each rectangle is equal to the fraction of the sample with each nominal size. The base of each rectangle is 2 cm, so the $p\{x\}$ for a line graph, ninth row, have to be divided by 2 to make each area correct and to make the total area equal to 1. This gives us Figure 1.19. Now suppose that the process is repeated indefinitely, larger and larger samples being taken and measured to finer and finer intervals. Then in the limit we will obtain a smooth curve for the histogram, as indicated in Figure 1.19. Such a curve is known as a *continuous probability density distribution*, and the function $p\{x\}$ defining the curve is known as the *probability density function*.

Table 1.11

Nominal length	24	28	32	36	40	44	48
Actually the interval	22–26	26–30	30–34	34–38	38–42	42–46	46–50
Number in sample	4	10	18	36	18	10	4
$p\{x\}$ for line graph	0.04	0.10	0.18	0.36	0.18	0.10	0.04
$p\{x\}$ for histogram	0.010	0.025	0.045	0.090	0.045	0.025	0.010

Nominal length	23	25	27	29	31	33	35	37	39	41	43	45	47	49
Actually the interval	22–4	24–6	26–8	28–30	30–2	32–4	34–6	36–8	38–40	40–2	42–4	44–6	46–8	48–50
Number in sample	2	6	8	12	16	20	36	36	20	16	12	8	6	2
$p\{x\}$ for line graph	0.01	0.03	0.04	0.06	0.08	0.10	0.18	0.18	0.10	0.08	0.06	0.04	0.03	0.01
$p\{x\}$ for histogram	0.005	0.015	0.020	0.030	0.040	0.050	0.090	0.090	0.050	0.040	0.030	0.020	0.015	0.005

SECT. 1.11 CONTINUOUS FREQUENCY FUNCTIONS 39

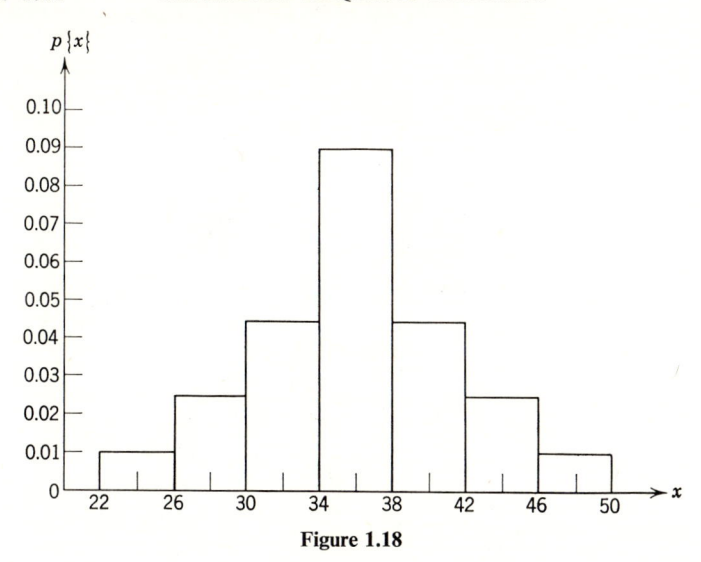

Figure 1.18

The probability that an observation X taken at random from a population with density function $p\{x\}$ lies between x_a and x_b is given by the area under the curve between x_a and x_b (Figure 1.20). The operation of finding such an area is handled mathematically by the technique of integration, denoted by the symbol

$$\int_{x_b}^{x_a} p\{x\}\, dx.$$

It follows that for the function $p\{x\}$ to be a probability density it must

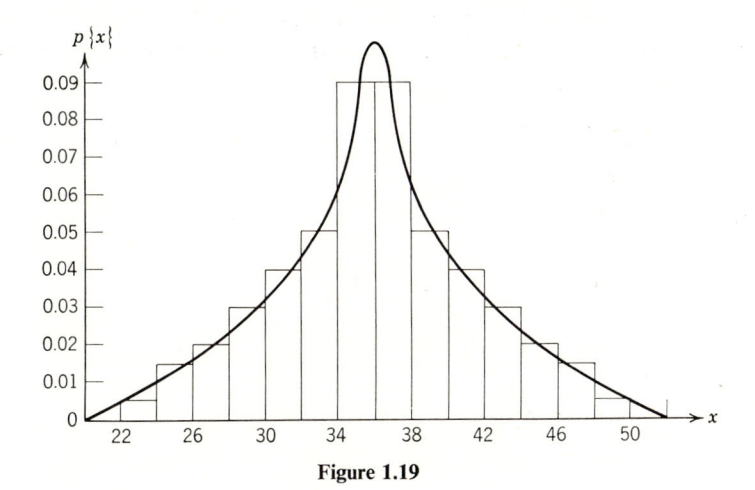

Figure 1.19

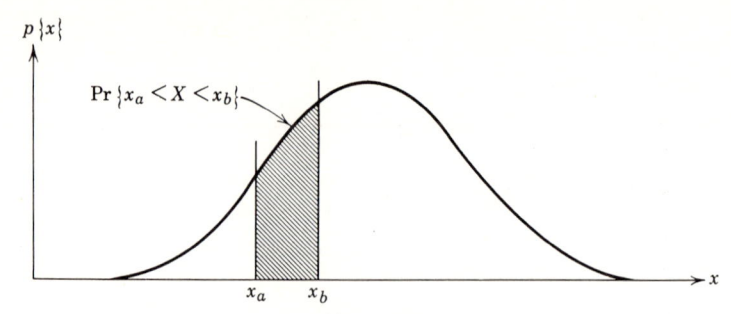

Figure 1.20

satisfy the condition that $p\{x\} \geq 0$ for all x and that

$$\int_{-\infty}^{\infty} p\{x\}\, dx = 1. \tag{11.1}$$

Also, we see from Figure 1.20 that

$$\Pr\{x_a < X < x_b\} = \int_{x_a}^{x_b} p\{x\}\, dx. \tag{11.2}$$

From the left-hand shaded area of Figure 1.21 we have

$$\Pr\{X < x_a\} = \int_{-\infty}^{x_a} p\{x\}\, dx, \tag{11.3}$$

and from the right-hand shaded area

$$\Pr\{X > x_b\} = \int_{x_b}^{\infty} p\{x\}\, dx. \tag{11.4}$$

In dealing with continuous distributions, we replace the summation operation that sufficed for discrete distributions by the integration operation. Thus the *cumulative distribution function* in the continuous case, analogous to (8.1) in the discrete case, is

$$P\{x\} = \Pr\{X < x\} = \int_{-\infty}^{x} p\{t\}\, dt. \tag{11.5}$$

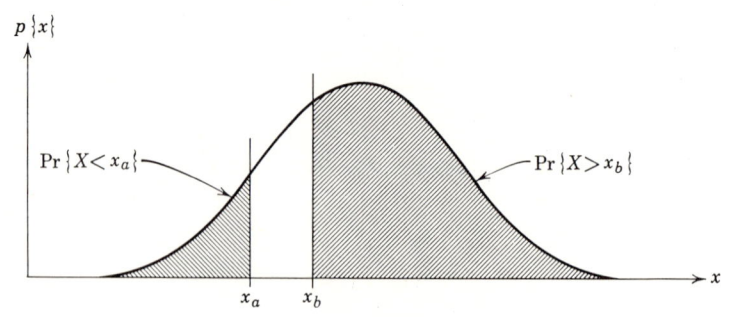

Figure 1.21

SECT. 1.11 CONTINUOUS FREQUENCY FUNCTIONS

From a given probability density function $p\{x\}$ we can compute $P\{x\}$ for every x, and construct its graphical form. $P\{x\}$ must start at zero on the left-hand end, since

$$\int_{-\infty}^{-\infty} p\{x\}\, dx = 0,$$

and reach 1 on the right-hand side, since

$$\int_{-\infty}^{\infty} p\{x\}\, dx = 1$$

by (11.1). The upper part of Figure 1.22 gives the cumulative distribution $P\{x\}$ corresponding to the density function $p\{x\}$ in the lower part of the figure. A cumulative distribution function graph has the property that

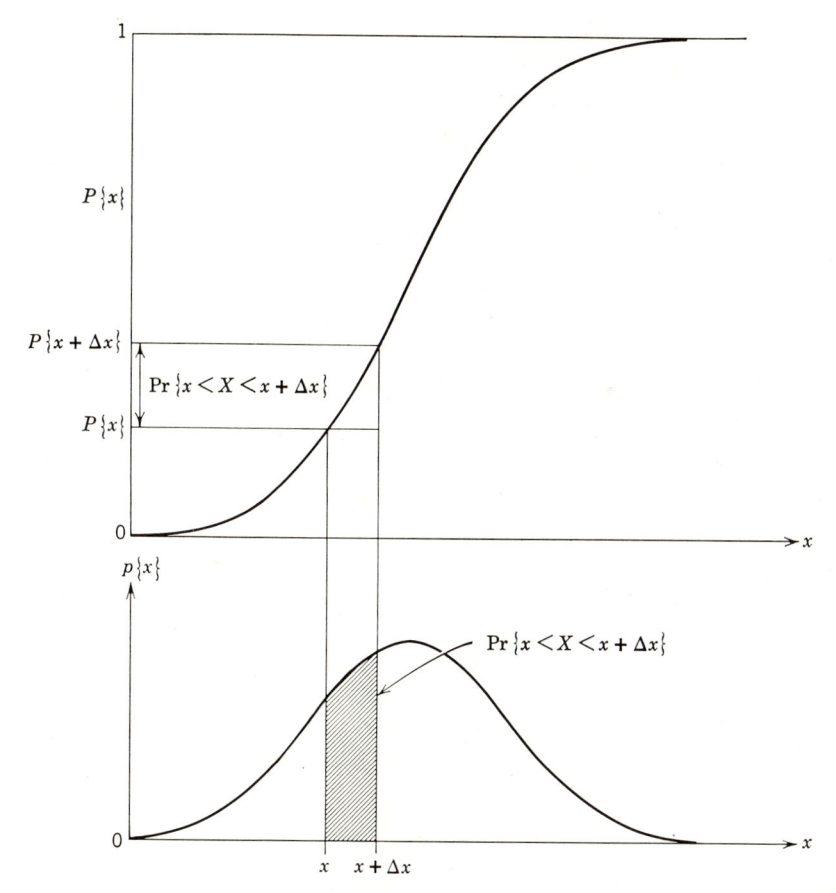

Figure 1.22

its slope can never be negative, since the probability density function from which it is derived can never be negative.

By the elementary rules of calculus, the derivative of a function $f(x)$, denoted by the symbol $df(x)/dx$, is equal to the slope of the function at the point x. Furthermore, the derivative of an indefinite integral of a function is the function itself; i.e., the derivative of (11.5) with respect to x is

$$\frac{dP\{x\}}{dx} = \frac{d}{dx}\int_{-\infty}^{x} p\{t\}\,dt = p\{x\}, \qquad (11.6)$$

so the slope of the cumulative distribution function is equal to the probability density function at that point.

To see this graphically, in the upper part of Figure 1.22,

$$\Pr\{x < X < x + \Delta x\} = P\{x + \Delta x\} - P\{x\}, \qquad (11.7)$$

and in the lower part of Figure 1.22,

$$\Pr\{x < X < x + \Delta x\} = \int_{x}^{x+\Delta x} p\{t\}\,dt \simeq p\{x\}\,\Delta x. \qquad (11.8)$$

Since the left-hand sides of (11.7) and (11.8) are identical, we can equate the right-hand sides, whence

$$\frac{P\{x + \Delta x\} - P\{x\}}{\Delta x} \simeq p\{x\}. \qquad (11.9)$$

When we take the limit of Δx tending to zero, the approximate equality sign tends to an equality sign, and the limit of the left-hand side is just the definition of the derivative of $P\{x\}$:

$$\lim_{\Delta x \to 0} \frac{P\{x + \Delta x\} - P\{x\}}{\Delta x} = \frac{dP\{x\}}{dx} = p\{x\}. \qquad (11.10)$$

1.12. Examples of Continuous Distributions

Any continuous function $f(x)$ which is never negative and for which

$$\int_{-\infty}^{\infty} f(x)\,dx = 1$$

can be regarded as a probability density function.

The *rectangular* or *uniform* distribution has the density function

$$p\{x\} = \frac{1}{c - b}, \qquad b < x < c,$$
$$= 0, \qquad \text{otherwise.} \qquad (12.1)$$

SECT. 1.12   EXAMPLES OF CONTINUOUS DISTRIBUTIONS

The parameters b and c must be such that $c - b > 0$. For the special case of $b = -a/2$, $c = a/2$, this becomes

$$p\{x\} = \frac{1}{a}, \quad -\frac{a}{2} < x < \frac{a}{2},$$
$$= 0, \quad \text{otherwise,} \qquad (12.2)$$

and is graphed in the upper part of Figure 1.23. The cumulative distribution function is

$$P\{x\} = \int_{-\infty}^{x} p\{t\}\, dt = \frac{1}{a}\int_{-a/2}^{x} dt = \frac{t}{a}\Big|_{-a/2}^{x}$$
$$= \frac{1}{a}\left[x - \left(-\frac{a}{2}\right)\right] = \frac{x}{a} + \frac{1}{2} \qquad (12.3)$$

for x satisfying the inequality $-a/2 < x < a/2$. For $x = -a/2$, $P\{x\} = 0$; for $x = 0$, $P\{x\} = 1/2$; and for $x = a/2$, $P\{x\} = 1$. The cumulative distribution function is thus zero up to $-a/2$, a straight line with slope $1/a$ from $(-a/2, 0)$ to $(a/2, 1)$, and 1 for $x > a/2$, as shown in the lower part of Figure 1.23.

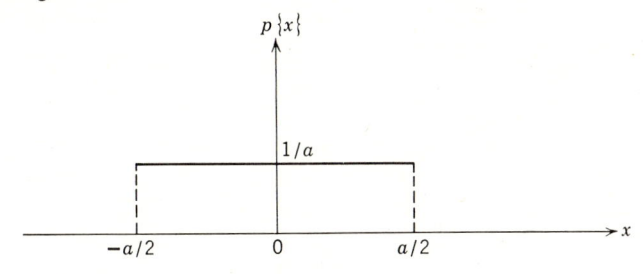

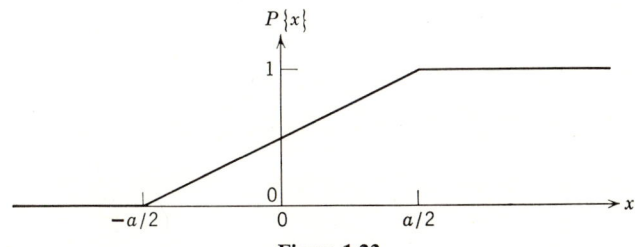

Figure 1.23

Another simple family of continuous probability density functions is the negative exponential:

$$p\{x\} = \theta e^{-\theta x}, \quad 0 \leq x < \infty,$$
$$= 0, \quad \text{otherwise,} \qquad (12.4)$$

where θ is a fixed parameter greater than zero, and e is the base of natural logarithms. The cumulative distribution function is

$$P\{x\} = \theta \int_0^x e^{-\theta t}\, dt = \theta \left(-\frac{1}{\theta} e^{-\theta t}\right)\bigg|_0^x = -e^{-\theta t}\bigg|_0^x$$

$$= -\frac{1}{e^{\theta x}} - \left(-\frac{1}{e^0}\right) = 1 - \frac{1}{e^{\theta x}}. \qquad (12.5)$$

The probability density function (12.4) and the cumulative distribution function (12.5) are graphed in Figure 1.24 for the case $\theta = 0.5$. Each value of θ will give a different but similar distribution.

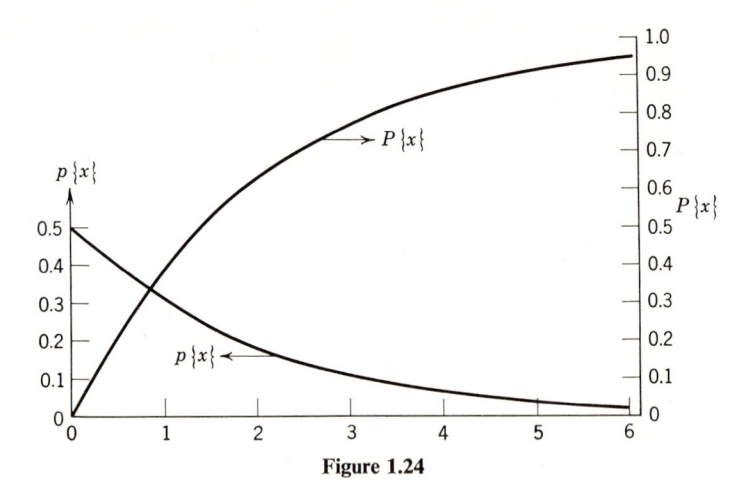

Figure 1.24

A particularly important family of continuous probability density functions is the so-called normal or gaussian:

$$p\{x\} = \frac{1}{\sqrt{2\pi}\,\sigma} e^{-(x-\xi)^2/2\sigma^2}, \qquad (12.6)$$

where ξ and σ are fixed parameters, π has its traditional meaning, and e is the base of natural logarithms. The cumulative distribution function is

$$P\{x\} = \frac{1}{\sqrt{2\pi}\,\sigma} \int_{-\infty}^x e^{-(t-\xi)^2/2\sigma^2}\, dt, \qquad (12.7)$$

involving an integration that does not lead to a standard explicit form, and the integration has to be performed numerically. We will often write (12.6) as $N(\xi, \sigma^2)$.

1.13. Transformations of Probability Functions and Density Functions

We are sometimes faced with the problem of finding the distribution of a function $Y = f(X)$ of a random variable X, already knowing the distribution of X itself. For example, suppose that the distribution of diameters D of a certain population of ball bearings is normal. The volume of a sphere is $\frac{4}{3}\pi r^3 = \pi d^3/6$ and if the density of the material is ρ then the weight $w = \rho \pi d^3/6$. We may now want to know the form of the distribution of the weights W.

We assume that $y = f(x)$ is a strictly monotonic function of x, and therefore $x = g(y)$ is a strictly monotonic function of y.

In the discrete case things are simple. Let $p_Y\{y\}$ be the probability function of Y. Whenever X takes a particular value x, which it does with probability $p_X\{x\}$, then Y takes the corresponding value $y = f\{x\}$, also with the same probability $p_X\{x\}$, so

$$p_X\{x\} = p_X\{g(y)\} = p_Y\{y\}. \tag{13.1}$$

As an example, consider the probability function of Table 1.4. This can be represented by the formula

$$p_Y\{y\} = \frac{1}{16}(4 - |y - 5|), \qquad y = 2, 3, \ldots, 8. \tag{13.2}$$

Consider the function $v = f(y) = y^2$, which has the inverse function $y = g(v) = \sqrt{v}$. Then

$$p_V\{v\} = p_Y\{g(v)\} = \frac{1}{16}(4 - |\sqrt{v} - 5|), \qquad v = 4, 9, \ldots, 64. \tag{13.3}$$

To illustrate this, consider the case when $y = 3$. Then $v = 9$. From (13.2),

$$p_Y\{y = 3\} = \frac{1}{16}(4 - |3 - 5|) = \frac{2}{16}, \tag{13.4}$$

and from (13.3),

$$p_V\{v = 9\} = \frac{1}{16}(4 - |\sqrt{9} - 5|) = \frac{2}{16}. \tag{13.5}$$

The continuous case is more troublesome. Figure 1.25a shows y as a function of x, $y = f\{x\}$, and x as a function of y, $x = g\{y\}$. Figure 1.25b shows the density function of x, $p_X\{x\}$. Now whenever y falls in the interval $(y_1, y_1 + \Delta y_1)$, then x must fall in the interval $(x_1, x_1 + \Delta x_1)$, i.e., in the interval $(g(y_1), g(y_1 + \Delta y_1))$. Therefore the probabilities of these

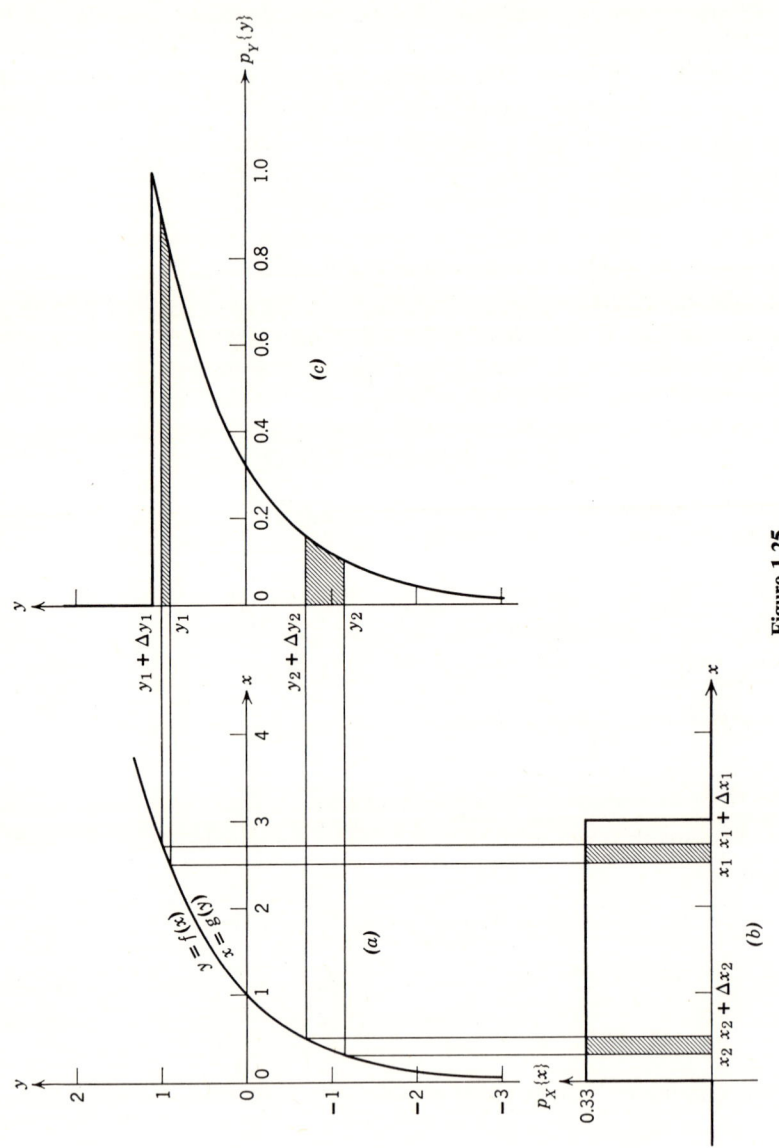

Figure 1.25

SECT. 1.13   TRANSFORMATIONS OF PROBABILITY FUNCTIONS   47

two events must be equal:

$$p_Y\{y_1\} \Delta y_1 = p_X\{x_1\}[g(y_1 + \Delta y_1) - g(y_1)], \tag{13.6}$$

whence, dropping the subscript and substituting $g(y)$ for x:

$$p_Y\{y\} = p_X\{g(y)\} \frac{g(y + \Delta y) - g(y)}{\Delta y}. \tag{13.7}$$

In the limit $\Delta y \to 0$ we obtain

$$p_Y\{y\} = p_X\{g(y)\} \frac{dg}{dy}. \tag{13.8}$$

In words, the probability density function for Y equals the formula for the probability density for X, with $g(y) = x$ substituted for x, multiplied by the derivative of $g(y)$ with respect to y. The foregoing discussion assumed that y was a strictly increasing function of x everywhere. The same result is readily obtained if y is a strictly decreasing function of x everywhere, the only difference being that in (13.8) in place of dg/dy the absolute value of dg/dy, namely $|dg/dy|$, appears:

$$p_Y\{y\} = p_X\{g(y)\} \left| \frac{dg}{dy} \right|. \tag{13.9}$$

As an example, consider the normal density function (12.6). As it stands, it is a different function for every pair of values of ξ and σ, and it is obviously impossible to tabulate an infinity of normal distributions. However, all these normal distributions can be reduced to a common form, the standardized normal distribution, by a simple transformation. Define

$$y = f(x) = \frac{x - \xi}{\sigma} = \frac{x}{\sigma} - \frac{\xi}{\sigma}. \tag{13.10}$$

The inverse function $x = g(y)$ is obtained by solving (13.10) for x:

$$x = g(y) = \sigma y + \xi. \tag{13.11}$$

The derivative of $g(y)$ with respect to y is $dg(y)/dy = \sigma$. We now substitute in (13.8):

$$p_Y(y) = \frac{1}{\sqrt{2\pi}\,\sigma} e^{-y^2/2} \cdot \sigma = \frac{1}{\sqrt{2\pi}} e^{-y^2/2}$$

This is the standardized normal distribution, for which we reserve the symbol $\phi(u)$:

$$\phi(u) = \frac{1}{\sqrt{2\pi}} e^{-u^2/2}. \tag{13.12}$$

The cumulative form, for which we use the symbol $\Phi(u)$, is

$$\Phi(u) = \int_{-\infty}^{u} \frac{1}{\sqrt{2\pi}} e^{-t^2/2} \, dt. \tag{13.13}$$

A random variable with the probability density (13.12) is often referred to as a *unit* or *standardized normal deviate*. The properties of $\phi(u)$ and of $\Phi(u)$ are discussed in Section 1.18.

1.14. Another Example of the Transformation of a Density Function

If $y = f(x)$ is a function such that two (or more) values of x can correspond to the same value of y, then (13.8) can be applied to each section of the function over which monotonicity holds and then the resulting density functions added together.

As an example, consider the function $y = f(x) = x^2$, sketched in Figure 1.26a, when x has the density function sketched in Figure 1.26b. The inverse functions are

$$x = g_1(y) = -\sqrt{y} \quad \text{when } -\infty < x < 0,$$
$$= g_2(y) = \sqrt{y} \quad \text{when } 0 < x < \infty. \tag{14.1}$$

When x is in the interval $g_1(y), g_1(y + \Delta y)$, then y is in the interval $y, y + \Delta y$, and also when x is in the interval $g_2(y), g_2(y + \Delta y)$, then y is again in the interval $y, y + \Delta y$. The corresponding probabilities must be equal:

$$p_Y\{y\} \Delta y = p_X\{g_1(y)\} |g_1(y + \Delta y) - g_1(y)|$$
$$+ p_X\{g_2(y)\} |g_2(y + \Delta y) - g_2(y)|, \tag{14.2}$$

whence, dividing by Δy and taking the limit as $\Delta y \to 0$,

$$p_Y\{y\} = p_X\{g_1(y)\} \left|\frac{dg_1}{dy}\right| + p_X\{g_2(y)\} \left|\frac{dg_2}{dy}\right|. \tag{14.3}$$

As an example, consider the function $y = f(x) = x^2$, Figure 1.27a, when x has the density function (Figure 1.27b)

$$p_X\{x\} = \frac{2}{9a}\left(1 - \frac{x}{a}\right), \quad -2a < x < a,$$
$$= 0, \quad \text{otherwise}. \tag{14.4}$$

Figure 1.27 is drawn with $a = \frac{1}{3}$. The inverse functions are

$$x = g_1(y) = -\sqrt{y}, \quad -2a < x < 0, \tag{14.5}$$
$$x = g_2(y) = \sqrt{y}, \quad 0 < x < a. \tag{14.6}$$

SECT. 1.14 TRANSFORMATION OF A DENSITY FUNCTION

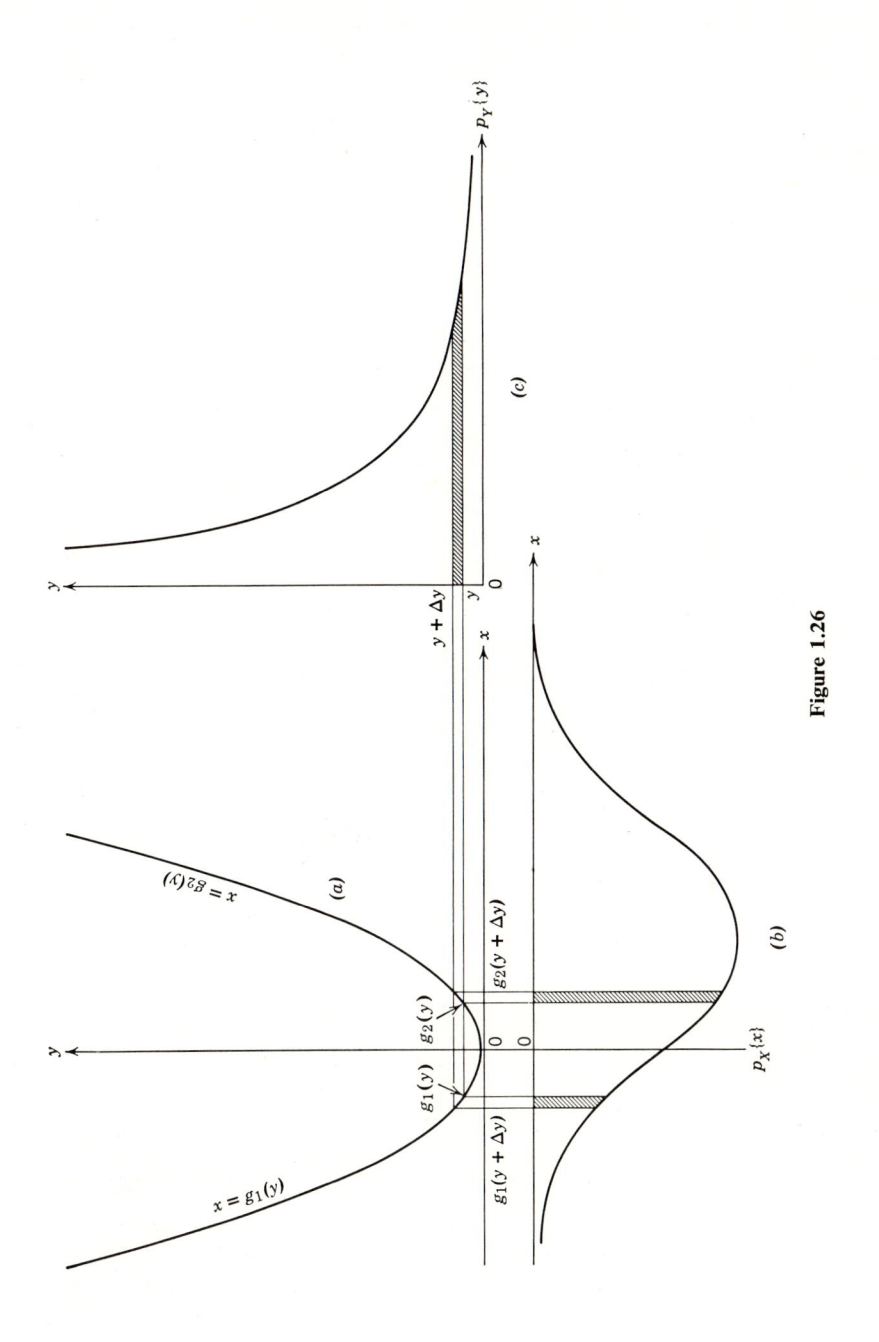

Figure 1.26

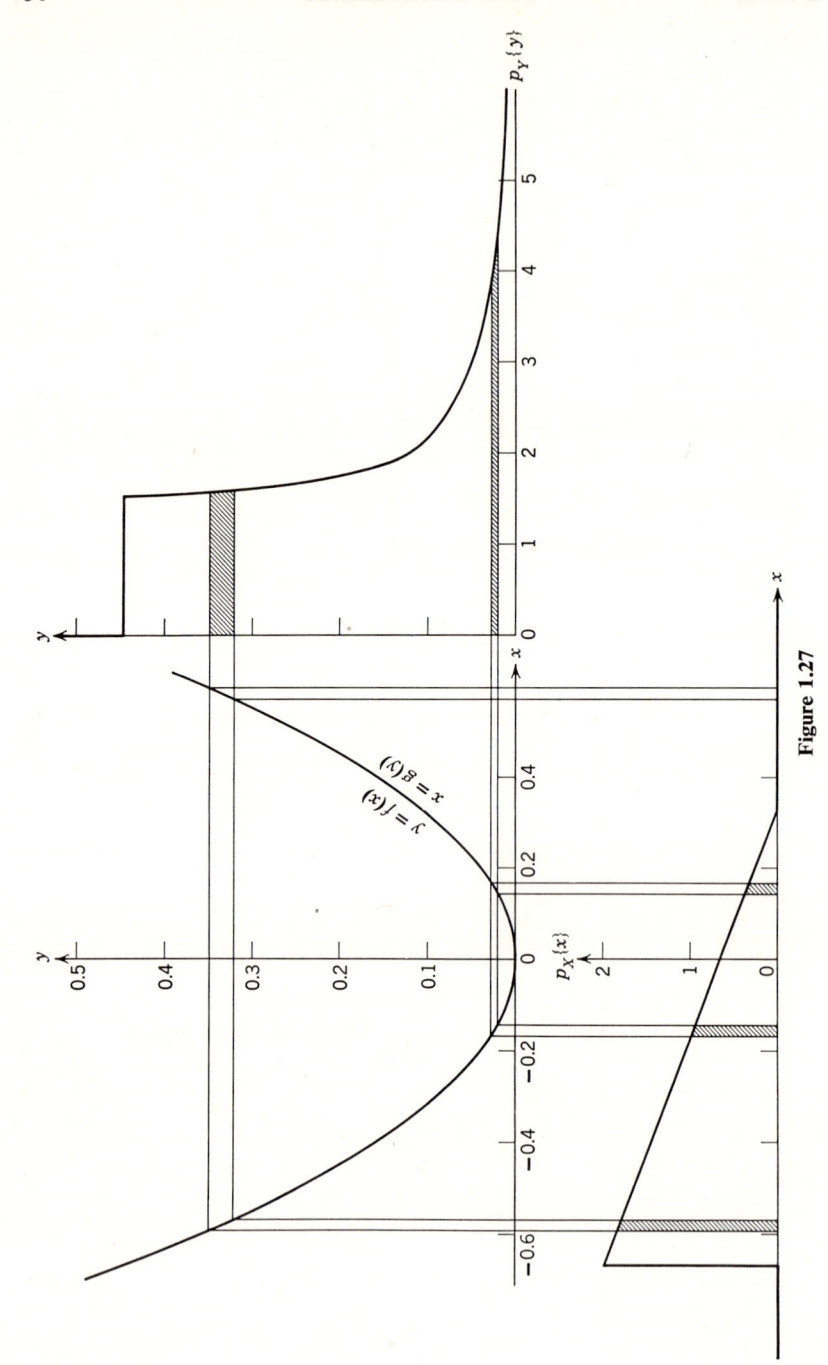

Figure 1.27

SECT. 1.15   THE CONCEPT OF EXPECTATION

Application of (14.3) gives

$$p_{Y(1)}\{y\} = \frac{2}{9a}\left(1 - \frac{(-\sqrt{y})}{a}\right)\left|-\frac{1}{2}y^{-\frac{1}{2}}\right| \tag{14.7}$$

$$= \frac{1}{9a\sqrt{y}}\left(1 + \frac{\sqrt{y}}{a}\right), \quad \begin{cases} -2a < x < 0 \\ 0 < y < 4a^2, \end{cases} \tag{14.8}$$

and

$$p_{Y(2)}\{y\} = \frac{2}{9a}\left(1 - \frac{\sqrt{y}}{a}\right)\left|\frac{1}{2}y^{-\frac{1}{2}}\right| \tag{14.9}$$

$$= \frac{1}{9a\sqrt{y}}\left(1 - \frac{\sqrt{y}}{a}\right), \quad \begin{cases} 0 < x < a \\ 0 < y < a^2. \end{cases} \tag{14.10}$$

Adding these two functions gives

$$p_Y\{y\} = \frac{2}{9a\sqrt{y}}, \qquad\qquad 0 < y < a^2,$$

$$= \frac{1}{9a\sqrt{y}}\left(1 + \frac{\sqrt{y}}{a}\right) = \frac{1}{9a\sqrt{y}} + \frac{1}{9a^2}, \quad a^2 < y < 4a^2,$$

$$= 0, \qquad\qquad\qquad \text{otherwise.} \tag{14.11}$$

This density function is plotted in Figure 1.27c.

1.15. The Concept of Expectation

Two of the most useful properties of a random variable are its *expectation* (or *expected value* or *mean*) and its *variance*. In this section we will discuss expectation, defined as

$$E[X] = \sum_i x_i p\{x_i\}, \qquad \text{in the discrete case,} \tag{15.1}$$

$$= \int_{-\infty}^{\infty} xp\{x\}\,dx, \qquad \text{in the continuous case.} \tag{15.2}$$

The usefulness of the concept of expectation is that it corresponds to our intuitive idea of average. Consider the binomial distribution of Figure 1.15 with $n = 9$, $\theta = 0.1$. The random variable x could be the number of defective electronic tubes found in random samples of 9 from a population of tubes whose fraction defective is 0.1. The numerical values of $p\{x\}$ calculated with (9.3) are given in the first column of Table 1.12. If we imagine drawing 1,000,000 samples, we would expect to find 0 defectives in the sample 1,000,000 × 0.387,420 = 387,420 times, etc. Thus the total number of defectives found in the 1,000,000 samples would be

$$0 \times 387{,}420 + 1 \times 387{,}420 + 2 \times 172{,}187 + \cdots = 899{,}999,$$

so the average number of defectives per sample is 899,999/1,000,000 = 0.9. This calculation is exactly that of the expected value, (15.1). The expected value is not necessarily the most frequent value (which is known as the *mode* of the distribution). In fact, for a discrete distribution the expected

Table 1.12

x	$p\{x\}$	$1{,}000{,}000 p\{x\}$	$x \times 1{,}000{,}000 p\{x\}$
0	0.387420	387,420	0
1	0.387420	387,420	387,420
2	0.172187	172,187	344,374
3	0.044641	44,641	133,923
4	0.007440	7,440	29,760
5	0.000827	827	4,135
6	0.000061	61	366
7	0.000003	3	21
8	0.000000	0	0
9	0.000000	0	0

value may never occur at all. For example, the binomial distribution is confined to the integers 0, 1, 2, ..., n, and there is no reason in general why its expectation, which we shall show is $n\theta$, should be an integer. In the present example, for instance, there are actually two most-frequent values, 0 and 1, and the expected value 0.9 is equal to neither of them.

If we visualize a distribution plotted on stiff card and cut out, and then balanced on a knife edge parallel to the $p\{x\}$ axis, it will balance at the expected value of X. The expected value is equal to the center of gravity of the distribution along the x axis.

A constant can be regarded as a discrete distribution entirely at one point. Thus in $E[a] = \Sigma\, ap\{a\}$, the summation is just a single term and $p\{a\} = 1$; hence $E[a] = a$. Thus the expectation of a constant is that constant. Also, since $E[X]$ is a constant,

$$E[E[X]] = E[X]. \tag{15.3}$$

To consider a simple example of the expected value of a distribution, Table 1.13 shows the calculation of the expectation of the random variable Y equal to the sum of two 4-sided dice whose frequency distribution was given in Table 1.4.

Table 1.13

y_i	$p\{y_i\}$	$y_i p\{y_i\}$
2	1/16	2/16
3	2/16	6/16
4	3/16	12/16
5	4/16	20/16
6	3/16	18/16
7	2/16	14/16
8	1/16	8/16

$$E[Y] = \sum_i y_i p\{y_i\} = 80/16 = 5$$

A more interesting example is the expectation of the binomial distribution (9.3). By the definition of expectation for a discrete random variable, (15.1),

$$E[X] = \sum_{x=0}^{n} x \binom{n}{x} \theta^x (1-\theta)^{n-x}. \tag{15.4}$$

We note that

$$x\binom{n}{x} = \frac{xn!}{x!(n-x)!} = \frac{(n-1)!}{(x-1)!(n-x)!} n = \binom{n-1}{x-1} n, \tag{15.5}$$

so (15.4) can be written as

$$E[X] = n\theta \sum_{x=1}^{n} \binom{n-1}{x-1} \theta^{x-1} (1-\theta)^{n-x}. \tag{15.6}$$

We have changed the lower limit of the summation from 0 in (15.4) to 1 in (15.6), for when $x = 0$ the corresponding term in the summation is zero and adds nothing to the summation, and hence can be omitted. Equation (15.6) will appear in a more satisfactory form if we write $x = y + 1$, so $x - 1 = y$, and $n = m + 1$, so $n - 1 = m$. In (15.6), x ranges over 1 to n, or 1 to $m + 1$, so y ranges over 0 to m; thus

$$E[X] = n\theta \sum_{y=0}^{m} \binom{m}{y} \theta^y (1-\theta)^{m-y}. \tag{15.7}$$

The summation following $n\theta$ is the sum of all the terms of a binomial distribution for samples of size m, and the sum of any probability function must equal 1. Hence

$$E[X] = n\theta. \tag{15.8}$$

To turn to continuous distributions, the rectangular distribution, (12.2), has the expectation, using the definition (15.2),

$$E[X] = \int_{-a/2}^{a/2} x \cdot \frac{1}{a} \, dx = \frac{1}{a} \frac{x^2}{2} \bigg|_{-a/2}^{a/2} = 0. \tag{15.9}$$

The expectation of the exponential distribution, (12.4), is

$$E[X] = \int_0^\infty x\theta e^{-\theta x} \, dx. \tag{15.10}$$

If we use the rule for integration by parts,

$$\int f(x)g'(x) \, dx = f(x)g(x) - \int g(x)f'(x) \, dx, \tag{15.11}$$

and identify $f(x)$ with x so that $f'(x) = 1$, and $g'(x)$ with $\theta e^{-\theta x}$ so that $g(x) = -e^{-\theta x}$, we get

$$E[X] = \int_0^\infty x\theta e^{-\theta x} \, dx = x(-e^{-\theta x})\bigg|_0^\infty - \int_0^\infty (-e^{-\theta x}) \cdot 1 \cdot dx$$

$$= 0 - \left(\frac{1}{\theta} e^{-\theta x}\right)\bigg|_0^\infty = \frac{1}{\theta}. \tag{15.12}$$

For the normal distribution, (12.6),

$$E[X] = \int_{-\infty}^\infty x p\{x\} \, dx = \int_{-\infty}^\infty [\xi + (x - \xi)] p\{x\} \, dx$$

$$= \xi \int_{-\infty}^\infty p\{x\} \, dx + \int_{-\infty}^\infty (x - \xi) \frac{1}{\sqrt{2\pi}\,\sigma} e^{-(x-\xi)^2/2\sigma^2} \, dx. \tag{15.13}$$

Since the integral over the whole line of any probability density function is 1, the first term on the right-hand side is ξ. To evaluate the second integral, we make a change of variable to $y = x - \xi$ and obtain

$$\frac{1}{\sqrt{2\pi}\,\sigma} \int_{-\infty}^\infty y e^{-y^2/2\sigma^2} \, dy = -\frac{\sigma}{\sqrt{2\pi}} e^{-y^2/2\sigma^2} \bigg|_{-\infty}^\infty = 0. \tag{15.14}$$

Thus for the normal distribution

$$E[X] = \xi. \tag{15.15}$$

We have defined two of the classical so-called measures of central tendency, the expected value or the mean and the mode. The third, the median, say x_m, is that value of x which has half the mass of the distribution below it and half the mass above it. Thus if we pick an X at random it is equally likely to lie above as to lie below the median x_m. For symmetric distributions, e.g., the rectangular or the normal, the median coincides with the expectation, but for asymmetric distributions this will not usually be the case. For example, for the exponential distribution (12.4) we find the median x_m by requiring that x_m satisfy the condition that $\Pr\{X < x_m\} = 1/2$. But from (12.5) we have

$$\Pr\{X < x_m\} = P\{x_m\} = 1 - \frac{1}{e^{\theta x_m}}. \tag{15.16}$$

Equating these and solving for x_m, we obtain

$$x_m = \frac{1}{\theta} \log_e 2 = \frac{0.69315}{\theta}. \tag{15.17}$$

Incidentally, we recall from (15.12) that the expectation of the exponential distribution is $1/\theta$, so the median is $0.693E[X]$, and Figure 1.24 shows that the mode of the exponential distribution is zero.

1.16. The Expectation of a Function of a Random Variable

Suppose that $Y = f(X)$ is a monotonic function of X and $X = g(Y)$ is likewise monotonic. We will need to determine the expected value of Y, given the density function of X: by the definition (15.2),

$$E[Y] = \int_{-\infty}^{\infty} y p_Y\{y\}\, dy. \tag{16.1}$$

To evaluate $E[Y]$ in this form involves finding $p_Y\{y\}$. However, for functions with the properties specified in Section 1.13 on the transformation of distributions, so that $y = f(x)$ is a single-valued function of x and $x = g(y)$ is a single-valued function of y, we can substitute $f(x)$ for y and $p_X\{g(y)\}\,|dg/dy|$ for $p_Y\{y\}$, from (13.9), in (16.1). We also need to change the variable of integration from y to x. The rule for change of variable when $v = \phi(u)$, $u = \psi(v)$ is

$$\int_a^b h(v)\, dv = \int_{\psi(a)}^{\psi(b)} h(\phi(u)) \phi'(u)\, du. \tag{16.2}$$

To apply this formula, replace v by y, u by x, $\phi(u)$ by $f(x)$, $\psi(v)$ by $g(y)$, and $h(v)$ by $y p_Y\{y\}$. Changing the variable in $y p_Y\{y\}$ to x gives $f(x) p_X\{g(y)\}\, dx/dy$, corresponding to $h(\phi(u))$. Corresponding to $\phi'(u) = dv/du$ we have dy/dx. Also when $y = \infty$, $x = g(\infty) = \infty$, and when $y = -\infty$, $x = -\infty$. Therefore

$$E[f(X)] = \int_{-\infty}^{\infty} y p_Y\{y\}\, dy = \int_{-\infty}^{\infty} f(x) p_X\{x\} \left|\frac{dx}{dy}\right| \left|\frac{dy}{dx}\right| dx$$

$$= \int_{-\infty}^{\infty} f(x) p_X\{x\}\, dx. \tag{16.3}$$

In other words, we can obtain $E[f(X)]$ directly from $p_X\{x\}$ and we do not need to determine $p_{f(X)}\{f(x)\}$. The analogous formula holds for discrete distributions:

$$E[f(X)] = \sum_i f(x_i)p\{x_i\}. \tag{16.4}$$

The foregoing proof of (16.3) is of course valid only under the stated conditions of monotonicity. Equation (16.3) is, however, valid quite generally, without the restrictions of monotonicity. A proof of this can be found in Cramér [13], Sections 7.4 and 7.5.

As an example, consider $Y = f(X) = X^2$ where X has the density function (14.4) and Y the density function (14.11). We could find $E[Y]$ literally from its definition as

$$\begin{aligned} E[Y] &= \int_{-\infty}^{\infty} yp\{y\}\,dy \\ &= \int_0^{a^2} y \cdot \frac{2}{9a\sqrt{y}}\,dy + \int_{a^2}^{4a^2} y \cdot \left(\frac{1}{9a\sqrt{y}} + \frac{1}{9a^2}\right)dy = \frac{3a^2}{a}. \end{aligned} \tag{16.5}$$

Alternatively, using (16.3),

$$\begin{aligned} E[X^2] &= \int_{-\infty}^{\infty} x^2 p\{x\}\,dx \\ &= \int_{-2a}^{a} x^2 \cdot \frac{2}{9a}\left(1 - \frac{x}{a}\right)dx = \frac{3a^2}{2}. \end{aligned} \tag{16.6}$$

For any linear function of a random variable, say $a + bX$, where a and b are constants,

$$\begin{aligned} E[a + bX] &= \int_{-\infty}^{\infty} (a + bx)p\{x\}\,dx = a\int_{-\infty}^{\infty} p\{x\}\,dx + b\int_{-\infty}^{\infty} xp\{x\}\,dx \\ &= a + bE[X]. \end{aligned} \tag{16.7}$$

If we put $b = 0$, then $E[a] = a$, so the expectation of a constant is that constant, and if we put $a = 0$, then $E[bX] = bE[X]$. Further, the expected value of the deviation of a random variable from its expectation is

$$E[X - E[X]] = E[X] - E[E[X]] = E[X] - E[X] = 0; \tag{16.8}$$

i.e., the expected value of a random variable has the property that the expected value of the deviations of the random variable about it is zero.

As another example, the standardized normal distribution (13.12) was obtained from the general normal distribution (12.6) by the substitution $u = (x - \xi)/\sigma$. We could obtain $E[U]$ directly from its definition as

$$\int_{-\infty}^{\infty} u\,\phi(u)\,du.$$

SECT. 1.17 THE CONCEPT OF VARIANCE

Alternatively, since u is a linear function of x and since $E[X] = \xi$,

$$E[U] = E\left[\frac{X - \xi}{\sigma}\right] = \frac{E[X] - \xi}{\sigma} = \frac{\xi - \xi}{\sigma} = 0, \tag{16.9}$$

so that standardized normal distribution has expectation zero.

1.17. The Concept of Variance

As a measure of the spread of a distribution the *variance*, defined as the expected value of the square of the deviation of the random variable X from its expectation, has many mathematical and statistical advantages:

$$V[X] = E[(X - E[X])^2]. \tag{17.1}$$

The units of measurement of variance are squared units on the original scale. The square root of the variance, commonly represented by the symbol σ, is known as the *standard deviation*. For calculating variances the following identity is often convenient:

$$V[X] = E[X^2 + (E[X])^2 - 2XE[X]] = E[X^2] + E[(E[X])^2] - 2E[XE[X]]$$
$$= E[X^2] + (E[X])^2 - 2(E[X])^2 = E[X^2] - (E[X])^2, \tag{17.2}$$

i.e., the variance of the random variable X is equal to the expectation of the square of X minus the square of the expectation of X. An alternative identity is sometimes more convenient:

$$V[X] = E[X^2] - (E[X])^2 = E[X^2] - E[X] - (E[X])^2 + E[X]$$
$$= E[X(X - 1)] - E[X](E[X] - 1). \tag{17.3}$$

If a and b are constants, then the variance of a linear function of X, say $a + bX$, is

$$V[a + bX] = E[(a + bX)^2] - (E[a + bX])^2$$
$$= E[a^2 + 2abX + b^2X^2] - (a + bE[X])^2$$
$$= E[a^2] + 2abE[X] + b^2E[X^2] - a^2 - 2abE[X] - b^2(E[X])^2$$
$$= b^2\{E[X^2] - (E[X])^2\} = b^2V[X]. \tag{17.4}$$

Thus adding a constant a to a random variable leaves the variance unchanged, but the variance of bX is b^2 times the variance of X.

To use (17.2) to calculate the variance of the random variable Y with the distribution given in Table 1.4, we need $E[Y^2]$, Y^2 being a function of Y. Using (16.4), $E[Y^2] = \sum_i y_i^2 p\{y_i\}$. This summation is obtained as the sum of the third column of Table 1.14. In Table 1.13 we found $E[Y] = 5$. Substituting in (17.2) gives $V[Y] = 27.5 - 5^2 = 2.5$.

Table 1.14

y_i	$p\{y_i\}$	$y_i^2 p\{y_i\}$
2	1/16	4/16
3	2/16	18/16
4	3/16	48/16
5	4/16	100/16
6	3/16	108/16
7	2/16	98/16
8	1/16	64/16

$$E[Y^2] = \sum_i y_i^2 p\{y_i\} = 440/16 = 27.5$$

To calculate the variance of the binomial distribution, (9.3), we will use (17.3). In computing $E[X(X-1)]$, $X(X-1)$ is a function of X, and by (16.4)

$$E[X(X-1)] = \sum_i x_i(x_i - 1)p\{x_i\} = \sum_{x=0}^{n} x(x-1)\binom{n}{x}\theta^x(1-\theta)^{n-x}. \quad (17.5)$$

We note that

$$x(x-1)\binom{n}{x} = x(x-1) \cdot \frac{n!}{x!(n-x)!} = n(n-1) \cdot \frac{(n-2)!}{(x-2)!(n-x)!}$$

$$= n(n-1) \cdot \binom{n-2}{x-2}. \quad (17.6)$$

Substituting in (17.5),

$$E[X(X-1)] = n(n-1)\theta^2 \sum_{x=2}^{n} \binom{n-2}{x-2}\theta^{x-2}(1-\theta)^{n-x}. \quad (17.7)$$

We have changed the lower limit of summation from 0 in (17.5) to 2 in (17.7), for clearly when $x = 0$ or 1 the corresponding terms in the summation are zero and add nothing to the summation, and hence can be omitted. Equation (17.7) will appear in a more satisfactory form if we write $x = y + 2$, so $x - 2 = y$, and $n = m + 2$, so $n - 2 = m$. In (17.7), x ranges over 2 to n, so y ranges over 0 to m; thus

$$E[X(X-1)] = n(n-1)\theta^2 \sum_{y=0}^{m} \binom{m}{y}\theta^y(1-\theta)^{m-y}. \quad (17.8)$$

The summation is just the sum of all the terms of a binomial distribution, and the sum of any probability function must equal 1. Hence

$$E[X(X-1)] = n(n-1)\theta^2. \quad (17.9)$$

From (15.8), $E[X] = n\theta$. Making these substitutions in (17.3), we obtain for the variance of the binomial distribution:

$$V[X] = n(n-1)\theta^2 - n\theta(n\theta - 1) = n\theta(1 - \theta). \qquad (17.10)$$

If instead of considering the number of "successes" X in the binomial distribution, we consider the proportion of successes $H = X/n$, then by (17.4) the variance of H is

$$V[H] = V\left[\frac{X}{n}\right] = \frac{1}{n^2} V[X] = \frac{\theta(1-\theta)}{n}. \qquad (17.11)$$

To consider some examples of the calculation of variances of continuous distributions, for the rectangular distribution, (12.2), we first obtain $E[X^2]$ by substituting for $p\{x\}$ in (16.3):

$$E[X^2] = \int_{-\infty}^{\infty} x^2 p_X\{x\}\, dx = \int_{-a/2}^{a/2} x^2 \left(\frac{1}{a}\right) dx$$

$$= \frac{1}{a} \frac{x^3}{3} \bigg|_{-a/2}^{a/2} = \frac{a^2}{12}. \qquad (17.12)$$

Substituting this in (17.2), and also substituting $E[X] = 0$ from (15.9), we get

$$V[X] = E[X^2] - (E[X])^2 = \frac{a^2}{12}. \qquad (17.13)$$

For the exponential distribution, we first obtain $E[X^2]$ as

$$E[X^2] = \int_0^{\infty} x^2 \theta e^{-\theta x}\, dx. \qquad (17.14)$$

Using the formula for integration by parts, (15.11), and identifying $f(x)$ with x^2, so that $f'(x) = 2x$, and $g'(x)$ with $\theta e^{-\theta x}$, so that $g(x) = -e^{-\theta x}$, we have

$$E[X^2] = x^2(-e^{-\theta x})\bigg|_0^{\infty} - \int_0^{\infty} (-e^{-\theta x}) 2x\, dx$$

$$= 0 + 2\int_0^{\infty} xe^{-\theta x}\, dx. \qquad (17.15)$$

In (15.12) we found

$$E[X] = \theta \int_0^{\infty} xe^{-\theta x}\, dx = \frac{1}{\theta}, \qquad (17.16)$$

so the integral in (17.15) equals $1/\theta^2$ and we get

$$E[X^2] = \frac{2}{\theta^2}. \qquad (17.17)$$

Substituting in (17.2), we obtain, for the variance of the exponential distribution,

$$V[X] = \frac{2}{\theta^2} - \left(\frac{1}{\theta}\right)^2 = \frac{1}{\theta^2}. \tag{17.18}$$

To find $E[X^2]$ for the normal distribution (12.6), the change of variable $x = \sigma u + \xi$ is convenient:

$$E[X^2] = \int_{-\infty}^{\infty} x^2 \cdot \frac{1}{\sqrt{2\pi}\,\sigma} e^{-(x-\xi)^2/2\sigma^2}\,dx \tag{17.18}$$

$$= \int_{-\infty}^{\infty} \frac{1}{\sqrt{2\pi}} (u\sigma + \xi)^2 e^{-u^2/2}\,du \tag{17.19}$$

$$= \sigma^2 \int_{-\infty}^{\infty} u^2 \cdot \frac{1}{\sqrt{2\pi}} e^{-u^2/2}\,du + 2\sigma\xi \int_{-\infty}^{\infty} u \cdot \frac{1}{\sqrt{2\pi}} e^{-u^2/2}\,du$$

$$+ \xi^2 \int_{-\infty}^{\infty} \frac{1}{\sqrt{2\pi}} e^{-u^2/2}\,du. \tag{17.20}$$

The second integral corresponds to $E[U]$ which from (16.9) we know to be zero. The third integral is $\Phi(\infty)$, (13.13), which must equal 1. To evaluate the first integral, in the formula for integration by parts, (15.11), we identify $f(x)$ with $u/\sqrt{2\pi}$, so that $f'(x) = 1/\sqrt{2\pi}$, and $g'(x)$ with $ue^{-u^2/2}$, so that $g(x) = -e^{-u^2/2}$:

$$\int_{-\infty}^{\infty} u^2 \cdot \frac{1}{\sqrt{2\pi}} e^{-u^2/2}\,du = \frac{u}{\sqrt{2\pi}}(-e^{-u^2/2})\bigg|_{-\infty}^{\infty} - \int_{-\infty}^{\infty} (-e^{-u^2/2}) \frac{1}{\sqrt{2\pi}}\,du \tag{17.21}$$

$$= 0 + 1 = 1, \tag{17.22}$$

since the latter integral, when the minus sign is moved in front of the integral, is $\Phi(\infty)$. Substituting these results in (17.20),

$$E[X^2] = \sigma^2 + \xi^2, \tag{17.23}$$

whence

$$V[X] = E[X^2] - (E[X])^2 = (\sigma^2 + \xi^2) - \xi^2$$
$$= \sigma^2. \tag{17.24}$$

We thus see that the two parameters of the normal distribution, ξ and σ^2, are actually its mean and variance respectively. For the standard normal distribution $\phi(u)$, since $u = (x - \xi)/\sigma$, by (17.4),

$$V[U] = \frac{1}{\sigma^2} V[X] = 1. \tag{17.25}$$

We have seen in (16.9) that $E[U] = 0$, so we will sometimes write $N(0, 1)$ for $\phi(u)$.

For any random variable X, the standardized form is defined as

$$\frac{X - E[X]}{\sqrt{V[X]}} = W, \quad \text{say.} \tag{17.26}$$

Then

$$E[W] = \frac{E[X] - E[E[X]]}{\sqrt{V[X]}} = 0, \tag{17.27}$$

and

$$V[W] = E[(W - E[W])^2] = E[W^2]$$
$$= \frac{E[(X - E[X])^2]}{V[X]} = \frac{V[X]}{V[X]} = 1. \tag{17.28}$$

Thus any random variable when put in standardized form using (17.26) has a zero expectation and a unit variance.

EXERCISES 1D

1D.1. A piggy bank contains 7 nickels, 8 dimes, 6 quarters, and 4 half dollars. You are permitted to withdraw one coin at random and then another without replacing the first. The random variable X is your gain in cents. What is (a) the distribution of X, (b) the probability that your gain will be more than 35 cents, (c) the expectation of X, (d) the variance of X? Assume that the probability of any coin being drawn is the same as for any other coin.

1D.2. In an eight-floor apartment house the elevator takes 10 seconds to get from one floor to the adjoining floor. Individuals leave and arrive with equal frequency, and the traffic arising from any floor is the same as for any other floor. The traffic density is low, so that the probability of the elevator being called by one individual while in use by another individual is to be regarded as zero. There is no traffic between floors, i.e., no tenant who visits any other tenant.

For a tenant (a) on the second floor, (b) on the eighth floor, what are (i) the distributions of waiting times? (ii) The expected values of the waiting times? (iii) The variances of the waiting times?

1D.3. A soap company distributes entry blanks to a lottery requiring nothing but the filling in of one's name and the mailing of the blank. The prize schedule is: first prize, $25,000; second prize, $10,000; third prize, $5000; next 5 prizes, $1000 each; next 10 prizes, $500 each; next 50 prizes, $250 each; next 100 prizes, $100 each; next 1100 prizes, $25 each. Assume that 10 million entry blanks are returned. Let the random variable X be your gain from participation. (a) What is the distribution of X? (b) What is its expected value? (c) Supposing that the only cost of entry is the 5-cent stamp to mail in the entry, does it make sense to participate?

1D.4. "The word 'love' in the title of 'For Love or Money' is meant to be a synonym for prizes. The show is unusual among daytime programs in that it offers cash as an alternative to love. The money is hard to come by in any serious amount. A kind of electronic roulette ball ... darts from side to side of a stated number, such as 01400 and determines the payoff as it comes to rest: $0.01, $0.14, $1.40, $14, $140, or $1400. As any bookmaker's infant child could tell you, the chances of winning a respectable bundle are only two in six. The odds, therefore, are two to one against the player who goes for the cash instead of for a prize that is worth ... $140. I'll detain you no longer with the laws of Pascal."—John Lardner in *The New Yorker*, July 19, 1958.

Comment. [By "odds of n to 1 against" is meant a probability of $1/(1 + n)$. Assume that the "electronic roulette ball," i.e., the decimal point, runs back and forth between .01400 and 01400., moving instantaneously over each digit and after each move pausing for an equal interval of time. Assume that it stops after a random number of moves.]

1D.5. The random variable x has the density function

$$p\{x\} = \frac{2}{b}\left(1 - \frac{x}{b}\right), \quad 0 < x < b,$$
$$= 0, \quad \text{otherwise}$$

Find (a) $P\{x\}$, (b) $E[x]$, (c) $E[x^2]$, (d) $V[x]$, (e) the mode, (f) the median. Sketch the graphs of the density function and the cumulative distribution function, and mark on the graph of the density function the positions of $E[x]$, the mode, and the median.

1D.6. The Pareto distribution,

$$p\{x\} = \alpha\beta^\alpha x^{-(\alpha+1)}, \quad \beta \leq x < \infty,$$
$$= 0, \quad \text{otherwise,}$$

with the parameters α and β both greater than zero, has been proposed as a representation of, e.g., data on incomes from tax returns when only those with incomes in excess of some specified figure file returns. (a) Find the expected value of X (i) when $\alpha \leq 1$, (ii) when $\alpha > 1$. (b) Find the variance of X (i) when $\alpha \leq 2$, (ii) when $\alpha > 2$. (c) Find the median of X. (d) Consider the variable Y defined as $Y = \log_e X$. Find the density function of Y. (e) Find the median of Y.

1D.7. X is a random variable with expectation 10 and standard deviation 2. Obtain numerical answers for (a) $E[X^2]$, (b) $E[E[X^2]]$, (c) $V[E[X^2]]$, (d) $V[V[X^2]]$.

1D.8. Let X be a random variable whose logarithm Y is normally distributed with mean η and variance σ^2, i.e., $y = \log x$ and

$$p\{y\} = \frac{1}{\sqrt{2\pi}\sigma} e^{-(y-\eta)^2/2\sigma^2}, \quad -\infty < y < \infty.$$

Then X is said to have a *logarithmic normal distribution*. Define ξ as e^η, so $\log \xi = \eta$. Find the density function of X.

Show that
(a) the median of the distribution of x is ξ,
(b) the mode of the distribution of x is $\xi e^{-\sigma^2}$,
(c) $E[X] = \xi e^{\sigma^2/2}$,
(d) $V[X] = e^{\sigma^2 + 2\eta}(e^{\sigma^2} - 1)$,
(e) $V[Y] = \log_e(1 + V[x]/(E[x])^2)$,
(f) $E[Y] = \log_e\left(\dfrac{E[x]}{\sqrt{1 + V[x]/(E[x])^2}}\right)$.

1D.9. A box contains five electron tubes of a certain type, and you recall that two are good and three are bad, though they are unmarked. You need two good tubes, so you draw one tube at random and test it, and then draw another at random and test it, etc., until you have two good tubes, when you quit. (a) What is the probability that you have to test all five tubes? (b) What is the expected value of the number of tubes tested?

1D.10. Suppose that X is a random variable with the density function

$$p_X\{x\} = \frac{1}{a}, \quad -\frac{a}{3} < x < \frac{2a}{3},$$
$$= 0, \quad \text{otherwise.}$$

Suppose that y is a function of x, namely $y = x^2$. (a) What is the density function of Y? (b) What is the median of Y, say y_m? Does $y_m = x_m^2$? If so, why? If not, why not? (c) What is the expected value of Y? Compute this in two ways.

1D.11. For the geometric distribution, (problem 1C.7), show that (a) $E[X] = 1/\theta$, (b) $V[X] = (1-\theta)/\theta^2$.

1D.12. For the Pascal distribution, (1C.8), show that $E[Y] = a/\theta$.

1D.13. What is the value of the constant c which makes $E[(x-c)^2]$ a minimum?

1D.14. Show that the expected value of $|x-c|$, where c is a constant, is a minimum when $c = x_m$, where x_m is the median.

1D.15. Suppose that Y has a density function $p_Y\{y\}$. Define Z as the cumulative distribution function

$$\int_{-\infty}^{Y} p_Y\{t\} \, dt.$$

What is the density function of Z?

1.18. The Properties of the Standardized Normal Distribution

We saw in Section 1.13 that the substitution $u = (x - \xi)/\sigma$ transforms the general normal distribution, (12.6), into the standardized normal distribution $\phi(u)$, (13.12). We saw in (16.9) that the standardized normal distribution has expectation zero, and in (17.22) that it has unit variance. We now examine in more detail the properties of

$$\phi(u) = \frac{1}{\sqrt{2\pi}} e^{-u^2/2} \tag{18.1}$$

and

$$\Phi(u) = \int_{-\infty}^{u} \frac{1}{\sqrt{2\pi}} e^{-t^2/2} \, dt \tag{18.2}$$

Firstly, since $-(-u)^2 = -(u)^2$, $\phi(u)$ is symmetric about $u = 0$. Therefore

$$\phi(-u) = \phi(u). \tag{18.3}$$

Secondly, the larger the absolute value of u, $|u|$, the smaller is $\phi(u)$, i.e., $\phi(u)$ tends to zero as u tends to $\pm\infty$, and conversely $\phi(u)$ takes its maximum at $u = 0$, when $\phi(u) = 1/\sqrt{2\pi} = 0.3989$. More formally,

$$\frac{d\phi(u)}{du} = \frac{1}{\sqrt{2\pi}} e^{-u^2/2}\left(-\frac{1}{2}\right) \cdot 2u = -u\phi(u), \tag{18.4}$$

and

$$\frac{d^2\phi(u)}{du^2} = -\phi(u) + (-u)[-u\phi(u)] = (u^2 - 1)\phi(u), \tag{18.5}$$

which by the usual rules imply that $\phi(u)$ has a maximum at $u = 0$ and points of inflection at $u = \pm 1$. The function $\phi(u)$ is graphed in the upper part of Figure 1.28.

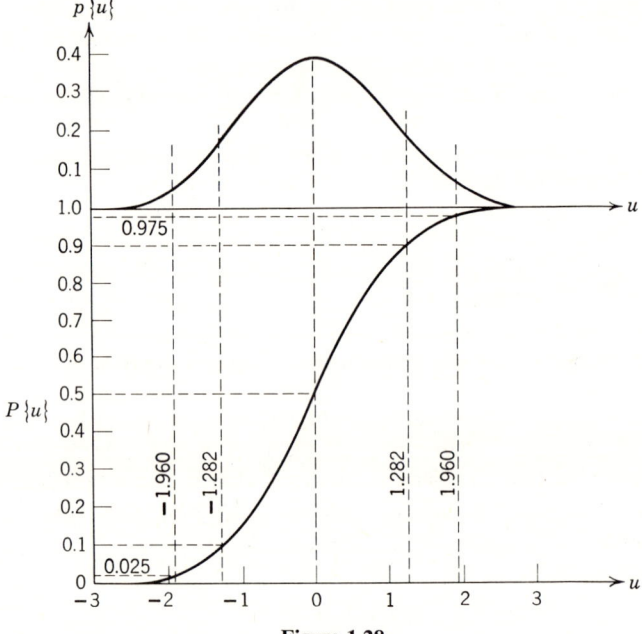

Figure 1.28

Certain properties of $\Phi(u)$ can be immediately inferred. From the symmetry about zero of $\phi(u)$, the area in the lower tail below $-u$ (where u is a positive number) must equal the area in the upper tail above $+u$, i.e.,

$$\int_{-\infty}^{-u} \phi(t)\, dt = \int_{u}^{\infty} \phi(t)\, dt. \tag{18.6}$$

SECT. 1.18   STANDARDIZED NORMAL DISTRIBUTION

But

$$\int_u^\infty \phi(t)\,dt = 1 - \int_{-\infty}^u \phi(t)\,dt, \qquad (18.7)$$

so

$$\Phi(-u) = 1 - \Phi(u). \qquad (18.8)$$

Let u_P be that value of u corresponding to the P point of the cumulative distribution function; i.e., if we take an observation at random from a standardized normal distribution the probability is P that the observation is less than u_P:

$$\Pr\{u < u_P\} = P. \qquad (18.9)$$

But $\Pr\{u < u_P\} = \Phi(u_P)$, i.e.,

$$\Phi(u_P) = P. \qquad (18.10)$$

From (18.8), $\Phi(u_P) = 1 - \Phi(-u_P)$, so $P = 1 - \Phi(-u_P)$, and $\Phi(-u_P) = 1 - P$. But $\Phi(u_{1-P}) = 1 - P$, so

$$-u_P = u_{1-P}. \qquad (18.11)$$

Table I in the Appendix gives the values of P corresponding to specified values of u_P. For example, if $u_P = -2$, $P = 0.02275$, and if $u_P = 2$, $P = 0.97725$. Table I can be used conversely to find u_P for a specified value of P, but Table VII does this directly for the more commonly used values of P. For example, if $P = 0.025$, $u_P = -1.960$, and if $P = 0.975$, $u_P = 1.960$. These points are plotted in Figure 1.28.

These two operations, namely given u_P to find P and given P to find u_P, can also be performed readily for any normal distribution if we know its mean ξ and its variance σ^2. In the equation for the cumulative distribution function of the normal distribution,

$$P\{x\} = \frac{1}{\sqrt{2\pi}\sigma} \int_{-\infty}^x e^{-(t-\xi)^2/2\sigma^2}\,dt, \qquad (18.12)$$

change the variable from t to $u = (t - \xi)/\sigma$. Then

$$P\{x\} = \frac{1}{\sqrt{2\pi}\sigma} \int_{-\infty}^{(x-\xi)/\sigma} e^{-u^2/2}\sigma\,du = \Phi\!\left(\frac{x - \xi}{\sigma}\right). \qquad (18.13)$$

For example, suppose that we are given that $\xi = 100$, $\sigma = 10$, and we want the probability that an observation taken at random from this distribution is less than 120. We have

$$\Pr\{X < 120\} = P\{120\} = \Phi\!\left(\frac{120 - 100}{10}\right) = \Phi(2) = 0.97725. \qquad (18.14)$$

Conversely, given the same distribution, what is the value of x_P that a fraction P of all observations are less than? We solve the equation

$$\Phi\left(\frac{x_P - \xi}{\sigma}\right) = P. \qquad (18.15)$$

For example, if P is specified as 0.95, we know that the solution of $u_{0.95}$ in $\Phi(u_{0.95}) = 0.95$ is $u_{0.95} = 1.645$, so

$$\Phi(1.645) = 0.95 = \Phi\left(\frac{x_{0.95} - \xi}{\sigma}\right). \qquad (18.16)$$

Thus $1.645 = (x_{0.95} - \xi)/\sigma = (x_{0.95} - 100)/10$, or $x_{0.95} = 116.45$.

Equation (18.13) will give the probability that an observation will lie k or more times the standard deviation below the mean:

$$\Pr\{X < \xi - k\sigma\} = \Phi\left(\frac{(\xi - k\sigma) - \xi}{\sigma}\right) = \Phi(-k). \qquad (18.17)$$

The probability that an observation will lie below k times the standard deviation above the mean is $\Phi(k)$. The probability that an observation will lie above k times the standard deviation above the mean is

$$\Pr\{X > \xi + k\sigma\} = 1 - \Pr\{X < \xi + k\sigma\} = 1 - \Phi(k) = \Phi(-k). \qquad (18.18)$$

We can also ask for the probability that an observation deviates from the mean by more than k times the standard deviation in either direction, i.e., that X lies outside the interval $\xi \pm k\sigma$. This is

$$\Pr\{X < \xi - k\sigma\} + \Pr\{X > \xi + k\sigma\} = \Phi(-k) + \Phi(-k)$$
$$= 2\Phi(-k) = 2[1 - \Phi(k)]. \qquad (18.19)$$

For example, for $k = 1.96$, $2\Phi(-1.96) = 2 \times 0.025 = 0.05$, or alternatively $2[1 - \Phi(1.96)] = 2(1 - 0.975) = 0.05$. The left-hand side of (18.17) can be written in an alternative form:

$$\Pr\{X < \xi - k\sigma\} + \Pr\{X > \xi + k\sigma\}$$
$$= \Pr\{X - \xi < -k\sigma\} + \Pr\{X - \xi > k\sigma\}$$
$$= \Pr\{-(X - \xi) > k\sigma\} + \Pr\{X - \xi > k\sigma\}$$
$$= \Pr\{|X - \xi| > k\sigma\} = 2\Phi(-k). \qquad (18.20)$$

where k is a positive number. Complimentarily,

$$\Pr\{|X - \xi| < k\sigma\} = 1 - 2\Phi(-k). \qquad (18.21)$$

1.19. Discrete Bivariate Distributions

Consider the experiment consisting of dropping three light bulbs in sequence with possible outcomes U = undamaged, F = filament broken, and G = glass envelope broken. The sample space contains 27 sample points. If the successive drops are independent, then for example

$$\Pr\{U, U, U\} = \Pr\{U\} \Pr\{U\} \Pr\{U\}.$$

Define two random variables, X = number of U's, Y = number of F's, and let $\Pr\{U\} = 1/2$, $\Pr\{F\} = 1/3$, $\Pr\{G\} = 1/6$. For each of the 27 points

Table 1.15

$(U, U, U)(3, 0)$	27	$(U, F, U)(2, 1)$	18	$(U, G, U)(2, 0)$	9
$(U, U, F)(2, 1)$	18	$(U, F, F)(1, 2)$	12	$(U, G, F)(1, 1)$	6
$(U, U, G)(2, 0)$	9	$(U, F, G)(1, 1)$	6	$(U, G, G)(1, 0)$	3
$(F, U, U)(2, 1)$	18	$(F, F, U)(1, 2)$	12	$(F, G, U)(1, 1)$	6
$(F, U, F)(1, 2)$	12	$(F, F, F)(0, 3)$	8	$(F, G, F)(0, 2)$	4
$(F, U, G)(1, 1)$	6	$(F, F, G)(0, 2)$	4	$(F, G, G)(0, 1)$	2
$(G, U, U)(2, 0)$	9	$(G, F, U)(1, 1)$	6	$(G, G, U)(1, 0)$	3
$(G, U, F)(1, 1)$	6	$(G, F, F)(0, 2)$	4	$(G, G, F)(0, 1)$	2
$(G, U, G)(1, 0)$	3	$(G, F, G)(0, 1)$	2	$(G, G, G)(0, 0)$	1

in the sample space we can tabulate the values taken by X and Y and also the probability of that point occurring; see Table 1.15. For example, for the sample point (U, U, U) we have $x = 3$, $y = 0$, and $\Pr\{U, U, U\} = (1/2)(1/2)(1/2) = 1/8 = 27/216$. This sample point is therefore labeled $(U, U, U)(3, 0)$ 27, the denominator 216 being omitted for conciseness.

From Table 1.15 we can construct Table 1.16 showing the probability of obtaining any pair of values of x and y.

Table 1.16

(x_i, y_j)	$216\, p\{x_i, y_j\}$
(0, 0)	1
(1, 0)	$3 + 3 + 3 = 9$
(2, 0)	$9 + 9 + 9 = 27$
(3, 0)	27
(0, 1)	$2 + 2 + 2 = 6$
(1, 1)	$6 + 6 + 6 + 6 + 6 + 6 = 36$
(2, 1)	$18 + 18 + 18 = 54$
(0, 2)	$4 + 4 + 4 = 12$
(1, 2)	$12 + 12 + 12 = 36$
(0, 3)	8

Table 1.17

$$216\, p\{x_i, y_j\}$$

x_i	y_j				$\sum_j 216\, p\{x_i, y_j\}$
	0	1	2	3	
0	1	6	12	8	27
1	9	36	36	0	81
2	27	54	0	0	81
3	27	0	0	0	27
$\sum_i 216\, p\{x_i, y_j\}$	64	96	48	8	

It is natural to express Table 1.16 in a two-way form (Table 1.17) and also to represent it graphically (Figure 1.29).

In general, a discrete bivariate distribution will appear as in Table 1.18, where x and y are confined to the discrete values $x_1, \ldots, x_n$ and $y_1, \ldots, y_m$. The probability of any particular pair of values, x_i, y_j, is $p\{x_i, y_j\}$. The marginal probabilities for x can be obtained by summing over y, and

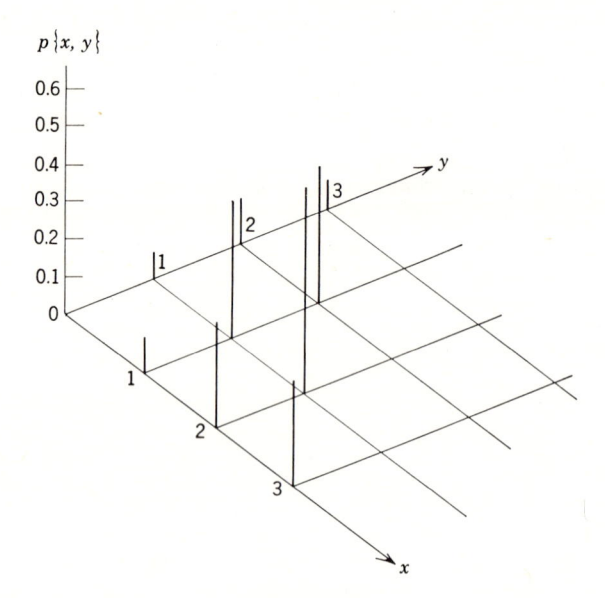

Figure 1.29

SECT. 1.19   DISCRETE BIVARIATE DISTRIBUTIONS

vice versa:

$$p_X\{x_i\} = \sum_j^m p\{x_i, y_j\}, \qquad (19.1)$$

$$p_Y\{y_j\} = \sum_i^n p\{x_i, y_j\}. \qquad (19.2)$$

For example, for Table 1.17,

$$p_Y\{2\} = \frac{12 + 36 + 0 + 0}{216} = \frac{48}{216} = \frac{2}{9}.$$

Table 1.18

	y_1	$\cdots$	y_j	$\cdots$	y_m	$\sum_j^m p\{x_i, y_j\}$
x_1	$p\{x_1, y_1\}$	$\cdots$	$p\{x_1, y_j\}$	$\cdots$	$p\{x_1, y_m\}$	$p_X\{x_1\}$
.	.					
.	.					
.	.					
x_i	$p\{x_i, y_1\}$		$p\{x_i, y_j\}$		$p\{x_i, y_m\}$	$p_X\{x_i\}$
.	.					
.	.					
.	.					
x_n	$p\{x_n, y_1\}$		$p\{x_n, y_j\}$		$p\{x_n, y_m\}$	$p_X\{x_n\}$
$\sum_i^n p\{x_i, y_j\}$	$p_Y\{y_1\}$		$p_Y\{y_j\}$		$p_Y\{y_m\}$	

This result can be checked by regarding Y as a binomially distributed variable with $n = 3$, $\theta = 1/3$, and using (9.3):

$$p_3\{Y = 2\} = \binom{3}{2}\left(\frac{1}{3}\right)^2\left(1 - \frac{1}{3}\right)^{3-2} = \frac{2}{9}.$$

The conditional probability that $X = x_i$, given that $Y = y_j$, can be found by using (4.3):

$$\Pr\{X = x_i | Y = y_j\} = \frac{\Pr\{X = x_i \text{ and } Y = y_j\}}{\Pr\{Y = y_j\}} = \frac{p\{x_i, y_j\}}{p\{y_j\}}. \qquad (19.3)$$

It is convenient to call this the conditional probability function and use the symbol $p\{x|y\}$. Also, if X and Y are independent, using (5.9), namely $\Pr\{E_1|E_2\} = \Pr\{E_1\}$, gives

$$\Pr\{X = x_i | Y = y_j\} = \Pr\{X = x_i\}. \qquad (19.4)$$

Substituting from (19.3) and writing $\Pr\{X = x_i\} = p\{x_i\}$ we find that in the case of x, y independent

$$p\{x_i, y_j\} = p\{x_i\}p\{y_j\}; \tag{19.5}$$

i.e., the joint probability function is the product of the two marginal probability functions. In the case of the bivariate distribution of Table 1.16, for example, we have just seen that $p\{Y = 2\} = 2/9$, whereas from the table, for example, $p\{Y = 2 | X = 0\} = (12/216)/(27/216) = 4/9$, so for this distribution $p\{y|x\} \neq p\{y\}$ and hence X and Y are not independent. Similarly, $p\{X = 3\} = 27/216$, so $p\{X = 3\}p\{Y = 2\} = (27/216)(2/9)$, which is not equal to $p\{X = 3, Y = 2\}$, which is 0.

1.20. Continuous Bivariate Distributions

Consider a function $p\{x, y\} \geq 0$ for all x, y such that

$$\int_{-\infty}^{\infty} \int_{-\infty}^{\infty} p\{x, y\} \, dy \, dx = 1. \tag{20.1}$$

This function $p\{x, y\}$ can be regarded as a two-dimensional, or bivariate, probability density function and is the analog of the univariate probability density functions we have considered hitherto. Analogously to (11.5) in the univariate case, we can define a cumulative distribution function

$$P\{x_i, y_j\} = \Pr\{X \leq x_i, Y \leq y_j\}$$
$$= \int_{-\infty}^{x_i} \int_{-\infty}^{y_j} p\{x, y\} \, dy \, dx. \tag{20.2}$$

Graphically, we can use the two horizontal dimensions to represent x, y and the vertical dimension to represent $p\{x, y\}$. Thus $p\{x, y\}$ generates a surface above the plane $p\{x, y\} = 0$. The total volume enclosed between this surface and this plane, by (20.1), is 1. $P\{x_i, y_j\}$ is the volume under the surface measured over the shaded area only (Figure 1.30).

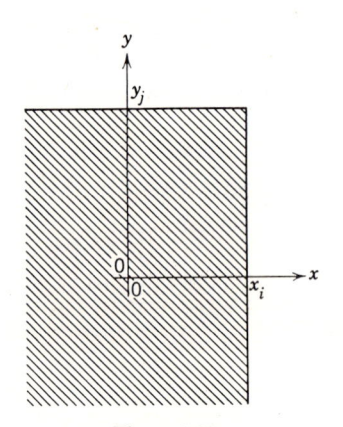

Figure 1.30

In manipulating bivariate probability density functions we will often find it convenient to reverse the order of integration, i.e., to assume

$$\int_{x_a}^{x_b} \int_{y_c}^{y_d} p\{x, y\} \, dy \, dx = \int_{y_c}^{y_d} \int_{x_a}^{x_b} p\{x, y\} \, dx \, dy. \tag{20.3}$$

This is always legitimate in the situation in which we are involved. Technically, it is permissible if the integral is absolutely convergent. The requirement that $p\{x, y\} \geq 0$ implies that if the integrals converge then they are absolutely convergent, and the requirement (20.1) implies that they are convergent, and hence they are absolutely convergent.

The only example of a continuous bivariate distribution we will encounter in this book is the bivariate normal:

$$p\{x, y\} = \frac{1}{2\pi\sigma_x\sigma_y\sqrt{1-\rho^2}} \exp\left\{-\frac{1}{2(1-\rho^2)}\right.$$
$$\left. \times \left[\left(\frac{x-\xi}{\sigma_x}\right)^2 - 2\rho\left(\frac{x-\xi}{\sigma_x}\right)\left(\frac{y-\eta}{\sigma_y}\right) + \left(\frac{y-\eta}{\sigma_y}\right)^2\right]\right\}. \quad (20.4)$$

This will be discussed in detail in Chapter 12.

We may wish to find the marginal probability density function of X alone, given $p\{x, y\}$. Intuitively, we would expect to get this by integrating $p\{x, y\}$ over y. More formally, we can proceed as follows. Define $Q_X(r)$ as

$$Q_X(r) = \int_{-\infty}^{\infty} p_{X,Y}\{r, y\} \, dy. \quad (20.5)$$

Then

$$\Pr\{-\infty < X < x\} = \Pr\{-\infty < X < x, -\infty < Y < \infty\}$$
$$= \int_{-\infty}^{x} \left(\int_{-\infty}^{\infty} p_{X,Y}\{r, y\} \, dy\right) dr = \int_{-\infty}^{x} Q_X(r) \, dr. \quad (20.6)$$

Also, considering X alone,

$$\Pr\{-\infty < X < x\} = \int_{-\infty}^{x} p_X\{r\} \, dr. \quad (20.7)$$

The left-hand sides of (20.6) and (20.7) are identical, so the right-hand sides are equal:

$$\int_{-\infty}^{x} p_X\{r\} \, dr = \int_{-\infty}^{x} Q_X(r) \, dr. \quad (20.8)$$

Intuitively, if we regard x as a variable we have here two functions of x which are equal for all values of x, and this implies that the functions must be identical. More formally, we can use a standard rule of calculus (see, e.g., Courant, *Differential and Integral Calculus*, Volume 1, p. 111),

$$\frac{d}{dx} \int_a^x f(u) \, du = f(x). \quad (20.9)$$

Differentiating both sides of (20.8) with respect to x, and substituting from (20.5) for Q, gives

$$p_X(x) = Q_X(x) = \int_{-\infty}^{\infty} p_{X,Y}\{x, y\} \, dy. \quad (20.10)$$

1.21. Conditional Continuous Density Functions

We want a function $p\{x|y\}$ which will be the probability density function of X when Y is known; i.e., we want a function $p\{x|y\}$ such that

$$\Pr\{x_a < X < x_b | y\} = \int_{x_a}^{x_b} p\{x|y\}\, dx. \tag{21.1}$$

We start from our definition of conditional probability, (4.3), $\Pr\{E_1|E_2\} =$

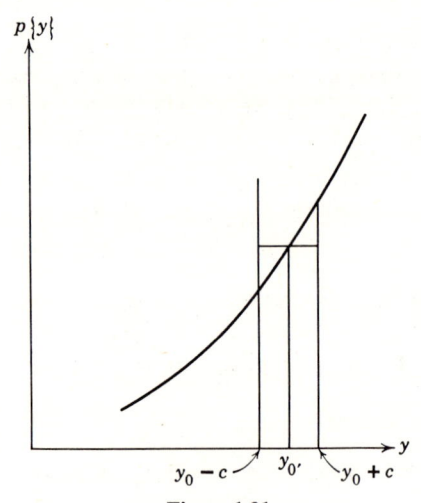

Figure 1.31

$\Pr\{E_1 \cap E_2\}/\Pr\{E_2\}$, and identify E_1 with the event $x_a < X < x_b$ and E_2 with the event $y_0 - c < Y < y_0 + c$. Thus

$$\Pr\{x_a < X < x_b | y_0 - c < Y < y_0 + c\}$$
$$= \frac{\Pr\{x_a < X < x_b,\, y_0 - c < Y < y_0 + c\}}{\Pr\{y_0 - c < Y < y_0 + c\}}$$
$$= \frac{\int_{x_a}^{x_b} \int_{y_0-c}^{y_0+c} p\{x, y\}\, dy\, dx}{\int_{y_0-c}^{y_0+c} p_Y\{y\}\, dy}. \tag{21.2}$$

Figure 1.31 shows that the area under the curve $p_Y\{y\}$ bounded by the lines $y = y_0 - c$, $y = y_0 + c$ can be approximated by a rectangle with the base of length $2c$ and the height $p_Y\{y_{0'}\}$, where $y_{0'}$ is some value of y

SECT. 1.21   CONDITIONAL CONTINUOUS DENSITY FUNCTIONS   73

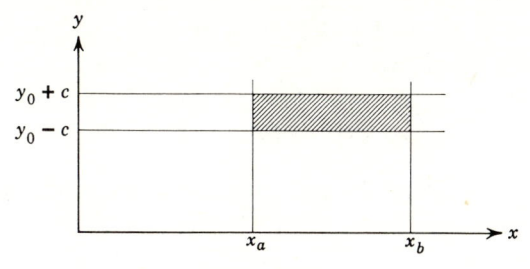

Figure 1.32

in the interval $(y_0 - c, y_0 + c)$. In other words, we can choose $y_{0'}$ so that

$$\int_{y_0-c}^{y_0+c} p_Y\{y\}\, dy = 2c p_Y\{y_{0'}\}. \tag{21.3}$$

The numerator of (21.2) is graphically represented in Figures 1.32 and 1.33. If we suppose that the x and y axes are in the plane of the paper and the $p\{x, y\}$ axis is vertical to the paper, the shaded area in Figure 1.32 is the base of the volume represented by the numerator of (21.2). Figure 1.33 is a three-dimensional sketch of this volume element, resting on this base. The volume of this element could be approximated as the area of the face marked $ABCD$ times the thickness, which is $(y_0 + c) - (y_0 - c) = 2c$. A better approximation would be given by using instead of $ABCD$ a similar area, say $A'B'C'D'$, not actually shown, lying between the two faces, say at $y_{0''}$, where $y_{0''}$, not actually shown, lies in the interval $(y_0 - c, y_0 + c)$. The upper edge $C'D'$, analogous to CD but moved from $y = y_0 - c$ to $y = y_{0''}$, has the functional form $p\{x, y_{0''}\}$, so the area $A'B'C'D'$ will be given by integrating this from x_a to x_b, to wit,

$$\int_{x_a}^{x_b} p\{x, y_{0''}\}\, dx.$$

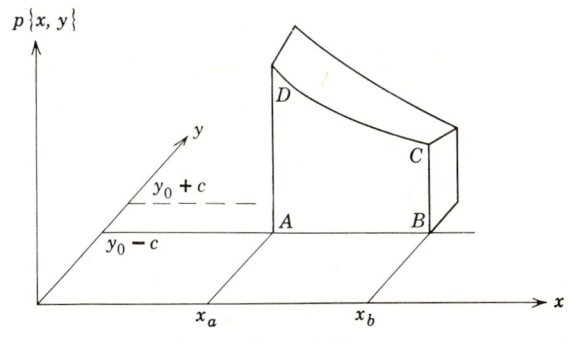

Figure 1.33

Hence the volume of this element is given by multiplying this area by the thickness, $2c$, giving

$$\int_{x_a}^{x_b} \int_{y_0-c}^{y_0-c} p\{x,y\}\,dy\,dx = 2c \int_{x_a}^{x_b} p\{x,y_{0''}\}\,dx. \qquad (21.4)$$

We now substitute (21.4) for the numerator and (21.3) for the denominator of (21.2) and cancel out the $2c$:

$$\Pr\{x_a < X < x_b | y_0 - c < Y < y_0 + c\} = \frac{\int_{x_a}^{x_b} p\{x, y_{0''}\}\,dx}{p_Y\{y_{0'}\}}. \qquad (21.5)$$

We now let c tend to 0, when both $y_{0'}$ and $y_{0''}$ will tend to y_0; thus in the limit,

$$\Pr\{x_a < X < x_b | Y = y_0\} = \frac{\int_{x_a}^{x_b} p\{x, y_0\}\,dx}{p_Y\{y_0\}}. \qquad (21.6)$$

This holds good for any x_a, x_b. In particular, we can let $x_a = -\infty$ and $x_b = x$, when the left-hand side becomes the cumulative form $P\{x|y = y_0\}$ of the probability density function $p\{x|y_0\}$. On differentiating a cumulative form we get the density form, (11.6), so we have

$$p\{x|y\} = \frac{p\{x,y\}}{p_Y\{y\}}. \qquad (21.7)$$

1.22. Independent Continuous Random Variables

Our definition of independence, (5.1), $\Pr\{E_1|E_2\} = \Pr\{E_1|E_2^c\}$, was shown to be equivalent to (5.9), $\Pr\{E_1|E_2\} = \Pr\{E_1\}$. We now identify E_1 with the event $y_c < Y < y_d$ and E_2 with the event $x_a < X < x_b$, so when X and Y are independent,

$$\Pr\{y_c < Y < y_d | x_a < X < x_b\} = \Pr\{y_c < Y < y_d\}. \qquad (22.1)$$

Using (4.3), $\Pr\{E_1|E_2\} = \Pr\{E_1 \cap E_2\}/\Pr\{E_2\}$, the left-hand side of (22.1) is

$$\Pr\{y_c < Y < y_d | x_a < X < x_b\} = \frac{\Pr\{y_c < Y < y_d, x_a < X < x_b\}}{\Pr\{x_a < X < x_b\}}$$

$$= \frac{\int_{y_c}^{y_d} \int_{x_a}^{x_b} p\{x, y\}\,dx\,dy}{\int_{x_a}^{x_b} p_X\{x\}\,dx}. \qquad (22.2)$$

The right-hand side of (22.1) is of course

$$\int_{y_c}^{y_d} p_Y\{y\}\, dy. \tag{22.3}$$

We therefore have, for X and Y independent,

$$\frac{\int_{y_c}^{y_d}\int_{x_a}^{x_b} p\{x,y\}\, dx\, dy}{\int_{x_a}^{x_b} p_X\{x\}\, dx} = \int_{y_c}^{y_d} p_Y\{y\}\, dy, \tag{22.4}$$

whence

$$\int_{y_c}^{y_d}\int_{x_a}^{x_b} p\{x,y\}\, dx\, dy = \int_{x_a}^{x_b} p_X\{x\}\, dx \int_{y_c}^{y_d} p_Y\{y\}\, dy$$

$$= \int_{x_a}^{x_b}\int_{y_c}^{y_d} p_Y\{x\} p_Y\{y\}\, dy\, dx. \tag{22.5}$$

This identity must hold for all x_a, x_b, y_c, y_d. Intuitively, this must imply that the functions being integrated are identical, and in fact this is the case, so when x and y are independent

$$p\{x,y\} = p_X\{x\} p_Y\{y\}. \tag{22.6}$$

1.23. Expectation in the Multivariate Case

We have seen, (16.3), that if X is a random variable with probability density function $p\{x\}$, and $f\{x\}$ is a function of x, then the expectation of $f(X)$ is

$$E[f(X)] = \int_{-\infty}^{\infty} f(x) p_X\{x\}\, dx. \tag{23.1}$$

Now consider the case of a function $h(X_1, \ldots, X_k)$ of several random variables $X_1, \ldots, X_k$ with joint probability density function $p\{x_1, \ldots, x_k\}$. It is natural to define the expectation of $h(X_1, \ldots, X_k)$ as

$$E[h(X_1, \ldots, X_k)] = \int_{-\infty}^{\infty}\cdots\int_{-\infty}^{\infty} h(x_1, \ldots, x_k)$$
$$\times p\{x_1, \ldots, x_k\}\, dx_1 \cdots dx_k. \tag{23.2}$$

We can use this to find the expectation of the sum of two random variables X, Y:

$$E[X+Y] = \int_{-\infty}^{\infty}\int_{-\infty}^{\infty} (x+y) p\{x,y\}\, dx\, dy \tag{23.3}$$

$$= \int_{-\infty}^{\infty}\int_{-\infty}^{\infty} x p\{x,y\}\, dy\, dx + \int_{-\infty}^{\infty}\int_{-\infty}^{\infty} y p\{x,y\}\, dx\, dy \tag{23.4}$$

$$= \int_{-\infty}^{\infty} x \left[\int_{-\infty}^{\infty} p\{x,y\}\, dy\right] dx + \int_{-\infty}^{\infty} y \left[\int_{-\infty}^{\infty} p\{x,y\}\, dx\right] dy. \tag{23.5}$$

We now use (20.10) for the two expressions in brackets and obtain

$$E[X + Y] = \int_{-\infty}^{\infty} x p_X\{x\}\, dx + \int_{-\infty}^{\infty} y p_Y\{y\}\, dy = E[X] + E[Y]. \quad (23.6)$$

Thus the expectation of the sum of two random variables is equal to the sum of their expectations. Incidentally, if X and Y are separate observations, say Z_1 and Z_2, from the same distribution with expectation ζ, then $E[Z_1 + Z_2] = E[Z_1] + E[Z_2] = 2\zeta$.

This generalizes to the case of n observations:

$$E\left[\sum_i^n Z_i\right] = \sum_i^n E[Z_i] = n\zeta, \quad (23.7)$$

and using (16.7),

$$E\left[\frac{1}{n}\sum_i^n Z_i\right] = \zeta, \quad (23.8)$$

i.e., the expected value of the mean of n observations from a distribution is the expectation of that distribution.

EXERCISES 1E

1E.1. The random variable X is normally distributed with a mean 100 and a standard deviation of 10. What are (a) $\Pr\{X < 95\}$, (b) $\Pr\{X > 90\}$, (c) $\Pr\{80 < X < 85\}$, (d) $\Pr\{|X - 100| < 20\}$? What are the values of a, b, and c such that (e) $\Pr\{X < a\} = 0.95$, (f) $\Pr\{X > b\} = 0.90$, (g) $\Pr\{|X - 100| < c\} = 0.90$?

1E.2. The random variable X is normally distributed with mean 100 and standard deviation 10. (a) What is the probability that a random observation does not deviate from 100 in either direction by more than 15? (b) What is the value of c such that $\Pr\{|X - 100| < c\} = 0.99$? (c) What is the probability that a random observation does not deviate from 80 in either direction by more than 15?

1E.3. Suppose that a population of men has a mean of 150 pounds and a standard deviation of 20 pounds, and that the weights are normally distributed. (i) What are the probabilities that a man selected at random is (a) less than 100 pounds, (b) greater than 190 pounds, (c) more than 30 pounds from the population mean? (ii) (a) What is the weight that 90 per cent of the population is less than? (b) What is the weight that 80 per cent of the population is greater than? (c) Give the interval, symmetrical about the mean, in which 50 per cent of the population lie.

1E.4. In a certain period of time on the average 25 per cent of make A of electric light bulbs will fail and 50 per cent of make B will fail. Three bulbs of type A and three bulbs of type B are mounted in a chandelier. What is the probability that after this specified period more of the A bulbs will have failed than the B bulbs? Assume independence.

1E.5. Suppose that the life in hours (X) of a brand of television picture tubes has the probability density function

$$p\{x\} = \theta e^{-\theta x}, \qquad 0 < x < \infty,$$
$$= 0, \qquad \text{otherwise,}$$

where θ is some fixed known parameter ($\theta > 0$). Obtain the relationship between (a) the probability that the life of a tube is less than b hours, and (b) the probability that the life of a tube is less than $2b$ hours, given that the tube has survived b hours.

1E.6. Consider the bivariate density function

$$p\{x_1, x_2\} = abe^{-ax_1 - bx_2}; \qquad x_1, x_2 > 0; \quad a, b > 0.$$
$$= 0, \qquad \text{otherwise.}$$

(a) Evaluate $p\{x_1\}$ and $p\{x_1|x_2\}$. (b) Determine whether X_1 and X_2 are independent, giving the reasons for your conclusion. (c) Evaluate $P\{x_1, x_2\}$.

1E.7. We have a joint density function $p\{x, y\} = 1$ for $0 < X < 1$, $0 < Y < 1$, and $p\{x, y\} = 0$ otherwise. Find the probabilities that (a) $X > 0.5$ and $Y > 0.7$, (b) $X > 0.5$, (c) $X > Y$, (d) $X > 0.5$, given that $Y = 0.5$, (e) $X > Y$, given that $Y < 0.5$, (f) $X + Y < 1$.

1E.8. Over a 2-mile length OA of pipe line a blockage occurs at a point B at random in the interval OA. The blockage causes an increase in pressure and the pipe breaks at a point C at random in the interval OB. (a) What is the probability that the break C is in the interval from the origin O to the 1-mile point? (b) What is the expected value of the length OC?

1E.9. As in 1E.8, except that the blockage occurs at a point B' at random in the interval from the 1-mile to the 2-mile point.

1E.10. Assuming that x and y are independent random variables, show that

$$\frac{V[xy]}{(E[x])^2 (E[y])^2} = C_x^2 C_y^2 + C_x^2 + C_y^2,$$

where $C_x = \sqrt{V[x]}/E[x]$, $C_y = \sqrt{V[y]}/E[y]$ are the so-called coefficients of variation of x and y.

1.24. Covariance and the Correlation Coefficient

The *covariance* of two random variables X and Y is defined as the expected value of the product of the deviations of X and Y from their expected values:

$$\text{Cov}[X, Y] = E[(X - E[X])(Y - E[Y])]. \tag{24.1}$$

For calculating a covariance, an equivalent form is often more convenient:

$$\text{Cov}[X, Y] = E[XY - YE[X] - XE[Y] + E[X]E[Y]]$$
$$= E[XY] - E[X]E[Y]. \tag{24.2}$$

If large positive deviations of X are associated with large positive deviations of Y, and likewise large negative deviations of the two variables occur together, then the covariance will be positive. Furthermore, if positive deviations of X are associated with negative deviations of Y, and vice versa, then the covariance will be negative. On the other hand, if positive and negative deviations of X occur equally frequently with positive and negative deviations of Y, then the covariance will tend to zero. Thus the covariance is a measure of a particular kind of association between two random variables.

It will be noted that the variance is the special case of the covariance of a random variable with itself:

$$\begin{aligned} \text{Cov}[X, X] &= E[(X - E[X])(X - E[X])] \\ &= E[(X - E[X])^2] = V[X]. \end{aligned} \quad (24.3)$$

If V, W are two random variables, and $X = a + bV$, $Y = c + dW$ are two linear functions of them, a, b, c, and d being constants, then $E[X] = a + bE[V]$ and $E[Y] = c + dE[W]$, and so

$$\begin{aligned} \text{Cov}[X, Y] &= E[(a + bV - a - bE[V])(c + dW - c - dE[W])] \\ &= bdE[(V - E[V])(W - E[W])] = bd\,\text{Cov}[V, W]. \end{aligned} \quad (24.4)$$

Equation (17.4) was a special case of this.

Suppose that X, Y are two random variables with a joint distribution. The covariance of their standardized forms is known as their *correlation coefficient*:

$$\rho_{XY} = \text{Cov}\left[\frac{X - E[X]}{\sqrt{V[X]}}, \frac{Y - E[Y]}{\sqrt{V[Y]}}\right]. \quad (24.5)$$

Using the definition of covariance, (24.1), this readily reduces to

$$\rho_{XY} = \frac{\text{Cov}[X, Y]}{\sqrt{V[X]V[Y]}}. \quad (24.6)$$

If $\rho_{XY} = 0$, we say that X and Y are uncorrelated, and this implies

$$\text{Cov}[X, Y] = 0.$$

Now consider the covariance of independent variables. We know from (22.6) that if X and Y are independent, $p\{x, y\} = p_X\{x\}p_Y\{y\}$. The definition of covariance, (24.1), involves $E[XY]$; using the definition of expectation in the multivariate case, (23.2), we have

$$E[XY] = \int_{-\infty}^{\infty}\int_{-\infty}^{\infty} xy p\{x, y\}\,dx\,dy, \quad (24.7)$$

SECT. 1.24   COVARIANCE AND THE CORRELATION COEFFICIENT   79

so for the case of X, Y independent,

$$E[XY] = \int_{-\infty}^{\infty} \int_{-\infty}^{\infty} xy p_X\{x\} p_Y\{y\} \, dx \, dy$$

$$= \int_{-\infty}^{\infty} x p_X\{x\} \, dx \int_{-\infty}^{\infty} y p_Y\{y\} \, dy = E[X]E[Y]. \quad (24.8)$$

Substituting this in (24.2) we see that $\text{Cov}[X, Y] = 0$ and by (24.6) also $\rho_{XY} = 0$. Thus independent variables are uncorrelated. The converse,

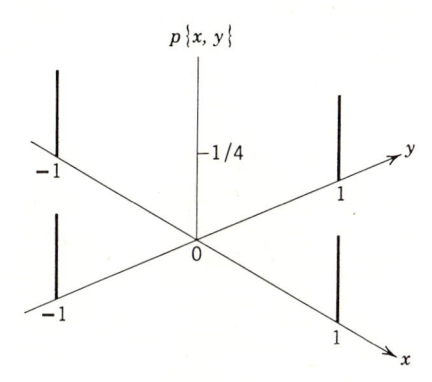

Figure 1.34

however, is generally not true. Two random variables can be uncorrelated but not independent. A simple example of this is to let $p\{x, y\} = 1/4$ at the points $(-1, 0)$, $(0, 1)$, $(0, -1)$, and $(1, 0)$; see Figure 1.34. Then by the discrete analogy of (23.2),

$$E[XY] = \sum_i \sum_j (x_i y_j) p\{x_i, y_j\}$$

$$= (-1) \times 0 \times \frac{1}{4} + 0 \times 1 \times \frac{1}{4} + 0 \times (-1) \times \frac{1}{4}$$

$$+ 1 \times 0 \times \frac{1}{4} = 0, \quad (24.9)$$

$$E[X] = \sum_i x_i p_X\{x_i\} = (-1) \times \frac{1}{4} + 0 \times \frac{1}{2} + 1 \times \frac{1}{4} = 0, \quad (24.10)$$

and likewise $E[Y] = 0$. The covariance of X and Y is thus

$$\text{Cov}[X, Y] = E[XY] - E[X]E[Y] = 0 - 0 \times 0 = 0. \quad (24.11)$$

Thus X, Y have zero covariance, but are obviously not independent. For example, at $x = -1$, $y = 0$, we have $p\{x, y\} = 1/4$, and $p_X\{x\} = 1/4$.

$p_Y\{y\} = 1/2$, so the relationship (22.6), $p\{x, y\} = p_X\{x\}p_Y\{y\}$, which is necessary for the independence of X and Y, is not satisfied.

1.25. The Variance of a Mean

We saw in (23.8) that the expectation of the mean of n observations from a distribution was the expectation of that distribution. We now want to consider the variance of a sample mean. Let us start with the sum of two random variables, $Z = X + Y$; its variance will be

$$\begin{aligned} V[Z] &= E[Z^2] - (E[Z])^2 = E[(X + Y)^2] - (E[X + Y])^2 \\ &= E[X^2] + 2E[XY] + E[Y^2] - (E[X])^2 - 2E[X]E[Y] - (E[Y])^2 \\ &= V[X] + V[Y] + 2 \operatorname{Cov}[X, Y] \quad (25.1) \\ &= V[X] + V[Y] + 2\rho\sqrt{V[X]V[Y]}, \quad (25.2) \end{aligned}$$

the last line being an alternative form given by using (24.6).

This result generalizes easily. Let $X_1, \ldots, X_n$ be random variables, and consider any linear combination

$$Z = a_0 + a_1 X_1 + \cdots + a_n X_n, \quad (25.3)$$

where the a_i are fixed constants. Then

$$E[Z] = a_0 + a_1 E[X_1] + \cdots + a_n E[X_n] \quad (25.4)$$

and

$$\begin{aligned} V[Z] &= E[(Z - E[Z])^2] \\ &= E[(a_0 + a_1 X_1 + \cdots + a_n X_n - a_0 - a_1 E[X_1] - \cdots \\ &\quad - a_n E[X_n])^2] \\ &= E[\{a_1(X_1 - E[X_1]) + \cdots + a_n(X_n - E[X_n])\}^2] \\ &= E\left[\sum_i^n a_i^2 (X_i - E[X_i])^2 + \sum_{\substack{i \ j \\ i \ne j}}^n \sum a_i a_j (X_i - E[X_i])(X_j - E[X_j]) \right] \\ &= \sum_i^n a_i^2 E[(X_i - E[X_i])^2] + \sum_{\substack{i \ j \\ i \ne j}}^n \sum a_i a_j E[(X_i - E[X_i])(X_j - E[X_j])] \\ &= \sum_i^n a_i^2 V[X_i] + \sum_{\substack{i \ j \\ i \ne j}}^n \sum a_i a_j \operatorname{Cov}[X_i, X_j]. \quad (25.5) \end{aligned}$$

An alternative form for (25.5), using (24.3), is

$$V[Z] = \sum_i^n \sum_j^n a_i a_j \operatorname{Cov}[X_i, X_j]; \quad (25.6)$$

SECT. 1.26   ADDITION THEOREM FOR NORMAL DISTRIBUTION   81

in this form the double summation includes the case $i = j$, which give the variance terms in (25.5). Also, the covariance term in (25.5) involves every combination of i with j, excluding $i = j$, and may be written as

$$2 \sum_{\substack{i=1 \\ i<j}}^{n-1} \sum_{j=2}^{n} a_i a_j \, \text{Cov}[X_i, X_j]. \tag{25.7}$$

If in (25.3) we put $a_0 = 0$, $a_1 = a_2 = \cdots = 1$, then Z is just the simple sum of the X_i, and

$$V[Z] = \sum_i^n V[X_i] + \sum_{\substack{i \\ i \neq j}}^{n} \sum_j^n \text{Cov}[X_i, X_j]. \tag{25.8}$$

If the variables are uncorrelated, then their covariances are zero and

$$V[Z] = \sum_i^n V[X_i]. \tag{25.9}$$

Often we are in the case where the variables X_i are independent, and since independence implies zero covariance, (25.9) will hold here also.

To consider the special, but important, case of the mean of n independent observations from the same distribution, the distribution having mean ξ and variance σ^2, in (25.3) put $a_0 = 0$ and $a_i = 1/n$, $i = 1, \ldots, n$. Then

$$Z = \frac{X_1}{n} + \cdots + \frac{X_n}{n} = \frac{1}{n} \sum_i^n X_i = \bar{X},$$

i.e., with these values for the coefficients a_i, Z is the mean, say $\bar{X}$. Using (25.4) and (25.5) we have

$$E[\bar{X}] = \frac{1}{n} E[X_1] + \cdots + \frac{1}{n} E[X_n] = \frac{\xi}{n} + \cdots + \frac{\xi}{n} = \xi, \tag{25.10}$$

and

$$V[\bar{X}] = \frac{1}{n^2} V[X_1] + \cdots + \frac{1}{n^2} V[X_n] = \frac{\sigma^2}{n^2} \cdot n = \frac{\sigma^2}{n}. \tag{25.11}$$

1.26. The Addition Theorem for the Normal Distribution

In the preceding section we have proved that if Z is a linear combination of random variables X_i (25.3) then it has expectation (25.4) and variance (25.5). It is lengthy with the techniques so far at our disposal to prove further that any linear combination Z of normally distributed random variables X_i is itself normally distributed. A proof will be given at the end of Section 12.4. In particular this applies to the mean of n independent identically normally distributed variables X_i from a population $N(\xi, \sigma^2)$:

the mean will be normally distributed $N(\xi, \sigma^2/n)$, i.e., will have a density function

$$p\{\bar{x}\} = \frac{1}{\sqrt{2\pi}\sigma/\sqrt{n}} e^{-(\bar{x}-\xi)^2/(2\sigma^2/n)} \tag{26.1}$$

and cumulative distribution function

$$P\{\bar{x}\} = \int_{-\infty}^{\bar{x}} \frac{1}{\sqrt{2\pi}\sigma/\sqrt{n}} e^{-(t-\xi)^2/(2\sigma^2/n)} dt. \tag{26.2}$$

Since $(\bar{x} - \xi)/(\sigma/\sqrt{n})$ is a unit normal deviate,

$$P\{\bar{x}\} = \Phi\left(\frac{\bar{x} - \xi}{\sigma/\sqrt{n}}\right), \tag{26.3}$$

analogous to (18.13), the change being the substitution of $\bar{x}$ for x and $\sigma/\sqrt{n}$ for σ. With the change of $\bar{X}$ for X, and $\sigma/\sqrt{n}$ for σ where necessary, (18.15) to (18.21) apply.

1.27. The χ^2 Distribution

Suppose that we have n independent observations $x_1, \ldots, x_n$ from a normal distribution $N(\xi, \sigma^2)$. The standardized variables $u_i = (x_i - \xi)/\sigma$ will also be independent, and the sum of their squares will have a distribution whose functional form can be determined. We define the $\chi^2(n)$ distribution as the distribution of the sum of the squares of n independent unit normal variables,

$$\chi^2(n) = \sum_i^n u_i^2. \tag{27.1}$$

The $\chi^2(n)$ distribution is different for each value of n, and the parameter n is known as the number of degrees of freedom. Percentage points of its cumulative distribution are given in Table III of the Appendix. Figure 1.35 shows the density function of χ^2 for degrees of freedom $n = 1, 2, 4$ and 20. Since u_i^2 can never be negative, all the χ^2 distributions are confined to the positive half of the χ^2 axis.

To obtain the expectation of the χ^2 distribution we need $E[u_i^2]$. Since u_i is a unit normal deviate, it has zero expectation and unit variance, and so

$$E[u_i^2] = E[(u_i - E[u_i])^2] = V[u_i] = 1. \tag{27.2}$$

Then

$$E[\chi^2(n)] = E\left[\sum_i^n u_i^2\right] = \sum_i^n E[u_i^2] = \sum_i^n (1) = n. \tag{27.3}$$

Since the u_i are assumed to be independent, their covariance is zero, and

SECT. 1.27   THE χ^2 DISTRIBUTION

the variance of $\chi^2(n)$ is

$$V[\chi^2(n)] = V\left[\sum_i^n u_i^2\right] = \sum_i^n V[u_i^2] = nV[u_i^2]. \quad (27.4)$$

We therefore need $V[u_i^2]$ which can be calculated in the form

$$V[u_i^2] = E[(u_i^2)^2] - (E[u_i^2])^2. \quad (27.5)$$

To obtain $E[u_i^4]$, we use the rule for integration by parts,

$$\int f(x)g'(x)\,dx = f(x)g(x) - \int g(x)f'(x)\,dx, \quad (27.6)$$

identifying $f(x)$ with u^3, so that $f'(x) = 3u^2$, and $g(x)$ with $-e^{-u^2/2}$, so that $g'(x) = ue^{-u^2/2}$. We now have

$$\begin{aligned}
E[u^4] &= \int_{-\infty}^{\infty} u^4 p\{u\}\,du = \int_{-\infty}^{\infty} u^4 \cdot \frac{1}{\sqrt{2\pi}} e^{-u^2/2}\,du \\
&= \frac{1}{\sqrt{2\pi}} \int_{-\infty}^{\infty} u^3 \cdot ue^{-u^2/2}\,du \\
&= \frac{1}{\sqrt{2\pi}} u^3(-e^{-u^2/2})\Big|_{-\infty}^{\infty} - \frac{1}{\sqrt{2\pi}} \int_{-\infty}^{\infty} (-e^{-u^2/2}) \cdot 3u^2\,du \\
&= 3 \cdot \frac{1}{\sqrt{2\pi}} \int_{-\infty}^{\infty} u^2 e^{-u^2/2}\,du = 3E[u^2] = 3. \quad (27.7)
\end{aligned}$$

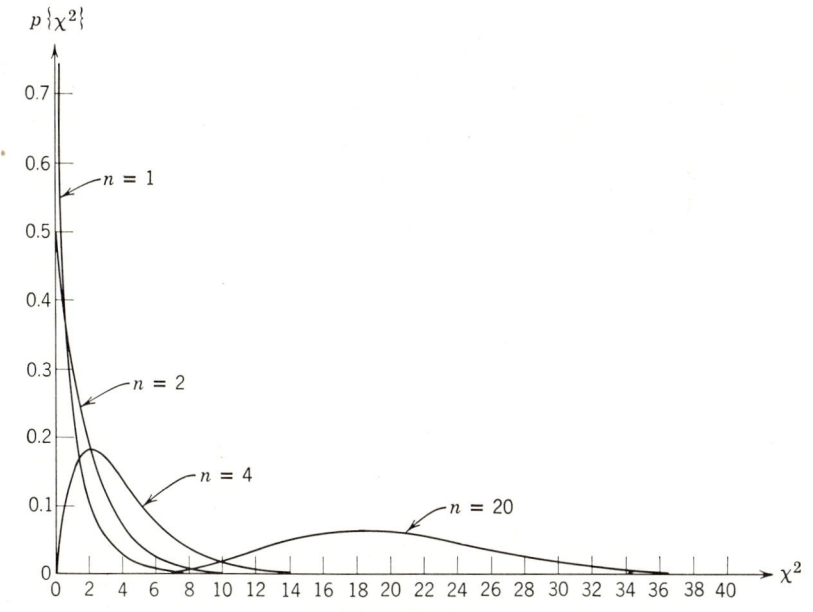

Figure 1.35

Hence, substituting (27.7) and (27.2) in (27.5),

$$V[u_i^2] = 3 - 1^2 = 2, \qquad (27.8)$$

and substituting this in (27.4),

$$V[\chi^2(n)] = 2n. \qquad (27.9)$$

From the central limit theorem, to be referred to in Section 7.1, $\chi^2(n)$ is asymptotically normal for large n. As can be seen from the distribution for $n = 20$ in Figure 1.35, the approach to normality is quite fast. We can thus obtain an approximation to the P point of the distribution from

$$\frac{\chi_P^2(n) - n}{\sqrt{2n}} \simeq u_P, \qquad (27.10)$$

whence

$$\chi_P^2(n) \simeq n + u_P\sqrt{2n}. \qquad (27.11)$$

A better approximation can be obtained from the fact, noted by Fisher [14], that $\sqrt{2\chi^2(n)}$ is approximately normally distributed with mean $\sqrt{2n-1}$ and variance 1. Thus the P point of $\chi^2(n)$ is obtained by solving

$$\sqrt{2\chi_P^2(n)} - \sqrt{2n-1} \simeq u_P, \qquad (27.12)$$

i.e.,

$$\chi_P^2(n) \simeq \tfrac{1}{2}(\sqrt{2n-1} + u_P)^2. \qquad (27.13)$$

If we have two independent χ^2-distributed random variables with degrees of freedom f_1 and f_2, then their sum has the χ^2 distribution with $f_1 + f_2$ degrees of freedom. For $\chi^2(f_1)$ can be written as the sum of squares of f_1 independent unit normal deviates:

$$\chi^2(f_1) = u_1^2 + \cdots + u_{f_1}^2, \qquad (27.14)$$

and $\chi^2(f_2)$ can be likewise written as

$$\chi^2(f_2) = u_{f_1+1}^2 + u_{f_1+2}^2 + \cdots + u_{f_1+f_2}^2, \qquad (27.15)$$

so

$$\chi^2(f_1) + \chi^2(f_2) = u_1^2 + \cdots + u_{f_1+f_2}^2 = \chi^2(f_1 + f_2). \qquad (27.16)$$

EXERCISES 1F

1F.1. For the discrete bivariate distribution of Table 1.17, (a) calculate $E[X + Y]$ from its definition

$$E[X + Y] = \sum_i \sum_j (x_i + y_j)\, p\{x_i, y_j\}.$$

(b) Calculate $E[X]$ and $E[Y]$ and check that equation (23.6) is satisfied. (c) Calculate ρ_{XY}.

1F.2. Two discrete random variables have a joint density function given by the probabilities in the table below.

y	x = −1	x = 0	x = 1
−1	4/15	1/15	4/15
0	1/15	2/15	1/15
1	0/15	2/15	0/15

(a) What is the probability that $X = -1$? (b) What is the probability that $X = -1$, given that $Y = 0$? (c) What is the probability that $X = -1$ and simultaneously $Y = 0$? (d) Are the variables uncorrelated? (e) Are the variables independent? [In (d) and (e), present some explanation and/or justification for your yes or no answer.]

1F.3. X, Y, and Z are random variables each with expectation 10 and variances 1, 4, and 9 respectively. The correlation coefficients are $\rho_{XY} = 0$, $\rho_{XZ} = 1/4$, and $\rho_{YZ} = 1/2$. Obtain numerical answers for the following: (a) $E[X+Y]$, (b) $V[X+Y]$, (c) $E[X+Z]$, (d) $V[X+Z]$, (e) $E[X-Z]$, (f) $V[X-Z]$, (g) $E[X+Y-2Z]$, (h) $V[X+Y-2Z]$, (i) $E[E[X]]$, (j) $V[E[X]]$, (k) $E[V[X]]$, (l) $V[V[X]]$.

1F.4. Suppose that among married couples in a certain population the weights of the husbands are normally distributed with a mean of 80 kilograms and a standard deviation of 9 kilograms, and the weights of the wives are normally distributed with a mean of 60 kilograms and a standard deviation of 4 kilograms. Suppose further that the correlation coefficient between the weight of a husband and the weight of a wife is 1/3. Obtain numerical answers for the following: (a) the probability that the total weight of a couple chosen at random is more than 162 kilograms; (b) the probability that a wife is heavier than her husband.

1F.5. The independent random variables X_i, $i = 1, 2, 3, 4$, are normally distributed with means the same, namely 10, and variances the same, namely 12. We define Z as $X_1 + X_2 + X_3 - 3X_4$. Obtain the numerical values of (a) the expectation of Z, (b) the variance of Z.

1F.6. Axles are manufactured so that their diameters are normally distributed with a mean of 1.00 inch and a standard deviation of 0.004 inch. The bearings in which they are to run are manufactured so that their internal diameters are normally distributed with a mean of 1.01 inch and a standard deviation of 0.003 inch. Operator A assembles axles and bearings at random. Operator B is able to visually pick out axles and bearings so that the dimensions of these two items have a correlation coefficient of 2/3.

The assemblies of axles and bearings are rejected if the gap between the axle and bearing lies outside the interval 0.008 to 0.013. What proportion of the assemblies of (a) operator A, (b) operator B, will be rejected?

1F.7. A small plane will take four passengers in addition to the pilot. The safe payload for the four passengers is 720 lb. Assuming that the passengers are selected at random from a normal population with mean weight 150 lb and standard deviation 32 lb, how often will four passengers overload the plane?

1F.8. You are packing by machine 16 cookies to a box. The label states that the box contains 1 pound of cookies. The weight of the individual cookies is normally distributed with a mean of 1 oz and a standard deviation of 0.1 oz.

If a customer buys a box at random, what are the probabilities that he receives (*a*) less than 1 pound, (*b*) less than 15 oz, (*c*) more than 16.5 oz? (*d*) If you wish to change your manufacturing process so that the mean weight of the cookies is such that only one customer in a hundred will receive less than 1 pound, what should the new mean weight of the cookies be, assuming that the standard deviation remain unchanged? (*e*) Further, if you could also reduce the standard deviation to 0.05 oz, what mean weight would satisfy the condition specified in the previous sentence?

1F.9. Suppose that you drive from New York to San Francisco, 3040 miles by a certain route, starting with new spark plugs in your eight-cylinder engine. Suppose that the satisfactory life of a plug is normally distributed with a mean of 5000 miles and a standard deviation of 1000 miles. What is the probability that you will roll over the Bay Bridge with your motor still purring (with the original plugs) on all eight cylinders?

1F.10. Pipes (for tobacco) are being packed in fancy plastic boxes. The length of the pipes is normally distributed with a mean of 5 inches and a standard deviation of 0.04 inch. The internal length of the boxes is normally distributed with a mean of 5.1 inches and a standard deviation of 0.03 inch. What proportion of the time will the box be too small for the pipe?

REFERENCES

1. Todhunter, I., *A History of the Mathematical Theory of Probability*. London: Macmillan and Co., 1865. New York: Chelsea Publishing Co., 1949.
2. Pearson, E. S., *Karl Pearson*. London: Cambridge University Press, 1938.
3. Pearson, E. S., and Wishart, J. (eds.), *"Student's" Collected Papers*. London: Biometrika Office, 1942.
4. Fisher, R. A., *Statistical Methods for Research Workers*. 1st ed. 1925, 13th ed. 1958. Edinburgh: Oliver and Boyd.
5. Fisher, R. A., *The Design of Experiments*. 1st ed. 1935, 7th ed. 1960. Edinburgh: Oliver and Boyd.
6. Fisher, R. A., *Contributions to Mathematical Statistics*, ed. W. A. Shewhart. New York: John Wiley and Sons, 1950.
7. Neyman, J., and Pearson, E. S., "On the Problem of the Most Efficient Tests of Statistical Hypotheses," *Philosophical Transactions of the Royal Society*, A, 231 (1933), 289–337.
8. Wald, A., *Sequential Analysis*. New York: John Wiley and Sons, 1947.
9. Wald, A., *Statistical Decision Functions*. New York: John Wiley and Sons, 1950.
10. Bayes, Thomas, "Essay towards Solving a Problem in the Doctrine of Chance," *Philosophical Transactions of the Royal Society*, 53 (1763), 370–418. Reprinted in *Biometrika*, 45 (1958), 293–315.
11. Wallis, W. Allen, and Roberts, Harry V., *Statistics: A New Approach*. New York: The Free Press of Glencoe, 1956.
12. Mosteller, Frederick, "The World Series Competition," *Journal of the American Statistical Association*, 4 (1952), 355–80.
13. Cramér, H., *Mathematical Methods of Statistics*. Princeton: Princeton University Press, 1946.
14. Fisher, R. A., and Yates, F., *Statistical Tables for Biological, Agricultural and Medical Research*. 6th ed. Edinburgh: Oliver and Boyd, 1963.

CHAPTER 2

Statistical Ideas

2.1. Statistical Inference

Statistics is frequently defined as the science of making wise decisions in the presence of uncertainty. To cite Savage's example in his review [1] of Wald's book *Statistical Decision Functions* [2], the decision to be made may be whether to take an umbrella on one's trip to the office. This approach requires a knowledge of the relative costs of carrying an umbrella when the day turns out to be fine and of getting wet by failing to carry an umbrella when the day turns out to be wet. The practical usefulness of this approach has been severely hindered by the rarity with which one can actually estimate with any confidence the cost functions. Whether this obstacle can be circumvented sufficiently to bring this decision theory approach into common use remains to be seen. For an elementary account, see Chernoff and Moses [3].

Classical statistical inference operates one stage further back from the decision-making process: very roughly speaking, it confines itself to establishing what can be said about the facts of the situation, and it leaves the decision as to what to actually do, if anything, to the common sense of the experimenter.

Two broad categories of problems that have received particular attention are *estimation* and the *testing of (statistical) hypotheses*. The first is subdivided into *point estimation* and *interval estimation* of the parameters of a distribution. For example, given a sample of n observations from a distribution assumed normal, we may wish to obtain point estimates of the parameter σ, or the parameter σ^2, or both the parameters, or conceivably some function such as e^ξ or $\xi + k\sigma$. We may, on the other hand, wish to obtain an interval which we are confident will include the actual value of the parameter or parameters: this is the problem of interval estimation.

The second problem, hypothesis testing, consists of making an assumption about the distribution function of a random variable, very often about the numerical values of one or more of the parameters of the distribution function, and deciding whether those values of the parameters are consistent in some sense with our sample of observations on that random variable. For example, in the case of the normal distribution, the hypothesis might be that $\xi = 0$, or that $\sigma^2 = 1$. Of course, if we could take infinitely large samples of observations we would be able, in an ordinary case, to determine the parameters of the distribution in question exactly, and there would be no statistical problem. The problems of statistical inference are to do the best we can with limited samples of observations.

Implicit in the treatment of the problems of statistical inference is the assumption that we are able to obtain random samples of observations. A *random sample* can be defined as consisting of statistically independent, identically distributed random variables; i.e., random variables with the same distribution function.

As an example of how we may generate a random sample, consider a sample space with all n points equiprobable. Let X be a random variable, so that associated with every point in the sample space is a characteristic x_i. Let $n(x_i)$ be the number of points with characteristic x_i. Now sample N points from the sample space, replacing each point obtained before taking the next sample. Then we will observe x_i with probability $n(x_i)/N$. Since the drawings are with replacement, they are independent. Since all observations come from the same sample space they will have the same distribution function. Thus our observations will satisfy our definition of a random sample.

Suppose we take a random sample of two observations on a random variable with distribution function $p_X\{x\}$. The pair of observations X_1, X_2 will have a bivariate distribution function $p\{x_1, x_2\}$. But if the sample was random, as supposed, the observations will be independent, and by (1.22.6)

$$p\{x_1, x_2\} = p_X\{x_1\} p_X\{x_2\}. \tag{1.1}$$

Clearly this will generalize to n observations, so

$$p\{x_1, \ldots, x_n\} = p_X\{x_1\} \cdots p_X\{x_n\} = \prod_i^n p_X\{x_i\}. \tag{1.2}$$

2.2. Some Principles of Point Estimation

Suppose that we have a random sample of n observations $x_1, \ldots, x_n$ from a population with distribution function of known form

$$p\{x:\theta_1, \ldots, \theta_k\},$$

involving k parameters θ_j, $j = 1, \ldots, k$. For example, $p\{\ \}$ could be the normal distribution which has the two parameters ξ and σ. We may wish to estimate ξ, or we may wish to estimate σ^2 either in the case where ξ is known or in the case where ξ is unknown. The general problem is to estimate one (or more) of the θ_j, the remaining θ_j being either known or unknown. The function of the observations we choose, $\hat{\theta}(x_1, \ldots, x_n)$ is known as the *estimator*, and when we insert a particular sample of numerical values for the x_i we obtain a numerical value of the function which is known as an *estimate*. Often several alternative functions will naturally suggest themselves as estimators: for example, as estimators of the mean of a normal distribution we might use the arithmetic mean, the median, the mode, the midrange (the arithmetic mean of the largest and smallest observations in the sample), etc.

What criteria should we use for choosing our estimator? Obviously, in principle the answer may depend on the particular purpose for which we want it. However, conventional statistics attempts to answer this question in general terms, in order to generate estimators of general utility, since it would be impractical to have to consider every separate problem completely from first principles. In practice, our choice is sometimes influenced by economic considerations; one estimator may be somewhat better than another, but if it requires $500.00 of computation whereas the alternative requires only $5.00, we may well decide that the margin of superiority of the former does not justify the additional expenditure and that the latter is adequate for our needs.

Confining our discussion to the one-parameter case, intuitively we want our estimator $\hat{\theta}$ to yield estimates whose distribution is close in some sense to θ. This broad criterion is not sufficient to resolve ambiguities, however. In Figure 2.1, which shows the distribution of three alternative estimators $\hat{\theta}_a$, $\hat{\theta}_b$ and $\hat{\theta}_c$, the first two have the advantage that their expected values are equal to θ. This property, namely that

$$E[\hat{\theta}] = \theta, \tag{2.1}$$

is known as *unbiasedness*. The *bias* of an estimator $\hat{\theta}$ is defined as

$$(E[\hat{\theta}] - \theta). \tag{2.2}$$

The estimator $\hat{\theta}_a$ is preferable to $\hat{\theta}_b$ in that medium-sized deviations occur less frequently; on the other hand, extreme deviations are more frequent with $\hat{\theta}_a$ than with $\hat{\theta}_b$. Using the variance, $V[\hat{\theta}] = E[(\hat{\theta} - E[\hat{\theta}])^2]$, as a measure of spread, the third estimator $\hat{\theta}_c$ is the best of the three, but since its expected value is not equal to θ, it is a biased estimator.

Unbiased estimators have the following desirable property: if we have a series of independent unbiased estimates then their average will also be unbiased. On the other hand, the average of biased estimates will be biased, no matter how large the number being averaged.

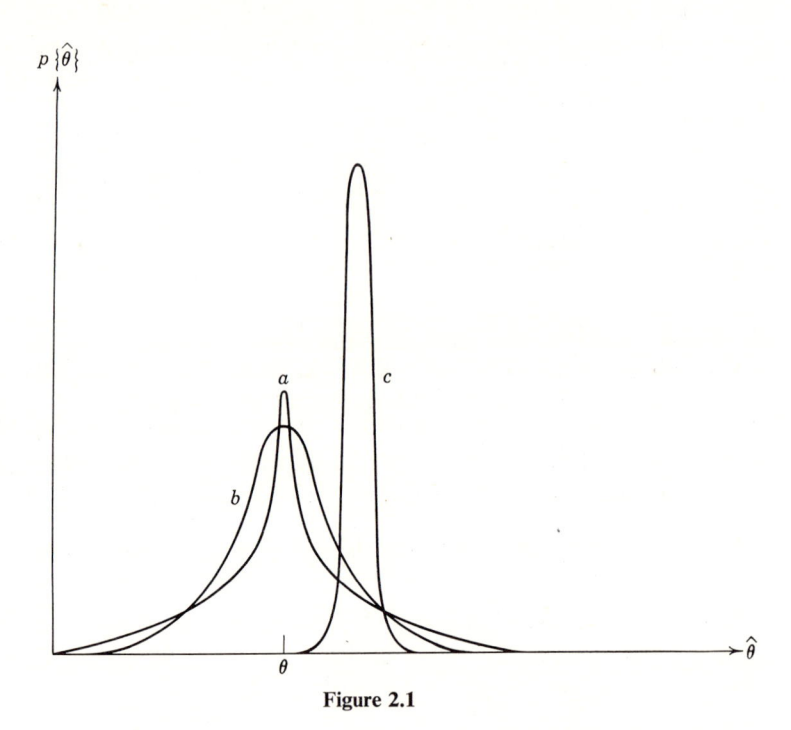

Figure 2.1

For comparing estimators, including biased estimators, a useful criterion is the *mean square error*, defined as the expected value of the square of the deviation of the estimate from the parameter $E[(\hat{\theta} - \theta)^2]$. This quantity is equal to the variance plus the square of the bias, as can be shown as follows:

$$E[(\hat{\theta} - \theta)^2] = E[\{(\hat{\theta} - E[\hat{\theta}]) + (E[\hat{\theta}] - \theta)\}^2]$$
$$= E[(\hat{\theta} - E[\hat{\theta}])^2] + E[(E[\hat{\theta}] - \theta)^2] + 2(E[\hat{\theta}] - \theta)E[\hat{\theta} - E[\hat{\theta}]]$$
$$= V[\hat{\theta}] + (\text{bias})^2, \qquad (2.3)$$

since

$$E[\hat{\theta} - E[\hat{\theta}]] = E[\hat{\theta}] - E[E[\hat{\theta}]] = E[\hat{\theta}] - E[\hat{\theta}] = 0 \qquad (2.4)$$

A further criterion, consistency, involves the behavior of an estimator as the sample size increases indefinitely Specifically, if for any small quantity ϵ, the probability that the absolute value of the deviation of $\hat{\theta}$

from θ is less than ϵ tends to 1 as n tends to infinity, i.e., if

$$\Pr\{|\hat{\theta} - \theta| < \epsilon\} \to 1 \quad \text{as } n \to \infty, \tag{2.5}$$

then we say that the estimator $\hat{\theta}$ is *consistent*.

Among the class of unbiased estimators, there will be one or more with minimum variance: this (or these) is (or are) the *efficient* estimator(s). The *efficiency* of any other estimator is defined as the ratio of the variance of the efficient estimator(s) to the variance of the other estimator.

2.3. Maximum Likelihood Estimation

A method of estimation which usually in practice works out satisfactorily is the method of maximum likelihood [4]; namely, to choose that value of θ which maximizes the likelihood function defined as

$$L = p\{x_1:\theta\} \cdots p\{x_n:\theta\} \tag{3.1}$$

where $p\{x:\theta\}$ is the distribution function of x, of known form but containing the unknown parameter θ. In maximizing the likelihood function, the observed x's are considered as constants and the parameter θ as a variable.

Incidentally, at this point we will cease to preserve the distinction between random variables X and the values which they can take, x. Strict consistency in this convention becomes clumsy and leads to uncomfortable contradictions with long-established usage; for example, Student's t would have to be written as T. This difficulty could be avoided by the notational device of using bold-face type for random variables, but other infelicities remain, and therefore we will use lower-case letters except on those occasions in which upper-case letters are necessary to avoid confusion.

Maximum likelihood estimators have the desirable properties of being consistent and asymptotically normal and asymptotically efficient for large samples under general conditions. Sections 33.2 and 33.3 of [5] and Chapter 18 of [6] contain extensive discussions of these questions. Maximum likelihood estimators are often biased, but frequently the bias is removable by a simple adjustment.

As one example of maximum likelihood estimation, suppose that we take a sample of size n from a binomial population with parameter θ and find x defectives in the sample. We wish to estimate θ, the proportion of defectives in the population. The likelihood function is

$$L = p\{x:n, \theta\} = \binom{n}{x}\theta^x(1-\theta)^{n-x}. \tag{3.2}$$

Figure 2.2 shows plots of L against θ for the two cases, $n = 10$, $x = 3$ and $n = 50$, $x = 15$. In maximizing this function, it is more convenient to maximize its logarithm, which amounts to the same thing; those

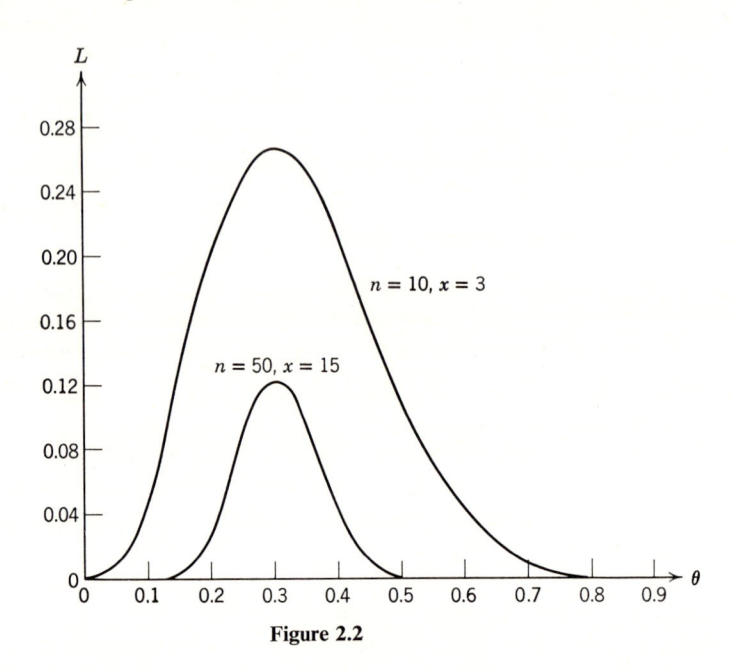

Figure 2.2

values of the parameters which maximize $\log L$ will maximize L. The logarithm of (3.2) is

$$\log L = \log \binom{n}{x} + x \log \theta + (n - x) \log(1 - \theta). \quad (3.3)$$

The usual method for maximization with respect to a parameter is to differentiate with respect to that parameter and equate the derivative to zero:

$$\frac{d \log L}{d\theta} = \frac{x}{\theta} + (n - x) \frac{-1}{1 - \theta}, \quad (3.4)$$

which yields $\hat{\theta} = x/n$ on equating to zero. The caret is conventionally used over a symbol to denote the maximum likelihood estimator. Thus $\hat{\theta}$ is the maximum likelihood estimator of θ.

When the density function has several parameters, we can usually find the values of the parameters that maximize $\log L$ by setting the partial derivatives of $\log L$ with respect to the parameters equal to zero; i.e.,

SECT. 2.3 MAXIMUM LIKELIHOOD ESTIMATION

we set
$$\frac{\partial \log L}{\partial \theta_1} = \frac{\partial \log L}{\partial \theta_2} = \cdots = 0. \tag{3.5}$$

Frequently, but not always, the value of, say, θ_1 that maximizes log L depends on the value of θ_2, so to estimate θ_1 we have also to estimate θ_2.

As an example, consider the estimation of the parameter ξ of a normal distribution from a sample $x_1, \ldots, x_n$. The likelihood function is obtained by substituting the normal density function in (3.1):

$$L = \frac{1}{\sqrt{2\pi}\sigma} e^{-(x_1-\xi)^2/2\sigma^2} \cdots \frac{1}{\sqrt{2\pi}\sigma} e^{-(x_n-\xi)^2/2\sigma^2}$$

$$= \left(\frac{1}{2\pi\sigma^2}\right)^{n/2} e^{-(1/2\sigma^2)\Sigma(x_i-\xi)^2}. \tag{3.6}$$

where the summation is over the index $i = 1, \ldots, n$, as also in the remainder of this section. The logarithm of the likelihood is

$$\log L = -\frac{n}{2} \log(2\pi\sigma^2) - \frac{1}{2\sigma^2} \Sigma (x_i - \xi)^2. \tag{3.7}$$

Differentiating with respect to ξ gives

$$\frac{\partial \log L}{\partial \xi} = -\frac{1}{2\sigma^2} \Sigma 2(x_i - \xi)(-1). \tag{3.8}$$

Equating to zero gives

$$\Sigma (x_i - \hat{\xi}) = \Sigma x_i - n\hat{\xi} = 0, \tag{3.9}$$

whence

$$\hat{\xi} = \frac{\Sigma x_i}{n}, \tag{3.10}$$

which is the sample mean, usually denoted by $\bar{x}$. We obtained $\hat{\xi}$ without having to estimate σ^2.

To obtain the maximum likelihood estimator of σ^2 we differentiate (3.7) with respect to σ^2:

$$\frac{\partial \log L}{\partial \sigma^2} = -\frac{n}{2} \frac{1}{\sigma^2} + \frac{1}{2(\sigma^2)^2} \Sigma (x_i - \xi)^2. \tag{3.11}$$

If ξ is known we equate this to zero and solve for $\widehat{\sigma^2}$:

$$\widehat{\sigma^2} = \frac{\Sigma (x_i - \xi)^2}{n}. \tag{3.12}$$

If ξ is unknown, we put the two partial derivatives (3.8) and (3.11) equal to zero, giving $\hat{\xi} = \bar{x}$ as before and $\sigma^2 = \Sigma(x_i - \hat{\xi})^2/n$. Substituting for $\hat{\xi}$ gives

$$\widehat{\sigma^2} = \frac{\Sigma(x_i - \bar{x})^2}{n}. \tag{3.13}$$

Here we had to obtain $\hat{\xi}$ in order to obtain σ^2.

In the foregoing we obtained the maximum likelihood estimator of σ^2, i.e., $\widehat{\sigma^2}$. We might have chosen instead to obtain the maximum likelihood estimator of σ, i.e., $\hat{\sigma}$. We would then have differentiated (3.7) with respect to σ:

$$\frac{\partial \log L}{\partial \sigma} = -\frac{n}{\sigma} + \frac{1}{\sigma^3}\Sigma(x_i - \xi)^2. \tag{3.14}$$

We equate to zero and solve for $\hat{\sigma}$:

$$\hat{\sigma} = \sqrt{\Sigma(x_i - \hat{\xi})^2/n} = \sqrt{\Sigma(x_i - \bar{x})^2/n}. \tag{3.15}$$

We thus see that

$$\hat{\sigma}^2 = \widehat{\sigma^2}. \tag{3.16}$$

This illustrates a general property of maximum likelihood estimators, and one which is highly desirable, namely *invariance*. Generally, if $f(\theta)$ is a single-valued function of θ, and $\hat{\theta}$ is the maximum likelihood estimator of θ, then $f(\hat{\theta})$ is the maximum likelihood estimator of $f(\theta)$; i.e., $\widehat{f(\theta)}$. In the foregoing example, $\sigma = \sqrt{\sigma^2}$ is a single-valued function of σ^2 and $\hat{\sigma} = \sqrt{\widehat{\sigma^2}}$.

Let us now check on the expected value of $\hat{\sigma}^2$ to see if it is a biased estimator. We have

$$n\hat{\sigma}^2 = \Sigma(x_i - \bar{x})^2 = \Sigma[(x_i - \xi) - (\bar{x} - \xi)]^2$$
$$= \Sigma(x_i - \xi)^2 + n(\bar{x} - \xi)^2 - 2(\bar{x} - \xi)\Sigma(x_i - \xi)$$
$$= \Sigma(x_i - \xi)^2 - n(\bar{x} - \xi)^2, \tag{3.17}$$

since

$$2(\bar{x} - \xi)\Sigma(x_i - \xi) = 2(\bar{x} - \xi)(\Sigma x_i - n\xi)$$
$$= 2(\bar{x} - \xi)(n\bar{x} - n\xi) = 2n(\bar{x} - \xi)^2. \tag{3.18}$$

Thus

$$E[n\hat{\sigma}^2] = \Sigma E[(x_i - \xi)^2] - nE[(\bar{x} - \xi)^2]. \tag{3.19}$$

Now

$$E[(x_i - \xi)^2] = E[(x_i - E[x_i])^2] = V[x_i], \tag{3.20}$$

and

$$E[(\bar{x} - \xi)^2] = E[(\bar{x} - E[\bar{x}])^2] = V[\bar{x}] = \frac{V[x_i]}{n}. \tag{3.21}$$

Hence

$$E[\hat{\sigma}^2] = \frac{1}{n} \cdot nV[x_i] - \frac{V[x_i]}{n} = \frac{n-1}{n} V[x_i]. \qquad (3.22)$$

In the case of the normal distribution, $V[x_i] = \sigma^2$, so $\hat{\sigma}^2$ defined as in (3.13) is a biased estimator of σ^2. On the other hand, if we define s^2 as

$$s^2 = \frac{\sum (x_i - \bar{x})^2}{n - 1} \qquad (3.23)$$

it will have expected value

$$E[s^2] = E\left[\frac{n}{n-1} \frac{\sum (x_i - \bar{x})^2}{n}\right] = \frac{n}{n-1} E[\hat{\sigma}^2] \qquad (3.24)$$

$$= V[x_i]. \qquad (3.25)$$

Therefore s^2 will be an unbiased estimator of the parameter σ^2 of the normal distribution.

It will be noted that, though (3.13) was derived specifically as an estimator of the parameter σ^2 of a normal distribution, the arguments of (3.17)–(3.22), showing that it was a biased estimator of the variance, made no reference to the distribution being sampled being normal. Likewise (3.25), showing that s^2 as defined in (3.23) is an unbiased estimator of the variance, is true for observations X_i from any distribution.

The general subject of estimation is rather controversial because it is possible to give different weights to the various criteria, and to make up criteria of one's own, depending on one's view as to what the estimate is to be used for. We will not explore this topic further, except in Chapter 11 where we introduce the method of *least squares*, which gives results identical with those of the method of maximum likelihood when the underlying distribution is normal.

2.4. A Weighted Mean Unbiased and of Minimum Variance

Suppose that we have k observations x_i, all with the same expectation ξ, but with variances σ_i^2. We wish to choose coefficients a_i so that a linear combination of the x_i, defined as

$$\bar{x} = \sum_i^k a_i x_i, \qquad (4.1)$$

will be unbiased and of minimum variance. For $\bar{x}$ to be unbiased, its expected value,

$$E[\bar{x}] = E\left[\sum_i^k a_i x_i\right] = \sum_i^k a_i E[x_i] = \xi \sum_i^k a_i, \qquad (4.2)$$

must equal ξ, so we require that $\sum_i^k a_i = 1$, which we can write as

$$a_k + \sum_i^{k-1} a_i = \sum_i^k a_i = 1, \qquad (4.3)$$

so

$$a_k = 1 - \sum_i^{k-1} a_i. \qquad (4.4)$$

The variance of $\bar{x}$, which we wish to minimize, is

$$V[\bar{x}] = V\left[\sum_i^k a_i x_i\right] = \sum_i^k a_i^2 V[x_i] = \sum_i^k a_i^2 \sigma_i^2 \qquad (4.5)$$

$$= \sum_i^{k-1} a_i^2 \sigma_i^2 + \left(1 - \sum_i^{k-1} a_i\right)^2 \sigma_k^2$$

$$= \sum_i^{k-1} a_i^2 \sigma_i^2 + \left[1 - 2\sum_i^{k-1} a_i + \left(\sum_i^{k-1} a_i\right)^2\right] \sigma_k^2. \qquad (4.6)$$

To find the values of a_i which make this a minimum we differentiate with respect to a_j and equate to zero:

$$\frac{\partial V[\bar{x}]}{\partial a_j} = 2a_j \sigma_j^2 - 2\sigma_k^2 + 2\left(\sum_i^{k-1} a_i\right)\sigma_k^2$$

$$= 2\left[a_j \sigma_j^2 - \left(1 - \sum_i^{k-1} a_i\right)\sigma_k^2\right] = 0. \qquad (4.7)$$

Substituting (4.4) in this, we get

$$a_j = a_k \frac{\sigma_k^2}{\sigma_j^2}, \quad j = 1, \ldots, k - 1. \qquad (4.8)$$

However, this relationship is obviously true for $j = k$ also. We can therefore sum over $j = 1, \ldots, k$ to get

$$\sum_j^k a_j = a_k \sigma_k^2 \sum_j^k \frac{1}{\sigma_j^2}. \qquad (4.9)$$

But $\sum_i^k a_i = 1$, so

$$a_k = \left(\sigma_k^2 \sum_i^k \frac{1}{\sigma_i^2}\right)^{-1}. \qquad (4.10)$$

Substituting (4.10) into (4.8) gives, for any j,

$$a_j = \left(\sigma_j^2 \sum_i^k \frac{1}{\sigma_i^2}\right)^{-1}. \qquad (4.11)$$

These a_i are the values which make $\bar{x} = \sum_i^k a_i x_i$ unbiased and of minimum variance. If we use these coefficients, the variance of $\bar{x}$, using (4.5), is

$$V[\bar{x}] = \sum_i^k a_i^2 \sigma_i^2 = \sum_i^k \left[\left(\sigma_i^2 \sum_i^k \frac{1}{\sigma_i^2}\right)^{-1}\right]^2 \sigma_i^2$$

$$= \left[\left(\sum_i^k \frac{1}{\sigma_i^2}\right)^{-1}\right]^2 \sum_i^k \left(\frac{\sigma_i^2}{\sigma_i^4}\right) = \left(\sum_i^k \frac{1}{\sigma_i^2}\right)^{-1}. \quad (4.12)$$

Sometimes it is convenient to define weights w_i as $w_i = 1/\sigma_i^2$. From (4.11),

$$a_j = \frac{1}{\sigma_j^2}\left(\sum_i^k \frac{1}{\sigma_i^2}\right)^{-1} = \frac{w_j}{\sum_i^k w_i}. \quad (4.13)$$

With this notation in (4.1) and (4.5),

$$\bar{x} = \frac{\sum_j^k w_j x_j}{\sum_i^k w_i}, \quad (4.14)$$

$$V[\bar{x}] = \sum_i^k \left(\frac{w_i}{\sum_i^k w_i}\right)^2 \frac{1}{w_i} = \frac{\sum_i^k w_i}{\left(\sum_i^k w_i\right)^2} = \frac{1}{\sum_i^k w_i}. \quad (4.15)$$

2.5. Some Principles of Hypothesis Testing

The simplest situation is the test of a hypothesis against a single alternative. We suppose that under the *null hypothesis* H_0 the density function is $p\{x:\theta_0\}$ and under the *alternative hypothesis* the density function is $p\{x:\theta_1\}$. The two hypotheses in question supposedly completely define the two distributions; i.e., θ_0 and θ_1 are both exactly specified, and if there are further parameters in the density functions they are assumed known. Hypotheses of this type are known as *simple hypotheses*. If any parameters are not specified completely the hypothesis is called a *composite hypothesis*. For example, if the distribution is the normal and the parameter in which we are interested is ξ, but the variance is unknown, then we would be concerned with a composite hypothesis. Again, if the alternative distribution is the normal with known variance but it is merely specified that $\xi_1 > \xi_0$, or that $\xi_1 \neq \xi_0$, then ξ_1 is not specified completely and so we are dealing with a composite alternative hypothesis. This and the three following sections will deal with simple hypotheses.

We are going to take an observation x and we want a criterion for accepting the null hypothesis or accepting the alternative hypothesis (and rejecting the null hypothesis).

We start by choosing a region on the line such that if the observation

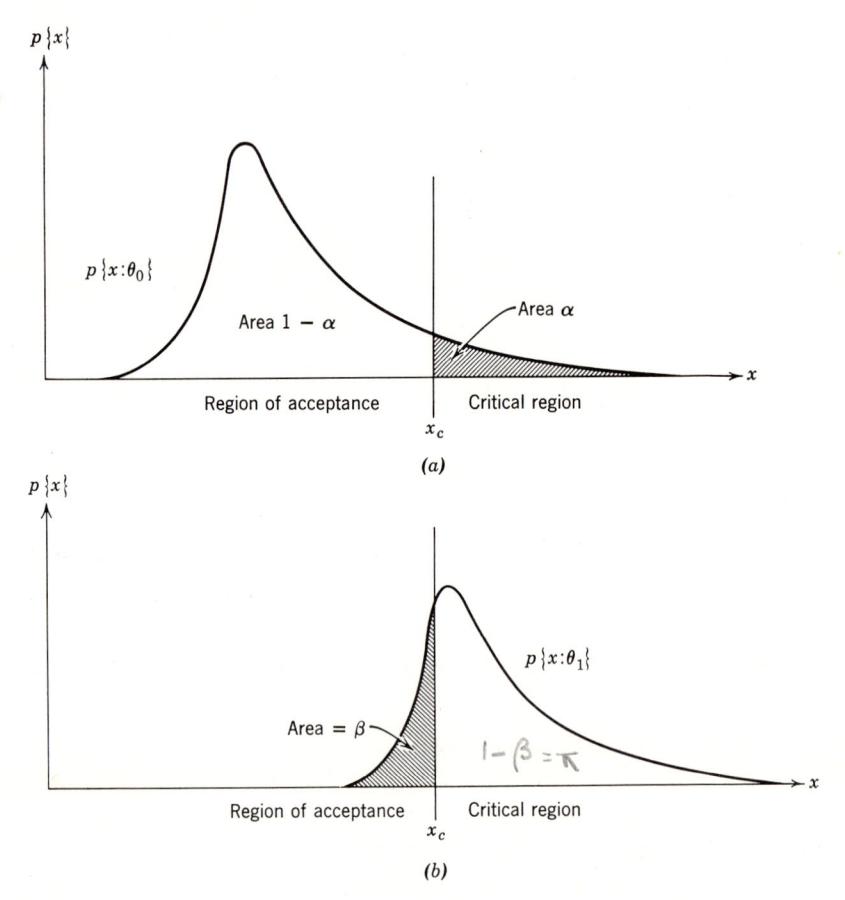

Figure 2.3

falls in this region then we accept the null hypothesis; this is the *region of acceptance*. The complementary region, where we reject the null hypothesis, is the *region of rejection* or the *critical region*.

On what basis shall we choose these regions? The first criterion is that only in a small fraction α of the time shall we commit a *Type I error* or an *error of the first kind*, which is to reject the null hypothesis when in fact it is true. Clearly we wish to commit such an error only rarely: common choices for α are 0.05 or 0.01. The numerical value selected for α is known as the *level of significance* of the test.

To be more specific, suppose that under the alternative hypothesis the distribution is shifted without change of shape to the right so that the expected value of x under the alternative hypothesis, $E_{\theta_1}[x]$, is greater than $E_{\theta_0}[x]$, the expected value under the null hypothesis. Then it is reasonable to choose as the critical region that part of the line to the right of some value x_c, where x_c is chosen (see Figure 2.3a), so that if the null hypothesis is true (so that x has the distribution $p\{x:\theta_0\}$), the probability of a random observation falling in the critical region is α; i.e., x_c satisfies the equation

$$\int_{x_c}^{\infty} p\{x:\theta_0\}\, dx = \alpha. \tag{5.1}$$

We now consider what will happen if actually H_1 is true and x has the frequency function $p\{x:\theta_1\}$. We supposed earlier that the difference between $p\{x:\theta_0\}$ and $p\{x:\theta_1\}$ was that the distribution was shifted to the right, so the situation is as in Figure 2.3b. Under H_1, the probability, say β, of our observation falling in the region of acceptance, $x < x_c$, is the shaded area in Figure 2.3b; i.e., β is determined by the equation

$$\int_{-\infty}^{x_c} p\{x:\theta_1\}\, dx = \beta. \tag{5.2}$$

To accept H_0 when it is false is an error, known as an *error of the second kind*, or a *Type II error*. The probability of the complementary event, namely of correctly rejecting the null hypothesis, is known as the *power* of the test, say π. The power is thus equal to the probability of x falling in the region of rejection when it has the alternative distribution:

$$\pi = 1 - \beta = \int_{x_c}^{\infty} p\{x:\theta_1\}\, dx. \tag{5.3}$$

We would like to have the power large, say 0.90 or 0.99, but restrictions of time and money may mean we have to settle for substantially less.

The result of a statistical test can be summarized in Table 2.1.

The usual procedure is to choose α small, say 0.05 or 0.01. For specified θ_0 and θ_1, and a given $p\{x:\theta\}$, then β will be determined, and often it will be substantially larger than what we would regard as a satisfactorily small value, say 0.1. We will then be chary of actually rejecting H_1; while we accept H_0, we do not rule out the possibility that H_1 is true. Such a situation is illustrated by Figure 2.4. Here, if x falls at the point indicated, it is clearly in the region of acceptance and so we accept H_0. However, such a value of x could very easily arise in sampling from the alternative

Table 2.1

Conclusion of experimenter	True situation	
	H_0 true H_1 false	H_0 false H_1 true
H_0 true H_1 false	Conclusion correct	Conclusion false Type II error committed
H_0 false H_1 true	Conclusion false Type I error committed	Conclusion correct

distribution $p\{x:\theta_1\}$; the probability

$$\int_{-\infty}^{x_c} p\{x:\theta_1\}\, dx$$

is by no means small, being about 3/16, and it would be hazardous to rule out the possibility that H_1 is true. Nevertheless, the customary procedure is to accept H_0 until we are forced by further data to revise our opinion.

This procedure is standard but clearly open to a variety of criticisms. For example, the conventional policy of choosing α and leaving β to fend for itself often appears as an arbitrary asymmetry. However, it will be noted that this is analogous to a broad principle of English common law: a jury is instructed to return a verdict of not guilty (corresponding to

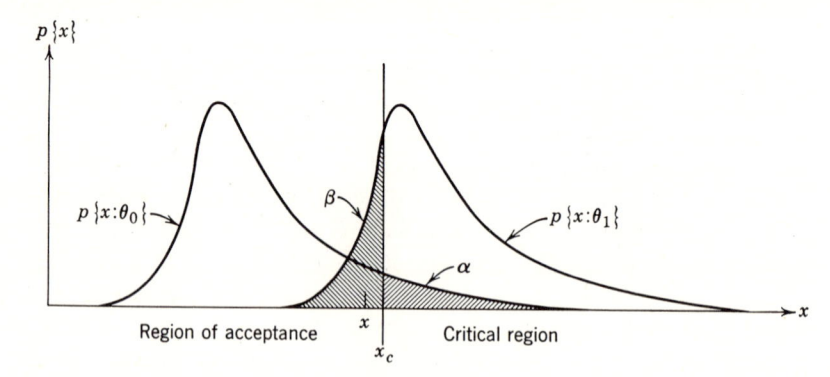

Figure 2.4

accepting the null hypothesis) unless it is satisfied beyond all reasonable doubt (corresponding to a very small α) that the defendant is guilty. Then it rejects the null hypothesis that the defendant is not guilty and accepts the alternative hypothesis that the defendant is guilty. If this policy results in a rather large proportion of guilty men going free, society nevertheless accepts this as a price it has to pay for achieving its prime objective; namely, very rarely convicting an innocent man. The acceptance of the null hypothesis does not imply a belief that it is true, merely that the evidence for rejecting it is insufficient. The hypothesis testing procedure itself does not directly distinguish between the case in which the null hypothesis is either true or close to being true, on the one hand, and on the other hand the case in which the data is really insufficient to draw any useful conclusion. *Confidence intervals*, to be discussed in Section 2.14, can be used to throw light on this question.

2.6. A Criterion for Choosing between Alternative Tests

We have seen that we construct a test by dividing the x axis into two regions, the region of acceptance and the critical region, and so far the only restriction we have imposed on this choice is that the probability of an error of the first kind should be

$$\int_R p\{x:\theta_0\}\, dx = \alpha, \qquad (6.1)$$

where R is the region of rejection. In the preceding section we stated that in the case in question a reasonable choice for the critical region was the upper tail of the distribution $p\{x:\theta_0\}$ without discussing whether this was the best choice. We now examine this question.

Consider an alternative critical region, for example that defined by $x_d < x < x_e$ in Figure 2.5, where x_d and x_e satisfy the condition that the probability of an error of the first kind continues to be α:

$$\int_{x_d}^{x_e} p\{x:\theta_0\}\, dx = \alpha. \qquad (6.2)$$

The obvious basis for comparing the two tests, since they have the same probability of a Type I error, is the relative magnitudes of the probabilities of their Type II errors.

Figure 2.6 shows the relation to the alternative distribution $p\{x:\theta_1\}$ of the two alternative critical regions. If β_1 and β_2 are the probabilities of

102   STATISTICAL IDEAS   CHAP. 2

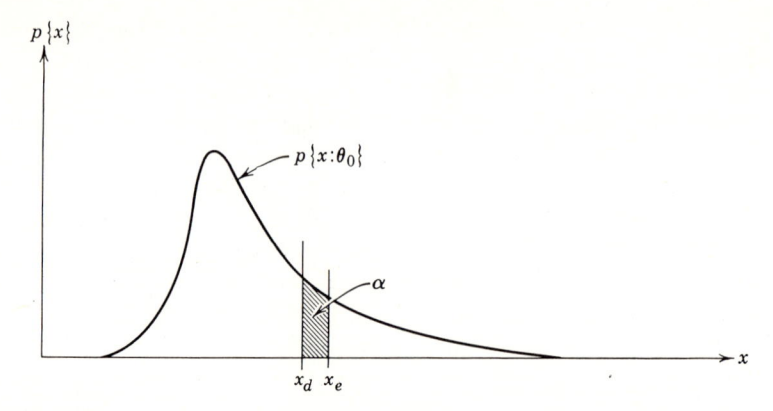

Figure 2.5

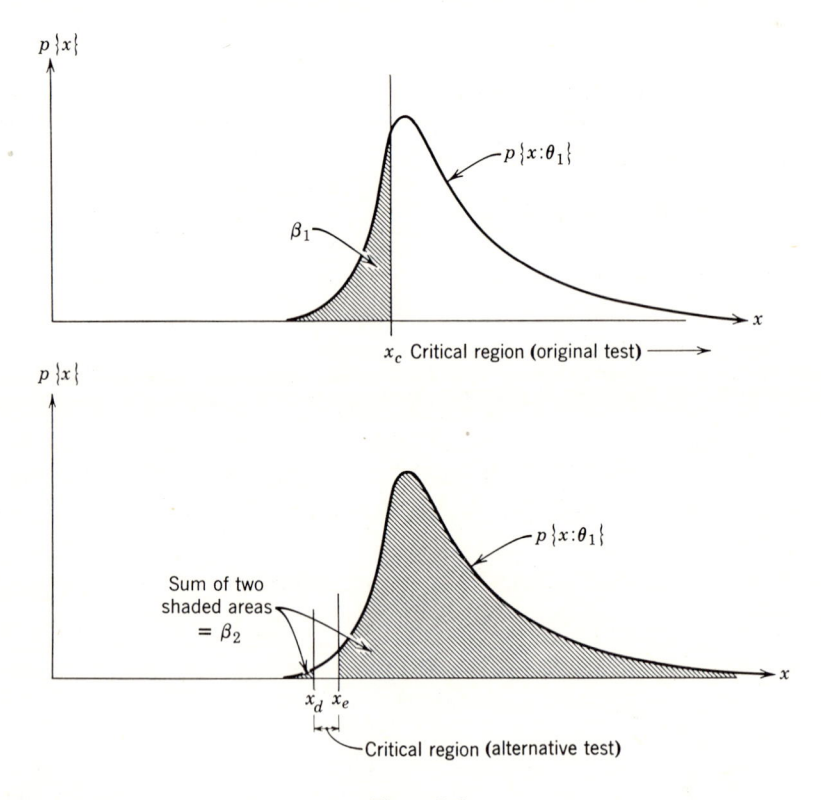

Figure 2.6

SECT. 2.6   CRITERION FOR CHOOSING BETWEEN ALTERNATIVE TESTS   103

error of the second kind of the two tests, then

$$\beta_1 = \int_{-\infty}^{x_c} p\{x:\theta_1\}\, dx, \tag{6.3}$$

$$\beta_2 = \int_{-\infty}^{x_d} p\{x:\theta_1\}\, dx + \int_{x_e}^{\infty} p\{x:\theta_1\}\, dx. \tag{6.4}$$

In Figure 2.6, it is clear that β_2 is much greater than β_1, so the first test is much to be preferred.

To proceed on a more rigorous basis, we use the Neyman-Pearson lemma [7], which states that the critical region should include those values of x for which $p\{x:\theta_1\}$ is as large as possible relative to $p\{x:\theta_0\}$. We choose those x's for which

$$\frac{p\{x:\theta_1\}}{p\{x:\theta_0\}} > K, \tag{6.5}$$

where K has to be adjusted so that the level of significance of the test is a preselected value α. In other words, (6.5) will define a region of x, say R, and we must adjust K so that

$$\int_R p\{x:\theta_0\}\, dx = \alpha. \tag{6.6}$$

The Neyman-Pearson lemma asserts that a test constructed in accordance with the above rule will have maximum possible power (and minimum probability of error of the second kind).

A proof is as follows. Suppose that our choice of tests following the Neyman-Pearson lemma, leads to a critical region R containing a small interval $\delta x'$ about a point x'. Consider whether we can do better, i.e., obtain a test with greater power, by replacing this small interval $\delta x'$ by an alternative interval $\delta x''$ about a point x'' not in the original critical region R. For the alternative test to have the same level of significance as the original test the amount of probability in the new interval added to R must equal that in the old interval which has been deleted from R:

$$p\{x'':\theta_0\}\delta x'' = p\{x':\theta_0\}\delta x'. \tag{6.7}$$

Multiplying both sides by K gives

$$Kp\{x'':\theta_0\}\delta x'' = Kp\{x':\theta_0\}\delta x'. \tag{6.8}$$

The power of the original test was, (5.3),

$$\int_R p\{x:\theta_1\}\, dx.$$

With the proposed change, we remove from this integral an amount

$p\{x':\theta_1\}\delta x'$ and substitute an amount $p\{x'':\theta_1\}\delta x''$. The increase in power, say Δ, is thus

$$\Delta = p\{x'':\theta_1\}\delta x'' - p\{x':\theta_1\}\delta x'. \tag{6.9}$$

We know that x' lay in the original critical region R, and so from (6.5)

$$\frac{p\{x':\theta_1\}}{p\{x':\theta_0\}} > K, \tag{6.10}$$

whence, on multiplying both numerator and denominator by $\delta x'$, we get

$$Kp\{x':\theta_0\}\delta x' < p\{x':\theta_1\}\delta x'. \tag{6.11}$$

Also we know that x'' lies in the region of acceptance of the original test, so

$$\frac{p\{x'':\theta_1\}}{p\{x'':\theta_0\}} < K, \tag{6.12}$$

whence, on multiplying both numerator and denominator by $\delta x''$, we get

$$p\{x'':\theta_1\}\delta x'' < Kp\{x'':\theta_0\}\delta x''. \tag{6.13}$$

By (6.8), the right-hand side of (6.13) is equal to the left-hand side of (6.11), so

$$p\{x'':\theta_1\}\delta x'' < p\{x':\theta_1\}\delta x', \tag{6.14}$$

and hence

$$p\{x'':\theta_1\}\delta x'' - p\{x':\theta_1\}\delta x' < 0. \tag{6.15}$$

The left-hand side of this inequality is identical with (6.9), the increase in power of the test given by the proposed substitution. Thus we have proved that the increase in power is negative, i.e., the change produces a decrease in the power of the test. Therefore the original test must have been optimum.

When we have a k-variate multivariate observation $x, y, \ldots$, then in (6.5) in place of $p\{x:\theta_1\}$ we would use $p\{x, y, \ldots:\theta_1\}$ and analogously for the denominator; i.e., the criterion becomes

$$\frac{p\{x, y, \ldots:\theta_1\}}{p\{x, y, \ldots:\theta_0\}} > K. \tag{6.16}$$

The proof that this criterion gives the most powerful test follows the same lines as for the univariate case, the difference being that the critical region is now a region in k-dimensional Euclidean space and the integrations determining α and π are now k-fold.

SECT. 2.7 A ONE-SIDED TEST FROM A NORMAL POPULATION

When we have a sample of n independent identically distributed random variables, the criterion becomes, using (1.2),

$$\frac{p\{x_1,\ldots,x_n:\theta_1\}}{p\{x_1,\ldots,x_n:\theta_0\}} = \frac{p\{x_1:\theta_1\}\cdots p\{x_n:\theta_1\}}{p\{x_1:\theta_0\}\cdots p\{x_n:\theta_0\}}$$

$$= \frac{\prod_i^n p\{x_i:\theta_1\}}{\prod_i^n p\{x_i:\theta_0\}} > K. \qquad (6.17)$$

It will be noted that although we used a notation implying a single parameter family of distributions, $p\{x:\theta\}$, at no point was this restriction to a single parameter necessary, and θ could be replaced throughout by $\theta_1,\ldots,\theta_r$: the only requirement is that the values of all the parameters be precisely specified under both the null and alternative hypotheses.

2.7. A One-Sided Test of an Observation from a Normal Population with Known Variance

In Section 2.5 we discussed the construction of tests of a null hypothesis against a simple alternative, and in Section 2.6 we saw that for this situation the Neyman-Pearson lemma (6.5) gave a method of constructing the most powerful test at a specified level of significance α. When the alternative hypothesis is not a simple hypothesis, e.g., $\theta = \theta_1$, but rather a composite hypothesis, e.g., $\theta > \theta_0$ or $\theta \neq \theta_0$, then usually there is no test which is more powerful than any other test for all possible alternative values of θ, i.e., usually a *uniformly most powerful test* does not exist.

One instance in which a uniformly most powerful test does exist is the problem of testing the null hypothesis that the parameter ξ of a normal population is ξ_0 against the alternative that $\xi > \xi_0$. For a particular value $\xi_1 > \xi_0$ for the alternative hypothesis, to apply the Neyman-Pearson lemma (6.5) we need to consider the ratio

$$\frac{p\{x:\xi_1,\sigma^2\}}{p\{x:\xi_0,\sigma^2\}} = \frac{(\sqrt{2\pi}\,\sigma)^{-1} e^{-(x-\xi_1)^2/2\sigma^2}}{(\sqrt{2\pi}\,\sigma)^{-1} e^{-(x-\xi_0)^2/2\sigma^2}}$$

$$= e^{-[(x-\xi_1)^2 - (x-\xi_0)^2]/2\sigma^2} = e^{x(\xi_1-\xi_0)/\sigma^2} \cdot e^{-(\xi_1^2-\xi_0^2)/2\sigma^2}. \qquad (7.1)$$

The second exponential here is some known positive constant, say c, since ξ_1 and ξ_0 are specified and σ^2 is known. The first exponential is of the form e^{ax} where $a = (\xi_1 - \xi_0)/\sigma^2$ is a positive constant since $\xi_1 - \xi_0 > 0$. Thus $p\{x:\xi_1,\sigma^2\}/p\{x:\xi_0,\sigma^2\}$ has the form ce^{ax} with both a and c positive:

therefore it increases with increasing x. Thus to select all x for which this function is greater than K, we start with x at $+\infty$ and allow it to decrease until we have taken in an amount of the null distribution $p\{x:\xi_0, \sigma^2\}$ equal to the required level of significance α.

Let the smallest x which lies in the critical region be x_c. Then x_c is determined by the equation

$$\Pr\{x > x_c | \xi = \xi_0\} = \alpha. \tag{7.2}$$

Using (1.18.13)

$$\Pr\{x < x_c | \xi = \xi_0\} = \Phi\left(\frac{x_c - \xi_0}{\sigma}\right). \tag{7.3}$$

Putting this equal to $1 - \alpha$, we get $\frac{x_c - \xi_0}{\sigma} = 1-\alpha$

$$x_c = \xi_0 + u_{1-\alpha}\sigma. \tag{7.4}$$

Thus in this instance the critical region is the same for all alternatives $\xi_1 > \xi_0$, so here we have a uniformly most powerful test.

For example, if we choose a level of significance $\alpha = 0.05$, Table I in the Appendix gives $u_{0.95} = 1.645$, and $x_c = \xi_0 + 1.645\sigma$, i.e., the bottom edge of the critical region is 1.645 times the standard deviation above the expectation under the null hypothesis.

The power of the foregoing test by definition is the probability that we reject the null hypothesis $\xi = \xi_0$ when ξ is equal to the alternative ξ_1; i.e., the power is the probability that a random observation x lies in the critical region, $x > x_c$:

$$\pi(\xi_1) = \Pr\{x > x_c | \xi = \xi_1\} = 1 - \Pr\{x < x_c | \xi = \xi_1\}$$

$$= 1 - \Phi\left(\frac{x_c - \xi_1}{\sigma}\right), \tag{7.5}$$

using (1.18.13). Substituting x_c from (7.4) gives

$$\pi(\xi_1) = 1 - \Phi\left(\frac{\xi_0 + \sigma u_{1-\alpha} - \xi_1}{\sigma}\right) = 1 - \Phi\left(u_{1-\alpha} + \frac{\xi_0 - \xi_1}{\sigma}\right)$$

$$= \Phi\left(-u_{1-\alpha} - \frac{\xi_0 - \xi_1}{\sigma}\right) = \Phi\left(u_\alpha + \frac{\xi_1 - \xi_0}{\sigma}\right), \tag{7.6}$$

since $1 - \Phi(u) = \Phi(-u)$ by (1.18.8), and $-u_{1-\alpha} = u_\alpha$ by (1.18.11).

We have so far considered tests based on a single observation. For n observations we use (6.17). Suppose we take a sample of n independent observations x_i from a normal distribution of known variance σ^2 and unknown mean ξ. We wish to test the null hypothesis $H_0: \xi = \xi_0$ against

SECT. 2.7   A ONE-SIDED TEST FROM A NORMAL POPULATION   107

the alternative $\xi > \xi_0$ at the level of significance α. Substituting for $p\{x_i\}$ in (6.17),

$$\frac{p\{x_1:\xi_1, \sigma^2\} \cdots p\{x_n:\xi_1, \sigma^2\}}{p\{x_1:\xi_0, \sigma^2\} \cdots p\{x_n:\xi_0, \sigma^2\}}$$

$$= \frac{(\sqrt{2\pi}\,\sigma)^{-1} e^{-(x_1-\xi_1)^2/2\sigma^2} \cdots (\sqrt{2\pi}\,\sigma)^{-1} e^{-(x_n-\xi_1)^2/2\sigma^2}}{(\sqrt{2\pi}\,\sigma)^{-1} e^{-(x_1-\xi_0)^2/2\sigma^2} \cdots (\sqrt{2\pi}\,\sigma)^{-1} e^{-(x_n-\xi_0)^2/2\sigma^2}}$$

$$= \frac{e^{-(2\sigma^2)^{-1} \Sigma(x_i-\xi_1)^2}}{e^{-(2\sigma^2)^{-1} \Sigma(x_i-\xi_0)^2}} = e^{\bar{x}(\xi_1-\xi_0)/(\sigma^2/n)} e^{-(\xi_1^2-\xi_0^2)/(2\sigma^2/n)}. \quad (7.7)$$

This is similar to (7.1) except that it is a function of $\bar{x}$ instead of x and of σ^2/n instead of σ^2. We must have the critical region of size α; i.e.,

$$\Pr\{\bar{x} > x_c \mid \xi = \xi_0\} = \alpha, \quad (7.8)$$

so, using (1.26.3), x_c must satisfy the equation

$$\Pr\{\bar{x} < x_c \mid \xi = \xi_0\} = \Phi\left(\frac{x_c - \xi_0}{\sigma/\sqrt{n}}\right) = 1 - \alpha, \quad (7.9)$$

whence

$$x_c = \xi_0 + u_{1-\alpha} \frac{\sigma}{\sqrt{n}}. \quad (7.10)$$

The power function is

$$\pi(\xi_1) = \Pr\{\bar{x} > x_c \mid \xi = \xi_1\} = 1 - \Phi\left(\frac{x_c - \xi_1}{\sigma/\sqrt{n}}\right) \quad (7.11)$$

$$= 1 - \Phi\left(\frac{\xi_0 + u_{1-\alpha}(\sigma/\sqrt{n}) - \xi_1}{\sigma/\sqrt{n}}\right)$$

$$= \Phi\left(u_\alpha + \frac{\xi_1 - \xi_0}{\sigma/\sqrt{n}}\right) = \Phi(u_\alpha + \delta), \quad (7.12)$$

if we define $\delta = (\xi_1 - \xi_0)/(\sigma/\sqrt{n})$. For example, for a test at the level of significance $\alpha = 0.05$, $u_\alpha = -1.645$, and when $\delta = 1$,

$$\pi(\xi_1) = \Phi(-1.645 + 1) = \Phi(-0.645) = 0.259. \quad (7.13)$$

Table 2.2, prepared in this manner, is plotted in Figure 2.7. In line with

Table 2.2. Power of One-Tailed Test at Level of Significance 0.05 of Mean of n Observations from a Normal Distribution

$\dfrac{\xi_1 - \xi_0}{\sigma/\sqrt{n}}$	−1.0	−0.5	0	0.5	1	1.5	2	2.5	3	3.5	4
$\pi(\xi_1)$	.004	.016	.050	.126	.259	.442	.639	.804	.912	.968	.999

the definitions, the power is equal to the level of significance when $\xi_1 = \xi_0$. Also when $\xi_1 < \xi_0$, there is some probability, but very slight, of rejecting $H_0: \xi = \xi_0$ in favor of the alternative $\xi = \xi_1 > \xi_0$.

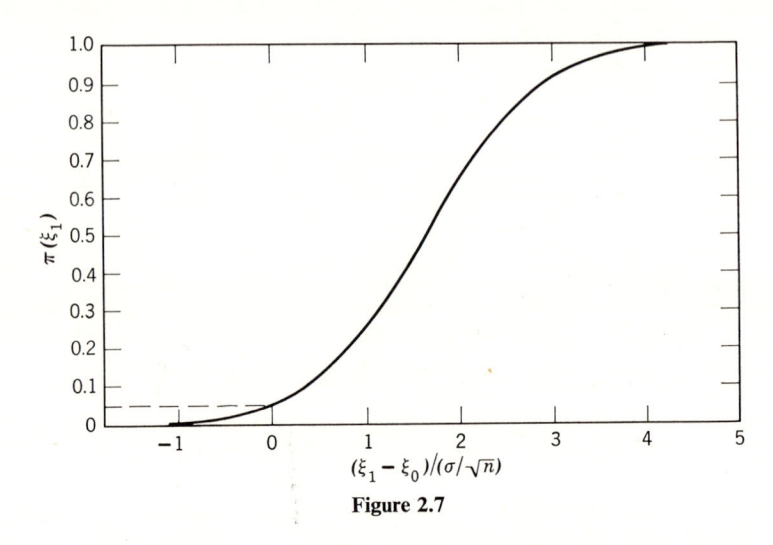

Figure 2.7

Figure 2.8 illustrates the basis of the power calculation for a test with $\alpha = 0.05$ when $\delta = 1$; i.e., $\xi_1 - \xi_0 = 1 \times \sigma/\sqrt{n}$. The critical region, corresponding to an area $\alpha = 0.05$ in the upper tail of the null distribution, is $\bar{x} > \xi_0 + 1.645\sigma/\sqrt{n}$. The power, calculated in (7.13) as 0.259, is the area of that part of the alternative distribution lying in the critical region.

We have been discussing the test with the alternative hypothesis that $\xi_1 > \xi_0$. When the alternative hypothesis is $\xi_1 < \xi_0$, the critical region is $x < \xi_0 + u_\alpha \sigma$ for a single observation, and

$$\bar{x} < \xi_0 + u_\alpha \frac{\sigma}{\sqrt{n}} \tag{7.14}$$

for the mean of n observations. In this latter case the power function is

$$\pi(\xi_1) = \Phi\left(u_\alpha + \frac{\xi_0 - \xi_1}{\sigma/\sqrt{n}}\right). \tag{7.15}$$

Thus for a test at the level of significance $\alpha = 0.05$, $u_\alpha = -1.645$, and for $(\xi_0 - \xi_1)/(\sigma/\sqrt{n}) = 1$, $\pi(\xi_1) = \Phi(-1.645 + 1) = 0.2594$. Therefore we can use Table 2.2 as it stands for the power of this other alternative hypothesis, $H_1: \xi = \xi_1 < \xi_0$, if we replace $(\xi_1 - \xi_0)/(\sigma/\sqrt{n})$ in the table by $(\xi_0 - \xi_1)/(\sigma/\sqrt{n})$.

SECT. 2.7 A ONE-SIDED TEST FROM A NORMAL POPULATION

We can use (7.12) to calculate the number of observations necessary to give a specified power, $1 - \beta$, assuming that σ is known. Putting (7.12) equal to $1 - \beta$,

$$\Phi\left(u_\alpha + \frac{\xi_1 - \xi_0}{\sigma/\sqrt{n}}\right) = 1 - \beta. \tag{7.16}$$

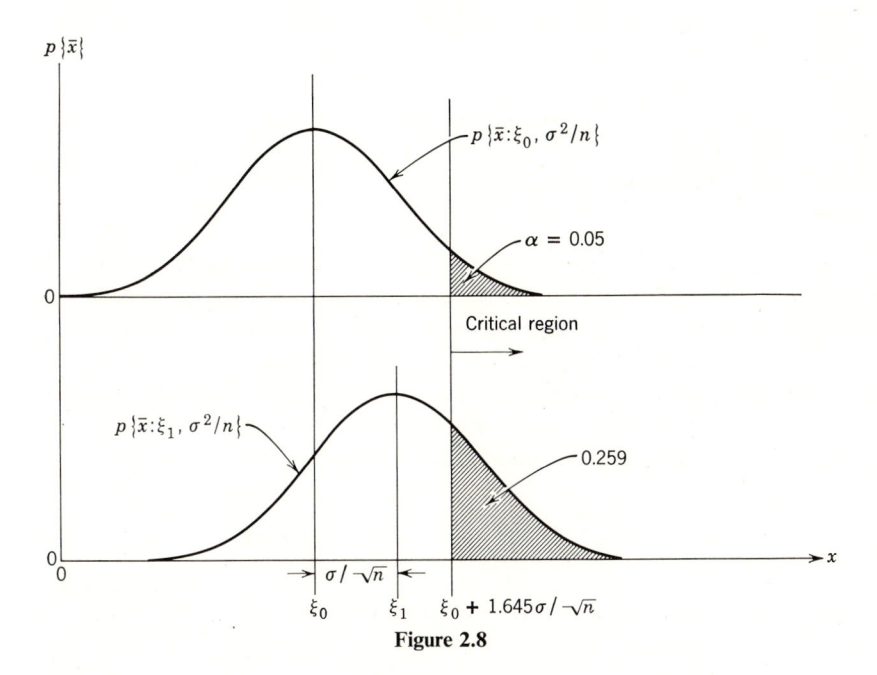

Figure 2.8

But, in general, $\Phi(u_P) = P$, and so $\Phi(u_{1-\beta}) = 1 - \beta$, whence

$$u_\alpha + \frac{\xi_1 - \xi_0}{\sigma/\sqrt{n}} = u_{1-\beta}. \tag{7.17}$$

Solving for n, and writing $u_{1-\alpha}$ for $-u_\alpha$,

$$n = (u_{1-\beta} + u_{1-\alpha})^2 \left(\frac{\sigma}{\xi_1 - \xi_0}\right)^2. \tag{7.18}$$

This equation gives surprisingly large values of n for powers that we might consider desirable. Suppose $\sigma = 0.12$, and we wish to test at the level of significance $\alpha = 0.01$, so $u_{1-\alpha} = u_{0.99} = 2.326$. Suppose that when $\xi_1 - \xi_0 = 0.02$, i.e., one-sixth of the standard deviation, we want a probability of 0.95 of rejecting the null hypothesis, so $u_{1-\beta} = u_{0.95} = 1.645$. These values give $n = 568$.

2.8. A One-Sided Test of an Observation from a Binomial Distribution

Suppose that we have a sample of size n from a binomial distribution and that the observed number of defectives is x. Our null hypothesis is that $\theta = \theta_0$ and the alternative hypothesis is that $\theta = \theta_1$, $\theta_1 > \theta_0$. Then from (6.5), we wish to maximize

$$\frac{p\{x:\theta_1\}}{p\{x:\theta_0\}} = \frac{\binom{n}{x}\theta_1^x(1-\theta_1)^{n-x}}{\binom{n}{x}\theta_0^x(1-\theta_0)^{n-x}} = \left(\frac{\theta_1}{\theta_0}\right)^x \left(\frac{1-\theta_1}{1-\theta_0}\right)^{n-x} \tag{8.1}$$

Since $\theta_1/\theta_0 > 1$, and $(1-\theta_1)/(1-\theta_0) < 1$, this will be maximized by selecting for the critical region those values of x as large as possible, i.e., $n, n-1, n-2, \ldots$, subject to the condition that the probability of x falling in the critical region under the null hypothesis is α. For a discrete distribution there is the difficulty that it will be impossible to get α exactly equal to the prechosen value, e.g., 0.05. For example, if $n = 10$ and $\theta_0 = 1/4$, if the critical region is $5 \leq x \leq 10$, then

$$\alpha = \sum_{x=5}^{10} \binom{10}{x}\left(\frac{1}{4}\right)^x\left(1-\frac{1}{4}\right)^{10-x} = 0.0781, \tag{8.2}$$

and if we reduce the size of the critical region to $6 \leq x \leq 10$, then

$$\alpha = \sum_{x=6}^{10} \binom{10}{x}\left(\frac{1}{4}\right)^x\left(1-\frac{1}{4}\right)^{10-x} = 0.0197. \tag{8.3}$$

It is possible to obtain exactly a prechosen level of significance, say $\alpha = 0.05$, by the following procedure. Let $\alpha_n (= 0.0781)$ and $\alpha_{n-1} (= 0.0197)$ be the probabilities under the null hypothesis of the observation falling in the critical region with n points and the critical region with $n - 1$ points respectively. Then $\alpha_n - \alpha_{n-1} = 0.0584$ is the probability of the observation falling on the nth point. Define γ as

$$\gamma = \frac{\alpha - \alpha_{n-1}}{\alpha_n - \alpha_{n-1}} = \frac{0.0500 - 0.0197}{0.0781 - 0.0197} = 0.519. \tag{8.4}$$

Then if the observation falls in the critical region with $n - 1 = 5$ points we reject the null hypothesis, and if the observation falls on the nth point we reject the null hypothesis with probability $\gamma = 0.519$. This procedure will give the desired probability of rejecting the null hypothesis, for

$$\Pr\{\text{reject } H_0\} = \alpha_{n-1} + \gamma(\alpha_n - \alpha_{n-1}) = \alpha \tag{8.5}$$

$$= 0.0197 + 0.519 \times 0.0584 = 0.050. \tag{8.6}$$

In most practical situations, however, it would be more satisfactory to quote the P value, as discussed in Section 2.13. The main use of this randomized test procedure is for comparing tests in terms of their power, since for this comparison we need to have the tests with an identical α. Using the critical region $5 \leq x \leq 10$, the power when $\theta_1 = 1/2$ is

$$\pi\left(\theta_1 = \frac{1}{2}\right) = \Pr\left\{x \geq 5 | \theta = \frac{1}{2}\right\} = \sum_{x=5}^{10} \binom{10}{x} \left(\frac{1}{2}\right)^x \left(1 - \frac{1}{2}\right)^{10-x}$$

$$= 0.6231, \tag{8.7}$$

and the power using the critical region $6 \leq x \leq 10$ is 0.3770. The power of the randomized test at level of significance $\alpha = 0.05$ is

$$\Pr\left\{\text{reject } H_0 | \theta = \theta_1 = \frac{1}{2}\right\}$$

$$= \Pr\{x \geq 6\} + \Pr\{x = 5\} \Pr\{\text{rejecting when } x = 6\}$$

$$= 0.3770 + 0.2461 \times 0.519 = 0.5047. \tag{8.8}$$

2.9. The Testing of Composite Hypotheses

In Section 2.6 we saw that the criterion (6.5) defined the best critical region for a test of a simple null hypothesis against a simple alternative. For multiparameter distributions (6.5) would become

$$\frac{p\{x: \theta_{1a}, \theta_{2a}, \ldots, \theta_{ka}\}}{p\{x: \theta_{10}, \theta_{20}, \ldots, \theta_{k0}\}} > K, \tag{9.1}$$

where the θ's take the values θ_{i0} under the null hypothesis and θ_{ia} under the alternative $(i = 1, \ldots, k)$. This test, namely, rejecting the null hypothesis when x falls in the critical region, is equivalent to using the left-hand side of (9.1) as the test statistic and rejecting the null hypothesis when it is large.

We can regard the parameters $\theta_1, \ldots, \theta_k$ as being represented in a k-dimensional space, the coordinates corresponding to the parameters. For a simple hypothesis, all the coordinates are specified, and we have a single point in the parameter space. For a composite hypothesis, a certain region in the parameter space is specified. For example, with a normal distribution there are two parameters, ξ and σ^2 (Figure 2.9). Specifying

$\xi = 0$, $\sigma^2 = 1$ and $\xi = 4$, $\sigma^2 = 1$, gives two simple hypotheses, represented by the points (0, 1) and (4, 1). $\xi < 0$, $\sigma^2 = 2$ is the line at $\sigma^2 = 2$ to the left of the ξ axis and is a composite hypothesis. $\xi > 0$ is the entire right-hand quadrant and is also a composite hypothesis.

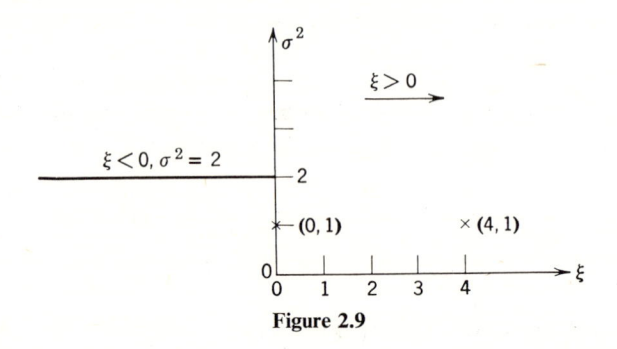

Figure 2.9

Now suppose that, though θ_{10} is fixed under the null hypothesis, θ_{1a} is not precisely specified under the alternative hypothesis, and the remaining parameters $\theta_2, \ldots, \theta_k$ are not specified under either hypothesis, so that we are comparing two composite hypotheses. The two hypotheses will define regions in the parameter space. The symbol ω is given to the region corresponding to the null hypothesis, and we will use the symbol Ω' to represent the region corresponding to the alternative hypothesis. We cannot compute the left-hand side of (9.1) to use as a test statistic, as the values of θ_{10} and $\theta_2, \ldots, \theta_k$ are all unspecified. However, we can compute an analog of (9.1), in which the unspecified parameters are given their maximum likelihood values. The numerator and denominator of (9.1) are both likelihood functions, and by definition the maximum likelihood estimates of the unspecified parameters will maximize the likelihoods. If $L(\omega)$ and $L(\Omega')$ are these two likelihood functions, then the analog of (9.1) is $L(\Omega')/L(\omega)$ and we would reject the null hypothesis for large values of this statistic.

The usual likelihood ratio test procedure is a slight modification of the above. If Ω represents the region in the parameter space made up of the union of the regions of the null and alternative hypotheses, i.e., $\Omega = \Omega' \cup \omega$, then we reject the null hypothesis for small values of the likelihood ratio λ,

$$\lambda = \frac{L(\omega)}{L(\Omega)}. \qquad (9.2)$$

[Note that λ is a function of the observations and hence is a random variable. Although using a Greek letter (λ) for a random variable violates our practice of confining the use of Greek letters to parameters, the use of λ to represent the likelihood ratio is such a widely established convention that we continue the practice.] Clearly λ is positive since it is a ratio of products of probability functions which must always be positive. Also λ cannot be greater than 1 since the maximum value for varying the parameters in a region ω cannot exceed the maximum value for L varying the parameters in a region Ω, where ω is a subset of Ω. Thus λ must lie in the interval 0 to 1. A small value of λ indicates that the likelihood computed using ω, corresponding to the null hypothesis, is relatively unlikely, and so we should reject the null hypothesis. Conversely, a value of λ close to 1 indicates that the null hypothesis is very plausible and should be accepted. We therefore define a critical region as

$$0 < \lambda < \lambda_c, \tag{9.3}$$

where λ_c is a constant chosen so that the level of significance of the test is at the desired level α.

In a two-parameter situation the test can be pictured graphically as follows. The two horizontal coordinates represent the two parameters and the vertical coordinate the likelihood. First, confined to region ω we wander round till we find as large a likelihood as possible: this is $L(\omega)$. Second, confined to a larger region Ω (which includes ω) we wander round till we find a likelihood as large as possible: this is $L(\Omega)$. If $L(\Omega)$ is not much larger than $L(\omega)$, i.e., if λ is close to 1, then the extra liberty of selection permitted under the alternative hypothesis has yielded small improvement in the likelihood, and so the null hypothesis is plausible. On the other hand, if $L(\Omega)$ is much larger than $L(\omega)$, then the null hypothesis appears implausible.

The likelihood ratio procedure produces a plausible statistic λ, and will indicate the general nature of the critical region. The critical region cannot be determined exactly for a test at the level of significance α unless we know the distribution of λ under the null hypothesis. Wilks [9] showed that for large sample size (and moderate restrictions on the continuity of the likelihood function) the distribution of $-2 \log \lambda$ tends to the $\chi^2(r - s)$ distribution where r is the number of parameters fitted under Ω and s the number of parameters fitted under ω.

2.10. A Two-Sided Test of an Observation from a Normal Population with Known Variance

To apply the procedure of the previous section to testing that a group of n observations came from a normal population with mean ξ_0 and known variance σ^2 against the alternative that the mean is $\xi_1 \neq \xi_0$, we write down the likelihood function (3.6):

$$L = \left(\frac{1}{2\pi\sigma^2}\right)^{n/2} e^{-(1/2\sigma^2)\Sigma(x_i-\xi)^2}. \qquad (10.1)$$

In Section 2.3 we saw that, allowing ξ to vary, L was maximized by putting $\xi = \Sigma x_i/n = \bar{x}$, (3.10). Thus

$$L(\Omega) = \left(\frac{1}{2\pi\sigma^2}\right)^{n/2} e^{-(1/2\sigma^2)\Sigma(x_i-\bar{x})^2}. \qquad (10.2)$$

Under the null hypothesis H_0 no parameters are allowed to vary, since we are assuming σ^2 to be fixed and known, and ξ is fixed at ξ_0; thus

$$L(\omega) = \left(\frac{1}{2\pi\sigma^2}\right)^{n/2} e^{-(1/2\sigma^2)\Sigma(x_i-\xi_0)^2}. \qquad (10.3)$$

Substituting these values for $L(\omega)$ and $L(\Omega)$ in the definition of the likelihood ratio, (9.2), and canceling out common factors gives

$$\lambda = \frac{e^{-(1/2\sigma^2)\Sigma(x_i-\xi_0)^2}}{e^{-(1/2\sigma^2)\Sigma(x_i-\bar{x})^2}}. \qquad (10.4)$$

But

$$\Sigma(x_i - \xi_0)^2 = \Sigma[(x_i - \bar{x}) + (\bar{x} - \xi_0)]^2 = \Sigma(x_i - \bar{x})^2 + n(\bar{x} - \xi_0)^2, \qquad (10.5)$$

since

$$2\Sigma(x_i - \bar{x})(\bar{x} - \xi_0) = 2(\bar{x} - \xi_0)\Sigma(x_i - \bar{x}) = 2(\bar{x} - \xi_0) \cdot 0 = 0. \qquad (10.6)$$

Thus the likelihood ratio is

$$\lambda = e^{-(n/2\sigma^2)(\bar{x}-\xi_0)^2}. \qquad (10.7)$$

The edge of the critical region, $\bar{x}_c$, is determined by

$$e^{-(n/2\sigma^2)(\bar{x}_c-\xi_0)^2} = \lambda_c, \qquad (10.8)$$

or, solving for $\bar{x}_c$,

$$\bar{x}_c = \xi_0 - \sqrt{-2\log\lambda_c}\frac{\sigma}{\sqrt{n}} \quad \text{and} \quad \xi_0 + \sqrt{-2\log\lambda_c}\frac{\sigma}{\sqrt{n}}. \qquad (10.9)$$

Since λ_c is less than 1, $\log\lambda_c$ is negative, so $\bar{x}_c$ is of the form

$$\bar{x}_c = \xi_0 \pm k\frac{\sigma}{\sqrt{n}} \qquad (10.10)$$

where $k = \sqrt{-2\log\lambda_c}$. From (10.7) we see that if $\bar{x}$ is far from ξ_0, in either direction, then $(\bar{x} - \xi_0)^2$ will be large, and hence λ small. Thus

SECT. 2.10   A TWO-SIDED TEST FROM A NORMAL POPULATION

large values of $|\bar{x} - \xi_0|$ call for rejection of the null hypothesis. The critical region is that part of the line below $\xi_0 - k\sigma/\sqrt{n}$ plus that part of the line above $\xi_0 + k\sigma/\sqrt{n}$; see Figure 2.10. The total area of the curve in the critical region has to equal α: since the normal distribution is symmetrical about its mean this implies that the area of each tail is $\alpha/2$. The critical region will therefore be

$$\bar{x} < \xi_0 + u_{\alpha/2} \frac{\sigma}{\sqrt{n}} \quad \text{and} \quad \bar{x} > \xi_0 + u_{1-\alpha/2} \frac{\sigma}{\sqrt{n}}. \qquad (10.11)$$

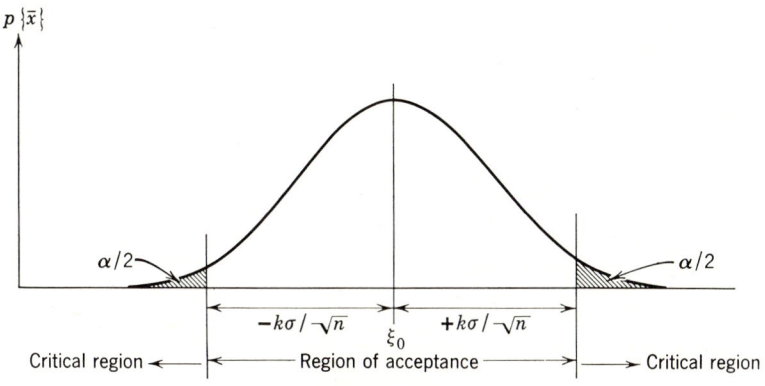

Figure 2.10

Since $u_{\alpha/2} = -u_{1-\alpha/2}$, the left-hand term can be written $\bar{x} < \xi_0 - u_{1-\alpha/2}\sigma/\sqrt{n}$, and (10.11) is equivalent to saying: reject if $(\bar{x} - \xi_0)/(\sigma/\sqrt{n})$ is less than $-u_{1-\alpha/2}$ or greater than $+u_{1-\alpha/2}$. This is equivalent to saying: reject if

$$\left| \frac{\bar{x} - \xi_0}{\sigma/\sqrt{n}} \right| > u_{1-\alpha/2}. \qquad (10.12)$$

The power of this test, when $\xi = \xi_1$, is

$$\pi(\xi_1) = \Pr\left\{ \frac{\bar{x} - \xi_0}{\sigma/\sqrt{n}} < -u_{1-\alpha/2} \right\} + \Pr\left\{ \frac{\bar{x} - \xi_0}{\sigma/\sqrt{n}} > u_{1-\alpha/2} \right\}$$

$$= \Pr\left\{ \frac{\bar{x} - \xi_1}{\sigma/\sqrt{n}} + \frac{\xi_1 - \xi_0}{\sigma/\sqrt{n}} < -u_{1-\alpha/2} \right\}$$

$$+ \Pr\left\{ \frac{\bar{x} - \xi_1}{\sigma/\sqrt{n}} + \frac{\xi_1 - \xi_0}{\sigma/\sqrt{n}} > u_{1-\alpha/2} \right\}$$

$$= \Pr\left\{ \frac{\bar{x} - \xi_1}{\sigma/\sqrt{n}} < u_{\alpha/2} - \frac{\xi_1 - \xi_0}{\sigma/\sqrt{n}} \right\} + 1$$

$$- \Pr\left\{ \frac{\bar{x} - \xi_1}{\sigma/\sqrt{n}} < -u_{\alpha/2} - \frac{\xi_1 - \xi_0}{\sigma/\sqrt{n}} \right\}. \qquad (10.13)$$

$$1 - N(-k) = N(k)$$

$$= N\left(z_{\alpha/2} + \frac{\xi_1 - \xi_0}{\sigma/\sqrt{n}} \right)$$

Now under the alternative hypothesis $\xi = \xi_1$, the random variable $(\bar{x} - \xi_1)/(\sigma/\sqrt{n})$ is a unit normal deviate. Each of these two probability statements is therefore of the form $\Pr\{u < k\} = \Phi(k)$. Let us define δ as

$$\delta = \frac{\xi_1 - \xi_0}{\sigma/\sqrt{n}}. \tag{10.14}$$

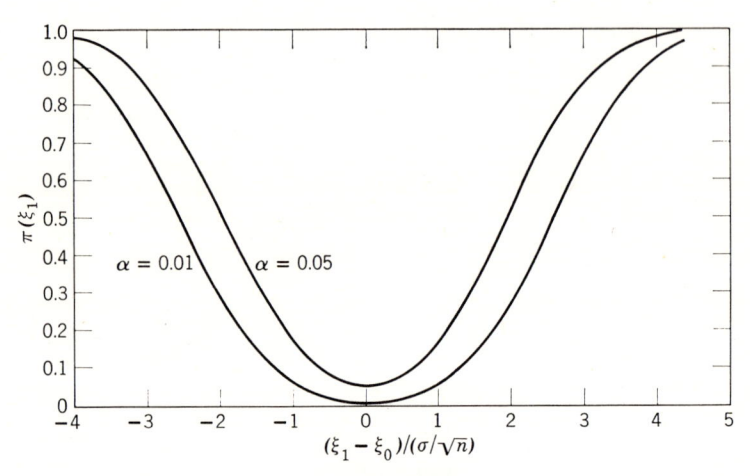

Figure 2.11

Then remembering that $1 - \Phi(-k) = \Phi(k)$, (1.18.8),

$$\pi(\xi_1) = \Phi(u_{\alpha/2} - \delta) + \Phi(u_{\alpha/2} + \delta). \tag{10.15}$$

For example, for $\alpha = 0.05$, $u_{0.05/2} = u_{0.025} = -1.96$, and for $\delta = 1$,

$$\pi(\xi_1) = \Phi(-1.96 - 1) + \Phi(-1.96 + 1) = \Phi(-2.96) + \Phi(-0.96)$$
$$= 0.0015 + 0.1685 = 0.1700. \tag{10.16}$$

Table 2.3, prepared in this manner, is plotted in Figure 2.11. The function is symmetrical about 0, and so only the first two negative values

Table 2.3. Power of Two-Tailed Test at Level of Significance 0.05 of Mean of n Observations from a Normal Distribution

$\dfrac{\xi_1 - \xi_0}{\sigma/\sqrt{n}}$	−1.0	−0.5	0	0.5	1	1.5	2	2.5	3	3.5	4.0	4.5	5.0
$\pi(\xi_1)$	.170	.079	.05	.079	.170	.323	.516	.705	.851	.938	.979	.994	.999

SECT. 2.10 A TWO-SIDED TEST FROM A NORMAL POPULATION

are tabulated. When $\xi_1 = \xi_0$, the power coincides with the level of significance. The power curve for $\alpha = 0.01$ is also plotted in Figure 2.11. We gain increased protection against the risk of committing an error of the first kind at the cost of decreased protection against the risk of committing an error of the second kind. For example, when $\delta = 3$, a test with $\alpha = 0.05$ has power 0.851, whereas a test with $\alpha = 0.01$ has power only 0.664.

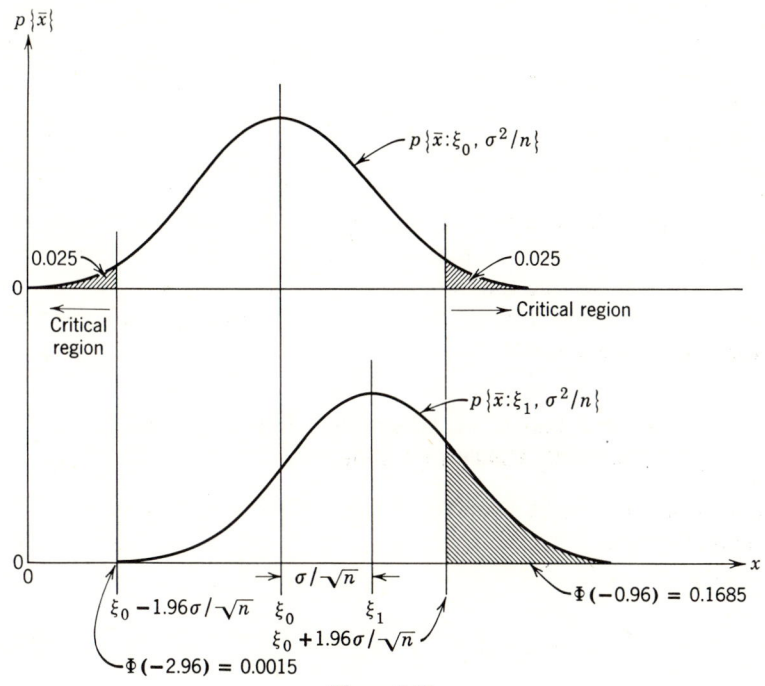

Figure 2.12

Figure 2.12 illustrates the basis of the power calculation for a test with $\alpha = 0.05$ when $\delta = 1$, i.e., $\xi_1 - \xi_0 = 1 \times \sigma/\sqrt{n}$. The critical region, corresponding to an area $\alpha/2 = 0.025$ in each of the tails of the null distribution, is $\bar{x} < \xi_0 - 1.96\sigma/\sqrt{n}$ and $\bar{x} > \xi_0 + 1.96\sigma/\sqrt{n}$. The power, calculated in (10.16) as 0.1700, is the area of the two parts of the alternative distribution lying in the two parts of the critical region.

We can use (10.13) to calculate the number of observations necessary to give a specified power $1 - \beta$, assuming that σ is known. Equation (10.13) can only be solved exactly for n by troublesome iterations. However, in a typical situation one term is much larger than the other: for example, with $\delta = 1$ and $\alpha = 0.05$, the term $\Phi(u_{\alpha/2} + \delta)$ at 0.1685 was more than 100 times as large as the other at 0.0015. Even at $\delta = 0.5$, this term is over 10 times the other. For any calculation involving δ greater than 0.5, therefore, we can neglect the other term in (10.15) and write

$$\pi(\xi_1) \simeq \Phi\left(u_{\alpha/2} + \frac{\xi_1 - \xi_0}{\sigma/\sqrt{n}}\right), \tag{10.17}$$

and putting $\pi(\xi_1) = 1 - \beta$, we get

$$u_{\alpha/2} + \frac{\xi_1 - \xi_0}{\sigma/\sqrt{n}} \simeq u_{1-\beta}, \tag{10.18}$$

whence

$$n \simeq (u_{1-\beta} + u_{1-\alpha/2})^2 \left(\frac{\sigma}{\xi_1 - \xi_0}\right)^2. \tag{10.19}$$

For example, suppose $\sigma = 0.12$, and we wish to make a test at the level of significance $\alpha = 0.01$, so that $u_{1-\alpha/2} = u_{0.995} = 2.58$. Suppose that if $\xi_1 - \xi_0 = 0.02$, i.e., one-sixth of the standard deviation, we wish to have a probability of 0.95 of rejecting the null hypothesis, so $u_{1-\beta} = u_{0.95} = 1.645$. These values give $n = 641$.

2.11. A Two-Sided Test of an Observation from a Normal Distribution with Unknown Variance

Let us now construct a test for the null hypothesis that the mean of a normal distribution is ξ_0 against the alternative $\xi_1 \neq \xi_0$, the variance σ_2 not being specified. The likelihood function (3.6) is

$$L = \left(\frac{1}{2\pi\sigma^2}\right)^{n/2} e^{-(1/2\sigma^2)\Sigma(x_i - \xi)^2}. \tag{11.1}$$

For the null hypothesis, the parameter ξ is specified to take the value ξ_0, but σ^2 is allowed to vary. We saw that (3.12) gave the maximum likelihood estimator for σ^2 for a fixed ξ as $\hat{\sigma}^2 = \Sigma(x_i - \xi)^2/n$. Substituting this, with $\xi = \xi_0$, in (11.1) gives

$$L(\omega) = \left[\frac{n}{2\pi \Sigma(x_i - \xi_0)^2}\right]^{n/2} e^{-n/2}. \tag{11.2}$$

For the entire parameter space Ω, with no restrictions on the parameters ξ and σ^2, we saw in (3.10) that $\hat{\xi} = \Sigma x_i/n$ and in (3.13) that $\hat{\sigma}^2 = \Sigma(x_i - \bar{x})^2/n$. Inserting these maximum likelihood estimators in (11.1) we get

$$L(\Omega) = \left[\frac{n}{2\pi \Sigma(x_i - \bar{x})^2}\right]^{n/2} e^{-n/2}. \tag{11.3}$$

Hence the likelihood ratio as defined in (9.2) is

$$\lambda = \left[\frac{\sum(x_i - \bar{x})^2}{\sum(x_i - \xi_0)^2}\right]^{n/2}. \tag{11.4}$$

Any monotone function of λ can be used instead of λ itself for defining the critical region: hence we may use the nth root of λ^2,

$$\lambda^{2/n} = \frac{\sum(x_i - \bar{x})^2}{\sum(x_i - \xi_0)^2} = \frac{\sum(x_i - \bar{x})^2}{\sum(x_i - \bar{x})^2 + n(\bar{x} - \xi_0)^2} = \left[1 + \frac{n(\bar{x} - \xi_0)^2}{\sum(x_i - \bar{x})^2}\right]^{-1}$$

$$= \left[1 + \frac{1}{n-1}\frac{(\bar{x} - \xi_0)^2}{[\sum(x_i - \bar{x})^2/(n-1)]/n}\right]^{-1} = \left[1 + \frac{t^2}{n-1}\right]^{-1}, \tag{11.5}$$

if we define t as

$$t = \frac{\bar{x} - \xi_0}{\sqrt{[\sum(x_i - \bar{x})^2/(n-1)]}/\sqrt{n}} = \frac{\bar{x} - \xi_0}{s/\sqrt{n}}, \tag{11.6}$$

with s defined as in (3.23).

We recall that we reject the null hypothesis for small values of λ, which is equivalent from (11.5) to large values of $|t|$. Thus t as defined by (11.6) can be used as a test statistic for the null hypothesis $\xi = \xi_0$ against the alternative $\xi \neq \xi_0$, σ^2 being unknown. We obtain this same result later, in Section 9.6, by a different route.

2.12. The Comparison of Two Means

Suppose that we have independent random samples, with means $\bar{x}_1$ and $\bar{x}_2$, and sample sizes n_1 and n_2, drawn from two normal distributions $p\{x:\xi_1, \sigma_1^2\}, p\{x:\xi_2, \sigma_2^2\}$, and that the variances σ_1^2, σ_2^2 are known. Define $d = \bar{x}_1 - \bar{x}_2$. Then by (1.25.4), $E[d] = \delta = E[\bar{x}_1 - \bar{x}_2] = \xi_1 - \xi_2$. The means $\bar{x}_1$ and $\bar{x}_2$ will have variances σ_1^2/n_1 and σ_2^2/n_2, and zero covariance, so by (1.25.5) the variance of d, $V[d]$, equals $\sigma_1^2/n_1 + \sigma_2^2/n_2$. Also by Section 1.26, d is normally distributed, so

$$\frac{d - E[d]}{\sqrt{V[d]}} = \frac{d - \delta}{\sqrt{\sigma_1^2/n_1 + \sigma_2^2/n_2}} \tag{12.1}$$

is a standardized normal variable u. Just as in the two preceding sections we outlined tests for the null hypothesis that a sample mean $\bar{x}$ with variance σ^2/n came from a normal distribution with expectation ξ_0, so we can test the null hypothesis that d with variance $\sigma_1^2/n_1 + \sigma_2^2/n_2$ comes from a normal distribution with expectation δ_0. For a one-sided test with $\delta = \delta_1 > \delta_0$, (7.4) gives the critical region as

$$d > \delta_0 + u_{1-\alpha}\sqrt{\sigma_1^2/n_1 + \sigma_2^2/n_2}, \tag{12.2}$$

120   STATISTICAL IDEAS   CHAP. 2

and for the two-sided test $\delta = \delta_1 \neq \delta_0$, (10.11) gives the critical region as

$$d < \delta_0 + u_{\alpha/2}\sqrt{\sigma_1^2/n_1 + \sigma_2^2/n_2} \quad \text{and} \quad d > \delta_0 + u_{1-\alpha/2}\sqrt{\sigma_1^2/n_1 + \sigma_2^2/n_2}. \tag{12.3}$$

The null hypothesis in which we are most frequently interested is, of course, $\delta = 0$, since this corresponds to $\xi_1 = \xi_2$, the two populations having the same expectation.

2.13. The Concept of P Value

We have seen that for a one-tailed test against the alternative $\xi_1 > \xi_0$ on an observation x from a normal distribution the critical region was defined by (7.4) as

$$x > \xi_0 + u_{1-\alpha}\sigma, \tag{13.1}$$

and for a two-tailed test, adapting (10.12) to the case of a single observation x with variance σ^2,

$$\left|\frac{x - \xi_0}{\sigma}\right| > u_{1-\alpha/2}. \tag{13.2}$$

The standard procedure is to observe x, and note whether it falls in the region of acceptance or rejection, and accept or reject the null hypothesis accordingly. There are often advantages to an inverse procedure. Instead of working to a fixed level of significance α, and merely recording whether H_0 is to be accepted or rejected at this level, we may choose to insert the observed value of the test statistic x in (13.1) or (13.2), replace the inequality sign by an equality, and solve for α. The value of α so found is known as the P value. The P value is thus the value of α at which the decision regarding H_0 would just be on the borderline between acceptance and rejection.

For example, suppose we observe $x = 125$ from a normal population with variance known to be 100, and test the null hypothesis $\xi_0 = 100$ at the level of significance $\alpha = 0.05$ against two-sided alternatives. Then

$$\left|\frac{125 - 100}{\sqrt{100}}\right| = 2.5 > u_{0.975} = 1.96.$$

so we reject the null hypothesis at the level of significance 0.05. Alternatively we write

$$\left|\frac{125 - 100}{\sqrt{100}}\right| = 2.5 = u_{1-P/2},$$

whence $1 - P/2 = 0.99379$, and $P = 0.012$. It is often more satisfactory to know that the null hypothesis can be just rejected at an α as small as 0.012 rather than rejected at $\alpha = 0.05$.

2.14. Confidence Limits: The General Method

As indicated in Section 2.2, a point estimate of a parameter may be obtained, but we know that this point estimate is a random variable distributed in some way around the true value of the parameter, and we may lead ourselves into error if we act as if the true value of the parameter were equal to our estimate. To give ourselves some guidance we want an interval which we are reasonably confident will actually include the true value of the parameter. The generally accepted method of handling this question is to construct what are known as *confidence limits*. The procedure which we will describe in this section will construct lower and upper $100(1 - \alpha)$ per cent confidence limits with the property that, when we say that these limits include the true value of the parameter, $100(1 - \alpha)$ per cent of all such statements will be correct (and 100α per cent will be incorrect). Obviously we choose α small: commonly used values are 0.05 and 0.01.

We suppose that we have a sample of observations $X_1, \ldots, X_n$ from a population with density function of known form $p\{x:\theta\}$, X being the random variable observed and θ the unknown parameter for which we want a confidence interval. We suppose that we have an estimator T to estimate θ, that T is a function of the observed X_i, and that we know the form of the density function of T, namely $p\{T:\theta\}$. We discuss in the following section the construction of a confidence interval for the parameter ξ of a normal population $N(\xi, \sigma^2)$ for which we have a sample of size n and for which the parameter σ^2 is known: in this case we know from (3.10) that $\bar{X}$ is an appropriate estimator for ξ with density function (1.26.1) and cumulative distribution function (1.26.3). Reverting to the general argument, if we assume that θ equals some particular value, say θ', we can insert this value in the formula for $p\{T:\theta\}$ and get the density function of T under this assumption.

Under the assumption that $\theta = \theta'$, the distribution of T will have a P_1 point, say $T_1(\theta')$, which will be determined by the equation

$$\Pr\{T < T_1(\theta') | \theta = \theta'\} = \int_{-\infty}^{T_1(\theta')} p\{T:\theta'\} \, dT = P_1. \qquad (14.1)$$

Under the same assumption $\theta = \theta'$, the distribution of T will also have a P_2 point, say $T_2(\theta')$, which will be determined by the equation

$$\Pr\{T < T_2(\theta') | \theta = \theta'\} = \int_{-\infty}^{T_2(\theta')} p\{T:\theta'\} \, dT = P_2. \qquad (14.2)$$

This equation, of course, implies that

$$\Pr\{T > T_2(\theta')|\theta = \theta'\} = \int_{T_2(\theta')}^{\infty} p\{T:\theta'\}\, dT = 1 - P_2. \quad (14.3)$$

We also have from (14.1) and (14.2) that

$$\Pr\{T_1(\theta') < T < T_2(\theta')|\theta = \theta'\} = \int_{T_1(\theta')}^{T_2(\theta')} p\{T:\theta'\}\, dT = P_2 - P_1. \quad (14.4)$$

The P_1 point $T_1(\theta')$ and the P_2 point $T_2(\theta')$ are indicated in Figure 2.13 for the assumption $\theta = \theta'$. If we change the assumed value of θ from θ'

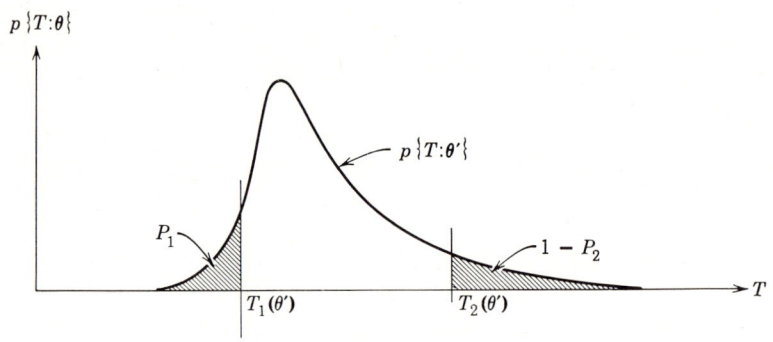

Figure 2.13

to some other value θ'' then we change the distribution of T and so the values of T_1 and T_2 will be changed. In other words, T_1 and T_2 are functions of θ, say $T_1(\theta)$ and $T_2(\theta)$. In principle, we can plot these two functions $T_1(\theta)$ and $T_2(\theta)$ against θ. In idealized form these are plotted in Figure 2.14.

Now assume that the true value of θ is θ_0. Then $T_1(\theta)$ and $T_2(\theta)$ take the values $T_1(\theta_0)$ and $T_2(\theta_0)$, respectively, and

$$\Pr\{T < T_1(\theta_0)\} = P_1,$$
$$\Pr\{T > T_2(\theta_0)\} = 1 - P_2,$$

which imply

$$\Pr\{T_1(\theta_0) < T < T_2(\theta_0)\} = P_2 - P_1. \quad (14.5)$$

Now suppose that we have taken a sample of observations and have calculated the numerical value of the estimate, say T_0. In Figure 2.14 let the horizontal line parallel to the θ axis through the point T_0 on the T axis intercept the two curves $T_2(\theta)$ and $T_1(\theta)$ at points A and B. Drop lines parallel to the T axis through the points A and B to intercept the θ

axis at points $\underline{\theta}$ and $\bar{\theta}$. We assert that the interval $(\underline{\theta}, \bar{\theta})$ is a $P_2 - P_1$ confidence interval for θ_0; i.e.,

$$\Pr\{\underline{\theta} < \theta_0 < \bar{\theta}\} = P_2 - P_1. \tag{14.6}$$

The justification for this assertion is as follows. Enter θ_0, the true value of θ, on the θ axis. Erect the perpendicular at this point to cut the curves $T_1(\theta)$ at C and $T_2(\theta)$ at D. At both these points θ has the value θ_0, so, at C, $T = T_1(\theta_0)$, and, at D, $T = T_2(\theta_0)$. Now draw the horizontal lines

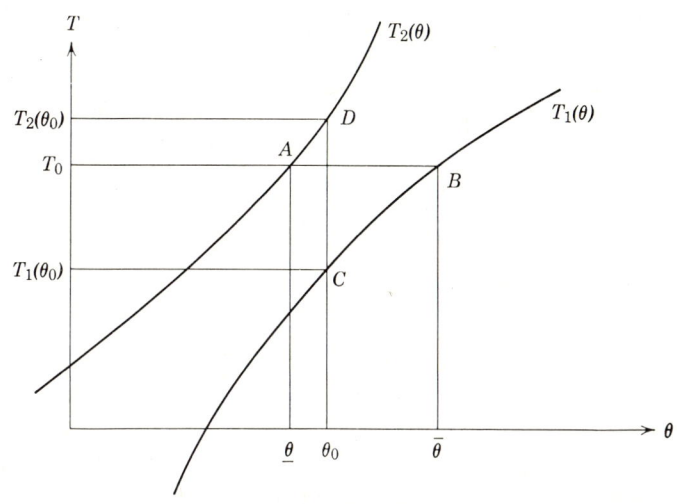

Figure 2.14

through C and D to cut the T axis at $T_1(\theta_0)$ and $T_2(\theta_0)$ respectively. As drawn, Figure 2.14 has three properties:

(a) AB intersects CD,
(b) T_0 lies in the interval $(T_1(\theta_0), T_2(\theta_0))$,
(c) The interval $(\underline{\theta}, \bar{\theta})$ includes θ_0.

Figure 2.15 is constructed by the same procedure as Figure 2.14 the difference being that in Figure 2.15 we assume that θ_0 is greater than $\bar{\theta}$. Figure 2.15 has three properties:

(d) AB does not intercept CD,
(e) T_0 does not lie in the interval $(T_1(\theta_0), T_2(\theta_0))$,
(f) The interval $(\underline{\theta}, \bar{\theta})$ does not include θ_0.

Thus the two statements

(b) T_0 lies in the interval $(T_1(\theta_0), T_2(\theta_0))$,
(c) The interval $(\underline{\theta}, \bar{\theta})$ includes θ_0,

are always true simultaneously or false simultaneously. But by (14.5), the event (b) has probability $P_2 - P_1$, so the event (c) must also have the same probability, namely $P_2 - P_1$. Hence we can write

$$\Pr\{\underline{\theta} < \theta_0 < \bar{\theta}\} = P_2 - P_1. \tag{14.7}$$

It will be noted that $\underline{\theta}$ and $\bar{\theta}$ are functions of T_0, which is a function of the observations and hence is a random variable, and therefore $\underline{\theta}$ and $\bar{\theta}$

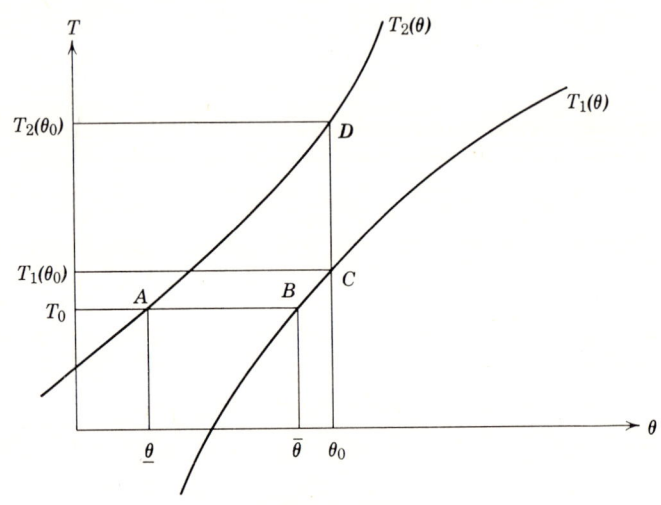

Figure 2.15

are random variables. The confidence interval $(\underline{\theta}, \bar{\theta})$ is thus a random variable. On repeating the experiment of taking the sample, calculating the estimate T_0, and constructing the confidence interval, in general we will get different numerical values for $\underline{\theta}, \bar{\theta}$. Nevertheless, our procedure guarantees that in a portion $P_2 - P_1$ of those experiments the intervals $(\underline{\theta}, \bar{\theta})$ will include the true value of θ.

2.15. Confidence Limits for the Mean of a Normal Distribution with Known Variance

We will now illustrate the above procedure by finding confidence limits for the mean ξ of a normal distribution with known variance σ^2. We assume that we have a sample $X_1, \ldots, X_n$. We know that the mean of the observations, say $\bar{X}$, is an unbiased estimator of ξ, with density function (1.26.1). We also know from (1.26.3) that the cumulative

SECT. 2.15 CONFIDENCE LIMITS OF A NORMAL DISTRIBUTION

distribution function of $\bar{X}$ is

$$\Pr\{\bar{X} < \bar{x}\} = \int_{-\infty}^{\bar{x}} p\{\bar{x}:\xi\}\, d\bar{x} = \Phi\left(\frac{\bar{x} - \xi}{\sigma/\sqrt{n}}\right). \tag{15.1}$$

For (14.1) we can write

$$\Pr\{\bar{X} < \bar{x}_1(\xi)\} = \int_{-\infty}^{\bar{x}_1(\xi)} p\{\bar{x}:\xi\}\, d\bar{x} = \Phi\left(\frac{\bar{x}_1(\xi) - \xi}{\sigma/\sqrt{n}}\right) = P_1. \tag{15.2}$$

Thus $\bar{x}_1(\xi)$, corresponding to $T_1(\theta)$ in the general case, is the solution to

$$\Phi\left(\frac{\bar{x}_1(\xi) - \xi}{\sigma/\sqrt{n}}\right) = P_1 \tag{15.3}$$

But we know that $\Phi(u_{P_1}) = P_1$, so

$$\frac{\bar{x}_1(\xi) - \xi}{\sigma/\sqrt{n}} = u_{P_1}, \tag{15.4}$$

whence

$$\bar{x}_1(\xi) = \xi + u_{P_1} \cdot \frac{\sigma}{\sqrt{n}}. \tag{15.5}$$

Thus $\bar{x}_1(\xi)$ is a linear function of ξ, with slope 1 and intercept $u_{P_1}\sigma/\sqrt{n}$. The graph of this function is plotted in Figure 2.16.

Likewise, for (14.2) we can write

$$\Pr\{\bar{X} < \bar{x}_2(\xi)\} = \int_{-\infty}^{\bar{x}_2(\xi)} p\{\bar{x}:\xi\}\, d\bar{x} = \Phi\left(\frac{\bar{x}_2(\xi) - \xi}{\sigma/\sqrt{n}}\right) = P_2, \tag{15.6}$$

whence

$$\bar{x}_2(\xi) = \xi + u_{P_2} \frac{\sigma}{\sqrt{n}}, \tag{15.7}$$

and this is also plotted in Figure 2.16.

For any value of the estimator $\bar{X} = \bar{x}$ calculated from the observations, the confidence limits are given by dropping perpendiculars from the points of interception A and B to the ξ axis. Clearly ξ is the solution to (15.7) when $\bar{x}_2(\xi) = \bar{x}$. Inserting this value for $\bar{x}_2(\xi)$ in (15.7) and solving for ξ, we get

$$\xi = \bar{x} - u_{P_2} \frac{\sigma}{\sqrt{n}}. \tag{15.8}$$

Similarly, putting $\bar{x}_1(\xi) = \bar{x}$ in (15.5), we get

$$\xi = \bar{x} - u_{P_1} \frac{\sigma}{\sqrt{n}}. \tag{15.9}$$

So far we have left P_2 and P_1 unspecified, other than that $P_2 - P_1 = 1 - \alpha$. One rational basis for particularizing the choice would be to make the length on the θ axis of the interval $(\underline{\theta}, \bar{\theta})$ as short as possible. In general the mechanics of actually doing this are not easy, and even if

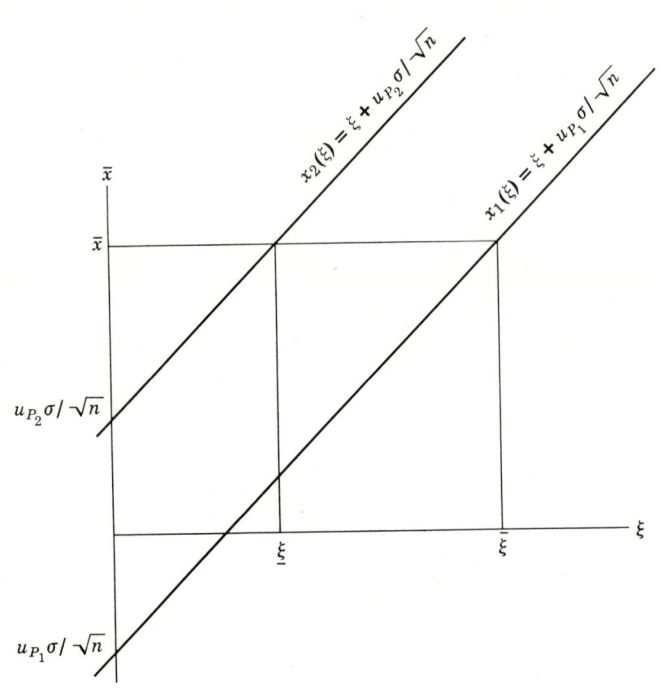

Figure 2.16

they were, most people would usually still prefer confidence limits symmetric in probability, so that $P_1 = 1 - P_2$, which implies $P_1 = 1 - P_2 = \alpha/2$. If the estimator has a symmetrical distribution, as it does in the present example, then the shortest interval coincides with the interval symmetric in probability.

To revert to our example of the mean of a normal distribution, if we want 95 per cent confidence, so that $1 - \alpha = 0.95$, we put

$$P_1 = 1 - P_2 = \alpha/2 = 0.025, \tag{15.10}$$

so we want $u_{P_2} = u_{0.975} = +1.96$ and $u_{P_1} = u_{0.025} = -1.96$. The 95 per cent confidence limits are

$$\underline{\xi} = \bar{x} - 1.96 \frac{\sigma}{\sqrt{n}}, \quad \bar{\xi} = \bar{x} + 1.96 \frac{\sigma}{\sqrt{n}}. \tag{15.11}$$

SECT. 2.16   CONFIDENCE LIMITS: THE PIVOTAL METHOD

It is often convenient to write this as

$$\bar{x} \pm 1.96 \frac{\sigma}{\sqrt{n}}. \tag{15.12}$$

Frequently in practice the explicit geometric construction is omitted, and the confidence limits $\underline{\theta}$, $\bar{\theta}$ are found algebraically. Referring to Figure 2.14, we see that at the point A the function $T_2(\theta)$ has $\theta = \underline{\theta}$ and takes the value T_0, i.e.,

$$T_2(\underline{\theta}) = T_0. \tag{15.13}$$

$T_2(\theta')$ was defined as the solution of (14.3) for a specified $\theta = \theta'$ (and P_2). We can use equation (14.3) the other way round to find θ as a function of T_2. Thus $\underline{\theta}$ is the solution when $T_2(\theta) = T_0$. In other words, $\underline{\theta}$ is the value of θ which satisfies the equation

$$\int_{T_0}^{\infty} p\{T:\underline{\theta}\}\, dT = 1 - P_2, \tag{15.14}$$

or equivalently

$$\int_{-\infty}^{T_0} p\{T:\underline{\theta}\}\, dT = P_2. \tag{15.15}$$

Similarly, in Figure 2.14 at the point B the function $T_1(\theta)$ has $\theta = \bar{\theta}$ and takes the value T_0, i.e.,

$$T_1(\bar{\theta}) = T_0. \tag{15.16}$$

$T_1(\theta')$ was defined as the solution of (14.1) for a specified $\theta = \theta'$ (and P_1). Conversely, (14.1) determines θ for a specified T_1. In particular, for $T_1 = T_0$, $\theta = \bar{\theta}$:

$$\int_{-\infty}^{T_0} p\{T:\bar{\theta}\}\, dT = P_1. \tag{15.17}$$

For our example of the mean of a normal distribution, (15.15) becomes

$$\int_{-\infty}^{\bar{x}} p\{\bar{x}:\xi\}\, d\bar{x} = \Phi\left(\frac{\bar{x} - \xi}{\sigma/\sqrt{n}}\right) = P_2, \tag{15.18}$$

whence

$$\xi = \bar{x} - u_{P_2}\frac{\sigma}{\sqrt{n}} \tag{15.19}$$

as before in (15.8), and from (15.17) we obtain (15.9) as before.

2.16. Confidence Limits: The Pivotal Method

In some situations an easier method can be used. This method requires that we can find a function, say Y, known as a *pivotal function*, of the sample observations and the parameter for which we want confidence limits with the property that its distribution does not involve the parameter in question or any other parameters. Then Y will have P_1 and P_2 points y_1 and y_2 such that

$$\Pr\{y_1 < Y < y_2\} = P_2 - P_1, \tag{16.1}$$

and we may be able to manipulate the inequality inside the braces to yield a confidence interval. For example, for the problem of finding confidence limits for the mean of a normal distribution with known variance we can choose

$$Y = \frac{\bar{X} - \xi}{\sigma/\sqrt{n}}. \tag{16.2}$$

This has the desired properties of being a function of the observations since it contains $\bar{X}$, and of the parameter in question since it contains ξ, and its distribution, being a unit normal distribution, is independent of the parameter ξ and the other parameter σ. We can therefore write

$$\Pr\left\{u_{P_1} < \frac{\bar{X} - \xi}{\sigma/\sqrt{n}} < u_{P_2}\right\} = P_2 - P_1. \tag{16.3}$$

Multiplying the inequality by $-\sigma/\sqrt{n}$, adding $\bar{X}$, and then reversing its direction yields

$$\Pr\left\{\bar{X} - u_{P_2}\frac{\sigma}{\sqrt{n}} < \xi < \bar{X} - u_{P_1}\frac{\sigma}{\sqrt{n}}\right\} = P_2 - P_1, \tag{16.4}$$

which is equivalent to (15.8) and (15.9).

This method will also work in the problem of finding confidence limits for the mean of a normal distribution with unknown variance. We use s^2, defined in (3.23), as an estimate of σ^2, and take as our function Y,

$$Y = \frac{\bar{X} - \xi}{s/\sqrt{n}}. \tag{16.5}$$

This is a function of the observations, since $\bar{X}$ and s are functions of the observations, and of the parameter ξ. It will be shown in Section 9.6 that the distribution of Y as defined in (16.5) does not involve ξ or σ^2 and is what is known as the t distribution with $n - 1$ degrees of freedom. This is well tabulated (e.g., Table II in the Appendix), so we can readily write

$$\Pr\left\{t_{P_1} < \frac{\bar{X} - \xi}{s/\sqrt{n}} < t_{P_2}\right\} = P_2 - P_1, \tag{16.6}$$

SECT. 2.17   CONFIDENCE LIMITS FOR THE PARAMETER θ 129

and by manipulations analogous to those performed on (16.3) we obtain

$$\Pr\left\{\bar{X} - t_{P_2}\frac{s}{\sqrt{n}} < \xi < \bar{X} - t_{P_1}\frac{s}{\sqrt{n}}\right\} = P_2 - P_1. \tag{16.7}$$

2.17. Confidence Limits for the Parameter θ of a Binomial Distribution

As an example for which the pivotal method cannot be made to work, consider the construction of confidence limits for a binomial parameter θ. The maximum likelihood estimator of θ is $\hat{\theta} = X/n$. We know from (1.9.3) that X has probability function

$$p\{x\} = \binom{n}{x}\theta^x(1-\theta)^{n-x}, \qquad x = 0, 1, \ldots, n, \tag{17.1}$$

and hence the probability function of $\hat{\theta} = x/n = h$, say, is

$$p\{h\} = \binom{n}{nh}\theta^{nh}(1-\theta)^{n-nh}, \qquad h = 0, \frac{1}{n}, \frac{2}{n}, \ldots, 1. \tag{17.2}$$

However, we cannot find a function of h and θ with the property that the distribution of this function does not involve θ. We therefore have to use the method of Section 2.14. For (14.1) we can write

$$\Pr\{H \leq h_1(\theta)\} = \sum_0^{h_1(\theta)}\binom{n}{nh}\theta^{nh}(1-\theta)^{n-nh} = P_1. \tag{17.3}$$

It is perhaps easier to consider the equivalent equation

$$\Pr\{X \leq x_1(\theta)\} = \sum_0^{x_1(\theta)}\binom{n}{x}\theta^x(1-\theta)^{n-x} = P_1. \tag{17.4}$$

For a fixed P_1, each value of θ will determine a corresponding value of $x_1(\theta)$.

We encounter a difficulty, however. The variable x is discrete, running over the integers 0 to n, and in general for a particular value of θ we will be able to find for the upper index of the summation the largest integer such that the summation is less than P_1 and for the next integer the summation will be greater than P_1. Thus when we attempt to construct the graphs of $x_1(\theta)$ against θ, solutions for $x_1(\theta)$ will only exist for a series of isolated points, namely those values of θ that correspond to integral values of $x_1(\theta)$ in (17.4). However, our use of this graph of $x_1(\theta)$ against θ is to read off the value of θ corresponding to an observed value of X, say x_0, and since x_0 must be an integer the fact that our graph exists only at the integers is no inconvenience.

The analog of (15.17) is

$$\sum_{x=0}^{x_0} p\{x:\bar{\theta}\} = \sum_{x=0}^{x_0} \binom{n}{x} \bar{\theta}^x (1-\bar{\theta})^{n-x} = P_1, \qquad (17.5)$$

and this determines $\bar{\theta}$ for a specified n, x_0, and P_1. The analog of (15.14) is

$$\sum_{x=x_0}^{n} p\{x:\underline{\theta}\} = \sum_{x=x_0}^{n} \binom{n}{x} \underline{\theta}^x (1-\underline{\theta})^{n-x} = 1 - P_2, \qquad (17.6)$$

which implies

$$\sum_{x=0}^{x_0-1} \binom{n}{x} \underline{\theta}^x (1-\underline{\theta})^{n-x} = P_2. \qquad (17.7)$$

The solution of these equations from first principles would be tedious. In Section 3.5 we give a rapid method that uses readily available tables.

2.18. The Relationship between Confidence Limits and Tests of Hypotheses

The construction of $1 - \alpha$ confidence intervals symmetric in probability has a close connection with the testing of hypotheses at the level of significance α against two-sided alternatives.

We will consider first the specific case of an observed mean $\bar{x}$, being an estimator of the parameter ξ of a normal distribution with known variance σ^2. For the case of $\alpha = 0.05$ we have from (15.11) that the lower and upper confidence limits for ξ are

$$\underline{\xi} = \bar{x} - 1.96 \frac{\sigma}{\sqrt{n}}, \qquad \bar{\xi} = \bar{x} + 1.96 \frac{\sigma}{\sqrt{n}}. \qquad (18.1)$$

These are sketched in Figure 2.17a. Now consider testing the null hypothesis that $\xi = \underline{\xi}$ against the two-sided alternative $\xi \neq \underline{\xi}$. From (10.11), with $\alpha = 0.05$, if $\bar{x}_{\text{CL}}(\underline{\xi})$ and $\bar{x}_{\text{CU}}(\underline{\xi})$ are the lower and upper edges of the critical region, then the critical region is

$$\bar{X} < \bar{x}_{\text{CL}}(\underline{\xi}) = \underline{\xi} - 1.96 \frac{\sigma}{\sqrt{n}}, \qquad \bar{X} > \bar{x}_{\text{CU}}(\underline{\xi}) = \underline{\xi} + 1.96 \frac{\sigma}{\sqrt{n}}. \qquad (18.2)$$

Similarly, if $\bar{x}_{\text{CL}}(\bar{\xi})$ and $\bar{x}_{\text{CU}}(\bar{\xi})$ are the lower and upper edges of the critical region for testing the null hypothesis that $\xi = \bar{\xi}$, then the critical region is

$$\bar{X} < \bar{x}_{\text{CL}}(\bar{\xi}) = \bar{\xi} - 1.96 \frac{\sigma}{\sqrt{n}}, \qquad \bar{X} > \bar{x}_{\text{CU}}(\bar{\xi}) + 1.96 \frac{\sigma}{\sqrt{n}}. \qquad (18.3)$$

Equations (18.2) and (18.3) are sketched in Figure 2.17b and c.

SECT. 2.18 CONFIDENCE LIMITS AND TESTS OF HYPOTHESES

It is apparent from (b) that if we tested the null hypothesis that ξ had some value less than $\underline{\xi}$, then the region of acceptance would move downwards, $\bar{X}$ would fall above the region of acceptance, and the null hypothesis would be rejected. Likewise, it is apparent from (c) that if we tested the null hypothesis that ξ had some value greater than $\bar{\xi}$, then the region of

(a) Confidence interval for ξ
$\underline{\xi} = \bar{x} - 1.96 \frac{\sigma}{\sqrt{n}}$ ... $\bar{x}$ ... $\bar{\xi} = \bar{x} + 1.96 \frac{\sigma}{\sqrt{n}}$

(b) $\alpha/2 = 0.025$
$\bar{x}_{CL} = \underline{\xi} - 1.96 \frac{\sigma}{\sqrt{n}}$ ... $\underline{\xi}$ ... $\bar{x}_{CU} = \underline{\xi} + 1.96 \frac{\sigma}{\sqrt{n}}$

(c) $\alpha/2 = 0.025$
$\bar{x}_{CL}(\bar{\xi}) = \bar{\xi} - 1.96 \frac{\sigma}{\sqrt{n}}$ ... $\bar{\xi}$ ... $\bar{x}_{CU}(\bar{\xi}) = \bar{\xi} + 1.96 \frac{\sigma}{\sqrt{n}}$

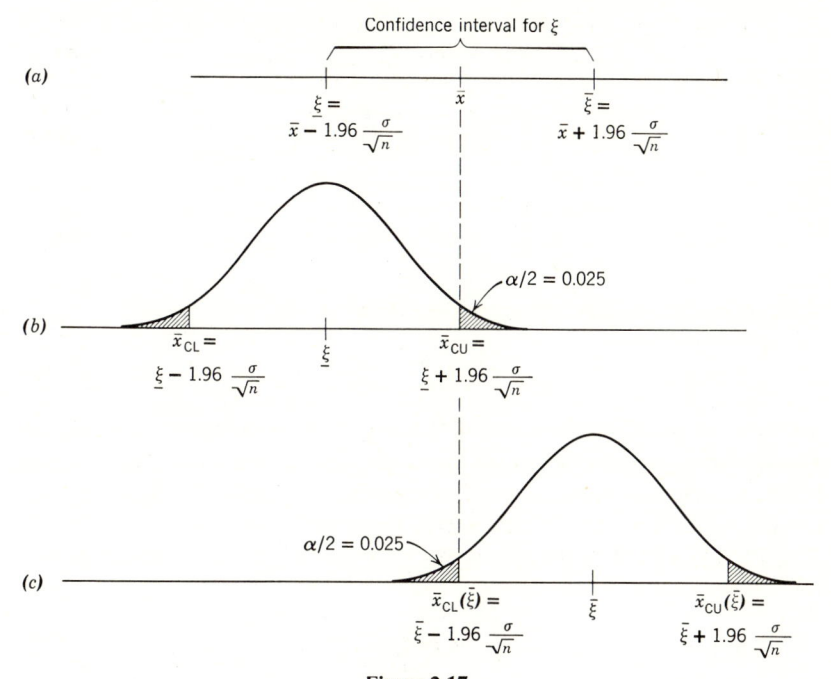

Figure 2.17

acceptance would move upwards and $\bar{x}_0$ would fall below the region of acceptance and the null hypothesis would be rejected. Conversely, if we tested the null hypothesis that ξ had any value in the interval $(\underline{\xi}, \bar{\xi})$, then the region of acceptance would cover $\bar{X}$ so the null hypothesis would be accepted. In other words, if ξ' is any ξ in the interval $(\underline{\xi}, \bar{\xi})$, then the null hypothesis that $\xi = \xi'$ will be accepted for all values of ξ', and if ξ'' is any ξ not in the interval $(\underline{\xi}, \bar{\xi})$, then the null hypothesis that $\xi = \xi''$ will be rejected for all values of ξ''.

In the general case, suppose that we have an observed value T_0 of an estimator T of a parameter θ. Then $\underline{\theta}$ is determined by (15.14) with $1 - P_2 = \alpha/2$:

$$\int_{T_0}^{\infty} p\{T:\underline{\theta}\}\, dT = \frac{\alpha}{2}, \qquad (18.4)$$

and $\bar{\theta}$ is determined by (15.17) with $P_1 = \alpha/2$:

$$\int_{-\infty}^{T_0} p\{T:\bar{\theta}\} \, dT = \frac{\alpha}{2}. \tag{18.5}$$

Suppose now that we make a two-sided test at the level of significance α of the null hypothesis that $\theta = \underline{\theta}$. The critical region is defined by $T < T_{\text{CL}}(\underline{\theta})$ and $T > T_{\text{CU}}(\underline{\theta})$, where $T_{\text{CL}}(\underline{\theta})$ and $T_{\text{CU}}(\underline{\theta})$ are determined by

$$\int_{-\infty}^{T_{\text{CL}}(\underline{\theta})} p\{T:\underline{\theta}\} \, dT = \frac{\alpha}{2}, \tag{18.6}$$

$$\int_{T_{\text{CU}}(\underline{\theta})}^{\infty} p\{T:\underline{\theta}\} \, dT = \frac{\alpha}{2}. \tag{18.7}$$

Comparing (18.4) with (18.7), we see that

$$T_0 = T_{\text{CU}}(\underline{\theta}). \tag{18.8}$$

Thus in a test of significance of the null hypothesis that $\theta = \underline{\theta}$, T_0 lies exactly on the upper edge of the critical region so that we would be on the borderline of accepting or rejecting this null hypothesis. Similarly, the critical region for the test of the null hypothesis that $\theta = \bar{\theta}$ is defined by $T < T_{\text{CL}}(\bar{\theta})$ and $T > T_{\text{CU}}(\bar{\theta})$ where $T_{\text{CL}}(\bar{\theta})$ and $T_{\text{CU}}(\bar{\theta})$ are determined by

$$\int_{-\infty}^{T_{\text{CL}}(\bar{\theta})} p\{T:\bar{\theta}\} \, dT = \frac{\alpha}{2}, \tag{18.9}$$

$$\int_{T_{\text{CU}}(\bar{\theta})}^{\infty} p\{T:\bar{\theta}\} \, dT = \frac{\alpha}{2}. \tag{18.10}$$

Comparing (18.5) with (18.9), we see that

$$T_0 = T_{\text{CL}}(\bar{\theta}). \tag{18.11}$$

Thus in a test of significance of the null hypothesis that $\theta = \bar{\theta}$, T_0 lies exactly on the lower edge of the critical region, so we would be on the border line of accepting or rejecting this null hypothesis.

Therefore, for a test of any null hypothesis that θ equals some value in the interval $(\underline{\theta}, \bar{\theta})$, the null hypothesis would be accepted; for a test of any null hypothesis that θ is outside the interval $(\underline{\theta}, \bar{\theta})$, the null hypothesis would be rejected.

EXERCISES

2.1. Suppose that $\hat{\theta}$ is an unbiased estimator of a parameter θ, and that this estimator $\hat{\theta}$ has a variance $V[\hat{\theta}]$ which is greater than zero. Show that $\hat{\theta}^2$ is a biased estimator of θ^2 and determine the bias.

2.2. (a) Suppose that $\widehat{\theta^2}$ is an unbiased estimator of a parameter θ^2, and that this estimator has a variance $V[\widehat{\theta^2}]$ which is greater than zero. Show that $\hat{\theta}$ is a biased estimator of θ. (b) For observations $x_1, \ldots, x_n$ from a normal distribution, s^2 as defined in (2.3.23) is an unbiased estimator of σ^2. It can be shown that, for observations from a normal distribution, $V[s] \simeq \sigma^2/2(n-1)$. Show that

$$E[s] \simeq \sigma \sqrt{1 - 1/2(n-1)}.$$

2.3. For observations from a normal distribution with variance σ^2,

$$s^2 = \sum_i^n (x_i - \bar{x})^2/(n-1)$$

has a variance $2(\sigma^2)^2/(n-1)$. Determine whether s^2 or $\hat{\sigma}^2 = \sum_i^n (x_i - \bar{x})^2/n$ has the smaller mean square by calculating either the difference between or the ratio of the two mean square errors.

2.4. (i) For the geometric distribution (1C.7), for a single observation x show that (a) the maximum likelihood estimator is $\hat{\theta} = 1/x$, and (b),

$$E[\hat{\theta}] = \theta \frac{-\log \theta}{1 - \theta}.$$

(ii) For the Pascal distribution (1C.8), for a single observation x show that the maximum likelihood estimator of θ is a/x. This is a biased estimator. Show that $(a-1)/(x-1)$ is an unbiased estimator of θ.

2.5. (a) Given a sample of size n, namely $X_1, \ldots, X_n$, from an exponential distribution,

$$p\{x\} = \theta e^{-\theta x}, \quad 0 \leq x < \infty,$$
$$= 0, \quad \text{otherwise,}$$

where θ is positive, find the maximum likelihood estimator of θ.

(b) Given a sample of size 1 from an exponential distribution, find the density function of the maximum likelihood estimator of θ. Find the expected value of this estimator.

(c) Suppose the exponential distribution in (a) is written in the form

$$p\{x\} = \frac{1}{\lambda} e^{-x/\lambda}.$$

Answer the questions in (a) and (b) as applied to the maximum likelihood estimator of λ.

2.6. Samples of size n_i, $i = 1, \ldots, k$, are taken from a population with fraction defective θ, and the number of defectives observed in the ith sample is

X_i. (a) Form the minimum variance unbiased estimator of θ. (b) What is its variance? (c) Form the maximum likelihood estimator of θ.

2.7. Construct the best test at the level of significance $\alpha = 0.05$ for the null hypothesis that

$$p_0\{x\} = \begin{cases} 1/2, & -1 < x < 1 \\ 0, & \text{otherwise,} \end{cases}$$

against the alternative hypothesis that

$$p_1\{x\} = N\left(0, \left(\frac{1}{2}\right)^2\right).$$

(a) State clearly the critical region for this test. (b) Calculate the power of this test.

2.8. Do the same as in exercise (2.7), but interchange the null and the alternative hypotheses.

2.9. (a) What is the best critical region for a test at the level of significance $\alpha = 0.05$ of the null hypothesis that an observation X comes from an exponential distribution

$$\begin{aligned} p\{x\} &= \theta e^{-\theta x}, & 0 \leq x < \infty \\ &= 0, & \text{otherwise,} \end{aligned}$$

with $\theta = 1/2$ against the alternative hypothesis that $\theta = 2$. (b) What is the power of this test?

2.10. From long experience with a process for manufacturing an alcoholic beverage, it is known that the yield is normally distributed with a mean of 500 units and a standard deviation of 96 units. We receive a proposal for a modification which it is claimed will increase the yield (leaving the standard deviation unchanged).

We propose to make a test of the null hypothesis that the yield remains unchanged at 500 units, using a level of significance 0.05. If the alternative hypothesis is $\xi > 500$, (a) with 50 observations, what is the critical region? (b) with 50 observations, if the yield actually is 535 units, what is the probability of rejecting the null hypothesis? (c) How many observations should we take to make the probability of rejecting the null hypothesis equal to 0.9 when the yield is actually 535 units?

2.11. Do the same as in exercise (2.10), but the proposal is now for a modification which may change the yield, in one direction or the other. If the alternative hypothesis is now $\xi \neq 500$, answer (a), (b) and (c) as in (2.10).

2.12. A material is obtained in nominal pound packages from two suppliers, A and B. From previous experience it is known that A and B have standard deviations 0.07 and 0.03 pound respectively. A sample of 100 packages from A is found to have a mean weight of 0.99 pound, and a sample of 400 packages from B has a mean weight of 1.01 pounds. (a) Find the P value for the null hypothesis that A and B are supplying the same weight, the alternative hypothesis being that $A \neq B$. (b) Give 95 per cent confidence limits for the difference $B - A$.

2.13. In a proposed test that the mean of a normal distribution is ξ_0 against the alternative that it is ξ_1, $\xi_1 > \xi_0$, the level of significance being α, a sample size n is chosen, the power of the test is calculated, and it comes out to be 0.5. This is regarded as unsatisfactory so the decision is made to change the sample size to $4n$. What will be the power of the new test?

2.14. The following is an example of a situation for which the likelihood ratio method of constructing a test proves unsatisfactory (the example is due to Charles Stein). X is a discrete random variable with probability functions under H_0 and H_1 as follows:

X	-2	-1	0	1	2
H_0	$\dfrac{\alpha}{2}$	$\dfrac{1}{2} - \alpha$	α	$\dfrac{1}{2} - \alpha$	$\dfrac{\alpha}{2}$
H_1	pc	$\dfrac{1-c}{1-\alpha}\left(\dfrac{1}{2}-\alpha\right)$	$\alpha\dfrac{1-c}{1-\alpha}$	$\dfrac{1-c}{1-\alpha}\left(\dfrac{1}{2}-\alpha\right)$	$(1-p)c$

α is a constant, $0 < \alpha < 1/2$, so H_0 is a simple hypothesis. c is a constant satisfying the conditions $\alpha/(2 - \alpha) < c < \alpha$. p is a parameter not specified other than that $0 \leq p \leq 1$, so H_1 is a composite hypothesis.

(a) Find the critical region given by the likelihood ratio test for a level of significance α. (b) What is the power of this test? (c) As an alternative test, consider rejecting H_0 with probability α irrespective of the observed value of X. What is the power of his test? (d) As another alternative test, consider rejecting H_0 if $X = 0$. How does the power of this test compare with the power of the tests in (b) and (c)?

2.15. Suppose a sample of observations x_{iv}, $v = 1, \ldots, n_i$ is taken from a normal distribution with mean ξ_i and variance σ^2, and then the sample estimator s_i^2 of the variance σ^2 is calculated. Suppose that this is repeated for a total of k samples (i.e., $i = 1, \ldots, k$). The variance of s_i^2 is known to be (see Section 9.8) $2(\sigma^2)^2/(n_i - 1)$. What is the minimum variance unbiased estimator of σ^2?

REFERENCES

1. Savage, L. J., "The Theory of Statistical Decision," *Journal of the American Statistical Association*, 46 (1951), 55–67.
2. Wald, A., *Statistical Decision Functions*. New York: John Wiley and Sons, 1950.
3. Chernoff, Herman, and Moses, Lincoln E., *Elementary Decision Theory*. New York: John Wiley and Sons, 1959.
4. Fisher, R. A., "The Mathematical Foundations of Theoretical Statistics," *Philosophical Transactions of the Royal Society*, A, 222 (1922), 306–368.
5. Cramér, H., *Mathematical Methods of Statistics*. Princeton: Princeton University Press, 1951.
6. Kendall, Maurice G., and Stuart, Alan, *The Advanced Theory of Statistics;* Volume 1: *Distribution Theory*, 1958, Volume 2: *Inference and Relationship*, 1961. New York: Hafner Publishing Company.
7. Neyman, J., and Pearson, E. S., "On the Problem of the Most Efficient Type of Statistical Hypotheses," *Philosophical Transactions of the Royal Society*, A, 231 (1933), 289–337.
8. Neyman, J., "On the Problem of Confidence Intervals," *Annals of Mathematical Statistics*, 6 (1935), 111–16.
9. Wilks, S. S., "The Large Sample Distribution of the Likelihood Ratio for Testing Composite Hypotheses," *Annals of Mathematical Statistics*, 9 (1938), 60–62.

CHAPTER 3

The Binomial, Hypergeometric, and Poisson Distributions

3.1. The Normal Approximation to the Binomial Distribution

For evaluating binomial probabilities, particularly sums in either the lower or upper tails, certain extensive tabulations are of great value [1–4]. The fact that the binomial distribution can be approximated by a normal distribution with mean $n\theta$ and variance $n\theta(1 - \theta)$, first demonstrated by Demoivre in 1733, is still of considerable theoretical and practical importance, however, and we will now sketch a proof.

In the factorials in the binomial coefficient $\binom{n}{x}$ in

$$p\{x\} = \binom{n}{x}\theta^x(1-\theta)^{n-x} = \frac{n!}{x!(n-x)!}\theta^x(1-\theta)^{n-x}, \quad (1.1)$$

we use Stirling's approximation,

$$n! \simeq n^{n+\frac{1}{2}}e^{-n}\sqrt{2\pi}. \quad (1.2)$$

Thus

$$\binom{n}{x} = \frac{n!}{x!(n-x)!}$$

$$\simeq \frac{n^{n+\frac{1}{2}}e^{-n}\sqrt{2\pi}}{x^{x+\frac{1}{2}}e^{-x}\sqrt{2\pi}(n-x)^{n-x+\frac{1}{2}}e^{-(n-x)}\sqrt{2\pi}}$$

$$\simeq \frac{1}{\sqrt{2\pi}}\frac{n^{n+\frac{1}{2}}}{x^{x+\frac{1}{2}}(n-x)^{n-x+\frac{1}{2}}}\frac{e^{-n}}{e^{-x-n+x}}. \quad (1.3)$$

The exponential terms cancel each other. We now multiply the numerator

SECT. 3.1   NORMAL APPROXIMATION TO THE BINOMIAL DISTRIBUTION   137

and denominator by $n^{1/2}$; the numerator is then

$$n^{n+1/2}n^{1/2} = n^{x+1/2}n^{n-x+1/2}. \tag{1.4}$$

Thus (1.3) becomes

$$\binom{n}{x} \simeq \frac{1}{\sqrt{2\pi}\sqrt{n}} \left(\frac{n}{x}\right)^{x+1/2} \left(\frac{n}{n-x}\right)^{n-x+1/2} \tag{1.5}$$

We can also write

$$\theta^x(1-\theta)^{n-x} = \frac{\theta^{x+1/2}}{\sqrt{\theta}} \frac{(1-\theta)^{n-x+1/2}}{\sqrt{(1-\theta)}}. \tag{1.6}$$

Substituting (1.5) and (1.6) in (1.1), we get

$$p\{x\} \simeq \frac{1}{\sqrt{2\pi}} \frac{1}{\sqrt{n\theta(1-\theta)}} \frac{\theta^{x+1/2}}{(x/n)^{x+1/2}} \frac{(1-\theta)^{n-x+1/2}}{[(n-x)/n]^{n-x+1/2}}$$

$$\simeq \frac{1}{\sqrt{2\pi}} \frac{1}{\sqrt{n\theta(1-\theta)}} \left[\left(\frac{x}{n\theta}\right)^{x+1/2}\right]^{-1} \left\{\left[\frac{n-x}{n(1-\theta)}\right]^{n-x+1/2}\right\}^{-1}. \tag{1.7}$$

Taking logarithms to the base e:

$$\log p\{x\} \simeq -\log\sqrt{2\pi n\theta(1-\theta)} - \left(x+\frac{1}{2}\right)\log\left(\frac{x}{n\theta}\right)$$

$$-\left(n-x+\frac{1}{2}\right)\log\left[\frac{n-x}{n(1-\theta)}\right]. \tag{1.8}$$

Now define

$$z = \frac{x - n\theta}{\sqrt{n\theta(1-\theta)}}. \tag{1.9}$$

We make the following substitutions in (1.8):

$$x = n\theta + z\sqrt{n\theta(1-\theta)}, \tag{1.10}$$

$$\frac{x}{n\theta} = 1 + z\sqrt{\frac{1-\theta}{n\theta}}, \tag{1.11}$$

$$n - x = n(1-\theta) - z\sqrt{n\theta(1-\theta)}, \tag{1.12}$$

$$\frac{n-x}{n(1-\theta)} = 1 - z\sqrt{\frac{\theta}{n(1-\theta)}}. \tag{1.13}$$

Now z as defined in (1.9) is approximately a unit normal deviate, which means that large values will occur only with small probability. For example, $\Pr\{|z| > 3\} \simeq 0.0027$. Further, $z\sqrt{(1-\theta)/n\theta}$ will be small for large n. It is therefore permissible to use the expansion

$$\log(1+y) = y - \frac{y^2}{2} + \frac{y^3}{3} - \cdots, \tag{1.14}$$

which is convergent for $|y| < 1$ and for which the first terms are an approximation of increasing accuracy as $|y|$ tends to zero, for the logarithm of (1.11) and similarly for the logarithm of (1.13). Thus

$$\log\left(\frac{x}{n\theta}\right) = \log\left(1 + z\sqrt{\frac{1-\theta}{n\theta}}\right) \simeq z\sqrt{\frac{1-\theta}{n\theta}} - z^2 \frac{1-\theta}{2n\theta} + \cdots \tag{1.15}$$

and $\log\left[\dfrac{n-x}{n(1-\theta)}\right] = \log\left[1 - z\sqrt{\dfrac{\theta}{n(1-\theta)}}\right]$

$$\simeq -z\sqrt{\frac{\theta}{n(1-\theta)}} - z^2 \frac{\theta}{2n(1-\theta)} - \cdots. \tag{1.16}$$

Making these substitutions in (1.8), we obtain

$\log p\{x\} \simeq -\log \sqrt{2\pi n\theta(1-\theta)}$

$$-\left[n\theta + z\sqrt{n\theta(1-\theta)} + \frac{1}{2}\right]\left[z\sqrt{\frac{1-\theta}{n\theta}} - z^2 \frac{1-\theta}{2n\theta} + \cdots\right]$$

$$-\left[n(1-\theta) - z\sqrt{n\theta(1-\theta)} + \frac{1}{2}\right]$$

$$\times \left[-z\sqrt{\frac{\theta}{n(1-\theta)}} - z^2 \frac{\theta}{2n(1-\theta)} - \cdots\right]. \tag{1.17}$$

Collecting terms in powers of z, the coefficient of z is zero except for $(1/2\sqrt{n})[\sqrt{\theta/(1-\theta)} - \sqrt{(1-\theta)/\theta}]$, which tends to zero as n tends to infinity. The coefficient of z^2 is $-1/2$ plus a component in $1/n$, which tends to zero as n tends to infinity. Higher terms in z also tend to zero; so

$$\log p\{x\} \simeq -\log\sqrt{2\pi n\theta(1-\theta)} - \frac{z^2}{2}. \tag{1.18}$$

Substituting (1.9) for z, we get

$$p\{x\} \simeq \frac{1}{\sqrt{2\pi}\sqrt{n\theta(1-\theta)}} e^{-(x-n\theta)^2/2n\theta(1-\theta)}, \tag{1.19}$$

which is the normal probability density function with the expectation $n\theta$ and variance $n\theta(1-\theta)$ of the binomial distribution. We have thus shown that the binomial distribution can be approximated by a normal distribution with the appropriate mean and variance.

SECT. 3.1 NORMAL APPROXIMATION TO THE BINOMIAL DISTRIBUTION

Sometimes we may prefer to deal with the observed proportion $h = x/n$. Since h is a function of x, we use (1.13.8);

$$p\{h\} \simeq \frac{1}{\sqrt{2\pi}\sqrt{\theta(1-\theta)/n}} e^{-(h-\theta)^2/[2\theta(1-\theta)/n]}. \qquad (1.20)$$

The corresponding cumulative distribution functions are

$$\Phi\left(\frac{x-n\theta}{\sqrt{n\theta(1-\theta)}}\right) \quad \text{and} \quad \Phi\left(\frac{h-\theta}{\sqrt{\theta(1-\theta)/n}}\right). \qquad (1.21)$$

However, we are approximating a discrete distribution by a continuous distribution. In the discrete distribution of x the probability is concentrated at the integers, and when we approximate it by a continuous

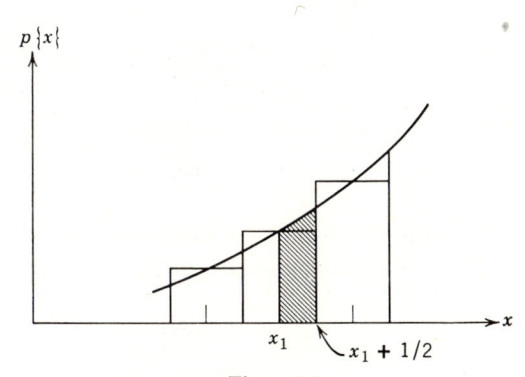

Figure 3.1

distribution the corresponding probability is spread over a figure approximately a rectangle with base stretching from $-1/2$ to $+1/2$ on either side of the integer. In Figure 3.1 the integral

$$\int_{-\infty}^{x} p\{x\}\, dx$$

will omit the shaded area from x to $x + 1/2$ which properly belongs to x. We therefore change the upper limit of integration to $x + 1/2$:

$$\Pr\{X \leq x\} \simeq \int_{-\infty}^{x+\frac{1}{2}} p\{x\}\, dx = \Phi\left(\frac{x + 1/2 - n\theta}{\sqrt{n\theta(1-\theta)}}\right). \qquad (1.22)$$

If on the other hand we wanted the probability that $X < x$, the integral

$$\int_{-\infty}^{x} p\{x\}\, dx$$

would improperly include the area between $x - 1/2$ and x. We therefore integrate to $x - 1/2$:

$$\Pr\{X < x\} \simeq \int_{-\infty}^{x-\frac{1}{2}} p\{x\}\, dx = \Phi\left(\frac{x - 1/2 - n\theta}{\sqrt{n\theta(1-\theta)}}\right). \quad (1.23)$$

This constant 1/2 that is added or subtracted to the limit of integration is known as the *correction for continuity*.

Formulas (1.22) and (1.23) can be combined to give

$$\Pr\{X = x\} = \Pr\{X \leq x\} - \Pr\{X < x\}$$
$$\simeq \Phi\left(\frac{x + 1/2 - n\theta}{\sqrt{n\theta(1-\theta)}}\right) - \Phi\left(\frac{x - 1/2 - n\theta}{\sqrt{n\theta(1-\theta)}}\right). \quad (1.24)$$

As an illustration, let $n = 100$, $\theta = 0.1$, $x = 10$; then

$$\Pr\{X = 10\} \simeq \Phi\left(\frac{10 + 1/2 - 100 \times 0.1}{\sqrt{100 \times 0.1 \times 0.9}}\right) - \Phi\left(\frac{10 - 1/2 - 100 \times 0.1}{\sqrt{100 \times 0.1 \times 0.9}}\right).$$

$$\simeq \Phi(0.1667) - \Phi(-0.1667) = 0.5662 - 0.4338$$

$$= 0.1324. \quad (1.25)$$

The exact answer is 0.1319.

The alternative forms of (1.22) and (1.23) referring to $h = x/n$, obtained by dividing the numerator and denominator of the argument of $\Phi(\ )$ by n, are

$$\Pr\{H \leq h\} \simeq \Phi\left(\frac{h + 1/2n - \theta}{\sqrt{\theta(1-\theta)/n}}\right), \quad (1.26)$$

$$\Pr\{H < h\} \simeq \Phi\left(\frac{h - 1/2n - \theta}{\sqrt{\theta(1-\theta)/n}}\right). \quad (1.27)$$

For a rigorous proof of the results of this section, with a careful attention to remainder terms, etc., the reader is referred to Uspensky [5] or Feller [6].

The approximations developed in this section are usually satisfactory if $n\theta(1-\theta) > 9$. Thus if $\theta = 1/2$, an n of 36 is large enough, but if $\theta = 1/10$, n needs to be ≥ 100.

3.2. Testing Hypotheses about the Binomial Distribution with a Normal Approximation

Suppose that we observe x defectives in a sample of size n and wish to test the null hypothesis that the fraction defective θ equals θ_0 against the alternative hypothesis $\theta = \theta_1$ where $\theta_1 > \theta_0$. This problem was discussed in Section 2.8, in terms of hypothesis testing at a stated level of

SECT. 3.2 TESTING HYPOTHESES ABOUT THE BINOMIAL DISTRIBUTION

significance. Alternatively, we can set

$$\Pr\{X \geq x\} = \sum_{v=x}^{n} \binom{n}{v} \theta_0^v (1 - \theta_0)^{n-v} = P, \quad (2.1)$$

and, for example, using the tables cited in [1], [2], [3], or [4], evaluate P. This will be the P value of the null hypothesis. To use the normal approximation to the binomial distribution, we note that

$$\Pr\{X < x\} + \Pr\{X \geq x\} = 1, \quad (2.2)$$

whence, using (1.23),

$$P = \Pr\{X \geq x\} = 1 - \Pr\{X < x\} \simeq 1 - \Phi\left(\frac{x - 1/2 - n\theta_0}{\sqrt{n\theta_0(1 - \theta_0)}}\right), \quad (2.3)$$

so the equation

$$u_{1-P} = \frac{x - 1/2 - n\theta_0}{\sqrt{n\theta_0(1 - \theta_0)}} \quad (2.4)$$

has to be solved for P. For example, if we observe 60 heads in 100 tosses of a coin, and are testing the null hypothesis that the coin is fair, i.e., $H_0 : \theta_0 = 1/2$, against the alternative that it is biased in favor of heads, we refer

$$u_{1-P} = \frac{60 - 1/2 - 100 \times 1/2}{\sqrt{100 \times (1/2)(1 - 1/2)}} = 1.900 \quad (2.5)$$

to Table I, the cumulative normal distribution, obtaining $1 - P \simeq 0.9713$, whence $P \simeq 0.0287$. The exact value, obtained from tables, is 0.02844.

If the alternative hypothesis is $\theta = \theta_1 < \theta_0$, we set

$$\Pr\{X \leq x\} = \sum_{v=0}^{x} \binom{n}{x} \theta_0^v (1 - \theta_0)^{n-v} = P, \quad (2.6)$$

whence, using (1.22),

$$P \simeq \Phi\left(\frac{x + 1/2 - n\theta_0}{\sqrt{n\theta_0(1 - \theta_0)}}\right), \quad (2.7)$$

and the equation

$$u_P = \left(\frac{x + 1/2 - n\theta_0}{\sqrt{n\theta_0(1 - \theta_0)}}\right) \quad (2.8)$$

has to be solved for P. For example, if we observe 40 heads in 100 tosses of a coin, and are testing the null hypothesis that the coin is fair against the alternative that it is biased against heads, we calculate

$$u_P = \frac{40 + 1/2 - 100 \times 1/2}{\sqrt{100 \times (1/2)(1 - 1/2)}} = -1.900, \quad (2.9)$$

whence $P \simeq 0.0287$.

The calculation of P values for two-sided alternatives is most easily carried out by observing whether the observed number x falls in the upper or lower tail, and calculating the appropriate single-tail P value as above, and doubling it to get the two-tailed P value. Thus if we observed 40 heads in 100 tosses of a coin, and are testing the null hypothesis that the coin is fair against the alternative that it is biased in either direction, the P value would be $2 \times 0.0287 = 0.0574$. Note that with the one-sided alternative the null hypothesis would be rejected at the 0.05 level of significance, whereas against the two-sided alternative the null hypothesis would be accepted at this significance level.

In computing the power of these tests, since H is approximately a normally distributed variable with mean θ and variance $\theta(1-\theta)/n$, we can use the methods of Section 2.7 for one-sided tests and Section 2.10 for two-sided tests. There is, however, a slight complication here; the variance is not a constant but instead is a function of θ. The calculation of the power of a test at a specified level of significance α for a specified alternative $\theta = \theta_1$, $\theta_1 > \theta_0$, proceeds as follows. We want the probability of X falling in the critical region to be α. Let x_c be the lower end of the critical region. Then we require

$$\Pr\{X \geq x_c\} = \alpha, \tag{2.10}$$

so

$$\Pr\{X < x_c\} \simeq \Phi\left(\frac{x_c - 1/2 - n\theta_0}{\sqrt{n\theta_0(1-\theta_0)}}\right) = 1 - \alpha, \tag{2.11}$$

and

$$\frac{x_c - 1/2 - n\theta_0}{\sqrt{n\theta_0(1-\theta_0)}} = u_{1-\alpha}. \tag{2.12}$$

Solving for x_c, we get

$$x_c = n\theta_0 + \tfrac{1}{2} + u_{1-\alpha}\sqrt{n\theta_0(1-\theta_0)}. \tag{2.13}$$

The power by definition is the probability that X falls in the region of rejection when the alternative hypothesis is true:

$$\pi(\theta_1) = \Pr\{X \geq x_c | \theta = \theta_1\} = 1 - \Pr\{X < x_c | \theta = \theta_1\} \tag{2.14}$$

$$\simeq 1 - \Phi\left(\frac{n\theta_0 + 1/2 + u_{1-\alpha}\sqrt{n\theta_0(1-\theta_0)} - 1/2 - n\theta_1}{\sqrt{n\theta_1(1-\theta_1)}}\right)$$

$$\simeq 1 - \Phi\left(\frac{\sqrt{n}(\theta_0 - \theta_1)}{\sqrt{\theta_1(1-\theta_1)}} + u_{1-\alpha}\frac{\sqrt{\theta_0(1-\theta_0)}}{\sqrt{\theta_1(1-\theta_1)}}\right). \tag{2.15}$$

If we define

$$\sigma_0 = \sqrt{\theta_0(1-\theta_0)/n}, \quad \sigma_1 = \sqrt{\theta_1(1-\theta_1)/n}, \tag{2.16}$$

SECT. 3.2 TESTING HYPOTHESES ABOUT THE BINOMIAL DISTRIBUTION

this can be written as

$$\pi(\theta_1) \simeq 1 - \Phi\left(\frac{\theta_0 - \theta_1}{\sigma_1} + u_{1-\alpha}\frac{\sigma_0}{\sigma_1}\right)$$

$$\simeq 1 - \Phi\left[\left(u_{1-\alpha} + \frac{\theta_0 - \theta_1}{\sigma_0}\right)\frac{\sigma_0}{\sigma_1}\right]$$

$$\simeq \Phi\left[\left(u_\alpha + \frac{\theta_1 - \theta_0}{\sigma_0}\right)\frac{\sigma_0}{\sigma_1}\right]. \quad (2.17)$$

When the alternative hypothesis is $\theta_1 < \theta_0$, similar manipulations yield

$$\pi(\theta_1) \simeq \Phi\left[\left(u_\alpha + \frac{\theta_0 - \theta_1}{\sigma_0}\right)\frac{\sigma_0}{\sigma_1}\right]. \quad (2.18)$$

For a two-sided test, the power is the probability that X falls in the critical region when $\theta = \theta_1$:

$$\pi(\theta_1) = \Pr\{X \leq n\theta_0 - \tfrac{1}{2} + u_{\alpha/2}\sqrt{n\theta_0(1-\theta_0)}\,|\,\theta = \theta_1\}$$

$$+ \Pr\{X \geq n\theta_0 + \tfrac{1}{2} + u_{1-\alpha/2}\sqrt{n\theta_0(1-\theta_0)}\,|\,\theta = \theta_1\} \quad (2.19)$$

$$\simeq \Phi\left[\left(u_{\alpha/2} + \frac{\theta_0 - \theta_1}{\sigma_0}\right)\frac{\sigma_0}{\sigma_1}\right] + \Phi\left[\left(u_{\alpha/2} - \frac{\theta_0 - \theta_1}{\sigma_0}\right)\frac{\sigma_0}{\sigma_1}\right] \quad (2.20)$$

by manipulations similar to those leading from (2.14) to (2.17). These formulas will give the sample size necessary for a power of $1 - \beta$ of rejecting the null hypothesis at a level of significance α when $\theta_1 - \theta_0$ has any specified value. For the one-sided alternative $\theta_1 > \theta_0$, putting (2.17) equal to $1 - \beta$, we get

$$\left(u_\alpha + \frac{\theta_1 - \theta_0}{\sigma_0}\right)\frac{\sigma_0}{\sigma_1} = u_{1-\beta}. \quad (2.21)$$

Substituting for σ_0 and σ_1 from (2.16) and solving for n gives

$$n = \frac{1}{(\theta_1 - \theta_0)^2}[u_{1-\beta}\sqrt{\theta_1(1-\theta_1)} + u_{1-\alpha}\sqrt{\theta_0(1-\theta_0)}]^2. \quad (2.22)$$

For example, if we wish to have a power $1 - \beta$ of 0.95 of rejecting the null hypothesis $\theta_0 = 0.05$ at the one-sided level of significance $\alpha = 0.01$ when actually θ is $\theta_1 = 0.10$, then

$$n = \frac{1}{(0.10 - 0.05)^2}[u_{0.95}\sqrt{0.10(1-0.10)} + u_{0.99}\sqrt{0.05(1-0.05)}]^2 = 400$$

$$(2.23)$$

3.3. The Angular Transformation and Other Variance Stabilizing Transformations

It is convenient to be able to assume that the variance of a random variable, say X, is a constant, say σ^2. However, situations do arise in which the variance is instead a function, say $g(\xi)$, of the expected value of X, ξ. For example, the variance of a binomial proportion H is $\theta(1-\theta)/n$, which is a function of θ. In such a situation, to permit the use of statistical techniques which assume a constant variance, we need to transform X into a function of X, say $\phi(X)$, where the function $\phi(\ )$ is chosen so that the random variable so defined has a constant variance. This we can do in the following manner.

Let $\phi(x)$ be a function of a real variable x. By a Taylor series, $\phi(x)$ can be approximated by a linear function near any point ξ:

$$\phi(x) \simeq \phi(\xi) + \phi'(\xi)(x-\xi) + \phi''(\xi)\frac{(x-\xi)^2}{2!}. \tag{3.1}$$

Let X be a random variable with an expected value $E[X] = \xi$. Then $Y = \phi(X)$ defines a new random variable Y:

$$Y \simeq \phi(\xi) + \phi'(\xi)(X-\xi) + \phi''(\xi)\frac{(X-\xi)^2}{2!}. \tag{3.2}$$

If X does not vary greatly about ξ, so that the variance of X is small, when we take expectations we may neglect $E[(X-\xi)^2]$:

$$E[Y] \simeq \phi(\xi) + \phi'(\xi)E[X-\xi] = \phi(\xi), \tag{3.3}$$

so

$$Y - E[Y] \simeq \phi'(\xi)(X-\xi), \tag{3.4}$$

and

$$V[Y] = E[(Y-E[Y])^2] \simeq \{\phi'(\xi)\}^2 E[(X-\xi)^2]$$
$$\simeq \{\phi'(\xi)\}^2 V[X]. \tag{3.5}$$

In general, $V[X]$ will depend on various parameters. If, however, it can be written as a function of the expected value ξ, say $g(\xi)$, then

$$V[Y] \simeq \{\phi'(\xi)\}^2 g(\xi). \tag{3.6}$$

If we choose $\phi(\xi)$ so that its derivative $\phi'(\xi)$ satisfies

$$\phi'(\xi) = \frac{1}{\sqrt{g(\xi)}}, \tag{3.7}$$

SECT. 3.3 THE ANGULAR TRANSFORMATION

then we will have made $V[Y] \simeq 1$. Equation (3.7) is equivalent to

$$\phi(\xi) = \int \frac{d\xi}{\sqrt{g(\xi)}}. \tag{3.8}$$

For example, for a binomial proportion H with expectation θ, the variance $V[H] = \theta(1 - \theta)/n$. Inserting this for $g(\xi)$ in (3.8), we have

$$\phi(\theta) = \int \frac{d\theta}{\sqrt{\theta(1 - \theta)/n}} = \sqrt{n} \int \frac{d\theta}{\sqrt{\theta(1 - \theta)}}. \tag{3.9}$$

This integral can be evaluated by changing the variable to $t = \sqrt{\theta}$, so that $t^2 = \theta$, that $2t\, dt = d\theta$, and that

$$\int \frac{d\theta}{\sqrt{\theta(1 - \theta)}} = \int \frac{2t\, dt}{\sqrt{t^2(1 - t^2)}} = 2 \int \frac{dt}{\sqrt{1 - t^2}}$$

$$= 2 \arcsin t = 2 \arcsin \sqrt{\theta}. \tag{3.10}$$

Thus, if we use the transformation $\phi(H) = 2\sqrt{n} \arcsin \sqrt{H}$, the variance of $\phi(H)$ will be 1. If we omit the factor $\sqrt{n}$ and instead use $\psi(H) = 2 \arcsin \sqrt{H}$, then the variance of this transformed variable will be $1/n$. Table V gives this latter transformation directly from a proportion H to $\psi(H) = Y$ in radians: for example, if we enter the table with $H = 0.500$, it gives directly $2 \arcsin \sqrt{H}$ as $Y = 1.5708$.

We will note here several other transformations of frequent utility. First, if the variance is proportional to the expected value, so that $V[X] = k\xi$, then

$$\phi(\xi) = \int \frac{d\xi}{\sqrt{k\xi}} = \frac{2}{\sqrt{k}} \sqrt{\xi}. \tag{3.11}$$

Thus a square root transformation will give a constant variance. In particular, if $k = 1$, as occurs with the Poisson distribution, to be discussed in Section 3.11, $2\sqrt{X}$ will have variance 1, and $\sqrt{X}$ will have variance $1/4$.

Second, if the standard deviation is proportional to the expected value, so that $V[X] = k^2\xi^2$,

$$\phi(\xi) = \int \frac{d\xi}{\sqrt{k^2\xi^2}} = \frac{1}{k} \log_e \xi, \tag{3.12}$$

so that $\log_e X$ will have a constant variance k^2, and $\log_{10} X$ a constant variance $0.189k^2$. We might note that if $\psi(\xi) = \log_e \xi$, then $\psi'(\xi) = 1/\xi$ and $\psi''(\xi) = -1/\xi^2$. Using the Taylor series up to the second-degree

term,
$$Y \simeq \psi(\xi) + \psi'(\xi)(X - \xi) + \psi''(\xi)\frac{(X - \xi)^2}{2}, \quad (3.13)$$

so

$$E[Y] \simeq \psi(\xi) + \frac{1}{2}\psi''(\xi)E[(X - \xi)^2] \simeq \log_e \xi - \frac{V[X]}{2\xi^2}. \quad (3.14)$$

This shows that when we include the second-degree term in the Taylor series the expected value of the transformed variable Y differs from (3.3), the transformation of the expected value of the original variable X, by an amount in this case $-V[X]/2(E[X])^2$. We might also note that on substituting $1/\xi$ for $\psi'(\xi)$ in (3.5) we get

$$V[Y] = \frac{V[X]}{(E[X])^2}. \quad (3.15)$$

Thirdly, if the standard deviation is proportional to the square of the expected value, so that $V[X] = k^2\xi^4$, then

$$\phi(\xi) = \int \frac{d\xi}{\sqrt{k^2\xi^4}} = \int \frac{d\xi}{k\xi^2} = -\frac{1}{k\xi}, \quad (3.16)$$

so that the reciprocal $1/X$ will have constant variance k^2.

To summarize these three results, to obtain constant variance, if $V[X] \propto \xi$ we use $\sqrt{X}$, if $V[X] \propto \xi^2$ we use $\log X$, and if $V[X] \propto \xi^4$ we use $1/X$.

Of course, since we have been neglecting the higher order terms in these various Taylor series, the results of this section are approximations.

We have discussed transformations chosen to give constant variance in the transformed variable. If the original variable is normally distributed, then the transformed variable cannot be. Frequently, however, the lack of constancy of variance (*heteroscedasticity*) is simultaneously associated with a nonnormality, and the transformation that gives a constant variance (*homoscedasticity*) also simultaneously gives a distribution closer to normal. In short, this is one case where usually we can both have our cake and eat it.

3.4. Testing Hypotheses about the Binomial Distribution with the Angular Transformation

If H is a binomial proportion with expectation θ based on a sample of n, then $Y = 2 \arcsin \sqrt{H}$ in radians is approximately normally distributed with approximate expectation $\eta = 2 \arcsin \sqrt{\theta}$ and variance $1/n$,

SECT. 3.4   TESTING HYPOTHESES ABOUT THE BINOMIAL DISTRIBUTION   147

and

$$\Pr\{H \leq h\} \simeq \int_{-\infty}^{2 \arcsin \sqrt{h+1/2n}} p\{y\}\, dy$$

$$\simeq \Phi\left(\frac{2 \arcsin \sqrt{h+1/2n} - \eta}{1/\sqrt{n}}\right), \qquad (4.1)$$

where the $1/2n$ is a correction for continuity analogous to that used with the normal approximation. For a one-sided test of the null hypothesis $\theta = \theta_0$ against the alternative $\theta = \theta_1 < \theta_0$, the critical region will be determined by putting (4.1) equal to α and writing h_c for h, $\eta_0 = 2 \arcsin \sqrt{\theta_0}$ for η; on rearrangement we get

$$2 \arcsin \sqrt{h_c + 1/2n} = 2 \arcsin \sqrt{\theta_0} + \frac{u_\alpha}{\sqrt{n}}, \qquad (4.2)$$

which for specified θ_0, α, and n will determine h_c. If $H \leq h_c$, we reject the null hypothesis. The other one-sided test and the two-sided test can be constructed similarly. However, the angular transformation appears to give approximations no better than the normal approximation, and these tests are not customarily used.

However, since the variance of the angular transformation is a constant, the calculation of powers and necessary sample sizes can be made more expeditiously with it than with the normal approximation, in which the variance is a function of θ. Ignoring the correction for continuity, the formula (2.7.12) for the power of a one-sided test applies immediately: for the alternative $\eta_1 > \eta_0$,

$$\pi(\eta_1) = \Phi\left(u_\alpha + \frac{\eta_1 - \eta_0}{1/\sqrt{n}}\right). \qquad (4.3)$$

The same formula, with η_1 and η_0 interchanged, applies for the alternative $\eta_1 < \eta_0$. For the two-sided test, the analog of (2.10.15) is

$$\pi(\eta_1) = \Phi\left(u_{\alpha/2} - \frac{\eta_1 - \eta_0}{1/\sqrt{n}}\right) + \Phi\left(u_{\alpha/2} + \frac{\eta_1 - \eta_0}{1/\sqrt{n}}\right). \qquad (4.4)$$

For calculating necessary sample sizes, for the one-sided test the analog of (2.7.18) is

$$n = (u_{1-\beta} + u_{1-\alpha})^2 \left(\frac{1}{\eta_1 - \eta_0}\right)^2, \qquad (4.5)$$

and for the two-sided test, the analog of (2.10.19) is

$$n \simeq (u_{1-\beta} + u_{1-\alpha/2})^2 \left(\frac{1}{\eta_1 - \eta_0}\right)^2. \qquad (4.6)$$

148 BINOMIAL, HYPERGEOMETRIC, AND POISSON DISTRIBUTIONS   CHAP. 3

For example, if we wish to have a power $1 - \beta$ of 0.95 of rejecting the null hypothesis $\theta_0 = 0.05$ at the level of significance $\alpha = 0.01$, making a one-sided test, when actually θ is $\theta_1 = 0.10$, we use (4.5) with $u_{1-\beta} = u_{0.95} = 1.645$, $u_{1-\alpha} = u_{0.99} = 2.326$, $\eta_0 = 2 \arcsin \sqrt{0.05} = 0.4510$, $\eta_1 = 2 \arcsin \sqrt{0.10} = 0.6435$; then

$$n = \frac{(1.645 + 2.326)^2}{(0.6435 - 0.4510)^2} = 425, \qquad (4.7)$$

which can be compared with the result $n = 400$ obtained for the same problem with the normal approximation in (2.23). Both of these are approximations; there is no obvious reason to prefer one to the other. An exact calculation would be difficult and not worth the trouble.

3.5. Confidence Limits for the Parameter of a Binomial Distribution

Suppose that in a sample of n light bulbs from a very large (infinite) lot we find x defective. The maximum likelihood estimator of θ is x/n. We wish to place confidence limits on θ. This problem was discussed in Section 2.17 and it remains to solve (2.17.5) for $\bar{\theta}$ and (2.17.6) for $\underline{\theta}$ for chosen values of P_1 and P_2 for observed values of x and n.

For moderately small n (i.e., $n < 100$), with some trouble in interpolation we can use the tables [1–4]. Alternatively, we can use the relationship, proved, e.g., in Section 21.3 of [7],

$$\sum_{v=0}^{x} \binom{n}{v} \theta^v (1-\theta)^{n-v} = 1 - \Pr\left\{F(f_1, f_2) < \frac{n-x}{x+1} \frac{\theta}{1-\theta}\right\}, \qquad (5.1)$$

where F is a random variable with the variance ratio distribution. The distribution will be discussed in Section 9.3; it is a function of two parameters known as the "degrees of freedom" (f_1, f_2) and is tabulated for a number of upper percentage points in Table IV. In (5.1) the variance ratio F has degrees of freedom $f_1 = 2(x+1)$, $f_2 = 2(n-x)$. In Section 9.3 we will see that we can obtain lower percentage points from the relation

$$F_\alpha(v_1, v_2) = \frac{1}{F_{1-\alpha}(v_2, v_1)}. \qquad (5.2)$$

For example, the 0.05 point of F with degrees of freedom 60 and 120 is

$$F_{0.05}(60, 120) = \frac{1}{F_{1-0.05}(120, 60)} = \frac{1}{1.47} = 0.680. \qquad (5.3)$$

SECT. 3.5   LIMITS FOR PARAMETER OF A BINOMIAL DISTRIBUTION   149

We can use (5.1) for (2.17.5):

$$1 - \Pr\left\{F(2(x+1), 2(n-x)) < \frac{n-x}{x+1}\frac{\bar{\theta}}{1-\bar{\theta}}\right\} = P_1, \quad (5.4)$$

so

$$\Pr\left\{F(2(x+1), 2(n-x)) < \frac{n-x}{x+1}\frac{\bar{\theta}}{1-\bar{\theta}}\right\} = 1 - P_1 \quad (5.5)$$

But the $1 - P_1$ point of F is F_{1-P_1}; i.e.,

$$\Pr\{F < F_{1-P_1}\} = 1 - P_1 \quad (5.6)$$

Thus

$$\frac{n-x}{x+1}\frac{\bar{\theta}}{1-\bar{\theta}} = F_{1-P_1}(2(x+1), 2(n-x)), \quad (5.7)$$

so solving for $\bar{\theta}$,

$$\bar{\theta} = \frac{(x+1)F_{1-P_1}(2(x+1), 2(n-x))}{n-x+(x+1)F_{1-P_1}(2(x+1), 2(n-x))}. \quad (5.8)$$

We can also use (5.1) for (2.17.7), noting that the summation in (2.17.7) is to $x-1$:

$$1 - \Pr\left\{F(2x, 2(n-x+1)) < \frac{n-x+1}{x}\frac{\underline{\theta}}{1-\underline{\theta}}\right\} = P_2. \quad (5.9)$$

By similar manipulations we obtain

$$\underline{\theta} = \frac{xF_{1-P_2}(2x, 2(n-x+1))}{n-x+1+xF_{1-P_2}(2x, 2(n-x+1))}. \quad (5.10)$$

However, when P_2 is, for example, 0.975, we cannot read $F_{1-0.975} = F_{0.025}$ directly from Table IV. We need to use (5.2) to substitute $1/F_{P_2}(2(n-x+1), 2x)$ for $F_{1-P_2}(2x, 2(n-x+1))$:

$$\underline{\theta} = \frac{x}{(n-x+1)F_{P_2}(2(n-x+1), 2x) + x}. \quad (5.11)$$

As an example, suppose that an automobile dealer observes that in a presumably random consignment of $n = 30$ automobiles $x = 8$ are characterized by inexcusably shoddy workmanship. For 95 per cent confidence limits we want $P_2 = 0.975$, $P_1 = 0.025$, $1 - P_1 = 0.975$. Then from Table IV

$$F_{1-P_1}(2(x+1), 2(n-x)) = F_{0.975}(2(8+1), 2(30-8))$$
$$= F_{0.975}(18, 44) = 2.07, \quad (5.12)$$

$$F_{P_2}(2(n-x+1), 2x) = F_{0.975}(2(30-8+1), 2 \times 8)$$
$$= F_{0.975}(46, 16) = 2.49, \quad (5.13)$$

150 BINOMIAL, HYPERGEOMETRIC, AND POISSON DISTRIBUTIONS CHAP. 3

giving from (5.8) and (5.11)

$$\bar{\theta} = \frac{(8+1) \times 2.07}{30 - 8 + (8+1) \times 2.07} = 0.459, \quad (5.14)$$

$$\underline{\theta} = \frac{8}{(30 - 8 + 1) \times 2.49 + 8} = 0.123. \quad (5.15)$$

For large n what is known as the quadratic normal approximation can be used. For the lower confidence limit $\underline{\theta}$ we use (1.23) in (2.17.7) to give

$$\Phi\left(\frac{x - \tfrac{1}{2} - n\underline{\theta}}{\sqrt{n\underline{\theta}(1 - \underline{\theta})}}\right) = P_2, \quad (5.16)$$

whence

$$\frac{x - \tfrac{1}{2} - n\underline{\theta}}{\sqrt{n\underline{\theta}(1 - \underline{\theta})}} = u_{P_2}. \quad (5.17)$$

This gives a quadratic equation in $\underline{\theta}$, with the solution

$$\underline{\theta} = \frac{1}{n + u_{P_2}^2}\left\{x - \frac{1}{2} + \frac{u_{P_2}^2}{2} - u_{P_2}\left[\frac{(x - \tfrac{1}{2})(n - x + \tfrac{1}{2})}{n} + \frac{u_{P_2}^2}{4}\right]^{1/2}\right\}. \quad (5.18)$$

For the upper limit $\bar{\theta}$ we use (1.22) in (2.17.5) to give

$$\Phi\left(\frac{x + \tfrac{1}{2} - n\bar{\theta}}{\sqrt{n\bar{\theta}(1 - \bar{\theta})}}\right) = P_1, \quad (5.19)$$

which likewise leads to

$$\bar{\theta} = \frac{1}{n + u_{P_1}^2}\left\{x + \frac{1}{2} + \frac{u_{P_1}^2}{2} - u_{P_1}\left[\frac{(x + \tfrac{1}{2})(n - x - \tfrac{1}{2})}{n} + \frac{u_{P_1}^2}{4}\right]^{1/2}\right\}. \quad (5.20)$$

For the example of 8 poor automobiles in a consignment of 30 ($n = 30$, used for purposes of illustration, is rather small to justify using this approximation), straightforward substitution and the use of $P_2 = 0.975$, $P_1 = 0.025$ gives 95 per cent confidence limits of (0.130, 0.462), to be compared with the exact result (0.123, 0.459).

3.6. Comparison of Two Observed Frequencies with the Normal Approximation

Suppose that from two infinite populations with fractions defective θ_1 and θ_2 we draw samples of sizes n_1 and n_2 and observe n_{11} and n_{21} defectives respectively. The data are as in Table 3.1.

COMPARISON OF TWO OBSERVED FREQUENCIES

Table 3.1

	Defective	Nondefective	Totals
Population 1	n_{11}	n_{12}	$n_{1.}$
Population 2	n_{21}	n_{22}	$n_{2.}$
Totals	$n_{.1}$	$n_{.2}$	n

We suppose that the row totals (sample sizes) are fixed by the experimenter, but the column total $n_{.1}$, being the sum of two random variables n_{11} and n_{21}, is a random variable, and likewise $n_{.2}$. We wish to test the null hypothesis that $\theta_1 = \theta_2 = \theta$, say. Define

$$h_1 = \frac{n_{11}}{n_{1.}}, \quad h_2 = \frac{n_{21}}{n_{2.}}. \tag{6.1}$$

Under the null hypothesis,

$$E[h_1 - h_2] = E[h_1] - E[h_2] = \theta_1 - \theta_2 = 0, \tag{6.2}$$

$$V[h_1 - h_2] = V[h_1] + V[h_2] = \frac{\theta(1-\theta)}{n_{1.}} + \frac{\theta(1-\theta)}{n_{2.}}$$

$$= \theta(1-\theta)\left(\frac{1}{n_{1.}} + \frac{1}{n_{2.}}\right). \tag{6.3}$$

To estimate $V[h_1 - h_2]$ we need an estimate of

$$\theta(1-\theta) = \theta - \theta^2. \tag{6.4}$$

Under the null hypothesis that $\theta_1 = \theta_2 = \theta$ we can use the column totals as referring to a single sample of size n from a population with fraction defective θ. From (1.15.8), $n_{.1}/n$ is an unbiased estimator of θ, and from (1.17.9),

$$\frac{n_{.1}(n_{.1}-1)}{n(n-1)} \tag{6.5}$$

is an unbiased estimator of θ^2. Thus an unbiased estimator of $\theta(1-\theta)$ is

$$\frac{n_{.1}}{n} - \frac{n_{.1}(n_{.1}-1)}{n(n-1)} = \frac{n_{.1}n_{.2}}{n(n-1)}, \tag{6.6}$$

whence

$$\hat{V}[h_1 - h_2] = \frac{n_{.1}n_{.2}}{n(n-1)}\left(\frac{1}{n_{1.}} + \frac{1}{n_{2.}}\right)$$

$$= \frac{n_{.1}n_{.2}}{n(n-1)} \frac{(n_{2.} + n_{1.})}{n_{1.}n_{2.}}$$

$$= \frac{n_{.1}n_{.2}}{(n-1)n_{1.}n_{2.}}. \qquad (6.7)$$

Therefore, under the null hypothesis that $E[h_1] - E[h_2] = 0$,

$$\frac{h_1 - h_2}{\sqrt{\hat{V}[h_1 - h_2]}} = \frac{\dfrac{n_{11}}{n_{1.}} - \dfrac{n_{21}}{n_{2.}}}{\left[\dfrac{n_{.1}n_{.2}}{(n-1)n_{1.}n_{2.}}\right]^{1/2}} \qquad (6.8)$$

$$= \frac{n_{11} - \dfrac{n_{1.}n_{.1}}{n}}{\left[\dfrac{n_{1.}n_{.1}n_{2.}n_{.2}}{n^2(n-1)}\right]^{1/2}} \qquad (6.9)$$

is a unit deviate asymptotically normal. The form (6.9) will be discussed in Section 3.10. Empirical investigation seems to indicate that the approximation is improved by replacing the $n-1$ in (6.8) by n. The statistic can then be written in the form

$$\frac{h_1 - h_2}{\sqrt{h(1-h)(1/n_{1.} + 1/n_{2.})}} \qquad (6.10)$$

where $h = n_{.1}/n$. The approximation is also improved by introducing corrections for continuity. If the alternative hypothesis is that $\theta_1 > \theta_2$, then the P value is derived from

$$u_{1-P} = \frac{(h_1 - 1/2n_{1.}) - (h_2 + 1/2n_{2.})}{\sqrt{h(1-h)(1/n_{1.} + 1/n_{2.})}}. \qquad (6.11)$$

If the alternative hypothesis is $\theta_1 < \theta_2$, then the P value is derived from

$$u_P = \frac{(h_1 + 1/2n_{1.}) - (h_2 - 1/2n_{2.})}{\sqrt{h(1-h)(1/n_{1.} + 1/n_{2.})}}. \qquad (6.12)$$

For a two-sided test, if $h_1 > h_2$ we use (6.11) with u_{1-P} replaced by $u_{1-P/2}$, and if $h_1 < h_2$ we use (6.12) with u_P replaced by $u_{P/2}$.

A criterion for deciding whether the approximation of this section is satisfactory is to compute the quantities $n_{i.}n_{.j}/n$ for all four combinations

SECT. 3.6   COMPARISON OF TWO OBSERVED FREQUENCIES

of i and j. If in every instance this quantity is greater than 5, then the approximation is good. The figure 5 is perhaps rather conservative, and something of the order of 3.5 will be usually adequate. If this criterion is not satisfied, so we cannot use this normal approximation, then this situation can be handled with Fisher's exact test, described in Section 3.10.

As an example, Table 3.2 shows the number of cases with reactions observed on using two types of rubber tubing for injection of a certain substance. If we assume that patients were allocated at random to the two "treatments," rubber A and rubber B, any difference between the groups will be attributable to a difference between the rubbers. (On the

Table 3.2

Number of cases

Type of rubber	With reactions	Without reactions	Totals
A	27	13	40
B	5	10	15
Totals	32	23	55

other hand, if random allocation was not used, it will probably be impossible to conclude anything useful from the data. If there is a significant difference, we will not know to what it is due.) The smallest of the four quantities $n_i n_{.j}/n$ is $23 \times 15/55 = 6.27$. Since this is greater than 5, the normal approximation of this section will be satisfactory. We calculate $h = 32/55 = 0.5818$ and then compute, for a two-tailed test,

$$\frac{\left(\frac{27}{40} - \frac{1}{2 \times 40}\right) - \left(\frac{5}{15} + \frac{1}{2 \times 15}\right)}{\left[0.5818(1 - 0.5818)\left(\frac{1}{40} + \frac{1}{15}\right)\right]^{1/2}} = 1.981 = u_{1-P/2}, \qquad (6.13)$$

whence $P = 0.0476$. We would thus conclude at the 5 per cent level of significance that the two groups differed in their percentage reactions, presumably on account of the different rubber tubing.

For calculating powers and necessary sample sizes, the angular transformation is convenient: $y_1 = 2 \arcsin \sqrt{h_1}$, $y_2 = \arcsin \sqrt{h_2}$ have variances $1/n_1$, $1/n_2$, writing $n_1 = n_{1.}$, $n_2 = n_{2.}$, so $V[y_1 - y_2] = 1/n_1 + 1/n_2$. Let η_1, η_2 be equal to $2 \arcsin \sqrt{\theta_1}$, $2 \arcsin \sqrt{\theta_2}$ respectively. The power of a two-sided test is given by appropriate substitutions in (2.10.15):

$$\pi(\theta_1 - \theta_2) = \Phi\left(u_{\alpha/2} - \frac{\eta_1 - \eta_2}{\sqrt{1/n_1 + 1/n_2}}\right) + \Phi\left(u_{\alpha/2} + \frac{\eta_1 - \eta_2}{\sqrt{1/n_1 + 1/n_2}}\right), \tag{6.14}$$

and for a one-sided test against the alternative $\theta_1 > \theta_2$, (2.7.12) gives

$$\pi(\theta_1 - \theta_2) = \Phi\left(u_\alpha + \frac{\eta_1 - \eta_2}{\sqrt{1/n_1 + 1/n_2}}\right). \tag{6.15}$$

For calculating necessary sample sizes we need to make some assumption about the relative magnitudes of n_1 and n_2. It is easy to show that $n_1 + n_2$ for a specified power, etc., is a minimum when $n_1 = n_2 = m$, say, so that the standard deviation of $y_1 - y_2$ is $\sqrt{2/m}$. For the two-sided test, (2.10.19) gives

$$m = (u_{1-\beta} + u_{1-\alpha/2})^2 \frac{2}{(\eta_1 - \eta_2)^2}, \tag{6.16}$$

and for the one-sided test, (2.7.18) gives

$$m = (u_{1-\beta} + u_{1-\alpha})^2 \frac{2}{(\eta_1 - \eta_2)^2}. \tag{6.17}$$

For example, if we wish to have a power $1 - \beta$ of 0.95 of rejecting the null hypothesis $\theta_1 = \theta_2$ at the level of significance $\alpha = 0.01$, making a one-sided test, when in fact $\theta_1 = 0.10$, $\theta_2 = 0.05$, then

$$m = \frac{2(1.645 + 2.326)^2}{(0.6435 - 0.4510)^2} = 850. \tag{6.18}$$

Note that $m = 850$ implies that $n_1 = n_2 = 850$, i.e., we need 850 observations on each population, making a total of 1700 observations.

3.7. The Correlated Two × Two Table

The standard way of presenting the results of two sets of independent trials is a 2 × 2 table such as Table 3.1 and the null hypothesis that the proportions of "successes" is the same in each population can be tested by the methods of Section 3.6. However, there are some experimental situations which give rise to data which may also be put in a 2 × 2 table which cannot correctly be analyzed in that way.

If we were given Table 3.3 (from Mosteller [8]) and asked to test the null hypothesis that the probability of nausea was the same with either

THE CORRELATED TWO × TWO TABLE

Table 3.3

Drug	Nausea	No nausea	
A	18	82	100
B	10	90	100
Totals	28	172	200

Table 3.4

Patient	Drug A	Drug B
1	N	N
2	N	$\bar{N}$
3	$\bar{N}$	N
4	$\bar{N}$	$\bar{N}$
5		
.		
.		
.		
100		

drug, we might be tempted to proceed with the normal approximation for the comparison of two proportions, Section 3.6, without pausing to inquire how the data was obtained. A naïve interpretation of Table 3.3 would be that we took two samples each of 100 patients and gave one set of 100 drug A and the other set of 100 drug B. In actual fact, the data was obtained from just 100 patients, each of whom received both drugs, with results as sketched in Table 3.4, where N and $\bar{N}$ mean nausea and no nausea. Nine patients, like patient number 1, had nausea with both drugs; 9 patients like number 2 had nausea with drug A but not with drug B; only 1 patient, number 3, had nausea with drug B but not with A; and 81 patients like patient number 4 had no nausea with either drug. The data of Table 3.4 should therefore be summarized as in Table 3.5.

Table 3.5

		Drug A		
		N	$\bar{N}$	Totals
Drug B	N	9	1	10
	$\bar{N}$	9	81	90
Totals		18	82	100

Table 3.6

		Drug A		
		N	$\bar{N}$	Totals
Drug B	N	π_{11}	π_{12}	$\pi_{1.}$
	$\bar{N}$	π_{21}	π_{22}	$\pi_{2.}$
Totals		$\pi_{.1}$	$\pi_{.2}$	1

As can be seen from the column totals, there were 18 cases of nausea and 82 without nausea with drug A, which is how the first row of Table 3.3 was formed. Likewise the row totals, 10 and 90, are the figures for drug B in Table 3.3. The essential features of the original data in Table 3.4 have been lost in the summarization of Table 3.3 but have been retained in Table 3.5. Table 3.3 can be constructed from Table 3.5, but the reverse is not true.

Table 3.6 gives the population proportions corresponding to the observed frequencies of Table 3.5. We are interested in the difference $\pi_{1.} - \pi_{.1}$, which is

$$\pi_{1.} - \pi_{.1} = (\pi_{11} + \pi_{12}) - (\pi_{11} + \pi_{21}) = \pi_{12} - \pi_{21}. \quad (7.1)$$

Thus in Table 3.5, the 9 patients who had nausea with both drugs, and the 81 who had nausea with neither, tell us nothing about the difference between the drugs. All the information on this question is contained in the other diagonal, presented in Table 3.7. If there was no difference

Table 3.7. Patients Who Responded Differently to the Two Drugs

Favorably to A and unfavorably to B	1
Unfavorably to A and favorably to B	9
Total	10

between the drugs, we would expect these 10 patients to be split on the average 50:50 between the two categories in Table 3.7. The one-sided P value for the null hypothesis is thus given by the sum of the terms in the binomial tail:

$$\Pr\{X \leq x | n, \theta\} = \sum_{v=0}^{x} \binom{n}{v} \theta^v (1-\theta)^{n-v}. \quad (7.2)$$

With $\theta = 1/2$, $n = 10$, $x = 1$, we have

$$\Pr\{X \leq x | n, \theta\} = \sum_{v=0}^{x} \binom{n}{v} \theta^v (1-\theta)^{n-v}$$

$$= \sum_{v=0}^{1} \binom{10}{v} \left(\frac{1}{2}\right)^v \left(1-\frac{1}{2}\right)^{10-v} = \frac{1}{2^{10}} \left(\frac{10!}{0!\, 10!} + \frac{10!}{1!\, 9!}\right)$$

$$= 0.01074, \quad (7.3)$$

or with the normal approximation (1.22),

$$\Pr\{X \leq x\} = \Phi\left(\frac{x + 1/2 - n\theta}{\sqrt{n\theta(1-\theta)}}\right) = \Phi(-2.214) = P, \quad (7.4)$$

whence $P = 0.0134$. Of course, since $n\theta(1 - \theta) = 10 \times (1/2) \times (1/2) = 2.25$, which is less than 9, the use of the normal approximation cannot be justified in this instance.

For the generalization of this test to the case of k drugs, $k > 2$, see Section 7.10.

EXERCISES 3A

3A.1. For the approximation (1.2), calculate the ratio of the right-hand side to the left-hand side for $n = 4$ and for $n = 9$.

3A.2. The manager of a large automobile repair shop suspects that in 6-cylinder engines, the valves of the front cylinder deteriorate faster than those of the other cylinders. Records are to be kept on 115 such jobs.

(a) If a test of the null hypothesis $\theta = 1/6$ is to be made at the level of significance $\alpha = 0.05$ against the alternative $\theta > 1/6$, what is the probability of the null hypothesis being rejected if in fact $\theta = 1/5$? Use both the methods of Sections 3.2 and 3.4.

(b) If instead of fixing the sample size at 115, the sample size is to be chosen so that the probability of rejecting the null hypothesis $\theta = 1/6$ when in fact $\theta = 1/5$ is 0.90, what should this sample size be? Use both the methods of Sections 3.2 and 3.4.

Suppose that the experiment is actually carried out and in 115 jobs 27 have the front cylinder in the worst condition.

(c) What is the P value of the null hypothesis that $\theta = 1/6$ (assuming that the alternative hypothsis is $\theta > 1/6$)?

(d) Give 95 per cent confidence limits for the proportion θ. Since the sample size is rather large, a normal approximation will be satisfactory.

3A.3. Fertilizer was stored in drums of a certain type. After a certain period, it was observed that in a sample of 63 drums 1 had split seams. Calculate 90 per cent confidence limits for the proportion of split drums in that population of drums (a) by a normal approximation (b) exactly.

3A.4. The Chevalier de Méré thought that it paid to bet evens on (i) getting one or more sixes in 4 throws of a die; but not on

(ii) getting one or more double sixes in 24 throws with a pair of dice. In point of fact, the true probabilities (assuming fair dice) for these events are 0.51775 and 0.49141 respectively.

Suppose that you are planning experiments to test empirically the null hypotheses

(a) that the probability of (i) is 0.5, against the alternative that it is 0.51775.

(b) that the probability of (i) is equal to the probability of (ii), against the alternative that they are 0.51775 and 0.49141 respectively.

Assuming one-sided tests of significance with $\alpha = 0.05$, in each case, (a) and (b), how many observations should be taken to give probability 0.9 of rejecting the null hypothesis?

3A.5. Suppose that you are planning a clinical trial for a proposed vaccine against a disease which has a low and variable incidence from year to year. Therefore it is necessary to run a control group. Suppose that the average incidence for a season is 1 per 50,000. Suppose that you wish the trial to have a probability of 0.99 of rejecting the null hypothesis that the vaccine is without effect if in fact the vaccine reduces the incidence by one-half. Suppose that a level of significance 0.01 is to be used, and only a one-sided alternative is to be considered. Assuming that the two groups will be made the same size, what is the total number of subjects required?

(Note that for very small values of x, $\sin x \simeq x$ and $\arcsin x \simeq x$.)

3A.6. In an experiment to test whether seeding clouds of a certain type causes them to produce radar echoes corresponding to the occurrence of rain (R. R. Braham, L. J. Battan, and H. R. Byers, "Artificial Nucleation of Cumulus Clouds," *Report* No. 24, Cloud Physics Project, University of Chicago), on each suitable day a plane flew through two clouds that met certain criteria and one of the pair, chosen at random, was seeded and the other not. For 46 flights, echoes occurred in both clouds 5 times, in the unseeded cloud only 6 times, in the seeded cloud only 17 times, and in neither cloud 18 times. Find the one-sided P value for the null hypothesis that seeding is without effect.

3.8. The Hypergeometric Distribution

Suppose that from a population of N elements, of which M are defective and $N - M$ are nondefective, we draw a sample of size n, without replacement. What is the probability that our sample contains exactly x defectives, $p\{x\}$?

The following equations are evident:

$$\Pr\{\text{first is defective}\} = \frac{M}{N}, \tag{8.1}$$

$$\Pr\{\text{second is defective} \mid \text{first is defective}\} = \frac{M-1}{N-1}, \tag{8.2}$$

$\vdots$

$\Pr\{x\text{th is defective} \mid \text{first, second}, \ldots, (x-1)\text{th are defective}\}$

$$= \frac{M - (x-1)}{N - (x-1)}, \tag{8.3}$$

$$\Pr\{(x+1)\text{th is nondefective} \mid \text{first } x \text{ were defective}\} = \frac{N-M}{N-x}, \tag{8.4}$$

$\Pr\{(x+2)\text{th is nondefective} \mid \text{first } x \text{ were defective and}$

$$\text{the } (x+1)\text{th was nondefective}\} = \frac{N-M-1}{N-x-1}, \tag{8.5}$$

$\vdots$

$\Pr\{[x + (n-x)]\text{th is a nondefective} \mid \text{first } x \text{ were defective}$
$\text{and } (x+1)\text{th}, \ldots, [x + (n-x-1)]\text{th were nondefective}\}$

$$= \frac{N - M - (n - x - 1)}{N - (x + n - x - 1)} = \frac{N - M - n + x + 1}{N - n + 1}. \tag{8.6}$$

SECT. 3.8   THE HYPERGEOMETRIC DISTRIBUTION

Thus the probability of drawing the sequence $D \cdots D \, \bar{D} \cdots \bar{D}$, in which D recurs n times and $\bar{D}$ recurs $n - x$ times, is the product of the probabilities (8.1), ..., (8.6):

$$\Pr\{D \cdots D \, \bar{D} \cdots \bar{D}\}$$

$$= \frac{M(M-1) \cdots (M-x+1) \times (N-M)(N-M-1) \cdots (N-M-n+x+1)}{N(N-1) \cdots (N-x+1) \times (N-x)(N-x-1) \cdots (N-n+1)} \quad (8.7)$$

If we multiply numerator and denominator by

$$(N-n)! \, (N-M-n+x)! \, (M-x)! \quad (8.8)$$

we obtain

$$\Pr\{D \cdots D \, \bar{D} \cdots \bar{D}\} = \frac{(N-n)! \, M! \, (N-M)!}{(M-x)! \, (N-M-n+x)! \, N!}. \quad (8.9)$$

This probability was derived for the specific sequence of x D's and $n - x$ $\bar{D}$'s, but will hold for any other sequence of the same numbers of D's and $\bar{D}$'s. By (1.7.7) the number of such sequences is $n!/x! \, (n-x)!$. Thus the probability of obtaining x D's and $n - x$ $\bar{D}$'s, the particular sequence not being specified and being regarded as irrelevant, is

$$p\{x\} = \frac{n!}{x! \, (n-x)!} \frac{(N-n)! \, M! \, (N-M)!}{(M-x)! \, (N-M-n+x)! \, N!} = \frac{\binom{M}{x}\binom{N-M}{n-x}}{\binom{N}{n}},$$

$$(8.10)$$

where there are certain restrictions on the variable x, namely

$$0 \leq x \leq n, \quad 0 \leq x \leq M, \quad 0 \leq n - x \leq N - M. \quad (8.11)$$

This result can be obtained more directly by the following argument. There are $\binom{N}{n}$ different ways, all assumed equally likely, in which to draw a sample of size n from a population of N elements. We want the number of ways which give samples with x defective elements. The x defective elements must have been drawn from the M defective elements in the population, and this can be done in $\binom{M}{x}$ ways. Likewise the $n - x$ nondefective elements must have been drawn from the $N - M$ nondefective elements in the population, and this can be done in $\binom{N-M}{n-x}$

160 BINOMIAL, HYPERGEOMETRIC, AND POISSON DISTRIBUTIONS CHAP. 3

ways. These two drawings are independent. Therefore there are $\binom{M}{x}\binom{N-M}{n-x}$ ways of drawing a sample of size n with x defectives. Thus $p\{x\}$, being the number of ways of drawing a sample of size n with x defectives divided by the total number of ways of drawing a sample of size n, is

$$\binom{M}{x}\binom{N-M}{n-x} \bigg/ \binom{N}{n},$$

which is the same result as (8.10).

The hypergeometric probability function (8.10) is tedious to handle numerically, except with the aid of a published table which goes up to $N \leq 100$ [9]. We might expect that in the limiting case in which the population size is large compared with the sample size it might be approximated by a binomial probability function, since in this case the distinction between sampling without replacement (hypergeometric) and with replacement (binomial) tends to zero. This we will now demonstrate. We write (8.10) in the form

$$p\{x\} = \frac{M!}{x!\,(M-x)!} \frac{(N-M)!}{(n-x)!\,(N-M-n+x)!} \frac{n!\,(N-n)!}{N!}$$

$$= \frac{M(M-1)\cdots(M-x+1)}{x!}$$

$$\times \frac{(N-M)(N-M-1)\cdots(N-M-n+x+1)}{(n-x)!}$$

$$\times \frac{n!}{N(N-1)\cdots(N-n+1)}$$

$$= \frac{n!}{x!\,(n-x)!}$$

$$\times \frac{M(M-1)\cdots(M-x+1)\times(N-M)(N-M-1)\cdots(N-M-n+x+1)}{N(N-1)\cdots(N-n+1)}. \quad (8.12)$$

Ignoring the first part of (8.12), $n!/x!\,(n-x)!$, the numerator is made up of two sequences of terms, the first sequence, $M(M-1)\cdots$, being x in number, and the second sequence, $(N-M)(N-M-1)\cdots$, being $n-x$ in number, so the total number of these terms is $x + (n-x) = n$. In the denominator, the sequence $N(N-1)\cdots$ is made up of n terms. Dividing both numerator and denominator by N^n, there will be one N

SECT. 3.8 THE HYPERGEOMETRIC DISTRIBUTION

for every term in the numerator and denominator. Denoting the proportion of defectives in the population, M/N, as θ, we get

$$p\{x\} = \frac{n!}{x!(n-x)!}$$

$$\times \frac{\theta\left(\theta - \frac{1}{N}\right)\cdots\left(\theta - \frac{x-1}{N}\right)(1-\theta)\left(1-\theta-\frac{1}{N}\right)\cdots\left(1-\theta-\frac{n-x-1}{N}\right)}{1\left(1-\frac{1}{N}\right)\cdots\left(1-\frac{n-1}{N}\right)}.$$

(8.13)

If now N tends to infinity with θ held constant, and n and x also fixed,

$$p\{x\} \simeq \binom{n}{x}\theta^x(1-\theta)^{n-x}, \qquad (8.14)$$

which is the usual binomial probability function. A rough criterion for the validity of the approximation is that $n/N < 0.1$; i.e., for the sample size to be less than 10 per cent of the population size.

As an illustration of the degree of approximation given in one case with $n/N = 0.1$, Table 3.8 gives the values of $p\{x\}$ for the hypergeometric probability function with $N = 1000$, $M = 20$, $n = 100$ along with the values of $p\{x\}$ for the binomial probability function with $\theta = M/N = 20/1000 = 0.02$, $n = 100$. The column for the binomial with $\theta = 0.01$, $n = 200$, and the column headed Poisson will be referred to in Section 3.11.

Table 3.8

x	Hypergeometric $N = 1000, M = 20, n = 100$	Binomial $\theta = 0.02, n = 100$	Binomial $\theta = 0.01, n = 200$	Poisson $\xi = 2$
0	0.1190	0.1326	0.1340	0.1353
1	0.2701	0.2707	0.2707	0.2707
2	0.2881	0.2734	0.2720	0.2707
3	0.1918	0.1823	0.1813	0.1804
4	0.0895	0.0902	0.0902	0.0902
5	0.0311	0.0353	0.0357	0.0361
6	0.0083	0.0114	0.0117	0.0120
7	0.0018	0.0031	0.0033	0.0034
8	0.0003	0.0007	0.0008	0.0009
9	0.0000	0.0002	0.0001	0.0002
10	0.0000	0.0000	0.0000	0.0000
.				
.				
.				
100	0.0000	0.0000	0.0000	0.0000

3.9. An Application of the Hypergeometric Distribution to Wild Life Population Estimation

Suppose that we have an enclosed lake containing N fish. We wish to estimate N. We take a sample of size M and mark the fish and return them to the lake. We now have a population of size N containing M marked elements.

Suppose that there exists a period sufficiently long to allow adequate mixing but not so long that births and deaths will have appreciable effects on N and M. After such a period we take a second sample of size n and find x marked fish. The frequency function of x is, by (8.10),

$$p\{x\} = \binom{M}{x}\binom{N-M}{n-x} \bigg/ \binom{N}{n}. \tag{9.1}$$

We know M, n, and x. We may estimate N by the method of maximum likelihood; i.e., we find that N which maximizes $L = p\{x\}$. We regard $p\{x\}$ as a function of N, say $p_N\{x\}$, and consider the ratio $p_N\{x\}/p_{N-1}\{x\}$. Increasing N from M we find the largest value of N for which this ratio is greater than 1. Since each successive $p_N\{x\}$ in this sequence is larger than its immediate predecessor, the last in the sequence must give the maximum value for $L = p_N\{x\}$. The ratio

$$\frac{p_N\{x\}}{p_{N-1}\{x\}} = \frac{\binom{M}{x}\binom{N-M}{n-x}}{\binom{N}{n}} \cdot \frac{\binom{N-1}{n}}{\binom{M}{x}\binom{N-1-M}{n-x}}$$

$$= \frac{N^2 - MN - nN + nM}{N^2 - MN - nN + Nx}, \tag{9.2}$$

is greater than one for $nM > Nx$, so the maximum likelihood estimator $\hat{N}$ is the integer just less than nM/x.

If we take $\hat{N} = nM/x$, we might note that maximum likelihood estimators sometimes have disconcerting properties. Thus

$$E[\hat{N}] = E\left[\frac{nM}{x}\right] = nME\left[\frac{1}{x}\right] = nM \sum_{x=0}^{\min n, M} \frac{1}{x} \cdot \frac{\binom{M}{x}\binom{N-M}{n-x}}{\binom{N}{n}}. \tag{9.3}$$

Since the summation includes the term for $x = 0$, for which $1/x = \infty$,

SECT. 3.10   FISHER'S EXACT TEST FOR TWO × TWO TABLES

the expected value of $\hat{N}$ is ∞. However, the expected value of $1/\hat{N}$ is better behaved, being unbiased:

$$E\left[\frac{1}{\hat{N}}\right] = E\left[\frac{x}{nM}\right] = \frac{1}{nM} E[x] = \frac{1}{nM} \cdot \frac{nM}{N} = \frac{1}{N}, \qquad (9.4)$$

using the result of exercise (3B.2a).

For a detailed examination of these topics see Chapman [10].

3.10. Fisher's Exact Test for Two × Two Tables

In his *Design of Experiments* [11] Fisher discussed an experimental investigation of a lady's claim to be able to tell by taste whether the tea was added to the milk or the milk was added to the tea. In one form of such an experiment, four cups would be prepared by each method, making a total of eight cups, and presented to the lady for tasting. She would be informed that there were four of each. Each cup could then be categorized (A), according to how it was made, and (B), according to how the lady says it was made. The data from such an experiment could be represented generally as in Table 3.9.

Table 3.9

		Category B		
		B_1	B_2	Totals
Category A	A_1	n_{11}	n_{12}	$n_{1.}$
	A_2	n_{21}	n_{22}	$n_{2.}$
Totals		$n_{.1}$	$n_{.2}$	n

An important feature of Table 3.9 is that the row totals $n_{1.}$ and $n_{2.}$ were fixed by the experimenter, and also the column totals $n_{.1}$ and $n_{.2}$ are fixed, since presumably the lady, knowing that in fact there are precisely $n_{1.}$ cups with tea added to the milk, will adjust her judgements so that the sum of her n_{11} and n_{21}, equal to $n_{.1}$, equals the known number $n_{1.}$.

Fisher's example has, as stated above, the feature that $n_{.1} = n_{1.}$, and hence $n_{.2} = n_{2.}$, but this is special to his example. More generally, consider an urn containing n balls of which $n_{1.}$ are marked A_1 and $n_{2.}$ are marked A_2. Imagine that we have a row of n cells, $n_{.1}$ marked B_1 and $n_{.2}$ marked B_2. Then before the sampling starts $n_{1.}, n_{2.}, n_{.1}$, and $n_{.2}$ are all fixed, and there is no requirement that $n_{1.} = n_{.1}$. We now sample the balls one at a time, without replacement, placing them serially in the cells, till all the balls have been withdrawn. Let n_{ij} be the number of type A_i balls which were placed in type B_j cells. Then the results of this sampling experiment can be assembled as in Table 3.9.

Since all the marginal totals are fixed, knowing say n_{11} implies that we know all the other n_{ij}. The probability of obtaining a particular value of n_{11} can be calculated immediately from the hypergeometric probability function (8.10). We can suppose that we have a finite population of size $N = n$ in which $M = n_{1.}$ elements are defective. We take a sample of size $n = n_{.1}$, and in this sample we observe $x = n_{11}$ defectives. Then

$$N - M = n - n_{1.} = n_{2.}, \quad n - x = n_{.1} - n_{11} = n_{21}, \quad (10.1)$$

and (8.10) gives

$$p\{n_{11}\} = \frac{\binom{n_{1.}}{n_{11}}\binom{n_{2.}}{n_{21}}}{\binom{n}{n_{.1}}} = \frac{n_{1.}!\, n_{2.}!\, n_{.1}!\, n_{.2}!}{n_{11}!\, n_{12}!\, n_{21}!\, n_{22}!\, n!}. \quad (10.2)$$

This is the probability of obtaining precisely that value for n_{11}. For a test of significance, we want not only this probability but also the sum of the probabilities of the possible results more extreme in the same direction; i.e., we need to sum the tail of the distribution. For a long tail this calculation will be tedious, but it is some help to note that the factor

$$\frac{n_{1.}!\, n_{2.}!\, n_{.1}!\, n_{.2}!}{n!} = C, \quad \text{say}, \quad (10.3)$$

is common to all terms in the series.

The data of Table 3.2 will be used to illustrate the arithmetic, though it was not collected under the condition of both sets of marginal totals fixed which we have been supposing in this section. In Table 3.2 the row totals could have been fixed, but the column totals would be random variables and would therefore not be fixed. This point will be discussed further at the end of this Section. Table 3.10 contains the arithmetic. The logarithm of C, (10.3), is

$$\log \frac{40!\, 15!\, 32!\, 23!}{55!}$$

$$= 47.911645 + 12.116500 + 35.420172 + 22.412494 - 73.103681$$
$$= 44.757130. \quad (10.4)$$

In constructing the upper part of Table 3.10, in this instance the observed proportion of reactions with rubber B, 5/15, is less than 27/40, and so we

SECT. 3.10   FISHER'S EXACT TEST FOR TWO × TWO TABLES   165

write down all possible tables in which this proportion is smaller than 5/15, always subject to the restriction that the marginal totals are unchanged. When the entry in this cell has gone from 5 to 0, it can go no further. This gives the 2 × 2 tables across the upper part of Table 3.10. The sum of the probabilities in the last row is 0.02406. This is the P value for this tail. For a two-sided test, the usual procedure is to double it, setting 0.04812.

Table 3.10

Observed table and more extreme tables	27	13	28	12	29	11	30	10	31	9	32	8
	5	10	4	11	3	12	2	13	1	14	0	15
log n_{11}!	28.036983	29.484141	30.946539	32.423660	33.915022	35.420172
log n_{12}!	9.794280	8.680337	7.601156	6.559763	5.559763	4.605521
log n_{21}!	2.079181	1.380211	0.778151	0.301030	0.000000	0.000000
log n_{22}!	6.559763	7.601156	8.680337	9.794280	10.940408	12.116500
Sum	46.470207	47.145845	48.006183	49.078733	50.415193	52.142193
log C − sum	$\bar{2}$.286923	$\bar{3}$.611285	$\bar{4}$.750957	$\bar{5}$.678397	$\bar{6}$.341937	$\bar{8}$.614937
Probability	0.01936	0.00409	0.00056	0.00005	0.00000	0.00000

Calculation of P values by the Fisher exact test may be somewhat tedious, but tables have been prepared by Mainland [12] giving the probabilities of all possible samples for $n_1 = n_2 \leq 20$ and the probabilities of samples in the region of probabilities 0.005 and 0.025 for $n_1 < n_2 \leq 20$. Another set of tables by Finney [13] deals with all samples, equal and unequal, up to $n_1 = n_2 = 15$, and these were extended by Latsha [14] up to $n_1 = n_2 = 20$.

For large samples we can develop an approximate test. By exercise (3B.2) we know that

$$E[n_{11}] = \frac{n_{1.}n_{.1}}{n}, \qquad (10.5)$$

$$V[n_{11}] = \frac{n_{1.}n_{.1}n_{2.}n_{.2}}{n^2(n-1)}, \qquad (10.6)$$

so that under the null hypothesis of random sampling under the specified model we will have a unit deviate approximately normal:

$$u = \frac{n_{11} - E[n_{11}]}{\sqrt{V[n_{11}]}} = \frac{n_{11} - \dfrac{n_{1.}n_{.1}}{n}}{\left[\dfrac{n_{1.}n_{.1}n_{2.}n_{.2}}{n^2(n-1)}\right]^{1/2}}. \qquad (10.7)$$

It appears from empirical comparisons that the approximation is improved by replacing the $n-1$ in (10.7) by n, so we use

$$u = \frac{n_{11} - \dfrac{n_{1.}n_{.1}}{n}}{\left(\dfrac{n_{1.}n_{.1}n_{2.}n_{.2}}{n^3}\right)^{1/2}} \tag{10.8}$$

with a correction for continuity of $\pm 1/2$ with the sign chosen to reduce the absolute value of the numerator. An alternative form of the statistic (10.8) is

$$u = \frac{(n_{11}n_{22} - n_{12}n_{21})\sqrt{n}}{(n_{1.}n_{.1}n_{2.}n_{.2})^{1/2}} \tag{10.9}$$

which when corrected for continuity has its numerator written as

$$\left\{|n_{11}n_{22} - n_{21}n_{12}| - \frac{n}{2}\right\}\sqrt{n}. \tag{10.10}$$

For the data of Table 3.2, these statistics give a P value of 0.0476, to be compared with the exact value of 0.04812.

It will be noted that the statistic (10.7), developed for the 2×2 table with all margins fixed, is identical with the statistic (6.9), developed for the 2×2 table with one set of margins fixed. This suggests that the Fisher exact test can be used for the latter case when the sample sizes are too small to justify the normal approximation of Section 3.6. This in fact was shown to be the case by Tocher [15].

3.11. The Poisson Distribution

One approach to the Poisson distribution is to consider a limiting case of the binomial distribution. For the binomial, $E[x] \equiv \xi = n\theta$; we suppose that n tends to infinity and θ tends to zero in such a way that $n\theta = \xi$ remains a nonzero, noninfinite quantity. Then

$$p\{x\} = \binom{n}{x}\theta^x(1-\theta)^{n-x} = \frac{n!}{x!(n-x)!}\left(\frac{\xi}{n}\right)^x\left(1-\frac{\xi}{n}\right)^{n-x}$$

$$= \frac{n(n-1)\cdots(n-x+1)}{n^x}\frac{\xi^x}{x!}\left(1-\frac{\xi}{n}\right)^{n-x}$$

$$= \left[1\left(1-\frac{1}{n}\right)\cdots\left(1-\frac{x-1}{n}\right)\right]\cdot\left(1-\frac{\xi}{n}\right)^{-x}\frac{\xi^x}{x!}\left(1-\frac{\xi}{n}\right)^n. \tag{11.1}$$

SECT. 3.11   THE POISSON DISTRIBUTION

As n tends to infinity, all the terms in brackets tend to 1, and so does $(1 - \xi/n)^{-x}$, also the limit of $(1 - \xi/n)^n$ is known to be $e^{-\xi}$, so

$$p\{x\} \to \frac{\xi^x}{x!} e^{-\xi}, \quad x = 0, 1, \ldots, \quad (11.2)$$

and this is the frequency function of the Poisson distribution.

From the form of the above derivation, it is apparent that the Poisson distribution can be used as an approximation to the binomial for large n and small θ. Table 3.8 gives the values of $p\{x\}$ for the binomial with $\theta = 0.02$, $n = 100$ and $\theta = 0.01$, $n = 200$ and for the Poisson with $\xi = n\theta = 100 \times 0.02$. It will be noted that as n increases and θ decreases the Poisson probability function becomes a better approximation to the binomial.

The expectation of the Poisson distribution is easily found:

$$E[X] = \sum_{x=0}^{\infty} x p\{x\} = \sum_{x=0}^{\infty} x \cdot e^{-\xi} \cdot \frac{\xi^x}{x!}$$

$$= e^{-\xi}\left[0 \cdot \frac{\xi^0}{0!} + 1 \cdot \frac{\xi^1}{1!} + 2 \cdot \frac{\xi^2}{2!} + \cdots\right]$$

$$= e^{-\xi}\left[0 + \xi\left(1 + \frac{\xi^1}{1!} + \frac{\xi^2}{2!} + \cdots\right)\right] = e^{-\xi} \cdot \xi \cdot e^{\xi} = \xi \quad (11.3)$$

since

$$e^{\xi} = 1 + \frac{\xi^1}{1!} + \frac{\xi^2}{2!} + \cdots. \quad (11.4)$$

To find the variance we use (1.17.3) which requires finding

$$E[X(X-1)] = \sum_{x=0}^{\infty} x(x-1) e^{-\xi} \frac{\xi^x}{x!}$$

$$= \sum_{x=2}^{\infty} x(x-1) e^{-\xi} \frac{\xi^{x-2} \xi^2}{x(x-1)(x-2)!}$$

$$= \xi^2 \sum_{x=2}^{\infty} e^{-\xi} \frac{\xi^{x-2}}{(x-2)!} = \xi^2 \sum_{y=0}^{\infty} e^{-\xi} \frac{\xi^y}{y!}, \quad (11.5)$$

making the substitution $y = x - 2$ in the summation. Thus

$$E[X(X-1)] = \xi^2, \quad (11.6)$$

whence

$$V[X] = E[X(X-1)] - E[X](E[X] - 1)$$
$$= \xi^2 - \xi(\xi - 1) = \xi. \quad (11.7)$$

For a random sample of observations from a Poisson distribution, $x_1, \ldots, x_n$, the maximum likelihood estimator is found by maximizing the likelihood,

$$L = p\{x_1:\xi\} \cdots p\{x_n:\xi\}$$

$$= e^{-\xi} \cdot \frac{\xi^{x_1}}{x_1!} \cdots e^{-\xi} \cdot \frac{\xi^{x_n}}{x_n!} = e^{-n\xi} \cdot \frac{\xi^{\sum_{i}^{n} x_i}}{\prod_{i}^{n} x_i!}, \qquad (11.8)$$

or equivalently, maximizing the logarithm of the likelihood,

$$\log L = -n\xi + \left(\sum_{i}^{n} x_i\right) \log \xi - \log \left(\prod_{i}^{n} x_i!\right). \qquad (11.9)$$

To maximize, we differentiate with respect to ξ and equate to zero:

$$\frac{d \log L}{d\xi} = -n + \left(\sum_{i}^{n} x_i\right) \cdot \frac{1}{\xi} = 0 \qquad (11.10)$$

whence

$$\hat{\xi} = \frac{\sum_{i}^{n} x_i}{n} = \bar{x}. \qquad (11.11)$$

As an example of data with a distribution closely represented by the Poisson frequency function, R. D. Clarke [16] gave the numbers of flying bombs falling into areas of 0.25 sq. km in London over a certain period. There were 576 such areas; 229 received zero bombs, 211 received one bomb, etc. (Table 3.11); i.e., $x = 0$ on 229 occasions, $x = 1$ on 211 occasions, etc. No areas received more than seven bombs. Let n_x be the number of areas which received x bombs: $\sum_{x=0}^{\infty} n_x = n$. From (11.11) the maximum likelihood estimator of ξ is

$$\hat{\xi} = \frac{\sum_{i=1}^{n} x_i}{n} = \frac{\sum_{x=0}^{\infty} n_x x}{\sum_{x=0}^{\infty} n_x}$$

$$= \frac{229 \times 0 + 211 \times 1 + 93 \times 2 + 35 \times 3 + 7 \times 4 + 0 \times 5 + 0 \times 6 + 1 \times 7}{576} \qquad (11.12)$$

$$= \frac{537}{576} = 0.932292.$$

SECT. 3.12   DERIVATION OF THE POISSON DISTRIBUTION

Inserting $\hat{\xi}$ in place of ξ in (11.2) we get the estimated probability that a random area will have a particular value of x. Multiplying $p\{x\}$ by n gives the expected number of areas with particular values of x. For example,

$$p\{0\} = \frac{(0.932292)^0}{0!} e^{-0.932292} = 0.393650, \qquad (11.13)$$

and $np\{0\} = 226.742$. The agreement of n_x with $np\{x\}$ seems satisfactory. The last two columns of Table 3.11 are required for a method of testing that the n_x are consistent with the hypothesis that their expected values are the values $np\{x\}$ derived under the assumption that x is Poisson distributed, to be discussed in Section 5.2.

Table 3.11

x	n_x	$p\{x\}$	$np\{x\}$	d_i	d^2/e_i
0	229	0.393650	226.742	2.258	0.0225
1	211	0.366997	211.390	−0.390	0.0007
2	93	0.171074	98.539	−5.539	0.3114
3	35	0.053164	30.622	4.378	0.6259
4	7	0.012391	7.137	−0.706	0.0698
5	0	0.002310	1.331		
6	0	0.000359	0.207		
7	1	0.000048	0.028		
8	0	0.000006	0.003		
Totals	576	0.999999	575.999	0.001	1.0303

3.12. An Alternative Derivation of the Poisson Distribution

While the derivation of the density function of the Poisson distribution (11.2) as a limiting case of the binomial is simple, we may obtain more insight into its meaning and range of applicability from an alternative approach.

Let the probability of an event occurring in a time interval $(t, t + dt)$ be $\xi\, dt$, where ξ is a constant, and where the length of the time interval, dt, is so small that the probability of the event occurring more than once in this time interval is of a higher order of smallness than dt and may be neglected.

Let the probability that the event will occur x times in the interval $(0, t)$ be $p_x(t)$. With this notation $p_0(t + dt)$ is the probability that zero events will occur in the interval $(0, t + dt)$. To get zero events in this interval means that we must have zero events both in the interval $(0, t)$

and in the interval $(t, t + dt)$. The probability of the former is $p_0(t)$. The probability of the latter is $(1 - \xi\, dt)$. We assume that these probabilities are independent, so

$$p_0(t + dt) = p_0(t)(1 - \xi\, dt) = p_0(t) - \xi p_0(t)\, dt, \qquad (12.1)$$

whence

$$\frac{p_0(t + dt) - p_0(t)}{dt} = -\xi p_0(t). \qquad (12.2)$$

The limit of the left-hand side is just the derivative of $p_0(t)$ with respect to t, namely $dp_0(t)/dt$. We thus have a differential equation

$$\frac{dp_0(t)}{dt} = -\xi p_0(t), \qquad (12.3)$$

whose solution is

$$p_0(t) = e^{-\xi t}, \qquad (12.4)$$

since, as we can readily check,

$$\frac{dp_0(t)}{dt} = \frac{d}{dt}(e^{-\xi t}) = -\xi e^{-\xi t} = -\xi p_0(t). \qquad (12.5)$$

The constant of integration in (12.3) is 0, since we must have $p_0(0) = 1$, and $e^{-\xi \cdot 0} = 1$.

Now consider $p_x(t + dt)$ when $x > 0$:

$$\begin{aligned}
p_x(t + dt) &= \Pr\{x \text{ events in interval } (0, t + dt)\} \\
&= \Pr\{x \text{ in interval } (0, t)\} \Pr\{0 \text{ in interval } (t, t + dt)\} \\
&\quad + \Pr\{x - 1 \text{ in interval } (0, t)\} \Pr\{1 \text{ in interval } (t, t + dt)\} \\
&= p_x(t) \cdot (1 - \xi\, dt) + p_{x-1}(t) \cdot \xi\, dt. \qquad (12.6)
\end{aligned}$$

Rearranging gives

$$\frac{p_x(t + dt) - p_x(t)}{dt} = -\xi p_x(t) + \xi p_{x-1}(t). \qquad (12.7)$$

The limit of the left-hand side is the derivative of $p_x(t)$ with respect to t, so we have the differential equation

$$\frac{dp_x(t)}{dt} = -\xi p_x(t) + \xi p_{x-1}(t). \qquad (12.8)$$

A solution is

$$p_x(t) = \frac{(\xi t)^x}{x!} e^{-\xi t}, \qquad (12.9)$$

SECT. 3.12 DERIVATION OF THE POISSON DISTRIBUTION

as is easily checked, since

$$\frac{dp_x(t)}{dt} = \frac{\xi^x x t^{x-1}}{x!} e^{-\xi t} + \frac{(\xi t)^x}{x!}(-\xi)e^{-\xi t}$$

$$= \xi \cdot \frac{(\xi t)^{x-1}}{(x-1)!} e^{-\xi t} - \xi \cdot \frac{(\xi t)^x}{x!} e^{-\xi t}$$

$$= \xi p_{x-1}(t) - \xi p_x(t). \tag{12.10}$$

Thus (12.9) does satisfy (12.8). Therefore the distribution of the number of events in the time interval $(0, t)$ is given by (12.9), which is a Poisson distribution with parameter ξt. There is nothing special about the origin in the interval $(0, t)$, so (12.9) applies to any interval of length t.

From the present approach we see that if the probability of each radioactive atom in a mass disintegrating is a constant, then the number of atoms disintegrating in a time period t has the distribution (12.9). Similarly, if over a given part of the day the probability of a telephone call being received by a switchboard is constant, then the distribution of the number of calls per time interval is given by (12.9). The same would apply to the number of flaws per yard of insulated wire, the number of misprints per page, the number of blood cells on individual squares on a haemocytometer, etc.

The Poisson distribution, which is a discrete distribution, is closely related to the negative exponential distribution (1.12.4), $p\{x\} = \theta e^{-\theta x}$, $0 < x < \infty$, which is a continuous distribution. In the foregoing derivation of the Poisson we assumed that the probability of an event occurring in the interval $(t, t + dt)$ was $\xi\, dt$. The probability that the event occurs 0 times in the interval $(0, t)$ was then found to be $p_0(t) = e^{-\xi t}$, (12.4). We can write

Pr{interval between successive events $> t$}

$$= \text{Pr\{event occurs 0 times in interval } (0, t)\} = e^{-\xi t}. \tag{12.11}$$

Hence
$$\text{Pr\{interval between successive events} < t\} = 1 - e^{-\xi t}. \tag{12.12}$$

The left-hand side of this is in the form of a cumulative distribution function for a random variable T defined as the interval between successive events. By (1.11.6) the corresponding probability density function is obtained by differentiation with respect to t. Differentiating (12.12) we set

$$\frac{dP\{t\}}{dt} = p\{t\} = \xi e^{-\xi t} \tag{12.13}$$

which has the form of the negative exponential probability density function.

In other words, if the probability of an event in the time interval $(t, t + dt)$ is $\xi\, dt$, then the distribution of the number of events per interval of time t is Poisson of the form (12.9) and the distribution of time between successive events is negative exponential of the form (12.13).

3.13. Test of Hypotheses about the Poisson Distribution

To obtain sums of terms, $\sum_{v=0}^{n} p\{x\}$, of Poisson distributions we can use Molina's table [17]. Alternatively, we can use a relationship with the cumulative χ^2 distribution, tabulated in Table III. From (5.1) the cumulative sum of the terms of the binomial distribution is given exactly as

$$\Pr\{X \leq x\} = P\{x\} = 1 - \Pr\left\{F < \frac{n-x}{x+1}\cdot\frac{\theta}{1-\theta}\right\} \quad (13.1)$$

where the variance ratio F has degrees of freedom $2(x + 1)$ and $2(n - x)$. We have derived the Poisson distribution as the limiting case of the binomial with $\theta = \xi/n$ and $n \to \infty$. Taking these limits, for a Poisson variable,

$$P\{x\} = 1 - \Pr\left\{F < \frac{n-x}{n-\xi}\cdot\frac{\xi}{x+1}\right\} = 1 - \Pr\left\{F < \frac{\xi}{x+1}\right\}, \quad (13.2)$$

where the degrees of freedom are $f_1 = 2(x+1)$, $f_2 = \infty$. We will see in Section 9.3 that F with degrees of freedom f and ∞ is distributed as another quantity, χ^2 with f degrees of freedom, divided by f; i.e., $F(f, \infty) = \chi^2(f)/f$. Thus

$$P\{x\} = 1 - \Pr\left\{\frac{\chi^2}{2(x+1)} < \frac{\xi}{x+1}\right\} = 1 - \Pr\{\chi^2 < 2\xi\}, \quad (13.3)$$

where χ^2 has $2(x + 1)$ degrees of freedom. The χ^2 distribution is tabulated in Table III. For example, in the case of $\xi = 0.932292$, Table 4.4 gives the individual terms, so we find by summation $\Pr\{X \leq 3\} = 0.9848$. Using (13.3),

$$\Pr\{X \leq 3\} = 1 - \Pr\{\chi^2(8) < 2 \times 0.9323\}. \quad (13.4)$$

For 8 degrees of freedom, the 0.01 and 0.025 points of the χ^2 distribution are 1.65 and 2.18, so 1.86 must correspond to about the 0.015 point. Hence $\Pr\{X \leq 3\} \simeq 1 - 0.015 = 0.985$.

With such a simple formula as (13.3) for the cumulative Poisson distribution, there seems small practical need for approximations. However, substituting ξ for the expectation $n\theta$ and ξ for the variance $n\theta(1 - \theta)$ in (1.22) which is a good approximation to the cumulative binomial when

SECT. 3.14 CONFIDENCE LIMITS FOR A POISSON PARAMETER

$n\theta(1-\theta)$ is greater than 9, which corresponds in the Poisson case to $\xi > 9$, gives

$$P\{x\} \simeq \Phi\left(\frac{x+1/2-\xi}{\sqrt{\xi}}\right). \quad (13.5)$$

Another approximation is easily obtained. In (3.11) and following we saw that if the variance of a random variable was equal to the expected value, then the square root of the variable had a variance 1/4. Hence

$$P\{x\} \simeq \Phi\left(\frac{\sqrt{x+1/2}-\sqrt{\xi}}{\sqrt{1/4}}\right) = \Phi[2(\sqrt{x+1/2}-\sqrt{\xi})]. \quad (13.6)$$

To illustrate these formulas, suppose that we observe 4 telephone calls in an hour when we have the null hypothesis that the mean hourly rate is 8. Formulas (13.3), (13.5), and (13.6) give

$$\Pr\{X \le 4\} = 1 - \Pr\{\chi^2(10) < 16\} = 1 - 0.90 = 0.10, \quad (13.7)$$

$$\Pr\{X \le 4\} \simeq \Phi\left(\frac{4+1/2-8}{\sqrt{8}}\right) = \Phi(-1.238) = 0.109, \quad (13.8)$$

$$\Pr\{X \le 4\} \simeq \Phi[2(\sqrt{4+1/2}-\sqrt{8})] = \Phi(-1.414) = 0.079. \quad (13.9)$$

It is clear that $\xi = 8$ is still somewhat on the small side for the approximations to be accurate.

3.14. Confidence Limits for a Poisson Parameter

Equations (2.15.14) and (2.15.17) will give confidence limits for the population parameter for a Poisson distribution from an observation. Using (13.3), the upper confidence limit $\bar{\xi}$ is defined by the equation

$$\Pr\{X \le x | \xi = \bar{\xi}\} = P_1 = 1 - \Pr\{\chi^2(2(x+1)) < 2\bar{\xi}\}, \quad (14.1)$$

so

$$\Pr\{\chi^2(2(x+1)) < 2\bar{\xi}\} = 1 - P_1, \quad (14.2)$$

but in general

$$\Pr\{\chi^2(2(x+1)) < \chi^2_{1-P_1}(2(x+1))\} = 1 - P_1, \quad (14.3)$$

so

$$\bar{\xi} = \tfrac{1}{2}\chi^2_{1-P_1}(2(x+1)). \quad (14.4)$$

Likewise the lower confidence limit is defined by

$$\Pr\{X \le x - 1 | \xi = \underline{\xi}\} = P_2 = 1 - \Pr\{\chi^2(2x) < 2\underline{\xi}\}, \quad (14.5)$$

so

$$\Pr\{\chi^2(2x) < 2\underline{\xi}\} = 1 - P_2, \quad (14.6)$$

so
$$\xi = \frac{1}{2}\chi^2_{1-P_2}(2x). \qquad (14.7)$$

For example, if on an airplane coming off an assembly line we find one missing rivet, and if we can assume that the distribution of the number of missing rivets is Poisson, i.e., with constant probability and independent, then 99 per cent confidence limits for the average number of missing rivets per plane in the population of planes are

$$\xi = \frac{1}{2}\chi^2_{0.995}(2(1+1)) = \frac{14.9}{2} = 7.45,$$

$$\xi = \frac{1}{2}\chi^2_{0.005}(2\times 1) = \frac{0.010}{2} = 0.005.$$

3.15. Simple Sampling Inspection

Suppose that a *producer* is supplying to a *consumer* lots of N items. Each item can be inspected and the inspection will lead to the conclusion that the item is either good or defective. Suppose that the number of defective items in a lot is M, and define $\theta = M/N$ as the *fraction defective*. Suppose that the two parties agree that a sample of size n is to be taken, and if the number of defectives x is less than or equal to a specified integer c, then the lot is to be accepted; if $x > c$, the lot is to be rejected.

From the arguments of Section 3.8, we have

$$\Pr\{\text{lot is accepted}\} = \Pr\{x \leq c\}$$

$$= \sum_{x=0}^{c} \binom{M}{x}\binom{N-M}{n-x} \Big/ \binom{N}{n}. \qquad (15.1)$$

Under the usual industrial conditions, the lot size N is large and the sampling fraction n/N is small, say <0.1, so by the arguments that led to (8.14) we can use the binomial approximation to the hypergeometric distribution. Also, usually the sample size n is quite large and the fraction defective θ is quite small, $\theta < 0.1$, so we may use the Poisson approximation to the binomial to write the probability that the lot is accepted as a function of θ, say $A(\theta)$, as

$$A(\theta) = \Pr\{x \leq c\} \simeq \sum_{x=0}^{c} \binom{n}{x}\theta^x(1-\theta)^{n-x} \qquad (15.2)$$

$$\simeq \sum_{x=0}^{c} \frac{(n\theta)^x}{x!} e^{-n\theta}. \qquad (15.3)$$

SECT. 3.15 SIMPLE SAMPLING INSPECTION

For handling sums of Poisson distributions we can use Molina's table [17] or (13.3):

$$A(\theta) = \Pr\{x \le c\} = 1 - \Pr\{\chi^2 < 2n\theta\}, \qquad f = 2(c+1). \quad (15.4)$$

The graph of $A(\theta)$ against θ is known as the *operating characteristic* of the sampling plan defined by a specified n and c. For a fixed n and c, (15.4) shows that the probability of acceptance $A(\theta)$ equals 1 when $\theta = 0$ and tends towards zero as θ gets large. On what basis should we choose n and c?

The producer and consumer have differing requirements. The producer may demand that if the lot is relatively good, the probability of its being rejected should be low. Specifically, if $\theta = \theta_0$ where θ_0 is called the *acceptable quality level* (AQL) then the probability of the lot being rejected should be a small number α, where α is called the *producer's risk*. Thus the producer requires that $A(\theta_0) = 1 - \alpha$. The consumer may demand that if the lot is relatively bad, the probability of its being accepted should be low. Specifically, if $\theta = \theta_1$, where θ_1 is called the *lot tolerance per cent defective* (LTPD), then the probability of its being accepted is a small number β, where β is called the *consumer's risk*. Thus the consumer demands that $A(\theta_1) = \beta$. Using (15.4), the demands of the producer and the consumer can be written as

$$1 - \Pr\{\chi^2 < 2n\theta_0\} = 1 - \alpha, \quad (15.5)$$

$$1 - \Pr\{\chi^2 < 2n\theta_1\} = \beta, \quad (15.6)$$

where both the χ^2's have degrees of freedom $2(c+1)$. We readily obtain the two equivalent equations

$$2n\theta_0 = \chi^2_\alpha \quad (15.7)$$

$$2n\theta_1 = \chi^2_{1-\beta}. \quad (15.8)$$

We can solve for c by finding the smallest value of $2(c+1)$, the number of degrees of freedom of the χ^2's, which satisfies the inequality

$$\frac{\chi^2_{1-\beta}}{\chi^2_\alpha} \le \frac{\theta_1}{\theta_0}. \quad (15.9)$$

Having found c, n can then be determined from either (15.7) or (15.8). Thus the separate demands of the two parties, the producer and the consumer, can be satisfied simultaneously. The situation is shown in Figure 3.2. By a suitable choice of n and c, the operating characteristic curve can be made to pass through the points $(\theta_0, 1 - \alpha)$ and (θ_1, β), and of course it always passes through the point $(0, 1)$, since lots with 0 per cent defectives will be accepted with probability 1. Actually, because the distribution of x is discrete, in general an exact solution will be unobtainable, and we will have to settle for an actual α less than or equal to the desired value, and, likewise for β.

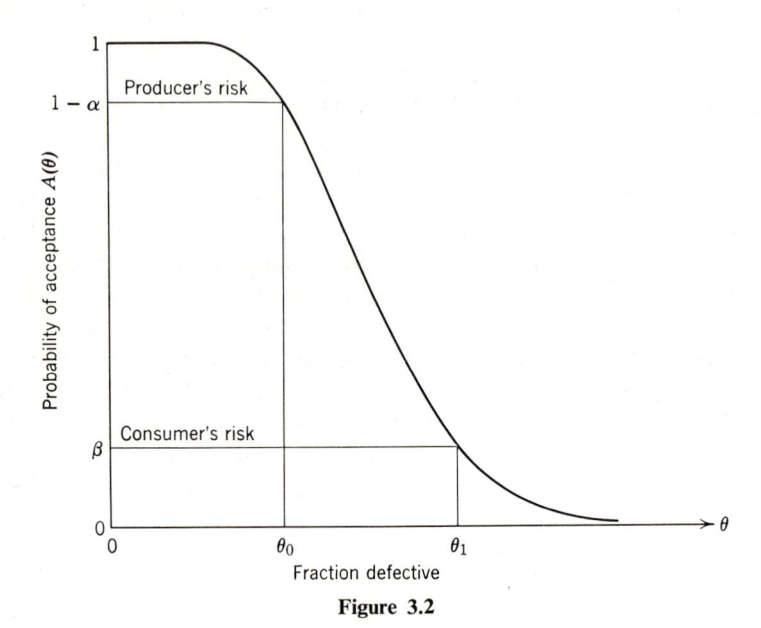

Figure 3.2

For example, if $\theta_0 = 0.03$, $\alpha = 0.05$, and $\theta_1 = 0.08$, $\beta = 0.10$, then we have

$$\frac{\chi^2_{0.90}}{\chi^2_{0.05}} = \frac{0.08}{0.03} = 2.67. \tag{15.10}$$

For 20 degrees of freedom, $\chi^2_{0.90}/\chi^2_{0.05} = 28.4/10.9 = 2.61$, and for 18 degrees of freedom $\chi^2_{0.90}/\chi^2_{0.05} = 26.0/9.39 = 2.77$. On account of the distribution of x being discrete, we cannot obtain an exact solution. We need to take the larger of the numbers of degrees of freedom, $20 = 2(c + 1)$, giving $c = 9$. From (15.8) we obtain

$$n = \frac{\chi^2_{0.90}(20)}{2 \times 0.08} = \frac{28.4}{0.16} = 177.5.$$

Thus if we take $c = 9$, $n = 178$ we will satisfy our requirements, in the sense that $\alpha \leq 0.05$, $\beta \leq 0.10$. Using (15.4), $A(\theta)$ can be calculated for a number of values of θ, and graphed as in Figure 3.3 to give the operating characteristic of this sampling plan.

SECT. 3.17   RECTIFYING INSPECTION   177

[Figure: OC curve showing Probability of acceptance, $A(\theta)$, vs. Fraction defective, θ]

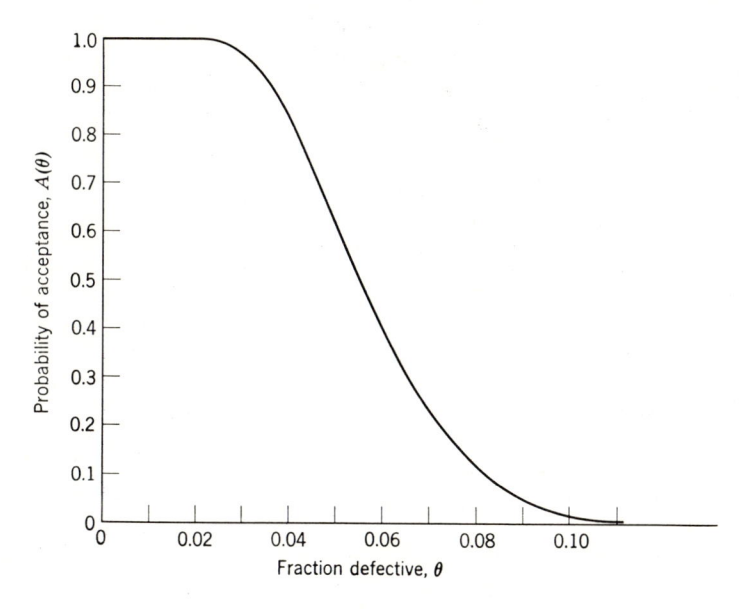

Figure 3.3

3.16. Relationship between Sampling Inspection and Hypothesis Testing

There is a one-to-one relationship between the terminologies of sampling inspection and the testing of a simple null hypothesis against a simple alternative, as summarized in Table 3.12. The parameters θ_0, θ_1, α, and β have closely analogous interpretations under the two situations. It is traditional, however, to plot the probability of *accepting* the lot as a function of θ to give the operating characteristic but to plot the probability of *rejecting* the null hypothesis as a function θ as the power function, so the operating characteristic and power function are complementary (for any specified θ, each is 1 minus the other).

3.17. Rectifying Inspection

The foregoing sampling scheme by itself affords inadequate protection for the consumer, for if the producer is permitted to resubmit rejected lots (possibly under new serial numbers, so that the consumer does not realize that these are lots which already have been rejected) even very bad lots will eventually be accepted. Also suppose that the producer is producing uniform lots with fraction defective θ, and disposing of the rejected lots through some other channel. Then, depending on θ and the operating characteristic of the sampling scheme, a fraction $A(\theta)$ of the lots will be accepted and $1 - A(\theta)$ of the lots will be rejected. However, the lots rejected will be identical in quality to the lots accepted.

Table 3.12

	Sampling inspection	Hypothesis testing
θ_0	Acceptable quality level (AQL)	Value of the parameter under H_0
θ_1	Lot tolerance per cent defective (LTPD)	Value of the parameter under H_1
decision	Accept lot	Accept null hypothesis that $\theta = \theta_0$
c	Acceptance number	Upper bound to region of acceptance
α	Producer's risk = Pr{lot being rejected$\|\theta = \theta_0$}	Level of significance = Pr{Type I error} = Pr{H_0:$\theta = \theta_0$ being rejected$\|\theta = \theta_0$}
β	Consumer's risk = Pr{lot being accepted$\|\theta = \theta_1$}	Pr{Type II error} = Pr{H_0:$\theta = \theta_0$ being accepted$\|\theta = \theta_1$}
	Operating characteristic = probability of acceptance as function of θ	1 − power function = 1 − probability of rejection of H_0 as function of θ

To guard against these possibilities, the producer may agree with the consumer that any lot rejected shall be inspected 100 per cent, item by item, and all items found defective replaced by good items. He may also agree to replace defective items found in the samples from lots which are accepted.

Suppose that the producer submits K lots, each lot of N items, and that the fraction defective in these lots is θ. The expected number of lots accepted is $KA(\theta)$. Assuming $N \gg n$, so that we can neglect the effect of replacement of defective items found in the samples, the expected number of defective items in these accepted lots is $N\theta KA(\theta)$. The expected number of lots rejected is $K[1 - A(\theta)]$, but these rejected lots are "rectified" and made 100 per cent good, so that (if the inspection is really 100 per cent efficient) they will contain 0 defectives.

The proportion of defectives in the K lots finally accepted, the so-called *average outgoing quality* (AOQ), is thus the total number of defectives

SECT. 3.17 RECTIFYING INSPECTION

in the lots accepted divided by the total number of items accepted:

$$\text{AOQ} = \frac{N\theta K A(\theta)}{NK} = \theta A(\theta). \tag{17.1}$$

From the operating characteristic curve we can readily compute the AOQ for any θ. For example, for $\theta = 0.04$, from Figure 3.3 we see that $A(0.04) = 0.82$, so the AOQ $= 0.04 \times 0.82 = 0.0328$. By allowing θ to

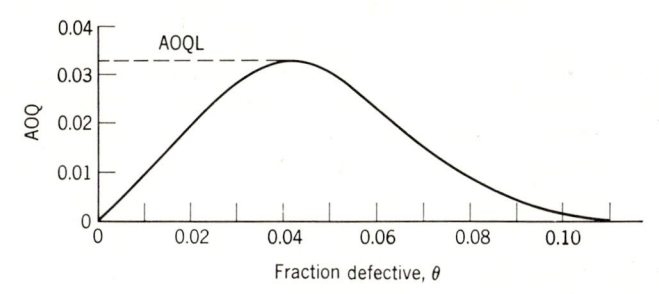

Figure 3.4

range over appropriate values, we can plot the AOQ as a function of θ, obtaining Figure 3.4. It will be seen that the AOQ has a maximum, close to 0.0328, known as the *average outgoing quality limit* (AOQL), which represents the worst average quality the consumer will find himself accepting under this rectifying scheme. Also, if $\theta = 0$, then there are no defective items submitted and so no defective items are accepted, and if θ is large then almost all the lots are inspected and made 100 per cent good, so the material finally delivered has a very low proportion of defectives.

Specifying n and c determines a sampling plan and its operating characteristic. For each plan we can compute the AOQ curve from the operating characteristic curve and hence determine the AOQL. In an extensive tabulation of plans, for example the Dodge-Romig tables [18], it will be found several pairs of values of (n, c) will give effectively identical AOQL's. If the AOQL is all that the consumer cares about, then he may be prepared to give the producer some leeway in the choice of sampling plan in order to minimize the total amount of sampling.

For example, the Dodge-Romig tables [18] give for large lots the following combinations of n and c for an AOQL of 3.0 per cent:

n	28	65	125	215	385	690
c	1	3	6	10	17	29

The operating characteristic curves for these plans are, of course, widely different. Suppose that the producer is submitting lots with a process average fraction defective θ. Then for the ith plan the fraction of lots accepted is $A_i(\theta)$; for these lots a sample of size n_i is inspected. A fraction $1 - A_i(\theta)$ of the lots is rejected and submitted to 100 per cent inspection; for these lots a "sample" of size N (i.e., the entire lot) is inspected. Thus the expected number of items inspected per lot, say a_i, is

$$a_i = nA_i(\theta) + N[1 - A_i(\theta)]. \tag{17.2}$$

For any specified θ, a_i can be determined, and it will be found that for one of the plans above a_i is a minimum. Appendix 6 of [18] shows that, e.g., if $\theta < 0.0006$, the plan with the smallest a_i is that with $n = 28$, $c = 1$; but if $\theta > 0.0241$, then the plan with the smallest a_i is that with $n = 690$, $c = 29$.

3.18. Double Sampling

It will usually be considered desirable to minimize as far as possible the amount of inspection. If the sample of size n is broken up into a first sample of size n_1 with x_1 defectives, and a second sample of size n_2 with x_2 defectives, $n_1 + n_2 = n$, if the lot is outstandingly good or outstandingly bad it may be possible to come to the decision to accept or reject solely on the basis of the first sample of size n_1. For lots of intermediate quality the second sample will be necessary for forming a decision. The Dodge-Romig tables [18] are for rectifying inspection and are set up as follows:

(a) If $x_1 \leq c_1$, accept the lot, and if $x_1 > c_2$, reject the lot.

(b) If $c_1 < x_1 \leq c_2$, take the second sample. If $x_1 + x_2 \leq c_2$ accept the lot, and if $x_1 + x_2 > c_2$, reject the lot (which implies 100 per cent inspection and rectification).

The Dodge-Romig tables [18] contain solutions for $n_1, n_2, c_1,$ and c_2 classified by the corresponding AOQL. These double sampling plans will typically decrease the total amount of inspection by at least 10 per cent, and in certain circumstances the reduction may be near 50 per cent. However, they are more troublesome to administer than a simple single sampling plan, and the increased efficiency may not be worth while.

The obvious extension of the idea of double sampling is sequential sampling (Wald [19]), in which items are taken one at a time and the decision to accept or reject the lot is made at each stage, on the basis of the cumulative record.

3.19. The Addition Theorem for the Poisson Distribution

Suppose that $X_1, \ldots, X_k$ are independently distributed according to the Poisson frequency function with parameters $\xi_1, \ldots, \xi_k$. Then $X = \sum_{i=1}^{k} X_i$ has the Poisson distribution with parameter $\sum_{i=1}^{k} \xi_i$. To prove this it will be sufficient to consider the case of $k = 2$.

The random variables X_1, X_2 take the values $0, 1, 2, \ldots$. We want the probability that their sum, $X_1 + X_2$, is equal to r. The probability that X_1 has the value s and X_2 the value $r - s$ is, since X_1, X_2 are independent,

$$\Pr\{X_1 = s\} \Pr\{X_2 = r - s\} = e^{-\xi_1} \frac{\xi_1^s}{s!} e^{-\xi_2} \frac{\xi_2^{r-s}}{(r-s)!} \qquad (19.1)$$

All values of s from 0 to r will give $X = X_1 + X_2 = r$, so the probability that $X = r$ is given by summing (19.1) over all permitted values of s, namely 0 to r:

$$\sum_{s=0}^{r} e^{-\xi_1} e^{-\xi_2} \frac{\xi_1^s \xi_2^{r-s}}{s!(r-s)!} = e^{-(\xi_1+\xi_2)} \sum_{s=0}^{r} \frac{\xi_1^s \xi_2^{r-s}}{s!(r-s)!}. \qquad (19.2)$$

To evaluate the summation in (19.2), consider the expansion of $(\xi_1 + \xi_2)^r$ by the binomial theorem [quoted in (1.9.4)]:

$$(\xi_1 + \xi_2)^r = \sum_{s=0}^{r} \binom{r}{s} \xi_1^s \xi_2^{r-s} = r! \sum_{s=0}^{r} \frac{\xi_1^s \xi_2^{r-s}}{s!(r-s)!}. \qquad (19.3)$$

Hence the summation in (19.2) is $(\xi_1 + \xi_2)^r / r!$, and

$$\Pr\{X = r\} = e^{-(\xi_1+\xi_2)} \frac{(\xi_1 + \xi_2)^r}{r!}, \qquad (19.4)$$

which is a Poisson frequency function with parameter $\xi_1 + \xi_2$. Thus the theorem is proved for the case of $k = 2$, and so it is obviously true for any k.

3.20. The Comparison of Two Poisson-Distributed Observations

Suppose we observe that in a certain yardage carpeting A has x_1 flaws and carpeting B has x_2 flaws. We wish to test the null hypothesis that the mean number of flaws per yard in the two populations of carpeting is the same, i.e., $H_0: \xi_1 = \xi_2 = \xi$, say. Under the null hypothesis X_1 and X_2 will both be approximately normally distributed independently with expectation ξ and variance ξ, so $X_1 - X_2$ will be approximately normally distributed with expectation zero and variance 2ξ. We can estimate 2ξ as $X_1 + X_2$. Thus under the null hypothesis $(X_1 - X_2)/\sqrt{X_1 + X_2}$ will be approximately a unit normal deviate. The approximation will be improved by introducing corrections for continuity analogous to those used in the two-sample binomial problem, (6.11). For a test against the alternative hypothesis $\xi_1 > \xi_2$ the null hypothesis is rejected if

$$\frac{(x_1 - 1/2) - (x_2 + 1/2)}{\sqrt{x_1 + x_2}} > u_{1-\alpha}. \tag{20.1}$$

An exact test can be constructed as follows. We identify E_1 with getting X_1 equal to x_1 and X_2 equal to x_2, and E_2 with getting $X_1 + X_2$ equal to $x_1 + x_2$. Then, under the null hypothesis,

$$\Pr\{E_1 \cap E_2\} = \Pr\{X_1 = x_1, X_2 = x_2 \text{ and } X_1 + X_2 = x_1 + x_2\}$$
$$= \Pr\{X_1 = x_1, X_2 = x_2\} = \Pr\{X_1 = x_1\} \Pr\{X_2 = x_2\}$$
$$= e^{-\xi} \frac{\xi^{x_1}}{x_1!} \cdot e^{-\xi} \frac{\xi^{x_2}}{x_2!} = e^{-2\xi} \frac{\xi^{x_1+x_2}}{x_1! \, x_2!}, \tag{20.2}$$

and, using (19.4),

$$\Pr\{E_2\} = \Pr\{X_1 + X_2 = x_1 + x_2\} = e^{-2\xi} \frac{(2\xi)^{x_1+x_2}}{(x_1 + x_2)!}. \tag{20.3}$$

Then by the formula for conditional probability, (1.4.3),

$$\Pr\{X_1 = x_1, X_2 = x_2 | X_1 + X_2 = x_1 + x_2\} = \frac{\Pr\{E_1 \cap E_2\}}{\Pr\{E_2\}}$$
$$= \frac{\xi^{x_1+x_2}(x_1 + x_2)!}{(2\xi)^{x_1+x_2} x_1! \, x_2!} = \binom{x_1 + x_2}{x_1}\left(\frac{1}{2}\right)^{x_1}\left(1 - \frac{1}{2}\right)^{(x_1+x_2)-x_1} \tag{20.4}$$

which is the $(x_1 + 1)$th term in the binomial expansion for $n = x_1 + x_2$, $\theta = 1/2$. Equation (20.4) gives the probability that $X_1 = x_1$, given that $X_1 + X_2 = x_1 + x_2$, and as in the Fisher exact test we also want the probabilities for all values of X_1 more extreme than the observed one, x_1. Thus if $x_1 > x_2$, we want the probabilities given by (20.4) for $X_1 = x_1 + 1$, $x_1 + 2, \ldots, x_1 + x_2$, the last being the maximum possible value for X_1 since it corresponds with $X_2 = 0$. The probability we want, the sum of these probabilities, is then

$$\Pr\{X_1 \geq x_1 | X_1 + X_2 = x_1 + x_2\}$$
$$= \sum_{\nu=x_1}^{x_1+x_2} \binom{x_1 + x_2}{\nu}\left(\frac{1}{2}\right)^{\nu}\left(1 - \frac{1}{2}\right)^{x_1+x_2-\nu} \tag{20.5}$$

We use (5.1) for the sum of the upper tail of a binomial with $\theta = 1/2$ so $\theta/(1 - \theta) = 1$:

$$\Pr\{X_1 \geq x_1 | X_1 + X_2 = x_1 + x_2\} = \Pr\left\{F < \frac{x_1 + x_2 - x_1 + 1}{x_1}\right\}$$

$$= \Pr\left\{F < \frac{x_2 + 1}{x_1}\right\}, \quad (20.6)$$

where the degrees of freedom for F are $2x_1$, $2(x_2 + 1)$. Our P value for a one-sided test against the alternative $\xi_1 > \xi_2$, is determined by

$$\Pr\left\{F(2x_1, 2(x_2 + 1)) < \frac{x_2 + 1}{x_1}\right\} = P \quad (20.7)$$

and, since $\Pr\{F < F_P\} = P$,

$$F_P(2x_1, 2(x_2 + 1)) = \frac{x_2 + 1}{x_1} \quad (20.8)$$

or

$$F_{1-P}(2(x_2 + 1), 2x_1) = \frac{x_1}{x_2 + 1}. \quad (20.9)$$

To revert to our initial example, suppose that the number of flaws in carpeting A is $X_1 = 9$ and in carpeting B is $X_2 = 2$. Then

$$F_{1-P}(2(2 + 1), 2 \times 9) = \frac{9}{2 + 1}$$

or $F_{1-P}(6, 18) = 3$. From Table IV, $F_{0.95}(6, 18) = 2.66$ and $F_{0.975}(6, 18) = 3.22$, so $1 - P \simeq 0.965$, and $P \simeq 0.035$. The normal approximation, (20.1), gives

$$\Phi\left[\frac{(9 - 1/2) - (2 + 1/2)}{\sqrt{9 + 2}}\right] = \Phi(1.81) = \Phi(u_{1-P})$$

so $1 - P = 0.965$ and $P = 0.035$.

3.21. The Comparison of Two Poisson-Distributed Observations with the Parameters in a Certain Hypothetical Ratio

Suppose that the probability of a breakdown on machine 1 in a time interval Δt is $\lambda_1 \Delta t$ and the probability of a breakdown on machine 2 in a time interval Δt is $\lambda_2 \Delta t$. Then the number of breakdowns of machine i in a time T_i has, by (12.9), a Poisson distribution with parameter $\lambda_i T_i \equiv \xi_i$, say. If $\lambda_1 = \lambda_2$, then $\xi_1/T_1 = \xi_2/T_2$, so $\xi_1/\xi_2 = T_1/T_2$. Thus a test of the null hypothesis $\lambda_1 = \lambda_2$ is equivalent to a test of the null hypothesis

184   BINOMIAL, HYPERGEOMETRIC, AND POISSON DISTRIBUTIONS   CHAP. 3

$\xi_1/\xi_2 = T_1/T_2$. The exact test of the previous section for the null hypothesis $\xi_1 = \xi_2$ can be extended to this new case. As before we identify E_1 with getting X_1 equal to x_1 and X_2 equal to x_2, and E_2 with getting $X_1 + X_2$ equal to $x_1 + x_2$. Then under the null hypothesis

$$\Pr\{E_1 \cap E_2\} = \Pr\{X_1 = x_1, X_2 = x_2 \text{ and } X_1 + X_2 = x_1 + x_2\}$$
$$= \Pr\{X_1 = x_1, X_2 = x_2\} = \Pr\{X_1 = x_1\} \Pr\{X_2 = x_2\}$$
$$= e^{-\xi_1} \frac{\xi_1^{x_1}}{x_1!} e^{-\xi_2} \frac{\xi_2^{x_2}}{x_2!} = e^{-(\xi_1+\xi_2)} \frac{\xi_1^{x_1} \xi_2^{x_2}}{x_1! \, x_2!}. \quad (21.1)$$

The sum of observations from two Poisson distributions has a Poisson distribution with parameter equal to the sum of the parameters of the two distributions, (19.4), so $X_1 + X_2$ has a Poisson distribution with parameter $\xi_1 + \xi_2$, and

$$\Pr\{E_2\} = \Pr\{X_1 + X_2 = x_1 + x_2\} = e^{-(\xi_1+\xi_2)} \frac{(\xi_1 + \xi_2)^{x_1+x_2}}{(x_1 + x_2)!}. \quad (21.2)$$

Then by the formula for conditional probability, (1.4.3),

$$\Pr\{X_1 = x_1, X_2 = x_2 | X_1 + X_2 = x_1 + x_2\} = \frac{\Pr\{E_1 \cap E_2\}}{\Pr\{E_2\}}$$

$$= \frac{(x_1 + x_2)! \, \xi_1^{x_1} \xi_2^{x_2}}{x_1! \, x_2! \, (\xi_1 + \xi_2)^{x_1+x_2}}$$

$$= \binom{x_1 + x_2}{x_1} \left(\frac{\xi_1}{\xi_1 + \xi_2}\right)^{x_1} \left(1 - \frac{\xi_1}{\xi_1 + \xi_2}\right)^{x_1+x_2-x_1}, \quad (21.3)$$

which is equal to the probability of x_1 successes in $x_1 + x_2$ binomial trials with $\theta = \xi_1/(\xi_1 + \xi_2)$.

We assume that the observed value of X_1 exceeds its expectation under the null hypothesis, i.e., that $x_1/T_1 > x_2/T_2$. We therefore need to sum the binomial series:

$$\Pr\{X_1 \geq x_1 | X_1 + X_2 = x_1 + x_2\}$$
$$= \sum_{v=x_1}^{x_1+x_2} \binom{x_1 + x_2}{v} \left(\frac{\xi_1}{\xi_1 + \xi_2}\right)^v \left(1 - \frac{\xi_1}{\xi_1 + \xi_2}\right)^{x_1+x_2-v}. \quad (21.4)$$

We use (5.1) for the sum of the upper tail of a binomial, where $\theta = \xi_1/(\xi_1 + \xi_2)$, so

$$\frac{\theta}{1-\theta} = \frac{\xi_1/(\xi_1 + \xi_2)}{\xi_2/(\xi_1 + \xi_2)} = \frac{\xi_1}{\xi_2}. \quad (21.5)$$

Thus

$$\Pr\{X_1 \geq x_1 | X_1 + X_2 = x_1 + x_2\} = \Pr\left\{F < \frac{x_1 + x_2 - x_1 + 1}{x_1} \frac{\xi_1}{\xi_2}\right\}$$

$$= \Pr\left\{F < \frac{x_2 + 1}{x_1} \frac{\xi_1}{\xi_2}\right\}, \quad (21.6)$$

where the degrees of freedom for F are $2x_1$, $2(x_2 + 1)$. Suppose that this probability is P. Then

and

$$\frac{x_2 + 1}{x_1} \frac{\xi_1}{\xi_2} = F_P(2x_1, 2(x_2 + 1)) = \frac{x_2 + 1}{x_1} \frac{T_1}{T_2} \quad (21.7)$$

$$\frac{x_1}{x_2 + 1} \frac{\xi_2}{\xi_1} = F_{1-P}(2(x_2 + 1), 2x_1) = \frac{x_1}{x_2 + 1} \frac{T_2}{T_1}. \quad (21.8)$$

3.22. An Application to Vaccine Testing

Suppose that we are testing lots of vaccine containing γ live particles per liter and we test a sample of Ω milliliters (ml) drawn from the well-stirred lot. Then on the average the sample will contain $\gamma\Omega/1000$ live particles: call this quantity ξ. Suppose that the test of the sample will find a live particle if it is present, and that if one or more live particles are found then the lot is rejected. The probability of rejection will be

$$\Pr\{x > 0\} = 1 - \Pr\{x = 0\} = 1 - e^{-\xi} \frac{\xi^x}{x!}\bigg|_{x=0} = 1 - e^{-\xi}.$$

Suppose that $\gamma = 5$ particles per liter and $\Omega = 60$ ml; then $\xi = 0.3$, and the probability of rejection is $(1 - e^{-0.3}) = 0.259$. Thus 25.9 per cent of such lots will be rejected.

Suppose that we wish to determine the size of sample that will accept only a fraction β of lots containing 5 live particles per liter; i.e., we require $\Pr\{x = 0\} = \beta$. But $\Pr\{x = 0\} = e^{-\xi}$, so $\xi = -\log_e \beta$. Suppose that we require $\beta = 0.05$; then $\log_e \beta = \log_e 5 - \log_e 100 = 1.60944 - 4.60517 = -2.99563$, from a table of natural logarithms, so $\xi = 2.99563$. Then $\Omega = \xi/\gamma = 2.99563/5 = 0.599$ liters $= 599$ ml.

EXERCISES 3B

3B.1. Interpret in words the conditions (8.11).

3B.2. Show that for the hypergeometric distribution (8.10)

(a) $E[x] = \dfrac{nM}{N}$, (b) $V[x] = \dfrac{nM}{N}\left(1 - \dfrac{M}{N}\right)\left(1 - \dfrac{n-1}{N-1}\right)$.

3B.3. You are dealt a hand of 13 cards from a well-shuffled bridge deck of 52 cards. What is the probability of receiving (a) exactly zero aces, (b) exactly two aces?

3B.4. Find an expression for the variance of the estimator $1/\hat{N} = x/nM$ discussed in Section 3.9.

3B.5. Fertilizer was stored in drums of two types. After a certain period it was observed that of 57 of the first type, 7 had split seams, and of 63 of the second type, 1 had split seams. Calculate the one-sided P value for the null hypothesis that the two types of drums do not differ in their liability to splitting (a) with the Fisher exact test, (b) with the normal approximation.

3B.6. A small car-hire company has two cars which it rents out by the day. Suppose that the number of demands for a car on each day is distributed as a Poisson distribution with mean 1.5. (a) On what proportion of days is neither car required? (b) On what proportion of days is the demand in excess of the company's capacity? (Note that $e^{-1.5} = 0.223$.)

3B.7. Suppose that a system involves n components in series, each of which must be operative for the system to function. Suppose that the probability of the ith component failing in the time interval $(t, t + dt)$, given that it has not already failed, is $\lambda_i\, dt$. What is the expected value of the length of time to failure of the system?

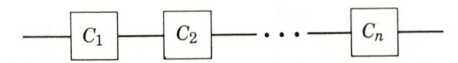

―□―□― · · · ―□―
   C_1 C_2 C_n

3B.8. (a) Suppose that a system requires a certain function to be performed at a certain stage, and that the component responsible for performing this function has probability of failure in the time interval $(t, t + dt)$ of $\lambda\, dt$. What is the expected value of the length of time before failure?

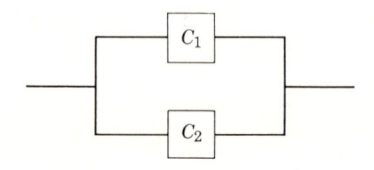

[diagram: two components C_1 and C_2 in parallel]

(b) Suppose that the component is duplicated, as in the sketch. Both components are operating, and the system functions if one or the other or both the components are functioning but fails if both components have failed. What is the expected value of the length of time before failure of the system?

(c) Do the same as in (b), but with n components in parallel, instead of two. If t is the time to failure of the system, show that

$$E[T] = \frac{1}{\lambda}\left[\binom{n}{1}\frac{1}{1} - \binom{n}{2}\frac{1}{2} + \cdots + (-1)^{n-1}\binom{n}{n}\frac{1}{n}\right].$$

Feller [6], Volume 1, p. 63, gives the identity

$$\binom{n}{1}\frac{1}{1} - \binom{n}{2}\frac{1}{2} + \cdots + (-1)^{n-1}\binom{n}{n}\frac{1}{n} = 1 + \frac{1}{2} + \frac{1}{3} + \cdots + \frac{1}{n}.$$

Prove this using Feller's hint of integrating the identity

$$\sum_{\nu=0}^{n-1}(1-t)^{\nu} = [1 - (1-t)^n]t^{-1}.$$

It follows that

$$E[T] = \frac{1}{\lambda}\left(1 + \frac{1}{2} + \frac{1}{3} + \cdots + \frac{1}{n}\right).$$

3B.9. (a) Do the same as in (3B.8b), but the system starts with C_1 only in operation, and C_1 has the property that when it fails it switches C_2 on. (b) As in (a), but with a total of n components functioning on a standby and takeover basis. Show that if t is the time to failure of the system the density function of t is

$$p_T\{t\} = \frac{\lambda^k}{(k-1)!} t^{k-1} e^{-\lambda t},$$

$$E[T] = \frac{k}{\lambda}.$$

3B.10. (a) Show that

$$\sum_{x=0}^{z}\binom{n}{x}\binom{m}{z-x} = \binom{m+n}{z}.$$

(b) Given that X is binomially distributed with parameters n, θ, and that Y is binomially distributed with parameters m, θ, show that $Z = X + Y$ is binomially distributed with parameters $(n + m, \theta)$.

3B.11. A company installed two compressors at the same time. These compressors are used continuously. By the end of a year one of them has had 13 breakdowns and the other 3. Can you say that the first compressor is significantly inferior to the second? Make both exact and approximate tests. Discuss the assumptions underlying your test.

3B.12. Suppose that the company in (3B.11) above is going to expand its plant and acquire more compressors of the second type. They would like to know within what limits the average number of breakdowns per compressor per year will lie, with 95 per cent confidence. Find these limits.

3B.13. W. Allen Wallis [20] found that for the 96-year period 1837–1932 there were 59 years in which no vacancies occurred in the U.S. Supreme Court, 27 years with 1 vacancy, 9 years with 2 vacancies, 1 year with 3 vacancies, and 0 years with more than 3 vacancies. (a) Calculate the expected numbers of 0, 1, 2, 3, and more than 3, vacancies on the assumption that the number of vacancies has a Poisson distribution. (If tables of natural logarithms or the exponential function are not readily available, note that if $z = e^y$, then $y = \log_e z = 2.3026 \log_{10} z$). (b) What is the probability that a President will serve out his (first) four-year term without being presented with the opportunity to make any appointments?

3B.14. A careful inspection shows 2 flaws in 1200 feet of Brand A magnetic tape and 10 flaws in 1800 feet of Brand B magnetic tape. Assuming that the probabilities of flaws in any length dx are $\xi_A\, dx$ and $\xi_B\, dx$, obtain exact bounds for the P value of the null hypothesis that $\xi_A = \xi_B$.

3B.15. You decide to replace the three 12AX7 tubes in the preamplifier of your hi-fi system. You purchase four such tubes from a retailer who has twelve of the tubes on his shelf, five of which are defective. What is the probability that you receive at least three good tubes, i.e., three or four good tubes. Reduce your answer to a simple numerical fraction.

3B.16. A consumer agrees to purchase large lots of items provided that samples of size n are to be taken from each lot and the lot will be accepted if the number of defectives $x \leq c$. The consumer requires that if the fraction defective in a lot is 4.5 per cent then that lot has a probability of 0.90 or more of being rejected. The producer requires that if the fraction defective in a lot is 2.25 per cent then that lot has a probability of 0.10 or less of being rejected. (*a*) What are the smallest c and n with the desired properties? (*b*) Suppose that the producer agrees to institute rectifying inspection. What is the worst possible average fraction defective that the consumer could find himself accepting?

3B.17. "(The committee) came up with 12 deaths from pulmonary embolism among 1.0 million Enovid users in 1962, compared with 203 deaths among the general population of 25.6 million women of child-bearing age, or a death rate of (7.9) per million," *Wall Street Journal*, September 18, 1963. Test the null hypothesis that the death rates among Enovid users and the general population are equal.

REFERENCES

1. National Bureau of Standards, *Table of the Binomial Probability Distribution*, Applied Mathematics Series 6 (1950).
2. Romig, Harry G., *50–100 Binomial Tables*. New York: John Wiley and Sons, 1953.
3. *Tables of the Cumulative Binomial Probabilities*. Ordnance Corps Pamphlet ORDP 20-1. U.S. Government Printing Office, 1952.
4. Staff of the Computation Laboratory, *Tables of the Cumulative Binomial Probability Distribution*. Cambridge: Harvard University Press, 1955.
5. Uspensky, J. V., *Introduction to Mathematical Probability*. New York: McGraw-Hill Book Co., 1937.
6. Feller, William, *An Introduction to Probability Theory and Its Applications*, Volume 1. 2nd ed. New York: John Wiley and Sons, 1957.
7. Hald, A., *Statistical Theory with Engineering Applications*. New York: John Wiley and Sons, 1952.
8. Mosteller, Frederick, "Some Statistical Problems in Measuring the Subjective Response to Drugs," *Biometrics*, 8 (1952), 220–26.
9. Lieberman, Gerald J., and Donald B. Owen, *Tables of the Hypergeometric Probability Distribution*. Stanford: Stanford University Press, 1961.
10. Chapman, Douglas G., "Some Properties of the Hypergeometric Distribution with Application to Zoological Sample Censuses," *University of California Publications in Statistics*, 1 (1951), 131–60.
11. Fisher, R. A., *The Design of Experiments*. 7th ed. Edinburgh: Oliver and Boyd, 1960.
12. Mainland, Donald, "Statistical Methods in Medical Research: I: Qualitative Statistics (Enumeration Data)," *Canadian Journal of Research*, E, 26 (1948), 1–166.
13. Finney, D. J., "The Fisher-Yates Test of Significance in 2×2 Contingency Tables," *Biometrika*, 35 (1948), 145–56.

14. Latscha, R., "Tests of Significance in a 2 × 2 Contingency Table: Extension of Finney's Table," *Biometrika*, 40 (1953), 74–86.
15. Tocher, K. D., "Extension of the Neyman-Pearson Theory of Tests to Discontinuous Variates," *Biometrika*, 37 (1950), 130–144.
16. Clarke, R. D., "An Application of the Poisson Distribution," *Journal of the Institute of Actuaries*, 72 (1946) p. 481.
17. Molina, E. C., *Poisson's Exponential Binomial Limit*. New York: Van Nostrand, 1942.
18. Dodge, Harold F., and Romig, Harry G., *Sampling Inspection Tables*. 2nd ed. New York: John Wiley and Sons, 1959.
19. Wald, A., *Sequential Analysis*. New York: John Wiley and Sons, 1947.
20. Wallis, W. Allen, "The Poisson Distribution and the Supreme Court," *Journal of the American Statistical Association*, 31 (1936), 376–80.

CHAPTER 4

An Introduction to Queuing Theory

4.1. Introduction

An important branch of probability theory deals with the behavior of queues. Customers waiting in a barber shop, airplanes waiting their turn for a runway at an airport, looms needing the attention of an operator in a spinning mill, are all examples of queues. Queues are classified according to:

(*a*) The time distribution of arrivals. Usually this is considered to be a Poisson process as discussed in Section 3.12.

(*b*) The distribution of service times. The assumption that this is exponential leads to the easiest mathematics, and in some instances, e.g., duration of calls from a telephone which is not a pay phone, reasonably realistic, but in other cases other distributions, which may lead to intractable mathematics, may be appropriate.

(*c*) The queue discipline. The simplest assumption is "first come, first served," i.e., the queue waits in line and the head of the line is the next to receive service. Sometimes, however, the service is at random. For example, the operator servicing looms can pick a loom at random from the group needing service rather than pick the one which has been waiting longest.

(*d*) The number of service channels. An airport with only one usable runway has only one channel; a barber shop with k barbers has k channels.

Queuing theory considers primarily such questions as the distribution of the length of the queue, the distribution of waiting times, and the number of customers lost because when they arrive they see that the queue is too long so they go away.

Historically, some of the earliest studies of these problems were in the context of a manual telephone exchange receiving calls from subscribers.

SECT. 4.2 SINGLE-CHANNEL, INFINITE, POISSON ARRIVAL

A. K. Erlang first published on this topic in 1909 and his most important paper appeared in 1917 (reprinted by Brockmeyer et al. [1]). The field was brought to the attention of modern statisticians by D. G. Kendall [2] in 1951; doubtless his interest was stimulated by the ubiquity of queues in all aspects of British existence in that grey and depressing era. For a monograph with many applications (and a bibliography of 910 items) see Saaty [3]. Other monographs are by Morse [4] and Takacs [5].

4.2. Single-Channel, Infinite, Poisson Arrival, Exponential Service Queues

In this section we consider the simplest case, in which the arrivals are Poisson with parameter λ, i.e., the probability of a new customer arriving in the interval $(t, t + \Delta t)$ is $\lambda \Delta t$, and there is a single server with service time having an exponential distribution with parameter μ. In other words, the probability of arriving in a time interval of length t is given by the Poisson frequency function with parameter λt, (3.12.9). The expected value for a variable with a Poisson distribution is equal to the parameter, (3.11.3). Thus the average number arriving per time t equals λt, and the average number arriving per unit time equals λ. Also, from (1.15.12), the expected value of an exponential distribution written as $p\{t\} = \mu e^{-\mu t}$ is $E[t] = 1/\mu$. Thus the average service time is $1/\mu$, so the average number which could be served per unit time is μ. Hence λ/μ is the ratio of arrival rate to potential service rate. In order to be able to reach a state of equilibrium it is necessary that $\lambda < \mu$, since otherwise the queue would grow indefinitely. We assume that there are no restrictions on the possible length of the queue, and that the queue discipline is "first come, first served." A customer is regarded as being a member of the queue until his waiting for service is completed; i.e., when receiving service he is still a member of the queue. Let n be the number of customers waiting in the queue at time t and $p_n(t)$ be the probability that at time t the queue contains n customers. For $n > 0$, and small Δt, we have

Pr{n customers in queue at $t + \Delta t$}
 = Pr{n customers in line at time t} Pr{0 customers arrive
   in $(t, t + \Delta t)$} Pr{0 customers discharged in $(t, t + \Delta t)$}
 + Pr{$n + 1$ customers in line at time t} Pr{0 customers arrive
   in $(t, t + \Delta t)$} Pr{1 customer discharged in $(t, t + \Delta t)$}
 + Pr{$n - 1$ customers in line at time t} Pr{1 customer arrives
   in $(t, t + \Delta t)$} Pr{0 customers discharged in $(t, t + \Delta t)$}
 + Pr{n customers in line at time t} Pr{1 customer arrives
   in $(t, t + \Delta t)$} Pr{1 customer discharged in $(t, t + \Delta t)$}. (2.1)

It is assumed, of course, that the probabilities are independent, e.g., that the probability of an arrival is independent of the probability of a customer being accepted. Thus (2.1) can be written as

$$p_n(t + \Delta t) = p_n(t)(1 - \lambda \Delta t)(1 - \mu \Delta t) + p_{n+1}(t)(1 - \lambda \Delta t)\mu \Delta t$$
$$+ p_{n-1}(t)\lambda \Delta t(1 - \mu \Delta t) + p_n(t)\lambda \Delta t \mu \Delta t \quad (2.2)$$
$$\simeq p_{n-1}(t)\lambda \Delta t + p_n(t)(1 - \lambda \Delta t - \mu \Delta t) + p_{n+1}(t)\mu \Delta t, \quad (2.3)$$

terms involving $(\Delta t)^2$ being neglected in (2.3). Equation (2.3) can be rearranged to give

$$\frac{p_n(t + \Delta t) - p_n(t)}{\Delta t} \simeq \lambda p_{n-1}(t) - (\lambda + \mu)p_n(t) + \mu p_{n+1}(t). \quad (2.4)$$

We now take the limit as Δt tends to zero:

$$\frac{dp_n(t)}{dt} = \lambda p_{n-1}(t) - (\lambda + \mu)p_n(t) + \mu p_{n+1}(t). \quad (2.5)$$

We now consider in exactly the same way Pr{0 customers in queue at $t + \Delta t$}, obtaining

$$p_0(t + \Delta t) = p_0(t)(1 - \lambda \Delta t) + p_1(t)(1 - \lambda \Delta t)\mu \Delta t, \quad (2.6)$$

$$\frac{p_0(t + \Delta t) - p_0(t)}{\Delta t} \simeq -\lambda p_0(t) + \mu p_1(t), \quad (2.7)$$

$$\frac{dp_0(t)}{dt} = -\lambda p_0(t) + \mu p_1(t). \quad (2.8)$$

We now assume that a stationary state is reached so that $p_n(t)$ is independent of t and can be denoted by p_n, i.e., we assume that $dp_n/dt = 0$ for $n = 0, 1, \ldots$. Equations (2.8) and (2.5) then become

$$-\lambda p_0 + \mu p_1 = 0 \quad \text{when } n = 0, \quad (2.9)$$
$$\lambda p_{n-1} - (\lambda + \mu)p_n + \mu p_{n+1} = 0 \quad \text{when } n > 0. \quad (2.10)$$

From (2.9),

$$p_1 = \frac{\lambda}{\mu} p_0. \quad (2.11)$$

From (2.10), with $n = 1$,

$$\lambda p_0 - (\lambda + \mu)p_1 + \mu p_2 = 0, \quad (2.12)$$

whence, solving for p_2 and substituting for p_1 from (2.11),

$$p_2 = \left(\frac{\lambda}{\mu}\right)^2 p_0. \quad (2.13)$$

SECT. 4.2   SINGLE-CHANNEL, INFINITE, POISSON ARRIVAL

Continuing for $n = 2, 3, \ldots$, it is apparent that

$$p_n = \left(\frac{\lambda}{\mu}\right)^n p_0. \tag{2.14}$$

Since the queue must be of some length,

$$\sum_{i=0}^{\infty} p_i = 1. \tag{2.15}$$

From (2.14)

$$\sum_{i=0}^{\infty} p_i = p_0 \sum_{i=0}^{\infty} \left(\frac{\lambda}{\mu}\right)^i. \tag{2.16}$$

If we assume that $\lambda/\mu < 1$, then the summation is the sum of an infinite geometric series, and so

$$\sum_{i=0}^{\infty} \left(\frac{\lambda}{\mu}\right)^i = \frac{1}{1 - \lambda/\mu}. \tag{2.17}$$

Substituting (2.17) and (2.15) in (2.16), we have

$$p_0 = 1 - \frac{\lambda}{\mu}, \tag{2.18}$$

and substituting this in (2.14) gives

$$p_n = \left(\frac{\lambda}{\mu}\right)^n \left(1 - \frac{\lambda}{\mu}\right). \tag{2.19}$$

Table 4.1 gives the first five terms of p_n for four values of λ/μ. The probability that a queue has more than 4 members is thus $1/1024 = 0.00098$ when $\lambda/\mu = 1/4$ and $525.22/1024 = 0.5129$ when $\lambda/\mu = 7/8$.

Table 4.1. $1024\, p_n$

n	λ/μ			
	1/4	1/2	3/4	7/8
0	768	512	256	128
1	192	256	192	112
2	48	128	144	98
3	12	64	108	85.75
4	3	32	81	75.03
≥5	1	32	243	525.22

The average value of the length of the queue is the simplest aspect of the distribution, though clearly not the entire story, for if two distributions had the same expected value, we would usually prefer the one which had fewer very large queues. The expected value of the length is

$$E[n] = \sum_{i=0}^{\infty} i p_i = \sum_{i=1}^{\infty} i \left(\frac{\lambda}{\mu}\right)^i \left(1 - \frac{\lambda}{\mu}\right)$$

$$= \left(1 - \frac{\lambda}{\mu}\right) \frac{\lambda}{\mu} \left[1 + 2\left(\frac{\lambda}{\mu}\right) + 3\left(\frac{\lambda}{\mu}\right)^2 + \cdots \right]. \quad (2.20)$$

We recall the formula for the sum of an infinite geometric series with $a < 1$:

$$1 + a + a^2 + a^3 + \cdots = \frac{1}{1-a}. \quad (2.21)$$

Differentiating both sides gives

$$1 + 2a + 3a^2 + \cdots = \frac{1}{(1-a)^2}. \quad (2.22)$$

Using this in (2.20) gives, for $\lambda/\mu < 1$,

$$E[n] = \left(1 - \frac{\lambda}{\mu}\right) \frac{\lambda}{\mu} \frac{1}{(1 - \lambda/\mu)^2} = \frac{\lambda/\mu}{1 - \lambda/\mu}. \quad (2.23)$$

As λ/μ approaches 1, the expected value of the queue length tends rapidly to infinity; for $\lambda/\mu = 1/2$, $E[n] = 1$, but for $\lambda/\mu = 15/16$, $E[n] = 15$.

A customer will be interested not only in the length of queue as measured by the number of customers in it, but also by the time waiting for service, say t_w. The average waiting for service time can be derived as follows. At any random instant the probability that the queue contains n customers is p_n, given by (2.19). The expected service time for each of these customers is $1/\mu$, since the service time has an exponential distribution with parameter μ. The expected total service time for these n customers will be n/μ. The expected waiting time $E[t_w]$ will be

$$E[t_w] = \sum_{n=0}^{\infty} (\text{probability of } n \text{ customers}) \times (\text{waiting time for } n \text{ customers})$$

$$= \sum_{n=0}^{\infty} p_n \left(\frac{n}{\mu}\right) = \sum_{n=0}^{\infty} \left(\frac{\lambda}{\mu}\right)^n \left(1 - \frac{\lambda}{\mu}\right) \frac{n}{\mu} = \frac{1}{\mu} \sum_{n=1}^{\infty} n \left(\frac{\lambda}{\mu}\right)^n \left(1 - \frac{\lambda}{\mu}\right). \quad (2.24)$$

Comparing the summation with (2.20), we see that

$$E[t_w] = \frac{1}{\mu} E[n] = \frac{1}{\mu} \frac{\lambda/\mu}{1 - \lambda/\mu} = \frac{\lambda}{\mu} \frac{1}{\mu - \lambda}. \quad (2.25)$$

If we add on the expected value of the service time for ourselves, $1/\mu$, we obtain for the expected value for the sum of time waiting for service plus time for service, say $E[t_q]$,

$$E[t_q] = \frac{\lambda}{\mu}\frac{1}{\mu - \lambda} + \frac{1}{\mu} = \frac{1}{\mu - \lambda}. \tag{2.26}$$

It will be noted that p_0, (2.18), is the fraction of the time there are no customers either waiting or being serviced and the service facility is being unused. It can be made close to zero by making λ/μ close to 1, but then the proportion of each customer's time that is wasted waiting in the queue rises drastically. This latter may be regarded as

$$\frac{E[t_w]}{E[t_q]} = \frac{\lambda}{\mu}. \tag{2.27}$$

Thus, for example, if λ/μ is 0.9, then 10 per cent of the server's time is wasted (resting!) but of the time each customer spends in the queue on the average 90 per cent is wasted (fuming!).

4.3. Queues with Arbitrary Service Time Distribution

In Section 4.2 we derived the distribution function of the length of a queue (2.19) where the distribution of service times was exponential, and from that we obtained the expected value of the length of the queue $E[n]$ (2.23) and the expected value of the waiting time $E[t_w]$ (2.25). In this section we relax the assumption about the form of the distribution of service time and merely suppose that it has an expected value $E[t_s] = \tau$ and variance σ^2. We will obtain formulas for $E[n]$ and $E[t_w]$. The general argument follows section 2 of Kendall's paper [2].

An essential concept in the argument is that at certain time instants, called by Kendall "points of regeneration," a knowledge of the state of the process at such an instant has the property that all relevant information is contained in that knowledge alone, and further knowledge of the past history is useless for predicting the future behavior of the process. For a Poisson process, all instants have this property and are thus points of regeneration. For a queuing process with Poisson input and arbitrary service time distribution, the instant at which service is completed on a customer is a point of regeneration. Also, all instants at which the queue is empty and no one is being serviced are points of regeneration.

Consider an instant at which customer C_i leaves. Let n be the size of the queue at this instant (n does not include the departing customer). Since on occasion the departing customer may leave the line empty, it is possible for n to equal zero. Let the next customer C_{i+1} to be served have service time t_s (t_s is a random variable with the service time distribution) and during this time suppose that r new customers arrive. Then, conditionally on the value of t_s, r is a Poisson variable with parameter $t_s\lambda$ and probability function analogous to (3.12.9). Using (3.11.3)

$$E[r] = t_s\lambda, \tag{3.1}$$

and from (3.11.6)

$$E[r(r-1)] = E[r^2] - E[r] = (t_s\lambda)^2, \tag{3.2}$$

whence it follows that

$$E[r^2] = (t_s\lambda)^2 + t_s\lambda. \tag{3.3}$$

Equations (3.1) and (3.3) are conditional on the particular value of t_s, and if we take expectations over time we obtain

$$E[r] = E[t_s\lambda] = \lambda\tau \tag{3.4}$$

and

$$E[r^2] = \lambda^2 E[t_s^2] + \lambda E[t_s]. \tag{3.5}$$

Now the variance of the service time distribution was defined as σ^2, so

$$\sigma^2 = V[t_s] = E[t_s^2] - (E[t_s])^2, \tag{3.6}$$

whence

$$E[t_s^2] = \sigma^2 + \tau^2; \tag{3.7}$$

and substituting in (3.5),

$$E[r^2] = \lambda^2(\sigma^2 + \tau^2) + \lambda\tau. \tag{3.8}$$

Now let n' be the length of the queue which customer C_{i+1} leaves behind him. We assume that statistical equilibrium will exist and therefore the marginal distributions of n and n' will be identical and in particular will have the same means and the same mean squares. We assume therefore that

$$E[n] = E[n'], \tag{3.9}$$

$$E[n^2] = E[n'^2]. \tag{3.10}$$

We now demonstrate that n and n' are related by the equation

$$n' = \max(n-1, 0) + r. \tag{3.11}$$

There are two cases to consider. First, when customer C_i leaves the queue length is zero; i.e., $n = 0$. Then we wait for the next customer C_{i+1} to arrive and eventually he does. He receives immediate service lasting a time t_s: in this time r further customers arrive and wait in line, so that in this case

$$n' = r. \tag{3.12}$$

Second, when customer C_i leaves the queue length is $n > 0$. Then the next in line moves into service immediately, leaving $n - 1$ waiting in line.

SECT. 4.3   QUEUES WITH ARBITRARY SERVICE TIME DISTRIBUTION   197

Customer C_{i+1} takes time t_s for service, in which time r customers arrive and add themselves to the line, so when C_{i+1} leaves the queue length is

$$n' = n - 1 + r. \tag{3.13}$$

It is easy to check that (3.12) and (3.13) can be written as (3.11).

We now define a variable d as a function of n, $\delta(n)$, with the properties

$$d = \delta(n) = 1 \quad \text{if } n = 0, \tag{3.14}$$
$$= 0 \quad \text{if } n > 0. \tag{3.15}$$

We can then write (3.11) as

$$n' = n - 1 + d + r. \tag{3.16}$$

It is easy to check that when $n = 0$, $d = 1$, and (3.16) gives $n' = r$ corresponding to (3.12), and that when $n > 0$, $d = 0$, and (3.16) gives $n' = n - 1 + r$ corresponding to (3.13). We note that in consequence of the definitions (3.14) and (3.15)

$$d^2 = d, \tag{3.17}$$
$$n(1 - d) = n, \tag{3.18}$$

as can be readily checked by considering the cases $n = 0, n > 0$. We now use the assumption (3.9) that $E[n] = E[n']$ and take expectations of (3.16) to get

$$E[d] = 1 - E[r] = 1 - \lambda\tau, \tag{3.19}$$

using (3.4) for $E[r]$.

We now square (3.16), $n' = n - (1 - d) + r$, to get

$$n'^2 = n^2 + 1 - 2d + d^2 + r^2 - 2n(1-d) + 2nr - 2(1-d)r, \tag{3.20}$$

and substitute from (3.17) for d^2 and from (3.18) for $n(1-d)$, to get

$$n'^2 - n^2 = 2n(r-1) + (r-1)^2 + d(2r-1). \tag{3.21}$$

We now take expectations and use the assumption (3.10) that $E[n^2] = E[n'^2]$ to get

$$2E[n(r-1)] + E[(r-1)^2] + E[d(2r-1)] = 0. \tag{3.22}$$

An essential part of the argument is that r is independent of n and d (d, of course, is a function of n): this permits us to write (3.22) as

$$2E[n]E[r-1] + E[(r-1)^2] + E[d]E[2r-1] = 0. \tag{3.23}$$

Solving for $E[n]$, this gives

$$E[n] = \frac{E[(r-1)^2] + E[d]E[2r-1]}{2E[1-r]}$$
$$= \frac{E[r^2] - 2E[r] + 1 + E[d]\{2E[r] - 1\}}{2(1 - E[r])}. \tag{3.24}$$

Substituting from (3.8) for $E[r^2]$, from (3.4) for $E[r]$, and from (3.19) for $E[d]$ gives

$$E[n] = \lambda\tau + \frac{\lambda^2\tau^2 + \lambda^2\sigma^2}{2(1 - \lambda\tau)}. \tag{3.25}$$

This equation expresses the average length of the queue in terms of the arrival rate λ and the service time mean τ and variance σ^2.

Let t_w be the time a customer waits in the queue for service: t_w does not include his service time t_s. Thus $t_w + t_s$ is the total time from arrival to discharge, and the average total time is

$$E[t_w + t_s] = E[t_w] + \tau. \tag{3.26}$$

Since the arrival rate is λ, the average number of arrivals in this time is $\lambda(E[t_w] + \tau)$. But this must equal the average queue length immediately following his discharge, $E[n]$, given by (3.25); thus

$$\lambda(E[t_w] + \tau) = \lambda\tau + \frac{\lambda^2\tau^2 + \lambda^2\sigma^2}{2(1 - \lambda\tau)}, \tag{3.27}$$

so

$$E[t_w] = \frac{\lambda\tau^2 + \lambda\sigma^2}{2(1 - \lambda\tau)}. \tag{3.28}$$

This shows that if we consider all service time distributions with the same average service time, that with σ^2 a minimum (i.e., zero), i.e., a constant service time, gives the smallest average waiting time.

4.4. Single-Channel, Finite, Poisson Arrival, Exponential Service Queues

The situation considered in this section is identical with that of Section 4.2 except for the difference that the maximum permissible queue length is N rather than infinity. This situation could arise, e.g., in a downtown gasoline station for which the available space will only accommodate a certain number of cars and customers arriving when the station is full are not permitted to wait on the street.

For n in the interval $(0, N - 1)$ the arguments of (2.1) to (2.14) apply unchanged in the present situation. We will consider now the special case of $n = N$. Similar to but not identical to (2.1), we have the equation

Pr{N customers in queue at $t + \Delta t$}
= Pr{N customers in line at time t} Pr{0 customers discharged in $(t, t + \Delta t)$}
+ Pr{$N - 1$ customers in line at time t} Pr{1 customer arrives in $(t, t + \Delta t)$} Pr{0 customers discharged in $(t, t + \Delta t)$}.

SECT. 4.4 SINGLE-CHANNEL, FINITE, POISSON ARRIVAL

This can be written as

$$p_N(t + \Delta t) = p_N(t)(1 - \mu \Delta t) + p_{N-1}(t) \cdot \lambda \Delta t \cdot (1 - \mu \Delta t) \quad (4.2)$$
$$\simeq p_N(t) - \mu p_N(t) \Delta t + \lambda p_{N-1}(t) \Delta t, \quad (4.3)$$

which rearranged gives

$$\frac{p_N(t + \Delta t) - p_N(t)}{\Delta t} = \lambda p_{N-1}(t) - \mu p_N(t). \quad (4.4)$$

When we take the limit of this as $\Delta t \to 0$, the left-hand side becomes $dp_N(t)/dt$, and if we assume that a stationary state is reached, so that $dp_N(t)/dt = 0$, we obtain

$$\lambda p_{N-1} = \mu p_N. \quad (4.5)$$

But for $n < N$, (2.14) applies, so

$$p_{N-1} = \left(\frac{\lambda}{\mu}\right)^{N-1} p_0. \quad (4.6)$$

Thus, substituting this in (4.5), we have

$$p_N = \frac{\lambda}{\mu} p_{N-1} = \frac{\lambda}{\mu}\left(\frac{\lambda}{\mu}\right)^{N-1} p_0 = \left(\frac{\lambda}{\mu}\right)^N p_0. \quad (4.7)$$

Therefore (2.14) is valid in the present case for $0 \leq n \leq N$:

$$p_n = \left(\frac{\lambda}{\mu}\right)^n p_0. \quad (4.8)$$

Analogous to (2.15), the queue must be of some length, so

$$1 = \sum_{i=0}^{N} p_i = p_0 \sum_{i=0}^{N} \left(\frac{\lambda}{\mu}\right)^i. \quad (4.9)$$

The formula for the sum of a finite geometric series is

$$1 + a + a^2 + \cdots + a^N = \frac{1 - a^{N+1}}{1 - a}, \quad (4.10)$$

so

$$\sum_{i=0}^{N} \left(\frac{\lambda}{\mu}\right)^i = \frac{1 - (\lambda/\mu)^{N+1}}{1 - \lambda/\mu}. \quad (4.11)$$

Substituting this in (4.9) gives

$$p_0 = \frac{1 - \lambda/\mu}{1 - (\lambda/\mu)^{N+1}}, \quad (4.12)$$

and substituting this in (4.8) gives

$$p_n = \frac{1 - \lambda/\mu}{1 - (\lambda/\mu)^{N+1}} \left(\frac{\lambda}{\mu}\right)^n, \qquad 0 \leq n \leq N. \tag{4.13}$$

Manipulations analogous to (2.20)–(2.23) give as the average length of the queue

$$E[n] = \rho \, \frac{1 - (N+1)\rho^N + N\rho^{N+1}}{(1-\rho)(1-\rho^{N+1})}, \tag{4.14}$$

where $\rho = \lambda/\mu$.

The proportion of the time customers are turned away because the queue is full is equal to the proportion of the time the queue is of size N, i.e.,

$$p_N = \frac{1 - \rho}{1 - \rho^{N+1}} \rho^N = 1 - \frac{1 - \rho^N}{1 - \rho^{N+1}}. \tag{4.15}$$

4.5. Multichannel, Infinite, Poisson Arrival, Exponential Service Queues

In our discussion (Section 4.2) of a single-channel queue, with Poisson arrivals and exponential service time distribution, we had to consider the two situations $n = 0, n > 0$. With k service channels we have to consider the three situations $n = 0, 1 \leq n < k, n \geq k$. The discussion for the case $n = 0$ leading to (2.9) remains unchanged and we continue to have

$$\lambda p_0 = \mu p_1, \qquad n = 0. \tag{5.1}$$

For the case $1 \leq n < k$, (2.1) applies as stated. The terms involving the probabilities of 0 or 1 customers being discharged need consideration. For example, if there are n customers in line at time t and the probability of any one being discharged in $(t, t + \Delta t)$ is $\mu \, \Delta t$, then the probability of 0 being discharged is given by the binomial probability function

$$\binom{n}{0}(\mu \, \Delta t)^0 (1 - \mu \, \Delta t)^{n-0} = (1 - \mu \, \Delta t)^n = 1 - \binom{n}{1}(\mu \, \Delta t)^1$$
$$+ \binom{n}{2}(\mu \, \Delta t)^2 - \cdots$$
$$\simeq 1 - n\mu \, \Delta t. \tag{5.2}$$

Similarly, if there are $n + 1$ customers in line the probability of 1 being discharged is

$$\binom{n+1}{1}(\mu \, \Delta t)^1 (1 - \mu \, \Delta t)^{n+1-1} \simeq (n+1)\mu \, \Delta t, \tag{5.3}$$

SECT. 4.5 MULTICHANNEL, INFINITE, POISSON ARRIVAL

and if there are $n - 1$ customers in line the probability of 0 being discharged is

$$\binom{n-1}{0}(\mu \Delta t)^0(1 - \mu \Delta t)^{n-1-0} \simeq 1 - (n-1)\mu \Delta t, \quad (5.4)$$

and if there are n customers in line the probability of 1 being discharged is

$$\binom{n}{1}(\mu \Delta t)^1(1 - \mu \Delta t)^{n-1} \simeq n\mu \Delta t. \quad (5.5)$$

Substituting (5.2)–(5.5) in (2.1) we get

$$\begin{aligned}p_n(t + \Delta t) &\simeq p_n(t)(1 - \lambda \Delta t)(1 - n\mu \Delta t) + p_{n+1}(t)(1 - \lambda \Delta t)(n+1)\mu \Delta t \\ &\quad + p_{n-1}(t)\lambda \Delta t[1 - (n-1)\mu \Delta t] + p_n(t)\lambda \Delta t n\mu \Delta t \\ &\simeq p_n(t)(1 - \lambda \Delta t - n\mu \Delta t) + p_{n+1}(t)(n+1)\mu \Delta t \\ &\quad + p_{n-1}(t)\lambda \Delta t. \end{aligned} \quad (5.6)$$

By the same manipulations that led from (2.3) to (2.5), this gives

$$(\lambda + n\mu)p_n = \lambda p_{n-1} + (n+1)\mu p_{n+1}, \quad 1 \leq n < k. \quad (5.7)$$

If $n > k$, (2.1) applies as stated, and in place of (5.2) we have $1 - k\mu \Delta t$, in place of (5.3) we have $k\mu \Delta t$, in place of (5.4) we have $1 - k\mu \Delta t$, and in place of (5.5) we have $k\mu \Delta t$. Substituting these expressions in (2.1) we get

$$\begin{aligned}p_n(t + \Delta t) &\simeq p_n(t)(1 - \lambda \Delta t)(1 - k\mu \Delta t) + p_{n+1}(t)(1 - \lambda \Delta t)k\mu \Delta t \\ &\quad + p_{n-1}(t)\lambda \Delta t(1 - k\mu \Delta t) + p_n(t)\lambda \Delta t\, k\mu \Delta t \quad (5.8) \\ &\simeq p_n(t)(1 - \lambda \Delta t - k\mu \Delta t) + p_{n+1}(t)k\mu \Delta t + p_{n-1}(t)\lambda \Delta t. \end{aligned}$$
$$(5.9)$$

If $n = k$, the changes listed above for the case $n > k$ for (5.2), (5.3), and (5.5) apply, but in place of the change for (5.4), namely $1 - k\mu \Delta t$, we have $1 - (k-1)\mu \Delta t$. Making this change in (5.8) leads to the same expression as (5.9), however. By the same manipulations that lead from (2.3) to (2.5) we obtain

$$(\lambda + k\mu)p_n = \lambda p_{n-1} + k\mu p_{n+1}, \quad k \leq n. \quad (5.10)$$

From (5.1) we obtain

$$p_1 = \frac{\lambda}{\mu} p_0. \quad (5.11)$$

Putting $n = 1$ in (5.7) gives

$$(\lambda + \mu)p_1 = \lambda p_0 + (1+1)\mu p_{1+1}, \quad (5.12)$$

whence
$$p_2 = \left(\frac{\lambda}{\mu}\right)^2 \frac{1}{2} p_0, \tag{5.13}$$

and more generally
$$p_n = \left(\frac{\lambda}{\mu}\right)^n \frac{1}{n!} p_0, \quad 1 \le n < k, \tag{5.14}$$

and this equation is also true for $n = 0$.

When we put $n = k$ in (5.10) we can derive
$$p_{k+1} = \left(\frac{\lambda}{\mu k}\right)^{k+1} \frac{k^k}{k!} p_0, \tag{5.15}$$

and when we put $n = k + 1$ we can derive
$$p_{k+2} = \left(\frac{\lambda}{\mu k}\right)^{k+2} \frac{k^k}{k!} p_0, \tag{5.16}$$

and in general for $n \ge k$,
$$p_n = \left(\frac{\lambda}{\mu k}\right)^n \frac{k^k}{k!} p_0 = \left(\frac{\lambda}{\mu}\right)^n \frac{1}{k!\, k^{n-k}} p_0, \quad k \le n. \tag{5.17}$$

We need to evaluate p_0. The condition $\sum_{n=0}^{\infty} p_n = 1$ must be satisfied, so
$$\sum_{n=0}^{k-1} \left(\frac{\lambda}{\mu}\right)^n \frac{1}{n!} p_0 + \sum_{n=k}^{\infty} \left(\frac{\lambda}{\mu}\right)^n \frac{1}{k!\, k^{n-k}} p_0 = 1, \tag{5.18}$$

and
$$\frac{1}{p_0} = \sum_{n=0}^{k-1} \left(\frac{\lambda}{\mu}\right)^n \frac{1}{n!} + \sum_{n=k}^{\infty} \left(\frac{\lambda}{k\mu}\right)^n \frac{k^k}{k!}. \tag{5.19}$$

The second term on the right-hand side can be written as
$$\frac{k^k}{k!} \sum_{n=k}^{\infty} \left(\frac{\lambda}{k\mu}\right)^n = \frac{k^k}{k!} \left\{ \sum_{n=0}^{\infty} \left(\frac{\lambda}{k\mu}\right)^n - \sum_{n=0}^{k-1} \left(\frac{\lambda}{k\mu}\right)^n \right\}. \tag{5.20}$$

For the right-hand side we use the formulas for the sums of infinite and finite geometric series to obtain
$$\frac{k^k}{k!} \sum_{n=k}^{\infty} \left(\frac{\lambda}{k\mu}\right)^n = \frac{k^k}{k!}\left[\frac{1}{1 - \lambda/k\mu} - \frac{1 - (\lambda/k\mu)^k}{1 - \lambda/k\mu}\right] = \frac{(\lambda/\mu)^k}{k!\,(1 - \lambda/k\mu)}. \tag{5.21}$$

Substituting in (5.19) we get
$$\frac{1}{p_0} = \sum_{n=0}^{k-1} \left(\frac{\lambda}{\mu}\right)^n \frac{1}{n!} + \frac{(\lambda/\mu)^k}{k!\,(1 - \lambda/k\mu)}. \tag{5.22}$$

Substituting the value for p_0 implied by this equation into (5.14) and (5.17) gives the solutions for all p_n.

As an application of these formulas, we have that the probability of a new random arrival having to wait in line is

$$\Pr\{n \geq k\} = \sum_{n=k}^{\infty} \left(\frac{\lambda}{\mu}\right)^n \frac{1}{k!\, k^{n-k}} p_0$$

$$= \frac{(\lambda/\mu)^k}{k!\,(1 - \lambda/k\mu)} p_0, \qquad (5.23)$$

where p_0 is given by (5.22).

4.6. Inventory Control

In this section we will merely indicate how the methods of queuing theory are applicable to inventory control. In Section 4.4 we discussed single channel queues of finite length N, and in Section 4.5 we discussed multichannel infinite queues. Suppose that we continued with the natural extension to multichannel finite queues, and than particularized to the case where the maximum queue length N equals the number of channels k.

Now consider a retailer of large, single, standard items, whose customers will purchase an item if he can deliver it from stock but otherwise will go away and look for it at a competitor's store. This retailer is assumed to place a reorder every time he makes a sale. This situation is the exact analogy of the queuing situation discussed in the previous paragraph. We have the relationships

Number of channels = k	$N = k$	Maximum size of inventory = N
Maximum length of queue = N		
Idle channel		Item in stock
Arrival of customer and start of service		Item purchased and order for replacement sent immediately
End of service		Delivery of ordered item
Service time		Time for reordered item to be delivered
All channels busy		No item in stock

It is apparent that the solution of the queuing problem is the solution of the inventory problem. The optimum inventory will depend on the relative costs of holding an item in inventory, the profit on a sale when made, and the loss in customer good will when a customer is turned away because there are no items in stock. The reader is referred to Chapter 10 of [4] for an examination of these questions.

EXERCISES

4.1. For a single-channel infinite queue with Poisson input with parameter λ and exponential service time with parameter μ, what is the mode of the distribution of the queue length n?

4.2. For a queue of the type discussed in Section 4.2, with Poisson input with parameter λ and exponential service time with parameter μ, show that

$$V[n] = E[n] + (E[n])^2,$$

where $E[n]$ is given by (2.23).

4.3. Consider a queuing situation in which the same corporation operates both the customers and the service facility; e.g., a large cab company owning and operating both cabs and a service facility for the cabs. Suppose the cabs arrive randomly with Poisson parameter λ and a single service channel is available for which the service times are exponential with parameter μ. Suppose that the cost per hour of providing a service facility with parameter μ is $M\mu$, and that the cost in lost time, etc., for a cab in waiting and being serviced is C per hour. The constants M and C are fixed, as is the parameter λ. Suppose that μ can be varied, e.g., by providing a larger service staff or more equipment. What value should μ be to minimize the total cost per hour to the corporation (owning both cabs and service facility)?

4.4. In a queuing situation with single server, with Poisson input with parameter λ and exponential service time with parameter μ, let n_w be the number waiting in line for service (i.e., the total queue length n minus the customer being served, if any). Find the expected value of n_w.

4.5. A manager operates a service facility in which customers arrive randomly with Poisson parameter λ and queue for service. The service times are exponential with parameter μ. The manager can vary μ. Suppose that he wishes to choose μ so that only in a fraction α of the time, on the average, will the total queue length equal or exceed n members. Express the value of μ that achieves this condition explicitly in terms of λ, α, and n.

4.6. For a single-channel finite queue of fixed maximum length N, prove (4.15) and show that the average length of the queue $E[n]$ has the following limits:

(a) $\lim\limits_{\rho \to 0} E[n] = \rho + \rho^2$, (b) $\lim\limits_{\rho \to 1} E[n] = N/2$, (c) $\lim\limits_{\rho \to \infty} E[n] = N - 1/\rho$.

4.7. Show that (3.25) is consistent with (2.23), and that (3.28) is consistent with (2.25), when the appropriate values of τ and σ are inserted in (3.25) and (3.28).

4.8. For a multichannel queue of the type discussed in Section 4.5, show that the average number waiting for service is

$$E[n_w] = \frac{\left(\dfrac{\lambda}{k\mu}\right)\left(\dfrac{\lambda}{\mu}\right)^k}{k!\,(1 - \lambda/k\mu)^2} p_0.$$

4.9. Consider two single-channel, Poisson arrival, infinite queuing situations. In queue a, the service time is a constant, say τ. In b, the service time has an exponential distribution with mean τ. Obtain a simple result for the ratio of the average waiting time in queue a to the average waiting time in queue b.

4.10. Consider two single-channel, Poisson arrival, infinite queuing situations. In queue a, the service time has a rectangular distribution over the interval $(0, T)$. In b, the service time has a constant value equal to the mean of the service time in a. Obtain a simple result for the ratio of the average waiting time in queue a to the average waiting time in queue (b).

4.11. Let $P_{0,1}$ be the probability of an arriving customer not having to wait for service with a single-channel infinite queue with Poisson arrivals with parameter λ and exponential service time distributed with parameter μ_1. Let $P_{0,2}$ be the probability of an arriving customer not having to wait for service with a two-channel infinite queue with Poisson arrivals with parameter λ and exponential service time distributed with parameter $\mu_2 = \mu_1/2$. Thus the average service time in the single-channel queue is one-half the average service time in the two channel queue. Obtain a simple expression for the ratio $P_{0,2}/P_{0,1}$ in terms of $\lambda/\mu_2 = \rho_2$. If $\rho_2 = 1$, what is $P_{0,2}/P_{0,1}$?

REFERENCES

1. Brockmeyer, E., Halmstrom, H. L., and Jensen, Arne, *The Life and Works of A. K. Erlang*. Transactions of the Danish Academy of Technical Sciences, Number 2. Copenhagen, 1948.
2. Kendall, David G., "Some Problems in the Theory of Queues," *Journal of the Royal Statistical Society*, B 13 (1951) 151–173.
3. Saaty, Thomas L., *Elements of Queuing Theory*. New York: McGraw-Hill Book Co., 1961.
4. Morse, Philip M., *Queues, Inventories and Maintenance*, New York: John Wiley and Sons, 1958.
5. Takacs, L., *Introduction to the Theory of Queues*, London: Oxford University Press, 1962.

CHAPTER 5

The Multinomial Distribution and Contingency Tables

5.1. The Multinomial Distribution

So-called contingency tables are the main topic of this chapter. Their analysis requires a consideration of the multinominal distribution, which we discuss in this section. Section 5.2 treats a method of obtaining approximate percentage points in terms of the χ^2 distribution. Contingency tables themselves are discussed in Section 5.3.

The multinomial distribution is a generalization of the binomial distribution in which instead of two possible outcomes A and $\bar{A}$ there are k mutually exclusive and exhaustive outcomes $A_1, \ldots, A_k$ with probabilities $\theta_1, \ldots, \theta_k$, where $\sum_i^k \theta_i = 1$. We want the probability that, on n trials, A_1 occurs exactly x_1 times, ..., A_k occurs exactly x_k times, where $\sum_i^k x_i = n$. The probability of getting the specific sequence

$$\underbrace{A_1 \cdots A_1}_{x_1 \text{ times}} \cdots \underbrace{A_k \cdots A_k}_{x_k \text{ times}} \tag{1.1}$$

is, since successive trials are independent, $\theta_1^{x_1} \cdots \theta_k^{x_k}$. The ordering of the sequence is irrelevant to our purpose, as we are merely interested in the total number of times A_1 occurs, etc. All sequences with a specified set of x_i have the same probability. It remains to evaluate the number of sequences with a specified set of x_i. Equation (1.7.6) gave the number of arrangements of x_1 objects of type A_1, x_2 objects of type A_2, etc., as $n!/x_1! x_2! \cdots x_k!$; so

$$\Pr\{x_1, \ldots, x_k\} = \frac{n!}{x_1! \cdots x_k!} \theta_1^{x_1} \cdots \theta_k^{x_k} \tag{1.2}$$

is the frequency function of the multinomial distribution.

SECT. 5.2   THE χ^2 APPROXIMATION

The multivariate distribution considered in Section 1.19 is an example of a multinomial distribution, with $\theta_U = 1/2$, $\theta_F = 1/3$, $\theta_G = 1/6$. In that section we calculated from first principles the entire distribution, giving the results in Table 1.17. Equation (1.2) will give the same results directly. For example,

$$\Pr\{2, 0, 1\} = \frac{3!}{2!\,0!\,1!}\left(\frac{1}{2}\right)^2\left(\frac{1}{3}\right)^0\left(\frac{1}{6}\right)^1 = \frac{1}{8} = \frac{27}{216}. \quad (1.3)$$

In the case of $k = 2$, the multinomial distribution reduces immediately to the binomial. In general, however, it is awkward to work with, and we outline in the next section the development of an approximation to (1.2) which can then be used to obtain certain cumulative probabilities.

5.2. The χ^2 Approximation for the Multinomial Distribution

We use the symbol P^* for the probability defined in (1.2). As in the derivation of an approximation to the binomial distribution, so here we use Stirling's approximation (3.1.2) for the factorials in (1.2). Thus

$$P^* \simeq \frac{\sqrt{2\pi}\, n^{n+\frac{1}{2}} e^{-n}}{\prod_i^k \sqrt{2\pi} x_i^{x_i+\frac{1}{2}} e^{-x_i}} \prod_i^k \theta_i^{x_i}$$

$$\simeq (2\pi)^{-\frac{1}{2}(k-1)} n^{n+\frac{1}{2}} \prod_i^k x_i^{-(x_i+\frac{1}{2})} \prod_i^k \theta_i^{x_i}. \quad (2.1)$$

This involves n to the $(n + 1/2)$th power. We can write

$$n + \frac{1}{2} = -\frac{1}{2}(k-1) + \sum_i^k \left(x_i + \frac{1}{2}\right), \quad (2.2)$$

and also

$$\prod_i^k \theta_i^{x_i} = \prod_i^k \theta_i^{-\frac{1}{2}} \theta_i^{(x_i+\frac{1}{2})}. \quad (2.3)$$

Substituting in (2.1) gives

$$P^* \simeq (2\pi n)^{-\frac{1}{2}(k-1)} \left(\prod_i^k \theta_i\right)^{-\frac{1}{2}} \prod_i^k \left(\frac{n\theta_i}{x_i}\right)^{x_i+\frac{1}{2}}. \quad (2.4)$$

Taking logarithms,

$$\log P^* \simeq -\frac{1}{2}(k-1)\log(2\pi n) - \frac{1}{2}\sum_i^k \log \theta_i - \sum_i^k \left(x_i + \frac{1}{2}\right)\log\left(\frac{x_i}{n\theta_i}\right). \quad (2.5)$$

The expected value for the ith cell is $n\theta_i = e_i$, say. Define the deviation of the observed value in the ith cell from its expected value as $d_i = x_i - e_i$. Then

$$\frac{x_i}{n\theta_i} = \frac{d_i + e_i}{e_i} = 1 + \frac{d_i}{e_i}, \quad (2.6)$$

and $(x_i + 1/2) = (e_i + d_i + 1/2)$. Substituting in (2.5),

$$\log P^* \simeq -\frac{1}{2}(k-1)\log(2\pi n) - \frac{1}{2}\sum_i^k \log \theta_i$$

$$- \sum_i^k \left(e_i + d_i + \frac{1}{2}\right)\log\left(1 + \frac{d_i}{e_i}\right). \quad (2.7)$$

Again as in the binomial case we use the expansion

$$\log(1 + y) = y - \frac{y^2}{2} + \frac{y^3}{3} - \cdots. \quad (2.8)$$

For the first terms of this series to give a good approximation we need $|y| \ll 1$. Here we are going to substitute $y = d_i/e_i$. We therefore need to check on the magnitude of $|d_i/e_i|$. From (1.18.21) we have, when x has the distribution $N(\xi, \sigma^2)$,

$$\Pr\{|x - \xi| > k\sigma\} = 2\Phi(-k). \quad (2.9)$$

We can regard x_i as a binomial variable which will be approximately normally distributed with expectation $n\theta_i = e_i$ and variance $n\theta_i(1 - \theta_i)$. Hence

$$\Pr\{|x_i - e_i| > k\sqrt{n\theta_i(1 - \theta_i)}\} = 2\Phi(-k). \quad (2.10)$$

Choose for k the value $\sqrt{n\theta_i/(1 - \theta_i)}$. Then we have

$$\Pr\left\{|d_i| > \sqrt{\frac{n\theta_i}{1 - \theta_i}}\sqrt{n\theta_i(1 - \theta_i)}\right\} = 2\Phi\left(-\sqrt{\frac{n\theta_i}{1 - \theta_i}}\right), \quad (2.11)$$

or, since $\sqrt{n\theta_i/(1 - \theta_i)}\sqrt{n\theta_i(1 - \theta_i)} = n\theta_i = e_i$,

$$\Pr\{|d_i| > e_i\} = 2\Phi\left(-\sqrt{\frac{n\theta_i}{1 - \theta_i}}\right). \quad (2.12)$$

For moderate values and beyond of $e_i = n\theta_i$, say 5 or greater, $\sqrt{n\theta_i/(1 - \theta_i)}$ will be greater than $\sqrt{5}$, and hence $\Phi(-\sqrt{n\theta_i/(1 - \theta_i)})$ will be very small. Hence $\Pr\{|d_i/e_i| > 1\}$ will be very small, and we will be justified in using the expansion (2.8). We note here that d_i will be of the order of its standard deviation $\sqrt{n\theta_i(1 - \theta_i)}$, or approximately $\sqrt{e_i}$. We now examine

SECT. 5.2 THE χ^2 APPROXIMATION

the second summation term in (2.7), using (2.8) to expand $\log(1 + d_i/e_i)$:

$$\sum_i^k \left(e_i + d_i + \frac{1}{2}\right) \left[\frac{d_i}{e_i} - \frac{1}{2}\left(\frac{d_i}{e_i}\right)^2 + \frac{1}{3}\left(\frac{d_i}{e_i}\right)^3 - \frac{1}{4}\left(\frac{d_i}{e_i}\right)^4 + \cdots\right]$$

$$= \sum_i^k \left(d_i - \frac{1}{2}\frac{d_i^2}{e_i} + \frac{1}{3}\frac{d_i^3}{e_i^2} - \cdots + \frac{d_i^2}{e_i} - \frac{1}{2}\frac{d_i^3}{e_i^2} + \cdots + \frac{1}{2}\frac{d_i}{e_i} - \frac{1}{4}\frac{d_i^2}{e_i^2} + \cdots\right). \quad (2.13)$$

We note that $\sum_i^k d_i = \sum_i^k (x_i - e_i) = \sum_i^k x_i - \sum_i^k e_i = 0$. Examining the terms in powers of e_i, recalling that d_i is of order $\sqrt{e_i}$, we see that the zero-order terms are

$$\sum_i^k \left(-\frac{1}{2}\frac{d_i^2}{e_i} + \frac{d_i^2}{e_i}\right) = \frac{1}{2}\sum_i^k \frac{d_i^2}{e_i}, \quad (2.14)$$

and the terms of order $1/\sqrt{e_i}$ are

$$\frac{1}{2}\sum_i^k \frac{d_i}{e_i} + \left(-\frac{1}{2} + \frac{1}{3}\right)\sum_i^k \frac{d_i^3}{e_i^2}. \quad (2.15)$$

For moderately large e_i, say greater than 5, all terms except those of zero order may be neglected. Hence, substituting back in (2.7) and taking antilogarithms, we get

$$P^* \simeq (2\pi n)^{-\frac{1}{2}(k-1)} \left(\prod_i^k \theta_i\right)^{-\frac{1}{2}} \exp\left[-\frac{1}{2}\sum_i^k \frac{d_i^2}{e_i}\right]. \quad (2.16)$$

Here all the terms preceding the exponential part, involving π, n, k, and the θ_i, are constants or parameters. Thus P^* is, to this approximation, determined by $\sum_i^k d_i^2/e_i$, and historically the symbol χ^2 was given to this statistic:

$$\chi^2 = \sum_i^k \frac{d_i^2}{e_i}. \quad (2.17)$$

For a test of significance based on this statistic, we need to be able to calculate the probability of obtaining a value of the statistic as large as or larger than the observed value. We can write (2.17) in the form

$$\chi^2 = \sum_i^k \frac{d_i^2}{e_i} = \sum_i^k \frac{(x_i - e_i)^2}{n\theta_i} = \sum_i^k \frac{(x_i - e_i)^2}{n\theta_i(1 - \theta_i)}(1 - \theta_i)$$

$$= \sum_i^k \left(\frac{x_i - e_i}{\sqrt{n\theta_i(1 - \theta_i)}}\right)^2 (1 - \theta_i). \quad (2.18)$$

If we consider a particular cell, say the ith, and regard ourselves as in a binomial situation, then

$$\frac{x_i - e_i}{\sqrt{n\theta_i(1 - \theta_i)}} \sim N(0, 1). \qquad (2.19)$$

Hence our "χ^2," as defined by (2.17), is a weighted sum, the weights being $1 - \theta_i$, of squares of approximate unit normal deviates. These approximate unit normal deviates are not quite independent, since $\sum_i^k (x_i - e_i) = 0$. Thus our "χ^2," because of this restriction, and on account of the weights, is not a true $\chi^2(k)$ as defined in (1.27.1). However, it may be shown that it is approximately a true $\chi^2(k - 1)$.

As an example, suppose that the lost-time accidents reported for a certain period for three shifts are 1, 7, and 7. We wish to test the null hypothesis that $\theta_1 = \theta_2 = \theta_3$, i.e., that $\theta_i = 1/3$. There are a total of $n = 15$ accidents; so the expected number for each shift is $e_i = n\theta_i = 15 \times 1/3 = 5$, and the corresponding values of $d_i = x_i - e_i$ for the three shifts are $1 - 5 = -4$, $7 - 5 = 2$, and $7 - 5 = 2$. The test statistic, with degrees of freedom $k - 1 = 2$, is

$$\chi^2 = \sum_i^3 \frac{d_i^2}{e_i} = \frac{(-4)^2}{5} + \frac{2^2}{5} + \frac{2^2}{5} = 4.80. \qquad (2.20)$$

The 0.90 and 0.95 points of χ^2 with 2 degrees of freedom are 4.61 and 5.99. The observed value of 4.80 being intermediate between these two points, our P value is approximately $1 - 0.91 = 0.09$.

As another example, consider the data of Table 3.11. Under the null hypothesis that the observations are Poisson distributed, we have a sample of size 576 which should be multinomially distributed with θ_i, given by the column headed $p\{x\}$. The columns headed $np\{x\}$ give the expected numbers e_i; the last two columns are $d_i = x_i - e_i$ and d_i^2/e_i. Since the χ^2 approximation for the multinomial distribution is not very satisfactory for $e_i < 5$, the cells for $x \geq 4$ are combined into a single cell. Summing the entries in the last column gives $\chi^2 = 1.03$. As regards the degrees of freedom for this χ^2, here we have five classes; so $k = 5$, and we have constrained Σd_i to be zero, and we have also estimated the parameter ξ of the Poisson distribution which we fitted to the data. The degrees of freedom are therefore $5 - 1 - 1 = 3$. Table III of the appendix gives for three degrees of freedom the 0.10 and 0.25 points of the χ^2 distribution as 0.58 and 1.21; so $1 - P \simeq 0.20$ and $P \simeq 0.8$. The data of Table 3.11 are thus very well fitted by a Poisson distribution.

5.3. Contingency Tables

Suppose we have a random sample of n objects, cross-classified according to two attributes A_i, B_j. Let the probability of an object having the attributes A_i, B_j be θ_{ij}, and the number observed in the sample be n_{ij}: $\sum_i^k \sum_j^m n_{ij} = n, \sum_i^k \sum_j^m \theta_{ij} = 1$. Let the marginal row probabilities be θ_i. and the marginal row sums be n_i. as in Tables 5.1 and 5.2. By (1.19.1) and (1.19.2),

$$\theta_{i\cdot} = \sum_j^m \theta_{ij}, \qquad \theta_{\cdot j} = \sum_i^k \theta_{ij}. \tag{3.1}$$

Table 5.1

	B_1	$\cdots$	B_j	$\cdots$	B_m	
A_1	θ_{11}		θ_{1j}		θ_{1m}	$\theta_{1\cdot}$
$\vdots$						
A_i	θ_{i1}		θ_{ij}		θ_{im}	$\theta_{i\cdot}$
$\vdots$						
A_k	θ_{k1}		θ_{kj}		θ_{km}	$\theta_{k\cdot}$
	$\theta_{\cdot 1}$		$\theta_{\cdot j}$		$\theta_{\cdot m}$	1

Table 5.2

	B_1	$\cdots$	B_j	$\cdots$	B_m	
A_1	n_{11}		n_{1j}		n_{1m}	$n_{1\cdot}$
$\vdots$						
A_i	n_{i1}		n_{ij}		n_{im}	$n_{i\cdot}$
$\vdots$						
A_k	n_{k1}		n_{kj}		n_{km}	$n_{k\cdot}$
	$n_{\cdot 1}$		$n_{\cdot j}$		$n_{\cdot m}$	$n_{\cdot\cdot}$

If the true probabilities θ_{ij} are known, the agreement between the observed and hypothetical distribution can be tested by the statistic (2.17) developed in the previous section,

$$\chi^2 = \sum_i^k \sum_j^m \frac{(n_{ij} - n\theta_{ij})^2}{n\theta_{ij}}, \qquad f = km - 1. \tag{3.2}$$

However, usually in practice the θ_{ij} have to be estimated from the data. We are usually interested in testing the hypothesis that the row and column classifications are independent, i.e., that

$$\Pr\{A_i, B_j\} = \Pr\{A_i\} \Pr\{B_j\}, \tag{3.3}$$

i.e.,
$$\theta_{ij} = \theta_{i\cdot}\theta_{\cdot j}. \tag{3.4}$$

We now find the maximum likelihood estimators of $\theta_{i\cdot}$ and $\theta_{\cdot j}$. We first find a suitable expression for the likelihood function. Assuming

212 MULTINOMIAL DISTRIBUTION AND CONTINGENCY TABLES CHAP. 5

that we have a multinomial distribution of the form (1.2), if we take a sample of size 1 then the x_{ij} are all zero except for one of them, which has the value 1. Thus the $x_{ij}!$ equal either $0! = 1$ or $1! = 1$. Thus the frequency function is

$$\frac{n!}{x_{11}! \cdots x_{km}!} \theta_{11}^{x_{11}} \cdots \theta_{km}^{x_{km}} = \prod_{i=1}^{k} \prod_{j=1}^{m} \theta_{ij}^{x_{ij}}. \tag{3.5}$$

Assume now that we take a sequence of n samples, each of size 1, and let n_{ij} be the sum of the x_{ij} summed over this sequence of n observations. Thus n_{ij} is equal to the number of occurrences in the ijth cell. The likelihood function (2.3.1) is

$$L = p\{x_1\} \cdots p\{x_n\} = \prod_{i}^{n} \prod_{j}^{k} \prod_{}^{m} \theta_{ij}^{x_{ij}} = \prod_{i}^{k} \prod_{j}^{m} \theta_{ij}^{n_{ij}}. \tag{3.6}$$

Under the null hypothesis of independence of the row and column classifications, (3.4), we have

$$L = \prod_{i}^{k} \prod_{j}^{m} (\theta_{i.}\theta_{.j})^{n_{ij}} = \left(\prod_{i}^{k} \prod_{j}^{m} \theta_{i.}^{n_{ij}} \right) \left(\prod_{j}^{m} \prod_{i}^{k} \theta_{.j}^{n_{ij}} \right). \tag{3.7}$$

Now we can write for the first parenthesis,

$$\prod_{i}^{k} \prod_{j}^{m} \theta_{i.}^{n_{ij}} = \prod_{i}^{k} (\theta_{i.}^{n_{i1}} \theta_{i.}^{n_{i2}} \cdots \theta_{i.}^{n_{im}}) = \prod_{i}^{k} \theta_{i.}^{\sum_{j}^{m} n_{ij}} = \prod_{i}^{k} \theta_{i.}^{n_{i\cdot}}, \tag{3.8}$$

and analogously for the second parenthesis. Thus

$$L = \prod_{i}^{k} \theta_{i.}^{n_{i\cdot}} \prod_{j}^{m} \theta_{.j}^{n_{.j}}. \tag{3.9}$$

Now since $\sum_{i=1}^{k} \theta_{i.} = 1$ we can write $\theta_{k.}$ as

$$\theta_{k.} = 1 - \sum_{i=1}^{k-1} \theta_{i.}. \tag{3.10}$$

Substituting in (3.9), we get

$$L = \left(1 - \sum_{i=1}^{k-1} \theta_{i.} \right)^{n_{k\cdot}} \prod_{i=1}^{k-1} \theta_{i.}^{n_{i\cdot}} \prod_{j=1}^{m} \theta_{.j}^{n_{.j}}, \tag{3.11}$$

and, taking logarithms,

$$\log L = n_{k.} \log\left(1 - \sum_{i=1}^{k-1} \theta_{i.} \right) + \sum_{i=1}^{k-1} n_{i.} \log \theta_{i.} + \sum_{j=1}^{m} n_{.j} \log \theta_{.j}. \tag{3.12}$$

To find the value of $\theta_{i.}$ which maximizes this, we differentiate with respect to $\theta_{i.}$ and equate to zero:

$$\frac{\partial \log L}{\partial \theta_{i.}} = n_{k.}(-1) \frac{1}{1 - \sum_{i=1}^{k-1} \theta_{i.}} + n_{i.} \frac{1}{\theta_{i.}} = 0. \tag{3.13}$$

SECT. 5.3   CONTINGENCY TABLES   213

Using (3.10), this gives

$$\frac{n_{i.}}{\theta_{i.}} = \frac{n_{k.}}{\theta_{k.}} ; \qquad (3.14)$$

so

$$\sum_{i=1}^{k} \theta_{i.} = \frac{\theta_{k.}}{n_{k.}} \sum_{i=1}^{k} n_{i.} = \frac{n\theta_{k.}}{n_{k.}} . \qquad (3.15)$$

But $\sum_{i=1}^{k} \theta_{i.} = 1$, so $\theta_{k.}/n_{k.} = 1/n$. Substituting in (3.14),

$$\theta_{i.} = n_{i.} \left(\frac{\theta_{k.}}{n_{k.}}\right) = \frac{n_{i.}}{n} . \qquad (3.16)$$

Similar arguments must apply to the estimation of $\theta_{.j}$; so $\hat\theta_{.j} = n_{.j}/n$. The maximum likelihood estimators of the θ_{ij} are thus

$$\hat\theta_{ij} = \frac{n_{i.}}{n} \frac{n_{.j}}{n}, \qquad (3.17)$$

and these can be inserted in (3.2) to give

$$\chi^2 = \sum_{i}^{k} \sum_{j}^{m} \frac{(n_{ij} - n_{i.}n_{.j}/n)^2}{n_{i.}n_{.j}/n} . \qquad (3.18)$$

However, this χ^2 does not have the degrees of freedom of the χ^2 in (3.2), namely $km - 1$, since we have estimated a number of parameters from the data. We have estimated k parameters $\theta_{i.}$, but, in view of the restriction that $\sum_{i}^{k} \theta_{i.} = 1$, only $k - 1$ of these are independent. Likewise $m - 1$ degrees of freedom are taken in estimation of the $\theta_{.j}$. The degrees of freedom for the χ^2 in (3.18) are thus

$$(km - 1) - (k - 1) - (m - 1) = (k - 1)(m - 1). \qquad (3.19)$$

As an illustration of a contingency table, Abrahamson et al. [1] present data on the bacterial count of three types of pastry (Table 5.3). We ask whether the distribution of class of bacterial count varies according to type of pastry. We estimate the expected number for each cell as $n_{i.}n_{.j}/n$. For $i = 1, j = 1$, for example, this is $175 \times 220/368 = 104.620$. The calculations are given in detail in Table 5.4. Summing all the entries in the third part of this table,

$$\sum_{i}^{k} \sum_{j}^{m} d_{ij}^2/e_{ij} = 11.389,$$

and this will be distributed as χ^2 with degrees of freedom $(3 - 1)(3 - 1) = 4$ under the null hypothesis. The 0.975 point of $\chi^2(4)$ is 11.1; so $P < 0.025$, and therefore we reject the null hypothesis that the distribution of bacterial count is independent of the type of pastry. In other words, the pastries do differ in their distributions of bacterial counts.

This is all that the χ^2 test as applied to a contingency table will do for us. It does not tell us in what specific way or ways the pastries differ. To form an opinion on that question we need to compare visually the table of

Table 5.3

Type of pastry	Low	Medium	High	Totals
Éclairs	92	37	46	175
Napoleons	53	15	19	87
Coconut custard pies	75	19	12	106
Totals	220	71	77	368

Table 5.4

Expectations e_{ij}

104.620	33.764	36.617
52.011	16.785	18.204
63.370	20.451	22.179

Observed minus expectation d_{ij}

−12.620	3.236	9.383
0.989	−1.785	0.796
11.630	−1.451	−10.179

d_{ij}^2/e_{ij}

1.5223	0.3101	2.4044
0.0188	0.1898	0.0348
2.1344	0.1029	4.6716

expectations with the table of observations and see if it is obvious in what way the discrepancy between expectation and observation is arising. This has to be done on a common-sense basis. If we attempt to formulate and test any particular hypothesis, its real significance level is distorted by the fact that we are making multiple tests suggested by the data. In the present instance, there are no obvious difficulties to the obvious interpretation of the d_{ij} in Table 5.4: Coconut custard pies have a relatively small number of high counts and a relatively large number of low counts, napoleons are average, and éclairs have a relatively large number of high counts and a small number of low counts. In other words, stay away from éclairs.

For a very extensive examination of contingency tables with particular emphasis on measures of association that are relevant to particular purposes, see Goodman and Kruskal [2–4]. For a general review of the χ^2 test see Cochran [5, 6]. The examination of three-dimensional contingency tables proves surprisingly difficult: for a recent review see Goodman [7].

5.4. The Two × Two Table

The 2 × 2 contingency table is a special, but frequently occurring, case of the $k \times m$ contingency table. We suppose that in an infinite population all elements are categorized as A_1 or A_2 and simultaneously as B_1 or B_2. For example, A_1 and A_2 could be fair hair or otherwise and B_1 and B_2 could be blue eyes or otherwise. We suppose that the fraction of the population classified as $A_i B_j$ is θ_{ij}. We take a random sample of size n from this population and obtain the results in Table 5.5.

Table 5.5

	B_1	B_2	Totals
A_1	n_{11}	n_{12}	$n_{1.}$
A_2	n_{21}	n_{22}	$n_{2.}$
Totals	$n_{.1}$	$n_{.2}$	n

The total number of observations n is fixed, but both the row totals and the column totals are random variables. We are interested in testing the null hypothesis (3.4), for which an appropriate statistic is (3.18), which in this case will have 1 degree of freedom. For Table 5.5, (3.18) can be written after some manipulation as

$$\chi^2 = \frac{(n_{11}n_{22} - n_{21}n_{12})^2 n}{n_{.1}n_{.2}n_{1.}n_{2.}}. \tag{4.1}$$

If the rows in Table 5.5 were labeled Population 1 and Population 2 and the columns were labeled Defective and Nondefective, then Table 5.5 would be identical, apart from the difference in sampling procedure, with Table 3.1. For Table 5.5 the null hypothesis is that $\theta_{ij} = \theta_{i.}\theta_{.j}$ for all i and j, and in particular $\theta_{11} = \theta_{1.}\theta_{.1}$ and $\theta_{21} = \theta_{2.}\theta_{.1}$, so that, under the null hypothesis of independence,

$$\frac{\theta_{11}}{\theta_{1.}} = \theta_{.1} = \frac{\theta_{21}}{\theta_{2.}}. \tag{4.2}$$

From the equation for conditional probability, (1.4.5), we can write

$$\text{Pr}\{\text{defective} \mid \text{item from population } i\}$$
$$= \frac{\text{Pr}\{\text{defective and from population } i\}}{\text{Pr}\{\text{item from population } i\}}. \tag{4.3}$$

Identifying the right-hand side of (4.3) with $i = 1, 2$, with the first and last terms in (4.2), we have equivalent to the null hypothesis of independence the relationship

$$\text{Pr}\{\text{defective} \mid \text{item from population } 1\}$$
$$= \text{Pr}\{\text{defective} \mid \text{item from population } 2\}. \tag{4.4}$$

Thus a test of the null hypothesis of independence $\theta_{ij} = \theta_{i.}\theta_{.j}$ is identical with a test that the proportion of defectives is the same in the two populations.

We have encountered three situations giving rise to similar 2×2 tables, namely Tables 3.1, 3.9, and 5.5. The differences between the three situations was first emphasized by Barnard [8] and Pearson [9]. In Pearson's nomenclature, Problem I is what we discussed in Section 3.10, where both row totals and column totals were fixed, Problem II is what we discussed in Section 3.6, where one set of marginal totals (rows) was fixed and the other a random variable, and Problem III is what we discussed in this section, where both sets of marginal totals are random variables. The large sample statistics for testing the appropriate null hypotheses are (3.10.7) or (3.10.9) for Problem I, (3.6.8) or (3.6.10) for Problem II, and (4.1) for Problem III.

We first note that (3.10.9) is algebraically identical with (3.6.10). Secondly, the distribution of the square root of (4.1) will be a unit normal deviate, since $\chi^2(1) = u^2$. But the square root of (4.1) is identical with (3.10.9). In all three cases the correction for continuity improves the approximation. For (4.1) the correction takes the form of bringing each n_{ij} closer to its expectation by $1/2$. This is equivalent to replacing the factor $(n_{11}n_{22} - n_{21}n_{12})^2$ in the numerator by

$$\left\{|n_{11}n_{22} - n_{21}n_{21}| - \frac{n}{2}\right\}^2, \tag{4.5}$$

the other terms in (4.1) remaining unchanged. In this form the adjustment is widely known as "Yates' correction."

SECT. 5.5 LIFE TESTING 217

These three large sample approximations are, of course, only valid for large samples. For most purposes, the approximation is satisfactory if the minimum expectation, calculated as $n_i n_{.j}/n$, regarding the 2 × 2 table as being Problem III whether it is or not, exceeds some number such as 5. There is some reason to suppose that this is rather conservative and that it would be satisfactory to use 3.5 as the minimum expectation.

If the minimum expectation is too small to allow the large sample approximation to be used, if we are dealing with a Problem I we can use the Fisher exact test of Section 3.10 as an exact solution. If we are dealing with a Problem II or III, it was shown by Tocher [10] and Sverdrup [11] that the Fisher exact test is an exact solution to these other situations. An exposition of their arguments is beyond the level of this book. See also Lehmann [12], Sections 4.4 and 4.5.

5.5. Life Testing

Suppose that n electron tubes are placed on life test and that we assume that their life has an exponential distribution $p\{t\} = \theta e^{-\theta t}$. Tubes will fail at varying times, but there is an appreciable probability that we will have to wait a very long time for the longest surviving tube to fail. The

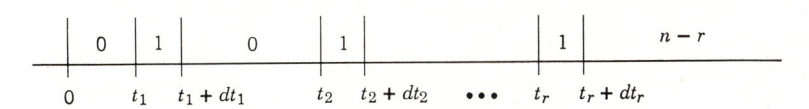

```
   | 0 | 1 |  0  | 1 |        |  1  | n − r
 ──┼───┼───┼─────┼───┼────────┼─────┼──────
   0  t₁  t₁+dt₁  t₂ t₂+dt₂ ···  tᵣ  tᵣ+dtᵣ
```

Figure 5.1

problem we discuss in this section is the derivation of the maximum likelihood estimator of θ from the observations $t_1, \ldots, t_r$, $r < n$, i.e., when the observations are terminated after the failure of the rth tube and we have no knowledge of what the lives of the remaining $n - r$ tubes would be other than that they are greater than t_r.

We imagine the t axis divided into intervals as in Figure 5.1. The numbers above the axis are the numbers of tubes whose lives terminate in the corresponding intervals.

The probability element $p\{t_1, t_2, \ldots, t_r\} \, dt_1 \, dt_2 \cdots dt_r$ is equal to the probability given by the multinomial probability function (1.2), where the x's are $0, 1, 0, \ldots, 1, n - r$, and the corresponding θ's are

$$\int_0^{t_1} p\{t\} \, dt, \ \int_{t_1}^{t_1+dt_1} p\{t\} \, dt, \ldots, \ \int_{t_r}^{t_r+dt_r} p\{t\} \, dt, \ \int_{t_r+dt_r}^{\infty} p\{t\} \, dt.$$

Thus

$$p\{t_1, t_2, \ldots, t_r\}\, dt_1\, dt_2 \cdots dt_r$$
$$= \frac{n!}{0!\, 1! \cdots 1!\, (n-r)!} \left(\int_0^{t_1} p\{t\}\, dt\right)^0 \left(\int_{t}^{t_1+dt_1} p\{t\}\, dt\right)^1 \cdots$$
$$\times \left(\int_{t_r+dt_r}^{\infty} p\{t\}\, dt\right)^{n-r} \quad (5.1)$$

$$= \frac{n!}{(n-r)!} \int_{t_1}^{t_1+dt_1} p\{t\}\, dt \cdots \int_{t_r}^{t_r+dt_r} p\{t\}\, dt \left(\int_{t_r+dt_r}^{\infty} p\{t\}\, dt\right)^{n-r}. \quad (5.2)$$

By the mean value theorem, $\int_a^b f(x)\, dx = (b-a)f(\xi)$ where $a \le \xi \le b$, so

$$\int_{t_i}^{t_i+dt_i} p\{t\}\, dt \simeq p\{t_i\}\, dt_i = \theta e^{-\theta t_i}\, dt_i, \quad i = 1, \ldots, r. \quad (5.3)$$

Also, using (1.12.5)

$$\int_{t_r+dt_r}^{\infty} p\{t\}\, dt \simeq \int_{t_r}^{\infty} p\{t\}\, dt = e^{-\theta t_r}. \quad (5.4)$$

Thus substituting (5.3) and (5.4) in (5.2), and canceling out the dt_i, $i = 1, \ldots, r$, we get

$$p\{t_1, \ldots, t_r\} = \frac{n!}{(n-r)!}\, \theta e^{-\theta t_1} \cdots \theta e^{-\theta t_r}(e^{-\theta t_r})^{n-r}$$
$$= \frac{n!}{(n-r)!}\, \theta^r \exp\left(-\theta \sum_i^r t_i\right) \exp\left[-(n-r)\theta t_r\right]. \quad (5.5)$$

This is also the likelihood function, so

$$\log L = \log n! - \log(n-r)! + r \log \theta - \theta \sum_i^r t_i - (n-r)\theta t_r \quad (5.6)$$

$$\frac{d \log L}{d\theta} = \frac{r}{\theta} - \sum_i^r t_i - (n-r)t_r. \quad (5.7)$$

Equating this to zero and solving for $\hat\theta$ gives

$$\hat\theta = \frac{r}{\sum_i^r t_i + (n-r)t_r}. \quad (5.8)$$

For a further discussion of this topic, see Epstein and Sobel [13], who show that $2r\, \hat\theta/\theta$ is distributed as $\chi^2(2r)$, which implies that $\hat\theta$ is an unbiased estimator of θ and that it has variance θ^2/r which is independent of n, and which permits tests to be made and confidence intervals to be constructed. Epstein and Sobel give a table which shows, for example, that the expected time to the tenth failure in a sample of twenty is 0.23 times the expected time to the tenth failure in a sample of ten.

EXERCISES

5.1. In a particular hour interval on four consecutive days the numbers of bugs of a certain type caught by a bug-catching device were 11, 25, 19, and 35. Test the null hypothesis that the expected numbers of bugs caught per hour were the same on the four days.

5.2. In intervals of 50, 70, 50, and 75 minutes on four consecutive days the numbers of bugs of a certain type caught by a bug catching device were 11, 25, 19, and 35. Test the null hypothesis that the expected numbers of bugs caught per hour were the same on the four days.

5.3. In a series of autopsies on 199 heavy smokers evidence of hypertension was found in 38.2 per cent of the cases. For moderate, light, and nonsmokers the corresponding numbers of cases were 288, 152, and 161 and the corresponding percentages 40.3, 45.5, and 50.3. Test the null hypothesis that the probability of hypertension is independent of the smoking category [Data from Wilens, Sigmund L., and Cassius M. Plais, "Cigarette Smoking and Arteriosclerosis," *Science*, 138 (1962), 975–977].

5.4. The number of window air conditioners in nine rows of row houses in an eastern city are as follows:

Row	1	2	3	4	5	6	7	8	9
Number of houses	23	43	43	41	41	42	42	39	36
Number of houses with air conditioners	5	8	18	3	17	11	25	19	18

Test the null hypothesis that the probability that a house has an air conditioner is independent of which row it is in.

5.5. In two high-altitude balloon flights near the north magnetic pole, the numbers of positive and negative electrons in cosmic rays were counted, and further each particle was categorized by the energy range into which it fell:

Energy interval	Number of electrons	
MEV	Positive	Negative
50–100	9	20
100–300	32	51
300–1000	23	117

[*Source:* De Shong, James A. Jr., Roger H. Hildebrand, and Peter Meyer, "Ratio of Electrons to Positrons in the Primary Cosmic Radiation," *Physical Review Letters* 12 (1964), 3–6.]

Test the null hypothesis that the relative proportions of positive and negative electrons are independent of the energy range.

REFERENCES

1. Abrahamson, Abraham E., Rubin Field, Leon Buchbinder, and Anna V. Catilli, "A Study of the Control of Sanitary Quality of Custard Filled Bakery Products in a Large City," *Food Research*, 17 (1952), 268–77.
2. Goodman, Leo A., and Williams H. Kruskal, "Measures of Association for Cross Classification," *Journal of the American Statistical Association*, 49 (1954), 723–64.
3. Goodman, Leo A., and William H. Kruskal, "Measures of Association for Cross Classifications. II: Further Discussion and References," *Journal of the American Statistical Association*, 54 (1959). 123–63.
4. Goodman, Leo A., and William H. Kruskal, "Measures of Association for Cross Classifications. III: Approximate Sampling Theory," *Journal of the American Statistical Association*, 58 (1963), 310–64.
5. Cochran, William G., "The χ^2 Test of Goodness of Fit," *Annals of Mathematical Statistics*, 23 (1952), 315–45.
6. Cochran, William G., "Some methods for strengthening the common χ^2 tests," *Biometrics*, 10 (1954), 417–51.
7. Goodman, Leo A., "Simple Methods for Analyzing Three-Factor Interaction in Contingency Tables," *Journal of the American Statistical Association*, 59 (1954), 319–52.
8. Barnard, G. A., "Significance Tests for 2×2 Tables," *Biometrika*, 34 (1947), 123–38.
9. Pearson, E. S., "The Choice of Statistical Tests Illustrated on the Interpretation of Data Classified in a 2×2 Table," *Biometrika*, 34 (1947), 139–67.
10. Tocher, K. D., "Extension of the Neyman-Pearson Theory of Tests to Discontinuous Variates," *Biometrika*, 37 (1950), 130–44.
11. Sverdrup, Erling, "Similarity, Unbiassedness, Minimaxibility, and Admissibility of Statistical Test Procedures," *Skandinavisk Aktuarietidskrift*, 36 (1953), 64–86.
12. Lehmann, E. L., *Testing Statistical Hypotheses*. New York: John Wiley and Sons, 1959.
13. Epstein, Benjamin, and Milton Sobel, "Life Testing," *Journal of the American Statistical Association*, 48 (1953), 486–502.

CHAPTER 6

Some Tests of the Hypothesis of Randomness: Control Charts

6.1. Introduction

Data are frequently obtained serially in time or space. For example, a series of determinations of the velocity of light may be spread over weeks or months. The quality of insulation of a long length of wire may be determined at a number of points along its length. In calculating the variance of the mean as σ^2/n, we are making the assumption that the observations are independent and are identically distributed. It is therefore desirable to have some method of checking on this assumption. In this chapter we will consider two such tests, the first appropriate for continuous observations with a normal distribution, and the second appropriate to a sequence of dissimilar elements of two types. This latter test is immediately adaptable to any continuous measurements by classifying them as above or below the median. The resulting test assumes continuity in the distribution but makes no assumptions about the form of the distribution, and is in fact an example of a nonparametric test, a class of tests to be discussed in Chapter 7.

6.2. The Mean Square Successive Difference Test

The mean square successive difference test is a test of the null hypothesis that we have a sequence of independent observations $x_1, \ldots, x_n$ from a population $N(\xi, \sigma^2)$. We compute estimates of σ^2 in two ways. The first is the unbiased estimator (2.3.23),

$$s^2 = \frac{1}{n-1} \sum_i^n (x_i - \bar{x})^2. \tag{2.1}$$

In computing this, it is usually convenient to use the identity

$$\sum_i^n (x_i - \bar{x})^2 = \sum_i^n x_i^2 - 2\bar{x}\sum_i^n x_i + n\bar{x}^2$$

$$= \sum_i^n x_i^2 - 2\left(\sum_i^n \frac{x_i}{n}\right)\sum_i^n x_i + n\left(\sum_i^n \frac{x_i}{n}\right)^2$$

$$= \sum_i^n x_i^2 - \frac{1}{n}\left(\sum_i^n x_i\right)^2. \quad (2.2)$$

The second estimator of σ^2 is $d^2/2$, where d^2 is defined as

$$d^2 = \frac{1}{n-1}\sum_{i=1}^{n-1}(x_{i+1} - x_i)^2. \quad (2.3)$$

It is easy to see that $E[d^2/2] = \sigma^2$, since

$$E[d^2] = \frac{1}{n-1} E\left[\sum_{i=1}^{n-1} x_{i+1}^2 + \sum_{i=1}^{n-1} x_i^2 - 2\sum_{i=1}^{n-1} x_{i+1}x_i\right]$$

$$= \frac{1}{n-1}\left\{\sum_{i=1}^{n-1} E[x_{i+1}^2] + \sum_{i=1}^{n-1} E[x_i^2] - 2\sum_{i=1}^{n-1} E[x_{i+1}]E[x_i]\right\}$$

$$= 2\{E[x_i^2] - (E[x_i])^2\} = 2V[x] = 2\sigma^2. \quad (2.4)$$

It was proved [1] that, under the null hypothesis,

$$E\left[\frac{d^2/2}{s^2}\right] = 1, \quad (2.5)$$

and

$$V\left[\frac{d^2/2}{s^2}\right] = \frac{n-2}{n^2-1}. \quad (2.6)$$

Thus the test statistic

$$\frac{\frac{d^2/2}{s^2} - 1}{\sqrt{(n-2)/(n^2-1)}} \quad (2.7)$$

is approximately distributed as a unit normal deviate under the null hypothesis. The exact distribution under the null hypothesis has been tabulated for n over the range 4 to 60 (but note that in [2] the sample estimate s^2 was defined with n in the denominator instead of $n-1$). This tabulation shows that even for n as small as 10 the normal approximation (2.7) is good.

The alternative to the null hypothesis is usually that consecutive observations tend to be correlated positively with their predecessors. The successive differences $x_{i+1} - x_i$ therefore tend to be smaller than they would

SECT. 6.2 THE MEAN SQUARE SUCCESSIVE DIFFERENCE TEST

be under complete randomness, and so the expected value of $d^2/2$ is less than σ^2. The numerator of (2.7) will tend to be negative, and the P value for the null hypothesis is obtained by putting (2.7) equal to u_P.

Table 6.1 gives the results of 23 determinations, ordered in time, of the density of the earth by Cavendish [3]. The right-hand column of the table is referred to in Section 6.5.

Table 6.1

i	x_i	d_i		i	x_i	d_i	
1	5.36		B	13	5.27	+0.17	B
2	5.29	−0.07	B	14	5.39	+0.12	B
3	5.58	+0.29	A	15	5.42	+0.03	B
4	5.65	+0.07	A	16	5.47	+0.05	A
5	5.57	−0.08	A	17	5.63	+0.16	A
6	5.53	−0.04	A	18	5.34	−0.29	B
7	5.62	+0.09	A	19	5.46	+0.12	Median
8	5.29	−0.33	B	20	5.30	−0.16	B
9	5.44	+0.15	B	21	5.75	+0.45	A
10	5.34	−0.10	B	22	5.68	−0.07	A
11	5.79	+0.45	A	23	5.85	+0.17	A
12	5.10	−0.69	B				

Using (2.1) and (2.2), s^2 is computed as

$$s^2 = \frac{\left[(5.36^2 + \cdots + 5.85^2) - \dfrac{(5.36 + \cdots + 5.85)^2}{23}\right]}{23 - 1} = 0.036260.$$

We compute d^2 from (2.3):

$$d^2 = \left[\frac{(-0.07)^2 + \cdots + (0.17)^2}{22}\right] = 0.061941.$$

From (2.6) we obtain

$$V\left[\frac{(d^2/2)}{s^2}\right] = \frac{23 - 2}{23^2 - 1} = 0.03977.$$

Thus our test statistic is

$$u_P = \frac{(0.061941/2)/0.036260 - 1}{\sqrt{0.03977}} = \frac{-0.14588}{0.1944} = -0.732,$$

whence $P = 0.23$. This is substantially greater than 0.05; so we would not reject the null hypothesis of randomness at the 5 per cent level of significance.

6.3. Runs of Elements of Two Types

Suppose that we have m elements of type A and n of type B, $m + n = N$, and these N elements are selected randomly one at a time without replacement and the sequence of A's and B's recorded. In this section we consider the distribution of the number of runs, say u, a run being a sequence of like elements. For example, if $m = n = 5$, and we observe any of the sequences

$ABBBBBAAAA$, $AABBBBBAAA$, $AAABBBBBAA$, $AAAABBBBBA$,

or $BAAAAABBBB$,   etc.,   (3.1)

then $u = 3$. We want $\Pr\{u = 3\}$.

We will consider first two combinatorial problems. We will determine the number of ways in which r indistinguishable objects can be placed in n identifiable cells, firstly with no restriction on the number of objects that can be put in any one cell (other than, of course, the obvious restriction that we cannot put in any one cell more objects than we have, namely r), and secondly with the restriction that no cell can be empty.

Consider a row of n cells with r objects to be placed in them. The n cells can be represented by the spaces between $n + 1$ bars; e.g.,

$|A\ A\ A|\ |A\ A|\ |\ |$

represents a row of 5 cells with 3, 0, 2, 0, and 0 objects A in the cells. Of the $n + 1$ bars, one must always be in the first position and one in the last, but the remaining $n - 1$ may be anywhere. Each arrangement of $n - 1$ objects of one type, namely bars, and r objects of a second type, namely A's, determines a different way of filling the n cells, and by (1.7.7) the number of such arrangements, and hence the number of ways of filling the n cells, is

$$\frac{[(n - 1) + r]!}{(n - 1)!\, r!}. \qquad (3.2)$$

Now suppose that the number of objects exceeds the number of cells, i.e., $r > n$, and we impose the condition that no cell is to be empty. Now no interval between objects can have more than one bar, since if it did have say two, then these two bars would define a cell which would be empty. Of the $r - 1$ spaces between the r objects, we can choose $n - 1$ of them as places to put the bars (we have a total of $n + 1$ bars with two of them committed to the two end positions). The number of ways in which we can make this choice is, by (1.7.7),

$$\binom{r-1}{n-1} = \frac{(r-1)!}{(n-1)!\,(r-n)!}. \tag{3.3}$$

This is the number of ways in which we can place r objects in n cells, $r \geq n$, with none of the cells empty.

An alternative argument is as follows. Given r objects, first place n of them in the n cells so that every cell contains precisely one object. This leaves $r - n$ objects which can be placed in the n cells now without any restriction. Using (3.2) with r replaced by $r - n$, the number of ways is

$$\frac{[(n-1) + (r-n)]!}{(n-1)!\,(r-n)!} = \frac{(r-1)!}{(n-1)!\,(r-n)!}, \tag{3.4}$$

as before in (3.3).

We now turn to obtaining $\Pr\{U = u\}$ given m objects of one kind and n objects of a second kind. From (1.7.7), the total number of arrangements is $\binom{m+n}{m} = \binom{m+n}{n}$. We assume that all these arrangements have equal probability, so

$$\Pr\{U = u\} = \frac{\text{number of arrangements giving } u \text{ runs}}{\text{total number of arrangements}}. \tag{3.5}$$

Now u is either odd or even. Let us consider the case where it is even, so that $u = 2v$ where v is an integer. Then there must be v runs of objects of the first kind and v runs of objects of the second kind. Consider the runs of objects of the first kind and regard each run as a cell. By (3.3), the number of ways we can fill these v cells from m objects in such a way that no cell is empty is $\binom{m-1}{v-1}$. Similarly, there are $\binom{n-1}{v-1}$ ways in which the n objects of the second kind can be placed in v cells, no cell being empty. Finally, given a sequence $A \cdots B \cdots A \cdots$, we can exchange every A group with the B group following it so that we have a sequence $B \cdots A \cdots B \cdots$, and this sequence will have the same number of runs as the first. Thus the number of arrangements giving u runs is

$$2\binom{m-1}{v-1}\binom{n-1}{v-1}. \tag{3.6}$$

Substituting this in (3.5) gives

$$\Pr\{U = u = 2v\} = \frac{2\binom{m-1}{v-1}\binom{n-1}{v-1}}{\binom{m+n}{m}}. \tag{3.7}$$

A similar argument for the case of u odd, say equal to $2v + 1$, gives

$$\Pr\{U = u = 2v + 1\} = \frac{\binom{m-1}{v}\binom{n-1}{v-1} + \binom{m-1}{v-1}\binom{n-1}{v}}{\binom{m+n}{m}}. \quad (3.8)$$

For the example of (3.1), $m = n = 5$, $u = 3$, and

$$\Pr\{U \leq 3\} = \Pr\{U = 2\} + \Pr\{U = 3\}$$

$$= \frac{2\binom{4}{0}\binom{4}{0}}{\binom{10}{5}} + \frac{\binom{4}{1}\binom{4}{0} + \binom{4}{0}\binom{4}{1}}{\binom{10}{5}} = \frac{2}{252} + \frac{8}{252} = 0.0397. \quad (3.9)$$

This problem was discussed by Stevens [4] and Wald and Wolfowitz [5]. The cumulative probability $\Pr\{U \leq u\}$ has been tabulated for $m \leq n \leq 20$ by Swed and Eisenhart [6].

6.4. An Approximation to the Distribution of the Number of Runs of Elements of Two Types

The formulas for the exact probabilities of numbers of runs of two types of elements obtained in the previous section are too cumbersome to use in practice, particularly when we are beyond the range of Swed and Eisenhart's tables [6]. In this section we obtain the expected value and the variance of the number of runs, u, and then assuming that u is normally distributed we can obtain P values for observed u's.

It is convenient to consider the number of transitions t rather than the number of runs u: A transition is defined as the point where one run ends and another begins. The number of transitions must be one less than the number of runs, as the last run ends at the end of the sequence, and this point is not counted as a transition. Hence

$$t = u - 1. \quad (4.1)$$

We want to find $E[u] = E[t] + 1$ and $V[u] = V[t]$ under the null hypothesis.

Denote the total number of gaps between elements where transitions could occur as $N' = N - 1$. Define t_i as the number of transitions at the ith gap, i.e.,

$$t_i = \begin{cases} 0 & \text{if either } A, A \text{ or } B, B \text{ on the two sides of the gap,} \\ 1 & \text{if either } A, B \text{ or } B, A \text{ on the two sides of the gap.} \end{cases} \quad (4.2)$$

SECT. 6.4 DISTRIBUTION OF THE NUMBER OF RUNS OF ELEMENTS

Then the total number of transitions $t = \sum_i^{N'} t_i$, and $E[t_i]$ is the probability that a pair of consecutive elements are dissimilar. We have

$$\Pr\{\text{first in a pair is an } A\} = \frac{m}{m+n}, \tag{4.3}$$

$$\Pr\{\text{second in a pair is a } B \mid \text{first was an } A\} = \frac{n}{m+n-1}; \tag{4.4}$$

so

$$\Pr\{\text{a pair is an } AB\} = \frac{m}{m+n}\frac{n}{m+n-1}. \tag{4.5}$$

Using these and similar results we can tabulate the probabilities of all possible types of pairs (Table 6.2), along with the corresponding values of t_i and t_i^2.

Table 6.2

Type of pair	t_i	t_i^2	Probability
AA	0	0	$m(m-1)/(m+n)(m+n-1)$
AB	1	1	$mn/(m+n)(m+n-1)$
BA	1	1	$mn/(m+n)(m+n-1)$
BB	0	0	$n(n-1)/(m+n)(m+n-1)$

It follows that

$$E[t_i] = 1 \times \frac{mn}{(m+n)(m+n-1)} + 1 \times \frac{mn}{(m+n)(m+n-1)}$$

$$= \frac{2mn}{(m+n)(m+n-1)}, \tag{4.6}$$

$$E[t_i^2] = \frac{2mn}{(m+n)(m+n-1)}. \tag{4.7}$$

We thus obtain

$$E[t] = E\left[\sum_i^{N'} t_i\right] = \sum_i^{N'} E[t_i] = N' \frac{2mn}{(m+n)(m+n-1)} = \frac{2mn}{m+n}, \tag{4.8}$$

since $N' = m+n-1$, and the expected number of runs is

$$E[u] = 1 + \frac{2mn}{m+n}. \tag{4.9}$$

We now want the variance of u:

$$V[u] = V[t] = V\left[\sum_i^{N'} t_i\right]$$

$$= \sum_i^{N'} V[t_i] + 2\sum_{i=1}^{N'-1}\sum_{j=i+1}^{N'} \text{Cov}[t_i, t_j]. \tag{4.10}$$

The first term is readily evaluated:

$$\sum_i^{N'} V[t_i] = N'V[t_i] = N'\{E[t_i^2] - (E[t_i])^2\}. \tag{4.11}$$

The second term in (4.10) involves the $\text{Cov}[t_i, t_j]$ which can be calculated as

$$\text{Cov}[t_i, t_j] = E[t_i t_j] - E[t_i]E[t_j] = E[t_i t_j] - (E[t_i])^2, \tag{4.12}$$

since $E[t_i] = E[t_j]$. The terms $t_i t_j$ are best considered in two groups:

1. The terms $t_i t_{i+1}$ which involve adjacent gaps, in which the pair of elements determining t_i has as its second element the first element of the second pair determining t_{i+1}.

2. The terms $t_i t_k$, where $k > i + 1$, for which the two pairs of elements do not have an element in common; i.e., the ith and kth gaps are separated by one or more other gaps.

We need the numbers of terms of these two types. The total number of pairs t_i, t_j, with $i < j$, is the number of combinations that can be formed from N' items taken two at a time, i.e.,

$$\binom{N'}{2} = \frac{N'!}{2!(N'-2)!} = \frac{N'(N'-1)}{2}. \tag{4.13}$$

The number of pairs of type 1 is $N - 2 = N' - 1$, since, if we consider a typical sequence of elements 1, 2, 3, 4, 5, then the only adjacent pairs of t's that can be formed are t_1, t_2 from elements 1, 2, 3; t_2, t_3 from elements 2, 3, 4; t_3, t_4 from elements 3, 4, 5. The number of pairs of type 2 can then be obtained as the total number of all pairs minus the number of pairs of type 1:

$$\frac{N'(N'-1)}{2} - (N'-1) = \frac{(N'-1)(N'-2)}{2}. \tag{4.14}$$

To compute the $\text{Cov}[t_i, t_j]$ from (4.12) we need $E[t_i t_j]$ for the two types of pairs. For type 1, the pairs t_i, t_{i+1} are those pairs of transitions with one element in common. All possible examples are listed in Table 6.3. The only sequences giving nonzero values for $t_i t_{i+1}$ are ABA and BAB.

Table 6.3

Sequences of elements	t_i	t_{i+1}	$t_i t_{i+1}$
AAA	0	0	0
AAB	0	1	0
ABA	1	1	1
ABB	1	0	0
BAA	1	0	0
BAB	1	1	1
BBA	0	1	0
BBB	0	0	0

These have probabilities

$$\frac{m}{m+n} \cdot \frac{n}{m+n-1} \cdot \frac{m-1}{m+n-2} \quad \text{and} \quad \frac{n}{m+n} \cdot \frac{m}{m+n-1} \cdot \frac{n-1}{m+n-2}. \tag{4.15}$$

Thus

$$E[t_i t_{i+1}] = 1 \times \frac{mn(m-1)}{(m+n)(m+n-1)(m+n-2)}$$

$$+ 1 \times \frac{mn(n-1)}{(m+n)(m+n-1)(m+n-2)}$$

$$= \frac{mn}{(m+n)(m+n-1)}. \tag{4.16}$$

Inserting this in (4.12) we get for the covariances of the pairs of the type t_i, t_{i+1}

$$\text{Cov}[t_i, t_{i+1}] = \frac{mn}{(m+n)(m+n-1)} - (E[t_i])^2. \tag{4.17}$$

There are $N' - 1 = m + n - 2$ such terms.

To compute $\text{Cov}[t_i, t_k]$, $k > i + 1$, we need $E[t_i t_k]$ for the pairs of t's formed by the types of pairs of elements listed in Table 6.4. The only types giving nonzero values for $t_i t_k$ are $AB \cdots AB$, $AB \cdots BA$, $BA \cdots AB$, and $BA \cdots BA$, all of which involve two A's and two B's: These types all have the same probability

$$\frac{m}{m+n} \cdot \frac{n}{m+n-1} \cdot \frac{m-1}{m+n-2} \cdot \frac{n-1}{m+n-3}. \tag{4.18}$$

Thus

$$E[t_i t_k] = \frac{4mn(m-1)(n-1)}{(m+n)(m+n-1)(m+n-2)(m+n-3)}. \tag{4.19}$$

Inserting this in (4.12), we get of the covariances of pairs of the type $t_i, t_k, k > i + 1$,

$$\text{Cov}[t_i, t_k] = \frac{4mn(m-1)(n-1)}{(m+n)(m+n-1)(m+n-2)(m+n-3)} - (E[t_i])^2. \quad (4.20)$$

By (4.14), there are $(m+n-2)(m+n-3)/2$ such terms.

Table 6.4

Types of pairs	t_i	t_k	$t_i t_k$	Types of pairs	t_i	t_k	$t_i t_k$
$AA \cdots AA$	0	0	0	$BA \cdots AA$	1	0	0
$AA \cdots AB$	0	1	0	$BA \cdots AB$	1	1	1
$AA \cdots BA$	0	1	0	$BA \cdots BA$	1	1	1
$AA \cdots BB$	0	0	0	$BA \cdots BB$	1	0	0
$AB \cdots AA$	1	0	0	$BB \cdots AA$	0	0	0
$AB \cdots AB$	1	1	1	$BB \cdots AB$	0	1	0
$AB \cdots BA$	1	1	1	$BB \cdots BA$	0	1	0
$AB \cdots BB$	1	0	0	$BB \cdots BB$	0	0	0

We now substitute in (4.12) the variance term (4.11) and the two covariance terms (4.17) and (4.20), the two latter with the appropriate coefficients, namely, the numbers of terms of the two types:

$$V[u] = (m+n-1)\{E[t_i^2] - (E[t_i])^2\}$$
$$+ 2(m+n-2)\left\{\frac{mn}{(m+n)(m+n-1)} - (E[t_i])^2\right\}$$
$$+ 2 \times \frac{1}{2}(m+n-2)(m+n-3)$$
$$\times \left\{\frac{4mn(m-1)(n-1)}{(m+n)(m+n-1)(m+n-2)(m+n-3)} - (E[t_i])^2\right\}. \quad (4.21)$$

The sum of the coefficients of $(E[t_i])^2$ is easily shown to be $-(m+n-1)^2$. Substituting for $E[t_i]$ from (4.6) and for $E[t_i^2]$ from (4.7), (4.21) reduces to

$$V[u] = \frac{2mn(2mn-m-n)}{(m+n)^2(m+n-1)}. \quad (4.22)$$

Thus, if u is an observed number of runs, the statistic

$$\frac{u - [2mn/(m+n) + 1]}{\sqrt{2mn(2mn-m-n)/(m+n)^2(m+n-1)}} \quad (4.23)$$

is under the null hypothesis a standardized variable which for large m and n is approximately normal.

The above statistic has been studied by Stevens [4] and Wald and Wolfowitz [5]. Wallis [7] suggested making a correction for continuity by bringing the observed u closer to its expectation by 1/2. For very small values of m and n the normal approximation will be unreliable, and the exact values of the distribution tabulated by Swed and Eisenhart [6] should be used.

Usually the alternative hypothesis envisaged is one-sided: Usually we anticipate the runs of like elements to be greater in length and hence fewer in number than under the hypothesis of randomness. For example, if a row of tomato plants contains diseased plants we might expect these to occur in groups. The usual critical region for the statistic (4.23) is therefore $<u_\alpha$.

As an example, for (3.1) $m = 5$, $n = 5$, $u = 3$, whence

$$E[u] = 1 + \frac{2 \times 5 \times 5}{5 + 5} = 6, \qquad (4.24)$$

$$V[u] = \frac{2 \times 5 \times 5 \times (2 \times 5 \times 5 - 5 - 5)}{(5 + 5)^2(5 + 5 - 1)} = 2.222, \qquad (4.25)$$

and the approximate unit normal deviate is

$$\frac{u + 1/2 - E[u]}{\sqrt{V[u]}} = \frac{3 + 1/2 - 6}{\sqrt{2.222}} = 1.677, \qquad (4.26)$$

whence $P = 0.047$, to be compared with the exact figure 0.0397 in (3.9). Of course, as m and n increase the approximation improves. For example, for $m = n = 20$, $\Pr\{U \leq 15\}$ equals 0.0388 by the approximation to be compared with the exact figure 0.0380 from [6].

The foregoing treatment of runs of two kinds of elements has been extended to the case of three kinds of elements: If the numbers of elements of the three types are a, b, and c,

$$E[u] = \frac{2(ab + ac + bc)}{a + b + c} + 1, \qquad (4.27)$$

$$V[u] = \frac{[2(ab + ac + bc)]^2}{(a + b + c)^2(a + b + c - 1)} - \frac{2(ab + ac + bc) + 6abc}{(a + b + c)(a + b + c - 1)}. \qquad (4.28)$$

6.5. Runs Above and Below the Median

The test of the previous section can readily be adapted to test the randomness of a sequence of continuous observations, $x_1, \ldots, x_N$. By classifying the observations as being above or below the sample median, each observation will be labeled either A or B. If the number of observations is odd, we ignore the observation which falls on the median. The number of observations above the median m equals the number of observations below the median n; so $m = n$. Equations (4.9) and (4.22) become

$$E[u] = 1 + m, \quad (5.1)$$

$$V[u] = \frac{m(m-1)}{2m-1}. \quad (5.2)$$

For the data of Table 6.1, the median is 5.46, and the observations are marked A or B accordingly in the last column. The number of runs $u = 8$, $m = n = 11$; $E[u] = 1 + 11 = 12$, and

$$V[u] = \frac{11 \times (11-1)}{2 \times 11 - 1} = 5.2381, \quad u_P = \frac{8 + 1/2 - 12}{\sqrt{5.2381}} = -1.529, \quad (5.3)$$

whence $P = 0.063$.

This test is an example of a so-called nonparametric test; its only assumptions under the null hypothesis are that the observations are random and identically distributed from some continuous distribution whose form has not been specified. The mean square successive difference test, in contrast, assumed normality. Usually, if such a stronger assumption is justified, then the test making use of such an assumption is more powerful against a particular alternative than an analogous test not making use of the assumption, assuming that both tests are oriented toward having power against this alternative. In the present instance, the assumption of normality appears reasonable, and, if the null hypothesis had been appreciably false, we might have anticipated a smaller P value with the mean square successive difference test than the test for runs above and below the median. Actually the reverse occurred, though with both tests the null hypothesis was acceptable at the 5 per cent level of significance.

Other studies have been made of the distributions of runs of various types. The distributions of runs above and below the median of specified lengths, of runs up and down by number and by length, etc., are available (see [8–11]).

6.6. Control Charts for the Mean and Range

The statistical control chart, due to Shewhart [12, 13], is a device for keeping a check on the stability of a repetitive process. For example, we may be filling cans with lubricating oil and wish to maintain the contents

SECT. 6.6   CONTROL CHARTS FOR THE MEAN AND RANGE

at a stable level. If x_i is the weight of the contents of the ith can, if the x_i are independent observations from a population normally distributed with known mean ξ and variance σ^2, then if we take samples of n cans the mean weighs $\bar{x}$ will satisfy (1.18.19) with $\bar{x}$ written for x and $\sigma/\sqrt{n}$ written for σ:

$$\Pr\left\{\bar{x} < \xi - \frac{k\sigma}{\sqrt{n}}\right\} + \Pr\left\{\bar{x} > \xi + \frac{k\sigma}{\sqrt{n}}\right\} = 2[1 - \Phi(k)]. \tag{6.1}$$

With $k = 3.09$, for example, 99.8 per cent of all sample means will lie in the interval $\xi \pm 3.09\sigma/\sqrt{n}$. Should a sample mean lie outside this interval, since this will only happen twice in a thousand times under the stated assumptions, the natural conclusion is to suspect that the assumptions are incorrect in some respect. Usually the most likely way in which the system has deviated from the assumptions is for the mean to have shifted. So long as only the stated proportion of points lies outside the interval, the process is said to be in a *state of statistical control*, and, if more than that proportion of points is outside the interval, then the process is said to be *out of control*.

The sample means are plotted on a chart serially as they are obtained, and lines known as *control limits* are drawn in at $\xi \pm k\sigma/\sqrt{n}$. Usually ξ is estimated by the mean of the previous 30 or more sample means. The standard deviation σ can be estimated by (2.3.23), but almost invariably a quick but not fully efficient method is used, based on the *ranges*. The range w of a sample of n is defined as the difference between the largest and the smallest observations in the sample. For samples from a normal population $E[w] = d_n \sigma$, where d_n is a constant, tabulated in Table VI, dependent on n. The standard deviation is estimated by

$$\hat{\sigma} = \frac{\bar{w}}{d_n} \tag{6.2}$$

where $\bar{w}$ is the mean of 30 or more ranges. For example, if ξ is estimated as 100, and $\bar{w} = 10$ for a large number of samples of 5, then $\hat{\sigma} = 10/2.326$. For 99 per cent control limits, we have $2[1 - \Phi(k)] = 0.01$; so $\Phi(k) = 0.995$ and $k = 2.576$. The control limits are

$$100 \pm 2.576 \times \frac{10/2.326}{\sqrt{5}} = 100.00 \pm 4.95.$$

The object of this procedure is to enable the operator to distinguish between random variation and variation in excess of what would reasonably occur at random. The operator has to accept the variation represented by the fluctuation of the sample means within the control limits as inevitable, given ξ and σ. However, the occurrence of an out-of-control point is a signal for him to suspect that something has changed, to find out what, and to restore the status quo.

If σ increases, points on the mean chart can go out of control without any change in ξ. If the standard deviation increases by a factor of 4, and we are using 99 per cent control limits for the means, so that in (6.1) $k = 2.58$, the limits would now be effectively at $\pm 2.58(\sigma/4)/\sqrt{n} = \pm 0.645\sigma/\sqrt{n}$; so the probability of a point falling outside these limits is $2[1 - \Phi(0.645)] = 2(1 - 0.7405) = 0.519$, a drastic change from the supposed 0.01.

To guard against this ambiguity we can keep a control chart on the ranges. For samples of size n from a normal population with standard deviation σ, the sampling distribution of the range w is known,

$$\Pr\{w < \sigma W_P\} = P, \qquad (6.3)$$

where W_P is tabulated in Table VI of the Appendix. Thus $P_2 - P_1$ control limits for w are given by

$$\Pr\{\sigma W_{P_1} < w < \sigma W_{P_2}\} = P_2 - P_1. \qquad (6.4)$$

For example, if $n = 10$, and we want 95 per cent control limits, then we need $P_2 = 0.975$, $P_1 = 0.025$. From Table VI for $n = 10$, $W_{0.975} = 4.79$, $W_{0.025} = 1.67$, and the limits are $(1.67\sigma, 4.79\sigma)$. If σ is estimated as $\bar{w}/d_n = \bar{w}/3.078$, then the lower control limit is $0.542\bar{w}$, and the upper control limit $1.556\bar{w}$. A control chart for ranges is kept in an analogous manner to that for means. The sample ranges are plotted from left to right as they occur in time, and the control lines drawn in. If a point lies outside a control limit, this is evidence that the standard deviation of the population has changed.

Control limits are not the same as specification limits. If a process is in a state of statistical control, the sample averages with rare exceptions will be fluctuating inside the control limits $\xi \pm k\sigma/\sqrt{n}$ and the individual observations will be fluctuating with rare exceptions in the interval $\xi \pm k\sigma$: These limits, $+k\sigma$ and $-k\sigma$, will only coincide with the process specification limits, if it has any, by accident. The limits for the individual observations are wider than the control limits for the sample means by the factor $\sqrt{n}$.

To revert to our example of filling cans with lubricating oil, if ξ is equal to the claimed quantity, say ξ_0, then the individual observations x will be distributed around ξ_0 with standard deviation σ, and 50 per cent of all cans will have less than the claimed amount. If only 1 per cent of all cans are to have less than the claimed amount, we require that

$$\Pr\{x < \xi_0\} = 0.01 = \Phi\left(\frac{\xi_0 - \xi}{\sigma}\right)$$

by (1.18.13); so $(\xi_0 - \xi)/\sigma = u_{0.01} = -2.326$, and so the required overfill $\xi - \xi_0 = 2.326\sigma$. It may be economic to make quite an effort to reduce σ.

6.7. Control Charts for Poisson Distributed Observations

Suppose that we wish to keep a control chart on the number x of defects in square-yard samples of carpeting. If the process is in control, then x will be a Poisson distributed variable with parameter ξ. We assume that ξ can be estimated accurately by (3.11.11) as $\bar{x} = \sum_i^n x_i/n$ where n is large.

The usual procedure is to use the normal approximation to the Poisson, (3.13.5). We assume that x is normally distributed with mean ξ and variance ξ, where ξ is estimated by $\bar{x}$, and the so-called three sigma limits are $\bar{x} \pm 3\sqrt{\bar{x}}$. Continuity corrections are usually omitted.

It may sometimes be justifiable to be more precise. Equating (3.13.3) with P gives

$$\Pr\{\chi^2 < 2\xi\} = 1 - P, \qquad f = 2(x_P + 1). \tag{7.1}$$

But, since $\Pr\{\chi^2 < \chi^2_{1-P}\} = 1 - P$,

$$2\xi = \chi^2_{1-P}, \qquad f = 2(x_P + 1). \tag{7.2}$$

This equation will determine x_P for a specified ξ and P: By changing x we change f and hence χ^2_{1-P} until it equals 2ξ. Since x has to change by integers, f will change by jumps of two units, and in general we will not be able to get an exact solution.

As an example, suppose that $\xi = 9$ (there is no reason, of course, why ξ should be an integer). If we want 95 per cent control limits, we will want P_1 to be as close as possible to 0.025 from the lower side. Substituting in (7.2), we want $2 \times 9 = \chi^2_{1-0.025}$. From the χ^2 table, $\chi^2_{0.975} = 17.5$, 19.0, and 20.5 for $f = 8$, 9, and 10, respectively. We cannot use an odd value of f, because that would make x fractional. We have to settle for $f = 8$, whence $x = 3$, and $\Pr\{x \leq 3\} = 1 - \Pr\{\chi^2(8) < 18\} \simeq 1 - 0.976 = 0.024$, actually very close to the desired value of 0.025. If we used $f = 10$, to give $x = 4$, $\Pr\{x \leq 4\} = 1 - \Pr\{\chi^2(10) < 18\} \simeq 1 - 0.94 = 0.06$, much larger than the desired figure. For the upper limit, we want

$$\Pr\{x \geq x_{P_2}\} = 1 - \Pr\{x \leq x_{P_2} - 1\} = \Pr\{\chi^2(2x_{P_2}) < 2\xi\}, \tag{7.3}$$

to be less than or equal to $1 - P_2 = 0.025$. We try $f = 30$, when $x = 15$,

and
$$\Pr\{\chi^2(30) < 2 \times 9\} \simeq 0.035, \tag{7.4}$$
which is too large; so, trying $f = 32$, we have
$$\Pr\{\chi^2(32) < 2 \times 9\} \simeq 0.02, \tag{7.5}$$
and so we use our upper control limit, $x_{0.98} = 16$.

The crude limits $\bar{x} \pm 1.96\sqrt{\bar{x}}$ in this case, for $\bar{x} = 9$, are 3.12 and 14.88, which would be rounded outward to 3 and 15.

EXERCISES

6.1. A zoo has ten lions and three cages. Assuming that the lions are indistinguishable, in how many ways can the lions be placed in the cages (*a*) with no restriction on the number of lions per cage, (*b*) with no cage empty, (*c*) with no lion to be alone by himself and no cage empty? In each case give the appropriate general formula for the case of r lions and n cages before particularizing to the given numerical case.

6.2. In a street of row houses X represents the presence of an air conditioner and 0 the absence of an air conditioner:

00X0X000000000000XXXXXX000000000X000X00X00

There are 31 0's and 11 X's. Does the observed number of runs differ significantly from the number expected under the null hypothesis of randomness?

6.3. A physician running a clinical trial on a weight-reducing product, C, included in his experiment two other substances, A and B, intended for use as placebos. The initial weights of the patients assigned to the three treatments are given below. Rank the patients by order of increasing weight. If the patients had been allocated to the three treatments at random, then the sequence of A's. B's, and C's would be a random sequence. Consider whether the observed number of runs is consistent with the hypothesis that randomization had been employed.

A: 147, 183.5, 150, 167, 180.25, 216.5, 127.5, 222.5, 132, 163, 221.5, 203.5
B: 180, 161.5, 157, 155, 146.5, 131.5, 136.25, 159.5, 162.5, 225.5, 159.
C: 175, 168, 144.5, 125, 250.5, 123.75, 124.25, 117, 118, 162.25.

6.4. The number of hurricanes on the East Coast for the years 1930 through 1954 were reported as follows:

2,2,6,10,5,5,5,2,4,2,4,4,2,5,6,4,2,4,5,8,11,8,6,5,6.

Test the null hypothesis that this a random sequence (*a*) with the mean square successive difference test, assuming that the square root of the numbers observed is normally distributed (why?); (*b*) with the test for runs of two kinds of elements (Let years with 4 or fewer hurricanes be "good" and with 5 or more be "bad"); (*c*) with the test for runs of three kinds of elements (Let years with 4 or fewer hurricanes be "good," with 5 be "medium," and with 6 or more be "bad"). Report one-sided P values.

6.5. Construct a control chart for the data in the preceding example, using 99 per cent control limits.

6.6. We have a machine automatically filling tubes of toothpaste. We take a large number of samples of five tubes, find the weights of the individual tubes, and take the range of weights in each sample of 5. The mean weight is 16 grams, and the mean range is 0.7 gram.

(*a*) Suppose we want control limits that will contain 98 per cent of all sample means, on the average, when the system is under control. What should the control limits be? (*b*) What are 98 per cent control limits for the ranges of the samples of five? (*c*) If the label claims that the tube contains 16 grams, what percentage of the customers are receiving less than they have a right to expect? (*d*) What percentage of the customers get less than 15.8 grams? (*e*) To give 99.9 per cent of the customers at least what the label claims, where should the process average be?

6.7. A mining company finds a body of ore, approximately rectangular. At equally spaced intervals along the length they bore through the body, and the cores are analyzed for a certain mineral. In this sample the minimum is 0.005, the median 0.05, and the maximum 1.32. It is apparent that this distribution is exceedingly skew, since the distance from the minimum to the median is 0.045 whereas the distance from the median to the maximum is 1.27. If we use logarithms, or more conveniently 100 times the (logarithms + 3), say x, the minimum, median, and maximum are 70, 170, and 312. It appears that the logarithm of the percentage is much more symmetrically distributed than the percentage itself.

Test the null hypothesis that this sequence of observations is a random sequence with (*a*) the mean-square successive difference test, (*b*) the test for number of runs above and below the median.

Bore	x	Bore	x	Bore	x
1	170	16	148	31	130
2	178	17	130	32	178
3	263	18	100	33	190
4	185	19	70	34	291
5	311	20	100	35	241
6	312	21	160	36	130
7	190	22	148	37	70
8	178	23	130	38	215
9	160	24	300	39	223
10	308	25	160	40	195
11	223	26	148	41	160
12	130	27	130	42	100
13	195	28	100	43	130
14	170	29	70	44	252
15	160	30	100	45	240
				46	274

What practical inferences might you draw if the hypothesis of randomness was (c) acceptable? (d) Rejected at some reasonable significance level?

6.8. Construct a control chart for means and ranges for the data of the preceding exercise. Use samples of size 5 made up by grouping consecutive observations, and discard the 46th bore. Give 99 per cent control limits.

6.9. A process for purification of a fine chemical involved passing it in solution through a column containing a resin on which the chemical was adsorbed. A specified volume of solution constituted a batch, after which the flow was switched to another column. The figures in Table A give the concentration escaping from the outgoing end of the column at the conclusion of each batch operation.

(a) Construct a control chart for means and ranges of samples of 4 with 99 per cent control limits. Note that a chart of totals is equivalent for all practical

Table A

Batches	1	5	9	13	17	21	25	29	33	37
	0.5	2.9	1.0	1.9	3.5	1.2	1.7	2.8	2.3	4.2
	3.0	3.0	2.5	4.6	0.7	2.0	2.2	2.9	1.7	3.0
	3.8	1.7	6.7	0.8	2.1	1.4	1.1	1.9	4.0	2.2
	1.1	3.1	1.9	3.7	3.0	1.6	2.7	3.2	0.8	2.1
Totals	8.4	10.7	12.1	11.0	9.3	6.2	7.7	10.8	8.8	11.5
Ranges	3.3	1.4	5.7	3.8	2.8	0.8	1.6	1.3	3.2	2.1

Batches	41	45	49	53	57	61	65	69	73	77
	2.3	1.8	1.3	4.2	0.5	0.8	1.2	2.3	1.2	0.7
	1.4	4.0	5.2	2.4	1.8	2.7	2.9	1.5	0.7	0.5
	2.2	2.6	0.9	1.0	0.6	0.9	1.0	0.3	3.4	1.3
	1.5	1.2	0.8	1.9	0.8	1.4	1.0	0.3	1.2	0.3
Totals	7.4	9.6	8.2	9.4	3.7	5.8	6.1	4.4	6.5	2.8
Ranges	0.9	2.8	4.4	3.2	1.3	1.9	1.9	2.0	2.7	1.0

Batches	81	85	89	93	97	101	105	109	113	117
	1.3	0.5	1.1	1.2	0.9	1.6	0.3	0.8	0.7	0.6
	0.1	0.9	0.5	1.2	1.3	0.6	0.7	0.4	0.8	1.4
	2.1	0.8	0.5	0.8	0.6	1.0	0.3	0.9	3.2	0.4
	2.0	0.4	0.7	0.6	1.1	0.9	0.8	1.3	0.5	1.1
Totals	5.5	2.6	2.8	3.8	3.9	4.1	2.1	3.4	5.2	3.5
Ranges	2.0	0.5	0.6	0.6	0.7	1.0	0.5	0.9	2.7	1.0

Table B

Batch	1	5	9	13	17	21	25	29	33	37
	0.70	1.46	1.00	1.28	1.54	1.08	1.23	1.45	1.36	1.62
	1.48	1.48	1.40	1.65	0.85	1.30	1.34	1.46	1.23	1.48
	1.58	1.23	1.83	0.90	1.32	1.15	1.04	1.28	1.60	1.34
	1.04	1.49	1.28	1.57	1.48	1.20	1.43	1.51	0.90	1.32
Totals	4.80	5.66	5.51	5.40	5.19	4.73	5.04	5.70	5.09	5.76
Ranges	0.99	0.26	0.83	0.75	0.69	0.22	0.39	0.39	0.23	0.70

Batch	41	45	49	53	57	61	65	69	73	77
	1.36	1.26	1.11	1.62	0.70	0·90	1.08	1.36	1.08	0.85
	1.15	1.60	1.72	1.38	1.25	1.43	1.46	1.18	0.85	0.70
	1.34	1.41	0.95	1.00	0.78	0.95	1.00	0.48	1.53	1.11
	1.18	1.08	0.90	1.26	0.90	1.15	1.00	0.48	1.08	0.48
Totals	5.03	5.35	4.68	5.26	3.63	4.43	4.54	3.50	4.54	3.14
Ranges	0.21	0.52	0.82	0.62	0.55	0.53	0.46	0.88	0.68	0.63

Batch	81	85	89	93	97	101	105	109	113	117
	1.11	0.70	1.04	1.08	0.95	1.20	0.48	0.09	0.85	0.78
	0.00	0.95	0.70	1.08	1.11	0.78	0.85	0.60	0.90	1.15
	1.32	0.90	0.70	0.90	0.78	1.00	0.48	0.95	1.51	0.60
	1.30	0.60	0.85	0.78	1.04	0.95	0.90	1.11	0.70	1.04
Totals	3.73	3.15	3.29	3.84	3.88	3.93	2.71	3.56	3.96	3.57
Ranges	1.32	0.35	0.34	0.30	0.33	0.42	0.42	0.51	0.81	0.55

purposes to a chart for means, with the obvious adjustment to the control limits, and saves some arithmetic. Comment on the charts.

(b) Comment on a graph of the ranges against the totals for each batch.

(c) Table B gives the logarithms of the data of Table A multiplied by a factor of 10. Construct charts as in (a) and comment.

REFERENCES

1. von Neumann, J., R. H. Kent, H. R. Bellinson, and B. I. Hart, "The Mean Square Successive Difference," *Annals of Mathematical Statistics*, 12 (1941), 153–162.
2. Hart, B. I., "Significance Levels for the Ratio of the Mean Square Successive Difference to the Variance," *Annals of Mathematical Statistics*, 13 (1942), 445–47.

3. Cavendish, H., "Experiments to Determine the Density of the Earth," *Philosophical Transactions of the Royal Society*, 88 (1798), 469–526.
4. Stevens, W. L., "Distribution of Groups in a Sequence of Alternatives," *Annals of Eugenics*, 9 (1939), 10–17.
5. Wald, A., and J. Wolfowitz, "On a Test Whether Two Samples are from the Same Population," *Annals of Mathematical Statistics*, 11 (1940), 147–62.
6. Swed, F. S., and C. Eisenhart, "Tables for Testing Randomness of Grouping in a Sequence of Alternatives," *Annals of Mathematical Statistics*, 14 (1943), 66–87.
7. Wallis, W. Allen, "Rough-and-Ready Statistical Tests," *Industrial Quality Control*, 8 (1952), 35–40.
8. Mosteller, Frederick, "Note on an Application of Runs to Quality Control Charts," *Annals of Mathematical Statistics*, 12 (1941), 228–32.
9. Olmstead, P. S., "Distribution of Sample Arrangements for Runs Up and Down," *Annals of Mathematical Statistics*, 17 (1946), 24–33.
10. Wolfowitz, J., "Asymptotic Distribution of Runs Up and Down," *Annals of Mathematical Statistics*, 15 (1944), 163–72.
11. Moore, G. H., and W. Allen Wallis, "Time Series Significance Tests Based on Signs of Differences," *Journal of the American Statistical Association*, 38 (1943), 153–64.
12. Shewhart, W. A., *Economic Control of Quality of Manufactured Product*. Princeton, N.J.: D. Van Nostrand Co., 1931.
13. Shewhart, W. A., *Statistical Method from the Viewpoint of Quality Control*. Washington, D.C.: Department of Agriculture, 1939.

CHAPTER 7

Some Nonparametric Tests

7.1. The Assumption of Normality

A large proportion of present-day statistical techniques for dealing with continuous variables relies on the assumption that the variable has an underlying normal distribution. This assumption is not so restrictive as it may seem at first sight, for, first, we can often transform a variable, if we know the general form of its distribution, into a variable which is approximately normally distributed. Second, we can often arrange to deal with means, and the central limit theorem assures us, roughly, that if a population has a finite variance then the distribution of the sample mean approaches normality as n increases. The central limit theorem has a long history dating back to Demoivre, La Place, and Gauss; for a modern review see Cramér [1], sections 17.4 and 17.5. It is presumably on this foundation that applied statisticians have found empirically that usually there is no great need to fuss about the normality assumption. After a statistician has analyzed several quite widely differing transformations of a variable in a fair number of specific instances and found that the conclusions reached are substantially identical for all the transformations, then he ceases to worry unduly about the normality assumption in most situations.

This is a convenient place to interpolate a few more remarks about the importance of the assumption of normality. The importance of the assumption depends on

1. The nature of the departure from normality
2. The statistical technique being used
3. The ultimate purpose of the analysis.

For example, marked skewness can badly upset the significance level of a one-sided test but have only a small effect on a two-sided test. Again, deviation from normality in the extreme tails is rather unimportant in significance testing: To think that we are rejecting a null hypothesis at the level of significance 0.0001 when in fact the true level of significance is 0.001 is rarely going to tarnish our reputation, but to have 10 vacuum tubes failing per week in a system involving 10,000 when we have predicted only 1 could be embarrassing.

It is probable that deviations from normality cause fewer gross errors than two other departures from the usual assumptions:

1. Lack of constancy of variance
2. Lack of independence.

Some of the effects of (1) are explored in Section 9.8 and of (2) in Section 10.5.

Parenthetically, we might remark that there is some reason to believe that in some areas of research gross errors, e.g. reading the wrong gauge, reading off the wrong scale, transposing digits in writing down numbers, mistranscribing data, losing part of the sample, collecting the sample in a dirty container, making a mistake in the analytical procedure, are far commoner than ordinarily realized.

In recent years techniques have been developed which make no assumption about the form of the underlying distribution except that it be continuous. These methods are known as *nonparametric* or *distribution-free* methods, neither name being particularly satisfactory. The observations certainly do have a distribution, with parameters: what we are free of is assumptions about the form of that distribution.

The literature of nonparametric methods has grown rapidly: see I. R. Savage [2]. An advanced text is that of Fraser [3]. A general text on some ranking methods is that of Kendall [4].

7.2. The Sign Test

Consider tomato plants grown in pairs at a number of sites, one pair at each of n sites. Let the yields at the ith site be x_i, y_i. Then (x, y) will have a joint probability density function $p\{x, y\}$. Imagine that a supplementary fertilizer be applied to one member of each pair, and let y correspond to the yield of this member. If the fertilizer is without effect, it is reasonable to assume that the two yields x_i, y_i are identically and symmetrically distributed so that

$$p\{a, b\} = p\{b, a\}. \qquad (2.1)$$

If the fertilizer does have an effect, we will suppose that the effect is a constant amount τ. Now every y will be greater than what it would have been in the absence of fertilizer by the amount τ, so if we subtract τ from every y we will be back in the original situation (2.1); i.e., we have

$$p\{x, y - \tau\} = p\{y - \tau, x\}. \tag{2.2}$$

The assumptions made imply that τ is the median of $y - x$. To see this, we proceed as follows. Substitute $w = y - \tau$ in (2.2), giving

$$p\{x, w\} = p\{w, x\}; \tag{2.3}$$

i.e., the joint density function of x, w is symmetric about the line $w = x$. The region above this line corresponds to $x < w$, and hence the integral of the joint density function over this region gives $\Pr\{x < w\}$. Likewise the region below this line corresponds to $w < x$, and hence the integral over this region gives $\Pr\{w < x\}$. Now from the symmetry property of (2.3), these two integrals must be equal numerically, and therefore

$$\Pr\{x < w\} = \Pr\{w < x\}, \tag{2.4}$$

or, substituting $y - \tau$ for w,

$$\Pr\{x < y - \tau\} = \Pr\{y - \tau < x\}. \tag{2.5}$$

The following two identities are always true:

$$\Pr\{y - x < \tau\} = \Pr\{y - \tau < x\}, \tag{2.6}$$

$$\Pr\{\tau < y - x\} = \Pr\{x < y - \tau\}. \tag{2.7}$$

But by (2.5), the right-hand sides of (2.6) and (2.7) are equal, and hence the left-hand sides are equal, i.e.,

$$\Pr\{y - x < \tau\} = \Pr\{\tau > y - x\}. \tag{2.8}$$

In other words, τ is the median of $y - x = z$, say. Thus a test of the null hypothesis $\tau = 0$ is a test of the null hypothesis that the median of z is zero, and likewise, under the alternative hypothesis $\tau > 0$, the median of z will be greater than zero.

To make the test, therefore, we define a variable

$$\begin{aligned} Z_i &= 1 \quad \text{if } z_i > 0, \\ &= 0 \quad \text{if } z_i < 0. \end{aligned} \tag{2.9}$$

We assume continuity in the original joint distribution $p\{x, y\}$ so that the distribution of z is also continuous, and "ties," in which $x_i = y_i$, so that $z_i = 0$, should occur with zero probability. The Z_i are independent, so we are in the binomial situation of making n independent trials in which the probability of success, namely the occurrence $Z_i = 1$, is $1/2$ on each trial. Thus $\sum_i^n Z_i$ has under the null hypothesis a binomial distribution with parameters n, $\theta = 1/2$. Thus the sign test, assuming that the alternative hypothesis is $\tau > 0$, when we have m positive differences in a sample of size n gives a P value of

$$\Pr\left\{\sum_{i}^{n} Z_i \geq m \Big| n, \theta = \frac{1}{2}\right\} = \sum_{x=m}^{n} \binom{n}{x}\left(\frac{1}{2}\right)^x\left(1 - \frac{1}{2}\right)^{n-x}$$

$$= \frac{1}{2^n} \sum_{x=m}^{n} \binom{n}{x} = \frac{1}{2^n} \sum_{x=0}^{n-m} \binom{n}{x}. \quad (2.10)$$

For moderate n and m, this can be easily computed directly, and for larger n and m we can use the normal approximation (3.2.3).

The foregoing argument remains valid if the joint density function $p\{x, y\}$ is a function of i; i.e., $p_i\{x, y\}$ can be different for different i.

As an example of the use of the sign test, Table 7.1 gives the differences $A - B$ in potency of a series of lots of a pharmaceutical product as

Table 7.1. Differences between Two Analytical Methods for 16 Lots

| 0.3, | 6.3, | 3.7, | 2.8, | 5.8, | −1.4, | 1.7, | 2.3, |
| −1.7, | 1.6, | −1.8, | 0.6, | 4.5, | | 1.9, | 2.4, | 6.8. |

measured by two different methods A and B. The original observations were on each lot by each method: For the first lot the potencies were 89.7 and 89.4 by the methods A and B, but only the difference 0.3 is relevant. We have $Z_i = 1$ for 13 lots and 0 for 3 lots. Using (2.10),

$$\Pr\left\{\sum_{i}^{n} Z_i \geq 13 \Big| n = 16, \theta = \frac{1}{2}\right\} = \frac{1}{2^{16}} \sum_{x=0}^{16-13} \binom{16}{x}$$

$$= \frac{1}{65,536}\left(\frac{16!}{0!\,16!} + \frac{16!}{1!\,15!} + \frac{16!}{2!\,14!} + \frac{16!}{3!\,13!}\right) = 0.01064, \quad (2.11)$$

or, using (3.2.4),

$$u_{1-P} = \frac{13 - 1/2 - 16 \times 1/2}{\sqrt{16 \times (1/2)(1 - 1/2)}} = 2.25, \quad (2.12)$$

whence $1 - P = 0.9878$ and $P = 0.0122$.

The sign test assumes that the underlying distributions are continuous and hence the probability of a tie occurring, giving rise to a zero difference, is zero. However, in practice all continuous measurements are only recorded to a finite number of decimal places, and ties may occur. The best procedure when this happens is to delete the ties from all consideration.

THE SIGN TEST

The tie is ignored in computing $\sum_i^n Z_i$, and the tie does not contribute to the sample size n either [5].

Our discussion so far has proceeded under the assumption that the null hypothesis was that the median of the differences $x_i - y_i = z_i$ was zero. If our null hypothesis is that the median of the z_i is ζ_0, then we can define a new variable $w_i = z_i - \zeta_0$ and make the foregoing sign test on the w_i.

This device immediately suggests a method of constructing $1 - \alpha$ confidence intervals for ζ. By trial and error we find that value for ζ, say $\underline{\zeta}$, which leads to rejection of the null hypothesis that the median of $z = \underline{\zeta}$ at the $\alpha/2$ level, and that value of ζ, say $\bar{\zeta}$, which leads to the rejection of the null hypothesis that the median of $z = \bar{\zeta}$ at the $\alpha/2$ level. We therefore put

$$\Pr\left\{\sum_i^n Z_i \geq r \mid n, \theta = \frac{1}{2}\right\} = \frac{1}{2^n} \sum_{x=0}^{n-r} \binom{n}{x} \leq \frac{\alpha}{2}, \quad (2.13)$$

and

$$\Pr\left\{\sum_i^n Z_i \leq s \mid n, \theta = \frac{1}{2}\right\} = \frac{1}{2^n} \sum_{x=0}^{s} \binom{n}{x} \leq \frac{\alpha}{2}, \quad (2.14)$$

and solve for r and s. Because of the discreteness of the binomial distribution we may not be able to approach very closely the desired value of $\alpha/2$. In the present example,

$$\Pr\left\{\sum_i^n Z_i \leq 4\right\} = 0.0384, \quad (2.15)$$

and

$$\Pr\left\{\sum_i^n Z_i \leq 3\right\} = 0.0106. \quad (2.16)$$

For 95 per cent confidence limits, we would want $\alpha/2 = 0.025$. To be conservative, we have to choose $s = 3$, which will give us $(1 - 2 \times 0.0106) \times 100 = 97.88$ per cent confidence. The choice of $s = 4$ would give us $(1 - 2 \times 0.0384) \times 100 = 92.32$ per cent confidence, which is far below our desired value of 95 per cent. From the symmetry of the binomial distribution with $\theta = 1/2$, $r = n - s = 16 - 3 = 13$. We now order the sample as in the first column of Table 7.2. We then select the maximum value of ζ, $\bar{\zeta}$, which gives $\Sigma Z_i = 13$, and the minimum value of ζ, $\underline{\zeta}$, which gives $\Sigma Z_i = 3$. Choosing $\underline{\zeta} = 0.2$, $\bar{\zeta} = 4.6$ gives the results in the second and third and fifth and sixth columns of Table 7.2. We could actually choose $\underline{\zeta}$ as large as 0.2999 and still have only three negative signs for $z - \underline{\zeta}$, and $\bar{\zeta}$ as small as 4.50001 and still only have three positive signs for $z - \bar{\zeta}$. Thus the 97.88 per cent confidence limits are roughly (0.29, 4.51), or more accurately just under 0.3 and just over 4.5. In practice, of course, we just order the sample and count in from the bottom end to the $(s + 1)$th observation and down from the top end likewise.

Table 7.2

z	$z - 0.2$	$z - 4.6$	z	$z - 0.2$	$z - 4.6$
−1.8	−2.0	−6.4	2.3	2.1	−2.3
−1.7	−1.9	−6.3	2.4	2.2	−2.2
−1.4	−1.6	−6.0	2.8	2.6	−1.8
0.3	0.1	−4.3	3.7	3.5	−0.9
0.6	0.4	−4.0	4.5	4.3	−0.1
1.6	1.4	−3.0	5.8	5.6	1.2
1.7	1.5	−2.9	6.3	6.1	1.7
1.9	1.7	−2.7	6.8	6.6	2.2

7.3. The Median Test

The sign test discussed in the previous section is appropriate when we have equal numbers of observations from the two distributions and natural pairing is present. In the median test we have samples of n_1 observations x_i from a distribution $p_1\{x\}$ and n_2 observations y_i from a distribution $p_2\{y\}$ and there is no natural pairing. We arrange the observations in a common sequence of increasing magnitude:

$$x_1, x_2, y_1, y_2, y_3, x_3, x_4, x_5, x_6, y_4, \ldots$$

The null hypothesis is that the x's and y's are independent and identically distributed. The alternative hypothesis strictly is that the observations are not identically distributed. In practice, however, the (one-sided) alternative usually envisaged is that the distribution of the x's is slipped towards the right compared with the distribution of the y's, so that the x's tend to be larger than the y's.

Suppose that the two samples have been taken and that each observation is categorized as lying either above or below the sample median (see the notation of Table 7.3). We can picture the situation as follows. Under

Table 7.3

	Below median	Above median	Totals
Sample 1	n_{1b}	n_{1a}	n_1
Sample 2	n_{2b}	n_{2a}	n_2
Totals	$n_{1b} + n_{2b} = n_b$	$n_{1a} + n_{2a} = n_a$	$n_1 + n_2$

the null hypothesis we have a finite population of $n_1 + n_2$ elements of which n_a can be classified as "above." We take a sample of size n_1. We ask for the probability that this sample contains n_{1a} or more "aboves."

SECT. 7.3   THE MEDIAN TEST   247

Just as in the Fisher exact test in Section 3.10, the answer is immediately given by appropriate summing of the probability function for the hypergeometric distribution. Substituting in (3.8.10) $M = n_a$, $x = n_{1a}$, $N - M = n_a + n_b - n_a = n_b$, $n - x = n_1 - n_{1a} = n_{1b}$, $N = n_1 + n_2$, $n = n_1$, we have

$$p\{n_{1a}\} = \frac{\binom{n_a}{n_{1a}}\binom{n_b}{n_{1b}}}{\binom{n_1 + n_2}{n_1}} = \frac{n_a!}{n_{1a}!\,n_{2a}!} \cdot \frac{n_b!}{n_{1b}!\,n_{2b}!} \cdot \frac{n_1!\,n_2!}{(n_1 + n_2)!}, \quad (3.1)$$

similar, with the change of notation, to (3.10.2). The one-sided P value is $p\{n_{1a}\}$ plus the similar probabilities for all possible integers greater than n_{1a}. For small samples the tables referred to in Section 3.10 will avoid the calculations, and for larger samples (3.10.9) can be used as an approximation.

If $n_1 + n_2$ is odd, then the median of the joint sample will be actually one of the observations: Suppose that it occurs in the first sample. This observation, since it lies on the joint sample median, contributes no information on the question of whether the distribution of the first sample has its median above or below the joint sample median. It appears reasonable, therefore, to delete this observation from all consideration, excluding it also from the sample total.

As an example of the application of the median test, Table 7.4 gives the lives in hundreds of hours of samples of electron tubes of two brands A and B. Incidentally, survival time data are typically skewed with a long tail to the right, and usually quite appreciably nonnormal, so a test assuming normality would be inappropriate.

Table 7.4

A	32, 34, 35, 37, 42, 43, 47, 58, 59, 62, 69, 71, 78, 84	$n_1 = 14$
B	39, 48, 54, 65, 70, 76, 87, 90, 111, 118, 126, 127	$n_2 = 12$

The median in Table 7.4 falls between 62 and 65, and so we have Table 7.5. By Fisher's exact test the two-tailed P value is 0.0472: The normal approximation, which we can consider reliable since the minimum expectation in any cell is 6, gives $P = 0.0492$.

Table 7.5

	Below median	Above median	Totals
Brand A	10	4	14
Brand B	3	9	12
Totals	13	13	26

7.4. The Mean and Variance of a Sample from a Finite Population

In the section to follow this, on the Wilcoxon two-sample rank test, we need the mean and variance of a sample of size n from a finite population of N elements, the elements having attached to them numbers $x_1, x_2, \ldots, x_N$. We wish to express them in terms of the mean and variance of the population, which we define as

$$\xi = E[x] = \sum_i^N x_i p\{x_i\} = \frac{1}{N} \sum_i^N x_i, \qquad (4.1)$$

since, for a finite population of size N, $p\{x_i\} = 1/N$, and

$$\sigma^2 = V[x] = E[x^2] - (E[x])^2 = \sum_i^N x_i^2 p\{x_i\} - (E[x])^2$$

$$= \frac{1}{N}(x_1^2 + \cdots + x_N^2) - \left[\frac{1}{N}(x_1 + \cdots + x_N)\right]^2. \qquad (4.2)$$

This can be written in the form

$$\sigma^2 = (x_1^2 + \cdots + x_N^2)\left(\frac{1}{N} - \frac{1}{N^2}\right) - (x_1 x_2 + x_1 x_3 + \cdots + x_{N-1} x_N)\frac{2}{N^2}. \qquad (4.3)$$

The set of all possible samples of size n from the population will include

$$\begin{aligned} &(x_1, x_2, \ldots, x_{n-1}, x_n) \\ &(x_1, x_2, \ldots, x_{n-1}, x_{n+1}) \\ &\qquad \cdot \\ &\qquad \cdot \\ &\qquad \cdot \\ &(x_{N-n+1}, x_{N-n+2}, \ldots, x_N) \end{aligned} \qquad (4.4)$$

These samples are formed by picking n elements at a time from N; by (1.7.8) there are $\binom{N}{n}$ ways of picking such a sample. It is axiomatic that every possible sample is equally likely, and so the probability of any particular sample being picked is $1/\binom{N}{n}$.

SECT. 7.4 THE MEAN AND VARIANCE OF A SAMPLE 249

Suppose that the samples in (4.4) have means $\bar{x}_j$, $j = 1, 2, \ldots, \binom{N}{n}$. The expected value of $\bar{x}$ is

$$E[\bar{x}] = \sum_j^{\binom{N}{n}} \bar{x}_j p\{\bar{x}_j\} = \binom{N}{n}^{-1} \sum_j^{\binom{N}{n}} \bar{x}_j$$

$$= \binom{N}{n}^{-1} \left[\frac{1}{n}(x_1 + x_2 + \cdots + x_n) + \cdots + \frac{1}{n}(x_{N-n+1} + \cdots + x_N) \right]. \quad (4.5)$$

Now consider the number of times any particular x_i, say x_1, will occur in (4.5). The samples containing x_1 are made up by selecting $n-1$ other elements from the available population of $N-1$ elements, and this can be done in $\binom{N-1}{n-1}$ ways. There will therefore be $\binom{N-1}{n-1}$ samples containing x_1. In other words, x_1 occurs $\binom{N-1}{n-1}$ times in (4.5). The same will apply to every other x_i. Thus

$$E[\bar{x}] = \binom{N}{n}^{-1} \left[\frac{1}{n} \binom{N-1}{n-1} \sum_i^N x_i \right] = \frac{1}{N} \sum_i^N x_i = \xi \quad (4.6)$$

by (4.1). The expected value of the sample mean is thus the population mean.

The variance of $\bar{x}$ is

$$V[\bar{x}] = E[\bar{x}^2] - (E[\bar{x}])^2. \quad (4.7)$$

We have already found $E[\bar{x}]$. Now consider $E[\bar{x}^2]$:

$$E[\bar{x}^2] = \sum_j^{\binom{N}{n}} \bar{x}_j^2 p\{\bar{x}_j\} = \binom{N}{n}^{-1} \sum_j^{\binom{N}{n}} \bar{x}_j^2. \quad (4.8)$$

But

$$\sum_j^{\binom{N}{n}} \bar{x}_j^2 = \left[\frac{1}{n}(x_1 + x_2 + \cdots + x_n) \right]^2 + \cdots + \left[\frac{1}{n}(x_{N-n+1} + \cdots + x_N) \right]^2. \quad (4.9)$$

When we square each term, each x_i will give rise to an x_i^2, and we have already seen that in the similar expression (4.5) each x_i occurs $\binom{N-1}{n-1}$ times; so the squared part of (4.9) is

$$\frac{1}{n^2} \binom{N-1}{n-1} (x_1^2 + \cdots + x_N^2). \quad (4.10)$$

250 SOME NONPARAMETRIC TESTS CHAP. 7

The expression (4.9) will also give rise to product terms $x_i x_j$. Any particular x_i and x_j will occur together in a given sequence in $\binom{N-2}{n-2}$ of the samples; so the product part of (4.9) is

$$\frac{2}{n^2}\binom{N-2}{n-2}(x_1 x_2 + x_1 x_3 + \cdots + x_{N-1} x_N), \quad (4.11)$$

the factor 2 arising from the fact that $x_i x_j = x_j x_i$. Substituting these back into (4.8) gives

$$E[\bar{x}^2] = \binom{N}{n}^{-1}\left[\frac{1}{n^2}\binom{N-1}{n-1}(x_1^2 + \cdots + x_N^2)\right.$$
$$\left. + \frac{2}{n^2}\binom{N-2}{n-2}(x_1 x_2 + \cdots + x_{N-1} x_N)\right]. \quad (4.12)$$

We thus have $E[\bar{x}^2]$ ready for substitution into (4.7) to give $V[\bar{x}]$. Equation (4.7) also requires $(E[\bar{x}])^2$. In (4.6) we found $E[\bar{x}])$ to be $(1/N)\sum_i^N x_i$; so

$$(E[\bar{x}])^2 = \frac{(x_1 + \cdots + x_N)^2}{N^2} = \frac{x_1^2 + \cdots + x_N^2}{N^2} + \frac{2(x_1 x_2 + \cdots + x_{N-1} x_N)}{N^2}.$$
$$(4.13)$$

Substituting (4.12) and (4.13) in (4.7), we get

$$V[\bar{x}] = \left[\binom{N}{n}^{-1}\frac{1}{n^2}\binom{N-1}{n-1} - \frac{1}{N^2}\right](x_1^2 + \cdots + x_N^2)$$
$$+ \left[\binom{N}{n}^{-1}\frac{2}{n^2}\binom{N-2}{n-2} - \frac{2}{N^2}\right](x_1 x_2 + \cdots + x_{N-1} x_N). \quad (4.14)$$

The coefficient of $x_1^2 + \cdots + x_N^2$ can be written as

$$\frac{\binom{N-1}{n-1}}{n^2 \binom{N}{n}} - \frac{1}{N^2} = \frac{1}{n^2}\frac{(N-1)!}{(n-1)!(N-n)!}\frac{n!(N-n)!}{N!} - \frac{1}{N^2} = \frac{1}{nN} - \frac{1}{N^2}$$
$$= \frac{N-n}{N^2 n} = \frac{N-1}{N^2}\frac{N-n}{n(N-1)} = \left(\frac{1}{N} - \frac{1}{N^2}\right)\frac{N-n}{n(N-1)},$$
$$(4.15)$$

and the coefficient of $(x_1 x_2 + \cdots + x_{N-1} x_N)$ is

$$\frac{2\binom{N-2}{n-2}}{n^2 \binom{N}{n}} - \frac{2}{N^2} = \frac{2}{n^2}\frac{(N-2)!}{(n-2)!(N-n)!}\frac{n!(N-n)!}{N!} - \frac{2}{N^2}$$
$$= \frac{2(n-1)}{nN(N-1)} - \frac{2}{N^2} = -\frac{2(N-n)}{N^2 n(N-1)}. \quad (4.16)$$

Then, inserting these results in (4.14), we get

$$V[\bar{x}] = \frac{N-n}{n(N-1)}\left[\left(\frac{1}{N} - \frac{1}{N^2}\right)(x_1^2 + \cdots + x_N^2) - \frac{2}{N^2}(x_1 x_2 + \cdots + x_{N-1} x_N)\right].$$
(4.17)

The part in brackets is identical with the expression for σ^2, (4.3), so

$$V[\bar{x}] = \frac{\sigma^2}{n}\frac{N-n}{N-1}$$
(4.18)

$$= \frac{\sigma^2}{n}\left(1 - \frac{n-1}{N-1}\right).$$
(4.19)

Clearly, if N tends to infinity, then $V[\bar{x}]$ tends to σ^2/n, its customary form for an infinite population.

7.5. The Wilcoxon Two-Sample Rank Test

The Wilcoxon two-sample rank test [6] is a test of the null hypothesis that two populations are identical, against the alternative hypothesis that they differ by a linear translation. We substitute ranks for the actual observations. As an example, Table 7.6 lists five determinations of the atomic weight of carbon from one preparation and four determinations from another preparation [8]. Ranks are allocated to the observations in order of increasing magnitude without regard to the division into two samples.

Table 7.6

Preparation A		Preparation B	
Determination	Rank	Determination	Rank
12.0072	8	11.9853	1
12.0064	7	11.9949	2
12.0054	5	11.9985	3
12.0016	4	12.0061	6
12.0077	9		

Suppose that one sample is of size n and the other of size $N - n$. The test assumes that any combination of the ranks into these two groups is equally likely. The total number of ways of grouping the ranks, given N and n, is the number of ways of picking n elements out of N, $\binom{N}{n}$. The test then counts how many of the possible combinations give a rank sum as extreme as or more extreme than that observed.

In Table 7.6, regarding the observations from preparation B as the sample of size n, the rank sum is $1 + 2 + 3 + 6 = 12$. The only ways we could get a rank sum as small as or smaller than this, given $n = 4$, are

$$1 + 2 + 3 + 4 = 10, \quad 1 + 2 + 3 + 5 = 11,$$
$$1 + 2 + 3 + 6 = 12, \quad 1 + 2 + 4 + 5 = 12.$$

For example, $1 + 3 + 4 + 5 = 13$ is greater than our observed rank sum 12. The P value is equal to the ratio of the number of ways we can form a rank sum as extreme as or more extreme than that observed, namely, 4 ways, to the total possible number of ways of forming sums of $n = 4$ ranks, namely, $\binom{N}{n} = \binom{9}{4} = 126$ ways. Thus $P = 4/126 = 0.0317$ for a one-sided test. The rationale of this procedure is that, if one distribution is displaced relative to the other, the low ranks will tend to fall in one sample and the high ranks in the other sample, and so the rank sums will be relatively low or high.

In the case of small N and n, it is relatively easy to compute the P value directly as in the above example. For large samples, an approximate test is available based on the fact that the mean of the ranks of a sample is distributed around its expected value approximately normally.

Let R be the rank sum and $\bar{R}$ the mean of the ranks of the sample of size n. By (4.6), the expected value for $\bar{R}$ is $E[\bar{R}] = (1/N) \sum_i^N x_i$ where the x_i are the elements of the finite population, here the integers 1 to N. The sum of the first N integers is

$$1 + 2 + \cdots + N = \frac{N(N + 1)}{2}, \tag{5.1}$$

and also the sum of their squares is

$$1^2 + 2^2 + \cdots + N^2 = \frac{N(N + 1)(2N + 1)}{6}. \tag{5.2}$$

Using (4.1) and (5.1),

$$E[\bar{R}] = \frac{1}{N} \cdot \frac{N(N + 1)}{2} = \frac{N + 1}{2}. \tag{5.3}$$

The variance of $\bar{R}$, $V[\bar{R}]$, will be given by (4.18) where σ^2 is given by substituting (5.1) and (5.2) in (4.2):

$$\sigma^2 = \frac{1}{N} \cdot \frac{N(N + 1)(2N + 1)}{6} - \left[\frac{1}{N} \cdot \frac{N(N + 1)}{2}\right]^2 = \frac{N^2 - 1}{12}. \tag{5.4}$$

Thus, substituting this in (4.18),

$$V[\bar{R}] = \frac{(N^2 - 1)/12}{n} \cdot \frac{N - n}{N - 1} = \frac{(N + 1)(N - n)}{12n}. \tag{5.5}$$

THE ADJUSTMENT FOR TIES

We then have

$$\frac{\bar{R} - E[\bar{R}]}{\sqrt{V[\bar{R}]}} = \frac{\bar{R} - (N+1)/2}{\sqrt{(N+1)(N-n)/12n}} \quad (5.6)$$

$$= \frac{2R - n(N+1)}{\sqrt{n(N+1)(N-n)/3}} \quad (5.7)$$

asymptotically a unit normal deviate. Kruskal and Wallis [11] have observed that the approximation is improved when the one-sided P value is found to be greater than 0.02 by introducing a correction for continuity by bringing $\bar{R}$ closer to its expectation by $1/2n$, or $2R$ closer to its expectation by 1. If the one-sided P value is less than 0.02, this correction for continuity should be omitted.

In the example in Table 7.6, if we consider the results with preparation B as the sample of size n, then $n = 4$, $N = 9$, $R = 12$, $\bar{R} = 12/4 = 3$, and (5.6) is

$$u_P = \frac{3 - (9+1)/2}{\sqrt{(9+1)(9-4)/12 \times 4}} = -1.96; \quad (5.8)$$

so $P = 0.025$. This implies that we should use the continuity correction:

$$u_P = \frac{3 + (1/2 \times 4) - (9+1)/2}{\sqrt{(9+1)(9-4)/12 \times 4}} = -1.837; \quad (5.9)$$

so the one-sided $P = 0.033$. Even though N and n are small in this example, the normal approximation gives a P value close to the exact value, 0.0317, calculated earlier.

A careful development of the Wilcoxon test was given by Mann and Whitney [9]. For the history of the test see Kruskal [10].

7.6. The Adjustment for Ties in the Wilcoxon Two-Sample Rank Test

If ties occur, so that two or more of the observations are identical, the best procedure is to allocate to these tied observations the mean of the ranks they would receive if they were not tied. Table 7.7 gives two series of determinations of the conversion efficiency of an ammonia oxidation plant for the production of nitric acid. If we allocate ranks to the observations in increasing order of magnitude, 90.0, 90.1, 92.1, and 93.3 receive ranks 1, 2, 3, and 4, respectively. We then encounter two observations at 94.7; these receive the ranks 5 and 6, so that the mean rank $5\frac{1}{2}$ is allocated to each of them. Later on, two observations at 95.6 both receive ranks $(9 + 10)/2 = 9\frac{1}{2}$. The effect of this procedure is to leave the sum of the ranks used unchanged, and so $E[\bar{R}]$ (5.3) is unchanged. The variance is somewhat affected, however.

Table 7.7

A		B	
Determination	Rank	Determination	Rank
95.6	$9\frac{1}{2}$	93.3	4
94.9	7	92.1	3
96.2	12	94.7	$5\frac{1}{2}$
95.1	8	90.1	2
95.8	11	95.6	$9\frac{1}{2}$
96.3	13	90.0	1
		94.7	$5\frac{1}{2}$

The variance of the ranks, see (4.2), is formed from $E[x^2]$ and $(E[x])^2$. The latter involves the sum of the ranks, which is unchanged, and hence is unaltered. The former is the sum of the squares of the ranks, divided by N; this is affected by the substitution of mean ranks for individual ranks.

Consider one group of t ties. The integers $(x+1), (x+2), \ldots, (x+t)$ are replaced by their mean

$$\frac{(x+1)+(x+2)+\cdots+(x+t)}{t} = \frac{xt + t(t+1)/2}{t} = x + \frac{t+1}{2}. \tag{6.1}$$

The sum of squares $x_1^2 + \cdots + x_N^2$ in (4.2) is thus reduced by

$$(x+1)^2 + \cdots + (x+t)^2 - t\left(x + \frac{t+1}{2}\right)^2 \tag{6.2}$$

which, after some simplification, can be written as

$$\frac{(t-1)t(t+1)}{12} = \frac{T}{12}, \tag{6.3}$$

if we define $T = (t-1)t(t+1)$. The variance of the ranks is no longer given by (5.4). Now the sum of squares of the ranks is

$$\frac{N(N+1)(2N+1)}{6} - \frac{T}{12} \tag{6.4}$$

and this is substituted for $x_1^2 + \cdots + x_N^2$ in the formula for σ^2 (4.2). The

SECT. 7.6 THE ADJUSTMENT FOR TIES

sum of the ranks is unchanged at $N(N + 1)/2$, and this is substituted for $x_1 + \cdots + x_N$: Thus

$$\sigma^2 = \frac{1}{N}\left[\frac{N(N + 1)(2N + 1)}{6} - \frac{T}{12}\right] - \left[\frac{1}{N}\frac{N(N + 1)}{2}\right]^2$$

$$= \frac{1}{12N}[N(N^2 - 1) - T]. \tag{6.5}$$

Using (4.18), the variance of $\bar{R}$ is

$$V[\bar{R}] = \frac{N(N^2 - 1) - T}{12Nn} \cdot \frac{N - n}{N - 1}. \tag{6.6}$$

The term $T = (t - 1)t(t + 1)$ occurs for each group of ties, if there is more than one such group. In the example in Table 7.7, there are two groups of two ties; so the correction term $\sum_j T_j$ is

$$\sum_j T_j = (2 - 1) \cdot 2 \cdot (2 + 1) + (2 - 1) \cdot 2 \cdot (2 + 1) = 12. \tag{6.7}$$

Then

$$V[\bar{R}] = \frac{13(13^2 - 1) - 12}{12 \times 13 \times 6} \cdot \frac{13 - 6}{13 - 1} = 1.3536, \tag{6.8}$$

and

$$\bar{R} = \frac{9\frac{1}{2} + 7 + \cdots + 13}{6} = 10.083; \tag{6.9}$$

so we have an approximate unit normal deviate

$$u_{1-P} = \frac{10.083 - (13 + 1)/2}{\sqrt{1.3536}} = 2.650, \tag{6.10}$$

giving a one-sided P value of 0.0040. Since this is less than 0.02, we omit the correction for continuity.

We can find the level of significance by a direct enumeration as we did in the example without ties in Section 7.5. In Table 7.7 the rank sum for the smaller sample A is $60\frac{1}{2}$. The various ways in which a rank sum of $60\frac{1}{2}$ or greater can be formed from the ranks listed in Table 7.7 are given in Table 7.8, where tied ranks are distinguished from each other by the letters a and b.

The total number of ways 6 ranks can be selected from 13 is $\binom{13}{6} = 1716$. The one-sided P value is thus $6/1716 = 0.00350$. The normal approximation, which gave $P = 0.0040$, is thus reasonably close in this instance.

Table 7.8. Ways in Which Six Ranks Can Be Selected from the Ranks of Table 7.7 Subject to Condition That Their Sum Is Greater than or Equal to $60\frac{1}{2}$

	13	13	13	13	13	13
	12	12	12	12	12	12
	11	11	11	11	11	11
	$9\frac{1}{2}a$	$9\frac{1}{2}a$	$9\frac{1}{2}a$	$9\frac{1}{2}a$	$9\frac{1}{2}a$	$9\frac{1}{2}b$
	$9\frac{1}{2}b$	$9\frac{1}{2}b$	$9\frac{1}{2}b$	$9\frac{1}{2}b$	8	8
	8	7	$5\frac{1}{2}a$	$5\frac{1}{2}b$	7	7
Rank sum	63	62	$60\frac{1}{2}$	$60\frac{1}{2}$	$60\frac{1}{2}$	$60\frac{1}{2}$

7.7. The H Test

The H test, due to Kruskal and Wallis [11], is a generalization of the two-sample Wilcoxon test to the case of k samples, $k > 2$. As in the Wilcoxon test, the entire set of observations, here in k groups of size n_i rather than two groups as in the Wilcoxon test, are ranked, and mean ranks $\bar{R}_i$ are calculated for each group. $\bar{R}_i$ has an expectation $(N + 1)/2$ (5.3), and a variance $(N + 1)(N - n_i)/12n_i$ (5.5). The ratios $\{\bar{R}_i - E[\bar{R}_i]\}/\sqrt{V[\bar{R}_i]}$ will be standardized variables approximately normal. Kruskal and Wallis denoted by H the sum of their squares multiplied by a weighting factor $1 - n_i/N$, and showed that H has approximately a $\chi^2(k - 1)$ distribution; i.e.,

$$H = \sum_i^k \frac{[\bar{R}_i - (N + 1)/2]^2}{(N + 1)(N - n_i)/12n_i} \cdot \left(1 - \frac{n_i}{N}\right) \underset{\text{approx}}{\sim} \chi^2(k - 1). \quad (7.1)$$

Two identical forms for H, more convenient for calculation, are

$$H = \frac{N - 1}{N} \sum_i^k \frac{[\bar{R}_i - (N + 1)/2]^2}{(N^2 - 1)/12n_i} \quad (7.2)$$

$$= \frac{12}{N(N + 1)} \sum_i^k \left(\frac{R_i^2}{n_i}\right) - 3(N + 1). \quad (7.3)$$

If ties occur, H should be divided by the factor

$$1 - \frac{\sum T}{N^3 - N} \quad (7.4)$$

where $T = (t - 1)t(t + 1)$ is calculated and included in the sum for each group of ties. While H is distributed asymptotically as $\chi^2(k - 1)$ for large k and n_i, in small samples the approximation is not very good, and Kruskal and Wallis [11] provided tables of the exact distribution for the

SECT. 7.7   THE H TEST   257

case of $k = 3$, $n_i \leq 5$. For intermediate cases they proposed approximations based on the incomplete gamma and incomplete beta distributions, for details of which see their paper. Wallace [12] has discussed several approximations, and Box [13] suggested an approximation based on the F distribution.

As an example of the application of the H test, Table 7.9 gives the terminal digits of observations on six days on the mechanical equivalent of heat [14]. The first observation was 4.1849, but only the last two digits are given in Table 7.9. There are several groups of ties, the first being

Table 7.9

	Day 1		Day 2		Day 3		Day 4		Day 5		Day 6	
	Obs.	Rank	Obs.	Rank	Obs.	Rank	Obs.	Rank	Obs.	Rank	Obs.	Rank
	49	18	42	12½	46	17	11	1	38	8	24	3
	52	21½	43	15	52	21½	27	5	50	19	40	9
	43	15	42	12½	27	5	71	23	41	10½	27	5
			43	15	51	20	23	2	41	10½	37	7
n_i	3		4		4		4		4		4	
R_i		54½		55		63½		31		48		24

three observations at 27 which receive the mean rank $(4 + 5 + 6)/3 = 5$. Substituting in (7.3),

$$H = \frac{12}{23(23 + 1)} \left[\frac{(54\frac{1}{2})^2}{3} + \frac{(55)^2}{4} + \cdots \right] - 3 \times (23 + 1) = 8.753. \quad (7.5)$$

However, we need the correction for ties, there being two groups of three tied ranks and three groups of two tied ranks. For each of the triplets the correction $(t - 1)t(t + 1)$ is $(3 - 1) \cdot 3 \cdot (3 + 1) = 24$, and for each of the doublets the correction is $(2 - 1) \cdot 2 \cdot (2 + 1) = 6$. The correction factor (7.4) is

$$1 - \frac{24 \times 2 + 6 \times 3}{23^3 - 23} = 0.99457; \quad (7.6)$$

so the corrected H is $8.753/0.99457 = 8.801$ with $6 - 1 = 5$ degrees of freedom. The 0.90 point of $\chi^2(5)$ is 9.24, and so the null hypothesis is acceptable at the 0.10 level.

We can apply the H test in the case where there are only two samples, so that $k = 2$. The H statistic (7.1) will then have approximately the χ^2 distribution with $2 - 1 = 1$ degree of freedom. In Section 1.27 we saw that $\chi^2(n)$ was defined as $\sum_i^n u_i^2$; so $\chi^2(1)$ is just the square of a single unit normal deviate. We shall see in Section 9.4 that specifically $\chi^2_{1-\alpha}(1) = u^2_{1-\alpha/2}$.

It is easy to show that the H statistic in the case of $k = 2$ is identically equal to the square of the Wilcoxon statistic (5.7). In other words, the H test for the case of $k = 2$ is identical with the two-sample Wilcoxon test.

7.8. The Wilcoxon One-Sample Test

Wilcoxon [7] proposed a test for the median of a single sample, in which we give ranks to the absolute magnitudes of the observations and then give to the ranks the signs of the corresponding observations. Essentially the test is of the null hypothesis that the distribution of the observations is symmetric about zero, so that any rank is equally likely to be positive or negative.

Frequently in application the observations are differences between paired observations, as in Table 7.10 which reproduces the data of Table

Table 7.10

Difference	0.3	6.3	3.7	2.8	5.8	−1.4	1.7	2.3	−1.7	1.6	−1.8	0.6	4.5	1.9	2.4	6.8
Rank	1	15	12	11	14	−3	$5\frac{1}{2}$	9	$-5\frac{1}{2}$	4	−7	2	13	8	10	16

7.1 on the difference in potency for 16 lots of a pharmaceutical product reported by two methods of analysis, here with ranks attached to the absolute magnitude of the differences. Table 7.10 includes the complication of two differences 1.7 and −1.7 tying in absolute magnitude. As in the unpaired Wilcoxon test, such ties receive the mean of the ranks necessary for the group of ties, here $\frac{1}{2}(5 + 6) = 5\frac{1}{2}$. The test statistic is the sum of the ranks of either sign, $15\frac{1}{2}$ for the negative ranks or $120\frac{1}{2}$ for the positive ranks, and the P value is the probability of getting a rank sum equal to or more extreme than the observed value.

Under the null hypothesis any rank is equally likely to be positive or negative. The total number of ways rank sums can be produced is thus 2^N, 2^{16} in the case of Table 7.10. In moderate situations it is possible to enumerate all the rank sums less than or equal to the observed rank sum. Here the observed negative rank sum is $3 + 5\frac{1}{2} + 7 = 15\frac{1}{2}$. We proceed to write down all ways in which we can form rank sums less than or equal to $15\frac{1}{2}$. Starting with $0, 1, \ldots, 15$; continuing with $1 + 2, \ldots, 1 + 14$, $2 + 3, \ldots, 2 + 13$; continuing on up to $7 + 8$; then counting triplets such as $1 + 2 + 3$, quadruplets such as $1 + 2 + 3 + 4$, and the quintuplets $1 + 2 + 3 + 4 + 5\frac{1}{2}a$ and $1 + 2 + 3 + 4 + 5\frac{1}{2}b$; there are a total of 140 combinations of ranks with sums $\leq 15\frac{1}{2}$. The one-sided P value is thus $140/2^{16} = 0.00214$.

SECT. 7.8 THE WILCOXON ONE-SAMPLE TEST

Obviously, direct enumeration can be excessively tedious and a normal approximation is useful. Consider the ranks R_i, $i = 1, 2, \ldots, N$. Construct subsidiary variables d_i, where d_i is attached to the ith rank. These variables d_i take the values 0 when a rank is negative and 1 when a rank is positive. Under the null hypothesis a rank is equally likely to be positive as negative. Then

$$E[d_i] = 1 \times \frac{1}{2} + 0 \times \frac{1}{2} = \frac{1}{2}, \tag{8.1}$$

$$E[d_i^2] = 1^2 \times \frac{1}{2} + 0^2 \times \frac{1}{2} = \frac{1}{2}, \tag{8.2}$$

$$\mathop{E}_{i \neq j}[d_i d_j] = 0 \times 0 \times \frac{1}{4} + 0 \times 1 \times \frac{1}{4} + 1 \times 0 \times \frac{1}{4} + 1 \times 1 \times \frac{1}{4} = \frac{1}{4}; \tag{8.3}$$

The sum of the positive ranks, say S, is $\sum_i^N d_i R_i$. Under the null hypothesis,

$$E[S] = E\left[\sum_i^N d_i R_i\right] = \sum_i^N R_i E[d_i] = \frac{1}{2}\sum_i^N R_i, \tag{8.4}$$

$$E[S^2] = E\left[\left(\sum_i^N d_i R_i\right)^2\right] = E\left[\sum_i^N \sum_j^N R_i R_j d_i d_j\right]$$

$$= \sum_{\substack{i \ j \\ i=j}}^{N\ N} R_i^2 E[d_i^2] + \sum_{\substack{i \ j \\ i \neq j}}^{N\ N} R_i R_j E[d_i d_j]$$

$$= \frac{1}{2}\sum_i^N R_i^2 + \frac{1}{4}\left[\left(\sum_i^N R_i\right)^2 - \sum_i^N R_i^2\right]$$

$$= \frac{1}{4}\sum_i^N R_i^2 + \frac{1}{4}\left(\sum_i^N R_i\right)^2. \tag{8.5}$$

Thus

$$V[S] = E[S^2] - (E[S])^2 = \frac{1}{4}\sum_i^N R_i^2. \tag{8.6}$$

If the R_i are the integers 1 to N, then using (5.1) and (5.2),

$$E[S] = \frac{N(N+1)}{4}, \tag{8.7}$$

$$V[S] = \frac{N(N+1)(2N+1)}{24}. \tag{8.8}$$

If, instead of the integers 1 to N, the ranks contain a set of t ties, as in Section 7.6 the sum of the ranks is unchanged, so $E[S]$ continues to be given by (8.7). The sum of squares of the ranks is changed, however. In place of the ranks $R_j + 1, R_j + 2, \ldots, R_j + t$ we have the mean rank $R_j + (t + 1)/2$ a total of t times [see (6.1)], so the sum of squares of the ranks is increased by

$$t\left(R_j + \frac{t+1}{2}\right)^2 - [(R_j + 1)^2 + \cdots + (R_j + t)^2], \qquad (8.9)$$

which reduces to $-(t-1)t(t+1)/12$. Making this change in $\sum_i^N R_i^2$ in (8.6) and (8.8) gives

$$V[S] = \frac{N(N+1)(2N+1)}{24} - \frac{(t-1)t(t+1)}{48}. \qquad (8.10)$$

For the data of Table 7.10, the sum of the positive ranks $S = 120\frac{1}{2}$, and there is one pair of ties; so

$$E[S] = \frac{N(N+1)}{4} = \frac{16 \times (16+1)}{4} = 68, \qquad (8.11)$$

$$V[S] = \frac{16 \times (16+1)(2 \times 16+1)}{24} - \frac{(2-1) \times 2 \times (2+1)}{48}$$

$$= 374 - 0.125 = 373.875, \qquad (8.12)$$

$$u_{1-P} = \frac{S - E[S]}{\sqrt{V[S]}} = \frac{120.5 - 68}{\sqrt{373.875}} = 2.715, \qquad (8.13)$$

whence $P = 0.0033$, to be compared with the exact figure 0.0021 previously obtained. While nothing generally appears to be known about the use of a continuity correction with this approximation, its use does not seem to be indicated.

We have indicated how to handle ties in the absolute values of the ranks. However, if the observations are differences between paired samples, some samples may be tied in one or more pairs, giving rise to differences which are zero. It is not clear how these zeros should be handled. One procedure will be to ignore their existence completely, i.e., to delete them from the sample.

7.9. The Friedman Rank Test

Consider the data of Table 7.11, which gives a function of the daily determination of the efficiency of a chemical plant for each of six runs, each run lasting seven days. We ask whether the null hypothesis that the median efficiencies for the different runs are the same should be rejected. At first glance we might consider using the H test of Section 7.7, but this

THE FRIEDMAN RANK TEST

is not appropriate to the present problem; it assumes under the null hypothesis that all observations are identically distributed, whereas in the present problem we postulate as the null hypothesis merely that all observations on day 1 are identically distributed and that all observations on day 2 are identically distributed, etc., but we do not postulate that the day 2 distribution is the same as the day 1 distribution, etc.

Table 7.11

Day	Run number					
	1	2	3	4	5	6
1	60(4)	64(5)	14(1)	30(2)	72(6)	35(3)
2	62(5)	63(5)	46(4)	41(3)	38(2)	35(1)
3	58(5)	63(6)	47(4)	40(2)	46(3)	33(1)
4	52(6)	36(1)	39(2)	41(3)	47(5)	46(4)
5	31(1)	34(2)	42(5)	37(3)	38(4)	47(6)
6	23(2)	32(3)	43(4)	17(1)	60(6)	47(5)
7	26(2)	27(3)	57(6)	12(1)	41(5)	38(4)
$\sum_{i}^{r} R_{ij}$	25	26	26	15	31	24

In general, suppose that there are r rows and c columns, that we wish to test for column differences, and that the rank in the ijth cell, the ranking being within rows, is R_{ij}. For Table 7.11, for the first row the observations are 60, 64, 14, 30, 72, and 35, so these are allocated the ranks 4, 5, 1, 2, 6, and 3 given in parentheses beside the corresponding observations. For the ith row for the ranks R_{ij} we have the integers $1, \ldots, c$, so $E[R_{ij}] = (c + 1)/2$, $V[R_{ij}] = (c^2 - 1)/12$ [see (5.3) and (5.4)]. Then since $\bar{R}_{.j}$, the mean of the ranks in the jth column, is the mean of r R_{ij}'s,

$$V[\bar{R}_{.j}] = \frac{c^2 - 1}{12r}. \tag{9.1}$$

If we assume that $\bar{R}_{.j}$ is asymptotically normal we have

$$\frac{\bar{R}_{.j} - E[\bar{R}_{.j}]}{\sqrt{V[\bar{R}_{.j}]}} \sim N(0, 1), \tag{9.2}$$

and the sum of squares of c such quantities will have approximately a $\chi^2(c)$ distribution. However, the $\bar{R}_{.j}$ are not independent, since

$$\sum_{j}^{c} \bar{R}_{.j} = \sum_{j}^{c} \frac{1}{r} \sum_{i}^{r} R_{ij} = \frac{1}{r} \sum_{i}^{r} \sum_{j}^{c} R_{ij} = \frac{c(c + 1)}{2}. \tag{9.3}$$

Along these lines Friedman [15] derived the statistic which he called χ_r^2,

$$\chi_r^2 = \frac{c-1}{c} \frac{\sum_{j}^{c}(\bar{R}_{\cdot j} - E[\bar{R}_{\cdot j}])^2}{V[\bar{R}_{\cdot j}]}, \tag{9.4}$$

and showed that under the null hypothesis it has approximately the $\chi^2(c-1)$ distribution. The statistic can be put in the form

$$\chi_r^2 = \frac{12}{rc(c+1)} \sum_{j}^{c} \left(\sum_{i}^{r} R_{ij}\right)^2 - 3r(c+1). \tag{9.5}$$

For Table 7.11,

$$\chi_r^2 = \frac{12}{7 \times 6(6+1)} (25^2 + \cdots + 24^2) - 3 \times 7 \times (6+1)$$
$$= 5.612, \tag{9.6}$$

which is substantially less than $\chi_{0.90}^2(5) = 9.24$, so the null hypothesis can be accepted.

We could, of course, use the same procedure to test whether the median efficiencies for the different days are equal.

An alternative, but essentially identical, form of this test was introduced by M. G. Kendall under the name coefficient of concordance [4].

7.10. The Cochran Q Test

Consider the data of Table 7.12 taken from Cochran [16]. A number of specimens, 69 in all, were tested on four different media A, B, C, and D for the presence of a certain organism. For a particular specimen on a particular medium the outcome could be growth or no growth, represented by 0 or 1. For a particular specimen, therefore, the results can be 1111, 1110, 1101, ..., 1000, 0000. Table 7.12 gives the number of specimens

Table 7.12

	A	B	C	D	Number of cases
	1	1	1	1	4
	1	1	0	1	2
	0	1	1	1	3
	0	1	0	1	1
	0	0	0	0	59
T_j	6	10	7	10	

with particular results: for example, there were 4 1111's, 0 1110's (not

SECT. 7.10 THE COCHRAN Q TEST

shown in the table), 2 1101's, etc. We are interested in testing the null hypothesis that the probabilities of growth with the different media, averaged over all specimens, are equal. This situation is the generalization to k columns of the situation discussed in Section 3.7. There, if each patient had been tested on k drugs rather than two, then we would have the situation discussed here.

Cochran proposed for a test of the null hypothesis the statistic Q defined as

$$Q = \frac{c(c-1) \sum_{j}^{c} (T_j - \bar{T})^2}{c \sum_{i}^{r} u_i - \sum_{i}^{r} u_i^2}, \tag{10.1}$$

where u_i is the number of 1's in the ith row and T_j is the sum of the entries in the jth column, allowing, of course, for the fact that in Table 7.12 each row is really repeated a total number of times equal to the corresponding number of cases. A sketch of the proof that the distribution of Q under the null hypothesis tends to $\chi^2(c-1)$ as the number of rows other than those all 0 and all 1 tends to infinity is quite involved, and we can obtain this result more simply by regarding the Cochran Q test as a special case of the Friedman test with ties in the ranks.*

Let x_{ij} be a variable with the property that

$$\begin{aligned} x_{ij} &= 1 \quad \text{if } ij\text{th cell has a success,} \\ &= 0 \quad \text{if } ij\text{th cell has a failure.} \end{aligned} \tag{10.2}$$

Then since T_j is the number of successes in the jth column,

$$\sum_{i}^{r} x_{ij} = T_j, \tag{10.3}$$

and since u_i is the number of successes in the ith row,

$$\sum_{j}^{c} x_{ij} = u_i. \tag{10.4}$$

It follows that

$$\bar{T} = \frac{1}{c} \sum_{j}^{c} T_j = \frac{1}{c} \sum_{j}^{c} \sum_{i}^{r} x_{ij} = \frac{1}{c} \sum_{i}^{r} \sum_{j}^{c} x_{ij} = \frac{1}{c} \sum_{i}^{r} u_i. \tag{10.5}$$

Consider a given row with u_i successes. The successes are allocated ranks $1, \ldots, u_i$ with sum $u_i(u_i + 1)/2$ and hence mean rank $(u_i + 1)/2$. The $c - u_i$ cells with failures are allocated ranks $u_i + 1, \ldots, c$, and the mean

---

* This was demonstrated to the author by Nancy D. Bailey following a surmise by William H. Kruskal at a seminar by Bailey.

of these ranks is $(c + u_i + 1)/2$. From (4.2), the variance of the ranks R_{ij} is

$$V[R_{ij}] = \frac{1}{c}\sum_j^c R_{ij}^2 - \left(\frac{1}{c}\sum_j^c R_{ij}\right)^2. \qquad (10.6)$$

In $\sum_j R_{ij}$ we have the mean rank $(u_i + 1)/2$ occurring u_i times and the mean rank $(c + u_i + 1)/2$ occurring $c - u_i$ times. Thus

$$V[R_{ij}] = \frac{1}{c}\left[u_i\left(\frac{u_i+1}{2}\right)^2 + (c-u_i)\left(\frac{c+u_i+1}{2}\right)^2\right]$$
$$- \left\{\frac{1}{c}\left[u_i\frac{u_i+1}{2} + (c-u_i)\frac{c+u_i+1}{2}\right]\right\}^2$$
$$= \frac{cu_i - u_i^2}{4}. \qquad (10.7)$$

Therefore

$$V[\bar{R}_{\cdot j}] = V\left[\frac{1}{r}\sum_i^r R_{ij}\right] = \frac{1}{4r^2}\sum_i^r (cu_i - u_i^2). \qquad (10.8)$$

In the ith row the ranks are R_{ij} equal to $(u_i + 1)/2$ or to $(c + u_i + 1)/2$ depending on whether $x_{ij} = 1$ or 0. We can write

$$R_{ij} = \frac{1}{2}[u_i + 1 + c(1 - x_{ij})], \qquad (10.9)$$

so

$$\bar{R}_{\cdot j} = \frac{1}{r}\sum_i^r R_{ij} = \frac{1}{2r}\sum_i^r u_i + \frac{1}{2}(c+1) - \frac{c}{2r}\sum_i^r x_{ij}. \qquad (10.10)$$

Now $\bar{R}_{\cdot\cdot} = (c+1)/2$, and using (10.3) and (10.5) for the first and last terms on the right-hand side we get

$$\bar{R}_{\cdot j} - \bar{R}_{\cdot\cdot} = -\frac{c}{2r}(T_j - \bar{T}). \qquad (10.11)$$

Therefore

$$\sum_j^c (\bar{R}_{\cdot j} - \bar{R}_{\cdot\cdot})^2 = \frac{c^2}{4r^2}\sum_j^c (T_j - \bar{T})^2. \qquad (10.12)$$

We now substitute (10.12) and (10.8) in (9.4) to get

$$\chi_r^2 = \frac{c-1}{c}\frac{\frac{c^2}{4r^2}\sum_j^c (T_j - \bar{T})^2}{\frac{1}{4r^2}\sum_i^r (cu_i - u_i^2)} = \frac{c(c-1)\sum_j^c (T_j - \bar{T})^2}{c\sum_i^r u_i - \sum_i^r u_i^2}, \qquad (10.13)$$

which is identical with Cochran's Q, (10.1).

To compute Q for the data of Table 7.12 we need a table showing the number of specimens having each possible value of u_i (Table 7.13) from which we get

$$\sum_i^r u_i = 4 \times 4 + 3 \times 5 + 2 \times 1 + 1 \times 0 + 0 \times 59 = 33, \qquad (10.14)$$

$$\sum_i^r u_i^2 = 4^2 \times 4 + 3^2 \times 5 + 2^2 \times 1 + 1^2 \times 0 + 0^2 \times 59 = 113. \qquad (10.15)$$

We also need $\sum_j^c (T_j - \bar{T})^2$ which can be calculated as

$$\sum_j^c T_j^2 - \frac{1}{c}\left(\sum_j^c T_j\right)^2 = 6^2 + 10^2 + 7^2 + 10^2 - \frac{33^2}{4} = 12.75. \qquad (10.16)$$

Thus

$$Q = \frac{4(4-1) \times 12.75}{4 \times 33 - 113} = 8.05. \qquad (10.17)$$

Since $\chi^2_{0.95}(3) = 7.81$, $P < 0.05$.

Table 7.13

u_i	4	3	2	1	0
Number of specimens	4	5	1	0	59

EXERCISES

7.1. Apply the appropriate Wilcoxon rank test to the data of Table 7.4.

7.2. A group of mice are allocated to individual cages randomly. The cages are allocated in equal numbers, randomly, to two treatments, a control A and a certain drug B. All animals are infected, in a random sequence, with tuberculosis [Note: the experimenter usually wants to infect all the controls and then all the B group, but this is terrible]. The mice die on the following days following infection [one mouse got lost].

Control A: 5, 6, 7, 7, 8, 8, 8, 9, 12
Drug B: 7, 8, 8, 8, 9, 9, 12, 13, 14, 17

A preliminary experiment having established that the drug is not toxic it can be assumed that the test group cannot be worse (die sooner) than the control group under any reasonable alternative hypothesis. Report the P value for the null hypothesis that the drug is without effect, using the appropriate Wilcoxon test.

7.3. Acid is concentrated continuously in a certain type of plant. Part of the plant corrodes and eventually fails. The throughput in hundreds of tons obtained between installation and failure is recorded. These parts were obtained from three separate foundries. Test the hypothesis that the median life is the same for the three foundries.

Foundry	Throughputs obtained
A	84, 60, 40, 47, 34, 46
B	67, 92, 95, 40, 98, 60, 59, 108, 86, 117
C	46, 93, 100, 92, 92

7.4. In a rain-making (?) experiment, rainfall measurements were made on 16 pairs of days. On one day in each pair the clouds were seeded and on the other day no seeding was done. The choice of which day in a pair to seed was made randomly. The total rainfall over the network of gauges for the 16 pairs of days is below. Test the null hypothesis that seeding is without effect with (a) the sign test, (b) the appropriate Wilcoxon test. Report one-sided P values.

Pair no.	S	NS	Pair no.	S	NS
1	0	1.37	9	0	0
2	2.09	0	10	1.87	0.62
3	0.07	0	11	2.50	0
4	0.30	0.10	12	3.15	5.54
5	0	0.44	13	0.15	0.01
6	2.55	0	14	2.96	0
7	1.62	1.01	15	0	0
8	0	0.54	16	0	0.75

7.5. In a trial of two types of rain gauge, 69 of type A and 12 of type B were distributed at random over a certain area. In a certain period 14 storms occurred, and the average amounts of rain found in the two types of gauge were as shown in the accompanying table.

Storm	Type A	Type B	Storm	Type A	Type B
1	1.38	1.42	8	2.63	2.69
2	9.69	10.37	9	2.44	2.68
3	0.39	0.39	10	0.56	0.53
4	1.42	1.46	11	0.69	0.72
5	0.54	0.55	12	0.71	0.72
6	5.94	6.15	13	0.95	0.93
7	0.59	0.61	14	0.50	0.53

Data from E. L. Hamilton, "The Problem of Sampling Rainfall in Mountainous Areas," pp. 469–475 of *Proceedings of the Berkeley Symposium on Mathematical Statistics and Probability*, J. Neyman (ed.), University of California Press, Berkeley and Los Angeles, 1949.

Obtain the one-sided P value for the hypothesis that the two types of gauge are giving similar results, using (a) the appropriate Wilcoxon test by exact enumeration, (b) the appropriate Wilcoxon test using a normal approximation, (c) the sign test.

7.6. On a number of days coffee is prepared by two different electric coffee makers, and the time in minutes and tenths of a minute for the coffee-making operation to be completed by each machine is recorded. The results were as below.

Machine	Day							
	1	2	3	4	5	6	7	8
A	9.9	9.7	8.8	9.8	6.8	7.3	12.0	11.0
B	14.3	11.5	8.8	13.5	8.2	10.1	10.1	11.9

It is probable that the time required varies from day to day due to variation in such factors as the temperature of the water or line voltage. Use the appropriate Wilcoxon test to find the exact P value for the null hypothesis that the median times for the two machines are the same, against the one-sided alternative that machine B takes longer than machine A. Make a similar test with the sign test.

7.7. Fruit juice is stored for a number of months in four types of container and then rated for quality by eight panels of tasters. The taste scores assigned by the panels were as below.

Container	Panel							
	1	2	3	4	5	6	7	8
A	6.14	5.72	6.90	5.80	6.23	6.06	5.42	6.04
B	6.55	6.29	7.40	6.40	6.28	6.26	6.22	6.76
C	5.54	5.61	6.60	5.70	5.31	5.58	5.57	5.84
D	4.81	5.09	6.61	5.03	5.15	5.05	5.77	6.17

(a) Test the null hypothesis that there is no difference between the containers. (b) Test the null hypothesis that there is no difference between the panels.

7.8. Samples of soil were taken at five locations on a farm and tested for the presence of a certain fungus. The test was of the form that yields only yes or no answers, represented by 1 or 0 in the table below. The same five locations were sampled on a total of 18 occasions. Test the null hypothesis that the probability of a sample being positive is the same for all five locations.

Location	Occasion																	
	1	2	3	4	5	6	7	8	9	10	11	12	13	14	15	16	17	18
1	0	0	0	1	1	0	0	1	1	1	0	0	0	0	0	0	0	1
2	0	1	0	1	1	0	0	1	0	0	0	0	0	0	0	0	1	1
3	1	1	1	1	1	1	1	1	1	0	0	0	0	0	0	1	1	
4	1	1	1	1	0	1	1	0	1	0	0	0	0	1	0	1	0	
5	0	1	0	0	1	0	0	0	0	0	0	0	0	0	0	1	0	

7.9. A sample of five observations, $x_1, \ldots, x_5$ is taken from one population and a sample of five observations $y_1, \ldots, y_5$ is taken from another population. It is found that four of the x's lie below the joint sample median.

(a) Using the median test, what is the one-sided P value for the null hypothesis that the samples came from populations with the same medians?

(b) Suppose that the density function of y is

$$p_Y\{Y\} = 1 \qquad -\tfrac{1}{2} < y < \tfrac{1}{2},$$
$$= 0 \qquad \text{otherwise,}$$

and that the density function of x is

$$p_X\{x\} = 1 \qquad -1 < x < -\tfrac{1}{2}, \tfrac{1}{2} < x < 1,$$
$$= 0 \qquad \text{otherwise.}$$

What is the probability of observing four or more x's below the joint sample median under these assumptions?

(The relevance of this exercise is that it demonstrates that the median test does assume under the null hypothesis indentity of the two distributions.)

7.10. In the context of Section 7.4, consider a finite population of size N in which M of the elements have x_i taking the value 1 and the remaining $N - M$ elements have x_i taking the value 0. If $x_i = 1$ call the element defective and if $x_i = 0$ call the element nondefective. Take a sample of size n from this population. Then $\sum_i^n x_i = n\bar{x}$ is equivalent to the number of defectives in the sample. Show that $E\left[\sum_i^n x_i\right] = nM/N$, and

$$V\left[\sum_i^n x_i\right] = \frac{nM}{N}\left(1 - \frac{M}{N}\right)\left(1 - \frac{n-1}{N-1}\right).$$

Relate these results to those of exercise (3B.2).

7.11. Consider the median test of Section 7.3. Suppose that the numerical values of all observations below the median are lost and all that is known is which sample they came from and that they are below the median: analogously for all observations above the median. Now analyze the data as in a two-sample Wilcoxon test with adjustment for ties. Show that the unit deviate approximately normal of the Wilcoxon test is identical with the large sample statistic for the median test in its unmodified form (3.10.7).

7.12. Suppose that we consider taking a sample of size n from a normal distribution with known variance σ^2 and testing, with the usual test at level of significance α assuming normality and knowledge of the variance, the null hypothesis that the mean is ξ_0 against the alternative that it is ξ_1, $\xi_1 > \xi_0$, and that we require that n be such that the power be some value $1 - \beta$ when $(\xi_1 - \xi_0)/\sigma$ is some small value δ.

Now consider taking a sample of size n' from the same normal distribution and testing at level of significance α with the sign test the null hypothesis that the median is ξ_0 against the alternative that it is ξ_1, $\xi_1 > \xi_0$, and that we require n'

be such that the power is the same value $1 - \beta$ when $(\xi_1 - \xi_0)/\sigma$ is the same small value δ as in the previous paragraph.

Obtain a simple expression for n/n'. This is known as the asymptotic relative efficiency of the sign test.

Where appropriate use a "rectangular" approximation to the integral of a normal curve over a small interval. For the power of the sign test use a formula that assumes that the binomial distribution can be approximated by a normal distribution. Where appropriate approximate by discarding terms in δ^2.

7.13. The statistics (5.6) was derived by picking one of the two samples and calculating its observed mean rank $\bar{R}$, $E[\bar{R}]$, and $V[\bar{R}]$. Show that if the other sample is selected, the absolute value of the corresponding statistic is identical with the absolute value of (5.6).

7.14. Suppose that in a two-sample Wilcoxon test one sample of observations is $X_1, \ldots, X_n$ and the other sample is $Y_1, \ldots, Y_m$. Consider all possible pairings (X_i, Y_j) and let U be the number of pairs in which $X_i < Y_j$. Let R_{Y_j} be the ranks of the Y's. Show that

$$U = \sum_{j=1}^{m} R_{Y_j} - \frac{m(m+1)}{2}.$$

[Since $m(m+1)/2$ is a constant, $\sum_{j}^{m} R_{Y_j}$ (the sum of the ranks of the Y's) is a linear function of U. Since U is an intuitively appealing statistic, this provides a justification for the use of the rank sum as a test statistic. This is the approach taken by Mann and Whitney [9]].

REFERENCES

1. Cramér, H., *Mathematical Methods of Statistics*. Princeton: Princeton University Press, 1951.
2. Savage, I. Richard, *Bibliography of Nonparametric Statistics*. Cambridge, Mass.: Harvard University Press, 1962.
3. Fraser, D. A. S., *Nonparametric Methods in Statistics*. New York: John Wiley and Sons, 1957.
4. Kendall, M. G., *Rank Correlation Methods*. 2nd ed.; London: Griffin and Co., 1955.
5. Putter, J., "The Treatment of Ties in Some Nonparametric Tests," *Annals of Mathematical Statistics*, 26 (1955), 368–86.
6. Wilcoxon, F., "Individual Comparisons by Ranking Methods," *Biometrics Bulletin*, 1 (1947), 80–83.
7. Wilcoxon, F., "Probability Tables for Individual Comparisons by Ranking Methods," *Biometrics*, 3 (1947), 119–22.
8. Dean, G., "The Atomic Weight of Carbon and Silver," *Journal of the Chemical Society of London*, 125 (1924), 2656–72.
9. Mann, H. B., and D. R. Whitney, "On a Test of Whether One of Two Random Variables is Stochastically Larger than the Other," *Annals of Mathematical Statistics*, 18 (1947), 50–60.
10. Kruskal, W. H., "Historical Notes on the Wilcoxon Unpaired Two-Sample Test," *Journal of the American Statistical Association*, 52 (1957), 356–60.

11. Kruskal, W. H., and W. Allen Wallis, "Use of Ranks in One-Criterion Analysis of Variance," *Journal of the American Statistical Association*, 47 (1952), 583–621.
12. Wallace, D. L., "Simplified Beta-Approximations to the Kruskal-Wallis H Test." *Journal of the American Statistical Association*, 54 (1959), 225–30.
13. Box, G. E. P., and S. L. Andersen, "Permutation Theory in the Derivation of Robust Criteria and the Study of Departure from Assumption," *Journal of the Royal Statistical Society*, B (Methodological), 17 (1955), 1–26.
14. Laby, T. H., and E. O. Hercus, "The Mechanical Equivalent of Heat," *Philosophical Transactions of the Royal Society*, A, 227 (1928), 63–91.
15. Friedman, M., "The Use of Ranks to Avoid the Assumption of Normality in the Analysis of Variance," *Journal of the American Statistical Association*, 32 (1937), 675–701.
16. Cochran, W. G., "The Comparison of Percentages in Matched Samples," *Biometrika*, 37 (1950), 256–66.

CHAPTER 8

The Partitioning of Sums of Squares

8.1. The Distribution of Sample Estimates of Variance

This chapter, largely algebraic, is devoted to a proof of two theorems. The theorem of this section is the basis of the Student t test to be discussed in Section 9.6 and that of the following section is the basis of the analysis of variance discussed in Chapter 10. Some readers may prefer to omit this chapter temporarily. The account given here is based on an exposition by A. Hald [1].

Suppose that we have n independent observations $x_1, \ldots, x_n$ from a normal population of unknown mean ξ and variance σ^2. In this section we will show that the usual unbiased estimator of the variance

$$s^2 = \frac{1}{n-1} \sum_{i=1}^{n} (x_i - \bar{x})^2 \sim \sigma^2 \frac{\chi^2(n-1)}{n-1}, \tag{1.1}$$

where $\sim$ is used to denote "is distributed as," and that s^2 is independent of $\bar{x}$. These two results are the basis of the Student t test to be discussed in Section 9.6.

We can write

$$\sum_{i}^{n} (x_i - \xi)^2 = \sum_{i}^{n} [(x_i - \bar{x}) + (\bar{x} - \xi)]^2 = \sum_{i}^{n} (x_i - \bar{x})^2 + n(\bar{x} - \xi)^2. \tag{1.2}$$

Dividing by σ^2,

$$\sum_{i}^{n} \left(\frac{x_i - \xi}{\sigma}\right)^2 = \sum_{i}^{n} \left(\frac{x_i - \bar{x}}{\sigma}\right)^2 + \left(\frac{\bar{x} - \xi}{\sigma/\sqrt{n}}\right)^2. \tag{1.3}$$

Define $u_i = (x_i - \xi)/\sigma$, so that $x_i = \sigma u_i + \xi$. Then

$$\bar{x} = \frac{1}{n}\sum_i^n x_i = \sigma\left(\frac{1}{n}\sum_i^n u_i\right) + \xi = \sigma\bar{u} + \xi, \quad (1.4)$$

so

$$\frac{x_i - \bar{x}}{\sigma} = \frac{\sigma u_i + \xi - (\sigma\bar{u} + \xi)}{\sigma} = u_i - \bar{u}, \quad (1.5)$$

and

$$\frac{\bar{x} - \xi}{\sigma/\sqrt{n}} = \frac{\sigma\bar{u} + \xi - \xi}{\sigma/\sqrt{n}} = \frac{\bar{u}}{1/\sqrt{n}} = \sqrt{n}\bar{u}. \quad (1.6)$$

Thus (1.3) can be written as

$$\sum_i^n u_i^2 = \sum_i^n (u_i - \bar{u})^2 + (\sqrt{n}\bar{u})^2 \quad (1.7)$$

$$= Q_2 + Q_1, \quad \text{say}. \quad (1.8)$$

The left-hand side $\sum_i^n u_i^2$ is distributed as $\chi^2(n)$. On the right-hand side, $\sqrt{n}\,\bar{u} = \bar{u}(1/\sqrt{n})$ is a unit normal deviate, and hence its square Q_1 is distributed as $\chi^2(1)$. We shall now prove that Q_2 is distributed as $\chi^2(n-1)$ and is independent of Q_1. This will establish that $\sum_i^n (x_i - \bar{x})^2$ is distributed as $\sigma^2\chi^2(n-1)$ and is independent of $(\bar{x} - \xi)^2$.

Define $l_i = u_i - \bar{u}$, so that $Q_2 = \sum_i^n l_i^2$, and

$$\sum_i^n l_i = \sum_i^n u_i - n\bar{u} = \sum_i^n u_i - n\left(\sum_i^n u_i/n\right) = 0. \quad (1.9)$$

The number of degrees of freedom for a set of variables is defined as the number of variables minus the number of independent linear relations or constraints between them. The number of degrees of freedom of the sum of squares of a set of variables is the same as the number of degrees of freedom of the variables themselves. In the present instance, $\sum_i^n u_i^2$ involves n variables u_i with no linear relationship between them, and so it has n degrees of freedom; but Q_2 involves n variables l_i with the restriction $\sum_i^n l_i = 0$, and so Q_2 has $n - 1$ degrees of freedom. The n variables l_i are not independent [see exercise (8.1)], but we can construct from them $n - 1$ variables v_i ($i = 2, 3, \ldots, n$) with the properties that

(a) $\sum_{i=1}^n l_i^2 = \sum_{i=2}^n v_i^2$,
(b) the v_i are independent unit normal deviates,
(c) the v_i ($i = 2, \ldots, n$) are independent of v_1 defined as $\sqrt{n}\bar{u}$.

SECT. 8.1 THE DISTRIBUTION OF SAMPLE ESTIMATES OF VARIANCE

Thus the distribution of $\sum_{i=1}^{n} v_i^2$ is $\chi^2(n-1)$, and therefore the distribution of $Q_2 = \sum_{i=2}^{n} l_i^2$ is also $\chi^2(n-1)$ and is independent of Q_1.

The first step is to eliminate l_1^2 from $\sum_{i=1}^{n} l_i^2$ by using the relation $\sum_{i=1}^{n} l_i = 0$, which implies that

$$l_1 = -(l_2 + l_3 + \cdots + l_n), \tag{1.10}$$

so

$$\begin{aligned} l_1^2 = \; & l_2^2 + 2(l_2 l_3 + l_2 l_4 + \cdots + l_2 l_n) \\ & + l_3^2 + 2(l_3 l_4 + \cdots + l_3 l_n) \\ & + \cdots \qquad\qquad\qquad + \\ & \qquad\qquad\qquad\qquad \vdots \\ & + l_n^2. \end{aligned} \tag{1.11}$$

Substituting this for l_1^2 in $Q_2 = \sum_{i=1}^{n} l_i^2$ will give Q_2 in the form of a function of the $n-1$ variables l_i, $i = 2, 3, \ldots, n$:

$$\begin{aligned} Q_2 = \; & 2(l_2^2 + l_2 l_3 + l_2 l_4 + \cdots + l_2 l_n \\ & + l_3^2 + l_3 l_4 + \cdots + l_3 l_n \\ & + \cdots \qquad\qquad \cdots + \\ & \qquad\qquad\qquad \vdots \\ & + l_n^2). \end{aligned} \tag{1.12}$$

This can be expressed as the sum of $n-1$ squares, by first collecting all terms that involve l_2, the first row, and writing them as a perfect square plus whatever is left over:

$$\begin{aligned} & 2(l_2^2 + l_2 l_3 + l_2 l_4 + \cdots + l_2 l_n) \\ & = \left\{ \sqrt{2} \left[l_2 + \frac{1}{2}(l_3 + l_4 + \cdots + l_n) \right] \right\}^2 \\ & \quad - \frac{1}{2} l_3^2 - l_3 l_4 - \cdots - l_3 l_n \\ & \qquad\quad - \frac{1}{2} l_4^2 - \cdots - l_4 l_n \\ & \qquad\qquad\qquad\qquad \vdots \\ & \qquad\qquad\qquad\qquad - \frac{1}{2} l_n^2. \end{aligned} \tag{1.13}$$

Substituting this in (1.12),

$$Q_2 = \left\{\sqrt{2}\left[l_2 + \frac{1}{2}(l_3 + l_4 + \cdots + l_n)\right]\right\}^2$$

$$+ \frac{3}{2}l_3^2 + l_3 l_4 + \cdots + l_3 l_n$$

$$\vdots$$

$$+ \frac{3}{2}l_n^2. \qquad (1.14)$$

The next step is to collect all the terms in l_3 excluding those in the first row: They are set out in the second row of (1.14). We write them as a perfect square plus whatever is left over, just as we did for l_2. The square part is

$$\left\{\sqrt{\frac{3}{2}}\left[l_3 + \frac{1}{3}(l_4 + l_5 + \cdots + l_n)\right]\right\}^2. \qquad (1.15)$$

This procedure can be continued until we are finally left with only l_n^2. These squares can be denoted by v_i^2, $i = 2, \ldots, n$:

$$v_2 = \sqrt{2}\left[l_2 + \frac{1}{2}(l_3 + l_4 + \cdots + l_n)\right],$$

$$v_3 = \sqrt{\frac{3}{2}}\left[l_3 + \frac{1}{3}(l_4 + l_5 + \cdots + l_n)\right],$$

$$\vdots$$

$$v_i = \sqrt{\frac{i}{i-1}}\left[l_i + \frac{1}{i}(l_{i+1} + l_{i+2} + \cdots + l_n)\right],$$

$$\vdots$$

$$v_n = \sqrt{\frac{n}{n-1}}\, l_n. \qquad (1.16)$$

We have thus expressed $Q_2 = \sum_{i=1}^{n} l_i^2$ as $\sum_{i=2}^{n} v_i^2$. It remains to show that these v_i are unit normal deviates and are independent of each other and of v_1.

SECT. 8.1 THE DISTRIBUTION OF SAMPLE ESTIMATES OF VARIANCE 275

To do this we express the v_i, $i > 1$, in terms of the u_i by the substitution $l_i = u_i - \bar{u}$:

$$\begin{aligned}
v_i &= \frac{1}{\sqrt{i(i-1)}}(il_i + l_{i+1} + \cdots + l_n) \\
&= \frac{1}{\sqrt{i(i-1)}}(iu_i - i\bar{u} + u_{i+1} - \bar{u} + \cdots + u_n - \bar{u}) \\
&= \frac{1}{\sqrt{i(i-1)}}(iu_i + u_{i+1} + \cdots + u_n - n\bar{u}) \\
&= \frac{1}{\sqrt{i(i-1)}}(iu_i + u_{i+1} + \cdots + u_n - u_1 - u_2 - \cdots - u_{i-1} \\
&\qquad\qquad\qquad - u_i - u_{i+1} - \cdots - u_n) \\
&= -\frac{1}{\sqrt{i(i-1)}}[u_1 + u_2 + \cdots + u_{i-1} - (i-1)u_i]. \quad (1.17)
\end{aligned}$$

The v_i will be normally distributed since they are linear functions of the u_i which are normally distributed, and

$$E[v_i] = -\frac{1}{\sqrt{i(i-1)}}\{E[u_1] + \cdots + E[u_{i-1}] - (i-1)E[u_i]\} = 0, \quad (1.18)$$

$$V[v_i] = \frac{1}{i(i-1)}\{V[u_1] + \cdots + V[u_{i-1}] + (i-1)^2 V[u_i]\} = 1, \quad (1.19)$$

$$\begin{aligned}
\mathrm{Cov}[v_i, v_j] &= E[v_i v_j] - E[v_i]E[v_j] \\
&= \frac{1}{\sqrt{i(i-1)j(j-1)}} E[(u_1 + \cdots + u_{i-1} - (i-1)u_i) \\
&\qquad\qquad \times (u_1 + \cdots + u_{j-1} - (j-1)u_j)]. \quad (1.20)
\end{aligned}$$

For $i < j$, the expectation $E[\ ]$ will include the squared terms u_i^2 for $i < j$, and their expectation is

$$E[u_1^2 + \cdots + u_{i-1}^2 - (i-1)u_i^2] = 0. \quad (1.21)$$

The expectation $E[\ ]$ will also include cross products of the form $k_{rs}u_r u_s$, $r \neq s$, where k_{rs} is some constant. Their expectation is

$$E[k_{rs}u_r u_s] = k_{rs}E[u_r]E[u_s] = 0. \quad (1.22)$$

Thus $\mathrm{Cov}[v_i, v_j] = 0$.

It will be shown in Section 12.3 that, if v_1, v_2 are linear functions of normally distributed variables u_1, u_2, then v_1, v_2 are jointly distributed in the bivariate normal distribution, and that, if $\mathrm{Cov}[v_1, v_2] = 0$, then v_1, v_2

are independent. Thus the v_i are independent, and since they have zero means and unit variances, and are normally distributed,

$$Q_2 = \sum_{i=2}^{n} v_i^2 \sim \chi^2(n-1), \tag{1.23}$$

where as before the symbol $\sim$ is used to denote "is distributed as." It is easy to show that $v_1, v_i, i = 2, \ldots, n$, are independent, and hence Q_1 is independent of Q_2.

To recapitulate, if we write

$$\sum_{i=1}^{n} u_i^2 = (\sqrt{n}\,\bar{u})^2 + \sum_{i=1}^{n} (u_i - \bar{u})^2 = Q_1 + Q_2, \tag{1.24}$$

then Q_1 and Q_2 have independent χ^2 distributions with degrees of freedom 1 and $n-1$. Substituting $u_i = (x_i - \xi)/\sigma$ and multiplying both sides by σ^2 gives

$$\sum_{i}^{n}(x_i - \xi)^2 = n(\bar{x} - \xi)^2 + \sum_{i}^{n}(x_i - \bar{x})^2, \tag{1.25}$$

for which the left-hand side is distributed as $\sigma^2\chi^2$ with n degrees of freedom and the two terms on the right-hand side are distributed as $\sigma^2\chi^2$ with degrees of freedom 1 and $n-1$, and are independent. This implies that for normally distributed random variables

$$s^2 = \frac{1}{n-1}\sum_{i}^{n}(x_i - \bar{x})^2 \sim \sigma^2 \frac{\chi^2(n-1)}{n-1}, \tag{1.26}$$

and also that $\bar{x}$ is independent of s^2.

8.2. The Partitioning of Sums of Squares into Independent Components

The result of the preceding section will be used for the Student t test in Chapter 9. For the comparison of k means, in Chapter 10 and following, we need a stronger result, Cochran's theorem [2]. A restricted form of this theorem is as follows.

We have n unit normally distributed and independent random variables $u_i, i = 1, \ldots, n$. The sum of their squares is distributed as $\chi^2(n)$. Suppose that $Q_j, j = 1, \ldots, k$, are sums of squares with f_j degrees of freedom. Then, if

$$\sum_{j}^{k} Q_j = Q_1 + \cdots + Q_k = \sum_{i}^{n} u_i^2 \tag{2.1}$$

and

$$\sum_{j}^{k} f_j = f_1 + \cdots + f_k = n, \tag{2.2}$$

SECT. 8.2 PARTITIONING INTO INDEPENDENT COMPONENTS

then the theorem states that the Q_j are independently distributed as $\chi^2(f_j)$. Actually the theorem is somewhat stronger in that the Q_j can be quadratic forms,

$$\sum_i \sum_j a_{ij} x_i x_j = a_{11} x_1^2 + a_{12} x_1 x_2 + \cdots + a_{1n} x_1 x_n$$
$$+ a_{21} x_1 x_2 + a_{22} x_2^2 + a_{23} x_2 x_3 + \cdots, \quad (2.3)$$

where $a_{ij} = a_{ji}$.

We assume that each Q_j is the sum of the squares of m_j variables l_{ij}, $i = 1, \ldots, m_j$; i.e.,

$$Q_j = l_{1j}^2 + l_{2j}^2 + \cdots + l_{m_j j}^2 = \sum_i^{m_j} l_{ij}^2. \quad (2.4)$$

We assume that, among the m_j variables l_{ij}, there are r_j linear relations, so that the number of degrees of freedom for Q_j is $f_j = m_j - r_j$. We are going to show that each $Q_j = \sum_i^{m_j} l_{ij}^2$ can be written in the form $Q_j = \sum_i^{f_j} v_{ij}^2$, in which the v_{ij} are independent unit normal deviates. This will show that the Q_j have $\chi^2(f_j)$ distributions and are independent.

If there are r_j linear relations among the m_j variables l_{ij}, then we can use these relations to eliminate r_j of the l_{ij} and convert Q_j into a quadratic form in only $m_j - r_j = f_j$ variables l_{ij}. Thus it is possible to obtain

$$Q_j = \sum_i^{f_j} \sum_{i'}^{f_j} a_{ii'} l_{ij} l_{i'j}. \quad (2.5)$$

Further, this quadratic form can be linearly transformed into another quadratic form in f_j variables $v_{1j}, \ldots, v_{f_j j}$ involving only squares

$$Q_j = \sum_i^{f_j} b_{ij} v_{ij}^2, \quad (2.6)$$

in which the $b_{ij} = \pm 1$ (see, e.g., Section 51 of [3]). Combining (2.6) and (2.1), we have

$$\sum_i^n u_i^2 = \sum_j^k Q_j = \sum_j^k \sum_i^{f_j} b_{ij} v_{ij}^2. \quad (2.7)$$

Now, if the condition (2.2) for Cochran's theorem is satisfied, $\sum_j^k f_j = n$, so that the number of terms on the left-hand side of (2.7) equals the number of terms on the right-hand side. The theory of quadratic forms contains the result (see, e.g., Section 50 of [3]) that, if a real quadratic form of rank r is reduced by two nonsingular transformations to the forms

$$(c_1 x_1'^2 + \cdots + c_r x_r'^2) \quad \text{and} \quad (k_1 x_1''^2 + \cdots + k_r x_r''^2), \quad (2.8)$$

then the number of positive c's equals the number of positive k's. In (2.7) all the coefficients of the u_i^2 are positive, in fact being all $+1$, and hence all the coefficients of the v_{ij}^2 must also be positive. They were already known to be ± 1; so it follows that they are all $+1$, and (2.6) becomes

$$Q_j = \sum_j^{f_j} v_{ij}^2. \tag{2.9}$$

We now have two sets of transformations of the quadratic form $\sum_j^k Q_j$, where Q_j is written as in (2.5), one leading to $\sum_i^n u_i^2$ and the other to $\sum_j^k \sum_i^{f_j} v_{ij}^2$. In other words, $\sum_i^n u_i^2$ can be linearly transformed to $\sum_j^k \sum_i^{f_j} v_{ij}^2$, where $\sum_j^k f_j = n$; i.e., the n v_{ij}'s are linear functions of the n u_i's. It will be convenient at this point to change the index on v from ij, $i = 1, \ldots, k$, $j = 1, \ldots, f_j$, to $g = 1, \ldots, n$. If the transformation is

$$v_g = c_{g1}u_1 + c_{g2}u_2 + \cdots + c_{gn}u_n = \sum_j^n c_{gj}u_j, \quad g = 1, \ldots, n, \tag{2.10}$$

then

$$\sum_g^n v_g^2 = \sum_g^n \left(\sum_j^n c_{gj}u_j\right)^2 = \sum_g^n \sum_j^n \sum_{j'}^n c_{gj}c_{gj'}u_ju_{j'} = \sum_j^n \sum_{j'}^n \left(\sum_g^n c_{gj}c_{gj'}\right)u_ju_{j'} \tag{2.11}$$

We know that $\sum_g^n v_g^2 = \sum_i^n u_i^2$; so

$$\sum_i^n u_i^2 = \sum_j^n \sum_{j'}^n \left(\sum_g^n c_{gj}c_{gj'}\right)u_ju_{j'}, \tag{2.12}$$

and the coefficients of the u's on the two sides of this equation must be equal for any $i = j = j'$,

$$\sum_g^n c_{gi}^2 = c_{1i}^2 + c_{2i}^2 + \cdots + c_{ni}^2 = 1. \tag{2.13}$$

There are no cross products $u_ju_{j'}$, $j \neq j'$, in the left-hand side of (2.12); so on the right-hand side the coefficient of $u_ju_{j'}$, $j \neq j'$, must be zero.

$$c_{1j}c_{1j'} + c_{2j}c_{2j'} + \cdots + c_{nj}c_{nj'} = \sum_g^n c_{gj}c_{gj'} = 0. \tag{2.14}$$

SECT. 8.2   PARTITIONING INTO INDEPENDENT COMPONENTS

If we multiply the first of the n equations (2.10) by c_{11}, the second by c_{21}, etc., we get

$$c_{11}v_1 = c_{11}^2 u_1 + c_{11}c_{12}u_2 + \cdots + c_{11}c_{1n}u_n$$
$$c_{21}v_2 = c_{21}^2 u_1 + c_{21}c_{22}u_2 + \cdots + c_{21}c_{2n}u_n$$
$$\vdots \qquad (2.15)$$

Adding these n equations gives

$$c_{11}v_1 + c_{21}v_2 + \cdots + c_{n1}v_n$$
$$= u_1(c_{11}^2 + c_{21}^2 + \cdots + c_{n1}^2) + u_2(c_{11}c_{12} + c_{21}c_{22} + \cdots + c_{n1}c_{n2}) + \cdots$$
$$+ u_n(c_{11}c_{1n} + c_{21}c_{2n} + \cdots + c_{n1}c_{nn})$$
$$= u_1, \qquad (2.16)$$

since by (2.13) the coefficient of u_1 equals 1 and by (2.14) the coefficients of $u_2, \ldots, u_n$ are all zero. Proceeding in this manner, we multiply the n equations (2.10) by c_{12}, c_{22}, etc., to get

$$c_{12}v_1 + c_{22}v_2 + \cdots + c_{n2}v_n = u_2, \qquad (2.17)$$

and so on. Thus in general,

$$u_j = c_{1j}v_1 + c_{2j}v_2 + \cdots + c_{nj}v_n = \sum_g^n c_{gj}v_g, \qquad (2.18)$$

and so

$$\sum_j^n u_j^2 = \sum_j^n \left(\sum_g^n c_{gj}v_g\right)^2 = \sum_j^n \sum_g^n \sum_{g'}^n c_{gj}c_{g'j}v_g v_{g'} = \sum_g^n \sum_{g'}^n \left(\sum_j^n c_{gj}c_{g'j}\right)v_g v_{g'}. \qquad (2.19)$$

But $\sum_j^n u_j^2 = \sum_g^n v_g^2$; so the coefficients of the v_g's on the two sides of the equation

$$\sum_g^n v_g^2 = \sum_g^n \sum_{g'}^n \left(\sum_j^n c_{gj}c_{g'j}\right)v_g v_{g'} \qquad (2.20)$$

are equal. Thus, for $g = g'$,

$$\sum_j^n c_{gj}c_{g'j} = \sum_j^n c_{gj}^2 = c_{g1}^2 + c_{g2}^2 + \cdots + c_{gn}^2 = 1. \qquad (2.21)$$

and, for $g \neq g'$,

$$\sum_j^n c_{gj}c_{g'j} = c_{g1}c_{g'1} + c_{g2}c_{g'2} + \cdots + c_{gn}c_{g'n} = 0. \qquad (2.22)$$

We will now use these relations to show that the v_g are independent unit normal deviates.

From the definition of v_g in (2.10), it follows that

$$E[v_g] = E[c_{g1}u_1 + \cdots + c_{gn}u_n] = 0, \tag{2.23}$$

$$V[v_g] = c_{g1}^2 V[u_1] + \cdots + c_{gn}^2 V[u_n] = c_{g1}^2 + \cdots + c_{gn}^2 = 1, \tag{2.24}$$

using (2.21). The v_g are thus unit normal deviates, and it remains to show that they are independent. This we do by showing that they have zero covariance, this implying independence by the theorem of Section 12.3. The covariance is

$$\begin{aligned}\text{Cov}[v_g, v_{g'}] &= E[v_g v_{g'}] - E[v_g]E[v_{g'}] \\ &= E[(c_{g1}u_1 + \cdots + c_{gn}u_n)(c_{g'1}u_1 + \cdots + c_{g'n}u_n)] \\ &= E[c_{g1}c_{g'1}u_1^2 + \cdots + c_{gn}c_{g'n}u_n^2] + E[\text{cross products in } u_g, u_{g'}].\end{aligned} \tag{2.25}$$

But $E[u_g u_{g'}] = E[u_g]E[u_{g'}] = 0$, since $u_g, u_{g'}$ are independent and have zero expectation. Hence

$$\begin{aligned}\text{Cov}[v_g, v_{g'}] &= c_{g1}c_{g'1}E[u_1^2] + \cdots + c_{gn}c_{g'n}E[u_n^2] \\ &= c_{g1}c_{g'1} + \cdots + c_{gn}c_{g'n} = 0,\end{aligned} \tag{2.26}$$

by (2.22). Since the v_g are independent unit normal deviates, each $Q_j = \sum_i v_{ji}^2$, changing the index on v back to ij from g, has the $\chi^2(f_j)$ distribution, and is independent of the other Q_j. This completes the proof of the slightly restricted form of Cochran's theorem which we stated in (2.1) and (2.2)

The independence of the sample mean and variance, established at the end of Section 8.1, was required for Student's original exposition of the t test in 1908 [4]. A formal proof was given by Fisher in 1925 [5], an earlier proof by Helmert in 1876 being overlooked. Cochran's theorem was implicit in Fisher's early use of the analysis of variance [6, 7], but apparently did not receive a formal statement until 1934 [2]. Two papers by Irwin [8, 9] reviewed the mathematical basis of the analysis of variance. For a modern proof see Section 11.11 of Cramer [10].

EXERCISE

8.1. Show that l_i, defined in Section 8.1 as $u_i - \bar{u}$, has the properties $E[l_i] = 0$, $V[l_i] = (n-1)/n$, $\text{Cov}[l_i, l_j] = -1/n$.

REFERENCES

1. Hald, A., *Statistical Theory with Engineering Applications*. New York: John Wiley and Sons, 1952.
2. Cochran, William G., "The Distribution of Quadratic Forms in a Normal System," *Proceedings of the Cambridge Philosophical Society*, 30 (1934), 178–91.
3. Bocher, Maxime, *Introduction to Higher Algebra*. New York: The Macmillan Co., 1907.
4. "Student." "The Probable Error of a Mean," *Biometrika*, 6 (1908), 1–25.
5. Fisher, R. A., "Applications of Student's Distribution," *Metron*, 5 (1925), 90–104.
6. Fisher, R. A., "The Goodness of Fit and Regression Formulae, and the Distribution of Regression Coefficients," *Journal of the Royal Statistical Society*, 85 (1922), 597–612.
7. Fisher, R. A., *Statistical Methods for Research Workers*. 1st ed.: Edinburgh: Oliver and Boyd, 1925.
8. Irwin, J. O., "Mathematical Theorems Involved in the Analysis of Variance," *Journal of the Royal Statistical Society*, 94 (1931), 284–300.
9. Irwin, J. O., "On the Independence of the Constituent Items in the Analysis of Variance," *Supplement to the Journal of the Royal Statistical Society*, 1 (1934), 236–52.
10. Cramér, H., *Mathematical Methods of Statistics*. Princeton: Princeton University Press, 1951.

CHAPTER 9

Tests of Equality of Variances and Means

9.1. Introduction

In this chapter we discuss tests as follows. Suppose that we have a sample $x_{11}, \ldots, x_{1n_1}$, distributed normally with mean ξ_1 and variance σ_1^2. In Section 9.2 we give the test for the null hypothesis $\sigma_1^2 = \sigma_0^2$. In Section 9.7 we give the test for the null hypothesis that $\xi_1 = \xi_0$. When we have a second sample, $x_{21}, \ldots, x_{2n_2}$, distributed normally with mean ξ_2 and variance σ_2^2, we may wish to test the null hypothesis that $\sigma_1^2 = \sigma_2^2$ (Section 9.3), or that $\xi_1 = \xi_2$ assuming that $\sigma_1^2 = \sigma_2^2$ (Section 9.7), or that $\xi_1 = \xi_2$ without any assumption about σ_1^2 and σ_2^2 (Section 9.8). Supposing that we have k samples, $k > 2$, the test for the equality of variances is given in Section 9.5 and the test for the equality of means is given in Chapter 10. Section 9.9 reviews the various tests for means in this chapter and for medians in Chapter 7.

9.2. Uses of the Sample Estimate of Variance

We saw in Section 8.1 that $s^2 = \sum_i^n (x_i - \bar{x})^2/(n-1)$ is distributed as $\sigma^2 \chi^2(n-1)/(n-1)$. If we use f for the number of degrees of freedom, it follows that fs^2/σ^2 is distributed as $\chi^2(f)$. We can obtain confidence limits for σ^2 from

$$\Pr\{\chi^2_{P_1}(f) < \chi^2(f) < \chi^2_{P_2}(f)\} = P_2 - P_1, \qquad (2.1)$$

whence on substituting fs^2/σ^2 for $\chi^2(f)$, taking reciprocals of the terms of the inequality, multiplying by s^2f, and reversing the order of the inequality,

SECT. 9.2 USES OF THE SAMPLE ESTIMATE OF VARIANCE

we get

$$\Pr\left(\frac{s^2 f}{\chi^2_{P_2}} < \sigma^2 < \frac{s^2 f}{\chi^2_{P_1}}\right) = P_2 - P_1. \tag{2.2}$$

As discussed in Section 2.15, we might choose P_1 and P_2 to make the confidence interval as short as possible in some sense, but most people would prefer that the limits be symmetric in probability so that $P_1 = 1 - P_2 = \alpha/2$. For example, if we observe $s^2 = 23.394$ with degrees of freedom $f = 66$, and want 90 per cent confidence limits, we need $\chi^2_{0.95}(66) = 86.0$ and $\chi^2_{0.05}(66) = 48.3$, whence the limits are

$$\left(23.394 \times \frac{66}{86.0},\ 23.394 \times \frac{66}{48.3}\right) = (17.95,\ 31.97). \tag{2.3}$$

To derive a likelihood ratio test of the null hypothesis that $\sigma^2 = \sigma_0^2$ against the alternative hypothesis that $\sigma^2 \neq \sigma_0^2$, we need the logarithm of the likelihood function (2.3.7),

$$\log L = -\frac{n}{2}\log 2\pi\sigma^2 - \frac{1}{2\sigma^2}\sum(x_i - \xi)^2. \tag{2.4}$$

For ω, σ^2 is fixed as σ_0^2, and we need the maximum likelihood estimator of ξ. Differentiating with respect to ξ and equating to zero gives $\hat{\xi} = \bar{x}$, whence

$$L(\omega) = \left(\frac{1}{2\pi\sigma_0^2}\right)^{n/2} \exp\left[-\frac{1}{2\sigma_0^2}\sum(x_i - \bar{x})^2\right]. \tag{2.5}$$

For Ω, both σ^2 and ξ are allowed to vary, and we know from (2.3.13) that $\hat{\sigma}^2 = \sum(x_i - \bar{x})^2/n$ and from (2.3.10) that $\hat{\xi} = \bar{x}$. Hence

$$L(\Omega) = \left(\frac{1}{2\pi\sum(x_i - \bar{x})^2/n}\right)^{n/2} \exp\left[-\frac{1}{2\sum(x_i - \bar{x})^2/n}\sum(x_i - \bar{x})^2\right]. \tag{2.6}$$

The likelihood ratio $\lambda = L(\omega)/L(\Omega)$ can be reduced to

$$\lambda = \left(\frac{F}{e^F}\right)^{n/2} e^{n/2} \tag{2.7}$$

if we define $F = \hat{\sigma}^2/\sigma_0^2$. The likelihood ratio λ (2.7) tends to zero as $F \to 0$ and as $F \to \infty$. Since we know the distribution of s^2, in principle we can find the distribution of $\hat{\sigma}^2$, of F, and of λ. We could then make our critical region correspond to equal tail areas in the distribution of λ. There is no theorem that states we have to follow the likelihood ratio procedure exactly, however, and in practice we use equal tail areas in the distribution of s^2. The usual critical region is thus made up of

$$s^2 < \sigma_0^2 \frac{\chi_{\alpha/2}^2(f)}{f} \tag{2.8}$$

and

$$s^2 > \sigma_0^2 \frac{\chi_{1-\alpha/2}^2(f)}{f}. \tag{2.9}$$

For one-sided tests, $\alpha/2$ in the above formulas is replaced by α.

For the alternative $\sigma^2 > \sigma_0^2$, the power of the test is

$$\pi(\sigma_1^2) = \Pr\left\{s^2 > \frac{\sigma_0^2 \chi_{1-\alpha}^2(f)}{f} \,\Big|\, E[s^2] = \sigma_1^2\right\}$$

$$= \Pr\left\{\frac{fs^2}{\sigma_1^2} > \frac{\sigma_0^2}{\sigma_1^2} \chi_{1-\alpha}^2(f) \,\Big|\, E[s^2] = \sigma_1^2\right\}$$

$$= \Pr\left\{\chi^2 > \frac{\sigma_0^2}{\sigma_1^2} \chi_{1-\alpha}^2(f)\right\}. \tag{2.10}$$

For example, suppose that we are making a test with $\alpha = 0.05$, using $f = 19$. We want the probability of rejecting the null hypothesis if $\sigma_1^2/\sigma_0^2 = 3/2$. Substituting $\chi_{0.95}^2(19) = 30.1$,

$$\pi\left(\sigma_1^2 = \frac{3\sigma_0^2}{2}\right) = \Pr\left\{\chi^2(19) > \frac{2}{3} \times 30.1\right\} = \Pr\{\chi^2(19) > 20.0\} \simeq 0.39. \tag{2.11}$$

Equation (2.10) can be used to calculate the number of degrees of freedom necessary to give specified power. When the alternative hypothesis is $E[s^2] = \sigma_1^2 > \sigma_0^2$, we put (2.10) equal to $1 - \beta$:

$$\pi(\sigma_1^2) = \Pr\left\{\chi^2 > \frac{\sigma_0^2}{\sigma_1^2} \chi_{1-\alpha}^2(f)\right\} = 1 - \beta. \tag{2.12}$$

But $\Pr\{\chi^2 > \chi_\beta^2\} = 1 - \beta$; so

$$\frac{\sigma_1^2}{\sigma_0^2} = \frac{\chi_{1-\alpha}^2(f)}{\chi_\beta^2(f)}. \tag{2.13}$$

For specified values of the ratio σ_1^2/σ_0^2, α, and β, this can be solved for f with the χ^2 table. For example, for $\sigma_1^2/\sigma_0^2 = 3/2$, $\alpha = 0.05$, $1 - \beta = 0.90$, we find that, for $f = 100$, $\chi_{0.95}^2(100) = 124.3$ and $\chi_{0.10}^2(100) = 82.4$; so $\chi_{0.95}^2(100)/\chi_{0.10}^2 = 124.3/82.4 = 1.508$, very close to the required value of

1.500. Thus the solution is f slightly greater than 100. For large values of f, we can use the approximation (1.27.13)

$$\chi_P^2(f) \simeq \tfrac{1}{2}(\sqrt{2f-1} + u_P)^2. \tag{2.14}$$

Substitute this in (2.13):

$$\frac{\sigma_1^2}{\sigma_0^2} \simeq \frac{\tfrac{1}{2}(\sqrt{2f-1} + u_{1-\alpha})^2}{\tfrac{1}{2}(\sqrt{2f-1} + u_\beta)^2}, \tag{2.15}$$

and solve for f:

$$f \simeq \frac{1}{2} + \frac{1}{2}\left(\frac{u_{1-\alpha} + u_{1-\beta}\sqrt{(\sigma_1^2/\sigma_0^2)}}{\sqrt{(\sigma_1^2/\sigma_0^2)} - 1}\right)^2. \tag{2.16}$$

For $\alpha = 0.05$, $u_{1-\alpha} = 1.645$, $1 - \beta = 0.90$, $u_{1-\beta} = 1.282$, and $\sigma_1^2/\sigma_0^2 = 3/2$, we obtain $f \simeq 102.9$.

9.3. The Variance Ratio

Let s_1^2, s_2^2 be independent sample estimates of σ^2 based on f_1, f_2 degrees of freedom. We have seen that s_i^2 is distributed as $\sigma^2 \chi^2(f_i)/f_i$. Denote by F the ratio of two such independent mean squares which are estimates of the same σ^2:

$$F = \frac{s_1^2}{s_2^2}. \tag{3.1}$$

A variance ratio will have associated with it two numbers of degrees of freedom, one for the numerator sample variance and one for the denominator sample variance. We will, when necessary, attach these in parentheses following the F: For the F in (3.1), e.g., we write $F(f_1, f_2)$. If we substitute $\sigma^2 \chi^2(f_i)/f_i$ for s_i^2 in (3.1), we obtain

$$F = \frac{\sigma^2 \chi^2(f_1)/f_1}{\sigma^2 \chi^2(f_2)/f_2} = \frac{\chi^2(f_1)/f_1}{\chi^2(f_2)/f_2}. \tag{3.2}$$

The distribution of χ^2 is known, and the distribution of the ratio of two χ^2's, and hence of F, can be found. The cumulative form of F is tabulated in Table IV. Since χ^2 is never less than zero, F is distributed from 0 to ∞. It can be shown that $E[F] = f_2/(f_2 - 2)$, which tends to 1 as f_2 tends to ∞, and the mode is at $f_2(f_1 - 2)/f_1(f_2 + 2)$.

Table IV of the Appendix gives only the upper tail of the F distribution. We obtain points in the lower tail as follows. We have

$$\Pr\left\{\frac{s_1^2}{s_2^2} < F_{1-P}(f_1, f_2)\right\} = 1 - P. \tag{3.3}$$

Taking reciprocals of the inequality inside the braces will reverse the inequality sign:

$$\Pr\left\{\frac{s_2^2}{s_1^2} > \frac{1}{F_{1-P}(f_1, f_2)}\right\} = 1 - P; \tag{3.4}$$

so

$$\Pr\left\{\frac{s_2^2}{s_1^2} < \frac{1}{F_{1-P}(f_1, f_2)}\right\} = P. \tag{3.5}$$

But

$$\Pr\left\{\frac{s_2^2}{s_1^2} < F_P(f_2, f_1)\right\} = P; \tag{3.6}$$

so, comparing the last two expressions,

$$F_P(f_2, f_1) = \frac{1}{F_{1-P}(f_1, f_2)}. \tag{3.7}$$

For example, the 0.05 point of F for degrees of freedom 6 and 12 is found as $1/F_{0.95}(12, 6) = 1/4.00 = 0.250$.

If s_1^2, s_2^2 are sample estimates of σ_1^2, σ_2^2 based on f_1, f_2 degrees of freedom, their ratio will be distributed as

$$\frac{s_1^2}{s_2^2} \sim \frac{\sigma_1^2 \chi^2(f_1)/f_1}{\sigma_2^2 \chi^2(f_2)/f_2} = \frac{\sigma_1^2}{\sigma_2^2} F(f_1, f_2). \tag{3.8}$$

We can write

$$\Pr\left\{\frac{\sigma_1^2}{\sigma_2^2} F_{P_1}(f_1, f_2) < \frac{s_1^2}{s_2^2} < \frac{\sigma_1^2}{\sigma_2^2} F_{P_2}(f_1, f_2)\right\} = P_2 - P_1. \tag{3.9}$$

Taking reciprocals and multiplying by $(\sigma_1^2/\sigma_2^2)(s_1^2/s_2^2)$ gives

$$\Pr\left\{\frac{s_1^2}{s_2^2} \frac{1}{F_{P_2}(f_1, f_2)} < \frac{\sigma_1^2}{\sigma_2^2} < \frac{s_1^2}{s_2^2} \frac{1}{F_{P_1}(f_1, f_2)}\right\}$$

$$= \Pr\left\{\frac{s_1^2}{s_2^2} \frac{1}{F_{P_2}(f_1, f_2)} < \frac{\sigma_1^2}{\sigma_2^2} < \frac{s_1^2}{s_2^2} F_{1-P_1}(f_2, f_1)\right\} = P_2 - P_1, \tag{3.10}$$

and hence $P_2 - P_1$ confidence limits for a variance ratio. Here again it is customary to set $P_1 = 1 - P_2 = \alpha/2$.

To test the null hypothesis $\sigma_1^2 = \sigma_2^2$, as in the previous section we can express the likelihood ratio statistic as a function of $F = s_1^2/s_2^2$ [see exercise (9.9)]. Here again it is more convenient, and perhaps more meaningful, to use equal tail areas of the distribution of F for the critical region.

The critical region is thus made up of

$$\frac{s_1^2}{s_2^2} < F_{\alpha/2}(f_1, f_2) \tag{3.11}$$

and

$$\frac{s_1^2}{s_2^2} > F_{1-\alpha/2}(f_1, f_2). \tag{3.12}$$

In practice we need never obtain the lower percentage points of the F distribution as implied by (3.11), for if $s_1^2 > s_2^2$ then we need only consider whether (3.12) is satisfied, and if $s_1^2 < s_2^2$ we can take reciprocals of (3.11) to give

$$\frac{s_2^2}{s_1^2} > \frac{1}{F_{\alpha/2}(f_1, f_2)} = F_{1-\alpha/2}(f_2, f_1), \tag{3.13}$$

and now consider whether this inequality is satisfied. For one-sided tests, $\alpha/2$ in (3.12) and (3.13) is replaced by α.

For the alternative $\sigma_1^2 > \sigma_2^2$, the power of the test for a specified value of the ratio $\sigma_1^2/\sigma_2^2 = \phi$ is

$$\pi(\phi) = \Pr\left\{\frac{s_1^2}{s_2^2} > F_{1-\alpha}(f_1, f_2) \middle| E[s_1^2] = \sigma_1^2 = \phi\sigma_2^2 = \phi E[s_2^2]\right\}$$

$$= \Pr\left\{\frac{s_1^2/\sigma_1^2}{s_2^2/\sigma_2^2} > \frac{1}{\phi} F_{1-\alpha}(f_1, f_2)\right\}. \tag{3.14}$$

But, by (3.8),

$$\frac{s_1^2/\sigma_1^2}{s_2^2/\sigma_2^2} \sim F(f_1, f_2). \tag{3.15}$$

Hence (3.14) is equivalent to

$$\pi(\phi) = \Pr\left\{F(f_1, f_2) > \frac{1}{\phi} F_{1-\alpha}(f_1, f_2)\right\}. \tag{3.16}$$

For example, if we are making a test of the null hypothesis $\sigma_1^2 = \sigma_2^2$ at the level of significance $\alpha = 0.05$, with $f_1 = 30$, $f_2 = 10$, then $F_{0.95}(30, 10) = 2.70$, and the power for $\phi = 5$ is

$$\Pr\left\{F(30, 10) > \frac{2.70}{5}\right\} = \Pr\left\{F(10, 30) < \frac{5}{2.70}\right\} \simeq 0.90, \tag{3.17}$$

and the power for $\phi = 1.25$ is

$$\Pr\left\{F(30, 10) > \frac{2.70}{1.25}\right\} = 1 - \Pr\{F(30, 10) < 2.16\}$$

$$\simeq 1 - 0.90 = 0.10. \tag{3.18}$$

To find the number of degrees of freedom necessary to achieve a specified power, we put (3.16) equal to $1 - \beta$. But also

$$\Pr\{F(f_1, f_2) > F_\beta(f_1, f_2)\} = 1 - \beta; \tag{3.19}$$

so

$$\phi = \frac{F_{1-\alpha}(f_1, f_2)}{F_\beta(f_1, f_2)} = F_{1-\alpha}(f_1, f_2) F_{1-\beta}(f_2, f_1), \tag{3.20}$$

which can be solved iteratively with the F tables. For example, with $\alpha = 0.05$, $1 - \beta = 0.90$, $F_{0.95}(80, 80) = 1.45$ and $F_{0.90}(80, 80) = 1.33$; so their product is 1.93. The solution for $\phi = 2$ will therefore require $f_1 = f_2$ slightly smaller than 80, about 75. For a given sum $f_1 + f_2$, it can be shown that an equal allocation of the total number of observations to the two samples so that $f_1 = f_2$ is not exactly optimum but so close that further consideration is unnecessary.

9.4. The Interrelations of Various Distributions

In (1.27.1), $\chi^2(n)$ was defined as $\sum_i^n u_i^2$, where the u_i were independent unit normal deviates. When $n = 1$, $\chi^2(1) = u^2$. To get corresponding probability levels for the two distributions u and χ^2, we proceed as follows. Consider small areas α in the lower and upper tails of the standardized normal distribution: These will be defined as $u < u_\alpha$ and $u > u_{1-\alpha}$. The sum of the areas in the two tails is 2α, and the area between u_α and $u_{1-\alpha}$ is $1 - 2\alpha$. Then

$$\Pr\{u_\alpha < u < u_{1-\alpha}\} = 1 - 2\alpha. \tag{4.1}$$

From the symmetry of the normal distribution, $u_\alpha = -u_{1-\alpha}$, and so (4.1) becomes

$$\Pr\{-u_{1-\alpha} < u < u_{1-\alpha}\} = 1 - 2\alpha. \tag{4.2}$$

This implies

$$\Pr\{u^2 < u_{1-\alpha}^2\} = 1 - 2\alpha. \tag{4.3}$$

Now put $1 - 2\alpha = P$, so that $1 - \alpha = (1 + P)/2$: Then (4.3) becomes

$$\Pr\{u^2 < u_{(1+P)/2}^2\} = P. \tag{4.4}$$

Also,

$$\Pr\{\chi^2(1) < \chi_P^2(1)\} = P. \tag{4.5}$$

Comparing (4.4) and (4.5), and, since $u^2 = \chi^2(1)$,

$$\chi_P^2(1) = u_{(1+P)/2}^2. \tag{4.6}$$

The exponents 2 in (4.6) need careful interpretation. The left-hand side, $\chi_P^2(1)$, is the P point of the distribution of χ^2 with 1 degree of freedom;

the right-hand side, $u^2_{(1+P)/2}$, is the square of the $(1 + P)/2$ point of the distribution of u. For example, if $P = 0.95$, $(1 + P)/2 = 0.975$, and

$$\chi^2_{0.95}(1) = 3.84 = (1.96)^2 = u^2_{0.975}. \tag{4.7}$$

Or, if $P = 0.10$, $(1 + P)/2 = 0.55$, and

$$\chi^2_{0.10}(1) = 0.0158 = (0.126)^2 = u^2_{0.55}. \tag{4.8}$$

In (1.27.3) we noted that $E[\chi^2(f)] = f$, and in (1.27.9) that $V[\chi^2(f)] = 2f$. It follows from the former that $E[\chi^2(f)/f] = f/f = 1$, and from the latter that

$$V\left[\frac{\chi^2(f)}{f}\right] = \frac{2f}{f^2} = \frac{2}{f}. \tag{4.9}$$

Thus, as f tends to infinity, $\chi^2(f)/f$ becomes closer and closer to 1 with high probability. In (3.2) put $f_2 = \infty$; the denominator $\chi^2(f_2)/f_2$ becomes 1 and we get

$$F(f_1, \infty) = \frac{\chi^2(f_1)}{f_1}. \tag{4.10}$$

For example, the 0.99 point of χ^2 with 10 degrees of freedom is 23.2: the 0.99 point of F with degrees of freedom 10 and ∞ is 2.32, which equals 23.2/10.

The distribution of the ratio of a unit normal deviate to the square root of an independent χ^2 with f degrees of freedom, divided by f, is known as the t distribution with f degrees of freedom:

$$t(f) = \frac{u}{\sqrt{\chi^2(f)/f}}. \tag{4.11}$$

As stated earlier, $\chi^2(f)/f$ tends to 1 as f tends to infinity. Thus the t distribution with infinite degrees of freedom is identical with the standardized normal distribution.

The t distribution is related to the F distribution, for, if we put $f_1 = 1$ in (3.2), the numerator becomes $\chi^2(1)/1$ which is just u^2. Hence

$$F(1, f_2) = \frac{u^2}{\chi^2(f_2)/f_2}. \tag{4.12}$$

Comparing (4.11) with (4.12), we see that $t^2 = F$. Corresponding probability levels of $t(f)$ and $F(1,f)$ are obtained in the same way that we found the relationship for u and $\chi^2(1)$. The t distribution is symmetric about zero; so, with $t(f)$ replacing u and $F(1, f)$ replacing $\chi^2(1)$, the argument proceeds exactly analogously to (4.1) through (4.6) and gives

$$F_P(1, f) = t^2_{(1+P)/2}(f). \qquad (4.13)$$

For example, for $f = 12$ and $P = 0.95$,

$$F_{0.95}(1, 12) = 4.75 = (2.179)^2 = t^2_{0.975}(12). \qquad (4.14)$$

9.5. A Test for the Equality of Several Variances

We saw in Section 9.3 that the null hypothesis that two sample variances are estimates of a common variance can be tested with the F test. Neyman constructed a test for the k sample case by the likelihood ratio procedure.

Suppose that we have observations x_{ij}, $i = 1, \ldots, k$, $j = 1, \ldots, n_i$, which are distributed normally with means ξ_i and variances σ_i^2. We wish to test the null hypothesis

$$\sigma_1^2 = \sigma_2^2 = \cdots = \sigma_k^2 = \sigma^2, \qquad (5.1)$$

against the alternative that the σ_i^2 are in general different. The density function of x_{ij} is

$$p\{x_{ij}\} = \frac{1}{\sqrt{2\pi}\,\sigma_i} e^{-(x_{ij} - \xi_i)^2/2\sigma_i^2}. \qquad (5.2)$$

The likelihood function, defined as in (2.3.1), is

$$L = \frac{1}{(2\pi)^{n/2} \sigma_1^{n_1} \cdots \sigma_k^{n_k}} \exp\left[-\frac{1}{2} \sum_i^k \sum_j^{n_i} \left(\frac{x_{ij} - \xi_i}{\sigma_i}\right)^2\right], \qquad (5.3)$$

in which $\sum_i^k n_i = n$. When maximizing L it is easier to deal with the logarithm:

$$\log L = -\frac{n}{2} \log 2\pi - n_1 \log \sigma_1 - \cdots - n_k \log \sigma_k$$

$$-\frac{1}{2} \sum_i^k \frac{1}{\sigma_i^2} \sum_j^n (x_{ij} - \xi_i)^2. \qquad (5.4)$$

For computing $L(\Omega)$, Ω is the entire parameter space of both the null and the alternative hypotheses. In Ω there are no restrictions on the ranges of any of the parameters other than that $\sigma_i^2 > 0$. We find the

SECT. 9.5 A TEST FOR THE EQUALITY OF SEVERAL VARIANCES

values of ξ_i and σ_i which maximize L, or $\log L$, by differentiating and equating to zero in the usual way:

$$\frac{\partial \log L}{\partial \xi_i} = \frac{1}{\sigma_i^2} \sum_j^{n_i} (x_{ij} - \xi_i) = 0, \tag{5.5}$$

$$\frac{\partial \log L}{\partial \sigma_i} = -\frac{n_i}{\sigma_i} + \frac{1}{\sigma_i^3} \sum_j^{n_i} (x_{ij} - \xi_i)^2 = 0, \tag{5.6}$$

whence the maximum likelihood estimators, for Ω, are

$$\hat{\xi}_i = \frac{1}{n_i} \sum_j^{n_i} x_{ij} = \bar{x}_{i.}, \tag{5.7}$$

$$\hat{\sigma}_i^2 = \frac{1}{n_i} \sum_j^{n_i} (x_{ij} - \bar{x}_{i.})^2. \tag{5.8}$$

Substituting these in (5.3), we obtain

$$L(\Omega) = \frac{1}{(2\pi)^{n/2} \hat{\sigma}_1^{n_1} \cdots \hat{\sigma}_k^{n_k}} \exp\left\{-\frac{1}{2} \sum_i^k \sum_j^{n_i} \left[\frac{(x_{ij} - \bar{x}_{i.})^2}{\sum_j (x_{ij} - \bar{x}_{i.})^2 / n_i}\right]\right\}$$

$$= \frac{e^{-n/2}}{(2\pi)^{n/2} \hat{\sigma}_1^{n_1} \cdots \hat{\sigma}_k^{n_k}}. \tag{5.9}$$

For computing $L(\omega)$, ω is the parameter space under the null hypothesis, in which the ξ_i are allowed to vary but the σ_i^2 are subject to the constraint (5.1). We obtain

$$\frac{\partial \log L}{\partial \xi_i} = \frac{1}{\sigma^2} \sum_j^{n_i} (x_{ij} - \xi_i) = 0, \tag{5.10}$$

$$\frac{\partial \log L}{\partial \sigma} = -\frac{n}{\sigma} + \frac{1}{\sigma^3} \sum_i^k \sum_j^{n_i} (x_{ij} - \xi_i)^2 = 0, \tag{5.11}$$

whence the maximum likelihood estimators, for ω, are

$$\hat{\xi}_i = \frac{1}{n_i} \sum_j^{n_i} x_{ij} = \bar{x}_{i.}, \tag{5.12}$$

$$\hat{\sigma}^2 = \frac{1}{n} \sum_i^k \sum_j^{n_i} (x_{ij} - \bar{x}_{i.})^2 \tag{5.13}$$

$$= \frac{1}{n} \sum_i^k n_i \hat{\sigma}_i^2, \tag{5.14}$$

(5.14) following on substituting (5.8) in (5.13). Substituting (5.12) and (5.13) in (5.3), we obtain

$$L(\omega) = \left[(2\pi)^{n/2}\left(\sum_i^k n_i \hat{\sigma}_i^2/n\right)^{n/2}\right]^{-1} \exp\left[-\frac{1}{2}\sum_i^k\sum_j^{n_i}\frac{(x_{ij} - \bar{x}_{i.})^2}{\sum_i^k\sum_j^{n_i}(x_{ij} - \bar{x}_{i.})^2/n}\right]$$

$$= \frac{e^{-n/2}}{(2\pi)^{n/2}\left(\sum_i^k n_i \hat{\sigma}_i^2/n\right)^{n/2}}.$$

(5.15)

Substituting (5.9) and (5.15) in (2.9.2), we obtain

$$\lambda = \frac{\hat{\sigma}_1^{n_1} \cdots \hat{\sigma}_k^{n_k}}{\left(\sum_i^k n_i \hat{\sigma}_i^2/n\right)^{n/2}} = \frac{\prod_i^k \hat{\sigma}_i^{n_i}}{\hat{\sigma}^n}.$$

(5.16)

In Ω there are $2k$ parameters (k ξ_i's and k σ_i^2's) and in ω there are $k + 1$ parameters (k ξ_i's and σ^2). Thus from Wilks' result that $-2 \log \lambda$ has the $\chi^2(r - s)$ distribution asymptotically, where r and s are the numbers of parameters in Ω and ω, here

$$-2 \log \lambda = -2 \log \frac{\prod_i^k \hat{\sigma}_i^{n_i}}{\hat{\sigma}^n} = -\sum_i^k n_i \log \hat{\sigma}_i^2 + n \log \hat{\sigma}^2 \quad (5.17)$$

$$= -\sum_i^k n_i \log \frac{\hat{\sigma}_i^2}{\hat{\sigma}^2} \quad (5.18)$$

will have approximately a $\chi^2(k - 1)$ distribution.

The above statistic was modified by Bartlett [1] by substituting the conventional unbiased estimators of the variances for the biased maximum likelihood estimators and substituting the degrees of freedom $n_i - 1$ for the n_i. Thus Bartlett proposed using the quantity

$$B = -\sum_i^k (n_i - 1) \log \frac{s_i^2}{s^2}, \quad (5.19)$$

where

$$s_i^2 = \frac{1}{n_i - 1}\sum_j^{n_i}(x_{ij} - \bar{x}_{i.})^2, \quad (5.20)$$

$$s^2 = \frac{\sum_i^k (n_i - 1)s_i^2}{\sum_i^k (n_i - 1)} = \frac{\sum_i^k\sum_j^{n_i}(x_{ij} - \bar{x}_{i.})^2}{\sum_i^k (n_i - 1)}. \quad (5.21)$$

SECT. 9.5 A TEST FOR THE EQUALITY OF SEVERAL VARIANCES

A closer approximation to the $\chi^2(k-1)$ distribution was obtained by using the statistic B/C, where

$$C = 1 + \frac{1}{3(k-1)}\left[\sum_i^k \frac{1}{n_i - 1} - \frac{1}{\sum_i^k (n_i - 1)}\right]. \quad (5.22)$$

The final form of the test statistic is therefore

$$\frac{1}{C}\left[\sum_i^k (n_i - 1) \log s^2 - \sum_i^k (n_i - 1) \log s_i^2\right], \quad (5.23)$$

and in this form it is commonly referred to as Bartlett's test. If the logarithms are taken to the base 10 then (5.23) is multiplied by 2.3026. Hartley [2] has shown that the approximation involved in using the χ^2 distribution for the distribution of B/C is poor for small n_i and has given a modification with the necessary tables. Hartley [3] has also proposed an alternative test applicable when the n_i are all equal. This test uses the statistic the ratio of the largest to the smallest sample variance. A tabulation by H. A. David of the 0.95 and 0.99 points of the distribution for 12 or fewer sample variances is reproduced in the *Biometrika Tables* [4].

Box and Andersen [5] have concluded that this test is sensitive to departures from the assumption of normality: in fact, if the statistic is found to be lying in the critical region, it is as likely to be because the distributions are nonnormal as because the variances are different.

As an example, the data of Table 9.1 are the final digits of determinations of the velocity of light by Michelson [6] made with six different rotating mirrors. The lower part of the table details the calculation of the s_i^2. Table 9.2 continues the calculation of B and C. s^2 is obtained from Table 9.2 as the sum of the sums of squares divided by the sum of the degrees of freedom, $22{,}191.317/83 = 267.365$, and from a table of natural logarithms $\log_e s^2 = 5.58860$. Thus

$$B = 83 \times 5.58860 - (11 \times 5.54953 + \cdots + 15 \times 4.75214) = 9.95023,$$

$$C = 1 + \frac{1}{3(6-1)}\left(0.4532 - \frac{1}{83}\right) = 1.0294,$$

and under the null hypothesis $B/C = 9.95023/1.0294 = 9.666$ is distributed as $\chi^2(5)$. For 5 degrees of freedom, the 0.90 and 0.95 points of χ^2 are 9.236 and 11.070; hence $P \simeq 0.08$, and we cannot reject the null hypothesis at the 0.05 level of significance.

It is suggestive that four of the six mirrors were made of glass and the remaining two of steel, and that there is not much variation in the s_i^2 within each group. Forming pooled sample variances with (5.20), we get

Table 9.1. Determinations of the Velocity of Light with Different Rotating Mirrors*

Table number Material Number of sides	II Glass 8	III Glass 12	IV Glass 16	V Glass 16	VI Steel 12	VII Steel 8
	47 47	42 18	3 39	66 21	18 9	30 21
	38 62	36 45	27 66	27 33	12 30	33 18
	29 59	33 30	48 15	9 24	30 27	12 33
	92 44	0 27	3 7	6 39	30 39	24 23
	41 47	18 27	27 27	42 18	18 27	57 39
	44 41	57 66	42 37	12 63	48 24	44 33
		48 24	69 24		18	30 24
		15	63 15			24 30
			30 27			
			42 42			
			60			
n_i	12	15	21	12	13	16
$\sum_{v}^{n_i} x_{iv}$	591	486	713	360	330	475
$\sum_{v}^{n_i} x_{iv}^2$	31,935	19,890	32,081	15,030	9756	15,839
$\left(\sum_{v}^{n_i} x_{iv}\right)^2 / n_i$	29,106.750	15,746.400	24,208.048	10,800.000	8376.923	14,101.562
$\sum_{v}^{n_i} (x_{iv} - \bar{x}_i)^2$	2,828.250	4,143.600	7,872.952	4,230.000	1379.077	1,737.438
s_i^2	257.114	295.971	393.648	384.545	114.923	115.829

* Data from [6].

Table 9.2

Table number	Sums of squares	Degrees of freedom (f_i)	Mean squares (s_i^2)	$\log_e s_i^2$	$1/f_i$
II	2,828.250	11	257.114	5.54953	0.0909
III	4,143.600	14	295.971	5.69026	0.0714
IV	7,872.952	20	393.648	5.97545	0.0500
V	4,230.000	11	384.545	5.95208	0.0909
VI	1,379.077	12	114.923	4.74426	0.0833
VII	1,737.438	15	115.829	4.75214	0.0667
Totals	22,191.317	83			0.4532

estimates of 340.621 with 56 degrees of freedom for the glass mirrors and 115.426 with 27 degrees of freedom for the steel mirrors. The variance ratio 2.951 is at about the 0.9975 point of the F distribution. A two-sided test is called for, since there is no a priori reason to expect either variance to be less than the other; so the P value is about 0.005. However, since we are testing a null hypothesis to some extent suggested by the data, this P value is not legitimate, but, if we knew how to allow for this fact, probably the result would still be significant.

9.6. The One-Sample t Test

Suppose that we have a sample of n independent observations $x_1, \ldots, x_n$ from a normal population with mean ξ and variance σ^2. We wish to test the null hypothesis $\xi = \xi_0$ against the alternative $\xi \neq \xi_0$. The parameter σ^2 is not known.

We saw in Section 2.11 that the likelihood ratio procedure led to large absolute values of the statistic (2.11.6),

$$\frac{\bar{x} - \xi_0}{s/\sqrt{n}} \qquad (6.1)$$

as the critical region. In Section 8.1 we saw that $\bar{x}$ was independent of $s^2 = \Sigma (x_i - \bar{x})^2/(n-1)$, and that s^2 was distributed as $\sigma^2 \chi^2(n-1)/(n-1)$. In (4.11) we defined the t distribution with f degrees of freedom as the distribution of the ratio $u/\sqrt{\chi^2(f)/f}$ where the numerator and denominator were independent. If we write (6.1) as

$$\frac{\dfrac{\bar{x} - \xi_0}{\sigma/\sqrt{n}}}{\sqrt{s^2/\sigma^2}}, \qquad (6.2)$$

then under the null hypothesis its numerator is a unit normal deviate and independent of the denominator which has the distribution of the square root of $\chi^2(n-1)/(n-1)$, and so (6.2) has the $t(n-1)$ distribution and likewise (6.1). Thus under the null hypothesis

$$\frac{\bar{x} - \xi_0}{s/\sqrt{n}} \sim t(n-1), \qquad (6.3)$$

and for the two-sided test against the alternative $\xi \neq \xi_0$ the critical region is equivalent to

$$\left| \frac{\bar{x} - \xi_0}{s/\sqrt{n}} \right| > t_{1-\alpha/2}(n-1). \qquad (6.4)$$

For the one-sided tests against the alternatives $\xi > \xi_0$, $\xi < \xi_0$, the critical regions are

$$\bar{x} > \xi_0 + t_{1-\alpha}(n-1)\frac{s}{\sqrt{n}}, \tag{6.5}$$

$$\bar{x} < \xi_0 + t_\alpha(n-1)\frac{s}{\sqrt{n}}. \tag{6.6}$$

These critical regions are the analogs of those obtained when σ was assumed known. The difference is that the use of s in place of σ leads to the use of the $t(n-1)$ distribution instead of the normal distribution.

Confidence limits for ξ were given in (2.16.7) as

$$\underline{\xi} = \bar{x} - t_{P_2}\frac{s}{\sqrt{n}}, \qquad \bar{\xi} = \bar{x} - t_{P_1}\frac{s}{\sqrt{n}}. \tag{6.7}$$

As an example, we consider the data of Table 7.1 on the difference in potency of a series of lots of a pharmaceutical analyzed by two methods, A and B. These data were used in Section 7.2 to illustrate the sign test and in Section 7.8 to illustrate the Wilcoxon one-sample test, the one-sided P values for the null hypothesis that the median was zero being 0.0106 and 0.00214 by exact calculation and 0.0122 and 0.0033 by normal approximations to the exact nonparametric probabilities. To apply the t test, we need $\bar{x} = 2.2375$ and

$$s^2 = \frac{\sum_i^n (x_i - \bar{x})^2}{n-1} = \frac{\sum_i^n x_i^2 - \left(\sum_i^n x_i\right)^2/n}{n-1}$$

$$= \frac{(0.3)^2 + \cdots + (6.8)^2 - (0.3 + \cdots + 6.8)^2/16}{16-1} = 7.3265. \tag{6.8}$$

We thus obtain for (6.4)

$$\left|\frac{\bar{x}-\xi_0}{s/\sqrt{n}}\right| = \left|\frac{2.2375-0}{\sqrt{7.3265}/\sqrt{16}}\right| = \frac{2.2375}{0.67669} = 3.3065,$$

and refer this value to the t table with 15 degrees of freedom. The 0.995 and 0.999 levels of t with these degrees of freedom are 2.947 and 3.733. The two-sided P value is between 0.010 and 0.002. We can construct 95 per cent confidence limits for ξ with (6.7): $t_{0.975}(15) = 2.131$, $t_{0.025}(15) = -2.131$, $s/\sqrt{n} = 0.67669$, and $\bar{x} = 2.2375$; so the confidence limits are $2.2375 \pm 2.131 \times 0.67669 = (0.796, 3.679)$.

9.7. The Two-Sample t Test

Suppose that we have two samples, $x_{11}, \ldots, x_{1n_1}$ and $x_{21}, \ldots, x_{2n_2}$, from normal populations with means ξ_1 and ξ_2 and both with the same variance σ^2. We wish to test the null hypothesis that $\xi_1 = \xi_2$: We do not assume knowledge of σ^2.

We calculate s_i^2, the sample estimate of variance for the ith sample, $i = 1, 2$. From (8.1.26),

$$(n_1 - 1)s_1^2 = \sum_{v}^{n_1} (x_{1v} - \bar{x}_1)^2 \sim \sigma^2 \chi^2(n_1 - 1), \tag{7.1}$$

$$(n_2 - 1)s_2^2 = \sum_{v}^{n_2} (x_{2v} - \bar{x}_2)^2 \sim \sigma^2 \chi^2(n_2 - 1). \tag{7.2}$$

From (1.27.16), the sum of two χ^2's has a χ^2 distribution:

$$\sum_{v}^{n_1} (x_{1v} - \bar{x}_1)^2 + \sum_{v}^{n_2} (x_{2v} - \bar{x}_2)^2 \sim \sigma^2 \chi^2(n_1 + n_2 - 2). \tag{7.3}$$

If we now define s^2 as

$$s^2 = \frac{\sum_{v}^{n_1} (x_{1v} - \bar{x}_1)^2 + \sum_{v}^{n_2} (x_{2v} - \bar{x}_2)^2}{n_1 + n_2 - 2} = \frac{\sum_{i}^{2} \sum_{v}^{n_i} (x_{iv} - \bar{x}_i)^2}{\sum_{i}^{2} (n_i - 1)}, \tag{7.4}$$

it is distributed as

$$\sigma^2 \frac{\chi^2(n_1 + n_2 - 2)}{n_1 + n_2 - 2}, \tag{7.5}$$

and it has an expected value σ^2. This generalizes to the case of k sample variances s_i^2 with f_i degrees of freedom:

$$s^2 = \frac{\sum_{i}^{k} f_i s_i^2}{\sum_{i}^{k} f_i} = \frac{\sum_{i}^{k} \sum_{v}^{n_i} (x_{iv} - \bar{x}_i)^2}{\sum_{i}^{k} f_i} \sim \sigma^2 \frac{\chi^2 \left(\sum_{i}^{k} f_i \right)}{\sum_{i}^{k} f_i}. \tag{7.6}$$

Since s_1^2 is independent of $\bar{x}_1$ and s_2^2 is independent of $\bar{x}_2$, s^2 will be independent of $\bar{x}_1$ and $\bar{x}_2$.

A likelihood ratio argument similar to that of Section 2.11 leads to the result that

$$\lambda^{2/(n_1+n_2)} = \left(1 + \frac{t^2}{n_1 + n_2 - 2}\right)^1, \tag{7.7}$$

where

$$t = \frac{(\bar{x}_1 - \bar{x}_2) - (\xi_1 - \xi_2)}{s\sqrt{1/n_1 + 1/n_2}}. \qquad (7.8)$$

For a two-sided test, the critical region will be large absolute values of the statistic (7.8). It is easy to show that (7.8) has the $t(n_1 + n_2 - 2)$ distribution, since it can be written as

$$\frac{\dfrac{(\bar{x}_1 - \bar{x}_2) - (\xi_1 - \xi_2)}{\sigma\sqrt{1/n_1 + 1/n_2}}}{\sqrt{s^2/\sigma^2}}. \qquad (7.9)$$

In this form the numerator is a unit normal deviate and independent of the denominator which is the square root of a $\chi^2(n_1 + n_2 - 2)/(n_1 + n_2 - 2)$ variate. Therefore (7.9) has a $t(n_1 + n_2 - 2)$ distribution. For the null hypothesis $\xi_1 = \xi_2$ we reject at the level of significance α if

$$\left| \frac{\bar{x}_1 - \bar{x}_2}{s\sqrt{1/n_1 + 1/n_2}} \right| > t_{1-\alpha/2}(n_1 + n_2 - 2). \qquad (7.10)$$

Confidence limits can be obtained analogously to Section 2.16 as

$$\Pr\left\{ (\bar{x}_1 - \bar{x}_2) - t_{P_2}s\sqrt{\frac{1}{n_1} + \frac{1}{n_2}} < \xi_1 - \xi_2 < (\bar{x}_1 - \bar{x}_2) - t_{P_1}s\sqrt{\frac{1}{n_1} + \frac{1}{n_2}} \right\}$$
$$= P_2 - P_1. \qquad (7.11)$$

As an illustration of the two-sample t test, we will use two series of determinations of the atomic weight of scandium by Honigschmid [7] (Table 9.3). The figures are given in units in the third decimal place; so 79 corresponds to 45.079. Certain calculations are given in Table 9.4.

Table 9.3

Series A	79, 84, 108, 114, 120, 103, 122, 120,
Series B	91, 103, 90, 113, 108, 87, 100, 80, 99, 54.

Table 9.4

	n_i	$\sum\limits_{v}^{n_i} x_{iv}$	$\bar{x}_i$	$\sum\limits_{v}^{n_i} x_{iv}^2$	$\dfrac{1}{n_i}\left(\sum\limits_{v}^{n_i} x_{iv}\right)^2$	$\sum\limits_{v}^{n_i} (x_{iv} - \bar{x}_i)^2$
Series A	8	850	106.25	92,250	90,312.50	1,937.50
Series B	10	925	92.50	88,109	85,562.50	2,546.50

SECT. 9.8   THE TWO-SAMPLE TEST WITH UNEQUAL VARIANCES   299

From (7.4),
$$s^2 = \frac{1937.50 + 2546.50}{8 - 1 + 10 - 1} = 280.25. \tag{7.12}$$

and for the test statistic (7.10) we have

$$\left| \frac{106.25 - 92.50}{\sqrt{280.25}\sqrt{1/8 + 1/10}} \right| = \frac{13.75}{7.9408} = 1.732 \tag{7.13}$$

which is referred to the t table with 16 degrees of freedom. The 0.90 and 0.95 points of $t(16)$ are 1.337 and 1.746, and so the two-sided P value is just greater than 0.10.

For 95 per cent confidence limits we need $t_{0.975}(16) = 2.120$, $t_{0.025}(16) = -2.120$, $\bar{x}_1 - \bar{x}_2 = 13.75$, and $s\sqrt{1/n_1 + 1/n_2} = 7.9408$, to get $13.75 \pm 2.120 \times 7.9408 = (-3.08, 30.58)$.

9.8. The Two-Sample Test with Unequal Variances

Suppose that we have two independent samples $x_{11}, \ldots, x_{1n_1}$ and $x_{21}, \ldots, x_{2n_1}$ from normal distributions with means ξ_1 and ξ_2 and variances σ_1^2 and σ_2^2. We wish to test the null hypothesis that $\xi_1 = \xi_2$: We do not assume knowledge of σ_1^2 or σ_2^2, and in distinction to the previous section we do not assume that $\sigma_1^2 = \sigma_2^2$. For example, we may measure the same quantity with two different instruments and wish to test the null hypothesis that the difference between the instruments is zero: There is, in general, no reason to suppose that the measurements made by the two instruments have the same variance.

In this problem both the null and the alternative hypotheses are composite. The likelihood ratio procedure for constructing a test fails in this instance. The maximum likelihood estimator for ξ in ω turns out to be a solution to a cubic polynomial, and the distribution of λ involves the ratio σ_1^2/σ_2^2, which is unknown (see Mood and Graybill [8]). No generally accepted solution to this problem, often called the Behrens-Fisher problem on account of a solution proposed by Behrens, exists. We will discuss a treatment by Welch [9, 10].

We saw in Section 2.12 that the means $\bar{x}_1, \bar{x}_2$ are normally distributed with variances σ_1^2/n_1, σ_2^2/n_2, and

$$\frac{(\bar{x}_1 - \bar{x}_2) - (\xi_1 - \xi_2)}{\sqrt{\sigma_1^2/n_1 + \sigma_2^2/n_2}} \tag{8.1}$$

is a unit normal deviate. However, we do not know the σ_i^2, and the problem is to determine the distribution of

$$\frac{(\bar{x}_1 - \bar{x}_2) - (\xi_1 - \xi_2)}{\sqrt{s_1^2/n_1 + s_2^2/n_2}} \tag{8.2}$$

formed by substituting sample estimates s_i^2 with degrees of freedom $n_i - 1$ for the σ_i^2 in (8.1).

We will first discuss a more general question. Suppose that s_i^2, $i = 1, \ldots, k$ are independent mean squares with degrees of freedom f_i and expected values σ_i^2. Suppose that we are concerned with a linear combination of these mean squares, S^2, defined as

$$S^2 = a_1 s_1^2 + \cdots + a_k s_k^2 = \sum_i^k a_i s_i^2, \tag{8.3}$$

where the a_i are known constants. We have

$$E[S^2] = E\left[\sum_i^k a_i s_i^2\right] = \sum_i^k a_i E[s_i^2] = \sum_i^k a_i \sigma_i^2. \tag{8.4}$$

From (8.1.26), $s_i^2 \sim \sigma_i^2 \chi^2(f_i)/f_i$, and from (4.9), $V[\chi^2(f_i)/f_i] = 2/f_i$, so

$$V[s_i^2] = V\left[\frac{\sigma_i^2 \chi^2(f_i)}{f_i}\right] = (\sigma_i^2)^2 V\left[\frac{\chi^2(f_i)}{f_i}\right] = \frac{2(\sigma_i^2)^2}{f_i}, \tag{8.5}$$

and

$$V[S^2] = V\left[\sum_i^k a_i s_i^2\right] = \sum_i^k a_i^2 V[s_i^2] = \sum_i^k a_i^2 \frac{2(\sigma_i^2)^2}{f_i}. \tag{8.6}$$

We propose to approximate the distribution of S^2 by the distribution of a mean square, say S'^2, where S'^2 has some number of degrees of freedom, say f', by choosing S'^2 and f' so that S^2 and S'^2 have the same expectation and variance. Thus we put

$$E[S'^2] = E[S^2] = \sum_i^k a_i \sigma_i^2. \tag{8.7}$$

From (8.5), which gives the variance of a variance estimate,

$$V[S'^2] = (E[S'^2])^2 \frac{2}{f'} = \left(\sum_i^k a_i \sigma_i^2\right)^2 \frac{2}{f'}. \tag{8.8}$$

Equating $V[S^2]$, (8.6), and $V[S'^2]$, (8.8), and solving for f' gives

$$f' = \frac{\left(\sum_i^k a_i \sigma_i^2\right)^2}{\sum_i^k a_i^2 \frac{(\sigma_i^2)^2}{f_i}}. \tag{8.9}$$

SECT. 9.8 THE TWO-SAMPLE TEST WITH UNEQUAL VARIANCES

In practice, we do not know the values of the σ_i^2, and so we have to substitute the sample estimates s_i^2; so f' is estimated as

$$f' \simeq \frac{\left(\sum\limits_{i}^{k} a_i s_i^2\right)^2}{\sum\limits_{i}^{k} a_i^2 \frac{(s_i^2)^2}{f_i}}. \tag{8.10}$$

To revert to our particular problem, we are concerned with the linear combination of two variances s_1^2 and s_2^2, namely, $s_1^2/n_1 + s_2^2/n_2$, and so our coefficients are $a_1 = 1/n_1$, $a_2 = 1/n_2$. Substituting these values of the coefficients in (8.10), we get

$$f' \simeq \frac{[(s_1^2/n_1) + (s_2^2/n_2)]^2}{\dfrac{(1/n_1)^2(s_1^2)^2}{n_1 - 1} + \dfrac{(1/n_2)^2(s_2^2)^2}{n_2 - 1}}$$

$$\simeq \frac{[(s_1^2/n_1) + (s_2^2/n_2)]^2}{\dfrac{(s_1^2/n_1)^2}{n_1 - 1} + \dfrac{(s_2^2/n_2)^2}{n_2 - 1}}. \tag{8.11}$$

If we define

$$c = \frac{s_1^2/n_1}{s_1^2/n_1 + s_2^2/n_2}, \tag{8.12}$$

we can derive

$$\frac{1}{f'} = \frac{c^2}{f_1} + \frac{(1-c)^2}{f_2}. \tag{8.13}$$

It is then easy to show, by differentiating $1/f'$ with respect to c and then equating to zero, that the maximum value that f' can take is $f_1 + f_2$: This occurs when

$$\frac{s_1^2}{n_1(n_1 - 1)} = \frac{s_2^2}{n_2(n_2 - 1)}. \tag{8.14}$$

The smallest value that f' can approach is the minimum of f_1 and f_2: This occurs when either $1 - c$ or c approaches zero, i.e., when $(s_2^2/n_2)/(s_1^2/n_1)$ or $(s_1^2/n_1)/(s_2^2/n_2)$ approaches zero.

As an example of this procedure we will use the data of Dean on the atomic weight of carbon, quoted in Table 7.6, for an illustration of the Wilcoxon two-sample test which gave an exact one-sided P value of 0.0317 and a normal approximation of 0.033. Here we need to compute the separate s_i^2. Using (6.8), for the first sample A, we can subtract a constant,

12.0000, from all observations:

$$s_1^2 = \frac{(0.0072)^2 + \cdots + (0.0077)^2 - (0.0072 + \cdots + 0.0077)^2/5}{5-1}$$

$$= \frac{(18{,}381 - 16{,}017.80) \times 10^{-8}}{4} = 590.80 \times 10^{-8}. \qquad (8.15)$$

Similarly $s_2^2 = 7460.00 \times 10^{-8}$. Also $\bar{x}_1 = 12.00566$ and $\bar{x}_2 = 11.99620$. For the null hypothesis $\xi_1 = \xi_2$, the test statistic (8.2) is

$$\frac{(12.00566 - 11.99620) - 0}{\sqrt{590.80 \times 10^{-8}/5 + 7460.00 \times 10^{-8}/4}} = 2.124. \qquad (8.16)$$

The approximate number of degrees of freedom of this t-like statistic is given by (8.11): First calculating

$$\frac{s_1^2}{n_1} = \frac{590.80 \times 10^{-8}}{5} = 118.16 \times 10^{-8}, \qquad (8.17)$$

$$\frac{s_2^2}{n_2} = \frac{7460.00 \times 10^{-8}}{4} = 1865.00 \times 10^{-8}, \qquad (8.18)$$

we get

$$f' \simeq \frac{(118.16 + 1865.00)^2}{(118.16)^2/(5-1) + (1865.00)^2/(4-1)} = 3.38. \qquad (8.19)$$

The t table (Table II of the Appendix) shows that for degrees of freedom 3 and 4 the 0.95 point is 2.353 and 2.132. For 3.38 degrees of freedom the 0.95 point will be approximately 2.27. The one-sided P value for the observed value of the statistic, 2.124, is thus greater than 0.05.

If we had treated this problem as an ordinary two-sample t test we would have obtained $t = 2.372$ with 7 degrees of freedom corresponding to a one-sided P value of just less than 0.025, so making the assumption that the variances are from the same population makes a substantial difference in the conclusions reached. The two-sample Wilcoxon test agrees closely with the two-sample t test, but it too makes the assumption that the variances of the two populations are the same.

It is interesting to note the results of falsely assuming that the two sample variances are samples of a common variance and using (7.8) instead of (8.2). The numerators of these two statistics are identical and they differ only in their denominators. If $f_i = n_i - 1$, and if $s_1^2/s_2^2 = F$, so that $s_1^2 = Fs_2^2$, the square of the denominator of (7.8) is

$$\frac{f_1 s_1^2 + f_2 s_2^2}{f_1 + f_2}\left(\frac{1}{f_1 + 1} + \frac{1}{f_2 + 1}\right), \qquad (8.20)$$

SECT. 9.8 THE TWO-SAMPLE TEST WITH UNEQUAL VARIANCES

and the square of the denominator of (8.2) is

$$\frac{s_1^2}{f_1+1} + \frac{s_2^2}{f_2+1}. \tag{8.21}$$

The ratio of (8.20) to (8.21) is reducible to

$$\frac{(Ff_1+f_2)(f_1+f_2+2)}{(f_1+f_2)(f_1+Ff_2+F+1)}. \tag{8.22}$$

If we are using equal sample sizes, so that $f_1 = f_2 = f$, say, then the ratio (8.22) equals

$$\frac{(Ff+f)(2f+2)}{2f(Ff+F+f+1)} = 1 \tag{8.23}$$

no matter what the value of F. Thus, for equal sample sizes, the test statistic has the same numerical value, and the only difference would be that we would refer (7.8) to the t table with $2f$ degrees of freedom whereas we would refer (8.2) to the t table with degrees of freedom given by (8.11), which in the case of $f_1 = f_2 = f$ becomes

$$f' = f\frac{(F+1)^2}{F^2+1}, \tag{8.24}$$

which will always be less than $2f$ except when $F = 1$. But, for $0.5 < F < 2$, the reduction in the number of degrees of freedom does not exceed 10 per cent; for $0.333 < F < 3$, not 20 per cent; so that, when the sample sizes are equal and sample variances nearly equal, there is little difference between the procedures.

When the sample sizes are unequal, however, e.g., when $f_1 \gg f_2$, (8.22) tends to F; i.e., the test statistic will be in error by a ratio approaching $\sqrt{F}$. Since there are no theoretical bounds on F, the test statistic could be in error by any amount.

We conclude, therefore, that the two-sample t test is rather sensitive to the assumption that the sample variances come from a common population, unless the sample sizes are close to equality. For markedly unequal sample sizes, and when the assumption that the sample variances are from a common population cannot be justified, a preferable procedure would be to use the methods of this section. A further conclusion is that the sample sizes should be made equal if possible.

The treatment of the two-sample test with unequal variances is subject to disagreements which are still unresolved; see Fisher [11]. However important the controversy from the point of view of statistical theory, it seems that the Welch procedure described here is close enough to the truth to be used in practice without qualms. The k-sample form appears to have been first published by Satterthwaite [12].

9.9. A Comparison of Simple Tests for Means and Medians

We have discussed seven tests for means and medians, and Table 9.5 is intended to assist in choosing the most appropriate for a particular situation. In general, we should use as powerful a test as we feel can be justified. Definitions and discussion of the power of these tests are beyond

Table 9.5. Assumptions Involved in Various Tests

All tests assume that the observations are independent and have continuous distributions

Test	Two samples: $x_{11}, \ldots, x_{1n_1}$, $x_{21}, \ldots, x_{2n_2}$	One sample: $y_1, \ldots, y_n$	One sample formed as differences between paired observations: $d_i = x_{1i} - x_{2i}$, $i = 1, \ldots, n$
t tests	Normality and equality of variances	Normality	The parent populations must be normally distributed but may have different variances
Wilcoxon tests	Identity of distributions (which implies) equality of variances)	Symmetry about zero of the distribution	Necessary and sufficient condition is that $p\{x_1, x_2\}$ is symmetric, so that $p\{a, b\} = p\{b, a\}$.
Median test (two samples)	Identity of distributions	Observations have median zero	A sufficient condition is that $p_i\{x_{1i}, x_{2i}\}$ is symmetric. The $p_i\{\ ,\ \}$ can be different for different i.
Sign test (one sample)		Not necessary for the d_i to have identical distributions, nor that the distribution of any d_i be symmetrical	
Welch test	Normality. Inequality of variances permitted		

the scope of this book, but it is not misleading to state that when the observations are normally distributed the powers of the Wilcoxon tests are of the order of $3/\pi$, and the powers of the median and sign tests are of the order of $2/\pi$, of the corresponding t tests.

An important topic in applied statistics is the question of the *robustness* of statistical procedures. A robust procedure is one which is affected only slightly by appreciable departures from the assumptions involved. Implicit in the concept is the feeling that conclusions in error by so much are not going to make us look foolish. For example, with a certain amount of a certain type of nonnormality the 0.05 point of the t statistic may actually be the 0.055 point, but that would not harm us appreciably. Also implicit is the feeling that in many areas of application the departures from the assumption will rarely exceed a certain degree. To discuss robustness usefully we would need to quantify these various feelings.

We will not attempt this. We merely remark that, e.g., at the end of Section 9.8 we saw that in the two-sample t test when the two sample sizes are equal the test is very little affected by large departures from the assumption of equality of variances in the two populations. On the other hand, at the end of Section 9.5 we referred to Box and Andersen's conclusion [5] that Bartlett's test for the equality of k variances was very sensitive to nonnormality. These authors found, on the other hand, that the test for the comparison of k means (the analysis of variance, to be discussed in Chapter 10) was quite robust against nonnormality.

EXERCISES

9.1. Construct 95 per cent confidence limits (*a*) for the variance, and (*b*) for the mean, of Cavendish's measurements of the density of the earth given in Table 6.1.

9.2. Construct 95 per cent confidence limits for the ratio of the variances of the series *A* and series *B* measurements in Table 9.3.

9.3. Test the null hypotheses that (*a*) the variances are equal and (*b*) that the means are equal, and (*c*) construct 95 per cent confidence limits for the difference between the means, for the data of Table 7.4. Do this (i) on the data as it stands, (ii) on the logarithms of the observations, and (iii) on the reciprocals of the observations. In the case of (ii) and (iii), transform the confidence limits for the transformed variable back into the original scale.

9.4. Samples of very pure iron prepared by two different methods had the following melting points:

A: 1493, 1519, 1518, 1512, 1512, 1514, 1489, 1508, 1508, 1494
B: 1509, 1494, 1512, 1483, 1507, 1491

(a) Test the null hypothesis that the two methods give iron with the same melting point. (b) Construct 95 per cent confidence limits for the difference $A - B$.

Assume normality, and (i) assume the variances are the same, and (ii) do not assume that the variances are the same.

9.5. For the data of exercise (7.5), obtain the one-sided P value for the null hypothesis that the difference between the two types of gauges is zero, using (a) the data as it stands, (b) the logarithms of the data. Give an explanation for the difference between the results, and indicate which you would prefer.

9.6.1. For the data of exercise (7.2), (a) test the null hypothesis that the two samples could have come from populations with the same variance. (b) Test the null hypothesis that the means are the same, assuming normality, (i) assuming that the variances are the same and (ii) not assuming that the two variances are the same.

Data for Exercise 9.7

Region A	Region B	Region C	Region D
84.0	82.4	83.2	80.2
83.5	82.4	82.8	82.9
84.0	83.4	83.4	84.6
85.0	83.3	80.2	84.2
83.1	83.1	82.7	82.8
83.5	83.3	83.0	83.0
81.7	82.4	85.0	82.9
85.4	83.3	83.0	83.4
84.1	82.6	85.0	83.1
83.0	82.0	83.7	83.5
85.8	83.2	83.6	83.6
84.0	83.1	83.3	86.7
84.2	82.5	83.8	82.6
82.2		85.1	82.4
83.6		83.1	83.4
84.9		84.2	82.7
		80.6	82.9
		82.3	83.7
			81.5
			81.9
			81.7
			82.5

Data from O. C. Blade, "National Motor-Gasoline Survey," *Bureau of Mines Report of Investigation* 5041.

II. The table below gives the reciprocals of the observations of exercise (7.2). (a), (b) Perform the same tests on these data as in (a) and (b) above. (c) In exercise (7.2), the original data were tested with the appropriate Wilcoxon test: do the same on the reciprocals.

III. Compare Ia with IIa, Ib(i) with Ib(ii), Ib(i) with IIb(i), IIc with exercise (7.2). Comment on similarities and differences in the results.

Control A: 0.200, 0.167, 0.143, 0.143, 0.125, 0.125, 0.125, 0.111, 0.083
Drug B: 0.143, 0.125, 0.125, 0.125, 0.111, 0.111, 0.083, 0.077, 0.071, 0.059

9.7. The data on p. 306 are the results of octane determinations on samples of gasoline obtained in four regions of the northeastern United States in the summer of 1953.

Test the null hypothesis that the variability in octane number is the same for all four regions.

Some calculations which may be useful are summarized below.

Region	A	B	C	D
n_i	16	13	18	22
$\sum_{v}^{n_i} x_{iv}$	62.0	37.0	58.0	66.2
$\sum_{v}^{n_i} x_{iv}^2$	258.06	107.98	215.86	232.24

A constant 80 has been subtracted from all observations before making these calculations.

9.8. Rosa and Dorsey [see exercise (10.3)] measured the ratio of the electromagnetic to the electrostatic unit of electricity with great precision. In a long series of observations they on occasion disassembled their apparatus, cleaned it, and reassembled it. The variances of the groups of observations, multiplied by 10^8, and numbers of observations in each group, were as follows.

Group	Number of observations	Variance
1	11	1.5636
2	8	1.1250
3	6	3.7666
4	24	4.1721
5	15	4.2666

Test the null hypothesis that these sample variances could come from a common population.

9.9. Let s_1^2, s_2^2 be independent unbiased estimators of σ_1^2, σ_2^2 with $n_1 - 1$, $n_2 - 1$ degrees of freedom respectively. Show that the likelihood ratio statistic for a test of the null hypothesis $\sigma_1^2 = \sigma_2^2$ can be written as

$$\lambda = \frac{(n_1 + n_2)^{(n_1+n_2)/2}}{n_1^{n_1/2} n_2^{n_2/2}} \left[1 + \frac{(n_2 - 1)s_2^2}{(n_1 - 1)s_1^2}\right]^{-n_1/2} \left[1 + \frac{(n_1 - 1)s_1^2}{(n_2 - 1)s_2^2}\right]^{-n_2/2}.$$

Thus λ is small for large values of s_1^2/s_2^2 and also for small values of s_1^2/s_2^2. (Hint: The derivation of λ in (5.16) for comparing k variances is valid for $k = 2$.)

9.10. With reference to Section 9.7 on the two-sample t test, show that, in Ω

$$\hat{\xi}_1 = \bar{x}_1, \; \hat{\xi}_2 = \bar{x}_2, \; \hat{\sigma} = \frac{1}{n_1 + n_2}\left[\sum_\nu^{n_1}(x_{1\nu} - \bar{x})^2 + \sum_\nu^{n_2}(x_{2\nu} - \bar{x}_2)^2\right],$$

and in ω,

$$\hat{\xi} = \frac{1}{n_1 + n_2}\left(\sum_\nu^{n_1} x_{1\nu} + \sum_\nu^{n_2} x_{2\nu}\right),$$

$$\hat{\sigma}^2 = \frac{1}{n_1 + n_2}\left[\sum_\nu^{n_1}(x_{1\nu} - \bar{x}_1)^2 + \sum_\nu^{n_2}(x_{2\nu} - \bar{x}_2)^2 + \frac{n_1 n_2}{n_1 + n_2}(\bar{x}_1 - \bar{x}_2)^2\right],$$

whence λ is as determined by equations (7.7) and (7.8).

REFERENCES

1. Bartlett, M. S., "Properties of Sufficiency and Statistical Tests," *Proceedings of the Royal Society of London*, A, 160 (1937), 268–82.
2. Hartley, H. O., "Testing the Homogeneity of a Set of Variances," *Biometrika*, 31 (1940), 249–55.
3. Hartley, H. O., "The Maximum F Ratio as a Short-Cut Test for Heterogeneity of Variance," *Biometrika*, 37 (1950), 308–312.
4. Pearson, E. S., and H. O. Hartley (eds.), *Biometrika Tables for Statisticians*, Vol. 1. London: Cambridge University Press, 1954.
5. Box, G. E. P., and S. L. Andersen, "Permutation Theory in the Derivation of Robust Criteria and the Study of the Departures from Assumption," *Journal of the Royal Statistical Society*, B (Methodological), 17 (1955), 1–26.
6. Michelson, A. A., "Measurement of the Velocity of Light between Mount Wilson and Mount San Antonio," *Astrophysical Journal*, LXV (1927), 1–14.
7. Honigschmid, O., "Neure Atomgewichtsbestimmungen," *Zeitschrift fur Electrochemie*, 25 (1919), 91–96.
8. Mood, Alexander M., and Franklin A. Graybill, *Introduction to the Theory of Statistics*, 2nd edition. New York: McGraw-Hill Book Co., 1963.
9. Welch, B. L., "The Significance of the Difference Between Two Means When the Population Variances are Unequal," *Biometrika*, 29 (1937), 350–62.
10. Welch, B. L., "The Generalization of 'Student's' Problem when Several Different Population Variances are Involved," *Biometrika*, 34 (1947), 28–35.
11. Fisher, R. A., "Comment on the Notes by Neyman, Bartlett, and Welch in This Journal," *Journal of the Royal Statistical Society*, B, 19 (1957), 179.
12. Satterthwaite, F. E., "An Approximate Distribution of Estimates of Variance Components," *Biometrics Bulletin*, 2 (1946), 110–14.

CHAPTER 10

One-Way Analysis of Variance

10.1. Introduction: Models I and II

We have seen in Section 9.7 that two sample means can be compared with the two-sample t test. The generalization of this problem to k means, $k > 2$, brings us to the body of techniques known as the analysis of variance. In this chapter we shall be concerned with the case in which the data are subject to only one dimension of classification. There are two somewhat different situations. In the first, known as model I, the individuals in the sample represent the particular individuals in which we are interested. In the second, known as model II, we have no particular interest in the particular individuals that happen to be in the sample. Our concern is to estimate the variance of the infinite population from which our sample has been randomly selected.

As an illustration of the difference between models I and II, consider a machine tool manufacturer producing a standard model in quantity who is interested in some variable associated with the quality of the items produced by the tool. A customer may purchase k tools, and the manufacturer may supply him with a sample taken at random from his current production. The measurements are made on a sample of the items produced by these k tools, and the data analyzed by both the customer and the manufacturer. From the point of view of the customer, he is concerned solely with these k tools sitting on his floor, and he uses a model I approach. From the point of view of the manufacturer, these k tools are merely a random sample, and he is only concerned with using these measurements to estimate the variance of the population of tools; therefore he uses a model II approach.

The problem of whether any particular situation is model I or model II is often clarified by asking the question, "If we were to repeat the experiment, would we have the same individuals or not?" Clearly in the model I case we would; in the model II case, the probability of getting the identical sample, or even any single individual, a second time is zero.

Model I can be regarded as the case where the sample consists of all in the population, and model II as the case where the interest is in the infinite population from which the sample came. In Section 14.8 we shall consider the intermediate case in which the population is finite; there, by letting the population size decrease to the sample size or increase to infinity, we will get models I and II as special cases.

10.2. One-Way Analysis of Variance: Model I

Suppose that we have k groups of independent observations $x_{11}, \ldots, x_{1n_1}, x_{21}, \ldots, x_{2n_2}, \ldots, x_{k1}, \ldots, x_{kn_k}$ from normally distributed populations with means $\xi_1, \ldots, \xi_k$, all with the same variance σ^2. Thus the model is

$$x_{iv} = \xi_i + z_{iv}; \quad i = 1, \ldots, k, \quad v = 1, \ldots, n_i, \quad (2.1)$$

where the ξ_i are fixed constants and the z_{iv} are independent random normal deviates with zero mean and variance σ^2.

It is convenient to reparameterize the model (2.1). We define ξ as the weighted average of the ξ_i,

$$\xi = \left(\sum_i^k n_i\right)^{-1} \left(\sum_i^k n_i \xi_i\right), \quad (2.2)$$

and then introduce new parameters η_i defined as

$$\eta_i = \xi_i - \xi. \quad (2.3)$$

The model (2.1) can now be written as

$$x_{iv} = \xi + \eta_i + z_{iv}. \quad (2.4)$$

The weighted sum of the η_i is zero:

$$\sum_i^k n_i \eta_i = \sum_i^k n_i(\xi_i - \xi) = \sum_i^k n_i \xi_i - \xi \sum_i^k n_i = 0. \quad (2.5)$$

It is often helpful, but not always essential, when averaging over a suffix to replace that suffix by a dot. Thus $\bar{x}_{i.} = (1/n_i) \sum_v^{n_i} x_{iv}$. We define $\bar{x}_{..}$ as the weighted average of the $\bar{x}_{i.}$, or what comes to the same thing, as the grand average of all the x_{iv}, since $n_i \bar{x}_{i.} = \sum_v^{n_i} x_{iv}$:

$$\bar{x}_{..} = \frac{\sum_i^k n_i \bar{x}_{i.}}{\sum_i^k n_i} = \frac{\sum_i^k \sum_v^{n_i} x_{iv}}{\sum_i^k n_i}. \quad (2.6)$$

In consequence of these definitions,

$$\sum_i^k n_i(\bar{x}_{i.} - \bar{x}_{..}) = \sum_i^k n_i \bar{x}_{i.} - \bar{x}_{..} \sum_i^k n_i = 0. \qquad (2.7)$$

From (8.1.26), for each group we can write

$$\sum_\nu^{n_i} (x_{i\nu} - \xi_i)^2 = n_i(\bar{x}_{i.} - \xi_i)^2 + \sum_\nu^{n_i} (x_{i\nu} - \bar{x}_{i.})^2, \qquad (2.8)$$

where the sums of squares are distributed as $\sigma^2 \chi^2$ with degrees of freedom n_i, 1, and $n_i - 1$ respectively, and the two terms on the right-hand side are independent. Now sum (2.8) over all k groups:

$$\sum_i^k \sum_\nu^{n_i} (x_{i\nu} - \xi_i)^2 = \sum_i^k n_i(\bar{x}_{i.} - \xi_i)^2 + \sum_i^k \sum_\nu^{n_i} (x_{i\nu} - \bar{x}_{i.})^2. \qquad (2.9)$$

We saw in (1.27.16) that the sum of a number of $\chi^2(f_i)$ is itself distributed as $\chi^2\left(\sum_i^k f_i\right)$, so the sums of squares in (2.9) are distributed as $\sigma^2 \chi^2$ with degrees of freedom $\sum_i^k n_i$, k, $\sum_i^k (n_i - 1) = \left(\sum_i^k n_i\right) - k$ respectively. If we define

$$s_1^2 = \frac{\sum_i^k \sum_\nu^{n_i} (x_{i\nu} - \bar{x}_{i.})^2}{\left(\sum_i^k n_i\right) - k}, \qquad (2.10)$$

then as discussed in (9.7.6) it will be distributed as $\sigma^2 \chi^2 \left(\sum_i^k n_i - k\right) / \left(\sum_i^k n_i - k\right)$ and have expected value σ^2. The first term on the right-hand side of (2.9) involves $\bar{x}_{i.} - \xi_i$, which we can write as

$$\bar{x}_{i.} - \xi_i = (\bar{x}_{i.} - \bar{x}_{..}) - (\xi_i - \xi) + (\bar{x}_{..} - \xi)$$
$$= (\bar{x}_{i.} - \bar{x}_{..} - \eta_i) + (\bar{x}_{..} - \xi). \qquad (2.11)$$

When we square this and sum over i and ν the cross product term is zero by (2.7) and (2.5):

$$2(\bar{x}_{..} - \xi) \sum_i^k n_i(\bar{x}_{i.} - \bar{x}_{..} - \eta_i) = 2(\bar{x}_{..} - \xi)\left[\sum_i^k n_i(\bar{x}_{i.} - \bar{x}_{..}) - \sum_i^k n_i \eta_i\right]$$
$$= 0. \qquad (2.12)$$

Therefore

$$\sum_i^k n_i(\bar{x}_{i.} - \xi_i)^2 = \sum_i^k n_i(\bar{x}_{i.} - \bar{x}_{..} - \eta_i)^2 + (\bar{x}_{..} - \xi)^2 \sum_i^k n_i. \qquad (2.13)$$

In (2.9) we saw that the left-hand side is distributed as $\sigma^2\chi^2(k)$. We have partitioned this sum of squares in two components. The first involves k variables $\bar{x}_{i.} - \bar{x}_{..}$ subject to the restriction (2.7), so it will have $k - 1$ degrees of freedom. The second involves the single variable $x_{..}$, on which there is no restriction, so it will have one degree of freedom. By Cochran's theorem of Section 8.2 these two sums of squares will be distributed as $\sigma^2\chi^2$ and be independent. If we define

$$s_2'^2 = \frac{1}{k-1} \sum_i^k n_i(\bar{x}_{i.} - \bar{x}_{..} - \eta_i)^2, \tag{2.14}$$

then it will be distributed as $\sigma^2\chi^2(k-1)/(k-1)$, have expected value σ^2, and be independent of s_1^2. Hence the ratio $s_2'^2/s_1^2$ has the F distribution with degrees of freedom $k - 1, \sum_i^k n_i - k$. Now define

$$s_2^2 = \frac{1}{k-1} \sum_i^k n_i(\bar{x}_{i.} - \bar{x}_{..})^2. \tag{2.15}$$

To find its expected value, consider the expected value of the numerator of $s_2'^2$, noting that $E[\bar{x}_{i.} - \bar{x}_{..}] = \xi_i - \xi = \eta_i$:

$$E\left[\sum_i^k n_i(\bar{x}_{i.} - \bar{x}_{..} - \eta_i)^2\right]$$

$$= E\left[\sum_i^k n_i(\bar{x}_{i.} - \bar{x}_{..})^2\right] + \sum_i^k n_i\eta_i^2 - 2\sum_i^k n_i\eta_i E[\bar{x}_{i.} - \bar{x}_{..}]$$

$$= E[(k-1)s_2^2] - \sum_i^k n_i\eta_i^2. \tag{2.16}$$

The left-hand side equals $(k-1)\sigma^2$, whence it follows that

$$E[s_2^2] = \sigma^2 + \frac{1}{k-1}\sum_i^k n_i\eta_i^2. \tag{2.17}$$

If the null hypothesis that $\xi_i = \xi$ for all i is true, then $\eta_i = 0$ for all i, $s_2^2 = s_2'^2$, and so s_2^2 will have the distribution $\sigma^2\chi^2(k-1)/(k-1)$, and

$$\frac{s_2^2}{s_1^2} \sim F\left(k-1, \sum_i^k n_i - k\right). \tag{2.18}$$

If the null hypothesis is false, so that some $\eta_i \neq 0$, then $E[s_2^2] > \sigma^2$, and the ratio s_2^2/s_1^2 will not have the F distribution but instead a distribution displaced upwards in the direction of larger values of s_2^2/s_1^2. The critical region is therefore large values of s_2^2/s_1^2.

SECT. 10.2   ONE-WAY ANALYSIS OF VARIANCE: MODEL I   313

These results are conventionally and conveniently summarized in an analysis of variance table (Table 10.1).

Table 10.1

Source of variance	Sums of squares	Degrees of freedom	Mean squares	$E[\text{M. S.}]$
Between groups	$\sum\limits_{i}^{k} n_i(\bar{x}_{i.} - \bar{x}_{..})^2$	$k - 1$	s_2^2	$\sigma^2 + \dfrac{1}{k-1}\sum\limits_{i}^{k} n_i(\xi_i - \xi)^2$
Within groups	$\sum\limits_{i}^{k}\sum\limits_{v}^{n_i}(x_{iv} - \bar{x}_{i.})^2$	$\left(\sum\limits_{i}^{k} n_i\right) - k$	s_1^2	σ^2
Total	$\sum\limits_{i}^{k}\sum\limits_{v}^{n_i}(x_{iv} - \bar{x}_{..})^2$	$\left(\sum\limits_{i}^{k} n_i\right) - 1$		

An alternative model is sometimes preferable. In (2.2) we defined ξ as the average of the ξ_i weighted by the n_i. The n_i may be quite arbitrary numbers, and it may be more satisfactory to define a mean ξ' as the unweighted mean

$$\xi' = \frac{1}{k}\sum_{i}^{k} \xi_i. \tag{2.19}$$

Corresponding to the η_i of (2.3) we define τ_i as

$$\tau_i = \xi_i - \xi'. \tag{2.20}$$

Thus the original model (2.1) is written as

$$x_{iv} = \xi' + \tau_i + z_{iv}. \tag{2.21}$$

The two models are related by the equation

$$\xi_i = \xi + \eta_i = \xi' + \tau_i. \tag{2.22}$$

We have, substituting ξ_i from (2.22) in (2.2):

$$\xi = \frac{\sum\limits_{i}^{k} n_i \xi_i}{\sum\limits_{i}^{k} n_i} = \frac{\sum\limits_{i}^{k} n_i(\xi' + \tau_i)}{\sum\limits_{i}^{k} n_i} = \xi' + \frac{\sum\limits_{i}^{k} n_i \tau_i}{\sum\limits_{i}^{k} n_i}. \tag{2.23}$$

Therefore

$$\eta_i = \xi_i - \xi = (\xi' + \tau_i) - \left(\xi' + \frac{\sum\limits_{i}^{k} n_i \tau_i}{\sum\limits_{i}^{k} n_i}\right) = \tau_i - \frac{\sum\limits_{i}^{k} n_i \tau_i}{\sum\limits_{i}^{k} n_i}. \tag{2.24}$$

Substituting this for η_i in (2.17), the alternative expression for $E[s_2^2]$ is

$$E[s_2^2] = \sigma^2 + \frac{1}{k-1} \sum_i^k n_i \left(\tau_i - \frac{\sum_i^k n_i \tau_i}{\sum_i^k n_i} \right)^2. \qquad (2.25)$$

If the τ_i are zero for all i, then the second term on the right-hand side is zero and $E[s_2^2] = \sigma^2$ as before. Of course, if the n_i are all equal, then the two models are identical.

We may wish to construct a confidence interval for the difference between two population means, $\xi_i - \xi_{i'}$. The conventional procedure is to note that

$$E[\bar{x}_{i.} - \bar{x}_{i'.}] = \xi_i - \xi_{i'}, \qquad (2.26)$$

$$V[\bar{x}_{i.} - \bar{x}_{i'.}] = \sigma^2 \left(\frac{1}{n_i} + \frac{1}{n_{i'}} \right), \qquad (2.27)$$

whence

$$\frac{(\bar{x}_{i.} - \bar{x}_{i'.}) - (\xi_i - \xi_{i'})}{s_1 \left(\frac{1}{n_i} + \frac{1}{n_{i'}} \right)^{1/2}} \sim t\left(\sum_i^k n_i - k \right), \qquad (2.28)$$

and $1 - \alpha$ confidence limits for $\xi_i - \xi_{i'}$ are

$$\bar{x}_{i.} - \bar{x}_{i'.} \pm t_{1-\alpha/2} s_1 \sqrt{\frac{1}{n_i} + \frac{1}{n_{i'}}}. \qquad (2.29)$$

This differs from the interval derived from a two-sample t test, (9.7.11), by the use of the s_1 from Table 10.1, which is an estimate pooled over all k groups rather than just the i and i'th. Clearly, if there is reason to doubt the assumption of this section that σ is constant over all k groups, then (9.7.11) should be used (and if we cannot assume that σ is constant even over the i and i'th groups, we should use the methods of Section 9.8).

As an example of one-way Model I analysis of variance, Table 10.2 gives the units in the third decimal place of determinations by Heyl [1] of the gravitational constant G; e.g., 83 corresponds to an observation of 6.683. Balls of three different materials were used. While the sums of squares in Table 10.1 can be calculated in the forms given there, it is usually more satisfactory to use identities that involve totals rather than means. We need

$$\left(\sum_i^k n_i \right)^{-1} \left(\sum_i^k \sum_v^{n_i} x_{iv} \right)^2 = \frac{(1159)^2}{16} = 83{,}955.062, \qquad (2.30)$$

SECT. 10.2   ONE-WAY ANALYSIS OF VARIANCE: MODEL I   315

Table 10.2

	Gold	Platinum	Glass	Sums
	83	61	78	
	81	61	71	
	76	67	75	
	78	67	72	
	79	64	74	
	72			
n_i	6	5	5	$16 = \sum_{i}^{k} n_i$
$\sum_{v}^{n_i} x_{iv}$	469	320	370	$1{,}159 = \sum_{i}^{k}\sum_{v}^{n_i} x_{iv}$
$\sum_{v}^{n_i} x_{iv}^2$	36,735	20,516	27,410	$84{,}661 = \sum_{i}^{k}\sum_{v}^{n_i} x_{iv}^2$
$\frac{1}{n_i}\left(\sum_{v}^{n_i} x_{iv}\right)^2$	36,660.167	20,480.000	27,380.000	$84{,}520.167 = \sum_{i}^{k}\frac{1}{n_i}\left(\sum_{v}^{n_i} x_{iv}\right)^2$

and then

$$\sum_{i}^{k} n_i(\bar{x}_{i.} - \bar{x}_{..})^2 = \sum_{i}^{k} n_i \bar{x}_{i.}^2 + \sum_{i}^{k} n_i \bar{x}_{..}^2 - 2\bar{x}_{..}\sum_{i}^{k} n_i \bar{x}_{i.}$$

$$= \sum_{i}^{k} n_i \left(\frac{\sum_{v}^{n_i} x_{iv}}{n_i}\right)^2 + \sum_{i}^{k} n_i \left(\frac{\sum_{i}^{k}\sum_{v}^{n_i} x_{iv}}{\sum_{i}^{k} n_i}\right)^2$$

$$- 2\left(\frac{\sum_{i}^{k}\sum_{v}^{n_i} x_{iv}}{\sum_{i}^{k} n_i}\right)\sum_{i}^{k} n_i\left(\frac{\sum_{v}^{n_i} x_{iv}}{n_i}\right)$$

$$= \sum_{i}^{k} \frac{1}{n_i}\left(\sum_{v}^{n_i} x_{iv}\right)^2 - \left(\sum_{i}^{k} n_i\right)^{-1}\left(\sum_{i}^{k}\sum_{v}^{n_i} x_{iv}\right)^2 \qquad (2.31)$$

$$= 84{,}520.167 - 83{,}955.062 = 565.105. \qquad (2.32)$$

By similar manipulations,

$$\sum_{i}^{k}\sum_{v}^{n_i}(x_{iv} - \bar{x}_{i.})^2 = \sum_{i}^{k}\sum_{v}^{n_i} x_{iv}^2 - \sum_{i}^{k}\frac{1}{n_i}\left(\sum_{v}^{n_i} x_{iv}\right)^2 \qquad (2.33)$$

$$= 84{,}661 - 84{,}502.167 = 140.833, \qquad (2.34)$$

$$\sum_{i}^{k}\sum_{v}^{n_i}(x_{iv} - \bar{x}_{..})^2 = \sum_{i}^{k}\sum_{v}^{n_i} x_{iv}^2 - \left(\sum_{i}^{k} n_i\right)^{-1}\left(\sum_{i}^{k}\sum_{v}^{n_i} x_{iv}\right)^2 \qquad (2.35)$$

$$= 84{,}661 - 83{,}955.062 = 705.938. \qquad (2.36)$$

We assemble these results in Table 10.3.

Table 10.3

Source of variance	Sums of squares	Degrees of freedom	Mean squares
Materials	565.105	2	282.553
Within materials	140.833	13	10.833
Total	705.938	15	

The test of the null hypothesis that the ξ_i are all equal is given by the variance ratio $282.553/10.833 = 26.08$ with degrees of freedom 2 and 13; this is overwhelmingly significant as the 0.999 point for these degrees of freedom is 12.31.

10.3. The Problem of Multiple Comparisons

An F test as performed in the previous section may reject the null hypothesis that the ξ_i are all equal, but it does not tell us which ξ_i are significantly different from which. A single prechosen pair may be compared by an ordinary two-sample t test, either using a within-group mean square calculated only from the two groups in question, or using the within-group mean square from all the groups, and confidence limits for the difference constructed in the usual way. This is valid only for one prechosen comparison; if we start making comparisons suggested by the data, and several of them, the significance level becomes hopelessly incorrect. Several procedures have been proposed for this problem. We will discuss those offered by Scheffé [2] and Tukey [3].

Scheffé's system is more general than simple comparison between pairs of means. Suppose that we have estimates $\bar{x}_i$ of true means ξ_i, with variances σ^2/n_i estimated as s^2/n_i, s^2 being estimated with f degrees of freedom. We are interested in *contrasts*, defined as

$$\theta = \sum_i^k c_i \xi_i, \tag{3.1}$$

where $\sum_i^k c_i = 0$. The contrast θ is estimated as

$$H = \sum_i^k c_i \bar{x}_i. \tag{3.2}$$

Assuming that the $\bar{x}_i$ are independent,

$$V[H] = \sum_i^k c_i^2 \cdot \frac{\sigma^2}{n_i} = \sigma^2 \sum_i^k \frac{c_i^2}{n_i}, \tag{3.3}$$

SECT. 10.3   THE PROBLEM OF MULTIPLE COMPARISONS   317

and the estimated variance of H is

$$\hat{V}[H] = s^2 \sum_i^k \frac{c_i^2}{n_i}. \tag{3.4}$$

Scheffé's result is that we can construct $1 - \alpha$ confidence limits for all imaginable contrasts θ,

$$\Pr\{H - S\sqrt{\hat{V}[H]} < \theta < H + S\sqrt{\hat{V}[H]}\} = 1 - \alpha, \tag{3.5}$$

where

$$S^2 = (k-1)F_{1-\alpha}(k-1, f). \tag{3.6}$$

In this formula, k is the number of means which might be entering into the contrast, rather than the number of means actually entering into any particular contrast. If, for each experiment we perform, we construct confidence limits according to (3.5), then, in a fraction $1 - \alpha$ of these experiments, all the confidence statements will be correct: In a fraction α, one or more of the statements will be incorrect.

Tukey's procedure is somewhat similar but requires that the $\bar{x}_i$ have equal variances. We construct confidence limits for each contrast as

$$\Pr\{H - Ts < \theta < H + Ts\} = 1 - \alpha, \tag{3.7}$$

where s^2 is the estimated variance of individual observations, as before, and T is defined as

$$T = \frac{1}{2} \sum_i^k |c_i| \cdot q \cdot \frac{1}{\sqrt{n}}, \tag{3.8}$$

where q is the $1 - \alpha$ point of the studentized range for a sample of k and f degrees of freedom (Table IX of the Appendix). The function q is the distribution of $(x_{\max} - x_{\min})/s$, where s is estimated with f degrees of freedom.

These two procedures have somewhat different properties. In the first place, Scheffé's can be used when the n_i are different; Tukey's requires that the n_i be all equal to n. Second, Tukey's gives somewhat shorter confidence intervals for simple differences, e.g., a contrast formed by coefficients $c_i = -1, 1, 0, \ldots, 0$, whereas Scheffé's gives shorter confidence intervals for more complex contrasts, e.g., the difference between the sum of the first three means minus three times the mean of the fourth, which would be given by coefficients $c_i = 1, 1, 1, -3, 0, \ldots, 0$.

To illustrate the use of these methods we will use the data of Table 10.2. So that the results of the different methods will be comparable, and since Tukey's method requires equal n_i, we will omit the last observation from the gold balls, so that the three means will be 79.4, 64.0, and 74.00, respectively, but we will use the estimate of variance of a single observation unchanged at 10.833 with 13 degrees of freedom.

Suppose that we wish to construct confidence limits for the differences between the metal balls and the glass ball, i.e., the contrast

$$\theta = \xi_1 + \xi_2 - 2\xi_3, \qquad (3.9)$$

which will be defined by the coefficients c_i taking the values $c_1 = 1$, $c_2 = 1$, $c_3 = -2$. Then

$$H = 1 \times 79.4 + 1 \times 64.0 - 2 \times 74.0 = -4.6, \qquad (3.10)$$

$$\hat{V}[H] = \frac{10.833}{5}[1^2 + 1^2 + (-2)^2] = 13.00, \qquad (3.11)$$

$$S^2 = (3-1)F_{0.95}(2, 13) = 2 \times 3.81 = 7.62, \qquad (3.12)$$

$$S\sqrt{\hat{V}[H]} = \sqrt{7.62}\sqrt{13.00} = 9.951; \qquad (3.13)$$

so the Scheffé limits are -4.6 ± 9.95. If this were the only contrast for which we wanted confidence limits, and the choice had been made before we saw the data, it would be legitimate to use $t_{0.975}(13) = 2.160$ in place of S, which would give limits $-46. \pm 7.8$. The Tukey limits involve q for three means and a variance estimated on 13 degrees of freedom. From Table IX, $q = 3.73$ for these values of the parameters. We need

$$T = \frac{1}{2}\sum_i^k |c_i| \cdot q \cdot \frac{1}{\sqrt{n}} = \frac{1}{2}(|1| + |1| + |-2|) \times 3.73 \times \frac{1}{\sqrt{5}} = 3.336; \qquad (3.14)$$

so $Ts = 3.336 \times \sqrt{10.833} = 10.98$, and the confidence limits are -4.6 ± 11.0.

A third type of multiple confidence intervals was developed by Dunnett [5] for the special but important case where we have tested $1 + k$ treatments, of which one is a control and we wish to compare the other k with the control. These limits are easy to construct, being $\pm ds\sqrt{1/n_0 + 1/n_i}$ where n_0 is the number of observations on the control, n_i on the treatments, and d is a parameter analogous to t tabulated in his paper.

10.4. One-Way Analysis of Variance: Model II

In model I analysis of variance we defined the model in (2.1) as $x_{iv} = \xi_i + z_{iv}$, and in (2.20) we defined $\tau_i = \xi_i - \xi'$; so the model was

$$x_{iv} = \xi' + \tau_i + z_{iv} \qquad (4.1)$$

where $\sum_i^k \tau_i = 0$ and $z_{iv} \sim N(0, \sigma^2)$. The τ_i were fixed constants. A model II analysis is based on the model

$$x_{iv} = \xi + y_i + z_{iv} \qquad (4.2)$$

SECT. 10.4 ONE-WAY ANALYSIS OF VARIANCE: MODEL II

where the $y_i \sim N(0, \omega^2)$ and the $z_{iv} \sim N(0, \sigma^2)$. Regarding the relevant populations as infinite, such a model could correspond to the situation where we take a number of sacks of wool from a large consignment and the sack means are distributed about a mean ξ with variance ω^2: We then take a sample from the sack which is distributed about the sack mean with variance σ^2. Both y_i and z_{iv} are random samples from infinite populations, and our only interest in the particular y_i and z_{iv} we happen to get in the sample is insofar as they enable us to estimate ξ, ω^2 and σ^2. The parameters ω^2 and σ^2 are known as *components of variance*.

Since the model is so similar to model I, much of the analysis proceeds along similar lines. The total sum of squares about the grand mean is split up as before into two components:

$$\sum_i^k \sum_v^{n_i} (x_{iv} - \bar{x}_{..})^2 = \sum_i^k n_i(\bar{x}_{i.} - \bar{x}_{..})^2 + \sum_i^k \sum_v^{n_i} (x_{iv} - \bar{x}_{i.})^2, \quad (4.3)$$

where the two terms on the right-hand side are the numerators of s_2^2 (2.15) and s_1^2 (2.10), with degrees of freedom $k - 1$ and $\sum_i^k n_i - k$. The mean square s_1^2 as before has expected value σ^2, but the change in the model affects the expected value and the distribution of s_2^2. To find this we proceed as follows:

$$E\left[\sum_i^k n_i(\bar{x}_{i.} - \bar{x}_{..})^2\right] = E\left[\sum_i^k n_i \bar{x}_{i.}^2\right] + E\left[\bar{x}_{..}^2 \sum_i^k n_i\right] - 2E\left[\bar{x}_{..} \sum_i^k n_i \bar{x}_{i.}\right]$$

$$= \sum_i^k n_i E[\bar{x}_{i.}^2] - \left(\sum_i^k n_i\right) E[\bar{x}_{..}^2]. \quad (4.4)$$

To evaluate this we need $E[\bar{x}_{i.}^2]$ and $E[\bar{x}_{..}^2]$. The averages $\bar{x}_{i.}$ and $\bar{x}_{..}$ are formed by averaging the model (4.2) first over v to give $\bar{x}_{i.}$; we then average $\bar{x}_{i.}$ over i to get $\bar{x}_{..}$:

$$\bar{x}_{i.} = \xi + y_i + \frac{1}{n_i} \sum_v^{n_i} z_{iv}, \quad (4.5)$$

$$\bar{x}_{..} = \frac{\sum_i^k n_i \bar{x}_{i.}}{\sum_i^k n_i} = \xi + \frac{\sum_i^k n_i y_i}{\sum_i^k n_i} + \frac{\sum_i^k \sum_v^{n_i} z_{iv}}{\sum_i^k n_i}. \quad (4.6)$$

We see that $E[\bar{x}_{i.}] = \xi$ and likewise $E[\bar{x}_{..}] = \xi$. From the definition of variance, $V[\bar{x}_{i.}] = E[\bar{x}_{i.}^2] - (E[\bar{x}_{i.}])^2$, we have

$$E[\bar{x}_{i.}^2] = V[\bar{x}_{i.}] + (E[\bar{x}_{i.}])^2 = V[y_i] + \frac{1}{n_i^2} V\left[\sum_v^{n_i} z_{iv}\right] + \xi^2 = \omega^2 + \frac{\sigma^2}{n_i} + \xi^2.$$

$$(4.7)$$

Similarly,

$$E[\bar{x}_{..}^2] = V[\bar{x}_{..}] + (E[\bar{x}_{..}])^2$$

$$= \left[\left(\sum_i^k n_i\right)^2\right]^{-1}\left\{V\left[\sum_i^k n_i y_i\right] + V\left[\sum_i^k \sum_v^{n_i} z_{iv}\right]\right\} + \xi^2$$

$$= \left[\left(\sum_i^k n_i\right)^2\right]^{-1}\left(\omega^2 \sum_i^k n_i^2 + \sigma^2 \sum_i^k n_i\right) + \xi^2. \qquad (4.8)$$

We now substitute (4.7) and (4.8) in (4.4):

$$E\left[\sum_i^k n_i(\bar{x}_{i.} - \bar{x}_{..})^2\right] = \sum_i^k n_i\left(\omega^2 + \frac{\sigma^2}{n_i} + \xi^2\right)$$

$$- \left(\sum_i^k n_i\right)\left\{\left[\left(\sum_i^k n_i\right)^2\right]^{-1}\left(\omega^2 \sum_i^k n_i^2 + \sigma^2 \sum_i^k n_i\right) + \xi^2\right\}$$

$$= (k-1)\sigma^2 + \left(\sum_i^k n_i - \frac{\sum_i^k n_i^2}{\sum_i^k n_i}\right)\omega^2; \qquad (4.9)$$

so the expected value of s_2^2 is

$$E[s_2^2] = E\left[\frac{\sum_i^k n_i(\bar{x}_{i.} - \bar{x}_{..})^2}{k-1}\right] = \sigma^2 + \frac{1}{k-1}\left(\sum_i^k n_i - \frac{\sum_i^k n_i^2}{\sum_i^k n_i}\right)\omega^2. \qquad (4.10)$$

In the case when the n_i are all equal, say to n, then (4.10) becomes

$$E[s_2^2] = \sigma^2 + n\omega^2. \qquad (4.11)$$

It is apparent that model I and II one-way analyses of variance are very similar. The partitioning of the total sum of squares and the arithmetic are identical, and the only difference that emerges is the change in the expectation and distribution of s_2^2. In the case of equal n_i, the change in the expectation of s_2^2 is the substitution of ω^2 for $\sum_i^k (\xi_i - \xi)^2/(k-1)$. For equal $n_i = n$, (4.5) is

$$\bar{x}_{i.} = \xi + y_i + \bar{z}_{i.}, \qquad (4.12)$$

and so $\bar{x}_{i.}$ has expectation $E[\bar{x}_{i.}] = \xi$ and variance

$$V[\bar{x}_{i.}] = V[y_i] + V[\bar{z}_{i.}] = \omega^2 + \frac{\sigma^2}{n}. \qquad (4.13)$$

Also, since y_i and z_i are normally distributed, $\bar{x}_{i.}$ is normally distributed. Therefore $\sum_{i}^{k} (\bar{x}_{i.} - \bar{x}_{..})^2/(k-1)$ is an ordinary sample estimate of variance, where the variance is $\omega^2 + \sigma^2/n$, and will have the distribution $(\omega^2 + \sigma^2/n)\chi^2(k-1)/(k-1)$. It follows that s_2^2 has the distribution $(\sigma^2 + n\omega^2)\chi^2(k-1)/(k-1)$.

10.5. Interpretation of a Model II One-Way Analysis of Variance

Under the null hypothesis that $\omega^2 = 0$, s_2^2/s_1^2 will be distributed as F with degrees of freedom $k - 1$ and $\sum_{i}^{k} n_i - k$; so this is the test for this null hypothesis.

We have seen that $E[\bar{x}_{..}] = \xi$; so $\bar{x}_{..}$ is an obvious estimator of ξ. The expectation of $\bar{x}_{..}^2$ (4.8), in the case $n_i = n$, reduces to

$$\frac{n\omega^2 + \sigma^2}{kn} + \xi^2, \tag{5.1}$$

and so the variance of $\bar{x}_{..}$ in the case of equal n_i is

$$V[\bar{x}_{..}] = \frac{\sigma^2 + n\omega^2}{kn}. \tag{5.2}$$

Hence
$$\frac{\bar{x}_{..} - E[\bar{x}_{..}]}{\sqrt{V[\bar{x}_{..}]}} = \frac{\bar{x}_{..} - \xi}{\sqrt{(\sigma^2 + n\omega^2)/kn}} \sim N(0, 1). \tag{5.3}$$

Substituting the sample estimate of $\sigma^2 + n\omega^2$, namely, s_2^2, based on $k - 1$ degrees of freedom, gives

$$\frac{\bar{x}_{..} - \xi}{\sqrt{s_2^2/kn}} \sim t(k - 1), \tag{5.4}$$

which will give confidence limits for ξ as in (9.6.7).

The variance of the z_{iv}, σ^2, is estimated by s_1^2 and ω^2 is estimated as

$$\hat{\omega}^2 = \frac{s_2^2 - s_1^2}{n}. \tag{5.5}$$

Confidence limits for σ^2 can be obtained as in (9.2.2). Confidence limits for ω^2 are considerably more troublesome. We can use either a large sample approximation or a somewhat more exact approximation. The large sample treatment applies (9.8.5), $V[s^2] = 2(\sigma^2)^2/f$, to s_2^2 and s_1^2:

$$V[s_2^2] = \frac{2(n\omega^2 + \sigma^2)^2}{k - 1}, \quad V[s_1^2] = \frac{2(\sigma^2)^2}{k(n - 1)}, \tag{5.6}$$

and so

$$V[\hat{\omega}^2] = V\left[\frac{1}{n}(s_2^2 - s_1^2)\right] = \frac{2(n\omega^2 + \sigma^2)^2}{n^2(k-1)} + \frac{2(\sigma^2)^2}{n^2k(n-1)}. \quad (5.7)$$

Substituting the sample estimates s_2^2 and s_1^2 for $n\omega^2 + \sigma^2$ and σ^2, we get

$$\hat{V}[\hat{\omega}^2] = \frac{2}{n^2}\left[\frac{(s_2^2)^2}{k-1} + \frac{(s_1^2)^2}{k(n-1)}\right]. \quad (5.8)$$

We then assume $\hat{\omega}^2$ to be normally distributed with this variance, and obtain confidence limits in the usual way. This approximation is poor except for large k. Probably k should be greater than 50 before the approximation ceases to be crude.

The better approximation is due to Bross [6], and the reader is referred to his article for the derivation of what strictly are known as fiducial limits. At the present level of sophistication we will regard these limits as effectively the same as confidence limits. Bross's results are that $1 - \alpha$ approximate confidence limits for $\hat{\omega}^2$ are $\underline{L}\hat{\omega}^2$, $\overline{L}\hat{\omega}^2$, where

$$\underline{L} = \frac{F/F_{1-\alpha/2} - 1}{F'_{1-\alpha/2}F/F_{1-\alpha/2} - 1}, \quad \overline{L} = \frac{F/F_{\alpha/2} - 1}{F'_{\alpha/2}F/F_{\alpha/2} - 1}. \quad (5.9)$$

where F is the observed variance ratio s_2^2/s_1^2; $F_{1-\alpha/2}$ and $F_{\alpha/2}$ have degrees of freedom the same as F, namely $k-1$ and $k(n-1)$; and $F'_{1-\alpha/2}$ and $F'_{\alpha/2}$ have degrees of freedom $k-1$ and ∞.

Frequently the observed F will be less than $F_{1-\alpha/2}$, which will make $\underline{L}$ as given in (5.9) negative: Since a component of variance cannot be negative, it is not easy to interpret a negative value for the confidence limit, and in these circumstances $\underline{L}$ may be taken as zero. Procedures for this situation are discussed in Section 7.2 of Scheffé [7]. An alternative technique is given by Williams [8].

Although we have only approximations for confidence limits for ω^2, we are able to obtain exact confidence limits for the ratio ω^2/σ^2. In the derivation of (9.3.10), s_1^2 and s_2^2 were sample estimates of σ_1^2 and σ_2^2 with f_1 and f_2 degrees of freedom. Here s_1^2 is an estimate of σ^2 with the distribution $\sigma^2\chi^2(k(n-1))/k(n-1)$ and s_2^2 is an estimate of $\sigma^2 + n\omega^2$ with the distribution $(\sigma^2 + n\omega^2)\chi^2(k-1)/(k-1)$. The arguments of (9.3.10) are valid here; so, substituting s_2^2 here for the s_1^2 in (9.3.10) and vice versa, we have

$$\Pr\left\{\frac{s_2^2}{s_1^2}\frac{1}{F_{P_2}(k-1, k(n-1))} < \frac{\sigma^2 + n\omega^2}{\sigma^2} < \frac{s_2^2}{s_1^2}F_{1-P_1}(k(n-1), k-1)\right\}$$

$$= P_2 - P_1, \quad (5.10)$$

SECT. 10.5 INTERPRETATION OF A MODEL II ANALYSIS

which rearranges to

$$\Pr\left\{\frac{1}{n}\left[\frac{s_2^2}{s_1^2}\frac{1}{F_{P_2}(k-1,k(n-1))}-1\right]<\frac{\omega^2}{\sigma^2}\right.$$

$$\left.<\frac{1}{n}\left[\frac{s_2^2}{s_1^2}F_{1-P_1}(k(n-1),k-1)-1\right]\right\}$$

$$=P_2-P_1 \qquad (5.11)$$

If the observed variance ratio s_2^2/s_1^2 is less than F_{P_2}, then the lower confidence limit will be negative. Since both ω^2 and σ^2 can never be negative, their ratio can never be negative, and zero might be substituted for the negative confidence limit. Scheffé (Section 7.2 of [7]) suggests nevertheless that the unmodified results of (5.11) give a more informative picture.

It is interesting to note what can happen if we are presented with kn observations, without being informed that they are really k groups of n observations, and asked to calculate confidence limits for the mean. We would start by computing as s^2,

$$s^2=\sum_{i,v}^{k,n}(x_{iv}-\bar{x}_{..})^2/(kn-1). \qquad (5.12)$$

But

$$E\left[\sum_{i,v}^{k,n}(x_{iv}-\bar{x}_{..})^2\right]=E\left[n\sum_{i}^{k}(\bar{x}_{i.}-\bar{x}_{..})^2\right]+E\left[\sum_{i}^{k}\sum_{v}^{n}(x_{iv}-\bar{x}_{i.})^2\right]$$

$$=(k-1)(\sigma^2+n\omega^2)+k(n-1)\sigma^2; \qquad (5.13)$$

so

$$E[s^2]=\frac{(k-1)(\sigma^2+n\omega^2)+k(n-1)\sigma^2}{kn-1}=\frac{n(k-1)}{kn-1}\omega^2+\sigma^2, \quad (5.14)$$

and the incorrectly estimated variance of $\bar{x}_{..}$ would have expected value

$$V_{\text{inc}}[\bar{x}_{..}]=\frac{[n(k-1)/(kn-1)]\omega^2+\sigma^2}{kn}. \qquad (5.15)$$

But we saw in (5.2) that the correct variance of $\bar{x}_{..}$, say $V_{\text{cor}}[\bar{x}_{..}]$, equals

$$V_{\text{cor}}[\bar{x}_{..}]=\frac{\sigma^2+n\omega^2}{kn}. \qquad (5.16)$$

The ratio of incorrect to correct variances is the ratio of (5.15) to (5.16), which can be written in the form

$$\frac{V_{\text{inc}}[\bar{x}_{..}]}{V_{\text{cor}}[\bar{x}_{..}]}=1-\left(\frac{1-1/n}{1-1/nk}\right)\frac{1}{1+(1/n)(\sigma^2/\omega^2)}. \qquad (5.17)$$

The magnitude of the error is going to depend on the values of the various parameters and particularly on σ^2/ω^2. If $\sigma^2/\omega^2 \to \infty$, then the ratio (5.17) tends to 1, but, if $\sigma^2/\omega^2 \to 0$ and n is large, then the ratio tends to $(k-1)/(nk-1)$, which for large k will tend to $1/n$. Thus a very serious error may be made by assuming that we have kn independent observations when in point of fact we do not.

In this section we have so far made the simplification that the n_i were all equal to n. As an illustration of the difficulties that arise when this is not the case we will compute $V[\bar{x}_{..}]$. From the expression (4.6) for $\bar{x}_{..}$, we get

$$V[\bar{x}_{..}] = \left[\left(\sum_i^k n_i\right)^2\right]^{-1} \sum_i^k n_i^2 V[y_i] + \left[\left(\sum_i^k n_i\right)^2\right]^{-1} \sum_i^k n_i V[z_{iv}]$$

$$= \frac{\sum_i^k n_i^2}{\left(\sum_i^k n_i\right)^2} \omega^2 + \left(\sum_i^k n_i\right)^{-1} \sigma^2. \qquad (5.18)$$

Whereas, in the case of equal n_i, $V[\bar{x}_{..}]$ was found in (5.2) to be $(\sigma^2 + n\omega^2)/kn$, where we had a mean square, s_2^2, for estimating $\sigma^2 + n\omega^2$, here we do not have a mean square to estimate (5.18). An approximate procedure would be to insert the appropriate estimators of ω^2 and σ^2, involving s_2^2 and s_1^2, and reduce the resulting expression to a linear combination of these two mean squares, and then estimate the approximate degrees of freedom of this linear combination by (9.8.10). This is clearly an awkward business of unknown accuracy. All this trouble can be avoided by the use of equal n_i.

An alternative approach to the estimation of ξ is to use the results of Section 2.4 on the formation of weighted means of minimum variance. There we saw that $\bar{x}$ defined as $\Sigma w_i x_i / \Sigma w_i$ had minimum variance, actually $1/\Sigma w_i$, if the weights w_i were chosen as $1/\sigma_i^2$. Here, from (4.5),

$$\bar{x}_{i.} = \xi + y_i + \sum_v^{n_i} \frac{z_{iv}}{n_i}, \qquad (5.19)$$

and so

$$V[\bar{x}_{i.}] = V[y_i] + \sum_v^{n_i} \frac{V[z_{iv}]}{n_i^2} = \omega^2 + \frac{\sigma^2}{n_i}; \qquad (5.20)$$

so we might use weights based on the estimates of ω^2 and σ^2:

$$\hat{w}_i = \left(\hat{\omega}^2 + \frac{\hat{\sigma}^2}{n_i}\right)^{-1}. \qquad (5.21)$$

For the construction of approximate confidence limits for ξ, Cochran [9] suggests using $\bar{x} \pm t\sqrt{\hat{V}[\bar{x}]}$ where t is given $(k-1)$ degrees of freedom.

Cochran, in the same paper [9], also discusses how to handle the still more awkward situation where in the model

$$x_{iv} = \xi + y_i + z_{iv} \qquad (5.22)$$

the z_{iv} are distributed normally with mean zero and variances σ_i^2, i.e., where the within-group component of variance varies from group to group. This situation can arise, for example, when different laboratories determine some quantity. There is no a priori reason why the variance of the measurements within a laboratory should be the same from laboratory to laboratory. The reader is referred to Cochran's paper for details.

10.6. An Example of a Model II One-Way Analysis of Variance with Equal Group Sizes

Table 10.4 gives the measurements of a certain physical property on 88 successive sub-batches of a plastic-like material. The raw material goes through a number of stages of processing in batches, which then are

Table 10.4

Batch	1	2	3	4	5	6	7	8	9	10	11
	58	49	45	28	54	47	45	49	43	37	48
	48	41	44	55	49	45	54	47	48	43	52
	47	46	44	50	53	47	50	46	49	47	57
	65	46	44	41	52	47	57	50	47	27	51
Totals	218	182	177	174	208	186	206	192	187	154	208

Batch	12	13	14	15	16	17	18	19	20	21	22
	45	55	42	45	41	43	53	41	43	34	50
	43	42	41	43	46	42	44	43	45	34	48
	44	47	46	48	41	38	49	41	44	40	48
	44	52	50	45	30	35	52	35	46	40	48
Totals	176	196	179	181	158	158	198	160	178	148	194

split into four sub-batches, which go through several more stages of processing. In Table 10.4 each column gives the measurements on the four sub-batches from one batch. The variation was in excess of that which could be tolerated. If we suppose that the individual observations x_{iv} are represented by the model $x_{iv} = \xi + y_i + z_{iv}$, then the variance of the y_i,

ω^2, will represent the variation due to the earlier stages and the variance of the z_{iv}, σ^2, the variation due to the later stages.

The analysis of variance follows the same lines as in the model I example discussed in Section 10.2, except that the n_i being all equal to n makes the calculation slightly simpler. We need

$$A = \sum_i^k \sum_v^n x_{iv}^2 = 58^2 + 48^2 + \cdots + 48^2 = 186{,}922,$$

$$B = \frac{1}{n} \sum_i^k \left(\sum_v^n x_{iv} \right)^2 = \frac{1}{4}(218^2 + 182^2 + \cdots 194^2) = 185{,}378.$$

$$C = \frac{1}{kn} \left(\sum_i^k \sum_v^n x_{iv} \right)^2 = \frac{(4018)^2}{22 \times 4} = 183{,}458.227.$$

With these figures we construct Table 10.5.

Table 10.5

Source of variance	Sums of squares	Degrees of freedom	Mean squares	[EM. S.]
Between batches	$B - C = 1919.773$	21	91.418	$\sigma^2 + 4\omega^2$
Between sub-batches	$A - B = 1544.000$	66	23.394	σ^2
Total	$A - C = 3463.733$	87		

The succeeding analysis runs as follows. Under the null hypothesis that $\omega^2 = 0$, $s_2^2/s_1^2 = 91.418/23.394 = 3.91 \sim F(21, 66)$. The 0.9995 point of F with these degrees of freedom is 2.94, and so we reject the null hypothesis at the level of significance $\alpha = 0.0005$. The mean square $s_1^2 = 23.394$ is an estimate of σ^2, and

$$\hat{\omega}^2 = \frac{91.418 - 23.394}{4} = 17.006. \tag{6.1}$$

It appears, therefore, that the variability is arising in roughly equal amounts from the two parts of the process. Application of (9.2.2) gives (17.95, 31.97) as 90 per cent confidence limits for σ^2, as were calculated in (9.2.3). The large sample approach to confidence limits for ω^2 uses (5.8):

$$\hat{V}[\hat{\omega}^2] = \frac{2}{4^2} \left[\frac{(91.418)^2}{22 - 1} + \frac{(23.296)^2}{22(4 - 1)} \right] = 50.78; \tag{6.2}$$

so 90 per cent confidence limits for ω^2 are $17.006 \pm 1.65 \times 7.126 = (5.29, 28.7)$.

Alternatively, and better, Bross's formulas (5.9) involve
$F = 91.418/23.394 = 3.908$, $F_{0.95}(21, 66) = 1.72$, $F'_{0.95}(21, \infty) = 1.56$,
$F_{0.05}(21, 66) = 1/F_{0.95}(66, 21) = 1/1.91 = 0.5236$, $F'_{0.05}(21, \infty) = 1/F_{0.95}(\infty, 21) = 1/1.81 = 0.5525$:

$$\underline{L} = \frac{3.908/1.72 - 1}{(1.56 \times 3.908)/1.72 - 1} = 0.500,$$

$$\overline{L} = \frac{3.908/0.5236 - 1}{(0.5525 \times 3.908)/0.5236 - 1} = 2.069.$$

Since $\hat{\omega}^2 = 17.006$, the limits are $\underline{L}\hat{\omega}^2 = 0.500 \times 17.006 = 8.503$ and $\overline{L}\hat{\omega}^2 = 2.069 \times 17.006 = 35.185$. Comparing these with the cruder approximate limits, we see that the crude limits fall down particularly in being, from their very method of construction, symmetric about the point estimate $\hat{\omega}^2$.

Confidence limits for the ratio ω^2/σ^2 are obtained with (5.11). Inserting $s_2^2/s_1^2 = 91.418/23.394 = 3.91$, $k(n-1) = 22(4-1) = 66$, $k-1 = 22-1 = 21$, $F_{0.95}(21, 66) = 1.72$, $F_{0.95}(66, 21) = 1.91$, we get

$$\frac{1}{4}\left(3.91 \times \frac{1}{1.72} - 1\right) < \frac{\omega^2}{\sigma^2} < \frac{1}{4}(3.91 \times 1.91 - 1) = (0.32, 1.62).$$

This has the somewhat disagreeable implication that, though the point estimate of ω^2/σ^2 is $17.006/23.394 = 0.727$, we have determined this ratio with rather poor precision, even in spite of having quite a lot of data, since the 90 per cent confidence limits range from less than half to more than twice the point estimate.

Finally, if we wanted 90 per cent confidence limits for the grand mean, we would use (5.4), inserting $\bar{x}_{..} = 4018/88 = 45.659$, $s_2^2 = 91.418$, $kn = 88$, and using $t_{0.05}(21) = -1.721 = -t_{0.95}(21)$: $\pm t\sqrt{s_2^2/kn} = \pm 1.721\sqrt{91.418/88} = \pm 1.754$, whence the 90 per cent confidence limits for ξ are (43.9, 47.4).

10.7. An Example of Model II One-Way Analysis of Variance with Unequal Group Sizes

To illustrate a model II one-way analysis of variance with unequal group sizes we will use the data of Table 9.1, assuming that the different groups correspond to random replications. This may not actually be the case, as the groups have mirrors with identifiably different properties. For the purpose of illustrating the arithmetical procedures, however, we will assume that the mirrors were drawn at random from a large population of mirrors. A straightforward analysis of variance proceeds by obtaining from the calculations in the lower part of Table 9.1 the following quantities:

$$\sum_i^k \sum_v^{n_i} x_{iv}^2 = 124{,}531, \qquad \sum_i^k \frac{1}{n_i}\left(\sum_v^{n_i} x_{iv}\right)^2 = 102{,}339.683,$$

$$\left(\sum_i^k n_i\right)^{-1}\left(\sum_i^k \sum_v^{n_i} x_{iv}\right)^2 = \frac{(2955)^2}{89} = 98{,}112.640$$

These are inserted in the identities (2.31), (2.33), and (2.35) to give Table 10.6. The coefficient of ω^2 in the expected mean square for between groups is, by (4.10),

$$\frac{1}{k-1}\left(\sum_i^k n_i - \frac{\sum_i^k n_i^2}{\sum_i^k n_i}\right) = \frac{1}{6-1}\left(89 - \frac{1379}{89}\right) = 14.701. \qquad (7.1)$$

Table 10.6

Source of variance	Sums of squares	Degrees of freedom	Mean squares	E[M. S.]
Between groups	4,227.043	5	845.409	$\sigma^2 + 14.701\omega^2$
Within groups	22,191.317	83	267.365	σ^2
Total	26,418.360	88		

The null hypothesis that $\omega^2 = 0$ is tested by the variance ratio

$$\frac{845.409}{267.365} = 3.16.$$

Since $F_{0.975}(5, 83) = 2.72$, we reject the null hypothesis and estimate ω^2 as $(845.409 - 267.365)/14.701 = 39.320$.

To form a weighted mean with approximately minimum variance, we compute the weights $\hat{w}_i$ from (5.21). For $i = 1$ for example,

$$\hat{w}_1 = \frac{1}{39.320 + 267.365/12} = \frac{1}{61.60} = 0.016234. \qquad (7.2)$$

We then form

$$\bar{x} = \frac{\sum_i^k \hat{w}_i \bar{x}_{i.}}{\sum_i^k \hat{w}_i} = \frac{3.459562}{0.103726} = 33.353. \qquad (7.3)$$

This will have a variance estimated as

$$\hat{V}[\bar{x}] = \frac{1}{\sum_{i}^{k} \hat{w}_i} = \frac{1}{0.103726} = 9.6408. \tag{7.4}$$

Making the conservative assumption that this has the usual distribution with $k - 1 = 5$ degrees of freedom, confidence limits for ξ are $33.353 \pm 2.571\sqrt{9.6408} = 33.35 \pm 7.98$. If we made the incorrect assumption that we had 89 independent observations we would have calculated $\bar{x}_{..} = 2{,}955/89 = 33.202$ and $s^2 = 26{,}418.360/88 = 300.209$, whence $\hat{V}[\bar{x}_{..}] = 300.209/89 = 3.373$ and the confidence limits for ξ would be $33.202 \pm 1.987\sqrt{3.373} = 33.20 \pm 3.65$. The length of this (incorrect) confidence interval would thus be a serious underestimate of the better estimate, being too short by a factor of more than 2.

10.8. Simple Sampling Theory

In this section we will consider a simple sampling problem. Suppose that we wish to estimate the mean fat content of a large consignment of wool delivered in many bales. Suppose that it costs c_1 to get hold of a bale, and that once a bale is obtained it costs c_2 to take each sample. Thus if we take n samples from a bale, the cost is $c_1 + c_2 n$, and if we take n samples from each of k bales the total cost is $k(c_1 + c_2 n) = kc_1 + knc_2$. Suppose that we have to operate so that the total cost is some fixed constant, say C, and we wish to choose k and n, subject to this limitation, so that the variance of the estimated mean fat content is a minimum. In other words, we wish to minimize

$$V[\bar{x}_{..}] = \frac{\sigma^2 + n\omega^2}{kn}, \tag{8.1}$$

using the notation of (5.2), subject to the condition that

$$kc_1 + knc_2 = C. \tag{8.2}$$

Substituting for n from (8.2) in (8.1) we obtain

$$V[\bar{x}_{..}] = \frac{\omega^2}{k} + \frac{\sigma^2 c_2}{C - c_1 k}. \tag{8.3}$$

The value of k that makes this a minimum can be found by differentiating with respect to k and equating to zero:

$$\frac{dV[\bar{x}_{..}]}{dk} = -\frac{\omega^2}{k^2} + \sigma^2 c_2 \frac{(-1)(-c_1)}{(C - c_1 k)^2} = 0. \tag{8.4}$$

We can substitute knc_2 for $C - c_1 k$, from (8.2), obtaining as the optimum value of n,

$$n = \frac{\sigma \sqrt{c_1}}{\omega \sqrt{c_2}}. \tag{8.5}$$

The corresponding optimum value of k is found from (8.2). Use of these formulas requires estimates of σ and ω in addition to c_1 and c_2. The formulas will give nonintegral values for n and k and in practice it will be adequate to use the nearest integers, though of course we cannot use an n of zero.

For a full study of sampling techniques, see Cochran [10].

10.9. The Power Function of Model II One-Way Analysis of Variance

In (9.3.14) we found the power function $\pi(\phi)$ for a ratio of variances $\sigma_1^2/\sigma_2^2 = \phi$, when the null hypothesis was $\sigma_1^2 = \sigma_2^2$,

$$\pi(\phi) = \Pr\left\{F(f_1, f_2) > \frac{1}{\phi} F_{1-\alpha}(f_1, f_2)\right\}. \tag{9.1}$$

Here we are dealing with mean squares s_2^2 and s_1^2 with expected values $\sigma^2 + n\omega^2$ and σ^2: We put ϕ equal to the ratio of the expected values as before:

$$\phi = \frac{\sigma^2 + n\omega^2}{\sigma^2} = 1 + n\frac{\omega^2}{\sigma^2}. \tag{9.2}$$

The procedure is best illustrated by an example. Suppose we are using $k = 22$ groups of $n = 4$ observations, with a level of significance, $\alpha = 0.05$. Then $f_1 = 21, f_2 = 66$. We ask what is the probability of rejecting the null hypothesis when in fact $\omega^2/\sigma^2 = 3/4$. Then $\phi = 1 + 4 \times 3/4 = 4$, and $F_{0.95}(21, 66) = 1.72$, and

$$\pi\left(\frac{\omega^2}{\sigma^2} = \frac{3}{4}\right) = \Pr\left\{F(21, 66) > \frac{1}{4} \times 1.72\right\} = \Pr\{F(21, 66) > 0.43\}$$
$$= \Pr\{F(66, 21) < 2.326\}, \tag{9.3}$$

taking reciprocals and reversing the sign of the inequality. Since $\Pr\{F(66, 21) < 2.173\} = 0.975$, the power is somewhat greater than 0.975.

EXERCISES

10.1. For the data of exercise (9.7), irrespective of the outcome of that exercise:

(a) Test the null hypothesis that the mean octane number is the same in the four regions.

(b) Construct 95 per cent confidence limits for the difference in means of regions A and B (i) assuming that it had been your original intention so to do, (ii) assuming that the idea occurred to you after looking at the data.

(c) Construct 95 per cent confidence limits for the contrast defined by the difference between region A and the mean of the other three regions. Assume that this contrast was suggested by the data.

10.2. The table below gives 100 times the logarithm to the base 10 of one-tenth the throughputs listed in exercise (7.3). The logarithmic transformation is selected as it seems likely to stabilize the variance as a function of the mean: The specific form mentioned gives numbers easy to work with.

Foundry	Transformed throughputs
A	92, 78, 60, 67, 53, 66
B	83, 96, 98, 60, 99, 78, 77, 103, 93, 107
C	66, 97, 100, 96, 96

(a) Test the null hypothesis that the means of the three foundries are the same.
(b) Construct 95 per cent confidence limits for the difference between foundry A and the mean of foundries B and C, assuming (i) that this had been your original intent, and (ii) that this contrast was suggested to you by the data. Quote these limits in terms of the transformed numbers and also in terms of the original scale.

10.3. The data below give some of the results of Rosa and Dorsey ["A New Determination of the Ratio of the Electromagnetic to the Electrostatic Unit of

	Group						
	1	2	3	4		5	$\sum\limits_{i}^{k}$
	62	65	65	62	65	66	64
	64	64	64	66	63	65	65
	62	63	67	64	63	65	64
	62	62	62	64	63	66	
	65	65	65	63	61	67	
	64	63	62	62	56	66	
	65	64		64	64	69	
	62	63		64	64	70	
	62			66	65	68	
	63			64	64	69	
	64			66	64	63	
				63	65	65	
n_i	11	8	6	24		15	64
$\sum\limits_{v}^{n_i} x_{iv}$	695	509	385	1,525		992	4,106
$\sum\limits_{v}^{n_i} x_{iv}^2$	43,927	32,393	24,723	96,997		65,664	263,704

Electricity," *Bulletin of the National Bureau of Standards*, 3 (1907), 433–604] on the ratio of electromagnetic to electrostatic units of electricity, a constant which is equal to the velocity of light. The figures below have had 2.99 subtracted from them and have been multiplied by 10,000 to give numbers simple to work with. The groups correspond to successive dismantling and reassembly of the apparatus. Certain sums which may be useful are given in the lower part of the table. (a) Make a conventional analysis of variance of these data, giving the expectations of the mean squares. (b) Obtain estimates of the components of variance for within groups and between groups. Test the null hypothesis that the latter is zero. (c) Form the weighted mean which has minimum variance. (d) What is the estimated variance of this mean? (e) Supposing that all 64 observations were regarded as 64 independent observations, what would the variance of the simple mean be?

10.4. A manufacturer has been making all his product from a single large uniform batch of raw material and has achieved a reputation for uniformity of product. This reputation has brought him more business, and he now needs to consider a much larger output. The raw material is no longer obtainable in very large batches, and he must now use relatively large numbers of small batches.

He considers that he will lose his reputation for uniformity if the standard deviation of his new output exceeds by 20 per cent the standard deviation of the old. In other words, if the new standard deviation is $\sigma_{T'}$ and the old σ_T, then $\sigma_{T'}$ must not exceed $1.2\sigma_T$.

He decides to run a trial on a random sample of five batches of raw material. He is going to make a number, say n, of parts from each batch and test for batch differences with a one-way analysis of variance using α as his level of significance. (a) Suppose he chooses $n = 9$, $\alpha = 0.01$; what is the probability of his detecting a deterioration, i.e., an increase in total standard deviation of the magnitude specified above? (b) Suppose he uses $\alpha = 0.1$, what then? (c) Suppose he requires $\alpha = 0.01$ and a probability of detecting the specified deterioration in uniformity of 0.99, what should n be?

REFERENCES

1. Heyl, Paul R., "A Redetermination of the Constant of Gravitation," *Journal of Research of the Bureau of Standards*, 5 (1930), 1243–50.
2. Scheffé, H., "A Method for Judging All Contrasts in the Analysis of Variance," *Biometrika*, 40 (1953), 87–104.
3. Tukey, John W., "The Problem of Multiple Comparisons." Unpublished dittoed manuscript.
4. Pearson, E. S., and H. O. Hartley (eds.), *Biometrika Tables for Statisticians*, Vol. 1. London: Cambridge University Press, 1954.
5. Dunnett, Charles W., "A Multiple Comparison Procedure for Comparing Several Treatments with a Control," *Journal of the American Statistical Association*, 50 (1955). 1096–1121.
6. Bross, Irwin, "Fiducial Intervals for Variance Components," *Biometrics*, 6 (1950), 136–44.

7. Scheffé, Henry, *Analysis of Variance*. New York: John Wiley and Sons, 1959.
8. Williams, J. S., "A Confidence Interval for Variance Components," *Biometrika*, 49 (1962), 278–81
9. Cochran, W. G., "The Combination of Estimates from Different Experiments," *Biometrics*, 10 (1954), 101–129.
10. Cochran, William G., *Sampling Techniques*, 2nd ed. New York: John Wiley and Sons, 1963

CHAPTER 11

Simple Linear Regression

11.1. Introduction

When an investigator observes simultaneously two variables x and y, usually with good reason he plots the observations on a graph. If there is any sign of an association, he is usually seized with the impulse to fit a line, usually a straight line or, rather infrequently, a parabola or cubic. The purpose of this arithmetic penance of curve fitting is often not very clearly defined; one purpose, however, might be to predict x from a new observed y or vice versa. Another purpose is to use the route of testing the significance of the parameters of the line as a means of testing for association between x and y. The standard technique for fitting a line is known as "least squares," and the line so fitted is known as a regression line for curious historical reasons (see Section 12.5).

In this chapter we shall consider the case in which a series of values of x have been selected by the experimenter and he observes y at those values of x. The so-called independent variable x is assumed to be measured without appreciable error. The situation in which the variables x and y vary at random outside the control of the experimenter and are only observed will be discussed in the next chapter.

The present chapter is of unusual length, and some guidance to the reader is called for. Sections 11.2 and 11.3 give the usual fitting of a straight line to data by the method of least squares, and Section 11.4 is a numerical example. This is as much as is found in some elementary textbooks. Section 11.5 deals with finding confidence limits for x from an observed y. In Section 11.6 the problem of comparing two regression lines is covered. An important application of this statistical technique is to parallel-line biological assay (Section 11.7); a numerical example follows in

Section 11.8. The line discussed thus far is the two-parameter line $Y = a + b(x - \bar{x})$. In Section 11.9 the one-parameter line through the origin $Y = bx$ is described, with its use in reverse in Section 11.10. The construction of joint confidence regions for (α, β) is considered in Section 11.11. Sections 11.12 and 11.13 discuss the case where we have several observations on y at some of the x's and it becomes possible to check the line for goodness of fit. Section 11.14 extends the methods of Section 11.6, for comparing two regression lines, to the case of more than two lines: This technique is also known as the analysis of covariance as it amounts to making an analysis of variance of y adjusted for concomitant variation in x.

For a thorough review of linear regression see Acton [1].

In general we assume that we have observations y_{iv} as follows:

$$y_{11}, \ldots, y_{1n_1} \quad \text{at } x_1, \quad y_{i1}, \ldots, y_{in_i} \quad \text{at } x_i, \qquad (1.1)$$

where $i = 1, \ldots, k$. If all the $n_i = 1$, so that there is only one observation on y at each x, we have a special, and important case, for which the analysis, both theoretical and arithmetical, is simpler. We will therefore deal with this case first. The general case, where all the n_i are not equal to 1, can always be treated as the special case by merely ignoring the fact that some of the x_i happen to be identical. For example, if $n_1 = 2$, $n_2 = 3$ and $n_3 = 1$, we can regard the observations

$$(y_{11}, x_1), (y_{12}, x_1), (y_{21}, x_2), (y_{22}, x_2), (y_{23}, x_2), (y_{31}, x_3) \qquad (1.2)$$

as

$$(y_1, x_1), (y_2, x_2), (y_3, x_3), (y_4, x_4), (y_5, x_5), (y_6, x_6). \qquad (1.3)$$

The fact that in this second set of observations $x_1 = x_2$, etc., can in general be disregarded. The only case in which it would matter is where all the x's are identical; then it is obviously meaningless to attempt to fit a line.

For the present we will deal with the simpler situation and suppose that we have observations (x_i, y_i), $i = 1, \ldots, k$. Except where otherwise obvious or explicitly stated, all summation operations, $\sum_i^k$, will be over $i = 1, \ldots, k$, and so we will omit the index of the summation and write merely Σ.

11.2. The Model

We assume that y is distributed normally about an expected value η with variance σ^2, and that all observations are independent. We further assume that η is a simple linear function of x:

$$\eta = \alpha + \beta(x - \bar{x}). \qquad (2.1)$$

The problem is to obtain, from the data, sample estimates a, b and s^2 of α, β and σ^2 and to determine the distribution of these estimates. The estimated regression equation is

$$Y = a + b(x - \bar{x}) \tag{2.2}$$

where $\bar{x} = \sum x_i/k$. We write (2.1) and (2.2) in the forms given rather than as $\eta = \alpha' + \beta x$, $Y = a' + bx$ because in this latter form a', b are dependent whereas in the form (2.2) a, b are independent, and this property is convenient when we come to consider $V[Y]$.

The standard method of estimation in regression is the *method of least squares*; this is to use those values of a, b which will minimize the sum of squares of deviations, say R, between the observed values y_i and the predictions Y_i given by inserting the values of x_i in the estimated equation (2.2). Thus we minimize

$$R = \sum (y_i - Y_i)^2 = \sum [y_i - a - b(x_i - \bar{x})]^2. \tag{2.3}$$

The method of least squares appears to be largely due to Gauss. As far as estimation of the parameters is concerned, it does not require the assumption of normality, but this assumption is necessary for construction of confidence intervals for or tests of hypotheses about the parameters. With the assumption of normality, the method of maximum likelihood gives results identical with those of the method of least squares. The method of least squares has the desirable properties that the estimators it gives are unbiased and, among all unbiased linear estimators, have minimum variance. Detailed discussions have been given by David and Neyman [2] and Plackett [3].

To find the values of a and b that minimize R we differentiate (2.3) with respect to a and b and equate to zero:

$$\frac{\partial R}{\partial a} = -2 \sum [y_i - a - b(x_i - \bar{x})] = 0, \tag{2.4}$$

$$\frac{\partial R}{\partial b} = -2 \sum [y_i - a - b(x_i - \bar{x})](x_i - \bar{x}) = 0. \tag{2.5}$$

These two equations can be written as

$$\sum (y_i - Y_i) = 0, \tag{2.6}$$

$$\sum (y_i - Y_i)(x_i - \bar{x}) = 0. \tag{2.7}$$

Rearranging (2.4) and (2.5) gives

$$ka + b \sum (x_i - \bar{x}) = \sum y_i, \tag{2.8}$$

$$a \sum (x_i - \bar{x}) + b \sum (x_i - \bar{x})^2 = \sum (x_i - \bar{x}) y_i. \tag{2.9}$$

SECT. 11.2 THE MODEL

Since $\sum (x_i - \bar{x}) = 0$, we have as estimators for α and β:

$$a = \frac{\sum y_i}{k} = \bar{y}, \tag{2.10}$$

$$b = \frac{\sum (x_i - \bar{x})y_i}{\sum (x_i - \bar{x})^2}. \tag{2.11}$$

The numerator of this expression for b can be written slightly differently: Since $\sum (x_i - \bar{x}) = 0$, then $\bar{y} \sum (x_i - \bar{x}) = 0$, and

$$\sum (x_i - \bar{x})y_i = \sum (x_i - \bar{x})y_i - \bar{y} \sum (x_i - \bar{x}) = \sum (x_i - \bar{x})(y_i - \bar{y}). \tag{2.12}$$

Thus an alternative form for b is

$$b = \frac{\sum (x_i - \bar{x})(y_i - \bar{y})}{\sum (x_i - \bar{x})^2}. \tag{2.13}$$

We can readily check that b is an unbiased estimator of β. We assumed that the expected value of y_i was η_i, given by (2.1) with $x = x_i$. Then

$$E[b] = \frac{\sum (x_i - \bar{x})E[y_i]}{\sum (x_i - \bar{x})^2} = \frac{\sum (x_i - \bar{x})[\alpha + \beta(x_i - \bar{x})]}{\sum (x_i - \bar{x})^2}$$

$$= \alpha \frac{\sum (x_i - \bar{x})}{\sum (x_i - \bar{x})^2} + \beta \frac{\sum (x_i - \bar{x})^2}{\sum (x_i - \bar{x})^2} = \beta. \tag{2.14}$$

The variances of a and b can be obtained directly, for inspection of (2.10) and (2.11) shows that they are linear functions of the y_i, which are assumed to be independent and have a normal distribution with variance σ^2:

$$V[a] = V\left[\frac{\sum y_i}{k}\right] = \frac{1}{k^2} \sum V[y_i] = \frac{\sigma^2}{k}, \tag{2.15}$$

$$V[b] = V\left[\frac{\sum (x_i - \bar{x})y_i}{\sum (x_i - \bar{x})^2}\right] = \frac{\sum (x_i - \bar{x})^2 V[y_i]}{[\sum (x_i - \bar{x})^2]^2} = \frac{\sigma^2}{\sum (x_i - \bar{x})^2}. \tag{2.16}$$

We will defer the estimation of σ^2 to the next section.

A demonstration that in general the method of least squares produces estimators of smallest variance among all unbiased linear estimators is somewhat involved [2, 3], but it is often quite easy to show that a least squares estimator, when it has been obtained, is of minimum variance.

We shall show that the estimator b (2.11) has the smallest variance of all unbiased linear estimators. Suppose that there exists an alternative linear estimator b',

$$b' = \sum c_i y_i. \tag{2.17}$$

We have
$$E[b'] = \sum c_i E[y_i] = \sum c_i[\alpha + \beta(x_i - \bar{x})] = \alpha \sum c_i + \beta \sum (x_i - \bar{x})c_i. \quad (2.18)$$

For b' to be an unbiased estimator, so that $E[b'] = \beta$, we require
$$\sum c_i = 0, \quad (2.19)$$
$$\sum (x_i - \bar{x})c_i = 1. \quad (2.20)$$

The variance of this alternative estimator b' is
$$V[b'] = \sum c_i^2 V[y_i] = \sigma^2 \sum c_i^2 = \sigma^2 \sum \left[c_i - \frac{x_i - \bar{x}}{\sum (x_i - \bar{x})^2} + \frac{x_i - \bar{x}}{\sum (x_i - \bar{x})^2} \right]^2$$
$$= \sigma^2 \sum \left[c_i - \frac{x_i - \bar{x}}{\sum (x_i - \bar{x})^2} \right]^2 + \sigma^2 \frac{\sum (x_i - \bar{x})^2}{[\sum (x_i - \bar{x})^2]^2}, \quad (2.21)$$

since the cross product term is zero, for
$$\sum \left[c_i - \frac{x_i - \bar{x}}{\sum (x_i - \bar{x})^2} \right] \frac{(x_i - \bar{x})}{\sum (x_i - \bar{x})^2} = \frac{\sum c_i(x_i - \bar{x})}{\sum (x_i - \bar{x})^2} - \frac{\sum (x_i - \bar{x})^2}{[\sum (x_i - \bar{x})^2]^2} = 0, \quad (2.22)$$

using (2.20). Thus
$$V[b'] = \sigma^2 \sum \left[c_i - \frac{x_i - \bar{x}}{\sum (x_i - \bar{x})^2} \right]^2 + \frac{\sigma^2}{\sum (x_i - \bar{x})^2}, \quad (2.23)$$

in which the last term is a constant. Hence to minimize $V[b']$ we can only make adjustments to the first term; by putting
$$c_i = \frac{x_i - \bar{x}}{\sum (x_i - \bar{x})^2} \quad (2.24)$$

we make the first term zero and hence make $V[b']$ a minimum. But, with this value of c_i, our alternative estimator (2.17) is
$$b' = \sum c_i y_i = \frac{\sum (x_i - \bar{x})y_i}{\sum (x_i - \bar{x})^2} \quad (2.25)$$

which is our original least squares estimator b (2.11). Therefore $b' = b$, and b is the minimum variance unbiased linear estimator. Incidentally, from (2.23) we see that when c_i is given the value in (2.24) $V[b] = \sigma^2/\sum (x_i - \bar{x})^2$, as found earlier in (2.16).

11.3. An Analysis of Variance Representation

We will now consider regression analysis from the point of view of analysis of variance. From this approach we will obtain the variances of

SECT. 11.3 AN ANALYSIS OF VARIANCE REPRESENTATION

a and b (which we have already found directly), and in addition we will be able to show that a and b are independent of each other and of s^2, our estimate of σ^2.

The deviation of an observation y_i from the value predicted by the true regression equation (2.1) can be written as

$$\begin{aligned} y_i - \eta_i &= (y_i - Y_i) + (Y_i - \eta_i) \\ &= (y_i - Y_i) + [a + b(x_i - \bar{x}) - \{\alpha + \beta(x_i - \bar{x})\}] \\ &= (y_i - Y_i) + (a - \alpha) + (b - \beta)(x_i - \bar{x}). \end{aligned} \quad (3.1)$$

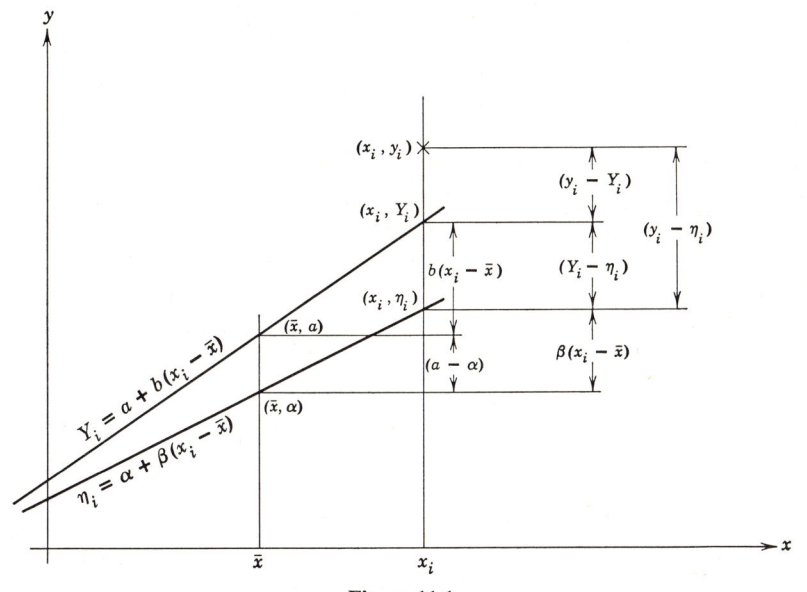

Figure 11.1

This equation is represented graphically in Figure 11.1. Squaring and summing over i gives

$$\sum (y_i - \eta_i)^2 = k(a - \alpha)^2 + (b - \beta)^2 \sum (x_i - \bar{x})^2 + \sum (y_i - Y_i)^2, \quad (3.2)$$

using (2.6) and (2.7) to show that two of the cross products are zero. On the left-hand side of (3.2), $\sum (y_i - \eta_i)^2$ is a sum of squares with k degrees of freedom and distributed as $\sigma^2 \chi^2(k)$. It is partitioned into three components. The first and second each involve one variable, a and b respectively, and will each have one degree of freedom. The third involves k variables $y_i - Y_i$, but these are subject to the two restrictions (2.6) and (2.7), so the degrees of freedom are $k - 2$. Thus the sum of the three sums of squares on the right-hand side of (3.2) equals the sum of squares on the left-hand side, and the degrees of freedom likewise, so by Cochran's theorem the sums of squares on the right-hand side are distributed as $\sigma^2 \chi^2$ with the corresponding degrees of freedom and are independent. Since $\Sigma (y_i - Y_i)^2$ is distributed as $\sigma^2 \chi^2 (k-2)$, s^2, defined as

$$s^2 = \frac{1}{k-2} \Sigma (y_i - Y_i)^2, \tag{3.3}$$

will be distributed as $\sigma^2 \chi^2 (k-2)/(k-2)$, will have expected value σ^2, and will be independent of a and b. Also, since $k(a-\alpha)^2$ is distributed as $\sigma^2 \chi^2(1)$ it has expected value σ^2, and therefore

$$V[a] = E[(a - \alpha)^2] = \frac{\sigma^2}{k}. \tag{3.4}$$

By a similar argument, $V[b] = \sigma^2 / \Sigma (x_i - \bar{x})^2$. We can make a test of the null hypothesis $\beta = 0$ by substituting s^2 for σ^2 in the expression for $V[b]$. Alternatively, since the last two terms on the right-hand side of (3.2) are independent and have distributions $\sigma^2 \chi^2(1)$, $\sigma^2 \chi^2(k-2)$ respectively, we have that

$$\frac{(b-\beta)^2 \Sigma (x_i - \bar{x})^2}{s^2} \sim F(1, k-2). \tag{3.5}$$

Thus under the null hypothesis $\beta = 0$,

$$\frac{b^2 \Sigma (x_i - \bar{x})^2}{s^2} \sim F(1, k-2). \tag{3.6}$$

To calculate the numerator of s^2, (3.3), we usually use an identity obtained as follows. We note that

$$Y_i - \bar{y} = [a + b(x_i - \bar{x})] - a = b(x_i - \bar{x}), \tag{3.7}$$

so by (2.7)

$$\Sigma (y_i - Y_i)(Y_i - \bar{y}) = b \Sigma (y_i - Y_i)(x_i - \bar{x}) = 0. \tag{3.8}$$

Thus when we square and sum over i the identity

$$y_i - \bar{y} = (y_i - Y_i) + (Y_i - \bar{y}), \tag{3.9}$$

the cross product is zero. Therefore

$$\Sigma (y_i - \bar{y})^2 = \Sigma (y_i - Y_i)^2 + \Sigma (Y_i - \bar{y})^2. \tag{3.10}$$

This equation is entered in the second column of Table 11.1.

SECT. 11.3 AN ANALYSIS OF VARIANCE REPRESENTATION

To calculate $\Sigma (Y_i - \bar{y})^2$, known as the sum of squares due to regression, we use (3.7):

$$\Sigma (Y_i - \bar{y})^2 = b^2 \Sigma (x_i - \bar{x})^2 = b \Sigma (x_i - \bar{x})(y_i - \bar{y}) \quad (3.11)$$

$$= \frac{[\Sigma (x_i - \bar{x})(y_i - \bar{y})]^2}{\Sigma (x_i - \bar{x})^2}. \quad (3.12)$$

Table 11.1

Source of variance	Degrees of freedom	Sums of squares	Mean squares	$E[\text{M. S.}]$
Due to regression	1	$\Sigma(Y_i - \bar{y})^2$	s_2^2	$\sigma^2 + \beta^2 \Sigma(x_i - \bar{x})^2$
Remainder	$k - 2$	$\Sigma(y_i - Y_i)^2$	s^2	σ^2
Total	$k - 1$	$\Sigma(y_i - \bar{y})^2$		

The other term on the right-hand side of (3.10), $\Sigma (y_i - Y_i)^2$, is the sum of squares of deviations of observed values about the estimated line, and is commonly known as the *residual* or *remainder* sum of squares. It is, of course, the numerator of s^2 defined as in (3.3). Using (3.10) and (3.12), it can be calculated as

$$\Sigma (y_i - Y_i)^2 = \Sigma (y_i - \bar{y})^2 - \frac{[\Sigma (x_i - \bar{x})(y_i - \bar{y})]^2}{\Sigma (x - \bar{x})^2}. \quad (3.13)$$

To find the expected value of s_2^2 defined as in Table 11.1, we note that $(b - \beta)^2 \Sigma (x_i - \bar{x})^2$ is distributed as $\sigma^2 \chi^2(1)$ and hence has expected value σ^2. Thus

$$\sigma^2 = \Sigma (x_i - \bar{x})^2 E[b^2] - 2\beta \Sigma (x_i - \bar{x})^2 E[b] + \beta^2 \Sigma (x_i - \bar{x})^2. \quad (3.14)$$

Now from (2.14), $E[b] = \beta$, and from (3.11),

$$\Sigma (x_i - \bar{x})^2 E[b^2] = E[\Sigma (Y_i - \bar{y})^2]. \quad (3.15)$$

Thus substituting in (3.14) and rearranging,

$$E[\Sigma (Y_i - \bar{y})^2] = \sigma^2 + \beta^2 \Sigma (x_i - \bar{x})^2 \quad (3.16)$$

$$= \sigma^2 \left(1 + \frac{\beta^2}{V[b]}\right). \quad (3.17)$$

The latter form makes it clear that $E[s_2^2]$ is a function of the ratio of β^2 to the variance of b.

Using (2.2) for Y, (2.15) and (2.16) for $V[a]$ and $V[b]$, and the fact that a and b have zero covariance, we can write, for any fixed x,

$$V[Y] = V[a + b(x - \bar{x})] = V[a] + (x - \bar{x})^2 V[b]$$
$$= \sigma^2 \left[\frac{1}{k} + \frac{(x - \bar{x})^2}{\sum(x_i - \bar{x})^2} \right]. \qquad (3.18)$$

The expected value of Y is $\alpha + \beta(x - \bar{x}) = \eta$. Y is a linear function of a and b, and a and b are linear functions of the y_i which are normally distributed. So Y is normally distributed; inserting s^2 for σ^2 in (3.18), we have

$$\frac{Y - \eta}{\sqrt{\hat{V}[Y]}} \sim t(k - 2). \qquad (3.19)$$

This gives confidence limits for η, the true value at some specified x:

$$\Pr\{Y - t_{P_2}\sqrt{\hat{V}[Y]} < \eta < Y - t_{P_1}\sqrt{\hat{V}[Y]}\} = P_2 - P_1. \qquad (3.20)$$

A new single observation at x will be distributed about η, with a variance σ^2, independently of Y, so

$$E[y - Y] = E[y] - E[Y] = \eta - \eta = 0, \qquad (3.21)$$

$$V[y - Y] = V[y] + V[Y] = \sigma^2 \left[1 + \frac{1}{k} + \frac{(x - \bar{x})^2}{\sum(x_i - \bar{x})^2} \right], \qquad (3.22)$$

and

$$\frac{y - Y}{\sqrt{\hat{V}[y - Y]}} \sim t(k - 2). \qquad (3.23)$$

Thus we have the conclusion

$$\Pr\{Y + t_{P_1}\sqrt{\hat{V}[y - Y]} < y < Y + t_{P_2}\sqrt{\hat{V}[y - Y]}\} = P_2 - P_1. \qquad (3.24)$$

This resembles a confidence interval statement, but differs, for whereas a confidence interval statement is an interval for a parameter, (3.24) is an interval for a random variable y. The interval (3.24) is known as a *prediction interval* and represents the limits between which we are $P_2 - P_1$ confident that a new single observation y taken at the specified x will lie. The interval (3.20) represents the limits between which we are $P_2 - P_1$ confident that the true value of the parameter will lie.

11.4. An Example of Linear Regression

The data of Table 11.2 (personal communication from Dr. D. W. Cugel), plotted in Figure 11.2, give the results of an experiment to determine the

AN EXAMPLE OF LINEAR REGRESSION

Table 11.2

x_i	y_i	x_i	y_i	x_i	y_i
1190	1115	1900	1830	2720	2630
1455	1425	1920	1920	2710	2740
1550	1515	1960	1970	2530	2390
1730	1795	2295	2300	2900	2800
1745	1715	2335	2280	2760	2630
1770	1710	2490	2520	3010	2970

behavior of a method of measuring blood flow. The y_i are rates of flow estimated by this method for a series of x_i; the x_i were accurately determined by a direct method.

We need the following:

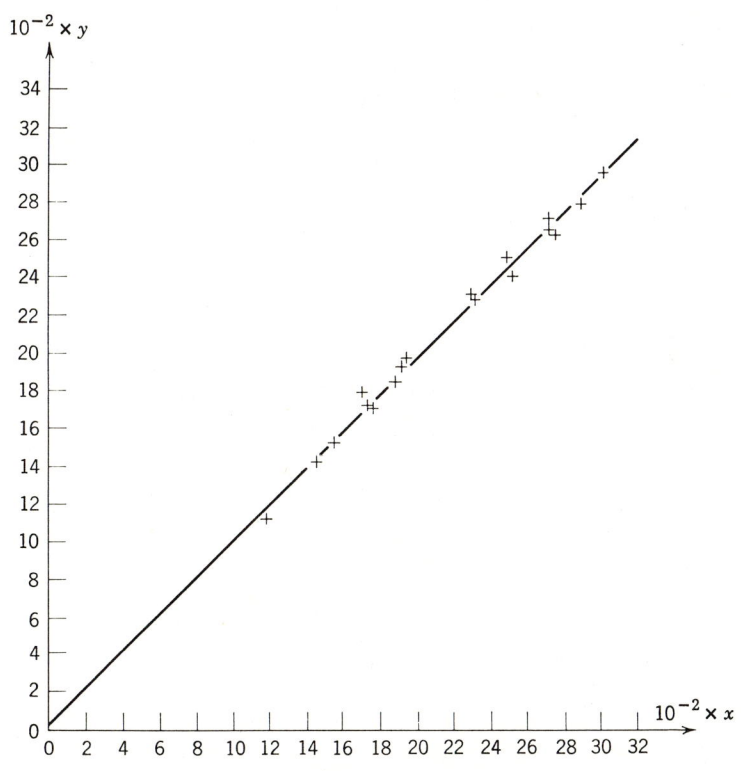

$\sum x_i = 38{,}970,$ $\qquad \sum y_i = 38{,}255,$ $\qquad k = 18,$

$\sum x_i^2 = 89{,}394{,}900,$ $\qquad \sum y_i^2 = 86{,}125{,}825,$ $\qquad \sum x_i y_i = 87{,}719{,}100,$

Figure 11.2

from which we derive

$$\sum (x_i - \bar{x})^2 = \sum x_i^2 - \frac{(\sum x_i)^2}{k} = 89{,}394{,}900 - \frac{(38{,}970)^2}{18} = 5{,}024{,}850,$$

$$\sum (y_i - \bar{y})^2 = \sum y_i^2 - \frac{(\sum y_i)^2}{k} = 86{,}125{,}825 - \frac{(38{,}255)^2}{18} = 4{,}823{,}323.6,$$

$$\sum (x_i - \bar{x})(y_i - \bar{y}) = \sum x_i y_i - \frac{\sum x_i \sum y_i}{k}$$

$$= 87{,}719{,}100 - \frac{38{,}970 \times 38{,}255}{18} = 4{,}897{,}025.0.$$

The sum of squares due to regression is, from (3.12),

$$\sum (Y_i - \bar{y})^2 = \frac{(4{,}897{,}025.0)^2}{5{,}024{,}850.0} = 4{,}772{,}451.7. \qquad (4.1)$$

We can now assemble Table 11.3, finding the residual sum of squares by difference [see (3.13)].

Table 11.3

Source of variance	Sums of squares	Degrees of freedom	Mean squares	E[M. S.]
Due to regression	4,772,451.7	1	4,772,451.7	$\sigma^2 + \beta^2 \Sigma(x_i - \bar{x})^2$
Residual	50,871.9	16	3,179.49	σ^2
Total	4,823,323.6	17		

Under the null hypothesis $\beta = 0$ the variance ratio $4{,}772{,}451.7/3179.49 = 1501.0$ is distributed as $F(1, 16)$. Here the result is obviously significant. An alternative test would be to use the fact that

$$\frac{b - \beta}{\sqrt{\hat{V}[b]}} \sim t(k - 2), \qquad (4.2)$$

for which we need b, from (2.13),

$$b = \frac{\sum (x_i - \bar{x})(y_i - \bar{y})}{\sum (x_i - \bar{x})^2} = \frac{4{,}897{,}025.0}{5{,}024{,}850.0} = 0.974561, \qquad (4.3)$$

and $\hat{V}[b]$, which we get by replacing σ^2 in (2.16) by s^2:

$$\hat{V}[b] = \frac{s^2}{\sum (x_i - \bar{x})^2} = \frac{3179.49}{5{,}024{,}850.0} = 6.32753 \times 10^{-4}. \qquad (4.4)$$

SECT. 11.4 AN EXAMPLE OF LINEAR REGRESSION

A test of the null hypothesis that $\beta = 0$ is given by

$$\frac{b - 0}{\sqrt{\hat{V}[b]}} = \frac{0.974561 - 0}{\sqrt{6.32753 \times 10^{-4}}} = 38.74, \qquad (4.5)$$

which will be distributed as $t(16)$. The null hypothesis obviously has to be rejected. Of course, $t^2 = (38.74)^2 = 1501.0 = F$ of the previous test.

In this particular example there is no reason to doubt the significance of the regression. A more interesting null hypothesis is that $\beta = 1$; for this, (4.2) gives

$$\frac{0.974561 - 1}{\sqrt{6.32753 \times 10^{-4}}} = -1.012, \qquad (4.6)$$

which is distributed as $t(16)$ under this null hypothesis. Clearly the null hypothesis that $\beta = 1$ can be accepted. We may wish to construct 95 per cent confidence limits for β; for these, $t_{0.975}(16) = 2.120$ and $\sqrt{\hat{V}[b]} = 0.02515$; so $t\sqrt{\hat{V}[b]} = 0.05333$, and the 95 per cent confidence limits are 0.97456 ± 0.05333 or $(0.9212, 1.028)$.

To construct the estimated regression line we need $\bar{y} = 38{,}255/18 = 2125.278$, $\bar{x} = 38{,}970/18 = 2{,}165.000$, and $b = 0.974561$, whence the estimated regression line is

$$Y = 2125.278 + 0.974561(x - 2165.000). \qquad (4.7)$$

At $x = 0$, $(Y)_{x=0} = 15.352$. From (3.18),

$$\hat{V}[(Y)_{x=0}] = 3179.49 \left[\frac{1}{18} + \frac{(0 - 2165.000)^2}{5{,}024{,}850.0} \right] = 3142.493. \qquad (4.8)$$

Under the hypothesis that $(\eta)_{x=0} = 0$, the ratio

$$\frac{15.352 - 0}{\sqrt{3142.493}} = 0.274 \qquad (4.9)$$

is distributed as $t(16)$: Clearly the null hypothesis of a zero intercept is acceptable. Confidence limits for the intercept are

$$15.352 \pm 2.120 \times \sqrt{3142.493} = (-103.5, 134.2). \qquad (4.10)$$

Let us summarize what has been so far established.

(i) The estimated regression line of y on x as given in (4.7).

(ii) 95 per cent confidence limits for the regression coefficient β are $(0.921, 1.028)$; so the null hypothesis $\beta = 1$ is acceptable.

(iii) The intercept on the y axis has 95 per cent confidence limits $(-103, 134)$; so the null hypothesis that the intercept is zero is acceptable.

(iv) The estimated variance of an observation around its true value is 3179.49, corresponding to a standard deviation of 56.83.

We might ask, if we observe a new value of y, what is our estimate of x, and what are confidence limits on the true value of x corresponding to this observed y? This question is investigated in the following section.

A further question arising from items (ii) and (iii) above is the following: While the null hypothesis that $\beta = 1$, the intercept unspecified, is acceptable, and also the null hypothesis that the intercept is zero, β being unspecified, is acceptable, is the null hypothesis that $\beta = 1$ and the intercept is zero simultaneously acceptable? This question is discussed from the testing point of view in Section 11.9 and from the confidence region point of view in Section 11.11.

11.5. The Use of the Regression Line in Reverse

Suppose that we have a regression line $Y = a + b(x - \bar{x})$, based on k observations (x_i, y_i). Suppose that we now observe a new $\bar{y}'$, the mean of m new observations known to have arisen from the same x, and we wish to predict the x corresponding to this $\bar{y}'$, and to construct confidence limits for this prediction. Of course, m may equal 1, so that we just have a single observation y'. We can solve the estimated regression equation (2.2) for x, inserting $\bar{y}'$ for Y, where $\bar{y}'$ is the mean of the new set of observations on y, to get

$$\hat{x} = \bar{x} + \frac{\bar{y}' - a}{b}, \quad (5.1)$$

a point estimate of the value of x corresponding to the new observed value $\bar{y}'$. The expected value of the new $\bar{y}'$ is $E[\bar{y}'] = \eta$. Corresponding to this value of η is a value of x given by solving the true regression equation (2.1) for x: Denote this value of x by ξ. Then

$$\xi = \bar{x} + \frac{\eta - \alpha}{\beta} \quad (5.2)$$

and

$$\eta - \alpha - \beta(\xi - \bar{x}) = 0. \quad (5.3)$$

We now define a new variable z as

$$z = \bar{y}' - a - b(\xi - \bar{x}). \quad (5.4)$$

This variable will have expected value

$$E[z] = E[\bar{y}'] - E[a] - (\xi - \bar{x})E[b] = \eta - \alpha - (\xi - \bar{x})\beta = 0 \quad (5.5)$$

by (5.3). Its variance is

$$V[z] = V[\bar{y}'] + V[a] + (\xi - \bar{x})^2 V[b] = \frac{\sigma^2}{m} + \frac{\sigma^2}{k} + (\xi - \bar{x})^2 \frac{\sigma^2}{\sum (x_i - \bar{x})^2}$$

$$= \sigma^2 \left[\frac{1}{m} + \frac{1}{k} + \frac{(\xi - \bar{x})^2}{\sum (x_i - \bar{x})^2} \right]. \quad (5.6)$$

SECT. 11.5   THE USE OF THE REGRESSION LINE IN REVERSE

The random variable z is a linear function of three random normally distributed variables $\bar{y}'$, a and b, and hence will itself be normally distributed. Thus $z/\sqrt{V[z]}$ is $N(0, 1)$, and, on replacing σ^2 in (5.6) by its estimate s^2 from (3.3), we have

$$\frac{\bar{y}' - a - b(\xi - \bar{x})}{s\sqrt{1/m + 1/k + (\xi - \bar{x})^2/\sum(x_i - \bar{x})^2}} \sim t(k - 2). \qquad (5.7)$$

We can insert the above expression in place of t in the statement $\Pr\{t_1 < t < t_2\} = P_2 - P_1$, to get confidence limits for ξ. If $\underline{\xi}$ is the lower confidence limit, it is given by the equation

$$\frac{\bar{y}' - a - b(\underline{\xi} - \bar{x})}{s\sqrt{1/m + 1/k + (\underline{\xi} - \bar{x})^2/\sum(x_i - \bar{x})^2}} = t_2, \qquad (5.8)$$

where t_2 is the P_2 point of t with the degrees of freedom of s, namely $k - 2$. Squaring and expanding and collecting terms in $\underline{\xi}^2$, $\underline{\xi}$, we get a quadratic equation in $\underline{\xi}$:

$$\underline{\xi}^2\left[b^2 - \frac{t_2^2 s^2}{\sum(x_i - \bar{x})^2}\right] + 2\underline{\xi}\left[\frac{t_2^2 s^2}{\sum(x_i - \bar{x})^2}\bar{x} - b^2\bar{x} - b(\bar{y}' - a)\right]$$
$$+ (\bar{y}' - a + b\bar{x})^2 - t_2^2 s^2\left[\frac{1}{m} + \frac{1}{k} + \frac{\bar{x}^2}{\sum(x_i - \bar{x})^2}\right] = 0. \qquad (5.9)$$

Using the usual formula for the solution to a quadratic equation, using the negative sign for the square root term, we get

$$\underline{\xi} = \bar{x} + \frac{b(\bar{y}' - a)}{b^2 - t_2^2 s^2/\sum(x_i - \bar{x})^2} - \frac{t_2 s}{b^2 - t_2^2 s^2/\sum(x_i - \bar{x})^2}$$
$$\times\left\{\left[b^2 - \frac{t_2^2 s^2}{\sum(x_i - \bar{x})^2}\right]\left(\frac{1}{m} + \frac{1}{k}\right) + \frac{(\bar{y}' - a)^2}{\sum(x_i - \bar{x})^2}\right\}^{1/2}. \qquad (5.10)$$

The upper confidence limit $\bar{\xi}$ is obtained in the identical manner, using t_1 in place of t_2, and the solution is the same as (5.10) with this change.

Now let us suppose that we choose P_1 and P_2 so that the limits are symmetric in probability, i.e., $t_1 = t_{\alpha/2}$, $t_2 = t_{1-\alpha/2}$, and where there is no danger of confusion we will omit the suffix on the t's.

The behavior of (5.10) is determined by the quantity we define as g:

$$g = \left(\frac{t}{b/\sqrt{V[b]}}\right)^2 = \frac{t^2 s^2}{b^2 \sum(x_i - \bar{x})^2}. \qquad (5.11)$$

First, suppose that $g < 1$. Then

$$\left|\frac{b}{\sqrt{V[b]}}\right| > t, \qquad (5.12)$$

and so b is significantly different from zero at the level of significance α when tested against the two-sided alternative. Also, when $g < 1$,

$$b^2 - \frac{t^2 s^2}{\sum (x_i - \bar{x})^2} > 0, \tag{5.13}$$

so the quantity under the square root sign in (5.10), say Q, is positive and we obtain a real solution for ξ.

Second, suppose that $g > 1$. Then in (5.12) the inequality sign is reversed and b is not significantly different from zero. Also, the inequality sign in (5.13) is reversed. We will get imaginary solutions to (5.11) if $Q < 0$, i.e., if

$$\left[b^2 - \frac{t^2 s^2}{\sum (x_i - \bar{x})^2}\right]\left(\frac{1}{m} + \frac{1}{k}\right) + \frac{(\bar{y}' - a)^2}{\sum (x_i - \bar{x})^2} < 0, \tag{5.14}$$

i.e., if

$$|\bar{y}' - a| < \left\{\sum (x_i - \bar{x})^2 \left[\frac{t^2 s^2}{\sum (x_i - \bar{x})^2} - b^2\right]\left(\frac{1}{m} + \frac{1}{k}\right)\right\}^{1/2}. \tag{5.15}$$

Thus if $\bar{y}'$ is rather close to $a = \bar{y}$, the confidence limits are imaginary, i.e., $(-\infty, \infty)$. However, if $\bar{y}'$ is rather far from $a = \bar{y}$, then the inequality in (5.15) is reversed, and then $Q > 0$ and (5.10) gives real solutions.

Thirdly, if g is small, say $g < 0.1$, then

$$b^2 - \frac{t^2 s^2}{\sum (x_i - \bar{x})^2} = b^2\left[1 - \frac{t^2 s^2}{b^2 \sum (x_i - \bar{x})^2}\right] = b^2(1 - g) \simeq b^2, \tag{5.16}$$

and (5.10) and its analog for $\bar{\xi}$ become

$$\xi \simeq \bar{x} + \frac{\bar{y}' - a}{b} - \frac{t_2 s}{|b|}\left[\left(\frac{1}{m} + \frac{1}{k}\right) + \frac{(\bar{y}' - a)^2}{b^2 \sum (x_i - \bar{x})^2}\right]^{1/2} \tag{5.17}$$

$$\bar{\xi} \simeq \bar{x} + \frac{\bar{y}' - a}{b} - \frac{t_1 s}{|b|}\left[\left(\frac{1}{m} + \frac{1}{k}\right) + \frac{(\bar{y}' - a)^2}{b^2 \sum (x_i - \bar{x})^2}\right]^{1/2} \tag{5.18}$$

as approximate confidence limits for ξ. These are usually considered valid for most purposes when $g < 0.1$.

To illustrate these results, suppose that in the example of Section 11.4 we observe a single new observation $y = 3000$. To construct 95 per cent confidence limits for ξ we need $t_{0.975} = -t_{0.025}$. For that example $s^2 = 3179.49$, $b = 0.974561$, $\sum (x_i - \bar{x})^2 = 5{,}024{,}850$. Inserting these values in (5.11) we obtain $g = 0.00299$, which permits use of the approximations

SECT. 11.6   THE COMPARISON OF TWO REGRESSION LINES   349

(5.17) and (5.18). The 95 per cent confidence limits for ξ are

$$2165.000 + \frac{3000.000 - 2125.277}{0.974561}$$

$$\pm \frac{2.120\sqrt{3179.49}}{0.974561} \left[\left(\frac{1}{1} + \frac{1}{18}\right) + \frac{(3000.000 - 2125.277)^2}{(0.974561)^2 \times 5{,}024{,}850} \right]^{1/2}$$

$$= 3062.5 \pm 135.2.$$

Thus if we observe a flow rate of 3000 by our new method, we can be 95 per cent confident that the true flow rate is in the interval (2927, 3198).

11.6. The Comparison of Two Regression Lines

We suppose that we have two sets of observations, (x_{iv}, y_{iv}), $i = 1, 2$, $v = 1, \ldots, n_i$:

$$(x_{11}, y_{11}), (x_{12}, y_{12}), \ldots, (x_{1n_1}, y_{1n_1})$$

and

$$(x_{21}, y_{21}), (x_{22}, y_{22}), \ldots, (x_{2n_2}, y_{2n_2}).$$

We will discuss the procedure for deciding whether a single common regression line is an adequate fit, or whether separate regression lines

$$\begin{aligned} Y_1 &= a_1 + b_1(x - \bar{x}_1) \\ Y_2 &= a_2 + b_2(x - \bar{x}_2) \end{aligned} \quad (6.1)$$

are necessary.

We start by fitting separate lines, obtaining estimates a_i, b_i and s_i^2, $i = 1, 2$. If the lines are identical, the s_i^2 will be estimates of a common σ^2, and their ratio will be distributed as F. It is easier to put the larger s_i^2 in the numerator of the variance ratio; a two-sided test will usually be appropriate. If the null hypothesis is rejected, then the lines differ in this regard, but further examination is difficult because the dissimilar variances involve the Behrens–Fisher problem. If the null hypothesis of a common residual variance is accepted, we can form a joint estimate of σ^2 [cf. (9.7.6)],

$$s^2 = \frac{(n_1 - 2)s_1^2 + (n_2 - 2)s_2^2}{n_1 - 2 + n_2 - 2}. \quad (6.2)$$

If the null hypothesis $\beta_1 - \beta_2 = 0$ is true, $b_1 - b_2$ will be normally distributed about 0 with a variance

$$V[b_1 - b_2] = V[b_1] + V[b_2] = \frac{\sigma^2}{\sum\limits_{v}^{n_1}(x_{1v} - \bar{x}_1)^2} + \frac{\sigma^2}{\sum\limits_{v}^{n_2}(x_{2v} - \bar{x}_2)^2} \quad (6.3)$$

where σ^2 will be estimated by (6.2). Thus under the null hypothesis, $\beta_1 - \beta_2 = 0$,

$$\frac{b_1 - b_2}{s\left\{\left[\sum_{\nu}^{n_1}(x_{1\nu} - \bar{x}_1)^2\right]^{-1} + \left[\sum_{\nu}^{n_2}(x_{2\nu} - \bar{x}_2)^2\right]^{-1}\right\}^{1/2}} \sim t(n_1 + n_2 - 4). \quad (6.4)$$

If we reject this null hypothesis, then the lines differ in slope and hence are different. If, on the other hand, we accept this null hypothesis, then we fit a joint estimate of the common slope and proceed to test whether the lines are coincident as well as parallel.

We next need to estimate the common slope. We have two true equations for the two parallel lines,

$$\eta_1 = \alpha_1 + \beta(x - \bar{x}_1), \qquad \eta_2 = \alpha_2 + \beta(x - \bar{x}_2), \quad (6.5)$$

and two estimated equations,

$$Y_1 = a_1 + b(x - \bar{x}_1), \qquad Y_2 = a_2 + b(x - \bar{x}_2). \quad (6.6)$$

The sum of squares of deviations of the observations from the two parallel estimated lines is

$$R = \sum_{\nu}^{n_1}(y_{1\nu} - Y_{1\nu})^2 + \sum_{\nu}^{n_2}(y_{2\nu} - Y_{2\nu})^2$$

$$= \sum_{\nu}^{n_1}[y_{1\nu} - a_1 - b(x_{1\nu} - \bar{x}_1)]^2 + \sum_{\nu}^{n_2}[y_{2\nu} - a_2 - b(x_{2\nu} - \bar{x}_2)]^2. \quad (6.7)$$

The least squares estimates are those which make this a minimum. Differentiating with respect to a_1, a_2 and b and equating to zero gives

$$\frac{\partial R}{\partial a_1} = -2\sum_{\nu}^{n_1}[y_{1\nu} - a_1 - b(x_{1\nu} - \bar{x}_1)] = 0, \quad (6.8)$$

$$\frac{\partial R}{\partial a_2} = -2\sum_{\nu}^{n_2}[y_{2\nu} - a_2 - b(x_{2\nu} - \bar{x}_2)] = 0, \quad (6.9)$$

$$\frac{\partial R}{\partial b} = -2\sum_{\nu}^{n_1}[y_{1\nu} - a_1 - b(x_{1\nu} - \bar{x}_1)](x_{1\nu} - \bar{x}_1)$$

$$-2\sum_{\nu}^{n_2}[y_{2\nu} - a_2 - b(x_{2\nu} - \bar{x}_2)](x_{2\nu} - \bar{x}_2) = 0. \quad (6.10)$$

The first two of these equations give

$$a_1 = \frac{1}{n_1}\sum_{\nu}^{n_1} y_{1\nu}, \qquad a_2 = \frac{1}{n_2}\sum_{\nu}^{n_2} y_{2\nu}, \quad (6.11)$$

SECT. 11.6 THE COMPARISON OF TWO REGRESSION LINES

and the third gives

$$b = \frac{\sum_{v}^{n_1} y_{1v}(x_{1v} - \bar{x}_1) + \sum_{v}^{n_2} y_{2v}(x_{2v} - \bar{x}_2)}{\sum_{v}^{n_1} (x_{1v} - \bar{x}_1)^2 + \sum_{v}^{n_2} (x_{2v} - \bar{x}_2)^2}. \qquad (6.12)$$

The same arguments that were used to obtain (2.16) give

$$V[b] = \frac{\sigma^2}{\sum_{i}^{2} \sum_{v}^{n_i} (x_{iv} - \bar{x}_i)^2}. \qquad (6.13)$$

To estimate σ^2 for the model (6.5), the sum of squares of deviations from the two parallel lines is given by (6.7). Inserting the solutions for a_1, a_2, and b, straightforward manipulation leads to

$$R = \left[\sum_{i}^{2}\sum_{v}^{n_i} y_{iv}^2 - \sum_{i}^{2} \frac{\left(\sum_{v}^{n_i} y_{iv}\right)^2}{n_i}\right] - \frac{\left[\sum_{i}^{2}\sum_{v}^{n_i} y_{iv}(x_{iv} - \bar{x}_i)\right]^2}{\sum_{i}^{2}\sum_{v}^{n_i}(x_{iv} - \bar{x}_i)^2}. \qquad (6.14)$$

Since we have fitted three parameters to the data, this sum of squares has $n_1 + n_2 - 3$ degrees of freedom.

We now proceed to test whether the two parallel lines are identical, i.e., lie on top of each other. If the true lines (6.5) are identical, then $\eta_1 = \eta_2$ for all x, and hence

$$\alpha_1 - \beta\bar{x}_1 = \alpha_2 - \beta\bar{x}_2, \qquad (6.15)$$

and

$$(\alpha_1 - \alpha_2) - \beta(\bar{x}_1 - \bar{x}_2) = 0. \qquad (6.16)$$

It follows that the quantity

$$(a_1 - a_2) - b(\bar{x}_1 - \bar{x}_2) \qquad (6.17)$$

will have expected value zero, and be distributed normally with variance

$$\frac{\sigma^2}{n_1} + \frac{\sigma^2}{n_2} + (\bar{x}_1 - \bar{x}_2)^2 V[b] = \sigma^2 \left[\frac{1}{n_1} + \frac{1}{n_2} + \frac{(\bar{x}_1 - \bar{x}_2)^2}{\sum_{i}^{2}\sum_{v}^{n_i}(x_{iv} - \bar{x}_i)^2}\right]. \qquad (6.18)$$

Thus, if the lines are identical,

$$\frac{(a_1 - a_2) - b(\bar{x}_1 - \bar{x}_2)}{s\left[1/n_1 + 1/n_2 + (\bar{x}_1 - \bar{x}_2)^2 \Big/ \sum_{i}^{2}\sum_{v}^{n_i}(x_{iv} - \bar{x}_i)^2\right]^{1/2}} \sim t(n_1 + n_2 - 3) \qquad (6.19)$$

where s is derived from the sum of squares in (6.14). A numerical example will be discussed in Section 11.8.

11.7. Parallel Line Biological Assay

An important application of the foregoing section is to a common form of biological assay for vitamins, hormones, etc., in which the response of the organism, usually an animal, over a certain range is linearly proportional to the logarithm of the dose. For complicated substances not readily susceptible of chemical analysis this provides a method of assaying the potency of an unknown preparation in terms of a standard.

Suppose that animals receive various known log doses x_{1v} of the standard and other animals receive various known log doses x_{2v} of the unknown. Then the responses y_1, y_2 may be fitted by two straight lines, one for the standard and one for the unknown, with common slope b:

$$Y_1 = a_1 + b(x - \bar{x}_1), \qquad Y_2 = a_2 + b(x - \bar{x}_2). \tag{7.1}$$

These lines are estimates of the corresponding true lines:

$$\eta_1 = \alpha_1 + \beta(x - \bar{x}_1), \qquad \eta_2 = \alpha_2 + \beta(x - \bar{x}_2). \tag{7.2}$$

If the basic preparations of the standard and the unknown from which the various doses of each have been prepared are of the same potency, then the two lines (7.2) will be identical, but if, e.g., the unknown is ρ times as potent as the standard then it will take $1/\rho$ units of the unknown to give the same response as is given by 1 unit of the standard. Graphically, the line for the unknown will be displaced horizontally relative to the line for the standard by an amount equal to $\log \rho = \mu$, say. Since the lines have the same slope, they are parallel, and therefore the horizontal distance between them, μ, is the same for all values of the response η. Let ξ_1 be the value of x_1 when η_1 takes some convenient value, say $(\alpha_1 + \alpha_2)/2$, and let ξ_2 be the value of x_2 when η_2 takes the same value. Then $\xi_1 - \xi_2 = \mu$, and

$$\alpha_1 + \beta(\xi_1 - \bar{x}_1) = \frac{\alpha_1 + \alpha_2}{2} = \alpha_2 + \beta(\xi_2 - \bar{x}_2), \tag{7.3}$$

whence

$$\mu = \xi_1 - \xi_2 = \bar{x}_1 - \bar{x}_2 - \frac{\alpha_1 - \alpha_2}{\beta}. \tag{7.4}$$

The difference $\xi_1 - \xi_2 = \mu$ is the difference in the logarithms of equivalent quantities of the standard and unknown; i.e., μ is the logarithm of the potency ratio, and the antilogarithm of μ, ρ, is the potency ratio.

To obtain an estimate M of μ we replace α_1, α_2 and β in (7.4) by the estimates a_1, a_2 and b. From (6.11), $a_1 = \bar{y}_1$, $a_2 = \bar{y}_2$, and b is given by (6.12):

$$M = \bar{x}_1 - \bar{x}_2 - \frac{\bar{y}_1 - \bar{y}_2}{b}. \tag{7.5}$$

SECT. 11.7 PARALLEL LINE BIOLOGICAL ASSAY

The estimated potency ratio, say r, is the antilogarithm of M. To obtain confidence limits for the logarithm of the potency ratio μ, consider the variable z defined as

$$z = -(\bar{y}_1 - \bar{y}_2) - b[(\xi_1 - \xi_2) - (\bar{x}_1 - \bar{x}_2)]. \tag{7.6}$$

Its expected value is

$$E[z] = -(\alpha_1 - \alpha_2) - \beta[(\xi_1 - \xi_2) - (\bar{x}_1 - \bar{x}_2)] = 0, \tag{7.7}$$

substituting for $\xi_1 - \xi_2$ from (7.4). The variance of z is

$$V[z] = V[\bar{y}_1] + V[\bar{y}_2] + [(\xi_1 - \xi_2) - (\bar{x}_1 - \bar{x}_2)]^2 \, V[b]$$

$$= \sigma^2 \left[\frac{1}{n_1} + \frac{1}{n_2} + \frac{[(\xi_1 - \xi_2) - (\bar{x}_1 - \bar{x}_2)]^2}{\sum\limits_i^2 \sum\limits_v^{n_i} (x_{iv} - \bar{x}_i)^2} \right]. \tag{7.8}$$

Then, substituting the sample estimate s^2 derived from (6.14) for σ^2,

$$\frac{-(\bar{y}_1 - \bar{y}_2) - b[(\xi_1 - \xi_2) - (\bar{x}_1 - \bar{x}_2)]}{s \left\{ \dfrac{1}{n_1} + \dfrac{1}{n_2} + \dfrac{[(\xi_1 - \xi_2) - (\bar{x}_1 - \bar{x}_2)]^2}{\sum\limits_i^2 \sum\limits_v^{n_i} (x_{iv} - \bar{x}_i)^2} \right\}^{1/2}} \sim t(n_1 + n_2 - 3). \tag{7.9}$$

This is similar to (5.7), with a replaced by $\bar{y}_1 - \bar{y}_2$, ξ by $\xi_1 - \xi_2$, $\bar{x}$ by $\bar{x}_1 - \bar{x}_2$, $1/k$ by $1/n_1 + 1/n_2$, and $\Sigma (x_i - \bar{x})^2$ by $\sum\limits_i^2 \sum\limits_v^{n_i} (x_{iv} - \bar{x}_i)^2$, and with $\bar{y}'$ and $1/m$ omitted. Equation (7.9) can thus be handled in the same way as (5.7). If we define g as

$$g = \frac{t^2 s^2}{b^2 \sum\limits_i^2 \sum\limits_v^{n_i} (x_{iv} - \bar{x}_i)^2}, \tag{7.10}$$

analogous to (5.11), we get as the confidence limits for $\xi_1 - \xi_2 = \mu$,

$$(\bar{x}_1 - \bar{x}_2) + \frac{-(\bar{y}_1 - \bar{y}_2)/b}{1 - g}$$

$$- \frac{ts}{b(1-g)} \left[(1-g)\left(\frac{1}{n_1} + \frac{1}{n_2}\right) + \frac{(\bar{y}_1 - \bar{y}_2)^2}{b^2 \sum\limits_i^k \sum\limits_v^{n_i} (x_{iv} - \bar{x}_i)^2} \right]^{1/2}, \tag{7.11}$$

where t takes the probability levels P_2 and P_1 to give $P_2 - P_1$ confidence limits.

For a comprehensive review of the statistical problems in biological assay see two books by Finney [4, 5]. The first deals mainly with the awkward situation where the response at each x is not a continuous variable but instead an all-or-none affair, e.g., alive or dead. At each dose we have a proportion h_i of animals surviving. The fitting of a regression line of h on x is not straightforward since the h_i are binomial variables with variances $\theta_i(1 - \theta_i)/n_i$ which are not constant but instead a function of θ. In fitting the line the points h_i have to be weighted inversely as their variances. Furthermore, the variances involve the θ_i which are unknown but which can be estimated from a provisional line. This will give a better line, which will give better estimates of the θ_i, which give a still better line. This iterative procedure converges, but a number of theoretical problems are involved, and the calculations in practice are tedious. The second text of Finney is a comprehensive examination of all types of bioassay. See also Emmens [6].

11.8. An Example of Parallel Line Biological Assay

In an assay of an estrogenic hormone [6], three groups of rats received 0.2, 0.3 and 0.4 mg of the standard and two groups received 1 and 2.5 mg of the unknown. Table 11.4 gives a linear function of the logarithm of the weight of the rats' uteri. The vth ($v = 1, \ldots, n_{ij}$) observation at the jth level ($j = 1, \ldots, m_i$) with the ith preparation ($i = 1$ for the standard and $i = 2$ for the unknown) is (x_{ijv}, y_{ijv}). The lower part of Table 11.4 assembles certain sums, sums of squares and sums of products. We further need

$$\sum_{j}^{m_1}\sum_{v}^{n_{1j}}(x_{1jv} - \bar{x}_{1..})^2 = \sum_{j}^{m_1}\sum_{v}^{n_{1j}} x_{1jv}^2 - \frac{\left(\sum_{j}^{m_1}\sum_{v}^{n_{1j}} x_{1jv}\right)^2}{\sum_{j}^{m_1} n_{1j}} \quad (8.1)$$

$$= 4.175858 - \frac{(8.632)^2}{19} = 0.254205,$$

$$\sum_{j}^{m_1}\sum_{v}^{n_{1j}}(y_{1jv} - \bar{y}_{1..})^2 = \sum_{j}^{m_1}\sum_{v}^{n_{1j}} y_{1jv}^2 - \frac{\left(\sum_{j}^{m_1}\sum_{v}^{n_{1j}} y_{1jv}\right)^2}{\sum_{j}^{m_1} n_{1j}} \quad (8.2)$$

$$= 160{,}163 - \frac{(1721)^2}{19} = 4276.632,$$

$$\sum_{j}^{m_1}\sum_{v}^{n_{1j}}(x_{1jv} - \bar{x}_{1..})(y_{1jv} - \bar{y}_{1..}) = \sum_{j}^{m_1}\sum_{v}^{n_{1j}} x_{1jv}y_{1jv} - \frac{\sum_{j}^{m_1}\sum_{v}^{n_{1j}} x_{1jv} \sum_{j}^{m_1}\sum_{v}^{n_{1j}} y_{1jv}}{\sum_{j}^{m_1} n_{1j}} \quad (8.3)$$

$$= 794.598 - \frac{8.632 \times 1721}{19} = 12.720526$$

SECT. 11.8 EXAMPLE OF PARALLEL LINE BIOLOGICAL ASSAY 355

Table 11.4*

	Standard				Unknown		
Dose, mg	0.2	0.3	0.4		1.0	2.5	
$\log(\text{dose} \times 10) = x$	0.301	0.477	0.602		1.000	1.398	
i	1				2		
j	1	2	3	$\sum_j^{m_1}$	1	2	$\sum_j^{m_2}$
Response = y_{ijv}	73	77	118		79	101	
	69	93	85		87	86	
	71	116	105		71	105	
	91	78	76		78	111	
	80	87	101		92	102	
	110	86			92	107	
		101				102	
		104				112	
n_{ij}	6	8	5	19	6	8	14
$\sum_v^{n_{ij}} y_{ijv}$	494	742	485	1,721	499	826	1,325
$\sum_v^{n_{ij}} y_{ijv}^2$	41,912	70,100	48,151	160,163	41,863	85,744	127,607
$\sum_v^{n_{ij}} x_{ijv}$	$6 \times .301$	$8 \times .477$	$5 \times .602$	8.632	6×1.000	8×1.398	17.184
$\sum_v^{n_{ij}} x_{ijv}^2$	$6 \times .301^2$	$8 \times .477^2$	$5 \times .602^2$	4.175858	6×1.000^2	8×1.398^2	21.635232
$\sum_v^{n_{ij}} x_{ijv} y_{ijv}$	$494 \times .301$	$742 \times .477$	$485 \times .602$	794.598	499×1.000	826×1.398	1653.748

* Data derived from [6].

The similar quantities for the unknown are 0.543100, 2205.214, and 27.405143. The sum of squares due to regression for the standard is

$$\frac{(12.720526)^2}{0.254205} = 636.543, \qquad (8.4)$$

and the residual sum of squares about the regression line is $4276.632 - 636.543 = 3640.089$; so $s_1^2 = 3640.089/17 = 214.123$. Likewise $s_2^2 = 68.528$. The variance ratio $214.123/68.528 = 3.12$ is rather close to $F_{0.975}(17, 12)$, 3.13, but the null hypothesis is acceptable at the two-sided 0.05 level of significance. The joint s^2 (6.2) is $(3640.089 + 822.334)/(17 + 12) = 153.877$.

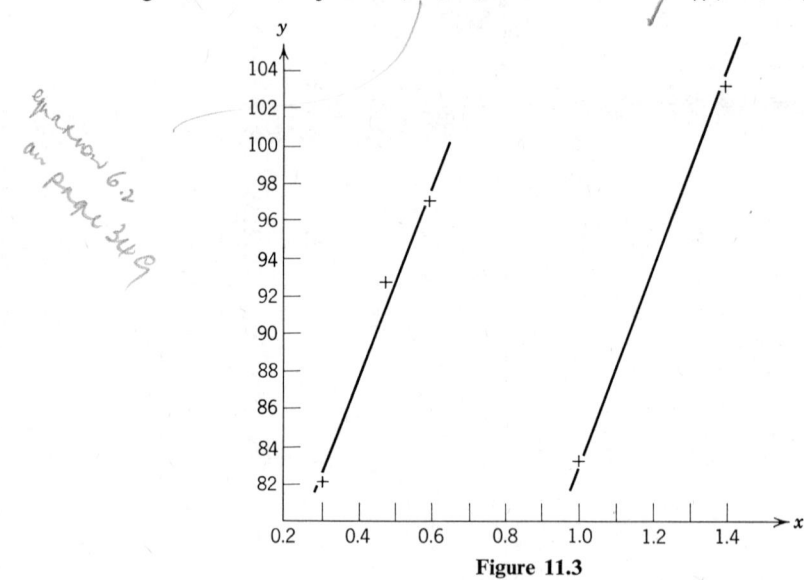

Figure 11.3

The next step is to compute $b_1 = 12.720526/0.254204 = 50.041$ and $b_2 = 27.405143/0.543100 = 50.461$. The estimated variance of $b_1 - b_2$, using (6.3), is

$$\hat{V}[b_1 - b_2] = 153.877 \left(\frac{1}{0.254204} + \frac{1}{0.543100} \right) = 888.660 \qquad (8.5)$$

whence the statistic for testing the null hypothesis $\beta_1 = \beta_2$ (6.4) is

$$\frac{50.041 - 50.461}{\sqrt{888.660}} = -0.014,$$

which is distributed as $t(29)$ and is obviously nonsignificant. We therefore form a joint b as given by (6.12),

$$b = \frac{12.720526 + 27.405143}{0.254204 + 0.54310} = \frac{40.125669}{0.797304} = 50.326687, \qquad (8.6)$$

SECT. 11.8 EXAMPLE OF PARALLEL LINE BIOLOGICAL ASSAY 357

and a new residual sum of squares about the two parallel regression lines as given by (6.14):

$$R = 4276.632 + 2205.214 - \frac{(40.125669)^2}{0.797304} = 4462.454. \quad (8.7)$$

This has $19 + 14 - 3 = 30$ degrees of freedom; so the new $s^2 = 4462.454/30 = 148.748$.

The test for whether these two parallel lines can be regarded as a single coincident line is given by (6.19), requiring $\bar{x}_{1..} = 8.632/19 = 0.454316$, $\bar{x}_{2..} = 17.184/14 = 1.227429$, $\bar{y}_{1..} = 1721/19 = 90.578947$, and $\bar{y}_{2..} = 1325/14 = 94.642857$. The statistic (6.19) has the value

$$\frac{(90.578947 - 94.642857) - 50.326687(0.454316 - 1.227429)}{\sqrt{148.748}\sqrt{1/19 + 1/14 + (0.454316 - 1.227429)^2/0.797304}} = 3.057$$

$t(30)_{.01} = 2.75$ (8.8)

and is distributed as t with 30 degrees of freedom.

The foregoing concludes our analysis of these data according to the procedures described in Section 11.6. The null hypothesis that the lines are parallel can be accepted, but the null hypothesis that they are coincident must be rejected. We will now apply the methods of Section 11.7 to calculate the potency ratio and its confidence limits.

The logarithm of the potency ratio is given by (7.5):

$$M = (0.454316 - 1.227429) - \frac{90.578947 - 94.642857}{50.326687}$$

$$= -0.773113 - (-0.080751) = -0.692362 = \bar{1}.3076. \quad (8.9)$$

The antilogarithm of this, 0.203, is the point estimate of the potency ratio.

The exact confidence limits are given by (7.11). We first calculate g as defined in (7.10) to see if approximate limits would be acceptable. For 95 per cent confidence limits we need $t_{0.975}(30) = 2.042$, and

$$g = \frac{(2.042)^2 \times 148.748}{(50.326687)^2 \times 0.797304} = 0.307144. \quad (8.10)$$

If g was less than 0.05 we would consider an approximation acceptable, given by putting $g = 0$ in (7.11), but with $g = 0.307$ the exact formula (7.11) must be used:

$$-0.773113 + \frac{-(-0.080751)}{1 - 0.307144} \pm \frac{2.042\sqrt{148.748}}{50.326687 \times (1 - 0.307144)}$$

$$\times \left[(1 - 0.307144)\left(\frac{1}{19} + \frac{1}{14}\right) + \frac{(-0.080751)^2}{0.797304}\right]^{\frac{1}{2}}$$

$$= -0.4374 \text{ and } -0.8757 = \bar{1}.5626 \text{ and } \bar{1}.1243. \quad (8.11)$$

These are confidence limits for the logarithm of the potency ratio. Their antilogarithms, (0.133, 0.365), are the 95 per cent confidence limits for the potency ratio ρ.

11.9. Regression through the Origin

There are occasions when it appears appropriate for a regression line to pass through the origin, i.e., for the true regression line to be

$$\eta = \beta x. \tag{9.1}$$

In the numerical example considered in Section 11.4, where blood flow rate was measured by a new method y and by a standard method x, it would be reasonable to expect η to equal zero when $x = 0$. We did find in fact that the null hypothesis that the intercept was zero was acceptable. In this section we study the fitting of a line through the origin. We assume that y is distributed normally about η as given by (9.1) with variance σ^2, and that the observations are independent. The estimated regression equation is

$$Y = bx. \tag{9.2}$$

The sum of squares of deviations between the observed values y_i and the predicted values Y_i is

$$R = \sum (y_i - Y_i)^2 = \sum (y_i - bx_i)^2. \tag{9.3}$$

Differentiating with respect to b and equating to zero to make R a minimum gives

$$\frac{dR}{db} = -2 \sum (y_i - bx_i)x_i = 0, \tag{9.4}$$

whence

$$b = \frac{\sum x_i y_i}{\sum x_i^2}. \tag{9.5}$$

It is clear that b is a linear function of the y_i, and its variance is

$$V[b] = \frac{\sum x_i^2 V[y_i]}{(\sum x_i^2)^2} = \frac{\sigma^2}{\sum x_i^2}. \tag{9.6}$$

Analogous to (3.1), we write

$$y_i - \eta_i = (y_i - Y_i) + (Y_i - \eta_i) = (y_i - Y_i) + (b - \beta)x_i. \tag{9.7}$$

Squaring and summing over i gives

$$\sum (y_i - \eta_i)^2 = \sum (y_i - Y_i)^2 + (b - \beta)^2 \sum x_i^2, \tag{9.8}$$

SECT. 11.9   REGRESSION THROUGH THE ORIGIN

the terms being distributed as $\sigma^2\chi^2$ with k, $k-1$, and 1 degrees of freedom respectively. It follows that s^2 defined as $s^2 = \Sigma(y_i - Y_i)^2/(k-1)$ has expected value σ^2 and is independent of b. We have

$$V[Y] = V[bx] = x^2 V[b] = \frac{x^2\sigma^2}{\Sigma x_i^2}. \tag{9.9}$$

We now write

$$y_i = (y_i - Y_i) + Y_i = (y_i - Y_i) + bx_i \tag{9.10}$$

and square and sum over i:

$$\Sigma y_i^2 = \Sigma(y_i - Y_i)^2 + \frac{(\Sigma x_i y_i)^2}{\Sigma x_i^2}. \tag{9.11}$$

Thus we can calculate $\Sigma(y_i - Y_i)^2$, which we want as the numerator of s^2, as

$$\Sigma(y_i - Y_i)^2 = \Sigma y_i^2 - \frac{(\Sigma x_i y_i)^2}{\Sigma x_i^2}. \tag{9.12}$$

To find the expected value of $(\Sigma x_i y_i)^2/\Sigma x_i^2$, we note from (9.8) that $E[(b-\beta)^2 \Sigma x_i^2] = \sigma^2$, so

$$E[b^2 \Sigma x_i^2] - 2\beta \Sigma x_i^2 E[b] + \beta^2 \Sigma x_i^2 = \sigma^2. \tag{9.13}$$

But

$$b^2 \Sigma x_i^2 = \left(\frac{\Sigma x_i y_i}{\Sigma x_i^2}\right)^2 \Sigma x_i^2 = \frac{(\Sigma x_i y_i)^2}{\Sigma x_i^2}. \tag{9.14}$$

Thus

$$E\left[\frac{(\Sigma x_i y_i)^2}{\Sigma x_i^2}\right] = \sigma^2 + \beta^2 \Sigma x_i^2. \tag{9.15}$$

We can construct a table of analysis of variance (Table 11.5) corresponding to (9.11).

Applying these results to the data of Table 11.2, we have as the regression coefficient, using (9.5),

$$b = \frac{\Sigma x_i y_i}{\Sigma x_i^2} = \frac{87{,}719{,}100}{89{,}394{,}900} = 0.981253, \tag{9.16}$$

Table 11.5

Source of variance	Sums of squares	Degrees of freedom	E[M. S.]
Due to line	$(\Sigma x_i y_i)^2/\Sigma x_i^2$	1	$\sigma^2 + \beta^2 \Sigma x_i^2$
Residual	$\Sigma(y_i - Y_i)^2$	$k-1$	σ^2
Total about origin	Σy_i^2	k	

as the sum of squares due to the regression line,

$$\frac{(\sum x_i y_i)^2}{\sum x_i^2} = \frac{(87,719,100)^2}{89,394,900} = 86,074,714.6, \quad (9.17)$$

and as the residual sum of squares, using (9.12),

$$\sum (y_i - Y_i)^2 = 86,125,825.0 - 86,074,714.6 = 51,110.4. \quad (9.18)$$

We enter these results in Table 11.6.

Table 11.6

Source of variance	Sums of squares	Degrees of freedom	Mean squares	E[M. S.]
Due to line	86,074,714.6	1	86,074,714.6	$\sigma^2 + \beta^2 \Sigma x_i^2$
Residual	51,110.4	17	3,006.5	σ^2
Total about origin	86,125,825.0	18		

We can combine Tables 11.3 and 11.6 to give a test of whether a line $Y = bx$ through the origin is an adequate fit (Table 11.7).

A test of the null hypothesis that there is no improvement in fit when using the two-parameter line in place of the one-parameter line is given by the variance ratio $238.5/3179.5 = 0.075$. If this null hypothesis was to

Table 11.7

Source of variance	Sums of squares	Degrees of freedom	Mean squares
Remainder using line $Y = bx$	51,110.4	17	
Remainder using line $Y = a + b(x - \bar{x})$	50,871.9	16	3179.5
Difference: attributable to improvement in fit through using two parameters in place of one	238.5	1	238.5

be rejected at the α level of significance, this variance ratio would have to be not less than $F_{1-\alpha}(1, 16)$. Clearly the null hypothesis here is acceptable. This test is identical with the test that the intercept of the two-parameter line could be zero. For that test we found $t = 0.2739$; so $[t(16)]^2 = (0.2739)^2 = 0.0750 = F(1, 16)$, as we obtained here.

SECT. 11.10   REGRESSION LINE THROUGH THE ORIGIN IN REVERSE   361

To revert to Table 11.6, there is clearly no doubt that the null hypothesis $\beta = 0$ has to be rejected. We will be more interested in the null hypothesis $\beta = 1$. Using (9.6),

$$\hat{V}[b] = \frac{s^2}{\sum x_i^2} = \frac{3006.5}{89{,}394{,}900} = 0.3363 \times 10^{-4} \qquad (9.19)$$

and, under the null hypothesis that $\beta = 1$,

$$\frac{b - 1}{\sqrt{\hat{V}[b]}} = \frac{0.981253 - 1}{\sqrt{0.3363 \times 10^{-4}}} = 3.23 \qquad (9.20)$$

is distributed as $t(17)$. For the line constrained to pass through the origin we thus have to reject the null hypothesis that $\beta = 1$.

For the unconstrained line $Y = a + b(x - \bar{x})$ we found that the null hypothesis that $\beta = 1$ was acceptable, and that the null hypothesis that the intercept is zero was acceptable. We might have expected on this basis that, if we made the intercept zero, i.e., switched to the line constrained to pass through the origin, then we could continue to accept the null hypothesis that $\beta = 1$. However, the above result shows that this is not the case. We will gain greater insight by constructing a joint confidence region for α and β, and for the intercept and β. This we will proceed to do in Section 11.11.

11.10. The Use of the Regression Line through the Origin in Reverse

Suppose that we observe a new $\bar{y}'$, and we wish to predict the corresponding x and to construct confidence limits for this prediction. We can solve the estimated regression equation (9.2) to obtain a point estimate, $x = \bar{y}'/b$. The expected value of the new $\bar{y}'$ is η. Corresponding to this value of η is a value of x given by solving the true regression equation (9.1) for x, $x = \eta/\beta$. Denote this value of x by ξ, so that $\xi = \eta/\beta$, or $\eta - \beta\xi = 0$. We now define a new variable z,

$$z = \bar{y}' - b\xi. \qquad (10.1)$$

This variable will have expected value

$$E[z] = \eta - \xi E[b] = \eta - \xi\beta = 0, \qquad (10.2)$$

and variance

$$V[z] = V[\bar{y}'] + \xi^2 \, V[b] = \frac{\sigma^2}{m} + \xi^2 \frac{\sigma^2}{\sum x_i^2} \qquad (10.3)$$

Substituting the residual mean square in Table 11.5 as an estimate of σ^2, we have that

$$\frac{\bar{y}' - b\xi}{s\sqrt{1/m + \xi^2/\sum x_i^2}} \sim t(k - 1). \qquad (10.4)$$

The subsequent manipulation proceeds along lines similar to Section 11.5, and leads to

$$\frac{b\bar{y}'}{b^2 - t_2^2 s^2/\sum x_i^2} - \frac{t_2 s}{b^2 - t_2^2 s^2/\sum x_i^2}\left[\left(b^2 - \frac{t_2^2 s^2}{\sum x_i^2}\right)\frac{1}{m} + \frac{\bar{y}'^2}{\sum x_i^2}\right]^{1/2} \quad (10.5)$$

as the solution for ξ_2. Use of t_1 in place of t_2 gives ξ_1.

If we define g as

$$g = \left(t_2 \frac{\sqrt{\hat{V}[b]}}{b}\right)^2 = \frac{t_2^2 s^2}{b^2 \sum x_i^2}, \quad (10.6)$$

analogous to (5.11), then, when g is less than 0.1, b is highly significant and (10.5) can be approximated by

$$\xi_2 = \frac{\bar{y}'}{b} - \frac{t_2 s}{b}\left(\frac{1}{m} + \frac{\bar{y}'^2}{b^2 \sum x_i^2}\right)^{1/2}. \quad (10.7)$$

Applying this result to the example of Section 11.4, we will suppose that we observe a single new observation, $y' = 3000$. For 95 per cent confidence limits, $t_{0.975}(17) = 2.110$, and, from Table 11.6, $s^2 = 3006.5$. We have $\Sigma x_i^2 = 89{,}394{,}900$ and $b = 0.981253$. Thus, using (10.6), the value of g is

$$g = \frac{(2.110)^2 \times 3006.5}{(0.981253)^2 \times 89{,}394{,}900} = 0.000156,$$

which clearly permits us to use the approximation (10.7). The 95 per cent confidence limits are

$$\frac{3000}{0.981253} \pm \frac{2.110 \times \sqrt{3006.5}}{0.981253}\left[\frac{1}{1} + \frac{(3000)^2}{86{,}074{,}714}\right]^{1/2} = 3057.3 \pm 128.4.$$

The resulting interval (2929, 3186) compares closely with that obtained using the two-parameter line in Section 11.5 (2927, 3198).

11.11. A Joint Confidence Region for α, β

As indicated in Section 11.9, we may need a joint confidence region for α, β to show those pairs of values which are compatible with the data.

By the discussion of (3.2), $k(a - \alpha)^2$ and $(b - \beta)^2 \Sigma(x_i - \bar{x})^2$ are distributed independently both as $\sigma^2 \chi^2(1)$. From (1.27.16) their sum will be distributed as $\sigma^2 \chi^2(2)$. Also, s^2 is independently distributed as $\sigma^2 \chi^2(k - 2)$. Therefore

$$\frac{[k(a - \alpha)^2 + (b - \beta)^2 \sum (x_i - \bar{x})^2]/2}{s^2}$$

$$\sim \frac{\sigma^2 \chi^2(2)/2}{\sigma^2 \chi^2(k-2)/(k-2)} \sim F(2, k - 2). \quad (11.1)$$

A JOINT CONFIDENCE REGION FOR α, β

In $\Pr\{F < F_{1-\alpha}\} = 1 - \alpha$, we replace F by the left-hand side of (11.1):

$$\Pr\left\{\frac{k(a-\alpha)^2 + (b-\beta)^2 \sum(x_i - \bar{x})^2}{2s^2} < F_{1-\alpha}(2, k-2)\right\} = 1 - \alpha. \quad (11.2)$$

All pairs of values of (α, β) which satisfy this inequality lie inside the $100(1-\alpha)$ per cent confidence region, and the boundary of the region is given by substituting an equality for the inequality:

$$\frac{k(a-\alpha)^2 + (b-\beta)^2 \sum(x_i - \bar{x})^2}{2s^2} = F_{1-\alpha}(2, k-2). \quad (11.3)$$

To determine the boundary of the confidence region, we have to find those pairs (α, β) which satisfy (11.3).

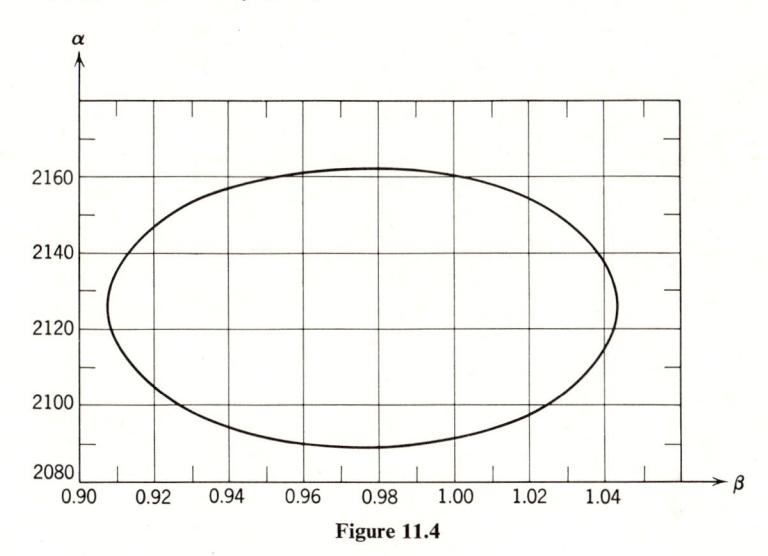

Figure 11.4

For the data of the example in Section 11.4:

$k = 18$, $\quad a = \bar{y} = 2125.277$, $\quad b = 0.974561$
$\sum(x_i - \bar{x})^2 = 5{,}024{,}850.0$, $\quad s^2 = 3179.49$, $\quad F_{0.95}(2, 16) = 3.63$.

Inserting these values in (11.3) gives the equation

$$18(2125.277 - \alpha)^2 + 5{,}024{,}850 \times (0.974561 - \beta)^2 = 23{,}083.1. \quad (11.4)$$

When $\beta = 0.974561$, $\alpha = 2089.468$ or 2161.088. When $\alpha = 2125.277$, $\beta = 0.906784$ or 1.042338. Choosing values of β in this range, we get pairs of solutions for α, and, plotting these and connecting them up, we get the ellipse in Figure 11.4. All pairs of values of α, β inside this ellipse are jointly compatible with the data at the 0.05 level of significance.

We are, however, more interested in a joint confidence region for the intercept, say η_0, and β. This is easily obtained, since η_0 is given in terms of α and β by inserting $x = 0$ in (2.1):

$$\eta_0 = \alpha - \beta\bar{x}. \tag{11.5}$$

Thus, for all our pairs of solutions of α and β we compute η_0, and then

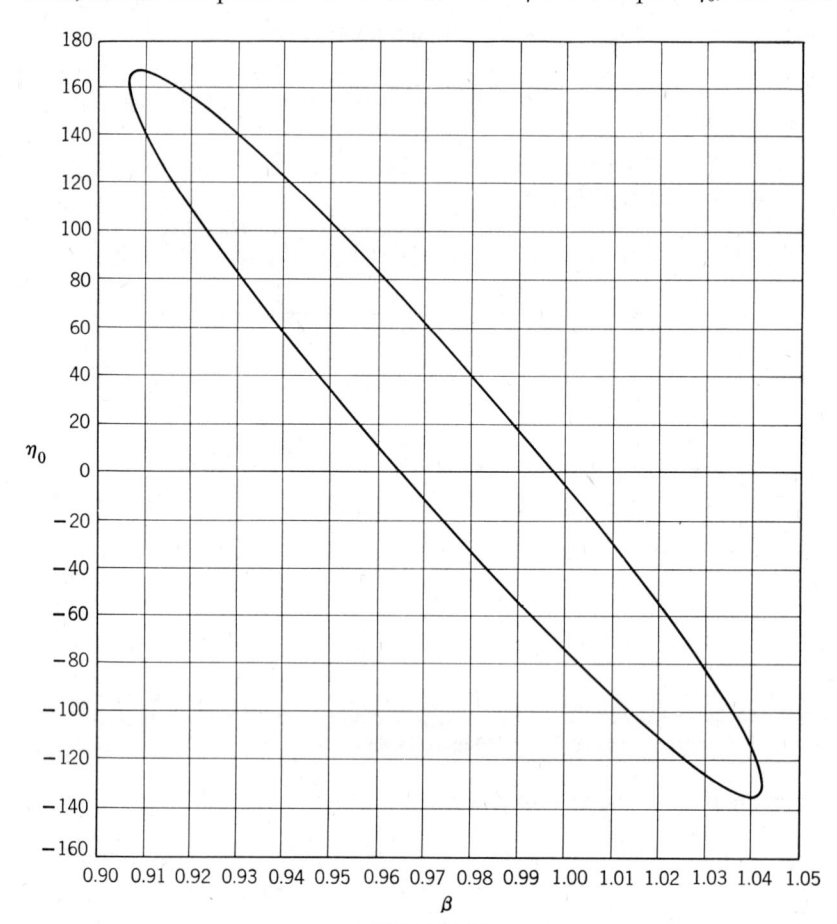

Figure 11.5

plot η_0 against β and again come up with an ellipse (Figure 11.5). This shows that, if we want a large β, say $\beta = 1.03$, then we must have η_0 in the range -122, -87. If we want a zero intercept η_0, we must have β in the range 0.967 to 0.9965, or, if we want $\beta = 1$, we must have an intercept in the range -71 to -9. The ellipse excludes the point $\beta = 1, \eta_0 = 0$. In other words, we can have a zero intercept but not a slope of 1, or we can have a slope of 1 but not a zero intercept; we cannot have a slope of 1 and a zero intercept simultaneously.

Having constructed the ellipse for the 95 per cent confidence region for α and β, Figure 11.4, we know that any point (α, β) that lies outside the ellipse corresponds to a line that is inadmissible in the sense that it lies outside the 95 per cent confidence region for the line. Any point (α, β) that lies on the ellipse gives a line that is just admissible. If we took a whole sequence of points all round the ellipse and drew the corresponding lines we would generate two envelopes, and all lines lying inside the envelopes lie inside the 95 per cent confidence region for the line.

We can construct the boundary of the confidence region for the line more easily by obtaining an explicit formula for it. Points on the boundary will be given by finding maximum and minimum values of

$$\eta = \alpha + \beta(x - \bar{x}) \tag{11.6}$$

for any and all fixed values of x, with α and β subject to the condition

$$k(a - \alpha)^2 + (b - \beta)^2 \sum (x_i - \bar{x})^2 - 2F_{1-\alpha}(2, k - 2)s^2 = 0, \tag{11.7}$$

derived from (11.3). The standard procedure for finding the extreme value of a function $f(x, y)$ subject to the subsidiary condition $\phi(x, y) = 0$ is Lagrange's method of undetermined multipliers. This involves solving the equations

$$\frac{\partial f(x, y)}{\partial x} + \lambda \frac{\partial \phi(x, y)}{\partial x} = 0, \tag{11.8}$$

$$\frac{\partial f(x, y)}{\partial y} + \lambda \frac{\partial \phi(x, y)}{\partial y} = 0, \tag{11.9}$$

where λ is a constant, the undetermined multiplier, along with the subsidiary condition

$$\phi(x, y) = 0. \tag{11.10}$$

Here for $f(x, y)$ we have $\eta = f(\alpha, \beta)$ given by (11.6) and for $\phi(x, y)$ we have (11.7) considered as a function of α and β. For (11.8) and (11.9) we obtain

$$1 + \lambda(-1) \cdot 2k(a - \alpha) = 0, \tag{11.11}$$

$$(x - \bar{x}) + \lambda(-1) \cdot 2(b - \beta) \sum (x_i - \bar{x})^2 = 0, \tag{11.12}$$

whence

$$a - \alpha = \frac{1}{2k\lambda}, \tag{11.13}$$

$$b - \beta = \frac{x - \bar{x}}{2\lambda \sum (x_i - \bar{x})^2}. \tag{11.14}$$

Inserting these expressions for $a - \alpha$ and $b - \beta$ in (11.7) and solving the resulting equation for λ gives

$$\lambda = \pm \frac{1}{2\sqrt{2Fs}} \left[\frac{1}{k} + \frac{(x - \bar{x})^2}{\sum (x_i - \bar{x})^2} \right]^{1/2}. \tag{11.15}$$

Substituting this solution for λ in (11.3) and (11.4) gives

$$\alpha = a \pm \frac{\sqrt{2Fs}}{k} \left[\frac{1}{k} + \frac{(x - \bar{x})^2}{\sum (x_i - \bar{x})^2} \right]^{-1/2}, \tag{11.16}$$

$$\beta = b \pm \frac{(x - \bar{x})\sqrt{2Fs}}{\sum (x_i - \bar{x})^2} \left[\frac{1}{k} + \frac{(x - \bar{x})^2}{\sum (x_i - \bar{x})^2} \right]^{-1/2}. \tag{11.17}$$

Finally, substituting these solutions for α and β in (11.7) gives

$$\eta = a + b(x - \bar{x}) \pm \sqrt{2Fs} \left[\frac{1}{k} + \frac{(x - \bar{x})^2}{\sum (x_i - \bar{x})^2} \right]^{1/2}. \tag{11.18}$$

For our values of a, b, s, k, $\bar{x}$, $\sum (x_i - \bar{x})^2$, and $F_{1-\alpha}(2, k - 2)$, this will give a pair of points for any x, and by moving x over the line we generate the hyperbolas which are identical with the envelopes to the admissible lines.

Equation (11.18) is similar to (3.20), the difference being the use of $\sqrt{2F}$ in place of t. The difference in interpretation is that while (3.20) gives a confidence interval for η at one, and only one, specified value of x, (11.18) gives confidence intervals for η at all values of x, and can therefore be used repeatedly.

11.12. Linear Regression with Several Observations on y at Each x

In this section we assume that at x_i, $i = 1, \ldots, k$, we have n_i observations $y_{i\nu}$, $\nu = 1, \ldots, n_i$. We define $\bar{x}$ as the mean of the x_i weighted in proportion to the numbers of observations at each point:

$$\bar{x} = \frac{\sum_{i}^{k} n_i x_i}{\sum_{i}^{k} n_i}. \tag{12.1}$$

We define $\bar{y}_i$ as $\sum_{\nu}^{n_i} y_{i\nu}/n_i$ and compute the sample variance within each group of replicate observations:

$$s_{1i}^2 = \frac{1}{n_i - 1} \sum_{\nu}^{n_i} (y_{i\nu} - \bar{y}_i)^2. \tag{12.2}$$

SECT. 11.12 LINEAR REGRESSION WITH SEVERAL OBSERVATIONS

In principle, we might test the null hypothesis that the s_{1i}^2 are drawn from a population with common parameter σ^2 with Bartlett's test. In practice, this will be frequently unrewarding since the n_i are often small and the test will be of low power. Also the s_{1i}^2 are ordered by the magnitude of the x_i from which they were obtained, and Bartlett's test pays no attention to this ordering. If there is a departure from the null hypothesis, it is likely to be that σ^2 increases with x, instead of varying irregularly and it may be more profitable to make a rough graph of s_{1i}^2 against x_i and inspect this with common sense and judgment. Frequently, we must admit, no attempt is made to check this assumption, and one proceeds directly to form a pooled estimate of σ^2, according to (9.7.6):

$$s_1^2 = \frac{\sum_i^k (n_i - 1)s_i^2}{\sum_i^k (n_i - 1)} = \frac{\sum_i^k \sum_v^{n_i} (y_{iv} - \bar{y}_i)^2}{\sum_i^k n_i - k}. \tag{12.3}$$

The sum of squares of deviations between the observed values y_{iv} and the predicted values Y_i is

$$R = \sum_i^k \sum_v^{n_i} (y_{iv} - Y_i)^2 = \sum_i^k \sum_v^{n_i} [y_{iv} - a - b(x_i - \bar{x})]^2. \tag{12.4}$$

Partially differentiating R with respect to a and to b, and equating to zero gives

$$\frac{\partial R}{\partial a} = -2 \sum_i^k \sum_v^{n_i} [y_{iv} - a - b(x_i - \bar{x})] = 0, \tag{12.5}$$

$$\frac{\partial R}{\partial b} = -2 \sum_i^k \sum_v^{n_i} [y_{iv} - a - b(x_i - \bar{x})](x_i - \bar{x}) = 0. \tag{12.6}$$

Rearranging,

$$a \sum_i^k n_i + b \sum_i^k n_i(x_i - \bar{x}) = \sum_i^k \sum_v^{n_i} y_{iv}, \tag{12.7}$$

$$a \sum_i^k n_i(x_i - \bar{x}) + b \sum_i^k n_i(x_i - \bar{x})^2 = \sum_i^k n_i(x_i - \bar{x})\bar{y}_i, \tag{12.8}$$

since

$$\sum_i^k \sum_v^{n_i} (x_i - \bar{x})y_{iv} = \sum_i^k (x_i - \bar{x}) \sum_v^{n_i} y_{iv} = \sum_i^k n_i(x_i - \bar{x})\bar{y}_i. \tag{12.9}$$

The definition of $\bar{x}$ in (12.1) implies that

$$\sum_i^k n_i(x_i - \bar{x}) = \sum_i^k n_i x_i - \bar{x} \sum_i^k n_i = 0; \tag{12.10}$$

so (12.7) gives

$$a = \frac{\sum_i^k \sum_v^{n_i} y_{iv}}{\sum_i^k n_i} = \frac{\sum_i^k n_i \bar{y}_i}{\sum_i^k n_i} = \bar{y}, \quad (12.11)$$

and (12.8) gives

$$b = \frac{\sum_i^k n_i(x_i - \bar{x})\bar{y}_i}{\sum_i^k n_i(x_i - \bar{x})^2} = \frac{\sum_i^k n_i(x_i - \bar{x})(\bar{y}_i - \bar{y})}{\sum_i^k n_i(x_i - \bar{x})^2}, \quad (12.12)$$

the second form following from the identity

$$\sum_i^k n_i(x_i - \bar{x})(\bar{y}_i - \bar{y}) = \sum_i^k n_i(x_i - \bar{x})\bar{y}_i. - \sum_i^k n_i(x_i - \bar{x})\bar{y}$$

$$= \sum_i^k n_i(x_i - \bar{x})\bar{y}_i. \quad (12.13)$$

We will now consider an analysis of variance representation. The deviation of an observation y_{iv} from the value η_i predicted by the true regression equation (2.1) can be written as

$$y_{iv} - \eta_i = (y_{iv} - \bar{y}_i) + (\bar{y}_i - \eta_i) = (y_{iv} - \bar{y}_i) + (\bar{y}_i - Y_i) + (Y_i - \eta_i)$$
$$= (y_{iv} - \bar{y}_i) + (\bar{y}_i - Y_i) + (a - \alpha) + (b - \beta)(x_i - \bar{x}). \quad (12.14)$$

This equation is represented in Figure 11.6. Squaring and summing over i and v gives

$$\sum_i^k \sum_v^{n_i} (y_{iv} - \eta_i)^2 = (a - \alpha)^2 \sum_i^k n_i + (b - \beta)^2 \sum_i^k n_i(x_i - \bar{x})^2$$
$$+ \sum_i^k n_i(\bar{y}_i - Y_i)^2 + \sum_i^k \sum_v^{n_i} (y_{iv} - \bar{y}_i.)^2. \quad (12.15)$$

In this equation, we have partitioned a sum of squares with $\sum_i^k n_i$ degrees of freedom into four sums of squares. The first and second components each involve only one variable, a and b, respectively, and these each have one degree of freedom. The third component involves k variables, but equating (12.5) and (12.6) to zero imposed two restrictions, and so the degrees of freedom are $k - 2$. The fourth component is the numerator of (12.3), which has $\left(\sum_i^k n_i\right) - k$ degrees of freedom. Thus the sum of the sums of squares equals the sum of squares on the left-hand side, and the sum of the degrees of freedom, likewise; so, by Cochran's theorem,

SECT. 11.12 LINEAR REGRESSION WITH SEVERAL OBSERVATIONS

the sums of squares are distributed as $\sigma^2\chi^2$ and are independent. If $(a - \alpha)^2 \sum_i^k n_i$ is distributed as $\sigma^2\chi^2$ with one degree of freedom, analogously to (3.4),

$$V[a] = E[(a - \alpha)^2] = \frac{\sigma^2}{\sum_i^k n_i}. \tag{12.16}$$

Likewise,

$$V[b] = E[(b - E[b])^2] = \frac{\sigma^2}{\sum_i^k n_i(x_i - \bar{x})^2}. \tag{12.17}$$

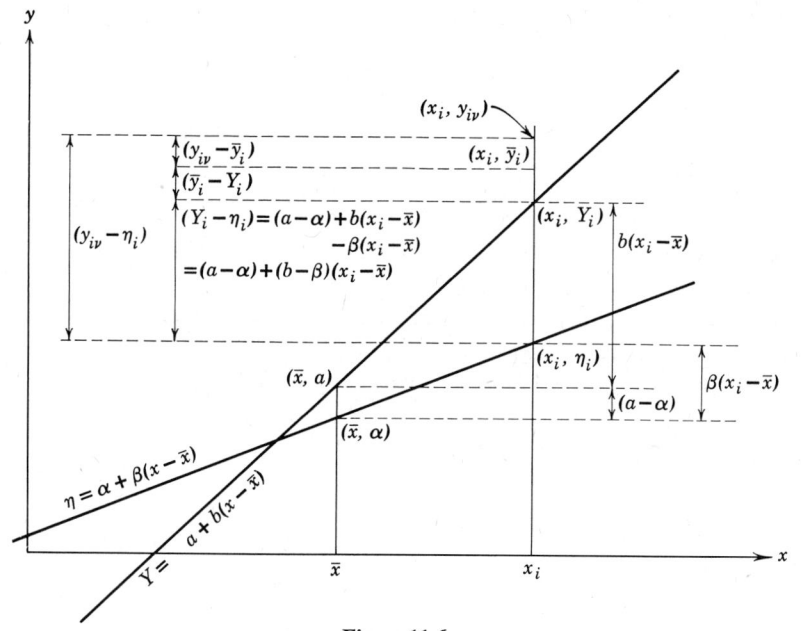

Figure 11.6

Since a and b are independent,

$$V[Y] = V[a + b(x - \bar{x})] = V[a] + (x - \bar{x})^2 V[b]$$

$$= \sigma^2 \left[\frac{1}{\sum_i^k n_i} + \frac{(x - \bar{x})^2}{\sum_i^k n_i(x_i - \bar{x})^2} \right]. \tag{12.18}$$

We now write

$$y_{iv} - \bar{y} = (y_{iv} - \bar{y}_i) + (\bar{y}_i - Y_i) + (Y_i - \bar{y}), \tag{12.19}$$

and square and sum over i and v:

$$\sum_i^k \sum_v^{n_i} (y_{iv} - \bar{y})^2 = \sum_i^k \sum_v^{n_i} (y_{iv} - \bar{y}_i)^2 + \sum_i^k n_i(\bar{y}_i - Y_i)^2 + \sum_i^k n_i(Y_i - \bar{y})^2. \tag{12.20}$$

The first item on the right-hand side is the numerator of s_1^2 in (12.3), distributed as $\sigma^2 \chi^2$ with $\left(\sum_i^k n_i\right) - k$ degrees of freedom, and the corresponding mean square has expected value σ^2. The second item is the third item in (12.15), and if the η_i really lie on the regression line $\alpha + \beta(x_i - \bar{x})$, then this sum of squares is distributed as $\sigma^2 \chi^2$ with $k - 2$ degrees of freedom. It is possible, however, that the η_i do not lie on this line. Even if the η_i do not lie on a straight line, it will be possible to fit a least squares line to the points (x_i, η_i), and the parameters will be, by analogy with (12.11) and (12.12),

$$\alpha = \bar{\eta} = \frac{\sum_i^k n_i \eta_i}{\sum_i^k n_i}, \qquad \beta = \frac{\sum_i^k n_i(x_i - \bar{x}) \eta_i}{\sum_i^k n_i(x_i - \bar{x})^2}. \tag{12.21}$$

We can write

$$\begin{aligned}
\bar{y}_i - \eta_i &= (\bar{y}_i - Y_i) + (Y_i - \eta_i) \\
&= (\bar{y}_i - Y_i) + [a + b(x_i - \bar{x}) - \bar{\eta} - \beta(x_i - \bar{x})] \\
&\quad - [\eta_i - \bar{\eta} - \beta(x_i - \bar{x})] \\
&= (\bar{y}_i - Y_i) - [\eta_i - \bar{\eta} - \beta(x_i - \bar{x})] + (a - \bar{\eta}) \\
&\quad + (b - \beta)(x_i - \bar{x}).
\end{aligned} \tag{12.22}$$

Square and sum over i and v:

$$\sum_i^k n_i(\bar{y}_i - \eta_i)^2 = \sum_i^k n_i\{(\bar{y}_i - Y_i) - [\eta_i - \bar{\eta} - \beta(x_i - \bar{x})]\}^2 \\
+ (a - \bar{\eta})^2 \sum_i^k n_i + (b - \beta)^2 \sum_i^k n_i(x_i - \bar{x})^2. \tag{12.23}$$

The left-hand side will be distributed as $\sigma^2 \chi^2$ with k degrees of freedom. The terms on the right-hand side will be distributed $\sigma^2 \chi^2$ with degrees of freedom $k - 2$, 1, and 1, respectively; so, considering the first term,

$$\begin{aligned}
E\left[\sum_i^k n_i\{(\bar{y}_i - Y_i) - [\eta_i - \bar{\eta} - \beta(x_i - \bar{x})]\}^2\right] \\
= (k - 2)\sigma^2 \\
= E\left[\sum_i^k n_i(\bar{y}_i - Y_i)^2\right] + E\left[\sum_i^k n_i\{\eta_i - \bar{\eta} - \beta(x_i - \bar{x})\}^2\right] \\
- 2E\left[\sum_i^k n_i(\bar{y}_i - Y_i)\{\eta_i - \bar{\eta} - \beta(x_i - \bar{x})\}\right]. \tag{12.24}
\end{aligned}$$

SECT. 11.13 LINEAR REGRESSION WITH SEVERAL OBSERVATIONS

The last term here can be written as

$$-2\sum_i^k n_i\{\eta_i - \bar{\eta} - \beta(x_i - \bar{x})\}E[\bar{y}_i - Y_i]$$

$$= -2\sum_i^k n_i\{\eta_i - \bar{\eta} - \beta(x_i - \bar{x})\}\{\eta_i - \alpha - \beta(x_i - \bar{x})\}$$

$$= -2\sum_i^k n_i\{\eta_i - \bar{\eta} - \beta(x_i - \bar{x})\}^2, \qquad (12.25)$$

since $\alpha = \bar{\eta}$. Then (12.24) can be rearranged to give

$$E\left[\sum_i^k n_i(\bar{y}_i - Y_i)^2\right] = (k-2)\sigma^2 + \sum_i^k n_i\{\eta_i - \bar{\eta} - \beta(x_i - \bar{x})\}^2. \qquad (12.26)$$

The same arguments that gave (3.16) here give

$$E\left[\sum_i^k n_i(Y_i - \bar{y})^2\right] = \sigma^2 + \beta^2 \sum_i^k n_i(x_i - \bar{x})^2. \qquad (12.27)$$

We can now put (12.20) in a tabular form (Table 11.8).

Table 11.8

Source of variance	Sums of squares	Degrees of freedom	Mean squares	E[M.S.]
Slope of line	$\sum_i^k n_i(Y_i - \bar{y}_i)^2$	1	s_3^2	$\sigma^2 + \beta^2 \sum_i^k n_i(x_i - \bar{x})^2$
Variation of true group means about line	$\sum_i^k n_i(\bar{y}_i - Y_i)^2$	$k - 2$	s_2^2	$\sigma^2 + \dfrac{\sum_i^k n_i(\eta_i - \bar{\eta} - \beta(x_i - \bar{x}))^2}{k-2}$
Within groups	$\sum_i^k \sum_v^{n_i} (y_{iv} - \bar{y}_i)^2$	$\left(\sum_i^k n_i\right) - k$	s_1^2	σ^2
Totals	$\sum_i^k \sum_v^{n_i} (y_{iv} - \bar{y})^2$	$\left(\sum_i^k n_i\right) - 1$		

A test of the null hypothesis that the η_i do lie on a straight line is given by the variance ratio s_2^2/s_1^2, and a test of the null hypothesis that $\beta = 0$ is given by the variance ratio s_3^2/s_1^2.

11.13. An Example of Linear Regression with Several Observations on y at Each x

The data of Table 11.9 give the square root of the stopping distance in feet y of an automobile when traveling on a road with a certain surface at a number of speeds in miles per hour x. The results are only directly applicable to that automobile on that road; if we want to make a general

Table 11.9

x_i	20.5	30.5	40.5	48.8	57.8	
y_{iv}	$\begin{cases} 3.92 \\ 3.65 \end{cases}$	$\begin{matrix} 5.82 \\ 5.20 \end{matrix}$	8.55	10.63	11.94	
n_i	2	2	1	1	1	$\sum_i^k n_i = 7$
$\sum_v^{n_i} y_{iv}$	7.57	11.02	8.55	10.63	11.94	$\sum_i^k \sum_v^{n_i} y_{iv} = 49.71$

inference about other automobiles of the same model or about other roads, we can only do it with data either from a sample of automobiles and from a sample of roads, or from a substantial body of experience that tells us that the variation between automobiles of a certain model and between roads is very slight.

The reasons for choosing the square root of the stopping distance as the dependent variable are that a plot of the distance itself against speed showed obvious signs of curvature, whereas the square root appears to be linear (Figure 11.7). Since the energy of a moving object is proportional to the square of its velocity, this is reasonable. We could have chosen the stopping distance as the dependent variable, and the square of the speed as the independent variable, and this would have come to almost the same thing. However, one of the assumptions of the regression analysis is that

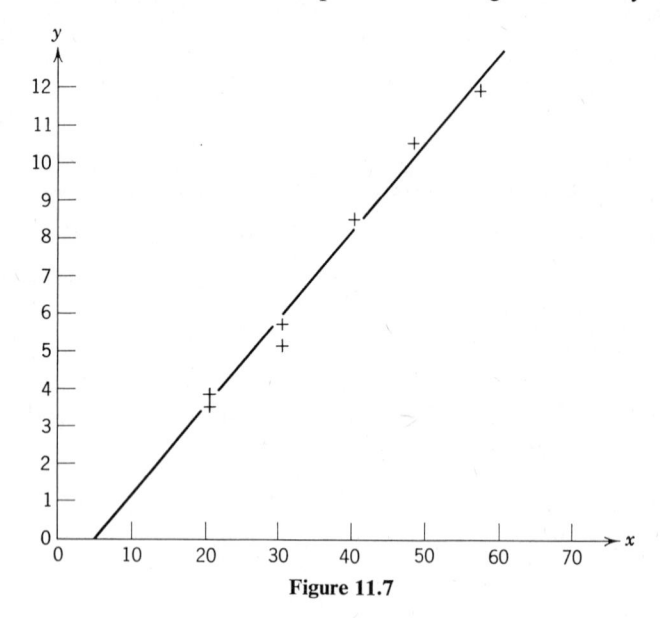

Figure 11.7

SECT. 11.13 LINEAR REGRESSION WITH SEVERAL OBSERVATIONS

the variance of the dependent variable, given the independent variable, is constant, and this is much more likely to be so when we use the square root than the stopping distance itself. It is comparatively rarely that we have sufficient data to discriminate objectively between different possible models, and usually all we can do is to make plausible guesses based on previous experience in similar fields.

Table 11.8 involves four sums of squares which we will now compute. The general procedure is to convert averages into sums over the appropriate index. The total sum of squares is, analogous to (10.2.35),

$$\sum_i^k \sum_v^{n_i} (y_{iv} - \bar{y})^2 = (3.92)^2 + \cdots + (11.94)^2 - \frac{(49.71)^2}{7}$$

$$= 418.2643 - 353.012014 = 65.252286. \quad (13.1)$$

The within-groups sum of squares is, analogous to (10.2.33),

$$\sum_i^k \sum_v^{n_i} (y_{iv} - \bar{y}_i)^2 = 418.2643 - \left[\frac{(7.57)^2}{2} + \frac{(11.02)^2}{2} + \cdots + \frac{(11.94)^2}{1}\right]$$

$$= 418.2643 - 418.035650 = 0.228650. \quad (13.2)$$

The sum of squares for the slope of the line is, analogous to (3.12),

$$\sum_i^k n_i(Y_i - \bar{y})^2 = b^2 \sum_i^k n_i(x_i - \bar{x})^2 = \frac{\left[\sum_i^k n_i(x_i - \bar{x})(\bar{y}_i - \bar{y})\right]^2}{\sum_i^k n_i(x_i - \bar{x})^2}. \quad (13.3)$$

For this we need

$$\sum_i^k n_i(x_i - \bar{x})^2 = \sum_i^k n_i x_i^2 - \frac{\left(\sum_i^k n_i x_i\right)^2}{\sum_i^k n_i} \quad (13.4)$$

$$= [2 \times (20.5)^2 + 2 \times (30.5)^2 + \cdots + 1 \times (57.8)^2]$$
$$- \frac{(2 \times 20.5 + 2 \times 30.5 + \cdots + 1 \times 57.8)^2}{7}$$

$$= 1199.128572$$

and

$$\sum_i^k n_i(x_i - \bar{x})(\bar{y}_i - \bar{y}) = \sum_i^k x_i \sum_v^{n_i} y_{iv} - \frac{\left(\sum_i^k \sum_v^{n_i} y_{iv}\right)\left(\sum_i^k n_i x_i\right)}{\sum_i^k n_i} \quad (13.5)$$

$$= (20.5 \times 7.57 + 30.5 \times 11.02 + \cdots + 57.8 \times 11.94)$$
$$- \frac{49.71 \times 249.1}{7}$$

$$= 277.480143,$$

whence, substituting in (13.3),

$$\sum_{i}^{k} n_i(Y_i - \bar{y})^2 = \frac{(277.480143)^2}{1199.128572} = 64.209320. \tag{13.6}$$

Finally we want the sum of squares for the variation of the true group means about the true line:

$$\sum_{i}^{k} n_i(\bar{y}_i - Y_i)^2 = \sum_{i}^{k} n_i[\bar{y}_i - \bar{y} - b(x_i - \bar{x})]^2$$

$$= \left[\sum_{i}^{k} \frac{\left(\sum_{v}^{n_i} y_{iv}\right)^2}{n_i} - \frac{\left(\sum_{i}^{k}\sum_{v}^{n_i} y_{iv}\right)^2}{\sum_{i}^{k} n_i}\right] - \frac{\left[\sum_{i}^{k} n_i(x_i - \bar{x})(\bar{y}_i - \bar{y})\right]^2}{\sum_{i}^{k} n_i(x_i - \bar{x})^2}$$

$$\tag{13.7}$$

$$= (418.035650 - 353.012014) - 64.209320 = 0.814316.$$

We now have the numerical values of all the mean squares, and can enter them in Table 11.10.

Table 11.10

Source of variance	Sums of squares	Degrees of freedom	Mean squares
Slope of line	64.209320	1	64.209320
Variation of true group means about the line	0.814316	3	0.271439
Within groups	0.228650	2	0.114325
Total	65.252286	6	

The test of linearity is given by $0.271439/0.114325 = 2.37$ which under the null hypothesis is distributed as F with degrees of freedom 3 and 2. The 0.90 point is 9.16; so obviously the null hypothesis is acceptable. The test of the null hypothesis $\beta = 0$ is given by $64.209320/0.114325 = 562$, which is distributed as F with degrees of freedom 1 and 2. The 0.995 point is 199; so obviously we reject the null hypothesis. However, many would take a point of view that either the true regression is linear or it is not. If it is, then the expected value of s_2^2 is σ^2, and they would pool the sums of squares and degrees of freedom of s_2^2 and s_1^2 to get a new estimate of σ^2, say $s_1'^2$, with degrees of freedom $\left(\sum_{i}^{k} n_i\right) - 2 = 5$. On the other hand, if the test of linearity leads to the rejection of the null hypothesis, then there is little point to a test of the null hypothesis $\beta = 0$. Deviation from

SECT. 11.13 LINEAR REGRESSION WITH SEVERAL OBSERVATIONS 375

linearity could be of two types. The η_i could lie erratically on either side of a line, the deviation having no systematic pattern, or η_i could lie on some more complicated curve such as a parabola. One would plot the points and inspect them to decide what the situation was.

The estimates of the parameters for the regression line are $a = 49.71/7 = 7.101429$ from (12.11) and $b = 277.480143/1199.128572 = 0.231401$ from (12.12). Also $\bar{x} = 249.7/7 = 35.585714$ from (12.1). Thus the estimated line is

$$Y = 7.101429 + 0.231401(x - 35.585714) = -1.133141 + 0.231401x. \tag{13.8}$$

The pooled estimate $s_1'^2$ of σ^2 is

$$s_1'^2 = \frac{0.814316 + 0.228650}{3 + 2} = 0.208593. \tag{13.9}$$

A test of the null hypothesis $\beta = 0$ equivalent to the one above can be made by substituting $s_1'^2$ for σ^2 in (12.17) which gives the estimated variance of b as $\hat{V}[b] = 0.208593/1199.128 = 0.0001740$. Then

$$\frac{b - \beta}{\sqrt{\hat{V}[b]}} \sim t\left(\sum_i^k n_i - 2\right). \tag{13.10}$$

Putting $\beta = 0$, we have $t(5) = (0.2314 - 0)/\sqrt{0.0001740} = 17.5$.

Ninety-five per cent confidence limits for β are $0.2314 \pm 2.571 \times 0.01319$ or $(0.1975, 0.2653)$.

We might ask what is the predicted square root stopping distance when $x = 50$:

$$Y = -1.133141 + 0.231401 \times 50 = 10.437. \tag{13.11}$$

Using $s'^2 = 0.208593$ with 5 degrees of freedom in place of σ^2 in (12.18),

$$\hat{V}[Y] = 0.208593\left[\frac{1}{7} + \frac{(50 - 35.5857)^2}{1199.128}\right] = 0.065942, \tag{13.12}$$

whence 95 per cent confidence limits for η at $x = 50$ are $\pm 2.571 \times \sqrt{0.065942} = \pm 0.660$ on either side of Y, i.e., $(9.777, 11.097)$.

In this case, if we are interested in not hitting something, a one-sided confidence limit might be more reasonable; for example, using $t_{0.01}(5) = -3.365$ to get an upper confidence limit.

$$10.437 - (-3.365) \times \sqrt{0.065942} = 11.301. \tag{13.13}$$

Thus we are 99 per cent confident that $\eta < 11.301$. However, we are probably more interested in a prediction limit for an individual observation, for which we use the equivalent of (3.23), which gives $\hat{V}[y - Y] = 0.274535$. The one-sided 99 per cent prediction limit is $10.437 + 3.365\sqrt{0.274575} = 12.200$.

11.14. The Comparison of Several Regression Lines: Simple Analysis of Covariance

The comparison of two regression lines (Section 11.6) fell into three parts; first, testing that the variance around the separate lines could be regarded as homogeneous; second, testing whether parallel lines through the respective means could be regarded as an acceptable fit; and third, testing whether these separate parallel lines could be regarded as coincident, i.e., as a single line.

This last operation is subject to a slightly different interpretation. Suppose that the two estimated parallel lines are

$$Y_1 = \bar{y}_1 + b(x - \bar{x}_1), \qquad Y_2 = \bar{y}_2 + b(x - \bar{x}_2). \qquad (14.1)$$

The observed averages of the y's of the two samples are $\bar{y}_1$ and $\bar{y}_2$. However, the x averages of the two samples were in general different, being $\bar{x}_1$ and $\bar{x}_2$. We might ask what the y averages would have been if the x averages had been the same, say equal to the weighted mean for the two samples,

$$\bar{x} = \frac{n_1\bar{x}_1 + n_2\bar{x}_2}{n_1 + n_2} = \frac{\sum\limits_{v}^{n_1} x_{1v} + \sum\limits_{v}^{n_2} x_{2v}}{n_1 + n_2}. \qquad (14.2)$$

Inserting this value of x in the two equations (14.1),

$$Y_{1(\bar{x})} = \bar{y}_1 + b(\bar{x} - \bar{x}_1), \qquad Y_{2(\bar{x})} = \bar{y}_2 + b(\bar{x} - \bar{x}_2); \qquad (14.3)$$

so

$$Y_{1(\bar{x})} - Y_{2(\bar{x})} = (\bar{y}_1 - \bar{y}_2) - b(\bar{x}_1 - \bar{x}_2) \qquad (14.4)$$

is the difference between the y averages, adjusted for differences in the x averages. But this is precisely the same quantity as (6.17), which we developed for testing whether the lines are identical. In other words, the test that the true lines are identical is the same as a test of whether the η averages are the same after adjustment for differences in the x averages. A test of whether a group of population means is identical is known as the analysis of variance. Here we are making an analysis of variance

SECT. 11.14 COMPARISON OF SEVERAL REGRESSION LINES

with adjustment for variation in x; this is called, perhaps not very felicitously, the analysis of covariance, the variable x being called the covariate or concomitant variable (see Figure 11.8).

An example suitable for covariance analysis is a study of the marketable weight of hogs fed different rations; it might be appropriate to use covariance on the weight of each hog at the start of the feeding trial. It would be most inappropriate to use as a covariate the amount of ration consumed per day, because this might be influenced by the ration itself.

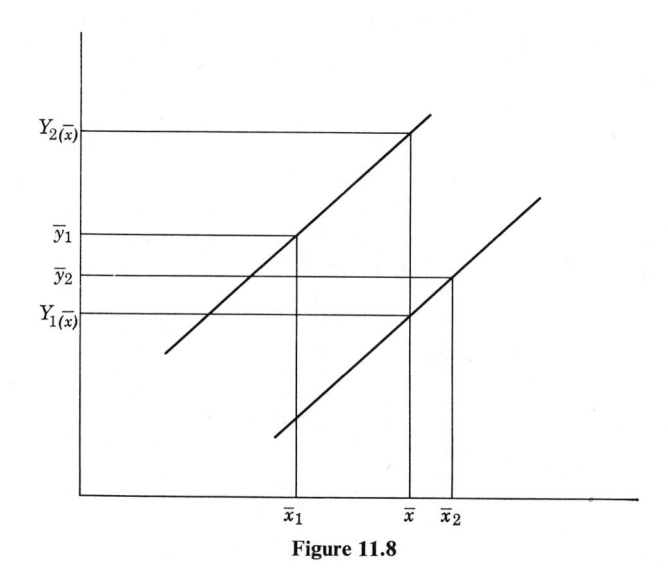

Figure 11.8

In pharmacological experiments, some initial measurement on each experimental subject might be used as a covariate. In experiments on performance of tests by human subjects after taking drugs, or after receiving instruction, measurements made on the same or similar tests before the administration of the treatment might be good covariates. All that is required of a covariate is that it be independent of the treatments under study, and that it be correlated with the variable we are analyzing. If the covariate x selected is actually uncorrelated with y, then there is no significant loss in precision compared with a simple analysis of variance of y. The only consequence is the wasted effort that goes into the additional arithmetic.

We assume that we have k groups of observations (x_{iv}, y_{iv}), $i = 1, \ldots, k$, $v = 1, \ldots, n_i$. A separate line can be fitted to each group, $Y = \bar{y}_{i.} + b_i(x - \bar{x}_{i.})$, and a sum of squares for variation about each line s_{i1}^2 will be obtained. These may be tested for heterogeneity by Bartlett's test, and, if the null hypothesis is acceptable, pooled to give

$$s_1^2 = \frac{\sum_i^k (n_i - 2)s_{i1}^2}{\sum_i^k (n_i - 2)}. \tag{14.5}$$

There are four sets of lines to be considered:

1. The k individual lines,

$$Y = \bar{y}_{i.} + b_i(x - \bar{x}_{i.}), \tag{14.6}$$

where b_i is, of course,

$$b_i = \frac{\sum_v^{n_i} (x_{iv} - \bar{x}_{i.})y_{iv}}{\sum_v^{n_i} (x_{iv} - \bar{x}_{i.})^2}. \tag{14.7}$$

2. The k parallel lines with an average slope $\bar{b}$;

$$Y = \bar{y}_{i.} + \bar{b}(x - \bar{x}_{i.}), \tag{14.8}$$

where, by analogy with (6.12),

$$\bar{b} = \frac{\sum_i^k \sum_v^{n_i} (x_{iv} - \bar{x}_{i.})y_{iv}}{\sum_i^k \sum_v^{n_i} (x_{iv} - \bar{x}_{i.})^2}. \tag{14.9}$$

3. The least squares line for the group means $(\bar{x}_{i.}, \bar{y}_{i.})$,

$$Y = \bar{y}_{..} + \hat{b}(x - \bar{x}_{..}), \tag{14.10}$$

where

$$\hat{b} = \frac{\sum_i^k n_i(\bar{x}_{i.} - \bar{x}_{..})\bar{y}_{i.}}{\sum_i^k n_i(\bar{x}_{i.} - \bar{x}_{..})^2}. \tag{14.11}$$

4. The overall regression line which assumes that all observations come from a single population,

$$Y = \bar{y}_{..} + b(x - \bar{x}_{..}), \tag{14.12}$$

where

$$b = \frac{\sum_i^k \sum_v^{n_i} (x_{iv} - \bar{x}_{..})y_{iv}}{\sum_i^k \sum_v^{n_i} (x_{iv} - \bar{x}_{..})^2}. \tag{14.13}$$

SECT. 11.14   COMPARISON OF SEVERAL REGRESSION LINES

The analysis of variance is based on the identity

$$y_{iv} - \bar{y}_{..} = (y_{iv} - Y_{iv}) + (Y_{iv} - \bar{y}_{..}), \qquad (14.14)$$

where Y_{iv} is the Y given by the overall regression line (14.12). When squared and summed over i and v, (14.14) gives

$$\sum_i^k \sum_v^{n_i} (y_{iv} - \bar{y}_{..})^2 = \sum_i^k \sum_v^{n_i} (y_{iv} - Y_{iv})^2 + \sum_i^k \sum_v^{n_i} (Y_{iv} - \bar{y}_{..})^2, \qquad (14.15)$$

where the last term is the sum of squares due to regression on the overall regression line (14.12), as in (3.10). The first term on the right-hand side of (14.14) represents the deviations of the individual observations from the values Y_{iv} predicted by the overall regression line. This deviation can be written as

$$\begin{aligned}
y_{iv} - Y_{iv} &= y_{iv} - [\bar{y}_{..} + b(x_{iv} - \bar{x}_{..})] \\
&= \{y_{iv} - [\bar{y}_{i.} + b_i(x_{iv} - \bar{x}_{i.})]\} + (b_i - \bar{b})(x_{iv} - \bar{x}_{i.}) \\
&\quad + \{\bar{y}_{i.} - [\bar{y}_{..} + \hat{b}(\bar{x}_{i.} - \bar{x}_{..})]\} \\
&\quad + [(\bar{b} - \hat{b})(x_{iv} - \bar{x}_{i.}) + (\hat{b} - b)(x_{iv} - \bar{x}_{..})]. \qquad (14.16)
\end{aligned}$$

The result of squaring this equation and summing over i and v is written as the second column in Table 11.11, with the following identity being used for the last term:

$$\sum_i^k \sum_v^{n_i} [(\bar{b} - \hat{b})(x_{iv} - \bar{x}_{i.}) + (\hat{b} - b)(x_{iv} - \bar{x}_{..})]^2$$

$$= \frac{(\hat{b} - \bar{b})^2}{\left[\sum_i^k n_i(\bar{x}_{i.} - \bar{x}_{..})^2\right]^{-1} + \left[\sum_i^k \sum_v^{n_i} (x_{iv} - \bar{x}_{i.})^2\right]^{-1}}. \qquad (14.17)$$

Proof of this identity is left as an exercise.

Table 11.11

Source of variance	Sums of squares	Degrees of freedom	Mean squares
Between $\hat{b}$ and $\bar{b}$	$\dfrac{(\hat{b} - \bar{b})^2}{\left[\sum_i^k n_i(\bar{x}_{i.} - \bar{x}_{..})^2\right]^{-1} + \left[\sum_i^k \sum_v^{n_i} (x_{iv} - \bar{x}_{i.})^2\right]^{-1}}$	1	s_4^2
Deviations of the group means about their regression line	$\sum_i^k n_i[\bar{y}_{i.} - \{\bar{y}_{..} + \hat{b}(\bar{x}_{i.} - \bar{x}_{..})\}]^2$	$k - 2$	s_3^2
Between the individual slopes b_i	$\sum_i^k (b_i - \bar{b})^2 \sum_v^{n_i} (x_{iv} - \bar{x}_{i.})^2$	$k - 1$	s_2^2
About the individual lines	$\sum_i^k \sum_v^{n_i} \{y_{iv} - [\bar{y}_{i.} + b_i(x_{iv} - \bar{x}_{i.})]\}^2$	$\sum_i^k n_i - 2k$	s_1^2
About the overall line	$\sum_i^k \sum_v^{n_i} \{y_{iv} - [\bar{y}_{..} + b(x_{iv} - \bar{x}_{..})]\}^2$	$\sum_i^k n_i - 2$	

Each term in (14.16) has a useful interpretation.

1. $y_{iv} - [\bar{y}_{i.} + b_i(x_{iv} - \bar{x}_{i.})]$ is the deviation between y_{iv} and the value predicted by the ith individual regression line (14.6). The corresponding sum of squares is the numerator of s_1^2 defined in (14.5).

2. $(b_i - \bar{b})(x_{iv} - \bar{x}_{i.})$ is the deviation between the slope of the ith individual line (14.6) and the parallel lines (14.8), weighted by the deviation of x_{iv} from $\bar{x}_{i.}$.

3. $\bar{y}_{i.} - [\bar{y}_{..} + \hat{b}(\bar{x}_{i.} - \bar{x}_{..})]$ is the deviation between the mean of the ith group and the value predicted by the regression line for group means, (14.10).

4. From the identity (14.17) we see that the sum of squares derived from the last term in (14.16) is a function of the difference between $\hat{b}$, the regression coefficient for the group means, and $\bar{b}$, the regression coefficient for the parallel lines.

Table 11.12 gives the results of observations on three lime kilns. The variables x and y were daily observations on the tons of lime made per day x and a measure of the quality of the lime y. The mean qualities $\bar{y}_{1.}$, $\bar{y}_{2.}$, $\bar{y}_{3.}$ (column 4) were 70.767, 69.933, and 79.514. A simple analysis of variance could be made on y_{iv} to test the null hypothesis that there was no difference between the kilns as regards quality, but it was known that y was roughly linearly related to x, and the tonnage means $\bar{x}_{1.}$, $\bar{x}_{2.}$, and $\bar{x}_{3.}$ (column 6) were 74.100, 69.733, and 66.541. We therefore want to compare the y means adjusted for variation in the x means. We need the sums of squares and products of x_{iv} and y_{iv}, and these are given in columns 7, 8, and 9. We next calculate $\sum_v^{n_i} (y_{iv} - \bar{y}_{i.})^2$, etc., in columns 10 through 15 of Table 11.12.

The various sums of squares can be calculated as follows.

The sum of squares for s_1^2 is the sum of the sums of squares of deviations about the separate lines: Each of these sums of squares is

$$\sum_v^{n_i} (y_{iv} - \bar{y}_{i.})^2 - \frac{\left[\sum_v^{n_i} (x_{iv} - \bar{x}_{i.})(y_{iv} - \bar{y}_{i.})\right]^2}{\sum_v^{n_i} (x_{iv} - \bar{x}_{i.})^2} ; \qquad (14.18)$$

so the sum over i is

$$\sum_i^k \sum_v^{n_i} (y_{iv} - \bar{y}_{i.})^2 - \sum_i^k \left\{ \frac{\left[\sum_v^{n_i} (x_{iv} - \bar{x}_{i.})(y_{iv} - \bar{y}_{i.})\right]^2}{\sum_v^{n_i} (x_{iv} - \bar{x}_{i.})^2} \right\}. \qquad (14.19)$$

SECT. 11.14 COMPARISON OF SEVERAL REGRESSION LINES 381

This calculation is carried out in Table 11.12. The separate sums of squares for each line, (14.18), are tabulated in column 17, and their sum over i, (14.19), is given in the last row of column 17.

The sum of squares for s_2^2 is

$$\sum_i^k (b_i - \bar{b})^2 \sum_v^{n_i} (x_{iv} - \bar{x}_{i.})^2$$

$$= \sum_i^k \frac{\left[\sum_v^{n_i} (x_{iv} - \bar{x}_{i.})(y_{iv} - \bar{y}_{i.})\right]^2}{\sum_v^{n_i} (x_{iv} - \bar{x}_{i.})^2} - \frac{\left[\sum_i^k \sum_v^{n_i} (x_{iv} - \bar{x}_{i.})(y_{iv} - \bar{y}_{i.})\right]^2}{\sum_i^k \sum_v^{n_i} (x_{iv} - \bar{x}_{i.})^2}.$$

(14.20)

$$= [16] - \frac{[15]^2}{[13]} = 13{,}158.245 - \frac{(21{,}972.630)^2}{38{,}196.689} = 518.498$$

where the numbers in square brackets are the column totals from Table 11.12. For the sum of squares for s_3^2 we need

$$\sum_i^k n_i(\bar{y}_{i.} - \bar{y}_{..})^2 = \sum_i^k \frac{\left(\sum_v^{n_i} y_{iv}\right)^2}{n_i} - \frac{\left(\sum_i^k \sum_v^{n_i} y_{iv}\right)^2}{\sum_i^k n_i}$$

(14.21)

$$= [10] - \frac{[3]^2}{[2]} = 604{,}246.590 - \frac{(8212)^2}{112} = 2131.019,$$

$$\sum_i^k n_i(\bar{x}_{i.} - \bar{x}_{..})(\bar{y}_{i.} - \bar{y}_{..})$$

$$= \sum_i^k \frac{\left(\sum_v^{n_i} x_{iv} \sum_v^{n_i} y_{iv}\right)}{n_i} - \frac{\left(\sum_i^k \sum_v^{n_i} x_{iv}\right)\left(\sum_i^k \sum_v^{n_i} y_{iv}\right)}{\sum_i^k n_i}$$

(14.22)

$$= [14] - \frac{[5][3]}{[2]} = 572{,}527.370 - \frac{7823 \times 8212}{112} = -1066.166,$$

$$\sum_i^k n_i(\bar{x}_{i.} - \bar{x}_{..})^2 = \sum_i^k \frac{\left(\sum_v^{n_i} x_{iv}\right)^2}{n_i} - \frac{\left(\sum_i^k \sum_v^{n_i} x_{iv}\right)^2}{\sum_i^k n_i}$$

(14.23)

$$= [12] - \frac{[5]^2}{[2]} = 547{,}370.311 - \frac{(7823)^2}{112} = 947.731.$$

Table 11.12

1	2	3	4	5	6	7	8	9	10	11
i	n_i	$\sum_v^{n_i} y_{iv}$	$\bar{y}_{i.}$	$\sum_v^{n_i} x_{iv}$	$\bar{x}_{i.}$	$\sum_v^{n_i} y_{iv}^2$	$\sum_v^{n_i} x_{iv}^2$	$\sum_v^{n_i} y_{iv} x_{iv}$	$\dfrac{\left(\sum_v^{n_i} y_{iv}\right)^2}{n_i}$	$[7] - [10] =$ $\sum_v^{n_i}(y_{iv} - \bar{y}_{i.})^2$
1	30	2123	70.767	2223	74.100	159,813	176,675	162,518	150,237.633	9,575.367
2	45	3147	69.933	3138	69.733	232,975	233,698	227,882	220,080.200	12,894.800
3	37	2942	79.514	2462	66.541	247,854	175,194	204,100	233,928.757	13,925.243
$\sum_i^k n_i$ $=112$		$\sum_i^k \sum_v^{n_i} y_{iv}$ $=8212$		$\sum_i^k \sum_v^{n_i} x_{iv}$ $=7823$		$\sum_i^k \sum_v^{n_i} y_{iv}^2$ $=640{,}642$	$\sum_i^k \sum_v^{n_i} x_{iv}^2$ $=585{,}567$	$\sum_i^k \sum_v^{n_i} y_{iv} x_{iv}$ $=594{,}500$	$\sum_i^k \dfrac{\left(\sum_v^{n_i} y_{iv}\right)^2}{n_i}$ $=604{,}246.590$	$\sum_i^k \sum_v^{n_i} (y_{iv}-\bar{y}_{i.})^2$ $=36{,}395.410$

Table 11.12 (Continued)

1	12	13	14	15	16	17
i	$\dfrac{\left(\sum\limits_{v}^{n_i} x_{iv}\right)^2}{n_i}$	$[8] - [12] =$ $\sum\limits_{v}^{n_i}(x_{iv} - \bar{x}_{i.})^2$	$\dfrac{\sum\limits_{v}^{n_i} x_{iv} \sum\limits_{v}^{n_i} y_{iv}}{n_i}$	$[9] - [14] =$ $\sum\limits_{v}^{n_i}(x_{iv} - \bar{x}_{i.})(y_{iv} - \bar{y}_{i.})$	$[15]^2/[13] =$ $\dfrac{\left[\sum\limits_{v}^{n_i}(x_{iv} - \bar{x}_{i.})(y_{iv} - \bar{y}_{i.})\right]^2}{\sum\limits_{v}^{n_i}(x_{iv} - \bar{x}_{i.})^2}$	$[11] - [16]$
1	164,724.300	11,950.700	157,314.300	5203.700	2265.850	7309.517
2	218,823.200	14,874.800	219,450.800	8431.200	4778.897	8115.903
3	163,822.811	11,371.189	195,762.270	8337.730	6113.498	7811.745
	$\sum\limits_{i}^{k}\dfrac{\left(\sum\limits_{v}^{n_i} x_{iv}\right)^2}{n_i}$	$\sum\limits_{i}^{k}\sum\limits_{v}^{n_i}(x_{iv} - \bar{x}_{i.})^2$	$\sum\limits_{i}^{k}\dfrac{\sum\limits_{v}^{n_i} x_{iv} \sum\limits_{v}^{n_i} y_{iv}}{n_i}$	$\sum\limits_{i}^{k}\sum\limits_{v}^{n_i}(x_{iv} - \bar{x}_{i.})(y_{iv} - \bar{y}_{i.})$	$\sum\limits_{i}^{k}\dfrac{\left[\sum\limits_{v}^{n_i}(x_{iv} - \bar{x}_{i.})(y_{iv} - \bar{y}_{i.})\right]^2}{\sum\limits_{v}^{n_i}(x_{iv} - \bar{x}_{i.})^2}$	Sum of squares for s_1^2
	$= 547,370.311$	$= 38,196.689$	$= 572,527.370$	$= 21,972.630$	$= 13,158.245$	$= 23,237.165$

The sum of squares for s_3^2 is

$$\sum_i^k n_i[\bar{y}_{i.} - \{\bar{y}_{..} + \hat{b}(\bar{x}_{i.} - \bar{x}_{..})\}]^2$$

$$= \sum_i^k n_i(\bar{y}_{i.} - \bar{y}_{..})^2 - \frac{\left[\sum_i^k n_i(\bar{x}_{i.} - \bar{x}_{..})(\bar{y}_{i.} - \bar{y}_{..})\right]^2}{\sum_i^k n_i(\bar{x}_{i.} - \bar{x}_{..})^2} \quad (14.24)$$

$$= 2131.019 - \frac{(-1066.166)^2}{947.731} = 931.618.$$

For the sum of squares for s_4^2 we first substitute [15] and [13] in (14.9),

$$\bar{b} = \frac{21{,}972.630}{38{,}196.689} = 0.575250,$$

and (14.22) and (14.23) in (14.11),

$$\hat{b} = \frac{-1066.166}{947.731} = -1.24967.$$

We can now calculate the sum of squares for s_4^2 from (14.17) as

$$(-1.124967 - 0.575250)^2 \left(\frac{1}{947.731} + \frac{1}{38{,}196.689}\right)^{-1} = 2673.310.$$

For the sum of squares about the overall line we first need

$$\sum_i^k \sum_v^{n_i} (y_{iv} - \bar{y}_{..})^2 = \sum_i^k \sum_v^{n_i} y_{iv}^2 - \frac{\left(\sum_i^k \sum_v^{n_i} y_{iv}\right)^2}{\sum_i^k n_i} \quad (14.25)$$

$$= [7] - \frac{[3]^2}{[2]} = 640{,}642 - \frac{(8212)^2}{112} = 38{,}526.429,$$

$$\sum_i^k \sum_v^{n_i} (y_{iv} - \bar{y}_{..})(x_{iv} - \bar{x}_{..}) = \sum_i^k \sum_v^{n_i} x_{iv} y_{iv} - \frac{\sum_i^k \sum_v^{n_i} x_{iv} \sum_i^k \sum_v^{n_i} y_{iv}}{\sum_i^k n_i} \quad (14.26)$$

$$= [9] - \frac{[5][3]}{[2]} = 594{,}500 - \frac{7823 \times 8212}{112} = 20{,}906.464,$$

SECT. 11.14   COMPARISON OF SEVERAL REGRESSION LINES   385

and

$$\sum_i^k \sum_v^{n_i} (x_{iv} - \bar{x}_{..})^2 = \sum_i^k \sum_v^{n_i} x_{iv}^2 - \frac{\left(\sum_i^k \sum_v^{n_i} x_{iv}\right)^2}{\sum_i^k n_i} \quad (14.27)$$

$$= [8] - \frac{[5]^2}{[2]} = 585{,}567 - \frac{(7823)^2}{112} = 39{,}144.420.$$

Then the sum of squares of deviations about the overall line is

$$\sum_i^k \sum_v^{n_i} (y_{iv} - Y_{iv})^2 = \sum_i^k \sum_v^{n_i} \{y_i - [\bar{y}_{..} + b(x_{iv} - \bar{x}_{..})]\}^2$$

$$= \sum_i^k \sum_v^{n_i} (y_{iv} - \bar{y}_{..})^2 - \frac{\left[\sum_i^k \sum_v^{n_i} (y_{iv} - \bar{y}_{..})(x_{iv} - \bar{x}_{..})\right]^2}{\sum_i^k \sum_v^{n_i} (x_{iv} - \bar{x}_{..})^2} \quad (14.28)$$

$$= 38{,}526.429 - \frac{(20{,}906.464)^2}{39{,}144.420} = 27{,}360.591.$$

The sum of squares due to regression on the overall line is

$$\sum_i^k \sum_v^{n_i} (Y_{iv} - \bar{y}_{..})^2 = \frac{\left[\sum_i^k \sum_v^{n_i} (y_{iv} - \bar{y}_{..})(x_{iv} - \bar{x}_{..})\right]^2}{\sum_i^k \sum_v^{n_i} (x_{iv} - \bar{x}_{..})^2} \quad (14.29)$$

$$= \frac{(20{,}906.464)^2}{39{,}144.420} = 11{,}165.838.$$

Finally, the total sum of squares about the grand mean is

$$\sum_i^k \sum_v^{n_i} (y_{iv} - \bar{y}_{..})^2 = 38{,}526.429.$$

We now assemble all these sums of squares in Table 11.13.

Various interpretations of Tables 11.11 and 11.13 are illustrated in Figure 11.9.

In Figure 11.9a the slopes β_i of the individual lines are different and in general not equal to the average slope $\bar{\beta}$ of the separate parallel lines. The test of the null hypothesis $\beta_i = \bar{\beta}$ is given by $s_2^2/s_1^2 = 259.249/219.219 = 1.18$ which under the null hypothesis is distributed here as $F(2, 106)$. Clearly here the null hypothesis of parallelism of the separate lines is acceptable.

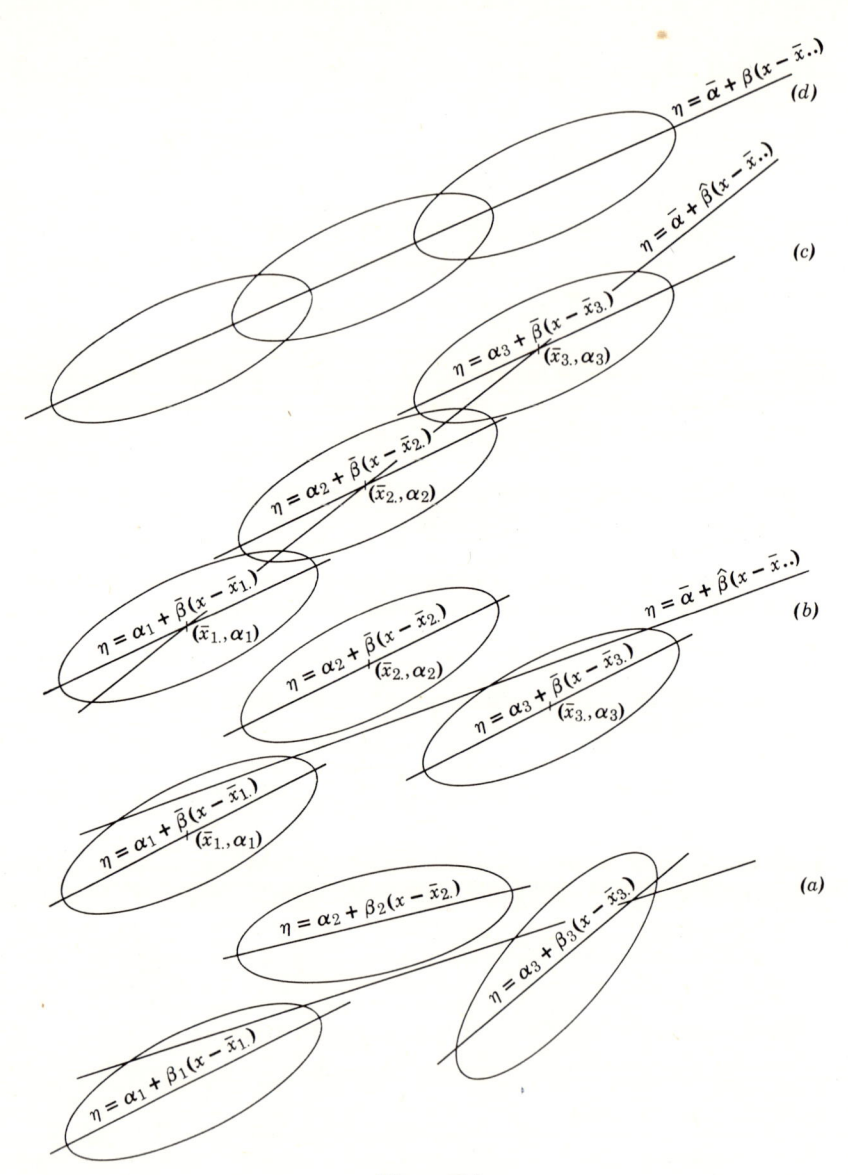

Figure 11.9

SECT. 11.14 COMPARISON OF SEVERAL REGRESSION LINES

If we can accept the foregoing null hypothesis we then proceed to test whether the group means can be regarded as lying on a least squares line. In Figure 11.9*b* they do not, whereas in Figure 11.9*c* they do; the test is $s_3^2/s_1^2 = 931.618/219.219 = 4.25$, which under the null hypothesis is distributed here as $F(1, 106)$. In this instance this null hypothesis is rejected. This establishes that the lines for the groups do differ in the way illustrated by Figure 11.9*b*.

Table 11.13

Source of variance	Sums of squares	Degrees of freedom	Mean squares
Between $\hat{b}$ and $\bar{b}$	2,673.310	1	$2673.310 = s_4^2$
Deviations of the group means about their regression line	931.618	1	$931.618 = s_3^2$
Between the individual slopes	518.498	2	$259.249 = s_2^2$
About the individual lines	23,237.165	106	$219.219 = s_1^2$
About the over-all line	27,360.591	110	
Due to the over-all line	11,165.838	1	
Total	38,526.429	111	

If this null hypothesis had been accepted, then there would remain the possibility that though the individual lines are parallel with slope $\bar{\beta}$ and the group means do lie on a line with slope $\hat{\beta}$, yet $\bar{\beta} \neq \hat{\beta}$, as illustrated in Figure 11.9*c*. The alternative is that $\bar{\beta} = \hat{\beta}$, as illustrated in Figure 11.9*d*, and this implies that a single line, the overall regression line, is an adequate fit to all groups. The test for this in Tables 11.11 and 11.13 is s_4^2/s_1^2.

In some forms of analysis of covariance, the parallelism of the separate lines is assumed, so that s_1^2 and s_2^2 are pooled, and also the null hypotheses involved in s_3^2 and s_4^2 are tested jointly, by pooling these. This will be discussed in the next section.

If we accept the null hypothesis that the individual lines are parallel, we can construct the adjusted means as follows. The individual lines with common slope (14.8) are

$$Y_i = \bar{y}_{i.} + \bar{b}(x - \bar{x}_{i.}) \tag{14.30}$$

and the *y* mean adjusted for *x* equal to $\bar{x}_{..}$ is

$$Y_{i(\bar{x})} = \bar{y}_{i.} + \bar{b}(\bar{x}_{..} - \bar{x}_{i.}). \tag{14.31}$$

For example, $\bar{x}_{..} = 7823/112 = 69.848$, and

$$Y_{1(\bar{x})} = 70.767 + 0.57525(69.848 - 74.100) = 68.321.$$

The variance between two adjusted means is

$$\begin{aligned}
V[Y_{i(\bar{x})} - Y_{i'(\bar{x})}] &= V[\bar{y}_{i.} + \bar{b}(\bar{x}_{..} - \bar{x}_{i.}) - \bar{y}_{i'.} - \bar{b}(\bar{x}_{..} - \bar{x}_{i'.})] \\
&= V[\bar{y}_{i.}] + V[\bar{y}_{i'.}] + (\bar{x}_{i.} - \bar{x}_{i'.})^2 V[\bar{b}] \\
&= \sigma^2 \left[\frac{1}{n_i} + \frac{1}{n_{i'}} + \frac{(\bar{x}_{i.} - \bar{x}_{i'.})^2}{\sum_i^k \sum_v^{n_i} (x_{iv} - \bar{x}_{i.})^2} \right],
\end{aligned} \qquad (14.32)$$

where $V[\bar{b}]$ is given by a formula analogous to (6.13).

For example, the estimated variance between the adjusted means for kilns 1 and 2 is

$$\hat{V}[Y_{1(\bar{x})} - Y_{2(\bar{x})}] = 219.219 \left[\frac{1}{30} + \frac{1}{45} + \frac{(74.100 - 69.733)^2}{38{,}196.689} \right] = 12.29,$$

and the confidence limits can be immediately constructed.

Table 11.14

Source of variance	Sums of squares	Degrees of freedom	Mean squares
Between kilns	2,131.019	2	1065.509
Within kilns	36,395.410	109	333.903
Total	38,526.429	111	

It is natural to inquire whether the analysis of covariance of these data has achieved any advantages over a simple analysis of variance of y. From the calculations given, we can readily assemble Table 11.14. The variance ratio is 3.191, which can be compared with 8.222 obtained from Table 11.13 by pooling s_4^2 and s_3^2. We can also compute the variances between the unadjusted means as

$$\hat{V}[Y_1 - Y_2] = 333.903(\tfrac{1}{30} + \tfrac{1}{45}) = 18.550$$

which is some 50 per cent larger than the variance between the adjusted means.

11.15. Simple Analysis of Covariance

Quite frequently the analysis of the previous section is simplified. Two changes are made:

1. The sums of squares and degrees of freedom for s_4^2 and s_3^2 in Table

SECT. 11.15 SIMPLE ANALYSIS OF COVARIANCE

11.11 are combined into a single line measuring differences between the adjusted y means.

2. The test for parallelism of the individual slopes involving s_2^2 is omitted.

The effect of these two changes is to simplify the arithmetic considerably. This modified analysis starts from a table of sums of squares and products (Table 11.15).

Table 11.15

Source of variance	Degrees of freedom	Sums of squares and products for x^2	for xy	for y^2
Groups	$k-1$	$\sum_i^k n_i(\bar{x}_i. - \bar{x}..)^2 = T_{xx}$	$\sum_i^k n_i(\bar{x}_i. - \bar{x}..)(\bar{y}_i. - \bar{y}..)^2 = T_{xy}$	$\sum_i^k n_i(\bar{y}_i. - \bar{y}..)^2 = T_{yy}$
Error	$\sum_i^k n_i - k$	$\sum_i^k \sum_v^{n_i} (x_{iv} - \bar{x}_i.)^2 = E_{xx}$	$\sum_i^k \sum_v^{n_i} (x_{iv} - \bar{x}_i.)(y_{iv} - \bar{y}_i.) = E_{xy}$	$\sum_i^k \sum_v^{n_i} (y_{iv} - \bar{y}_i.)^2 = E_{yy}$
Total	$\sum_i^k n_i - 1$	$\sum_i^k \sum_v^{n_i} (x_{iv} - \bar{x}..)^2 = S_{xx}$	$\sum_i^k \sum_v^{n_i} (x_{iv} - \bar{x}..)(y_{iv} - \bar{y}..) = S_{xy}$	$\sum_i^k \sum_v^{n_i} (y_{iv} - \bar{y}..)^2 = S_{yy}$

To pool s_4^2 and s_3^2 in Table 11.11 involves pooling the degrees of freedom, $1 + (k - 2) = k - 1$, and the corresponding sums of squares. Call the pooled mean square s_6^2. Then the corresponding sums of squares will be $(k-1)s_6^2$. Straightforward manipulation gives for the sum of squares for the adjusted y means

$$(k-1)s_6^2 = T_{yy} - \frac{(E_{xy} + T_{xy})^2}{E_{xx} + T_{xx}} + \frac{E_{xy}^2}{E_{xx}}, \qquad (15.1)$$

changing from the notation of Table 11.11 to that of Table 11.15.

To dispense with the test for parallelism of the individual lines amounts to assuming that the individual lines are parallel, when s_2^2 of Table 11.11 will have expected value σ^2. Pooling the degrees of freedom of s_2^2 and s_1^2 gives

$$(k-1) + \left(\sum_i^k n_i - 2k\right) = \sum_i^k n_i - k - 1. \qquad (15.2)$$

Straightforward manipulation gives the error sum of squares as

$$\left(\sum_i^k n_i - k - 1\right)s_5^2 = E_{yy} - \frac{E_{xy}^2}{E_{xx}} \qquad (15.3)$$

changing from the notation of Table 11.11 to that of Table 11.15.

Under the null hypothesis that the adjusted means are equal, s_6^2/s_5^2 will be distributed as $F\left(k - 1, \sum_i^k n_i - k - 1\right)$.

To apply this simplified procedure to the data of the example of the previous section, Table 11.16 gives the numerical values corresponding to the data of Table 11.12.

The T's and the S's have been calculated earlier, the E's are most easily obtained by difference. Using (15.1), the sum of squares for adjusted y means is

$$2s_6^2 = 2131.019 - \frac{(20,906.464)^2}{39,144.420} + \frac{(21,972.630)^2}{38,196.689} = 3604.927;$$

so $s_6^2 = 1802.463$. It will be noted that, as a check, the sum of the sums of squares for s_4^2 and s_3^2 in Table 11.13 is $2673.310 + 931.618 = 3604.928$. Using (15.3), the sum of squares for error is

$$(112 - 3 - 1)s_5^2 = 36,395.410 - \frac{(21,972.630)^2}{38,196.689} = 23,755.664;$$

so $s_5^2 = 219.960$. It will be noted, as a check, that the sum of squares for s_2^2 and s_1^2 in Table 11.13 is $518.498 + 23,237.165 = 23,755.663$.

Table 11.16

Source of variance	Degrees of freedom	Sums of squares and sum of products of deviations		
		for x^2	for xy	for y^2
Groups	2	$T_{xx} = 947.731$	$T_{xy} = -1,066.166$	$T_{yy} = 2,131.019$
Error	109	$E_{xx} = 38,196.689$	$E_{xy} = 21,972.630$	$E_{yy} = 36,395.410$
Total	111	$S_{xx} = 39,144.420$	$S_{xy} = 20,906.464$	$S_{yy} = 38,526.429$

Hence the test of the null hypothesis of equality of the adjusted means is

$$\frac{s_6^2}{s_5^2} = \frac{1802.463}{219.960} = 8.19 \sim F(2, 108).$$

The arithmetic necessary for this simplified analysis of covariance is substantially less complex than in the full analysis of the previous section. Nevertheless, the full analysis would ordinarily be indicated except in routine applications where a substantial body of previous experience had established that the separate lines, if not truly parallel, at least must be very nearly so. Nonparallelism of the lines is an important feature and should not be overlooked.

The interpretation of an analysis of covariance can prove remarkably tricky, and a paper by Fairfield Smith [7] should be studied in this context. For a general discussion see Cochran [8].

11.16. Exponential Regression

Suppose that our model is

$$\eta = \alpha e^{\beta x}. \tag{16.1}$$

The sum of squares of deviations between the observations y_i and the predictions Y_i given by the estimated equation $Y = ae^{bx}$ is

$$R = \sum (y_i - Y_i)^2 = \sum (y_i - ae^{bx_i})^2. \tag{16.2}$$

Differentiating this with respect to a and b and equating to zero gives

$$\frac{\partial R}{\partial a} = -2 \sum y_i e^{bx_i} + 2a \sum e^{2bx_i} = 0, \tag{16.3}$$

$$\frac{\partial R}{\partial b} = -2a \sum x_i y_i e^{bx_i} + 2a^2 \sum x_i e^{2bx_i} = 0, \tag{16.4}$$

whence we have the two simultaneous equations

$$\sum y_i e^{bx_i} = a \sum e^{2bx_i}, \tag{16.5}$$

$$\sum x_i y_i e^{bx_i} = a \sum x_i e^{2bx_i}, \tag{16.6}$$

in the two unknowns a and b. An exact solution can only be approximated to by a tedious iterative procedure.

An alternative approach is to take logarithms of (16.1):

$$\log \eta = \log \alpha + \beta x, \tag{16.7}$$

and obtain a least squares solution for $\log \alpha$ and β by minimizing

$$R = \sum (\log y_i - \log Y_i)^2 \tag{16.8}$$

in the usual way, i.e., handle the problem as if it was to regress $\log y$ on x. The use of $\log y$ in place of y means that we are minimizing the sums of squares of deviations of $\log y$ from $\log Y$ instead of y from Y; so we will obtain a different solution. Also, if $V[y|x] = \sigma^2$, a constant, then $V[\log y|x]$ will not be a constant, and the least-squares analysis based on $\log y$ will be incorrect. Quite often, however, $V[y|x] = k^2\eta^2$; i.e., the standard deviation is proportional to the mean, and then, as discussed in Section 3.3, $\log y$ will have a constant variance. In these circumstances, then, we will be correct in regressing $\log y$ on x.

11.17. Regression with Error in the Independent Variable

Throughout this chapter we have assumed that the independent variable x was observed without error. We have further supposed that y was distributed normally about η with variance σ^2, and it is irrelevant whether this variation in y is in some sense genuine or represents measurement error. For example, if we were measuring the current y in a circuit for various values of the applied voltage x, then presumably variation in y is largely measurement error. On the other hand, if we were measuring the weights of hogs y fed various quantities of a ration supplement x, then the larger part of the variation in y for a fixed x would represent genuine variation in the hogs' weight. The theory of this chapter is the same whether the variation in y is measurement error or genuine variation. The assumption that x is known without error is, however, fundamental.

Suppose that there is a true linear relation

$$v = \alpha + \beta u \qquad (17.1)$$

where α and β are constants. Suppose that we obtain the various values of x in the following manner. The controls of the plant are set to bring u into roughly the desired region, and we then measure u with error d, independent of u, so that we record the measurement as x' where

$$x' = u + d. \qquad (17.2)$$

The variable v is observed and measured with error e, independent of v, so that we record

$$y' = v + e. \qquad (17.3)$$

Thus $v = y' - e$, $u = x' - d$. Substituting in (17.1),

$$y' = \alpha + \beta x' + (e - \beta d). \qquad (17.4)$$

This appears at first sight to be a standard regression model, y' being given by a linear relation $\alpha + \beta x'$ plus a random error $e - \beta d$. However, in standard regression analysis it is assumed that the random error is independent of the independent variable. In the present case this condition is not satisfied. We demonstrate this as follows:

$$\begin{aligned} \text{Cov}\,[x', e - \beta d] &= E[(u + d)(e - \beta d)] - E[u + d]E[e - \beta d] \\ &= E[ue] + E[de] - E[ud] - \beta E[d^2] \\ &\quad - \{E[u] + E[d]\}\{E[e] - \beta E[d]\}. \end{aligned} \qquad (17.5)$$

Now we are assuming that d is independent of u and of e, and e to be independent of u, and d and e to have zero expectations. It follows that

$$\text{Cov}\,[x', e - \beta d] = -\beta E[d^2] = -\beta V[d] \neq 0, \qquad (17.6)$$

and therefore x' and $e - \beta d$ are not independent. For reviews of what can be done in this situation see Madansky [9] and Keeping [10].

Berkson [11] pointed out that if we operate the controls to bring a gauge recording u to a selected value X', it is true that due to random errors in the gauge, say d, we do not get the plant set at X' but instead at

$$u = X' - d. \qquad (17.7)$$

If we substitute this value of u and $v = y' - e$ from (17.3) in (17.1), on rearranging we get

$$y' = \alpha + \beta X' + (e - \beta d). \qquad (17.8)$$

This is a standard linear regression situation, since X' is a fixed, chosen variable and the error term $e - \beta d$ is independent of X'. Hence our sample estimate of β will be unbiased.

For a review of Berkson's model, see Lindley [12], and for a generalization, see Scheffé [13].

EXERCISES

11.1. The solubility of nitrous oxide in nitrogen dioxide was determined with results as below for temperature ranging from 263 to 283 degrees absolute. The reciprocal temperature is expressed as $1000/T$. A number of independent determinations were made at each temperature. [Data from W. Arthur Rocker, "Solubility and freezing point depression of nitrous oxide in liquid nitrogen dioxide," *Analytical Chemistry*, 24 (1952), 1322–1324.]

Reciprocal temperature	3.801	3.731	3.662	3.593	3.533
Solubility, % by weight	1.28 1.33 1.52	1.21 1.27	1.11 1.04	0.81 0.82	0.65 0.59 0.63

(a) Fit a straight line of the regression of solubility on reciprocal temperature. (b) Test this line for deviations from linearity. (c) If the hypothesis of linearity is acceptable, form a pooled estimate of the variance of the solubility measurements. (d) What is your estimate of the true solubility for a reciprocal temperature of 3.78? (e) What are the 95 per cent confidence limits for this estimate? (f) What are the 95 per cent confidence limits for the slope of the line? (g) Suppose you took a sample and found its solubility to be 1.30. Between what limits would you have 95 per cent confidence that the reciprocal temperature lay (assuming the sample to be saturated)? Use (i) an exact method, (ii) an approximate method.

11.2. The data below are similar to those of Table 11.9 but on a sample of a different make of automobile.

x_i	19.65	31.15	35.95	50.15	59.65
y_i	3.44 3.93	4.98 5.45	6.40	8.88	11.22

I. (*a*) Obtain the regression line of y on x. (*b*) Test the null hypothesis of linearity for this line. (*c*) Extrapolate the line to $x = 0$, and construct 95 per cent confidence limits for η at this value of x.

II. Compare this line with that for the data of Table 11.9. (*a*) Compare the variances about the regression lines. (*b*) Compare the slopes. (*c*) Test whether the lines can be regarded as coincident.

11.3. In a comparison of a new method of gas analysis with a standard method, the following results were obtained on a series of samples:

Standard method (x):	2.97	3.56	6.45	1.12	6.66	1.37	6.80
New method (y):	2.94	3.54	6.48	1.08	6.73	1.33	6.86

Data from Jere Mead, "A critical orifice CO_2 analysis suitable for student use," *Science*, 121 (1955), 103–104.

Fit the line $y = a + b(x - \bar{x})$, and test at the level of significance $\alpha = 0.05$ the null hypotheses (*a*) $\beta = 1$; (*b*) the intercept on the y axis equals zero; (*c*) items (*a*) and (*b*) jointly.

11.4. In an assay of a preparation of insulin of unknown potency against a standard, three doses of the unknown and three doses of the standard were injected into rabbits, and the percentage fall in blood sugar after a certain period was observed; these are the data below. In insulin assay of this type, it is usually assumed that the plot of the above variable against log dose is a straight line. (*a*) Test the parallelism of the two lines. (*b*) Calculate the point estimate of the potency ratio. (*c*) Calculate 95 per cent confidence limits for the potency ratio.

Preparation

Standard log dose			Unknown log dose		
0.36	0.56	0.76	0.36	0.56	0.76
17	64	62	33	41	56
21	48	72	37	64	62
49	34	61	40	34	57
54	63	91	16	64	72
			21	48	73
			18	34	72
			25		81
					60

11.5. A sample of 56 subjects were given a test involving mental addition, x. They were divided into four groups randomly, and each group drank one of four beverages, which could not be distinguished by the subject. After a short time interval to allow the drugs in the beverages to act, the subjects were retested by a replicate of the first test, y. The scores are as below (data from H. Nash).

Drug A		Drug B		Drug C		Drug D	
x	y	x	y	x	y	x	y
24	24	23	18	27	35	27	28
28	30	33	32	27	31	44	40
38	39	39	33	44	55	39	34
42	41	36	35	38	43	27	27
24	27	18	19	32	44	59	47
39	46	28	28	32	28	36	30
45	56	43	41	24	33	19	24
19	25	37	37	13	13	34	28
19	18	30	33	39	39	22	21
22	25	49	39	52	58	28	28
34	31	37	38	17	18	39	39
52	52	40	41	20	17	29	26
27	38	36	38	49	41	55	46
42	45	41	36	29	25	49	42

I. Make a simple analysis of variance on the y's.

II. Make a simple analysis of variance on the differences $y - x$.

III. (a) Make an analysis of covariance of y, including a test for the parallelism of the separate regression lines. (b) Discuss the difference between I, II, and IIIa. (c) Construct a simple (nonmultiple) comparison 95 per cent confidence interval for the difference between the adjusted means for drugs A and B. (d) B is a placebo and C and D are two levels of a certain drug, where the level of D is twice the level of C. The contrast $B - 2C + D$ will measure the linearity of response. Construct a 95 per cent multiple comparison confidence interval for this contrast.

Certain sums and sums of squares and products which may be useful are below

i	n_i	$\sum_{v}^{n_i} y_{iv}$	$\sum_{v}^{n_i} x_{iv}$	$\sum_{v}^{n_i} y_{iv}^2$	$\sum_{v}^{n_i} x_{iv}^2$	$\sum_{v}^{n_i} x_{iv} y_{iv}$
1	14	497	455	19,367	16,249	17,623
2	14	468	490	16,332	18,008	17,066
3	14	480	443	18,842	15,787	17,018
4	14	460	507	16,040	20,265	17,941
$\sum_{i}^{k}$	56	1905	1895	70,581	70,309	69,648

REFERENCES

1. Acton, Forman S., *Analysis of Straight-Line Data*. New York: John Wiley and Sons, 1959.
2. David, F. N., and J. Neyman, "Extension of the Markov Theorem of Least Squares," *Statistical Research Memoirs*, 2 (1938), 105–116.
3. Plackett, R. L., "A Historical Note on Least Squares," *Biometrika*, 36 (1949), 458–60.
4. Finney, D. J., *Probit Analysis*. 2nd ed.; London: Cambridge University Press, 1952.
5. Finney, D. J., *Statistical Methods in Biological Assay*. New York: Hafner Publishing Co., 1952.
6. Emmens, C. W., *Principles of Biological Assay*. London: Chapman and Hall, 1948.
7. Smith, H. Fairfield, "Interpretation of Adjusted Treatment Means and Regressions in Analysis of Covariance," *Biometrics*, 13 (1957), 282–308.
8. Cochran, William G., "Analysis of Covariance: Its Nature and Uses," *Biometrics*, 13 (1957), 261–81.
9. Madansky, Albert, "The Fitting of Straight Lines When Both Variables are Subject to Error," *Journal of the American Statistical Association*, 54 (1959), 173–205.
10. Keeping, E. S., *Introduction to Statistical Inference*. Princeton, N.J.: D. Van Nostrand, 1962.
11. Berkson, J., "Are There Two Regressions?" *Journal of the American Statistical Association*, 45 (1950), 164–80.
12. Lindley, D. V., "Estimation of a Functional Relationship," *Biometrika*, 40 (1953), 47–49.
13. Scheffé, H., "Fitting Straight Lines When One Variable Is Controlled," *Journal of the American Statistical Association*, 53 (1958), 106–117.

CHAPTER 12

The Bivariate Normal Distribution and the Correlation Coefficient

12.1. Introduction

In the preceding chapter we supposed that we observed y at a number of selected values of x. The values of x used were what we cared to make them, and x was not a random variable. In this chapter we discuss the case where both x and y are random variables, drawn from some hypothetical population. For example, x could be the girth of a hog and y its marketable weight; or x could be the "intelligence" of a brother and y the "intelligence" of his sister; or x could be the grade average of members of a class and y their income in dollars after Federal income taxes, 10 years later. In every case care should be taken to define quite precisely the population from which the sample is taken, and to recognize that any inferences possible are strictly applicable only to that population.

12.2. Transformations of Bivariate Distributions

In Section 1.14 we saw how to obtain the distribution of a function of x, given the distribution of x. In this section we do the analogous thing for a bivariate distribution.

We are given a bivariate distribution with the probability density determined by the function $p_X(x_1, x_2)$. We are also given that y_1 is some function of x_1, x_2, namely, $y_1 = f_1(x_1, x_2)$, and likewise y_2 is another function of x_1, x_2, namely, $y_2 = f_2(x_1, x_2)$. We assume that these functions have continuous first partial derivatives, and that to each point in the (x_1, x_2) plane there is one and only one point in the (y_1, y_2) plane and vice versa. Let the inverse functions be $x_1 = g_1(y_1, y_2)$, $x_2 = g_2(y_1, y_2)$.

Now, if X_1, X_2 are random variables, then Y_1, Y_2 will be random variables. Our problem is to determine

$$\Pr\{y_1 < Y_1 < y_1 + dy_1, y_2 < Y_2 < y_2 + dy_2\} \simeq p_Y(y_1, y_2)\, dy_1\, dy_2 \quad (2.1)$$

where $p_Y(y_1, y_2)$ is the joint probability density function of y_1, y_2, given that we know $p_X(x_1, x_2)$ and the functions f_1 and f_2.

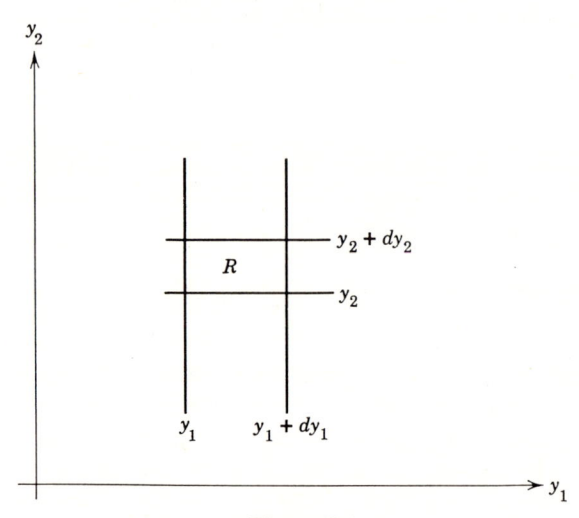

Figure 12.1

Consider the area R in the (y_1, y_2) plane defined by the four lines $y_1 = y_1$, $y_1 = y_1 + dy_1$, $y_2 = y_2$, $y_2 = y_2 + dy_2$ (Figure 12.1). The probability that a random point falls in the rectangle R is approximately equal to the product of the probability density $p_Y(y_1, y_2)$ and the area $dy_1\, dy_2$:

$$p_Y(y_1, y_2)\, dy_1\, dy_2. \quad (2.2)$$

Now, for a fixed y_1, the equation $y_1 = f_1(x_1, x_2)$ will determine a line in the (x_1, x_2) plane, say A. Similarly the equations $y_1 + dy_1 = f_1(x_1, x_2)$, $y_2 = f_2(x_1, x_2)$, $y_2 + dy_2 = f_2(x_1, x_2)$ will determine three more lines B, C, and D (Figure 12.2). These four lines will enclose an area S. Now, because of the one-to-one correspondence of points (y_1, y_2) with points (x_1, x_2), whenever a random point (Y_1, Y_2) falls inside the rectangle R in Figure 12.1, the corresponding point (X_1, X_2) falls inside the figure S in Figure 12.2. The probability of (X_1, X_2) falling inside S is approximately equal to the product of the probability density $p_X(x_1, x_2)$ times the area

SECT. 12.2 TRANSFORMATIONS OF BIVARIATE DISTRIBUTIONS

of S; hence
$$p_Y(y_1, y_2)\, dy_1\, dy_2 \simeq p_X(x_1, x_2)(\text{area of } S). \tag{2.3}$$

We therefore need to find the area of S. S is approximately a parallelogram. It is known from coordinate geometry that, if (x_1, x_2), (x_1', x_2'), and (x_1'', x_2'') are three of the vertices of a parallelogram, then the area of the parallelogram is given by the absolute value of the determinant

$$\begin{vmatrix} 1 & x_1 & x_2 \\ 1 & x_1' & x_2' \\ 1 & x_1'' & x_2'' \end{vmatrix}. \tag{2.4}$$

We therefore need the coordinates of three of the vertices of S.

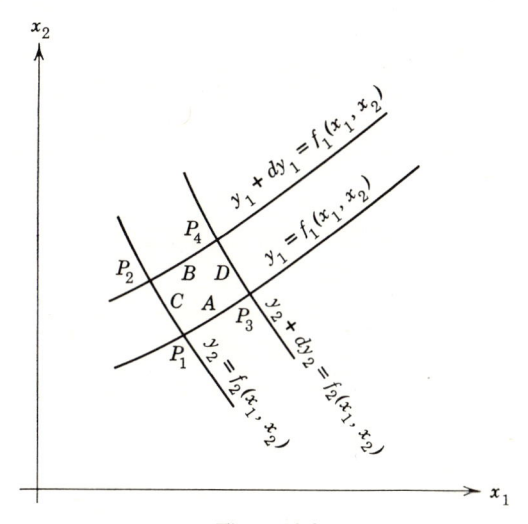

Figure 12.2

To obtain the coordinates of P_1, the intersection of the lines A and C, we note that along the line A we have values of (x_1, x_2) satisfying the equation $y_1 = f_1(x_1, x_2)$ and along the line C we have values of (x_1, x_2) satisfying the equation $y_2 = f_2(x_1, x_2)$. At the intersection of these two lines these two equations must be satisfied simultaneously; i.e., the coordinates of P_1 are the solutions for x_1, x_2 in

$$f_1(x_1, x_2) = y_1, \qquad f_2(x_1, x_2) = y_2. \tag{2.5}$$

But we know that when $y_1 = y_1, y_2 = y_2$,

$$x_1 = g_1(y_1, y_2), \qquad x_2 = g_2(y_1, y_2), \tag{2.6}$$

so these x values are the coordinates of P_1. Similarly, the point P_2 is the intersection of the lines B and C, and along the line B we have values of (x_1, x_2) satisfying the equation $y_1 + dy_1 = f_1(x_1, x_2)$, so the coordinates of P_2 are the solutions for x_1, x_2 in

$$f_1(x_1, x_2) = y_1 + dy_1, \quad f_2(x_1, x_2) = y_2, \tag{2.7}$$

and we know that when $y_1 = y_1 + dy_1, y_2 = y_2,$

$$x_1 = g_1(y_1 + dy_1, y_2), \quad x_2 = g_2(y_1 + dy_1, y_2), \tag{2.8}$$

so these x values are the coordinates of P_2.

But, by Taylor series,

$$g_1(y_1 + dy_1, y_2) = g_1(y_1, y_2) + \frac{\partial g_1}{\partial y_1} dy_1 + \text{higher order terms}; \tag{2.9}$$

$$g_2(y_1 + dy_1, y_2) = g_2(y_1, y_2) + \frac{\partial g_2}{\partial y_1} dy_1 + \text{higher order terms}; \tag{2.10}$$

so the coordinates of P_2 can be written, ignoring the higher-order terms, as approximately

$$\left(g_1(y_1, y_2) + \frac{\partial g_1}{\partial y_1} dy_1, \ g_2(y_1, y_2) + \frac{\partial g_2}{\partial y_1} dy_1 \right). \tag{2.11}$$

Similarly, the coordinates of P_3 are approximately

$$\left(g_1(y_1, y_2) + \frac{\partial g_1}{\partial y_2} dy_2, \ g_2(y_1, y_2) + \frac{\partial g_2}{\partial y_2} dy_2 \right). \tag{2.12}$$

Substituting these three coordinates in (2.4), we get for the area of S the absolute value of

$$\begin{vmatrix} 1 & g_1(y_1, y_2) & g_2(y_1, y_2) \\ 1 & g_1(y_1, y_2) + \dfrac{\partial g_1}{\partial y_1} dy_1 & g_2(y_1, y_2) + \dfrac{\partial g_2}{\partial y_1} dy_1 \\ 1 & g_1(y_1, y_2) + \dfrac{\partial g_1}{\partial y_2} dy_2 & g_2(y_1, y_2) + \dfrac{\partial g_2}{\partial y_2} dy_2 \end{vmatrix}. \tag{2.13}$$

Expanding this determinant gives

$$\left(\frac{\partial g_1}{\partial y_1} \frac{\partial g_2}{\partial y_2} - \frac{\partial g_1}{\partial y_2} \frac{\partial g_2}{\partial y_1} \right) dy_1 \, dy_2 = \begin{vmatrix} \dfrac{\partial g_1}{\partial y_1} & \dfrac{\partial g_2}{\partial y_1} \\ \dfrac{\partial g_1}{\partial y_2} & \dfrac{\partial g_2}{\partial y_2} \end{vmatrix} dy_1 \, dy_2. \tag{2.14}$$

Substituting this for the area of S in (2.3) gives

$$p_Y(y_1, y_2)\, dy_1\, dy_2 = p_X(x_1, x_2) \begin{vmatrix} \dfrac{\partial g_1}{\partial y_1} & \dfrac{\partial g_2}{\partial y_1} \\ \dfrac{\partial g_1}{\partial y_2} & \dfrac{\partial g_2}{\partial y_2} \end{vmatrix} dy_1\, dy_2 \qquad (2.15)$$

and

$$p_Y(y_1, y_2) = p_X(g_1(y_1, y_2), g_2(y_1, y_2)) \begin{vmatrix} \dfrac{\partial g_1}{\partial y_1} & \dfrac{\partial g_2}{\partial y_1} \\ \dfrac{\partial g_1}{\partial y_2} & \dfrac{\partial g_2}{\partial y_2} \end{vmatrix} \qquad (2.16)$$

where the absolute value of the determinant is used.

12.3. The Bivariate Normal Distribution

In this section we shall postulate a certain model which will lead us to the bivariate normal distribution.

Let x_1, x_2 be independent normally distributed variables with zero means and unit variances. Let y_1', y_2' be linear functions of x_1, x_2 defined by constants η_i, l_{ij}:

$$\begin{aligned} y_1' &= \eta_1 + l_{11}x_1 + l_{12}x_2, \\ y_2' &= \eta_2 + l_{21}x_1 + l_{22}x_2. \end{aligned} \qquad (3.1)$$

It will be more convenient to deal with $y_1 = y_1' - \eta_1$, $y_2 = y_2' - \eta_2$, since these new variables will have expected values zero. Thus y_1 and y_2 are functions of x_1 and x_2:

$$\begin{aligned} y_1 &= f_1(x_1, x_2) = l_{11}x_1 + l_{12}x_2, \\ y_2 &= f_2(x_1, x_2) = l_{21}x_1 + l_{22}x_2. \end{aligned} \qquad (3.2)$$

The variables y_1, y_2 will be normally distributed with expectations zero, and

$$V[y_1] = l_{11}^2 + l_{12}^2, \qquad V[y_2] = l_{21}^2 + l_{22}^2, \qquad (3.3)$$

$$\begin{aligned} \text{Cov}[y_1, y_2] &= E[y_1 y_2] - E[y_1]E[y_2] \\ &= E[l_{11}l_{21}x_1^2 + l_{12}l_{22}x_2^2 + l_{11}l_{22}x_1 x_2 + l_{12}l_{21}x_1 x_2] \\ &= l_{11}l_{21} + l_{12}l_{22}, \end{aligned} \qquad (3.4)$$

since $E[x_i^2] = 1$, and since x_1, x_2 are independent, $E[x_1 x_2] = E[x_1]E[x_2] = 0$.

We can solve the equations (3.2) to give the inverse functions of x in terms of y_1, y_2:

$$x_1 = g_1(y_1, y_2) = \frac{l_{22}y_1 - l_{12}y_2}{l_{11}l_{22} - l_{12}l_{21}} = \frac{l_{22}y_1 - l_{12}y_2}{\lambda}, \quad (3.5)$$

$$x_2 = g_2(y_1, y_2) = \frac{-l_{21}y_1 + l_{11}y_2}{l_{11}l_{22} - l_{12}l_{21}} = \frac{-l_{21}y_1 + l_{11}y_2}{\lambda}, \quad (3.6)$$

if we define

$$\lambda = l_{11}l_{22} - l_{12}l_{21}. \quad (3.7)$$

The random variables x_1, x_2 by definition are independent and $N(0, 1)$; so

$$p\{x_1, x_2\} = p\{x_1\}p\{x_2\} = \frac{1}{\sqrt{2\pi}} e^{-(x_1)^2/2} \frac{1}{\sqrt{2\pi}} e^{-(x_2)^2/2}$$

$$= \frac{1}{2\pi} e^{-\frac{1}{2}(x_1^2 + x_2^2)}. \quad (3.8)$$

To get the distribution of (y_1, y_2) we use (2.16). We need

$$\frac{\partial g_1}{\partial y_1} = \frac{l_{22}}{\lambda}, \quad \frac{\partial g_2}{\partial y_1} = -\frac{l_{21}}{\lambda}, \quad \frac{\partial g_1}{\partial y_2} = -\frac{l_{12}}{\lambda}, \quad \frac{\partial g_2}{\partial y_2} = \frac{l_{11}}{\lambda}; \quad (3.9)$$

so

$$\begin{vmatrix} \dfrac{\partial g_1}{\partial y_1} & \dfrac{\partial g_2}{\partial y_1} \\ \dfrac{\partial g_1}{\partial y_2} & \dfrac{\partial g_2}{\partial y_2} \end{vmatrix} = \frac{l_{22}}{\lambda} \frac{l_{11}}{\lambda} - \frac{(-l_{12})}{\lambda} \frac{(-l_{21})}{\lambda} = \frac{1}{\lambda}. \quad (3.10)$$

We now use (2.16):

$$p\{y_1, y_2\} = \frac{1}{2\pi} \exp\left\{-\frac{1}{2}\left[\left(\frac{l_{22}y_1 - l_{12}y_2}{\lambda}\right)^2 + \left(\frac{-l_{21}y_1 + l_{11}y_2}{\lambda}\right)^2\right]\right\} \frac{1}{\lambda}. \quad (3.11)$$

Define ρ as the correlation coefficient between y_1 and y_2:

$$\rho = \frac{\text{Cov}[y_1, y_2]}{\sqrt{V[y_1]V[y_2]}} = \frac{l_{11}l_{21} + l_{12}l_{22}}{\sqrt{(l_{11}^2 + l_{12}^2)(l_{21}^2 + l_{22}^2)}}. \quad (3.12)$$

Let $V[y_1] = \sigma_1^2$, $V[y_2] = \sigma_2^2$. Then

$$\sigma_1^2 \sigma_2^2 (1 - \rho^2) = (l_{11}^2 + l_{12}^2)(l_{21}^2 + l_{22}^2)\left[1 - \frac{(l_{11}l_{21} + l_{12}l_{22})^2}{(l_{11}^2 + l_{12}^2)(l_{21}^2 + l_{22}^2)}\right]$$

$$= (l_{11}l_{22} - l_{12}l_{21})^2 = \lambda^2, \quad (3.13)$$

SECT. 12.3   THE BIVARIATE NORMAL DISTRIBUTION   403

and the constant part of (3.11) outside the exponent is

$$\frac{1}{2\pi\lambda} = \frac{1}{2\pi\sigma_1\sigma_2\sqrt{1-\rho^2}}. \quad (3.14)$$

The exponent of (3.11) is

$$-\frac{1}{2\lambda^2}\{(l_{22}^2 + l_{21}^2)y_1^2 - 2(l_{11}l_{21} + l_{12}l_{22})y_1y_2 + (l_{11}^2 + l_{12}^2)y_2^2\}$$

$$= -\frac{1}{2\sigma_1^2\sigma_2^2(1-\rho^2)}(\sigma_2^2 y_1^2 - 2\rho\sigma_1\sigma_2 y_1 y_2 + \sigma_1^2 y_2^2)$$

$$= -\frac{1}{2(1-\rho^2)}\left(\frac{y_1^2}{\sigma_1^2} - \frac{2\rho y_1 y_2}{\sigma_1\sigma_2} + \frac{y_2^2}{\sigma_2^2}\right). \quad (3.15)$$

Substituting in (3.11),

$$p\{y_1, y_2\} = \frac{1}{2\pi\sigma_1\sigma_2\sqrt{1-\rho^2}}$$

$$\exp\left\{-\frac{1}{2(1-\rho^2)}\left[\left(\frac{y_1}{\sigma_1}\right)^2 - 2\rho\frac{y_1}{\sigma_1}\frac{y_2}{\sigma_2} + \left(\frac{y_2}{\sigma_2}\right)^2\right]\right\}. \quad (3.16)$$

Finally, we may make the further transformation back to y_1', y_2' which is very simple since the determinant is merely 1:

$$p\{y_1', y_2'\} = \frac{1}{2\pi\sigma_1\sigma_2\sqrt{1-\rho^2}}$$

$$\exp\left\{-\frac{1}{2(1-\rho^2)}\left[\left(\frac{y_1'-\eta_1}{\sigma_1}\right)^2 - 2\rho\frac{y_1'-\eta_1}{\sigma_1}\frac{y_2'-\eta_2}{\sigma_2} + \left(\frac{y_2'-\eta_2}{\sigma_2}\right)^2\right]\right\}, \quad (3.17)$$

and this is the general form for the bivariate normal distribution.

We can note at once an important result. If the covariance of y_1', y_2' is zero, then $\rho = 0$, and (3.17) becomes

$$p\{y_1', y_2'\} = \frac{1}{2\pi\sigma_1\sigma_2}\exp\left\{-\frac{1}{2}\left[\left(\frac{y_1'-\eta_1}{\sigma_1}\right)^2 + \left(\frac{y_2'-\eta_2}{\sigma_2}\right)^2\right]\right\}$$

$$= \frac{1}{\sqrt{2\pi}\sigma_1}\exp\left[-\frac{1}{2}\left(\frac{y_1'-\eta_1}{\sigma_1}\right)^2\right]\frac{1}{\sqrt{2\pi}\sigma_2}\exp\left[-\frac{1}{2}\left(\frac{y_2'-\eta_2}{\sigma_2}\right)^2\right]$$

$$= p\{y_1'\}p\{y_2'\}, \quad (3.18)$$

so under this circumstance y_1' and y_2' are independent. This is the result which was assumed in the discussion in Chapter 8.

12.4. Some Properties of the Bivariate Normal Distribution

The general form is given in (3.17). Just as with the univariate normal distribution we found it convenient to have a standardized form, so it will be here. We define new variables

$$u_1 = f_1(y_1', y_2') = \frac{y_1' - \eta_1}{\sigma_1}, \quad u_2 = f_2(y_1', y_2') = \frac{y_2' - \eta_2}{\sigma_2}, \quad (4.1)$$

with inverse functions

$$y_1' = g_1(u_1, u_2) = u_1\sigma_1 + \eta_1, \quad y_2' = g_2(u_1, u_2) = u_2\sigma_2 + \eta_2, \quad (4.2)$$

so that

$$\frac{\partial g_1}{\partial u_1} = \sigma_1, \quad \frac{\partial g_1}{\partial u_2} = 0, \quad \frac{\partial g_2}{\partial u_1} = 0, \quad \frac{\partial g_2}{\partial u_2} = \sigma_2. \quad (4.3)$$

The probability density of (u_1, u_2) will be, using (2.16),

$$p\{u_1, u_2\} = \frac{1}{2\pi\sigma_1\sigma_2\sqrt{1-\rho^2}} \exp\left[-\frac{1}{2(1-\rho^2)}(u_1^2 - 2\rho u_1 u_2 + u_2^2)\right]\sigma_1\sigma_2$$

$$= \frac{1}{2\pi\sqrt{1-\rho^2}} \exp\left[-\frac{1}{2(1-\rho^2)}(u_1^2 - 2\rho u_1 u_2 + u_2^2)\right]. \quad (4.4)$$

It will be convenient to use the symbol $\phi(u_1, u_2)$ for this standardized form. Of course, $\phi(u_1, u_2)$ is a function of ρ.

In studying the properties of the standardized bivariate normal distribution (4.4), it will be convenient to make a further pair of transformations. We define new variables

$$u_1' = f_1(u_1, u_2) = u_1, \quad (4.5)$$

$$u_2' = f_2(u_1, u_2) = \frac{u_2 - \rho u_1}{\sqrt{1-\rho^2}}. \quad (4.6)$$

The inverse functions are

$$u_1 = g_1(u_1', u_2') = u_1', \quad (4.7)$$

$$u_2 = g_2(u_1', u_2') = \rho u_1' + \sqrt{1-\rho^2}\, u_2', \quad (4.8)$$

so that

$$\frac{\partial g_1}{\partial u_1'} = 1, \quad \frac{\partial g_1}{\partial u_2'} = 0, \quad \frac{\partial g_2}{\partial u_1'} = \rho, \quad \frac{\partial g_2}{\partial u_2'} = \sqrt{1-\rho^2}, \quad (4.9)$$

SECT. 12.4   PROPERTIES OF BIVARIATE NORMAL DISTRIBUTION

and the determinant is

$$\begin{vmatrix} \dfrac{\partial g_1}{\partial u_1'} & \dfrac{\partial g_2}{\partial u_1'} \\ \dfrac{\partial g_1}{\partial u_2'} & \dfrac{\partial g_2}{\partial u_2'} \end{vmatrix} = \begin{vmatrix} 1 & \rho \\ 0 & \sqrt{1-\rho^2} \end{vmatrix} = \sqrt{1-\rho^2}. \qquad (4.10)$$

Also

$$u_1^2 - 2\rho u_1 u_2 + u_2^2 = u_1'^2 - 2\rho u_1'(\rho u_1' + \sqrt{1-\rho^2}\, u_2')$$
$$+ (\rho u_1' + \sqrt{1-\rho^2}\, u_2')^2 = (1-\rho^2)(u_1'^2 + u_2'^2). \qquad (4.11)$$

We now write down the probability density of (u_1', u_2'), using (2.16) again:

$$p\{u_1', u_2'\} = \frac{1}{2\pi\sqrt{1-\rho^2}} e^{-\frac{1}{2}(u_1'^2 + u_2'^2)} \sqrt{1-\rho^2}$$
$$= \frac{1}{\sqrt{2\pi}} e^{-u_1'^2/2} \frac{1}{\sqrt{2\pi}} e^{-u_2'^2/2}. \qquad (4.12)$$

Thus u_1', u_2' are independent. We get the marginal distribution of u_1' by integrating $p\{u_1', u_2'\}$ over u_2' [see (1.20.10)]:

$$p\{u_1'\} = \int_{-\infty}^{\infty} p\{u_1', u_2'\}\, du_2'$$
$$= \frac{1}{\sqrt{2\pi}} e^{-u_1'^2/2} \int_{-\infty}^{\infty} \frac{1}{\sqrt{2\pi}} e^{-u_2'^2/2}\, du_2' = \frac{1}{\sqrt{2\pi}} e^{-u_1'^2/2}, \qquad (4.13)$$

since the integral is just the integral of a unit normal distribution which must equal 1. Hence the marginal distribution of $u_1' = u_1$ is a unit normal distribution, and so the marginal distribution of y_1' will be a normal distribution with mean η_1 and variance σ_1^2. The same argument shows that the marginal distribution of y_2' is normal with mean η_2 and variance σ_2^2.

The conditional distribution of u_2, given u_1 [see (1.21.7)], is

$$p\{u_2 | u_1\} = \frac{p\{u_1, u_2\}}{p\{u_1\}}$$
$$= \frac{(2\pi\sqrt{1-\rho^2})^{-1} \exp\{-[2(1-\rho^2)]^{-1}(u_1^2 - 2\rho u_1 u_2 + u_2^2)\}}{(\sqrt{2\pi})^{-1} \exp(-u_1^2/2)}$$
$$= \frac{1}{\sqrt{2\pi}\sqrt{1-\rho^2}} \exp\left[-\frac{1}{2}\left(\frac{u_2 - \rho u_1}{\sqrt{1-\rho^2}}\right)^2\right], \qquad (4.14)$$

which can be regarded as a normal distribution of u_2 with mean ρu_1 and variance $1 - \rho^2$. We now transform this by defining $x_2 = f_2(u_1, u_2) = u_2 \sigma_2 + \xi_2$, so that the inverse function is $u_2 = g_2(x_1, x_2) = (x_2 - \xi_2)/\sigma_2$, and $dg_2/dx_2 = 1/\sigma_2$. We also define $x_1 = u_1 \sigma_1 + \xi_1$. Then (4.14) becomes

$$p\{x_2|x_1\} = \frac{1}{\sqrt{2\pi}\sqrt{1-\rho^2}} \exp\left\{-\frac{1}{2}\left[\frac{\frac{x_2 - \xi_2}{\sigma_2} - \rho\left(\frac{x_1 - \xi_1}{\sigma_1}\right)}{\sqrt{1-\rho^2}}\right]^2\right\}\frac{1}{\sigma_2}$$

$$= \frac{1}{\sqrt{2\pi}\sigma_2\sqrt{1-\rho^2}} \exp\left[-\frac{1}{2}\left\{\frac{x_2 - [\xi_2 + \rho(\sigma_2/\sigma_1)(x_1 - \xi_1)]}{\sigma_2\sqrt{1-\rho^2}}\right\}^2\right],$$

(4.15)

which can be regarded as a normal distribution of a random variable x_2 with mean

$$E[x_2|x_1] = \xi_2 + \rho\frac{\sigma_2}{\sigma_1}(x_1 - \xi_1), \qquad (4.16)$$

and variance

$$V[x_2|x_1] = \sigma_2^2(1 - \rho^2). \qquad (4.17)$$

The system is, of course, symmetric in x_1 and x_2, and so we have

$$E[x_1|x_2] = \xi_1 + \rho\frac{\sigma_1}{\sigma_2}(x_2 - \xi_2), \qquad (4.18)$$

$$V[x_1|x_2] = \sigma_1^2(1 - \rho^2). \qquad (4.19)$$

Thus the means of the conditional distributions are linear functions of the other variable, and the variances are constants. We recall that in Section 11.2 our model for linear regression was that y was normally distributed around its expected value with a constant variance, and this expected value was a simple linear function of another variable x. Therefore the conditions for a conditional regression analysis of x_1 on x_2, and for a conditional regression analysis of x_2 on x_1, are both satisfied. Here there are two true regression lines, (4.16) and (4.18), with regression coefficients

$$\beta_{x_2|x_1} = \rho\frac{\sigma_2}{\sigma_1}, \qquad \beta_{x_1|x_2} = \rho\frac{\sigma_1}{\sigma_2}, \qquad (4.20)$$

The product of the two regression coefficients is ρ^2. To find the point of intersection of the two regression lines, we can substitute x_2 from (4.16) into (4.18) which gives $x_1 - \xi_1 = \rho^2(x_1 - \xi_1)$, which is only true if $x_1 = \xi_1$,

SECT. 12.4 PROPERTIES OF BIVARIATE NORMAL DISTRIBUTION

and similarly we obtain $x_2 = \xi_2$. The point of intersection is therefore (ξ_1, ξ_2).

We find the angle between the two regression lines as follows. In Figure 12.3,

$$\beta_{x_1|x_2} = \tan A, \qquad \beta_{x_2|x_1} = \tan C, \qquad (4.21)$$

and B is the angle between the two regression lines. For three angles,

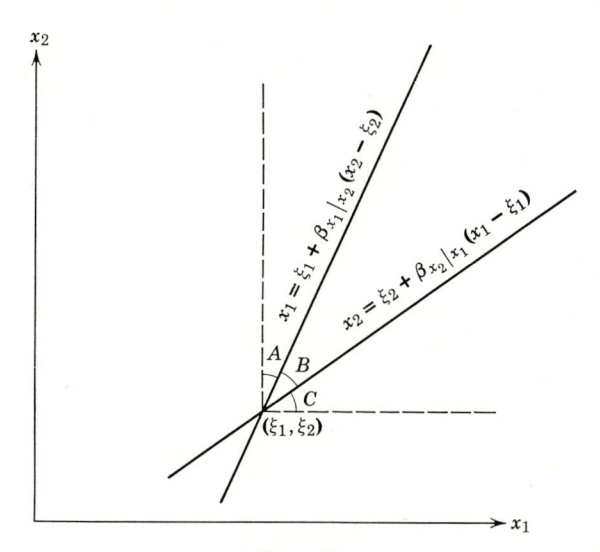

Figure 12.3

say A, $B + 90°$, and C, whose sum is $180°$,

$$\tan A + \tan(B + 90°) + \tan C = \tan A \tan(B + 90°) \tan C, \qquad (4.22)$$

whence

$$\tan(B + 90°) = \frac{\rho(\sigma_1/\sigma_2) + \rho(\sigma_2/\sigma_1)}{\rho(\sigma_1/\sigma_2)\rho(\sigma_2/\sigma_1) - 1} = \frac{\rho}{\rho^2 - 1} \frac{\sigma_1^2 + \sigma_2^2}{\sigma_1 \sigma_2}, \qquad (4.23)$$

so

$$\tan B = -\frac{1}{\tan(B + 90°)} = \frac{1 - \rho^2}{\rho} \frac{\sigma_1 \sigma_2}{\sigma_1^2 + \sigma_2^2}. \qquad (4.24)$$

When $\rho = 1$, $\tan B = 0$, and so the two regression lines are identical. When $\rho = 0$, $\tan B = \infty$, and so the lines are at right angles to each other.

We can write (4.17) and (4.19) as

$$\frac{V[x_2|x_1]}{V[x_2]} = 1 - \rho^2 = \frac{V[x_1|x_2]}{V[x_1]}. \tag{4.25}$$

Thus, when $\rho = 1$, the conditional variance $V[x_2|x_1] = 0$, and, when $\rho = 0$, the conditional variance equals the unconditional variance. Thus ρ^2 can be regarded as measuring the fraction of the variance of x_2 "explained" by the regression on x_1, and vice versa. This is one of the most useful interpretations of the correlation coefficient.

The nature of the surface generated by the bivariate normal distribution can be seen from the equation for its probability density (3.17). If we place this equal to a constant, this implies

$$\left(\frac{y_1 - \eta_1}{\sigma_1}\right)^2 - 2\rho \frac{y_1 - \eta_1}{\sigma_1} \frac{y_2 - \eta_2}{\sigma_2} + \left(\frac{y_2 - \eta_2}{\sigma_2}\right)^2 = \text{constant}, \tag{4.26}$$

dropping the primes from the y's. This equation defines ellipses, for different values of the constant, at an angle to the axes. When $\rho = 0$, this equation becomes

$$\left(\frac{y_1 - \eta_1}{\sigma_1}\right)^2 + \left(\frac{y_2 - \eta_2}{\sigma_2}\right)^2 = \text{constant}, \tag{4.27}$$

which defines ellipses whose principal axes are parallel to the (y_1, y_2) axes.

We can use the results of this section to indicate the proof of an important theorem we assumed in Section 1.26, namely, that any linear combination of independent random normal variables is itself normally distributed. To prove this for n random variables, it will be sufficient to prove it for two random variables. The proof is along the following lines.

In (3.2) we defined y_1 as $l_{11}x_1 + l_{12}x_2$ where l_{11} and l_{12} are constants and x_1 and x_2 are independent random variables normally distributed with means zero and unit variances. In (3.16) we found the joint density function $p\{y_1, y_2\}$, where y_2 was another linear combination $l_{21}x_1 + l_{22}x_2$. We defined u_1 as $(y_1' - \eta_1)/\sigma_1$, which is equal to y_1/σ_1. We subsequently defined u_1' as u_1, and found in (4.13) that u_1' was normally distributed with mean zero and unit variance. It follows that the linear combination $l_{11}x_1 + l_{12}x_2 = y_1 = u_1\sigma_1$ will be normally distributed, with zero mean and variance $\sigma_1^2 = l_{11}^2 + l_{12}^2$. The arguments are changed only in detail if, instead of being distributed $N(0, 1)$, the x_i are distributed $N(\xi_i, \sigma_{x_i}^2)$.

12.5. The Regression "Fallacy"

Equations (4.16) and (4.18) are the basis of the phenomenon of *regression* noted by Galton. Galton observed that on the average the sons of tall fathers are not as tall as their fathers, and similarly the sons of short fathers are not as short as their fathers; i.e., the second generation tended to regress towards the mean. But if we look at the data the other way round, we find that on the average the fathers of tall sons are not as tall as their sons and the fathers of short sons are not as short as their sons, so the first generation tends to regress towards the mean. It seems implausible that both statements can be true simultaneously, so this phenomenon has been called the *regression fallacy*.

In (4.16) let x_1 be the height of a father and x_2 be the height of his son:

$$E[x_2|x_1] = E[x_2] + \rho \frac{\sigma_2}{\sigma_1}(x_1 - E[x_1]), \qquad (5.1)$$

so

$$\frac{E[x_2|x_1] - E[x_2]}{\sigma_2} = \rho \frac{x_1 - E[x_1]}{\sigma_1}. \qquad (5.2)$$

For convenience, assume that the population of fathers and sons is stable, one generation to the next, so that $E[x_1] = E[x_2]$, $\sigma_1 = \sigma_2$. Then (5.2) becomes

$$E[x_2|x_1] - x_1 = -(1 - \rho)(x_1 - E[x_1]). \qquad (5.3)$$

Suppose that the correlation coefficient between x_1 and x_2 is positive and less than 1. Consider a particular value of x_1 greater than the mean, $E[x_1]$, so that $x_1 - E[x_1] > 0$. Then the right-hand side of (5.3) is negative, and we have

$$E[x_2|x_1] < x_1. \qquad (5.4)$$

Thus the expected value for the son's height x_2 for fathers of a particular height x_1 (greater than the average of x_1) is less than that particular father's height. In other words, "on the average, sons of tall fathers are not as tall as their fathers."

The foregoing arguments are symmetrical in x_1 and x_2, so for a particular x_2 greater than $E[x_2]$

$$E[x_1|x_2] < x_2, \qquad (5.5)$$

so "on the average, fathers of tall sons are not as tall as their sons."

The situation is illustrated in Figure 12.4, in which a single constant probability density ellipse, (4.26), is drawn for a bivariate normal distribution with means $E[x_1] = E[x_2] = 0$, variance $\sigma_1^2 = \sigma_2^2$, and $\rho = 0.6$. It is apparent that $BA < A0$, which is (5.4), and $DC < C0$, which is (5.5).

The fallacy in the regression fallacy consists in supposing that there is a fallacy.

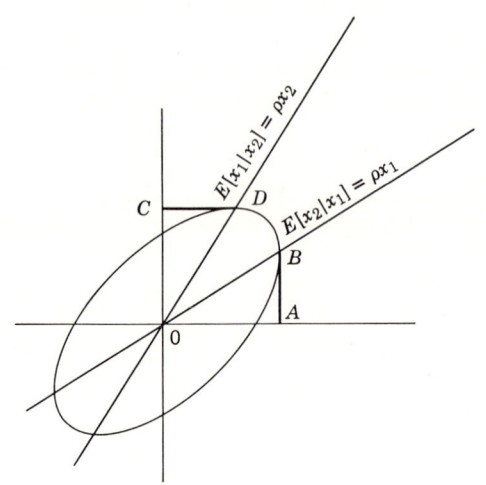

Figure 12.4

12.6. Estimation of the Parameters of the Bivariate Normal Distribution

We use the method of maximum likelihood to obtain estimators of the bivariate normal distribution

$$p\{x_{1v}, x_{2v}\} = \frac{1}{2\pi\sigma_1\sigma_2\sqrt{1-\rho^2}}$$
$$\exp\left\{-\frac{1}{2(1-\rho^2)}\left[\left(\frac{x_{1v}-\xi_1}{\sigma_1}\right)^2 - 2\rho\frac{x_{1v}-\xi_1}{\sigma_1}\frac{x_{2v}-\xi_2}{\sigma_2} + \left(\frac{x_{2v}-\xi_2}{\sigma_2}\right)^2\right]\right\}. \tag{6.1}$$

The likelihood $L = \prod_{v}^{n} p\{x_{1v}, x_{2v}\}$ is

$$L = \left(\frac{1}{2\pi\sigma_1\sigma_2\sqrt{1-\rho^2}}\right)^n$$
$$\exp\left\{-\frac{1}{2(1-\rho^2)}\sum\left[\left(\frac{x_{1v}-\xi_1}{\sigma_1}\right)^2 - 2\rho\frac{x_{1v}-\xi_1}{\sigma_1}\frac{x_{2v}-\xi_2}{\sigma_2} + \left(\frac{x_{2v}-\xi_2}{\sigma_2}\right)^2\right]\right\}, \tag{6.2}$$

SECT. 12.6 ESTIMATION OF THE PARAMETERS

where the summation is over v. As is usually the case, it is easier to maximize the logarithm of the likelihood:

$$\log L = -n \log (2\pi\sigma_1\sigma_2\sqrt{1-\rho^2})$$
$$- \frac{1}{2(1-\rho^2)} \left[\frac{\sum (x_{1v} - \xi_1)^2}{\sigma_1^2} - 2\rho \frac{\sum (x_{1v} - \xi_1)(x_{2v} - \xi_2)}{\sigma_1 \sigma_2} + \frac{\sum (x_{2v} - \xi_2)^2}{\sigma_2^2} \right]. \quad (6.3)$$

We differentiate with respect to $\xi_1, \xi_2, \sigma_1, \sigma_2$, and ρ:

$$\frac{\partial \log L}{\partial \xi_1} = -\frac{1}{2(1-\rho^2)} \left[-\frac{2}{\sigma_1^2} \sum (x_{1v} - \xi_1) + \frac{2\rho}{\sigma_1 \sigma_2} \sum (x_{2v} - \xi_2) \right], \quad (6.4)$$

$$\frac{\partial \log L}{\partial \xi_2} = -\frac{1}{2(1-\rho^2)} \left[\frac{2\rho}{\sigma_1 \sigma_2} \sum (x_{1v} - \xi_1) - \frac{2}{\sigma_2^2} \sum (x_{2v} - \xi_2) \right], \quad (6.5)$$

$$\frac{\partial \log L}{\partial \sigma_1} = -\frac{n}{\sigma_1} - \frac{1}{2(1-\rho^2)}$$
$$\times \left[-\frac{2 \sum (x_{1v} - \xi_1)^2}{\sigma_1^3} + \frac{2\rho \sum (x_{1v} - \xi_1)(x_{2v} - \xi_2)}{\sigma_1^2 \sigma_2} \right], \quad (6.6)$$

$$\frac{\partial \log L}{\partial \sigma_2} = -\frac{n}{\sigma_2} - \frac{1}{2(1-\rho^2)}$$
$$\times \left[\frac{2\rho \sum (x_{1v} - \xi)(x_{2v} - \xi_2)}{\sigma_1 \sigma_2^2} - \frac{2 \sum (x_{2v} - \xi_2)^2}{\sigma_2^3} \right], \quad (6.7)$$

$$\frac{\partial \log L}{\partial \rho} = \frac{n\rho}{1-\rho^2} + \frac{1}{1-\rho^2} \frac{\sum (x_{1v} - \xi_1)(x_{2v} - \xi_2)}{\sigma_1 \sigma_2} - \frac{\rho}{(1-\rho^2)^2}$$
$$\times \left[\frac{\sum (x_{1v} - \xi_1)^2}{\sigma_1^2} - 2\rho \frac{\sum (x_{1v} - \xi_1)(x_{2v} - \xi_2)}{\sigma_1 \sigma_2} + \frac{\sum (x_{2v} - \xi_2)^2}{\sigma_2^2} \right]. \quad (6.8)$$

Equating (6.4) and (6.5) to zero and rearranging gives

$$-\frac{1}{\hat\sigma_1^2} \sum (x_{1v} - \hat\xi_1) + \frac{\hat\rho}{\hat\sigma_1 \hat\sigma_2} \sum (x_{2v} - \hat\xi_2) = 0, \quad (6.9)$$

$$\frac{\hat\rho}{\hat\sigma_1 \hat\sigma_2} \sum (x_{1v} - \hat\xi_1) - \frac{1}{\hat\sigma_2^2} \sum (x_{2v} - \hat\xi_2) = 0. \quad (6.10)$$

Conventional manipulation leads to $\sum (x_{1v} - \hat\xi_1) = 0$, $\sum (x_{2v} - \hat\xi_2) = 0$, whence

$$\hat\xi_1 = \frac{1}{n} \sum x_{1v}, \quad \hat\xi_2 = \frac{1}{n} \sum x_{2v}. \quad (6.11)$$

Equating (6.6) and (6.7) to zero and rearranging gives

$$\frac{\sum (x_{1\nu} - \hat{\xi}_1)^2}{\hat{\sigma}_1^2} = \hat{\rho}\frac{\sum (x_{1\nu} - \hat{\xi}_1)(x_{2\nu} - \hat{\xi}_2)}{\hat{\sigma}_1\hat{\sigma}_2} + n(1 - \hat{\rho}^2), \quad (6.12)$$

$$\frac{\sum (x_{2\nu} - \hat{\xi}_2)^2}{\hat{\sigma}_2^2} = \hat{\rho}\frac{\sum (x_{1\nu} - \hat{\xi}_1)(x_{2\nu} - \hat{\xi}_2)}{\hat{\sigma}_1\hat{\sigma}_2} + n(1 - \hat{\rho}^2), \quad (6.13)$$

which when added give

$$\frac{\sum (x_{1\nu} - \hat{\xi}_1)^2}{\hat{\sigma}_1^2} - 2\hat{\rho}\frac{\sum (x_{1\nu} - \hat{\xi}_1)(x_{2\nu} - \hat{\xi}_2)}{\hat{\sigma}_1\hat{\sigma}_2} + \frac{\sum (x_{2\nu} - \hat{\xi}_2)^2}{\hat{\sigma}_2^2} = 2n(1 - \hat{\rho}^2). \quad (6.14)$$

Equating (6.8) to zero and multiplying by $1 - \hat{\rho}^2$ gives

$$n\hat{\rho} + \frac{\sum (x_{1\nu} - \hat{\xi}_1)(x_{2\nu} - \hat{\xi}_2)}{\hat{\sigma}_1\hat{\sigma}_2} - \frac{\hat{\rho}}{1 - \hat{\rho}^2}$$
$$\times \left[\frac{\sum (x_{1\nu} - \hat{\xi}_1)^2}{\hat{\sigma}_1^2} - 2\hat{\rho}\frac{\sum (x_{1\nu} - \hat{\xi}_1)(x_{2\nu} - \hat{\xi}_2)}{\hat{\sigma}_1\hat{\sigma}_2} + \frac{\sum (x_{2\nu} - \hat{\xi}_2)}{\hat{\sigma}_2^2}\right] = 0.$$
(6.15)

Substituting (6.14) in (6.15) gives

$$\hat{\rho}\frac{\sum (x_{1\nu} - \hat{\xi}_1)(x_{2\nu} - \hat{\xi}_2)}{\hat{\sigma}_1\hat{\sigma}_2} = n\hat{\rho}^2. \quad (6.16)$$

Substituting this in (6.12) and (6.13) gives

$$\hat{\sigma}_1^2 = \frac{1}{n}\sum (x_{1\nu} - \hat{\xi}_1)^2, \quad \hat{\sigma}_2^2 = \frac{1}{n}\sum (x_{2\nu} - \hat{\xi}_2)^2, \quad (6.17)$$

and since $\hat{\xi}_1 = \bar{x}_1$, $\hat{\xi}_2 = \bar{x}_2$

$$\hat{\sigma}_1^2 = \frac{1}{n}\sum (x_{1\nu} - \bar{x}_1)^2, \quad \hat{\sigma}_2^2 = \frac{1}{n}\sum (x_{2\nu} - \bar{x}_2)^2. \quad (6.18)$$

As might have been expected, the maximum likelihood estimators of the σ_i^2 ($i = 1, 2$) are biased, but of course we can obtain unbiased estimators, say s_i^2, by substituting $n - 1$ for n in the denominators in (6.18).

Substituting (6.18) in (6.16) and solving for $\hat{\rho}$, for which the symbol r is commonly used, gives

$$r = \hat{\rho} = \frac{\sum (x_{1\nu} - \bar{x}_1)(x_{2\nu} - \bar{x}_2)}{\sqrt{\sum (x_{1\nu} - \bar{x}_1)^2 \sum (x_{2\nu} - \bar{x}_2)^2}}. \quad (6.19)$$

SECT. 12.7 TESTS OF SIGNIFICANCE FOR CORRELATION COEFFICIENT 413

It can be shown that

$$E[r] = \rho - \frac{\rho(1-\rho^2)}{2n} + \cdots, \qquad (6.20)$$

so r is a biased estimator of ρ except when $\rho = 0$.

The regression coefficients $\beta_{x_i|x_j} = \rho(\sigma_i/\sigma_j)$ can be estimated as

$$\hat{\rho}\frac{\hat{\sigma}_i}{\hat{\sigma}_j} = r\frac{s_i}{s_j} = \frac{\sum (x_{iv} - \bar{x}_i)(x_{jv} - \bar{x}_j)}{\sqrt{\sum (x_{iv} - \bar{x}_i)^2 \sum (x_{jv} - \bar{x}_j)^2}} \frac{\sqrt{\sum (x_{iv} - \bar{x}_i)^2/(n-1)}}{\sqrt{\sum (x_{jv} - \bar{x}_j)^2/(n-1)}}$$

$$= \frac{\sum (x_{iv} - \bar{x}_i)(x_{jv} - \bar{x}_j)}{\sum (x_{jv} - \bar{x}_j)^2}, \qquad (6.21)$$

which is identical with the ordinary estimator of a regression coefficient [c.f. (11.2.13)].

Inserting maximum likelihood estimators into (4.17) gives

$$\hat{V}[x_i|x_j] = \hat{\sigma}_i^2(1 - \hat{\rho}^2) = \frac{\sum (x_{iv} - \bar{x}_i)^2}{n} \left\{ 1 - \frac{[\sum (x_{iv} - \bar{x}_i)(x_{jv} - \bar{x}_j)]^2}{\sum (x_{iv} - \bar{x}_i)^2 \sum (\bar{x}_{jv} - \bar{x}_j)^2} \right\}$$

$$= \frac{1}{n}\left\{ \sum (x_{iv} - \bar{x}_i)^2 - \frac{[\sum (x_{iv} - \bar{x}_i)(x_{jv} - \bar{x}_j)]^2}{\sum (x_{jv} - \bar{x}_j)^2} \right\}. \qquad (6.22)$$

If we replace the factor $1/n$ by $1/(n-2)$ this would be the usual regression estimator, say $s^2_{x_i|x_j}$, (11.3.13). It follows that (6.22) is a biased estimator of $V[x_i|x_j]$.

12.7. Tests of Significance for the Correlation Coefficient

Since b is normally distributed about β with a variance given by (11.2.16),

$$\frac{b_{x_j|x_i} - \beta_{x_j|x_i}}{s_{x_j|x_i}/\sqrt{\sum (x_{iv} - \bar{x}_i)^2}} \sim t(n-2). \qquad (7.1)$$

From (11.3.13) we have

$$s^2_{x_j|x_i} = \frac{1}{n-2}\left\{ \sum (x_{jv} - \bar{x}_j)^2 - \frac{[\sum (x_{iv} - \bar{x}_i)(x_{jv} - \bar{x}_j)]^2}{\sum (x_{iv} - \bar{x}_i)^2} \right\}$$

$$= \frac{1}{n-2}\sum (x_{jv} - \bar{x}_j)^2 \left\{ 1 - \frac{[\sum (x_{iv} - \bar{x}_i)(x_{jv} - \bar{x}_j)]^2}{\sum (x_{iv} - \bar{x}_i)^2 \sum (x_{jv} - \bar{x}_j)^2} \right\}$$

$$= \frac{n-1}{n-2} s_j^2 (1 - r^2). \qquad (7.2)$$

Substituting this in (7.1), and substituting $r(s_j/s_i) = b_{x_j|x_i}$, then under the null hypothesis $\beta_{x_j|x_i} = 0$,

$$\frac{r\dfrac{s_j}{s_i}}{\left[\dfrac{n-1}{n-2}\dfrac{s_j^2(1-r^2)}{(n-1)s_i^2}\right]^{1/2}} = \frac{r\sqrt{n-2}}{\sqrt{1-r^2}} \sim t(n-2). \tag{7.3}$$

The null hypothesis $\beta_{x_j|x_i} = 0$ is identical with the null hypothesis $\rho = 0$. Therefore (7.3) referred to the t table with $n-2$ degrees of freedom gives a test of the null hypothesis $\rho = 0$.

Alternatively we can use a very good approximation due to Fisher:

$$z = \frac{1}{2}\log_e \frac{1+r}{1-r} = 1.1513 \log_{10} \frac{1+r}{1-r} \tag{7.4}$$

is approximately normally distributed about

$$\zeta = \frac{1}{2}\log_e \frac{1+\rho}{1-\rho} \tag{7.5}$$

with variance

$$V[z] \simeq \frac{1}{n-3}. \tag{7.6}$$

Thus, under the null hypothesis that $\rho = 0$, $z\sqrt{n-3}$ is a unit normal deviate. Also, the null hypothesis that two independent sample correlation coefficients come from the same population ρ can be tested by referring

$$\frac{z_1 - z_2}{\sqrt{1/(n_1-3) + 1/(n_2-3)}} \tag{7.7}$$

to tables of the normal distribution.

12.8. The Effects of Errors of Measurement

Suppose that we sample x from a normal distribution $N(\xi, \sigma_x^2)$. Further suppose that y is normally distributed about an expected value

$$E[y|x] = \eta + \gamma(x - \xi) \tag{8.1}$$

with variance $V[y|x] = \sigma_{y|x}^2$. We will first demonstrate that the joint distribution of x, y is a bivariate normal distribution, and then study the effects of being only able to observe y with error, and then of being only able to observe both x and y with error.

SECT. 12.8 THE EFFECTS OF ERRORS OF MEASUREMENT

From (1.21.7),

$$p\{x, y\} = p\{y|x\}p\{x\}$$

$$= \frac{1}{\sqrt{2\pi}\,\sigma_{y|x}} \exp\left\{-\frac{\{y - [\eta + \gamma(x - \xi)]\}^2}{2\sigma_{y|x}^2}\right\}$$

$$\times \frac{1}{\sqrt{2\pi}\,\sigma_x} \exp\left[-\frac{(x - \xi)^2}{2\sigma_x^2}\right]$$

$$= \frac{1}{2\pi\sigma_x\sigma_{y|x}} \exp\left\{-\frac{1}{2}\left[(x - \xi)^2\left(\frac{1}{\sigma_x^2} + \frac{\gamma^2}{\sigma_{y|x}^2}\right)\right.\right.$$

$$\left.\left. - \frac{2(x - \xi)(y - \eta)}{\sigma_{y|x}^2/\gamma} + \frac{(y - \eta)^2}{\sigma_{y|x}^2}\right]\right\}. \tag{8.2}$$

Now define σ_y^2 and ρ_{xy} as

$$\sigma_y^2 = \sigma_{y|x}^2 + \gamma^2\sigma_x^2, \tag{8.3}$$

$$\rho_{xy}^2 = \frac{\gamma^2\sigma_x^2}{\sigma_{y|x}^2 + \gamma^2\sigma_x^2}. \tag{8.4}$$

We now eliminate $\sigma_{y|x}^2$ and γ from (8.2). From (8.3)

$$\gamma^2 = \frac{\sigma_y^2 - \sigma_{y|x}^2}{\sigma_x^2}, \tag{8.5}$$

and from (8.4) we obtain another expression for γ^2:

$$\gamma^2 = \frac{\rho_{xy}^2\sigma_{y|x}^2}{\sigma_x^2(1 - \rho_{xy}^2)}. \tag{8.6}$$

Equating (8.5) and (8.6) we derive

$$\sigma_{y|x}^2 = \sigma_y^2(1 - \rho_{xy}^2), \tag{8.7}$$

and substituting this in (8.6) gives

$$\gamma^2 = \rho_{xy}^2\frac{\sigma_y^2}{\sigma_x^2}. \tag{8.8}$$

These expressions for $\sigma_{y|x}^2$ and γ^2 are substituted in (8.2), giving

$$p\{x, y\} = \frac{1}{2\pi\sigma_x\sigma_y\sqrt{(1 - \rho_{xy}^2)}}$$

$$\exp\left\{-\frac{1}{2(1 - \rho_{xy}^2)}\left[\left(\frac{x - \xi}{\sigma_x}\right)^2 - 2\rho_{xy}\frac{x - \xi}{\sigma_x}\frac{y - \eta}{\sigma_y} + \left(\frac{y - \eta}{\sigma_y}\right)^2\right]\right\}, \tag{8.9}$$

which is the standard form of the density function of a bivariate normal distribution, (3.17), with parameters ξ, η, σ_x^2, $\sigma_y^2 = \sigma_{y|x}^2 + \gamma^2\sigma_x^2$ as defined by (8.3), and ρ_{xy} as defined by (8.4). We note that

$$\beta_{y|x} = \rho_{xy}\frac{\sigma_y}{\sigma_x} = \left(\frac{\gamma^2\sigma_x^2}{\sigma_{y|x}^2 + \gamma^2\sigma_x^2}\right)^{1/2}\frac{(\sigma_{y|x}^2 + \gamma^2\sigma_x^2)^{1/2}}{\sigma_x} = \gamma, \qquad (8.10)$$

so $b_{y|x}$, being an unbiased estimator of $\beta_{y|x}$, is an unbiased estimator of γ, the regression coefficient of y on x in the model (8.1). Thus if the data we observe are generated by this model, then the parameters are estimable, γ by $b_{y|x}$, σ_x^2 by s_x^2, and $\sigma_{y|x}^2$ by (7.2).

Now suppose that we observe, not y, but $y' = y + v$, where v is a random error with the distribution $N(0, \sigma_v^2)$. Then y' will be normally distributed about an expected value

$$E[y'|x] = \eta + \gamma(x - \xi) \qquad (8.11)$$

with a variance

$$V[y'|x] = \sigma_{y|x}^2 + \sigma_v^2. \qquad (8.12)$$

Repeating the arguments of the first part of this section, we find that the essential change is the replacement of $\sigma_{y|x}^2$ by $(\sigma_{y|x}^2 + \sigma_v^2)$, and the joint density function of x, y' is a bivariate normal distribution with parameters $\xi, \eta, \sigma_x^2, \sigma_{y'}^2 = \sigma_{y|x}^2 + \sigma_v^2 + \gamma^2\sigma_x^2$, and correlation coefficient $\rho_{xy'}$, given by the modified form of (8.4) as

$$\rho_{xy'} = \left(\frac{\gamma^2\sigma_x^2}{\sigma_{y|x}^2 + \sigma_v^2 + \gamma^2\sigma_x^2}\right)^{1/2} = \left(\frac{\gamma^2\sigma_x^2}{\sigma_y^2 + \sigma_v^2}\right)^{1/2} = \left(\frac{\gamma^2\sigma_x^2}{\sigma_y^2}\right)^{1/2}\left(\frac{\sigma_y^2}{\sigma_y^2 + \sigma_v^2}\right)^{1/2}$$

$$= \rho_{xy}\left(\frac{\sigma_y^2}{\sigma_y^2 + \sigma_v^2}\right)^{1/2}. \qquad (8.13)$$

Thus $r_{xy'}$ is not the maximum likelihood estimator of ρ_{xy}. On the other hand,

$$\beta_{y'|x} = \rho_{xy'}\frac{\sigma_{y'}}{\sigma_x} = \left(\frac{\gamma^2\sigma_x^2}{\sigma_{y|x}^2 + \sigma_v^2 + \gamma^2\sigma_x^2}\right)^{1/2}\frac{(\sigma_{yx}^2 + \sigma_v^2 + \gamma^2\sigma_x^2)^{1/2}}{\sigma_x} = \gamma, \qquad (8.14)$$

so introducing error into the observation of y leaves $b_{y'|x}$ an unbiased estimator of γ.

Now suppose that, in addition to the error in y, we observe not x but $x' = x + u$, where u is a random error with the distribution $N(0, \sigma_u^2)$. We assume, of course, that the errors of measurement u, v, are independent of each other and of x and y. We have $E[x'] = \xi$, $V[x'] = \sigma_x^2 + \sigma_u^2$. Since the bivariate normal distribution is symmetrical in form, if adding error in y changed σ_y^2 into $\sigma_{y'}^2 = \sigma_y^2 + \sigma_v^2$, left σ_x^2 unchanged, and multiplied the correlation coefficient by

$$\frac{\rho_{xy'}}{\rho_{xy}} = \left(\frac{\sigma_y^2}{\sigma_y^2 + \sigma_v^2}\right)^{1/2}, \qquad (8.15)$$

then adding error in x will have the analogous effects, i.e., changing σ_x^2 into $\sigma_{x'}^2 = \sigma_x^2 + \sigma_u^2$ and changing the correlation coefficient into $\rho_{x'y'}$ given by

$$\frac{\rho_{x'y'}}{\rho_{xy'}} = \left(\frac{\sigma_x^2}{\sigma_x^2 + \sigma_u^2}\right)^{1/2}. \tag{8.16}$$

Thus, substituting for $\rho_{xy'}$ from (8.13),

$$\rho_{x'y'} = \rho_{xy}\left(\frac{\sigma_x^2}{\sigma_x^2 + \sigma_u^2}\right)^{1/2}\left(\frac{\sigma_y^2}{\sigma_y^2 + \sigma_v^2}\right)^{1/2} = \rho_{xy}\left\{\left[\left(1 + \frac{\sigma_u^2}{\sigma_x^2}\right)\left(1 + \frac{\sigma_v^2}{\sigma_y^2}\right)\right]^{1/2}\right\}^{-1} \tag{8.17}$$

Thus $r_{x'y'}$ is not the maximum likelihood estimator of ρ_{xy}. Also,

$$\beta_{y'|x'} = \rho_{x'y'}\frac{\sigma_{y'}}{\sigma_{x'}} = \rho_{xy}\left(\frac{\sigma_x^2}{\sigma_x^2 + \sigma_u^2}\right)^{1/2}\left(\frac{\sigma_y^2}{\sigma_y^2 + \sigma_v^2}\right)^{1/2}\left(\frac{\sigma_y^2 + \sigma_v^2}{\sigma_x^2 + \sigma_u^2}\right)^{1/2}. \tag{8.18}$$

From (8.3) and (8.4),

$$\rho_{xy} = \frac{\gamma\sigma_x}{\sigma_y}, \tag{8.19}$$

so

$$\beta_{y'|x'} = \gamma\frac{\sigma_x^2}{\sigma_x^2 + \sigma_u^2}. \tag{8.20}$$

Thus introducing error into the observation of x makes $b_{y'|x'}$ a biased estimator of γ, the regression coefficient of y on x in the original model.

It is possible for the model of this section, with different values of the parameters σ_x^2, σ_u^2, $\sigma_{y|x}^2$, σ_v^2 and γ, to lead to identical bivariate normal distributions with the same values for the parameters $\sigma_{x'}^2$, $\sigma_{y'}^2$ and $\rho_{x'y'}$. Thus the same bivariate normal population can be produced by sampling from different regression situations.

EXERCISES

12.1. For a number of storms, the amounts of rain falling at two sites were observed. The amounts, transformed in a certain way to give better bivariate normality, were as follows:

x_1	1.05	1.40	0.69	1.41	0.51	1.49	1.38	2.00	0.96	1.31	2.07	1.02	0.89	1.51
x_2	0.66	1.16	0.64	1.07	0.33	1.59	1.11	1.33	0.96	1.40	1.71	0.75	0.75	0.92

For these data, $n = 14$, $\Sigma x_1 = 17.69$, $\Sigma x_2 = 14.38$, $\Sigma x_1^2 = 24.9465$, $\Sigma x_2^2 = 16.7508$, $\Sigma x_1 x_2 = 20.1135$.

(a) Obtain estimates of (i) ρ, (ii) $V[x_2]$, (iii) $V[x_2|x_1]$. (b) Test the null hypothesis that $\rho = 0$. (c) Obtain the regression equation of x_2 on x_1. (d) Obtain the regression equation of x_1 on x_2. (e) If we observe $x_1 = 1.4$, what is the predicted value of x_2? (f) If we observe $x_2 = 1.13$, what is the predicted value of x_1? (g) Another set of 18 storms gave a sample correlation coefficient between another pair of sites of 0.703. Test the null hypothesis that the correlations between the two sites in each pair are equal.

12.2. For the model of Section 12.8, suppose that (a) $\sigma_x^2 = 2/3$, $\sigma_{y|x}^2 = 55/96$, $\gamma = 3/8$, $\sigma_u^2 = 1/3$, $\sigma_v^2 = 1/3$, and alternatively that (b) $\sigma_x^2 = 1/2$, $\sigma_{y|x}^2 = 3/8$, $\gamma = 1/2$, $\sigma_u^2 = 1/2$, $\sigma_v^2 = 1/2$. Compare for the two bivariate normal distributions so produced $\sigma_{x'}^2$, $\sigma_{y'}^2$, $\rho_{x'y'}$. Also compare $\beta_{y'|x'}$ with γ for (a) and (b).

12.3. Suppose that x, y are independently normally distributed with zero means and unit variances. What is the density function of x/y?

CHAPTER 13

Regression on Several Independent Variables

13.1. Introduction

Chapter 11 dealt with the regression of a dependent variable y on a single independent variable x. This chapter will deal with the regression of y on r independent variables x_i. Although it is merely a special case, we will deal with $r = 2$ before the general case of any r, but before that we will establish an essential result.

13.2. Linear Transformation of the Variables in a Bivariate Normal Distribution to Give Independent Variables

We suppose that x_1, x_2 are distributed in a bivariate normal distribution such as (12.3.17). Now introduce new variables y_1, y_2 defined as

$$y_1 = f_1(x_1, x_2) = (x_1 - \xi_1) \cos \alpha + (x_2 - \xi_2) \sin \alpha,$$
$$y_2 = f_2(x_1, x_2) = -(x_1 - \xi_1) \sin \alpha + (x_2 - \xi_2) \cos \alpha. \quad (2.1)$$

The y's correspond to a new set of coordinates centered at $x_1 = \xi_1, x_2 = \xi_2$, and rotated with respect to the original coordinates through an angle α. The inverse functions are

$$x_1 = g_1(y_1, y_2) = \xi_1 + y_1 \cos \alpha - y_2 \sin \alpha,$$
$$x_2 = g_2(y_1, y_2) = \xi_2 + y_1 \sin \alpha + y_2 \cos \alpha. \quad (2.2)$$

We now use (12.2.16) for the probability density function of a transformation:

$$p\{y_1, y_2\} = p_x\{g_1(y_1, y_2), g_2(y_1, y_2)\} \begin{vmatrix} \dfrac{\partial g_1}{\partial y_1} & \dfrac{\partial g_2}{\partial y_1} \\ \dfrac{\partial g_1}{\partial y_2} & \dfrac{\partial g_2}{\partial y_2} \end{vmatrix}. \qquad (2.3)$$

Here p_x is the usual bivariate normal distribution (12.3.17) for variables x_1, x_2. Differentiating (2.2) gives

$$\dfrac{\partial g_1}{\partial y_1} = \cos\alpha, \quad \dfrac{\partial g_1}{\partial y_2} = -\sin\alpha, \quad \dfrac{\partial g_2}{\partial y_1} = \sin\alpha, \quad \dfrac{\partial g_2}{\partial y_2} = \cos\alpha; \qquad (2.4)$$

so the determinant is

$$\cos\alpha \cdot \cos\alpha - (-\sin\alpha)(\sin\alpha) = 1. \qquad (2.5)$$

Hence

$$p\{y_1, y_2\} = \dfrac{1}{2\pi\sigma_1\sigma_2\sqrt{1-\rho^2}}$$
$$\times \exp\left\{-\dfrac{1}{2(1-\rho^2)}\left[\left(\dfrac{y_1\cos\alpha - y_2\sin\alpha}{\sigma_1}\right)^2 + \left(\dfrac{y_1\sin\alpha + y_2\cos\alpha}{\sigma_2}\right)^2 \right.\right.$$
$$\left.\left. - 2\rho\dfrac{(y_1\cos\alpha - y_2\sin\alpha)(y_1\sin\alpha + y_2\cos\alpha)}{\sigma_1\sigma_2}\right]\right\}. \qquad (2.6)$$

Denote the exponent of this function by G. Recalling that $2\sin\alpha\cos\alpha = \sin 2\alpha$, $\cos^2\alpha - \sin^2\alpha = \cos 2\alpha$, G can be written as

$$G = -\dfrac{1}{2(1-\rho^2)}\left[y_1^2\left(\dfrac{\cos^2\alpha}{\sigma_1^2} + \dfrac{\sin^2\alpha}{\sigma_2^2} - \rho\dfrac{\sin 2\alpha}{\sigma_1\sigma_2}\right)\right.$$
$$+ y_2^2\left(\dfrac{\sin^2\alpha}{\sigma_1^2} + \dfrac{\cos^2\alpha}{\sigma_2^2} + \rho\dfrac{\sin 2\alpha}{\sigma_1\sigma_2}\right)$$
$$\left. - y_1 y_2\left(\dfrac{\sin 2\alpha}{\sigma_1^2} - \dfrac{\sin 2\alpha}{\sigma_2^2} + 2\rho\dfrac{\cos 2\alpha}{\sigma_1\sigma_2}\right)\right]. \qquad (2.7)$$

Thus $p\{y_1, y_2\}$ has the form of a bivariate normal distribution with mean $(0, 0)$ and variances and correlation coefficient which are functions of $\sigma_1^2, \sigma_2^2, \rho$, and α. If we make the coefficient of $y_1 y_2$ in (2.7) zero, we will have y_1, y_2 with zero correlation. Putting this coefficient equal to zero requires

$$\dfrac{\sin 2\alpha}{\sigma_1^2} - \dfrac{\sin 2\alpha}{\sigma_2^2} + 2\rho\dfrac{\cos 2\alpha}{\sigma_1\sigma_2} = 0, \qquad (2.8)$$

or

$$\tan 2\alpha = \dfrac{2\rho\sigma_1\sigma_2}{\sigma_1^2 - \sigma_2^2} \qquad (2.9)$$

SECT. 13.2 LINEAR TRANSFORMATION OF THE VARIABLES

If we use the value of α determined by this equation, we will have $\rho_{y_1 y_2} = 0$. Now the probability density function of y_1, y_2 with zero correlation is

$$p\{y_1, y_2\} = \frac{1}{2\pi \sigma_{y_1} \sigma_{y_2}} \exp\left\{-\frac{1}{2}\left[\left(\frac{y_1}{\sigma_{y_1}}\right)^2 + \left(\frac{y_2}{\sigma_{y_2}}\right)^2\right]\right\}. \qquad (2.10)$$

But we already have an equation for $p\{y_1, y_2\}$, namely, (2.6). These must be identical for all values of y_1, y_2. This includes $y_1 = 0, y_2 = 0$, so we can insert these values in the two equations and equate the results. This gives

$$\sigma_{y_1} \sigma_{y_2} = \sigma_1 \sigma_2 \sqrt{1 - \rho^2}. \qquad (2.11)$$

Also (2.6) and (2.10) must be identical for $y_1 = 1, y_2 = 1$, which implies

$$\frac{1}{\sigma_{y_1}^2} + \frac{1}{\sigma_{y_2}^2} = \frac{1}{1 - \rho^2}\left[\left(\frac{\cos^2 \alpha}{\sigma_1^2} + \frac{\sin^2 \alpha}{\sigma_2^2} - \rho \frac{\sin 2\alpha}{\sigma_1 \sigma_2}\right)\right.$$

$$\left. + \left(\frac{\sin^2 \alpha}{\sigma_1^2} + \frac{\cos^2 \alpha}{\sigma_2^2} + \rho \frac{\sin 2\alpha}{\sigma_1 \sigma_2}\right)\right]$$

$$= \frac{1}{1 - \rho^2}\left(\frac{1}{\sigma_1^2} + \frac{1}{\sigma_2^2}\right); \qquad (2.12)$$

so, if we multiply each side by the square of the corresponding side of (2.11), we get

$$\sigma_{y_1}^2 + \sigma_{y_2}^2 = \sigma_1^2 + \sigma_2^2. \qquad (2.13)$$

Adding and subtracting (2.11) gives

$$(\sigma_{y_1} + \sigma_{y_2})^2 = \sigma_1^2 + \sigma_2^2 + 2\sigma_1 \sigma_2 \sqrt{1 - \rho^2},$$
$$(\sigma_{y_1} - \sigma_{y_2})^2 = \sigma_1^2 + \sigma_2^2 - 2\sigma_1 \sigma_2 \sqrt{1 - \rho^2}. \qquad (2.14)$$

Thus, if we know σ_1, σ_2, and ρ for the original distribution of (x_1, x_2), we can determine σ_{y_1} and σ_{y_2} to use in the equation for the probability density of (y_1, y_2), (2.10).

If we substitute back for x_1, x_2 in (2.6), we get

$$p\{y_1, y_2\} = \frac{1}{2\pi \sigma_1 \sigma_2 \sqrt{1 - \rho^2}}$$

$$\times \exp\left\{-\frac{1}{2(1 - \rho^2)}\left[\left(\frac{x_1 - \xi_1}{\sigma_1}\right)^2 - 2\rho \frac{x_1 - \xi_1}{\sigma_1} \frac{x_2 - \xi_2}{\sigma_2} + \left(\frac{x_2 - \xi_2}{\sigma_2}\right)^2\right]\right\}.$$
$$(2.15)$$

But $p\{y_1, y_2\}$ is also given by (2.10). Equating these two, and using (2.11), we get

$$\frac{1}{(1-\rho^2)}\left[\left(\frac{x_1-\xi_1}{\sigma_1}\right)^2 - 2\rho\frac{x_1-\xi_1}{\sigma_1}\frac{x_2-\xi_2}{\sigma_2} + \left(\frac{x_2-\xi_2}{\sigma_2}\right)^2\right]$$
$$= \left(\frac{y_1}{\sigma_{y_1}}\right)^2 + \left(\frac{y_2}{\sigma_{y_2}}\right)^2. \quad (2.16)$$

The y's have zero means and zero covariance; so the right-hand side is the sum of squares of two independent unit normal deviates, which must have the χ^2 distribution with 2 degrees of freedom. Hence the left-hand side of (2.16) has the same distribution:

$$\frac{1}{1-\rho^2}\left[\left(\frac{x_1-\xi_1}{\sigma_1}\right)^2 - 2\rho\frac{x_1-\xi_1}{\sigma_1}\frac{x_2-\xi_2}{\sigma_2} + \left(\frac{x_2-\xi_2}{\sigma_2}\right)^2\right] \sim \chi^2(2).$$
(2.17)

We will need this result in the following section.

13.3. Regression on Two Independent Variables

We assume that y is distributed normally about an expected value η with variance σ^2, and that the observations are independent. We assume that η is a simple linear function of two *independent variables* x_1 and x_2:

$$\eta = \alpha + \beta_1(x_1 - \bar{x}_1) + \beta_2(x_2 - \bar{x}_2). \quad (3.1)$$

Although this is the standard terminology for x_1 and x_2, it is misleading in that there is no requirement that x_1, x_2 be independent in the statistical sense. All that is required is that they be variables whose values $x_{1\nu}, x_{2\nu}$ be known for each value of ν.

We assume that we have n triplets of observations $(y_\nu, x_{1\nu}, x_{2\nu})$. We wish to obtain sample estimates a, b_1, b_2 and s^2 of the parameters α, β_1, β_2 and σ^2.

The estimated equation is

$$Y = a + b_1(x_1 - \bar{x}_1) + b_2(x_2 - \bar{x}_2), \quad (3.2)$$

and the sum of squares of deviations between the observed values y_ν and the values predicted by the estimated equation is

$$R = \sum_\nu^n (y_\nu - Y_\nu)^2 = \sum_\nu^n \{y_\nu - [a + b_1(x_{1\nu} - \bar{x}_1) + b_2(x_{2\nu} - \bar{x}_2)]\}^2. \quad (3.3)$$

SECT. 13.3 REGRESSION ON TWO INDEPENDENT VARIABLES

To minimize this we differentiate with respect to a, b_1, b_2 and equate to zero:

$$\frac{\partial R}{\partial a} = -2 \sum_{v}^{n} [y_v - a - b_1(x_{1v} - \bar{x}_1) - b_2(x_{2v} - \bar{x}_2)] = 0, \quad (3.4)$$

$$\frac{\partial R}{\partial b_1} = -2 \sum_{v}^{n} [y_v - a - b_1(x_{1v} - \bar{x}_1) - b_2(x_{2v} - \bar{x}_2)](x_{1v} - \bar{x}_1) = 0, \quad (3.5)$$

$$\frac{\partial R}{\partial b_2} = -2 \sum_{v}^{n} [y_v - a - b_1(x_{1v} - \bar{x}_1) - b_2(x_{2v} - \bar{x}_2)](x_{2v} - \bar{x}_2) = 0. \quad (3.6)$$

These three equations imply

$$\sum_{v}^{n} (y_v - Y_v) = 0, \quad (3.7)$$

$$\sum_{v}^{n} (y_v - Y_v)(x_{1v} - \bar{x}_1) = 0, \quad (3.8)$$

$$\sum_{v}^{n} (y_v - Y_v)(x_{2v} - \bar{x}_2) = 0. \quad (3.9)$$

Since $\sum_{v}^{n} (x_{1v} - \bar{x}_1) = 0 = \sum_{v}^{n} (x_{2v} - \bar{x}_2)$, (3.4) gives us

$$\sum_{v}^{n} y_v - na - b_1 \sum_{v}^{n} (x_{1v} - \bar{x}_1) - b_2 \sum_{v}^{n} (x_{2v} - \bar{x}_2) = \sum_{v}^{n} y_v - na = 0, \quad (3.10)$$

whence

$$a = \frac{1}{n} \sum_{v}^{n} y_v. \quad (3.11)$$

From (3.5) and (3.6) we get a pair of simultaneous equations, known as the *normal equations*, for the two unknown b's with coefficients involving sums of squares and sums of products which can be calculated from the data:

$$b_1 \sum_{v}^{n} (x_{1v} - \bar{x}_1)^2 + b_2 \sum_{v}^{n} (x_{1v} - \bar{x}_1)(x_{2v} - \bar{x}_2) = \sum_{v}^{n} y_v(x_{1v} - \bar{x}_1), \quad (3.12)$$

$$b_1 \sum_{v}^{n} (x_{1v} - \bar{x}_1)(x_{2v} - \bar{x}_2) + b_2 \sum_{v}^{n} (x_{2v} - \bar{x}_2)^2 = \sum_{v}^{n} y_v(x_{2v} - \bar{x}_2). \quad (3.13)$$

Space can be saved by using the definitions

$$\sum' x_1^2 = \sum_v^n (x_{1v} - \bar{x}_1)^2, \qquad \sum' x_2^2 = \sum_v^n (x_{2v} - \bar{x}_2)^2,$$

$$\sum' x_1 x_2 = \sum_v^n (x_{1v} - \bar{x}_1)(x_{2v} - \bar{x}_2), \qquad (3.14)$$

$$\sum' y x_1 = \sum_v^n y_v (x_{1v} - \bar{x}_1), \qquad \sum' y x_2 = \sum_v^n y_v (x_{2v} - \bar{x}_2).$$

with which the normal equations (3.12) and (3.13) read

$$b_1 \sum' x_1^2 + b_2 \sum' x_1 x_2 = \sum' y x_1, \qquad (3.15)$$
$$b_1 \sum' x_1 x_2 + b_2 \sum' x_2^2 = \sum' y x_2. \qquad (3.16)$$

If we multiply (3.15) by $\sum' x_2^2$ and (3.16) by $\sum' x_1 x_2$ we get

$$b_1 \sum' x_1^2 \sum' x_2^2 + b_2 \sum' x_1 x_2 \sum' x_2^2 = \sum' y x_1 \sum' x_2^2, \qquad (3.17)$$
$$b_1 (\sum' x_1 x_2)^2 + b_2 \sum' x_1 x_2 \sum' x_2^2 = \sum' y x_2 \sum' x_1 x_2. \qquad (3.18)$$

Solving for b_1 gives

$$b_1 = \frac{\sum' y x_1 \sum' x_2^2 - \sum' y x_2 \sum' x_1 x_2}{\sum' x_1^2 \sum' x_2^2 - (\sum' x_1 x_2)^2}. \qquad (3.19)$$

By similar manipulations,

$$b_2 = \frac{\sum' y x_2 \sum' x_1^2 - \sum' y x_1 \sum' x_1 x_2}{\sum' x_1^2 \sum' x_2^2 - (\sum' x_1 x_2)^2}. \qquad (3.20)$$

The solution for b_1, (3.19), can be written in the form

$$b_1 = [\sum' x_1^2 \sum' x_2^2 - (\sum' x_1 x_2)^2]^{-1}$$
$$\times \left[\sum' x_2^2 \sum_v^n (x_{1v} - \bar{x}_1) y_v - \sum' x_1 x_2 \sum_v^n (x_{2v} - \bar{x}_2) y_v \right]$$
$$= [\sum' x_1^2 \sum' x_2^2 - (\sum' x_1 x_2)^2]^{-1}$$
$$\times \left\{ \sum_v^n [(\sum' x_2^2)(x_{1v} - \bar{x}_1) - (\sum' x_1 x_2)(x_{2v} - \bar{x}_2)] y_v \right\}, \qquad (3.21)$$

which shows that b_1 is a linear function of the y's. Since the y's are normally distributed, b_1 will be normally distributed, with variance

$$V[b_1] = \frac{\sum_v^n [(\sum' x_2^2)(x_{1v} - \bar{x}_1) - (\sum' x_1 x_2)(x_{2v} - \bar{x}_2)]^2 V[y_v]}{[\sum' x_1^2 \sum' x_2^2 - (\sum' x_1 x_2)^2]^2}$$

$$= \sigma^2 \frac{(\sum' x_2^2)^2 (\sum' x_1^2) - 2(\sum' x_2^2)(\sum' x_1 x_2)(\sum' x_1 x_2) + (\sum' x_1 x_2)^2 (\sum' x_2^2)}{[\sum' x_1^2 \sum' x_2^2 - (\sum' x_1 x_2)^2]^2}$$

$$= \sigma^2 \frac{\sum' x_2^2}{\sum' x_1^2 \sum' x_2^2 - (\sum' x_1 x_2)^2}. \qquad (3.22)$$

SECT. 13.3   REGRESSION ON TWO INDEPENDENT VARIABLES

If we define $\rho_{x_1 x_2}$ as the "correlation coefficient" between x_1 and x_2, i.e.,

$$\rho_{x_1 x_2} = \frac{\sum' x_1 x_2}{\sqrt{\sum' x_1^2 \sum' x_2^2}}, \tag{3.23}$$

we can write (3.22) as

$$V[b_1] = \frac{\sigma^2}{\sum' x_1^2} \cdot \left[1 - \frac{(\sum' x_1 x_2)^2}{\sum' x_1^2 \sum' x_2^2}\right]^{-1} = \frac{\sigma^2}{\sum' x_1^2} \frac{1}{1 - \rho_{x_1 x_2}^2}. \tag{3.24}$$

This can be compared with the expression for the variance of the regression coefficient of y on x_1 alone, $\sigma^2/\sum' x_1^2$, (11.2.16). Similarly

$$V[b_2] = \sigma^2 \frac{\sum' x_1^2}{\sum' x_1^2 \sum' x_2^2 - (\sum' x_1 x_2)^2} = \frac{\sigma^2}{\sum' x_2^2} \frac{1}{1 - \rho_{x_1 x_2}^2}. \tag{3.25}$$

The same type of manipulation leads to

$$\mathrm{Cov}[b_1, b_2] = -\sigma^2 \frac{\sum' x_1 x_2}{\sum' x_1^2 \sum' x_2^2 - (\sum' x_1 x_2)^2}. \tag{3.26}$$

whence

$$\rho_{b_1 b_2} = -\frac{\sum' x_1 x_2}{\sqrt{\sum' x_1^2 \sum' x_2^2}}. \tag{3.27}$$

If in (2.17) we substitute b_1 for x_1, b_2 for x_2, etc., we get

$$\frac{1}{1 - \rho_{b_1 b_2}^2}\left[\left(\frac{b_1 - \beta_1}{\sqrt{V[b_1]}}\right)^2 - 2\rho_{b_1 b_2}\frac{b_1 - \beta_1}{\sqrt{V[b_1]}}\frac{b_2 - \beta_2}{\sqrt{V[b_2]}} + \left(\frac{b_2 - \beta_2}{\sqrt{V[b_2]}}\right)\right] \sim \chi^2(2). \tag{3.28}$$

We now substitute (3.22) for $V[b_1]$, (3.25) for $V[b_2]$, and use (3.27) to get

$$1 - \rho_{b_1 b_2}^2 = 1 - \frac{(\sum' x_1 x_2)^2}{\sum' x_1^2 \sum' x_2^2} = \frac{\sum' x_1^2 \sum' x_2^2 - (\sum' x_1 x_2)^2}{\sum' x_1^2 \sum' x_2^2}, \tag{3.29}$$

and obtain

$$[(b_1 - \beta_1)^2 \sum' x_1^2 + 2(b_1 - \beta_1)(b_2 - \beta_2)\sum' x_1 x_2 + (b_2 - \beta_2)^2 \sum' x_2^2] \sim \sigma^2 \chi^2(2). \tag{3.30}$$

We will assume without proof the generalization of this to r independent variables $x_1, \ldots, x_r$:

$$\sum_i^r (b_i - \beta_i)^2 \sum' x_i^2 + 2\sum_{i=1}^{r-1}\sum_{j=i+1}^{r} (b_i - \beta_i)(b_j - \beta_j)\sum' x_i x_j \sim \sigma^2 \chi^2(r). \tag{3.31}$$

We can write the deviation between the observation y_v and the true value η_v as

$$y_v - \eta_v = (y_v - Y_v) + (Y_v - \eta_v)$$
$$= (y_v - Y_v) + (a - \alpha)$$
$$+ (b_1 - \beta_1)(x_{1v} - \bar{x}_1) + (b_2 - \beta_2)(x_{2v} - \bar{x}_2). \quad (3.32)$$

Squaring and summing, and using (3.7), (3.8), and (3.9) to dispose of cross products,

$$\sum_v^n (y_v - \eta_v)^2 = \sum_v^n (y_v - Y_v)^2 + n(a - \alpha)^2 + (b_1 - \beta_1)^2 \sum_v^n (x_{1v} - \bar{x}_1)^2$$
$$+ 2(b_1 - \beta_1)(b_2 - \beta_2) \sum_v^n (x_{1v} - \bar{x}_1)(x_{2v} - \bar{x}_2)$$
$$+ (b_2 - \beta_2)^2 \sum_v^n (x_{2v} - \bar{x}_2)^2. \quad (3.33)$$

The left-hand side of this equation is distributed as $\sigma^2 \chi^2(n)$. On the right-hand side $\sum_v^n (y_v - Y_v)^2$ has $n - 3$ degrees of freedom since the $y_v - Y_v$ have to satisfy the three linear restrictions (3.7), (3.8) and (3.9). The second term, involving a, has one degree of freedom. Third, we showed in (3.30) that the last three terms jointly are distributed as $\sigma^2 \chi^2(2)$. Thus the conditions for Cochran's theorem are satisfied, and the three component sums of squares, namely, $\sum_v^n (y_v - Y_v)^2$, $n(a - \alpha)^2$ and (3.30) are independently distributed as $\sigma^2 \chi^2$. If we define s^2 as

$$s^2 = \frac{1}{n-3} \sum_v^n (y_v - Y_v)^2, \quad (3.34)$$

it will be distributed as $\sigma^2 \chi^2(n-3)/(n-3)$ and have expected value σ^2. We can make separate tests of the null hypotheses $\beta_1 = 0$ and $\beta_2 = 0$ by substituting this estimate s^2 for σ^2 in (3.22) and (3.25), but in general these tests are not independent since usually $\text{Cov}[b_1, b_2] \neq 0$. We can make a joint test of the null hypothesis $\beta_1 = \beta_2 = 0$ as follows. Since (3.30) is distributed as $\sigma^2 \chi^2(2)$,

$$\tfrac{1}{2}[(b_1 - \beta_1)^2 \sum' x_1^2 + 2(b_1 - \beta_1)(b_2 - \beta_2) \sum' x_1 x_2 + (b_2 - \beta_2)^2 \sum' x_2^2]$$
$$\sim \frac{\sigma^2 \chi^2(2)}{2} \quad (3.35)$$

SECT. 13.3 REGRESSION ON TWO INDEPENDENT VARIABLES

and has expected value σ^2, and the distribution of the ratio of it to s^2 will be $F(2, n - 3)$. Hence, under the null hypothesis $\beta_1 = \beta_2 = 0$,

$$\frac{1}{2s^2}(b_1^2 \sum' x_1^2 + 2b_1 b_2 \sum' x_1 x_2 + b_2^2 \sum' x_2^2) \sim F(2, n - 3). \quad (3.36)$$

Both the numerator of s^2, $\sum\limits_{v}^{n}(y_v - Y_v)^2$, and the expression in parentheses in (3.36), known as the sum of squares due to regression, can be computed in the forms given. However, alternative identities are convenient. We obtain them as follows. Squaring and summing the identity

$$y_v - \bar{y} = (y_v - Y_v) + (Y_v - \bar{y}) \quad (3.37)$$

gives

$$\sum_{v}^{n}(y_v - \bar{y})^2 = \sum_{v}^{n}(y_v - Y_v)^2 + \sum_{v}^{n}(Y_v - \bar{y})^2, \quad (3.38)$$

since the cross product

$$2\sum_{v}^{n}(y_v - Y_v)(Y_v - \bar{y})$$

$$= 2\sum_{v}^{n}(y_v - Y_v)[\bar{y} + b_1(x_{1v} - \bar{x}_1) + b_2(x_{2v} - \bar{x}_2) - \bar{y}]$$

$$= 2b_1 \sum_{v}^{n}(y_v - Y_v)(x_{1v} - \bar{x}_1) + 2b_2 \sum_{v}^{n}(y_v - Y_v)(x_{2v} - \bar{x}_2)$$

$$= 0, \quad (3.39)$$

by (3.8) and (3.9). Rearranged, (3.38) becomes

$$\sum_{v}^{n}(y_v - Y_v)^2 = \sum_{v}^{n}(y_v - \bar{y})^2 - \sum_{v}^{n}(Y_v - \bar{y})^2. \quad (3.40)$$

The first term on the right-hand side is simply the sum of squares of deviations about the grand mean, and so we are left with finding a convenient form for $\sum\limits_{v}^{n}(Y_v - \bar{y})^2$. We note that

$$\sum_{v}^{n}(Y_v - \bar{y})^2 = \sum_{v}^{n}[a + b_1(x_{1v} - \bar{x}_1) + b_2(x_{2v} - \bar{x}_2) - a]^2$$

$$= \sum_{v}^{n}[b_1(x_{1v} - \bar{x}_1) + b_2(x_{2v} - \bar{x}_2)]^2$$

$$= b_1^2 \sum_{v}^{n}(x_{1v} - \bar{x}_1)^2 + 2b_1 b_2 \sum_{v}^{n}(x_{1v} - \bar{x}_1)(x_{2v} - \bar{x}_2)$$

$$+ b_2^2 \sum_{v}^{n}(x_{2v} - \bar{x}_2)^2 \quad (3.41)$$

$$= b_1^2 \sum' x_1^2 + 2b_1 b_2 \sum' x_1 x_2 + b_2^2 \sum' x_2^2. \quad (3.42)$$

We can obtain an alternative expression for the right-hand side as follows. Multiply the normal equations (3.12) and (3.13) by b_1 and b_2 respectively:

$$b_1^2 \sum_v^n (x_{1v} - \bar{x}_1)^2 + b_1 b_2 \sum_v^n (x_{1v} - \bar{x}_1)(x_{2v} - \bar{x}_2) = b_1 \sum_v^n y_v(x_{1v} - \bar{x}_1), \qquad (3.43)$$

$$b_1 b_2 \sum_v^n (x_{1v} - \bar{x}_1)(x_{2v} - \bar{x}_2) + b_2^2 \sum_v^n (x_{2v} - \bar{x}_2)^2 = b_2 \sum_v^n y_v(x_{2v} - \bar{x}_2), \qquad (3.44)$$

and add:

$$b_1^2 \sum_v^n (x_{1v} - \bar{x}_1)^2 + 2 b_1 b_2 \sum_v^n (x_{1v} - \bar{x}_1)(x_{2v} - \bar{x}_2) + b_2^2 \sum_v^n (x_{2v} - \bar{x})^2$$

$$= b_1 \sum_v^n y_v(x_{1v} - \bar{x}_1) + b_2 \sum_v^n y_v(x_{2v} - \bar{x}_2). \qquad (3.45)$$

Thus the sum of squares for regression is conveniently calculated from the right-hand side of (3.45) and the remainder sum of squares is then found from (3.40). The test implicit in (3.36) is conveniently put in tabular form (Table 13.1).

Table 13.1

Source of variance	Sums of squares	Degrees of freedom	Mean squares
Due to regression	$b_1 \Sigma' yx_1 + b_2 \Sigma' yx_2$	2	s_2^2
Remainder	$\sum_v^n (y_v - Y_v)^2$	$n - 3$	s^2
Total	$\sum_v^n (y_v - \bar{y})^2$	$n - 1$	

Finally, the predicted value Y,

$$Y = a + b_1(x_1 - \bar{x}_1) + b_2(x_2 - \bar{x}_2) \qquad (3.46)$$

has expected value

$$\eta = \alpha + \beta_1(x_1 - \bar{x}_1) + \beta_2(x_2 - \bar{x}_2). \qquad (3.47)$$

Since a is independent of b_1 and b_2,

$$[Y] = V[a] + (x_1 - \bar{x}_1)^2 V[b_1] + (x_2 - \bar{x}_2)^2 V[b_2]$$
$$+ 2(x_1 - \bar{x}_1)(x_2 - \bar{x}_2) \operatorname{Cov}[b_1, b_2]$$

$$\sigma^2 \left[\frac{1}{n} + \frac{(x_1 - \bar{x}_1)^2 \Sigma' x_2^2 - 2(x_1 - \bar{x}_1)(x_2 - \bar{x}_2) \Sigma' x_1 x_2 + (x_2 - \bar{x}_2)^2 \Sigma' x_1^2}{\Sigma' x_1^2 \Sigma' x_2^2 - (\Sigma' x_1 x_2)^2} \right].$$

$$(3.48)$$

13.4. The Partial Correlation Coefficient

In the preceding discussion in this chapter the so-called independent variables x_1, x_2 were regarded as fixed variables. They may, however, be random variables, in which case (y, x_1, x_2) will have a trivariate distribution. An important trivariate distribution is the trivariate normal:

$$p\{x_1, x_2, x_3\} = \frac{1}{\sigma_1 \sigma_2 \sigma_3 \sqrt{(2\pi)^3 \omega}} e^{-\phi/2}, \tag{4.1}$$

where ω is the determinant

$$= \begin{vmatrix} 1 & \rho_{21} & \rho_{31} \\ \rho_{12} & 1 & \rho_{32} \\ \rho_{13} & \rho_{23} & 1 \end{vmatrix} \tag{4.2}$$

$$= 1 - \rho_{12}^2 - \rho_{13}^2 - \rho_{23}^2 + 2\rho_{12}\rho_{13}\rho_{23}, \tag{4.3}$$

since $\rho_{ij} = \rho_{ji}$, and ϕ is defined as

$$\phi = \frac{1}{\omega}\left(\omega_{11}\frac{x_1'^2}{\sigma_1^2} + \omega_{22}\frac{x_2'^2}{\sigma_2^2} + \omega_{33}\frac{x_3'^2}{\sigma_3^2} + 2\omega_{12}\frac{x_1' x_2'}{\sigma_1 \sigma_2} + 2\omega_{13}\frac{x_1' x_3'}{\sigma_1 \sigma_3} + 2\omega_{23}\frac{x_2' x_3'}{\sigma_2 \sigma_3}\right) \tag{4.4}$$

in which $x_i' = x_i - \xi_i$, $i = 1, 2, 3$, and ω_{ij} is the cofactor of the ijth element in ω. Thus

$$\omega_{11} = 1 - \rho_{23}^2, \quad \omega_{22} = 1 - \rho_{13}^2, \quad \omega_{33} = 1 - \rho_{12}^2,$$
$$\omega_{12} = -(\rho_{12} - \rho_{13}\rho_{23}), \quad \omega_{13} = \rho_{12}\rho_{23} - \rho_{13}, \quad \omega_{23} = -(\rho_{23} - \rho_{12}\rho_{13}). \tag{4.5}$$

The trivariate normal is the generalization of the bivariate normal to three variables. Geometrically it can be represented by concentric ellipsoids of constant density in three-dimensional space.

We showed in Section 12.4 that when a bivariate normal distribution in x_1, x_2 is integrated over x_2 it gives a univariate normal distribution in x_1. Likewise, a trivariate normal in x_1, x_2, x_3 when integrated over x_3 gives a bivariate normal distribution in x_1, x_2 with parameters ξ_1, ξ_2, σ_1, σ_2, ρ_{12}.

Now suppose that we have a trivariate normal distribution in x_1, x_2, x_3 and we choose to consider the correlation coefficient between x_1 and x_2 with x_3 "held constant," i.e., we take a thin slice through the trivariate distribution parallel to the x_1, x_2 plane and consider the distribution of x_1, x_2. In other words, we consider the distribution function $p\{x_1, x_2|x_3\}$. By a simple extension of (1.21.7),

$$p\{x_1, x_2|x_3\} = \frac{p\{x_1, x_2, x_3\}}{p\{x_3\}}. \tag{4.6}$$

For simplicity, but with no loss of generality, we will assume that the means ξ_1, ξ_2, ξ_3 are zero. The substitutions are straightforward. The function $p\{x_1, x_2, x_3\}$ is given by (4.1)–(4.5). Since integrating $p\{x_1, x_2, x_3\}$ over x_1 gives a bivariate normal distribution in x_2, x_3, when we further integrate over x_2 we get as the distribution of x_3 a univariate normal distribution with parameters $(0, \sigma_3^2)$. After some manipulation, we can get (4.6) in the form

$$p\{x_1, x_2 | x_3\}$$
$$= \left\{ 2\pi\sigma_1 \sqrt{1 - \rho_{13}^2} \sigma_2 \sqrt{1 - \rho_{23}^2} \left[1 - \left(\frac{\rho_{12} - \rho_{13}\rho_{23}}{\sqrt{(1 - \rho_{13}^2)(1 - \rho_{23}^2)}} \right)^2 \right]^{1/2} \right\}^{-1}$$
$$\times \exp\left\{ -\frac{1}{2}\left[1 - \left(\frac{\rho_{12} - \rho_{13}\rho_{23}}{\sqrt{(1 - \rho_{13}^2)(1 - \rho_{23}^2)}} \right)^2 \right]^{-1} \left[\frac{[x_1 - \rho_{13}(\sigma_1/\sigma_3) x_3]^2}{\sigma_1^2(1 - \rho_{13}^2)} \right.\right.$$
$$\left.\left. - 2 \frac{\rho_{12} - \rho_{13}\rho_{23}}{\sqrt{(1 - \rho_{13}^2)(1 - \rho_{23}^2)}} \cdot \frac{[x_1 - \rho_{13}(\sigma_1/\sigma_3)x_3][x_2 - \rho_{23}(\sigma_2/\sigma_3)x_3]}{\sigma_1 \sqrt{1 - \rho_{13}^2} \sigma_2 \sqrt{1 - \rho_{23}^2}} \right.\right.$$
$$\left.\left. + \frac{[x_2 - \rho_{23}(\sigma_2/\sigma_3)x_3]^2}{\sigma_2^2(1 - \rho_{23}^2)} \right] \right\}. \quad (4.7)$$

This has the form of a bivariate normal density function of random variables $x_1 | x_3$ and $x_2 | x_3$ with parameters

$$E[x_1 | x_3] = \rho_{13} \frac{\sigma_1}{\sigma_3} x_3 = \beta_{13} x_3, \quad (4.8)$$

$$E[x_2 | x_3] = \rho_{23} \frac{\sigma_2}{\sigma_3} x_3 = \beta_{23} x_3, \quad (4.9)$$

$$V[x_1 | x_3] = \sigma_1^2(1 - \rho_{13}^2), \quad (4.10)$$
$$V[x_2 | x_3] = \sigma_2^2(1 - \rho_{23}^2), \quad (4.11)$$

$$\rho_{(x_1|x_3)(x_2|x_3)} = \frac{\rho_{12} - \rho_{13}\rho_{23}}{\sqrt{(1 - \rho_{13}^2)(1 - \rho_{23}^2)}}, \quad (4.12)$$

using for (4.8) and (4.9) the relation $\rho_{ij}(\sigma_i/\sigma_j) = \beta_{ij}$ from (12.4.20). The correlation coefficient (4.12) is usually written as $\rho_{12.3}$ and $V[x_1|x_3]$ and $V[x_2|x_3]$ are usually written as $\sigma_{1.3}^2$ and $\sigma_{2.3}^2$. Thus we see that the joint distribution of x_1 and x_2 for a fixed x_3 is a bivariate normal. The mean of the distribution, $(\beta_{13}x_3, \beta_{23}x_3)$, is a function of x_3, but the variances (4.10) and (4.11) are independent of x_3, as is the correlation coefficient (4.12). Thus though we derived $\rho(x_1|x_3)(x_2|x_3)$ for a fixed x_3, we obtain the same expression (4.12) no matter what the value of x_3.

SECT. 13.5   CORRELATION COEFFICIENTS BETWEEN INDICES

The sample partial correlation coefficient $r_{12.3}$ is the analogous expression with r's in place of ρ's:

$$r_{12.3} = \frac{r_{12} - r_{13}r_{23}}{\sqrt{(1 - r_{13}^2)(1 - r_{23}^2)}}. \tag{4.13}$$

Thus we can calculate $r_{12.3}$ from the simple correlation coefficients r_{12}, etc. The null hypothesis that $\rho_{12.3} = 0$ can be tested by the analog of (12.7.3),

$$\frac{r_{12.3}\sqrt{n-3}}{\sqrt{1 - r_{12.3}^2}}, \tag{4.14}$$

will be distributed under the null hypothesis as $t(n-3)$.

We recall that there is a relationship between the simple correlation coefficient between x_1 and x_2, say ρ_{12}, and the simple regression coefficient of x_1 on x_2, say β_{12}. By (12.4.20), $\beta_{12} = \rho_{12}(\sigma_1/\sigma_2)$, where σ_1^2, σ_2^2 are the simple variances of x_1 and x_2. Let $\beta_{12.3}$ be the regression coefficient of x_1 on x_2 in the multiple regression equation of x_1 on x_2 and x_3. It can be shown that, analogous to (12.4.20),

$$\beta_{12.3} = \rho_{12.3} \frac{\sigma_{1.3}}{\sigma_{2.3}}. \tag{4.15}$$

Thus the partial correlation coefficient of x_1 on x_2, "holding x_3 constant," is directly related to the multiple regression coefficient of x_1 on x_2 in the multiple regression equation of x_1 on x_2 and x_3.

13.5. Correlation Coefficients between Indices

In certain correlation studies it may be plausible to consider indices. Suppose that we have random variables x_i, $i = 1, \ldots, 4$, and form indices

$$i_{13} = \frac{x_1}{x_3}, \qquad i_{24} = \frac{x_2}{x_4}. \tag{5.1}$$

It was pointed out by Karl Pearson in 1897 [1] that the interpretation of the correlation coefficient between such indices,

$$\rho_{13,24} = \frac{\text{Cov}[i_{13}, i_{24}]}{\sqrt{V[i_{13}]V[i_{24}]}}, \tag{5.2}$$

could present difficulties.

Suppose that $E[x_i] = \xi_i$, $V[x_i] = \sigma_i^2$, and the correlation coefficient between x_i and x_j is ρ_{ij}. We can represent the observations x_i as generated by the model

$$x_{iv} = \xi_i + z_{iv}, \tag{5.3}$$

where $E[z_{iv}] = 0$, $V[z_{iv}] = E[z_{iv}^2] = \sigma_i^2$. Also

$$\begin{aligned}\operatorname{Cov}[z_{iv}, z_{jv}] &= E[z_{iv}z_{jv}] = E[(x_{iv} - \xi_i)(x_{jv} - \xi_j)] \\ &= \operatorname{Cov}[x_{iv}, x_{jv}] = \rho_{ij}\sigma_i\sigma_j.\end{aligned} \quad (5.4)$$

We first obtain an expression for $E[i_{13}]$:

$$E[i_{13}] = E\left[\frac{x_{1v}}{x_{3v}}\right] = E\left[\frac{\xi_1 + z_{1v}}{\xi_3 + z_{3v}}\right] = E\left[\xi_1\left(1 + \frac{z_{1v}}{\xi_1}\right)\xi_3^{-1}\left(1 + \frac{z_{3v}}{\xi_3}\right)^{-1}\right]$$

$$= \frac{\xi_1}{\xi_3} E\left[\left(1 + \frac{z_{1v}}{\xi_1}\right)\left(1 - \frac{z_{3v}}{\xi_3} + \frac{z_{3v}^2}{\xi_3^2} - \cdots\right)\right]$$

$$= \frac{\xi_1}{\xi_3} E\left[1 - \frac{z_{3v}}{\xi_3} + \frac{z_{1v}}{\xi_1} - \frac{z_{1v}z_{3v}}{\xi_1\xi_3} + \frac{z_{3v}^2}{\xi_3^2} - \cdots\right]$$

$$\simeq \frac{\xi_1}{\xi_3}\left(1 - \frac{E[z_{1v}z_{3v}]}{\xi_1\xi_3} + \frac{E[z_{3v}^2]}{\xi_3^2}\right) = \frac{\xi_1}{\xi_3}\left(1 + \frac{\sigma_3^2}{\xi_3^2} - \rho_{13}\frac{\sigma_1\sigma_3}{\xi_1\xi_3}\right). \quad (5.5)$$

We obtain an expression for the variance of i_{13} as follows:

$$V[i_{13}] = E\left[\left(\frac{x_{1v}}{x_{3v}} - E[i_{13}]\right)^2\right]$$

$$= \{E[i_{13}]\}^2 E\left[\left\{\xi_1\left(1 + \frac{z_{1v}}{\xi_1}\right)\xi_3^{-1}\left(1 + \frac{z_{3v}}{\xi_3}\right)^{-1}\frac{\xi_3}{\xi_1}\right.\right.$$

$$\left.\left. \times \left(1 + \frac{\sigma_3^2}{\xi_3^2} - \rho_{13}\frac{\sigma_1\sigma_3}{\xi_1\xi_3}\right)^{-1} - 1\right\}^2\right]$$

$$= \{E[i_{13}]\}^2 E\left[\left(1 + \frac{\sigma_3^2}{\xi_3^2} - \rho_{13}\frac{\sigma_1\sigma_3}{\xi_1\xi_3}\right)^{-2}\left(1 + 2\frac{z_{1v}}{\xi_1} - 2\frac{z_{3v}}{\xi_3} + \frac{z_{1v}^2}{\xi_1^2}\right.\right.$$

$$\left.\left. + 3\frac{z_{3v}^2}{\xi_3^2} - 4\frac{z_{1v}z_{3v}}{\xi_1\xi_3}\right) - 2\left(1 + \frac{\sigma_3^2}{\xi_3^2} - \rho_{13}\frac{\sigma_1\sigma_3}{\xi_1\xi_3}\right)^{-1}\right.$$

$$\left. \times \left(1 + \frac{z_{1v}}{\xi_1} - \frac{z_{3v}}{\xi_3} - \frac{z_{1v}z_{3v}}{\xi_1\xi_3} + \frac{z_{3v}^2}{\xi_3^2}\right) + 1\right]$$

$$= (E[i_{13}])^2\left(\frac{\sigma_1^2}{\xi_1^2} + \frac{\sigma_3^2}{\xi_3^2} - 2\rho_{13}\frac{\sigma_1\sigma_3}{\xi_1\xi_3}\right). \quad (5.6)$$

By similar manipulations we get the covariance of i_{13} with i_{24} as

$$\operatorname{Cov}[i_{13}, i_{24}] = E\left[\left(\frac{x_{1v}}{x_{3v}} - E[i_{13}]\right)\left(\frac{x_{2v}}{x_{4v}} - E[i_{24}]\right)\right]$$

$$= E[i_{13}]E[i_{24}]\left(\rho_{12}\frac{\sigma_1\sigma_2}{\xi_1\xi_2} - \rho_{14}\frac{\sigma_1\sigma_4}{\xi_1\xi_4} - \rho_{23}\frac{\sigma_2\sigma_3}{\xi_2\xi_3} + \rho_{24}\frac{\sigma_3\sigma_4}{\xi_3\xi_4}\right).$$

$$(5.7)$$

SECT. 13.6 REGRESSION ON SEVERAL INDEPENDENT VARIABLES

Substituting (5.7) and (5.6) and its analog for $E[i_{24}]$ in (5.2) we get

$$\rho_{13,24} = \frac{\rho_{12}\dfrac{\sigma_1\sigma_2}{\xi_1\xi_2} - \rho_{14}\dfrac{\sigma_1\sigma_4}{\xi_1\xi_4} - \rho_{23}\dfrac{\sigma_2\sigma_3}{\xi_2\xi_3} + \rho_{34}\dfrac{\sigma_3\sigma_4}{\xi_3\xi_4}}{\left[\left(\dfrac{\sigma_1^2}{\xi_1^2} + \dfrac{\sigma_3^2}{\xi_3^2} - 2\rho_{13}\dfrac{\sigma_1\sigma_3}{\xi_1\xi_3}\right)\left(\dfrac{\sigma_2^2}{\xi_2^2} + \dfrac{\sigma_4^2}{\xi_4^2} - 2\rho_{24}\dfrac{\sigma_2\sigma_4}{\xi_2\xi_4}\right)\right]^{1/2}}. \quad (5.8)$$

This formula will give various special cases. For example, if $x_3 = x_4$, then $i_{13} = x_1/x_4$, $i_{24} = x_2/x_4$, $\rho_{34} = 1$, $\sigma_3 = \sigma_4$ and $\xi_3 = \xi_4$. Then (5.8) becomes the correlation coefficient between x_1/x_3 and x_2/x_3,

$$\rho_{13,23} = \frac{\rho_{12}\dfrac{\sigma_1\sigma_2}{\xi_1\xi_2} - \rho_{13}\dfrac{\sigma_1\sigma_3}{\xi_1\xi_3} - \rho_{23}\dfrac{\sigma_2\sigma_3}{\xi_2\xi_3} + \dfrac{\sigma_3^2}{\xi_3^2}}{\left[\left(\dfrac{\sigma_1^2}{\xi_1^2} + \dfrac{\sigma_3^2}{\xi_3^2} - 2\rho_{13}\dfrac{\sigma_1\sigma_3}{\xi_1\xi_3}\right)\left(\dfrac{\sigma_2^2}{\xi_2^2} + \dfrac{\sigma_3^2}{\xi_3^2} - 2\rho_{23}\dfrac{\sigma_2\sigma_3}{\xi_2\xi_3}\right)\right]^{1/2}}. \quad (5.9)$$

If the pairwise correlation coefficients between x_1, x_2 and x_3 are all zero, i.e., if $\rho_{12} = \rho_{13} = \rho_{23} = 0$, then (5.9) becomes

$$\rho_{13,23} = \frac{\sigma_3^2/\xi_3^2}{\left[\left(\dfrac{\sigma_1^2}{\xi_1^2} + \dfrac{\sigma_3^2}{\xi_3^2}\right)\left(\dfrac{\sigma_2^2}{\xi_2^2} + \dfrac{\sigma_3^2}{\xi_3^2}\right)\right]^{1/2}}, \quad (5.10)$$

which is never zero except in the trivial case of $\sigma_3 = 0$, which would imply that x_3 was a constant.

If the three coefficients of variation are equal, i.e., if

$$\frac{\sigma_1}{\xi_1} = \frac{\sigma_2}{\xi_2} = \frac{\sigma_3}{\xi_3}, \quad (5.11)$$

then (5.10) gives

$$\rho_{13,23} = \frac{1}{2}. \quad (5.12)$$

13.6. Regression on Several Independent Variables

The extension of regression analysis to r independent variables is straightforward. We have $(r + 1)$-tuples of observations, $(y_\nu, x_{1\nu}, \ldots, x_{r\nu})$, $\nu = 1, \ldots, n$. We assume that y is normally distributed with variance σ^2 about η, where η is a simple linear function:

$$\eta = \alpha + \beta_1(x_1 - \bar{x}_1) + \cdots + \beta_r(x_r - \bar{x}_r). \quad (6.1)$$

The estimated equation is

$$Y = a + b_1(x_1 - \bar{x}_1) + \cdots + b_r(x_r - \bar{x}_r), \quad (6.2)$$

and the sample estimates, $a, b_1, \ldots, b_r$ are obtained by minimizing the sum of squares of deviations between the observed and predicted values,

$$R = \sum_v^n (y_v - Y_v)^2 = \sum_v^n \{y_v - [a + b_1(x_{1v} - \bar{x}_1) + \cdots + b_r(x_{rv} - \bar{x}_r)]\}^2, \quad (6.3)$$

by differentiating with respect to $a, b_1, \ldots, b_r$ and equating to zero. This procedure gives

$$a = \frac{1}{n} \sum_v^n y_v = \bar{y} \quad (6.4)$$

and a set of r simultaneous linear equations, the so-called *normal equations*:

$$b_1 \sum{}' x_1^2 + b_2 \sum{}' x_1 x_2 + \cdots + b_r \sum{}' x_1 x_r = \sum{}' y x_1,$$
$$b_1 \sum{}' x_1 x_2 + b_2 \sum{}' x_2^2 + \cdots + b_r \sum{}' x_2 x_r = \sum{}' y x_2, \quad (6.5)$$
$$\cdot$$
$$\cdot$$
$$\cdot$$
$$b_1 \sum{}' x_1 x_r + b_2 \sum{}' x_2 x_r + \cdots + b_r \sum{}' x_r^2 = \sum{}' y x_r.$$

These equations can be solved for the b's. However, an alternative procedure which will also give us $V[b_i]$ and $\text{Cov}[b_i, b_j]$ is to be preferred.

Suppose that there exist constants $c_{11}, c_{12}, \ldots, c_{1r}$ with properties to be defined later. Multiply the first of the normal equations by c_{11}, the second by c_{12}, etc., sum the resulting equations, and rearrange so as to collect all the coefficients of b_1 together, all the coefficients of b_2 together, etc.:

$$b_1(c_{11} \sum{}' x_1^2 + c_{12} \sum{}' x_1 x_2 + \cdots + c_{1r} \sum{}' x_1 x_r)$$
$$+ b_2(c_{11} \sum{}' x_1 x_2 + c_{12} \sum{}' x_2^2 + \cdots + c_{1r} \sum{}' x_2 x_r)$$
$$\cdot$$
$$\cdot$$
$$\cdot$$
$$+ b_r(c_{11} \sum{}' x_1 x_r + c_{12} \sum{}' x_2 x_r + \cdots + c_{1r} \sum{}' x_r^2)$$
$$= c_{11} \sum{}' y x_1 + c_{12} \sum{}' y x_2 + \cdots + c_{1r} \sum{}' y x_r. \quad (6.6)$$

Let us require that the coefficient of b_1 in this equation is 1 and the coefficients of all the other b's are zero, i.e., that

$$c_{11} \sum{}' x_1^2 + c_{12} \sum{}' x_1 x_2 + \cdots + c_{1r} \sum{}' x_1 x_r = 1,$$
$$c_{11} \sum{}' x_1 x_2 + c_{12} \sum{}' x_2^2 + \cdots + c_{1r} \sum{}' x_2 x_r = 0, \quad (6.7)$$
$$\cdot$$
$$\cdot$$
$$\cdot$$
$$c_{11} \sum{}' x_1 x_r + c_{12} \sum{}' x_2 x_r + \cdots + c_{1r} \sum{}' x_r^2 = 0.$$

SECT. 13.6 REGRESSION ON SEVERAL INDEPENDENT VARIABLES

This is a set of r simultaneous linear equations for r unknowns, namely, the constants c_{1j}, $j = 1, \ldots, r$, and they can be solved to give solutions for the c_{1j} in terms of the observed x_{iv}, since the various sums of squares and products $\sum' x_i^2$, $\sum' x_i x_j$ are readily calculated. Substituting the equations (6.7) in (6.6) gives

$$b_1 = c_{11} \sum{}' yx_1 + c_{12} \sum{}' yx_2 + \cdots + c_{1r} \sum{}' yx_r; \tag{6.8}$$

so once the c_{1j} have been found b_1 can be calculated simply, since the $\sum' yx_j$ are known numbers.

For each b_i, we can find a similar set of c_{ij} ($i = 1, \ldots, r$) which will do the same trick for b_i as (6.8) does for b_1. For b_i we have the set of simultaneous equations

$$c_{i1} \sum{}' x_1^2 + c_{i2} \sum{}' x_1 x_2 + \cdots + c_{ir} \sum{}' x_1 x_r = 0,$$

.
.
.

$$c_{i1} \sum{}' x_1 x_i + c_{i2} \sum{}' x_2 x_i + \cdots + c_{ir} \sum{}' x_i x_r = 1, \tag{6.9}$$

.
.
.

$$c_{i1} \sum{}' x_1 x_r + c_{i2} \sum{}' x_2 x_r + \cdots + c_{ir} \sum{}' x_r^2 = 0,$$

where the right-hand sides are 1 for the ith equation and zero for all the others. The ith equation has $\sum' x_i^2$ as the coefficient of c_{ii}. Analogous to (6.8), using (6.9) in (6.6),

$$b_i = c_{i1} \sum{}' yx_1 + c_{i2} \sum{}' yx_2 + \cdots + c_{ir} \sum{}' yx_r. \tag{6.10}$$

Recalling that $\sum' yx_i = \sum_v^n y_v(x_{iv} - \bar{x}_i)$, we can write this as

$$b_i = \sum_v^n y_v[c_{i1}(x_{1v} - \bar{x}_1) + c_{i2}(x_{2v} - \bar{x}_2) + \cdots + c_{ir}(x_{rv} - \bar{x}_r)], \tag{6.11}$$

which shows that b_i is a linear function of the y_v. Since the y_v are normally distributed, b_i will be also. The quantity in square brackets in (6.11) is solely a function of the x's. It will be convenient to have a symbol for it, say

$$k_{iv} = c_{i1}(x_{1v} - \bar{x}_1) + c_{i2}(x_{2v} - \bar{x}_2) + \cdots + c_{ir}(x_{rv} - \bar{x}_r). \tag{6.12}$$

Then

$$b_i = \sum_v^n y_v k_{iv}, \tag{6.13}$$

and

$$V[b_i] = \sum_v^n k_{iv}^2 V[y_v] = \sigma^2 \sum_v^n k_{iv}^2. \tag{6.14}$$

Thus when we have found $\sum_v^n k_{iv}^2$, we will have $V[b_i]$. Now

$$\sum_v^n k_{iv}^2 = \sum_v^n k_{iv}k_{iv} = \sum_v^n k_{iv}[c_{i1}(x_{1v} - \bar{x}_1) + \cdots + c_{ir}(x_{rv} - \bar{x}_r)]$$
$$= c_{i1}\sum_v^n k_{iv}(x_{1v} - \bar{x}_1) + \cdots + c_{ir}\sum_v^n k_{iv}(x_{rv} - \bar{x}_r). \quad (6.15)$$

In the sequence of terms with the index ij on the c's, i fixed and $j = 1, \ldots, r$, examine a particular one, say that for $j = h$:

$$c_{ih}\sum_v^n k_{iv}(x_{hv} - \bar{x}_h)$$
$$= c_{ih}\sum_v^n [c_{i1}(x_{1v} - \bar{x}_1) + \cdots + c_{ih}(x_{hv} - \bar{x}_h)$$
$$+ \cdots + c_{ir}(x_{rv} - \bar{x}_r)](x_{hv} - \bar{x}_h)$$
$$= c_{ih}[c_{i1}\sum_v^n (x_{1v} - \bar{x}_1)(x_{hv} - \bar{x}_h) + \cdots + c_{ih}\sum_v^n (x_{hv} - \bar{x}_h)^2 + \cdots$$
$$+ c_{ir}\sum_v^n (x_{hv} - \bar{x}_h)(x_{rv} - \bar{x}_r)$$
$$= c_{ih}(c_{i1}\sum' x_1 x_h + c_{i2}\sum' x_2 x_h + \cdots + c_{ih}\sum' x_h^2 + \cdots + c_{ir}\sum' x_h x_r). \quad (6.16)$$

We have two cases to consider; $h = i$ and $h \neq i$. If $h = i$, (6.16) is

$$c_{ii}[c_{i1}\sum' x_1 x_i + c_{i2}\sum' x_2 x_i + \cdots + c_{ii}\sum' x_i^2 + \cdots + c_{ir}\sum' x_i x_r]$$

and the part in brackets is identically equal to the left-hand side of the ith equation in the set (6.9), for which the right-hand side is 1. Thus, when $h = i$, (6.16) equals c_{ii}. For all values of h other than i, the part in brackets of (6.16) is one of the equations (6.9) which equals zero. Thus in (6.15) all the terms for which $i \neq j$ are zero, and the one term for which $i = j$ is equal to c_{ii}:

$$\sum_v^n k_{iv}^2 = c_{ii}, \quad (6.17)$$

so, from (6.14),

$$V[b_i] = \sigma^2 c_{ii}. \quad (6.18)$$

To obtain the covariance of b_i, b_j, we proceed as follows:

$$2\,\text{Cov}[b_i, b_j] = V[b_i + b_j] - V[b_i] - V[b_j]. \quad (6.19)$$

From (6.13),

$$b_i + b_j = \sum_v^n y_v k_{iv} + \sum_v^n y_v k_{jv} = \sum_v^n y_v(k_{iv} + k_{jv}), \quad (6.20)$$

SECT. 13.6 REGRESSION ON SEVERAL INDEPENDENT VARIABLES

with variance

$$V[b_i + b_j] = \sum_v^n (k_{iv} + k_{jv})^2 V[y_v] = \sigma^2 \sum_v^n (k_{iv} + k_{jv})^2$$

$$= \sigma^2 \sum_v^n k_{iv}^2 + \sigma^2 \sum_v^n k_{jv}^2 + 2\sigma^2 \sum_v^n k_{iv} k_{jv}$$

$$= V[b_i] + V[b_j] + 2\sigma^2 \sum_v^n k_{iv} k_{jv}. \quad (6.21)$$

Substituting in (6.19) gives

$$\text{Cov}[b_i, b_j] = \sigma^2 \sum_v^n k_{iv} k_{jv}. \quad (6.22)$$

From the definition of k_{iv}, (6.12),

$$\sum_v^n k_{iv} k_{jv} = c_{i1} \sum_v^n k_{jv}(x_{1v} - \bar{x}_1) + \cdots + c_{ir} \sum_v^n k_{jv}(x_{rv} - \bar{x}_r). \quad (6.23)$$

In the sequence of these terms with the index il on the c's, i fixed and $l = 1, \ldots, r$, examine a particular one, say that for $l = h$:

$$c_{ih} \sum_v^n k_{jv}(x_{hv} - \bar{x}_h)$$

$$= c_{ih} \sum_v^n [c_{j1}(x_{1v} - \bar{x}_1) + \cdots + c_{jh}(x_{hv} - \bar{x}_h) + \cdots + c_{jr}(x_{rv} - \bar{x}_r)](x_{hv} - \bar{x}_h)$$

$$= c_{ih}[c_{j1} \sum' x_1 x_h + \cdots + c_{jh} \sum' x_h^2 + \cdots + c_{jr} \sum' x_h x_r]. \quad (6.24)$$

We have two cases to consider: $h = j$ and $h \neq j$. If $h = j$, (6.24) is

$$c_{ij}[c_{j1} \sum' x_1 x_j + \cdots + c_{jj} \sum' x_j^2 + \cdots + c_{jr} \sum' x_j x_r] \quad (6.25)$$

and, except that j appears in place of i, the part in brackets is identical with the ith equation in the set (6.9), for which the right-hand side is 1. For all values of h other than j, the part in brackets of (6.24) is one of the equations (6.9) for which the right-hand side is zero. Thus, in (6.23), all the terms are zero except one, which is c_{ij}. Therefore

$$\sum_v^n k_{iv} k_{jv} = c_{ij}, \quad (6.26)$$

and so, from (6.22),

$$\text{Cov}[b_i, b_j] = \sigma^2 c_{ij}. \quad (6.27)$$

We can write the deviation between the observation y_v and the true value η_v as

$$y_v - \eta_v = (y_v - Y_v) + (a - \alpha) + (b_1 - \beta_1)(x_{1v} - \bar{x}_1)$$
$$+ \cdots + (b_r - \beta_r)(x_{rv} - \bar{x}_r). \quad (6.28)$$

Squaring and summing gives

$$\sum_v^n (y_v - \eta_v)^2 = \sum_v^n (y_v - Y_v)^2 + n(a - \alpha)^2 + \sum_i^r (b_i - \beta_i)^2 \sum' x_i^2$$

$$+ 2\sum_{i=1}^{r-1} \sum_{j=i+1}^r (b_i - \beta_i)(b_j - \beta_j) \sum' x_i x_j. \quad (6.29)$$

The left-hand side is distributed as $\sigma^2 \chi^2(n)$. On the right-hand side $\sum_v^n (y_v - Y_v)^2$ is distributed as $\sigma^2 \chi^2(n - 1 - r)$, $n(a - \alpha)^2$ as $\sigma^2 \chi^2(1)$, and the remaining part, as surmised in (3.31), is distributed as $\sigma^2 \chi^2(r)$. Each of these components is independent of the other. If we define

$$s^2 = \frac{1}{n - 1 - r} \sum_v^n (y_v - Y_v)^2, \quad (6.30)$$

it will be distributed as $\sigma^2 \chi^2(n - 1 - r)/(n - 1 - r)$ and have expected value σ^2. We can make separate tests of the null hypotheses $\beta_i = 0$ by substituting this estimate s^2 for σ^2 in (6.18), but in general these tests are not independent since usually $\text{Cov}[b_i, b_j] \neq 0$. We can make a joint test of the null hypothesis $\beta_i = 0$ for all i as follows. Since (3.31) is distributed as $\sigma^2 \chi^2(r)$,

$$\frac{1}{r}\left[\sum_i^r (b_i - \beta_i)^2 \sum' x_i^2 + 2\sum_{i=1}^{r-1} \sum_{j=i+1}^r (b_i - \beta_i)(b_j - \beta_j) \sum' x_i x_j\right] \sim \frac{\sigma^2 \chi^2(r)}{r} \quad (6.31)$$

and has expected value σ^2, and the distribution of the ratio of it to s^2, (6.30), will be $F(r, n - 1 - r)$. Hence, under the null hypothesis $\beta_i = 0$ for all i,

$$\frac{1}{rs^2}\left(\sum_i^r b_i^2 \sum' x_i^2 + \sum_{i=1}^{r-1} \sum_{j=i+1}^r b_i b_j \sum' x_i x_j\right) \sim F(r, n - 1 - r). \quad (6.32)$$

We could calculate the quantity in parentheses, known as the sum of squares due to regression, in this form, but an identity is usually more convenient. We multiply the normal equations (6.5) by b_1, b_2, etc. and sum:

$$b_1^2 \sum' x_1^2 + b_2^2 \sum' x_2^2 + \cdots + b_r^2 \sum' x_r^2 + 2b_1 b_2 \sum' x_1 x_2 + \cdots$$
$$+ 2b_{r-1} b_r \sum' x_{r-1} x_r$$
$$= \sum_i^r b_i^2 \sum' x_i^2 + 2\sum_{i=1}^{r-1} \sum_{j=i+1}^r b_i b_j \sum' x_i x_j$$
$$= b_1 \sum' yx_1 + \cdots + b_r \sum' yx_r, \quad (6.33)$$

which is the usual form for computing the sum of squares due to regression.

To calculate $\sum_v^n (y_v - Y_v)^2$, arguments similar to those of (3.41) to (3.45)

will give
$$\sum_{v}^{n}(Y_v - \bar{y})^2 = b_1 \sum' yx_1 + \cdots + b_r \sum' yx_r, \qquad (6.34)$$
and as in (3.40),
$$\sum_{v}^{n}(y_v - Y_v)^2 = \sum_{v}^{n}(y_v - \bar{y})^2 - \sum_{v}^{n}(Y_v - \bar{y})^2. \qquad (6.35)$$

Finally, the predicted value Y, (6.2), has expected value η, (6.1), and variance

$$V[Y] = V[a] + \sum_{i=1}^{r}(x_i - \bar{x}_i)^2 V[b_i]$$
$$+ 2 \sum_{i=1}^{r-1} \sum_{j=i+1}^{r} (x_i - \bar{x}_i)(x_j - \bar{x}_j) \operatorname{Cov}[b_i, b_j]$$
$$= \sigma^2 \left[\frac{1}{n} + \sum_{i=1}^{r}(x_i - \bar{x}_i)^2 c_{ii} + 2 \sum_{i=1}^{n-1} \sum_{j=i+1}^{r} (x_i - \bar{x}_i)(x_j - \bar{x}_j) c_{ij} \right]. \qquad (6.36)$$

13.7. A Matrix Representation

The set of equations (6.9) gives a set of $c_{ij}, j = 1, \ldots, r$, for each value of i, $i = 1, \ldots, r$. These c_{ij} can be written in a square matrix, say C, which is known as the c matrix:

$$C = \begin{bmatrix} c_{11} & c_{12} & \cdots & c_{1r} \\ c_{21} & c_{22} & & c_{2r} \\ \vdots & & & \\ c_{r1} & c_{r2} & & c_{rr} \end{bmatrix}. \qquad (7.1)$$

This section, which uses matrix notation, is not used explicitly in the remainder of this chapter and may be omitted. Its purpose is to show that C is actually the inverse of the matrix of the coefficients in the normal equations (6.5).

Let the $n \times r$ matrix of values of $x_{iv} - \bar{x}_i$, corresponding to the values of x_i at which observations were made on y, by X:

$$X = \begin{bmatrix} x_{11} - \bar{x}_1 & x_{21} - \bar{x}_2 & \cdots & x_{r1} - \bar{x}_r \\ x_{12} - \bar{x}_1 & x_{22} - \bar{x}_2 & & x_{r2} - \bar{x}_r \\ \vdots & & & \\ x_{1n} - \bar{x}_1 & x_{2n} - \bar{x}_2 & & x_{rn} - \bar{x}_r \end{bmatrix}. \qquad (7.2)$$

Then the transpose of X, namely X', is

$$X' = \begin{bmatrix} x_{11} - \bar{x}_1 & x_{12} - \bar{x}_1 & \cdots & x_{1n} - \bar{x}_1 \\ x_{21} - \bar{x}_2 & x_{22} - \bar{x}_2 & & x_{2n} - \bar{x}_2 \\ \cdot & & & \\ \cdot & & & \\ \cdot & & & \\ x_{r1} - \bar{x}_r & x_{r2} - \bar{x}_r & & x_{rn} - \bar{x}_r \end{bmatrix} \tag{7.3}$$

and, using the notation of (3.14),

$$X'X = \begin{bmatrix} \sum' x_1^2 & \sum' x_1 x_2 & \cdots & \sum' x_1 x_r \\ \sum' x_1 x_2 & \sum' x_2^2 & & \sum' x_2 x_r \\ \cdot & & & \\ \cdot & & & \\ \cdot & & & \\ \sum' x_1 x_r & \sum' x_2 x_r & & \sum' x_r^2 \end{bmatrix} \tag{7.4}$$

is the matrix of the coefficients of the b's in the normal equations (6.5).

Define B and G as

$$B = \begin{bmatrix} b_1 \\ b_2 \\ \cdot \\ \cdot \\ \cdot \\ b_r \end{bmatrix}, \quad G = \begin{bmatrix} \sum' yx_1 \\ \sum' yx_2 \\ \cdot \\ \cdot \\ \cdot \\ \sum' yx_r \end{bmatrix} \tag{7.5}$$

Then the normal equations (6.5) can be written as

$$X'XB = G. \tag{7.6}$$

Premultiply this by $(X'X)^{-1}$. Since $(X'X)^{-1}(X'X) = I$, this gives

$$B = (X'X)^{-1}G. \tag{7.7}$$

Thus the regression coefficients b_i can be obtained by premultiplying G, the right-hand sides of the normal equations, by the inverse of $(X'X)$, $(X'X)$ being the matrix of the coefficients of the b's in the normal equations.

Suppose that $C = (X'X)^{-1}$. Then (7.7) is equivalent to

$$\begin{bmatrix} b_1 \\ b_2 \\ \cdot \\ \cdot \\ \cdot \\ b_r \end{bmatrix} = \begin{bmatrix} c_{11} & c_{12} & \cdots & c_{1r} \\ c_{21} & c_{22} & & c_{2r} \\ \cdot & & & \\ \cdot & & & \\ \cdot & & & \\ c_{r1} & c_{r2} & & c_{rr} \end{bmatrix} \begin{bmatrix} \sum' yx_1 \\ \sum' yx_2 \\ \cdot \\ \cdot \\ \cdot \\ \sum' yx_r \end{bmatrix}, \tag{7.8}$$

SECT. 13.8   A TEST COMPARING r VARIABLES AND q VARIABLES

which gives

$$b_k = c_{k1} \sum' yx_1 + c_{k2} \sum' yx_2 + \cdots + c_{kr} \sum' yx_r = \sum_j^r c_{kj} \sum' yx_j,$$

(7.9)

which is identical to (6.10). Substituting $C = (X'X)^{-1}$ in $(X'X)^{-1}(X'X) = I$ gives

$$\begin{bmatrix} c_{11} & c_{12} & \cdots & c_{1r} \\ c_{21} & c_{22} & & c_{2r} \\ \vdots & & & \vdots \\ c_{r1} & c_{r2} & & c_{rr} \end{bmatrix} \begin{bmatrix} \sum' x_1^2 & \sum' x_1 x_2 & \cdots & \sum' x_1 x_r \\ \sum' x_1 x_2 & \sum' x_2^2 & & \sum' x_2 x_r \\ \vdots & & & \vdots \\ \sum' x_1 x_r & \sum' x_2 x_r & & \sum' x_r^2 \end{bmatrix} = \begin{bmatrix} 1 & 0 & \cdots & 0 \\ 0 & 1 & & 0 \\ \vdots & & & \vdots \\ 0 & 0 & & 1 \end{bmatrix}.$$

(7.10)

Now two matrices are equal if and only if the corresponding elements are equal. If we carry out the matrix multiplication on the left-hand side of (7.10), we get a single matrix, and if we put each element in the first row equal to the corresponding element in the first row of the matrix on the right-hand side of (7.10), we get

$$c_{11} \sum' x_1^2 + c_{12} \sum' x_1 x_2 + \cdots + c_{1r} \sum' x_1 x_r = 1,$$

$$c_{11} \sum' x_1 x_2 + c_{12} \sum' x_2^2 + \cdots + c_{1r} \sum' x_2 x_r = 0,$$

$$\vdots$$

$$c_{11} \sum' x_1 x_r + c_{12} \sum' x_2 x_r + \cdots + c_{1r} \sum' x_r^2 = 0, \qquad (7.11)$$

which set of equations is identical with the set (6.7), and in general equating the ith columns gives (6.9). This shows that the matrix of the c_{ij} obtained by solving the sets of equations (6.9) is in fact the inverse of the $X'X$ matrix.

13.8. A Test of Whether Regression on r Variables Gives a Significantly Better Fit than Regression on q Variables

Clearly there is no point in using a regression equation of y on r variables x_i, $i = 1, \ldots, r$, unless it gives a significantly better fit than the regression equation of y on a subset of the x_i, $i = 1, \ldots, q$. In this section we derive a likelihood ratio test.

We first need the maximum likelihood estimators of α and the β_i. The density function of y is

$$p\{y_v\} = N\left(\alpha + \sum_i^r \beta_i(x_{iv} - \bar{x}_i), \sigma^2\right)$$

$$= \frac{1}{\sqrt{2\pi}\sqrt{\sigma^2}} \exp\left\{-\frac{1}{2} \frac{\left[y_v - \alpha - \sum_i^r \beta_i(x_{iv} - \bar{x}_i)\right]^2}{\sigma^2}\right\}. \quad (8.1)$$

The likelihood function is

$$L = \left(\frac{1}{\sqrt{2\pi}\sqrt{\sigma^2}}\right)^n \exp\left\{-\sum_v^n \frac{1}{2\sigma^2}\left[y_v - \alpha - \sum_i^r \beta_i(x_{iv} - \bar{x}_i)\right]^2\right\}. \quad (8.2)$$

The logarithm is easier to handle:

$$\log L = -n \log \sqrt{2\pi} - \frac{n}{2} \log \sigma^2 - \frac{1}{2\sigma^2} \sum_v^n \left[y_v - \alpha - \sum_i^r \beta_i(x_{iv} - \bar{x}_i)\right]^2. \quad (8.3)$$

As usual, we differentiate with respect to the parameters:

$$\frac{\partial \log L}{\partial \alpha} = -\frac{1}{2\sigma^2}(-1)(2) \sum_v^n \left[y_v - \alpha - \sum_i^r \beta_i(x_{iv} - \bar{x}_i)\right] = 0, \quad (8.4)$$

$$\frac{\partial \log L}{\partial \beta_i} = -\frac{1}{2\sigma^2}(-1)(2) \sum_v^n \left[y_v - \alpha - \sum_i^r \beta_i(x_{iv} - \bar{x}_i)\right](x_{iv} - \bar{x}_i) = 0, \quad (8.5)$$

$$\frac{\partial \log L}{\partial \sigma^2} = -\frac{n}{2\sigma^2} - \frac{1}{2}(-1) \frac{1}{(\sigma^2)^2} \sum_v^n \left[y_v - \alpha - \sum_i^r \beta_i(x_{iv} - \bar{x}_i)\right]^2 = 0. \quad (8.6)$$

From (8.4) we get $\hat{\alpha} = \sum^n y/n$, identical with the least squares solution for a in (6.4). From the set of r equations (8.5) we get a set of r simultaneous equations identical to those of (6.5) with $\hat{\beta}_i = b_i$. From (8.6) we get

$$\hat{\sigma}^2 = \frac{1}{n} \sum_v^n \left[y_v - \hat{\alpha} - \sum_i^r \hat{\beta}_i(x_{iv} - \bar{x}_i)\right]^2 = \frac{1}{n} \sum_v^n (y_v - Y_v)^2. \quad (8.7)$$

Thus the maximum likelihood estimator of σ^2 is biased due to the occurrence of the divisor n in place of $n - 1 - r$. The maximum likelihood estimators of α and β_i are identical with the least squares estimators, but whereas the former are derived under the assumption of normality, (8.1), the derivation of the least squares estimators involved no assumption about the form of the distribution.

SECT. 13.8 A TEST COMPARING r VARIABLES AND q VARIABLES

We now construct a likelihood ratio test of the null hypothesis that y can be fitted by a regression equation with parameters $\alpha, \beta_1, \ldots, \beta_q$ against the alternative hypothesis that additional parameters $\beta_{q+1}, \ldots, \beta_r$ are necessary.

Let σ_q^2 be the estimate of the residual variance when q β's are used, i.e., for ω, and let σ_r^2 be the same quantity when all r β's are used, i.e., for Ω. Similarly, let $\hat{\beta}_{iq}, \hat{\beta}_{ir}$ be the estimators of β_i when the regression equation includes q and r β's respectively. The likelihood ratio is

$$\lambda = \frac{L(\omega)}{L(\Omega)} = \frac{[(2\pi\hat{\sigma}_q^2)^{n/2}]^{-1} \exp\left\{-(2\hat{\sigma}_q^2)^{-1} \sum_i^n [y_v - \hat{\alpha} - \sum_i^q \hat{\beta}_{iq}(x_{iv} - \bar{x}_i)]^2\right\}}{[(2\pi\hat{\sigma}_r^2)^{n/2}]^{-1} \exp\left\{-(2\hat{\sigma}_r^2)^{-1} \sum_v^n [y_v - \hat{\alpha} - \sum_i^r \hat{\beta}_{ir}(x_{iv} - \bar{x}_i)]^2\right\}}. \quad (8.8)$$

The summations in the two exponents are identical with the summations in the expression for $\hat{\sigma}^2$, (8.7), so

$$\lambda = \left(\frac{\hat{\sigma}_r^2}{\hat{\sigma}_q^2}\right)^{n/2}. \quad (8.9)$$

Any monotonic function of λ will serve as our statistic. The function below on the left-hand side of (8.10) is a function of s_q^2/s_r^2 where s_q^2, s_r^2 are the usual unbiased estimators of the residual variance, and s_q^2, s_r^2 are, of course, functions of $\hat{\sigma}_q^2, \hat{\sigma}_r^2$. The statistic is usually calculated in the form given on the right-hand side, where G_r and G_q are as defined in Table 13.2:

$$\frac{(r-q)^{-1}[(n-1-q)s_q^2 - (n-1-r)s_r^2]}{s_r^2} = \frac{(G_r - G_q)/(r-q)}{s_r^2}. \quad (8.10)$$

Table 13.2

Source of variance	Degrees of freedom	Sums of squares	Mean squares
A. Regression on $x_1, \ldots, x_q, x_{q+1}, \ldots, x_r$	r	G_r	
B. Regression on $x_1, \ldots, x_q$	q	G_q	
C. Difference $A - B$ = difference $E - D$	$r - q$	$G_r - G_q$ $= (n-1-q)s_q^2$ $- (n-1-r)s_r^2$	$\dfrac{G_r - G_q}{r - q}$
D. Remainder using $x_1, \ldots, x_q, x_{q+1}, \ldots, x_r$	$n - 1 - r$	$(n-1-r)s_r^2$	s_r^2
E. Remainder using $x_1, \ldots, x_q$	$n - 1 - q$	$(n-1-q)s_q^2$	s_q^2
F. Total	$n - 1$		

While we have shown that this statistic is equivalent to the likelihood ratio statistic, we have not given any indication as to its distribution under the null hypothesis. In fact, under the null hypothesis it is distributed as $F(r - q, n - 1 - r)$. A proof of this for the general case is complicated (see, e.g., Section 14.3 of Anderson and Bancroft [2] and Section 5.8 of Kempthorne [3]) and we consider only the case of $r = 2, q = 1$. For this special case, Table 13.2 becomes Table 13.3.

Table 13.3

Source of variance	Sums of squares	Degrees of freedom	Mean squares
Regression on x_1, x_2 jointly	A	2	
Regression on x_1 only	B	1	
Difference due to adding x_2 to x_1	$C = A - B$	1	C
Remainder using regression on x_1, x_2 jointly	$D = F - A$	$n - 3$	s^2
Total	F	$n - 1$	

Our objective is to show that the difference, say C, between the sum of squares due to regression on x_1, x_2 jointly, say A, and the sum of squares due to regression on x_1 only, say B, is independent of the remainder sum of squares, say D, and that under the null hypothesis $\beta_2 = 0$ the ratio

$$\frac{C}{D/(n-3)} \sim F(1, n-3).$$

Using (3.45) for A and (11.3.12) for B we have

$$C = \sum{'} x_1 y \left[\frac{\sum{'} x_1 y \sum{'} x_2^2 - \sum{'} x_2 y \sum{'} x_1 x_2}{\sum{'} x_1^2 \sum{'} x_2^2 - (\sum{'} x_1 x_2)^2} \right]$$
$$+ \sum{'} x_2 y \left[\frac{\sum{'} x_2 y \sum{'} x_1^2 - \sum{'} x_1 y \sum{'} x_1 x_2}{\sum{'} x_1^2 \sum{'} x_2^2 - (\sum{'} x_1 x_2)^2} \right] - \frac{(\sum{'} x_1 y)^2}{\sum{'} x_1^2}$$
(8.11)

$$= \frac{[\sum{'} x_1 y \sum{'} x_1 x_2 - \sum{'} x_2 y \sum{'} x_1^2]^2}{\sum{'} x_1^2 [\sum{'} x_1^2 \sum{'} x_2^2 - (\sum{'} x_1 x_2)^2]}.$$
(8.12)

We will derive (8.12) by a different route, which will make it clear that it is independent of $s^2 = D/(n-3)$. Consider the regression of x_2 on x_1.

SECT. 13.8 A TEST COMPARING r VARIABLES AND q VARIABLES

The estimated regression equation is

$$X_2 = \bar{x}_2 + \frac{\sum' x_1 x_2}{\sum' x_2^1}(x_1 - \bar{x}_1). \tag{8.13}$$

We define $x_{2.1}$ as the deviation of x_2 from the value predicted by this equation, i.e.,

$$x_{2.1} = x_2 - \bar{x}_2 - \frac{\sum' x_1 x_2}{\sum' x_1^2}(x_1 - \bar{x}_1). \tag{8.14}$$

Similarly, the estimated equation for the regression of y on x_1 is

$$Y = \bar{y} + \frac{\sum' x_1 y}{\sum' x_1^2}(x_1 - \bar{x}_1), \tag{8.15}$$

and we define $y_{2.1}$ as

$$y_{2.1} = y - \bar{y} - \frac{\sum' x_1 y}{\sum' x_1^2}(x_1 - \bar{x}_1). \tag{8.16}$$

We now consider the regression of $y_{2.1}$ on $x_{2.1}$. Since $\sum x_{2.1} = 0$ and $\sum y_{2.1} = 0$ we can write

$$b_{y_{2.1} x_{2.1}} = \frac{\sum x_{2.1} y_{2.1}}{\sum x_{2.1}^2}. \tag{8.17}$$

From the definitions of $x_{2.1}$ and $y_{2.1}$ it is straightforward to show that

$$\sum x_{2.1} y_{2.1} = \frac{1}{\sum' x_1^2}[\sum' x_1^2 \sum' x_2 y - \sum' x_1 x_2 \sum' x_1 y], \tag{8.18}$$

$$\sum x_{2.1}^2 = \frac{1}{\sum' x_1^2}[\sum' x_1^2 \sum' x_2^2 - (\sum' x_1 x_2)^2]. \tag{8.19}$$

Making these substitutions in (8.17) and noting (3.20), we have

$$b_{y_{2.1} x_{2.1}} = \frac{(\sum' x_1^2)^{-1}[\sum' x_1^2 \sum' x_2 y - \sum' x_1 x_2 \sum' x_1 y]}{(\sum' x_1^2)^{-1}[\sum' x_1^2 \sum' x_2^2 - (\sum' x_1 x_2)^2]} = b_2. \tag{8.20}$$

The sum of squares due to regression of $y_{2.1}$ on $x_{2.1}$, say C', is, by (11.3.11),

$$b_{y_{2.1} x_{2.1}} \sum x_{2.1} y_{2.1} = \frac{(\sum x_{2.1} y_{2.1})^2}{\sum x_{2.1}^2}$$

$$= \frac{[\sum' x_1 x_2 \sum' x_1 y - \sum' x_1^2 \sum' x_2 y]^2}{\sum' x_1^2 [\sum' x_1^2 \sum' x_2^2 - (\sum' x_1 x_2)^2]}, \tag{8.21}$$

which is identical with (8.12); i.e., $C = C'$.

The remainder sum of squares for the regression of $y_{2.1}$ on $x_{2.1}$, say D', is

$$D' = \sum y_{2.1}^2 - \text{(sum of squares due to regression of } y_{2.1} \text{ on } x_{2.1})$$

$$= \sum \left[y - \bar{y} - \frac{\sum' x_1 y}{\sum' x_1^2} (x_1 - \bar{x}_1) \right]^2$$

$$- \frac{[\sum' x_1 x_2 \sum' x_1 y - \sum' x_1^2 \sum' x_2 y]^2}{\sum' x_1^2 [\sum' x_1^2 \sum' x_2^2 - (\sum' x_1 x_2)^2]}, \quad (8.22)$$

substituting for $y_{2.1}$ from (8.16) and using (8.21). It is straightforward to show that (8.22) can be written as

$$D' = \sum (y - \bar{y})^2 - \left\{ \frac{(\sum' x_1 y)^2}{\sum' x_1^2} + \frac{(\sum' x_1^2 \sum' x_2 y - \sum' x_1 x_2 \sum' x_1 y)^2}{\sum' x_1^2 [\sum' x_1^2 \sum' x_2^2 - (\sum' x_1 x_2)^2]} \right\}. \quad (8.23)$$

Now from the identity of (8.11) and (8.12),

$$\frac{(\sum' x_1 y)^2}{\sum' x_1^2} + \frac{[\sum' x_1 y \sum' x_1 x_2 - \sum' x_2 y \sum' x_1^2]^2}{\sum' x_1^2 [\sum' x_1^2 \sum' x_2^2 - (\sum' x_1 x_2)^2]}$$

$$= \text{sum of squares due to regression of } y \text{ on } x_1, x_2 \text{ jointly.} \quad (8.24)$$

Therefore

$$D' = \sum (y - \bar{y})^2 - \text{(sum of squares due to regression of } y \text{ on } x_1, x_2 \text{ jointly)}$$
$$= D. \quad (8.25)$$

By the usual arguments (see Section 11.3) for simple linear regression on one independent variable, under the null hypothesis that the regression coefficient is zero the remainder sum of squares D' is independent of the sum of squares due to regression C', and they both have the same expected value. It therefore follows under the null hypothesis that $D = D'$ is independent of $C = C'$, and that the ratio of the corresponding mean squares has the F distribution with the appropriate degrees of freedom.

The test of Table 13.3 of whether x_2 adds to the fit of the regression of y on x_1 is identical with the test of the null hypothesis that β_2 in the joint regression equation is zero. For the latter test we would use (3.20) for b_2 and (3.25), modified by the substitution of s^2 for σ^2, for $\hat{V}[b_2]$ for the statistic

$$\frac{b_2}{\sqrt{\hat{V}[b_2]}} = \frac{\sum' x_2 y \sum' x_1^2 - \sum' x_1 y \sum' x_1 x_2}{\sum' x_1^2 \sum' x_2^2 - (\sum' x_1 x_2)^2} \left[\frac{\sum' x_1^2 \sum' x_2^2 - (\sum' x_1 x_2)^2}{s^2 \sum' x_1^2} \right]^{1/2}$$

$$= \frac{1}{s} \frac{\sum' x_2 y \sum' x_1^2 - \sum' x_1 y \sum' x_1 x_2}{(\sum' x_1^2)^{1/2} [\sum' x_1^2 \sum' x_2^2 - (\sum' x_1 x_2)^2]^{1/2}}, \quad (8.26)$$

SECT. 13.10 FURTHER USES FOR THE c MATRIX 447

and this will have the $t(n-1-2)$ distribution under the null hypothesis. Its square is identical with the test of Table 13.3, the ratio of C as in (8.12) to s^2, which has the $F(1, n-1-2)$ distribution. The two tests are therefore identical.

13.9. Polynomial Regression

The conventional designation of x_1, x_2 as "independent" variables is unfortunate, for in general, except in suitably designed experiments, they are not independent, since usually their covariance is not zero. Nothing in the foregoing development is assumed about the x_i except that they are known variables measured without error. We are therefore quite at liberty to use as x_2 the square of x_1, i.e., to fit the equation

$$\eta = \alpha + \beta_1(x_1 - \bar{x}_1) + \beta_2[(x_1^2) - \overline{(x_1^2)}]$$
$$= \text{constant} + \beta_1 x_1 + \beta_2 x_1^2$$

The foregoing techniques can therefore be used to fit a second-degree curve if we think it necessary. The test of Table 13.3 enables us to test whether a second-degree curve gives a significantly better fit than a straight line.

13.10. Further Uses for the c Matrix

One advantage of the c matrix method of handling multiple regression calculations is that once the c matrix has been obtained it is a relatively trivial matter to carry out the regression analysis of another independent variable, say z, on the same x's. We merely need the $\sum' zx_i, i = 1, \ldots, r$, and substitute them in (6.10) to obtain the regression coefficients of z on the x's. In this way, e.g., we can readily compare the results of regressing on the x's various functions of y, e.g., $\log y$ or $1/y$, to find the functional form which gives the best fit. A statistic appropriate for comparing fits is the multiple correlation coefficient, the sample value of which is defined by

$$R^2 = 1 - \frac{\text{remainder sum of squares of } y}{\text{unconditional sum of squares of } y} \quad (10.1)$$

$$= \frac{\text{sum of squares due to regression}}{\text{unconditional sum of squares of } y}. \quad (10.2)$$

So far in this chapter, with the exception of Section 13.4 on the partial correlation coefficient, we have supposed that the $x_i, i = 1, \ldots, r$, be known fixed variables. In general, however, they may be obtained in any of three different ways.

1. They may be chosen deliberately in some specified pattern. In particular, suppose that there are three variables on numerical scales, x_1 taking only r values, x_2 only t values, and x_3 only u values, and we obtain an observation on y for every combination of x_1 with x_2 and with x_3. The total number of observations will be rtu. In this case the simple and multiple regression coefficients of each x on each of the other x's will be zero, and by (12.4.20) and (4.12) the corresponding correlation coefficients will be zero also.

2. Certain ranges for the variables x_i may be selected, and combinations of values of x_1, x_2 and x_3 chosen by some randomization procedure. So far the only difference from case 1 is that the x's are chosen at random instead of by some deliberate pattern or design. However, now the regression coefficients of the x's among themselves will be distributed about expected values of zero with some variance. Furthermore, if the original choices of the x_i were made from normal distributions, then we will have a multivariate normal distribution with the sample correlation coefficients $r_{x_i x_j}$ distributed around population values $\rho_{x_i x_j} = 0$.

3. We may observe a system from the outside, without exercising any control over it. If the x_i have normal distributions, then we may have a multivariate normal distribution. Unlike case 2, in general the expected values of the regression coefficients of the x's among themselves will not now be zero.

In cases 2 and 3 we may be prepared to assume the multivariate normality. As implied in Section 13.4, just as we can carry out a simple regression analysis on a bivariate normal population, so we can carry out a multiple regression analysis on a multivariate normal population. We may wish to make tests of significance and set confidence limits on the regression coefficients of x_μ on the other x's in the regression equation of x_μ on the other x's. The c matrix gives us directly these regression equations.

Write out the equations (6.9) with $i = \mu$, omitting that with 1 on the right-hand side; at the same time move over to the right-hand side the terms involving $c_{\mu\mu}$.

$$c_{\mu 1} \sum' x_1^2 + c_{\mu 2} \sum' x_1 x_2 + \cdots + c_{\mu r} \sum' x_1 x_r = -c_{\mu\mu} \sum' x_\mu x_1$$

$$c_{\mu 1} \sum' x_1 x_2 + c_{\mu 2} \sum' x_2^2 + \cdots + c_{\mu r} \sum' x_2 x_r = -c_{\mu\mu} \sum' x_\mu x_2$$

.
.

$$c_{\mu 1} \sum' x_1 x_r + c_{\mu 2} \sum' x_2 x_r + \cdots + c_{\mu r} \sum' x_r^2 = -c_{\mu\mu} \sum' x_\mu x_r. \quad (10.3)$$

SECT. 13.10   FURTHER USES FOR THE c MATRIX   449

Now divide throughout by $-c_{\mu\mu}$

$$\left(-\frac{c_{\mu 1}}{c_{\mu\mu}}\right)\sum' x_1^2 + \left(-\frac{c_{\mu 2}}{c_{\mu\mu}}\right)\sum' x_1 x_2 + \cdots + \left(-\frac{c_{\mu r}}{c_{\mu\mu}}\right)\sum' x_1 x_r = \sum' x_\mu x_1$$

$$\left(-\frac{c_{\mu 1}}{c_{\mu\mu}}\right)\sum' x_1 x_2 + \left(-\frac{c_{\mu 2}}{c_{\mu\mu}}\right)\sum' x_2^2 + \cdots + \left(-\frac{c_{\mu r}}{c_{\mu\mu}}\right)\sum' x_2 x_r = \sum' x_\mu x_2$$

.
.
.

$$\left(-\frac{c_{\mu 1}}{c_{\mu\mu}}\right)\sum' x_1 x_r + \left(-\frac{c_{\mu 2}}{c_{\mu\mu}}\right)\sum' x_2 x_r + \cdots + \left(-\frac{c_{\mu r}}{c_{\mu\mu}}\right)\sum' x_r^2 = \sum' x_\mu x_r.$$
(10.4)

Comparing this set of equations with a typical set of normal equations (6.5), it is apparent that these are the normal equations for the regression of x_μ on $x_1, \ldots, x_r$ (omitting x_μ), and the regression coefficient of x_μ on x_1 is $-c_{\mu 1}/c_{\mu\mu}$, etc. Thus, having found the c matrix (7.10), we can immediately write down the regression equation of x_μ on the other x's:

$$x_\mu = \bar{x}_\mu + \left(-\frac{c_{\mu 1}}{c_{\mu\mu}}\right)(x_1 - \bar{x}_1) + \cdots + \left(-\frac{c_{\mu r}}{c_{\mu\mu}}\right)(x_r - \bar{x}_r). \quad (10.5)$$

Obviously in the sequence $i = 1, \ldots, r$ on the right-hand side, $i = \mu$ is omitted. Each row in the c matrix gives us the regression equation of a different x on the remaining x's.

A more explicit notation for regression coefficients is sometimes desirable. Let x_j stand for the sequence $x_1, x_2, \ldots, x_r$ in which x_μ and x_k are omitted. Then by $b_{x_\mu x_k \cdot x_j}$ we mean the regression coefficient of x_μ on x_k in the regression equation of x_μ on all the x's, x_1 to x_r (but naturally excluding x_μ). Thus in (10.5)

$$-\frac{c_{\mu 1}}{c_{\mu\mu}} = b_{x_\mu x_1 \cdot x_j}, \quad j = 1, \ldots, r \text{ (but } j \neq 1, \mu\text{)}. \quad (10.6)$$

We can readily obtain from the c matrix the estimated variances of the regression coefficients. We first obtain the estimated residual variance of x_μ about the regression plane on the remaining x's, say s^2.

In the set of equations (10.3) we omitted the equation in (6.9) whose right-hand side was 1:

$$c_{\mu 1}\sum' x_1 x_\mu + c_{\mu 2}\sum' x_2 x_\mu + \cdots + c_{\mu r}\sum' x_\mu x_r = 1 - c_{\mu\mu}\sum' x_\mu^2.$$
(10.7)

Dividing by $(-c_{\mu\mu})$:

$$\left(-\frac{c_{\mu 1}}{c_{\mu\mu}}\right)\sum' x_1 x_\mu + \left(-\frac{c_{\mu 2}}{c_{\mu\mu}}\right)\sum' x_2 x_\mu + \cdots$$

$$+ \left(-\frac{c_{\mu r}}{c_{\mu\mu}}\right)\sum' x_\mu x_r = \sum' x_\mu^2 - \frac{1}{c_{\mu\mu}}. \quad (10.8)$$

Since $-c_{\mu 1}/c_{\mu\mu}$ is the regression coefficient of x_μ on x_1, etc., the left-hand side of this is exactly (6.33), the sum of squares due to regression. But we do not need to calculate it in that form, for (10.8) gives it as $\sum' x_\mu^2 - 1/c_{\mu\mu}$. And, comparing (6.35), it is obvious that the residual sum of squares of x_μ about the regression plane on the other x's is $1/c_{\mu\mu}$. This residual sum of squares will have $[n - 1 - (r - 1)] = n - r$ degrees of freedom; so $s_\mu^2 = (1/c_{\mu\mu})/(n - r)$.

We may note here another interesting relationship.* If R_i is the multiple correlation coefficient of x_i on the remaining x's, we can substitute the right-hand side of (10.8) in (10.2) to get

$$R_i^2 = \frac{\sum' x_i^2 - 1/c_{ii}}{\sum' x_i^2} = 1 - \frac{1}{c_{ii}}\frac{1}{\sum' x_i^2}. \quad (10.9)$$

Solving for c_{ii} and substituting this solution in (6.18) gives

$$V[b_i] = \frac{\sigma^2}{\sum' x_i^2}\frac{1}{1 - R_i^2}, \quad (10.10)$$

analogous to (3.24). This shows that $V[b_i]$ increases as x_i is more highly correlated with the other x's.

So far we have the regression coefficients of x_μ on the other x's, and also the residual variance, but to get the variance and covariance of these regression coefficients we need the c matrix corresponding to the equations (10.4). This can be obtained from the original c matrix by the formula

$$c'_{ij} = c_{ij} - \frac{c_{i\mu}c_{j\mu}}{c_{\mu\mu}}. \quad (10.11)$$

where c'_{ij} is the ijth element of the c matrix obtained when x is omitted.

To prove this formula, order the x's so that x_r is the variable to be eliminated. Then corresponding to (6.7), but omitting the last of those

---

* Pointed out to the author by Cuthbert Daniel.

SECT. 13.10   FURTHER USES FOR THE c MATRIX

equations, we have

$$c_{11} \sum{}' x_1^2 + c_{12} \sum{}' x_1 x_2 + \cdots + c_{1(r-1)} \sum{}' x_1 x_{r-1} + c_{1r} \sum{}' x_1 x_r = 1,$$
$$c_{11} \sum{}' x_1 x_2 + c_{12} \sum{}' x_2^2 + \cdots + c_{1(r-1)} \sum{}' x_2 x_{r-1} + c_{1r} \sum{}' x_2 x_r = 0,$$
$$\vdots$$
$$c_{11} \sum{}' x_1 x_{r-1} + c_{12} \sum{}' x_2 x_{r-1} + \cdots + c_{1(r-1)} \sum{}' x_{r-1}^2 + c_{1r} \sum{}' x_r x_{r-1} = 0. \quad (10.12)$$

The corresponding set of equations for the reduced c matrix is

$$c'_{11} \sum{}' x_1^2 + c'_{12} \sum{}' x_1 x_2 + \cdots + c'_{1(r-1)} \sum{}' x_1 x_{r-1} = 1,$$
$$c'_{11} \sum{}' x_1 x_2 + c'_{12} \sum{}' x_2^2 + \cdots + c'_{1(r-1)} \sum{}' x_2 x_{r-1} = 0,$$
$$\vdots$$
$$c'_{11} \sum{}' x_1 x_{r-1} + c'_{12} \sum{}' x_2 x_{r-1} + \cdots + c'_{1(r-1)} \sum{}' x_{r-1}^2 = 0. \quad (10.13)$$

Subtracting corresponding equations in (10.12) from (10.13) gives

$$(c'_{11} - c_{11}) \sum{}' x_1^2 + (c'_{12} - c_{12}) \sum{}' x_1 x_2 + \cdots$$
$$+ (c'_{1(r-1)} - c_{1(r-1)}) \sum{}' x_1 x_{r-1} - c_{1r} \sum{}' x_1 x_r = 0,$$
$$\vdots$$
$$(c'_{11} - c_{11}) \sum{}' x_1 x_{r-1} + (c'_{12} - c_{12}) \sum{}' x_2 x_{r-1} + \cdots$$
$$+ (c'_{1(r-1)} - c_{1(r-1)}) \sum{}' x_{r-1}^2 - c_{1r} \sum{}' x_r x_{r-1} = 0, \quad (10.14)$$

whence

$$\frac{c'_{11} - c_{11}}{c_{1r}} \sum{}' x_1^2 + \frac{c'_{12} - c_{12}}{c_{1r}} \sum{}' x_1 x_2 + \cdots$$
$$+ \frac{c'_{1(r-1)} - c_{1(r-1)}}{c_{1r}} \sum{}' x_1 x_{r-1} = \sum{}' x_1 x_r,$$
$$\vdots$$
$$\frac{c'_{11} - c_{11}}{c_{1r}} \sum{}' x_1 x_{r-1} + \frac{c'_{12} - c_{12}}{c_{1r}} \sum{}' x_2 x_{r-1} + \cdots$$
$$+ \frac{c'_{1(r-1)} - c_{1(r-1)}}{c_{1r}} \sum{}' x_{r-1}^2 = \sum{}' x_{r-1} x_r. \quad (10.15)$$

These equations are identical with the normal equations for the regression of x_r on $x_1, \ldots, x_{r-1}$. Thus

$$\frac{c'_{1j} - c_{1j}}{c_{1r}} = b_{x_r x_j \cdot x_k}, \quad (k \neq r, j). \tag{10.16}$$

Substituting for $b_{x_r x_j \cdot x_k}$ from (10.6) gives

$$\frac{c'_{1j} - c_{1j}}{c_{1r}} = -\frac{c_{rj}}{c_{rr}}, \tag{10.17}$$

whence

$$c'_{1j} = c_{1j} - \frac{c_{1r} c_{rj}}{c_{rr}}, \tag{10.18}$$

and in general, with x_μ rather than x_r as the eliminated variable,

$$c'_{ij} = c_{ij} - \frac{c_{i\mu} c_{\mu j}}{c_{\mu\mu}}. \tag{10.19}$$

Thus, to get the estimated variance of the regression coefficient of x_μ on x_k, $s_\mu^2 c_{kk}$, we need

$$c'_{kk} = c_{kk} - \frac{c_{k\mu} c_{k\mu}}{c_{\mu\mu}} = \frac{c_{kk} c_{\mu\mu} - c_{k\mu}^2}{c_{\mu\mu}}, \tag{10.20}$$

and then

$$\hat{V}[b_{x_\mu x_k \cdot x_j}] = \frac{1/c_{\mu\mu}}{n-r} \frac{c_{kk} c_{\mu\mu} - c_{k\mu}^2}{c_{\mu\mu}} = \frac{1}{n-r} \frac{c_{kk} c_{\mu\mu} - c_{k\mu}^2}{c_{\mu\mu}^2}. \tag{10.21}$$

The formula (10.19) can be used also to drop from a regression equation a variable, say x_μ, that appears, after construction of the regression equation, to be nonsignificant. We could, of course, start again from the beginning, but, if we have four or more independent variables, it is more expeditious to remove the μth row and column from the c matrix and compute the new b's from (6.10). Alternatively, it can be shown that, if b_i is the regression coefficient of y on x_i in the multiple regression equation of y on all the x's, and if b'_i is the regression coefficient of y on x_i in the multiple regression equation of y on all the x's excluding x_μ, then

$$b'_i = b_i - \frac{c_{i\mu}}{c_{\mu\mu}} b_\mu. \tag{10.22}$$

13.11. Biases in Multiple Regression

In (10.22), b'_i represents the regression coefficient of y on x_i, the regression equation containing $x_1, x_2, \ldots, x_m$ but excluding x_μ. We can write

SECT. 13.11   BIASES IN MULTIPLE REGRESSION   453

this as $b_{yx_i \cdot x_j}$, where x_j is understood to stand for the sequence of x's from x_1 to x_m but excluding x_i and x_μ. Also, b_i represents the regression coefficient of y on x_i, the regression equation containing all the x's. We can write this as $b_{yx_i \cdot x_j'}$, where x_j' is understood to stand for the sequence of x's from x_1 to x_m, excluding x_i, but including x_μ. Also, b_μ is the regression coefficient of y on x_μ, the regression equation containing all the x's. We can write this as $b_{yx_\mu \cdot x_j''}$, where x_j'' is understood to stand for the sequence of x's from x_1 to x_m but excluding x_μ.

The remaining item in (10.22) is $-c_{i\mu}/c_{\mu\mu}$. Since $c_{i\mu} = c_{\mu i}$, this item is equal to $-c_{\mu i}/c_{\mu\mu}$. Reference to (10.5) shows that this is the regression coefficient of x_μ on x_i, the regression equation containing as independent variables all the x's except x_μ. We can write this as $b_{x_\mu x_i \cdot x_j}$, where x_j is the same as in the preceding paragraph.

We thus write (10.22) as

$$b_{yx_i \cdot x_j} = b_{yx_i \cdot x_j'} + b_{x_\mu x_i \cdot x_j} b_{yx_\mu \cdot x_j''} \qquad (11.1)$$

where
$x_j = x_1, \ldots, x_m$ but excluding x_i, x_μ.
$x_j' = x_1, \ldots, x_m$ but excluding x_i.
$x_j'' = x_1, \ldots, x_m$ but excluding x_μ.

The implication of this equation may be clearer if we consider a simple specific instance, say $m = 3$, $i = 1$, $\mu = 3$. Then $x_j = x_2$, $x_j' = x_2 x_3$, $x_j'' = x_1 x_2$, and (11.1) reads

$$b_{yx_1 \cdot x_2} = b_{yx_1 \cdot x_2 x_3} + b_{x_3 x_1 \cdot x_2} b_{yx_3 \cdot x_1 x_2}. \qquad (11.2)$$

This equation shows that the regression coefficient of y on x_1, ignoring x_3, is a biased estimator of the regression coefficient of y on x_1, not ignoring x_3, by an amount a function of the product of the regression coefficient of y on x_3 and the regression coefficient of x_3 on x_1.

Equation (11.2) illustrates why the application of multiple regression techniques to observational data can be so treacherous and misleading. The apparent regression of y on x_1 may really be due to the fact that y is dependent on x_3, and x_3 is correlated with x_1. We may fail to observe x_3, and attribute the regression of y on x_1 to a functional dependence which may be wholly false.

In most circumstances, therefore, any indications produced by a multiple regression analysis of observational data are merely a good hint to try for confirmation by a proper experiment. In a true experiment the independent variables will be properly randomized with a table of random numbers and will have low correlations differing from zero by only random fluctuation, or else in a completely balanced experiment the correlations will be exactly zero.

The justification sometimes advanced that a multiple regression analysis on observational data can be relied upon if there is an adequate theoretical background is utterly specious and disregards the unlimited capability of the human intellect for producing plausible explanations by the carload lot. For attempts to investigate these difficulties, see Tukey [4] and Simon [5].

A further reason for being suspicious of inferences from a multiple regression analysis on observational data is that there is no guarantee that the residuals are independent.

13.12. An Example of Multiple Regression

The data of Table 13.4 will be used to illustrate the foregoing procedures. They were obtained from 21 days of operation of a plant for the oxidation of ammonia to nitric acid. The x_1 column represents the rate of operation

Table 13.4

x_1	x_2	x_3	y	x_1	x_2	x_3	y
80	27	89	42	58	18	89	14
80	27	88	37	58	17	88	13
75	25	90	37	58	18	82	11
62	24	87	28	58	19	93	12
62	22	87	18	50	18	89	8
62	23	87	18	50	18	86	7
62	24	93	19	50	19	72	8
62	24	93	20	50	19	79	8
58	23	87	15	50	20	80	9
58	18	80	14	56	20	82	15
				70	20	91	15

x_1 = air flow
x_2 = cooling water inlet temperature
x_3 = acid concentration
y = stack loss

of the plant. The nitric oxides produced are absorbed in a countercurrent absorption tower. The third variable is the concentration of acid circulating, minus 50, times 10: i.e., 89 corresponds to 58.9 per cent acid. The x_2 column is the temperature of cooling water circulated through coils in the absorption tower. The dependent variable y is 10 times the percentage of the ingoing ammonia to the plant that escapes from the absorption

SECT. 13.12 AN EXAMPLE OF MULTIPLE REGRESSION

column unabsorbed, i.e., an (inverse) measure of the overall efficiency of the plant.

We will fit a linear regression equation similar to (6.2). We need all the sums, sums of squares, and sums of products (Table 13.5), and these

Table 13.5

	y	x_1	x_2	x_3
y	8518	23,953	8,326	32,189
x_1		78,365	27,223	109,988
x_2			9,545	38,357
x_3				156,924
Totals	368	1,269	443	1,812

are expressed as sums of squares and products of deviations from the means in Table 13.6. We now set up the equations (6.9). To give more convenient numbers we will temporarily multiply the right-hand sides by 10,000. Also, although we can obtain the b_i from the c matrix from (6.10), we might as well add an additional set of right-hand sides $\sum' y x_i$. We are thus solving four separate sets of three simultaneous linear equations, in which the numerical coefficients on the left-hand sides, $\sum' x_1^2$, $\sum' x_1 x_2$, etc., are identical for the four sets, but those on the right-hand sides do differ.

Table 13.6

	y	x_1	x_2	x_3
y	2069.238	1715.286	562.952	435.857
x_1		1681.143	453.143	491.429
x_2			199.810	132.429
x_3				574.286

The equations (6.5) and (6.9) are repeated in rows 1 through 3 of Table 13.7, and the numerical values for the coefficients entered from Table 13.6 in rows 4 through 6. The problem of solving simultaneous linear equations, though simple in theory, is arduous in practice, and has a long history. For conventional desk calculation a method known as the Doolittle, though probably due to Gauss, is one of the most satisfactory. Various modifications have been proposed, but the effort in learning their details seems to outweigh the slight savings they achieve. For r greater than 5, the work becomes excessive, and recourse should be made to an electronic digital computer. Programs are available for the standard machines.

Table 13.7

	Coefficients of				Right-hand sides		
	c_{i1}	c_{i2}	c_{i3}		$i=1$	$i=2$	$i=3$
1	$\Sigma' x_1^2$	$\Sigma' x_1 x_2$	$\Sigma' x_1 x_3$	$\Sigma' y x_1$	10,000	0	0
2	$\Sigma' x_1 x_2$	$\Sigma' x_2^2$	$\Sigma' x_2 x_3$	$\Sigma' y x_2$	0	10,000	0
3	$\Sigma' x_1 x_3$	$\Sigma' x_2 x_3$	$\Sigma' x_3^2$	$\Sigma' y x_3$	0	0	10,000
4	1681.143	453.143	491.429	1715.286	10,000	0	0
5	453.143	199.810	132.429	562.952	0	10,000	0
6	491.429	132.429	574.286	435.857	0	0	10,000
7	−1.0	−0.269544590	−0.292318381	−1.020309396	−5.94833896	0	0
8	453.143	199.810	132.429	562.952	0	10,000	0
9	−453.143	−122.142244	−132.462028	−462.346062	−2,695.44590	0	0
10		77.667756	−0.033028	100.605938	−2,695.44590	10,000	0
11		−1.0	0.000425247	−1.295337256	34.704825	−128.753559	0

SECT. 13.12 AN EXAMPLE OF MULTIPLE REGRESSION

12	491.429	132.429	574.286	435.857	0	0	0
13	−491.429	−132.462028	−143.653730	−501.409626	−2,923.18381	0	10,000
14		0.033027	−0.000014	0.042782	−1.14623	4.25247	0
15		−0.000001		−65.509844	−2,924.33004	4.25247	10,000
16			430.632256	−0.152124796	−6.7907826	0.0098749	23.221669
			1				
17		−1.0	−0.000064691	−1.295337256			
18			−0.002887760		34.704825		
19			+0.000004199				
20			+0.009874945			−128.753559	0
21		1.0		1.295272565	−34.707713	128.753563	0.009874945
22	−1.0	−0.349133712	0.044468874	−1.020309396	−5.948339	0	
23		9.355276	1.985070				
24		−34.704837	−0.002887			0	
25		−0.002662	−6.788121			−34.707724	0
26	1.0			0.715644558	17.288615	−34.707724	−6.790783

The procedure for solving the equations is as follows.

1. In line 7 divide line 4 by minus the coefficient of c_{i1} in line 4, i.e., by -1681.143.

2. In line 8 write out line 5 again. In line 9 multiply line 4 by the coefficient of c_{i2} in line 7, i.e., by -0.269544590. Add lines 8 and 9 together; the coefficient of c_{i1} vanishes, and we get line 10.

3. In line 11 divide line 10 by minus the coefficient of c_{i2} in line 10, i.e., by -77.667756.

4. In line 12 write out line 6 again. In line 13 multiply line 4 by the coefficient of c_{i3} in line 7, i.e., by -0.292318381. In line 14 multiply line 10 by the coefficient of c_{i3} in line 11, i.e., by 0.000425247. Add lines 12, 13, and 14 together; the coefficients of c_{i1} and c_{i2} vanish, and we get line 15.

5. In line 16 divide line 15 by the coefficient of c_{i3} in line 15, i.e., by 430.632256. This gives successively, on the right-hand side, $b_3 = -0.152125$, $c_{13} = -6.790783$, $c_{23} = 0.009875$, and $c_{33} = 23.221669$. Of course, the three c_{i3} need multiplying by 10^{-4} to give the correct values.

6. Now go back to line 11. This line represents the following four equations:

$$-1.0b_2 + 0.000425247b_3 = -1.295337256,$$
$$-1.0c_{12} + 0.000425247c_{13} = 34.704825,$$
$$-1.0c_{22} + 0.000425247c_{23} = -128.753559,$$
$$-1.0c_{32} + 0.000425247c_{33} = 0.$$

Substituting the solution for b_3 from line 16, i.e., -0.152124796, gives

$$-1.0b_2 - 0.000064691 = -1.259337256,$$

and this is schematically given in line 17. Solving for b_2 gives $b_2 = 1.295272$, as is schematically given in line 21. Similarly, line 18 corresponds to substituting $c_{13} = -6.7907826$ in the second of the four equations above,

$$-1.0c_{12} - 0.002887760 = 34.704825,$$

whence $c_{12} = -34.707713$, as is given in line 21. The solutions for c_{22} and c_{32} are obtained similarly.

7. Now go back to line 7, which represents the following four equations:

$$-1.0b_1 - 0.269544590b_2 - 0.292318381b_3 = -1.020309396,$$
$$-1.0c_{11} - 0.269544590c_{12} - 0.292318381c_{13} = -5.94833896,$$
$$-1.0c_{21} - 0.269544590c_{22} - 0.292318381c_{23} = 0,$$
$$-1.0c_{31} - 0.269544590c_{32} - 0.292318381c_{33} = 0.$$

SECT. 13.12   AN EXAMPLE OF MULTIPLE REGRESSION   459

Substituting $b_2 = 1.295272$ and $b_3 = -0.152124796$ in the first of these gives

$$-1.0b_1 - 0.349133712 + 0.044468874 = -1.020309396,$$

which is represented schematically in line 22. The solution for b_1 is $b_1 = 0.715644558$, as is given in line 26. The three remaining equations above for c_{11}, c_{21}, and c_{31} give lines 23, 24, and 25, respectively, and the final solutions are in the last three columns of line 26.

8. Assemble these solutions in Table 13.8.

Table 13.8. $10^4 c_{ij}$

$c_{11} =$	17.288615	$c_{12} =$	−34.707713	$c_{13} =$	−6.790783
$c_{21} =$	−34.707724	$c_{22} =$	128.753563	$c_{23} =$	0.009875
$c_{31} =$	−6.790783	$c_{32} =$	0.009875	$c_{33} =$	23.221669
$b_1 =$	0.715645	$b_2 =$	1.295272	$b_3 =$	−0.152125

9. Check the accuracy of these solutions by inserting them in the left-hand side of line 6 and seeing how the right-hand sides coincide with the required values. Here we get as left-hand sides 435.8569994, −0.034, −0.005, 10,000.000, which compare very well with the values in line 6. However, the need for carrying a large number of significant figures is pointed up by the discrepancy in the fifth decimal place between c_{21} and c_{12}.

In the above calculations we obtained the b_i directly by carrying the column $\Sigma' yx_i$ as an additional right-hand side. This was not strictly necessary, for we can use (6.10) to obtain, e.g.,

$$b_1 = [1715.286 \times 17.288615 + 562.952 \times (-34.707713)$$
$$+ 435.857 \times (-6.790783)] \times 10^{-4} = 0.715633,$$

which differs from the direct solution in the fifth decimal place on account of rounding errors.

To make a joint test of the null hypothesis $\beta_i = 0$ for all i, we compute the sum of squares due to regression from (6.33):

$$0.715644 \times 1715.286 + 1.295273 \times 562.952 + (-0.152125) \times 435.857$$
$$= 1890.406.$$

The residual sum of squares about the regression plane is given by (6.35) as $2069.238 - 1890.406 = 178.832$, and with $21 - 1 - 3 = 17$ degrees of freedom this gives $s^2 = 10.520$. These results are assembled in Table 13.9. The variance ratio, $630.135/10.520 = 60$, being distributed as $F(3, 17)$ under the null hypothesis, is overwhelmingly significant.

Table 13.9

Source of variance	Sums of squares	Degrees of freedom	Mean squares
Due to regression	1890.406	3	630.135
About the regression plane	178.832	17	10.520
Total	2069.238		

Separate t tests on the individual b_i are made, using (6.18). In Table 13.10 tests of the individual null hypotheses $\beta_i = 0$ are performed. Under the null hypothesis, the ratios in the last column are distributed as $t(17)$. The first two are obviously very significant, and the last nonsignificant. The individual confidence intervals for the separate b_i can be constructed if desired.

Table 13.10

i	$\hat{V}[b_i] = s^2 c_{ii}$	$\sqrt{\hat{V}[b_i]}$	b_i	$t = b_i / \sqrt{\hat{V}[b_i]}$
1	$10.520 \times 17.288 \times 10^{-4}$	0.1349	0.7156	5.305
2	$10.520 \times 128.754 \times 10^{-4}$	0.3680	1.2953	3.520
3	$10.520 \times 23.222 \times 10^{-4}$	0.1563	-0.1521	-0.973

The regression equation of Y on x_1, x_2, x_3 is

$$Y = 17.524 + 0.715633(x_1 - 60.429) + 1.295273(x_2 - 21.095)$$
$$+ (-0.152125)(x_3 - 86.286)$$
$$= -39.919 + 0.7156 x_1 + 1.2953 x_2 - 0.1521 x_3.$$

To test whether x_3 adds significantly to the regression on x_1 and x_2, we need the latter regression. When we have only three independent variables, to drop one it is about as quick to start from scratch with the two we want. However, we will illustrate the procedure of Section 13.10. Since we are omitting x_3, in (10.20) $\mu = 3$, and

$$c'_{11} = \left[17.288615 - \frac{(-6.790783)^2}{23.221670} \right] \times 10^{-4} = 15.302766 \times 10^{-4},$$

$$c'_{22} = \left[128.753603 - \frac{(0.009875)^2}{23.221670} \right] \times 10^{-4} = 128.753599 \times 10^{-4},$$

and, from (10.19),

$$c'_{12} = \left[-34.707713 - \frac{(-6.790783)(0.009875)}{23.221670} \right] \times 10^{-4}$$
$$= -34.704825 \times 10^{-4} = c'_{21}.$$

SECT. 13.12 AN EXAMPLE OF MULTIPLE REGRESSION

We can calculate b_1' from (6.10) as

$$b_1' = [1715.286 \times 15.302766 + 562.952 \times (-34.704825)] \times 10^{-4}$$
$$= 0.671159$$

and similarly $b_2' = 1.295338$. Alternatively, we can use (10.22),

$$b_1' = 0.715645 - \frac{(-6.790783)(-0.152125)}{23.221669} = 0.671159$$

which comes to the same thing. The sum of squares due to regression on x_1 and x_2 only is, again using (6.33),

$$(0.671159 \times 1715.286 + 1.295338 \times 562.952) \times 10^{-4} = 1880.443.$$

We now construct Table 13.11 analogous to Table 13.3. The test of the null hypothesis that adding x_3 to x_1, x_2 does not improve the fit is given by

Table 13.11

Source of variance	Sums of squares	Degrees of freedom	Mean squares
Due to regression jointly on x_1, x_2, x_3	1890.406	3	
Due to regression jointly on x_1, x_2	1880.443	2	940.221
Due to adding x_3 to x_1, x_2	9.963	1	9.963
Deviations about regression plane on x_1, x_2, x_3	178.832	17	10.520
Total	2069.238	20	

the variance ratio 9.963/10.520, which is clearly nonsignificant. The test of the joint hypothesis $\beta_1' = \beta_2' = 0$ is given by the variance ratio $940.221/[(2069.238-1880.443)/(20-2)]$ which is clearly overwhelmingly significant.

The regression equation for x_1 and x_2 only is

$$Y = 17.524 + 0.671159(x_1 - 60.429) + 1.295338(x_2 - 21.095)$$
$$= -50.359 + 0.671159 x_1 + 1.295338 x_2.$$

We might ask for 95 per cent confidence limits for η at $x_1 = 50$, $x_2 = 18$. For these values,

$$Y = -50.359 + 0.671159 \times 50 + 1.295338 \times 18 = 6.516.$$

The estimated variance of Y can be calculated from (3.48), which is applicable to the special case of two independent variables, or from (6.36), which is applicable to the general case of r independent variables. We will use the latter form here. Since we are using only two variables, s^2 is given by pooling the last two lines in the body of Table 13.11: $s^2 = (9.963 + 178.832)/(1 + 17) = 10.489$. Also $x_1 - \bar{x}_1 = 50 - 60.4286 = -10.4286$, $x_2 - \bar{x}_2 = 18 - 21.0952 = -3.0952$. Then

$$\hat{V}[Y] = 10.489[(1/21) + \{15.302766 \times (-10.4286)^2 + 128.753603 \\ \times (-3.0952)^2 + 2(-34.704825)(-10.4286)(-3.0952)\} \times 10^{-4}] \\ = 1.18893.$$

The square root of this is 1.0904, and $t_{0.975}(18) = 2.101$; so confidence limits for η are at $6.516 \pm 2.101 \times 1.0904 = (4.23, 8.81)$.

Finally, we will illustrate the use of the c matrix to give the regression equation of x_3 on x_1, x_2. Reading off the third line of Table 13.8, we have, for (10.5),

$$x_3 = \bar{x}_3 + \left(-\frac{-6.790783}{23.221669}\right)(x_1 - \bar{x}_1) + \left(-\frac{0.009875}{23.221669}\right)(x_2 - \bar{x}_2)$$

$$= 86.286 + 0.292433(x_1 - 60.429) - 0.000425(x_2 - 21.095).$$

To test the significance, say, of the regression coefficient of x_3 on x_1, in this equation, we would use (10.21):

$$\hat{V}[b_{31.2}] = \frac{1}{21 - 3} \frac{17.288615 \times 23.221669 - (-6.790783)^2}{(23.221669)^2} = 0.03651.$$

A test of the null hypothesis $\beta_{31.2} = 0$ is given by $0.292433/\sqrt{0.03651} = 1.53$, which is distributed as $t(18)$.

EXERCISES

13.1. The following table gives data on death rate due to heart disease in males in the 55 to 59 age group, along with the proportionate number of telephones, and of fat and protein in the diet.

(a) Test the significance of the regression of y on x_1, in the regression of y on x_1 alone.
(b) Construct the multiple regression equation of y on x_1, x_2.
(c) Make a joint test of the null hypothesis $\beta_1 = \beta_2 = 0$.
(d) Test whether adding x_2 to the regression equation (on x_1) has significantly improved the fit.
(e) Construct the multiple regression equation of y on x_1, x_2, and x_3.
(f) Give 95 per cent confidence limits for β_3 in this equation.
(g) Give 95 per cent confidence limits for η at $x_1 = 221$, $x_2 = 39$, $x_3 = 7$.
(h) Test whether x_2 and x_3 together add anything to the regression of y on x_1.
(i) Construct the multiple regression equation of x_1 on x_2 and x_3.
(j) Give 95 per cent confidence limits for the regression coefficient of x_1 on x_3.

	x_1	x_2	x_3	y
Australia	124	33	8	81
Austria	49	31	6	55
Canada	181	38	8	80
Ceylon	4	17	2	24
Chile	22	20	4	78
Denmark	152	39	6	52
Finland	75	30	7	88
France	54	29	7	45
Germany	43	35	6	50
Ireland	41	31	5	69
Israel	17	23	4	66
Italy	22	21	3	45
Japan	16	8	3	24
Mexico	10	23	3	43
Netherlands	63	37	6	38
New Zealand	170	40	8	72
Norway	125	38	6	41
Portugal	15	25	4	38
Sweden	221	39	7	52
Switzerland	171	33	7	52
United Kingdom	97	38	6	66
United States	254	39	8	89

$x_1 = 1000$ (telephones per head)

$x_2 = $ fat calories as per cent of total calories

$x_3 = $ animal protein calories as per cent of total calories

$y = 100$ [log (number deaths from heart disease per 100,000 for males in 55 to 59 age group) $- 2$]

Sources: x_1 from *World Almanac and Book of Facts* (New York: New York World Telegram, 1951) except the figures for Ireland and Ceylon, which were obtained by private communication from the countries concerned.

x_2, x_3, and x_4 from J. Yerushalmy and Herman E. Hilleboe, "Fat in the Diet and Mortality from Heart Disease: a Methodological Note," *New York State Journal of Medicine*, 57 (1957), 2343–54.

Sums of Squares and Products

	y	x_1	x_2	x_3
y	78,624	123,591	39,409	7,504
x_1		288,068	68,838	13,226
x_2			21,807	4,042
x_3				772
Sums	1,248	1,926	667	124

Sums of Squares and Products of Deviations

	y	x_1	x_2	x_3
y	7828.364	14,334.273	1,571.909	469.818182
x_1		119,455.455	10,445.182	2370.363636
x_2			1,584.773	282.545455
x_3				73.090909

13.2. In the table below, referring to the year 1950, for 46 states,
y = standardized liver cirrhosis death rate
x_1 = per cent of population "urban" (1950 Census definition of urban)
x_2 = 100 (number of children ever born to women 45–49 years old)$^{-1}$
x_3 = wine consumption in hundredths of U.S. gallons of absolute alcohol per capita of toal population
x_4 = spirits consumption, likewise.

Sources: y, x_3, and x_4 from Wolfgang Schmidt and Jean Bronetto, "Death from Liver Cirrhosis and Specific Alcohol Consumption: An Ecological Study," *American Journal of Public Health*, 52 (1962), 1473–82.

x_1 and x_2 from *Statistical Abstract of the United States*, 1955, U.S. Department of Commerce.

Two states, Oklahoma and Mississippi, are excluded on account of legal restrictions on the sale of liquor.

	y	x_1	x_2	x_3	x_4
Alabama	41.2	44	33.2	5	30
Idaho	31.7	43	33.8	4	41
Iowa	39.4	48	40.6	3	38
Maine	57.5	52	39.2	7	48
Michigan	74.8	71	45.5	11	53
Montana	59.8	44	37.5	9	65
New Hampshire	54.3	57	44.2	6	73
N. Carolina	47.9	34	31.9	3	32
Ohio	77.2	70	45.6	12	56
Oregon	56.6	54	45.9	7	57
Pennsylvania	80.9	70	43.7	14	43

	y	x_1	x_2	x_3	x_4
Utah	34.3	65	32.1	12	33
Vermont	53.1	36	36.9	10	48
Virginia	55.4	47	38.9	10	69
Washington	57.8	63	47.6	14	54
W. Virginia	62.8	35	33.0	9	47
Wyoming	67.3	50	38.9	7	68
Arizona	56.7	55	35.7	18	47
Arkansas	37.6	33	31.2	6	27
California	129.9	81	53.8	31	79
Colorado	70.3	63	42.5	13	59
Connecticut	104.2	78	53.3	20	97
Delaware	83.6	63	47.0	19	95
Florida	66.0	65	44.9	10	81
Georgia	52.3	45	35.6	4	26
Illinois	86.9	78	50.5	16	76
Indiana	66.6	60	42.3	9	37
Kansas	40.1	52	43.8	6	46
Kentucky	55.7	37	33.2	6	40
Louisiana	58.1	55	36.0	21	76
Maryland	74.3	69	47.6	15	70
Massachusetts	98.1	84	50.0	17	66
Minnesota	40.7	54	43.8	7	63
Missouri	66.7	61	45.0	13	59
Nebraska	48.0	47	42.2	8	55
Nevada	122.5	57	53.0	28	149
New Jersey	92.1	87	51.6	23	77
New Mexico	76.0	50	31.9	22	43
New York	97.5	85	56.1	23	74
N. Dakota	33.8	27	31.5	7	56
Rhode Island	90.5	84	50.0	16	63
S. Carolina	29.7	37	32.4	2	41
S. Dakota	28.0	33	36.1	6	59
Tennessee	51.6	44	35.3	3	32
Texas	55.7	63	39.3	8	40
Wisconsin	55.5	58	43.8	13	57
Sums	2920.7	2588	1907.9	533	

(a) Give 95 per cent confidence limits for the regression coefficient b_{yx_1}.
(b) Add x_2 to the regression equation. Test the null hypothesis $\beta_{yx_2 \cdot x_1} = 0$.
(c) Add x_3 to the regression equation. Test the null hypothesis $\beta_{yx_3 \cdot x_1 x_2} = 0$.
(d) Test the joint null hypothesis that $\beta_{xy_1 \cdot x_2 x_3} = \beta_{yx_2 \cdot x_1 x_3} = 0$.
(e) Give the regression equation of x_3 on x_1 and x_2. Give 95 per cent confidence limits for $\beta_{x_3 x_2 \cdot x_1}$.
(f) If you have strong views about hard liquor, make up your own exercises involving x_4.

Sums of Squares and Products of Deviations

	y	x_1	x_2	x_3
y	24,741.3481	12,446.4783	5817.9129	6167.47609
x_1		11,158.8696	4209.4870	3327.95658
x_2			2233.0237	1403.6457
x_3				2155.152174

13.3. Suppose that x_1, x_2, x_3 are distributed in a trivariate normal distribution. Let $\beta_{12.3}$ be the regression coefficient of x_1 on x_2 in the regression equation of x_1 on x_2 and x_3, and let β_{12} be the regression coefficient of x_1 on x_2 in the regression equation of x_1 on x_2 alone. (*a*) Express the relationship between $\beta_{12.3}$ and β_{12} as a function involving ρ_{12}, $\rho_{13.3}$, and ρ_{23}. (*b*) What relationships involving ρ_{12}, ρ_{13}, and ρ_{23} will make $\beta_{12.3} = \beta_{12}$?

13.4. Assume that x_1 and x_2 are random variables. (*a*) Obtain an expression for the correlation coefficient between x_1/x_2 and x_2, involving the parameters σ_{x_1}, σ_{x_2}, ξ_1, ξ_2, and $\rho_{x_1 x_2}$. (*b*) Suppose that the coefficients of variation of x_1 and x_2 are equal, i.e., that $\sigma_{x_1}/\xi_1 = \sigma_{x_2}/\xi_2$. Give a simple form for the correlation coefficient between x_1/x_2 and x_2. (*c*) Suppose further that $\rho_{x_1 x_2} = 0$. Obtain a numerical value for the correlation coefficient between x_1/x_2 and x_2.

13.5. Starting from equations of the form (11.2.13) for b_{yx_1} and $b_{x_1 x_2}$, and from equations of the form (3.19) of $b_{yx_1 \cdot y_2}$ and $b_{yx_2 \cdot y_1}$, show that

$$b_{yx_1} = b_{yx_1 \cdot x_2} + b_{x_1 x_2} b_{yx_2 \cdot x_1}.$$

REFERENCES

1. Pearson, Karl, "Mathematical Contributions to the Theory of Evolution. On a Form of Spurious Correlation Which May Arise When Indices are Used in the Measurement of Organs," *Proceedings of the Royal Society*, 60 (1897), 489–98.
2. Anderson, R. L., and T. A. Bancroft, *Statistical Theory in Research*. New York: McGraw-Hill Book Co., 1952.
3. Kempthorne, O., *The Design and Analysis of Experiments*. New York: John Wiley and Sons, 1952.
4. Tukey, John W., "Causation, Regression, and Path Analysis," Chapter 3, pp. 35–66, in *Statistics and Mathematics in Biology*, Oscar Kempthorne et al. (eds.). Ames, Iowa: Iowa State College Press, 1954.
5. Simon, Herbert A., "Spurious Correlation: a Causal Interpretation," *Journal of the American Statistical Association*, 49 (1954), 467–79.

CHAPTER 14

Two-Way and Nested Analysis of Variance

14.1. Introduction: The Model for Model I Analysis

In Chapter 10 we considered the analysis of variance where the data were classified in one way. In this chapter we will discuss the analysis of two-way tables, first when both classifications are model I, then when both are model II, and finally the mixed case where one classification is model I and the other model II.

We suppose that the data are in the form of Table 14.1. For example, rows could correspond to varieties of corn, and columns to quantity of some fertilizer, and we have n independent estimates x_{ijv} for each row × column combination. We assume that the rt sets of n observations are random samples from rt separate populations, each normally distributed about means ξ_{ij} but all with the same variance σ^2. The model is

$$x_{ijv} = \xi_{ij} + z_{ijv}: \quad z_{ijv} \sim N(0, \sigma^2), \tag{1.1}$$
$$i = 1, \ldots, r: \quad j = 1, \ldots, t: \quad v = 1, \ldots, n.$$

The means of the sample observations in each cell are $\bar{x}_{ij.} = (1/n)\sum_v^n x_{ijv}$. The mean of the sample means in the ith row is

$$\bar{x}_{i..} = \frac{1}{t}\sum_j^t \bar{x}_{ij.} = \frac{1}{tn}\sum_j^t \sum_v^n x_{ijv}, \tag{1.2}$$

and the mean of the sample means in the jth column is

$$\bar{x}_{.j.} = \frac{1}{r}\sum_i^r \bar{x}_{ij.} = \frac{1}{rn}\sum_i^r \sum_v^n x_{ijv}. \tag{1.3}$$

Table 14.1

		j			
i	1	2	$\cdots$	t	Averages
1	x_{11v}	x_{12v}		x_{1tv}	$\bar{x}_{1..}$
2	x_{21v}	x_{22v}		x_{2tv}	$\bar{x}_{2..}$
.					
.					
.					
r	x_{r1v}	x_{r2v}		x_{rtv}	$\bar{x}_{r..}$
Averages	$\bar{x}_{.1.}$	$\bar{x}_{.2.}$		$\bar{x}_{.t.}$	$\bar{x}_{...}$

Table 14.2 gives the population means ξ_{ij} for each cell, the row and column means, defined as $\bar{\xi}_{i.} = (1/t) \sum_{j}^{t} \xi_{ij}$, $\bar{\xi}_{.j} = (1/r) \sum_{i}^{r} \xi_{ij}$, and the grand mean defined as

$$\xi = \frac{1}{r} \sum_{i}^{r} \bar{\xi}_{i.} = \frac{1}{rt} \sum_{i}^{r} \sum_{j}^{t} \xi_{ij} = \frac{1}{t} \sum_{j}^{t} \bar{\xi}_{.j}. \qquad (1.4)$$

The deviations of each row mean from the grand mean are denoted by η_i,

$$\eta_i = \bar{\xi}_{i.} - \xi, \qquad (1.5)$$

and the deviations of each column mean from the grand mean by ζ_j:

$$\zeta_j = \bar{\xi}_{.j} - \xi. \qquad (1.6)$$

Clearly, both these sets of deviations sum to zero:

$$\sum_{i}^{r} \eta_i = 0 = \sum_{j}^{t} \zeta_j. \qquad (1.7)$$

Table 14.2

i	1	2	$\cdots$	t	Means	Deviations
1	ξ_{11}	ξ_{12}	$\cdots$	ξ_{1t}	$\bar{\xi}_{1.}$	$\bar{\xi}_{1.} - \xi = \eta_1$
2	ξ_{21}	ξ_{22}		ξ_{2t}	$\bar{\xi}_{2.}$	$\bar{\xi}_{2.} - \xi = \eta_2$
.						
.						
r	ξ_{r1}	ξ_{r2}		ξ_{rt}	$\bar{\xi}_{r.}$	$\bar{\xi}_{r.} - \xi = \eta_r$
Means	$\bar{\xi}_{.1}$	$\bar{\xi}_{.2}$		$\bar{\xi}_{.t}$	ξ	
Deviations	$\bar{\xi}_{.1} - \xi = \zeta_1$	$\bar{\xi}_{.2} - \xi = \zeta_2$		$\bar{\xi}_{.t} - \xi = \zeta_t$		

SECT. 14.1 INTRODUCTION: THE MODEL FOR MODEL I ANALYSIS

We define quantities θ_{ij} as the difference between the true mean for the ijth cell, ξ_{ij}, and what we would expect on the basis of an additive model,

$$\text{Grand mean + row effect + column effect} = \xi + \eta_i + \zeta_j; \quad (1.8)$$

i.e.

$$\theta_{ij} = \xi_{ij} - (\xi + \eta_i + \zeta_j). \quad (1.9)$$

Thus, if the true cell mean is equal to the prediction (1.8), then the additive model holds and $\theta_{ij} = 0$. In other words,

$$\xi_{ij} = \xi + \eta_i + \zeta_j + \theta_{ij}, \quad (1.10)$$

the θ_{ij} measuring the departure from the additive model (1.8). The θ_{ij} are known as the *interaction* constants. When we say that we have zero interaction, we mean that we have an additive model as in (1.8). The θ_{ij} sum to zero over each suffix, for each value of the other suffix; for the sum over i,

$$\sum_i^r \theta_{ij} = \sum_i^r \xi_{ij} - r\xi - \sum_i^r \eta_i - r\zeta_j. \quad (1.11)$$

But $\sum_i^r \eta_i = 0$, from (1.7), and, from (1.6),

$$r\zeta_j = r\bar{\xi}_{.j} - r\xi = \sum_i^r \xi_{ij} - r\xi; \quad (1.12)$$

so

$$\sum_i^r \theta_{ij} = \sum_i^r \xi_{ij} - r\xi - 0 - \sum_i^r \xi_{ij} + r\xi = 0. \quad (1.13)$$

Specifically, we have t relations

$$\sum_i^r \theta_{i1} = \sum_i^r \theta_{i2} = \cdots = \sum_i^r \theta_{it} = 0, \quad (1.14)$$

and r relations

$$\sum_j^t \theta_{1j} = \sum_j^t \theta_{2j} = \cdots = \sum_j^t \theta_{rj} = 0. \quad (1.15)$$

However, effectively there are only $r + t - 1$ independent restrictions on the θ_{ij}. This is because we have, say, the t restrictions (1.14), which when summed determine the relation $\sum_j^t \left(\sum_i^r \theta_{ij} \right) = 0$. But then the $\sum_i^r \theta_{ij}$ (1.15), whose sum is $\sum_j^r \left(\sum_i^t \theta_{ij} \right) = \sum_j^t \sum_i^r \theta_{ij}$, must also sum to zero. In other words, only $r - 1$ of the r relations (1.15) will be independent. Thus the total number of independent restrictions on the θ_{ij} is $r + t - 1$. Since the number of the θ_{ij} is rt, the number of independent constants in this group is

$$rt - (r + t - 1) = (r - 1)(t - 1). \quad (1.16)$$

We now rewrite the original model (1.1) as

$$x_{ijv} = \xi + \eta_i + \zeta_j + \theta_{ij} + z_{ijv}. \tag{1.17}$$

The original model involved rt independent cell means ξ_{ij}; this model involves the grand mean ξ, $r-1$ independent row constants η_i, $t-1$ independent column constants ζ_j, and $(r-1)(t-1)$ independent interaction constants θ_{ij}. The total number of independent parameters in the new model (1.17) is

$$1 + (r-1) + (t-1) + (r-1)(t-1) = rt, \tag{1.18}$$

the same as the original model (1.1). If the full number of parameters are needed, very little will be gained by the change in the model. However, if the null hypothesis of additivity can be accepted, we can regard the interaction constants θ_{ij} as zero, and then we have only to consider the grand mean and row and column parameters, a very substantial reduction in the number of parameters. Furthermore, it may happen that either the row or column parameters, or both, can be regarded as zero, which would allow further reduction in the number of parameters necessary to describe the situation. In fact, if both were zero, the only parameter left is the grand mean ξ.

Corresponding to the population parameters ξ, η_i, ζ_j and θ_{ij}, we will have sample analogs. The sample analog of ξ (1.4) is

$$\bar{x}_{...} = \frac{1}{rtn} \sum_i^r \sum_j^t \sum_v^n x_{ijv},$$

that of η_i (1.5) is $(\bar{x}_{i..} - \bar{x}_{...})$, that of ζ_j (1.6) is $(\bar{x}_{.j.} - \bar{x}_{...})$, and that of θ_{ij} (1.9), is

$$\bar{x}_{ij.} - [\bar{x}_{...} + (\bar{x}_{i..} - \bar{x}_{...}) + (\bar{x}_{.j.} - \bar{x}_{...})] = \bar{x}_{ij.} - \bar{x}_{i..} - \bar{x}_{.j.} + \bar{x}_{...}. \tag{1.19}$$

Using these expressions we can write an identity analogous to (1.10)

$$\bar{x}_{ij.} = \bar{x}_{...} + (\bar{x}_{i..} - \bar{x}_{...}) + (\bar{x}_{.j.} - \bar{x}_{...}) + (\bar{x}_{ij.} - \bar{x}_{i..} - \bar{x}_{.j.} + \bar{x}_{...}). \tag{1.20}$$

If we subtract this from (1.10), we get an expression for the deviation of the sample mean for the ijth cell from the true value for the mean of that cell:

$$\bar{x}_{ij.} - \xi_{ij} = (\bar{x}_{ij.} - \bar{x}_{i..} - \bar{x}_{.j.} + \bar{x}_{...} - \theta_{ij})$$
$$+ (\bar{x}_{i..} - \bar{x}_{...} - \eta_i) + (\bar{x}_{.j.} - \bar{x}_{...} - \zeta_j) + (\bar{x}_{...} - \xi). \tag{1.21}$$

This identity will be used in the following section.

14.2. The Analysis of Variance

We start with the identity

$$x_{ijv} - \bar{x}_{...} = (\bar{x}_{ij.} - \bar{x}_{i..} - \bar{x}_{.j.} + \bar{x}_{...}) + (\bar{x}_{i..} - \bar{x}_{...})$$
$$+ (\bar{x}_{.j.} - \bar{x}_{...}) + (x_{ijv} - \bar{x}_{ij.}), \quad (2.1)$$

and square and sum over i, j and v:

$$\sum_i^r \sum_j^t \sum_v^n (x_{ijv} - \bar{x}_{...})^2 = n \sum_i^r \sum_j^t (\bar{x}_{ij.} - \bar{x}_{i..} - \bar{x}_{.j.} + \bar{x}_{...})^2$$
$$+ nt \sum_i^r (\bar{x}_{i..} - \bar{x}_{...})^2 + nr \sum_j^t (\bar{x}_{.j.} - \bar{x}_{...})^2 + \sum_i^r \sum_j^t \sum_v^n (x_{ijv} - \bar{x}_{ij.})^2. \quad (2.2)$$

This equation is entered in the second column of Table 14.3. We wish to

Table 14.3

Source of variance	Sums of squares	Degrees of freedom	Mean squares	E[M. S.]
Rows	$nt \sum_i^r (\bar{x}_{i..} - \bar{x}_{...})^2$	$r - 1$	s_4^2	$\sigma^2 + \dfrac{nt \sum_i^r \eta_i^2}{r - 1}$
Columns	$nr \sum_j^t (\bar{x}_{.j.} - \bar{x}_{...})^2$	$t - 1$	s_3^2	$\sigma^2 + \dfrac{nr \sum_j^t \zeta_j^2}{t - 1}$
Interaction	$n \sum_i^r \sum_j^t (\bar{x}_{ij.} - \bar{x}_{i..} - \bar{x}_{.j.} + \bar{x}_{...})^2$	$(r - 1)(t - 1)$	s_2^2	$\sigma^2 + \dfrac{n \sum_i^r \sum_j^t \theta_{ij}^2}{(r - 1)(t - 1)}$
Within cells	$\sum_i^r \sum_j^t \sum_v^n (x_{ijv} - \bar{x}_{ij.})^2$	$rt(n - 1)$	s_1^2	σ^2
Total	$\sum_i^r \sum_j^t \sum_v^n (x_{ijv} - \bar{x}_{...})^2$	$rtn - 1$		

obtain the distributions of the various mean squares s_1^2, etc., under the various null hypotheses $\eta_i = 0$ for all i, etc. Consider the identity

$$x_{ijv} - \xi_{ij} = (x_{ijv} - \bar{x}_{ij.}) + (\bar{x}_{ij.} - \xi_{ij}). \quad (2.3)$$

We square this and then sum over v:

$$\sum_v^n (x_{ijv} - \xi_{ij})^2 = \sum_v^n (x_{ijv} - \bar{x}_{ij.})^2 + n(\bar{x}_{ij.} - \xi_{ij})^2. \quad (2.4)$$

The left-hand side is distributed as $\sigma^2\chi^2(n)$, and the two terms on the right-hand side are distributed as $\sigma^2\chi^2(n-1)$ and $\sigma^2\chi^2(1)$. Now sum over i and j.

$$\sum_i^r \sum_j^t \sum_v^n (x_{ijv} - \xi_{ij})^2 = \sum_i^r \sum_j^t \sum_v^n (x_{ijv} - \bar{x}_{ij.})^2 + n \sum_i^r \sum_j^t (\bar{x}_{ij.} - \xi_{ij})^2. \quad (2.5)$$

By the additivity of χ^2's, the left-hand side will be distributed as $\sigma^2\chi^2(rtn)$, and the two terms on the right-hand side as $\sigma^2\chi^2(rt(n-1))$ and $\sigma^2\chi^2(rt)$. If we define

$$s_1^2 = \frac{1}{rt(n-1)} \sum_i^r \sum_j^t \sum_v^n (x_{ijv} - \bar{x}_{ij.})^2, \quad (2.6)$$

it will have expected value σ^2 and be independent of the other term on the right-hand side of (2.5).

Now consider this other term. If we square the identity (1.21) and sum over i, j and v (summing over v amounts to multiplication by n), we get

$$n \sum_i^r \sum_j^t (\bar{x}_{ij.} - \xi_{ij})^2 = n \sum_i^r \sum_j^t (\bar{x}_{ij.} - \bar{x}_{i..} - \bar{x}_{.j.} + \bar{x}_{...} - \theta_{ij})^2$$

$$+ nt \sum_i^r (\bar{x}_{i..} - \bar{x}_{...} - \eta_i)^2 + nr \sum_j^t (\bar{x}_{.j.} - \bar{x}_{...} - \zeta_j)^2 + ntr(\bar{x}_{...} - \xi)^2. \quad (2.7)$$

The left-hand side is distributed as $\sigma^2\chi^2(rt)$. The degrees of freedom for the first term on the right-hand side follow from the fact that the random variables $\bar{x}_{ij.} - \bar{x}_{i..} - \bar{x}_{.j.} + \bar{x}_{...}$ are subject to the conditions

$$\sum_i^r (\bar{x}_{ij.} - \bar{x}_{i..} - \bar{x}_{.j.} + \bar{x}_{...}) = 0 \quad \text{for each } j, \quad (2.8)$$

$$\sum_j^t (\bar{x}_{ij.} - \bar{x}_{i..} - \bar{x}_{.j.} + \bar{x}_{...}) = 0 \quad \text{for each } i, \quad (2.9)$$

and, similar to the argument for the analogous θ_{ij}, these form only $r + t - 1$ independent relations. The degrees of freedom for this term are therefore

$$rt - (r + t - 1) = (r - 1)(t - 1). \quad (2.10)$$

For the second and third terms we have the conditions

$$\sum_i^r (\bar{x}_{i..} - \bar{x}_{...}) = 0 = \sum_j^t (\bar{x}_{.j.} - \bar{x}_{...}) \quad (2.11)$$

and so the degrees of freedom are $r - 1$ and $t - 1$, respectively. The last term involving the single random variable $\bar{x}_{...}$ has 1 degree of freedom. Hence, by Cochran's theorem, these sums of squares will be distributed as $\sigma^2\chi^2$ and be independent.

SECT. 14.2   THE ANALYSIS OF VARIANCE

If we define $s_2'^2$ as

$$s_2'^2 = \frac{n \sum_i^r \sum_j^t (\bar{x}_{ij} - \bar{x}_{i..} - \bar{x}_{.j.} + \bar{x}_{...} - \theta_{ij})^2}{(r-1)(t-1)}, \tag{2.12}$$

then

$$s_2'^2 \sim \sigma^2 \frac{\chi^2((r-1)(t-1))}{(r-1)(t-1)}, \tag{2.13}$$

and $s_2'^2$ will have expected value σ^2 and be independent of s_1^2. Hence the ratio $s_2'^2/s_1^2$ has the F distribution with degrees of freedom $(r-1)(t-1)$, $rt(n-1)$. Now define s_2^2 as

$$s_2^2 = \frac{n \sum_i^r \sum_j^t (\bar{x}_{ij} - \bar{x}_{i..} - \bar{x}_{.j.} + \bar{x}_{...})^2}{(r-1)(t-1)}. \tag{2.14}$$

To find its expected value, consider the expected value of the numerator of $s_2'^2$:

$$E\left[n \sum_i^r \sum_j^t (\bar{x}_{ij} - \bar{x}_{i..} - \bar{x}_{.j.} + \bar{x}_{...} - \theta_{ij})^2\right]$$

$$= E\left[n \sum_i^r \sum_j^t (\bar{x}_{ij} - \bar{x}_{i..} - \bar{x}_{.j.} + \bar{x}_{...})^2\right] + n \sum_i^r \sum_j^t \theta_{ij}^2$$

$$- 2n \sum_i^r \sum_j^t E\left[\theta_{ij}(\bar{x}_{ij} - \bar{x}_{i..} - \bar{x}_{.j.} + \bar{x}_{...})\right]$$

$$= E\left[(r-1)(t-1)s_2^2\right] - n \sum_i^r \sum_j^t \theta_{ij}^2. \tag{2.15}$$

The left-hand side equals $(r-1)(t-1)\sigma^2$, whence it follows that

$$E[s_2^2] = \sigma^2 + \frac{n \sum_i^r \sum_j^t \theta_{ij}^2}{(r-1)(t-1)}. \tag{2.16}$$

If the null hypothesis $\theta_{ij} = 0$ for all i, j is true, then $s_2^2 = s_2'^2$, and so

$$\frac{s_2^2}{s_1^2} \sim F((r-1)(t-1), rt(n-1)). \tag{2.17}$$

If the null hypothesis is false, so that some $\theta_{ij} \neq 0$, then $E[s_2^2] > \sigma^2$ and the ratio s_2^2/s_1^2 will not have the F distribution but instead a distribution displaced upwards in the direction of larger values of s_2^2/s_1^2. The critical region is therefore large values of s_2^2/s_1^2.

The other two mean squares in Table 14.3 can be treated similarly.

If the null hypothesis $\theta_{ij} = 0$ for all i, j is rejected, then the true cell means are not given by an additive model, and we might as well deal with the individual cell means. On the other hand, if the null hypothesis is acceptable, then we may assume that the θ_{ij} are zero, and proceed to test the row and column effects. If the $\eta_i = 0$ for all i, then s_4^2 is an estimate of σ^2 independent of s_1^2, and the ratio s_4^2/s_1^2 will be distributed as $F((r-1), rt(n-1))$.

We may wish to construct confidence limits for $\bar{\xi}_{i.} - \bar{\xi}_{i'.}$, the difference between two row means. Since, using (1.5),

$$\bar{\xi}_{i.} - \bar{\xi}_{i'.} = (\bar{\xi}_{i.} - \xi) - (\bar{\xi}_{i'.} - \xi) = \eta_i - \eta_{i'}, \quad (2.18)$$

confidence limits for $\bar{\xi}_{i.} - \bar{\xi}_{i'.}$ will be identical with confidence limits for $\eta_i - \eta_{i'}$. Averaging the model (1.17) over j and v gives

$$\bar{x}_{i..} = \xi + \eta_i + \bar{\zeta}_{.} + \bar{\theta}_{i.} + \bar{z}_{i..} = \xi + \eta_i + \bar{z}_{i..}, \quad (2.19)$$

since $\bar{\zeta}_{.} = (1/t)\sum_{j}^{t} \zeta_j = 0$ by (1.7) and $\bar{\theta}_{i.} = (1/t)\sum_{j}^{t} \theta_{ij} = 0$ by (1.15). Hence

$$\bar{x}_{i..} - \bar{x}_{i'..} = (\eta_i - \eta_{i'}) + (\bar{z}_{i..} - \bar{z}_{i'..}), \quad (2.20)$$

with expectation

$$E[\bar{x}_{i..} - \bar{x}_{i'..}] = \eta_i - \eta_{i'} \quad (2.21)$$

and variance

$$V[\bar{x}_{i..} - \bar{x}_{i'..}] = V[\bar{z}_{i..}] + V[\bar{z}_{i'..}] = \frac{2\sigma^2}{tn}. \quad (2.22)$$

We can therefore derive confidence limits for $\eta_i - \eta_{i'}$ from

$$\frac{(\bar{x}_{i..} - \bar{x}_{i'..}) - (\eta_i - \eta_{i'})}{\sqrt{2s_1^2/tn}} \sim t(rt(n-1)). \quad (2.23)$$

Usually, there is little or no point in constructing confidence limits for $\bar{\xi}_{i.} - \bar{\xi}_{i'.}$ unless $\xi_{ij} - \xi_{i'j}$ is constant over j, i.e., unless the difference between the two rows is the same for all columns. From (1.10),

$$\xi_{ij} - \xi_{i'j} = \eta_i - \eta_{i'} + \theta_{ij} - \theta_{i'j}. \quad (2.24)$$

Thus (2.23) will also give confidence limits for $\xi_{ij} - \xi_{i'j}$ if we can assume that the interaction constants θ_{ij} are zero. If we cannot make this assumption, we can obtain confidence limits for $\xi_{ij} - \xi_{i'j}$ as follows. Since

$$\bar{x}_{ij.} - \bar{x}_{i'j.} = \eta_i - \eta_{i'} + \theta_{ij} - \theta_{i'j} + \bar{z}_{ij.} - \bar{z}_{i'j.}. \quad (2.25)$$

has expectation

$$E[\bar{x}_{ij.} - \bar{x}_{i'j.}] = \eta_i - \eta_{i'} + \theta_{ij} - \theta_{i'j} = \xi_{ij} - \xi_{i'j}, \quad (2.26)$$

SECT. 14.3 FORMS FOR TWO-WAY ANALYSIS OF VARIANCE

from (2.24), and variance

$$V[\bar{x}_{ij.} - \bar{x}_{i'j.}] = V[\bar{z}_{ij.}] + V[\bar{z}_{i'j.}] = \frac{2\sigma^2}{n}, \quad (2.27)$$

confidence limits for $(\xi_{ij} - \xi_{i'j})$ can be obtained from

$$\frac{(\bar{x}_{ij.} - \bar{x}_{i'j.}) - (\xi_{ij} - \xi_{i'j})}{\sqrt{2s_1^2/n}} \sim t(rt(n-1)). \quad (2.28)$$

Comparison of the denominator of (2.28) with the denominator of (2.23) shows the advantage gained if the assumption of zero interaction is permissible.

14.3. Computing Forms for Two-Way Analysis of Variance

Table 14.4 gives the per cent reduction in blood sugar a certain time after injection of insulin into rabbits. A group of 24 rabbits was divided at random into six groups of four rabbits each, and each rabbit received an injection of insulin. Two factors were involved, the dose at three levels and the preparation of insulin, A and B, at two levels.

Table 14.4

Preparation	Dose 2.29	Dose 3.63	Dose 5.57	$\sum_j^t \sum_v^n x_{ijv}$
A	17	64	62	
	21	48	72	
	49	34	61	
	54	63	91	
$\sum_v^n x_{1jv}$	141	209	286	636
B	33	41	56	
	37	64	62	
	40	34	57	
	16	64	72	
$\sum_v^n x_{2jv}$	126	203	247	576
$\sum_i^r \sum_v^n x_{ijv}$	267	412	533	1212

While the sums of squares in Table 14.3 can be calculated in the forms given there, it is usually more satisfactory to use identities that involve totals rather than means. We need the following sums of squares:

$$\sum_{i}^{r}\sum_{j}^{t}\sum_{v}^{n} x_{ijv}^{2} = 17^{2} + 21^{2} + \cdots + 72^{2} = 69{,}358, \quad (3.1)$$

$$\frac{1}{n}\sum_{i}^{r}\sum_{j}^{t}\left(\sum_{v}^{n} x_{ijv}\right)^{2} = \frac{141^{2} + \cdots + 247^{2}}{4} = 65{,}863.00, \quad (3.2)$$

$$\frac{1}{nr}\sum_{j}^{t}\left(\sum_{i}^{r}\sum_{v}^{n} x_{ijv}\right)^{2} = \frac{267^{2} + \cdots + 533^{2}}{4 \times 2} = 65{,}640.25, \quad (3.3)$$

$$\frac{1}{nt}\sum_{i}^{r}\left(\sum_{j}^{t}\sum_{v}^{n} x_{ijv}\right)^{2} = \frac{636^{2} + 576^{2}}{4 \times 3} = 61{,}356.00, \quad (3.4)$$

$$\frac{1}{nrt}\left(\sum_{i}^{r}\sum_{j}^{t}\sum_{v}^{n} x_{ijv}\right)^{2} = \frac{1212^{2}}{4 \times 2 \times 3} = 61{,}206.00. \quad (3.5)$$

By manipulations similar to those of (10.2.31) we get for the total sum of squares

$$\sum_{i}^{r}\sum_{j}^{t}\sum_{v}^{n}(x_{ijv} - \bar{x}_{...})^{2} = \sum_{i}^{r}\sum_{j}^{t}\sum_{v}^{n} x_{ijv}^{2} - \frac{1}{nrt}\left(\sum_{i}^{r}\sum_{j}^{t}\sum_{v}^{n} x_{ijv}\right)^{2} \quad (3.6)$$

$$= 69{,}358.00 - 61{,}206.00 = 8152.00.$$

The within-cells of squares is

$$\sum_{i}^{r}\sum_{j}^{t}\sum_{v}^{n}(x_{ijv} - \bar{x}_{ij.})^{2} = \sum_{i}^{r}\sum_{j}^{t}\sum_{v}^{n} x_{ijv}^{2} - \frac{1}{n}\sum_{i}^{r}\sum_{j}^{t}\left(\sum_{v}^{n} x_{ijv}\right)^{2} \quad (3.7)$$

$$= 69{,}358.00 - 65{,}863.00 = 3495.00.$$

The rows sums of squares is

$$nt\sum_{i}^{r}(\bar{x}_{i..} - \bar{x}_{...})^{2} = \frac{1}{tn}\sum_{i}^{r}\left(\sum_{j}^{t}\sum_{v}^{n} x_{ijv}\right)^{2} - \frac{1}{rtn}\left(\sum_{i}^{r}\sum_{j}^{t}\sum_{v}^{n} x_{ijv}\right)^{2} \quad (3.8)$$

$$= 61{,}356.00 - 61{,}206.00 = 150.00$$

Similarly, the columns sum of squares is

$$nr\sum_{j}^{t}(\bar{x}_{.j.} - \bar{x}_{...})^{2} = \frac{1}{rn}\sum_{j}^{t}\left(\sum_{i}^{r}\sum_{v}^{n} x_{ijv}\right)^{2} - \frac{1}{rtn}\left(\sum_{i}^{r}\sum_{j}^{t}\sum_{v}^{n} x_{ijv}\right)^{2} \quad (3.9)$$

$$= 65{,}640.25 - 61{,}206.00 = 4434.25$$

SECT. 14.3 FORMS FOR TWO-WAY ANALYSIS OF VARIANCE

A convenient computing form for the interaction sum of squares is (see Exercise 14.5)

$$n \sum_{i}^{r} \sum_{j}^{t} (\bar{x}_{ij.} - \bar{x}_{i..} - \bar{x}_{.j.} + \bar{x}_{...})^2$$

$$= \frac{1}{n} \sum_{i}^{r} \sum_{j}^{t} \left(\sum_{v}^{n} x_{ijv} \right)^2 - \frac{1}{rtn} \left(\sum_{i}^{r} \sum_{j}^{t} \sum_{v}^{n} x_{ijv} \right)^2$$

$$- nt \sum_{i}^{r} (\bar{x}_{i..} - \bar{x}_{...})^2 - nr \sum_{j}^{t} (\bar{x}_{.j.} - \bar{x}_{...})^2 \qquad (3.10)$$

$$= 65{,}863.00 - 61{,}206.00 - 150.00 - 4434.25 = 72.75.$$

It will sometimes be worth while to calculate directly the quantities (1.19), because they are estimates of the θ_{ij} and a pattern in them may tell us something about the nature of the interaction. The cell means $\bar{x}_{ij.}$ are given in Table 14.5a. For $i = 1$, $j = 1$, for example, we have $\bar{x}_{11.} = 141/4 = 35.25$. Also $\bar{x}_{1..} = 636/4 \times 3 = 53.00$, $\bar{x}_{.1.} = 267/4 \times 2 = 33.75$, and $\bar{x}_{...} = 1212/4 \times 2 \times 3 = 50.50$, so

$$\bar{x}_{11.} - \bar{x}_{1..} - \bar{x}_{.1.} - \bar{x}_{...} = 35.25 - 53.00 - 33.75 + 50.50 = -0.625. \qquad (3.11)$$

The quantities $\bar{x}_{ij.} - \bar{x}_{i..} - \bar{x}_{.j.} + \bar{x}_{...}$ are tabulated in Table 14.5b. They have the property of summing to zero in each row and in each column [see (2.8) and (2.9)]. Their sum of squares, multiplied by n, is of course the interaction sum of squares, and this provides an alternative to the identity (3.10):

$$n \sum_{i}^{r} \sum_{j}^{t} (\bar{x}_{ij.} - \bar{x}_{i..} - \bar{x}_{.j.} + \bar{x}_{...})^2$$

$$= 4[(-0.625)^2 + \cdots + (-2.375)^2] = 72.75. \qquad (3.12)$$

Table 14.5

| | (a) $\bar{x}_{ij.}$ | | | (b) $\bar{x}_{ij.} - \bar{x}_{i..} - \bar{x}_{.j.} + \bar{x}_{...}$ | | |
| | j | | | j | | |
i	1	2	3	1	2	3
1	35.25	52.25	71.50	−0.625	−1.750	+2.375
2	31.50	50.75	61.75	+0.625	+1.750	−2.375

These results are assembled in Table 14.6. It is apparent that the null hypothesis that the interaction is zero is acceptable, and hence there is unlikely to be anything of interest in Table 14.5b. The null hypothesis that the difference between preparation is zero is acceptable since we have $F(1, 18) < 1$, but the dose effect, with a variance ratio $2217.125/194.167 = 11.4$ being distributed under the null hypothesis as $F(2, 18)$, is highly significant.

Table 14.6

Source of variance	Sums of squares	Degrees of freedom	Mean squares	$E[\text{M.S.}]$
Rows = preparations	150.00	1	150.000	$\sigma^2 + \dfrac{12}{1}\sum_i \eta_i^2$
Columns = doses	4434.25	2	2217.125	$\sigma^2 + \dfrac{8}{2}\sum_j^t \zeta_j^2$
Interaction	72.75	2	36.375	$\sigma^2 + \dfrac{4}{2}\sum_i^r\sum_j^t \theta_{ij}^2$
Within cells	3495.00	18	194.167	σ^2
Total	8152.00	23		

14.4. Two-Way Analysis of Variance: Model II

In model II two-way analysis of variance we assume that both rows and columns are random effects, sampled from infinite populations. For example, in a large factory with very many identical machines, machines could correspond to rows, columns to a random sample of batches of raw material, and the replicates in the cells are several items made from each batch on each machine. The model is

$$x_{ijv} = \xi + g_i + e_j + y_{ij} + z_{ijv} \tag{4.1}$$

where g_i, e_j, y_{ij} and z_{ijv} are independently sampled from normal populations with zero means and variances ψ_1^2, ψ_2^2, ω^2 and σ^2, respectively. The usual objective of the analysis is to estimate and construct confidence limits for the parameters of the model, namely, the grand mean and the four components of variance.

The analysis of variance involves the same equation (2.2) as in the model I analysis. The computing forms, the degrees of freedom, and the mean squares are all the same as in Table 14.3, and the only differences between the two models lie in the expectations and distributions of the mean squares.

The mean square s_1^2 continues to have the same expected value σ^2 and the same distribution as before.

SECT. 14.4   TWO-WAY ANALYSIS OF VARIANCE: MODEL II

To find the expected value of the interaction mean square s_2^2, we proceed as follows. We form various averages of the model (4.1),

$$\bar{x}_{ij.} = \xi + g_i + e_j + \bar{y}_{ij} + \bar{z}_{ij.}, \tag{4.2}$$
$$\bar{x}_{i..} = \xi + g_i + \bar{e}_. + \bar{y}_{i.} + \bar{z}_{i..}, \tag{4.3}$$
$$\bar{x}_{.j.} = \xi + \bar{g}_. + e_j + \bar{y}_{.j} + \bar{z}_{.j.}, \tag{4.4}$$
$$\bar{x}_{...} = \xi + \bar{g}_. + \bar{e}_. + \bar{y}_{..} + \bar{z}_{...}; \tag{4.5}$$

so we have the identity

$$\bar{x}_{ij.} - \bar{x}_{i..} - \bar{x}_{.j.} + \bar{x}_{...}$$
$$= (\bar{y}_{ij} - \bar{y}_{i.} - \bar{y}_{.j} + \bar{y}_{..}) + (\bar{z}_{ij.} - \bar{z}_{i..} - \bar{z}_{.j.} + \bar{z}_{...}). \tag{4.6}$$

Now

$$\frac{1}{n} E[(r-1)(t-1)s_2^2] = E\left[\sum_i^r \sum_j^t (\bar{x}_{ij.} - \bar{x}_{i..} - \bar{x}_{.j.} + \bar{x}_{...})^2\right]$$

$$= E\left[\sum_i^r \sum_j^t (\bar{y}_{ij} - \bar{y}_{i.} - \bar{y}_{.j} + \bar{y}_{..})^2\right] + E\left[\sum_i^r \sum_j^t (\bar{z}_{ij.} - \bar{z}_{i..} - \bar{z}_{.j.} + \bar{z}_{...})^2\right]$$
$$\tag{4.7}$$

the expectation of the cross product being zero since our model assumes independence of the y's and z's.

Consider the two parts of (4.7) separately. It is straightforward to show that

$$E\left[\sum_i^r \sum_j^t (\bar{z}_{ij.} - \bar{z}_{i..} - \bar{z}_{.j.} + \bar{z}_{...})^2\right]$$
$$= E\left[\sum_i^r \sum_j^t (\bar{z}_{ij.} - \bar{z}_{...})^2\right] - tE\left[\sum_i^r (\bar{z}_{i..} - \bar{z}_{...})^2\right]$$
$$- rE\left[\sum_j^t (\bar{z}_{.j.} - \bar{z}_{...})^2\right]. \tag{4.8}$$

Now $(rt-1)^{-1} \sum_i^r \sum_j^t (\bar{z}_{ij.} - \bar{z}_{...})^2$ is the ordinary sample estimate of the variance of the $\bar{z}_{ij.}$, which is σ^2/n, so

$$E\left[\sum_i^r \sum_j^t (\bar{z}_{ij.} - \bar{z}_{...})^2\right] = \frac{rt-1}{n} \sigma^2. \tag{4.9}$$

Analogously, $(r-1)^{-1} \sum_i^j (\bar{z}_{i..} - \bar{z}_{...})^2$ is the ordinary sample estimate of the variance of the $\bar{z}_{i..}$, which is σ^2/tn, so

$$E\left[\sum_i^r (\bar{z}_{i..} - \bar{z}_{...})^2\right] = \frac{r-1}{tn} \sigma^2. \tag{4.10}$$

Likewise,
$$E\left[\sum_{j}^{t}(\bar{z}_{.j.} - \bar{z}_{...})^2\right] = \frac{t-1}{rn}\sigma^2. \quad (4.11)$$

Thus
$$E\left[\sum_{i}^{r}\sum_{j}^{t}(\bar{z}_{ij.} - \bar{z}_{i..} - \bar{z}_{.j.} + \bar{z}_{...})^2\right]$$
$$= \left(\frac{rt-1}{n} - t\frac{r-1}{tn} - r\frac{t-1}{rn}\right)\sigma^2 = \frac{1}{n}(r-1)(t-1)\sigma^2. \quad (4.12)$$

The consideration of $E\left[\sum_{i}^{r}\sum_{j}^{t}(y_{ij} - \bar{y}_{i.} - \bar{y}_{.j} + \bar{y}_{..})^2\right]$, the other part of (4.7), will follow the analogous course, the only difference being that terms of the type $V[y_{ij}] = \omega^2$, $V[\bar{y}_{.j}] = \omega^2/r$, etc., involve ω^2 and not σ^2, and omit the factor $1/n$. We can thus assert

$$E\left[\sum_{i}^{r}\sum_{j}^{t}(y_{ij} - \bar{y}_{i.} - \bar{y}_{.j} + \bar{y}_{..})^2\right] = \omega^2(r-1)(t-1). \quad (4.13)$$

Substituting (4.12) and (4.13) in (4.7) gives

$$E\left[\sum_{i}^{r}\sum_{j}^{t}(\bar{x}_{ij.} - \bar{x}_{i..} - \bar{x}_{.j.} + \bar{x}_{...})^2\right]$$
$$= \frac{1}{n}(r-1)(t-1)\sigma^2 + (r-1)(t-1)\omega^2, \quad (4.14)$$

whence, multiplying by $n/(r-1)(t-1)$,

$$E[s_2^2] = \sigma^2 + n\omega^2. \quad (4.15)$$

Now consider $E[s_4^2]$. We have from (4.3) and (4.5) that
$$\bar{x}_{i..} - \bar{x}_{...} = (g_i - \bar{g}_.) + (\bar{y}_{i.} - \bar{y}_{..}) + (\bar{z}_{i..} - \bar{z}_{...}), \quad (4.16)$$

so
$$E\left[\sum_{i}^{r}(\bar{x}_{i..} - \bar{x}_{...})^2\right] = E\left[\sum_{i}^{r}(g_i - \bar{g}_.)^2\right]$$
$$+ E\left[\sum_{i}^{r}(\bar{y}_{i.} - \bar{y}_{..})^2\right] + E\left[\sum_{i}^{r}(\bar{z}_{i..} - \bar{z}_{...})^2\right], \quad (4.17)$$

the expectations of the cross products being zero since our model assumes independence of the g's, y's and z's. In (4.10) we have evaluated the last term, and the first two are analogously

$$E\left[\sum_{i}^{r}(g_i - \bar{g}_.)^2\right] = (r-1)\psi_1^2, \quad (4.18)$$

$$E\left[\sum_{i}^{r}(\bar{y}_{i.} - \bar{y}_{..})^2\right] = (r-1)\frac{\omega^2}{t}. \quad (4.19)$$

SECT. 14.5   THE INTERPRETATION OF A MODEL II ANALYSIS

Substituting in (4.17) and multiplying by $tn/(r-1)$ gives

$$E[s_4^2] = \sigma^2 + n\omega^2 + tn\psi_1^2. \tag{4.20}$$

Similarly,

$$E[s_3^2] = \sigma^2 + n\omega^2 + rn\psi_2^2. \tag{4.21}$$

These results are assembled in Table 14.7.

Table 14.7

Source of variance	Sums of squares	Degrees of freedom	Mean squares	E[M. S.]
Rows	$nt \sum_{i}^{r}(\bar{x}_{i..} - \bar{x}_{...})^2$	$r-1$	s_4^2	$\sigma^2 + n\omega^2 + tn\psi_1^2$
Columns	$nr \sum_{j}^{t}(\bar{x}_{.j.} - \bar{x}_{...})^2$	$t-1$	s_3^2	$\sigma^2 + n\omega^2 + rn\psi_2^2$
Interaction	$n \sum_{i}^{r}\sum_{j}^{t}(\bar{x}_{ij.} - \bar{x}_{i..} - \bar{x}_{.j.} + \bar{x}_{...})^2$	$(r-1)(t-1)$	s_2^2	$\sigma^2 + n\omega^2$
Within cells	$\sum_{i}^{r}\sum_{j}^{t}\sum_{\nu}^{n}(x_{ij\nu} - \bar{x}_{ij.})^2$	$rt(n-1)$	s_1^2	σ^2
Total	$\sum_{i}^{r}\sum_{j}^{t}\sum_{\nu}^{n}(x_{ij\nu} - \bar{x}_{...})^2$	$rtn-1$		

14.5. The Interpretation of a Model II Analysis

The tests of significance for the null hypotheses $\omega^2 = 0$, $\psi_1^2 = 0$, $\psi_2^2 = 0$ are obvious from the column of expected mean squares in Table 14.7. Whereas, in the model I analysis (Table 14.3), the main effects for rows and columns were tested against the within-cells mean square, here they are tested against the interaction mean square.

The parameters of the model are estimated in the obvious ways:

$$\hat{\xi} = \bar{x}_{...}, \quad \hat{\sigma}^2 = s_1^2, \quad \hat{\omega}^2 = \frac{s_2^2 - s_1^2}{n}, \quad \hat{\psi}_1^2 = \frac{s_4^2 - s_2^2}{tn}, \quad \hat{\psi}_2^2 = \frac{s_3^2 - s_2^2}{rn}. \tag{5.1}$$

Exact confidence limits for σ^2 and for ω^2/σ^2, and approximate confidence limits for ω^2, ψ_1^2 and ψ_2^2 can be obtained as in Section 10.5. For confidence limits for ξ, from (4.5) $E[\bar{x}_{...}] = \xi$, and

$$V[\bar{x}_{...}] = \frac{\psi_1^2}{r} + \frac{\psi_2^2}{t} + \frac{\omega^2}{rt} + \frac{\sigma^2}{rtn} = \frac{\sigma^2 + n\omega^2 + nt\psi_1^2 + nr\psi_2^2}{rtn}. \tag{5.2}$$

To obtain a mean square with expected value equal to the numerator in (5.2) we use the linear combination $s_4^2 + s_3^2 - s_2^2$, since it has expected value

$$E[s_4^2 + s_3^2 - s_2^2] = \sigma^2 + n\omega^2 + nt\psi_1^2 + nr\psi_2^2. \quad (5.3)$$

Thus

$$\frac{\bar{x}_{...} - \xi}{\sqrt{(s_4^2 + s_3^2 - s_2^2)/rtn}} \underset{\text{approx}}{\sim} t(f'), \quad (5.4)$$

where f' is given by application of (9.8.10). Confidence limits for ξ can be derived in the usual way, but these will be approximate on account of the approximation in (5.4).

14.6. Two-Way Analysis of Variance with Only One Observation per Cell

Sometimes we have data in a two-way classification with only one observation per cell. The analysis is similar to that with n observations per cell, but, with $n = 1$ the model becomes, in the model I case,

$$x_{ij} = \xi + \eta_i + \zeta_j + \theta_{ij} + z_{ij} \quad (6.1)$$

and in the model II case

$$x_{ij} = \xi + g_i + e_j + y_{ij} + z_{ij}. \quad (6.2)$$

In the table of analysis of variance there is no item "within cells," and the analysis is as in Table 14.8. The expectations of the mean squares for the two models are given in Table 14.9. In both models there is no test for interaction. In the model II analysis, the tests for the main effects of rows and columns are unchanged. In the model I analysis, the test for the row and column main effects may, if there is appreciable interaction so that $\sum_i^r \sum_j^t \theta_{ij}^2 \neq 0$, be inefficient, since the denominator mean square will be inflated by the extra component. On the other hand, if either variance ratio is significant, then it may be taken that the corresponding effect is real.

14.7. Nested or Hierarchical Analysis of Variance

In our discussion of one-way model II analysis of variance in Section 10.4 we postulated a sampling situation in which sacks of wool were taken from a large consignment, and then samples were taken from each sack at random. If we now suppose that several analyses are performed on each sample, an appropriate model would be

$$x_{ijv} = \xi + v_i + y_{ij} + z_{ijv} \quad (7.1)$$

SECT. 14.7 NESTED OR HIERARCHICAL ANALYSIS OF VARIANCE

Table 14.8

Source of variance	Sums of squares	Degrees of freedom	Mean squares
Rows	$t \sum_{i}^{r} (\bar{x}_{i.} - \bar{x}..)^2$	$r - 1$	s_4^2
	$= \frac{1}{t} \sum_{i}^{r} \left(\sum_{j}^{t} x_{ij} \right)^2 - \frac{1}{rt} \left(\sum_{i}^{r} \sum_{j}^{t} x_{ij} \right)^2$		
Columns	$r \sum_{j}^{t} (\bar{x}_{.j} - \bar{x}..)^2$	$t - 1$	s_3^2
	$= \frac{1}{r} \sum_{j}^{t} \left(\sum_{i}^{r} x_{ij} \right)^2 - \frac{1}{rt} \left(\sum_{i}^{r} \sum_{j}^{t} x_{ij} \right)^2$		
Remainder	(by difference)	$(r-1)(t-1)$	s_2^2
Total	$\sum_{i}^{r} \sum_{j}^{t} (x_{ij} - \bar{x}..)^2$	$rt - 1$	
	$= \sum_{i}^{r} \sum_{j}^{t} x_{ij}^2 - \frac{1}{rt} \left(\sum_{i}^{r} \sum_{j}^{t} x_{ij} \right)^2$		

where ξ is the grand mean, v_i corresponds to the sack effect, y_{ij} to the sample within sack effect, and z_{ijv} to analyses within samples. The random variables v_i, y_{ij}, and z_{ijv} are independently normally distributed with zero means and variances ψ^2, ω^2, and σ^2. Suppose there are r sacks, t samples per sack, and n analyses per sample.

Squaring and summing the identity

$$x_{ijv} - \bar{x}... = (\bar{x}_{i..} - \bar{x}...) + (\bar{x}_{ij.} - \bar{x}_{i..}) + (x_{ijv} - \bar{x}_{ij.}) \qquad (7.2)$$

Table 14.9

Source of variance	Mean squares	E[M.S.] Model 1	E[M.S.] Model II
Rows	s_4^2	$\sigma^2 + \frac{t}{r-1} \sum_{i}^{} \eta_i^2$	$\sigma^2 + \omega^2 + t\psi_1^2$
Columns	s_3^2	$\sigma^2 + \frac{r}{t-1} \sum_{j}^{t} \zeta_j^2$	$\sigma^2 + \omega^2 + r\psi_2^2$
Remainder	s_2^2	$\sigma^2 + \frac{1}{(r-1)(t-1)} \sum_{i}^{r} \sum_{j}^{t} \theta_{ij}^2$	$\sigma^2 + \omega^2$

gives

$$\sum_i^r \sum_j^t \sum_v^n (x_{ijv} - \bar{x}_{...})^2 = nt \sum_i^r (\bar{x}_{i..} - \bar{x}_{...})^2 + n \sum_i^r \sum_j^t (\bar{x}_{ij.} - \bar{x}_{i..})^2$$

$$+ \sum_i^r \sum_j^t \sum_v^n (x_{ijv} - \bar{x}_{ij.})^2. \quad (7.3)$$

These sums of squares are entered in Table 14.10, along with their degrees of freedom. We now determine the expected value of these mean squares, as given in the last column.

Table 14.10

Source of variance	Sums of squares	Degrees of freedom	Mean squares	E[M. S.]
Between sacks	$nt \sum_i^r (\bar{x}_{i..} - \bar{x}_{...})^2$	$r - 1$	s_3^2	$\sigma^2 + n\omega^2 + nt\psi^2$
Between samples within sacks	$n \sum_i^r \sum_j^t (\bar{x}_{ij.} - \bar{x}_{i..})^2$	$r(t - 1)$	s_2^2	$\sigma^2 + n\omega^2$
Between analyses within samples	$\sum_i^r \sum_j^t \sum_v^n (x_{ijv} - \bar{x}_{ij.})^2$	$rt(n - 1)$	s_1^2	σ^2
Total	$\sum_i^r \sum_j^t \sum_v^n (x_{ijv} - \bar{x}_{...})^2$	$rtn - 1$		

Considering s_1^2, averaging the model (7.1) over v gives

$$\bar{x}_{ij.} = \xi + v_i + y_{ij} + \bar{z}_{ij.}; \quad (7.4)$$

so

$$x_{ijv} - \bar{x}_{ij.} = z_{ijv} - \bar{z}_{ij.}. \quad (7.5)$$

Squaring and summing over v gives

$$\sum_v^n (x_{ijv} - \bar{x}_{ij.})^2 = \sum_v^n (z_{ijv} - \bar{z}_{ij.})^2. \quad (7.6)$$

Divided by $n - 1$, this is a sample estimate of the variance of the z_{ijv}, namely, σ^2. Pooling the sums of squares and degrees of freedom through summation over i and j leaves this unchanged; so we obtain

$$E[s_1^2] = E\left[\frac{\sum_i^r \sum_j^t \sum_v^n (x_{ijv} - \bar{x}_{ij.})^2}{rt(n - 1)} \right] = \sigma^2. \quad (7.7)$$

Now consider s_2^2: Averaging (7.4) over j gives

$$\bar{x}_{i..} = \xi + v_i + \bar{y}_{i.} + \bar{z}_{i..}; \quad (7.8)$$

so

$$\bar{x}_{ij.} - \bar{x}_{i..} = (y_{ij} - \bar{y}_{i.}) + (\bar{z}_{ij.} - \bar{z}_{i..}). \quad (7.9)$$

SECT. 14.7 NESTED OR HIERARCHICAL ANALYSIS OF VARIANCE

Squaring and summing over j and then taking expectations gives

$$E\left[\sum_j^t (\bar{x}_{ij.} - \bar{x}_{i..})^2\right] = E\left[\sum_j^t (y_{ij} - \bar{y}_{i.})^2\right] + E\left[\sum_j^t (\bar{z}_{ij.} - \bar{z}_{i..})^2\right], \quad (7.10)$$

the expectation of the cross product vanishing by reason of the independence of the y_{ij} and z_{ijv}. It is apparent that $\sum_j^t (y_{ij} - \bar{y}_{i.})^2/(t-1)$ is a sample estimate of the variance of the y_{ij}, namely, ω^2. Similarly $\sum_j^t (\bar{z}_{ij.} - \bar{z}_{i..})^2/(t-1)$ is a sample estimate of the variance of the $\bar{z}_{ij.}$. Since the z_{ijv} have variance σ^2, the $\bar{z}_{ij.}$ have variance σ^2/n, and so

$$E\left[\frac{\sum_j^t (\bar{x}_{ij.} - \bar{x}_{i..})^2}{t-1}\right] = \omega^2 + \frac{\sigma^2}{n}. \quad (7.11)$$

Pooling the sums of squares and degrees of freedom by summation over i, and multiplying by n, gives

$$E[s_2^2] = E\left[\frac{n \sum_i^r \sum_j^t (\bar{x}_{ij.} - \bar{x}_{...})^2}{r(t-1)}\right] = \sigma^2 + n\omega^2. \quad (7.12)$$

Now consider s_3^2: Averaging (7.8) over i gives

$$\bar{x}_{...} = \xi + \bar{v}_. + \bar{y}_{..} + \bar{z}_{...}; \quad (7.13)$$

so, subtracting this from (7.8) gives

$$\bar{x}_{i..} - \bar{x}_{...} = (v_i - \bar{v}_.) + (\bar{y}_{i.} - \bar{y}_{..}) + (\bar{z}_{i..} - \bar{z}_{...}). \quad (7.14)$$

Squaring and summing over i and then taking expectations gives

$$E\left[\sum_i^r (\bar{x}_{i..} - \bar{x}_{...})^2\right] = E\left[\sum_i^r (v_i - \bar{v}_.)^2\right] + E\left[\sum_i^r (\bar{y}_{i.} - \bar{y}_{..})^2\right]$$

$$+ E\left[\sum_i^r (\bar{z}_{i..} - \bar{z}_{...})^2\right], \quad (7.15)$$

the expectations of the cross products vanishing since our model assumes independence of the v's, y's, and z's. It is apparent that $\sum_i^r (\bar{z}_{i..} - \bar{z}_{...})^2/(r-1)$ is a sample estimate of the variance of the $\bar{z}_{i..}$, namely σ^2/tn.

Table 14.11

x' = quantity $\qquad x = 100(\log x' - 1)$

Batch	Sample	Subsamples		Sample totals	Batch totals	Subsamples		Sample totals	Batch totals
1	1 (1)	76	85	161		88	93	181	
	2 (1)	69	82	151		84	91	175	
	3 (1)	72	78	150		86	89	175	
	4 (1)	75	84	159	621	88	92	180	711
2	1 (2)	110	109	219		104	104	208	
	2 (2)	119	106	225		108	103	211	
	3 (2)	120	121	241		108	108	216	
	4 (2)	111	119	230	915	105	108	213	848
3	1 (3)	130	140	270		111	115	226	
	2 (3)	143	121	264		116	108	224	
	3 (3)	141	147	288		115	117	232	
	4 (3)	129	140	269	1091	111	115	226	908
4	1 (4)	62	67	129		79	83	162	
	2 (4)	50	61	111		70	79	149	
	3 (4)	71	74	145		85	87	172	
	4 (4)	66	67	133	518	82	83	165	648
5	1 (5)	62	64	126		79	81	160	
	2 (5)	48	50	98		68	70	138	
	3 (5)	80	86	166		90	93	183	
	4 (5)	87	91	178	568	94	96	190	671
6	1 (6)	91	97	188		96	99	195	
	2 (6)	87	90	177		94	95	189	
	3 (6)	78	74	152		89	87	176	
	4 (6)	87	83	170	687	94	92	186	746
7	1 (7)	101	97	198		100	99	199	
	2 (7)	89	96	185		95	98	193	
	3 (7)	78	96	174		89	98	187	
	4 (7)	76	87	163	720	88	94	182	761
8	1 (8)	136	123	259		113	109	222	
	2 (8)	108	131	239		103	112	215	
	3 (8)	128	119	247		111	108	219	
	4 (8)	96	82	178	923	98	91	189	845
9	1 (9)	140	136	276		115	113	228	
	2 (9)	92	80	172		96	90	186	
	3 (9)	107	114	221		103	106	209	
	4 (9)	84	113	197	866	92	105	197	820
10	1(10)	81	99	180		91	100	191	
	2(10)	86	83	169		93	92	185	
	3(10)	103	94	197		101	97	198	
	4(10)	85	87	172	718	93	94	187	761
11	1(11)	108	98	206		103	99	202	
	2(11)	102	102	204		101	101	202	
	3(11)	102	103	205		101	101	202	
	4(11)	109	111	220	835	104	105	209	815
12	1(12)	106	107	213		103	103	206	
	2(12)	100	104	204		100	102	202	
	3(12)	99	98	197		100	99	199	
	4(12)	102	91	193	807	101	96	197	804
13	1(13)	93	89	182		97	95	192	
	2(13)	85	89	174		93	95	188	
	3(13)	78	80	158		89	90	179	
	4(13)	89	87	176	690	95	94	189	748
14	1(14)	116	117	233		106	107	213	
	2(14)	104	116	220		102	106	208	
	3(14)	118	119	237		107	108	215	
	4(14)	112	109	221	911	105	104	209	845

SECT. 14.7 NESTED OR HIERARCHICAL ANALYSIS OF VARIANCE 487

Likewise $\sum_{i}^{r} (\bar{y}_{i.} - \bar{y}_{..})^2/(r-1)$ is a sample estimate of the variance of the $\bar{y}_{i.}$, namely ω^2/t, and $\sum_{i}^{r}(v_i - \bar{v}_.)^2/(r-1)$ is a sample estimate of the variance of the v's, namely ψ^2. Thus multiplying (7.15) by $tn/(r-1)$, we get

$$E[s_3^2] = E\left[\frac{nt\sum_{i}^{r}(\bar{x}_{i..} - \bar{x}_{...})^2}{r-1}\right] = \sigma^2 + n\omega^2 + nt\psi^2. \quad (7.16)$$

Equations (7.7), (7.12), and (7.16) are entered in the last column of Table 14.10.

The data of Table 14.11 give the results of taking four samples from each of 14 batches of a slurry. The quantity of matter in suspension in each sample x' was determined in duplicate by dividing each sample into two subsamples. The model for the analysis will be (7.1).

The range w_{ij} between the duplicates x'_{ijv} and $x'_{ijv'}$ can be used as an estimate of the standard deviation σ, since $\hat{\sigma}_{ij} = w_{ij}/d_2$; see (6.6.2). If we tabulate the ranges according as the batch total is in the intervals (500 − 599), (600 − 699), etc., we get mean ranges of 4.25, 5.50, 7.75, 6.83, 8.25 and 12.25. It appears that the standard deviation σ is increasing approximately linearly with the mean. The model (7.1) makes the assumption that the z_{ijv} are distributed normally with a constant variance σ^2. However, we saw in Section 3.3 that, when the variance is proportional to the square of the mean, the logarithm of the variable will have a constant variance. The analysis will therefore be performed on $x = 100[(\log x') - 1]$, this transformation producing numbers easy to handle.

Computing forms for the sums of squares in Table 14.10 are easily obtained. Defining

$$A = \sum_{i}^{r}\sum_{j}^{t}\sum_{v}^{n} x_{ijv}^2 = 88^2 + 93^2 + \cdots + 104^2 = 1{,}078{,}281, \quad (7.17)$$

$$B = \frac{1}{n}\sum_{i}^{r}\sum_{j}^{t}\left(\sum_{v}^{n} x_{ijv}\right)^2 = \frac{181^2 + \cdots + 209^2}{2} = 1{,}077{,}756.5, \quad (7.18)$$

$$C = \frac{1}{tn}\sum_{i}^{r}\left(\sum_{j}^{t}\sum_{v}^{n} x_{ijv}\right)^2 = \frac{711^2 + \cdots + 845^2}{4 \times 2} = 1{,}075{,}573.375, \quad (7.19)$$

$$D = \frac{1}{rtn}\left(\sum_{i}^{r}\sum_{j}^{t}\sum_{v}^{n} x_{ijv}\right)^2 = \frac{(10{,}931)^2}{14 \times 4 \times 2} = 1{,}066{,}846.080, \quad (7.20)$$

straightforward manipulation yields

$$nt \sum_{i}^{r} (\bar{x}_{i..} - \bar{x}_{...})^2 = C - D = 8727.295, \quad (7.21)$$

$$n \sum_{i}^{r} \sum_{j}^{t} (\bar{x}_{ij.} - \bar{x}_{i..})^2 = B - C = 2183.125, \quad (7.22)$$

$$\sum_{i}^{r} \sum_{j}^{t} \sum_{v}^{n} (x_{ijv} - \bar{x}_{ij.})^2 = A - B = 524.500, \quad (7.23)$$

$$\sum_{i}^{r} \sum_{j}^{t} \sum_{v}^{n} (x_{ijv} - \bar{x}_{...})^2 = A - D = 11{,}434.920. \quad (7.24)$$

The analysis of variance is in Table 14.12. The test of the null hypothesis $\omega^2 = 0$ is given by the variance ratio $51.979/9.366 = 5.55$: $F_{0.9995}(30, 50) = 2.86$; so clearly this null hypothesis is rejected. The test of the null hypothesis $\psi^2 = 0$ is given by the variance ratio $671.330/51.979 = 12.9$: $F_{0.9995}(10, 40) = 4.21$, so this null hypothesis is rejected. The point

Table 14.12

Source of variance	Sums of squares	Degrees of freedom	Mean squares	E[M. S.]
Between batches	8,727.295	13	671.330	$\sigma^2 + 2\omega^2 + 8\psi^2$
Between samples within batches	2,183.125	42	51.979	$\sigma^2 + 2\omega^2$
Between subsamples within samples	524.500	56	9.366	σ^2
Total	11,434.920	111		

estimates of the components of variance are

$$\hat{\sigma}^2 = 9.366, \quad \hat{\omega}^2 = \frac{51.979 - 9.366}{2} = 21.3, \quad \hat{\psi}^2 = \frac{671.330 - 51.979}{4 \times 2} = 77.4. \quad (7.25)$$

It is apparent that there is considerable variation between samples within a batch. The largest component of variance, however, is between batches. For estimating the mean of a batch, the estimated variance of one subsample from one sample would be $\hat{\sigma}^2 + \hat{\omega}^2 = 9.4 + 21.3 = 30.7$. The estimated variance of two subsamples from one sample would be $\hat{\sigma}^2/2 + \hat{\omega}^2 = 9.4/2 + 21.3 = 26.0$; so there is very little gain in the precision of the estimation of a batch mean through analyzing two subsamples instead of one. It might, nevertheless, be justifiable to analyze two subsamples as a check against gross errors and mistakes.

SECT. 14.8   THE TWO-WAY CROSSED FINITE POPULATION MODEL   489

Confidence limits for the overall mean of the process, averaged over batches, can be constructed as follows. The variance of (7.13) is

$$V[\bar{x}_{...}] = V[\bar{v}_.] + V[\bar{y}_{..}] + V[\bar{z}_{...}] = \frac{\psi^2}{r} + \frac{\omega^2}{rt} + \frac{\sigma^2}{rtn} = \frac{\sigma^2 + n\omega^2 + nt\psi^2}{rtn}, \quad (7.26)$$

and

$$\hat{V}[\bar{x}_{...}] = \frac{s_3^2}{rtn} = \frac{671.330}{14 \times 4 \times 2} = 5.994. \quad (7.27)$$

Since

$$\frac{\bar{x}_{...} - \xi}{\sqrt{\hat{V}[\bar{x}_{...}]}} \sim t(r-1), \quad (7.28)$$

we find 95 per cent confidence limits for ξ to be (92.3, 102.9). These are on our transformed scale. Transforming back, the 95 per cent confidence limits for the process average on the original scale are approximately (83.3, 106.9).

14.8. The Two-Way Crossed Finite Population Model

The model II analysis of Section 14.4 postulated random sampling from infinite populations. Random sampling from finite populations was first considered by Tukey [1], Cornfield and Tukey [2], and Bennett and Franklin [3]. This finite population model is of interest in itself, for sometimes the assumption that a population, e.g., of machines, is infinite is too gross. This model is also of interest because, if we let the population sizes go to infinity, with the additional assumption of normality, then we get model II, and, if we decrease the population size until it equals the sample size, so that the sample contains the entire population, then we get model I. Our main motivation for considering the finite population model, however, is that it will give us a procedure for handling the mixed model, in which one category, say rows, is model I and the other, columns, is model II. Such mixed models occur frequently in practice.

The arguments to follow only involve the ideas of expectation and of combinations but they are somewhat lengthy and involved, and some readers may be content to read only through (8.6) and then proceed to Section 14.9.

For a two-way crossed classification with replication in the cells the model is

$$x_{ijv} = \xi + \eta_i + \zeta_j + \theta_{ij} + z_{ijv}, \quad (8.1)$$

similar to (1.17), with $i = 1, \ldots, r$; $j = 1, \ldots, t$; $v = 1, \ldots, n$. However, here the η_i and ζ_j, referring to rows and columns, respectively, are random samples from populations of sizes R and T and satisfy the conditions

$$\sum_i^R \eta_i = 0 = \sum_j^T \zeta_j. \qquad (8.2)$$

Selecting a particular i and a particular j determines the row and column and hence the cell that forms their intersection, and with this cell is associated the interaction constant θ_{ij}. The interaction constants satisfy the conditions

$$\sum_i^R \theta_{ij} = 0 \text{ for each } j, \quad \sum_j^T \theta_{ij} = 0 \text{ for each } i. \qquad (8.3)$$

We make the following definitions:

$$\sigma_\eta^2 = \frac{1}{R-1} \sum_i^R \eta_i^2, \qquad (8.4)$$

$$\sigma_\zeta^2 = \frac{1}{T-1} \sum_j^T \zeta_j^2, \qquad (8.5)$$

$$\sigma_\theta^2 = \frac{1}{(R-1)(T-1)} \sum_i^R \sum_j^T \theta_{ij}^2. \qquad (8.6)$$

These definitions are not consistent with (7.4.2) which would give, e.g., $\sigma_\eta^2 = (1/R) \sum_i^R \eta_i^2$, but they are more convenient in the present instance.

The conventional partitioning of the total sum of squares is identical with that of Table 14.3. We will now evaluate the expectations of the corresponding mean squares under this different model. We will first need the expected values of the squares of certain sums of the z_{ij}, θ_{ij}, ζ_j, and η_i.

The z_{ijv} have zero expectation and are independent and hence have zero covariances, and so

$$V[z_{ijv}] = \sigma^2 = E[z_{ijv}^2].$$

Therefore

$$E\left[\sum_i^r \sum_j^t \sum_v^n z_{ijv}^2\right] = \sum_i^r \sum_j^t \sum_v^n E[z_{ijv}^2] = rtn\sigma^2. \qquad (8.7)$$

Also

$$V\left[\sum_v^n z_{ijv}\right] = E\left[\left(\sum_v^n z_{ijv}\right)^2\right].$$

But the variance of the sum of n independent observations each with variance σ^2 is $n\sigma^2$, and so

$$E\left[\sum_i^r \sum_j^t \left(\sum_v^n z_{ijv}\right)^2\right] = \sum_i^r \sum_j^t E\left[\left(\sum_v^n z_{ijv}\right)^2\right] = \sum_i^r \sum_j^t n\sigma^2 = rtn\sigma^2. \qquad (8.8)$$

SECT. 14.8 THE TWO-WAY CROSSED FINITE POPULATION MODEL

Similarly,

$$E\left[\sum_i^r\left(\sum_j^t\sum_v^n z_{ijv}\right)^2\right] = E\left[\sum_j^t\left(\sum_i^r\sum_v^n z_{ijv}\right)^2\right] = E\left[\left(\sum_i^r\sum_j^t\sum_v^n z_{ijv}\right)^2\right] = rtn\sigma^2. \tag{8.9}$$

We next find $E\left[\sum_i^r \eta_i^2\right]$. The total number of ways a sample of r can be taken from R is $\binom{R}{r}$, and these are all assumed equally likely. Thus

$$E\left[\sum_i^r \eta_i^2\right] = \binom{R}{r}^{-1}[(\eta_1^2 + \cdots + \eta_r^2) + \cdots + (\eta_{R-r+1}^2 + \cdots + \eta_R^2)]. \tag{8.10}$$

Any particular η_i will occur in $\binom{R-1}{r-1}$ samples and hence appear in the square brackets this number of times as η_i^2. Therefore, using (8.4),

$$E\left[\sum_i^r \eta_i^2\right] = \binom{R}{r}^{-1}\binom{R-1}{r-1}\sum_i^R \eta_i^2 = r\left(1 - \frac{1}{R}\right)\sigma_\eta^2. \tag{8.11}$$

We next find $E\left[\left(\sum_i^r \eta_i\right)^2\right]$. By similar arguments,

$$E\left[\left(\sum_i^r \eta_i\right)^2\right] = \binom{R}{r}^{-1}[(\eta_1 + \cdots + \eta_r)^2 + \cdots + (\eta_{R-r+1} + \cdots + \eta_R)^2]$$

$$= \binom{R}{r}^{-1}\left[\binom{R-1}{r-1}\sum_i^R \eta_i^2 + \binom{R-2}{r-2}\sum_{\substack{i\ j\\i\ne j}}^{R\ R}\eta_i\eta_j\right]. \tag{8.12}$$

Now

$$\left(\sum_i^R \eta_i\right)^2 = \sum_i^R \eta_i^2 + \sum_{\substack{i\ j\\i\ne j}}^{R\ R}\eta_i\eta_j \tag{8.13}$$

and by (8.2) the left hand is zero. Hence, substituting in (8.12),

$$E\left[\left(\sum_i^r \eta_i\right)^2\right] = \binom{R}{r}^{-1}\left[\binom{R-1}{r-1} - \binom{R-2}{r-2}\right]\sum_i^R \eta_i^2 = r\left(1 - \frac{r}{R}\right)\sigma_\eta^2. \tag{8.14}$$

Expressions for ζ_j similar to (8.11) and (8.14) are obtained by the same arguments.

We now find $E\left[\left(\sum_i^r\sum_j^t \theta_{ij}\right)^2\right]$. Specifying a particular row, say the pth, and a particular column, say the qth, determines a particular cell, and associated with this cell is the constant θ_{pq}. The total number of ways we can choose r rows out of a possible R, and t columns out of a possible T, is $\binom{R}{r}\binom{T}{t}$. However, if we specify that the sample of r rows is to include the pth row, and the sample of t columns is to include the qth column, the number of ways in which we can select the remaining $r-1$ rows and $t-1$ columns is $\binom{R-1}{r-1}\binom{T-1}{t-1}$. Thus, in the summation of all possible $\left(\sum_i^r \sum_j^t \theta_{ij}\right)^2$, the coefficient of the direct square of each element θ_{ij} is $\binom{R-1}{r-1}\binom{T-1}{t-1}$.

The cross products in $\left(\sum_i^r \sum_j^t \theta_{ij}\right)^2$ are of three types:

1. Those with both θ's in the same row but different columns, $2\theta_{pq}\theta_{pu}$, $q \neq u$.
2. Those with both θ's in the same column but different rows, $2\theta_{pq}\theta_{sq}$, $p \neq s$.
3. Those with the two θ's differing both in row and in column number, $2\theta_{pq}\theta_{su}$, $p \neq s$, $q \neq u$.

In how many of the possible $\left(\sum_i^r \sum_j^t \theta_{ij}\right)^2$ does a particular cross product of the first type, $2\theta_{pq}\theta_{pu}$, occur? A sample of the θ_{ij} will arise from a choice of r rows and t columns. Suppose that it contains a specified row, say the pth, and two specified columns, say the qth and the uth. Then the remaining $r-1$ rows can be selected from the $R-1$ available in $\binom{R-1}{r-1}$ ways, and the remaining $t-2$ columns from the $T-2$ available in $\binom{T-2}{t-2}$ ways. Thus a specified $2\theta_{pq}\theta_{pu}$ occurs $\binom{R-1}{r-1}\binom{T-2}{t-2}$ times when we consider all possible $\left(\sum_i^r \sum_j^t \theta_{ij}\right)^2$.

From (8.3) we can write

$$0 = \sum_j^T \theta_{pj} = \theta_{pq} + \sum_{j \neq q}^T \theta_{pj}; \tag{8.15}$$

so

$$-\theta_{pq}^2 = \theta_{pq}\sum_{j \neq q}^T \theta_{pj} = \theta_{pq}(\theta_{p1} + \cdots + \theta_{p(q-1)} + \theta_{p(q+1)} + \cdots + \theta_{pT}). \tag{8.16}$$

We now write down the $2\theta_{pq}\theta_{pu}$, $q \neq u$, for a fixed p:

$$\theta_{p1}(\theta_{p2} + \cdots + \theta_{pT}) + \theta_{p2}(\theta_{p1} + \theta_{p3} + \cdots + \theta_{pT}) + \cdots$$
$$+ \theta_{pq}(\theta_{p1} + \cdots + \theta_{p(q-1)} + \theta_{p(q+1)} + \cdots + \theta_{pT}) + \cdots$$
$$+ \theta_{pT}(\theta_{p1} + \cdots + \theta_{p(T-1)}). \tag{8.17}$$

SECT. 14.8   THE TWO-WAY CROSSED FINITE POPULATION MODEL

From (8.16) each term in (8.17) is equal to $-\theta_{pj}^2, j = 1, \ldots, T$, and so the sum of all terms in (8.17) is $-\sum_{j}^{T} \theta_{pj}^2$. Therefore the sum of all possible $2\theta_{pq}\theta_{pu}$, $q \neq u$, summed over all p, is $-\sum_{i}^{R}\sum_{j}^{T} \theta_{ij}^2$. But we saw above that each $2\theta_{pq}\theta_{pu}$ occurs $\binom{R-1}{r-1}\binom{T-2}{t-2}$ times in all possible $\left(\sum_{i}^{r}\sum_{j}^{t} \theta_{ij}\right)^2$, and so the sum of the $2\theta_{pq}\theta_{pu}$ over all possible $\left(\sum_{i}^{r}\sum_{j}^{t} \theta_{ij}\right)^2$ is

$$-\binom{R-1}{r-1}\binom{T-2}{t-2}\sum_{i}^{R}\sum_{j}^{T} \theta_{ij}^2. \tag{8.18}$$

For cross products of the second type, formed by θ's in the same column, the corresponding sum is

$$-\binom{R-2}{r-2}\binom{T-1}{t-1}\sum_{i}^{R}\sum_{j}^{T} \theta_{ij}^2. \tag{8.19}$$

With cross products of the third type, with θ's differing in both row and column number, a specified $2\theta_{pq}\theta_{su}$ will occur in $\binom{R-2}{r-2}\binom{T-2}{t-2}$ possible samples, since with two rows fixed the remaining $r-2$ can be selected from the $R-2$ available in $\binom{R-2}{r-2}$ ways, analogously for columns.

The sum of all possible cross products of the third type containing θ_{pq} is

$$\theta_{pq} \sum_{\substack{s \neq p}}^{R} \sum_{\substack{u \neq q}}^{T} \theta_{su}$$

$$= \theta_{pq}(\theta_{11} + \cdots + \theta_{1(q-1)} + \theta_{1(q+1)} + \cdots + \theta_{1T}$$
$$+ \theta_{21} + \cdots + \theta_{2(q-1)} + \theta_{2(q+1)} + \cdots + \theta_{2T}$$
$$\vdots$$
$$+ \theta_{(p-1)1} + \cdots + \theta_{(p-1)(q-1)} + \theta_{(p-1)(q+1)} + \cdots + \theta_{(p-1)T}$$
$$+ \theta_{(p+1)1} + \cdots + \theta_{(p+1)(q-1)} + \theta_{(p+1)(q+1)} + \cdots + \theta_{(p+1)T}$$
$$\vdots$$
$$+ \theta_{R1} + \cdots + \theta_{R(q-1)} + \theta_{R(q+1)} + \cdots + \theta_{RT})$$

$$= \theta_{pq}\left(\sum_{j \neq q}^{T} \theta_{1j} + \cdots + \sum_{j \neq q}^{T} \theta_{(p-1)j} + \sum_{j \neq q}^{T} \theta_{(p+1)j} + \cdots + \sum_{j \neq q}^{T} \theta_{Rj}\right)$$

$$= \theta_{pq}(-\theta_{1q} - \cdots - \theta_{(p-1)q} - \theta_{(p+1)q} - \cdots - \theta_{Rq})$$

$$= \theta_{pq}\left(-\sum_{i \neq p}^{R} \theta_{iq}\right) = \theta_{pq}^2. \tag{8.20}$$

This was for a specified pq. Therefore the sum of all possible cross products of the third type is

$$\sum_i^R \sum_j^T \theta_{ij}^2, \qquad (8.21)$$

and the sum of all possible cross products of the third type in all possible $\left(\sum_i^r \sum_j^t \theta_{ij}\right)$ is

$$\binom{R-2}{r-2}\binom{T-2}{t-2}\sum_i^R \sum_j^T \theta_{ij}^2. \qquad (8.22)$$

Hence the sum of all possible $\left(\sum_i^r \sum_j^t \theta_{ij}\right)^2$ is given by summing the pure squared terms and the three types of cross product:

$$\left[\binom{R-1}{r-1}\binom{T-1}{t-1} - \binom{R-1}{r-1}\binom{T-2}{t-2}\right.$$

$$\left. - \binom{R-2}{r-2}\binom{T-1}{t-1} + \binom{R-2}{r-2}\binom{T-2}{t-2}\right]\sum_i^R \sum_j^T \theta_{ij}^2$$

$$= \binom{R-1}{r-1}\binom{T-1}{t-1}\frac{(R-r)(T-t)}{(R-1)(T-1)}\sum_i^R \sum_j^T \theta_{ij}^2. \qquad (8.23)$$

Dividing by the number of possible samples $\binom{R}{r}\binom{T}{t}$, and substituting σ_θ^2 from (8.6), we get

$$E\left[\left(\sum_i^r \sum_j^t \theta_{ij}\right)^2\right] = rt\left(1 - \frac{r}{R}\right)\left(1 - \frac{t}{T}\right)\sigma_\theta^2. \qquad (8.24)$$

When we put $t = 1$ and $r = 1$ separately and then jointly, we get

$$E\left[\left(\sum_i^r \theta_{ij}\right)^2\right] = r\left(1 - \frac{r}{R}\right)\left(1 - \frac{1}{T}\right)\sigma_\theta^2, \qquad (8.25)$$

$$E\left[\left(\sum_j^t \theta_{ij}\right)^2\right] = t\left(1 - \frac{1}{R}\right)\left(1 - \frac{t}{T}\right)\sigma_\theta^2. \qquad (8.26)$$

$$E[\theta_{ij}^2] = \left(1 - \frac{1}{R}\right)\left(1 - \frac{1}{T}\right)\sigma_\theta^2. \qquad (8.27)$$

We can now evaluate the expectations of the various mean squares. From the model (8.1),

$$\bar{x}_{i..} = \xi + \eta_i + \frac{1}{t}\sum_j^t \zeta_j + \frac{1}{t}\sum_j^t \theta_{ij} + \frac{1}{tn}\sum_j^t \sum_v^n z_{ijv}, \qquad (8.28)$$

$$\bar{x}_{...} = \xi + \frac{1}{r}\sum_i^r \eta_i + \frac{1}{t}\sum_j^t \zeta_j + \frac{1}{rt}\sum_i^r \sum_j^t \theta_{ij} + \frac{1}{rtn}\sum_i^r \sum_j^t \sum_v^n z_{ijv}; \qquad (8.29)$$

SECT. 14.8   THE TWO-WAY CROSSED FINITE POPULATION MODEL   495

so

$$\bar{x}_{i..} - \bar{x}_{...} = \left(\eta_i - \frac{1}{r}\sum_i^r \eta_i\right) + \left(\frac{1}{t}\sum_j^t \theta_{ij} - \frac{1}{rt}\sum_i^r \sum_j^t \theta_{ij}\right)$$
$$+ \left(\frac{1}{tn}\sum_j^t \sum_v^n z_{ijv} - \frac{1}{rtn}\sum_i^r \sum_j^t \sum_v^n z_{ijv}\right). \quad (8.30)$$

When we square (8.30) and sum over i, the expectations of the sums of cross products are zero. For example,

$$E\left[\frac{1}{t}\sum_i^r \left(\eta_i - \frac{1}{r}\sum_i^r \eta_i\right)\left(\sum_j^t \theta_{ij} - \frac{1}{r}\sum_i^r \sum_j^t \theta_{ij}\right)\right]$$
$$= E\left[\frac{1}{t}\sum_i^r \left\{\eta_i \sum_j^t \theta_{ij} - \frac{1}{r}\eta_i \sum_i^r \sum_j^t \theta_{ij} - \frac{1}{r}\left(\sum_i^r \eta_i\right)\left(\sum_j^t \theta_{ji}\right)\right.\right.$$
$$\left.\left. + \frac{1}{r^2}\left(\sum_i^r \eta_i\right)\left(\sum_i^r \sum_j^t \theta_{ij}\right)\right\}\right]$$
$$= \frac{1}{t}E\left[\sum_i^r \eta_i \sum_j^t \theta_{ij} - \frac{1}{r}\left(\sum_i^r \eta_i\right)\left(\sum_i^r \sum_j^t \theta_{ij}\right) - \frac{1}{r}\left(\sum_i^r \eta_i\right)\left(\sum_i^r \sum_j^t \theta_{ij}\right)\right.$$
$$\left. + \frac{1}{r}\left(\sum_i^r \eta_i\right)\left(\sum_i^r \sum_j^t \theta_{ij}\right)\right]$$
$$= \frac{1}{t}E\left[\sum_i^r \eta_i \sum_j^t \theta_{ij}\right] - \frac{1}{rt}E\left[\left(\sum_i^r \eta_i\right)\left(\sum_i^r \sum_j^t \theta_{ij}\right)\right]. \quad (8.31)$$

For the first term, the products $\sum_i^r \eta_i \sum_j^t \theta_{ij}$ can be formed by picking r rows out of R, and t columns out of T; this can be done in $\binom{R}{r}\binom{T}{t}$ ways. Thus

$$E\left[\sum_i^r \eta_i \sum_j^t \theta_{ij}\right]$$
$$= \left[\binom{R}{r}\binom{T}{t}\right]^{-1}[\eta_1(\theta_{11} + \cdots + \theta_{1t}) + \cdots + \eta_1(\theta_{1(T-t+1)} + \cdots + \theta_{1T})$$
$$+ \eta_2(\theta_{21} + \cdots + \theta_{2t}) + \cdots + \eta_2(\theta_{2(T-t+1)} + \cdots + \theta_{2T}) + \cdots$$
$$+ \eta_R(\theta_{R1} + \cdots + \theta_{Rt}) + \cdots + \eta_R(\theta_{R(T-t+1)} + \cdots + \theta_{RT})]. \quad (8.32)$$

In any row in the square brackets, the θ_{ij} have a fixed i, say p, and in this row any particular value of j, say q, occurs $\binom{T-1}{t-1}$ times. Thus

$$E\left[\sum_i^r \eta_i \sum_j^t \theta_{ij}\right] = \left[\binom{R}{r}\binom{T}{t}\right]^{-1}\left[\eta_1\binom{T-1}{t-1}\sum_j^T \theta_{1j} + \cdots + \eta_R\binom{T-1}{t-1}\sum_j^T \theta_{Rj}\right]$$
$$= \frac{\binom{T-1}{t-1}}{\binom{R}{r}\binom{T}{t}}\sum_i^R \eta_i \sum_j^T \theta_{ij} = 0, \quad (8.33)$$

using (8.3). For the second term in (8.31) we have

$$E\left[\left(\sum_i^r \eta_i\right)\left(\sum_i^r \sum_j^t \theta_{ij}\right)\right]$$
$$= \left[\binom{R}{r}\binom{T}{t}\right]^{-1}[(\eta_1 + \cdots + \eta_r)\{(\theta_{11} + \cdots + \theta_{1t}) + \cdots + (\theta_{r1} + \cdots + \theta_{rt})$$
$$+ \cdots + (\theta_{1(T-t+1)} + \cdots + \theta_{1T}) + \cdots + (\theta_{r(T-t+1)} + \cdots + \theta_{rT})\}$$
$$+ \cdots$$
$$+ (\eta_{R-r+1} + \cdots + \eta_R)\{(\theta_{(R-r+1)1} + \cdots + \theta_{(R-r+1)t}) + \cdots$$
$$+ (\theta_{R1} + \cdots + \theta_{Rt}) + \cdots + (\theta_{(R-r+1)(T-t+1)} + \cdots + \theta_{(R-r+1)T})$$
$$+ (\theta_{R(T-t+1)} + \cdots + \theta_{RT})\}]$$
$$= (\text{constant}) \times \sum_i^R \eta_i \left(\sum_j^T \theta_{ij}\right) = 0, \qquad (8.34)$$

using (8.3). Hence (8.31) is zero, and so from (8.30) we have

$$E\left[nt \sum_i^r (\bar{x}_{i..} - \bar{x}_{...})^2\right]$$
$$= ntE\left[\sum_i^r \left(\eta_i - \frac{1}{r}\sum_i^r \eta_i\right)^2\right] + \frac{n}{t}E\left[\sum_i^r \left(\sum_j^t \theta_{ij} - \frac{1}{r}\sum_i^r \sum_j^t \theta_{ij}\right)^2\right]$$
$$+ \frac{1}{nt}E\left[\sum_i^r \left(\sum_j^t \sum_v^n z_{ijv} - \frac{1}{r}\sum_i^r \sum_j^t \sum_v^n z_{ijv}\right)^2\right]. \qquad (8.35)$$

The first term is

$$ntE\left[\sum_i^r \left(\eta_i - \frac{1}{r}\sum_i^r \eta_i\right)^2\right] = ntE\left[\sum_i^r \left\{\eta_i^2 - 2\frac{\eta_i}{r}\sum_i^r \eta_i + \frac{1}{r^2}\left(\sum_i^r \eta_i\right)^2\right\}\right]$$
$$= ntE\left[\sum_i^r \eta_i^2\right] - \frac{nt}{r}E\left[\left(\sum_i^r \eta_i\right)^2\right]$$
$$= nt \cdot r\left(1 - \frac{1}{R}\right)\sigma_\eta^2 - \frac{nt}{r} \cdot r\left(1 - \frac{r}{R}\right)\sigma_\eta^2 = nt(r-1)\sigma_\eta^2, \qquad (8.36)$$

using (8.11) and (8.14). The second term is

$$\frac{n}{t}E\left[\sum_i^r \left(\sum_j^t \theta_{ij} - \frac{1}{r}\sum_i^r \sum_j^t \theta_{ij}\right)^2\right]$$
$$= \frac{n}{t}\sum_i^r E\left[\left(\sum_j^t \theta_{ij}\right)^2\right] - \frac{n}{rt}E\left[\left(\sum_i^r \sum_j^t \theta_{ij}\right)^2\right]$$
$$= \frac{n}{t} \cdot r \cdot t\left(1 - \frac{1}{R}\right)\left(1 - \frac{t}{T}\right)\sigma_\theta^2 - \frac{n}{rt} \cdot rt\left(1 - \frac{r}{R}\right)\left(1 - \frac{t}{T}\right)\sigma_\theta^2$$
$$= n(r-1)\left(1 - \frac{t}{T}\right)\sigma_\theta^2, \qquad (8.37)$$

SECT. 14.8   THE TWO-WAY CROSSED FINITE POPULATION MODEL

using (8.24) and (8.26). The third term is

$$\frac{1}{nt} E\left[\sum_i^r \left(\sum_j^t \sum_v^n z_{ijv} - \frac{1}{r}\sum_i^r \sum_j^t \sum_v^n z_{ijv}\right)^2\right]$$

$$= \frac{1}{nt} E\left[\sum_i^r \left(\sum_j^t \sum_v^n z_{ijv}\right)^2\right] - \frac{1}{rtn} E\left[\left(\sum_i^r \sum_j^t \sum_v^n z_{ijv}\right)^2\right] = (r-1)\sigma^2, \tag{8.38}$$

using (8.9).

Inserting (8.36), (8.37), and (8.38) in (8.35) and dividing by $r-1$, we obtain for the expectation of the row mean square

$$E\left[\frac{nt}{r-1}\sum_i^r (\bar{x}_{i..} - \bar{x}_{...})^2\right] = nt\sigma_\eta^2 + n\left(1 - \frac{t}{T}\right)\sigma_\theta^2 + \sigma^2. \tag{8.39}$$

The expectation of the column mean square is similarly

$$E\left[\frac{nr}{t-1}\sum_j^t (\bar{x}_{.j.} - \bar{x}_{...})^2\right] = nr\sigma_\zeta^2 + n\left(1 - \frac{r}{R}\right)\sigma_\theta^2 + \sigma^2. \tag{8.40}$$

For the interaction sum of squares, after averaging the model (8.1) over the appropriate indices we get

$$\bar{x}_{ij.} - \bar{x}_{i..} - \bar{x}_{.j.} + \bar{x}_{...}$$

$$= \theta_{ij} - \frac{1}{r}\sum_i^r \theta_{ij} - \frac{1}{t}\sum_j^t \theta_{ij} + \frac{1}{rt}\sum_i^r \sum_j^t \theta_{ij} + \frac{1}{n}\sum_v^n z_{ijv} - \frac{1}{rn}\sum_i^r \sum_v^n z_{ijv}$$

$$- \frac{1}{tn}\sum_j^t \sum_v^n z_{ijv} + \frac{1}{rtn}\sum_i^r \sum_j^t \sum_v^n z_{ijv}. \tag{8.41}$$

When we square and sum and take expectations, the result is a set of terms involving θ and a set of terms involving z. The former reduces to

$$nE\left[\sum_i^r \sum_j^t \theta_{ij}^2 - \frac{1}{t}\sum_i^r \left(\sum_j^t \theta_{ij}\right)^2 - \frac{1}{r}\sum_j^t \left(\sum_i^r \theta_{ij}\right)^2 + \frac{1}{rt}\left(\sum_i^r \sum_j^t \theta_{ij}\right)^2\right]$$

$$= n\left[rt\left(1 - \frac{1}{R}\right)\left(1 - \frac{1}{T}\right) - \frac{r}{t} \cdot t\left(1 - \frac{1}{R}\right)\left(1 - \frac{t}{T}\right)\right.$$

$$\left. - \frac{t}{r}\cdot r\left(1 - \frac{r}{R}\right)\left(1 - \frac{1}{T}\right) + \frac{1}{rt}\cdot rt\left(1 - \frac{r}{R}\right)\left(1 - \frac{t}{T}\right)\right]\sigma_\theta^2$$

$$= n(r-1)(t-1)\sigma_\theta^2. \tag{8.42}$$

Similarly the expectation of the term involving the z's reduces to

$(r-1)(t-1)\sigma^2$. Hence the expected value of the interaction mean square is

$$E\left[\frac{n\sum_i^r \sum_j^t (\bar{x}_{ij.} - \bar{x}_{i..} - \bar{x}_{.j.} + \bar{x}_{...})^2}{(r-1)(t-1)}\right] = \sigma^2 + n\sigma_\theta^2. \qquad (8.43)$$

These results, (8.39), (8.40), and (8.43) are assembled in Table 14.13.

Table 14.13

Source of variance	Sums of squares	Mean squares	E[M. S.]
Rows	$nt \sum_i^r (\bar{x}_{i..} - \bar{x}_{...})^2$	s_4^2	$\sigma^2 + n\left(1 - \frac{t}{T}\right)\sigma_\theta^2 + nt\sigma_\eta^2$
Columns	$nr \sum_j^t (\bar{x}_{.j.} - \bar{x}_{...})^2$	s_3^2	$\sigma^2 + n\left(1 - \frac{r}{R}\right)\sigma_\theta^2 + nr\sigma_\zeta^2$
Interaction	$n \sum_i^r \sum_j^t (\bar{x}_{ij.} - \bar{x}_{i..} - \bar{x}_{.j.} + \bar{x}_{...})^2$	s_2^2	$\sigma^2 + n\sigma_\theta^2$
Within cells	$\sum_i^r \sum_j^t \sum_v^n (x_{ijv} - \bar{x}_{ij.})^2$	s_1^2	σ^2
Total	$\sum_i^r \sum_j^t \sum_v^n (x_{ijv} - \bar{x}_{...})^2$		

14.9. Discussion of the Two-Way Crossed Finite Population Model

In Table 14.13, if both the populations are infinite in extent, so that $1 - t/T$ and $1 - r/R$ both tend to 1, then we have exactly the expectations of the mean squares given in Table 14.7 for the model II case. If we further assume that the η_i, ζ_j, and θ_{ij} are normally distributed with variances σ_η^2, σ_ζ^2, and σ_θ^2, then we have exactly model II.

On the other hand, if the samples constitute the entire population, so that $t = T$ and $r = R$, then $1 - t/T = 1 - r/R = 0$ and the expectations of the mean squares become those given in Table 14.3 for model I, and the finite model becomes exactly model I.

If the rows are a sample from an infinite population and the sample of columns is the entire population, then we have the mixed model with the expectations of the mean squares as given in Table 14.14. The appropriate

Table 14.14

Source of variance	Type of effect	Mean squares	E[M. S.]
Rows	II	s_4^2	$\sigma^2 + nt\sigma_\eta^2$
Columns	I	s_3^2	$\sigma^2 + n\sigma_\theta^2 + nr\sigma_\zeta^2$
Interactions	Mixed	s_2^2	$\sigma^2 + n\sigma_\theta^2$
Within cells	II	s_1^2	σ^2

SECT. 14.10 NESTED CLASSIFICATIONS IN THE FINITE MODEL   499

denominator for the F test, the *error term*, for the random row effect is the within-cell mean square, whereas the error term for the fixed column effect is the interaction mean square. While σ_ζ^2 continues to be a sum of squares of a set of fixed constants, with an appropriate divisor, σ^2, σ_θ^2, and σ_η^2 are true components of variance and can be estimated in the usual way. The fixed column effects can be estimated from the column averages $\bar{x}_{.j.}$. We obtain confidence limits for the difference between two column means as follows. Averaging the model (8.1) over i and v gives

$$\bar{x}_{.j.} = \xi + \bar{\eta}_. + \zeta_j + \bar{\theta}_{.j} + \bar{z}_{.j.} \qquad (9.1)$$

where

$$\bar{\eta}_. = \frac{1}{r}\sum_i^r \eta_i, \quad \bar{\theta}_{.j} = \frac{1}{r}\sum_i^r \theta_{ij}, \quad \bar{z}_{.j.} = \frac{1}{rn}\sum_i^r\sum_v^n z_{ijv}.$$

Then

$$\bar{x}_{.j.} - \bar{x}_{.j'.} = (\zeta_j - \zeta_{j'}) + (\bar{\theta}_{.j} - \bar{\theta}_{.j'}) + (\bar{z}_{.j.} - \bar{z}_{.j'.}). \qquad (9.2)$$

If we now assume that θ_{ij} is distributed normally with zero mean and variance σ_θ^2 for each value of j, then $\bar{\theta}_{.j}$ is distributed normally with zero mean and variance σ_θ^2/r for each value of j. Thus $E[\bar{\theta}_{.j}] = 0$, and

$$E[\bar{x}_{.j.} - \bar{x}_{.j'.}] = \zeta_j - \zeta_{j'}, \qquad (9.3)$$

$$V[\bar{x}_{.j.} - \bar{x}_{.j'.}] = \frac{2\sigma_\theta^2}{r} + \frac{2\sigma^2}{rn} = \frac{2(\sigma^2 + n\sigma_\theta^2)}{rn}. \qquad (9.4)$$

Confidence limits can be obtained from the relation

$$\frac{(\bar{x}_{.j.} - \bar{x}_{.j'.}) - (\zeta_j - \zeta_{j'})}{\sqrt{2s_2^2/rn}} \sim t((r-1)(t-1)). \qquad (9.5)$$

With only one observation per cell, there is no within-cell mean square. Reference to Table 14.14, with $n = 1$, shows that the validity of the test for the model I effect, columns, is not affected by the change, the interaction being a satisfactory error term, but the test for the model II effect, rows, will only be satisfactory if the interaction component σ_θ^2 is small compared with σ^2.

14.10. Nested Classifications in the Finite Model

Similar to (7.1), we have the model

$$x_{ijv} = \xi + \eta_i + \lambda_{j(i)} + z_{ijv} \qquad (10.1)$$

where $i = 1, \ldots, r$; $j = 1, \ldots, t$; $v = 1, \ldots, n$. The η_i are random samples drawn from a population of size R, and $\sum_i^R \eta_i = 0$. Associated with each i is a population of $\lambda_{j(i)}$: For each of these populations, of size T, we have the condition that $\sum_j^T \lambda_{j(i)} = 0$. The complete array of $\lambda_{j(i)}$ is indicated in Table 14.15. For the $\lambda_{j(i)}$, the sampling procedure consists in selecting at random r of the columns (i) and then selecting at random t values of j and taking the corresponding $\lambda_{j(i)}$. As shown by the last line of the table, for each value of i the entire set of T $\lambda_{j(i)}$'s sum to zero, but of course in general the $\lambda_{j(i)}$ do not sum to zero for the sample of t unless $t = T$. The $\lambda_{j(i)}$ do not in general sum to zero within a row; i.e., in general $\sum_i^R \lambda_{j(i)} \neq 0$.

Table 14.15

	$i = 1,$	$i = 2,$	$\ldots,$	$i = i,$	$\ldots,$	$i = R$
$j = 1$	$\lambda_{1(1)}$	$\lambda_{1(2)}$		$\lambda_{1(i)}$		$\lambda_{1(R)}$
$j = 2$	$\lambda_{2(1)}$	$\lambda_{2(2)}$		$\lambda_{2(i)}$		$\lambda_{2(R)}$
$\cdot$						
$\cdot$						
$j = j$	$\lambda_{j(1)}$	$\lambda_{j(2)}$		$\lambda_{j(i)}$		$\lambda_{j(R)}$
$\cdot$						
$\cdot$						
$j = T$	$\lambda_{T(1)}$	$\lambda_{T(2)}$		$\lambda_{T(i)}$		$\lambda_{T(R)}$
	$\sum_j^T \lambda_{j(1)} = 0,$	$\sum_j^T \lambda_{j(2)} = 0,$		$\sum_j^T \lambda_{j(i)} = 0,$		$\sum_j^T \lambda_{j(R)} = 0$

The z_{ijv} are distributed independently $N(0, \sigma^2)$. We define

$$\sigma_\eta^2 = \frac{1}{R-1} \sum_i^R \eta_i^2, \qquad \sigma_\lambda^2 = \frac{1}{R(T-1)} \sum_i^R \sum_j^T \lambda_{j(i)}^2. \qquad (10.2)$$

The analysis of variance is based on the partitioning of the sum of squares in (7.3). The derivation of the expectations of the mean squares follows the same general lines of the crossed situation in Section 14.8, and leads

$$E[s_3^2] = \sigma^2 + n\left(1 - \frac{t}{T}\right)\sigma_\lambda^2 + nt\sigma_\eta^2, \tag{10.3}$$

$$E[s_2^2] = \sigma^2 + n\sigma_\lambda^2, \tag{10.4}$$

$$E[s_1^2] = \sigma^2. \tag{10.5}$$

If the population size of samples within sacks can be regarded as infinite, using the terminology of Table 14.10, $T = \infty$ and these expectations become identical with those of Table 14.10.

EXERCISES

14.1. The accompanying table gives the total acidities of samples of three types of brown coal determined in duplicate, using ethanolic NaOH of three concentrations.
(a) Make a conventional analysis of variance of these data. Regard both factors as model I effects. (b) Can the null hypothesis that there is no interaction between the three methods of analysis and the three types of coal be accepted? (c) Can the null hypothesis that there is no difference between the three methods of analysis be accepted? (d) Construct a simple 95 per cent confidence interval for the difference between $0.404N$ and $0.786N$ ethanolic NaOH, assuming that the factor type of coal is (i) model I, (ii) model II.

Ethanolic NaOH	Morwell		Yallourn		Maddingley	
$0.404N$	8.27,	8.17	8.66,	8.61	8.14,	7.96
$0.626N$	8.03,	8.21	8.42,	8.58	8.02,	7.89
$0.786N$	8.60,	8.20	8.61,	8.76	8.13,	8.07

Data from B. Sternhall, "Chemistry of Brown Coals, VI," *Australian Journal of Applied Science*, 9 (1958), 375–79.

14.2. The accompanying data give the compressive strength of concrete cylinders. A number of cylinders were made from each of five batches of concrete. From each batch, nine cylinders were selected at random. A capping treatment C_1 was applied to three of them, another capping treatment C_2 applied to another three, and a third capping treatment C_3 applied to the other three. The compressive strengths were then measured. The treatments are a model I effect and the batches a model II effect.
(a) Give bounds for the P values (e.g., $0.10 > P > 0.05$) for the null hypotheses that there are (i) no interaction between batches and treatments, (ii) no differences between batches, and (iii) no differences between treatments. (b) Give estimates of the components of variance (i) between cylinders in the same batch given the same treatment, (ii) for interaction between batches and treatments, and (iii)

between batches. (c) Give 95 per cent confidence limits for the difference between treatments C_2 and C_3.

	Batch				
	1	2	3	4	5
C_1	613	656	648	637	602
	631	637	638	637	585
	603	649	649	617	608
C_2	591	618	575	614	545
	591	613	608	591	534
	597	619	612	580	547
C_3	583	641	641	625	597
	609	617	634	639	566
	614	634	614	627	593

The sum of squares of all observations is 16,815,853.
[Source: George Werner, "The Effect of Type of Capping Material on the Compressive Strength of Concrete Cylinders," *Proceedings of the American Society for Testing and Materials*, 58 (1958), 1166–86.]

14.3. For the data of exercise (7.7), (a) test the null hypothesis that there is no difference between containers, (b) test the null hypothesis that there is no difference between panels, (c) construct 95 per cent confidence limits for the difference between containers A and B (i) assuming that that was your original intention and (ii) assuming that this comparison was suggested by the data. (d) What is the estimated variance of the difference between observations on two containers by a single panel, i.e., if x_{ij} is the observation on the ith container by the jth panel, what is $\hat{V}[x_{ij} - x_{i'j}]$? (e) What is the estimated variance of the difference between an observation on one container by one panel and an observation on another container by another panel, i.e., what is $\hat{V}[x_{ij} - x_{i'j'}]$?

14.4. Concrete beams were made with different "cement factors," namely 5, 6 and 7 sacks of cement per cubic yard. For each cement factor five replicate batches of concrete were prepared, and from each batch two replicate beams were cast. The modulus of rupture was determined on each beam. Thus in the table below, 671 and 595 are the results for the two beams from the first batch, and 648 and 618 are the results for the two beams from the second batch, etc., made with cement factor 5. The cement factor is a model I factor. Regard the five batches of concrete prepared for each level of the cement factor as a random sample from an infinite population, and the two beams cast from each batch as a random sample from an infinite population.
 (a) Give bounds for the P values (e.g., $0.10 > P > 0.05$) for the null hypotheses that there are no differences between (i) batches of concrete made with the same cement factor, and (ii) levels of the cement factor. (b) Give estimates of the components of variance (i) between duplicate beams from the same batch, and

(ii) between batches made with the same cement factor. (c) Give 95 per cent confidence limits for the difference between cement factors 6 and 7.

Moduli of rupture of concrete beams, in psi

Five batches made at each level of cement factor

Cement factor	Two beams cast from each batch				
5	671	648	548	604	519
	595	618	559	640	596
6	714	684	618	644	629
	618	688	628	657	624
7	708	683	633	725	634
	617	696	665	672	608

The sum of squares of all observations is 12,283,103.
[Source: Stanton Walker and Delmar L. Bloem, "Studies of Flexural Strength of Concrete. Part 3: Effects of Variations in Testing Procedure," *Proceedings of the American Society for Testing and Materials*, 57 (1957), 1127–1139.]

14.5. Prove the identity (3.10).
14.6. Prove the identity (4.8).

REFERENCES

1. Tukey, John W., "Interaction in a Row-by-Column Design," *Memorandum Report* 18, Statistical Research Group, Princeton University.
2. Cornfield, Jerome, and John W. Tukey, "Average Values of Mean Squares in Factorials," *Annals of Mathematical Statistics*, 27 (1956), 907–949.
3. Bennett, Carl A., and Norman L. Franklin, *Statistical Analysis in Chemistry and the Chemical Industry*. New York: John Wiley and Sons, 1954.

CHAPTER 15

Three-Way and Four-Way Analysis of Variance

15.1. The Model

The methods of analysis of two-way classification of data in the previous chapter generalize to the three-way case, in which observations can be classified according to three independent criteria. Imagine a three-dimensional lattice in which the index i refers to rows which might correspond to varieties of corn, j to columns which might correspond to quantity of fertilizer, and k to arrays, say date of harvesting. Suppose that in general in the population there are R rows, T columns, and U arrays, so that there will be RTU cells in the lattice. Suppose that in the sample there are rtu cells formed by the intersection of r rows, t columns, and u arrays. Let v be the index of the observation in each cell, going to n in the sample. Let ξ_{ijk} be the true mean for the ijkth cell. Then the model is

$$x_{ijkv} = \xi_{ijk} + z_{ijkv}, \tag{1.1}$$

where the z_{ijkv} are normally distributed with zero mean and variance σ^2.

To represent averaging of the ξ_{ijk} over any suffix, we will use a bar over the ξ and replace the suffix averaged over by an x. The overall average of the ξ_{ijk}, i.e., $\bar{\xi}_{xxx}$, we will however represent simply by ξ. The deviation of the ith row mean from the over-all mean we represent by $\eta_{i..}$:

$$\eta_{i..} = \bar{\xi}_{ixx} - \xi. \tag{1.2}$$

Similarly the column and array effects are

$$\eta_{.j.} = \bar{\xi}_{xjx} - \xi, \tag{1.3}$$

$$\eta_{..k} = \bar{\xi}_{xxk} - \xi. \tag{1.4}$$

SECT. 15.1   THE MODEL   505

The deviations of the cell means in the row and column table, formed by averaging over arrays, from the values expected on the assumption that they would be the grand mean ξ plus the row effect plus the column effect are denoted by $\zeta_{ij.}$:

$$\zeta_{ij.} = \xi_{ijx} - (\xi + \eta_{i..} + \eta_{.j.}). \tag{1.5}$$

The $\zeta_{ij.}$ are the constants for the row × column interaction. The row × array interaction will be represented by $\zeta_{i.k}$ and the column × array interaction by $\zeta_{.jk}$. The deviations of the cell means ξ_{ijk} from the values expected on the assumption that they would be the grand mean plus the row, column, and array effects plus the three two-way interactions are represented by θ_{ijk}:

$$\theta_{ijk} = \xi_{ijk} - (\xi + \eta_{i..} + \eta_{.j.} + \eta_{..k} + \zeta_{ij.} + \zeta_{i.k} + \zeta_{.jk}). \tag{1.6}$$

The θ_{ijk} are the constants for the three-way interaction among rows, columns, and arrays.

We can now rewrite the model (1.1) in the form

$$x_{ijkv} = \xi + \eta_{i..} + \eta_{.j.} + \eta_{..k} + \zeta_{ij.} + \zeta_{i.k} + \zeta_{.jk} + \theta_{ijk} + z_{ijkv}. \tag{1.7}$$

To represent averaging any of the constants we will use the same convention as for the ξ_{ijk}. Thus $\zeta_{.jx}$ is the average over arrays for the jth column of the column × array interaction constants.

We will consider the finite population model which will give the other models as special cases. The algebra of the partitioning of the sums of squares and the arithmetic of the calculation of the sums of squares are identical for all models. In the finite population model we suppose that the $\eta_{i..}$ are a sample of size r from a population of size R, and the $\eta_{.j.}$ and the $\eta_{..k}$ are samples of t and u from populations of size T and U, respectively. In the population, the various parameters sum to zero over each index:

$$\sum_i^R \eta_{i..} = \sum_j^T \eta_{.j.} = \sum_k^U \eta_{..k} = 0,$$

$$\sum_i^R \zeta_{ij.} = \sum_j^T \zeta_{ij.} = \sum_i^R \zeta_{i.k} = \sum_k^U \zeta_{i.k} = \sum_j^T \zeta_{.jk} = \sum_k^U \zeta_{.jk} = 0, \tag{1.8}$$

$$\sum_i^R \theta_{ijk} = \sum_j^T \theta_{ijk} = \sum_k^U \theta_{ijk} = 0.$$

We make the definitions

$$\sigma_A^2 = \frac{1}{(R-1)} \sum_i^R \eta_{i..}^2, \quad \text{etc.,}$$

$$\sigma_{AB}^2 = \frac{1}{(R-1)(T-1)} \sum_i^R \sum_j^T \zeta_{ij.}^2, \quad \text{etc.,} \tag{1.9}$$

$$\sigma_{ABC}^2 = \frac{1}{(R-1)(T-1)(U-1)} \sum_i^R \sum_j^T \sum_k^U \theta_{ijk}^2.$$

We can write the deviation of x_{ijkv} from the grand mean $\bar{x}_{....}$ as an identity in which the successive terms are sample estimates of the parameters:

$$x_{ijkv} - \bar{x}_{....} = (\bar{x}_{i...} - \bar{x}_{....}) + (\bar{x}_{.j..} - \bar{x}_{....}) + (\bar{x}_{..k.} - \bar{x}_{....})$$
$$+ (\bar{x}_{ij..} - \bar{x}_{i...} - \bar{x}_{.j..} + \bar{x}_{....}) + (\bar{x}_{i.k.} - \bar{x}_{i...} - \bar{x}_{..k.} + \bar{x}_{....})$$
$$+ (\bar{x}_{.jk.} - \bar{x}_{.j..} - \bar{x}_{..k.} + \bar{x}_{....})$$
$$+ (\bar{x}_{ijk.} - \bar{x}_{ij..} - \bar{x}_{i.k.} - \bar{x}_{.jk.} + \bar{x}_{i...} + \bar{x}_{.j..} + \bar{x}_{..k.} - \bar{x}_{....})$$
$$+ (x_{ijkv} - \bar{x}_{ijk.}). \tag{1.10}$$

If we write $\bar{x}_{ij..} - \bar{x}_{i...} - \bar{x}_{.j..} + \bar{x}_{....}$ in the form

$$\bar{x}_{ij..} - [\bar{x}_{....} + (\bar{x}_{i...} - \bar{x}_{....}) + (\bar{x}_{.j..} - \bar{x}_{....})], \tag{1.11}$$

it is more obviously a sample estimate of $\zeta_{ij.}$; see (1.5). Similarly, the penultimate term in (1.10) is more obviously a sample estimate of θ_{ijk}, see (1.6), if written as

$$\bar{x}_{ijk.} - [\bar{x}_{....} + (\bar{x}_{i...} - \bar{x}_{....}) + (\bar{x}_{.j..} - \bar{x}_{....}) + (\bar{x}_{..k.} - \bar{x}_{....})$$
$$+ (\bar{x}_{ij..} - \bar{x}_{i...} - \bar{x}_{.j..} + \bar{x}_{....}) + (\bar{x}_{i.k.} - \bar{x}_{i...} - \bar{x}_{..k.} + \bar{x}_{....})$$
$$+ (\bar{x}_{.jk.} - \bar{x}_{.j..} - \bar{x}_{..k.} + \bar{x}_{....})]. \tag{1.12}$$

Squaring and summing (1.10) over all indices gives an equation which is entered in column 2 of Table 15.1: the sums of all the cross products are zero. The last column gives the expectations of the mean squares, which can be derived by an extension of the methods of Section 14.8 [1].

The closed forms of sums of squares in Table 15.1 are inconvenient for calculation, and open forms involving totals instead of means are more satisfactory. For example, the sum of squares for the main effect for A is

$$tun \sum_i^r (\bar{x}_{i...} - \bar{x}_{....})^2 = \frac{1}{tun} \sum_i^r \left(\sum_j^t \sum_k^u \sum_v^n x_{ijkv} \right)^2 - \frac{1}{rtun} \left(\sum_i^r \sum_j^t \sum_k^u \sum_v^n x_{ijkv} \right)^2. \tag{1.13}$$

For the AB interaction

$$nu \sum_i^r \sum_j^t (\bar{x}_{ij..} - \bar{x}_{i...} - \bar{x}_{.j..} + \bar{x}_{....})^2$$
$$= \frac{1}{un} \sum_i^r \sum_j^t \left(\sum_k^u \sum_v^n x_{ijkv} \right)^2 - \frac{1}{rtun} \left(\sum_i^r \sum_j^t \sum_k^u \sum_v^n x_{ijkv} \right)^2$$
$$- ntu \sum_i^r (\bar{x}_{i...} - \bar{x}_{....})^2 - nru \sum_j^t (\bar{x}_{.j..} - \bar{x}_{....})^2 \tag{1.14}$$

Table 15.1

Source of variance	Sums of squares	Degrees of freedom	$E[\text{M.S.}]$
A	$ntu\sum_{i}^{r}(\bar{x}_{i\ldots}-\bar{x}_{\ldots\ldots})^2$	$r-1$	$\sigma^2+n\left(1-\dfrac{t}{T}\right)\left(1-\dfrac{u}{U}\right)\sigma_{ABC}^2+nu\left(1-\dfrac{t}{T}\right)\sigma_{AB}^2$ $+nt\left(1-\dfrac{u}{U}\right)\sigma_{AC}^2+ntu\sigma_A^2$
B	$nru\sum_{j}^{t}(\bar{x}_{\cdot j\ldots}-\bar{x}_{\ldots\ldots})^2$	$t-1$	$\sigma^2+n\left(1-\dfrac{r}{R}\right)\left(1-\dfrac{u}{U}\right)\sigma_{ABC}^2+nu\left(1-\dfrac{r}{R}\right)\sigma_{AB}^2$ $+nr\left(1-\dfrac{u}{U}\right)\sigma_{BC}^2+nru\sigma_B^2$
C	$nrt\sum_{k}^{u}(\bar{x}_{\cdot\cdot k\cdot}-\bar{x}_{\ldots\ldots})^2$	$u-1$	$\sigma^2+n\left(1-\dfrac{t}{T}\right)\left(1-\dfrac{r}{R}\right)\sigma_{ABC}^2+nt\left(1-\dfrac{r}{R}\right)\sigma_{AC}^2$ $+nr\left(1-\dfrac{t}{T}\right)\sigma_{BC}^2+nrt\sigma_C^2$
AB	$nu\sum_{i}^{r}\sum_{j}^{t}(\bar{x}_{ij\ldots}-\bar{x}_{i\ldots}-\bar{x}_{\cdot j\ldots}+\bar{x}_{\ldots\ldots})^2$	$(r-1)(t-1)$	$\sigma^2+n\left(1-\dfrac{u}{U}\right)\sigma_{ABC}^2+nu\sigma_{AB}^2$
AC	$nt\sum_{i}^{r}\sum_{k}^{u}(\bar{x}_{i\cdot k\cdot}-\bar{x}_{i\ldots}-\bar{x}_{\cdot\cdot k\cdot}+\bar{x}_{\ldots\ldots})^2$	$(r-1)(u-1)$	$\sigma^2+n\left(1-\dfrac{t}{T}\right)\sigma_{ABC}^2+nt\sigma_{AC}^2$
BC	$nr\sum_{j}^{t}\sum_{k}^{u}(\bar{x}_{\cdot jk\cdot}-\bar{x}_{\cdot j\ldots}-\bar{x}_{\cdot\cdot k\cdot}+\bar{x}_{\ldots\ldots})^2$	$(t-1)(u-1)$	$\sigma^2+n\left(1-\dfrac{r}{R}\right)\sigma_{ABC}^2+nr\sigma_{BC}^2$
ABC	$n\sum_{i}^{r}\sum_{j}^{t}\sum_{k}^{u}(\bar{x}_{ijk\cdot}-\bar{x}_{ij\ldots}-\bar{x}_{i\cdot k\cdot}-\bar{x}_{\cdot jk\cdot}+\bar{x}_{i\ldots}+\bar{x}_{\cdot j\ldots}+\bar{x}_{\cdot\cdot k\cdot}-\bar{x}_{\ldots\ldots})^2$	$(r-1)(t-1)(u-1)$	$\sigma^2+n\sigma_{ABC}^2$
Within cells	$\sum_{i}^{r}\sum_{j}^{t}\sum_{k}^{u}\sum_{v}^{n}(x_{ijkv}-\bar{x}_{ijk\cdot})^2$	$rtu(n-1)$	σ^2
Total	$\sum_{i}^{r}\sum_{j}^{t}\sum_{k}^{u}\sum_{v}^{n}(x_{ijkv}-\bar{x}_{\ldots\ldots})^2$	$rtun-1$	

where the last two terms are the sums of squares for the A and B main effects. The total sum of squares is

$$\sum_i^r \sum_j^t \sum_k^u \sum_v^n x_{ijkv}^2 - \frac{1}{rtun}\left(\sum_i^r \sum_j^t \sum_k^u \sum_v^n x_{ijkv}\right)^2, \qquad (1.15)$$

and the within-cells sum of squares is

$$\sum_i^r \sum_j^t \sum_k^u \sum_v^n x_{ijkv}^2 - \frac{1}{n}\sum_i^r \sum_j^t \sum_k^u \left(\sum_v^n x_{ijkv}\right)^2. \qquad (1.16)$$

The sum of squares for the ABC interaction is obtained by difference.

15.2. Models I and II

We will get the expected mean squares for a model I three-way analysis of variance by putting $r = R$, $t = T$, and $u = U$ in the coefficients of the components of variance in the last column in Table 15.1. All the factors in parentheses will be zero, giving the second column of Table 15.2, in

Table 15.2

$E[\text{M. S.}]$

Source of variance	Model I	Model II
A	$\sigma^2 + ntu\sigma_A^2$	$\sigma^2 + n\sigma_{abc}^2 + nu\sigma_{ab}^2 + nt\sigma_{ac}^2 + ntu\sigma_a^2$
B	$\sigma^2 + nru\sigma_B^2$	$\sigma^2 + n\sigma_{abc}^2 + nu\sigma_{ab}^2 + nr\sigma_{bc}^2 + nru\sigma_b^2$
C	$\sigma^2 + nrt\sigma_C^2$	$\sigma^2 + n\sigma_{abc}^2 + nt\sigma_{ac}^2 + nr\sigma_{bc}^2 + nrt\sigma_c^2$
AB	$\sigma^2 + nu\sigma_{AB}^2$	$\sigma^2 + n\sigma_{abc}^2 + nu\sigma_{ab}^2$
AC	$\sigma^2 + nt\sigma_{AC}^2$	$\sigma^2 + n\sigma_{abc}^2 + nt\sigma_{ac}^2$
BC	$\sigma^2 + nr\sigma_{BC}^2$	$\sigma^2 + n\sigma_{abc}^2 + nr\sigma_{bc}^2$
ABC	$\sigma^2 + n\sigma_{ABC}^2$	$\sigma^2 + n\sigma_{abc}^2$
Within cells	σ^2	σ^2

which all the components of variance are really sums of squares of constants, e.g., $\sigma_A^2 = \sum_i^R \eta_{i..}^2/(R-1)$, and are not true variances. All the effects are clearly to be tested against the within-cell mean square.

If there is only one observation per cell, the analysis will be unsatisfactory unless σ_{ABC}^2 is small compared with σ^2.

We will get the expected mean squares for a model II analysis by putting $R = T = U = \infty$ in the coefficients of the components of variance in the last column of Table 15.1. All the factors in parentheses will be equal to 1, giving the last column of Table 15.2. Here the components of variance are true variances, and we will adopt the convention of using lower-case letters in the subscript to denote this fact.

The usual testing procedure is to test the three-way interaction against the within-cells mean square. The next step depends on our point of view. A strict "nonpooler" proceeds to test the two-way interactions against the three-way interaction, irrespective of the outcome of this first test. Then he would test the main effects against appropriate linear combinations. For example, to test the A main effect he would use the mean squares for $AB + AC - ABC$, since the expected value for this combination is

$$\sigma^2 + n\sigma^2_{abc} + nu\sigma^2_{ab} + nt\sigma^2_{ac}. \tag{2.1}$$

This linear combination of three mean squares would have its approximate degrees of freedom estimated by (9.8.10).

Alternatively, some people would indulge in some judicious pooling. If at the first test the mean square for ABC was neither statistically significant at the chosen level of significance nor had a variance ratio exceeding 2, the "sometimes-pooler" would pool the sums of squares and degrees of freedom of the ABC and within-cells term, and use this as an estimate of σ^2. The assumption is being made that $\sigma^2_{abc} = 0$, and so σ^2_{abc} is stricken out of all the expected mean squares. Similarly, if one of the interactions, say AB, was statistically significant at the chosen level of significance, or if the variance ratio exceeded 2, the sometimes-pooler would leave this mean square untouched, but otherwise he would assume that σ^2_{ab} was zero, pool its sum of squares and degrees of freedom with those for ABC + within cells to get a better estimate of σ^2, and also strike σ^2_{ab} out of the expectations of the mean squares wherever it occurred. With this procedure, if none of the two-way interactions was significant nor had variance ratios exceeding 2, they would all end up by being pooled with the within-cells mean square, and the three main effects would be tested against this pooled error term.

The "never-pooler" can be confident that his errors of the first kind have the stated probability. The sometimes-pooler may be somewhat uncomfortable about this, but he will claim that his errors of the second kind have smaller probability than those of the never-pooler. If the sample sizes are large, so that degrees of freedom are plentiful, the motivation, or temptation, to be a sometimes-pooler are less. The rule about the factor 2 comes from Paull [2].

If, in a model II analysis, there is only one observation per cell, of course there is no within-cell mean square, but putting $n = 1$ in the expectations of mean squares in Table 15.2 does not affect the testing procedure.

A further complication in the testing of complicated analyses of variance is the multiplicity of tests being performed. For example, in a five-factor analysis there will be 5 main effects, 10 two-way interactions, and 10 three-way interactions. Thus, ignoring the four-way and the five-way interactions, we may be testing $5 + 10 + 10 = 25$ effects.

Suppose that $x_1, \ldots, x_n$ are identically distributed independent observations. Then one of the sample of n will be the largest: Call this $x_{\max}$. The condition that the largest is less than some value, say x, is the same as the condition that they are all less than x, i.e.,

$$\Pr\{x_1 < x, x_2 < x, \ldots\} = \Pr\{x_{\max} < x\}. \quad (2.2)$$

Also, since the observations are independent,

$$\Pr\{x_1 < x, x_2 < x, \ldots\} = \Pr\{x_1 < x\} \Pr\{x_2 < x\} \cdots$$
$$= (\Pr\{x_i < x\})^n; \quad (2.3)$$

so

$$\Pr\{x_{\max} < x\} = (\Pr\{x_i < x\})^n. \quad (2.4)$$

Now there will be a P point of the cumulative distribution of $x_{\max}$ such that

$$\Pr\{x_{\max} < x_{\max,P}\} = P. \quad (2.5)$$

Also, substituting $x_{\max,P}$ for x in (2.4),

$$\Pr\{x_{\max} < x_{\max,P}\} = (\Pr\{x_i < x_{\max,P}\})^n. \quad (2.6)$$

Comparing (2.5) and (2.6), we see that

$$\Pr\{x_i < x_{\max,P}\} = P^{1/n}, \quad (2.7)$$

or

$$\Pr\{x_i < x_{\max,P^n}\} = P. \quad (2.8)$$

In other words, the P^n point of the distribution of $x_{\max}$ is equal to the P point of the distribution of x. Thus, if we are testing 10 independent F ratios, all with the same degrees of freedom, so that they have the same distribution under the various null hypotheses, the 0.99 point of the distribution for the largest of the 10 is actually the $\sqrt[10]{0.99} \simeq 0.999$ point of the ordinary F distribution.

Of course, in the usual analysis-of-variance situation the F ratios are not independent since they use a common denominator mean square. Finney [3] showed that for moderately large, say greater than 10 or preferably 20, denominator degrees of freedom the F ratios could be assumed to be independent without serious error. For the special case where the numerator degrees of freedom are 1, Nair [4] tabulated the 0.95 and 0.99 points of the largest variance ratio for denominator degrees of freedom starting at

10, reproduced as Table X of the Appendix. Unfortunately his table only goes to the largest of 10 variance ratios.

Daniel [5] and Birnbaum [6] have developed a scheme for the significance testing of a large number of mean squares with single degrees of freedom which has promise. However, a completely satisfactory procedure must give weight to the relevant a priori probabilities. It is found by experience that main effects are more frequently significant than two-way interactions, and two-way interactions are more frequently significant than three-way interactions, and so on. Thus, if we find two effects, one a main effect and the other a four-way interaction, both significant at the 0.025 level, we would have little hesitation in accepting the former as real and dismissing the latter as an instance of random fluctuation. Also, the pattern of significance conveys relative information. If we find the main effects A, B, and C and their interactions AB, AC, and BC significant, we would not be surprised to find ABC significant, whereas, if ABC was significant without any of the other effects mentioned being significant, we would be tempted to regard this as an accident of random fluctuation.

It seems clear that an efficient analysis of a multi-factor experiment is at present somewhat subjective. One could certainly lay down certain rules, but they would lead to a higher proportion of errors, of the first and second kinds, than an intelligent and experienced practitioner would commit.

15.3. Mixed Models

In three-way analysis of variance there are two mixed models, one in which one factor is random and two factors are fixed, and vice versa. In the first case, if a is random and B and C are fixed, we put $R = \infty$, $t = T$, and $u = U$ in the expectations of mean squares in Table 15.1, and obtain the left-hand side of Table 15.3. On a nonpooling basis, the tests of significance are clear. For example, aB and aC are tested against within cells whereas BC is tested against aBC, and a is tested against within cells whereas B and C are tested against the aB and aC interactions. If there is only one observation per cell, then satisfactory tests for a, aB, and aC exist only if σ^2_{aBC} is small, but the tests for B, C, and BC remain valid.

When a and b are random and C fixed we put $R = T = \infty$, $u = U$ in Table 15.1, and this gives the right-hand side of Table 15.3. The tests are straightforward except that a linear combination of mean squares $aC + bC - abC$ is necessary to provide a satisfactory error term for C. If there is only one observation per cell, so that there is no within-cell mean square, the tests are unchanged except for ab, which requires σ^2_{abC} to be small for a satisfactory test.

Table 15.3

	a random, B and C fixed		a and b random, C fixed
Effect	E[M. S.]	Effect	E[M. S.]
a	$\sigma^2 + nt u\sigma_a^2$	a	$\sigma^2 + nu\sigma_{ab}^2 + ntu\sigma_a^2$
B	$\sigma^2 + nu\sigma_{aB}^2 + nru\sigma_B^2$	b	$\sigma^2 + nu\sigma_{ab}^2 + nru\sigma_b^2$
C	$\sigma^2 + nt\sigma_{aC}^2 + nrt\sigma_C^2$	C	$\sigma^2 + n\sigma_{abC}^2 + nt\sigma_{aC}^2 + nr\sigma_{bC}^2 + nrt\sigma_C^2$
aB	$\sigma^2 + nu\sigma_{aB}^2$	ab	$\sigma^2 + nu\sigma_{ab}^2$
aC	$\sigma^2 + nt\sigma_{aC}^2$	aC	$\sigma^2 + n\sigma_{abC}^2 + nt\sigma_{aC}^2$
BC	$\sigma^2 + n\sigma_{aBC}^2 + nr\sigma_{BC}^2$	bC	$\sigma^2 + n\sigma_{abC}^2 + nr\sigma_{bC}^2$
aBC	$\sigma^2 + n\sigma_{aBC}^2$	abC	$\sigma^2 + n\sigma_{abC}^2$
Within cells	σ^2	Within cells	σ^2

15.4. Confidence Limits in Three-Way Analysis

We will discuss the situation where there is only one observation per cell and it is assumed that the three-way interaction is zero; i.e., the model (1.7) with $\nu = 1$ and $\theta_{ijk} = 0$ becomes

$$x_{ijk} = \xi + \eta_{i..} + \eta_{.j.} + \eta_{..k} + \zeta_{ij.} + \zeta_{i.k} + \zeta_{.jk} + z_{ijk}. \quad (4.1)$$

We will discuss the construction of confidence limits for the difference between two row means. Using (1.2)

$$\eta_{i..} - \eta_{i'..} = (\bar{\xi}_{ixx} - \xi) - (\bar{\xi}_{i'xx} - \xi) = \bar{\xi}_{ixx} - \bar{\xi}_{i'xx}. \quad (4.2)$$

Thus confidence limits for $\eta_{i..} - \eta_{i'..}$ are identical with confidence limits for $\bar{\xi}_{ixx} - \bar{\xi}_{i'xx}$.

In the model I case, if we want confidence limits for the difference between two row means, then we will be making the assumption that the interaction involving rows, namely, the $\zeta_{ij.}$ and $\zeta_{i.k}$, are zero; so the model becomes

$$x_{ijk} = \xi + \eta_{i..} + \eta_{.j.} + \eta_{..k} + \zeta_{.jk} + z_{ijk}. \quad (4.3)$$

Averaging over j and k, we get

$$\bar{x}_{i..} = \xi + \eta_{i..} + \bar{\eta}_{.x.} + \bar{\eta}_{..x} + \bar{\zeta}_{.xx} + \bar{z}_{i..} = \xi + \eta_{i..} + \bar{z}_{i..}, \quad (4.4)$$

since

$$\bar{\eta}_{.x.} = \frac{1}{t}\sum_i^t \eta_{.j.} = \frac{1}{t}\sum_j^T \eta_{.j.} = 0, \quad (4.5)$$

since $t = T$, and similarly $\bar{\eta}_{..x} = \bar{\zeta}_{.xx} = 0$. Thus

$$\bar{x}_{i..} - \bar{x}_{i'..} = (\eta_{i..} - \eta_{i'..}) + (\bar{z}_{i..} - \bar{z}_{i'..}), \quad (4.6)$$

SECT. 15.4 CONFIDENCE LIMITS IN THREE-WAY ANALYSIS

with expectation and variance

$$E[\bar{x}_{i..} - \bar{x}_{i'..}] = \eta_{i..} - \eta_{i'..}, \qquad (4.7)$$

$$V[\bar{x}_{i..} - \bar{x}_{i'..}] = V[\bar{z}_{i..}] + V[\bar{z}_{i'..}] = \frac{2\sigma^2}{tu}. \qquad (4.8)$$

Confidence limits for $\eta_{i..} - \eta_{i'..}$ can be obtained by inserting in place of σ^2 the mean square for ABC, which is assumed to estimate σ^2.

In the mixed model of the type (a, B, C), if we are going to construct confidence limits for the difference between two column means, $\eta_{.j.} - \eta_{.j'.}$, we will be making the assumption that the BC interaction $\zeta_{.jk} = 0$, and so the model (4.1) becomes

$$x_{ijk} = \xi + \eta_{i..} + \eta_{.j.} + \eta_{..k} + \zeta_{ij.} + \zeta_{i.k} + z_{ijk}. \qquad (4.9)$$

Averaging over i and k, we get

$$\bar{x}_{.j.} = \xi + \bar{\eta}_{x..} + \eta_{.j.} + \bar{\eta}_{..x} + \bar{\zeta}_{xj.} + \bar{\zeta}_{x.x} + \bar{z}_{.j.}, \qquad (4.10)$$

whence

$$\bar{x}_{.j.} - \bar{x}_{.j'.} = (\eta_{.j.} - \eta_{.j'.}) + (\bar{\zeta}_{xj.} - \bar{\zeta}_{xj'.}) + (\bar{z}_{.j.} - \bar{z}_{.j'.}). \qquad (4.11)$$

The $\zeta_{ij.}$ is a mixed interaction subject to the conditions $\sum_{i}^{R} \zeta_{ij.} = \sum_{j}^{T} \zeta_{ij.} = 0$, but, since $R = \infty$ and $T = t$, these conditions become $\sum_{i}^{\infty} \zeta_{ij.} = \sum_{j}^{t} \zeta_{ij.} = 0$. Thus $\zeta_{ij.}$ is distributed normally with zero mean and variance σ_{aB}^2 for each level of j, and hence $\bar{\zeta}_{xj.}$ is distributed normally with zero mean and variance σ_{aB}^2/r for each level of j. Hence

$$E[\bar{x}_{.j.} - \bar{x}_{.j'.}] = (\eta_{.j.} - \eta_{.j'.}), \qquad (4.12)$$

$$V[\bar{x}_{.j.} - \bar{x}_{.j'.}] = \frac{2\sigma_{aB}^2}{r} + \frac{2\sigma^2}{ru} = \frac{2}{ru}(\sigma^2 + u\sigma_{aB}^2), \qquad (4.13)$$

$$\hat{V}[\bar{x}_{.j.} - \bar{x}_{.j'.}] = \frac{2}{ru}(\text{M. S. for } aB), \qquad (4.14)$$

and confidence limits follow in the usual way.

In the mixed model of the type (a, b, C), we have

$$\bar{x}_{..k} = \xi + \bar{\eta}_{x..} + \bar{\eta}_{.x.} + \eta_{..k} + \bar{\zeta}_{xx.} + \bar{\zeta}_{x.k} + \bar{\zeta}_{.xk} + \bar{z}_{..k}, \qquad (4.15)$$

$$\bar{x}_{..k} - \bar{x}_{..k'} = (\eta_{..k} - \eta_{..k'}) + (\bar{\zeta}_{x.k} - \bar{\zeta}_{x.k'}) + (\bar{\zeta}_{.xk} - \bar{\zeta}_{.xk'}) + (\bar{z}_{..k} - \bar{z}_{..k'}). \qquad (4.16)$$

The $\zeta_{i.k}$ and $\zeta_{.jk}$ are mixed interactions distributed normally with zero means and variances σ_{aC}^2, σ_{bC}^2 for each level of k. Hence

$$E[\bar{x}_{..k} - \bar{x}_{..k'}] = \eta_{..k} - \eta_{..k'}, \tag{4.17}$$

$$V[\bar{x}_{..k} - \bar{x}_{..k'}] = \frac{2\sigma_{aC}^2}{r} + \frac{2\sigma_{bC}^2}{t} + \frac{2\sigma^2}{rt} = \frac{2}{rt}(\sigma^2 + t\sigma_{aC}^2 + r\sigma_{bC}^2), \tag{4.18}$$

$$\hat{V}[\bar{x}_{..k} - \bar{x}_{..k'}] = \frac{2}{rt}\text{ [M. S. for } aC + bC - abC\text{]}, \tag{4.19}$$

and the linear combination of mean squares will have its approximate degrees of freedom given by (9.8.10).

It will be noticed from the foregoing results that it is unnecessary in practice to go through these calculations to obtain the estimated variance of the difference between two means, since the answer always comes out to be twice the appropriate error mean square for testing the corresponding effect divided by the number of original observations in each mean being compared.

15.5. An Example of Three-Way Analysis of Variance

The data of Table 15.4 (taken from [7]) were obtained in a research program aimed at developing procedures for the bacteriological testing of milk. Milk samples were tested in an apparatus which involved two major components, a bottle and a tube. The result of a single test is simply

Table 15.4

Bottle (k)		I			II		
Tube (j)		A	B	C	A	B	C
Milk sample (i)	1	1	1	1	1	3	2
	2	3	4	2	2	1	3
	3	3	2	4	3	3	6
	4	2	4	1	1	0	0
	5	2	1	3	2	4	6
	6	1	1	2	0	2	1
	7	5	5	5	3	5	5
	8	1	1	1	0	2	0
	9	0	1	2	2	2	2
	10	3	4	5	1	1	3
	11	0	0	4	0	2	1
	12	0	1	2	0	3	1

recorded as growth or failure to grow. All six combinations of two types of bottle and three types of tube were tested on each sample, and 10 tests were run with each sample × bottle × tube combination. Table 15.4 gives the number of positive tubes in each set of 10. As discussed in Section 3.3, this variable should be binomially distributed, and, to obtain a variable with a stable variance, we should use the inverse sine transformation. However, our main purpose in presenting this example is as an illustration of the calculations for a three-way analysis of variance, and this will be

SECT. 15.5 AN EXAMPLE OF THREE-WAY ANALYSIS OF VARIANCE

achieved better by using the simple integers of Table 15.4. It is, however, instructive to also carry out the analysis of variance on the transformed variable and see how little the conclusions are affected. Let i refer to samples, j to tubes, and k to bottles.

Regarding Table 15.4 as a three-way classification with one observation per cell, the operations of summing over cells and calculating a within-cells sum of squares do not arise.

The first step in the analysis is to form sums over every index and every combination of indices; e.g., we sum over samples (i) to obtain a tube

Table 15.5. Sums over Samples (i), $\sum\limits_{i}^{r} x_{ijk}$

Bottle (k)	Tube (j)			$\sum\limits_{i}^{r}\sum\limits_{j}^{t} x_{ijk}$
	A	B	C	
I	21	25	32	78
II	15	28	30	73
$\sum\limits_{i}^{r}\sum\limits_{k}^{u} x_{ijk}$	36	53	62	151

(j) × bottle (k) table containing $\sum\limits_{i}^{r} x_{ijk}$ (Table 15.5). This table is then summed over bottles (k) to give the tube totals $\sum\limits_{i}^{r}\sum\limits_{k}^{u} x_{ijk}$ and over tubes (j) to give the bottle totals $\sum\limits_{i}^{r}\sum\limits_{j}^{t} x_{ijk}$. The sum of the tube totals, equal to the sum of the bottle totals, is the grand total $\sum\limits_{i}^{r}\sum\limits_{j}^{t}\sum\limits_{k}^{n} x_{ijk}$. Tables 15.6 and 15.7 are obtained similarly.

Table 15.6. Sums over Tubes (j), $\sum\limits_{j}^{t} x_{ijk}$

Sample (i)	Bottle (k)		$\sum\limits_{j}^{t}\sum\limits_{k}^{u} x_{ijk}$
	I	II	
1	3	6	9
2	9	6	15
3	9	12	21
4	7	1	8
5	6	12	18
6	4	3	7
7	15	13	28
8	3	2	5
9	3	6	9
10	12	5	17
11	4	3	7
12	3	4	7
$\sum\limits_{i}^{r}\sum\limits_{j}^{t} x_{ijk}$	78	73	151

Table 15.7. Sums over Bottles (k), $\sum\limits_{k}^{u} x_{ijk}$

Sample (i)	Tube (j)			$\sum\limits_{j}^{t}\sum\limits_{k}^{u} x_{ijk}$
	A	B	C	
1	2	4	3	9
2	5	5	5	15
3	6	5	10	21
4	3	4	1	8
5	4	5	9	18
6	1	3	3	7
7	8	10	10	28
8	1	3	1	5
9	2	3	4	9
10	4	5	8	17
11	0	2	5	7
12	0	4	3	7
$\sum\limits_{i}^{r}\sum\limits_{k}^{u} x_{ijk}$	36	53	62	151

516   THREE-WAY AND FOUR-WAY ANALYSIS OF VARIANCE   CHAP. 15

With these preliminary summations the subsequent calculations are straightforward. The sum of squares for samples is given by (1.13) with the modification that $n = 1$ and summation over v is not involved.

$$\text{S.S. for samples} = \frac{9^2 + 15^2 + \cdots + 7^2}{2 \times 3} - \frac{(151)^2}{2 \times 3 \times 12} = 93.486,$$

$$\text{S.S. for tubes} = \frac{36^2 + 53^2 + 62^2}{12 \times 2} - \frac{(151)^2}{2 \times 3 \times 12} = 14.527,$$

$$\text{S.S. for bottles} = \frac{78^2 + 73^2}{12 \times 3} - \frac{(151)^2}{2 \times 3 \times 12} = 0.347.$$

For the sample × tube interaction, the sums of squares is given by (1.14):

$$\frac{2^2 + 5^2 + 6^2 + \cdots + 3^2}{2} - \frac{(151)^2}{2 \times 3 \times 12} - 93.486 - 14.527 = 22.806.$$

The other two interactions are calculated similarly. The total sum of squares is given by (1.15):

$$(1^2 + 3^2 + \cdots + 1^2) - \frac{(151)^2}{2 \times 3 \times 12} = 184.319.$$

All these items are entered in Table 15.8 and the three-way interaction is calculated by difference.

Table 15.8

Source of variance	Sums of squares	Degrees of freedom	Mean squares	E[M.S.]
Samples	93.486	11	8.499	$\sigma^2 + 3 \times 2\sigma_s^2$
Tubes	14.527	2	7.263	$\sigma^2 + 2\sigma_{sT}^2 + 2 \times 12\sigma_T^2$
Bottles	0.347	1	0.347	$\sigma^2 + 3\sigma_{sB}^2 + 3 \times 12\sigma_B^2$
Samples × tubes	22.806	22	1.037	$\sigma^2 + 2\sigma_{sT}^2$
Samples × bottles	27.153	11	2.468	$\sigma^2 + 3\sigma_{sB}^2$
Tubes × bottles	1.695	2	0.847	$\sigma^2 + 12\sigma_{TB}^2$
Samples × tubes × bottles	24.305	22	1.105	σ^2
Total	184.319	71		

The tube and bottle are fixed effects and the sample is a random effect. If s, T, and B refer to samples, tubes, and bottles, application of the left half of Table 15.3, with $n = 1$ and $\sigma_{sTB}^2 = 0$, gives the expectations of mean squares in the last column of Table 15.8.

Interpreting this table as a nonpooler, it is apparent that bottles, samples × tubes, and tubes × bottles are nonsignificant. Samples × bottles has a variance ratio 2.23, and $F_{0.95}(11, 22) = 2.26$; so it does not quite reach the 0.05 level of significance. The tube main effect, tested against the sample × tube interaction, has a variance ratio of 7.00, and $F_{0.975}(2, 22) = 6.81$; so there is no doubt as to the significance of the tube effect. The sample effect is also highly significant, and the component of variance σ_s^2 is estimated as $(8.499 - 1.105)/6 = 1.232$.

Confidence limits can be constructed with (4.14). For example, for 95 per cent confidence limits between the two bottles, we want $t_{0.975}(11) = 2.201$, and $(\bar{x}_{..\text{I}} - \bar{x}_{..\text{II}}) = (78 - 73)/12 \times 3 = 0.139$: Also

$$\hat{V}[\bar{x}_{..\text{I}} - \bar{x}_{..\text{II}}] = \frac{2}{12 \times 3} [\text{M.S. for samples} \times \text{bottles}] = 0.1371.$$

The confidence limits are $0.139 \pm 2.201\sqrt{0.1371}$, or $(-0.676, 0.954)$. Confidence limits for the difference between any two tube averages can be constructed similarly, although if we are interested in more than one comparison it would be advisable to use Tukey's multiple-comparison technique (cf. Section 10.3).

15.6. Orthogonal Contrasts

It is possible to split the $r - 1$ degrees of freedom of a model I factor up into $r - 1$ separate single degrees of freedom, each corresponding to a specific contrast, in such a way that the $r - 1$ contrasts are independent and the sum of the sums of squares corresponding to each contrast adds up to the original unpartitioned sum of squares.

Suppose that we have r means $\bar{x}_i$ distributed normally with means ξ_i and variances σ^2/n_i. We define a contrast as in (10.3.1) as $\theta = \sum_i^r c_i \xi_i$, where $\sum_i^r c_i = 0$. As in (10.3.2) the contrast is estimated as $H = \sum_i^r c_i \bar{x}_i$, and H is distributed normally with expectation θ and variance $V[H] = \sigma^2 \sum_i^r c_i^2/n_i$. Therefore

$$\frac{H - \theta}{\left(\sigma^2 \sum_i^r c_i^2/n_i\right)^{1/2}} \sim N(0, 1), \tag{6.1}$$

and

$$\frac{(H - \theta)^2}{\sum_i^r c_i^2/n_i} \sim \sigma^2 \chi^2(1). \tag{6.2}$$

Thus under the null hypothesis $\theta = 0$ the quantity M defined as

$$M = \frac{\left(\sum_i^r c_i \bar{x}_i\right)^2}{\sum_i^r c_i^2/n_i} \quad (6.3)$$

will be distributed as $\sigma^2 \chi^2(1)$, and the ratio of (6.3) to an independent estimate s^2 of σ^2 with f degrees of freedom will be distributed as $F(1,f)$. More generally, taking expectations of (6.2),

$$\sigma^2 \sum_i^n \frac{c_i^2}{n_i} = E[H^2] + \theta^2 - 2\theta E[H] = E[H^2] - \theta^2, \quad (6.4)$$

whence, substituting $H = \sum_i^r c_i \bar{x}_i$ and rearranging,

$$E\left[\frac{\left(\sum_i^r c_i \bar{x}_i\right)^2}{\sum_i^r c_i^2/n_i}\right] = E[M] = \sigma^2 + \frac{\theta^2}{\sum_i^r c_i^2/n_i}. \quad (6.5)$$

If the $\bar{x}_i$ are based on totals T_i of n_i observations, so that $\bar{x}_i = T_i/n_i$, we can write M, (6.3), as

$$M = \frac{\left(\sum_i^r c_i T_i/n_i\right)^2}{\sum_i^r c_i^2/n_i} \quad (6.6)$$

and, when the n_i all equal n, this becomes

$$M = \frac{\left(\sum_i^r c_i T_i\right)^2}{n \sum_i^r c_i^2}. \quad (6.7)$$

Suppose now that we have two contrasts,

$$H_1 = \sum_i^r c_{1i}\bar{x}_i, \qquad H_2 = \sum_i^r c_{2i}\bar{x}_i, \quad (6.8)$$

and we require these to be independent. We saw in Section 12.3 that for independence it is sufficient, when H_1, H_2 are jointly normal, to show that they have zero covariance. Now

$$V[H_1 + H_2] = V[H_1] + V[H_2] + 2\operatorname{Cov}[H_1, H_2]; \quad (6.9)$$

so

$$2\operatorname{Cov}[H_1, H_2] = V[H_1 + H_2] - V[H_1] - V[H_2]. \quad (6.10)$$

SECT. 15.6 ORTHOGONAL CONTRASTS

But
$$V[H_1 + H_2] = V\left[\sum_i^r c_{1i}\bar{x}_i + \sum_i^r c_{2i}\bar{x}_i\right]$$
$$= V\left[\sum_i^r (c_{1i} + c_{2i})\bar{x}_i\right] = \sum_i^r (c_{1i} + c_{2i})^2 V[\bar{x}_i]$$
$$= \sigma^2\left(\sum_i^r \frac{c_{1i}^2}{n_i} + \sum_i^r \frac{c_{2i}^2}{n_i} + 2\sum_i^r \frac{c_{1i}c_{2i}}{n_i}\right); \qquad (6.11)$$

so
$$2\,\text{Cov}[H_1, H_2] = 2\sigma^2 \sum_i^r \frac{c_{1i}c_{2i}}{n_i}. \qquad (6.12)$$

Thus independence between H_1 and H_2 implies

$$\sum_i^r \frac{c_{1i}c_{2i}}{n_i} = 0, \qquad (6.13)$$

or, when the n_i are all equal to n,

$$\sum_i^r c_{1i}c_{2i} = 0, \qquad (6.14)$$

For $r - 1$ degrees of freedom, it is possible to construct infinitely many sets of $r - 1$ orthogonal contrasts, but we are only interested in contrasts that are reasonable.

In the milk testing example in Section 15.5, the three tubes were such that tubes B and C were quite similar in size but A was much smaller. It is therefore reasonable to define contrasts with coefficients

$$c_{1j} = 0, -1, 1, \qquad c_{2j} = -2, 1, 1. \qquad (6.15)$$

These coefficients do define contrasts since $\sum_j^t c_{mj} = 0$ for $m = 1$ and 2. Also they are orthogonal as they satisfy (6.14):

$$\sum_j^t c_{1j}c_{2j} = 0 \times (-2) + (-1) \times 1 + 1 \times 1 = 0. \qquad (6.16)$$

The first contrast will measure the difference between B and C, and the second will measure twice the difference between A and the mean of B and C. By (6.7) the sum of squares for the contrast H_m will be

$$M_m = \frac{\left(\sum_j^t c_{mj} \sum_i^r \sum_k^u x_{ijk}\right)^2}{ru \sum_j^t c_{mj}^2}. \qquad (6.17)$$

For $m = 1$, this is

$$\frac{[0 \times 36 + (-1) \times 53 + 1 \times 62]^2}{12 \times 2[0^2 + (-1)^2 + 1^2]} = 1.687, \qquad (6.18)$$

and, for $m = 2$, it is

$$\frac{[(-2) \times 36 + 1 \times 53 + 1 \times 62]^2}{12 \times 2[(-2)^2 + 1^2 + 1^2]} = 12.840. \qquad (6.19)$$

Each of these sums of squares has one degree of freedom, and the sum $1.687 + 12.840 = 14.527$ is the unpartitioned sum of squares for tubes with two degrees of freedom. The appropriate error term for the partitioned mean square is the same as for the unpartitioned mean square, the sample × tube interaction in this case. For the two components the F's are $1.687/1.037 = 1.63$ and $12.840/1.037 = 12.4$. The first contrast, between the similar tubes, is completely nonsignificant, but the second contrast, between the small tube and the mean of the larger tubes, is highly significant.

The set of orthogonal contrasts in Table 15.9 is applicable to the case where the factor is a numerically valued variable for which the gaps between successive levels are equal. The coefficients ξ_1', ξ_2', etc., will give the sums of squares for linear, quadratic, cubic, etc., terms in a polynomial of the dependent variable y on the factor x. Obviously, for k levels only $k - 1$ terms can be fitted. To construct the polynomial regression equation is not difficult, but we will not deal with it here: See [8], Chapter 16. Coefficients up to the fifth degree for numbers of levels k up to 52 are given in [9].

Table 15.9

$k = 3$		$k = 4$			$k = 5$			
ξ_1'	ξ_2'	ξ_1'	ξ_2'	ξ_3'	ξ_1'	ξ_2'	ξ_3'	ξ_4'
−1	1	−3	1	−1	−2	2	−1	1
0	−2	−1	−1	3	−1	−1	2	−4
1	1	1	−1	−3	0	−2	0	+6
		3	1	1	1	−1	−2	−4
					2	2	1	1

15.7. The Partitioning of Interactions into Orthogonal Contrasts

A $t \times u$ two-way table will have $(t - 1)(u - 1)$ degrees of freedom for interaction, and, if both the classifications are fixed effects which have been partitioned into orthogonal contrasts, it is possible to compute sums of squares with single degrees of freedom corresponding to the pairwise

THE PARTITIONING OF INTERACTIONS

interaction of single degrees of freedom of the two sets of orthogonal contrasts. An example will make this much clearer.

Table 15.10

(a)

	c_{11} 0	c_{12} −1	c_{13} 1
$d_1 = -1$	0	1	−1
$d_2 = 1$	0	−1	1

(b)

	c_{21} −2	c_{22} 1	c_{23} 1
$d_1 = -1$	2	−1	−1
$d_2 = 1$	−2	1	1

For the milk testing example in Section 15.5, we partitioned the main effect of tubes into two contrasts in Section 15.6. The other fixed effect, bottles, has only two levels, and so only one degree of freedom, but we can regard this as a single contrast defined by coefficients d_k: $d_1 = -1$, $d_2 = 1$. We then set up Table 15.10. We form the products $d_k c_{mj}$ in the body of the table. The coefficients so formed are contrasts, since within each table they sum to zero, and they are orthogonal, since the sum of products of corresponding coefficients is zero. (If the factor bottles had four levels, and we had partitioned it into three contrasts, there would have been three sets of d's, namely, d_{1k}, d_{2k}, and d_{3k}, and we would have gotten 6 two-way tables of coefficients corresponding to the 6 individual degrees of freedom of the interaction.)

To get the sums of squares corresponding to these two degrees of freedom, we use (6.7) again, and get the sum of the products of the coefficients in Tables 15.10a and b with the totals in Table 15.5. From Table 15.10a,

$$\frac{[0 \times 21 + 1 \times 25 + (-1) \times 32 + 0 \times 15 + (-1) \times 28 + 1 \times 30]^2}{12[0^2 + 1^2 + (-1)^2 + 0^2 + (-1)^2 + 1^2]}$$

$$= \frac{(-5)^2}{12 \times 4} = 0.521. \quad (7.1)$$

Table 15.10b gives a sum of squares 1.173, and the sum of these two components is 1.694 with 2 degrees of freedom, which is equal to the unpartitioned sum of squares for the bottle × tube interaction.

In the example of Section 15.5, two of the two-way interactions are mixed model interactions. For example, the tube × sample interaction has tube as a fixed effect, which is partitionable into orthogonal contrasts, and samples as a random effect, which cannot be partitioned into individual degrees of freedom. However, the $(r-1)(t-1)$ degrees of freedom can be partitioned into $t-1$ components, each consisting of $r-1$ degrees of freedom, representing the interaction of each component of the tube effect with samples. We calculate the value of the contrast for each sample, and then find the variance of these.

For example, consider the contrast defined by the coefficients $c_{1j} = 0$, $-1, 1$. Let H_{1i} be the value of this contrast for the ith sample.

$$H_{1i} = \sum_j^t c_{1j}\bar{x}_{ij.} = \sum_j^t c_{1j} \sum_k^u x_{ijk}/u. \tag{7.2}$$

Then

$$E[H_{1i}] = \sum_j^t c_{1j} E[\bar{x}_{ij.}] = \sum_j^t c_{1j} \xi_{ijx} = \theta_{1i}, \tag{7.3}$$

$$V[H_{1i}] = \sum_j^t c_{1j}^2 V[\bar{x}_{ij.}] = \frac{\sigma^2}{u} \sum_j^t c_{1j}^2. \tag{7.4}$$

Suppose that the null hypothesis that all the $\theta_{1i} = \bar{\theta}_{1.} = \theta_1$ is true. Then $\sum_i^r (H_{1i} - \bar{H}_{1.})^2/(r-1)$ is the usual sample estimate of the variance of the H_{1i} and

$$\frac{1}{r-1}\sum_i^r (H_{1i} - \bar{H}_{1.})^2 \sim \frac{\sigma^2}{u}\sum_j^t c_{1j}^2 \frac{\chi^2(r-1)}{(r-1)}, \tag{7.5}$$

so if we define N as

$$N = \frac{u \sum_i^r (H_{1i} - \bar{H}_{1.})^2}{(r-1)\sum_j^t c_{1j}^2} \tag{7.6}$$

it is distributed as $\sigma^2 \chi^2(r-1)/(r-1)$. Thus under the null hypothesis $\theta_{1i} = \theta_1$, the ratio N/s^2, where s^2 is an independent estimate of σ^2 with f degrees of freedom, has the $F(r-1, f)$ distribution. Substituting (7.2) for H_{1i}, N can be calculated from the relationship

$$(r-1)N = \frac{u}{\sum_j^t c_{ij}^2}\sum_i^r (H_{1i} - \bar{H}_{1.})^2 = \frac{u}{\sum_j^t c_{ij}^2}\left[\sum_i^r H_{1i}^2 - \left(\sum_i^r H_{1i}\right)^2/r\right]$$

$$= \frac{\sum_i^r \left(\sum_j^t c_{1j}\sum_k^u x_{ijk}\right)^2}{u \sum_j^t c_{1j}^2} - \frac{\left(\sum_j^t c_{1j}\sum_i^r \sum_k^u x_{ijk}\right)^2}{ru \sum_j^t c_{1j}^2}. \tag{7.7}$$

We will now find $E[N]$. We have the identity

$$H_{1i} - \theta_{1i} = (H_{1i} - \bar{H}_{1.}) - (\theta_{1i} - \bar{\theta}_{1.}) + (\bar{H}_{1.} - \bar{\theta}_{1.}), \tag{7.8}$$

SECT. 15.7 THE PARTITIONING OF INTERACTIONS

whence

$$\sum_{i}^{r}(H_{1i} - \theta_{1i})^2 = \sum_{i}^{r}[(H_{1i} - \bar{H}_{1.}) - (\theta_{1i} - \bar{\theta}_{1.})]^2 + r(\bar{H}_{1.} - \bar{\theta}_{1.})^2, \quad (7.9)$$

since the cross product is zero:

$$2\sum_{i}^{r}(\bar{H}_{1.} - \bar{\theta}_{1.})[(H_{1i} - \bar{H}_{1.}) - (\theta_{1i} - \bar{\theta}_{1.})]$$

$$= (\bar{H}_{1.} - \bar{\theta}_{1.})\left[\sum_{i}^{r}(H_{1i} - \theta_{1i}) - r(\bar{H}_{1.} - \bar{\theta}_{1.})\right] = 0. \quad (7.10)$$

The left-hand side of (7.9) is distributed as $(\sigma^2/u)\sum_{j}^{t} c_{1j}^2 \chi^2(r)$. Thus taking expected values, we have

$$r\left(\frac{\sigma^2}{u}\right)\sum_{j}^{t} c_{1j}^2 = E\left[\sum_{i}^{r}(H_{1i} - \bar{H}_{1.})^2\right] + \sum_{i}^{r}(\theta_{1i} - \bar{\theta}_{1.})^2$$

$$- 2\sum_{i}^{r}(\theta_{1i} - \bar{\theta}_{1.})E[H_{1i} - \bar{H}_{1.}] + \frac{\sigma^2}{u}\sum_{j}^{t} c_{1j}^2. \quad (7.11)$$

Thus

$$E\left[\sum_{i}^{r}(H_{1i} - \bar{H}_{1.})^2\right] = (r-1)\frac{\sigma^2}{u}\sum_{j}^{t} c_{1j}^2 + \sum_{i}^{r}(\theta_{1i} - \bar{\theta}_{1.})^2, \quad (7.12)$$

whence, referring to (7.6),

$$E[N] = \sigma^2 + \frac{u\sum_{i}^{r}(\theta_{1i} - \bar{\theta}_{1.})^2}{(r-1)\sum_{j}^{t} c_{1j}^2}. \quad (7.13)$$

The sums $\sum_{k}^{u} x_{ijk}$ are obtained by summing over bottles and were given in Table 15.7. The sums $\sum_{k}^{u} x_{11k}$, $\sum_{k}^{u} x_{12k}$, and $\sum_{k}^{u} x_{13k}$ are given by the entries in the first row, $i = 1$, in that table: 2, 4, and 3, respectively. Then for $i = 1, 2, 3, \ldots, r$, we have uH_{1i} taking the values

$$uH_{11} = \sum_{j}^{t} c_{1j}\sum_{k}^{u} x_{1jk} = [0 \times 2 + (-1) \times 4 + 1 \times 3] = -1, \quad (7.14)$$

$$uH_{12} = \sum_{j}^{t} c_{1j}\sum_{k}^{u} x_{2jk} = [0 \times 5 + (-1) \times 5 + 1 \times 5] = 0, \quad (7.15)$$

.
.
.

$$uH_{1r} = \sum_{j}^{t} c_{1j}\sum_{k}^{u} x_{rjk} = [0 \times 0 + (-1) \times 4 + 1 \times 3] = -1. \quad (7.16)$$

Then, since $u = 2$, the first term in (7.7) is

$$\frac{\sum_{i}^{r}\left(\sum_{j}^{t} c_{1j} \sum_{k}^{u} x_{ijk}\right)^{2}}{u \sum_{j}^{t} c_{1j}^{2}} = \frac{(-1)^{2} + 0^{2} + 5^{2} + \cdots + (-1)^{2}}{2 \times [0^{2} + (-1)^{2} + 1^{2}]} = \frac{75}{2 \times 2} = 18.750, \quad (7.17)$$

whence the sum of squares for the interaction of this contrast with samples is $18.750 - 1.687 = 17.063$.

A similar calculation for the second contrast gives for the interaction sum of squares

$$\frac{3^{2} + 0^{2} + 3^{2} + \cdots + 7^{2}}{2[(-2)^{2} + 1^{2} + 1]^{2}} - 12.840 = 18.583 - 12.840 = 5.743. \quad (7.18)$$

The sum of these two components, $17.063 + 5.743 = 22.806$, equals the unpartitioned sum of squares for the sample $\times$ tube interaction.

15.8. Four-Way Analysis of Variance

The analysis of a four-way classification is the obvious extension of three-way analysis, and we will review it only briefly. The model is

$$x_{ijkmv} = \xi_{ijkm} + z_{ijkmv} \quad (8.1)$$

where the ξ_{ijkm} have the structure

$$\begin{aligned}\xi_{ijkm} = \xi &+ \eta_{i\ldots} + \eta_{.j..} + \eta_{..k.} + \eta_{\ldots m} \\ &+ \zeta_{ij..} + \zeta_{i.k.} + \zeta_{i..m} + \zeta_{.jk.} + \zeta_{.j.m} + \zeta_{..km} \\ &+ \theta_{ijk.} + \theta_{ij.m} + \theta_{i.km} + \theta_{.jkm} + \omega_{ijkm}\end{aligned} \quad (8.2)$$

and the z_{ijkmv}, $v = 1, \ldots, n$, are normally distributed with zero mean and variance σ^{2}. The sample sizes for i, j, k, m are r, t, u, v, and the population sizes are R, T, U, V. The $\eta_{i\ldots}$ are a sample of size r from a population of size R and sum to zero in the population

$$\sum_{i}^{R} \eta_{i\ldots} = 0; \quad (8.3)$$

similarly for the other main effects. The two-way terms sum to zero in the population over each index, e.g.,

$$\sum_{i}^{R} \zeta_{ij..} = \sum_{j}^{T} \zeta_{ij..} = 0. \quad (8.4)$$

The three-way terms and the four-way terms also sum to zero in the population over each index, e.g.,

$$\sum_{i}^{R} \theta_{ijk.} = \sum_{j}^{T} \theta_{ijk.} = \sum_{k}^{U} \theta_{ijk.} = 0 \quad (8.5)$$

and

$$\sum_{i}^{R} \omega_{ijkm} = \sum_{j}^{T} \omega_{ijkm} = \sum_{k}^{U} \omega_{ijkm} = \sum_{m}^{V} \omega_{ijkm} = 0. \quad (8.6)$$

SECT. 15.8   FOUR-WAY ANALYSIS OF VARIANCE   525

We define σ_A^2, σ_{AB}^2, etc., analogously to the definitions (1.9).
The usual identity $x_{ijkmv} - \bar{x}_{.....} = $ etc. has on its right-hand side the following groups of terms:

1. Sample estimates of the four main effects, e.g., $\bar{x}_{i....} - \bar{x}_{.....}$, which is an estimate of $\eta_{i...}$.
2. Sample estimates of the six two-way interactions, e.g., $\bar{x}_{ij...} - \bar{x}_{i....} - \bar{x}_{.j...} + \bar{x}_{.....}$, which is an estimate of $\zeta_{ij..}$.
3. Sample estimates of the four three-way interactions, e.g., $\bar{x}_{ijk..} - \bar{x}_{ij...} - \bar{x}_{i.k..} - \bar{x}_{.jk..} + \bar{x}_{i....} + \bar{x}_{.j...} + \bar{x}_{..k..} - \bar{x}_{.....}$, which is an estimate of $\theta_{ijk.}$.
4. The sample estimate of the single four-way interaction, which will have the form $\bar{x}_{ijkm.} - [\bar{x}_{.....} + \text{main effects} + \text{two-way interactions} + \text{three-way interactions}]$.
5. The deviations of the individual observations from the cell means, e.g., $x_{ijkmv} - \bar{x}_{ijkm.}$.

Squaring and summing over all indices gives the partitioning of the total sum of squares. Typical sums of squares and computing identities are

$$A = nvut \sum_{i}^{r} (\bar{x}_{i....} - \bar{x}_{.....})^2$$

$$= \frac{1}{tuvn} \sum_{i}^{r} \left(\sum_{j}^{t} \sum_{k}^{u} \sum_{m}^{v} \sum_{v}^{n} x_{ijkmv} \right)^2 - \frac{1}{rtuvn} \left(\sum_{i}^{r} \sum_{j}^{t} \sum_{k}^{u} \sum_{m}^{v} \sum_{v}^{n} x_{ijkmv} \right)^2, \quad (8.7)$$

$$AB = nvu \sum_{i}^{r} \sum_{j}^{t} (\bar{x}_{ij...} - \bar{x}_{i....} - \bar{x}_{.j...} + \bar{x}_{.....})^2$$

$$= \frac{1}{uvn} \sum_{i}^{r} \sum_{j}^{t} \left(\sum_{k}^{u} \sum_{m}^{v} \sum_{v}^{n} x_{ijkmv} \right)^2 - \frac{1}{rtuvn} \left(\sum_{i}^{r} \sum_{j}^{t} \sum_{k}^{u} \sum_{m}^{v} \sum_{v}^{n} x_{ijkmv} \right)^2$$

$$- \text{ sum of squares for } A - \text{ sum of squares for } B, \quad (8.8)$$

$$ABC = nv \sum_{i}^{r} \sum_{j}^{t} \sum_{k}^{u} (\bar{x}_{ijk..} - \bar{x}_{ij...} - \bar{x}_{i.k..} - \bar{x}_{.jk..} + \bar{x}_{i....} + \bar{x}_{.j...} + \bar{x}_{..k..} - \bar{x}_{.....})^2$$

$$= \frac{1}{vn} \sum_{i}^{r} \sum_{j}^{t} \sum_{k}^{u} \left(\sum_{m}^{v} \sum_{v}^{n} x_{ijkmv} \right)^2 - \frac{1}{rtuvn} \left(\sum_{i}^{r} \sum_{j}^{t} \sum_{k}^{u} \sum_{m}^{v} \sum_{v}^{n} x_{ijkmv} \right)^2$$

$$- (\text{sums of squares for } A, B, C, AB, AC, BC), \quad (8.9)$$

$$ABCD = \frac{1}{n} \sum_{i}^{r} \sum_{j}^{t} \sum_{k}^{u} \sum_{m}^{v} \left(\sum_{v}^{n} x_{ijkmv} \right)^2 - \frac{1}{rtuvn} \left(\sum_{i}^{r} \sum_{j}^{t} \sum_{k}^{u} \sum_{m}^{v} \sum_{v}^{n} x_{ijkmv} \right)^2$$

$$- \begin{pmatrix} \text{sums of squares for all main effects} \\ \text{two-way and three-way interactions} \end{pmatrix}, \quad (8.10)$$

$$\text{Within cells} = \sum_{i}^{r} \sum_{j}^{t} \sum_{k}^{u} \sum_{m}^{v} \sum_{v}^{n} x_{ijkmv}^2 - \frac{1}{n} \sum_{i}^{r} \sum_{j}^{t} \sum_{k}^{u} \sum_{m}^{v} \left(\sum_{v}^{n} x_{ijkmv} \right)^2. \quad (8.11)$$

The degrees of freedom for the foregoing are $r-1$, $(r-1)(t-1)$, $(r-1)(t-1)(u-1)$, $(r-1)(t-1)(u-1)(v-1)$, and $rtuv(n-1)$, respectively.

The expectations of the mean squares are as follows:

$$E[\text{M. S. for } A] = \sigma^2 + n\left(1 - \frac{v}{V}\right)\left(1 - \frac{u}{U}\right)\left(1 - \frac{t}{T}\right)\sigma^2_{ABCD}$$

$$+ nv\left(1 - \frac{u}{U}\right)\left(1 - \frac{t}{T}\right)\sigma^2_{ABC} + nu\left(1 - \frac{v}{V}\right)\left(1 - \frac{t}{T}\right)\sigma^2_{ABD}$$

$$+ nt\left(1 - \frac{v}{V}\right)\left(1 - \frac{u}{U}\right)\sigma^2_{ACD} + nuv\left(1 - \frac{t}{T}\right)\sigma^2_{AB}$$

$$+ ntv\left(1 - \frac{u}{U}\right)\sigma^2_{AC} + ntu\left(1 - \frac{v}{V}\right)\sigma^2_{AD} + ntuv\sigma^2_A, \quad (8.12)$$

$$E[\text{M. S. for } AB] = \sigma^2 + n\left(1 - \frac{u}{U}\right)\left(1 - \frac{v}{V}\right)\sigma^2_{ABCD} + nv\left(1 - \frac{u}{U}\right)\sigma^2_{ABC}$$

$$+ nu\left(1 - \frac{v}{V}\right)\sigma^2_{ABD} + nuv\sigma^2_{AB}, \quad (8.13)$$

$$E[\text{M. S. for } ABC] = \sigma^2 + n\left(1 - \frac{v}{V}\right)\sigma^2_{ABCD} + nv\sigma^2_{ABC}, \quad (8.14)$$

$$E[\text{M. S. for } ABCD] = \sigma^2 + n\sigma^2_{ABCD}. \quad (8.15)$$

The various models can be obtained from this finite population model.

EXERCISES

15.1. Four strains of a microorganism producing an antibiotic in a fermentation process were to be compared. The comparison was made on four batches of the main ingredient of the broth. A further factor was introduced into the experiment, namely, concentration of the broth, at three levels, equally spaced. The yields were as follows:

Batch	Strain	Concentration			Batch	Strain	Concentration		
		1	2	3			1	2	3
1	A	40	69	70	3	A	55	79	102
	B	52	71	91		B	61	83	94
	C	78	100	110		C	71	106	106
	D	59	76	108		D	78	103	127
2	A	47	76	91	4	A	44	77	85
	B	64	72	99		B	69	75	116
	C	73	122	143		C	87	106	131
	D	77	106	127		D	76	107	125

The strains are a model I effect, and in fact the main objective of the experiment is to select the best strain. The batches are a model II effect, and the concentration is a model I effect, partitionable into linear and quadratic components.

(a) Give the conventional analysis of variance with the expectations of the mean squares. Make tests of significance of the various effects. State succinctly your interpretation of the effects of the various factors.

(b) Give 95 per cent confidence limits for the difference between strain C and strain D, averaged over batches and concentrations.

15.2. The table below gives the results of an experiment on the amounts of niacin found in peas after various treatments. The factors were:

(a) A comparison between blanched peas P_0 and processed peas P_1.
(b) Two temperatures of cooking: $C_0 = 175°F$, $C_1 = 200°F$.
(c) Two times of cooking: $T_0 = 2\frac{1}{2}$ min, $T_1 = 8$ min.
(d) Three different sieve sizes of peas: S_1, S_2, S_3.

C	S	P_0		P_1	
		T_0	T_1	T_0	T_1
0	1	91	72	86	68
	2	92	68	85	72
	3	112	73	101	73
1	1	84	78	83	76
	2	94	78	90	71
	3	98	73	94	76

Source: R. Wagner, F. M. Strong, and C. A. Elvehyem, "Effects of Blenching on the Retention of Ascorbic Acid, Thiamine, and Niacin in Vegetables," *Industrial and Engineering Chemistry*, 39(1947), 990–93.

Make an analysis of variance of these data. Suppose that the levels of the factor sieve size are spaced equally, and partition the main effect of sieve size into components corresponding to linear and quadratic terms: likewise for the first-order interactions. Include in the analysis the second-order interactions, but do not bother with any partitioning of these. The highest-order interaction mean square will have too few degrees of freedom to be a satisfactory estimate of error (since there is no replication, there is no explicit estimate available). Therefore, for an estimate of error pool the second-order interactions with the highest-order interaction (i.e., assume that the second- and third-order interactions are all zero and hence the corresponding mean squares are all estimates of σ^2).

What effects do you consider to be statistically significant at the 0.05 level? For uniformity,

(a) be a never-pooler (apart from that recommended in the previous paragraph); (b) in testing the first-order interactions, make due allowance for the fact that there are quite a large number of them; (c) on the other hand, be more generous to the main effects, and test them individually.

Summarize in appropriate tables the effects you find statistically significant, and list the effects you consider nonsignificant.

15.3. In a comparison of three different compositions of mortar, three lots of cement were supplied to each of five laboratories. Each laboratory using each lot of cement made up batches of mortar according to the three compositions. Two-inch cubes of mortar were cast and the compressive strength determined. The factor composition is a model I effect, and the factors cements and laboratories are model II effects.

(*a*) Make a conventional analysis of variance of this data, presenting the results in standard tabular form, including the expectations of the mean squares. (*b*) Test the null hypotheses that the various main effects and interactions are zero. (*c*) Give estimates of the components of variance corresponding to the various random terms in your model. (*d*) Give 95 per cent confidence limits for the difference between compositions 1 and 2.

The compositions were such that it would be interesting to consider the following contrasts: (i) between compositions 1 and 2. (ii) between the mean of compositions 1 and 2 and composition 3.

(*e*) Partition the main effect for composition into single degrees of freedom corresponding to these two contrasts. Test the null hypotheses that each contrast is zero. (*f*) Partition the laboratory × composition interaction into two components and test the null hypotheses that they are zero.

Cement	1			2			3		
Composition	1	2	3	1	2	3	1	2	3
Lab 1	812	839	723	870	838	798	859	863	761
2	746	744	689	799	797	759	787	765	709
3	797	802	731	771	737	724	781	821	753
4	850	896	757	864	877	779	843	854	759
5	829	829	735	887	903	765	863	940	777

The sum of squares of all observations is 29,068,527.

Source: Working Committee on Plastic Mortar Tests, "Report on Investigation of Mortars by Seven Laboratories," *Proceedings of the American Society for Testing and Materials*, 40 (1940), 210–25.

REFERENCES

1. Cornfield, Jerome, and John W. Tukey, "Average Values of Mean Squares in Factorials," *Annals of Mathematical Statistics*, 27 (1956), 907–949.
2. Paull, A. E., "On a Preliminary Test for Pooling Mean Squares in the Analysis of Variance," *Annals of Mathematical Statistics*, 21 (1950), 539–56.
3. Finney, D. J., "The Joint Distribution of Variance Ratios Based on a Common Error Mean Square," *Annals of Eugenics*, 11 (1941), 136–40.
4. Nair, K. R., "The Studentized Form of the Extreme Mean Square Test in the Analysis of Variance," *Biometrika*, 35 (1948), 16–31.
5. Daniel, C., "Fractional Replication in Industrial Research," *Third Berkeley Symposium on Mathematical Statistics and Probability*, vol. 5, 87–98. J. Neyman (ed.). Berkeley: University of California Press, 1956.

REFERENCES

6. Birnbaum, A., "On the Analysis of Factorial Experiments without Replication." Contributed paper at Annual Meeting of the Institute of Mathematical Statistics, Cambridge, Massachusetts, August 25–28, 1958.
7. Barkworth, H., and J. O. Irwin, "Comparative Detection of Coliform Organisms in Milk and Water by the Presumptive Coliform Test," *Journal of Hygiene*, 43 (1943), 129–35.
8. Anderson, R. L., and T. A. Bancroft, *Statistical Theory in Research*. New York: McGraw-Hill Book Co., 1952.
9. Fisher, R. A., and F. Yates, *Statistical Tables for Biological, Agricultural, and Medical Research*. 3rd ed.; Edinburgh: Oliver and Boyd, 1948.

CHAPTER 16

Partially Hierarchical Situations

16.1. A Partially Hierarchical Situation and Its Model

In an investigation of the can-making properties of tin plate, two methods of annealing were studied. Three coils were selected at random out of a supposedly infinite population of coils made by each of these two methods. From each coil, samples were taken from two particular and reproducible locations, namely, the head and tail of each coil. From each sample, two sets of cans were made up independently, and from each set an estimate of the can life was obtained: These are the data in Table 16.1, taken from

Table 16.1

Location k	Duplicates v	Annealing method i					
		1			2		
		Coils within anneals $j(i)$					
		1(1)	2(1)	3(1)	1(2)	2(2)	3(2)
1	1	288	355	329	310	303	299
	2	295	369	343	282	321	328
2	1	278	336	320	288	302	289
	2	272	342	315	287	297	284

[1]. For a definitive study, one would require a substantially larger sample of coils, but the data of Table 16.1 will suffice to demonstrate the principles involved in the analysis.

The structure of this experiment is rather different from what we have previously encountered. If the coils were crossed across annealing method, so that the first coil with annealing method 1 corresponded in some way with the first coil with annealing method 2, and the second coils likewise, etc., then we would have a three-way analysis with replication in the cells. However, this is not the case: The coils are not so crossed, but instead are nested within the annealing methods. Alternatively, if the locations were random samples from each coil, so that they were nested within the coils, with no crossing of location 1 across coils or annealing methods, then we would have a purely nested or hierarchical situation, with four classifications, namely, annealing methods, coils within annealing methods, locations within coils, and replications within locations. However, this is not the case: The locations are a model I effect crossed across coils and annealing methods.

What we have is a *partially hierarchical* or *crossed nested* situation, which can be represented by the model

$$x_{ijkv} = \xi + \alpha_i + \{c(\alpha)\}_{j(i)} + \lambda_k + (\lambda\alpha)_{ik} + \{\lambda c(\alpha)\}_{kj(i)} + z_{ijkv}, \quad (1.1)$$

in which ξ is the grand mean, α_i is the annealing method effect, $\{c(\alpha)\}_{j(i)}$ represents the random coil effect within annealing method, λ_k represents the location effect, $(\lambda\alpha)_{ik}$ represents the interaction of locations with annealing methods, $\{\lambda c(\alpha)\}_{kj(i)}$ represents the interaction of locations with coils within anneals, and z_{ijkv} is a random error distributed normally with zero mean and variance σ^2.

In (1.1), single symbols could be used in place of $\{c(\alpha)\}$, $(\lambda\alpha)$, $\{\lambda c(\alpha)\}$, but the use of these multiple symbols is helpful in identifying immediately the meaning of each. It is also helpful to use Greek letters to denote fixed, model I effects, e.g., α and λ, and Roman letters for random, model II effects, e.g., c and z, and this has been done in (1.1), somewhat prematurely, as we will first consider the finite population model and then move to this particular case. Thus for the finite population model, i goes to r in the sample and R in the population, j to t in the sample and T in the population, k to u in the sample and U in the population, and v, which is from an infinite population, to n in the sample.

There are various side restrictions on the model (1.1). First,

$$\sum_i^R \alpha_i = 0, \quad \sum_k^U \lambda_k = 0, \quad \sum_i^R (\lambda\alpha)_{ik} = \sum_k^U (\lambda\alpha)_{ik} = 0. \quad (1.2)$$

These conditions are similar to those for a two-way model, (14.8.2) and (14.8.3). Second, the coils-within-annealing-methods term $\{c(\alpha)\}_{j(i)}$ is a standard nested term similar to the $\lambda_{j(i)}$ of Section 14.10 and Table 14.15, i.e.,

$$\sum_j^T \{c(\alpha)\}_{j(i)} = 0 \quad \text{for each } i. \quad (1.3)$$

The complete array of $\{\lambda c(\alpha)\}_{kj(i)}$ is indicated in Table 16.2. For each value of i we have a two-way table of interaction constants with the usual property of two-way interaction constants of summing to zero in each row and in each column [see (14.8.3)], i.e.,

$$\sum_{j}^{T} \{\lambda c(\alpha)\}_{kj(i)} = 0 \quad \text{for each } (k, i), \qquad (1.4)$$

$$\sum_{k}^{U} \{\lambda c(\alpha)\}_{kj(i)} = 0 \quad \text{for each } j(i). \qquad (1.5)$$

However, for a fixed k, i.e., in Table 16.2 for a fixed row, the $\{\lambda c(\alpha)\}_{kj(i)}$ do not sum to zero over i for a fixed j. In this respect they behave similarly to the $\lambda_{j(i)}$ of Table 14.15.

16.2. Calculation of Sums of Squares, Etc.

The identity corresponding to the model (1.1) is

$$\begin{aligned}
x_{ijkv} - \bar{x}_{....} &= (\bar{x}_{i...} - \bar{x}_{....}) + (\bar{x}_{ij..} - \bar{x}_{i...}) + (\bar{x}_{..k.} - \bar{x}_{....}) \\
&\quad + (\bar{x}_{i.k.} - \bar{x}_{i...} - \bar{x}_{..k.} + \bar{x}_{....}) + (\bar{x}_{ijk.} - \bar{x}_{ij..} - \bar{x}_{i.k.} + \bar{x}_{i...}) \\
&\quad + (x_{ijkv} - \bar{x}_{ijk.}). \qquad (2.1)
\end{aligned}$$

The terms on the right-hand side are the sample estimates of the terms on the right-hand side of the model (1.1), excluding the grand mean. The first and third terms need no comment. The second term is similar to an ordinary nested term such as the second term in (14.7.2). The fourth term is an ordinary two-way interaction resembling (15.1.11). The fifth term can be obtained by regarding it as the difference between $\bar{x}_{ijk.}$ and what would be predicted as the grand sum $\bar{x}_{....}$ plus the annealing method effect $\bar{x}_{i...} - \bar{x}_{....}$ plus the coils-within-annealing-method effect $\bar{x}_{ij..} - \bar{x}_{....}$ plus the location effect $\bar{x}_{..k.} - \bar{x}_{....}$ plus the location × anneal two-way interaction $\bar{x}_{i.k.} - \bar{x}_{i...} - \bar{x}_{..k.} + \bar{x}_{....}$; i.e.,

$$\begin{aligned}
\bar{x}_{ijk.} &- [\bar{x}_{....} + (\bar{x}_{i...} - \bar{x}_{....}) + (x_{ij..} - \bar{x}_{i...}) + (\bar{x}_{..k.} - \bar{x}_{....}) \\
&\quad + (\bar{x}_{i.k.} - \bar{x}_{i...} - \bar{x}_{..k.} + \bar{x}_{....})] \\
&= \bar{x}_{ijk.} - \bar{x}_{ij..} - \bar{x}_{i.k.} + \bar{x}_{i...}. \qquad (2.2)
\end{aligned}$$

An alternative way of constructing partially hierarchical models is to consider them as degenerate cases of fully crossed models. For example, we suppose momentarily that the coil effect is fully crossed, so that there will be a coil main effect $\bar{x}_{.j..} - \bar{x}_{....}$ and an anneal × coil interaction

Table 16.2

	$i = 1$		$\cdots$	$i = R$	
	$j(i) = 1(1) \cdots j(i) = T(1)$			$j(i) = 1(R) \cdots j(i) = T(R)$	
$k = 1$	$\{\lambda c(\alpha)\}_{11(1)} \cdots \{\lambda c(\alpha)\}_{1T(1)}$	$\sum_{j}^{T}\{\lambda c(\alpha)\}_{1j(1)} = 0$		$\{\lambda c(\alpha)\}_{11(R)} \cdots \{\lambda c(\alpha)\}_{1T(R)}$	$\sum_{j}^{T}\{\lambda c(\alpha)\}_{1j(R)} = 0$
$k = k$	$\{\lambda c(\alpha)\}_{kT(1)}$	$\sum_{j}^{T}\{\lambda c(\alpha)\}_{kj(1)} = 0$		$\{\lambda c(\alpha)\}_{k1(R)}$ $\{\lambda c(\alpha)\}_{kT(R)}$	$\sum_{j}^{T}\{\lambda c(\alpha)\}_{kj(R)} = 0$
$k = U$	$\{\lambda c(\alpha)\}_{U1(1)}$ $\{\lambda c(\alpha)\}_{UT(1)}$	$\sum_{j}^{T}\{\lambda c(\alpha)\}_{Uj(1)} = 0$		$\{\lambda c(\alpha)\}_{U1(R)}$ $\{\lambda c(\alpha)\}_{UT(R)}$	$\sum_{j}^{T}\{\lambda c(\alpha)\}_{Uj(R)} = 0$
	$\sum_{k}^{U}\{\lambda c(\alpha)\}_{k1(1)}$ $\sum_{k}^{U}\{\lambda c(\alpha)\}_{kT(1)}$			$\sum_{k}^{U}\{\lambda c(\alpha)\}_{k1(R)}$ $\sum_{k}^{U}\{\lambda c(\alpha)\}_{kT(R)}$	
	$= 0$ $= 0$			$= 0$ $= 0$	

$\bar{x}_{ij..} - \bar{x}_{i...} - \bar{x}_{.j..} + \bar{x}_{....}$. Now we admit that the coil effect is not a main effect and pool it with its interaction with anneals:

$$(\bar{x}_{.j..} - \bar{x}_{....}) + (\bar{x}_{ij..} - \bar{x}_{i...} - \bar{x}_{.j..} + \bar{x}_{....}) = \bar{x}_{ij..} - \bar{x}_{i...}, \quad (2.3)$$

which is the second term on the right-hand side of (2.1). Similarly, if coils was a crossed effect, then it would have an interaction with locations, and its interaction with anneals would also have an interaction with locations. But, since coils is not a crossed effect, these two interactions are pooled together:

$$(\bar{x}_{.jk.} - \bar{x}_{.j..} - \bar{x}_{..k.} + \bar{x}_{....})$$
$$+ (\bar{x}_{ijk.} - \bar{x}_{ij..} - \bar{x}_{i.k.} - \bar{x}_{.jk.} + \bar{x}_{i...} + \bar{x}_{.j..} + \bar{x}_{..k.} - \bar{x}_{....})$$
$$= \bar{x}_{ijk.} - \bar{x}_{ij..} - \bar{x}_{i.k.} + \bar{x}_{i...}, \quad (2.4)$$

which is identical with (2.2).

This viewpoint also applies to the degrees of freedom. For coils within anneals, each anneal contributes $t - 1$ degrees of freedom and there are r anneals; so the degrees of freedom are $r(t - 1)$. But, taking the viewpoint of (2.3), the degrees of freedom should be

$$(t - 1) + (r - 1)(t - 1) = r(t - 1), \quad (2.5)$$

which is the same result.

For the interaction of locations × coils within anneals, since locations have $u - 1$ degrees of freedom and coils within anneals have $r(t - 1)$ degrees of freedom, their interaction will have $r(t - 1)(u - 1)$ degrees of freedom. From the viewpoint of (2.4), the degrees of freedom will be

$$(t - 1)(u - 1) + (r - 1)(u - 1)(t - 1) = r(t - 1)(u - 1), \quad (2.6)$$

which is the same result.

Squaring and summing over all indices (2.1) gives an equation entered in the second column of Table 16.3. To calculate these sums of squares we form Table 16.4 by summing over v. We next sum over k to get the coils-within-annealing-method table. We also sum over j to get the locations × annealing method table. Summing this over i gives the location totals and over k gives the annealing method totals. The sum of squares for annealing methods is an ordinary main effect [see (15.1.13)]:

$$nut \sum_{i}^{r} (\bar{x}_{i...} - \bar{x}_{....})^2 = \frac{3842^2 + 3590^2}{2 \times 3 \times 2} - \frac{(7432)^2}{2 \times 3 \times 2 \times 2} = 2646.000. \quad (2.7)$$

Table 16.3

Source of variance	Sums of squares	Degrees of freedom	E[M. S.]
Annealing methods	$nut \sum_i^r (\bar{x}_{i\ldots} - \bar{x}_{\ldots})^2$	$r-1$	$\sigma^2 + \left(1 - \frac{t}{T}\right)\left(1 - \frac{u}{U}\right) n\sigma^2_{\lambda c(\alpha)} + t\left(1 - \frac{u}{U}\right) n\sigma^2_{\lambda \alpha} + \left(1 - \frac{t}{T}\right) un\sigma^2_{c(\alpha)} + tun\sigma^2_\alpha$
Coils within annealing methods	$nu \sum_i^r \sum_j^t (\bar{x}_{ij\ldots} - \bar{x}_{i\ldots})^2$	$r(t-1)$	$\sigma^2 + \left(1 - \frac{u}{U}\right) n\sigma^2_{\lambda c(\alpha)} + un\sigma^2_{c(\alpha)}$
Locations	$nrt \sum_k^u (\bar{x}_{\ldots k\cdot} - \bar{x}_{\ldots})^2$	$u-1$	$\sigma^2 + \left(1 - \frac{t}{T}\right) n\sigma^2_{\lambda c(\alpha)} + \left(1 - \frac{r}{R}\right) tn\sigma^2_{\lambda \alpha} + rtn\sigma_\lambda$
Locations × annealing methods	$nt \sum_i^r \sum_k^u (\bar{x}_{i\cdot k\cdot} - \bar{x}_{i\ldots} - \bar{x}_{\ldots k\cdot} + \bar{x}_{\ldots})^2$	$(r-1)(u-1)$	$\sigma^2 + n\left(1 - \frac{t}{T}\right)\sigma^2_{\lambda c(\alpha)} + tn\sigma^2_{\lambda \alpha}$
Locations × coils within annealing methods	$n \sum_i^r \sum_j^t \sum_k^u (\bar{x}_{ijk\cdot} - \bar{x}_{ij\cdot\cdot} - \bar{x}_{i\cdot k\cdot} + \bar{x}_{i\ldots})^2$	$r(t-1)(u-1)$	$\sigma^2 + n\sigma^2_{\lambda c(\alpha)}$
Within cells	$\sum_i^r \sum_j^t \sum_k^u \sum_v^n (x_{ijkv} - \bar{x}_{ijk\cdot})^2$	$rtu(n-1)$	σ^2
Total	$\sum_i^r \sum_j^t \sum_k^u \sum_v^n (x_{ijkv} - \bar{x}_{\ldots})^2$	$rtun-1$	

Table 16.4. The x_{ijkv} of Table 16.1 Summed over v, $\sum_{v}^{n} x_{ijkv}$

Annealing method i			$i=1$				$i=2$			Sum
Coils within annealing method $j(i)$	1(1)	2(1)	3(1)	$\sum_{j}^{t}\sum_{v}^{n} x_{1jkv}$	1(2)	2(2)	3(2)	$\sum_{j}^{t}\sum_{v}^{n} x_{2jkv}$	$\sum_{i}^{r}\sum_{j}^{t}\sum_{v}^{n} x_{ijkv}$
Location, $k=1$	583	724	672	1979	592	624	627	1843	3822
$k=2$	550	678	635	1863	575	599	573	1747	3610
$\sum_{k}^{u}\sum_{v}^{n} x_{ijkv}$	1133	1402	1307	$\sum_{k}^{u}\sum_{j}^{t}\sum_{v}^{n} x_{1jkv} = 3842$	1167	1223	1200	$\sum_{k}^{u}\sum_{j}^{t}\sum_{v}^{n} x_{2jkv} = 3590$	$\sum_{i}^{r}\sum_{j}^{t}\sum_{k}^{u}\sum_{v}^{n} x_{ijkv} = 7432$

SECT. 16.2   CALCULATION OF SUMS OF SQUARES, ETC.   537

The sum of squares for coils within anneals is an ordinary nested effect:

$$nu \sum_i^r \sum_j^t (\bar{x}_{ij..} - \bar{x}_{i...})^2$$

$$= \frac{1}{un} \sum_i^r \sum_j^t \left(\sum_k^u \sum_v^n x_{ijkv}\right)^2 - \frac{1}{tun} \sum_i^r \left(\sum_j^t \sum_k^u \sum_v^n x_{ijkv}\right)^2$$

$$= \frac{1133^2 + 1402^2 + \cdots + 1200^2}{2 \times 2} - \frac{3842^2 + 3590^2}{3 \times 2 \times 2}$$

$$= 9701.333. \tag{2.8}$$

The sum of squares for locations is an ordinary main effect [(see (15.1.13)]:

$$nrt \sum_k^u (\bar{x}_{..k.} - \bar{x}_{....})^2 = \frac{3822^2 + 3610^2}{2 \times 3 \times 2} - \frac{(7432)^2}{2 \times 3 \times 2 \times 2} = 1872.667. \tag{2.9}$$

The sum of squares for locations × annealing methods is an ordinary two-way interaction [see (15.1.14)]:

$$nt \sum_i^r \sum_k^u (\bar{x}_{i.k.} - \bar{x}_{i...} - \bar{x}_{..k.} + \bar{x}_{....})^2$$

$$= \frac{1979^2 + \cdots + 1747^2}{2 \times 3} - \frac{(7432)^2}{2 \times 3 \times 2 \times 2} - 2646.000 - 1872.667$$

$$= 16.667. \tag{2.10}$$

The sum of squares for locations × coils within annealing methods can be calculated from the identity

$$n \sum_i^r \sum_j^t \sum_k^u (\bar{x}_{ijk.} - \bar{x}_{ij..} - \bar{x}_{i.k.} + \bar{x}_{i...})^2$$

$$= n \sum_i^r \sum_j^t \sum_k^u (\bar{x}_{ijk.} - \bar{x}_{....})^2 - nut \sum_i^r (\bar{x}_{i...} - \bar{x}_{....})^2$$

$$- nu \sum_i^r \sum_j^t (\bar{x}_{ij..} - \bar{x}_{i...})^2 - nrt \sum_k^u (\bar{x}_{..k.} - \bar{x}_{....})^2$$

$$- nt \sum_i^r \sum_k^u (\bar{x}_{i.k.} - \bar{x}_{i...} - \bar{x}_{..k.} + \bar{x}_{....})^2 \tag{2.11}$$

where

$$n \sum_i^r \sum_j^t \sum_k^u (\bar{x}_{ijk.} - \bar{x}_{....})^2 = \frac{\sum_i^r \sum_j^t \sum_k^u \left(\sum_v^n x_{ijkv}\right)^2}{n} - \frac{\left(\sum_i^r \sum_j^t \sum_k^u \sum_v^n x_{ijkv}\right)^2}{rtun}.$$

$$\tag{2.12}$$

Numerically this is

$$\frac{(583^2 + \cdots + 573^2)}{2} - \frac{7432^2}{2 \times 3 \times 2 \times 2}$$
$$- 2646.000 - 9701.333 - 1872.667 - 16.667 = 211.667. \quad (2.13)$$

The sum of squares within cells is

$$(288^2 + \cdots + 284^2) - \frac{583^2 + \cdots + 573^2}{2} = 1269.000. \quad (2.14)$$

These sums of squares, and the corresponding degrees of freedom, are entered in Table 16.5. In the next section we shall discuss obtaining the expected values of the mean squares.

Table 16.5

Source of variance	Sums of squares	Degrees of freedom	Mean squares	E[M. S.]
Annealing methods	2,646.000	1	2646.000	$\sigma^2 + un\sigma^2_{c(\alpha)} + tun\sigma^2_\alpha$
Coils within annealing methods	9,701.333	4	2425.333	$\sigma^2 + un\sigma^2_{c(\alpha)}$
Locations	1,872.667	1	1872.667	$\sigma^2 + n\sigma^2_{\lambda c(\alpha)} + rtn\sigma^2_\lambda$
Locations × annealing methods	16.667	1	16.667	$\sigma^2 + n\sigma^2_{\lambda c(\alpha)} + tn\sigma^2_{\lambda\alpha}$
Locations × coils within annealing methods	211.667	4	52.917	$\sigma^2 + n\sigma^2_{\lambda c(\alpha)}$
Within cells	1,269.000	12	105.750	σ^2
Total	15,717.333	23		

16.3. The Expectations of Mean Squares in Partially Hierarchical Models

Bennett and Franklin [2] have given a procedure for obtaining the expected values of mean squares in partially hierarchical situations. Of course, wholly hierarchical and wholly crossed models are special cases.

The procedure is to construct a two-way table, columns corresponding to the indices used in the model, i, j, k, v in the present case, rows corresponding to the terms in the model. This has been done for the model (1.1) in Table 16.6. The numbers of elements in the sample and in the population are entered in parentheses. The orders of the rows and the columns are not important other than that a systematic order of some kind helps to avoid mistakes.

We now consider any row. For those columns whose indices are *not* in the suffix for the term defining that row, enter the number of elements in the sample. For example, the j, k, and v indices do *not* appear in the suffix to α_i; hence we enter t, u, and n in the corresponding columns opposite α_i.

Table 16.6

	i (r, R)	j (t, T)	k (u, U)	v n
z_{ijkv}	1	1	1	1
$\{\lambda c(\alpha)\}_{kj(i)}$	1	$1 - t/T$	$1 - u/U$	n
$(\lambda\alpha)_{ik}$	$1 - r/R$	t	$1 - u/U$	n
λ_k	r	t	$1 - u/U$	n
$\{c(\alpha)\}_{j(i)}$	1	$1 - t/T$	u	n
α_i	$1 - r/R$	t	u	n

Next, if any term is an unrestricted random variable, enter 1 in the cells left vacant after the previous stage. Here z_{ijkv} is the only restricted random variable, and 1's are entered in all columns.

Next, if any term contains a suffix inside parentheses, enter 1 in the column corresponding to the index inside the parentheses. Here $\{c(\alpha)\}_{j(i)}$ and $\{\lambda c(\alpha)\}_{kj(i)}$ each have i inside parentheses; so 1 goes in the i column opposite these terms.

Finally, wherever a cell is still empty after the preceding operations, enter $1 - c/C$, where c and C are the number of elements in the sample and in the population. This last step will fill up all the cells in the table. The expectation of a mean square will include all components of variance corresponding to those terms in the model which include in their suffices the index or indices which are in the suffix of the term in question. The expectation of the mean square for locations, e.g., will, since the location term is λ_k, include the components of variance corresponding to λ_k, $(\lambda\alpha)_{ik}$, $\{\lambda c(\alpha)\}_{kj(i)}$, and z_{ijk}, namely σ_λ^2, $\sigma_{\lambda\alpha}^2$, $\sigma_{\lambda c(\alpha)}^2$, and σ^2. Each component of variance has as coefficient the product of all the numbers in the row for the term corresponding to that component of variance excluding the number or numbers in the column or columns corresponding to the index or indices of the mean square in question.

For example, for the expected value of the mean square for locations, σ_λ^2 will have the coefficient rtn; $\sigma_{\lambda\alpha}^2$ the coefficient $(1 - r/R)tn$; $\sigma_{\lambda c(\alpha)}^2$ the coefficient $(1 - t/T)n$; and σ^2 the coefficient 1. The expected value for the location mean square is thus

$$\sigma^2 + \left(1 - \frac{t}{T}\right)n\sigma_{\lambda c(\alpha)}^2 + \left(1 - \frac{r}{R}\right)tn\sigma_{\lambda\alpha}^2 + rtn\sigma_\lambda^2.$$

This is entered in the last column of Table 16.3, and the other entries in that column are obtained similarly.

In the specific example we have been considering, the annealing methods and the locations were fixed effects; so the sample contained the entire population, and hence $1 - r/R = 1 - u/U = 0$. On the other hand, the coils were samples from infinite populations; so $1 - t/T = 1$. Inserting these values in the expectations of the mean squares in Table 16.3, we get the particular results in Table 16.5. The appropriate error term for testing each mean square is now obvious.

16.4. Confidence Limits in Partially Hierarchical Models

Calculation of confidence limits in a partially hierarchical model requires some care. They are derived from the model (1.1).

$$x_{ijkv} = \xi + \alpha_i + \{c(\alpha)\}_{j(i)} + \lambda_k + (\lambda\alpha)_{ik} + \{\lambda c(\alpha)\}_{kj(i)} + z_{ijkv}. \quad (4.1)$$

Two of the terms need particular attention. The term $\{c(\alpha)\}_{j(i)}$ is a standard nested term and by (1.3) sums to zero in the population T. However, $T = \infty$, so we make the further assumption of normality:

$$\{c(\alpha)\}_{j(i)} \sim N(0, \sigma^2_{c(\alpha)}). \quad (4.2)$$

Thus

$$\overline{\{c(\alpha)\}}_{.(i)} = \frac{1}{t}\sum_j^t \{c(\alpha)\}_{j(i)} \sim N(0, \sigma^2_{c(\alpha)}/t). \quad (4.3)$$

The term $\{\lambda c(\alpha)\}_{kj(i)}$ is more troublesome. As stated in (1.4) and (1.5),

$$\sum_k^U \{\lambda c(\alpha)\}_{kj(i)} = \sum_j^T \{\lambda c(\alpha)\}_{kj(i)} = 0; \quad (4.4)$$

i.e., it sums to zero in the population over j and k. However, the sample of locations u includes the entire population U; i.e., $u = U$; so

$$\overline{\{\lambda c(\alpha)\}}_{.j(i)} = \frac{1}{u}\sum_k^u \{\lambda c(\alpha)\}_{kj(i)} = \frac{1}{u}\sum_k^U \{\lambda c(\alpha)\}_{kj(i)} = 0. \quad (4.5)$$

Since this is zero, averaging over another suffix will leave it zero:

$$\overline{\{\lambda c(\alpha)\}}_{..(i)} = 0. \quad (4.6)$$

However, the sample of coils t is from an infinite population, $T = \infty$; so

$$\overline{\{\lambda c(\alpha)\}}_{k.(i)} \sim N\left(0, \frac{\sigma^2_{\lambda c(\alpha)}}{t}\right), \quad (4.7)$$

SECT. 16.4 LIMITS IN PARTIALLY HIERARCHICAL MODELS

and, if we further average over i,

$$\overline{\{\lambda c(\alpha)\}}_{k.(.)} \sim N\left(0, \frac{\sigma^2_{\lambda c(\alpha)}}{rt}\right). \tag{4.8}$$

We will now compute the variance of the difference between two annealing methods averaged over locations and of course over coils. We would only be looking at the annealing main effect if we assume that its interaction with the other fixed effect, locations, $(\lambda\alpha)_{ik}$, is zero. From the model (4.1)

$$\bar{x}_{i...} = \xi + \alpha_i + \overline{\{c(\alpha)\}}_{.(i)} + \bar{\lambda}_. + \overline{\{\lambda c(\alpha)\}}_{..(i)} + \bar{z}_{i...}. \tag{4.9}$$

However, by (4.6), $\overline{\{\lambda c(\alpha)\}}_{..(i)} = 0$; so

$$\bar{x}_{i...} - \bar{x}_{i'...} = (\alpha_i - \alpha_{i'}) + \overline{\{c(\alpha)\}}_{.(i)} - \overline{\{c(\alpha)\}}_{.(i')} + \bar{z}_{i...} - \bar{z}_{i'...}, \tag{4.10}$$

$$E[\bar{x}_{i...} - \bar{x}_{i'...}] = (\alpha_i - \alpha_{i'}), \tag{4.11}$$

$$V[\bar{x}_{i...} - \bar{x}_{i'...}] = 2\left(\frac{\sigma^2_{c(\alpha)}}{t} + \frac{\sigma^2}{tun}\right) = \frac{2}{tun}(\sigma^2 + un\sigma^2_{c(\alpha)}), \tag{4.12}$$

$$\hat{V}[\bar{x}_{i...} - \bar{x}_{i'...}] = \frac{2}{tun}\binom{\text{M. S. for coils within}}{\text{annealing methods}}. \tag{4.13}$$

We next compute the variance of the difference between two locations, averaged over annealing methods and coils, and again assuming $(\lambda\alpha)_{ik} = 0$:

$$\bar{x}_{..k.} = \xi + \bar{\alpha}_. + \overline{\{c(\alpha)\}}_{.(.)} + \lambda_k + \overline{\{\lambda c(\alpha)\}}_{k.(.)} + \bar{z}_{..k.}, \tag{4.14}$$

$$\bar{x}_{..k.} - \bar{x}_{..k'.} = (\lambda_k - \lambda_{k'}) + \overline{\{\lambda c(\alpha)\}}_{k.(.)} - \overline{\{\lambda c(\alpha)\}}_{k'.(.)} + \bar{z}_{..k.} - \bar{z}_{..k'.}, \tag{4.15}$$

$$E[\bar{x}_{..k.} - \bar{x}_{..k'.}] = \lambda_k - \lambda_{k'}, \tag{4.16}$$

$$V[\bar{x}_{..k.} - \bar{x}_{..k'.}] = 2\left(\frac{\sigma^2_{\lambda c(\alpha)}}{rt} + \frac{\sigma^2}{rtn}\right) = \frac{2}{rtn}(\sigma^2 + n\sigma^2_{\lambda c(\alpha)}), \tag{4.17}$$

$$\hat{V}[\bar{x}_{..k.} - \bar{x}_{..k'.}] = \frac{2}{rtn}\binom{\text{M. S. for locations} \times \text{coils}}{\text{within annealing methods}}. \tag{4.18}$$

If we are unwilling to assume that the location × annealing method interaction is zero, i.e., we admit the possibility that $(\lambda\alpha)_{ik} \neq 0$ in general, then it makes little sense to compare annealing methods averaged over locations or to compare locations averaged over annealing methods. We would rather compare annealing methods for a particular location and locations for a particular annealing method. To compute the variance of the difference between two locations for the same annealing method we start with

$$\bar{x}_{i.k.} = \xi + \alpha_i + \overline{\{c(\alpha)\}}_{.(i)} + \lambda_k + (\lambda\alpha)_{ik} + \overline{\{\lambda c(\alpha)\}}_{k.(i)} + \bar{z}_{i.k.}; \quad (4.19)$$

so

$$\bar{x}_{i.k.} - \bar{x}_{i.k'.} = \lambda_k - \lambda_{k'} + (\lambda\alpha)_{ik} - (\lambda\alpha)_{ik'}$$
$$+ \overline{\{\lambda c(\alpha)\}}_{k.(i)} - \overline{\{\lambda c(\alpha)\}}_{k'.(i)} + \bar{z}_{i.k.} - \bar{z}_{i.k'.}. \quad (4.20)$$

Thus

$$V[\bar{x}_{i.k.} - \bar{x}_{i.k'.}] = 2\left(\frac{\sigma^2_{\lambda c(\alpha)}}{t} + \frac{\sigma^2}{tn}\right) = \frac{2}{nt}(\sigma^2 + n\sigma^2_{\lambda c(\alpha)}), \quad (4.21)$$

$$\hat{V}[\bar{x}_{i.k.} - \bar{x}_{i.k'.}] = \frac{2}{nt}\begin{pmatrix}\text{M. S. for locations} \times \text{coils}\\ \text{within annealing methods}\end{pmatrix}. \quad (4.22)$$

Now we compute the variance of the difference between two annealing methods for the same location:

$$\bar{x}_{i.k.} - \bar{x}_{i'.k.} = (\alpha_i - \alpha_{i'}) + \overline{\{c(\alpha)\}}_{.(i)} - \overline{\{c(\alpha)\}}_{.(i')} + (\lambda\alpha)_{ik} - (\lambda\alpha)_{i'k}$$
$$+ \overline{\{\lambda c(\alpha)\}}_{k.(i)} - \overline{\{\lambda c(\alpha)\}}_{k.(i')} + \bar{z}_{i.k.} - \bar{z}_{i'.k.}, \quad (4.23)$$

$$V[\bar{x}_{i.k.} - \bar{x}_{i'.k.}] = 2\left(\frac{\sigma^2_{c(\alpha)}}{t} + \frac{\sigma^2_{\lambda c(\alpha)}}{t} + \frac{\sigma^2}{tn}\right) = \frac{2}{nt}[\sigma^2 + n\sigma^2_{\lambda c(\alpha)} + n\sigma^2_{c(\alpha)}]. \quad (4.24)$$

The analysis of variance table does not provide any mean square with the appropriate expected value. If, as is often the case, the term $\{\lambda c(\alpha)\}$ is omitted from the model, we have to construct a linear combination of mean squares with expected value $\sigma^2 + n\sigma^2_{c(\alpha)}$. This is given by

$$\frac{1}{u}[(u-1)(\text{M. S. for remainder})$$
$$+ \text{M. S. for coils within annealing methods}], \quad (4.25)$$

which has the expected value

$$= \frac{1}{u}[(u-1)\sigma^2 + \sigma^2 + un\sigma^2_{c(\alpha)}] = \sigma^2 + n\sigma^2_{c(\alpha)}. \quad (4.26)$$

The omission of $\{\lambda c(\alpha)\}$ from the model has the end result of pooling the sums of squares and degrees of freedom of this term with those for within cells to form the "remainder" sum of squares. If we are unwilling to make the foregoing simplifying assumption, we can obtain a linear combination with the desired expected value included in the brackets in (4.24) by using

$$\frac{1}{u}[-(\text{M. S. for within cells})$$

$$+ u(\text{M. S. for locations} \times \text{coils within annealing methods})$$

$$+ (\text{M. S. for coils within anneals})], \quad (4.27)$$

which has the expected value

$$\frac{1}{u}(-\sigma^2 + u\sigma^2 + u n\sigma^2_{\lambda c(\alpha)} + \sigma^2 + u n\sigma^2_{c(\alpha)}) = \sigma^2 + n\sigma^2_{\lambda c(\alpha)} + n\sigma^2_{c(\alpha)}. \quad (4.28)$$

Finally, the variance of the difference between the combination of the ith annealing method with the kth location and the combination of the i'th annealing method with the k'th location is the same as that just discussed, the difference between two annealing methods for the same location.

EXERCISES

16.1. Five laboratories cooperated in measuring the brightness of six lamps of each of two types. The lamps were sent from laboratory to laboratory for measurement. See p. 544.

(a) Make an appropriate analysis of variance of these data, including giving the $E[\text{M.S.}]$. We are particularly interested in testing the main effect of laboratories and the laboratory $\times$ type-of-lamp interaction.

(b) Construct 95 per cent confidence limits for the difference between types (for purposes of this question assume that laboratory $\times$ type-of-lamp interaction is zero).

(c) Construct 95 per cent confidence limits for the difference between laboratory A and laboratory E (again assuming laboratory $\times$ type-of-lamp interaction to be zero).

(d) Construct 95 per cent confidence limits for the difference between type 1 in laboratory A and type 2 in laboratory B.

(e) Estimate the component of variance for lamps within types.

Actually the lamps initially were measured in laboratory A (the Bureau of Standards), were then sent to laboratory B (National Physical Laboratory) who sent them on to laboratory C (Laboratoire Centrale), who returned them to the National Physical Laboratory (denoted this time by D), who returned them to the Bureau of Standards (denoted this time by E). Let the Bureau of Standards and the National Physical Laboratory on the second time around, E and D, be denoted by A' and B'. Then the following comparisons seem to be of particular interest:

(i) Early measurements versus late measurements: i.e., $(A + B) - (A' + B')$.
(ii) Change with time in difference between A and B, i.e. $(A - B) - (A' - B')$.
(iii) Difference between $(B + B')$ and C: i.e., $(B + B') - 2C$.

(iv) Difference between (mean of $B + B'$ and C) and (mean of A and A'), i.e., $2(B + B' + C) - 3(A + A')$.

(f) Construct contrasts to provide the above comparisons.

(g) Are these contrasts orthogonal?

(h) Partition the sums of squares for main effect for laboratories and for the interaction laboratory × type into components corresponding to these contrasts.

Values of Candlepower Obtained at Different Laboratories

All figures have been multiplied by 100 and then 1000 subtracted from them

Type	Lamp	\multicolumn{5}{c}{Laboratory}	
		A	B	C	D	E	Totals
I	1	741	768	770	772	738	3,789
	2	731	763	755	742	724	3,715
	3	731	763	757	760	728	3,739
	4	759	779	775	774	752	3,839
	5	738	758	750	750	730	3,726
	6	770	795	800	800	768	3,933
	Totals	4470	4626	4607	4598	4440	22,741
II	1	625	650	655	651	615	3,196
	2	590	611	605	625	588	3,019
	3	602	630	640	630	605	3,107
	4	578	607	640	608	581	3,014
	5	578	604	605	608	573	2,968
	6	625	673	670	664	631	3,263
	Totals	3598	3775	3815	3786	3593	18,567
	Totals	8068	8401	8422	8384	8033	41,308

Source: Edward P. Hyde, "A Comparison of the Unit of Luminous Intensity of the United States with Those of Germany, England, and France," *Bulletin of the Bureau of Standards*, 3(1907), 68–80.

16.2. Five laboratories cooperated in a comparison of their testing procedures for impact strength of a type of fiberboard. Panels from two batches of board were sent to the five laboratories. Each laboratory tested each batch in duplicate on three days. There is no correspondence between the three days in one laboratory and the three days in any other laboratory.

For notational consistency let

$i = 1, \ldots, r\ (= 5)$ refer to laboratories λ (model I),
$j = 1, \ldots, t\ (= 2)$ refer to batches β (model I),
$k = 1, \ldots, u\ (= 3)$ refer to days d (model II),
$m = 1, \ldots, v\ (= 2)$ refer to duplications of a lot within a day (model II).

The impact strengths reported were:

| | | Laboratory | | | | |
Day	Batch	A	B	C	D	E
1	1	1483	1449	1499	1428	1509
		1496	1400	1472	1401	1439
	2	1504	1465	1506	1407	1480
		1505	1423	1537	1416	1429
2	1	1441	1477	1483	1404	1416
		1416	1471	1509	1419	1441
	2	1477	1418	1578	1455	1364
		1457	1445	1486	1435	1441
3	1	1450	1446	1489	1414	1419
		1478	1398	1435	1446	1444
	2	1435	1424	1499	1423	1437
		1478	1426	1491	1442	1438

(a) Write down an appropriate linear model, and make an analysis of variance of these data, including the expected values of the mean squares. Make the appropriate tests of significance.

(b) Give simple 95 per cent confidence limits for the difference between laboratories B and C.

(c) Estimate the within-day component of variance averaged over laboratories.

(d) Estimate the between-day component of variance averaged over laboratories.

(e) A batch measured repeatedly by laboratory A had an average impact strength of 1420. If a single test is made on this batch in laboratory D, estimate the probability of this batch being rejected by this laboratory, if the specification is to reject if the observed impact strength is less than 1400.

If we subtract 1000 from every figure in the table, two sums of squares which may be useful are:

$$\sum_i^r \sum_j^t \sum_k^u \sum_m^v x_{ijkm}^2 = 12{,}414{,}257, \qquad \sum_i^r \sum_j^t \sum_k^u \left(\sum_m^v x_{ijkm} \right)^2 = 24{,}786{,}137.$$

16.3. Section 16.1 discusses an investigation of the can-making properties of tin plate. In that discussion u particular locations from each coil were used, so location was a model I effect. The same locations were used for all coils. Consider the following modifications.

(a) Instead of the two replicate measurements being obtained by randomization over the rtu samples of tin plate, suppose that one replicate was made immediately and the other 6 months later. Thus in place of duplicates we have a model I factor, age, say γ, at n levels.

(b) Instead of u particular locations (model I), a random sample of u locations, say $l_1, \ldots, l_u$, would be selected, so that locations would be a model II effect.

(c) Instead of the single random sample of locations $l_1, \ldots, l_u$ being taken for all coils for all annealing methods, as in (b), one random sample of locations is taken for the first annealing method, a second random sample of locations is taken for the second annealing method, and so on. All coils for a particular annealing method are sampled at the same locations.

(d) Instead of a single random sample of locations serving for all coils for a particular annealing method, as in (c), a separate random sample of locations is taken for every coil.

For each of these situations, using as far as possible the sample terminology and notation, but where necessary making appropriate changes, list the sources of variance for an analysis of variance table with the corresponding degrees of freedom and the expected values of the mean squares. State the error terms appropriate for testing the null hypotheses that there are no differences between annealing methods and between locations.

REFERENCES

1. Vaurio, V. W., and C. Daniel, "Evaluation of Several Sets of Constants and Several Sources of Variability," *Chemical Engineering Progress*, 50(1954), 81–86.
2. Bennett, Carl A., and Norman L. Franklin, *Statistical Analysis in Chemistry and the Chemical Industry*. New York: John Wiley and Sons, 1954.

CHAPTER 17

Some Simple Experimental Designs

17.1. Completely Randomized Designs

We have in previous chapters developed techniques suitable for analyzing the simpler experimental designs. The simplest experiment perhaps is to compare r levels of a single experimental factor: We may be comparing three brands of gasoline, or four thicknesses of shoe leather, or five quantities of supplement to a hog ration. If we make n_i independent observations on each level of the factor, in a completely random order, the model for the experiment will be

$$x_{ij} = \xi + \eta_i + z_{ij},$$

and the appropriate analysis will be model I one-way analysis of variance as discussed in Section 10.2. Usually it will be preferable to have the n_i all equal, since then the variances of the differences between any pair will be the same, and also since Tukey's method of multiple comparisons, which requires equal n_i and is more efficient than Scheffe's method for simple comparisons, can then be applied. However, if our objective is to compare all the other levels of the factor with one particular level, the "control," as can be done effectively with Dunnett's technique, it is advantageous to have the n_i for the control equal to $\sqrt{k}$ times the n_i for the other levels, where k is the number of other levels.

The next simplest experiment is to investigate two factors simultaneously in all combinations with n independent replicates per combination. For example, one factor could be brand of gasoline at r levels, and the other mean speed of automobile at t levels. Or one factor could be quantity of supplement to the hog ration and the other factor the breed of hog. The total number of observations required is rtn, and these should be obtained in a completely random order. The appropriate analysis will be two-way analysis of variance as discussed in Chapter 14. The model may be model I, or II, or mixed, depending on the nature of the factors. For example, in the hog example just given, the first factor, the quantity of supplement, is a fixed or model I factor, and the second factor, breed of hog, would be a model I factor if we were interested only in these particular breeds, but a model II factor if we were interested in generalizing to a larger population of breeds.

Table 17.1

Treatments	11	12	13	14	15	21	22	23	24	25	31	32	33	34	35
Random numbers	15	77	01	64	69(2)	69(8)	58	40	81	16	60	20	00	84	22
Ordering	3	13	2	10	11	12	8	7	14	4	9	5	1	15	6

In discussing the principles of experimental design, it is convenient to have a general word for the basic experimental unit that gives rise to the measurement which we analyze. In the preceding paragraph, a given trip with a particular automobile using a particular gasoline will give rise to a single determination of gasoline consumption and is the basic experimental unit. In the hog feeding example, the individual hog is the experimental unit. The great bulk of the theory of experimental design was developed in agronomy, in which the basic experimental unit is a plot of ground on which is grown a crop and to which is applied fertilizers, etc. It is convenient to use the word *plot* for basic experimental unit in general.

Randomization of treatments on to plots is best performed with a table of random numbers (Table XI). Suppose that we have an experiment involving five replicates of three treatments. We can denote the jth replicate of the ith treatment as ij. We write out in any order, systematic if convenient, these $3 \times 5 = 15$ treatments (Table 17.1, first row). Under each treatment we enter a two-digit random number from Table XI. We then order in increasing magnitude these random numbers. The particular set we chose happens to have a tie, two 69's. This tie is resolved by picking two further random digits and attaching one to each of the ties. The next two-digit random number is 28, and so the first 69 is regarded as 69.2 and the second as 69.8. The third row gives the ordering of the random numbers. Then plot 1 receives treatment (33), plot 2 receives treatment (13), etc.

17.2. Randomized-Block Designs

If we are studying a single factor at t levels, with r replicates on each level, it may be possible to arrange the observations in r blocks of t observations. In agricultural experimentation each observation of, say,

RANDOMIZED-BLOCK DESIGNS

yield, comes from a plot of ground, and we may group t adjacent plots to form a block. In executing the experiment, we randomly allocate the t levels to the t plots in the first block, repeat the randomization for the second block, and so on. This is quite different from the completely randomized experiment where there was a single randomization of rn treatments, actually r treatments repeated n times, on to rn plots.

Usually the blocks will be regarded as a random or model II factor, and the factor under study will be a model I factor. The appropriate analysis will be a mixed model with one observation per cell. A suitable modification of the model (14.8.1) to this circumstance would be

$$x_{ij} = \xi + b_i + \zeta_j + \theta_{ij} + z_{ij} \tag{2.1}$$

and Table 14.14 with no within-cell term and $n = 1$ becomes Table 17.2. The remainder mean square is an appropriate error term for testing the effect of the factor and for constructing confidence limits for differences. The test of the block effect is only satisfactory if it can be assumed that σ_θ^2 is small compared to σ^2. This limitation is usually of small import as our main objective is to study the factor.

Table 17.2

Source of variance	Type of effect	Mean square	$E[\text{M.S.}]$
Blocks	II	s_4^2	$\sigma^2 + t\sigma_b^2$
Factor	I	s_3^2	$\sigma^2 + \sigma_\theta^2 + r\sigma_\zeta^2$
Remainder		s_2^2	$\sigma^2 + \sigma_\theta^2$

The objective of using a randomized-block design instead of a completely randomized arrangement is to reduce experimental error. Adjacent plots clustered together in a block should be more alike in their response to the same treatment than plots at opposite ends of the field.

Let σ_{0b}^2 and σ_{0r}^2 be the error terms in the two forms. We define the more efficient design, the randomized blocks, as the standard, and the efficiency of the other is defined as

$$I = \frac{\sigma_{0b}^2}{\sigma_{0r}^2}. \tag{2.2}$$

This is a reasonable definition of efficiency, for to get the same accuracy on the comparison of treatment means we would have to use $1/I$ times as many replicates with the less efficient design; e.g., if the efficiency is 0.50, we need $1/0.5 = 2$ times as many observations with the inefficient design compared with the efficient design to get the same accuracy.

Suppose that we have t treatments and r blocks, or replicates. Let E be the error mean square and B be the block mean square, and let $F = B/E$. Then it can be shown that the estimated efficiency of the completely randomized design relative to the randomized-block design is

$$\hat{f} = \frac{\hat{\sigma}_{0b}^2}{\hat{\sigma}_{0r}^2} = \frac{E}{[(r-1)B + r(t-1)E]/(rt-1)} = \frac{rt-1}{F(r-1) + r(t-1)}.$$

(2.3)

As we would expect, the larger the F, the lower is the estimated relative efficiency of the completely randomized design.

If we have two factors, say B and C, at t and u levels, and r blocks containing tu plots, we can randomly allocate the tu treatment combinations to the plots in the first block, repeat the process for the second block, etc. If the blocks are regarded as a random effect and the two factors are fixed effects, the appropriate analysis is similar to that discussed in Section 15.3, and the expected values of the mean squares are like those given in the left-hand side of Table 15.3, where σ_a^2 corresponds to blocks, with the modification that $n = 1$ and there is no within-cells sum of squares. The appropriate error term for the factor B is its interaction with blocks, and analogously for C, and the two-way interaction $B \times C$ is to be tested against the remainder mean square.

Actually, many practitioners of the art pool the sums of squares and degrees of freedom for all the interactions with blocks, namely aB, aC, and aBC, and use this pooled mean square as an error term. This procedure has implicit in it the assumption that $\sigma_{aB}^2 = \sigma_{aC}^2 = \sigma_{aBC}^2 = 0$. It is not clear in what fields of experimentation such a set of assumptions is or is not valid.

17.3. The Split-Plot Situation

Suppose that we have two factors, say B corresponding to varieties of potato and C to quantity of fertilizer. We might plan the experiment as in the previous section, in r randomized blocks, each block containing tu plots.

Alternatively, suppose we group these tu plots into t groups of u plots, and now change the terminology so that the ultimate unit is a *subplot* and the groups of u subplots are *whole plots*, the block containing t such whole plots.

We now design the experiment as follows. We randomly allocate the t levels of factor B (variety of potato) to the t whole plots in the first block, repeat this procedure for the second block, etc. We now randomly allocate the u levels of factor C (quantity of fertilizer) to the u subplots contained

SECT. 17.3 THE SPLIT-PLOT SITUATION

in the first whole plot in the first block, repeat this procedure for the second whole plot, etc. If there are three varieties and four fertilizers, the first two blocks might have the arrangement shown in Table 17.3.

Table 17.3

Block I

v_3f_4	v_3f_2	v_1f_1	v_1f_3	v_2f_2	v_2f_1
v_3f_1	v_3f_3	v_1f_2	v_1f_4	v_2f_4	v_2f_3

Block II

v_1f_1	v_1f_3	v_3f_1	v_3f_4	v_2f_2	v_2f_1
v_1f_4	v_1f_2	v_3f_2	v_3f_3	v_2f_3	v_2f_4

Such an arrangement is known as a *split-plot* design, here in randomized blocks. We would be motivated to use it in the present example if, on the one hand, it was technically inconvenient to plant the varieties in small subplots, switching from variety to variety as we cover the four subplots in a whole plot, whereas on the other hand it was not troublesome to switch from fertilizer to fertilizer going from one subplot to another in the same whole plot.

The essential feature of a split-plot design is that instead of the rtu ultimate experimental units being obtained after randomization over the whole number of rtu units, as in a completely randomized design, or being obtained after r separate randizations over tu units, as in a simple randomized block design, they are obtained by first randomizing the treatments C on to the u subplots, this randomization being performed rt times, and then randomizing the treatments B on to the t whole plots, this randomization being performed r times, once for each of the r blocks.

An appropriate model for the experiment of Table 17.3 is

$$x_{ijk} = \xi + b_i + \psi_j + e_{j(i)} + \phi_k + (\phi\psi)_{jk} + (b\phi)_{ik} + z_{ijk}. \quad (3.1)$$

In this model, b_i is the random-block effect, ψ_j is the fixed variety effect, ϕ_k is the fixed fertilizer effect, $(\phi\psi)_{jk}$ is their interaction, and $(b\phi)_{ik}$ is the interaction of blocks with fertilizer. The motivation for writing $e_{j(i)}$ in this form is that if the experiment had been run with every whole plot receiving identical varieties and every subplot receiving identical fertilizers, then we would have a simple nested situation. The random variation of whole plots within the blocks is represented by the unrestricted error term $e_{j(i)}$, and the random variation of the subplots within the whole plots is represented by the unrestricted error term z_{ijk}. Let e and z have variances ω^2 and σ^2, respectively.

To obtain the expected values of the mean squares in the analysis of variance we follow the procedure of Section 16.3 and set up Table 17.4.

Table 17.4

	i (r, R)	j (t, T)	k (u, U)
z_{ijk}	1	1	1
$(b\phi)_{ik}$	$1 - r/R$	t	$1 - u/U$
$(\phi\psi)_{jk}$	r	$1 - t/T$	$1 - u/U$
ϕ_k	r	t	$1 - u/U$
$e_{j(i)}$	1	1	u
ψ_j	r	$1 - t/T$	u
b_i	$1 - r/R$	t	u

In general, in split-plot experiments the whole-plot treatments may be either model I or model II, and likewise the subplot treatments, though it is more usual for them both to be model I, as in the present case. Thus here $R = \infty$, so $1 - r/R = 1$, and $t = T$ and $u = U$, so $1 - t/T = 1 - u/U = 0$. We can now write down the expectations of the mean squares in Table 17.5. It is a matter of opinion in any particular instance

Table 17.5

Source of variance	Degrees of freedom	E[M.S.]
Blocks	$r - 1$	$\sigma^2 + u\omega^2 + tu\sigma_b^2$
Varieties	$t - 1$	$\sigma^2 + u\omega^2 + ru\sigma_\psi^2$
Whole-plot error	$(r - 1)(t - 1)$	$\sigma^2 + u\omega^2$
Fertilizers	$u - 1$	$\sigma^2 + t\sigma_{b\phi}^2 + rt\sigma_\phi^2$
Varieties × fertilizers	$(t - 1)(u - 1)$	$\sigma^2 + r\sigma_{\phi\psi}^2$
Blocks × fertilizers	$(r - 1)(u - 1)$	$\sigma^2 + t\sigma_{b\psi}^2$
Subplot error	$(r - 1)(t - 1)(u - 1)$	σ^2
Total	$rtu - 1$	

whether the term $(b\phi)_{ik}$ should or should not be included in the model. It is perhaps more usual to exclude it. In that case its sum of squares and degrees of freedom are pooled with subplot error to form a new estimate of σ^2 based on $t(r - 1)(k - 1)$ degrees of freedom, and of course $t\sigma_{b\phi}^2$ gets stricken out of the expectation of the fertilizer mean square.

17.4. Relationship of Split-Plot to Partially Hierarchical Situations

In our discussion of the split-plot experiment of the preceding section, there was nothing essential to the split-plot concept that the experiment be run in randomized blocks. As far as the whole-plot part of the experiment is concerned, it might just as well be run as r completely randomized replicates of the t whole-plot treatments. If we omit the block effects from the model (3.1), we get

$$x_{ijk} = \xi + \psi_j + e_{ij} + \phi_k + (\phi\psi)_{jk} + z_{ijk}. \tag{4.1}$$

If we now refer back to the model (16.1.1) for the partially hierarchical situation discussed in Section 16.1, and modify it to conform to the situation where there is only one replicate per cell by omitting the suffix v and the final error term z_{ijkv} and by substituting z_{ijk} for $\{\lambda c(\alpha)\}_{kj(i)}$, we get

$$x_{ijk} = \xi + \alpha_i + \{c(\alpha)\}_{j(i)} + \lambda_k + (\lambda\alpha)_{ik} + z_{ijk}, \tag{4.2}$$

which is essentially identical with (4.1).

We therefore see that the split-plot situation is an agricultural example of a partially hierarchical classification, and the two can be considered together. We can use the results of Section 16.4 on variances of various types of differences, with the afore-mentioned differences. Thus the analog of (16.4.13) becomes

$$\hat{V}[\bar{x}_{.j.} - \bar{x}_{.j'.}] = \frac{2}{ru} \text{ (M.S. for whole-plot error)}. \tag{4.3}$$

Since, with $v = 1$, the $\{\lambda c(\alpha)\}_{kj(i)}$ has been replaced by z_{ijk}, (16.4.18) becomes

$$\hat{V}[\bar{x}_{..k} - \bar{x}_{..k'}] = \frac{2}{rt} \text{ (M.S. for subplot error)}, \tag{4.4}$$

and (16.4.22) becomes

$$\hat{V}[\bar{x}_{.jk} - \bar{x}_{.jk'}] = \frac{2}{r} \text{ (M.S. for subplot error)}. \tag{4.5}$$

From (16.4.24) and (16.4.25),

$$\hat{V}[\bar{x}_{.jk} - \bar{x}_{.j'k}] = \frac{1}{ru} [(u-1)(\text{M.S. for subplot error})$$
$$+ (\text{M.S. for whole-plot error})]. \tag{4.6}$$

EXERCISES

17.1. Suppose that in a single experiment k treatments are to be compared only with a control treatment, and are not to be compared with each other. Suppose that n_0 replications are to be run on the control and n_t replicates are to be run on each of the k other treatments. The total number of replicates $N = n_0 + kn_t$ is fixed. Show that the choice of n_0 and n_t such that $n_0 = \sqrt{k}n_t$ makes $V[\bar{x}_0. - \bar{x}_i.]$, averaged over i, a minimum. Assume n_0 and n_t to be large enough to be regarded as continuous variables.

17.2. An experiment was run to compare three similar magnesium salts, A, B, C, in the production of an antibiotic by fermentation. In the first replication, three fermentations were started, one containing salt A, another salt B, and the third salt C. After five days, samples for analysis were withdrawn from each fermentation, and likewise after six days. The whole operation was repeated a total of four times. The replications should be regarded as blocks.

(a) Make an appropriate analysis of variance for these data, and report the F values, with the corresponding degrees of freedom, for the main effects of salt, age (five days versus six), and their interaction.

(b) Give 95 per cent confidence limits for (i) salt A − salt B, (ii) six days − five days, (iii) salt A − salt B, both at six days.

	Magnesium salt					
	A		B		C	
Replication	5 days	6 days	5 days	6 days	5 days	6 days
1	69	84	91	98	81	86
2	82	78	75	82	72	77
3	67	74	78	92	66	79
4	69	77	85	92	73	81

17.3. A comparison was made of the effects of two levels of temper, half and quarter, on the shearing modulus of elasticity of a certain stainless steel. From each of five random lots of this type of steel three tubes were chosen at random. Each tube was cut in half, and one portion given the quarter-temper treatment and the other portion the half-temper treatment.

Sample, $j(i)$	1(i)		2(i)		3(i)	
Temper, k	$k = 1$	$k = 2$	$k = 1$	$k = 2$	$k = 1$	$k = 2$
Lot, $i = 1$	1073	1024	1026	990	996	972
$i = 2$	1022	962	1009	1005	1150	985
$i = 3$	942	900	927	887	942	885
$i = 4$	1011	1000	1058	1006	1038	1022
$i = 5$	1044	1010	1027	1010	1035	1004

Sum of squares of all observations = 30,013,864.
Source: C. W. Muhlenbruch, V. N. Krivobok, and C. R. Mayne, "Mechanical Properties in Torsion and Poisson's Ratio for Certain Stainless Steel Alloys," *Proceedings of the American Society for Testing and Materials*, 51 (1951), 837–52.

(a) Write down an appropriate linear model and compute the corresponding analysis of variance. Give the expectations of the various mean squares. (b) Test the null hypothesis that the difference between tempering treatments is constant over lots. (c) Give a 95 per cent confidence limit of the difference between the two tempering treatments. (d) Estimate the various components of variance.

17.4. An experiment is run to compare r treatments τ_i, $i = 1, \ldots, r$ in t randomized blocks b_j, $j = 1, \ldots, t$. The treatments are randomized on to the plots in each block. Observations are made at the end of 1 year. The same treatments are used on the same plots for a total of u years y_k, $k = 1, \ldots, u$, and observations made each year. Thus no further randomization beyond the initial one is used. It is to be assumed, however, that the sequence of u years is in some sense a random sample of all years. The treatments are to be regarded as a model I effect, and the blocks as a model II effect.

(a) Write down a suitable linear model for this experiment. (b) Present a table listing the names of the mean squares you would compute, with the corresponding numbers of degrees of freedom and the expectations of the mean squares. (c) Indicate how you would test the main effect for treatments.

17.5. Suppose that the experiment in exercise (17.4) was replicated each year at several places. Let the index on the place symbol be m, $m = 1, \ldots, v$. Suppose that the places are (i) a random sample from an infinite population, and (ii) the only places of interest. (a) Write down suitable linear models for these two situations, and (b) present a table listing the names of the mean squares you would compute, with the corresponding degrees of freedom and the expectations of the mean squares for the two situations. (c) Under supposition (i), how would you test the main effect for treatments? (d) Under supposition (ii), how would you test the treatment × place interaction, and assuming that this was zero, the treatment main effect?

Appendix

Table I. The Cumulative Standardized Normal Distribution Function*

$$\Phi(u) = \frac{1}{\sqrt{2\pi}} \int_{-\infty}^{u} e^{-\frac{x^2}{2}} dx \quad \text{FOR} \quad -4.99 \leq u \leq 0.00.$$

u	·00	·01	·02	·03	·04	·05	·06	·07	·08	·09
− ·0	·5000	·4960	·4920	·4880	·4840	·4801	·4761	·4721	·4681	·4641
− ·1	·4602	·4562	·4522	·4483	·4443	·4404	·4364	·4325	·4286	·4247
− ·2	·4207	·4168	·4129	·4090	·4052	·4013	·3974	·3936	·3897	·3859
− ·3	·3821	·3783	·3745	·3707	·3669	·3632	·3594	·3557	·3520	·3483
− ·4	·3446	·3409	·3372	·3336	·3300	·3264	·3228	·3192	·3156	·3121
− ·5	·3085	·3050	·3015	·2981	·2946	·2912	·2877	·2843	·2810	·2776
− ·6	·2743	·2709	·2676	·2643	·2611	·2578	·2546	·2514	·2483	·2451
− ·7	·2420	·2389	·2358	·2327	·2297	·2266	·2236	·2206	·2177	·2148
− ·8	·2119	·2090	·2061	·2033	·2005	·1977	·1949	·1922	·1894	·1867
− ·9	·1841	·1814	·1788	·1762	·1736	·1711	·1685	·1660	·1635	·1611
−1·0	·1587	·1562	·1539	·1515	·1492	·1469	·1446	·1423	·1401	·1379
−1·1	·1357	·1335	·1314	·1292	·1271	·1251	·1230	·1210	·1190	·1170
−1·2	·1151	·1131	·1112	·1093	·1075	·1056	·1038	·1020	·1003	·09853
−1·3	·09680	·09510	·09342	·09176	·09012	·08851	·08691	·08534	·08379	·08226
−1·4	·08076	·07927	·07780	·07636	·07493	·07353	·07215	·07078	·06944	·06811
−1·5	·06681	·06552	·06426	·06301	·06178	·06057	·05938	·05821	·05705	·05592
−1·6	·05480	·05370	·05262	·05155	·05050	·04947	·04846	·04746	·04648	·04551
−1·7	·04457	·04363	·04272	·04182	·04093	·04006	·03920	·03836	·03754	·03673
−1·8	·03593	·03515	·03438	·03362	·03288	·03216	·03144	·03074	·03005	·02938
−1·9	·02872	·02807	·02743	·02680	·02619	·02559	·02500	·02442	·02385	·02330
−2·0	·02275	·02222	·02169	·02118	·02068	·02018	·01970	·01923	·01876	·01831
−2·1	·01786	·01743	·01700	·01659	·01618	·01578	·01539	·01500	·01463	·01426
−2·2	·01390	·01355	·01321	·01287	·01255	·01222	·01191	·01160	·01130	·01101
−2·3	·01072	·01044	·01017	·0²9903	·0²9642	·0²9387	·0²9137	·0²8894	·0²8656	·0²8424
−2·4	·0²8198	·0²7976	·0²7760	·0²7549	·0²7344	·0²7143	·0²6947	·0²6756	·0²6569	·0²6387
−2·5	·0²6210	·0²6037	·0²5868	·0²5703	·0²5543	·0²5386	·0²5234	·0²5085	·0²4940	·0²4799
−2·6	·0²4661	·0²4527	·0²4396	·0²4269	·0²4145	·0²4025	·0²3907	·0²3793	·0²3681	·0²3573
−2·7	·0²3467	·0²3364	·0²3264	·0²3167	·0²3072	·0²2980	·0²2890	·0²2803	·0²2718	·0²2635
−2·8	·0²2555	·0²2477	·0²2401	·0²2327	·0²2256	·0²2186	·0²2118	·0²2052	·0²1988	·0²1926
−2·9	·0²1866	·0²1807	·0²1750	·0²1695	·0²1641	·0²1589	·0²1538	·0²1489	·0²1441	·0²1395
−3·0	·0²1350	·0²1306	·0²1264	·0²1223	·0²1183	·0²1144	·0²1107	·0²1070	·0²1035	·0²1001
−3·1	·0³9676	·0³9354	·0³9043	·0³8740	·0³8447	·0³8164	·0³7888	·0³7622	·0³7364	·0³7114
−3·2	·0³6871	·0³6637	·0³6410	·0³6190	·0³5976	·0³5770	·0³5571	·0³5377	·0³5190	·0³5009
−3·3	·0³4834	·0³4665	·0³4501	·0³4342	·0³4189	·0³4041	·0³3897	·0³3758	·0³3624	·0³3495
−3·4	·0³3369	·0³3248	·0³3131	·0³3018	·0³2909	·0³2803	·0³2701	·0³2602	·0³2507	·0³2415
−3·5	·0³2326	·0³2241	·0³2158	·0³2078	·0³2001	·0³1926	·0³1854	·0³1785	·0³1718	·0³1653
−3·6	·0³1591	·0³1531	·0³1473	·0³1417	·0³1363	·0³1311	·0³1261	·0³1213	·0³1166	·0³1121
−3·7	·0³1078	·0³1036	·0⁴9961	·0⁴9574	·0⁴9201	·0⁴8842	·0⁴8496	·0⁴8162	·0⁴7841	·0⁴7532
−3·8	·0⁴7235	·0⁴6948	·0⁴6673	·0⁴6407	·0⁴6152	·0⁴5906	·0⁴5669	·0⁴5442	·0⁴5223	·0⁴5012
−3·9	·0⁴4810	·0⁴4615	·0⁴4427	·0⁴4247	·0⁴4074	·0⁴3908	·0⁴3747	·0⁴3594	·0⁴3446	·0⁴3304
−4·0	·0⁴3167	·0⁴3036	·0⁴2910	·0⁴2789	·0⁴2673	·0⁴2561	·0⁴2454	·0⁴2351	·0⁴2252	·0⁴2157
−4·1	·0⁴2066	·0⁴1978	·0⁴1894	·0⁴1814	·0⁴1737	·0⁴1662	·0⁴1591	·0⁴1523	·0⁴1458	·0⁴1395
−4·2	·0⁴1335	·0⁴1277	·0⁴1222	·0⁴1168	·0⁴1118	·0⁴1069	·0⁴1022	·0⁵9774	·0⁵9345	·0⁵8934
−4·3	·0⁵8540	·0⁵8163	·0⁵7801	·0⁵7455	·0⁵7124	·0⁵6807	·0⁵6503	·0⁵6212	·0⁵5934	·0⁵5668
−4·4	·0⁵5413	·0⁵5169	·0⁵4935	·0⁵4712	·0⁵4498	·0⁵4294	·0⁵4098	·0⁵3911	·0⁵3732	·0⁵3561
−4·5	·0⁵3398	·0⁵3241	·0⁵3092	·0⁵2949	·0⁵2813	·0⁵2682	·0⁵2558	·0⁵2439	·0⁵2325	·0⁵2216
−4·6	·0⁵2112	·0⁵2013	·0⁵1919	·0⁵1828	·0⁵1742	·0⁵1660	·0⁵1581	·0⁵1506	·0⁵1434	·0⁵1366
−4·7	·0⁵1301	·0⁵1239	·0⁵1179	·0⁵1123	·0⁵1069	·0⁵1017	·0⁶9680	·0⁶9211	·0⁶8765	·0⁶8339
−4·8	·0⁶7933	·0⁶7547	·0⁶7178	·0⁶6827	·0⁶6492	·0⁶6173	·0⁶5869	·0⁶5580	·0⁶5304	·0⁶5042
−4·9	·0⁶4792	·0⁶4554	·0⁶4327	·0⁶4111	·0⁶3906	·0⁶3711	·0⁶3525	·0⁶3348	·0⁶3179	·0⁶3019

Example: $\Phi(-3.57) = \cdot 0^3 1785 = 0.0001785$.

Table I. The Cumulative Standardized Normal Distribution Function (*continued*)

$$\Phi(u) = \frac{1}{\sqrt{2\pi}} \int_{-\infty}^{u} e^{-\frac{x^2}{2}} dx \quad \text{FOR} \quad 0.00 \le u \le 4.99.$$

u	·00	·01	·02	·03	·04	·05	·06	·07	·08	·09
·0	·5000	·5040	·5080	·5120	·5160	·5199	·5239	·5279	·5319	·5359
·1	·5398	·5438	·5478	·5517	·5557	·5596	·5636	·5675	·5714	·5753
·2	·5793	·5832	·5871	·5910	·5948	·5987	·6026	·6064	·6103	·6141
·3	·6179	·6217	·6255	·6293	·6331	·6368	·6406	·6443	·6480	·6517
·4	·6554	·6591	·6628	·6664	·6700	·6736	·6772	·6808	·6844	·6879
·5	·6915	·6950	·6985	·7019	·7054	·7088	·7123	·7157	·7190	·7224
·6	·7257	·7291	·7324	·7357	·7389	·7422	·7454	·7486	·7517	·7549
·7	·7580	·7611	·7642	·7673	·7703	·7734	·7764	·7794	·7823	·7852
·8	·7881	·7910	·7939	·7967	·7995	·8023	·8051	·8078	·8106	·8133
·9	·8159	·8186	·8212	·8238	·8264	·8289	·8315	·8340	·8365	·8389
1·0	·8413	·8438	·8461	·8485	·8508	·8531	·8554	·8577	·8599	·8621
1·1	·8643	·8665	·8686	·8708	·8729	·8749	·8770	·8790	·8810	·8830
1·2	·8849	·8869	·8888	·8907	·8925	·8944	·8962	·8980	·8997	·9^{0}147
1·3	·90320	·90490	·90658	·90824	·90988	·91149	·91309	·91466	·91621	·91774
1·4	·91924	·92073	·92220	·92364	·92507	·92647	·92785	·92922	·93056	·93189
1·5	·93319	·93448	·93574	·93699	·93822	·93943	·94062	·94179	·94295	·94408
1·6	·94520	·94630	·94738	·94845	·94950	·95053	·95154	·95254	·95352	·95449
1·7	·95543	·95637	·95728	·95818	·95907	·95994	·96080	·96164	·96246	·96327
1·8	·96407	·96485	·96562	·96638	·96712	·96784	·96856	·96926	·96995	·97062
1·9	·97128	·97193	·97257	·97320	·97381	·97441	·97500	·97558	·97615	·97670
2·0	·97725	·97778	·97831	·97882	·97932	·97982	·98030	·98077	·98124	·98169
2·1	·98214	·98257	·98300	·98341	·98382	·98422	·98461	·98500	·98537	·98574
2·2	·98610	·98645	·98679	·98713	·98745	·98778	·98809	·98840	·98870	·98899
2·3	·98928	·98956	·98983	·9^{2}0097	·9^{2}0358	·9^{2}0613	·9^{2}0863	·9^{2}1106	·9^{2}1344	·9^{2}1576
2·4	·9^{2}1802	·9^{2}2024	·9^{2}2240	·9^{2}2451	·9^{2}2656	·9^{2}2857	·9^{2}3053	·9^{2}3244	·9^{2}3431	·9^{2}3613
2·5	·9^{2}3790	·9^{2}3963	·9^{2}4132	·9^{2}4297	·9^{2}4457	·9^{2}4614	·9^{2}4766	·9^{2}4915	·9^{2}5060	·9^{2}5201
2·6	·9^{2}5339	·9^{2}5473	·9^{2}5604	·9^{2}5731	·9^{2}5855	·9^{2}5975	·9^{2}6093	·9^{2}6207	·9^{2}6319	·9^{2}6427
2·7	·9^{2}6533	·9^{2}6636	·9^{2}6736	·9^{2}6833	·9^{2}6928	·9^{2}7020	·9^{2}7110	·9^{2}7197	·9^{2}7282	·9^{2}7365
2·8	·9^{2}7445	·9^{2}7523	·9^{2}7599	·9^{2}7673	·9^{2}7744	·9^{2}7814	·9^{2}7882	·9^{2}7948	·9^{2}8012	·9^{2}8074
2·9	·9^{2}8134	·9^{2}8193	·9^{2}8250	·9^{2}8305	·9^{2}8359	·9^{2}8411	·9^{2}8462	·9^{2}8511	·9^{2}8559	·9^{2}8605
3·0	·9^{2}8650	·9^{2}8694	·9^{2}8736	·9^{2}8777	·9^{2}8817	·9^{2}8856	·9^{2}8893	·9^{2}8930	·9^{2}8965	·9^{2}8999
3·1	·9^{3}0324	·9^{3}0646	·9^{3}0957	·9^{3}1260	·9^{3}1553	·9^{3}1836	·9^{3}2112	·9^{3}2378	·9^{3}2636	·9^{3}2886
3·2	·9^{3}3129	·9^{3}3363	·9^{3}3590	·9^{3}3810	·9^{3}4024	·9^{3}4230	·9^{3}4429	·9^{3}4623	·9^{3}4810	·9^{3}4991
3·3	·9^{3}5166	·9^{3}5335	·9^{3}5499	·9^{3}5658	·9^{3}5811	·9^{3}5959	·9^{3}6103	·9^{3}6242	·9^{3}6376	·9^{3}6505
3·4	·9^{3}6631	·9^{3}6752	·9^{3}6869	·9^{3}6982	·9^{3}7091	·9^{3}7197	·9^{3}7299	·9^{3}7398	·9^{3}7493	·9^{3}7585
3·5	·9^{3}7674	·9^{3}7759	·9^{3}7842	·9^{3}7922	·9^{3}7999	·9^{3}8074	·9^{3}8146	·9^{3}8215	·9^{3}8282	·9^{3}8347
3·6	·9^{3}8409	·9^{3}8469	·9^{3}8527	·9^{3}8583	·9^{3}8637	·9^{3}8689	·9^{3}8739	·9^{3}8787	·9^{3}8834	·9^{3}8879
3·7	·9^{3}8922	·9^{3}8964	·9^{4}0039	·9^{4}0426	·9^{4}0799	·9^{4}1158	·9^{4}1504	·9^{4}1838	·9^{4}2159	·9^{4}2468
3·8	·9^{4}2765	·9^{4}3052	·9^{4}3327	·9^{4}3593	·9^{4}3848	·9^{4}4094	·9^{4}4331	·9^{4}4558	·9^{4}4777	·9^{4}4988
3·9	·9^{4}5190	·9^{4}5385	·9^{4}5573	·9^{4}5753	·9^{4}5926	·9^{4}6092	·9^{4}6253	·9^{4}6406	·9^{4}6554	·9^{4}6696
4·0	·9^{4}6833	·9^{4}6964	·9^{4}7090	·9^{4}7211	·9^{4}7327	·9^{4}7439	·9^{4}7546	·9^{4}7649	·9^{4}7748	·9^{4}7843
4·1	·9^{4}7934	·9^{4}8022	·9^{4}8106	·9^{4}8186	·9^{4}8263	·9^{4}8338	·9^{4}8409	·9^{4}8477	·9^{4}8542	·9^{4}8605
4·2	·9^{4}8665	·9^{4}8723	·9^{4}8778	·9^{4}8832	·9^{4}8882	·9^{4}8931	·9^{4}8978	·9^{5}0226	·9^{5}0655	·9^{5}1066
4·3	·9^{5}1460	·9^{5}1837	·9^{5}2199	·9^{5}2545	·9^{5}2876	·9^{5}3193	·9^{5}3497	·9^{5}3788	·9^{5}4066	·9^{5}4332
4·4	·9^{5}4587	·9^{5}4831	·9^{5}5065	·9^{5}5288	·9^{5}5502	·9^{5}5706	·9^{5}5902	·9^{5}6089	·9^{5}6268	·9^{5}6439
4·5	·9^{5}6602	·9^{5}6759	·9^{5}6908	·9^{5}7051	·9^{5}7187	·9^{5}7318	·9^{5}7442	·9^{5}7561	·9^{5}7675	·9^{5}7784
4·6	·9^{5}7888	·9^{5}7987	·9^{5}8081	·9^{5}8172	·9^{5}8258	·9^{5}8340	·9^{5}8419	·9^{5}8494	·9^{5}8566	·9^{5}8634
4·7	·9^{5}8699	·9^{5}8761	·9^{5}8821	·9^{5}8877	·9^{5}8931	·9^{5}8983	·9^{6}0320	·9^{6}0789	·9^{6}1235	·9^{6}1661
4·8	·9^{6}2067	·9^{6}2453	·9^{6}2822	·9^{6}3173	·9^{6}3508	·9^{6}3827	·9^{6}4131	·9^{6}4420	·9^{6}4696	·9^{6}4958
4·9	·9^{6}5208	·9^{6}5446	·9^{6}5673	·9^{6}5889	·9^{6}6094	·9^{6}6289	·9^{6}6475	·9^{6}6652	·9^{6}6821	·9^{6}6981

Example: $\Phi(3.57) = \cdot 9^3 8215 = 0 \cdot 9998215$.

* Abridged from Table II of *Statistical Tables and Formulas* by A. Hald, John Wiley & Sons, New York, 1952.

Table II. Fractional Points of the t Distribution*

P / f	0.750	0.900	0.950	0.975	0.990	0.995	0.999
1	1.000	3.078	6.314	12.706	31.821	63.657	318
2	0.816	1.886	2.920	4.303	6.965	9.925	22.3
3	0.765	1.638	2.353	3.182	4.541	5.841	10.2
4	0.741	1.533	2.132	2.776	3.747	4.604	7.173
5	0.727	1.476	2.015	2.571	3.365	4.032	5.893
6	0.718	1.440	1.943	2.447	3.143	3.707	5.208
7	0.711	1.415	1.895	2.365	2.998	3.499	4.785
8	0.706	1.397	1.860	2.306	2.896	3.355	4.501
9	0.703	1.383	1.833	2.262	2.821	3.250	4.297
10	0.700	1.372	1.812	2.228	2.764	3.169	4.144
11	0.697	1.363	1.796	2.201	2.718	3.106	4.025
12	0.695	1.356	1.782	2.179	2.681	3.055	3.930
13	0.694	1.350	1.771	2.160	2.650	3.012	3.852
14	0.692	1.345	1.761	2.145	2.624	2.977	3.787
15	0.691	1.341	1.753	2.131	2.602	2.947	3.733
16	0.690	1.337	1.746	2.120	2.583	2.921	3.686
17	0.689	1.333	1.740	2.110	2.567	2.898	3.646
18	0.688	1.330	1.734	2.101	2.552	2.878	3.610
19	0.688	1.328	1.729	2.093	2.539	2.861	3.579
20	0.687	1.325	1.725	2.086	2.528	2.845	3.552

Table II. Fractional Points of the t Distribution (*continued*)

f \ P	0.750	0.900	0.950	0.975	0.990	0.995	0.999
21	0.686	1.323	1.721	2.080	2.518	2.831	3.527
22	0.686	1.321	1.717	2.074	2.508	2.819	3.505
23	0.685	1.319	1.714	2.069	2.500	2.807	3.485
24	0.685	1.318	1.711	2.064	2.492	2.797	3.467
25	0.684	1.316	1.708	2.060	2.485	2.787	3.450
26	0.684	1.315	1.706	2.056	2.479	2.779	3.435
27	0.684	1.314	1.703	2.052	2.473	2.771	3.421
28	0.683	1.313	1.701	2.048	2.467	2.763	3.408
29	0.683	1.311	1.699	2.045	2.462	2.756	3.396
30	0.683	1.310	1.697	2.042	2.457	2.750	3.385
40	0.681	1.303	1.684	2.021	2.423	2.704	3.307
60	0.679	1.296	1.671	2.000	2.390	2.660	3.232
120	0.677	1.289	1.658	1.980	2.358	2.617	3.160
∞	0.674	1.282	1.645	1.960	2.326	2.576	3.090

*Abridged from Table 12 of *Biometrika Tables for Statisticians*, vol. I, edited by E. S. Pearson and H. O. Hartley, Cambridge University Press, Cambridge (1954), and Table III of *Statistical Tables for Biological, Agricultural, and Medical Research*, R. A. Fisher and F. Yates, Oliver & Boyd, Edinburgh, 1953.

Table III. Fractional

f	P							
	0.005	0.010	0.025	0.05	0.10	0.20	0.30	0.40
1	0.0^4393	0.0^3157	0.0^3982	0.0^2393	0.0158	0.0642	0.148	0.275
2	0.0100	0.0201	0.0506	0.103	0.211	0.446	0.713	1.02
3	0.0717	0.115	0.216	0.352	0.584	1.00	1.42	1.87
4	0.207	0.297	0.484	0.711	1.06	1.65	2.19	2.75
5	0.412	0.554	0.831	1.15	1.61	2.34	3.00	3.66
6	0.676	0.872	1.24	1.64	2.20	3.07	3.83	4.57
7	0.989	1.24	1.69	2.17	2.83	3.82	4.67	5.49
8	1.34	1.65	2.18	2.73	3.49	4.59	5.53	6.42
9	1.73	2.09	2.70	3.33	4.17	5.38	6.39	7.36
10	2.16	2.56	3.25	3.94	4.87	6.18	7.27	8.30
11	2.60	3.05	3.82	4.57	5.58	6.99	8.15	9.24
12	3.07	3.57	4.40	5.23	6.30	7.81	9.03	10.2
13	3.57	4.11	5.01	5.89	7.04	8.63	9.93	11.1
14	4.07	4.66	5.63	6.57	7.79	9.47	10.8	12.1
15	4.60	5.23	6.26	7.26	8.55	10.3	11.7	13.0
16	5.14	5.81	6.91	7.96	9.31	11.2	12.6	14.0
17	5.70	6.41	7.56	8.67	10.1	12.0	13.5	14.9
18	6.26	7.01	8.23	9.39	10.9	12.9	14.4	15.9
19	6.84	7.63	8.91	10.1	11.7	13.7	15.4	16.9
20	7.43	8.26	9.59	10.9	12.4	14.6	16.3	17.8
21	8.03	8.90	10.3	11.6	13.2	15.4	17.2	18.8
22	8.64	9.54	11.0	12.3	14.0	16.3	18.1	19.7
23	9.26	10.2	11.7	13.1	14.8	17.2	19.0	20.7
24	9.89	10.9	12.4	13.8	15.7	18.1	19.9	21.7
25	10.5	11.5	13.1	14.6	16.5	18.9	20.9	22.6
26	11.2	12.2	13.8	15.4	17.3	19.8	21.8	23.6
27	11.8	12.9	14.6	16.2	18.1	20.7	22.7	24.5
28	12.5	13.6	15.3	16.9	18.9	21.6	23.6	25.5
29	13.1	14.3	16.0	17.7	19.8	22.5	24.6	26.5
30	13.8	15.0	16.8	18.5	20.6	23.4	25.5	27.4
35	17.2	18.5	20.6	22.5	24.8	27.8	30.2	32.3
40	20.7	22.2	24.4	26.5	29.1	32.3	34.9	37.1
45	24.3	25.9	28.4	30.6	33.4	36.9	39.6	42.0
50	28.0	29.7	32.4	34.8	37.7	41.4	44.3	46.9
75	47.2	49.5	52.9	56.1	59.8	64.5	68.1	71.3
100	67.3	70.1	74.2	77.9	82.4	87.9	92.1	95.8

Points of the χ^2 Distribution*

0.50	0.60	0.70	0.80	0.90	0.95	0.975	0.990	0.995	0.999
0.455	0.708	1.07	1.64	2.71	3.84	5.02	6.63	7.88	10.8
1.39	1.83	2.41	3.22	4.61	5.99	7.38	9.21	10.6	13.8
2.37	2.95	3.67	4.64	6.25	7.81	9.35	11.3	12.8	16.3
3.36	4.04	4.88	5.99	7.78	9.49	11.1	13.3	14.9	18.5
4.35	5.13	6.06	7.29	9.24	11.1	12.8	15.1	16.7	20.5
5.35	6.21	7.23	8.56	10.6	12.6	14.4	16.8	18.5	22.5
6.35	7.28	8.38	9.80	12.0	14.1	16.0	18.5	20.3	24.3
7.34	8.35	9.52	11.0	13.4	15.5	17.5	20.1	22.0	26.1
8.34	9.41	10.7	12.2	14.7	16.9	19.0	21.7	23.6	27.9
9.34	10.5	11.8	13.4	16.0	18.3	20.5	23.2	25.2	29.6
10.3	11.5	12.9	14.6	17.3	19.7	21.9	24.7	26.8	31.3
11.3	12.6	14.0	15.8	18.5	21.0	23.3	26.2	28.3	32.9
12.3	13.6	15.1	17.0	19.8	22.4	24.7	27.7	29.8	34.5
13.3	14.7	16.2	18.2	21.1	23.7	26.1	29.1	31.3	36.1
14.3	15.7	17.3	19.3	22.3	25.0	27.5	30.6	32.8	37.7
15.3	16.8	18.4	20.5	23.5	26.3	28.8	32.0	34.3	39.3
16.3	17.8	19.5	21.6	24.8	27.6	30.2	33.4	35.7	40.8
17.3	18.9	20.6	22.8	26.0	28.9	31.5	34.8	37.2	42.3
18.3	19.9	21.7	23.9	27.2	30.1	32.9	36.2	38.6	43.8
19.3	21.0	22.8	25.0	28.4	31.4	34.2	37.6	40.0	45.3
20.3	22.0	23.9	26.9	29.6	32.7	35.5	38.9	41.4	46.8
21.3	23.0	24.9	27.3	30.8	33.9	36.8	40.3	42.8	48.3
22.3	24.1	26.0	28.4	32.0	35.2	38.1	41.6	44.2	49.7
23.3	25.1	27.1	29.6	33.2	36.4	39.4	43.0	45.6	51.2
24.3	26.1	28.2	30.7	34.4	37.7	40.6	44.3	46.9	52.6
25.3	27.2	29.2	31.8	35.6	38.9	41.9	45.6	48.3	54.1
26.3	28.2	30.3	32.9	36.7	40.1	43.2	47.0	49.6	55.5
27.3	29.2	31.4	34.0	37.9	41.3	44.5	48.3	51.0	56.9
28.3	30.3	32.5	35.1	39.1	42.6	45.7	49.6	52.3	58.3
29.3	31.3	33.5	36.3	40.3	43.8	47.0	50.9	53.7	59.7
34.3	36.5	38.9	41.8	46.1	49.8	53.2	57.3	60.3	66.6
39.3	41.6	44.2	47.3	51.8	55.8	59.3	63.7	66.8	73.4
44.3	46.8	49.5	52.7	57.5	61.7	65.4	70.0	73.2	80.1
49.3	51.9	54.7	58.2	63.2	67.5	71.4	76.2	79.5	86.7
74.3	77.5	80.9	85.1	91.1	96.2	100.8	106.4	110.3	118.6
99.3	102.9	106.9	111.7	118.5	124.3	129.6	135.6	140.2	149.4

* Abridged from Table V of *Statistical Tables and Formulas* by A. Hald, John Wiley and Sons, New York, 1952.

Table IV. Percentage Points of the F Distribution*
90 per cent points

f_2 \ f_1	1	2	3	4	5	6	7	8	9	10	12	15	20	24	30	40	60	120	∞
1	39.86	49.50	53.59	55.83	57.24	58.20	58.91	59.44	59.86	60.19	60.71	61.22	61.74	62.00	62.26	62.53	62.79	63.06	63.33
2	8.53	9.00	9.16	9.24	9.29	9.33	9.35	9.37	9.38	9.39	9.41	9.42	9.44	9.45	9.46	9.47	9.47	9.48	9.49
3	5.54	5.46	5.39	5.34	5.31	5.28	5.27	5.25	5.24	5.23	5.22	5.20	5.18	5.18	5.17	5.16	5.15	5.14	5.13
4	4.54	4.32	4.19	4.11	4.05	4.01	3.98	3.95	3.94	3.92	3.90	3.87	3.84	3.83	3.82	3.80	3.79	3.78	3.76
5	4.06	3.78	3.62	3.52	3.45	3.40	3.37	3.34	3.32	3.30	3.27	3.24	3.21	3.19	3.17	3.16	3.14	3.12	3.10
6	3.78	3.46	3.29	3.18	3.11	3.05	3.01	2.98	2.96	2.94	2.90	2.87	2.84	2.82	2.80	2.78	2.76	2.74	2.72
7	3.59	3.26	3.07	2.96	2.88	2.83	2.78	2.75	2.72	2.70	2.67	2.63	2.59	2.58	2.56	2.54	2.51	2.49	2.47
8	3.46	3.11	2.92	2.81	2.73	2.67	2.62	2.59	2.56	2.54	2.50	2.46	2.42	2.40	2.38	2.36	2.34	2.32	2.29
9	3.36	3.01	2.81	2.69	2.61	2.55	2.51	2.47	2.44	2.42	2.38	2.34	2.30	2.28	2.25	2.23	2.21	2.18	2.16
10	3.29	2.92	2.73	2.61	2.52	2.46	2.41	2.38	2.35	2.32	2.28	2.24	2.20	2.18	2.16	2.13	2.11	2.08	2.06
11	3.23	2.86	2.66	2.54	2.45	2.39	2.34	2.30	2.27	2.25	2.21	2.17	2.12	2.10	2.08	2.05	2.03	2.00	1.97
12	3.18	2.81	2.61	2.48	2.39	2.33	2.28	2.24	2.21	2.19	2.15	2.10	2.06	2.04	2.01	1.99	1.96	1.93	1.90
13	3.14	2.76	2.56	2.43	2.35	2.28	2.23	2.20	2.16	2.14	2.10	2.05	2.01	1.98	1.96	1.93	1.90	1.88	1.85
14	3.10	2.73	2.52	2.39	2.31	2.24	2.19	2.15	2.12	2.10	2.05	2.01	1.96	1.94	1.91	1.89	1.86	1.83	1.80
15	3.07	2.70	2.49	2.36	2.27	2.21	2.16	2.12	2.09	2.06	2.02	1.97	1.92	1.90	1.87	1.85	1.82	1.79	1.76
16	3.05	2.67	2.46	2.33	2.24	2.18	2.13	2.09	2.06	2.03	1.99	1.94	1.89	1.87	1.84	1.81	1.78	1.75	1.72
17	3.03	2.64	2.44	2.31	2.22	2.15	2.10	2.06	2.03	2.00	1.96	1.91	1.86	1.84	1.81	1.78	1.75	1.72	1.69
18	3.01	2.62	2.42	2.29	2.20	2.13	2.08	2.04	2.00	1.98	1.93	1.89	1.84	1.81	1.78	1.75	1.72	1.69	1.66
19	2.99	2.61	2.40	2.27	2.18	2.11	2.06	2.02	1.98	1.96	1.91	1.86	1.81	1.79	1.76	1.73	1.70	1.67	1.63
20	2.97	2.59	2.38	2.25	2.16	2.09	2.04	2.00	1.96	1.94	1.89	1.84	1.79	1.77	1.74	1.71	1.68	1.64	1.61
21	2.96	2.57	2.36	2.23	2.14	2.08	2.02	1.98	1.95	1.92	1.87	1.83	1.78	1.75	1.72	1.69	1.66	1.62	1.59
22	2.95	2.56	2.35	2.22	2.13	2.06	2.01	1.97	1.93	1.90	1.86	1.81	1.76	1.73	1.70	1.67	1.64	1.60	1.57
23	2.94	2.55	2.34	2.21	2.11	2.05	1.99	1.95	1.92	1.89	1.84	1.80	1.74	1.72	1.69	1.66	1.62	1.59	1.55
24	2.93	2.54	2.33	2.19	2.10	2.04	1.98	1.94	1.91	1.88	1.83	1.78	1.73	1.70	1.67	1.64	1.61	1.57	1.53
25	2.92	2.53	2.32	2.18	2.09	2.02	1.97	1.93	1.89	1.87	1.82	1.77	1.72	1.69	1.66	1.63	1.59	1.56	1.52
26	2.91	2.52	2.31	2.17	2.08	2.01	1.96	1.92	1.88	1.86	1.81	1.76	1.71	1.68	1.65	1.61	1.58	1.54	1.50
27	2.90	2.51	2.30	2.17	2.07	2.00	1.95	1.91	1.87	1.85	1.80	1.75	1.70	1.67	1.64	1.60	1.57	1.53	1.49
28	2.89	2.50	2.29	2.16	2.06	2.00	1.94	1.90	1.87	1.84	1.79	1.74	1.69	1.66	1.63	1.59	1.56	1.52	1.48
29	2.89	2.50	2.28	2.15	2.06	1.99	1.93	1.89	1.86	1.83	1.78	1.73	1.68	1.65	1.62	1.58	1.55	1.51	1.47
30	2.88	2.49	2.28	2.14	2.05	1.98	1.93	1.88	1.85	1.82	1.77	1.72	1.67	1.64	1.61	1.57	1.54	1.50	1.46
40	2.84	2.44	2.23	2.09	2.00	1.93	1.87	1.83	1.79	1.76	1.71	1.66	1.61	1.57	1.54	1.51	1.47	1.42	1.38
60	2.79	2.39	2.18	2.04	1.95	1.87	1.82	1.77	1.74	1.71	1.66	1.60	1.54	1.51	1.48	1.44	1.40	1.35	1.29
120	2.75	2.35	2.13	1.99	1.90	1.82	1.77	1.72	1.68	1.65	1.60	1.55	1.48	1.45	1.41	1.37	1.32	1.26	1.19
∞	2.71	2.30	2.08	1.94	1.85	1.77	1.72	1.67	1.63	1.60	1.55	1.49	1.42	1.38	1.34	1.30	1.24	1.17	1.00

95 per cent points

f_2 \ f_1	1	2	3	4	5	6	7	8	9	10	12	15	20	24	30	40	60	120	∞
1	161.4	199.5	215.7	224.6	230.2	234.0	236.8	238.9	240.5	241.9	243.9	245.9	248.0	249.1	250.1	251.1	252.2	253.3	254.3
2	18.51	19.00	19.16	19.25	19.30	19.33	19.35	19.37	19.38	19.40	19.41	19.43	19.45	19.45	19.46	19.47	19.48	19.49	19.50
3	10.13	9.55	9.28	9.12	9.01	8.94	8.89	8.85	8.81	8.79	8.74	8.70	8.66	8.64	8.62	8.59	8.57	8.55	8.53
4	7.71	6.94	6.59	6.39	6.26	6.16	6.09	6.04	6.00	5.96	5.91	5.86	5.80	5.77	5.75	5.72	5.69	5.66	5.63
5	6.61	5.79	5.41	5.19	5.05	4.95	4.88	4.82	4.77	4.74	4.68	4.62	4.56	4.53	4.50	4.46	4.43	4.40	4.36
6	5.99	5.14	4.76	4.53	4.39	4.28	4.21	4.15	4.10	4.06	4.00	3.94	3.87	3.84	3.81	3.77	3.74	3.70	3.67
7	5.59	4.74	4.35	4.12	3.97	3.87	3.79	3.73	3.68	3.64	3.57	3.51	3.44	3.41	3.38	3.34	3.30	3.27	3.23
8	5.32	4.46	4.07	3.84	3.69	3.58	3.50	3.44	3.39	3.35	3.28	3.22	3.15	3.12	3.08	3.04	3.01	2.97	2.93
9	5.12	4.26	3.86	3.63	3.48	3.37	3.29	3.23	3.18	3.14	3.07	3.01	2.94	2.90	2.86	2.83	2.79	2.75	2.71
10	4.96	4.10	3.71	3.48	3.33	3.22	3.14	3.07	3.02	2.98	2.91	2.85	2.77	2.74	2.70	2.66	2.62	2.58	2.54
11	4.84	3.98	3.59	3.36	3.20	3.09	3.01	2.95	2.90	2.85	2.79	2.72	2.65	2.61	2.57	2.53	2.49	2.45	2.40
12	4.75	3.89	3.49	3.26	3.11	3.00	2.91	2.85	2.80	2.75	2.69	2.62	2.54	2.51	2.47	2.43	2.38	2.34	2.30
13	4.67	3.81	3.41	3.18	3.03	2.92	2.83	2.77	2.71	2.67	2.60	2.53	2.46	2.42	2.38	2.34	2.30	2.25	2.21
14	4.60	3.74	3.34	3.11	2.96	2.85	2.76	2.70	2.65	2.60	2.53	2.46	2.39	2.35	2.31	2.27	2.22	2.18	2.13
15	4.54	3.68	3.29	3.06	2.90	2.79	2.71	2.64	2.59	2.54	2.48	2.40	2.33	2.29	2.25	2.20	2.16	2.11	2.07
16	4.49	3.63	3.24	3.01	2.85	2.74	2.66	2.59	2.54	2.49	2.42	2.35	2.28	2.24	2.19	2.15	2.11	2.06	2.01
17	4.45	3.59	3.20	2.96	2.81	2.70	2.61	2.55	2.49	2.45	2.38	2.31	2.23	2.19	2.15	2.10	2.06	2.01	1.96
18	4.41	3.55	3.16	2.93	2.77	2.66	2.58	2.51	2.46	2.41	2.34	2.27	2.19	2.15	2.11	2.06	2.02	1.97	1.92
19	4.38	3.52	3.13	2.90	2.74	2.63	2.54	2.48	2.42	2.38	2.31	2.23	2.16	2.11	2.07	2.03	1.98	1.93	1.88
20	4.35	3.49	3.10	2.87	2.71	2.60	2.51	2.45	2.39	2.35	2.28	2.20	2.12	2.08	2.04	1.99	1.95	1.90	1.84
21	4.32	3.47	3.07	2.84	2.68	2.57	2.49	2.42	2.37	2.32	2.25	2.18	2.10	2.05	2.01	1.96	1.92	1.87	1.81
22	4.30	3.44	3.05	2.82	2.66	2.55	2.46	2.40	2.34	2.30	2.23	2.15	2.07	2.03	1.98	1.94	1.89	1.84	1.78
23	4.28	3.42	3.03	2.80	2.64	2.53	2.44	2.37	2.32	2.27	2.20	2.13	2.05	2.01	1.96	1.91	1.86	1.81	1.76
24	4.26	3.40	3.01	2.78	2.62	2.51	2.42	2.36	2.30	2.25	2.18	2.11	2.03	1.98	1.94	1.89	1.84	1.79	1.73
25	4.24	3.39	2.99	2.76	2.60	2.49	2.40	2.34	2.28	2.24	2.16	2.09	2.01	1.96	1.92	1.87	1.82	1.77	1.71
26	4.23	3.37	2.98	2.74	2.59	2.47	2.39	2.32	2.27	2.22	2.15	2.07	1.99	1.95	1.90	1.85	1.80	1.75	1.69
27	4.21	3.35	2.96	2.73	2.57	2.46	2.37	2.31	2.25	2.20	2.13	2.06	1.97	1.93	1.88	1.84	1.79	1.73	1.67
28	4.20	3.34	2.95	2.71	2.56	2.45	2.36	2.29	2.24	2.19	2.12	2.04	1.96	1.91	1.87	1.82	1.77	1.71	1.65
29	4.18	3.33	2.93	2.70	2.55	2.43	2.35	2.28	2.22	2.18	2.10	2.03	1.94	1.90	1.85	1.81	1.75	1.70	1.64
30	4.17	3.32	2.92	2.69	2.53	2.42	2.33	2.27	2.21	2.16	2.09	2.01	1.93	1.89	1.84	1.79	1.74	1.68	1.62
40	4.08	3.23	2.84	2.61	2.45	2.34	2.25	2.18	2.12	2.08	2.00	1.92	1.84	1.79	1.74	1.69	1.64	1.58	1.51
60	4.00	3.15	2.76	2.53	2.37	2.25	2.17	2.10	2.04	1.99	1.92	1.84	1.75	1.70	1.65	1.59	1.53	1.47	1.39
120	3.92	3.07	2.68	2.45	2.29	2.17	2.09	2.02	1.96	1.91	1.83	1.75	1.66	1.61	1.55	1.50	1.43	1.35	1.25
∞	3.84	3.00	2.60	2.37	2.21	2.10	2.01	1.94	1.88	1.83	1.75	1.67	1.57	1.52	1.46	1.39	1.32	1.22	1.00

Table IV. Percentage Points of the F Distribution *(continued)*
97.5 per cent points

f_2 \ f_1	1	2	3	4	5	6	7	8	9	10	12	15	20	24	30	40	60	120	∞
1	647.8	799.5	864.2	899.6	921.8	937.1	948.2	956.7	963.3	968.6	976.7	984.9	993.1	997.2	1001	1006	1010	1014	1018
2	38.51	39.00	39.17	39.25	39.30	39.33	39.36	39.37	39.39	39.40	39.41	39.43	39.45	39.46	39.46	39.47	39.48	39.49	39.50
3	17.44	16.04	15.44	15.10	14.88	14.73	14.62	14.54	14.47	14.42	14.34	14.25	14.17	14.12	14.08	14.04	13.99	13.95	13.90
4	12.22	10.65	9.98	9.60	9.36	9.20	9.07	8.98	8.90	8.84	8.75	8.66	8.56	8.51	8.46	8.41	8.36	8.31	8.26
5	10.01	8.43	7.76	7.39	7.15	6.98	6.85	6.76	6.68	6.62	6.52	6.43	6.33	6.28	6.23	6.18	6.12	6.07	6.02
6	8.81	7.26	6.60	6.23	5.99	5.82	5.70	5.60	5.52	5.46	5.37	5.27	5.17	5.12	5.07	5.01	4.96	4.90	4.85
7	8.07	6.54	5.89	5.52	5.29	5.12	4.99	4.90	4.82	4.76	4.67	4.57	4.47	4.42	4.36	4.31	4.25	4.20	4.14
8	7.57	6.06	5.42	5.05	4.82	4.65	4.53	4.43	4.36	4.30	4.20	4.10	4.00	3.95	3.89	3.84	3.78	3.73	3.67
9	7.21	5.71	5.08	4.72	4.48	4.32	4.20	4.10	4.03	3.96	3.87	3.77	3.67	3.61	3.56	3.51	3.45	3.39	3.33
10	6.94	5.46	4.83	4.47	4.24	4.07	3.95	3.85	3.78	3.72	3.62	3.52	3.42	3.37	3.31	3.26	3.20	3.14	3.08
11	6.72	5.26	4.63	4.28	4.04	3.88	3.76	3.66	3.59	3.53	3.43	3.33	3.23	3.17	3.12	3.06	3.00	2.94	2.88
12	6.55	5.10	4.47	4.12	3.89	3.73	3.61	3.51	3.44	3.37	3.28	3.18	3.07	3.02	2.96	2.91	2.85	2.79	2.72
13	6.41	4.97	4.35	4.00	3.77	3.60	3.48	3.39	3.31	3.25	3.15	3.05	2.95	2.89	2.84	2.78	2.72	2.66	2.60
14	6.30	4.86	4.24	3.89	3.66	3.50	3.38	3.29	3.21	3.15	3.05	2.95	2.84	2.79	2.73	2.67	2.61	2.55	2.49
15	6.20	4.77	4.15	3.80	3.58	3.41	3.29	3.20	3.12	3.06	2.96	2.86	2.76	2.70	2.64	2.59	2.52	2.46	2.40
16	6.12	4.69	4.08	3.73	3.50	3.34	3.22	3.12	3.05	2.99	2.89	2.79	2.68	2.63	2.57	2.51	2.45	2.38	2.32
17	6.04	4.62	4.01	3.66	3.44	3.28	3.16	3.06	2.98	2.92	2.82	2.72	2.62	2.56	2.50	2.44	2.38	2.32	2.25
18	5.98	4.56	3.95	3.61	3.38	3.22	3.10	3.01	2.93	2.87	2.77	2.67	2.56	2.50	2.44	2.38	2.32	2.26	2.19
19	5.92	4.51	3.90	3.56	3.33	3.17	3.05	2.96	2.88	2.82	2.72	2.62	2.51	2.45	2.39	2.33	2.27	2.20	2.13
20	5.87	4.46	3.86	3.51	3.29	3.13	3.01	2.91	2.84	2.77	2.68	2.57	2.46	2.41	2.35	2.29	2.22	2.16	2.09
21	5.83	4.42	3.82	3.48	3.25	3.09	2.97	2.87	2.80	2.73	2.64	2.53	2.42	2.37	2.31	2.25	2.18	2.11	2.04
22	5.79	4.38	3.78	3.44	3.22	3.05	2.93	2.84	2.76	2.70	2.60	2.50	2.39	2.33	2.27	2.21	2.14	2.08	2.00
23	5.75	4.35	3.75	3.41	3.18	3.02	2.90	2.81	2.73	2.67	2.57	2.47	2.36	2.30	2.24	2.18	2.11	2.04	1.97
24	5.72	4.32	3.72	3.38	3.15	2.99	2.87	2.78	2.70	2.64	2.54	2.44	2.33	2.27	2.21	2.15	2.08	2.01	1.94
25	5.69	4.29	3.69	3.35	3.13	2.97	2.85	2.75	2.68	2.61	2.51	2.41	2.30	2.24	2.18	2.12	2.05	1.98	1.91
26	5.66	4.27	3.67	3.33	3.10	2.94	2.82	2.73	2.65	2.59	2.49	2.39	2.28	2.22	2.16	2.09	2.03	1.95	1.88
27	5.63	4.24	3.65	3.31	3.08	2.92	2.80	2.71	2.63	2.57	2.47	2.36	2.25	2.19	2.13	2.07	2.00	1.93	1.85
28	5.61	4.22	3.63	3.29	3.06	2.90	2.78	2.69	2.61	2.55	2.45	2.34	2.23	2.17	2.11	2.05	1.98	1.91	1.83
29	5.59	4.20	3.61	3.27	3.04	2.88	2.76	2.67	2.59	2.53	2.43	2.32	2.21	2.15	2.09	2.03	1.96	1.89	1.81
30	5.57	4.18	3.59	3.25	3.03	2.87	2.75	2.65	2.57	2.51	2.41	2.31	2.20	2.14	2.07	2.01	1.94	1.87	1.79
40	5.42	4.05	3.46	3.13	2.90	2.74	2.62	2.53	2.45	2.39	2.29	2.18	2.07	2.01	1.94	1.88	1.80	1.72	1.64
60	5.29	3.93	3.34	3.01	2.79	2.63	2.51	2.41	2.33	2.27	2.17	2.06	1.94	1.88	1.82	1.74	1.67	1.58	1.48
120	5.15	3.80	3.23	2.89	2.67	2.52	2.39	2.30	2.22	2.16	2.05	1.94	1.82	1.76	1.69	1.61	1.53	1.43	1.31
∞	5.02	3.69	3.12	2.79	2.57	2.41	2.29	2.19	2.11	2.05	1.94	1.83	1.71	1.64	1.57	1.48	1.39	1.27	1.00

APPENDIX

99 per cent points

f_2 \ f_1	1	2	3	4	5	6	7	8	9	10	12	15	20	24	30	40	60	120	∞
1	4052	4999.5	5403	5625	5764	5859	5928	5982	6022	6056	6106	6157	6209	6235	6261	6287	6313	6339	6366
2	98.50	99.00	99.17	99.25	99.30	99.33	99.36	99.37	99.39	99.40	99.42	99.43	99.45	99.46	99.47	99.47	99.48	99.49	99.50
3	34.12	30.82	29.46	28.71	28.24	27.91	27.67	27.49	27.35	27.23	27.05	26.87	26.69	26.60	26.50	26.41	26.32	26.22	26.13
4	21.20	18.00	16.69	15.98	15.52	15.21	14.98	14.80	14.66	14.55	14.37	14.20	14.02	13.93	13.84	13.75	13.65	13.56	13.46
5	16.26	13.27	12.06	11.39	10.97	10.67	10.46	10.29	10.16	10.05	9.89	9.72	9.55	9.47	9.38	9.29	9.20	9.11	9.02
6	13.75	10.92	9.78	9.15	8.75	8.47	8.26	8.10	7.98	7.87	7.72	7.56	7.40	7.31	7.23	7.14	7.06	6.97	6.88
7	12.25	9.55	8.45	7.85	7.46	7.19	6.99	6.84	6.72	6.62	6.47	6.31	6.16	6.07	5.99	5.91	5.82	5.74	5.65
8	11.26	8.65	7.59	7.01	6.63	6.37	6.18	6.03	5.91	5.81	5.67	5.52	5.36	5.28	5.20	5.12	5.03	4.95	4.86
9	10.56	8.02	6.99	6.42	6.06	5.80	5.61	5.47	5.35	5.26	5.11	4.96	4.81	4.73	4.65	4.57	4.48	4.40	4.31
10	10.04	7.56	6.55	5.99	5.64	5.39	5.20	5.06	4.94	4.85	4.71	4.56	4.41	4.33	4.25	4.17	4.08	4.00	3.91
11	9.65	7.21	6.22	5.67	5.32	5.07	4.89	4.74	4.63	4.54	4.40	4.25	4.10	4.02	3.94	3.86	3.78	3.69	3.60
12	9.33	6.93	5.95	5.41	5.06	4.82	4.64	4.50	4.39	4.30	4.16	4.01	3.86	3.78	3.70	3.62	3.54	3.45	3.36
13	9.07	6.70	5.74	5.21	4.86	4.62	4.44	4.30	4.19	4.10	3.96	3.82	3.66	3.59	3.51	3.43	3.34	3.25	3.17
14	8.86	6.51	5.56	5.04	4.69	4.46	4.28	4.14	4.03	3.94	3.80	3.66	3.51	3.43	3.35	3.27	3.18	3.09	3.00
15	8.68	6.36	5.42	4.89	4.56	4.32	4.14	4.00	3.89	3.80	3.67	3.52	3.37	3.29	3.21	3.13	3.05	2.96	2.87
16	8.53	6.23	5.29	4.77	4.44	4.20	4.03	3.89	3.78	3.69	3.55	3.41	3.26	3.18	3.10	3.02	2.93	2.84	2.75
17	8.40	6.11	5.18	4.67	4.34	4.10	3.93	3.79	3.68	3.59	3.46	3.31	3.16	3.08	3.00	2.92	2.83	2.75	2.65
18	8.29	6.01	5.09	4.58	4.25	4.01	3.84	3.71	3.60	3.51	3.37	3.23	3.08	3.00	2.92	2.84	2.75	2.66	2.57
19	8.18	5.93	5.01	4.50	4.17	3.94	3.77	3.63	3.52	3.43	3.30	3.15	3.00	2.92	2.84	2.76	2.67	2.58	2.49
20	8.10	5.85	4.94	4.43	4.10	3.87	3.70	3.56	3.46	3.37	3.23	3.09	2.94	2.86	2.78	2.69	2.61	2.52	2.42
21	8.02	5.78	4.87	4.37	4.04	3.81	3.64	3.51	3.40	3.31	3.17	3.03	2.88	2.80	2.72	2.64	2.55	2.46	2.36
22	7.95	5.72	4.82	4.31	3.99	3.76	3.59	3.45	3.35	3.26	3.12	2.98	2.83	2.75	2.67	2.58	2.50	2.40	2.31
23	7.88	5.66	4.76	4.26	3.94	3.71	3.54	3.41	3.30	3.21	3.07	2.93	2.78	2.70	2.62	2.54	2.45	2.35	2.26
24	7.82	5.61	4.72	4.22	3.90	3.67	3.50	3.36	3.26	3.17	3.03	2.89	2.74	2.66	2.58	2.49	2.40	2.31	2.21
25	7.77	5.57	4.68	4.18	3.85	3.63	3.46	3.32	3.22	3.13	2.99	2.85	2.70	2.62	2.54	2.45	2.36	2.27	2.17
26	7.72	5.53	4.64	4.14	3.82	3.59	3.42	3.29	3.18	3.09	2.96	2.81	2.66	2.58	2.50	2.42	2.33	2.23	2.13
27	7.68	5.49	4.60	4.11	3.78	3.56	3.39	3.26	3.15	3.06	2.93	2.78	2.63	2.55	2.47	2.38	2.29	2.20	2.10
28	7.64	5.45	4.57	4.07	3.75	3.53	3.36	3.23	3.12	3.03	2.90	2.75	2.60	2.52	2.44	2.35	2.26	2.17	2.06
29	7.60	5.42	4.54	4.04	3.73	3.50	3.33	3.20	3.09	3.00	2.87	2.73	2.57	2.49	2.41	2.33	2.23	2.14	2.03
30	7.56	5.39	4.51	4.02	3.70	3.47	3.30	3.17	3.07	2.98	2.84	2.70	2.55	2.47	2.39	2.30	2.21	2.11	2.01
40	7.31	5.18	4.31	3.83	3.51	3.29	3.12	2.99	2.89	2.80	2.66	2.52	2.37	2.29	2.20	2.11	2.02	1.92	1.80
60	7.08	4.98	4.13	3.65	3.34	3.12	2.95	2.82	2.72	2.63	2.50	2.35	2.20	2.12	2.03	1.94	1.84	1.73	1.60
120	6.85	4.79	3.95	3.48	3.17	2.96	2.79	2.66	2.56	2.47	2.34	2.19	2.03	1.95	1.86	1.76	1.66	1.53	1.38
∞	6.63	4.61	3.78	3.32	3.02	2.80	2.64	2.51	2.41	2.32	2.18	2.04	1.88	1.79	1.70	1.59	1.47	1.32	1.00

Table IV. Percentage Points of the F Distribution (*continued*)
99.5 per cent points

f_1 \ f_2	1	2	3	4	5	6	7	8	9	10	12	15	20	24	30	40	60	120	∞
1	16211	20000	21615	22500	23056	23437	23715	23925	24091	24224	24426	24630	24836	24940	25044	25148	25253	25359	25465
2	198.5	199.0	199.2	199.2	199.3	199.3	199.4	199.4	199.4	199.4	199.4	199.4	199.4	199.5	199.5	199.5	199.5	199.5	199.5
3	55.55	49.80	47.47	46.19	45.39	44.84	44.43	44.13	43.88	43.69	43.39	43.08	42.78	42.62	42.47	42.31	42.15	41.99	41.83
4	31.33	26.28	24.26	23.15	22.46	21.97	21.62	21.35	21.14	20.97	20.70	20.44	20.17	20.03	19.89	19.75	19.61	19.47	19.32
5	22.78	18.31	16.53	15.56	14.94	14.51	14.20	13.96	13.77	13.62	13.38	13.15	12.90	12.78	12.66	12.53	12.40	12.27	12.14
6	18.63	14.54	12.92	12.03	11.46	11.07	10.79	10.57	10.39	10.25	10.03	9.81	9.59	9.47	9.36	9.24	9.12	9.00	8.88
7	16.24	12.40	10.88	10.05	9.52	9.16	8.89	8.68	8.51	8.38	8.18	7.97	7.75	7.65	7.53	7.42	7.31	7.19	7.08
8	14.69	11.04	9.60	8.81	8.30	7.95	7.69	7.50	7.34	7.21	7.01	6.81	6.61	6.50	6.40	6.29	6.18	6.06	5.95
9	13.61	10.11	8.72	7.96	7.47	7.13	6.88	6.69	6.54	6.42	6.23	6.03	5.83	5.73	5.62	5.52	5.41	5.30	5.19
10	12.83	9.43	8.08	7.34	6.87	6.54	6.30	6.12	5.97	5.85	5.66	5.47	5.27	5.17	5.07	4.97	4.86	4.75	4.64
11	12.23	8.91	7.60	6.88	6.42	6.10	5.86	5.68	5.54	5.42	5.24	5.05	4.86	4.76	4.65	4.55	4.44	4.34	4.23
12	11.75	8.51	7.23	6.52	6.07	5.76	5.52	5.35	5.20	5.09	4.91	4.72	4.53	4.43	4.33	4.23	4.12	4.01	3.90
13	11.37	8.19	6.93	6.23	5.79	5.48	5.25	5.08	4.94	4.82	4.64	4.46	4.27	4.17	4.07	3.97	3.87	3.76	3.65
14	11.06	7.92	6.68	6.00	5.56	5.26	5.03	4.86	4.72	4.60	4.43	4.25	4.06	3.96	3.86	3.76	3.66	3.55	3.44
15	10.80	7.70	6.48	5.80	5.37	5.07	4.85	4.67	4.54	4.42	4.25	4.07	3.88	3.79	3.69	3.58	3.48	3.37	3.26
16	10.58	7.51	6.30	5.64	5.21	4.91	4.69	4.52	4.38	4.27	4.10	3.92	3.73	3.64	3.54	3.44	3.33	3.22	3.11
17	10.38	7.35	6.16	5.50	5.07	4.78	4.56	4.39	4.25	4.14	3.97	3.79	3.61	3.51	3.41	3.31	3.21	3.10	2.98
18	10.22	7.21	6.03	5.37	4.96	4.66	4.44	4.28	4.14	4.03	3.86	3.68	3.50	3.40	3.30	3.20	3.10	2.99	2.87
19	10.07	7.09	5.92	5.27	4.85	4.56	4.34	4.18	4.04	3.93	3.76	3.59	3.40	3.31	3.21	3.11	3.00	2.89	2.78
20	9.94	6.99	5.82	5.17	4.76	4.47	4.26	4.09	3.96	3.85	3.68	3.50	3.32	3.22	3.12	3.02	2.92	2.81	2.69
21	9.83	6.89	5.73	5.09	4.68	4.39	4.18	4.01	3.88	3.77	3.60	3.43	3.24	3.15	3.05	2.95	2.84	2.73	2.61
22	9.73	6.81	5.65	5.02	4.61	4.32	4.11	3.94	3.81	3.70	3.54	3.36	3.18	3.08	2.98	2.88	2.77	2.66	2.55
23	9.63	6.73	5.58	4.95	4.54	4.26	4.05	3.88	3.75	3.64	3.47	3.30	3.12	3.02	2.92	2.82	2.71	2.60	2.48
24	9.55	6.66	5.52	4.89	4.49	4.20	3.99	3.83	3.69	3.59	3.42	3.25	3.06	2.97	2.87	2.77	2.66	2.55	2.43
25	9.48	6.60	5.46	4.84	4.43	4.15	3.94	3.78	3.64	3.54	3.37	3.20	3.01	2.92	2.82	2.72	2.61	2.50	2.38
26	9.41	6.54	5.41	4.79	4.38	4.10	3.89	3.73	3.60	3.49	3.33	3.15	2.97	2.87	2.77	2.67	2.56	2.45	2.33
27	9.34	6.49	5.36	4.74	4.34	4.06	3.85	3.69	3.56	3.45	3.28	3.11	2.93	2.83	2.73	2.63	2.52	2.41	2.29
28	9.28	6.44	5.32	4.70	4.30	4.02	3.81	3.65	3.52	3.41	3.25	3.07	2.89	2.79	2.69	2.59	2.48	2.37	2.25
29	9.23	6.40	5.28	4.66	4.26	3.98	3.77	3.61	3.48	3.38	3.21	3.04	2.86	2.76	2.66	2.56	2.45	2.33	2.21
30	9.18	6.35	5.24	4.62	4.23	3.95	3.74	3.58	3.45	3.34	3.18	3.01	2.82	2.73	2.63	2.52	2.42	2.30	2.18
40	8.83	6.07	4.98	4.37	3.99	3.71	3.51	3.35	3.22	3.12	2.95	2.78	2.60	2.50	2.40	2.30	2.18	2.06	1.93
60	8.49	5.79	4.73	4.14	3.76	3.49	3.29	3.13	3.01	2.90	2.74	2.57	2.39	2.29	2.19	2.08	1.96	1.83	1.69
120	8.18	5.54	4.50	3.92	3.55	3.28	3.09	2.93	2.81	2.71	2.54	2.37	2.19	2.09	1.98	1.87	1.75	1.61	1.43
∞	7.88	5.30	4.28	3.72	3.35	3.09	2.90	2.74	2.62	2.52	2.36	2.19	2.00	1.90	1.79	1.67	1.53	1.36	1.00

99.9 per cent points

f_2 \ f_1	1	2	3	4	5	6	7	8	9	10	12	15	20	24	30	40	60	120	∞
1	4053†	5000†	5404†	5625†	5764†	5859†	5929†	5981†	6023†	6056†	6107†	6158†	6209†	6235†	6261†	6287†	6313†	6340†	6366†
2	998.5	999.0	999.2	999.2	999.3	999.3	999.4	999.4	999.4	999.4	999.4	999.4	999.4	999.5	999.5	999.5	999.5	999.5	999.5
3	167.0	148.5	141.1	137.1	134.6	132.8	131.6	130.6	129.9	129.2	128.3	127.4	126.4	125.9	125.4	125.0	124.5	124.0	123.5
4	74.14	61.25	56.18	53.44	51.71	50.53	49.66	49.00	48.47	48.05	47.41	46.76	46.10	45.77	45.43	45.09	44.75	44.40	44.05
5	47.18	37.12	33.20	31.09	29.75	28.84	28.16	27.64	27.24	26.92	26.42	25.91	25.39	25.14	24.87	24.60	24.33	24.06	23.79
6	35.51	27.00	23.70	21.92	20.81	20.03	19.46	19.03	18.69	18.41	17.99	17.56	17.12	16.89	16.67	16.44	16.21	15.99	15.75
7	29.25	21.69	18.77	17.19	16.21	15.52	15.02	14.63	14.33	14.08	13.71	13.32	12.93	12.73	12.53	12.33	12.12	11.91	11.70
8	25.42	18.49	15.83	14.39	13.49	12.86	12.40	12.04	11.77	11.54	11.19	10.84	10.48	10.30	10.11	9.92	9.73	9.53	9.33
9	22.86	16.39	13.90	12.56	11.71	11.13	10.70	10.37	10.11	9.89	9.57	9.24	8.90	8.72	8.55	8.37	8.19	8.00	7.81
10	21.04	14.91	12.55	11.28	10.48	9.92	9.52	9.20	8.96	8.75	8.45	8.13	7.80	7.64	7.47	7.30	7.12	6.94	6.76
11	19.69	13.81	11.56	10.35	9.58	9.05	8.66	8.35	8.12	7.92	7.63	7.32	7.01	6.85	6.68	6.52	6.35	6.17	6.00
12	18.64	12.97	10.80	9.63	8.89	8.38	8.00	7.71	7.48	7.29	7.00	6.71	6.40	6.25	6.09	5.93	5.76	5.59	5.42
13	17.81	12.31	10.21	9.07	8.35	7.86	7.49	7.21	6.98	6.80	6.52	6.23	5.93	5.78	5.63	5.47	5.30	5.14	4.97
14	17.14	11.78	9.73	8.62	7.92	7.43	7.08	6.80	6.58	6.40	6.13	5.85	5.56	5.41	5.25	5.10	4.94	4.77	4.60
15	16.59	11.34	9.34	8.25	7.57	7.09	6.74	6.47	6.26	6.08	5.81	5.54	5.25	5.10	4.95	4.80	4.64	4.47	4.31
16	16.12	10.97	9.00	7.94	7.27	6.81	6.46	6.19	5.98	5.81	5.55	5.27	4.99	4.85	4.70	4.54	4.39	4.23	4.06
17	15.72	10.66	8.73	7.68	7.02	6.56	6.22	5.96	5.75	5.58	5.32	5.05	4.78	4.63	4.48	4.33	4.18	4.02	3.85
18	15.38	10.39	8.49	7.46	6.81	6.35	6.02	5.76	5.56	5.39	5.13	4.87	4.59	4.45	4.30	4.15	4.00	3.84	3.67
19	15.08	10.16	8.28	7.26	6.62	6.18	5.85	5.59	5.39	5.22	4.97	4.70	4.43	4.29	4.14	3.99	3.84	3.68	3.51
20	14.82	9.95	8.10	7.10	6.46	6.02	5.69	5.44	5.24	5.08	4.82	4.56	4.29	4.15	4.00	3.86	3.70	3.54	3.38
21	14.59	9.77	7.94	6.95	6.32	5.88	5.56	5.31	5.11	4.95	4.70	4.44	4.17	4.03	3.88	3.74	3.58	3.42	3.26
22	14.38	9.61	7.80	6.81	6.19	5.76	5.44	5.19	4.99	4.83	4.58	4.33	4.06	3.92	3.78	3.63	3.48	3.32	3.15
23	14.19	9.47	7.67	6.69	6.08	5.65	5.33	5.09	4.89	4.73	4.48	4.23	3.96	3.82	3.68	3.53	3.38	3.22	3.05
24	14.03	9.34	7.55	6.59	5.98	5.55	5.23	4.99	4.80	4.64	4.39	4.14	3.87	3.74	3.59	3.45	3.29	3.14	2.97
25	13.88	9.22	7.45	6.49	5.88	5.46	5.15	4.91	4.71	4.56	4.31	4.06	3.79	3.66	3.52	3.37	3.22	3.06	2.89
26	13.74	9.12	7.36	6.41	5.80	5.38	5.07	4.83	4.64	4.48	4.24	3.99	3.72	3.59	3.44	3.30	3.15	2.99	2.82
27	13.61	9.02	7.27	6.33	5.73	5.31	5.00	4.76	4.57	4.41	4.17	3.92	3.66	3.52	3.38	3.23	3.08	2.92	2.75
28	13.50	8.93	7.19	6.25	5.66	5.24	4.93	4.69	4.50	4.35	4.11	3.86	3.60	3.46	3.32	3.18	3.02	2.86	2.69
29	13.39	8.85	7.12	6.19	5.59	5.18	4.87	4.64	4.45	4.29	4.05	3.80	3.54	3.41	3.27	3.12	2.97	2.81	2.64
30	13.29	8.77	7.05	6.12	5.53	5.12	4.82	4.58	4.39	4.24	4.00	3.75	3.49	3.36	3.22	3.07	2.92	2.76	2.59
40	12.61	8.25	6.60	5.70	5.13	4.73	4.44	4.21	4.02	3.87	3.64	3.40	3.15	3.01	2.87	2.73	2.57	2.41	2.23
60	11.97	7.76	6.17	5.31	4.76	4.37	4.09	3.87	3.69	3.54	3.31	3.08	2.83	2.69	2.55	2.41	2.25	2.08	1.89
120	11.38	7.32	5.79	4.95	4.42	4.04	3.77	3.55	3.38	3.24	3.02	2.78	2.53	2.40	2.26	2.11	1.95	1.76	1.54
∞	10.83	6.91	5.42	4.62	4.10	3.74	3.47	3.27	3.10	2.96	2.74	2.51	2.27	2.13	1.99	1.84	1.66	1.45	1.00

*Abridged from Table 18 of *Biometrika Tables for Statisticians*, vol. I, edited by E. S. Pearson and H. O. Hartley, Cambridge University Press, Cambridge, 1954, and Table V of *Statistical Tables for Biological, Agricultural, and Medical Research*, R. A. Fisher and F. Yates, Oliver & Boyd, Edinburgh, 1953.

†Multiply these entries by 100.

Table V. $y = 2 \arcsin \sqrt{x}$*

	·000	·001	·002	·003	·004	·005	·006	·007	·008	·009
·00	0·0000	0·0633	0·0895	0·1096	0·1266	0·1415	0·1551	0·1675	0·1791	0·1900
·01	0·2003	0·2101	0·2195	0·2285	0·2372	0·2456	0·2537	0·2615	0·2691	0·2766
·02	0·2838	0·2909	0·2977	0·3045	0·3111	0·3176	0·3239	0·3301	0·3362	0·3423
·03	0·3482	0·3540	0·3597	0·3653	0·3709	0·3764	0·3818	0·3871	0·3924	0·3976
·04	0·4027	0·4078	0·4128	0·4178	0·4227	0·4275	0·4323	0·4371	0·4418	0·4464
·05	0·4510	0·4556	0·4601	0·4646	0·4690	0·4734	0·4778	0·4822	0·4864	0·4907
·06	0·4949	0·4991	0·5033	0·5074	0·5115	0·5156	0·5196	0·5236	0·5276	0·5316
·07	0·5355	0·5394	0·5433	0·5472	0·5510	0·5548	0·5586	0·5624	0·5661	0·5698
·08	0·5735	0·5772	0·5808	0·5845	0·5881	0·5917	0·5953	0·5988	0·6024	0·6059
·09	0·6094	0·6129	0·6163	0·6198	0·6232	0·6266	0·6300	0·6334	0·6368	0·6402
·10	0·6435	0·6468	0·6501	0·6534	0·6567	0·6600	0·6632	0·6665	0·6697	0·6729
·11	0·6761	0·6793	0·6825	0·6857	0·6888	0·6920	0·6951	0·6982	0·7013	0·7044
·12	0·7075	0·7106	0·7136	0·7167	0·7197	0·7227	0·7258	0·7288	0·7318	0·7347
·13	0·7377	0·7407	0·7437	0·7466	0·7495	0·7525	0·7554	0·7583	0·7612	0·7641
·14	0·7670	0·7699	0·7727	0·7756	0·7785	0·7813	0·7841	0·7870	0·7898	0·7926
·15	0·7954	0·7982	0·8010	0·8038	0·8065	0·8093	0·8121	0·8148	0·8176	0·8203
·16	0·8230	0·8258	0·8285	0·8312	0·8339	0·8366	0·8393	0·8420	0·8446	0·8473
·17	0·8500	0·8526	0·8553	0·8579	0·8606	0·8632	0·8658	0·8685	0·8711	0·8737
·18	0·8763	0·8789	0·8815	0·8841	0·8867	0·8892	0·8918	0·8944	0·8969	0·8995
·19	0·9021	0·9046	0·9071	0·9097	0·9122	0·9147	0·9173	0·9198	0·9223	0·9248
·20	0·9273	0·9298	0·9323	0·9348	0·9373	0·9397	0·9422	0·9447	0·9471	0·9496
·21	0·9521	0·9545	0·9570	0·9594	0·9619	0·9643	0·9667	0·9692	0·9716	0·9740
·22	0·9764	0·9788	0·9812	0·9836	0·9860	0·9884	0·9908	0·9932	0·9956	0·9980
·23	1·0004	1·0027	1·0051	1·0075	1·0098	1·0122	1·0146	1·0169	1·0193	1·0216
·24	1·0239	1·0263	1·0286	1·0310	1·0333	1·0356	1·0379	1·0403	1·0426	1·0449
·25	1·0472	1·0495	1·0518	1·0541	1·0564	1·0587	1·0610	1·0633	1·0656	1·0679
·26	1·0701	1·0724	1·0747	1·0770	1·0792	1·0815	1·0838	1·0860	1·0883	1·0905
·27	1·0928	1·0951	1·0973	1·0995	1·1018	1·1040	1·1063	1·1085	1·1107	1·1130
·28	1·1152	1·1174	1·1196	1·1219	1·1241	1·1263	1·1285	1·1307	1·1329	1·1351
·29	1·1373	1·1396	1·1418	1·1440	1·1461	1·1483	1·1505	1·1527	1·1549	1·1571
·30	1·1593	1·1615	1·1636	1·1658	1·1680	1·1702	1·1723	1·1745	1·1767	1·1788
·31	1·1810	1·1832	1·1853	1·1875	1·1896	1·1918	1·1939	1·1961	1·1982	1·2004
·32	1·2025	1·2047	1·2068	1·2090	1·2111	1·2132	1·2154	1·2175	1·2196	1·2217
·33	1·2239	1·2260	1·2281	1·2303	1·2324	1·2345	1·2366	1·2387	1·2408	1·2430
·34	1·2451	1·2472	1·2493	1·2514	1·2535	1·2556	1·2577	1·2598	1·2619	1·2640
·35	1·2661	1·2682	1·2703	1·2724	1·2745	1·2766	1·2787	1·2807	1·2828	1·2849
·36	1·2870	1·2891	1·2912	1·2932	1·2953	1·2974	1·2995	1·3016	1·3036	1·3057
·37	1·3078	1·3098	1·3119	1·3140	1·3161	1·3181	1·3202	1·3222	1·3243	1·3264
·38	1·3284	1·3305	1·3325	1·3346	1·3367	1·3387	1·3408	1·3428	1·3449	1·3469
·39	1·3490	1·3510	1·3531	1·3551	1·3572	1·3592	1·3613	1·3633	1·3654	1·3674
·40	1·3694	1·3715	1·3735	1·3756	1·3776	1·3796	1·3817	1·3837	1·3857	1·3878
·41	1·3898	1·3918	1·3939	1·3959	1·3979	1·4000	1·4020	1·4040	1·4061	1·4081
·42	1·4101	1·4121	1·4142	1·4162	1·4182	1·4202	1·4222	1·4243	1·4263	1·4283
·43	1·4303	1·4324	1·4344	1·4364	1·4384	1·4404	1·4424	1·4445	1·4465	1·4485
·44	1·4505	1·4525	1·4545	1·4565	1·4586	1·4606	1·4626	1·4646	1·4666	1·4686
·45	1·4706	1·4726	1·4746	1·4767	1·4787	1·4807	1·4827	1·4847	1·4867	1·4887
·46	1·4907	1·4927	1·4947	1·4967	1·4987	1·5007	1·5027	1·5048	1·5068	1·5088
·47	1·5108	1·5128	1·5148	1·5168	1·5188	1·5208	1·5228	1·5248	1·5268	1·5288
·48	1·5308	1·5328	1·5348	1·5368	1·5388	1·5408	1·5428	1·5448	1·5468	1·5488
·49	1·5508	1·5528	1·5548	1·5568	1·5588	1·5608	1·5628	1·5648	1·5668	1·5688

Example: $2 \arcsin \sqrt{0 \cdot 296} = 1 \cdot 1505$.

Table V. $y = 2 \arcsin \sqrt{x}$ (continued)

	·000	·001	·002	·003	·004	·005	·006	·007	·008	·009
·50	1·5708	1·5728	1·5748	1·5768	1·5788	1·5808	1·5828	1·5848	1·5868	1·5888
·51	1·5908	1·5928	1·5948	1·5968	1·5988	1·6008	1·6028	1·6048	1·6068	1·6088
·52	1·6108	1·6128	1·6148	1·6168	1·6188	1·6208	1·6228	1·6248	1·6268	1·6288
·53	1·6308	1·6328	1·6348	1·6368	1·6388	1·6409	1·6429	1·6449	1·6469	1·6489
·54	1·6509	1·6529	1·6549	1·6569	1·6589	1·6609	1·6629	1·6649	1·6669	1·6690
·55	1·6710	1·6730	1·6750	1·6770	1·6790	1·6810	1·6830	1·6850	1·6871	1·6891
·56	1·6911	1·6931	1·6951	1·6971	1·6992	1·7012	1·7032	1·7052	1·7072	1·7092
·57	1·7113	1·7133	1·7153	1·7173	1·7193	1·7214	1·7234	1·7254	1·7274	1·7295
·58	1·7315	1·7335	1·7355	1·7376	1·7396	1·7416	1·7437	1·7457	1·7477	1·7498
·59	1·7518	1·7538	1·7559	1·7579	1·7599	1·7620	1·7640	1·7660	1·7681	1·7701
·60	1·7722	1·7742	1·7762	1·7783	1·7803	1·7824	1·7844	1·7865	1·7885	1·7906
·61	1·7926	1·7947	1·7967	1·7988	1·8008	1·8029	1·8049	1·8070	1·8090	1·8111
·62	1·8132	1·8152	1·8173	1·8193	1·8214	1·8235	1·8255	1·8276	1·8297	1·8317
·63	1·8338	1·8359	1·8380	1·8400	1·8421	1·8442	1·8463	1·8483	1·8504	1·8525
·64	1·8546	1·8567	1·8588	1·8608	1·8629	1·8650	1·8671	1·8692	1·8713	1·8734
·65	1·8755	1·8776	1·8797	1·8818	1·8839	1·8860	1·8881	1·8902	1·8923	1·8944
·66	1·8965	1·8986	1·9008	1·9029	1·9050	1·9071	1·9092	1·9113	1·9135	1·9156
·67	1·9177	1·9198	1·9220	1·9241	1·9262	1·9284	1·9305	1·9326	1·9348	1·9369
·68	1·9391	1·9412	1·9434	1·9455	1·9477	1·9498	1·9520	1·9541	1·9563	1·9584
·69	1·9606	1·9628	1·9649	1·9671	1·9693	1·9714	1·9736	1·9758	1·9780	1·9801
·70	1·9823	1·9845	1·9867	1·9889	1·9911	1·9932	1·9954	1·9976	1·9998	2·0020
·71	2·0042	2·0064	2·0087	2·0109	2·0131	2·0153	2·0175	2·0197	2·0219	2·0242
·72	2·0264	2·0286	2·0309	2·0331	2·0353	2·0376	2·0398	2·0420	2·0443	2·0465
·73	2·0488	2·0510	2·0533	2·0556	2·0578	2·0601	2·0624	2·0646	2·0669	2·0692
·74	2·0714	2·0737	2·0760	2·0783	2·0806	2·0829	2·0852	2·0875	2·0898	2·0921
·75	2·0944	2·0967	2·0990	2·1013	2·1037	2·1060	2·1083	2·1106	2·1130	2·1153
·76	2·1176	2·1200	2·1223	2·1247	2·1270	2·1294	2·1318	2·1341	2·1365	2·1389
·77	2·1412	2·1436	2·1460	2·1484	2·1508	2·1532	2·1556	2·1580	2·1604	2·1628
·78	2·1652	2·1676	2·1700	2·1724	2·1749	2·1773	2·1797	2·1822	2·1846	2·1871
·79	2·1895	2·1920	2·1944	2·1969	2·1994	2·2019	2·2043	2·2068	2·2093	2·2118
·80	2·2143	2·2168	2·2193	2·2218	2·2243	2·2269	2·2294	2·2319	2·2345	2·2370
·81	2·2395	2·2421	2·2446	2·2472	2·2498	2·2523	2·2549	2·2575	2·2601	2·2627
·82	2·2653	2·2679	2·2705	2·2731	2·2758	2·2784	2·2810	2·2837	2·2863	2·2890
·83	2·2916	2·2943	2·2970	2·2996	2·3023	2·3050	2·3077	2·3104	2·3131	2·3158
·84	2·3186	2·3213	2·3240	2·3268	2·3295	2·3323	2·3351	2·3378	2·3406	2·3434
·85	2·3462	2·3490	2·3518	2·3546	2·3575	2·3603	2·3631	2·3660	2·3689	2·3717
·86	2·3746	2·3775	2·3804	2·3833	2·3862	2·3891	2·3921	2·3950	2·3979	2·4009
·87	2·4039	2·4068	2·4098	2·4128	2·4158	2·4189	2·4219	2·4249	2·4280	2·4310
·88	2·4341	2·4372	2·4403	2·4434	2·4465	2·4496	2·4528	2·4559	2·4591	2·4623
·89	2·4655	2·4687	2·4719	2·4751	2·4783	2·4816	2·4849	2·4882	2·4915	2·4948
·90	2·4981	2·5014	2·5048	2·5082	2·5115	2·5149	2·5184	2·5218	2·5253	2·5287
·91	2·5322	2·5357	2·5392	2·5428	2·5463	2·5499	2·5535	2·5571	2·5607	2·5644
·92	2·5681	2·5718	2·5755	2·5792	2·5830	2·5868	2·5906	2·5944	2·5983	2·6022
·93	2·6061	2·6100	2·6140	2·6179	2·6220	2·6260	2·6301	2·6342	2·6383	2·6425
·94	2·6467	2·6509	2·6551	2·6594	2·6638	2·6681	2·6725	2·6770	2·6815	2·6860
·95	2·6906	2·6952	2·6998	2·7045	2·7093	2·7141	2·7189	2·7238	2·7288	2·7338
·96	2·7389	2·7440	2·7492	2·7545	2·7598	2·7652	2·7707	2·7762	2·7819	2·7876
·97	2·7934	2·7993	2·8053	2·8115	2·8177	2·8240	2·8305	2·8371	2·8438	2·8507
·98	2·8578	2·8650	2·8725	2·8801	2·8879	2·8960	2·9044	2·9131	2·9221	2·9314
·99	2·9413	2·9516	2·9625	2·9741	2·9865	3·0001	3·0150	3·0320	3·0521	3·0783
1·00	3·1416									

Example: $2 \arcsin \sqrt{0.724} = 2.0353$.

*Reproduced from Table XII of *Statistical Tables and Formulas* by A. Hald, John Wiley & Sons, New York, 1952.

Table VI. Values of d_n and Fractional Points of the Distribution of the Range*

n	d_n	0.001	0.005	0.025	0.050	0.95	0.975	0.995	0.999
2	1.128	0.00	0.01	0.04	0.09	2.77	3.17	3.97	4.65
3	1.693	0.06	0.13	0.30	0.43	3.31	3.68	4.42	5.06
4	2.059	0.20	0.34	0.59	0.76	3.63	3.98	4.69	5.31
5	2.326	0.37	0.55	0.85	1.03	3.86	4.20	4.89	5.48
6	2.534	0.54	0.75	1.06	1.25	4.03	4.36	5.03	5.62
7	2.704	0.69	0.92	1.25	1.44	4.17	4.49	5.15	5.73
8	2.847	0.83	1.08	1.41	1.60	4.29	4.61	5.26	5.82
9	2.970	0.96	1.21	1.55	1.74	4.39	4.70	5.34	5.90
10	3.078	1.08	1.33	1.67	1.86	4.47	4.79	5.42	5.97
11	3.173	1.20	1.45	1.78	1.97	4.55	4.86	5.49	6.04
12	3.258	1.30	1.55	1.88	2.07	4.62	4.92	5.54	6.09

*Abridged from Tables 20 and 22 of *Biometrika Tables for Statisticians*, vol. I, edited by E. S. Pearson and H. O. Hartley. Cambridge University Press, Cambridge (1954).

Table VII. u_P

P	u_P	P	u_P
0.20	−0.8416	0.80	0.8416
0.10	−1.2816	0.90	1.2816
0.05	−1.6449	0.95	1.6449
0.025	−1.9600	0.975	1.9600
0.01	−2.3263	0.99	2.3263
0.005	−2.5758	0.995	2.5758
0.001	−3.0902	0.999	3.0902
0.0005	−3.2905	0.9995	3.2905

Table VIII. Logarithms of $n!$*

n	$\log n!$	n	$\log n!$	n	$\log n!$	n	$\log n!$	n	$\log n!$	n	$\log n!$
1	0.0000	51	66.1906	101	159.9743	151	264.9359	201	377.2001		
2	0.3010	52	67.9066	102	161.9829	152	267.1177	202	379.5054		
3	0.7782	53	69.6309	103	163.9958	153	269.3024	203	381.8129		
4	1.3802	54	71.3633	104	166.0128	154	271.4899	204	384.1226		
5	2.0792	55	73.1037	105	168.0340	155	273.6803	205	386.4343		
6	2.8573	56	74.8519	106	170.0593	156	275.8734	206	388.7482		
7	3.7024	57	76.6077	107	172.0887	157	278.0693	207	391.0642		
8	4.6055	58	78.3712	108	174.1221	158	280.2679	208	393.3822		
9	5.5598	59	80.1420	109	176.1595	159	282.4693	209	395.7024		
10	6.5598	60	81.9202	110	178.2009	160	284.6735	210	398.0246		
11	7.6012	61	83.7055	111	180.2462	161	286.8803	211	400.3489		
12	8.6803	62	85.4979	112	182.2955	162	289.0898	212	402.6752		
13	9.7943	63	87.2972	113	184.3485	163	291.3020	213	405.0036		
14	10.9404	64	89.1034	114	186.4054	164	293.5168	214	407.3340		
15	12.1165	65	90.9163	115	188.4661	165	295.7343	215	409.6664		
16	13.3206	66	92.7359	116	190.5306	166	297.9544	216	412.0009		
17	14.5511	67	94.5619	117	192.5988	167	300.1771	217	414.3373		
18	15.8063	68	96.3945	118	194.6707	168	302.4024	218	416.6758		
19	17.0851	69	98.2333	119	196.7462	169	304.6303	219	419.0162		
20	18.3861	70	100.0784	120	198.8254	170	306.8608	220	421.3587		
21	19.7083	71	101.9297	121	200.9082	171	309.0938	221	423.7031		
22	21.0508	72	103.7870	122	202.9945	172	311.3293	222	426.0494		
23	22.4125	73	105.6503	123	205.0844	173	313.5674	223	428.3977		
24	23.7927	74	107.5196	124	207.1779	174	315.8079	224	430.7480		
25	25.1906	75	109.3946	125	209.2748	175	318.0509	225	433.1002		
26	26.6056	76	111.2754	126	211.3751	176	320.2965	226	435.4543		
27	28.0370	77	113.1619	127	213.4790	177	322.5444	227	437.8103		
28	29.4841	78	115.0540	128	215.5862	178	324.7948	228	440.1682		
29	30.9465	79	116.9516	129	217.6967	179	327.0477	229	442.5281		
30	32.4237	80	118.8547	130	219.8107	180	329.3030	230	444.8898		
31	33.9150	81	120.7632	131	221.9280	181	331.5606	231	447.2534		
32	35.4202	82	122.6770	132	224.0485	182	333.8207	232	449.6189		
33	36.9387	83	124.5961	133	226.1724	183	336.0832	233	451.9862		
34	38.4702	84	126.5204	134	228.2995	184	338.3480	234	454.3555		
35	40.0142	85	128.4498	135	230.4298	185	340.6152	235	456.7265		
36	41.5705	86	130.3843	136	232.5634	186	342.8847	236	459.0994		
37	43.1387	87	132.3238	137	234.7001	187	345.1565	237	461.4742		
38	44.7185	88	134.2683	138	236.8400	188	347.4307	238	463.8508		
39	46.3096	89	136.2177	139	238.9830	189	349.7071	239	466.2292		
40	47.9116	90	138.1719	140	241.1291	190	351.9859	240	468.6094		
41	49.5244	91	140.1310	141	243.2783	191	354.2669	241	470.9914		
42	51.1477	92	142.0948	142	245.4306	192	356.5502	242	473.3752		
43	52.7811	93	144.0632	143	247.5860	193	358.8358	243	475.7608		
44	54.4246	94	146.0364	144	249.7443	194	361.1236	244	478.1482		
45	56.0778	95	148.0141	145	251.9057	195	363.4136	245	480.5374		
46	57.7406	96	149.9964	146	254.0700	196	365.7059	246	482.9283		
47	59.4127	97	151.9831	147	256.2374	197	368.0003	247	485.3210		
48	61.0939	98	153.9744	148	258.4076	198	370.2970	248	487.7154		
49	62.7841	99	155.9700	149	260.5808	199	372.5959	249	490.1116		
50	64.4831	100	157.9700	150	262.7569	200	374.8969	250	492.5096		

*Abridged from Table XIII of *Statistical Tables and Formulas* by A. Hald, John Wiley & Sons, New York, 1952.

Table IX. Fractional Points of the Studentized Range, $q = (x_{max} - x_{min})/s^*$

$P = 0.95$

k \ f	2	3	4	5	6	7	8	9	10	11	12	13	14	15
1	18.0	27.0	32.8	37.1	40.4	43.1	45.4	47.4	49.1	50.6	52.0	53.2	54.3	55.4
2	6.09	8.3	9.8	10.9	11.7	12.4	13.0	13.5	14.0	14.4	14.7	15.1	15.4	15.7
3	4.50	5.91	6.82	7.50	8.04	8.48	8.85	9.18	9.46	9.72	9.95	10.1	10.3	10.5
4	3.93	5.04	5.76	6.29	6.71	7.05	7.35	7.60	7.83	8.03	8.21	8.37	8.52	8.66
5	3.64	4.60	5.22	5.67	6.03	6.33	6.58	6.80	6.99	7.17	7.32	7.47	7.60	7.72
6	3.46	4.34	4.90	5.31	5.63	5.89	6.12	6.32	6.49	6.65	6.79	6.92	7.03	7.14
7	3.34	4.16	4.68	5.06	5.36	5.61	5.82	6.00	6.16	6.30	6.43	6.55	6.66	6.76
8	3.26	4.04	4.53	4.89	5.17	5.40	5.60	5.77	5.92	6.05	6.18	6.29	6.39	6.48
9	3.20	3.95	4.42	4.76	5.02	5.24	5.43	5.60	5.74	5.87	5.98	6.09	6.19	6.28
10	3.15	3.88	4.33	4.65	4.91	5.12	5.30	5.46	5.60	5.72	5.83	5.93	6.03	6.11
11	3.11	3.82	4.26	4.57	4.82	5.03	5.20	5.35	5.49	5.61	5.71	5.81	5.90	5.99
12	3.08	3.77	4.20	4.51	4.75	4.95	5.12	5.27	5.40	5.51	5.62	5.71	5.80	5.88
13	3.06	3.73	4.15	4.45	4.69	4.88	5.05	5.19	5.32	5.43	5.53	5.63	5.71	5.79
14	3.03	3.70	4.11	4.41	4.64	4.83	4.99	5.13	5.25	5.36	5.46	5.55	5.64	5.72
15	3.01	3.67	4.08	4.37	4.60	4.78	4.94	5.08	5.20	5.31	5.40	5.49	5.58	5.65
16	3.00	3.65	4.05	4.33	4.56	4.74	4.90	5.03	5.15	5.26	5.35	5.44	5.52	5.59
17	2.98	3.63	4.02	4.30	4.52	4.71	4.86	4.99	5.11	5.21	5.31	5.39	5.47	5.55
18	2.97	3.61	4.00	4.28	4.49	4.67	4.82	4.96	5.07	5.17	5.27	5.35	5.43	5.50
19	2.96	3.59	3.98	4.25	4.47	4.65	4.79	4.92	5.04	5.14	5.23	5.32	5.39	5.46
20	2.95	3.58	3.96	4.23	4.45	4.62	4.77	4.90	5.01	5.11	5.20	5.28	5.36	5.43
24	2.92	3.53	3.90	4.17	4.37	4.54	4.68	4.81	4.92	5.01	5.10	5.18	5.25	5.32
30	2.89	3.49	3.84	4.10	4.30	4.46	4.60	4.72	4.83	4.92	5.00	5.08	5.15	5.21
40	2.86	3.44	3.79	4.04	4.23	4.39	4.52	4.63	4.74	4.82	4.91	4.89	5.05	5.11
60	2.83	3.40	3.74	3.98	4.16	4.31	4.44	4.55	4.65	4.73	4.81	4.88	4.94	5.00
120	2.80	3.36	3.69	3.92	4.10	4.24	4.36	4.48	4.56	4.64	4.72	4.78	4.84	4.90
∞	2.77	3.31	3.63	3.86	4.03	4.17	4.29	4.39	4.47	4.55	4.62	4.68	4.74	4.80

APPENDIX

$P = 0.99$

f \ k	2	3	4	5	6	7	8	9	10	11	12	13	14	15
1	90	135	164	186	202	216	227	237	246	253	260	266	272	277
2	14.0	19.0	22.3	24.7	26.6	28.2	29.5	30.7	31.7	32.6	33.4	34.1	34.8	35.4
3	8.26	10.6	12.2	13.3	14.2	15.0	15.6	16.2	16.7	17.1	17.5	17.9	18.2	18.5
4	6.51	8.12	9.17	9.96	10.6	11.1	11.5	11.9	12.3	12.6	12.8	13.1	13.3	13.5
5	5.70	6.97	7.80	8.42	8.91	9.32	9.67	9.97	10.2	10.5	10.7	10.9	11.1	11.2
6	5.24	6.33	7.03	7.56	7.97	8.32	8.61	8.87	9.10	9.30	9.49	9.65	9.81	9.95
7	4.95	5.92	6.54	7.01	7.37	7.68	7.94	8.17	8.37	8.55	8.71	8.86	9.00	9.12
8	4.74	5.63	6.20	6.63	6.96	7.24	7.47	7.68	7.87	8.03	8.18	8.31	8.44	8.55
9	4.60	5.43	5.96	6.35	6.66	6.91	7.13	7.32	7.49	7.65	7.78	7.91	8.03	8.13
10	4.48	5.27	5.77	6.14	6.43	6.67	6.87	7.05	7.21	7.36	7.48	7.60	7.71	7.81
11	4.39	5.14	5.62	5.97	6.25	6.48	6.67	6.84	6.99	7.13	7.25	7.36	7.46	7.56
12	4.32	5.04	5.50	5.84	6.10	6.32	6.51	6.67	6.81	6.94	7.06	7.17	7.26	7.36
13	4.26	4.96	5.40	5.73	5.98	6.19	6.37	6.53	6.67	6.79	6.90	7.01	7.10	7.19
14	4.21	4.89	5.32	5.63	5.88	6.08	6.26	6.41	6.54	6.66	6.77	6.87	6.96	7.05
15	4.17	4.83	5.25	5.56	5.80	5.99	6.16	6.31	6.44	6.55	6.66	6.76	6.84	6.93
16	4.13	4.78	5.19	5.49	5.72	5.92	6.08	6.22	6.35	6.46	6.56	6.66	6.74	6.82
17	4.10	4.74	5.14	5.43	5.66	5.85	6.01	6.15	6.27	6.38	6.48	6.57	6.66	6.73
18	4.07	4.70	5.09	5.38	5.60	5.79	5.94	6.08	6.20	6.31	6.41	6.50	6.58	6.65
19	4.05	4.67	5.05	5.33	5.55	5.73	5.89	6.02	6.14	6.25	6.34	6.43	6.51	6.58
20	4.02	4.64	5.02	5.29	5.51	5.69	5.84	5.97	6.09	6.19	6.29	6.37	6.45	6.52
24	3.96	4.54	4.91	5.17	5.37	5.54	5.69	5.81	5.92	6.02	6.11	6.19	6.26	6.33
30	3.89	4.45	4.80	5.05	5.24	5.40	5.54	5.65	5.76	5.85	5.93	6.01	6.08	6.14
40	3.82	4.37	4.70	4.93	5.11	5.27	5.39	5.50	5.60	5.69	5.77	5.84	5.90	5.96
60	3.76	4.28	4.60	4.82	4.99	5.13	5.25	5.36	5.45	5.53	5.60	5.67	5.73	5.79
120	3.70	4.20	4.50	4.71	4.87	5.01	5.12	5.21	5.30	5.38	5.44	5.51	5.56	5.61
∞	3.64	4.12	4.40	4.60	4.76	4.88	4.99	5.08	5.16	5.23	5.29	5.35	5.40	5.45

* Abridged from Table 29 of *Biometrika Tables for Statisticians*, vol. I, edited by E. S. Pearson and H. O. Hartley, Cambridge University Press, Cambridge, 1954.

Table X. Fractional Points of the Largest of k Variance Ratios with One Degree of Freedom in the Numerator*

$P = 0.95$

f \ k	1	2	3	4	5	6	7	8	9	10
10	4.96	6.79	8.00	8.96	9.78	10.52	11.18	11.79	12.36	12.87
12	4.75	6.44	7.53	8.37	9.06	9.68	10.20	10.68	11.12	11.53
15	4.54	6.12	7.11	7.86	8.47	8.98	9.43	9.82	10.19	10.52
20	4.35	5.81	6.72	7.40	7.94	8.39	8.79	9.13	9.44	9.71
30	4.17	5.52	6.36	6.97	7.46	7.87	8.21	8.51	8.79	9.03
60	4.00	5.25	6.02	6.58	7.02	7.38	7.68	7.96	8.20	8.41
∞	3.84	5.00	5.70	6.21	6.60	6.92	7.20	7.44	7.65	7.84

$P = 0.99$

f \ k	1	2	3	4	5	6	7	8	9	10
10	10.04	13.17	15.08	16.43	17.43	18.25	18.91	19.48	19.97	20.41
12	9.33	11.88	13.52	14.73	15.69	16.47	17.12	17.68	18.16	18.60
15	8.68	10.82	12.18	13.21	14.03	14.72	15.30	15.81	16.26	16.66
20	8.10	9.93	11.08	11.93	12.61	13.19	13.67	14.09	14.49	14.83
30	7.56	9.16	10.14	10.86	11.43	11.90	12.31	12.66	12.97	13.26
60	7.08	8.49	9.34	9.95	10.43	10.82	11.15	11.45	11.72	11.95
∞	6.63	7.88	8.61	9.15	9.54	9.87	10.16	10.41	10.62	10.82

*Reproduced from Table 19 of *Biometrika Tables for Statisticians*, vol. I, edited by E. S. Pearson and H. O. Hartley. Cambridge University Press, Cambridge (1954).

Table XI. Random Sampling Numbers*

15	77	01	64	69	69	58	40	81	16	60	20	00	84	22	28	26	46	66	36	86	66	17	34	49
85	40	51	40	10	15	33	94	11	65	57	62	94	04	99	05	57	22	71	77	99	68	12	11	14
47	69	35	90	95	16	17	45	86	29	16	70	48	02	00	59	33	93	28	58	34	32	24	34	07
13	26	87	40	20	40	81	46	08	09	74	99	16	92	99	85	19	01	23	11	74	00	79	41	69
10	55	33	20	47	54	16	86	11	16	59	34	71	55	84	03	48	17	60	13	38	71	23	91	83
05	06	67	26	77	14	85	40	52	68	60	41	94	98	18	62	20	94	03	71	60	26	45	17	92
65	50	89	18	74	42	07	50	15	69	86	97	40	25	88	14	17	73	92	07	93	11	93	45	15
59	68	53	31	55	73	47	16	49	79	69	80	76	16	60	58	53	07	04	53	66	94	94	18	13
31	31	05	36	48	75	16	00	21	11	42	44	84	46	84	83	20	49	17	12	21	93	34	61	16
91	59	46	44	45	49	25	36	12	07	25	90	89	55	25	83	47	17	23	93	99	56	14	39	16
63	59	73	21	67	80	00	25	58	25	72	06	12	86	74	54	79	70	85	88	71	58	21	98	48
89	72	47	46	94	78	56	10	65	97	84	79	42	31	49	94	15	31	13	09	45	43	03	82	81
70	51	21	03	18	50	21	99	49	73	06	99	19	24	96	39	43	10	14	12	94	08	55	54	70
14	15	99	60	44	62	72	38	18	36	63	92	61	55	93	77	66	82	10	91	81	51	67	01	47
92	46	90	39	99	64	08	00	97	27	54	96	63	40	54	34	70	27	48	18	68	59	91	83	32
81	23	17	13	01	37	57	92	16	34	15	80	90	25	64	67	77	29	95	84	80	84	84	87	22
87	54	42	46	56	28	89	02	06	98	59	90	74	13	38	98	66	23	20	23	90	55	31	83	48
74	73	84	98	13	11	48	25	33	39	27	36	08	99	57	60	42	88	68	25	22	89	67	83	16
94	55	14	00	97	32	51	92	47	03	92	33	73	20	21	29	77	37	06	98	64	63	34	31	43
69	21	94	26	20	73	90	70	92	76	49	14	60	34	43	90	51	72	11	07	75	94	19	49	40
82	36	36	89	29	87	70	08	71	98	49	00	89	89	99	29	08	02	72	32	68	16	29	82	19
25	06	22	30	87	87	44	48	90	91	38	53	10	60	29	40	07	58	97	84	09	04	33	56	72
82	37	97	60	92	76	39	17	84	34	67	65	52	89	90	62	97	04	33	81	91	27	56	46	35
83	71	07	22	15	17	55	56	82	62	88	83	86	38	14	63	89	39	81	90	25	62	58	68	87
73	13	79	15	12	18	34	22	24	75	56	47	45	22	81	30	82	38	34	52	57	48	30	34	17
91	28	00	57	30	92	12	38	95	21	15	70	78	50	88	01	07	90	72	77	99	53	04	34	73
33	47	55	62	57	08	21	77	31	05	64	74	04	93	42	20	19	09	71	46	37	32	69	69	89
56	66	25	32	38	64	70	26	27	67	77	40	04	34	63	98	99	89	31	16	12	90	50	28	96
88	40	52	02	29	82	69	34	50	21	74	00	91	27	52	98	72	03	45	65	30	89	71	45	91
87	63	88	23	62	51	07	69	59	02	89	49	14	98	53	41	92	36	07	76	85	37	84	37	47
32	25	21	15	08	82	34	57	57	35	22	03	33	48	84	37	37	29	38	37	89	76	25	09	69
44	61	88	23	13	01	59	47	64	04	99	59	96	20	30	87	31	33	69	45	58	48	00	83	48
94	44	08	67	79	41	61	41	15	60	11	88	83	24	82	24	07	78	61	89	42	58	88	22	16
13	24	40	09	00	65	46	38	61	12	90	62	41	11	59	85	18	42	61	29	88	76	04	21	80
78	27	84	05	99	85	75	67	80	05	57	05	71	70	21	31	99	99	06	96	53	99	25	13	63
42	39	30	02	34	99	46	68	45	15	19	74	15	50	17	44	80	13	86	38	40	45	82	13	44
04	52	43	96	38	13	83	80	72	34	20	84	56	19	49	59	14	85	42	99	71	16	34	33	79
82	85	77	30	16	69	32	46	46	30	84	20	68	72	98	94	62	63	59	44	00	89	06	15	87
38	48	84	88	24	55	46	48	60	06	90	08	83	83	98	40	90	88	25	26	85	74	55	80	85
91	19	05	68	22	58	04	63	21	16	23	38	25	43	32	98	94	65	35	35	16	91	07	12	43
54	81	87	21	31	40	46	17	62	63	99	71	14	12	64	51	68	50	60	78	22	69	51	98	37
65	43	75	12	91	20	36	25	57	92	33	65	95	48	75	00	06	65	25	90	16	29	34	14	43
49	98	71	31	80	59	57	32	43	07	85	06	64	75	27	29	17	06	11	30	68	70	97	87	21
03	98	68	89	39	71	87	32	14	99	42	10	25	37	30	08	27	75	43	97	54	20	69	93	50
56	04	21	34	92	89	81	52	15	12	84	11	12	66	87	47	21	06	86	08	35	39	52	28	09
48	09	36	95	36	20	82	53	32	89	92	68	50	88	17	37	92	02	23	43	63	24	69	80	91
23	97	10	96	57	74	07	95	26	44	93	08	43	30	41	86	45	74	33	78	84	33	38	76	73
43	97	55	45	98	35	69	45	96	80	46	26	39	96	33	60	20	73	30	79	17	19	03	47	28
40	05	08	50	79	89	58	19	86	48	27	98	99	24	08	94	19	15	81	29	82	14	35	88	03
66	97	10	69	02	25	36	43	71	76	00	67	56	12	69	07	89	55	63	31	50	72	20	33	36

Table XI. Random Sampling Numbers (*continued*)

```
15 62 38 72 92   03 76 09 30 75   77 80 04 24 54   67 60 10 79 26   21 60 03 48 14
77 81 15 14 67   55 24 22 20 55   36 93 67 69 37   72 22 43 46 32   56 15 75 25 12
18 87 05 09 96   45 14 72 41 46   12 67 46 72 02   59 06 17 49 12   73 28 23 52 48
08 58 53 63 66   13 07 04 48 71   39 07 46 96 40   20 86 79 11 81   74 11 15 23 17
16 07 79 57 61   42 19 68 15 12   60 21 59 12 07   04 99 88 22 39   75 16 69 13 84

54 13 05 46 17   05 51 24 53 57   46 51 14 39 17   21 39 89 07 35   47 87 44 36 62
95 27 23 17 39   80 24 44 48 93   75 94 77 09 23   48 75 91 69 03   55 51 09 74 47
22 39 44 74 80   25 95 28 63 90   41 19 48 46 72   51 12 97 39 83   35 83 23 17 29
69 95 21 30 11   98 81 38 00 53   41 40 04 16 78   67 29 83 41 18   30 90 44 37 64
75 75 63 97 12   11 57 05 86 52   82 72 47 72 14   37 72 69 75 48   72 21 52 51 81

08 74 79 30 80   70 11 66 79 25   88 01 94 52 31   38 57 98 71 62   12 56 61 01 54
04 88 45 98 60   90 92 74 77 87   40 18 65 87 37   08 68 62 39 52   84 74 90 68 18
97 35 74 05 75   42 13 49 48 38   74 19 06 42 60   20 79 90 81 77   18 51 71 27 27
53 09 93 28 29   80 19 68 30 45   94 49 49 71 21   93 93 71 30 34   52 65 83 40 13
26 36 68 48 09   37 69 26 22 80   23 34 10 45 70   83 51 07 37 44   62 96 74 42 64

49 16 57 15 79   56 63 22 94 28   11 39 69 55 38   53 06 97 20 42   09 14 90 43 48
03 51 79 78 74   75 23 73 75 98   47 85 07 26 02   61 28 01 22 16   14 12 15 67 22
21 88 87 28 48   23 44 03 03 80   53 89 07 87 93   30 17 84 17 74   16 53 31 39 01
56 41 73 33 41   59 16 59 50 98   24 24 87 06 75   99 52 09 88 05   86 25 43 50 94
72 39 19 70 17   01 04 01 22 33   04 84 63 27 65   84 39 45 55 31   95 88 93 90 37

97 28 25 81 49   71 69 22 04 51   56 46 56 15 10   69 59 99 50 29   33 50 16 93 09
18 87 02 72 08   74 52 16 03 82   20 19 66 23 62   37 51 04 89 31   32 19 59 85 57
53 40 11 75 45   13 56 85 31 37   09 17 71 96 79   39 50 79 27 62   71 14 95 53 03
60 49 03 41 56   78 33 77 28 92   21 90 10 62 01   97 06 45 01 19   95 12 24 18 52
09 16 12 75 04   39 69 95 00 48   26 85 28 73 08   66 92 10 66 75   62 61 27 82 57

64 20 19 87 54   88 15 12 54 24   06 99 57 07 28   51 34 54 98 50   70 88 02 86 48
31 28 07 58 77   03 98 26 76 09   10 44 57 61 28   60 29 85 70 79   80 29 19 98 92
80 04 28 47 76   35 73 67 78 28   09 39 88 63 74   41 26 92 42 33   06 80 06 33 84
24 60 22 51 19   34 54 08 24 73   86 72 11 44 69   76 90 81 17 85   57 47 35 16 84
59 16 11 26 29   18 97 78 44 43   58 92 78 70 80   09 65 32 68 26   65 73 90 50 46

58 54 29 98 27   40 51 92 07 13   58 41 59 56 94   16 32 51 42 54   77 37 13 85 19
20 18 34 22 73   57 40 67 17 28   63 57 74 36 18   65 55 25 50 68   35 90 00 03 38
53 90 46 56 19   50 58 33 84 53   14 74 17 40 73   86 11 04 02 04   02 28 49 62 36
97 16 93 94 65   70 95 95 83 20   91 42 57 95 63   00 86 29 02 53   02 27 80 70 95
72 55 71 70 92   04 22 53 19 29   67 29 13 56 70   45 73 45 05 04   32 43 30 93 41

99 19 72 58 35   49 09 26 00 74   26 42 94 52 02   83 31 85 65 66   31 97 67 52 15
48 21 49 72 97   79 19 64 81 82   78 92 51 96 51   28 79 13 20 82   34 81 39 46 86
52 37 68 15 53   22 98 30 16 31   83 24 87 69 29   24 85 44 25 50   75 62 83 95 41
97 50 52 53 52   26 78 21 68 69   57 79 42 40 89   55 81 75 24 52   51 32 79 97 05
36 05 09 18 11   71 01 63 17 60   11 65 19 43 07   44 86 19 58 92   23 71 32 96 19

20 79 70 09 30   81 14 53 80 93   71 94 10 18 14   83 69 76 53 25   27 36 65 65 05
13 07 89 72 08   00 37 75 14 94   83 85 06 72 66   07 47 30 17 11   16 02 63 97 30
94 26 82 37 43   34 23 00 14 50   96 85 41 17 71   69 20 15 98 82   79 69 68 50 31
13 55 88 38 43   75 37 43 83 85   53 74 54 62 99   68 93 74 43 95   06 26 79 78 87
02 44 24 97 71   97 93 12 70 89   42 52 33 24 91   05 87 53 15 77   49 92 83 97 80

34 90 96 63 54   22 84 36 38 99   85 36 25 03 27   49 24 72 10 50   95 14 18 26 64
13 67 06 34 98   04 20 80 12 54   01 18 54 20 76   92 10 47 04 65   54 45 82 42 90
18 75 55 82 66   34 77 27 71 79   67 65 85 92 68   16 43 83 18 74   12 48 68 87 22
91 25 52 57 15   21 54 40 05 50   67 51 66 45 69   84 72 74 32 30   17 70 40 90 24
76 24 00 14 92   14 29 12 17 73   77 46 44 24 30   48 50 36 30 24   93 08 01 39 37
```

*Abridged from Table XIX of *Statistical Tables and Formulas* by A. Hald, John Wiley & Sons, New York, 1952.

Partial Answers to Selected Exercises

1A.1. (a) Yes. (b) No. (c) No. (d) Yes. (e) No. (f) No.

1A.2. (a) $0 = \Pr\{E_1 \cap E_2\} = \Pr\{E_1|E_2\} < \Pr\{E_1\} < \Pr\{E_1 \cup E_2\} = \Pr\{E_1\} + \Pr\{E_2\}$.
(b) $0 < \Pr\{E_1 \cap E_2\} < \Pr\{E_1|E_2\} = \Pr\{E_1\} < \Pr\{E_1 \cup E_2\} < \Pr\{E_1\} + \Pr\{E_2\}$.

1A.3. $0 < \Pr\{E_1 \cap E_2\} = \Pr\{E_1\} < \Pr\{E_2\} < \Pr\{E_1 \cup E_2\} < \Pr\{E_2|E_1\} = 1$.

1A.6. (a) 1/3. (b) 3/11.

1A.8. $1 - (5/6)^6 = 0.665$.

1A.9. Probability of not being fired when Jones drives Monday, etc., is $\theta_1^2 \theta_2^2 (2 - \theta_1)$. Smith should drive Monday, etc.

1A.10. (a) Yes. (b) No.

1B.1. 1/4.

1B.3. (a) $\binom{10}{3} = 120$. (b) $P_3^{10} = 720$.

1B.5. $10!/5!\,3!\,2! = 2520$.

1B.6. (a) $\binom{12}{5} = 792$. (b) $\binom{4}{2}\binom{5}{2}\binom{3}{1} = 180$.

1B.8. $12!/3!\,3!\,3!\,3! = 369{,}600$.

1B.10. (a) $\binom{6}{3} = 20$. (b) $P_3^6 = 120$.

1C.2. (a) 0.0037. (b) 0.0199.

1C.3. (a) $1 - (5/6)^4 = 0.51775$. (b) $1 - (35/36)^{24} = 0.49140$.

1C.4. $694/4096 = 0.169$.

1C.6. (a) $\theta = 0.5$. (b) $\theta = 0.59$.

1D.1. (b) 0.35. (c) 37.2. (d) 465.8.

1D.2. (a ii) 2. (b ii) 5. (a iii) 3. (b iii) 6.

1D.4. Expected value of cash reward is $171.109.

1D.5. (a) $2x/b - x^2/b^2$. (b) $b/3$. (c) $b^2/6$. (d) $b^2/18$. (e) 0. (f) $(1 - 1/\sqrt{2})b = 0.2929b$.

1D.6. (a i) ∞. (a ii) $\alpha\beta/(\alpha - 1)$. (b i) ∞. (b ii) $\alpha\beta^2/(\alpha - 1)^2(\alpha - 2)$. (c) $2^{1/\alpha}\beta$. (d) $p_Y\{y\} = \alpha\beta^\alpha e^{-\alpha y} = \alpha e^{-\alpha(y - \log \beta)}$. (e) $(1/\alpha)\log 2 + \log \beta$.

1D.7. (a) 104. (b) 104. (c) 0. (d) 0.

1D.13. $E[x]$.

1D.15. $p_Z\{z\} = 1, 0 < z < 1, p_Z\{z\} = 0$ otherwise.

1E.1. (a) 0.3085. (b) 0.8413. (c) 0.0441. (d) 0.9545. (e) 116.45. (f) 87.18. (g) 16.45.

1E.3. (i a) 0.0062. (i b) 0.02275. (i c) 0.1336. (ii a) 175.64. (ii b) 133.17. (ii c) 136.61, 163.49.

1E.4. 35/256.

1E.5. Both (a) and (b) equal $1 - e^{-b\theta}$.

1E.7. (a) 0.15. (b) 0.5. (c) 0.5. (d) 0.5. (e) 0.75. (f) 0.5.

1E.8. $(1 + \log 2)/2$.

1F.1. (a) 2.5. (c) $-1/\sqrt{2}$.

1F.3. (a) 20. (b) 5. (c) 20. (d) 11.5. (e) 0. (f) 8.5. (g) 0. (h) 26. (i) 10. (j) 0. (k) 1. (l) 0.

1F.4. (a) 0.02275. (b) 0.0096.

1F.8. (a) 0.5. (b) 0.0062. (c) 0.1056. (d) 1.058. (e) 1.029.

1F.9. 0.8167.

1F.10. 0.02275.

2.1. $E[\hat{\theta}^2] = \theta^2 + V[\hat{\theta}]$.

2.3. (MSE s^2)/(MSE $\hat{\sigma}^2$) = $1/[1 - (3n - 1)/2n^2]$.

2.5. (a) $\hat{\theta} = 1/\bar{x}$. (b) $E[1/x] = \infty$. (c) $\hat{\lambda} = \bar{x}$. (d) $E[x] = \lambda$.

2.7. (a) $-\infty < x < -1, -0.05 < x < 0.05, 1 < x < \infty$. (b) 0.1251.

2.8. (a) $-1 < x < -0.8335, 0.8335 < x < 1$. (b) 0.167.

2.9. (a) $0 < x < 0.1024$. (b) 0.1852.

2.10. (a) $\bar{x} > 522.3$. (b) 0.8245. (c) 64.4.

2.11. (a) $\bar{x} < 473.4, \bar{x} > 522.6$. (b) 0.732. (c) 79.1.

2.12. (a) 0.0052. (b) (0.006, 0.034).

2.13. $1 - \alpha$.

2.14. (a) $x = -2, 2$. (b) c. (c) α. (d) Power is $\alpha(1 - c)/(1 - \alpha)$. The powers of the three tests have the relation $c < \alpha < \alpha(1 - c)/(1 - \alpha)$.

3A.2. (a) 0.261, 0.235. (b) 1140, 1155. (c) 0.033. (d) (0.163, 0.326).

3A.3. (0.0011, 0.0800). (b) (0.00081, 0.0730).

3A.4. (a) 6800. (b) 29,000.

3A.5. 12,600,000.

3A.6. 0.018.

3B.2. (a) 0.3038. (b) 0.2135.

3B.5. (a) 0.0218. (b) 0.0238.
3B.6. (a) 0.223. (b) 0.192.
3B.7. $1/\Sigma \lambda_i$.
3B.8. (a) $1/\lambda$. (b) $3/2\lambda$.
3B.9. (a) $2/\lambda$.
3B.11. (a) 0.0106. (b) 0.012.
3B.12. (0.62, 8.75).
3B.13. (b) 0.1353.
3B.14. $F_{1-P}(6, 20) = 2.22$; $0.10 > P > 0.05$.
3B.15. 14/33.
3B.16. (a) $c = 14, n = 448$. (b) $AOQL = 0.021$.

4.1. $n = 0$.
4.3. $\mu = \lambda + \sqrt{\lambda}\sqrt{C/M}$.
4.5. $\mu = \lambda \alpha^{-1/n}$.

5.1. $\chi^2(3) = 13.64$.
5.2. $\chi^2(3) = 6.25$.
5.4. $\chi^2(8) = 41.38$.

6.1. (a) $\dfrac{[(n-1)+r]!}{(n-1)!\,r!} = 66$. (b) $\dfrac{(r-1)!}{(n-1)!\,(r-n)!} = 36$.
(c) $\dfrac{(r-n-1)!}{(n-1)!\,(r-2n)!} = 15$.
6.2. $P = 0.064$.
6.3. $P = 0.012$.
6.4. $P = 0.0053$. (b) 0.0023. (c) 0.0028.
6.7. (a) $P = 0.0009$. (c) $P = 0.0009$.

7.1. $P \simeq 0.0044$.
7.2. $P \simeq 0.0186$.
7.3. $H = 6.452 \sim \chi^2(2)$.
7.4. (a) $P = 0.212$ (exact), 0.211 (approx.). (b) $P = 0.150$.
7.5. (a) 0.0043. (b) 0.0058. (c) 0.0112 (exact), 0.013 (approx.).
7.12 $2/\pi$.

9.1. (a) (0.0217, 0.0725). (b) (5.401, 5.566).
9.2. (0.233, 4.715).
9.4. (a i) $t(14) = 1.283$. (b i) $(-4.95, 19.68)$. (a ii) $t(10.0) = 1.258$. (b ii) $(-5.68, 20.41)$.
9.6. I. (a) $F(9, 8) = 2.775$, $P \simeq 0.10$ (two-sided). (b i) $t(17) = 2.142$. (b ii) $t(14.95) = 2.199$.
9.7. $\chi^2(3) = 12.04$.

9.8. $\chi^2(4) = 6.08$.

9.10. (a) 117.4. (b) 128.0.

10.1. (a) $F(3, 65) = 2.53$, $P \simeq 0.05$. (b i) (0.19, 1.87). (b ii) (-0.18, 2.24).
(c) (-0.08, 1.78).

10.2. (a) $F(2, 18) = 4.50$. (b i) (-35.6, -6.2). (b ii) (-39.5, -2.2).

10.3. (a) $F(4, 59) = 5.99$. (b) 3.357, 1.394. (c) 64.14. (d) 0.3423. (e) 0.0691.

11.1. (a) $Y = -9.402 + 2.8845x$. (b) $F(3, 7) = 0.86$. (c) $s^2 = 0.005235$.
(d) 1.350. (e) (1.28, 1.42). (f) (2.39, 3.30). (g i) (3.703, 3.827). (g ii) (3.701, 3.823).

11.3. Estimated line is $Y = 4.1371 + 1.01835(x - 4.1329)$. (a) $t(5) = 7.15$.
(b) $t(5) = 5.90$.

11.5.

Source of variance	S.S.	D.F.	M.S.
Between b and $\bar{b}$	322.207	1	322.207
Deviations of group means about their regression line	18.256	2	9.132
Between individual slopes	152.058	3	50.686
About individual lines	938.161	48	19.545
About overall line	1430.691	54	
Due to overall line	4346.291	1	
Total	5776.982	55	

12.1. (a) $r = 0.8574$, $\hat{V}[x_2] = 1523.4$, $\hat{V}[x_2|x_1] = 437.1$. (b) $t(12) = 5.771$.
(c) $X_2 = 0.0805 + 0.7492x_1$. (d) $X_1 = 0.2557 + 0.9813x_2$. (e) 1.13. (f) 1.37.
(g) $u = 1.033$.

12.3. $1/\pi[1 + (x/y)^2]$. Hint: Define $u = x$, $v = x/y$, then obtain joint density function of (u, v), then integrate over u to get density function of v. Remember that (2.16) uses the absolute value of the determinant.

13.1. (a) $t(20) = 2.373$.
(b) $Y = 56.727 + 0.07852(x_1 - 87.545) - 0.47438(x_2 - 30.318)$.
(c) $F(2, 19) = 2.98$.   (d) $F(1, 19) = 0.48$.
(e) $Y = 56.727 - 0.006784(x_1 - 87.545) - 0.47824(x_2 - 30.318) + 8.49662(x_3 - 5.636)$.
(f) (0.421, 16.572). (g) (46.0, 80.5). (h) $F(2, 18) = 2.73$. (i) $X_1 = 87.545 + 2.6031(x_2 - 30.318) + 22.367(x_3 - 5.636)$. (j) (2.41, 42.33).

13.3. (a) $\beta_{12.3} = \beta_{12} \dfrac{1 - \rho_{13}\rho_{23}/\rho_{12}}{1 - \rho_{23}^2}$. (b) $\beta_{12.3} = \beta_{12}$ if either $\rho_{23} = 0$ or $\rho_{13} = \rho_{12}\rho_{23}$.

13.4. (b) $\rho_{x_1/x_2, x_2} = -\sqrt{1 - \rho_{x_1 x_2}}/\sqrt{2}$. (c) $\rho_{x_1/x_2, x_2} = -1/\sqrt{2}$.

PARTIAL ANSWERS TO SELECTED EXERCISES 583

14.1. (b) $F(4, 9) = 0.21$. (b) $F(2, 9) = 3.66$. (d i) $(-0.263, 0.077)$. (d ii) $(-0.190, 0.003)$.

14.2. (a i) $F(8, 30) = 1.38$. (a ii) $F(4, 30) = 28.5$. (a iii) $F(2, 8) = 26.7$. (b i) 157.2. (b ii) 19.9. (b iii) 480.6. (c) $(-39.0, -14.2)$.

15.1.

Source of variance	D.F.	S.S.	M.S.
Concentration: linear	1	15,051.125	15,051.125
quadratic	1	104.167	104.167
Batches	3	1,712.500	570.833
Strains	3	8,701.667	2,900.556
Batch × concentration (linear)	3	168.625	56.208
(quadratic)	3	56.250	18.750
Strain × concentration (linear)	3	140.125	46.708
(quadratic)	3	369.583	123.194
Batch × strain	9	1,001.833	111.315
Remainder	18	882.792	49.044
Total	47	28,188.667	

Confidence limits for $C - D$, using batch × strain interaction as error term, are $(-4.41, 15.08)$. A "pooler" who pooled all interactions to form an error term would obtain $(-1.43, 12.10)$.

16.1. (a) Model might be

$$x_{ijk} = \xi + \tau_i + \{l(\tau)\}_{j(i)} + \lambda_k + (\tau\lambda)_{ik} + z_{ijk}.$$

Source of variance	S.S.	D.F.	M.S.	E[M.S.]
Types of lamp	290,371.2	1	290,371.2	$\sigma^2 + 5\sigma^2_{l(\tau)} + 30\sigma^2_\tau$
Lamps within type	20,441.3	10	2,044.1	$\sigma^2 + 5\sigma^2_{l(\tau)}$
Laboratories	12,490.1	4	3,122.5	$\sigma^2 + 12\sigma^2_\lambda$
Types × laboratories	345.6	4	84.6	$\sigma^2 + 6\sigma^2_{\tau\lambda}$
Remainder	1,652.7	40	41.3	σ^2
Total	325,300.9	59		

(b) (113, 165). (c) $(-2.39, 8.22)$. (d) (89.3, 142.4). (e) $\hat{\sigma}^2_{l(\tau)} = 400.6$. (h) Sums of squares for contrasts between laboratories:

Contrast	Main effect of contrast	Interaction of contrast with type
(i)	56.33	85.33
(ii)	6.75	4.08
(iii)	48.35	86.68
(iv)	12,378.67	169.46

17.3. (a) $x_{ijk} = \xi + l_i + \{s(l)\}_{j(i)} + \tau_k + (l\tau)_{ik} + z_{ijk}$

Source of variance	S.S.	D.F.	M.S.	E[M.S.]
Lots	54,395.9	4	13,599.0	$\sigma^2 + 2\sigma^2_{s(l)} + 6\sigma^2_l$
Samples within lots	11,795.0	10	11,795.5	$\sigma^2 + 2\sigma^2_{s(l)}$
Temper	13,568.2	1	13,568.2	$\sigma^2 + 3\sigma^2_{l\tau} + 15\sigma^2_\tau$
Lots × temper	2,533.1	4	633.3	$\sigma^2 + 3\sigma^2_{l\tau}$
Remainder	7,505.7	10	750.6	σ^2
Total	89,797.9	29		

(b) $F(4, 10) = 0.84$. (c) (17.0, 68.0). (d) $\hat{\sigma}^2 = 751$, $\hat{\sigma}^2_{l\tau} = 0$, $\hat{\sigma}^2_{s(l)} = 214$, $\hat{\sigma}^2_l = 2070$.

Index

Abrahmson, Abraham E., 213, 220
Acceptable quality-level, 175
Acceptance, region of, 98
Acton, Forman S., 335, 396
Additive model, 469
Analysis of covariance, 376
Analysis of variance:
   crossed nested, 531
   four-way, 524
   hierarchical, 482
   nested, 482
   one-way, model I, 310
   one-way, model II, 318
   partially hierarchical, 531
   three-way, 504
   two-way, model I, 467
   two-way, model II, 478
   two-way, mixed model, 498
Andersen, S. L., 270, 293, 308
Anderson, R. L., 444, 466, 529
Angular transformation, 144
Arcsin transformation, 144
Average outgoing quality, 178
   limit, 179

Bailey, Nancy D., 263
Bancroft, T. A., 444, 466, 529
Barkworth, H., 529
Barnard, G. A., 216, 220
Bartlett, M. S., 292, 308
Bartlett's test, 292
Battan, L. J., 158

Bayes, Thomas, 86
Bayes' theorem, 18
Behrens-Fisher problem, 299
Bellinson, H. R., 239
Bennett, Carl A., 489, 503, 538, 546
Berkson, J., 393, 396
Bias, 89
   in multiple regression, 452
Binomial distribution, 30, 136
   and angular transformation, 144
   and hypergeometric distribution, 160
   and Poisson distribution, 166
   expectation of, 53
   normal approximation to, 136
   variance of, 59
Biological assay, 352
Birnbaum, A., 511, 529
Bivariate distribution:
   continuous, 70
   discrete, 67
   normal, 401
Blade, O. C., 306
Blocks, randomized, 548
Bloem, Delmar L., 503
Bocher, Maxime, 281
Box, G. E. P., 257, 270, 293, 308
Braham, R. R., 158
Brockmeyer, E., 191, 205
Bronetto, Jean, 464
Bross, Irwin, 322, 332
Byers, H. R., 158

Cavendish, H., 223, 240
Chapman, Douglas G., 163, 188
Chernoff, Herman, 87, 135
Chevalier de Méré, 35, 137
χ^2 distribution, 82, 288
  test, 207
Clarke, R. D., 168, 189
c matrix, 439, 447
Cochran, William G., 215, 220, 262, 270, 281, 324, 325, 330, 333, 390, 396
Cochran Q test, 262
Cochran's theorem, 276
Combinations, 22
Comparison of several observed:
  means, 310
  medians, 256
  regression lines, 376
  variances, 290
Comparison of two observed:
  correlation coefficients, 414
  frequencies, 150, 216
  means, 297, 299
  medians, 242, 246
  Poisson-distributed observations, 181, 183
  regression lines, 349
  variances, 286
Complementary event, 3
Completely randomized design, 547
Components of variance, 319
Compound event, 3
Compound experiment, 12
Concomitant variable, 377
Conditional density function, 72
Conditional probability, 9
Conditional probability function, 69
Confidence limits, 121
  for α and β jointly, 362
  for binomial parameter, 129, 148
  for components of variance, 322
  for differences, in means, 314, 474, 512, 540, 553
    in medians, 245
  for mean, 126, 128, 321
  for Poisson parameter, 173
  for predicted x, 361
  for predicted η, 342
  for variance, 282

Confidence limits, for variance ratio, 286
  multiple, 316
Consistency, 90
Consumer's risk, 175
Contingency tables, 211
Continuity, correction for, 140
Contrast, 316
Control charts:
  for means, 232
  for Poisson-distributed observations, 235
  for ranges, 234
Cornfield, Jerome, 489, 503
Correlated two $\times$ two table, 154
Correlation coefficient, 78, 408, 413
  estimator of, 410
  multiple, 447
  partial, 429
Covariance, 77
  analysis of, 376
Cramér, H., 56, 86, 241, 269, 280, 281
Critical region, 98
Cugel, D. W., 342
Cumulative distribution function:
  continuous, 26
  discrete, 40
Curtailed binomial sampling, 32

Daniel, Cuthbert, 450, 511, 528, 546
David, F. N., 336, 396
David, H. A., 293, 308
Dean, G., 269
Degrees of freedom, 272
Demoivre, 136
Density function, 37
De Shong, James A., Jr., 219
Distribution:
  bivariate, 67, 70
  conditional, 69, 72
  continuous, 36
  cumulative, 28, 40
  discrete, 24
  marginal, 68, 71
Distribution-free methods, 241
Dodge, Harold F., 180, 189
Doolittle method, 455
Dorsey, N. E., 307, 331

Double sampling, 180
Dunnett, Charles W., 218, 332

Efficiency:
  of estimator, 91
  of randomized block design, 548
Eisenhart, C., 226, 231, 240
Elvehyem, C. A., 527
Emmens, C. W., 354, 396
Epstein, Benjamin, 218, 220
Erlang, A. K., 191
Error:
  mean square, 90
  type I, 98
  type II, 99
Errors of measurement, 414
Estimator, 89
  maximum likelihood, 91
Events, 3
  exhaustive, 6, 12
  independent, 11, 15
  mutually exclusive, 3
Expectation, 51
  of a function, 55
  of a multivariate function, 75
  of binomial distribution, 53
  of χ^2 distribution, 82
  of exponential distribution, 54
  of geometric distribution, 63
  of hypergeometric distribution, 185
  of logarithmic normal distribution, 62
  of normal distribution, 54
  of Pareto distribution, 62
  of Pascal distribution, 63
  of rectangular distribution, 53
Exponential distribution, 43

F distribution, 285, 289
Feller, William, 140, 186, 188
Fermat, 2
Finite population, 248
Finite population model, 489, 499
Finney, D. J., 165, 188, 353, 396, 510, 528
Fisher, R. A., 2, 86, 135, 163, 188, 280, 281, 303, 308, 529
Fisher exact test, 163

Fit:
  in multiple regression, 441
  in simple linear regression, 366
Franklin, Norman L., 489, 503, 538, 546
Fraser, D. A. S., 242, 269
Friedman, M., 270
Friedman test, 260

Geometric distribution, 36, 63
Goodman, L. A., 215, 220
Gossett, W. S., *see* Student
Graybill, Franklin A., 299, 308

Hald, A., 188, 271, 281
Halmstrom, H. L., 205
Hamilton, E. L., 266
Hart, B. I., 239
Hartley, H. O., 293, 308, 332
Hercus, E. O., 270
Heteroscedasticity, 146
Heyl, Paul R., 314, 332
Hildebrand, Roger H., 219
Hilleboe, Herman E., 463
Histogram, 37
Homoscedasticity, 146
Honigschmid, O., 298, 308
H test, 256
Hyde, Edward P., 544
Hypergeometric distribution, 158
Hypothesis:
  alternative, 97
  composite, 97, 111
  null, 97
  simple, 97

Independence, 10, 12
  complete, 15
  pairwise, 15
Independent variable, 422
Indices, 431
Interaction:
  in three-way analysis, 505
  in two-way analysis, 469
Intersection, 3
Invariance, 94
Inventory control, 203
Irwin, J. O., 280, 281, 529

Jensen, Arne, 205
Joint confidence region, 362

Keeping, E. S., 392, 396
Kempthorne, O., 444, 466
Kendall, D. G., 195, 205
Kendall, Maurice G., 135, 242, 262, 269
Kent, R. H., 239
Krivobok, V. N., 554
Kruskal, W. H., 215, 220, 253, 263, 269

Laby, T. H., 270
Latscha, R., 165, 188
Least squares, 95, 336
Lehman, E. L., 217, 220
Level of significance, 99
Lieberman, Gerald J., 188
Life testing, 217
Likelihood function, 91
Likelihood ratio, 112
Lindley, D. V., 393, 396
Linear combination, 80
Logarithmic normal distribution, 62
Lot tolerance per cent defective, 175

Madansky, Albert, 392, 396
Mainland, Donald, 165, 188
Mann, H. B., 253, 269
Maximum likelihood, 91
Mayne, C. R., 554
Mead, Jere, 394
Mean square error, 90
Mean square successive difference, 221
Median, 54
Median test, 246, 304
Meyer, Peter, 219
Michelson, A. A., 293, 308
Mixed models, 467, 498, 511
Mode, 52
Model, additive, 409
Model, finite population, 489, 499
Model I and model II, 309
Molina, E. C., 175, 189
Mood, Alexander M., 299, 308
Moore, G. H., 240
Morse, Philip M., 191, 205
Moses, Lincoln E., 87, 135

Mosteller, Frederick, 35, 86, 231
Muhlenbruch, C. W., 554
Multinomial distribution, 206
Multiple comparisons, 316
Multiple correlation coefficient, 447
Mutually exclusive events, 3

Nair, K. R., 510, 528
National Bureau of Standards, 188
Negative exponential distribution, 43
Neyman, J., 2, 86, 135, 290, 336, 396
Neyman-Pearson lemma, 103
Nonparametric tests, 241
Normal distribution, 44
 addition theorem for, 81, 408
 approximation to binomial, 136
 bivariate, 401
 properties of standardized, 63
 standardized, 47
 trivariate, 429
Normal equations, 423, 434
Normality, assumption of, 241

Olmstead, P. S., 240
Operating characteristic, 175
Ordnance Corps, 188
Orthogonal contrasts, 517
Owen, Donald B., 188

Pairwise independence, 15
Pareto distribution, 62
Partial correlation coefficient, 429
Partially hierarchical situations, 530
Pascal, 2
Pascal distribution, 36, 63
Paull, A. E., 509, 528
Pearson, E. S., 2, 86, 135, 216, 220, 332
Pearson, Karl, 2, 43, 466
Permutations, 20
Pivotal function, 127
Plackett, R. L., 336, 396
Plais, Cassius M., 219
Plot, 548
Poisson distribution, 166, 169
 addition theorem for, 181
Pooling, 509
Power, 99
Prediction interval, 342

INDEX

Probability density function, 37
Probability function, 25
Producer's risk, 175
Putter, J., 269
P value, 120

Queues, 190
  finite, 198
  infinite, 191
  multichannel, 200
  single-channel, 191

Randomization, 548
Randomized blocks, 540
Randomized test, 110
Randomness, tests for, 221
Random numbers, 548
Random variable, 24
Range, 233
Rectangular distribution, 42
Rectifying inspection, 177
Region of acceptance, 98
Region of rejection, 98
Regression, 334, 409
  comparison of several lines, 376
  comparison of two lines, 349
  exponential, 391
  fallacy, 409
  in bivariate normal distribution, 406
  in reverse, 346, 361
  multiple, 419
  on several independent variables, 433
  on two independent variables, 422
  polynomial, 447
  simple linear, 334
  through origin, 358
Rejection, region of, 98
Roberts, H. V., 86
Robustness, 305
Rocker, W. Arthur, 393
Romig, Harry G., 180, 188, 189
Rosa, E. B., 307, 331
Runs:
  above and below median, 231
  of three types of elements, 231
  of two types of elements, 224, 226
  of various types, 232

Saaty, Thomas L., 191, 205
Sample space, 2

Sampling, 329
Sampling inspection, 174
  and hypothesis testing, 177
Satterthwaite, F. E., 303, 308
Savage, I. R., 242, 269
Savage, L. J., 87, 135
Scheffé, Henry, 316, 322, 323, 333, 393, 396
Schmidt, Wolfgang, 464
Sequential analysis, 2, 180
Service time distribution:
  arbitrary, 195
  exponential, 191
Shewhart, W. A., 232, 246
Significance, level of, 99
Sign test, 242, 304
Simon, Herbert A., 454, 466
Smith, H. Fairfield, 390, 396
Sobel, Milton, 218, 220
Space:
  parameter, 112
  sample, 2
Split-plot design, 550
Standard deviation, 57
Standardized normal distribution, 47, 63
Standardized variable, 61
Statistical control, 233
Statistical inference, 87
Stein, Charles, 135
Stevens, W. L., 226, 231, 240
Strong, F. M., 527
Stuart, Alan, 135
Student, 2, 86, 280, 281
Subplot, 550
Sverdrup, Erling, 217, 220
Swed, F. S., 226, 231, 240

Takacs, L., 191, 205
t distribution, 289
Tests:
  likelihood ratio, 112
  of hypotheses, 97
  uniformly most powerful, 105
Ties:
  in H test, 256
  in sign test, 244
  in Wilcoxon one-sample test, 259
  in Wilcoxon two-sample test, 253

Tocher, K. D., 166, 185
Todhunter, I., 2, 86
Transformations:
  angular, 144
  of bivariate distributions, 397
  of density functions, 45
  of probability functions, 45
  variance stabilizing, 144
  z, 414
Trivariate normal distribution, 429
t test:
  one-sample, 295, 304
  two-sample, 297, 304
Tukey, J. W., 316, 332, 454, 466, 489, 503
Two-sample test with unequal variances, 299, 304
Two × two table, 215
Type I error, 98
Type II error, 99

Unbiasedness, 89
Uniform distribution, 42
Uniformly most powerful test, 105
Union, 5
Unit normal deviate, 48
Uspensky, J. V., 140, 188

Variable:
  independent, 422
  random, 24
Variance, 57
  of binomial distribution, 58
  of χ^2 distribution, 84
  of exponential distribution, 59
  of geometric distribution, 63
  of hypergeometric distribution, 185
  of linear combination, 80
  of logarithmic distribution, 62
  of mean, 81

Variance, of mean of sample from finite population, 248
  of multiple regression coefficient, 424, 436, 450, 452
  of normal distribution, 60
  of Pareto distribution, 62
  of Poisson distribution, 167
  of rectangular distribution, 59
  of regression coefficient, 337, 340
  of variance, 300
Variance ratio distribution, 285
Variance stabilizing transformations, 144
Vaurio, V. W., 546
Von Neuman, J., 239

Wagner, R., 527
Wald, A., 2, 86, 87, 135, 180, 189, 226, 231, 240
Walker, Stanton, 503
Wallace, D. L., 257, 269
Wallis, W. Allen, 86, 187, 189, 231, 240
Weighted mean, 95
Welch, B. L., 299, 308
Whitney, D. R., 253, 269
Wilcoxon, F., 269
Wilcoxon:
  one-sample test, 258, 304
  two-sample test, 251, 304
Wild life estimation, 162
Wilens, Sigmund L., 219
Wilks, S. S., 113, 135
Williams, J. S., 322, 333
Wolfowitz, J., 226, 231, 240

Yates, F., 529
Yates' correction, 216
Yerushalmy, J., 463

z transformation, 414